INVESTIGATIVE CRIMINAL PROCEDURE AND RACIAL INJUSTICE

ASPEN CASEBOOK SERIES

INVESTIGATIVE CRIMINAL PROCEDURE AND RACIAL INJUSTICE

JAMES C. REHNQUIST

TRACEY MACLIN
Raymond & Miriam Ehrlich Chair in
U.S. Constitutional Law
University of Florida Levin College of Law

To contact Customer Service, e-mail customer.service@aspenpublishing.com, call 1-800-950-5259, or mail correspondence to:

Aspen Publishing
Attn: Order Department
1 Wall Street
Burlington, MA 01803

Printed in the United States of America.

1 2 3 4 5 6 7 8 9 0

ISBN 979-8-8890-6117-5

Library of Congress Cataloging-in-Publication Data

Names: Rehnquist, James C., author. | Maclin, Tracey, author.
Title: Investigative criminal procedure and racial injustice / James C. Rehnquist, Tracey Maclin, Raymond & Miriam Ehrlich Chair in U.S. Constitutional law, University of Florida Levin College of Law.
Description: First edition. | Burlington, MA: Aspen Publishing, 2024. | Series: Aspen casebook series | Includes bibliographical references and index. | Summary: "Criminal Procedure (Investigative) casebook for law students with an emphasis on race"—Provided by publisher.
Identifiers: LCCN 2024034259 (print) | LCCN 2024034260 (ebook) | ISBN 9798889061175 (paperback) | ISBN 9798889061182 (ebook)
Subjects: LCSH: Race discrimination—Law and legislation—United States. | Civil rights—United States. | Criminal procedure—United States. | Criminal investigation—United States. | Right to counsel—United States. | Exclusionary rule (Evidence)—United States. | Tort liability of police—United States. | Police misconduct—Law and legislation—United States. | LCGFT: Casebooks (Law)
Classification: LCC KF4755.R455 2024 (print) | LCC KF4755 (ebook) | DDC 345.73/052—dc23/eng/20240725
LC record available at https://lccn.loc.gov/2024034259
LC ebook record available at https://lccn.loc.gov/2024034260

About Aspen Publishing

Aspen Publishing is a leading provider of educational content and digital learning solutions to law schools in the U.S. and around the world. Aspen provides best-in-class solutions for legal education through authoritative textbooks, written by renowned authors, and breakthrough products such as Connected eBooks, Connected Quizzing, and PracticePerfect.

The Aspen Casebook Series (famously known among law faculty and students as the "red and black" casebooks) encompasses hundreds of highly regarded textbooks in more than eighty disciplines, from large enrollment courses, such as Torts and Contracts to emerging electives such as Sustainability and the Law of Policing. Study aids such as the *Examples & Explanations* and the *Emanuel Law Outlines* series, both highly popular collections, help law students master complex subject matter.

Major products, programs, and initiatives include:

- **Connected eBooks** are enhanced digital textbooks and study aids that come with a suite of online content and learning tools designed to maximize student success. Designed in collaboration with hundreds of faculty and students, the Connected eBook is a significant leap forward in the legal education learning tools available to students.
- **Connected Quizzing** is an easy-to-use formative assessment tool that tests law students' understanding and provides timely feedback to improve learning outcomes. Delivered through CasebookConnect.com, the learning platform already used by students to access their Aspen casebooks, Connected Quizzing is simple to implement and integrates seamlessly with law school course curricula.
- **PracticePerfect** is a visually engaging, interactive study aid to explain commonly encountered legal doctrines through easy-to-understand animated videos, illustrative examples, and numerous practice questions. Developed by a team of experts, PracticePerfect is the ideal study companion for today's law students.
- The **Aspen Learning Library** enables law schools to provide their students with access to the most popular study aids on the market across all of their courses. Available through an annual subscription, the online library consists of study aids in e-book, audio, and video formats with full text search, note-taking, and highlighting capabilities.
- Aspen's **Digital Bookshelf** is an institutional-level online education bookshelf, consolidating everything students and professors need to ensure success. This program ensures that every student has access to affordable course materials from day one.
- **Leading Edge** is a community centered on thinking differently about legal education and putting those thoughts into actionable strategies. At the core of the program is the Leading Edge Conference, an annual gathering of legal education thought leaders looking to pool ideas and identify promising directions of exploration.

SUMMARY OF CONTENTS

CONTENTS

PREFACE

This casebook brings a sustained emphasis on race to the traditional content of criminal procedure. To be clear, the book is not intended as a wholesale revision of the standard criminal procedure fare: It amply covers all the familiar subject matter areas, as the Table of Contents should make clear. But it integrates into these and other materials, wherever possible, the roles that racial prejudice and racial disparities have played and continue to play in our criminal justice system. For example, in a chapter on jury trials, the book has a focus on *Batson v. Kentucky* and its progeny that is more extensive than counterpart books. For another example, in connection with *Terry v. Ohio*, the book looks deeply into the role that race — mostly implicitly — played not only in the Court's written decision but also in the trial court and appellate advocacy that produced that decision, including the direct and cross-examinations of Detective McFadden in the suppression hearing. The book also includes four race-orientated chapters not found in other criminal procedure casebooks: The Roots of Modern Constitutional Criminal Procedure (Chapter II), Race and Juries (Chapter XV), The Department of Justice and the Prosecution of Civil Rights Crimes (Chapter X), and Discriminatory Enforcement (Chapter XII).

An argument could be made that the DOJ prosecution chapter and another atypical chapter, Addressing Police Misconduct (Chapter VI), focusing on § 1983 and other civil remedies, aren't really "criminal procedure" topics. Fair enough. They are included for other reasons: the DOJ chapter because it permits an important historical and contemporary look into race and federal criminal enforcement, and the police misconduct chapter because, among other reasons, of the subject's increasing invocation by the Court as an alternative to the exclusionary rule.

These five unconventional chapters are not a package deal. They do not depend on each other or on any other chapters. A professor could fruitfully use some or all of these chapters, in whole or in part. Because the book aspires to something novel it does so modestly, aiming to permit maximum flexibility.

A secondary overarching goal of the book is to emphasize the role and power of prosecutors in the contemporary criminal justice system. As many scholars and judges have recognized, in our contemporary landscape of minimum mandatory sentences and unfettered plea bargaining, prosecutors not only exercise their historical function of making charging decisions but also, in the exercise of that power, significantly impact and even effectively determine the length of sentences. Chapter IX, The Prosecution Function, focuses on the powers, responsibilities, and obligations of prosecutors in this system. In keeping with this emphasis, and recognizing the reality that due to the prevalence of the notorious "trial penalty" in the modern plea-bargaining and sentencing regimes most criminal justice happens outside of a trial setting, the book also devotes more attention than most books to the grand jury (Chapter VII), pleas and plea bargaining (Chapter XI), and incarceration (Chapter XVI).

The book also focuses, more generally, on lawyering. Should the prosecutor have presented that piece of exculpatory information to the grand jury even if she wasn't required to under *Williams v. United States*? How could the cross-examination of the bank teller–cooperator in *Giglio v. United States* be improved? This emphasis comes from a conviction that encouraging students to think about what the lawyers did or did not do in the cases only enhances their understanding of the cases' doctrinal significance. Advocacy is not the enemy of the doctrine. Ideally, such a focus may even encourage a few students to pursue a career that includes time spent as a responsible and ethical prosecutor and/or a creative and aggressive defense attorney.

The book's pedagogical approach is conventional. The book consists primarily of cases followed by a numbered Notes and Questions section. There are many Notes and Questions for each case, in keeping with the book's themes to encourage thinking and discussion not only about the case's doctrinal situation but also about racial implications where applicable, the decisions made or forgone by the lawyers in the case, and also (again where applicable) the historical context of the case. The expectation is that professors will assign to students only the Notes and Questions that they anticipate to be most fruitful based on their own interests and emphases.

The book also contains approximately 80 photographs, mostly of defendants, lawyers, or images establishing relevant historical, cultural, or geographical context.

The cases have been edited for space and relevance. Almost all case citations within cases have been removed except where the citation was of contextual relevance. Unlike these omissions, the removal of more substantial matter — e.g., sections, paragraphs, or sentences in cases — are noted by ellipses (. . .).

There are three versions of this casebook: a hardcover volume (which includes everything) and two paperback volumes, one for use in courses focusing on the investigative phase of criminal procedure and the other for use in courses focusing on the adjudicative phase. Both of the paperback volumes include the entirety of Chapter I, Introductory Principles, and Chapter II, Roots of Modern Constitutional Criminal Procedure. The chapter numbering and pagination of both paperback volumes remains identical to the pagination in the hardcover volume. In other words, the investigative volume includes Chapters I through VII of the hardcover volume, while the adjudicative volume begins with Chapters I and II of the main volume and then picks up with Chapter VIII of the main volume.

Mr. Rehnquist thanks his coauthor Tracey Maclin for believing in and joining this venture, and for the insight, expertise, and credibility he has brought to bear on it; Aspen Publishing, especially Joe Terry, who gave a non-academic lawyer the opportunity to take a shot at this book, as well as editors Anton Yakovlev and Kathy Langone for their excellent assistance throughout and Corinne Pulicay for her photograph procurement; the many reviewers who gave helpful comments and suggestions on early drafts, especially David Sklansky, William Ortman, Dan Medwed, and Barry Friedman; and to his former law firm Goodwin Procter LLP, and his good friends there, who provided both institutional and personal support for this effort, especially his former Goodwin assistant Shannen Flanagan. Lastly, and above all, he thanks his family — his wife Anna; children Andy, Dana, Peter, Grace, and Thomas; and daughters-in-law Leah, MK, Molly, and Erica — for their continuous and loyal support.

ACKNOWLEDGMENTS

The authors gratefully acknowledge permission to reprint excerpts from the following:

A chain gang, ca. 1898. Photograph. Library of Congress, https://www.loc.gov/resource/det.4a10700/.

A choke hold. Photograph. Expert Infantry via Flickr. Licensed under CC BY 2.0 DEED, https://creativecommons.org/licenses/by/2.0/.

A segregated bus terminal in Memphis, Tennessee. Photograph. Library of Congress, https://www.loc.gov/item/2017862145/.

Alexander Butterfield. Photograph. Richard M. Nixon Presidential Library via Wikimedia Commons.

Attorney General Edwin Meese. Photograph. Wikimedia Commons.

Bar-Gill, Oren, et al. "Taking Warrants Seriously." *Northwestern University Law Review*, vol. 106, no. 4, 2012. Northwestern University Pritzker School of Law. Reprinted with permission from the authors.

Brown v. Mississippi Defendants on the cover of the NAACP's The Crisis. Photograph, April 1935. Vieilles Annonces via Flickr, www.flickr.com/photos/vieilles_annonces/5045426107.

Classic phone booth. Photograph. N9LXI via Wikimedia Commons. Licensed under CC BY-SA 3.0 DEED, https://creativecommons.org/licenses/by-sa/3.0/deed.en.

EJI Memorial in Montgomery, Alabama. Photograph. Copyright © Roy Johnson/ Alamy Stock Photo.

Elise and Roy Olmstead, Seattle, 1925. Photograph. Museum of History & Industry Collection, https://digitalcollections.lib.washington.edu/digital/collection/imlsmohai/id/892.

Eric Foner. Photograph. Wikimedia Commons.

Fountains of Wayne Lawn Ornament Store in Wayne, New Jersey. Photograph. Courtesy of the Manhattan Chowder Blog, 3.bp.blogspot.com/_XkZRvEeVzGA/Rl9TreEcTMI/AAAAAAAAASY/nMMhyjrDTiA/s1600-h/IMG_3569.JPG.

Frank Costello. Photograph. Library of Congress, http://loc.gov/pictures/resource/cph.3c20716/.

Fred T. Korematsu. Photograph. Courtesy of the family of Fred T. Korematsu via Wikimedia Commons. Licensed under CC BY 2.0, https://creativecommons.org/licenses/by/2.0.

Handheld Thermal Imaging Device. Photograph. Copyright © Ivan Smuk/Shutterstock.

Harold Cox. Photograph. Courtesy of Open Jurist, https://openjurist.org/judge/william-harold-cox.

Irvin Younger. Photograph. Library of Congress, https://www.loc.gov/item/2020734212/.

John Adams. Painting. National Gallery of Art, https://www.nga.gov/collection/art-object-page.42933.html.

Klarman, Michael. "The Racial Origins of Modern Criminal Procedure." *Michigan Law Review*, vol. 99, no. 1, Oct. 2000. University of Michigan Law School. Reprinted with permission of the author.

Kenneth Starr. Photograph. Gage Skidmore via Wikimedia Commons. Licensed under CC BY-SA 2.0 DEED, https://creativecommons.org/licenses/by-sa/2.0/deed.en.

Larry Dudley Hiibel. Photograph. Copyright © ZUMA Press, Inc. / Alamy Stock Photo.

Louis Stokes. Photograph. Via Wikimedia Commons.

Members of the Wickersham Commission. Photograph. Library of Congress, https://www.loc.gov/pictures/item/2016889308/.

Moorefield Storey. Photograph. Wikimedia Commons.

NAACP Headquarters Flag. Photograph. Library of Congress, https://www.loc.gov/resource/ppmsca.09705/.

New Jersey Turnpike, Exit 3. Photograph. Famartin via Wikimedia Commons. Licensed under CC BY-SA 4.0 DEED, https://creativecommons.org/licenses/by-sa/4.0/deed.en.

Nick Katzenbach. Photograph. John F. Kennedy Presidential Library and Museum via Wikimedia Commons.

Officer Elton Hymon. Photograph. The National Newspaper Publishers Association (NNPA), nnpa.org/nnpa_newswire/wp-content/uploads/2019/03/Rev.-Elton-Hymon-corrected-731x1024.jpg.

Roy Wilkins, Walter White, and Thurgood Marshall. Photograph. Library of Congress, www.loc.gov/item/95518993/.

Schmidt, Benno C. Jr. "Juries, Jurisdiction, and Race Discrimination: The Lost Promise of Strauder v. West Virginia." *Texas Law Review*, vol. 61, no. 8, May 1982. University of Texas School of Law. Reprinted with permission.

Schmidt, Benno C. Jr. "Principle and Prejudice: The Supreme Court and Race in the Progressive Era. Part 2: The Peonage Cases." *Columbia Law Review*, vol. 82, 1982. Columbia Law School.

Scottsboro Defendants with Their Lawyer, Samuel Leibowitz. Photograph, 1932. Courtesy of the Morgan County (AL) Archives.

Veronia High School. Photograph. Tedder via Wikimedia Commons. Licensed under CC BY 3.0 DEED, https://creativecommons.org/licenses/by/3.0/deed.en.

W.D. Lyons, NAACP defendant, handcuffed and standing next to six arresting officers and attorneys. Photograph. Library of Congress, www.loc.gov/item/95518936/.

Walter White. Photograph. Library of Congress, https://www.loc.gov/item/2017765010/.

Wesley McKinley. Video screenshot. Boulder Public Library.

William A. Dunning. Photograph. *A History of Political Theories, Recent Times: Essays on Contemporary Developments in Political Theory*. The Macmillan Company, 1924.

INVESTIGATIVE CRIMINAL PROCEDURE AND RACIAL INJUSTICE

CHAPTER I

INTRODUCTORY PRINCIPLES

The history of American freedom is, in no small measure, the history of procedure.

Malinski v. New York, 324 U.S. 401 (1945) (Frankfurter, J.)

A. STAGES OF THE CRIMINAL PROCESS

Investigation. Almost all criminal prosecutions are preceded by some degree of government investigation. At one end of the spectrum are complex investigations featuring the use of the grand jury and/or electronic surveillance to develop evidence in complex fraud or racketeering cases. These investigations can take months or even years before any charges are brought. At the other end are more "reactive" cases, where police or other law enforcement agents respond in real time to facts they observe or information they receive from witnesses and proceed quickly to an arrest after perhaps only a handful of interviews. Generally speaking, during the investigative phase of a case—before any charges are brought—the police have more powers and criminal suspects have fewer rights than they do once charges are brought.

Arrest. An arrest is an indefinite curtailment by police of the liberty of a criminal suspect. An arrest usually but not always results in a criminal charge against the arrestee. An arrest has constitutional significance in two important respects. First, when a suspect is under arrest the suspect can only be interrogated by police after receiving *Miranda* warnings and waiving his rights to remain silent and to be represented by counsel in connection with the interrogation. Second, a person under arrest must either be released, or brought to court within 48 hours of the arrest where his detention must be justified by a showing of probable cause that he has committed a crime.

The Criminal Charge. The forms in which a criminal charge is brought vary by state and even within the federal system. The federal system requires a grand jury indictment for serious crimes, but approximately half the states have no such requirement. In the states without a grand jury indictment requirement, charges can be brought by "complaints" or "informations" that sometimes will require a subsequent preliminary hearing where a judge will make a determination whether the charge is supported by probable cause. The filing of criminal charges leads to the formal engagement of the judiciary in a criminal case for the first time.

Arraignment/Initial Appearance. Most states require some sort of an initial appearance in a criminal case, often called an arraignment, where several things usually happen: (1) the judge will ensure the defendant is aware of the charges against him, sometimes reading the defendant the written charges; (2) the defendant will enter an initial plea to the charges, almost always a plea of not guilty unless the defendant has already agreed to cooperate with the government's continuing investigation; (3) a hearing will be held as to the terms of the defendant's pretrial release, if any; and (4) arrangements will be made for the retention or appointment of counsel for the defendant, if they haven't already been made. (If defendant does have not have counsel at this initial appearance, steps (1) through (3) may be deferred until defendant is represented.)

Scheduling Conferences. At some point early in the case the court will set scheduling deadlines, often with input from the parties. The critical deadlines, in addition to a trial date, will be a deadline for motions to suppress and for the parties to discharge their disclosure obligations under the applicable federal or state rules. The court also may set deadlines for other motions, such as motions to dismiss the indictment or to obtain a bill of particulars (adding detail to the charges), or more specific trial-related deadlines regarding evidence, such as for the filing of motions in limine or for turning over witness and exhibit lists.

Plea Bargaining. Plea bargaining is not a "stage" of a criminal case, exactly, but it needs to be included here because over 95 percent of all criminal cases are resolved by a guilty plea by defendant. Plea bargaining can take place at any time, including during the investigative phase, at one extreme, and during or even after trial, at the other. Timing can be crucial to the plea bargaining process. Defendants will often be reluctant to plead guilty unless and until they know enough about the strength of the government's case, usually through reviewing discovery provided by the government (including exculpatory information), in order to negotiate effectively with the prosecutor and to make an intelligent decision as to their best interests. Prosecutors, on the other hand, are often most amenable to negotiating a plea early in the case, before they have invested significant effort in the case beyond what was necessary to bring charges.

If the parties reach an agreement the defendant will enter a plea of guilty before a judge, who will normally accept the plea, without considering its substantive fairness or merit, as long as she is convinced the defendant is making a voluntary, knowing, and intelligent waiver of his constitutional right to a jury trial and the attendant rights that go along with that right. A guilty plea is a criminal "conviction," the equivalent for almost all legal purposes of being found guilty by a jury at trial.

Trial. Trial will usually be before a jury, which must find defendant guilty beyond a reasonable doubt. The jury's decision must be unanimous. Federal law and most state law require a twelve-person jury but the constitutional minimum is only six. A federal defendant can waive his right to a jury trial and have the case tried before the judge (a "bench trial"), but only if the prosecutor and judge both agree. State practice on jury waivers varies. Many constitutional rights come into play at trial. For example, the Sixth Amendment requires that defendants be permitted to cross-examine the government's witnesses and to demand the attendance of their own witnesses, and the Fifth Amendment requires that if the defendant declines to testify the government cannot comment on that lack of evidence.

Sentencing. If defendant is convicted he will thereafter be sentenced, with the timing and content of that procedure largely a matter of state law and practice in state courts. In federal court sentencings usually occur two to three months after verdict. During the interim period the probation department prepares an often lengthy presentence report, which includes a personal history of the defendant, including any aggravating or mitigating information; a complete explanation of the defendant's criminal history; and an analysis of how the United States Sentencing Guidelines apply to the defendant's conduct. A sentencing hearing will be held where the parties will have an opportunity to dispute any aspect of the presentence report, including the opportunity to make arguments as to how the Guidelines should be applied in the case and what sentence is appropriate. The judge will resolve the disputes and impose the sentence.

Appeals. Defendants have a right to appeal from their conviction. They may challenge the jury's verdict on any of several grounds, including the following: the evidence was insufficient to support the jury's verdict; the trial judge made errors in her evidentiary rulings or instructions to the jury or erroneously admitted evidence that was illegally obtained by the government; the theory of the case was legally flawed, that is, the facts proven did not violate the statute that was charged; and so on. The defendant can also appeal his sentence as being too harsh although many prosecuting authorities, including the Department of Justice, will usually require a defendant who pleads guilty to agree to waive any sentencing appeal he may have. It is extremely difficult to prevail on appeal on any issue that was not contested at trial. Indeed, the record on appeal is confined to the record of what took place during the trial. It is also difficult to have the sentence stayed (delayed) while an appeal is pending.

Post-Conviction Relief. A defendant who loses on his "direct appeal," as most do, can subsequently bring a claim for post-conviction relief in either state or federal court, wherever his trial was. Post-conviction motions are commonly although not exclusively based on information that was not presented at trial, such as ineffective assistance of trial or appellate counsel or newly discovered physical evidence or witnesses. At the federal level and in some state systems the potential grounds for post-conviction relief have been substantially narrowed in the last few decades by statute as well as by judicial decisions.

B. PLAYERS IN THE CRIMINAL JUSTICE SYSTEM

Police and Other Law Enforcement Agents. Primary responsibility for investigating criminal activity and apprehending criminal suspects lies with local and other state and federal law enforcement agents. There are an estimated 18,000 separate police and law enforcement agencies in the United States, including local municipal police departments, county sheriff's offices, state troopers, and federal law enforcement agencies. The police department is the nation's largest, with approximately 36,000 officers; many small towns have their own independent police officers with fewer than ten officers. In most local police departments the senior police officer is called the chief of police; in larger cities the title is usually police commissioner. Both commissioners and chiefs are usually appointed by the mayor or an equivalent local municipal authority. Approximately 80 percent of police officers nationwide are members of a union.

Prosecutors. There are approximately 2,300 separate state prosecutor's offices in the United States, typically corresponding to a county or other local subdivision of a state. In Rhode Island the attorney general is responsible for all prosecutions in the entire state. In all but three states (Connecticut, Hawaii, and New Jersey) prosecutors are elected. The United States is the only country in the world where prosecutors are elected. The elected prosecutor in charge of the office is usually called the district attorney (or state's attorney or commonwealth's attorney) and the "line" prosecutors underneath her are usually called assistant district attorneys (ADAs).

At the federal level the President appoints the senior prosecutors, called United States attorneys, for each of the country's 94 judicial districts. While United States attorneys largely operate independently they are part of, and are ultimately responsible to, the Department of Justice. New United States attorneys are usually appointed each time there is a change in the political party of the President. The "line" attorneys under the U.S. attorney are called assistant United States attorneys (AUSAs).

Judges and Magistrates. All federal judges—including the trial judges of the 94 United States District Courts, the judges of the 12 United States Circuit Courts of Appeals, and the Supreme Court—are appointed by the President and must be confirmed by the Senate. State judges are selected by a variety of methods, including election, appointment, and combined methods that can include appointment from candidates recommended by a panel. At the federal level United States magistrate judges, appointed by the district court, are empowered to handle minor criminal cases and pretrial matters, including arraignments and conferences. They also authorize search warrants. Many states also have magistrate judges or their equivalent, who have authority over minor criminal and pretrial matters.

Defendants. Persons who have been charged with crimes are called defendants. Unless and until charges are brought by a prosecutor, persons on law enforcement radar may be called "suspects" or "targets" (in DOJ parlance) but it is the formal act of filing charges that makes someone a defendant. It is this formality that establishes a right to counsel, although the Supreme Court's *Miranda* decision also provides that persons subjected to custodial interrogation by police also have a right to counsel even if they have not been charged.

Defense Counsel. Defendants charged with felonies or lesser offenses that could result in substantial jail time have a constitutional right to counsel, including a right to court-appointed counsel if they cannot afford to pay for a lawyer. In federal court approximately 66 percent of felony defendants are represented by appointed counsel; in state courts 88 percent of felony defendants have appointed counsel. There are two main types of court-appointed counsel: employees of state-funded public defender organizations or members of the bar who are appointed to represent defendants in specific cases and are reimbursed on a schedule for the type of case and/or the amount of time spent on the case.

Jurors. Jurors are drawn at random from public sources such as residence lists, voter rolls, or automobile registries. For each criminal trial, a large pool of potential jurors (often called a "panel" or "venire") is summoned to court and the judge and parties engage in a "jury selection" process to cull from the pool the jurors who will actually hear the case. Potential jurors may be excused because of personal hardship, actual or apparent bias, or without any expressed reason based on a limited number of "peremptory" challenges by either party.

It is sometimes said that the jury is "the judge of the facts." Jurors "deliberate"—discuss the case—in secret after all the evidence has been heard and the judge has given the jury instructions on the law that governs the case. Juries are not supposed to discuss the case even among themselves until they have heard all of the evidence; the judge will also instruct them that they are not to seek to acquire any information about the case from sources (e.g., the internet or television) other than the evidence at trial. Jurors take an oath to follow the judge's instructions, including that they will not decide the case based on sympathy for or prejudice against any party.

Probation Officers. As noted above, probation officers in the federal system and in some state systems prepare pre-sentence reports, which are used at sentencing. Probation officers also "supervise" criminal defendants who are serving a term of probation as part of a criminal sentence. Probation officers are generally considered to be part of the judicial branch. Probation officers' supervision of the persons reporting to them includes regular in-person meetings or telephone communication and ensuring that probationers comply with any conditions of their probation or release, such as drug testing or making restitution payments to crime victims.

C. CRIMINAL PROCEDURE VERSUS CIVIL PROCEDURE

Unlike civil procedure, the law of criminal procedure is almost entirely constitutional. In the investigative phase of criminal cases, almost all of what police and prosecutors do—conduct searches for evidence, talk to suspects, employ technology in surveillance or search efforts, call witnesses to the grand jury—is regulated to some degree by the Constitution, usually the Fourth and Fifth Amendments. When investigations result in charges, the process by which the persons charged are brought to court, beginning with the arrest, and the standards for initially evaluating those charges are constitutional. If, as is the case over 95 percent of the time, the defendant pleads guilty rather than going to trial, his guilty plea must be accepted by a judge who is charged with ensuring that the defendant is making a knowing and voluntary waiver of his Sixth and Fifth Amendment rights.

When a defendant chooses to go to trial, the manner in which that trial must be conducted is driven by the Fourth, Fifth, and Sixth Amendments. The jury, for example, must be drawn from a fair cross-section of the community, in a nondiscriminatory manner, and peremptory challenges to jurors based on race and other impermissible reasons are prohibited. Evidence that was obtained by the government by illegal means is normally inadmissible under the Fourth Amendment. The defendant has a Sixth Amendment right to both cross-examine the government's witnesses and to require the testimony of defense witnesses. By virtue of the Fifth Amendment, the defendant is not required to testify in his own defense, and the jury must be instructed not to draw an adverse inference against the defendant who chooses not to testify. *See generally* William J. Stuntz, *Substance, Process and the Civil-Criminal Line*, 7 J. Contemp. L. Issues 1, 3-4 (1996).

Consider, by contrast, the law of civil procedure. While some constitutional requirements form the deep backdrop for issues regarding notice, personal and subject matter jurisdiction, and jury trial rights, these issues form a minor part of even a law school civil procedure curriculum, and are much less significant in practice. The bulk of the raw material of civil procedure—service of process, venue, removal, pleadings, joinder, class actions, challenges to pleadings and other motion practice, discovery, trial practice, etc.—are regulated primarily or only by statutes and federal and state rules of civil procedure. *Id.* at 4.

Another manifestation of this phenomenon is the degree to which judicial management can affect how a case proceeds. In civil cases judges have wide discretion to manage the scope and length of the discovery process, and are able to put limits on the sort of information to which the parties are entitled and the length of time the parties will have for discovery. In a criminal case, on the other hand, the scope and content of discovery is largely driven by constitutional (the government's obligation to turn over exculpatory information) or statutory (witness statements) requirements, and courts have less discretion. Similarly, a judge in a civil trial has broad discretion to make evidentiary rulings and to control the presentation of evidence, whereas the judge in a criminal case must always be mindful of the defendant's Sixth Amendment rights. William J. Stuntz, *The Uneasy Relationship Between Criminal Procedure and Criminal Justice*, 107 Yale L.J. 1, 13-14 (1997).

How is it that criminal procedure became the special concern of constitutional regulation? And is that a good thing?

As to the first question, no theory is perfect, but Professor Stuntz has observed that the universe of criminal suspects and defendants as a group—politically unpopular and disproportionately poor and minority—is the classic sort of group that has been and should be the subject of constitutional protection on account of their comparative political powerlessness. As to whether this is a good thing, Professor Stuntz says no: He contends that the cause of criminal justice would be (would have been?) better served by less constitutional criminal procedure and more constitutional substantive criminal law in areas—such as requiring specified levels of funding for indigent defense, regulating crime definition and sentencing, and bolstering the mens rea requirement—where the Supreme Court has largely stayed away. *Id.* at 76.

Professor Barry Friedman shares the view that constitutional law is a less than ideal means for regulating criminal procedure, and not just because the scope of that regulation may have deterred forays into criminal substance. Professor Friedman and Maria Ponomarenko argue that policing is too important and too pervasive to be subject only to the sort of ad hoc regulation afforded by judicial review, and should instead be regulated by substantive rules promulgated by the municipal and other accountable political bodies that operate police forces, under a model similar to that governing federal administrative agencies. Barry Friedman & Maria Ponomarenko, *Democratic Policing*, 90 N.Y.U. L. Rev. 1827 (2015).

D. INCORPORATION

Much of modern constitutional criminal procedure has resulted from the Supreme Court's "incorporation" of particular rights found in the Bill of Rights into the Due Process Clause of the Fourteenth Amendment, thereby making those rights applicable to the states. That history will be outlined here and will be largely omitted from the discussion of the cases in the following chapters.

The Bill of Rights originally was held to apply only to the federal government. *Barron ex rel. Tiernan v. Mayor of Baltimore*, 7 Pet. 243 (1833). The constitutional Amendments adopted in the aftermath of the Civil War fundamentally altered the country's federal system, however. Section 1 of the Fourteenth Amendment provides, among other things, that a State may not abridge "the privileges or immunities of citizens of the United States" or deprive "any person of life, liberty, or property, without due process of law." Although the Supreme Court originally restricted the application of these clauses, *see Slaughter-House Cases*, 16 Wall. 36, 79 (1873) (the privileges and immunities protected by the Fourteenth Amendment were only the rights that were uniquely of national citizenship); *United States v. Cruikshank*, 92 U.S. 542 (1876) (First Amendment right of peaceful assembly only protects against infringement by Congress), beginning in the late nineteenth century the Court began to consider whether other rights in the Bill of Rights applied to the states. *See Hurtado v. California*, 110 U.S. 516 (1884) (due process does not require grand jury indictment); *Twining v. New Jersey*, 211 U.S. 78 (1908) (Fifth Amendment right against compelled incrimination does not apply to the states); *Powell v. Alabama*, 287 U.S. 45 (1932) (right to counsel apples to states in certain capital cases).

In the 1960s, the Warren Court accelerated the process of incorporation, holding that the Due Process Clause fully incorporates most of the particular rights contained in the Bill of Rights. *See, e.g., Mapp v. Ohio*, 367 U.S. 643 (1961) (Fourth Amendment exclusionary rule); *Gideon v. Wainwright*, 372 U.S. 335 (1963) (Sixth Amendment right to counsel in *Malloy v. Hogan*, 378 U.S. 1 (1964) (Fifth Amendment right against compelled incrimination); *Pointer v. Texas*, 380 U.S. 400 (1965) (Sixth Amendment right to confrontation); *Washington v. Texas*, 388 U.S. 14 (1967) (Sixth Amendment right to compulsory process); *Duncan v. Louisiana*, 391 U.S. 145 (1968) (Sixth Amendment right to jury trial). By the end of that decade, only a handful of rights in the Bill of Rights had not been incorporated into the Due Process Clause.

Another, shorter series of incorporation cases began in 2010. In *McDonald v. City of Chicago*, 561 U.S. 742 (2010), the Court considered whether the Due Process Clause incorporated

Gary Duncan, the defendant in *Duncan v. Louisisana*

the Second Amendment right to keep and bear arms for self-defense purposes, a right that the Court had recently recognized as a matter of federal law in *District of Columbia v. Heller*, 554 U.S. 570 (2008). The Court held the Second Amendment right was incorporated because the right was "fundamental to our scheme of ordered liberty" and was "deeply rooted in this Nation's history and tradition." *McDonald*, 561 U.S. at 767. The Court has since applied this test to two of the last remaining unincorporated rights in the criminal procedure area. In *Timbs v. Indiana*, 586 U.S. 146 (2019), the Court held that the Eighth Amendment's Excessive Fines Clause was incorporated under the *McDonald* test. The Court noted, among other things, that even though almost all state constitutions had prohibited excessive fines by the time of the ratification of the Fourteenth Amendment, draconian fines in the Black Codes enacted following the Civil War had been instrumental in the schemes of peonage and involuntary servitude used to re-enslave southern Black people in that era and beyond. *Id.* at 153. *See* Chapter II *infra*. And in *Ramos v. Louisiana*, 140 S. Ct. 1390 (2020), the Court held that the Sixth Amendment's right to jury unanimity in criminal cases applied to the states, invalidating procedures in Louisiana and Oregon, whose origin the Court traced to efforts by those states to dilute the influence of Black people on juries. *Id.* at 87-88.

Today the only significant criminal procedure right that has not been incorporated is the Fifth Amendment's right to grand jury indictment. *See* Chapter VII *infra*. *See* Roger A. Fairfax Jr., *Interrogating the Nonincorporation of the Grand Jury Clause*, 43 Cardozo L. Rev. 855 (2022) (analyzing the case for incorporation of the grand jury right).

E. STATE CONSTITUTIONAL CRIMINAL PROCEDURE

This book focuses largely but not exclusively on federal law, specifically, federal courts' interpretations of the federal constitution as the source of the rules of criminal procedure. But it must always be remembered that the states have their own constitutions, often with identical or similar provisions as the federal constitution, and that state judges are not bound by federal courts' interpretations of the federal constitution in interpreting identical or analogous terms of state constitutions.

The focus on state constitutional law has increased in the last 50 years. By the early 1970s the Warren Court's wholesale expansion of individual rights was plainly over. President Nixon had by then substantially succeeded in remaking the Court in the form that he had promised in his law-and-order presidential campaigns of 1968 and 1972. This trend was acknowledged by Justice Brennan in an important 1977 law review article, William Brennan Jr., *State Constitutions and the Protection of Individual Rights*, 90 Harv. L. Rev. 489 (1977), in which he noted the Supreme Court's recent proclivities and encouraged state judges to view their own constitutions as robust sources of individual rights:

> But the point I want to stress here is that state courts cannot rest when they have afforded their citizens the full protections of the federal Constitution. State constitutions, too, are a font of individual liberties, their protections often extending beyond those required by the Supreme Court's interpretation of federal law. The legal revolution which has brought federal law to the fore must not be allowed to inhibit the independent protective force of state law—for without it the full realization of our liberties cannot be guaranteed.

Id. at 491.

Even by 1977, Justice Brennan was able to point to multiple examples where state courts had interpreted their own state constitutions to be more protective of individual rights than the federal constitution as interpreted by Nixon's Burger Court. For example, in 1971 the Supreme Court held in *Harris v. New York*, 401 U.S. 222 (1971), that statements taken by police officers from a defendant without first giving *Miranda* warnings were nonetheless admissible to impeach a testifying defendant. *See* Chapter III *infra*. Justice Brennan noted that the California Supreme Court had explicitly renounced the United States Supreme Court's decision in *Harris*. In that case, after explaining its own view of the privilege against self-incrimination in the California Constitution, the court concluded: "We pause finally to reaffirm the independent nature of the California Constitution and our responsibility to separately define and protect the rights of California citizens despite conflicting decisions of the United States Supreme Court interpreting the federal Constitution." *People v. Disbrow*, 545 P.2d 272, 280 (Cal. 1976).

Another example was the nature of the consent required to authorize a police officer to conduct a motor vehicle search. In *Schneckloth v. Bustamonte*, 412 U.S. 218 (1973), the Supreme Court rejected any requirement that such a consent must be intelligent and knowing, and that the individual must be aware of his right to refuse to consent. In New Jersey, however, the state's highest court construed language in the New Jersey Constitution that was identical to the federal Fourth Amendment to require informed consent. "Under Art. I, par. 7 of our State Constitution the validity of a consent to search, even in a non-custodial situation, must be measured in terms of waiver, i.e., where the state seeks to justify a search on the basis of consent it has the burden of showing that the consent was voluntary, an essential element of which is knowledge of the right to refuse consent." *State v. Johnson*, 346 A.2d 66, 68 (N.J. 1975).

This trend continued long after in part because of Justice Brennan's influential article. For example, in 1984 the Supreme Court announced a major exception to its prior ruling in *Mapp v. Ohio*, 367 U.S. 643 (1961), which had held that illegally obtained evidence was inadmissible in state as well as federal court. In *United States v. Leon*, 469 U.S. 897 (1984), the Court held that *Mapp*'s exclusionary rule did not apply where the police officers acted in "good faith." A decade later, courts in eight states had rejected the *Leon* good faith exception. *See* Leigh A. Morrissey, *State Courts Reject Leon on State Constitutional Grounds: A Defense of Reactive Rulings*, 47 Vand. L. Rev. 917, 919 (1994). According to a 2023 survey in the Mississippi Law Journal, more states (17) have refused to follow *Leon* than any other Supreme Court criminal procedure decision. Christopher R. Green, et. al., *State-Court Departures from the Supreme Court: A Comprehensive Survey*, 92 Miss. L.J. 329, 330 (2023).

The availability of state constitutional law as a source of expanded individual rights should not be exaggerated, however. The vast majority of state courts follow federal Supreme Court precedent interpreting constitutional terms and principles that are common to both

John Adams

federal and state constitutions, either as a matter of deference or as a matter of independent agreement. For example, in *Whren v. United States*, 517 U.S. 806 (1996), the Supreme Court flatly and controversially rejected the argument that a police stop of a vehicle for a traffic violation could be challenged on the basis that the stop was "pretextual"—that is, that the stop was motivated by a reason other than enforcing traffic laws. *Id.* at 816-19. It declined to adopt a test that the validity of the stop depended on whether a reasonable officer "would have" made the stop regardless of the ulterior motive. *Id.* In the decades following *Whren*, 47 out of 50 states have followed the Supreme Court in also rejecting the "would have" test. *Commonwealth v. Long*, 485 Mass. 711, 727 & n.13 (2020). By contrast, only two states adopted some version of a "would have" test after *Whren*. *See State v. Gonzales*, 150 N.M. 74, 257 P.3d 894, 898 (2011) (question is whether, based on totality of circumstances, "the officer who made the stop would have done so even without the unrelated motive"); *State v. Ladson*, 138 Wash. 2d 343, 358-59, 979 P.2d 833 (1999) ("When determining whether a given stop is pretextual, the court should consider the totality of the circumstances, including both the subjective intent of the officer as well as the objective reasonableness of the officer's behavior.").

One of the most defendant-protective state constitutions is that of Massachusetts, which was the model on which the federal Constitution was based. Its author, more widely known as the second U.S. President, was John Adams, who also warrants a place in the criminal procedure pantheon on account of his successful trial defense of the British soldiers charged with murder arising out of the 1770 Boston Massacre.

CHAPTER II

THE ROOTS OF MODERN CONSTITUTIONAL CRIMINAL PROCEDURE: THE SUPREME COURT, RACE, AND THE POST-BELLUM SOUTH

The Supreme Court under the tenure of Chief Justice Earl Warren (1953-1969) has been widely credited with effecting a revolution in the American law of criminal procedure. Much of this was accomplished by the "incorporation" of constitutional rights into the Due Process Clause of the Fourteenth Amendment, thereby making them applicable to the states. *See* Chapter I *supra*. Not all of the criminal defendants in the seminal cases of the Warren Court revolution were Black, and the race of the defendant was only mentioned in one of them, *Duncan v. Louisiana*, 391 U.S. 145 (1968).

Nonetheless it is generally accepted that the Warren Court revolution was actually, albeit implicitly, driven by race, specifically by the Court's concerns about racial injustice. *See* Burt Newborne, *The Gravitational Pull of Race on the Warren Court*, 2010 Sup. Ct. Rev. 59, 60 (2010) ("concern over racial injustice and state institutional failure was so intense during . . . [the] "Warren years" that it played a significant role in shaping many of the most important constitutional decisions of the Supreme Court"); Gabriel J. Chin, *Race and the Disappointing Right to Counsel*, 122 Yale L.J. 2236, 2239 (2013) (although Clarence Gideon was white, "*Gideon* was a race case, in that *Gideon* and the Court's other criminal procedure cases of the era were concerned with institutional racism"); Dan M. Kahan & Tracey L. Meares, *Foreword: The Coming Crisis of Criminal Procedure*, 86 Geo. L.J. 1153, 1153 (1998) ("Law enforcement was a key instrument of racial repression, in both the North and the South, before the 1960s civil rights revolution. Modern criminal procedure reflects the Supreme Court's admirable contribution to eradicating this incidence of American apartheid."); David Alan Sklansky, *Police and Democracy*, 103 Mich. L. Rev. 1699, 1805 (2005) ("[C]riminal procedure in the Warren Court era was famously preoccupied with issues of illegitimate inequality, particularly those associated with race."); William J. Stuntz, *The Uneasy Relationship Between Criminal Procedure and Criminal Justice*, 107 Yale L.J. 1, 5 (1997) ("The post-1960 constitutionalization of criminal procedure arose, in large part, out of the sense that the system was treating black suspects and defendants much worse than white ones. Warren-era constitutional criminal procedure began as a kind of antidiscrimination law.").

This chapter looks at a handful of seeds that were sown in race cases in the decades preceding the advent of the Warren Court. These cases sometimes provided precedent for important Warren Court decisions. This is not to suggest that these cases necessarily represent an awakening on the part of the Supreme Court at any particular point in time. The development of the Supreme Court's case law on matters of criminal procedure and race has always been and continues to be belated, halting, regressive, and inconsistent.

Section A looks at cases where the Court considers state exclusion of Black people from juries. Section B considers the Court's invalidation of certain state mechanisms for enforcing a regime of peonage in the South long after the Thirteenth Amendment was passed, a regime of involuntary servitude largely enabled by criminal law and procedure. Section C looks at cases where the Supreme Court invalidated state court "trials" that were dominated by the shadow of the mobs outside the courthouse. Section D examines the Court's initial consideration of coerced confessions.

The focus of this chapter borrows heavily from the concept developed in Professor Michael J. Klarman's article *The Racial Origins of Modern Criminal Procedure*, 99 Mich. L. Rev. 48 (2000). Professor Klarman writes:

> The constitutional law of state criminal procedure was born between the First and Second World Wars. Prior to 1920, the Supreme Court had upset the results of the state criminal justice system in just a handful of cases, all involving race discrimination in jury selection. By 1940, however, the Court had interpreted the Due Process Clause of the Fourteenth Amendment to invalidate state criminal convictions in a wide variety of settings: mob-dominated trials, violation of the right to counsel, coerced confessions, financially-biased judges, and knowingly perjured testimony by prosecution witnesses.
>
> . . .
>
> Altogether, the Supreme Court decided six landmark state criminal procedure cases during the interwar period. Four of these cases involved black defendants from southern states. This Article contends that the linkage between the birth of modern criminal procedure and southern black defendants is no fortuity. For the Court to assume the function of superintending the state criminal process required a departure from a century and a half of tradition and legal precedent, both grounded in federalism concerns. The Justices were not prepared to embark on such a novel enterprise in cases of marginal unfairness — where the police had interrogated a suspect a bit too vigorously or permitted defense counsel a little less time than optimal for preparing a case. On the contrary, the Court was willing to take this leap only when confronted with cases in which defendants were brutally tortured into confessing or the appointment of defense counsel in a capital case was a complete sham. Such flagrant injustices were not frequent occurrences in the United States during the 1920s and 1930s — except in the South, in cases involving black defendants charged with serious interracial crimes, usually rape or murder.

Id. at 48-49.

The four cases Professor Klarman refers to above — *Moore v. Dempsey*, 261 U.S. 86 (1923); *Powell v. Alabama*, 287 U.S. 45 (1932); *Norris v. Alabama*, 294 U.S. 587 (1935); and *Brown v. Mississippi*, 297 U.S. 278 (1936) — are considered below, among others.

A. INVALIDATION OF CONVICTIONS WHERE BLACK PEOPLE WERE EXCLUDED FROM JURIES

Strauder v. West Virginia

100 U.S. 303 (1879)

Mr. Justice STRONG delivered the opinion of the court.

The plaintiff in error, a colored man, was indicated for murder in the Circuit Court of Ohio County, in West Virginia, on the 20th of October, 1874, and upon trial was convicted and sentenced. The record was then removed to the Supreme Court of the State, and there the judgment of the Circuit Court was affirmed. The present case is a writ of error to that court, and it is now, in substance, averred that at the trial in the State court the defendant (now plaintiff in error) was denied rights to which he was entitled under the Constitution and laws of the United States.

• • •

The law of the State to which reference was made in the petition for removal and in the several motions was enacted on the 12th of March, 1873, and it is as follows: "All white male persons who are twenty-one years of age and who are citizens of this State shall be liable to serve as jurors, except as herein provided." The persons excepted are State officials.

In this court, several errors have been assigned, and the controlling questions underlying them all are, first, whether, by the Constitution and laws of the United States, every citizen of the United States has a right to a trial of an indictment against him by a jury selected and impanelled without discrimination against his race or color, because of race or color; and, second, if he has such a right, and is denied its enjoyment by the State in which he is indicted, may he cause the case to be removed into the Circuit Court of the United States?

It is to be observed that the first of these questions is not whether a colored man, when an indictment has been preferred against him, has a right to a grand or a petit jury composed in whole or in part of persons of his own race or color, but it is whether, in the composition or selection of jurors by whom he is to be indicted or tried, all persons of his race or color may be excluded by law, solely because of their race or color, so that by no possibility can any colored man sit upon the jury.

The questions are important, for they demand a construction of the recent amendments of the Constitution. If the defendant has a right to have a jury selected for the trial of his case without discrimination against all persons of his race or color, because of their race or color, the right, if not created, is protected by those amendments, and the legislation of Congress under them. The Fourteenth Amendment ordains that "all persons born or naturalized in the United States and subject to the jurisdiction thereof are citizens of the United States and of the State wherein they reside. No State shall make or enforce any laws which shall abridge the privileges or immunities of citizens of the United States, nor shall any State deprive any person of life, liberty, or property, without due process of law, nor deny to any person within its jurisdiction the equal protection of the laws."

This is one of a series of constitutional provisions having a common purpose; namely, securing to a race recently emancipated, a race that through many generations had been held in slavery, all the civil rights that the superior race enjoy. The true spirit and meaning of the amendments, as we said in the *Slaughter-House Cases*, cannot be understood without keeping in view the history of the times when they were adopted, and the general objects they plainly sought to accomplish. At the time when they were incorporated into the Constitution, it required little knowledge of human nature to anticipate that those who had long been regarded as an inferior and subject race would, when suddenly raised to the rank of citizenship, be looked upon with jealousy and positive dislike, and that State laws might be enacted or enforced to perpetuate the distinctions that had before existed. Discriminations against them had been habitual. It was well known that in some States laws making such discriminations then existed, and others might well be expected. The colored race, as a race, was abject and ignorant, and in that condition was unfitted to command the respect of those who had superior intelligence. Their training had left them mere children, and as such they needed the protection which a wise government extends to those who are unable to protect themselves. They especially needed protection against unfriendly action in the States where they were resident. It was in view of these considerations the Fourteenth Amendment was framed and adopted. It was designed to assure to the colored race the enjoyment of all the civil rights that under the law are enjoyed by white persons, and to give to that race the protection of the general government, in that enjoyment, whenever it should be denied by the States. It not only gave citizenship and the privileges of citizenship to persons of color, but it denied to any State the power to withhold from them the equal protection of the laws, and authorized Congress to enforce its provisions by appropriate legislation. To quote the language used by us in the *Slaughter-House Cases*, "No one can fail to be impressed with the one pervading purpose found in all the amendments, lying at the foundation of each, and without which none of them would have been suggested,—we mean the freedom of the slave race, the security and firm establishment of that freedom, and the protection of the newly made freeman and citizen from the oppressions of those who had formerly exercised unlimited dominion over them." So again: "The existence of laws in the States where the newly emancipated negroes resided, which discriminated with gross injustice and hardship against them as a class, was the evil to be remedied, and by it [the Fourteenth Amendment] such laws were forbidden. If, however, the States did not conform their laws to its requirements, then, by the fifth section of the article of amendment, Congress was authorized to enforce it by suitable legislation." And it was added, "We doubt very much whether any action of a State, not directed by way of discrimination against the negroes, as a class, will ever be held to come within the purview of this provision."

If this is the spirit and meaning of the amendment, whether it means more or not, it is to be construed liberally, to carry out the purposes of its framers. It ordains that no State shall make or enforce any laws which shall abridge the privileges or immunities of citizens of the United States (evidently referring to the newly made citizens, who, being citizens of the United States, are declared to be also citizens of the State in which they reside). It ordains that no State shall deprive any person of life, liberty, or property, without due process of law, or deny to any person within its jurisdiction the equal protection of the laws. What is this but declaring that the law in the States shall be the same for the black as for the white; that all persons, whether colored or white, shall stand equal before the laws of the States, and, in regard to the colored race, for whose protection the amendment was primarily designed, that no discrimination shall be made against them by law because of their color? The words of the amendment, it is true, are prohibitory, but they contain a necessary implication of a positive immunity, or right, most valuable to the colored race,—the right to exemption from unfriendly legislation against them distinctively as colored,—exemption from legal discriminations, implying inferiority in civil society, lessening the security of their enjoyment of the rights which others enjoy, and discriminations which are steps towards reducing them to the condition of a subject race.

That the West Virginia statute respecting juries—the statute that controlled the selection of the grand and petit jury in the case of the plaintiff in error—is such a discrimination ought not to be doubted. Nor would it be if the persons excluded by it were white men. If in those States where the colored people constitute a majority of the entire population a law should be enacted excluding all white men from jury service, thus denying to them the privilege of participating equally with the blacks in the administration of justice, we apprehend no one would be heard to claim that it would not be a denial to white men of the equal protection of the laws. Nor if a law should be passed excluding all naturalized Celtic Irishmen, would there be any doubt of its inconsistency with the spirit of the amendment. The very fact that colored people are singled out and expressly denied by a statute all right to participate in the administration of the law, as jurors, because of their color, though they are citizens, and may be in other respects fully qualified, is practically a brand upon them, affixed by the law, an assertion of their inferiority, and a stimulant to that race prejudice which is an impediment to securing to individuals of the race that equal justice which the law aims to secure to all others.

The right to a trial by jury is guaranteed to every citizen of West Virginia by the Constitution of that State, and the constitution of juries is a very essential part of the protection such a mode of trial is intended to secure. The very idea of a jury is a body of men composed of the peers or equals of the person whose rights it is selected or summoned to determine; that is, of his neighbors, fellows, associates, persons having the same legal status in society as that which he holds. Blackstone, in his Commentaries, says, "The right of trial by jury, or the country, is a trial by the peers of every Englishman, and is the grand bulwark of his liberties, and is secured to him by the Great Charter." It is also guarded by statutory enactments intended to make impossible what Mr. Bentham called "packing juries." It is well known that prejudices often exist against particular classes in the community, which sway the judgment of jurors, and which, therefore, operate in some cases to deny to persons of those classes the full enjoyment of that protection which others enjoy. Prejudice in a local community is held to be a reason for a change of venue. The framers of the constitutional amendment must have known full well the existence of such prejudice and its likelihood to continue against the manumitted slaves and their race, and that knowledge was doubtless a motive that led to the amendment. By their manumission and citizenship the colored race became entitled to the equal protection of the laws of the States in which they resided; and the apprehension that through prejudice they might be denied that equal protection, that is, that there might be discrimination against them, was the inducement to bestow upon the national government the power to enforce the provision that no State shall deny to them the equal protection of the laws. Without the apprehended existence of prejudice that portion of the amendment would have been unnecessary, and it might have been left to the States to extend equality of protection.

In view of these considerations, it is hard to see why the statute of West Virginia should not be regarded as discriminating against a colored man when he is put upon trial for an alleged criminal offence against the State. It is not easy to comprehend how it can be said that while every white man is entitled to a trial by a jury selected from persons of his own race or color, or, rather, selected without discrimination against his color, and a negro is not, the latter is equally protected by the law with the former. Is not protection of life and liberty against race or color prejudice, a right, a legal right, under the constitutional amendment? And how can it be maintained that compelling a colored man to submit to a trial for his life by a jury drawn from a panel from which the State has expressly excluded every man of his race, because of color alone, however well qualified in other respects, is not a denial to him of equal legal protection?

We do not say that within the limits from which it is not excluded by the amendment a State may not prescribe the qualifications of its jurors, and in so doing make discriminations. It may confine the selection to males, to freeholders, to citizens, to persons within certain ages, or to persons having educational qualifications. We do not believe the Fourteenth Amendment was ever intended to prohibit this. Looking at its history, it is clear it had no such purpose. Its aim was against discrimination because of race or color.

• • •

The Fourteenth Amendment makes no attempt to enumerate the rights it designed to protect. It speaks in general terms, and those are as comprehensive as possible. Its language is prohibitory; but every prohibition implies the existence of rights and immunities, prominent among which is an immunity from inequality of legal protection, either for life, liberty, or property. Any State action that denies this immunity to a colored man is in conflict with the Constitution.

[Justices Field and Clifford dissented.]

NOTES AND QUESTIONS

1. *Strauder* marks the first time the Supreme Court invalidated a state court criminal conviction. In one sense it is an easy case, as the West Virginia statute at issue explicitly excluded Black people from serving on juries. The opinion nonetheless reflects an expansive view of the Fourteenth Amendment—"[i]t speaks in general terms, and those areas are as comprehensive as possible"—and notably recognizes the "stigmatizing" effect of racial discrimination (the statute is "practically a brand upon [Black people], affixed by law").

2. What do you make of the caveats the Court includes? For example, the Court is careful to note that the issue "is not whether a colored man, when an indictment has been preferred against him, has a right to a grand or petit jury composed in whole or part of persons of his own race or color." The Court also notes that under the Fourteenth Amendment a state is free to "prescribe the qualifications of its jurors, and in doing so may make discriminations. It may confine the selection to males, to freeholders, to citizens, to persons within certain ages, or to persons having educational qualifications." Do these caveats dilute the significance of *Strauder*?

3. The Court just a year later considered a claim of racial discrimination in juror panels in a much different context in *Neal v. Delaware*, 130 U.S. 370 (1880), inasmuch as no facially discriminatory statute was at issue. In *Neal*, the state conceded that no Black people had *ever* served on grand or petit juries in the state courts of Delaware. That concession was accompanied, moreover, by the following statement from the Delaware chief justice: "[T]hat none but white men were selected is in nowise remarkable in view of the fact—too notorious to be ignored—that the great body of black men residing in this State are utterly unqualified by want of intelligence, experience, or moral integrity to sit on juries." *Id.* at 393-94. The state made no effort to rebut the defendant's allegation that, although Black people were approximately 20 percent of the population of Delaware, not a single Black person had ever served on a grand or petit jury; the state just contended that this evidence did not amount to discrimination. The state court agreed, concluding that defendant had failed to prove that Black people had been excluded from jury panels "because of their color." *Id.* at 395.

The Supreme Court held otherwise, invoking the reasoning of *Strauder*. The Court noted that the defendant's allegations coupled with the state's concession established a prima facie case of a Fourteenth Amendment violation, which the state had failed to rebut. *Id.* at 397. As to the state court's conclusion that defendant had not shown that Black people had been excluded because of their race, the Court observed:

> It was, we think, under all the circumstances, a violent presumption which the State court indulged, that such uniform exclusion of that race from juries, during a period of many years, was solely because, in the judgment of those officers, fairly exercised, the black race in Delaware were utterly disqualified, by want of intelligence, experience, or moral integrity, to sit on juries. The action of those officers in the premises is to be deemed the act of the State; and the refusal of the State court to redress the wrong by them committed was a denial of a right secured to the prisoner by the Constitution and laws of the United States.

Id. Why do you think the State might have made such an extraordinary concession in *Neal*?

4. The burden-shifting framework employed by the Court in *Neal*—where the government must rebut a prima facie case of discrimination to prove its absence—is a methodology that lay dormant for 50 years before being employed implicitly in *Norris v. Alabama*, 294 U.S. 587 (1935). And it has been used intermittently by courts in discrimination cases for the past several decades. What do you see as its pros and cons from a methodological standpoint? Are there certain factual scenarios where it makes more or less sense?

5. A less enduring aspect of *Neal*, declining over the years but never totally eliminated, is the evidence of overt racial animus by the Delaware chief justice. For another example of a law enforcement official saying the quiet part out loud, *see infra Brown v. Mississippi*, 297 U.S. 278 (1936) (conviction obtained by police admission of brutally coerced confessions violated due process).

6. In two other cases from the same approximate time period the Supreme Court overturned the convictions of Black defendants indicted by grand juries from which Black people had been systematically excluded, in circumstances where state courts had thrown transparently bogus procedural roadblocks in front of their discrimination claims. In *Carter v. Texas*, 177 U.S. 442 (1900), the trial court denied defendant's motion for leave to introduce witnesses in support of his well-founded motion to quash the indictment, noting that the defendant should have presented his claim to the grand jury at the time of its empanelment (i.e., before he was indicted and when he was presumably unaware of the existence of the empanelment of the grand jury). In *Rogers v. Alabama*, 192 U.S. 226 (1904), the trial court struck defendant's motion because the motion—at two pages—was "unnecessarily prolix."

Generally, however, challenges to discriminatory administration of juror selection practices were unsuccessful. The sad truth is that *Strauder* and *Neal* and their progeny had virtually no direct effect on the racial composition of juries in the South. Their teachings were ignored by state courts and, in the rare instances where Black people were empaneled, they could be eliminated through the exercise of peremptory challenges. *See* Benno C. Schmidt Jr., *Juries, Jurisdiction, and Race Discrimination: The Lost Promise of* Strauder v. West Virginia, 61 Tex. L. Rev. 1401, 1406-08 (1983) (footnotes omitted):

> "In the whole of Georgia & Alabama, and other Southern states not a negro juror is allowed to sit in the jury box in state courts," lamented Booker T. Washington toward the end of the nineteenth century. After his travels through the South the young Harvard historian Albert B. Hart wrote in 1912 that "Negroes, although still eligible to jury service, are rarely impaneled, even for the trial of a Negro." As late as World War II, Gunnar Myrdal could treat as a reality too obvious and accepted to require documentation that "if, as in the South, Negroes are kept out of jury service, the democratic safeguard of the jury system is easily turned into a means of minority subjugation."
>
> The exclusion of blacks was virtually total. Gilbert T. Stephenson, author of the informative 1910 study, Race Distinctions in American Law, attempted to determine how many blacks served on Southern juries by sending questionnaires to the court clerks in every Southern county in which blacks comprised more than half the population. The replies from Alabama, Florida, and Georgia indicated uniform exclusion. The court clerks from Virginia, South Carolina, Louisiana, Mississippi, and Missouri reported occasional black jurors in some counties, although uniform exclusion was said to be the rule. Kentucky and Oklahoma indicated occasional black participation on juries. Stephenson's survey was impressionistic, but it supports other reports by observers of the South in the period from roughly 1890 to 1930 that black jurors were rare indeed. Certainly the federal and state court reports are filled with cases in which black defendants protested to no avail against the unfairness of all-white grand and petit juries.

B. PEONAGE CONVICTIONS

In the 1910s the Supreme Court decided two cases involving Alabama criminal statutes that were part and parcel of the regimes of "peonage" through which most southern states had substantially re-enslaved Black people after the Civil War. State criminal justice systems were the engines of these regimes, as it was through convictions on trumped-up charges under vaguely worded and cynically targeted statutes (e.g., vagrancy) that Black people typically entered the peonage system. It is a mistake, however, to think of these cases as criminal convictions in any conventional sense: The defendants were almost always unrepresented, there were seldom jury trials, and the adjudicators were often small-town mayors or justices of the peace with connections to local business interests. *See* Benno C. Schmidt Jr., *Principle and Prejudice in the Progressive Era. Part 2: The Peonage Cases*, 82 Colum. L. Rev. 646, 650-53 (1983) (footnotes omitted):

> A more or less unbroken momentum of law and history carried peonage into the twentieth century. Despite the thirteenth amendment's command that "[n]either slavery nor involuntary servitude, except as a punishment for crime . . . shall exist within the United States," forcing blacks to work was the paramount concern of the Black Codes passed in the relaxed years of presidential reconstruction following the Civil War. Under the Codes, black males who did not enter employment contracts could be charged as criminal vagrants. Those who quit jobs for which they had contracted could be arrested and returned to their employers. Enticement laws prohibited other employers from hiring laborers already under contract. Black children could be "apprenticed" to their former masters by order of the probate courts. Indigents fined for petty offenses such as vagrancy avoided harsh punishment by contracting to work for private employers who paid their fines, and the force of the state's criminal law fell behind the employment obligation.
>
> . . .
>
> The pinnacle of the system of servitude during Reconstruction and after was convict labor. The convicts were leased to private interests by the state, toiled on state or county chain gangs,

Chain gang circa 1898

or were forced into criminal surety contracts under which a period of servitude for a private employer was exchanged for the wherewithal to pay a fine levied as a result of a criminal conviction often based on petty or trumped-up charges. The practice of leasing convicts began during Reconstruction when large numbers of blacks became convicts for the first time. Leased convict labor was the shame of the South.

...

The exhausting cruelty of the penal system made almost any private servitude preferable. To avoid the chain gang, black convicts signed up with private employers who would pay their fines in return for much longer periods of forced labor. But the chain gang buttressed the system of involuntary servitude even with regard to those blacks never caught in the toils of Southern justice. Contract breaches, switching jobs, failure to pay debts and simple idleness were surrounded with the threat of false accusations and criminal sanctions—a potent weapon in the hands of white employers who sought to bend blacks to their bidding.

Bailey v. Alabama

219 U.S. 219 (1911)

Mr. Justice Hughes delivered the opinion of the court:

This is a writ of error to review a judgment of the supreme court of the state of Alabama, affirming a judgment of conviction in the Montgomery city court. The statute upon which the conviction was based is assailed as in violation of the 14th Amendment of the Constitution of the United States upon the ground that it deprived the plaintiff in error of his liberty without due process of law and denied him the equal protection of the laws, and also of the 13th Amendment, and of the act of Congress providing for the enforcement of that Amendment, in that the effect of the statute is to enforce involuntary servitude by compelling personal service in liquidation of a debt.

The statute in question is § 4730 of the Code of Alabama of 1896, as amended in 1903 and 1907. The section of the Code as it stood before the amendments provided that any person who, with intent to injure or defraud his employer, entered into a written contract for service, and thereby obtained from his employer money or other personal property, and with like intent and without just cause, and without refunding the money or paying for the property, refused to perform the service, should be punished as if he had stolen it. In 1903 the section was amended so as to make the refusal or failure to perform the service, or to refund the money, or pay for the property, without just cause, prima facie evidence of the intent to injure or defraud. This amendment was enlarged by that of 1907. The section, thus amended, reads as follows:

> Any person who, with intent to injure or defraud his employer, enters into a contract in writing for the performance of any act of service, and thereby obtains money or other personal property from such employer, and with like intent, and without just cause, and without refunding such money, or paying for such property, refuses or fails to perform such act or service, must on conviction be punished by a fine in double the damage suffered by the injured party, but not more than $300, one half of said fine to go to the county and one half to the party injured; and any person who, with intent to injure or defraud his landlord, enters into any contract in writing for the rent of land, and thereby obtains any money or other personal property from such landlord, and with like intent, without just cause, and without refunding such money, or paying for such property, refuses or fails to cultivate such land, or to comply with his contract relative thereto, must on conviction be punished by fine in double the damage suffered by the injured party, but not more than $300, one half of said fine to go to the county and one half to the party injured. And the refusal or failure of any person, who enters into such contract, to perform such act or service, or to cultivate such land, or refund such money, or pay for such property, without just

> cause, shall be prima facie evidence of the intent to injure his employer or landlord or defraud him. That all laws and parts of laws in conflict with the provisions hereof be and the same are hereby repealed.

There is also a rule of evidence enforced by the courts of Alabama which must be regarded as having the same effect as if read into the statute itself, that the accused, for the purpose of rebutting the statutory presumption, shall not be allowed to testify "as to his uncommunicated motives, purpose, or intention."

Bailey, the plaintiff in error, was committed for detention on the charge of obtaining $15 under a contract in writing with intent to injure or defraud his employer. He sued out a writ of habeas corpus, challenging the validity of the statute. His discharge was refused, and the supreme court of the state affirmed the order, holding the statute to be constitutional. On writ of error from this court it was held that the case was brought here prematurely, and the questions now presented were expressly reserved.

Having failed to obtain his release on habeas corpus, Bailey was indicted on the following charge:

> The grand jury of said county charge that before the finding of this indictment Alonzo Bailey, with intent to injure or defraud his employer, the Riverside Company, a corporation, entered into a written contract to perform labor or services for the Riverside Company, a corporation, and obtained thereby the sum of $15 from the said the Riverside Company, and afterwards with like intent, and without just cause, failed or refused to perform such labor or services, or to refund such money, against the peace and dignity of the state of Alabama.

Motion to quash and a demurrer to the indictment were overruled. Upon the trial the following facts appeared: On December 26, 1907, Bailey entered into a written contract with the Riverside Company, which provided:

> That I, Lonzo Bailey, for and in consideration of the sum of $15 in money, this day in hand paid to me by said the Riverside Company, the receipt whereof I do hereby acknowledge, I, the said Lonzo Bailey, do hereby consent, contract, and agree to work and labor for the said Riverside Company as a farm hand on their Scott's Bend place in Montgomery county, Alabama, from the 30 day of December, 1907, to the 30 day of December, 1908, at and for the sum of $12 per month.
>
> And the said Lonzo Bailey agrees to render respectful and faithful service to the said the Riverside Company, and to perform diligently and actively all work pertaining to such employment, in accordance with the instructions of the said the Riverside Company or agent.
>
> And the said the Riverside Company, in consideration of the agreement above mentioned of the said Lonzo Bailey, hereby employs the said Lonzo Bailey as such farm hand for the time above set out, and agrees to pay the said Lonzo Bailey the sum of $10.75 per month.

The manager of the employing company testified that at the time of entering into this contract there were present only the witness and Bailey, and that the latter then obtained from the company the sum of $15; that Bailey worked under the contract throughout the month of January and for three or four days in February, 1908, and then, "without just cause, and without refunding the money, ceased to work for said Riverside Company, and has not since that time performed any service for said company in accordance with or under said contract, and has refused and failed to perform any further service thereunder, and has, without just cause, refused and failed to refund said $15." He also testified, in response to a question from the attorney for the defendant, and against the objection of the state, that Bailey was a negro. No other evidence was introduced.

The court, after defining the crime in the language of the statute, charged the jury, in accordance with its terms, as follows:

> And the refusal of any person who enters into such contract to perform such act or service, or refund such money, or pay for such property, without just cause, shall be prima facie evidence of the intent to injure his employer, or to defraud him.

Bailey excepted to these instructions, and requested the court to instruct the jury that the statute and the provision creating the presumption were invalid, and further that "the refusal or failure of the defendant to perform the service alleged in the indictment, or to refund the money obtained from the Riverside Company under the contract between it and the defendant, without cause, does not of itself make out a prima facie case of the defendant's intent to injure or defraud said Riverside Company."

The court refused these instructions and Bailey took exception.

The jury found the accused guilty, fixed the damages sustained by the injured party at $15, and assessed a fine of $30. Thereupon Bailey was sentenced by the court to pay the fine of $30 and the costs, and in default thereof to hard labor "for twenty days in lieu of said fine, and one hundred and sixteen days on account of said costs."

On appeal to the supreme court of the state, the constitutionality of the statute was again upheld and the judgment affirmed.

We at once dismiss from consideration the fact that the plaintiff in error is a black man. While the action of a state, through its officers charged with the administration of a law fair in appearance, may be of such a character as to constitute a denial of the equal protection of the laws (*Yick Wo v. Hopkins*), such a conclusion is here neither required nor justified. The statute, on its face, makes no racial discrimination, and the record fails to show its existence in fact. No question of a sectional character is presented, and we may view the legislation in the same manner as if it had been enacted in New York or in Idaho. Opportunities for coercion and oppression, in varying circumstances, exist in all parts of the Union, and the citizens of all the states are interested in the maintenance of the constitutional guaranties, the consideration of which is here involved.

Prior to the amendment of the year 1903, enlarged in 1907, the statute did not make the mere breach of the contract, under which the employee had obtained from his employer money which was not refunded or property which was not paid for, a crime. The essential ingredient of the offense was the intent of the accused to injure or defraud. To justify conviction, it was necessary that this intent should be established by competent evidence, aided only by such inferences as might logically be derived from the facts proved, and should not be the subject of mere surmise or arbitrary assumption.

This was the construction which the supreme court of Alabama placed upon the statute, as it then stood. . . .

We pass, then, to the consideration of the amendment, through the operation of which under the charge of the trial court this conviction was obtained. No longer was it necessary for the prosecution to comply with the rule of the Riley Case (supra) in order to establish the intent to injure or defraud which, as the court said, constituted the gist of the offense. It was "the difficulty in proving the intent, made patent by that decision," which "suggested the amendment of 1903." By this amendment it was provided, in substance, that the refusal or failure to perform the service contracted for, or to refund the money obtained, without just cause, should be prima facie evidence of the intent to injure or defraud.

But the refusal or failure to perform the service, without just cause, constitutes the breach of the contract. The justice of the grounds of refusal or failure must, of course, be determined by the contractual obligation assumed. Whatever the reason for leaving the service, if, judged by the terms of the contract, it is insufficient in law, it is not "just cause." The money received and repayable, nothing more being shown, constitutes a mere debt. The asserted difficulty of proving the intent to injure or defraud is thus made the occasion for dispensing with such proof so far as the prima facie case is concerned. And the mere breach of a contract for personal service, coupled with the mere failure to pay a debt which was to be liquidated in the course of such service, is made sufficient to warrant a conviction.

It is no answer to say that the jury must find, and here found, that a fraudulent intent existed. The jury by their verdict cannot add to the facts before them. If nothing be shown but a mere breach of a contract of service and a mere failure to pay a debt, the jury have nothing else to go upon, and the evidence becomes nothing more because of their finding. Had it not been for this statutory presumption, supplied by the amendment, no one would be heard to say that Bailey could have been convicted.

Prima facie evidence is sufficient evidence to outweigh the presumption of innocence, and if not met by opposing evidence, to support a verdict of guilty. "It is such as, in judgment of law, is sufficient to establish the fact; and, if not rebutted, remains sufficient for the purpose."

We are not impressed with the argument that the supreme court of Alabama has construed the amendment to mean that the jury is not controlled by the presumption, if unrebutted, and still may find the accused not guilty. That court, in its opinion, said: "Again, it must be borne in mind that the rule of evidence fixed by the statute does not make it the duty of the jury to convict on the evidence referred to in the enactment, if unrebutted, whether satisfied thereby of the guilt of the accused beyond a reasonable doubt or not. On the contrary, with such evidence before them, the jury are still left free to find the accused guilty or not guilty, according as they may be satisfied of his guilt or not, by the whole evidence."

But the controlling construction of the statute is the affirmance of this judgment of conviction. It is not sufficient to declare that the statute does not make it the duty of the jury to convict, where there is no other evidence but the breach of the contract and the failure to pay the debt. The point is that, in such a case, the statute authorizes the jury to convict. It is not enough to say that the jury may not accept that evidence as alone sufficient; for the jury may accept it, and they have the express warrant of the statute to accept it as a basis for their verdict. And it is in this light that the validity of the statute must be determined.

It is urged that the time and circumstances of the departure from service may be such as to raise not only an inference, but a strong inference, of fraudulent intent. There was no need to create a statutory presumption, and it was not created for such a case. Where circumstances are shown permitting a fair inference of fraudulent purpose, the case falls within the rule of *Ex parte Riley* (supra), which governed prosecutions under the statute before the amendment was made. The "difficulty," which admittedly the amendment was intended to surmount, did not exist where natural inferences sufficed. Plainly, the object of the statute was to hit cases which were destitute of such inferences, and to provide that the mere breach of the contract and the mere failure to pay the debt might do duty in their absence.

While, in considering the natural operation and effect of the statute, as amended, we are not limited to the particular facts of the case at the bar, they present an illuminating illustration. We may briefly restate them. Bailey made a contract to work for a year at $12 a month. He received $15, and he was to work this out, being entitled monthly only to $10.75 of his wages. No one was present when he made the contract but himself and the manager of the employing company. There is not a particle of evidence of any circumstance indicating that he made the contract or received the money with any intent to injure or defraud his employer. On the contrary, he actually worked for upwards of a month. His motive in leaving does not appear, the only showing being that it was without legal excuse and that he did not repay the money received. For this he is sentenced to a fine of $30 and to imprisonment at hard labor, in default of the payment of the fine and costs, for 136 days. Was not the case the same in effect as if the statute had made it a criminal act to leave the service without just cause and without liquidating the debt? To say that he has been found guilty of an intent to injure or defraud his employer, and not merely for breaking his contract and not paying his debt, is a distinction without a difference to Bailey.

Consider the situation of the accused under this statutory presumption. If, at the outset, nothing took place but the making of the contract and the receipt of the money, he could show nothing else. If there was no legal justification for his leaving his employment, he could show none. If he had not paid the debt, there was nothing to be said as to that. The law of the state did not permit him to testify that he did not intend to injure or defraud. Unless he were fortunate enough to be able to command evidence of circumstances affirmatively showing good faith, he was helpless. He stood, stripped by the statute of the presumption of innocence, and exposed to conviction for fraud upon evidence only of breach of contract and failure to pay.

It is said that we may assume that a fair jury would convict only where the circumstances sufficiently indicated a fraudulent intent. Why should this be assumed in the face of the statute and upon this record? In the present case the jury did convict, although there is an absence of evidence sufficient to establish fraud under the familiar rule that fraud will not be presumed, and the obvious explanation of the verdict is that the trial court, in accordance with the statute, charged the jury that refusal to perform the service, or to repay the money, without just cause, constituted prima facie evidence of the commission of the offense which the statute defined. That is, the jury were told in effect that the evidence, under the statutory rule, was sufficient, and hence they treated it as such. There is no basis for an assumption that the jury would have acted differently if Bailey had worked for three months, or six months, or nine months, if in fact his debt had not been paid. The normal assumption is that the jury will follow the statute, and, acting in accordance with the authority it confers, will accept as sufficient what the statute expressly so describes.

It may further be observed that under the statute, there is no punishment for the alleged fraud if the service is performed or the money refunded. If the service is rendered in liquidation of the debt, there is no punishment; and if it is not rendered, and the money is not refunded, that fact alone is sufficient for conviction. By a statute passed by the legislature of Alabama in 1901, it was made a misdemeanor for any person who had made a written contract to labor for or serve another for any given time, to leave the service before the expiration of the contract, and without the consent of the employer, and to make a second contract of similar nature with another person without giving the second employer notice of the existence of the first contract. This was held unconstitutional upon the ground that it interfered with freedom of contract. But, judging it by its necessary operation and obvious effect, the fundamental purpose plainly was to compel, under the sanction of the criminal law, the enforcement of the contract for personal service, and the same purpose, tested by like criteria, breathes despite its different phraseology through the amendments of 1903 and 1907 of the statute here in question.

We cannot escape the conclusion that, although the statute in terms is to punish fraud, still its natural and inevitable effect is to expose to conviction for crime those who simply fail or refuse to perform contracts for personal service in liquidation of a debt; and judging its purpose by its effect, that it seeks in this way to provide the means of compulsion through which performance of such service may be secured. The question is whether such a statute is constitutional.

This court has frequently recognized the general power of every legislature to prescribe the evidence which shall be received, and the effect of that evidence, in the courts of its own government. In the exercise of this power numerous statutes have been enacted providing that proof of one fact shall be prima facie evidence of the main fact in issue; and where the inference is not purely arbitrary, and there is a rational relation between the two facts, and the accused is not deprived of a proper opportunity to submit all the facts bearing upon the issue, it has been held that such statutes do not violate the requirements of due process of law.

The latest expression upon this point is found in the case last cited, where the court, by Mr. Justice Lurton, said: "That a legislative presumption of one fact from evidence of another may not constitute a denial of due process of law, or a denial of the equal protection of the law, it is only essential that there shall be some rational connection between the fact proved and the ultimate fact presumed, and that the inference of one fact from proof of another shall not be so unreasonable as to be a purely arbitrary mandate. So, also, it must not, under guise of regulating the presentation of evidence, operate to preclude the party from the right to present his defense to the main fact thus presumed. If a legislative provision not unreasonable in itself, prescribing a rule of evidence, in either criminal or civil cases, does not shut out from the party affected a reasonable opportunity to submit to the jury in his defense all of the facts bearing upon the issue, there is no ground for holding that due process of law has been denied him."

In this class of cases where the entire subject-matter of the legislation is otherwise within state control, the question has been whether the prescribed rule of evidence interferes with the guaranteed equality before the law, or violates those fundamental rights and immutable principles of justice which are embraced within the conception of due process of law. But where the conduct or fact, the existence of which is made the basis of the statutory presumption, itself falls within the scope of a provision of the Federal Constitution, a further question arises. It is apparent that a constitutional prohibition cannot be transgressed indirectly by the creation of a statutory presumption any more than it can be violated by direct enactment. The power to create presumptions is not a means of escape from constitutional restrictions. And the state may not in this way interfere with matters withdrawn from its authority by the Federal Constitution, or subject an accused to conviction for conduct which it is powerless to proscribe.

In the present case it is urged that the statute as amended, through the operation of the presumption for which it provides, violates the 13th Amendment of the Constitution of the United States and the act of Congress passed for its enforcement.

The 13th Amendment provides:

> Section 1. Neither slavery nor involuntary servitude, except as a punishment for crime whereof the party shall have been duly convicted, shall exist within the United States, or any place subject to their jurisdiction.
>
> Section 2. Congress shall have power to enforce this article by appropriate legislation.

Pursuant to the authority thus conferred, Congress passed the [Antipeonage Act], as follows:

> Sec. 1990. The holding of any person to service or labor under the system known as peonage is abolished and forever prohibited in the territory of New Mexico, or in any other territory or state of the United States; and all acts, laws, resolutions, orders, regulations, or usages of the territory of New Mexico, or of any other territory or state, which have heretofore established, maintained, or enforced, or by virtue of which any attempt shall hereafter be made to establish, maintain, or enforce, directly or indirectly, the voluntary or involuntary service or labor of any persons as peons, in liquidation of any debt or obligation, or otherwise, are declared null and void.
>
> Sec. 5526. Every person who holds, arrests, returns, or causes to be held, arrested, or returned, or in any manner aids in the arrest or return, of any person to a condition of peonage, shall be punished by a fine of not less than one thousand nor more than five thousand dollars, or by imprisonment not less than one year nor more than five years, or by both.

The language of the 13th Amendment was not new. It reproduced the historic words of the ordinance of 1787 for the government of the Northwest territory, and gave them unrestricted application within the United States and all places subject to their jurisdiction. While the immediate concern was with African slavery, the Amendment was not limited to that. It was a charter of universal civil freedom for all persons, of whatever race, color, or estate, under the flag.

The words involuntary servitude have a "larger meaning than slavery."

"It was very well understood that, in the form of apprenticeship for long terms, as it had been practiced in the West India Islands, on the abolition of slavery by the English government, or by reducing the slaves to the condition of serfs attached to the plantation, the purpose of the article might have been evaded, if only the word 'slavery' had been used." The plain intention was to abolish slavery of whatever name and form and all its badges and incidents; to render impossible any state of bondage; to make labor free, by prohibiting that control by which the personal service of one man is disposed of or coerced for another's benefit, which is the essence of involuntary servitude.

While the Amendment was self-executing, so far as its terms were applicable to any existing condition, Congress was authorized to secure its complete enforcement by appropriate legislation. As was said in the Civil Rights Cases: "By its own unaided force and effect it abolished slavery, and established universal freedom. Still, legislation may be necessary and proper to meet all the various cases and circumstances to be affected by it, and to prescribe proper modes of redress for its violation in letter or spirit. And such legislation may be primary and direct in its character; for the Amendment is not a mere prohibition of state laws establishing or upholding slavery, but an absolute declaration that slavery or involuntary servitude shall not exist in any part of the United States."

The [Antipeonage Act] was a valid exercise of this express authority. It declared that all laws of any state, by virtue of which any attempt should be made "to establish, maintain, or enforce, directly or indirectly, the voluntary or involuntary service or labor of any person as peons, in liquidation of any debt or obligation, or otherwise," should be null and void.

Peonage is a term descriptive of a condition which has existed in Spanish America, and especially in Mexico. The essence of the thing is compulsory service in payment of a debt. A peon is one who is compelled to work for his creditor until his debt is paid. And in this explicit and comprehensive enactment, Congress was not concerned with mere names or manner of description, or with a particular place or section of the country. It was concerned with a fact, wherever it might exist; with a condition, however named and wherever it might be established, maintained, or enforced.

The fact that the debtor contracted to perform the labor which is sought to be compelled does not withdraw the attempted enforcement from the condemnation of the statute. The full intent of the constitutional provision could be defeated with obvious facility if, through the guise of contracts under which advances had been made, debtors could be held to compulsory service. It is the compulsion of the service that the statute inhibits, for when that occurs, the condition of servitude is created, which would be not less involuntary because of the original agreement to work out the indebtedness. The contract exposes the debtor to liability for the loss due to the breach, but not to enforced labor.

• • •

The act of Congress, nullifying all state laws by which it should be attempted to enforce the "service or labor of any persons as peons, in liquidation of any debt or obligation, or otherwise," necessarily embraces all legislation which seeks to compel the service or labor by making it a crime to refuse or fail to perform it. Such laws would furnish the readiest means of compulsion. The 13th Amendment prohibits involuntary servitude except as punishment for crime. But the exception, allowing full latitude for the enforcement of penal laws, does not destroy the prohibition. It does not permit slavery or involuntary servitude to be established or maintained through the operation of the criminal law by making it a crime to refuse to submit to the one or to render the service which would constitute the other. The state may impose involuntary servitude as a punishment for crime, but it may not compel one man to labor for another in payment of a debt, by punishing him as a criminal if he does not perform the service or pay the debt.

If the statute in this case had authorized the employing company to seize the debtor, and hold him to the service until he paid the $15, or had furnished the equivalent in labor, its invalidity would not be questioned. It would be equally clear that the state could not authorize its constabulary to prevent the servant from escaping, and to force him to work out his debt. But the state could not avail itself of the sanction of the criminal law to supply the compulsion any more than it could use or authorize the use of physical force. "In contemplation of the law, the compulsion to such service by the fear of punishment under a criminal statute is more powerful than any guard which the employer could station."

What the state may not do directly it may not do indirectly. If it cannot punish the servant as a criminal for the mere failure or refusal to serve without paying his debt, it is not permitted to accomplish the same result by creating a statutory presumption which, upon proof of no other fact, exposes him to conviction and punishment. Without imputing any actual motive to oppress, we must consider the natural operation of the statute here in question, and it is apparent that it furnishes a convenient instrument for the coercion which the Constitution and the act of Congress forbid; an instrument of compulsion peculiarly effective as against the poor and the ignorant, its most likely victims. There is no more important concern than to safeguard the freedom of labor upon which alone can enduring prosperity be based. The provision designed to secure it would soon become a barren form if it were possible to establish a statutory presumption of this sort, and to hold over the heads of laborers the threat of punishment for crime, under the name of fraud, but merely upon evidence of failure to work out their debts. The act of Congress deprives of effect all legislative measures of any state through which, directly or indirectly, the prohibited thing, to wit, compulsory service to secure the payment of a debt, may be established or maintained; and we conclude that § 4730, as amended, of the Code of Alabama, in so far as it makes the refusal or failure to perform the act or service, without refunding the money or paying for the property prima facie evidence of the commission received of the crime which the section defines, is in conflict with the 13th Amendment, and the legislation authorized by that Amendment, and is therefore invalid.

• • •

Mr. Justice HOLMES, dissenting:

We all agree that this case is to be considered and decided in the same way as if it arose in Idaho or New York. Neither public document nor evidence discloses a law which, by its administration, is made something different from what it appears on its face, and therefore the fact that in Alabama it mainly concerns the blacks does not matter. *Yick Wo v. Hopkins* does not apply. I shall begin, then, by assuming for the moment what I think is not true, and shall try to show not to be true, that this statute punishes the mere refusal to labor according to contract as a crime, and shall inquire whether there would be anything contrary to the 13th Amendment or the statute if it did, supposing it to have been enacted in the state of New York. I cannot believe it. The 13th Amendment does not outlaw contracts for labor. That would be at least as great a misfortune for the laborer as for the man that employed him. For it certainly would affect the terms of the bargain unfavorably for the laboring man if it were understood that the employer could do nothing in case the laborer saw fit to break his word. But any legal liability for breach of a contract is a disagreeable consequence which tends to make the contractor do as he said he would. Liability to an action for damages has that tendency as well a fine. If the mere imposition of such consequences as tend to make a man keep to his promise is the creation of peonage when the contract happens to be for labor, I do not see why the allowance of a civil action is not, as well as an indictment ending in fine. Peonage is service to a private master at which a man is kept by bodily compulsion against his will. But the creation of the ordinary legal motives for right conduct does not produce it. Breach of a legal contract without excuse is wrong conduct, even if the contract is for labor; and if a state adds to civil liability a criminal liability to fine, it simply intensifies the legal motive for doing right; it does not make the laborer a slave.

But if a fine may be imposed, imprisonment may be imposed in case of a failure to pay it. Nor does it matter if labor is added to the imprisonment. Imprisonment with hard labor is not stricken from the statute books. On the contrary, involuntary servitude as a punishment for crime is excepted from the prohibition of the 13th Amendment in so many words. Also the power of the states to make breach of contract a crime is not done away with by the abolition of slavery. But if breach of contract may be made a crime at all, it may be made a crime with all the consequences usually attached to crime. There is produced a sort of illusion if a contract to labor ends in compulsory labor in a prison. But compulsory work for no private master in a jail is not peonage. If work in a jail is not condemned in itself, without regard to what the conduct is it punishes, it may be made a consequence of any conduct that the state has power to punish at all. I do not blink the fact that the liability to imprisonment may work as a motive when a fine without it would not, and that it may induce the laborer to keep on when he would like to leave. But it does not strike me as an objection to a law that it is effective. If the contract is one that ought not to be made, prohibit it. But if it is a perfectly fair and proper contract, I can see no reason why the state should not throw its weight on the side of performance. There is no relation between its doing so in the manner supposed, and allowing a private master to use private force upon a laborer who wishes to leave.

But all that I have said so far goes beyond the needs of the case as I understand it. I think it a mistake to say that this statute attaches its punishment to the mere breach of a contract to labor. It does not purport to do so; what it purports to punish is fraudulently obtaining money by a false pretense of an intent to keep the written contract in consideration of which the money is advanced. (It is not necessary to cite cases to show that such an intent may be the subject of a material false representation.) But the import of the statute is supposed to be changed by the provision, that a refusal to perform, coupled with a failure to return the money advanced, shall be prima facie evidence of fraudulent intent. I agree that if the statute created a conclusive presumption, it might be held to make a disguised change in the substantive law. But it only makes the conduct prima facie evidence—a very different matter. Is it not evidence that a man had a fraudulent intent if he receives an advance upon a contract over night and leaves in the morning? I should have thought that it very plainly was. Of course, the statute is in general terms, and applies to a departure at any time without excuse or repayment, but that does no harm except on a tacit assumption that this law is not administered as it would be in New York, and that juries will act with prejudice against the laboring man. For prima facie evidence is only evidence, and as such may be held by the jury insufficient to make out guilt. This was decided by the supreme court of Alabama in this case, and we should be bound by their construction of the statute, even if we thought it wrong. But I venture to add that I think it entirely right. This being so, I take it that a fair jury would acquit, if the only evidence were a departure after eleven months' work, and if it received no color from some special well-known course of events. But the matter well may be left to a jury, because their experience as men of the world may teach them that in certain conditions it is so common for laborers to remain during a part of the season, receiving advances, and then to depart at the period of need, in the hope of greater wages at a neighboring plantation, that when a laborer follows that course there is a fair inference of fact that he intended it from the beginning.

The Alabama statute, as construed by the state court and as we must take it, merely says, as a court might say, that the prosecution may go to the jury. This means, and means only, that the court cannot say, from its knowledge of the ordinary course of events, that the jury could not be justified by its knowledge in drawing the inference from the facts proved. In my opinion, the statute embodies little if anything more than what I should have told the jury was the law without it. The right of the state to regulate laws of evidence is admitted, and the statute does not go much beyond the common law.

I do not see how the result that I have reached thus far is affected by the rule laid down by the court, but not contained in the statute, that the prisoner cannot testify to his uncommunicated intentions, and therefore, it is assumed, would not be permitted to offer a naked denial of an intent to defraud. If there is an excuse for breaking the contract, it will be found in external circumstances, and can be proved. So the sum of the wrong supposed to be inflicted is that the intent to go off without repaying may be put further back than it would be otherwise. But if there is a wrong it lies in leaving the evidence to the jury—a wrong that is not affected by the letting in or keeping out an item of evidence on the other side. I have stated why I think it was not a wrong.

To sum up, I think that obtaining money by fraud may be made a crime as well as murder or theft; that a false representation, expressed or implied, at the time of making a contract of labor, that one intends to perform it, and thereby obtaining an advance, may be declared a case of fraudulently obtaining money as well as any other; that if made a crime it may be punished like any other crime; and that an unjustified departure from the promised service without repayment may be declared a sufficient case to go to the jury for their judgment; all without in any way infringing the 13th Amendment or the statutes of the United States.

Mr. Justice LURTON concurs in this dissent.

NOTES AND QUESTIONS

1. The Court is at pains to ignore the elephant in the room: that *Bailey* is a race case. Indeed, *Bailey* is not just a case about race but a case where the conviction at the heart of the case is emblematic of the means by which Black people were re-enslaved after the Civil War. It would be odd enough if the Court simply ignored the racial dimension of the case but it goes further, affirmatively denying that race is a factor. *See id.* at 231 ("We at once dismiss from consideration the fact that the plaintiff in error is a black man. . . . The statute, on its face, makes no racial discrimination, and the record fails to show its existence in fact. No question of a sectional character is presented and we may view the legislation in the same manner as if it had been enacted in New York or in Idaho."). Idaho had been admitted to the Union in 1890, 25 years after the end of the Civil War, as the forty-third state. The dissent also accepts this premise: "that in Alabama [the statute] mainly concerns the blacks does not matter." *Id.* at 245 (Holmes, J., dissenting).

2. Why did the Court pretend this was not a race case? The southern peonage system at issue had by the time *Bailey* was decided in 1911 been the subject of wide reporting. The racial aspect of this particular case was no secret, moreover. The press covered it as a race case. And both the defendant and the United States as amicus in their briefs emphasized the racial impact of the Alabama statute. As the Court points out, at trial Bailey's attorney asked just one question of the government's sole witness, the manager of the company that had employed Bailey: whether Bailey was a Negro. And the United States' brief argued that all reported convictions under the statute were of farm laborers, the majority of whom were Black, and that the law thus violated the rule of *Yick Wo v. Hopkins*, 118 U.S. 356 (1886), imposing coercive legal burdens on a particular class "with an evil eye and an unequal hand."

3. Before reaching the federal statutory and constitutional issues, the Court addressed the statute's rebuttable presumption—that intent to defraud can be inferred from the mere fact of the breach of a labor contract—a presumption that the Alabama legislature had added to the statute after a prior version that criminalized a contractual breach itself was struck down by the Alabama Supreme Court. *Ex parte Riley*, 94 Ala. 82, 83 (1891). The Court concludes that inasmuch as the statute *authorizes* conviction without evidence of fraud that "its natural purpose and effect is to expose to conviction for crime those who simply fail or refuse to perform contracts for personal service . . . [and thereby] provide[s] the means of compulsion through which performance of such service is secured." 219 U.S. at 238. In his dissent Justice Holmes takes issue with this characterization, and points out factual scenarios where "a fair jury would acquit" notwithstanding the presumption. Does the dissent have a valid point? Is it possible for defendants to rebut the presumption? How so? Are these hypotheticals relevant given that in Bailey's case the only evidence of fraud was his breach of the contract? Note that Justice Holmes also chastises the majority, despite its disclaimers, for proceeding on "the tacit assumption that this law is not administered as it would be in New York, and that juries will act with prejudice against the laboring men." Fair point?

4. Once the Court had declared the "natural and inevitable effect" of the statute it had little trouble finding that it violated both the Antipeonage Act and the Thirteenth Amendment. In consecutive sentences the Court was able to both hint at the known but unstated premises of the statute and also dress its decision in the garb of laissez-faire economics:

> What the state may not do directly it may not do indirectly. If it cannot punish the servant as a criminal for the mere failure or refusal to serve without paying his debt, it is not permitted to accomplish the same result by creating a statutory presumption which, upon proof of no other fact, exposes him to conviction and punishment. Without imputing any actual motive to oppress, we must consider the natural operation of the statute here in question . . ., and it is apparent that it furnishes a convenient instrument for coercion which the Constitution and the act of Congress forbid; an instrument of compulsion peculiarly effective as against the poor and the ignorant, its most likely victims. There is no more important concern than to safeguard the freedom of labor upon which alone can enduring prosperity be based.

Id. at 244-45. Why the paean to "freedom of labor," a theme that had scarcely been implied in the opinion prior to this punch line?

5. Justice Holmes rejected the premise that the state could not criminalize the breach of a labor contract. *Id.* at 246-47. In rigidly moralistic fashion he reasoned, "[b]reach of a legal contract without excuse is wrong conduct, even if the contract is for labor; and if a state adds to civil liability a criminal liability to fine, it simply intensifies the legal motive for doing right; it does not make the laborer a slave." *Id.* at 246. Does this strike you as correct? Are there constitutional limits on the type of conduct a state can criminalize?

Just three years after *Bailey*, in *United States v. Reynolds*, 235 U.S. 133 (1914), the Court considered a different aspect of Alabama's neoslavery regime, namely, its criminal-surety system. Under this system a criminal defendant would "confess judgment" to a charge and an employer would step in to pay the defendant's fines and court costs in exchange for entering into a labor contract with the employer to pay off the debt. Breach of such a labor contract was itself a crime, enforceable by the employer. The defendant's motivation in agreeing to the surety arrangement was usually to avoid the alternative of the dreaded chain gang.

In *Reynolds*, the defendant employer was indicted for violating the federal Antipeonage Act. He had entered into a surety relationship on behalf of Rivers, who had been convicted of petit larceny and fined $15 with $43.75 of costs. Reynolds paid these amounts to the court and Rivers contracted with Reynolds to work for him as a farmhand for 9 months and 24 days at the rate of $6 a month. After about a month, Rivers stopped working and was arrested upon a warrant initiated by Reynolds, charging him with violating the labor contract. He was convicted on the charge, and fined one cent with $87.05 in costs. He again confessed judgment and entered into contract with a second defendant employer to work for 14 months and 15 days at the same rate. *Id.* at 139-40.

While acknowledging that the Thirteenth Amendment explicitly authorized involuntary servitude as punishment for crime, the Court found the surety arrangement in violation of both the Amendment and the statute, as by criminalizing a breach of a labor contract the state requires the worker "under pain of recurring prosecutions [to] be kept at labor, to satisfy the demands of the employer." *Id.* at 150. The majority opinion did not say a word about race.

The decision was unanimous, although Holmes added a one-paragraph concurrence, apparently to explain his deviation from his position in *Bailey*:

> There seems to me nothing in the 13th Amendment or the Revised Statutes that prevents a state from making a breach of contract, as well a reasonable contract for labor as for other matters, a crime and punishing it as such. But impulsive people with little intelligence or foresight may be expected to lay hold of anything that affords a relief from present pain, even though it will cause greater trouble by and by. The successive contracts, each for a longer term than the last, are the inevitable, and must be taken to have been the contemplated, outcome of the Alabama laws. On this ground I am inclined to agree that the statutes in question disclosed the attempt to maintain service that the Revised Statutes forbid.

Justice Holmes's petulant little paragraph is remarkable. Having been unwilling to acknowledge and explicitly disavowing the racial backdrop of the criminal regime at issue in *Bailey*, he relies overtly on a repugnant racial stereotype to justify his agreement with the majority in *Reynolds*. Rather than condemn the white Alabamans who established the criminal-surety system — a system that he seems to acknowledge was intended to doom Black people to successive periods of servitude — he castigates Black people for needing special dispensation from otherwise sound economic principles.

The Court's decisions in *Bailey* and *Reynolds* did not, to say the least, put an end to peonage in the South. While the Great Migration of Black people from the South to the North and a lessened demand for manual labor in the following decades decreased the extent of the practice, vestiges of the practice continued into the 1960s. *See* Tamar R. Birckhead, *The New Peonage*, 72 Wash. & Lee L. Rev. 1595, 1625-26 (2015).

As the next case shows, not only did peonage systems continue into the middle of the twentieth century, some southern courts and legislatures aided and abetted their survival by ignoring or disingenuously interpreting Supreme Court precedent.

Pollock v. Williams

322 U.S. 4 (1942)

Mr. Justice Jackson delivered the opinion of the Court.

Appellant Pollock questions the validity of a statute of the State of Florida making it a misdemeanor to induce advances with intent to defraud by a promise to perform labor and further making failure to perform labor for which money has been obtained prima facie evidence of intent to defraud. It conflicts, he says, with the Thirteenth Amendment to the Federal Constitution and with the antipeonage statute enacted by Congress thereunder. Claims also are made under the due process and equal protection clauses of the Fourteenth Amendment which we find it unnecessary to consider.

Pollock was arrested January 5, 1943, on a warrant issued three days before which charged that on the 17th of October, 1942, he did "with intent to injure and defraud under and by reason of a contract and promise to perform labor and service, procure and obtain money, to-wit: the sum of $5.00, as advances from one J. V. O'Albora, a corporation, contrary to the statute in such cases made and provided, and against the peace and dignity of the State of Florida." He was taken before the county judge on the same day, entered a plea of guilty, and was sentenced to pay a fine of $100 and in default to serve sixty days in the county jail. He was immediately committed.

On January 11, 1943, a writ of habeas corpus was issued by the judge of the circuit court, directed to the jail keeper, who is appellee here. Petition for the writ challenged the constitutionality of the statutes under which Pollock was confined and set forth that "at the trial aforesaid, he was not told that he was entitled to counsel, and that counsel would be provided for him if he wished, and he did not know that he had such right. Petitioner was without funds and unable to employ counsel. He further avers that he did not understand the nature of the charge against him, but understood that if he owed any money to his prior employer and had quit his employment without paying the same, he was guilty, which facts he admitted." The Sheriff's return makes no denial of these allegations, but merely sets forth that he holds the prisoner by virtue of the commitment "based upon the judgment and conviction as set forth in the petition." The Supreme Court of Florida has said that "undenied allegations of the petition are taken as true."

The Circuit Court held the statutes under which the case was prosecuted to be unconstitutional and discharged the prisoner. The Supreme Court of Florida reversed. It read our decisions in *Bailey v. Alabama* and *Taylor v. Georgia* to hold that similar laws are not in conflict with the Constitution in so far as they denounce the crime, but only in declaring the prima facie evidence rule. It stated that its first impression was that the entire Florida act would fall, as did that of Georgia, but on reflection it concluded that our decisions were called forth by operation of the presumption, and did not condemn the substantive part of the statute where the presumption was not brought into play. As the prisoner had pleaded guilty, the Florida court thought the presumption had played no part in this case, and therefore remanded the prisoner to custody. An appeal to this Court was taken and probable jurisdiction noted.

Florida advances no argument that the presumption section of this statute is constitutional, nor could it plausibly do so in view of our decisions. It contends, however, (1) that we can give no consideration to the presumption section because it was not in fact brought into play in the case, by reason of the plea of guilty; (2) that so severed the section denouncing the crime is constitutional.

These issues emerge from an historical background against which the Florida legislation in question must be appraised.

The Thirteenth Amendment to the Federal Constitution, made in 1865, declares that involuntary servitude shall not exist within the United States and gives Congress power to enforce the article by appropriate legislation. Congress on March 2, 1867, enacted that all laws or usages of any state "by virtue of which any attempt shall hereafter be made to establish, maintain, or enforce, directly or indirectly, the voluntary or involuntary service or labor of any persons as peons, in liquidation of any debt or obligation, or otherwise," are null and void, and denounced it as a crime to hold, arrest, or return a person to the condition of peonage. Congress thus raised both a shield and a sword against forced labor because of debt.

Clyatt v. United States was a case from Florida in which the Federal Act was used as a sword and an employer convicted under it. This Court sustained it as constitutional and said of peonage: "It may be defined as a status or condition of compulsory service, based upon the indebtedness of the peon to the master. The basal fact is indebtedness. Peonage is sometimes classified as voluntary or involuntary; but this implies simply a difference in the mode of origin, but none in the character of the servitude. The one exists where the debtor voluntarily contracts to enter the service of his creditor. The other is forced upon the debtor by some provision of law. . . . A clear distinction exists between peonage and the voluntary performance of labor or rendering of services in payment of a debt. In the latter case the debtor, though contracting to pay his indebtedness by labor or service, and subject, like any other contractor, to an action for damages for breach of that contract, can elect at any time to break it, and no law or force compels performance or a continuance of the service."

Then came the twice-considered case of *Bailey v. Alabama*, in which the Act and the Constitution were raised as a shield against conviction of a laborer under an Alabama act substantially the same as the one before us now. Bailey, a Negro, had obtained $15 from a corporation on a written agreement to work for a year at $12 per month, $10.75 to be paid him and $1.25 per month to apply on his debt. In about a month he quit. He was convicted, fined $30, or in default sentenced to hard labor for 20 days in lieu of the fine and 116 days on account of costs. The Court considered that the portion of the state law defining the crime would require proof of intent to defraud, and so did not strike down that part; nor was it expressly sustained, nor was it necessarily reached, for the prima facie evidence provision had been used to obtain a conviction. This Court held the presumption, in such a context, to be unconstitutional.

Later came *United States v. Reynolds* and *United States v. Broughton* in which the Act of 1867 was sword again. Reynolds and Broughton were indicted under it. The Alabama Code authorized one under some circumstances to become surety for a convict, pay his fine, and be reimbursed by labor. Reynolds and Broughton each got himself a convict to work out fines and costs as a farm hand at $6.00 per month. After a time each convict refused to labor further and, under the statute, each was convicted for the refusal. This Court said, "Thus, under pain of recurring prosecutions, the convict may be kept at labor, to satisfy the demands of his employer." It held the Alabama statute unconstitutional and employers under it subject to prosecution.

In *Taylor v. Georgia* the Federal Act was again applied as a shield, against conviction by resort to the presumption, of a Negro laborer, under a Georgia statute in effect like the one before us now. We made no effort to separate valid from invalid elements in the statute, although the substantive and procedural provisions were, as here, in separate, and separately numbered, sections. We said, "We think that the sections of the Georgia Code upon which this conviction rests are repugnant to the Thirteenth Amendment and to the Act of 1867, and that the conviction must therefore be reversed." Only recently in a case from Northern Florida a creditor-employer was indicted under the Federal Act for arresting a debtor to peonage, and we sustained the indictment. *United States v. Gaskin.*

These cases decided by this Court under the Act of 1867 came either from Florida or one of the adjoining states. And these were but a part of the stir caused by the Federal Antipeonage Act and its enforcement in this same region. This is not to intimate that this section, more than others, was sympathetic with peonage, for this evil has never had general approval anywhere, and its sporadic appearances have been neither sectional nor racial. It is mentioned, however, to indicate that the Legislature of Florida acted with almost certain knowledge in designing its successive "labor fraud" acts in relation to our series of peonage decisions. The present Act is the latest of a lineage, in which its antecedents were obviously associated with the practice of peonage. This history throws some light on whether the present state act is one "by virtue of which any attempt shall hereafter be made" to "enforce involuntary servitude," in which event the Federal Act declares it void.

In 1891, the Legislature created an offense of two elements: obtaining money or property upon a false promise to perform service, and abandonment of service without just cause and without restitution of what had been obtained. In 1905, this Court decided *Clyatt*, indicating that any person, including public officers, even if acting under state law, might be guilty of violating the Federal Act. In 1907, the Florida Legislature enacted a new statute, nearly identical in terms with that of Alabama. In 1911, in *Bailey v. Alabama*, this Court held such an act unconstitutional. In 1913, the Florida Legislature repealed the 1907 act, but reenacted in substance the section denouncing the crime, omitting the presumption of intent from the failure to perform the service or make restitution. In 1919, the Florida Supreme Court held this act, standing alone, void under the authority of *Bailey v. Alabama*. Whereupon, at the session of 1919, the present statute was enacted, including the prima facie evidence provisions, notwithstanding these decisions by the Supreme Court of Florida and by this Court. The Supreme Court of Florida later upheld a conviction under this statute on a plea of guilty, but declined to pass on the presumption section, because, as in the present case, the plea of guilty was thought to make its consideration unnecessary. The statute was re-enacted without substantial change in 1941. Again in 1943 it was re-enacted despite the fact that the year before we held a very similar Georgia statute unconstitutional in its entirety.

II

The State contends that we must exclude the prima facie evidence provision from consideration because in fact it played no part in producing this conviction. Such was the holding of the State Supreme Court. We are not concluded by that holding, however, but under the circumstances are authorized to make an independent determination.

What the prisoner actually did that constituted the crime cannot be gleaned from the record. The charge is cast in the words of the statute and is largely a conclusion. It affords no information except that Pollock obtained $5 from a corporation in connection with a promise to work which he failed to perform, and that his doing so was fraudulent. If the conclusion that the prisoner acted with intent to defraud rests on facts and not on the prima facie evidence provisions of the statute, none are stated in the warrant or appear in the record. None were so set forth that he could deny them. He obtained the money on the 14th of October, 1942, and the warrant was not sought until January 2, 1943. Whether the original advancement was more or less than $5, what he represented or promised in obtaining it, whether he worked a time and quit, or whether he never began work at all are undisclosed. About all that appears is that he obtained an advancement of $5 from a corporation and failed to keep his agreement to work it out. He admitted those facts and the law purported to supply the element of intent. He admitted the conclusion of guilt which the statute made prima facie thereon. He was fined $20 for each dollar of his debt, and in default of payment was required to atone for it by serving time at the rate of less than 9¢ per day.

Especially in view of the undenied assertions in Pollock's petition we cannot doubt that the presumption provision had a coercive effect in producing the plea of guilty. The statute laid its undivided weight upon him. The legislature had not even included a separability clause. Of course the function of the prima facie evidence section is to make it possible to convict where proof of guilt is lacking. No one questions that we clearly have held that such a presumption is prohibited by the Constitution and the federal statute. The Florida Legislature has enacted and twice re-enacted it since we so held. We cannot assume it was doing an idle thing. Since the presumption was known to be unconstitutional and of no use in a contested case, the only explanation we can find for its persistent appearance in the statute is its extra-legal coercive effect in suppressing defenses. It confronted this defendant. There was every probability that a law so recently and repeatedly enacted by the legislature would be followed by the trial court, whose judge was not required to be a lawyer. The possibility of obtaining relief by appeal was not bright, as the event proved, for Pollock had to come all the way to this Court and was required, and quite regularly, to post a supersedeas bond of $500, a hundred times the amount of his debt. He was an illiterate Negro laborer in the toils of the law for the want of $5. Such considerations bear importantly on the decision of a prisoner even if aided by counsel, as Pollock was not, whether to plead guilty and hope for leniency or to fight. It is plain that, had his plight after conviction not aroused outside help, Pollock himself would have been unheard in any appellate court.

In the light of its history, there is no reason to believe that the law was generally used or especially useful merely to punish deceit. Florida has a general and comprehensive statute making it a crime to obtain money or property by false pretenses or commit "gross fraud or cheat at common law." These appear to authorize prosecution for even the petty amount involved here. We can conceive reasons, even if unconstitutional ones, which might lead well-intentioned persons to apply this Act as a means to make otherwise shiftless men work, but if in addition to this general fraud protection employers as a class are so susceptible to imposition that they need extra legislation, or workmen so crafty and subtle as to constitute a special menace, we do not know it, nor are we advised of such facts.

We think that a state which maintains such a law in face of the court decisions we have recited may not be heard to say that a plea of guilty under the circumstances is not due to pressure of its statutory threat to convict him on the presumption.

As we have seen, Florida, persisted in putting upon its statute books a provision creating a presumption of fraud from the mere nonperformance of a contract for labor service three times after the courts ruled that such a provision violates the prohibition against peonage. To attach no meaning to such action, to say that legally speaking there was no such legislation, is to be blind to fact. Since the Florida Legislature deemed these repeated enactments to be important, we take the Legislature at its own word. Such a provision is on the statute books for those who are arrested for the crime, and it is on the statute books for us in considering the practical meaning of what Florida has done.

III

We are induced by the evident misunderstanding of our decisions by the Florida Supreme Court, in what we are convinced was a conscientious and pains-taking study of them, to make more explicit the basis of constitutional invalidity of this type of statute.

• • •

We impute to the Legislature no intention to oppress, but we are compelled to hold that the Florida Act of 1919 [is] by virtue of the Thirteenth Amendment and the Antipeonage Act of the United States, null and void. The judgment of the court below is reversed and the cause is remanded for further proceedings not inconsistent with this opinion.

[Chief Justice Stone and Justice Reed dissented.]

NOTES AND QUESTIONS

1. Justice Jackson memorably describes the federal Antipeonage Act as "both a shield and a sword" against forced labor because of debt. As to the sword, he references *Clyatt v. United States*, 197 U.S. 207 (1905), where the Court upheld the statute as constitutional although it reversed the conviction on evidentiary grounds. Although the Court in *Clyatt* defined the concept of peonage, *Clyatt*, and its definition of peonage, are barely mentioned in either *Bailey* or *Reynolds*.

2. The Florida Supreme Court found Pollock's conviction lawful because, inasmuch as he pleaded guilty, the statutory presumption that was found fatal in *Bailey* never went into operation. Does this reasoning have any superficial plausibility? What if the record in the case showed that Pollock had admitted to obtaining identical advances from multiple employers at the same time and then left town? Would the result be different?

3. The Court concludes that the presumption provision of the Florida statute "had a coercive effect in producing the plea of guilty." How can this be true given that Pollock appears to claim on appeal—which is almost certainly true, given his lack of counsel—that he "did not understand the nature of the charge against him"? Pollock does say that he understood that "if he owed any money to his prior employer and had quit his employment without paying the same" he would be guilty. Is this understanding tantamount to an understanding of the charge against him?

4. Justice Jackson's opinion is restrained in some respects, yet he is plainly "frustrated"—to put it mildly—with the Florida Supreme Court and the Florida legislature. He walks though the relevant Supreme Court case law—*Bailey*, *Reynolds*, and the 1942 case of *Taylor v. Georgia*, in which the Court struck down a virtually identical Georgia statute—as if providing a remedial tutorial for the Florida court. As to the Florida legislature his displeasure is more overt. He observes that "the Legislature acted with almost certain knowledge in designing its successive 'labor fraud' acts in relation to our series of peonage decisions," and suggests that the legislature's purpose was the presumption's "extra-legal coercive effect in suppressing defenses." He even has a sentence suggesting that Florida's conduct "estops" it from defending the statute:

> We think that a state which maintains such a law in face of the court decisions we have recited may not be heard to say that a plea of guilty under the circumstances is not due to pressure of its statutory threat to convict him on the presumption.

This is unusually forceful language for the Supreme Court to use in any context. Do you see any evidence that Justice Jackson's "frustration" extends to the actual operation of the state's criminal justice system?

5. Note also Justice Jackson's expressed sympathy to Pollock as compared to the Court's opinions in *Bailey* and *Reynolds*. Not only does he mention Pollock's race multiple times but he notes that without "outside help" Pollock would have been unheard in any appellate court, and the Florida statute would have affected him the same way it affected countless other uncounseled defendants.

The vagrancy statutes that fueled the peonage system in the South, and provided other avenues for assertions of white supremacy, were not outlawed by the Supreme Court until the 1970s in the following case, *Papachristou v. Jacksonville*, although the Court does so without critically examining their pedigree. But vagrancy prosecutorial regimes were not limited to the South. By the 1960s all 50 states and the District of Columbia had vagrancy statutes, which were often enforced against disfavored groups—civil rights activists, gays and lesbians, political dissidents, and, of course, hippies. Risa Goluboff, Vagrant Nation: Police Power, Constitutional Change and the Making of the 1960s 2-3 (2016). And by the time *Papachristou* was decided in 1972, the Supreme Court had already held in *Terry v. Ohio*, 392 U.S. 1 (1968), that police could stop and frisk persons based on "reasonable suspicion," which substantially compensated the police for any loss of authority due to the invalidation of vagrancy laws. *Id.* at 11. *See* Chapter IV *infra*.

Papachristou v. Jacksonville

405 U.S. 156 (1972)

Mr. Justice Douglas delivered the opinion of the Court.

This case involves eight defendants who were convicted in a Florida municipal court of violating a Jacksonville, Florida, vagrancy ordinance. Their convictions, entailing fines and jail sentences (some of which were suspended), were affirmed by the Florida Circuit The case is here on a petition for certiorari, which we granted. For reasons which will appear, we reverse.

At issue are five consolidated cases. Margaret Papachristou, Betty Calloway, Eugene Eddie Melton, and Leonard Johnson were all arrested early on a Sunday morning, and charged with vagrancy—"prowling by auto."

Jimmy Lee Smith and Milton Henry were charged with vagrancy—"vagabonds."

Henry Edward Heath and a codefendant were arrested for vagrancy—"loitering" and "common thief."

Thomas Owen Campbell was charged with vagrancy—"common thief."

Hugh Brown was charged with vagrancy—"disorderly loitering on street" and "disorderly conduct—resisting arrest with violence."

The facts are stipulated. Papachristou and Calloway are white females. Melton and Johnson are black males. Papachristou was enrolled in a job-training program sponsored by the State Employment Service at Florida Junior College in Jacksonville. Calloway was a typing and shorthand teacher at a state mental institution located near Jacksonville. She was the owner of the automobile in which the four defendants were arrested. Melton was a Vietnam war veteran who had been released from the Navy after nine months in a veterans' hospital. On the date of his arrest he was a part-time computer helper while attending college as a full-time student in Jacksonville. Johnson was a tow-motor operator in a grocery chain warehouse and was a lifelong resident of Jacksonville.

At the time of their arrest the four of them were riding in Calloway's car on the main thoroughfare in Jacksonville. They had left a restaurant owned by Johnson's uncle where they had eaten and were on their way to a nightclub. The arresting officers denied that the racial mixture in the car played any part in the decision to make the arrest. The arrest, they said, was made because the defendants had stopped near a used-car lot which had been broken into several times. There was, however, no evidence of any breaking and entering on the night in question.

Of these four charged with "prowling by auto" none had been previously arrested except Papachristou who had once been convicted of a municipal offense.

Jimmy Lee Smith and Milton Henry (who is not a petitioner) were arrested between 9 and 10 a.m. on a weekday in downtown Jacksonville, while waiting for a friend who was to lend them a car so they could apply for a job at a produce company. Smith was a part-time produce worker and part-time organizer for a Negro political group. He had a common-law wife and three children supported by him and his wife. He had been arrested several times but convicted only once. Smith's companion, Henry, was an 18-year-old high school student with no previous record of arrest.

This morning it was cold, and Smith had no jacket, so they went briefly into a dry cleaning shop to wait, but left when requested to do so. They thereafter walked back and forth two or three times over a two-block stretch looking for their friend. The store owners, who apparently were wary of Smith and his companion, summoned two police officers who searched the men and found neither had a weapon. But they were arrested because the officers said they had no identification and because the officers did not believe their story.

Heath and a codefendant were arrested for "loitering" and for "common thief." Both were residents of Jacksonville, Heath having lived there all his life and being employed at an automobile body shop. Heath had previously been arrested but his codefendant had no arrest record. Heath and his companion were arrested when they drove up to a residence shared by Heath's girl friend and some other girls. Some police officers were already there in the process of arresting another man. When Heath and his companion started backing out of the driveway, the officers signaled to them to stop and asked them to get out of the car, which they did. Thereupon they and the automobile were searched. Although no contraband or incriminating evidence was found, they were both arrested, Heath being charged with being a "common thief" because he was reputed to be a thief. The codefendant was charged with "loitering" because he was standing in the driveway, an act which the officers admitted was done only at their command.

Campbell was arrested as he reached his home very early one morning and was charged with "common thief." He was stopped by officers because he was traveling at a high rate of speed, yet no speeding charge was placed against him.

Brown was arrested when he was observed leaving a downtown Jacksonville hotel by a police officer seated in a cruiser. The police testified he was reputed to be a thief, narcotics pusher, and generally opprobrious character. The officer called Brown over to the car, intending at that time to arrest him unless he had a good explanation for being on the street. Brown walked over to the police cruiser, as commanded, and the officer began to search him, apparently preparatory to placing him in the car. In the process of the search he came on two small packets which were later found to contain heroin. When the officer touched the pocket where the packets were, Brown began to resist. He was charged with "disorderly loitering on street" and "disorderly conduct—resisting arrest with violence." While he was also charged with a narcotics violation, that charge was nolled.

Jacksonville's ordinance and Florida's statute were derived from early English law. . . .

This ordinance is void for vagueness, both in the sense that it "fails to give a person of ordinary intelligence fair notice that his contemplated conduct is forbidden by the statute," and because it encourages arbitrary and erratic arrests and convictions.

Living under a rule of law entails various suppositions, one of which is that "(all persons) are entitled to be informed as to what the State commands or forbids."

Lanzetta is one of a well-recognized group of cases insisting that the law give fair notice of the offending conduct. In the field of regulatory statutes governing business activities, where the acts limited are in a narrow category, greater leeway is allowed.

The poor among us, the minorities, the average householder are not in business and not alerted to the regulatory schemes of vagrancy laws; and we assume they would have no understanding of their meaning and impact if they read them. Nor are they protected from being caught in the vagrancy net by the necessity of having a specific intent to commit an unlawful act.

The Jacksonville ordinance makes criminal activities which by modern standards are normally innocent. "Nightwalking" is one. Florida construes the ordinance not to make criminal one night's wandering, only the "habitual" wanderer or, as the ordinance describes it, "common night walkers." We know, however, from experience that sleepless people often walk at night, perhaps hopeful that sleep-inducing relaxation will result.

Luis Munoz-Marin, former Governor of Puerto Rico, commented once that "loafing" was a national virtue in his Commonwealth and that it should be encouraged. It is, however, a crime in Jacksonville.

"(P)ersons able to work but habitually living upon the earnings of their wives or minor children"—like habitually living "without visible means of support"—might implicate unemployed pillars of the community who have married rich wives.

"(P)ersons able to work but habitually living upon the earnings of their wives or minor children" may also embrace unemployed people out of the labor market, by reason of a recession or disemployed by reason of technological or so-called structural displacements.

Persons "wandering or strolling" from place to place have been extolled by Walt Whitman and Vachel Lindsay. The qualification "without any lawful purpose or object" may be a trap for innocent acts. Persons "neglecting all lawful business and habitually spending their time by frequenting . . . places where alcoholic beverages are sold or served" would literally embrace many members of golf clubs and city clubs.

Walkers and strollers and wanderers may be going to or coming from a burglary. Loafers or loiterers may be "casing" a place for a holdup. Letting one's wife support him is an intra-family matter, and normally of no concern to the police. Yet it may, of course, be the setting for numerous crimes.

The difficulty is that these activities are historically part of the amenities of life as we have known them. They are not mentioned in the Constitution or in the Bill of Rights. These unwritten amenities have been in part responsible for giving our people the feeling of independence and self-confidence, the feeling of creativity. These amenities have dignified the right of dissent and have honored the right to be nonconformists and the right to defy submissiveness. They have encouraged lives of high spirits rather than hushed, suffocating silence.

They are embedded in Walt Whitman's writings, especially in his "Song of the Open Road." They are reflected too, in the spirit of Vachel Lindsay's "I Want to Go Wandering," and by Henry D. Thoreau.

This aspect of the vagrancy ordinance before us is suggested by what this Court said in 1876 about a broad criminal statute enacted by Congress: "It would certainly be dangerous if the legislature could set a net large enough to catch all possible offenders, and leave it to the courts to step inside and say who could be rightfully detained, and who should be set at large."

• • •

Where the list of crimes is so all-inclusive and generalized as the one in this ordinance, those convicted may be punished for no more than vindicating affronts to police authority:

> The common ground which brings such a motley assortment of human troubles before the magistrates in vagrancy-type proceedings is the procedural laxity which permits "conviction" for almost any kind of conduct and the existence of the House of Correction as an easy and convenient dumping-ground for problems that appear to have no other immediate solution.

Foote, *Vagrancy-Type Law and Its Administration*, 104 U. Pa. L. Rev. 603, 631.

Another aspect of the ordinance's vagueness appears when we focus, not on the lack of notice given a potential offender, but on the effect of the unfettered discretion it places in the hands of the Jacksonville police. Caleb Foote, an early student of this subject, has called the vagrancy-type law as offering "punishment by analogy." Such crimes, though long common in Russia, are not compatible with our constitutional system. We allow our police to make arrests only on "probable cause," a Fourth and Fourteenth Amendment standard applicable to the States as well as to the Federal Government. Arresting a person on suspicion, like arresting a person for investigation, is foreign to our system, even when the arrest is for past criminality. Future criminality, however, is the common justification for the presence of vagrancy statutes. Florida has, indeed, construed her vagrancy statute "as necessary regulations," inter alia, "to deter vagabondage and prevent crimes."

A direction by a legislature to the police to arrest all "suspicious" persons would not pass constitutional muster. A vagrancy prosecution may be merely the cloak for a conviction which could not be obtained on the real but undisclosed grounds for the arrest.

Those generally implicated by the imprecise terms of the ordinance—poor people, nonconformists, dissenters, idlers—may be required to comport themselves according to the life style deemed appropriate by the Jacksonville police and the courts. Where, as here, there are no standards governing the exercise of the discretion granted by the ordinance, the scheme permits and encourages an arbitrary and discriminatory enforcement of the law. It furnishes a convenient tool for "harsh and discriminatory enforcement by local prosecuting officials, against particular groups deemed to merit their displeasure." It results in a regime in which the poor and the unpopular are permitted to "stand on a public sidewalk . . . only at the whim of any police officer." Under this ordinance, "(I)f some carefree type of fellow is satisfied to work just so much, and no more, as will pay for one square meal, some wine, and a flophouse daily, but a court thinks this kind of living subhuman, the fellow can be forced to raise his sights or go to jail as a vagrant."

A presumption that people who might walk or loaf or loiter or stroll or frequent houses where liquor is sold, or who are supported by their wives or who look suspicious to the police are to become future criminals is too precarious for a rule of law. The implicit presumption in these generalized vagrancy standards—that crime is being nipped in the bud—is too extravagant to deserve extended treatment. Of course, vagrancy statutes are useful to the police. Of course, they are nets making easy the roundup of so-called undesirables. But the rule of law implies equality and justice in its application. Vagrancy laws of the Jacksonville type teach that the scales of justice are so tipped that even-handed administration of the law is not possible. The rule of law, evenly applied to minorities as well as majorities, to the poor as well as the rich, is the great mucilage that holds society together.

The Jacksonville ordinance cannot be squared with our constitutional standards and is plainly unconstitutional.

NOTES AND QUESTIONS

1. Although vagrancy statutes were a central driver of the peonage system in the South, the Court fails to acknowledge as much, rooting their pedigree only in "early English law." This may be true insofar as it goes, although recent research demonstrates that vagrancy laws were passed and reinvigorated in southern states as an explicit response to Reconstruction. *See* D. Blackmon, Slavery by Another Name: The Re-enslavement of Black America from the Civil War to World War II (2009), at 53 ("Every Southern state except Arkansas and Tennessee had passed laws by the end of 1865 outlawing vagrancy and so vaguely defining it that virtually any freed slave not under the protection of a white man could be arrested for the crime."). Assuming the Court was aware of this traditional use of vagrancy laws, why not mention that fact in the opinion? The Court is not otherwise reticent about race in the opinion.

2. The Court notes two evils of unduly vague criminal statutes: (a) they fail to provide fair notice of the conduct that is forbidden by the statute, and (b) they encourage arbitrary enforcement. Which are the lesser and greater of these two evils? As to the former, the Court observes that "the poor among us, the minorities, the average householder are not in business and not alerted to the regulatory schemes of vagrancy laws; and we assume they would have no understanding of their meaning and impact if they read them." What is the point here? Would whites or "above average householders" understand these laws and their potential impact? The Court also points out that the Jacksonville ordinance criminalizes "normally innocent" conduct, and in a riff on "the amenities of life" extols the virtues of loafing, wandering, strolling, etc. Is this a function of the ordinance's vagueness or is it a different problem?

3. The facts of *Papachristou* could hardly better demonstrate the dangers of arbitrary enforcement. Not only are the charges ludicrous but the defendants include a pair of mixed-race couples (white females and black males) and "an organizer for a Negro political group." The Court notes that one of the black males was a Vietnam war veteran and the other was a lifelong Jacksonville resident, and that the "organizer" had been arrested several times but convicted only once.

Just a few years after *Papachristou*, in *Kolender v. Lawson*, 461 U.S. 352 (1983), the Court considered a void-for-vagueness challenge to a California statute that made it a crime for a person who is loitering or wandering on the streets, if approached by a police officer, to fail to present "credible and reliable" identification and to "account for their presence." Appellee Lawson (the case was a civil rights action; Lawson filed a lawsuit challenging the constitutionality of the statute) had been arrested or detained under this statute on 15 occasions, but prosecuted only twice and convicted once. *Id.* at 354-55. As interpreted by California courts, the statute vested the inquiring police officer with full discretion to determine whether a suspect had sufficiently identified himself and accounted for his presence. The Supreme Court found the statute unconstitutional "because it encourages arbitrary enforcement by failing to describe with sufficient particularity what a suspect must do in order to satisfy the statute." *Id.* at 361.

Despite grounding its decision on the evil of arbitrary enforcement the Court avoided mentioning that Lawson was a Black man. Why not, in 1983?

The Court explicitly roots its holding in the evil of "arbitrary enforcement" rather than "fair notice." How does the statute fare as to "fair notice"? Would "an average householder" reading the statute know what conduct is prohibited?

C. MOB CONVICTIONS

The next set of cases involve Black defendants who were prosecuted for crimes against white victims. The "trials" were held within days of the crimes, in courthouses that were surrounded by white mobs that surely would have lynched the defendants but for the presence of armed militia. The all-white juries deliberated for just minutes before imposing the death penalty. In each case there was a substantial question as to the defendants' innocence.

The first case, *Moore v. Dempsey*, 261 U.S. 86 (1923), arose out of a large-scale racial altercation in Phillips County, Arkansas in the fall of 1919. Phillips County was a typical Deep South cotton county with a Black majority of approximately three to one. When local Black sharecroppers after World War I held meetings to consider unionization and to seek legal redress for their landlords' peonage practices, the white community became enraged and spread rumors of a Black conspiracy to murder white planters throughout the county. Whites fired shots into a Black union meeting at a church; Black people returned the gunfire, killing a white man; widespread mayhem ensued. Marauding bands of whites, some of whom came to the county from adjoining counties, went on a rampage against Black people, killing as many as 250 of them. Seventy-nine Black people (and no whites) were prosecuted as a result of the riot, including Frank Moore. *See generally* Klarman, *The Racial Origins of Modern Criminal Procedure*, *supra* at 50-51.

Moore v. Dempsey

261 U.S. 86 (1923)

Mr. Justice HOLMES delivered the opinion of the Court.

This is an appeal from an order of the District Court for the Eastern District of Arkansas dismissing a writ of habeas corpus upon demurrer, the presiding judge certifying that there was probable cause for allowing the appeal. There were two cases originally, but by agreement they were consolidated into one. The appellants are five negroes who were convicted of murder in the first degree and sentenced to death by the Court of the State of Arkansas. The ground of the petition for the writ is that the proceedings in the State Court, although a trial in form, were only a form, and that the appellants were hurried to conviction under the pressure of a mob without any regard for their rights and without according to them due process of law.

The case stated by the petition is as follows, and it will be understood that while we put it in narrative form, we are not affirming the facts to be as stated but only what we must take them to be, as they are admitted by the demurrer: On the night of September 30, 1919, a number of colored people assembled in their church were attacked and fired upon by a body of white men. and in the disturbance that followed a white man was killed. The report of the killing caused great excitement and was followed by the hunting down and shooting of many negroes and also by the killing on October 1 of one Clinton Lee, a white man, for whose murder the petitioners were indicted. They seem to have been arrested with many others on the same day. The petitioners say that Lee must have been killed by other whites, but that we leave on one side as what we have to deal with is not the petitioners' innocence or guilt but solely the question whether their constitutional rights have been preserved. They say that their meeting was to employ counsel for protection against extortions practiced upon them by the landowners and that the landowners tried to prevent their effort, but that again we pass by as not directly bearing upon the trial. It should be mentioned, however, that O. S. Bratton, a son of the counsel who is said to have been contemplated and who took part in the argument here, arriving for consultation on October 1, is said to have barely escaped being mobbed; that he was arrested and confined during the month on a charge of murder and on October 31 was indicted for barratry, but later in the day was told that he would be discharged but that he must leave secretly by a closed automobile to take the train at West Helena, four miles away, to avoid being mobbed. It is alleged that the judge of the Court in which the petitioners were tried facilitated the departure and went with Bratton to see him safely off.

A Committee of Seven was appointed by the Governor in regard to what the committee called the "insurrection" in the county. The newspapers daily published inflammatory articles. On the 7th a statement by one of the committee was made public to the effect that the present trouble was "a deliberately planned insurrection of the negroes against the whites, directed by an organization known as the 'Progressive Farmers' and 'Household Union of America' established for the purpose of banding negroes together for the killing of white people." According to the statement the organization was started by a swindler to get money from the blacks.

Shortly after the arrest of the petitioners a mob marched to the jail for the purpose of lynching them but were prevented by the presence of United States troops and the promise of some of the Committee of Seven and other leading officials that if the mob would refrain, as the petition puts it, they would execute those found guilty in the form of law. The Committee's own statement was that the reason that the people refrained from mob violence was "that this Committee gave our citizens their solemn promise that the law would be carried out." According to affidavits of two white men and the colored witnesses on whose testimony the petitioners were convicted, produced by the petitioners since the last decision of the Supreme Court hereafter mentioned, the Committee made good their promise by calling colored witnesses and having them whipped and tortured until they would say what was wanted, among them being the two relied on to prove the petitioners' guilt. However this may be, a grand jury of white men was organized on October 27 with one of the Committee of Seven and, it is alleged, with many of a posse organized to fight the blacks, upon it, and on the morning of the 29th the indictment was returned. On November 3 the petitioners were brought into Court, informed that a certain lawyer was appointed their counsel and were placed on trial before a white jury—blacks being systematically excluded from both grand and petit juries. The Court and neighborhood were thronged with an adverse crowd that threatened the most dangerous consequences to anyone interfering with the desired result. The counsel did not venture to demand delay or a change of venue, to challenge a juryman or to ask for separate trials. He had had no preliminary consultation with the accused, called no witnesses for the defence although they could have been produced, and did not put the defendants on the stand. The trial lasted about three-quarters of an hour and in less than five minutes the jury brought in a verdict of guilty of murder in the first degree. According to the allegations and affidavits there never was a chance for the petitioners to be acquitted; no juryman could have voted for an acquittal and continued to live Phillips County and if any prisoner by any chance had been acquitted by a jury he could not have escaped the mob.

The averments as to the prejudice by which the trial was environed have some corroboration in appeals to the Governor, about a year later, earnestly urging him not to interfere with the execution of the petitioners. One came from five members of the Committee of Seven, and stated in addition to what has been quoted heretofore that "all our citizens are of the opinion that the law should take its course." Another from a part of the American Legion protests against a contemplated commutation of the sentence of four of the petitioners and repeats that a "solemn promise was given by the leading citizens of the community that it the guilty parties were not lynched, and let the law take its course, that justice would be done and the majesty of the law upheld." A meeting of the Helena Rotary Club attended by members representing, as it said, seventy-five of the leading industrial and commercial enterprises of Helena, passed a resolution approving and supporting the action of the American Legion post. The Lions Club of Helena at a meeting attended by members said to represent sixty of the leading industrial and commercial enterprises of the city passed a resolution to the same effect. In May of the same year, a trial of six other negroes was coming on and it was represented to the Governor by the white citizens and officials of Phillips County that in all probability those negroes would be lynched. It is alleged that in order to appease the mob spirit and in a measure secure the safety of the six the Governor fixed the date for the execution of the petitioners at June 10, 1921, but that the execution was stayed by proceedings in Court; we presume the proceedings before the Chancellor to which we shall advert.

In *Frank v. Mangum*, it was recognized of course that if in fact a trial is dominated by a mob so that there is an actual interference with the course of justice, there is a departure from due process of law; and that "if the State, supplying no corrective process, carries into execution a judgment of death or imprisonment based upon a verdict thus produced by mob domination, the State deprives the accused of his life or liberty without due process of law." We assume in accordance with that case that the corrective process supplied by the State may be so adequate that interference by habeas corpus ought not to be allowed. It certainly is true that mere mistakes of law in the course of a trial are not to be corrected in that way. But if the case is that the whole proceeding is a mask—that counsel, jury and judge were swept to the fatal end by an irresistible wave of public passion, and that the State Courts failed to correct the wrong, neither perfection in the machinery for correction nor the possibility that the trial court and counsel saw no other way of avoiding an immediate outbreak of the mob can prevent this Court from securing to the petitioners their constitutional rights.

In this case a motion for a new trial on the ground alleged in this petition was overruled and upon exceptions and appeal to the Supreme Court the judgment was affirmed. The Supreme Court said that the complaint of discrimination against petitioners by the exclusion of colored men from the jury came too late and by way of answer to the objection that no fair trial could be had in the circumstances, stated that it could not say "that this must necessarily have been the case"; that eminent counsel was appointed to defend the petitioners, that the trial was had according to law, the jury correctly charged, and the testimony legally sufficient. On June 8, 1921, two days before the date fixed for their execution, a petition for habeas corpus was presented to the Chancellor and he issued the writ and an injunction against the execution of the petitioners; but the Supreme Court of the State held that the Chancellor had no jurisdiction under the state law whatever might be the law of the United States. The present petition perhaps was suggested by the language of the Court: "What the result would be of an application to a Federal Court we need not inquire." It was presented to the District

Court on September 21. We shall not say more concerning the corrective process afforded to the petitioners than that it does not seem to us sufficient to allow a Judge of the United States to escape the duty of examining the facts for himself when if true as alleged they make the trial absolutely void. We have confined the statement to facts admitted by the demurrer. We will not say that they cannot be met, but it appears to us unavoidable that the District Judge should find whether the facts alleged are true and whether they can be explained so far as to leave the state proceedings undisturbed.

Order reversed. The case to stand for hearing before the District Court.

[Justices Sutherland and McReynolds dissented.]

NOTES AND QUESTIONS

1. Both the majority and dissenting opinions mention *Frank v. Magnum*, 237 U.S. 309 (1915), in which just eight years earlier on somewhat comparable facts the Supreme Court had affirmed the denial of a writ of habeas corpus. Leo Frank, a Jewish businessman in Atlanta, was charged with the murder of a girl who worked at the factory he managed. His trial was also dominated by the threat of mob violence. After Frank failed in the Supreme Court, Georgia's governor commuted his sentence to life imprisonment, whereafter a mob seized him from the state prison farm where he was held and lynched him.

The two cases are difficult to reconcile. Professor Klarman attributes the transformation to a heightened national sensitivity to the evils of lynching to which the Court—even though its membership was more conservative in 1923 than 1915—was not immune. Klarman, *The Racial Origins of Modern Criminal Procedure*, *supra* at 60. After a resurgence in lynchings after World War I the NAACP waged a large-scale publicity campaign in support of a proposed federal anti-lynching act, the Dyer Bill. Although the bill passed in the House it was killed by filibuster in the Senate, as over two hundred such proposals were to do in the first half of

The Equal Justice Initiative's National Memorial for Peace and Justice, Montgomery, Alabama. Each of the Memorial's 800 metal plates represents a county where one of the known 4,400 terror lynchings in the United States between 1877 and 1950 occurred, along with the victims' names.

the twentieth century. But the bill had received wide recognition and had been endorsed by President Coolidge and other prominent politicians.

The Equal Justice Initiative has documented at least 4,742 lynchings in the United States between 1882 and 1968. Seven presidents petitioned Congress for anti-lynching legislation and the House passed three bills but the Senate blocked all efforts. Congress finally based the largely symbolic Emmit Till Act in 2022, codified at 18 U.S.C. § 249(a), adding lynching to the actions prohibited by the federal Hate Crimes Act.

2. The NAACP played an active role in *Moore v. Dempsey*. The facts on the ground were developed by Walter White, the organization's investigator par excellence, who was able to get local witnesses to open up to him in part because he was so light-skinned and fair that he was not perceived as Black. The NAACP also gave financial support to the appellate litigation, and Boston lawyer Moorefield Storey, the NAACP's first president and its leading advocate for the Dyer Bill, argued *Moore* before the Supreme Court. This was one of the NAACP's earliest and most successful litigation efforts, and helped shape its strategy for the coming decades. The NAACP continued to be cautious, however, about the cases that it took on.

Moorfield Storey

This flag was flown from the New York City headquarters of the NAACP from 1936-1938.

3. Note that the Court in *Moore*, in attempting to distinguish *Frank*, condemns the entire state judicial system of Arkansas, including its appellate courts, requiring federal judicial intervention where "the whole proceeding is a mask—that counsel, jury and judge were swept to the fatal end by an irresistible wave of public passion, and that the State courts failed to correct the wrong." Magdalen Zier argues that whatever limited effect *Moore* may have as a criminal procedure precedent, this aspect of *Moore*'s reasoning served as an important development in state action doctrine, helping pave the way for such landmark cases as *Shelley v. Kraemer*, 334 U.S. 1, 15-16, 20 (1948) (citing *Moore* in finding state action in judicial enforcement of racially restrictive housing covenants) and *Monroe v. Pape*, 365 U.S. 167, 171-87 (1961) (finding state action where even low-level state actors, such as police officers, could violate 42 U.S.C. § 1983). *See* Comment, *Crimes of Omission: State Action Doctrine and Anti-Lynching Legislation in the Jim Crow Era*, 73 Stan. L. Rev. 777, 815-17 (2021).

Walter White, NAACP investigator

The Supreme Court's next major venture into criminal procedure came in appeals from the convictions of nine young Black men in Scottsboro, Alabama.

Powell v. Alabama

287 U.S. 45 (1932)

Mr. Justice SUTHERLAND delivered the opinion of the Court.

The petitioners, hereinafter referred to as defendants, are negroes charged with the crime of rape, committed upon the persons of two white girls. The crime is said to have been committed on March 25, 1931. The indictment was returned in a state court of first instance on March 31, and the record recites that on the same day the defendants were arraigned and entered pleas of not guilty. There is a further recital to the effect that upon the arraignment they were represented by counsel. But no counsel had been employed, and aside from a statement made by the trial judge several days later during a colloquy immediately preceding the trial, the record does not disclose when, or under what circumstances, an appointment of counsel was made, or who was appointed. During the colloquy referred to, the trial judge, in response to a question, said that he had appointed all the members of the bar for the purpose of arraigning the defendants and then of course anticipated that the members of the bar would continue to help the defendants if no counsel appeared. Upon the argument here both sides accepted that as a correct statement of the facts concerning the matter.

There was a severance upon the request of the state, and the defendants were tried in three several groups, as indicated above. As each of the three cases was called for trial, each defendant was arraigned, and, having the indictment read to him, entered a plea of not guilty. Whether the original arraignment and pleas were regarded as ineffective is not shown. Each of the three trials was completed within a single day. Under the Alabama statute the punishment for rape is to be fixed by the jury, and in its discretion may be from ten years imprisonment to death. The juries found defendants guilty and imposed the death penalty upon all. The trial court overruled motions for new trials and sentenced the defendants in accordance with the verdicts. The judgments were affirmed by the state supreme court. Chief Justice Anderson thought the defendants had not been accorded a fair trial and strongly dissented.

In this court the judgments are assailed upon the grounds that the defendants, and each of them, were denied due process of law and the equal protection of the laws, in contravention of the Fourteenth Amendment, specifically as follows: (1) They were not given a fair, impartial, and deliberate trial; (2) they were denied the right of counsel, with the accustomed incidents of consultation and opportunity of preparation for trial; and (3) they were tried before juries from which qualified members of their own race were systematically excluded. These questions were properly raised and saved in the courts below.

The only one of the assignments which we shall consider is the second, in respect of the denial of counsel; and it becomes unnecessary to discuss the facts of the case or the circumstances surrounding the prosecution except in so far as they reflect light upon that question.

The record shows that on the day when the offense is said to have been committed, these defendants, together with a number of other negroes, were upon a freight train on its way through Alabama. On the same train were seven white boys and the two white girls. A fight took place between the negroes and the white boys, in the course of which the white boys, with the exception of one named Gilley, were thrown off the train. A message was sent ahead, reporting the fight and asking that every negro be gotten off the train. The participants in the fight, and the two girls, were in an open gondola car. The two girls testified that each of them was assaulted by six different negroes in turn, and they identified the seven defendants as having been among the number. None of the white boys was called to testify, with the exception of Gilley, who was called in rebuttal.

Before the train reached Scottsboro, Ala., a sheriff's posse seized the defendants and two other negroes. Both girls and the negroes then were taken to Scottsboro, the county seat. Word of their coming and of the alleged assault had preceded them, and they were met at Scottsboro by a large crowd. It does not sufficiently appear that the defendants were seriously threatened with, or that they were actually in danger of, mob violence; but it does appear that the attitude of the community was one of great hostility. The sheriff thought it necessary to call for the militia to assist in safeguarding the prisoners. Chief Justice Anderson pointed out in his opinion that every step taken from the arrest and arraignment to the sentence was accompanied by the military. Soldiers took the defendants to Gadsden for safe-keeping, brought them back to Scottsboro for arraignment, returned them to Gadsden for safe-keeping while awaiting trial, escorted them to Scottsboro for trial a few days later, and guarded the courthouse and grounds at every stage of the proceedings. It is perfectly apparent that the proceedings, from beginning to end, took place in an atmosphere of tense, hostile, and excited public sentiment. During the entire time, the defendants were closely confined or were under military guard. The record does not disclose their ages, except that one of them was nineteen; but the record clearly indicates that most, if not all, of them were youthful, and they are constantly referred to as "the boys." They were ignorant and illiterate. All of them were residents of other states, where alone members of their families or friends resided.

However guilty defendants, upon due inquiry, might prove to have been, they were, until convicted, presumed to be innocent. It was the duty of the court having their cases in charge to see that they were denied no necessary incident of a fair trial. With any error of the state court involving alleged contravention of the state statutes or Constitution we, of course, have nothing to do. The sole inquiry which we are permitted to make is whether the federal Constitution was contravened, and as to that, we confine ourselves, as already suggested, to the inquiry whether the defendants were in substance denied the right of counsel, and if so, whether such denial infringes the due process clause of the Fourteenth Amendment.

First. The record shows that immediately upon the return of the indictment defendants were arraigned and pleaded not guilty. Apparently they were not asked whether they had, or were able to employ, counsel, or wished to have counsel appointed; or whether they had friends or relatives who might assist in that regard if communicated with. That it would not have been an idle ceremony to have given the defendants reasonable opportunity to communicate with their families and endeavor to obtain counsel is demonstrated by the fact that very soon after conviction, able counsel appeared in their behalf. This was pointed out by Chief Justice Anderson in the course of his dissenting opinion. "They were nonresidents," he said, "and had little time or opportunity to get in touch with their families and friends who were scattered throughout two other states, and time has demonstrated that they could or would have been represented by able counsel had a better opportunity been given by a reasonable delay in the trial of the cases judging from the number and activity of counsel that appeared immediately or shortly after their conviction."

It is hardly necessary to say that the right to counsel being conceded, a defendant should be afforded a fair opportunity to secure counsel of his own choice. Not only was that not done here, but such designation of counsel as was attempted was either so indefinite or so close upon the trial as to amount to a denial of effective and substantial aid in that regard. This will be amply demonstrated by a brief review of the record.

April 6, six days after indictment, the trials began. When the first case was called, the court inquired whether the parties were ready for trial. The state's attorney replied that he was ready to proceed. No one answered for the defendants or appeared to represent or defend them. Mr. Roddy, a Tennessee lawyer not a member of the local bar, addressed the court, saying that he had not been employed, but that people who were interested had spoken to him about the case. He was asked by the court whether he intended to appear for the defendants, and answered that he would like to appear along with counsel that the court might appoint. The record then proceeds:

The Court: If you appear for these defendants, then I will not appoint counsel; if local counsel are willing to appear and assist you under the circumstances all right, but I will not appoint them.

Mr. Roddy: Your Honor has appointed counsel, is that correct?

The Court: I appointed all the members of the bar for the purpose of arraigning the defendants and then of course I anticipated them to continue to help them if no counsel appears.

Mr. Roddy: Then I don't appear then as counsel but I do want to stay in and not be ruled out in this case.

The Court: Of course I would not do that—

Mr. Roddy: I just appear here through the courtesy of Your Honor.

The Court: Of course I give you that right. . . .

And then, apparently addressing all the lawyers present, the court inquired:

. . . Well are you all willing to assist?

Mr. Moody: Your Honor appointed us all and we have been proceeding along every line we know about it under Your Honor's appointment.

The Court: The only thing I am trying to do is, if counsel appears for these defendants I don't want to impose on you all, but if you feel like counsel from Chattanooga—

Mr. Moody: I see his situation of course and I have not run out of anything yet. Of course, if Your Honor purposes to appoint us, Mr. Parks, I am willing to go on with it. Most of the bar have been down and conferred with these defendants in this case; they did not know what else to do.

The Court: The thing, I did not want to impose on the members of the bar if counsel unqualifiedly appears; if you all feel like Mr. Roddy is only interested in a limited way to assist, then I don't care to appoint—

Mr. Parks: Your Honor, I don't feel like you ought to impose on any member of the local bar if the defendants are represented by counsel.

The Court: That is what I was trying to ascertain, Mr. Parks.

Mr. Parks: Of course if they have counsel, I don't see the necessity of the Court appointing anybody; if they haven't counsel, of course I think it is up to the Court to appoint counsel to represent them.

The Court: I think you are right about it Mr. Parks and that is the reason I was trying to get an expression from Mr. Roddy.

Mr. Roddy: I think Mr. Parks is entirely right about it, if I was paid down here and employed, it would be a different thing, but I have not prepared this case for trial and have only been called into it by people who are interested in these boys from Chattanooga. Now, they have not given me an opportunity to prepare the case and I am not familiar with the procedure in Alabama, but I merely came down here as a friend of the people who are interested and not as paid counsel, and certainly I haven't any money to pay them and nobody I am interested in had me to come down here has put up any fund of money to come down here and pay counsel. If they should do it I would be glad to turn it over—a counsel but I am merely here at the solicitation of people who have become interested in this case without any payment of fee and without any preparation for trial and I think the boys would be better off if I step entirely out of the case according to my way of looking at it and according to my lack of preparation for it and not being familiar with the procedure in Alabama. . . .

Mr. Roddy later observed:

If there is anything I can do to be of help to them, I will be glad to do it; I am interested to that extent.

The Court: Well gentlemen, if Mr. Roddy only appears as assistant that way, I think it is proper that I appoint members of this bar to represent them, I expect that is right. If Mr. Roddy will appear, I wouldn't of course, I would not appoint anybody. I don't see, Mr. Roddy, how I can make a qualified appointment or a limited appointment. Of course, I don't mean to cut off your assistance in any way—Well gentlemen, I think you understand it.

Mr. Moody: I am willing to go ahead and help Mr. Roddy in anything I can do about it, under the circumstances.

The Court: All right, all the lawyers that will; of course I would not require a lawyer to appear if—

Mr. Moody: I am willing to go ahead and help Mr. Roddy in anything I can do about it, under the circumstances.

The Court: All right, all the lawyers that will, of course, I would not require a lawyer to appear if—

Mr. Moody: I am willing to do that for him as a member of the bar; I will go ahead and help do anything I can do.

The Court: All right.

And in this casual fashion the matter of counsel in a capital case was disposed of.

It thus will be seen that until the very morning of the trial no lawyer had been named or definitely designated to represent the defendants. Prior to that time, the trial judge had "appointed all the members of the bar" for the limited "purpose of arraigning the defendants." Whether they would represent the defendants thereafter, if no counsel appeared in their behalf, was a matter of speculation only, or, as the judge indicated, of mere anticipation on the part of the court. Such a designation, even if made for all purposes, would, in our opinion, have fallen far short of meeting, in any proper sense, a requirement for the appointment of counsel. How many lawyers were members of the bar does not appear; but, in the very nature of things, whether many or few, they would not, thus collectively named, have been given that clear appreciation of responsibility or impressed with that individual sense of duty which should and naturally would accompany the appointment of a selected member of the bar, specifically named and assigned.

That this action of the trial judge in respect of appointment of counsel was little more than an expansive gesture, imposing no substantial or definite obligation upon any one, is borne out by the fact that prior to the calling of the case for trial on April 6, a leading member of the local bar accepted employment on the side of the prosecution and actively participated in the trial. It is true that he said that before doing so he had understood Mr. Roddy would be employed as counsel for the defendants. This the lawyer is question, of his own accord, frankly stated to the court; and no doubt he acted with the utmost good faith. Probably other members of the bar had a like understanding. In any event, the circumstance lends emphasis to the conclusion that during perhaps the most critical period of the proceedings against these defendants, that is to say, from the time of their arraignment until the beginning of their trial, when consultation, thorough-going investigation and preparation were vitally important, the defendants did not have the aid of counsel in any real sense, although they were as much entitled to such aid during that period as at the trial itself.

Nor do we think the situation was helped by what occurred on the morning of the trial. At that time, as appears from the colloquy printed above, Mr. Roddy stated to the court that he did not appear as counsel, but that he would like to appear along with counsel that the court might appoint; that he had not been given an opportunity to prepare the case; that he was not familiar with the procedure in Alabama, but merely came down as a friend of the people who were interested; that he thought the boys would be better off if he should step entirely out of the case. Mr. Moody, a member of the local bar, expressed a willingness to help Mr. Roddy in anything he could do under the circumstances. To this the court responded: "All right, all the lawyers that will; of course I would not require a lawyer to appear if—." And Mr. Moody continued: "I am willing to do that for him as a member of the bar; I will go ahead and help do anything I can do." With this dubious understanding, the trials immediately proceeded. The defendants, young, ignorant, illiterate, surrounded by hostile sentiment, haled back and forth under guard of soldiers, charged with an atrocious crime regarded with especial horror in the community where they were to be tried, were thus put in peril of their lives within a few moments after counsel for the first time charged with any degree of responsibility began to represent them.

It is not enough to assume that counsel thus precipitated into the case thought there was no defense, and exercised their best judgment in proceeding to trial without preparation. Neither they nor the court could say what a prompt and thorough-going investigation might disclose as to the facts. No attempt was made to investigate. No opportunity to do so was given. Defendants were immediately hurried to trial. Chief Justice Anderson, after disclaiming any intention to criticize harshly counsel who attempted to represent defendants at the trials, said: ". . . The record indicates that the appearance was rather pro forma than zealous and active. . . ." Under the circumstances disclosed, we hold that defendants were not accorded the right of counsel in any substantial sense. To decide otherwise, would simply be to ignore actualities. This conclusion finds ample support in the reasoning of an overwhelming array of state decisions. . . .

It is true that great and inexcusable delay in the enforcement of our criminal law is one of the grave evils of our time. Continuances are frequently granted for unnecessarily long periods of time, and delays incident to the disposition of motions for new trial and hearings upon appeal have come in many cases to be a distinct reproach to the administration of justice. The prompt disposition of criminal cases is to be commended and encouraged. But in reaching that result a defendant, charged with a serious crime, must not be stripped of his right to have sufficient time to advise with counsel and prepare his defense. To do that is not to proceed promptly in the calm spirit of regulated justice but to go forward with the haste of the mob.

• • •

Second. The Constitution of Alabama (Const. 1901, s 6) provides that in all criminal prosecutions the accused shall enjoy the right to have the assistance of counsel; and a state statute (Code 1923, s 5567) requires the court in a capital case, where the defendant is unable to employ counsel, to appoint counsel for him. The state Supreme Court held that these provisions had not been infringed, and with that holding we are powerless to interfere. The question, however, which it is our duty, and within our power, to decide, is whether the denial of the assistance of counsel contravenes the due process clause of the Fourteenth Amendment to the Federal Constitution.

If recognition of the right of a defendant charged with a felony to have the aid of counsel depended upon the existence of a similar right at common law as it existed in England when our Constitution was adopted, there would be great difficulty in maintaining it as necessary to due process. Originally, in England, a person charged with treason or felony was denied the aid of counsel, except in respect of legal questions which the accused himself might suggest. At the same time parties in civil cases and persons accused of misdemeanors were entitled to the full assistance of counsel. After the revolution of 1688, the rule was abolished as to treason, but was otherwise steadily adhered to until 1836, when by act of Parliament the full right was granted in respect of felonies generally.

An affirmation of the right to the aid of counsel in petty offenses, and its denial in the case of crimes of the gravest character, where such aid is most needed, is so outrageous and so obviously a perversion of all sense of proportion that the rule was constantly, vigorously and sometimes passionately assailed by English statesmen and lawyers. As early as 1758, Blackstone, although recognizing that the rule was settled at common law, denounced it as not in keeping with the rest of the humane treatment of prisoners by the English law. "For upon what face of reason," he says "can that assistance be denied to save the life of a man, which yet is allowed him in prosecutions for every petty trespass?" One of the grounds upon which Lord Coke defended the rule was that in felonies the court itself was counsel for the prisoner. But how can a judge, whose functions are purely judicial, effectively discharge the obligations of counsel for the accused? He can and should see to it that in the proceedings before the court the accused shall be dealt with justly and fairly. He cannot investigate the facts, advise and direct the defense, or participate in those necessary conferences between counsel and accused which sometimes partake of the inviolable character of the confessional.

The [English] rule was rejected by the colonies. . . .

• • •

It never has been doubted by this court, or any other so far as we know, that notice and hearing are preliminary steps essential to the passing of an enforceable judgment, and that they, together with a legally competent tribunal having jurisdiction of the case, constitute basic elements of the constitutional requirement of due process of law. The words of Webster, so often quoted, that by "the law of the land" is intended "a law which hears before it condemns," have been repeated in varying forms of expression in a multitude of decisions. . . .

What, then, does a hearing include? Historically and in practice, in our own country at least, it has always included the right to the aid of counsel when desired and provided by the party asserting the right. The right to be heard would be, in many cases, of little avail if it did not comprehend the right to be heard by counsel. Even the intelligent and educated layman has small and sometimes no skill in the science of law. If charged with crime, he is incapable, generally, of determining for himself whether the indictment is good or bad. He is unfamiliar with the rules of evidence. Left without the aid of counsel he may be put on trial without a proper charge, and convicted upon incompetent evidence, or evidence irrelevant to the issue or otherwise inadmissible. He lacks both the skill and knowledge adequately to prepare his defense, even though he have a perfect one. He requires the guiding hand of counsel at every step in the proceedings against him. Without it, though he be not guilty, he faces the danger of conviction because he does not know how to establish his innocence. If that be true of men of intelligence, how much more true is it of the ignorant and illiterate, or those of feeble intellect. If in any case, civil or criminal, a state or federal court were arbitrarily to refuse to hear a party by counsel, employed by and appearing for him, it reasonably may not be doubted that such a refusal would be a denial of a hearing, and, therefore, of due process in the constitutional sense.

• • •

In the light of the facts outlined in the forepart of this opinion — the ignorance and illiteracy of the defendants, their youth, the circumstances of public hostility, the imprisonment and the close surveillance of the defendants by the military forces, the fact that their friends and families were all in other states and communication with them necessarily difficult, and above all that they stood in deadly peril of their lives — we think the failure of the trial court to give them reasonable time and opportunity to secure counsel was a clear denial of due process.

But passing that, and assuming their inability, even if opportunity had been given, to employ counsel, as the trial court evidently did assume, we are of opinion that, under the circumstances just stated, the necessity of counsel was so vital and imperative that the failure of the trial court to make an effective appointment of counsel was likewise a denial of due process within the meaning of the Fourteenth Amendment. Whether this would be so in other criminal prosecutions, or under other circumstances, we need not determine. All that it is necessary now to decide, as we do decide, is that in a capital case, where the defendant is unable to employ counsel, and is incapable adequately of making his own defense because of ignorance, feeble-mindedness, illiteracy, or the like, it is the duty of the court, whether requested or not, to assign counsel for him as a necessary requisite of due process of law; and that duty is not discharged by an assignment at such a time or under such circumstances as to preclude the giving of effective aid in the preparation and trial of the case. To hold otherwise would be to ignore the fundamental postulate, already adverted to, "that there are certain immutable principles of justice which inhere in the very idea of free government which no member of the Union may disregard." In a case such as this, whatever may be the rule in other cases, the right to have counsel appointed, when necessary, is a logical corollary from the constitutional right to be heard by counsel. . . .

• • •

Let us suppose the extreme case of a prisoner charged with a capital offense, who is deaf and dumb, illiterate, and feeble-minded, unable to employ counsel, with the whole power of the state arrayed against him, prosecuted by counsel for the state without assignment of counsel for his defense, tried, convicted, and sentenced to death. Such a result, which, if carried into execution, would be little short of judicial murder, it cannot be doubted would be a gross violation of the guarantee of due process of law; and we venture to think that no appellate court, state or federal, would hesitate so to decide. The duty of the trial court to appoint counsel under such circumstances is clear, as it is clear under circumstances such as are disclosed by the record here; and its power to do so, even in the absence of a statute, can not be questioned. Attorneys are officers of the court, and are bound to render service when required by such an appointment.

The United States by statute and every state in the Union by express provision of law, or by the determination of its courts, make it the duty of the trial judge, where the accused is unable to employ counsel, to appoint counsel for him. In most states the rule applies broadly to all criminal prosecutions, in others it is limited to the more serious crimes, and in a very limited number, to capital cases. A rule adopted with such unanimous accord reflects, if it does not establish the inherent right to have counsel appointed at least in cases like the present, and lends convincing support to the conclusion we have reached as to the fundamental nature of that right.

The judgments must be reversed and the causes remanded for further proceedings not inconsistent with this opinion.

[Justices Butler and McReynolds dissented.]

NOTES AND QUESTIONS

1. Of the three grounds for appeal presented to it — mob-dominated trial, insufficient right to counsel, discrimination in jury selection — the Supreme Court chose right to counsel. Why that choice? There was recent precedent in *Moore v. Dempsey* on the first ground, although the trials in *Powell* were not quite as egregious as in *Moore*: the trials lasted hours not 45 minutes; the prosecution severed the defendants into three groups; defense counsel cross-examined prosecution witnesses. There was also some constitutional precedent in the juror discrimination arena, although far from consistent, in *Strauder* and *Neal*. *See supra*. Assuming the Court wanted to take the most cautious path to reversal, which is likely, which ground for decision would be the least threatening to white supremacist criminal justice regimes?

2. It is unclear from the Court's opinion what lawyer or lawyers actually conducted the meager defense at the trials. But the Court has little trouble finding that the defendants were "in substance denied the right to counsel." It notes the "casual fashion" in which the trial court dealt with the issue — appointing all members of the local bar at the arraignment as counsel and apparently again on the morning of trial — and that, inasmuch as none of the "appointees" joined the prosecution team the appointment was nothing but an "expansive gesture." Why do you think the trial court might have handled the appointment in this manner?

3. The trials were held just 6 days after the indictment and arraignment and just 12 days after young men were arrested. The Court says nothing critical about this accelerated schedule, which was presumably due to the mob atmosphere, although it does state that defendants "should have been afforded a fair opportunity to secure counsel of their own choosing," and implies that defendants would have been entitled to a reasonable delay in order to do so. How important is this observation to the Court's decision? What if defendants had not been able to secure their own counsel and the trial court had unambiguously appointed counsel for defendants at their arraignment? Different result? If these had been the facts might the Court have decided the case on a different ground? Putting aside the obvious conflicts of interest with a lawyer or multiple lawyers representing nine defendants charged in a single criminal episode, is six days enough time to prepare a defense, which the Court acknowledges requires "consultation, thoroughgoing investigation and preparation"? The Court doesn't shed any light on this question—it didn't need to—but it does generally acknowledge "that great and inexcusable delays in the enforcement of our criminal law is one of the grave evils of our time." *Id.* at 59.

4. The Court recognizes that the Alabama Constitution enshrines the right to counsel in a criminal case and that a state statute requires the appointment of counsel for an indigent defendant in a capital case. *Id.* at 59-60. Because the Alabama Supreme Court had found these provisions satisfied in *Powell,* however, the Court could only reverse the conviction on the right-to-counsel issue by finding a violation of a new federal right to counsel that would bind states under the Fourteenth Amendment. The two dissenters take no issue with the majority's conclusion that the Sixth Amendment right should be "incorporated" into the Fourteenth Amendment. Was the Court's conclusion in this regard compelling? Why or why not? What about the Court's related conclusion—which it called a "logical corollary" of the first conclusion—that under certain circumstances courts were required to appoint counsel for indigent defendants? What bases were available to the Court in reaching these two conclusions?

5. The Court finds the right to counsel to be fundamental in part because it is derivative of, and essential to, the undoubtedly fundamental "right to be heard." *Id.* at 68. The Court continues:

> What, then, does a hearing include? Historically and in practice, in our own country at least, it has always included the right to the aid of counsel when desired and provided by the party asserting the right. The right to be heard would be, in many cases, of little avail if it did not comprehend the right to be heard by counsel. Even the intelligent and educated layman has small and sometimes no skill in the science of law. If charged with crime, he is incapable, generally, of determining for himself whether the indictment is good or bad. He is unfamiliar with the rules of evidence. Left without the aid of counsel he may be put on trial without a proper charge, and convicted upon incompetent evidence, or evidence irrelevant to the issue or otherwise inadmissible. He lacks both the skill and knowledge adequately to prepare his defense, even though he have a perfect one. He requires the guiding hand of counsel at every step in the proceedings against him. Without it, though he be not guilty, he faces the danger of conviction because he does not know how to establish his innocence. If that be true of men of intelligence, how much more true is it of the ignorant and illiterate, or those of feeble intellect. If in any case, civil or criminal, a state or federal court were arbitrarily to refuse to hear a party by counsel, employed by and appearing for him, it reasonably may not be doubted that such a refusal would be a denial of a hearing, and, therefore, of due process in the constitutional sense.

Id. at 68-69. While perhaps a statement of the obvious, this is powerful and compelling language, a ringing endorsement of the right to and necessity of counsel. Yet the Court in *Powell* narrowly limits its holding to the exceptional circumstances of the case: "the ignorance and illiteracy of the defendants, their youth, the circumstances of public hostility, the imprisonment and the close surveillance of the defendants by the military forces, the fact that their friends and families were all in other states and communication with them necessarily difficult, and above all that they stood in peril of their lives." *Id.* at 70. These are serious limitations. Presumably the Court was hesitant to impose on courts the burden, and perhaps cost, of an obligation to appoint counsel for indigent defendants in all capital cases or some subset of non-capital cases. But did it need to make the limited nature of its holding so explicit? Wouldn't the "holding" of *Powell* be tied to the circumstances of the case in any event?

6. Given this caveat, what does the federal right recognized in *Powell* truly accomplish? Is it that the right to counsel must be of meaningful substance, and "not discharged by an assignment at such a time or circumstances as to preclude the giving of effective aid in the trial of the case"?

Norris v. Alabama

294 U.S. 587 (1935)

Mr. Chief Justice HUGHES delivered the opinion of the Court.

Petitioner, Clarence Norris, is one of nine negro boys who were indicted in March, 1931, in Jackson county, Ala., for the crime of rape. On being brought to trial in that county, eight were convicted. The Supreme Court of Alabama reversed the conviction of one of these and affirmed that of seven, including Norris. This Court reversed the judgments of conviction upon the ground that the defendants had been denied due process of law in that the trial court had failed in the light of the circumstances disclosed, and of the inability of the defendants at that time to obtain counsel, to make an effective appointment of counsel to aid them in preparing and presenting their defense. *Powell v. Alabama*.

After the remand, a motion for change of venue was granted and the cases were transferred to Morgan county. Norris was brought to trial in November, 1933. At the outset, a motion was made on his behalf to quash the indictment upon the ground of the exclusion of negroes from juries in Jackson county where the indictment was found. A motion was also made to quash the trial venire in Morgan county upon the ground of the exclusion of negroes from juries in that county. In relation to each county, the charge was of long-continued, systematic, and arbitrary exclusion of qualified negro citizens from service on juries, solely because of their race and color, in violation of the Constitution of the United States. The state joined issue on this charge and after hearing the evidence, which we shall presently review, the trial judge denied both motions, and exception was taken. The trial then proceeded and resulted in the conviction of Norris who was sentenced to death. On appeal, the Supreme Court of the state considered and decided the federal question which Norris had raised and affirmed the judgment. We granted a writ of certiorari.

First. There is no controversy as to the constitutional principle involved. That principle, long since declared, was not challenged, but was expressly recognized, by the Supreme Court of the state. Summing up precisely the effect of earlier decisions, this Court thus stated the principle in *Carter v. Texas*, in relation to exclusion from service on grand juries: "Whenever by any action of a state, whether through its Legislature, through its courts, or through its executive or administrative officers, all persons of the African race are excluded, solely because of their race or color, from serving as grand jurors in the criminal prosecution of a person of the African race, the equal protection of the laws is denied to him, contrary to the Fourteenth Amendment of the Constitution of the United States." *Strauder v. West Virginia*; *Neal v. Delaware*. This statement was repeated in the same terms in *Rogers v. Alabama*, 192 U.S. 226, 231, 24 S. Ct. 257, 48 L. Ed. 417, and again in *Martin v. Texas*, 200 U.S. 316, 319, 26 S. Ct. 338, 50 L. Ed. 497. The principle is equally applicable to a similar exclusion of negroes from service on petit juries. And although the state statute defining the qualifications of jurors may be fair on its face, the constitutional provision affords protection against action of the state through its administrative officers in effecting the prohibited discrimination.

The question is of the application of this established principle to the facts disclosed by the record. That the question is one of fact does not relieve us of the duty to determine whether in truth a federal right has been denied. When a federal right has been specially set up and claimed in a state court, it is our province to inquire not merely whether it was denied in express terms but also whether it was denied in substance and effect. If this requires an examination of evidence, that examination must be made. Otherwise, review by this Court would fail of its purpose in safeguarding constitutional rights. Thus, whenever a conclusion of law of a state court as to a federal right and findings of fact are so intermingled that the latter control the former, it is incumbent upon us to analyze the facts in order that the appropriate enforcement of the federal right may be assured.

Second. The evidence on the motion to quash the indictment. In 1930, the total population of Jackson county, where the indictment was found, was 36,881, of whom 2,688 were negroes. The male population over twenty-one years of age numbered 8,801, and of these 666 were negroes.

The qualifications of jurors were thus prescribed by the state statute: "The jury commission shall place on the jury roll and in the jury box the names of all male citizens of the county who are generally reputed to be honest and intelligent men, and are esteemed in the community for their integrity, good character and sound judgment, but no person must be selected who is under twenty-one or over sixty-five years of age, or, who is an habitual drunkard, or who, being afflicted with a permanent disease or physical weakness is unfit to discharge the duties of a juror, or who cannot read English, or who has ever been convicted of any offense involving moral turpitude. If a person cannot read English and has all the other qualifications prescribed herein and is a freeholder or householder, his name may be placed on the jury roll and in the jury box."

Defendant adduced evidence to support the charge of unconstitutional discrimination in the actual administration of the statute in Jackson county. The testimony, as the state court said, tended to show that "in a long number of years no negro had been called for jury service in that county." It appeared that no negro had served on any grand or petit jury in that county within the memory of witnesses who had lived there all their lives. Testimony to that effect was given by men whose ages ran from fifty to seventy-six years. Their testimony was uncontradicted. It was supported by the testimony of officials. The clerk of the jury commission and the clerk of the circuit court had never known of a negro serving on a grand jury in Jackson county. The court reporter, who had not missed a session in that county in twenty-four years, and two jury commissioners testified to the same effect. One of the latter, who was a member of the commission which made up the jury roll for the grand jury which found the indictment, testified that he had "never known of a single instance where any negro sat on any grand or petit jury in the entire history of that county."

That testimony in itself made out a prima facie case of the denial of the equal protection which the Constitution guarantees. *See Neal v. Delaware, supra.* The case thus made was supplemented by direct testimony that specified negroes, thirty or more in number, were qualified for jury service. Among these were negroes who were members of school boards, or trustees, of colored schools, and property owners and householders. It also appeared that negroes from that county had been called for jury service in the federal court. Several of those who were thus described as qualified were witnesses. While there was testimony which cast doubt upon the qualifications of some of the negroes who had been named, and there was also general testimony by the editor of a local newspaper who gave his opinion as to the lack of "sound judgment" of the "good negroes" in Jackson county, we think that the definite testimony as to the actual qualifications of individual negroes, which was not met by any testimony equally direct, showed that there were negroes in Jackson county qualified for jury service.

The question arose whether names of negroes were in fact on the jury roll. The books containing the jury roll for Jackson county for the year 1930-31 were produced. They were produced from the custody of a member of the jury commission which, in 1931, had succeeded the commission which had made up the jury roll from which the grand jury in question had been drawn. On the pages of this roll appeared the names of six negroes. They were entered, respectively, at the end of the precinct lists which were alphabetically arranged. The genuineness of these entries was disputed. It appeared that after the jury roll in question had been made up, and after the new jury commission had taken office, one of the new commissioners directed the new clerk to draw lines after the names which had been placed on the roll by the preceding commission. These lines, on the pages under consideration, were red lines, and the clerk of the old commission testified that they were not put in by him. The entries made by the new clerk, for the new jury roll, were below these lines.

The names of the six negroes were in each instance written immediately above the red lines. An expert of long experience testified that these names were superimposed upon the red lines, that is, that they were written after the lines had been drawn. The expert was not cross-examined and no testimony was introduced to contradict him. In denying the motion to quash, the trial judge expressed the view that he would not "be authorized to presume that somebody had committed a crime" or to presume that the jury board "had been unfaithful to their duties and allowed the books to be tampered with." His conclusion was that names of negroes were on the jury roll.

We think that the evidence did not justify that conclusion. The Supreme Court of the state did not sustain it. That court observed that the charge that the names of negroes were fraudulently placed on the roll did not involve any member of the jury board, and that the charge "was, by implication at least, laid at the door of the clerk of the board." The court, reaching its decision irrespective of that question, treated that phase of the matter as "wholly immaterial" and hence passed it by "without any expression of opinion thereon."

The state court rested its decision upon the ground that even if it were assumed that there was no name of a negro on the jury roll, it was not established that race or color caused the omission. The court pointed out that the statute fixed a high standard of qualifications for and that the jury commission was vested with a wide discretion. The court adverted to the fact that more white citizens possessing age qualifications had been omitted from the jury roll than the entire negro population of the county, and regarded the testimony as being to the effect that "the matter of race, color, politics, religion or fraternal affiliations" had not been discussed by the commission and had not entered into their consideration, and that no one had been excluded because of race or color.

The testimony showed the practice of the jury commission. One of the commissioners who made up the jury roll in question, and the clerk of that commission, testified as to the manner of its preparation. The other two commissioners of that period did not testify. It was shown that the clerk, under the direction of the commissioners, made up a preliminary list which was based on the registration list of voters, the polling list and the tax list, and apparently also upon the telephone directory. The clerk testified that he made up a list of all male citizens between the ages of twenty-one and sixty-five years without regard to their status or qualifications. The commissioner testified that the designation "col." was placed after the names of those who were colored. In preparing the final jury roll, the preliminary list was checked off as to qualified jurors with the aid of men whom the commissioners called in for that purpose from the different precincts. And the commissioner testified that in the selections for the jury roll no one was "automatically or systematically" excluded, or excluded on account of race or color; that he "did not inquire as to color," that was not discussed.

But, in appraising the action of the commissioners, these statements cannot be divorced from other testimony. As we have seen, there was testimony, not overborne or discredited, that there were in fact negroes in the county qualified for jury service. That testimony was direct and specific. After eliminating those persons as to whom there was some evidence of lack of qualifications, a considerable number of others remained. The fact that the testimony as to these persons, fully identified, was not challenged by evidence appropriately direct, cannot be brushed aside. There is no ground for an assumption that the names of these negroes were not on the preliminary list. The inference to be drawn from the testimony is that they were on that preliminary list, and were designated on that list as the names of negroes, and that they were not placed on the jury roll. There was thus presented a test of the practice of the commissioners. Something more than mere general asseverations was required. Why were these names excluded from the jury roll? Was it because of the lack of statutory qualifications? Were the qualifications of negroes actually and properly considered?

The testimony of the commissioner on this crucial question puts the case in a strong light. That testimony leads to the conclusion that these or other negroes were not excluded on account of age, or lack of esteem in the community for integrity and judgment, or because of disease or want of any other qualification. The commissioner's answer to specific inquiry upon this point was that negroes were "never discussed."

We are of the opinion that the evidence required a different result from that reached in the state court. We think that the evidence that for a generation or longer no negro had been called for service on any jury in Jackson county, that there were negroes qualified for jury service, that according to the practice of the jury commission their names would normally appear on the preliminary list of male citizens of the requisite age but that no names of negroes were placed on the jury roll, and the testimony with respect to the lack of appropriate consideration of the qualifications of negroes, established the discrimination which the Constitution forbids. The motion to quash the indictment upon that ground should have been granted.

Third. The evidence on the motion to quash the trial venire. The population of Morgan county, where the trial was had, was larger than that of Jackson county, and the proportion of negroes was much greater. The total population of Morgan county in 1930 was 46,176, and of this number 8,311 were negroes.

Within the memory of witnesses, long resident there, no negro had ever served on a jury in that county or had been called for such service. Some of these witnesses were over fifty years of age and had always lived in Morgan county. Their testimony was not contradicted. A clerk of the circuit court, who had resided in the county for thirty years, and who had been in office for over four years, testified that during his official term approximately 2,500 persons had been called for jury service and that not one of them was a negro; that he did not recall "ever seeing any single person of the colored race serve on any jury in Morgan County."

There was abundant evidence that there were a large number of negroes in the county who were qualified for jury service. Men of intelligence, some of whom were college graduates, testified to long lists (said to contain nearly 200 names) of such qualified negroes, including many business men, owners of real property and householders. When defendant's counsel proposed to call many additional witnesses in order to adduce further proof of qualifications of negroes for jury service, the trial judge limited the testimony, holding that the evidence was cumulative.

We find no warrant for a conclusion that the names of any of the negroes as to whom this testimony was given, or of any other negroes, were placed on the jury rolls. No such names were identified. The evidence that for many years no negro had been called for jury service itself tended to show the absence of the names of negroes from the jury rolls, and the state made no effort to prove their presence. The trial judge limited the defendant's proof "to the present year, the present jury roll." The sheriff of the county, called as a witness for defendants, scanned the jury roll and after "looking over every single name on that jury roll, from A to Z," was unable to point out "any single negro on it."

For this long-continued, unvarying, and wholesale exclusion of negroes from jury service we find no justification consistent with the constitutional mandate. We have carefully examined the testimony of the jury commissioners upon which the state court based its decision. One of these commissioners testified in person and the other two submitted brief affidavits. By the state act in force at the time the jury roll in question was made up, the clerk of the jury board was required to obtain the names of all male citizens of the county over twenty-one and under sixty-five years of age, and their occupation, place of residence, and place of business. The qualifications of those who were to be placed on the jury roll were the same as those prescribed by the earlier statute which we have already quoted. The member of the jury board, who testified orally, said that a list was made up which included the names of all male citizens of suitable age; that black residents were not excluded from this general list; that in compiling the jury roll he did not consider race or color; that no one was excluded for that reason; and that he had placed on the jury roll the names of persons possessing the qualifications under the statute. The affidavits of the other members of the board contained general statements to the same effect.

We think that this evidence failed to rebut the strong prima facie case which defendant had made. That showing as to the long-continued exclusion of negroes from jury service, and as to the many negroes qualified for that service, could not be met by mere generalities. If, in the presence of such testimony as defendant adduced, the mere general assertions by officials of their performance of duty were to be accepted as in adequate justification for the complete exclusion of negroes from jury service, the constitutional provision—adopted with special reference to their protection—would be but a vain and illusory requirement. The general attitude of the jury commissioner is shown by the following extract from his testimony: "I do not know of any negro in Morgan County over twenty-one and under sixty-five who is generally reputed to be honest and intelligent and who is esteemed in the community for his integrity, good character and sound judgment, who is not an habitual drunkard, who isn't afflicted with a permanent disease or physical weakness which would render him unfit to discharge the duties of a juror, and who can read English, and who has never been convicted of a crime involving moral turpitude." In the light of the testimony given by defendant's witnesses, we find it impossible to accept such a sweeping characterization of the lack of qualifications of negroes in Morgan county. It is so sweeping, and so contrary to the evidence as to the many qualified negroes, that it destroys the intended effect of the commissioner's testimony.

In *Neal v. Delaware, supra,* decided over fifty years ago, this Court observed that it was a "violent presumption," in which the state court had there indulged, that the uniform exclusion of negroes from juries, during a period of many years, was solely because, in the judgment of the officers, charged with the selection of grand and petit jurors, fairly exercised, "the black race in Delaware were utterly disqualified by want of intelligence, experience, or moral integrity, to sit on juries." Such a presumption at the present time would be no less violent with respect to the exclusion of the negroes of Morgan county. And, upon the proof contained in the record now before us, a conclusion that their continuous and total exclusion from juries was because there were none possessing the requisite qualifications, cannot be sustained.

We are concerned only with the federal question which we have discussed, and in view of the denial of the federal right suitably asserted, the judgment must be reversed and the cause remanded for further proceedings not inconsistent with this opinion.

It is so ordered.

Mr. Justice McReynolds did not hear the argument and took no part in the consideration and decision of this case.

NOTES AND QUESTIONS

1. The retrials of the Scottsboro defendants were led by New York lawyer Samuel Leibowitz, who had been retained by the Internal Labor Defense (ILD), the legal arm of the Communist Party. After the original convictions the cases of the "Scottsboro Boys" became a national and even international cause célèbre. In addition, a bitter feud arose between the Communist Party and the NAACP over which organization would lead the appeals and

Scottsboro defendants with their lawyer, Samuel Leibowitz

(if any) retrials. The Communist Party had immediately denounced the convictions while the NAACP had moved more cautiously, and the Communists ultimately gained the upper hand and litigation control, simultaneously launching protests and supporting rallies in the North. *See* Michael Klarman, Powell v. Alabama: The Supreme Court Confronts "Legal Lynchings," at 5-6, 16 in Criminal Procedure Stories (Carol S. Steiker ed., 2006).

2. Leibowitz was able to launch vigorous challenges to the racial composition of both the grand jury in Jackson County, where defendants had been indicted, and the petit jury in Morgan County, where the new trials would be held. He was able to put on dozens of witnesses, including current and former jury commissioners, court clerks, a handwriting expert, and Black witnesses who were plainly qualified for jury service but had never been called for jury duty. Although it is true that the judges that oversaw this pretrial litigation ultimately denied the defendants' motions to quash, unwilling to reach the conclusions the factual records warranted, the defendants' ability to compile such a record was itself something of an achievement. It marked progress from the turn-of-the-century cases, *see supra*, where many such challenges were shut off without any factual inquiry whatsoever.

3. The coup de grace of this pretrial litigation was the discovery that a jury commissioner had falsified the addition of names of Black persons to one of the juror rolls. At oral argument in the Supreme Court Leibowitz made inspired use of this evidence:

> He brought to the counsel table the actual books containing the jury roll for Jackson County, Alabama, which had been made part of the record below and had been filed with the Clerk's office. During his argument, Leibowitz piqued the Chief Justice's curiosity about the books. Leibowitz declared that the forgery in the jury rolls was fraud "not only against the defendants but against this very court itself." At this point, Hughes asked whether Leibowitz could prove

> the forgery, and Leibowitz offered to exhibit the jury rolls. "Let's see them," demanded Hughes. According to Professor Don Carter, "One by one, the eight justices examined the names in question under a magnifying glass while Leibowitz explained the mechanics of the forgery." For the first time in the history of the United States a federal judge laid his hands directly on hard evidence of jury discrimination by state jury selection officials. At Hughes' right shoulder, the fastidious Willis Van Devanter, the senior Associate Justice, craned to look at the books. In the expectant hush of the courtroom, Van Devanter was heard to whisper to Hughes: "Why it's as plain as punch."

See Benno C. Schmidt Jr., *Juries, Jurisdiction, and Race Discrimination: The Lost Promise of* Strauder v. West Virginia, 61 Tex. L. Rev. 1401, 1478-79 (1983) (footnotes omitted).

4. As in *Neal, supra*, the Supreme Court found that defendants had made out a prima facie case of discrimination as to both the petit and grand juries, which the state failed to rebut. 294 U.S. at 591, 598. The means to that end was a thorough and independent review of the facts, which was far from standard practice. The Court stated at the outset of its opinion:

> That the question is one of fact does not relieve us of the duty to determine whether in truth a federal right has been denied. When a federal right has been specially set up and claimed in a state court, it is our province to inquire not merely whether it was denied in express terms but also whether it was denied in substance and effect. If this requires an examination of evidence, that examination must be made. Otherwise, review by this Court would fail of its purpose in safeguarding constitutional rights. Thus, whenever a conclusion of law of a state court as to a federal right and findings of fact are so intermingled that the latter control the former, it is incumbent upon us to analyze the facts in order that the appropriate enforcement of the federal right may be assured.

Id. at 589. Are there any reasonable limits that, in more normal circumstances, should be placed on appellate courts' review of lower courts' factfinding? In what ways in *Norris* are the legal right and the findings of fact "intermingled"? Did the Supreme Court essentially draw different inferences from the facts than the trial court did?

D. COERCED CONFESSIONS

Brown v. Mississippi

297 U.S. 278 (1936)

Mr. Chief Justice Hughes delivered the opinion of the Court.

The question in this case is whether convictions, which rest solely upon confessions shown to have been extorted by officers of the state by brutality and violence, are consistent with the due process of law required by the Fourteenth Amendment of the Constitution of the United States.

Petitioners were indicted for the murder of one Raymond Stewart, whose death occurred on March 30, 1934. They were indicted on April 4, 1934, and were then arraigned and pleaded not guilty. Counsel were appointed by the court to defend them. Trial was begun the next morning and was concluded on the following day, when they were found guilty and sentenced to death.

Aside from the confessions, there was no evidence sufficient to warrant the submission of the case to the jury. After a preliminary inquiry, testimony as to the confessions was received over the objection of defendants' counsel. Defendants then testified that the confessions were false and had been procured by physical torture. The case went to the jury with instructions, upon the request of defendants' counsel, that if the jury had reasonable doubt as to the confessions having resulted from coercion, . . . they were not to be considered as evidence. On their [appeal] to the Supreme Court of the State, defendants assigned as error the inadmissibility of the confessions. The judgment was affirmed.

Defendants then moved in the Supreme Court of the State to arrest the judgment and for a new trial on the ground that all the evidence against them was obtained by coercion and brutality known to the court and to the district attorney, and that defendants had been denied the benefit of counsel or opportunity to confer with counsel in a reasonable manner. The motion was supported by affidavits. At about the same time, defendants filed in the Supreme Court a "suggestion of error" explicitly challenging the proceedings of the trial, in the use of the confessions and with respect to the alleged denial of representation by counsel, as violating the due process clause of the Fourteenth Amendment of the Constitution of the United States. The state court entertained the suggestion of error, considered the federal question, and decided it against defendants' contentions. Two judges dissented. We granted a writ of certiorari.

The grounds of the decision were (1) that immunity from self-incrimination is not essential to due process of law; and (2) that the failure of the trial court to exclude the confessions after the introduction of evidence showing their incompetency, in the absence of a request for such exclusion, did not deprive the defendants of life or liberty without due process of law; and that even if the trial court had erroneously overruled a motion to exclude the confessions, the ruling would have been mere error reversible on appeal, but not a violation of constitution right.

The opinion of the state court did not set forth the evidence as to the circumstances in which the confessions were procured. That the evidence established that they were procured by coercion was not questioned. The state court said: "After the state closed its case on the merits, the appellants, for the first time, introduced evidence from which it appears that the confessions were not made voluntarily but were coerced." There is no dispute as to the facts upon this point, and as they are clearly and adequately stated in the dissenting opinion of Judge Griffith (with whom Judge Anderson concurred), showing both the extreme brutality of the measures to extort the confessions and the participation of the state authorities, we quote this part of his opinion in full, as follows:

> The crime with which these defendants, all ignorant negroes, are charged, was discovered about 1 o'clock p.m. on Friday, March 30, 1934. On that night one Dial, a deputy sheriff, accompanied by others, came to the home of Ellington, one of the defendants, and requested him to accompany them to the house of the deceased, and there a number of white men were gathered, who began to accuse the defendant of the crime. Upon his denial they seized him, and with the participation of the deputy they hanged him by a rope to the limb of a tree, and, having let him down, they hung him again, and when he was let down the second time, and he still protested his innocence, he was tied to a tree and whipped, and, still declining to accede to the demands that he confess, he was finally released, and he returned with some difficulty to his home, suffering intense pain and agony. The record of the testimony shows that the signs of the rope on his neck were plainly visible during the so-called trial. A day or two thereafter the said deputy, accompanied by another, returned to the home of the said defendant and arrested him, and departed with the prisoner towards the jail in an adjoining county, but went by a route which led into the state of Alabama; and while on the way, in that state, the deputy stopped and again severely whipped the defendant, declaring that he would continue the whipping until he confessed, and the defendant then agreed to confess to such a statement as the deputy would dictate, and he did so, after which he was delivered to jail.
>
> The other two defendants, Ed Brown and Henry Shields, were also arrested and taken to the same jail. On Sunday night, April 1, 1934, the same deputy, accompanied by a number of white men, one of whom was also an officer, and by the jailer, came to the jail, and the two last

named defendants were made to strip and they were laid over chairs and their backs were cut to pieces with a leather strap with buckles on it, and they were likewise made by the said deputy definitely to understand that the whipping would be continued unless and until they confessed, and not only confessed, but confessed in every matter of detail as demanded by those present; and in this manner the defendants confessed the crime, and, as the whippings progressed and were repeated, they changed or adjusted their confession in all particulars of detail so as to conform to the demands of their torturers. When the confessions had been obtained in the exact form and contents as desired by the mob, they left with the parting admonition and warning that, if the defendants changed their story at any time in any respect from that last stated, the perpetrators of the outrage would administer the same or equally effective treatment.

Further details of the brutal treatment to which these helpless prisoners were subjected need not be pursued. It is sufficient to say that in pertinent respects the transcript reads more like pages torn from some medieval account than a record made within the confines of a modern civilization which aspires to an enlightened constitutional government.

All this having been accomplished, on the next day, that is, on Monday, April 2, when the defendants had been given time to recuperate somewhat from the tortures to which they had been subjected, the two sheriffs, one of the county where the crime was committed, and the other of the county of the jail in which the prisoners were confined, came to the jail, accompanied by eight other persons, some of them deputies, there to hear the free and voluntary confession of these miserable and abject defendants. The sheriff of the county of the crime admitted that he had heard of the whipping, but averred that he had no personal knowledge of it. He admitted that one of the defendants, when brought before him to confess, was limping and did not sit down, and that this particular defendant then and there stated that he had been strapped so severely that he could not sit down, and, as already stated, the signs of the rope on the neck of another of the defendants were plainly visible to all. Nevertheless the solemn farce of hearing the free and voluntary confessions was gone through with, and these two sheriffs and one other person then present were the three witnesses used in court to establish the so-called confessions, which were received by the court and admitted in evidence over the objections of the defendants duly entered of record as each of the said three witnesses delivered their alleged testimony. There was thus enough before the court when these confessions were first offered to make known to the court that they were not, beyond all reasonable doubt, free and voluntary; and the failure of the court then to exclude the confessions is sufficient to reverse the judgment, under every rule of procedure that has heretofore been prescribed, and hence it was not necessary subsequently to renew the objections by motion or otherwise.

The spurious confessions having been obtained—and the farce last mentioned having been gone through with on Monday, April 2d—the court, then in session, on the following day, Tuesday, April 3, 1934, ordered the grand jury to reassemble on the succeeding day, April 4, 1934, at 9 o'clock, and on the morning of the day last mentioned the grand jury returned an indictment against the defendants for murder. Late that afternoon the defendants were brought from the jail in the adjoining county and arraigned, when one or more of them offered to plead guilty, which the court declined to accept, and, upon inquiry whether they had or desired counsel, they stated that they had none, and did not suppose that counsel could be of any assistance to them. The court thereupon appointed counsel, and set the case for trial for the following morning at 9 o'clock, and the defendants were returned to the jail in the adjoining county about thirty miles away.

The defendants were brought to the courthouse of the county on the following morning, April 5th, and the so-called trial was opened, and was concluded on the next day, April 6, 1934, and resulted in a pretended conviction with death sentences. The evidence upon which the conviction was obtained was the so-called confessions. Without this evidence, a peremptory instruction to find for the defendants would have been inescapable. The defendants were put on the stand, and by their testimony the facts and the details thereof as to the manner by which the confessions were extorted from them were fully developed, and it is further disclosed by the record that the same deputy, Dial, under whose guiding hand and active participation the tortures to coerce the confessions were administered, was actively in the performance of

> the supposed duties of a court deputy in the courthouse and in the presence of the prisoners during what is denominated, in complimentary terms, the trial of these defendants. This deputy was put on the stand by the state in rebuttal, and admitted the whippings. It is interesting to note that in his testimony with reference to the whipping of the defendant Ellington, and in response to the inquiry as to how severely he was whipped, the deputy stated, "Not too much for a negro; not as much as I would have done if it were left to me." Two others who had participated in these whippings were introduced and admitted it—not a single witness was introduced who denied it. The facts are not only undisputed, they are admitted, and admitted to have been done by officers of the state, in conjunction with other participants, and all this was definitely well known to everybody connected with the trial, and during the trial, including the state's prosecuting attorney and the trial judge presiding.

The state stresses the statement in *Twining v. New Jersey* that "exemption from compulsory self-incrimination in the courts of the states is not secured by any part of the Federal Constitution," and the statement in *Snyder v. Massachusetts* that "the privilege against self-incrimination may be withdrawn and the accused put upon the stand as a witness for the state." But the question of the right of the state to withdraw the privilege against self-incrimination is not here involved. The compulsion to which the quoted statements refer is that of the processes of justice by which the accused may be called as a witness and required to testify. Compulsion by torture to extort a confession is a different matter.

The state is free to regulate the procedure of its courts in accordance with its own conceptions of policy, unless in so doing it "offends some principle of justice so rooted in the traditions and conscience of our people as to be ranked as fundamental." The state may abolish trial by jury. It may dispense with indictment by a grand jury and substitute complaint or information. But the freedom of the state in establishing its policy is the freedom of constitutional government and is limited by the requirement of due process of law. Because a state may dispense with a jury trial, it does not follow that it may substitute trial by ordeal. The rack and torture chamber may not be substituted for the witness stand. The state may not permit an accused to be hurried to conviction under mob domination—where the whole proceeding is but a mask—without supplying corrective process. *Moore v. Dempsey*. The state may not deny to the accused the aid of counsel. *Powell v. Alabama*. Nor may a state, through the action of its officers, contrive a conviction through the pretense of a trial which in truth is "but used as a means of depriving a defendant of liberty through a deliberate deception of court and jury by the presentation of testimony known to be perjured." *Mooney v. Holohan*. And the trial equally is a mere pretense where the state authorities have contrived a conviction resting solely upon confessions obtained by violence. The due process clause requires "that state action, whether through one agency or another, shall be consistent with the fundamental principles of liberty and justice which lie at the base of all our civil and political institutions." It would be difficult to conceive of methods more revolting to the sense of justice than those taken to procure the confessions of these petitioners, and the use of the confessions thus obtained as the basis for conviction and sentence was a clear denial of due process.

It is in this view that the further contention of the State must be considered. That contention rests upon the failure of counsel for the accused, who had objected to the admissibility of the confessions, to move for their exclusion after they had been introduced and the fact of coercion had been proved. It is a contention which proceeds upon a misconception of the nature of petitioners' complaint. That complaint is not of the commission of mere error, but of a wrong so fundamental that it made the whole proceeding a mere pretense of a trial and rendered the conviction and sentence wholly void. We are not concerned with a mere question of state practice, or whether counsel assigned to petitioners were competent or mistakenly assumed that their first objections were sufficient. In an earlier case the Supreme Court of the State had recognized the duty of the court to supply corrective process where due process of law had been denied. In *Fisher v. State,* 145 Miss. 116, the court said: "Coercing the supposed state's criminals into confessions and using such confessions so coerced from them against them in trials has been the curse of all countries. It was the chief iniquity, the crowning infamy of the Star Chamber, and the Inquisition, and other similar institutions. The Constitution recognized the evils that lay behind these practices and prohibited them in this country. . . . The duty of maintaining constitutional rights of a person on trial for his life rises above mere rules of procedure, and wherever the court is clearly satisfied that such violations exist, it will refuse to sanction such violations and will apply the corrective."

In the instant case, the trial court was fully advised by the undisputed evidence of the way in which the confessions had been procured. The trial court knew that there was no other evidence upon which conviction and sentence could be based. Yet it proceeded to permit conviction and to pronounce sentence. The conviction and sentence were void for want of the essential elements of due process, and the proceeding thus vitiated could be challenged in any appropriate manner. It was challenged before the Supreme Court of the State by the express invocation of the Fourteenth Amendment. That court entertained the challenge, considered the federal question thus presented, but declined to enforce petitioners' constitutional right. The court thus denied a federal right fully established and specially set up and claimed, and the judgment must be reversed.

It is so ordered.

NOTES AND QUESTIONS

1. One of the remarkable aspects of *Brown* is that the coerced confessions were the only evidence the prosecution offered against the three defendants. There are at least two possible explanations for this: (a) no other evidence against them could be found after investigation; or (b) the state simply didn't bother to look for evidence once it had the confessions. As to the latter explanation, consider that the Mississippi Supreme Court had previously reversed convictions based on confessions coerced by violence, *Brown v. State,* 36 So. 73 (Miss. 1904), a fact that the U.S. Supreme Court notes in its opinion. Of course, from the state's perspective, there was always a chance that the facts of the coercion would never come to light, or that the defendant would not appeal. Or that the defendant would be lynched before trial. In any event, the lack of any non-confession evidence against the defendants suggests the likelihood of their innocence, which—as in the cases above—made it more likely that there would be potential financial support for appellate litigation and that the U.S. Supreme Court would hear the case.

2. The Mississippi Supreme Court affirms on two grounds, one of which is a procedural default by defense counsel. What error did defense counsel make? What does the U.S. Supreme Court make of this reasoning?

3. For the facts of the case the Court relies almost entirely on the dissenting opinion of Mississippi Supreme Court Justice Griffith, which it quotes at length. Why might the Supreme Court have done this?

4. Another remarkable aspect of *Brown* is that the only real issue in the case—whether the confessions were coerced—was not the subject of a swearing contest. The facts of the coercion, testified to by the defendants, were admitted by the law enforcement and civilian assailants. In light of this factual record, what is the likely effect, if any, of *Brown* on law enforcement tactics? *See* Mark Tushnet, Making Civil Rights Law: Thurgood Marshall and the Supreme Court, 1936-1961 (1994), at 57 ("The police did not stop using those tactics;

instead, having been told that they could not use the third degree, the police began to deny that the confessions they obtained resulted from improper tactics.").

Four of the cases highlighted in this chapter—*Moore*, *Powell*, *Norris*, and *Brown*—are widely regarded as landmark cases in the Supreme Court's constitutionalization of criminal procedure. Yet their actual impact is uncertain. *Moore* did not end mob-dominated trials. *Powell*, narrow to begin with, could be complied with by appointing counsel for a defendant just a few days before trial. *Norris* did not do much at all to change the racial composition of juries in the South, and to the extent any Black persons made their way on to grand juries, they could be outvoted and they could be removed from petit juries though peremptory challenges. *Brown* did not end coerced confessions, although it may have taught the police not to admit to them. *See* Klarman, *The Racial Origins of Modern Criminal Procedure*, *supra* at 78-83. And it wasn't as if counsel was readily available to help impecunious Black criminal defendants take advantage of the legal precedent that began to emerge, even at trial not to mention appellate litigation:

> The criminal procedure cases that reached the Supreme Court were atypical in this regard. The NAACP financed the appellate litigation in *Moore*; the ILD in *Powell* and *Norris*; and the NAACP, the CIC, and the ASWPL in *Brown*. None of these cases could have gotten to the Supreme Court without outside financial assistance. The Phillips County race riot and

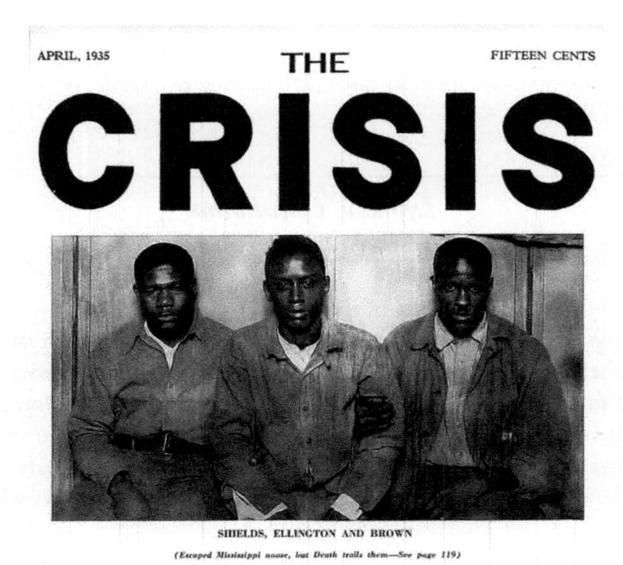

Brown v. Mississippi defendants Henry Shields, Arthur Ellington, and Ed Brown on the cover of the NAACP's April 1935 edition of *The Crisis*. The magazine's first editor was W.E.B. DuBois. It has been in continuous circulation since 1910.

> the alleged rapes and ensuing trials at Scottsboro captured national attention. Because these criminal cases revealed southern Jim Crow at its worst, they provided outstanding fundraising opportunities. The NAACP and the ILD, respectively, became involved at the early stages of litigation and raised large sums of money to finance appeals. *Brown v. Mississippi* was more of a garden variety murder case. Only the extraordinary efforts of local appointed counsel, who covered some of the legal costs from his own pocket, kept the case alive long enough for outside organizations to become involved and finance an appeal to the Supreme Court.
>
> In the run-of-the-mill criminal case, indigent black defendants were represented not by elite legal talent hired by the NAACP or the ILD, but rather by court-appointed lawyers. Generally these lawyers were white, and they could not always be counted upon to defend aggressively the rights of their black clients, since doing so could be injurious to their careers as well as potentially hazardous to their health. For example, a tacit agreement existed among prosecutors and defense counsel in many southern counties not to raise the issue of black exclusion from juries. When a white ILD lawyer challenged that tacit agreement in a Maryland murder case in 1931, he had to endure death threats and subsequent retaliatory disbarment proceedings. The ILD lawyer representing the Scottsboro Boys in their first round of retrials, Samuel Leibowitz, was besieged with death threats after he questioned in court the honesty of county jury commissioners and of the white women who had alleged rape. The court-appointed white defense attorney in *Brown v. Mississippi* ruined a promising political career by pursuing the case so aggressively. In the wake of Scottsboro, two white ILD lawyers lost their lives for defending three blacks charged with raping and killing a white woman in Tuscaloosa, Alabama.

Id. at 84-85.

Nor was it a sure thing that getting a case to the Supreme Court would result in a faithful application of the principles set forth in cases such as *Moore*, *Powell*, *Norris*, and *Brown*, as the next two cases will show.

Lyons v. Oklahoma

322 U.S. 596 (1944)

Mr. Justice Reed delivered the opinion of the Court.

This writ brings to this Court for review a conviction obtained with the aid of a confession which furnished, if voluntary, material evidence to support the conviction. As the questioned confession followed a previous confession which was given on the same day and which was admittedly involuntary, the issue is the voluntary character of the second confession under the circumstances which existed at the time and place of its signature and, particularly, because of the alleged continued influence of the unlawful inducements which vitiated the prior confession.

The petitioner was convicted in the state district court of Choctaw County, Oklahoma, on an information charging him and another with the crime of murder. The jury fixed his punishment at life imprisonment. The conviction was affirmed by the Criminal Court of Appeals, and this Court granted certiorari upon the petitioner's representation that there had been admitted against him an involuntary confession procured under circumstances which made its use in evidence a violation of his rights under the due process clause of the Fourteenth Amendment.

Prior to Sunday, December 31, 1939, Elmer Rogers lived with his wife and three small sons in a tenant house situated a short distance northwest of Fort Towson, Choctaw County, Oklahoma. Late in the evening of that day Mr. and Mrs. Rogers and a four year old son Elvie were murdered at their home and the house was burned to conceal the crime.

Suspicion was directed toward the petitioner Lyons and a confederate, Van Bizzell. On January 11, 1940. Lyons was arrested by a special policeman and another officer whose exact official status is not disclosed by the record. The first formal charge that appears is at Lyons' hearing before a magistrate on January 27, 1940. Immediately after his arrest there was an interrogation of about two hours at the jail. After he had been in jail eleven days he was again questioned, this time in the county prosecutor's office. This interrogation began about six-thirty in the evening, and on the following morning between two and four produced a confession. This questioning is the basis of the objection to the introduction as evidence of a second confession which was obtained later in the day at the state penitentiary at McAlester by Warden Jess Dunn and introduced in evidence at the trial. There was also a third confession, oral, which was admitted on the trial without objection by petitioner. This was given to a guard at the penitentiary two days after the second. Only the petitioner, police, prosecuting and penitentiary officials were present at any of these interrogations, except that a private citizen who drove the car that brought Lyons to McAlester witnessed this second confession.

William Douglas Lyons, handcuffed and in the company of the six arresting police officers

Lyons is married and was twenty-one or two years of age at the time of the arrest. The extent of his education or his occupation does not appear. He signed the second confession. From the transcript of his evidence, there is no indication of a subnormal intelligence. He had served two terms in the penitentiary—one for chicken stealing and one for burglary. Apparently he lived with various relatives.

While petitioner was competently represented before and at the trial, counsel was not supplied him until after his preliminary examination, which was subsequent to the confessions. His wife and family visited him between his arrest and the first confession. There is testimony by Lyons of physical abuse by the police officers at the time of his arrest and first interrogation on January 11th. His sister visited him in jail shortly afterwards and testified as to marks of violence on his body and a blackened eye. Lyons says that this violence was accompanied by threats of further harm unless he confessed. This evidence was denied in toto by officers who were said to have participated.

Eleven days later the second interrogation occurred. Again the evidence of assault is conflicting. Eleven or twelve officials were in and out of the prosecutor's small office during the night. Lyons says that he again suffered assault. Denials of violence were made by all the participants accused by Lyons except the county attorney, his assistant, the jailer and a highway patrolman. Disinterested witnesses testified to statements by an investigator which tended to implicate that officer in the use of force, and the prosecutor in cross-examination used language which gave color to defendant's charge. It is not disputed that the inquiry continued until two-thirty in the morning before an oral confession was obtained and that a pan of the victims' bones was placed in Lyon's lap by his interrogators to bring about his confession. As the confession obtained at this time was not offered in evidence, the only bearing these events have here is their tendency to show that the later confession at McAlester was involuntary.

After the oral confession in the early morning hours of January 23, Lyons was taken to the scene of the crime and subjected to further questioning about the instruments which were used to commit the murders. He was returned to the jail about eight-thirty a.m. and left there until early afternoon. After that the prisoner was taken to a nearby town of Antlers, Oklahoma. Later in the day a deputy sheriff and a private citizen took the petitioner to the penitentiary. There, sometime between eight and eleven o'clock on that same evening, the petitioner signed the second confession.

When the confession which was given at the penitentiary was offered, objection was made on the ground that force was practiced to secure it and that even if no force was then practiced, the fear instilled by the prisoner's former treatment at Hugo on his first and second interrogations continued sufficiently coercive in its effect to require the rejection of the second confession.

The judge in accordance with Oklahoma practice and, after hearing evidence from the prosecution and the defense in the absence of the jury, first passed favorably upon its admissibility as a matter of law, and then, after witnesses testified before the jury as to the voluntary character of the confession, submitted the guilt or innocence of the defendant to the jury under a full instruction, approved by the Criminal Court of Appeals, to the effect that voluntary confessions are admissible against the person making them but are to be "carefully scrutinized and received with great caution" by the jury and rejected if obtained by punishment, intimidation or threats. It was added that the mere fact that a confession was made in answer to inquiries "while under arrest or in custody" does not prevent consideration of the evidence if made "freely and voluntarily." The instruction did not specifically cover the defendant's contention, embodied in a requested instruction, that the second confession sprang from the fear engendered by the treatment he had received at Hugo.

The mere questioning of a suspect while in the custody of police officers is not prohibited either as a matter of common law or due process. The question of how specific an instruction in a state court must be upon the involuntary character of a confession is, as a matter of procedure or practice, solely for the courts of the state. When the state-approved instruction fairly raises the question of whether or not the challenged confession was voluntary, as this instruction did, the requirements of due process, under the Fourteenth Amendment, are satisfied and this Court will not require a modification of local practice to meet views that it might have as to the advantages of concreteness. The instruction given satisfies the legal requirements of the State of Oklahoma as to the particularity with which issues must be presented to its juries, and in view of the scope of that instruction, it was sufficient to preclude any claim of violation of the Fourteenth Amendment.

The federal question presented is whether the second confession was given under such circumstances that its use as evidence at the trial constitutes a violation of the due process clause of the Fourteenth Amendment, which requires that state criminal proceedings "shall be consistent with the fundamental principles of liberty and justice."

No formula to determine this question by its application to the facts of a given case can be devised. Here improper methods were used to obtain a confession, but that confession was not used at the trial. Later, in another place and with different persons present, the accused again told the facts of the crime. Involuntary confessions, of course, may be given either simultaneously with or subsequently to unlawful pressures, force or threats. The question of whether those confessions subsequently given are themselves voluntary depends on the inferences as to the continuing effect of the coercive practices which may fairly be drawn from the surrounding circumstances. The voluntary or involuntary character of a confession is determined by a conclusion as to whether the accused, at the time he confesses, is in possession of "mental freedom" to confess to or deny a suspected participation in a crime.

When conceded facts exist which are irreconcilable with such mental freedom, regardless of the contrary conclusions of the triers of fact, whether judge or jury, this Court cannot avoid responsibility for such injustice by leaving the burden of adjudication solely in other hands. But where there is a dispute as to whether the acts which are charged to be coercive actually occurred, or where different inferences may fairly be drawn from admitted facts, the trial judge and the jury are not only in a better position to appraise the truth or falsity of the defendant's assertions from the demeanor of the witnesses but the legal duty is upon them to make the decision.

Review here deals with circumstances which require examination into the possibility as to whether the judge and jury in the trial court could reasonably conclude that the McAlester confession was voluntary. The fact that there is evidence which would justify a contrary conclusion is immaterial. To triers of fact is left the determination of the truth or error of the testimony of prisoner and official alike. It is beyond question that if the triers of fact accepted as true the evidence of the immediate events at McAlester, which were detailed by Warden Dunn and the other witnesses, the verdict would be that the confession was voluntary, so that the petitioner's case rests upon the theory that the McAlester confession was the unavoidable outgrowth of the events at Hugo.

The Fourteenth Amendment does not protect one who has admitted his guilt because of forbidden inducements against the use at trial of his subsequent confessions under all possible circumstances. The admissibility of the later confession depends upon the same test—is it voluntary. Of course the fact that the earlier statement was obtained from the prisoner by coercion is to be considered in appraising the character of the later confession. The effect of earlier abuse may be so clear as to forbid any other inference than that it dominated the mind of the accused to such an extent that the later confession is involuntary. If the relation between the earlier and later confession is not so close that one must say the facts of one control the character of the other, the inference is one for the triers of fact and their conclusion, in such an uncertain situation, that the confession should be admitted as voluntary, cannot be a denial of due process.

• • •

Petitioner suggests a presumption that earlier abuses render subsequent confessions involuntary unless there is clear and definite evidence to overcome the presumption. We need not analyze this contention further than to say that in this case there is evidence for the state which, if believed, would make it abundantly clear that the events at Hugo did not bring about the confession at McAlester.

In our view, the earlier events at Hugo do not lead unescapably to the conclusion that the later McAlester confession was brought about by the earlier mistreatments. The McAlester confession was separated from the early morning statement by a full twelve hours. It followed the prisoner's transfer from the control of the sheriff's force to that of the warden. One person who had been present during a part of the time while the Hugo interrogation was in progress was present at McAlester, it is true, but he was not among those charged with abusing Lyons during the questioning at Hugo. There was evidence from others present that Lyons readily confessed without any show of force or threats within a very short time of his surrender to Warden Dunn and after being warned by Dunn that anything he might say would be used against him and that he should not "make a statement unless he voluntarily wanted to." Lyons, as a former inmate of the institution, was acquainted with the warden. The petitioner testified to nothing in the past that would indicate any reason for him to fear mistreatment there. The fact that Lyons, a few days later, frankly admitted the killings to a sergeant of the prison guard, a former acquaintance from his own locality, under circumstances free of coercion suggests strongly that the petitioner had concluded that it was wise to make a clean breast of his guilt and that his confession to Dunn was voluntary. The answers to the warden's questions, as transcribed by a prison stenographer, contain statements correcting and supplementing the questioner's information and do not appear to be mere supine attempts to give the desired response to leading questions.

The Fourteenth Amendment is a protection against criminal trials in state courts conducted in such a manner as amounts to a disregard of "that fundamental fairness essential to the very concept of justice," and in a way that "necessarily prevent(s) a fair trial." A coerced confession is offensive to basic standards of justice, not because the victim has a legal grievance against the police, but because declarations procured by torture are not premises from which a civilized forum will infer guilt. The Fourteenth Amendment does not provide review of mere error in jury verdicts, even though the error concerns the voluntary character of a confession. We cannot say that an inference of guilt based in part upon Lyons' McAlester confession is so illogical and unreasonable as to deny the petitioner a fair trial.

Affirmed.

Mr. Justice Douglas concurs in the result.

Mr. Justice Rutledge dissents.

Mr. Justice Murphy, dissenting.

This flagrant abuse by a state of the rights on an American citizen accused of murder ought not to be approved. The Fifth Amendment prohibits the federal government from convicting a defendant on evidence that he was compelled to give against himself. Decisions of this Court in effect have held that the Fourteenth Amendment makes this prohibition applicable to the states. It is our duty to apply that constitutional prohibition in this case.

Even though approximately twelve hours intervened between the two confessions and even assuming that there was no violence surrounding the second confession, it is inconceivable under these circumstances that the second confession was free from the coercive atmosphere that admittedly impregnated the first one. The whole confession technique used here constituted one single, continuing transaction. To conclude that the brutality inflicted at the time of the first confession suddenly lost all of its effect in the short space of twelve hours is to close one's eyes to the realities of human nature. An individual does not that easily forget the type of torture that accompanied petitioner's previous refusal to confess, nor does a person like petitioner so quickly recover from the gruesome effects of having had a pan of human bones placed on his knees in order to force incriminating testimony from him. Moreover, the trial judge refused petitioner's request that the jury be charged that the second confession was not free and voluntary if it was obtained while petitioner was still suffering from the inhuman treatment he had previously received. Thus it cannot be said that we are confronted with a finding by the trier of facts that the coercive effect of the prior brutality had completely worn off by the time the second confession was signed.

Presumably, therefore, this decision means that state officers are free to force a confession from an individual by ruthless methods, knowing full well that they dare not use such a confession at the trial, and then, as a part of the same continuing transaction and before the effects of the coercion can fairly be said to have completely worn off, procure another confession without any immediate violence being inflicted. The admission of such a tainted confession does not accord with the Fourteenth Amendment's command that a state shall not convict a defendant on evidence that he was compelled to give against himself.

Mr. Justice Black concurs in this opinion.

NOTES AND QUESTIONS

1. The Court concludes that deference must be given to the judge and jury's conclusion that the confession admitted into evidence at trial was voluntary. How does this square with the *Norris* Court's statements on the Supreme Court's obligations with respect to state-court factfinding?

Lyons's trial defense team, led by 32-year-old Thurgood Marshall (on the right)

2. The Court's discussion of the facts tells you right where this is headed. Perhaps most remarkable is the Court's statement that, with respect to the interrogation that produced the confession, "the evidence of assault is conflicting." Yet in the very next sentence we learn that "[denials] of violence were made by all of the [11 or 12] interrogation participants accused by Lyons *except the county attorney, his assistant, the jailer, and a highway patrolman.*" That is not disputed evidence. Four representatives of the state admitted that violence occurred; the other seven or eight lied.

3. Note that the ultimate question of voluntariness was an issue for the jury, not a preliminary matter for the court to decide. Does it make sense that the jury and not the court should decide this issue, which is at bottom an evidentiary issue—should the confession be admitted into evidence for the jury's consideration? The court also refused to give the jury the instruction requested by the defendant, that the second confession could not be considered voluntary if it was attributable to the defendant's inhumane treatment during the physically coerced confession made earlier. Do you think the relationship between the two confessions is a matter of common sense and that therefore a specific instruction was not necessary inasmuch as the jury was instructed that confessions must be "carefully scrutinized and received with great caution" and rejected if obtained by intimidation or threats? What effect, if any, might the instruction requested by the defendant have had?

4. The Court notes that the second confession was given to, among others, the warden of the penitentiary to which Lyons had been transferred, and that the warden had warned him that anything he said would be used against him. What effect might that have had on the voluntariness of Lyons's subsequent statements? What do you make of the Court's observation that Lyons "was acquainted with the warden"?

5. The dissent states that "it is inconceivable under these circumstances that the second confession was free from the coercive atmosphere that admittedly tainted the first one." Can you disagree with that point and still agree with the dissent?

Akins v. Texas

325 U.S. 398 (1945)

Mr. Justice Reed delivered the opinion of the Court.

This certiorari brings here for review a judgment of the Criminal District Court of Dallas County, Texas, sentencing petitioner to execution on a jury verdict which found petitioner guilty of murder with malice and assessed the penalty at death.

Certiorari was sought to the Court of Criminal Appeals of the State of Texas, which had affirmed the judgment, on a petition which claimed discrimination on account of his race, against the petitioner, who is a Negro, under the equal protection and due process clauses of the Fourteenth Amendment of the Constitution of the United States. Certiorari was allowed because of the importance in the administration of criminal justice of the alleged racial discrimination which was relied upon to support the claim of violation of constitutional rights. This discrimination was said to consist of an arbitrary and purposeful limitation by the Grand Jury Commissioners of the number of Negroes to one who was to be placed upon the grand jury panel of sixteen for the term of court at which the indictment against petitioner was found. This is petitioner's only complaint as to racial discrimination. No other errors in the proceedings are pointed out.

The Fourteenth Amendment forbids any discrimination against a race in the selection of a grand jury. An allegation of discriminatory practices in selecting a grand jury panel challenges an essential element of proper judicial procedure—the requirement of fairness on the part of the judicial arm of government in dealing with persons charged with criminal offenses. It cannot lightly be concluded that officers of the courts disregard this accepted standard of justice.

The order overruling the motion to quash the indictment was made after evidence and without opinion. That motion set out the alleged purposeful limitation on racial representation which is pressed here. The Court of Criminal Appeals, however, without a written analysis of the testimony, said in an opinion that it failed "to find any evidence of discrimination. On the contrary, the evidence shows an effort on the part of the authorities to comply with the holding of this court and of the Supreme Court of the United States upon the question of discrimination." Although this opinion of the Court of Criminal Appeals does not refer to proportional racial representation on juries, recent decisions of that court had previously disapproved that procedure. We think, therefore, that the conclusions of the state courts show that in their judgment there was no proven racial discrimination by limitation in this case. Otherwise there would have been a reversal by the Court of Criminal Appeals.

As will presently appear, the transcript of the evidence presents certain inconsistencies and conflicts of testimony in regard to limiting the number of negroes on the grand jury. Therefore, the trier of fact who heard the witnesses in full and observed their demeanor on the stand has a better opportunity than a reviewing court to reach a correct conclusion as to the existence of that type of discrimination. While our duty, in reviewing a conviction upon a complaint that the procedure through which it was obtained violates due process and equal protection under the Fourteenth Amendment, calls for our examination of evidence to determine for ourselves whether a federal constitutional right has been denied, expressly or in substance and effect, *Norris v. State of Alabama*, we accord in that examination great respect to the conclusions of the state judiciary. That respect leads us to accept the conclusion of the trier on disputed issues "unless it is so lacking in support in the evidence that to give it effect would work that fundamental unfairness which is at war with due process."

The regular statutory practice for the selection of grand jurors was followed in this case. Under the Texas statutes jury commissioners appointed by the judge of the trial court select a list of sixteen grandjurymen from which list twelve are chosen as a grand jury. Qualifications for grandjurymen are set out in Article 339. The Commissioners are instructed by the court as to their duties. This method of selection leaves a wide range of choice to the commissioners. Its validity, however, has been accepted by this Court. Petitioner does not attack it now. Its alternative would be a list composed of all eligibles within the trial court's jurisdiction and selection of the panel by lot.

Petitioner's sole objection to the grand jury is that the "commissioners deliberately, intentionally and purposely limited the number of the Negro race that should be selected on said grand jury panel to one member." Fairness in selection has never been held to require proportional representation of races upon a jury. Purposeful discrimination is not sustained by a showing that on a single grand jury the number of members of one race is less than that race's proportion of the eligible individuals. The number of our races and nationalities stands in the way of evolution of such a conception of due process or equal protection. Defendants under our criminal statutes are not entitled to demand representatives of their racial inheritance upon juries before whom they are tried. But such defendants are entitled to require that those who are trusted with jury selection shall not pursue a course of conduct which results in discrimination "in the selection of jurors on racial grounds." Our directions that indictments be quashed when Negroes, although numerous in the community, were excluded from grand jury lists have been based on the theory that their continual exclusion indicated discrimination and not on the theory that racial groups must be recognized. The mere fact of inequality in the number selected does not in itself show discrimination. A purpose to discriminate must be present which may be proven by systematic exclusion of eligible jurymen of the proscribed race or by unequal application of the law to such an extent as to show intentional discrimination. Cf. *Snowden v. Hughes*, 321 U.S. 1, 8, 64 S. Ct. 397, 401. Any such discrimination which affects an accused will make his conviction unlawful.

The history and record of this case gives evidence that the courts of Texas which are charged with the trial of petitioner endeavored to comply with the federal constitutional requirements as to the selection of grand juries, according to the interpretation of this Court in *Hill v. Texas, supra*. Not only did the Court of Criminal Appeals reverse a former conviction of petitioner on its authority but the judge, now deceased, of the criminal district court of Dallas instructed the three jury commissioners, who selected this grand jury list, as testified to by each of them, that there should be no discrimination against anyone because of his color.

Hill v. Texas, supra, was decided June 1, 1942. The trial court has four terms a year — January, April, July and October. After the *Hill* decision, the jury commissioners who were appointed at the July 1942 term to select grand jurors for the October 1942 term, placed a Negro on the grand jury list although he did not serve. Under the instructions of the judge as just detailed, the commissioners for the January 1943 term, at which petitioner was indicted, placed a Negro on the list and he served as a grand juror. Prior to the decision in the *Hill* case, it does not appear that any colored person had ever served on a grand jury in Dallas County.

On the precise act of discrimination by the jury commissioners which is asserted by petitioner, that is the deliberate, intentional and purposeful limitation to one of the number of Negroes on the grand jury panel, the record shows as follows. About fifteen and one-half per cent of the population of Dallas County, Texas, is negro. A substantial percentage of them are qualified to serve as grand jurors. No exact comparison can be made between the white and negro citizens as to the percentage of each race which is eligible. On the strictly mathematical basis of population, a grand jury of twelve would have 1.8552 negro members on the average. Of course, the qualifications for grand jury service would affect the proportion of eligibles from the two races. As one member of the Negro race served upon the grand jury which indicted petitioner and one had appeared upon the other grand jury list which had been selected after the decision in *Hill v. Texas, supra*, we cannot say that the omission from each of the two lists of all but one of the members of a race which composed some fifteen per cent of the population alone proved racial discrimination.

In connection with that fact of omission, we must appraise the testimony offered to show the intentional limitation. Besides the language quoted in note 4, supra, which relates particularly to the court's instructions, other relevant evidence of such intention is found only in the testimony of the commissioners. They made these statements as to their intentions:

Commissioner Wells: "There was nothing said about the number and nothing was said about the number on the panel. . . . We had no intention of placing more than one negro on the panel. When we did that we had finished with the negro. That was the suggestion of the others and what Judge Adams thought about the selection of the grand jury. . . . Judge Adams did not tell us to put one negro or five negroes on the grand jury. Yes, we just understood to see that negroes had representation on the grand jury, and we went out to see this particular one because we did not know him. . . . Among the white people whose names might go on the grand jury, unless I knew them personally and knew their qualifications, we went out and talked to them. No, we did not discriminate against a white man or a negro. I attempted not to."

Commissioner Tennant: "We three did not go to see any other negroes, that is the only one. I did not have any intention of putting more than one on the list; I could not think of anybody; I would have if I could have thought of another one, and putting one on."

Commissioner Douglas: "Yes, sir, there were other negroes' names mentioned besides the one we selected; we did not go talk to them; we liked this one, and our intentions were to get just one negro on the grand jury; that is right. No, I did not have any intention of placing more than one negro on the grand jury. . . . We never agreed to select any certain number, but when we found one with all the qualifications of a grand juror we felt like that was satisfactory representation. . . . No, sir, we did not have in mind to put any set number of representatives of the various races. . . . We did not agree to put eleven negroes and one white man on, no. That is right, all that we were endeavoring to get a fair and impartial grand jury without any discrimination against any race on earth. We did not have in mind, or the other commissioners, to put any set number on of any race, white, yellow or what-not."

A careful examination of these statements in connection with all the other evidence leaves us unconvinced that the commissioners deliberately and intentionally limited the number of Negroes on the grand jury list. The judge who heard the witnesses on the motion to quash did not find that type of discrimination. The law of their state, the instructions of the judge, their oath of office required them to choose prospective jurors on their statutory qualifications and without regard to their color or the number of representatives of various races who might appear upon the list. We cannot say the commissioners violated these obligations.

This conclusion makes it unnecessary to decide whether a purposeful limitation of jurors by race to the approximate proportion that the eligible jurymen of the race so limited bears to the total eligibles is invalid under the Fourteenth Amendment.

The judgment is affirmed.

Affirmed.

Mr. Justice Rutledge concurs in the result.

The Chief Justice and Mr. Justice Black dissent.

Mr. Justice Murphy, dissenting.

The equal protection clause of the Fourteenth Amendment entitles every person, whose life, liberty or property is in issue, to the benefits of grand and petit juries chosen without regard to race, color or creed. This constitutional principle is a fundamental tenet of the American faith in the jury system. The absence of such a principle would give free rein to those who wittingly or otherwise act to undermine the very foundations of this system and would make juries ready weapons for officials to oppress those accused individuals who by chance are numbered among unpopular or inarticulate minorities.

The State of Texas in this instance appears to have made a sincere effort to obey this constitutional mandate in selecting the grand jury which indicted the Negro petitioner. Until this Court's decision in 1942 in *Hill v. State of Texas*, no Negro ever served on a grand jury in Dallas County, Texas, where this case arose. In an attempt to comply with that decision the three jury commissioners were careful here to appoint one Negro to the sixteen-member grand jury panel; he qualified and served on the twelve-man jury. Thus it cannot be said that Texas has systematically and completely excluded Negroes from the grand jury. But that fact alone does not guarantee compliance with the Fourteenth Amendment, however commendable may be the attempt. Racial limitation no less than racial exclusion in the formation of juries is an evil condemned by the equal protection clause. "The Amendment nullifies sophisticated as well as simple-minded modes of discrimination." This case must therefore be reviewed with that in mind.

Petitioner, as a Negro, "cannot claim, as matter of right, that his race shall have a representation on the jury," inasmuch as "a mixed jury in a particular case is not essential to the equal protection of the laws." But petitioner, as a human being endowed with all the rights specified in the Constitution, can claim that no racial or religious exclusion, limitation or other form of discrimination shall enter into the selection of any jury which indicts or tries him.

It follows that the State of Texas, in insisting upon one Negro representative on the grand jury panel, has respected no right belonging to petitioner. On the contrary, to the extent that this insistence amounts to a definite limitation of Negro grand jurors, a clear constitutional right has been directly invaded. The equal protection clause guarantees petitioner not only the right to have Negroes considered as prospective veniremen but also the right to have them considered without numerical or proportional limitation. If a jury is to be fairly chosen from a cross section of the community it must be done without limiting the number of persons of a particular color, racial background or faith — all of which are irrelevant factors in setting qualifications for jury service. This may in a particular instance result in the selection of one, six, twelve or even no Negroes on a jury panel. The important point, however, is that the selections must in no way be limited or restricted by such irrelevant factors.

In this case the State of Texas has candidly admitted before us "that none of the three (jury commissioners) intended to place more than one Negro upon the grand jury drawn by them." Commissioner Wells testified that "We had no intention of placing more than one Negro on the panel. When we did that we had finished with the Negro." In the words of Commissioner Tennant, "We three did not go to see any other Negroes, that is the only one. I did not have any intention of putting more than one on the list." Finally, as Commissioner Douglas stated, "Yes, sir, there were other Negroes' names mentioned besides the one we selected; we did not go talk to them; we liked this one, and our intentions were to get just one Negro on the grand jury; that is right. No, I did not have any intention of placing more than one Negro on the grand jury."

Clearer proof of intentional and deliberate limitation on the basis of color would be difficult to produce. The commissioners' declarations that they did not intend to discriminate and their other inconsistent statements cited by the Court fade into insignificance beside the admitted and obvious fact that they intended to and did limit the number of Negroes on the jury panel. By limiting the number to one they thereby excluded the possibility that two or more Negroes might be among the persons qualified to serve. All those except the one Negro were required to be of white color. At the same time, by insisting upon one Negro, they foreclosed the possibility of choosing sixteen white men on the panel. They refused, in brief, to disregard the factor of color in selecting the jury personnel. To that extent they have disregarded petitioner's right to the equal protection of the laws. To that extent they have ignored the ideals of the jury system. Our affirmance of this judgment thus tarnishes the fact that we of this nation are one people undivided in ability or freedom by differences in race, color or creed.

NOTES AND QUESTIONS

1. After describing the Fourteenth Amendment principle and legal precedents at issue, the Court states that it "cannot lightly be concluded that officers of the courts disregard this accepted standard of justice." Why not? Is there some kind of a presumption of regularity when state officials are accused of unconstitutional conduct? Would such a presumption affect the result here?

2. The Court also notes that because the evidence contains "certain inconsistencies and conflicts of testimony" it must show deference to "the trier of fact who heard the witnesses in full and observed their demeanor." This point is largely uncontroversial as a general matter. But is the predicate — testimonial inconsistencies and conflicts — accurate here?

CHAPTER III

POLICE INTERROGATION AND THE FIFTH AMENDMENT

This chapter focuses on the Fifth Amendment, particularly as it is implicated in the context of police interrogations of suspects and arrestees.

Section A examines the overall scope of the Fifth Amendment right—or as some would say, privilege—against self-incrimination. This section looks at the Supreme Court's requirement that the Amendment's protection applies only to conduct that is "testimonial or communicative" in nature; the extent to which the right can be abrogated by a government grant of immunity to a witness, compelling the witness to testify; and the rule preventing a prosecutor from impairing the exercise of the right by commenting on a defendant's decision not to testify in a criminal trial.

Section B considers the backdrop to the Supreme Court's seminal decision in *Miranda v. Arizona*, 384 U.S. 436 (1966), which imposed certain requirements on police interrogation in order to protect the Fifth Amendment rights of suspects and arrestees in police custody. The backdrop includes a look at a series of cases leading up to *Miranda* in which the Court considered due process challenges to confessions on the grounds that they were "involuntary," a mode of analysis mostly—but not totally—displaced by *Miranda*.

Section C looks at the *Miranda* decision.

Sections D and E examine how the *Miranda* decision was implemented in practice, largely in a manner that can charitably be described as "grudging." Section D looks at how the Court recognized exceptions to the *Miranda* requirements, and diluted the threshold prerequisites of the doctrine by narrowly defining the terms "interrogation" and "custody." Section E looks at the how the Court further weakened *Miranda*—or confined it, if you will—by making it easy to "waive" *Miranda* rights while at the same time making it hard to "invoke" *Miranda* rights.

Section F looks at the consequences of *Miranda* violations, including cases where police employed a "successive interrogation" technique designed to circumvent the obligation to provide *Miranda* warnings until they were essentially useless. This section also looks at cases where the Court held there could be no violation of *Miranda* unless a suspect's unwarned statement was introduced into evidence against the suspect in a trial.

Section G considers the durability of *Miranda*. Despite the stingy implementation of the doctrine in the decades after it squeaked into existence, and efforts by Congress to legislate it away, the core of *Miranda* was affirmed—almost enthusiastically—by a 7-2 vote of the Court in 2000, in a decision noting that *Miranda* warnings have become "part of our national culture." A 2022 decision by a much different Court, finding in a civil rights action that the constitutional requirement of *Miranda* warnings is not "law" under 42 U.S.C. § 1983, raises the prospect that the apparent entrenchment of *Miranda* in 2000 may have been fleeting.

A. SCOPE OF THE RIGHT AGAINST SELF-INCRIMINATION

This first case considers the requirement that the Fifth Amendment only applies to conduct that is "testimonial or communicative."

Schmerber v. California

384 U.S. 757 (1966)

Mr. Justice BRENNAN delivered the opinion of the Court.

Petitioner was convicted in Los Angeles Municipal Court of the criminal offense of driving an automobile while under the influence of intoxicating liquor. He had been arrested at a hospital while receiving treatment for injuries suffered in an accident involving the automobile that he had apparently been driving. At the direction of a police officer, a blood sample was then withdrawn from petitioner's body by a physician at the hospital. The chemical analysis of this sample revealed a percent by weight of alcohol in his blood at the time of the offense which indicated intoxication, and the report of this analysis was admitted in evidence at the trial. Petitioner objected to receipt of this evidence of the analysis on the ground that the blood had been withdrawn despite his refusal, on the advice of his counsel, to consent to the test. He contended that in that circumstance the withdrawal of the blood and the admission of the analysis in evidence denied him due process of law under the Fourteenth Amendment, as well as specific guarantees of the Bill of Rights secured against the States by that Amendment: his privilege against self-incrimination under the Fifth Amendment; his right to counsel under the Sixth Amendment; and his right not to be subjected to unreasonable searches and seizures in violation of the Fourth Amendment. The Appellate Department of the California Superior Court rejected these contentions and affirmed the conviction. We affirm.

THE PRIVILEGE AGAINST SELF-INCRIMINATION CLAIM

We therefore must now decide whether the withdrawal of the blood and admission in evidence of the analysis involved in this case violated petitioner's privilege. We hold that the privilege protects an accused only from being compelled to testify against himself, or otherwise provide the State with evidence of a testimonial or communicative nature, and that the withdrawal of blood and use of the analysis in question in this case did not involve compulsion to these ends.

It could not be denied that in requiring petitioner to submit to the withdrawal and chemical analysis of his blood the State compelled him to submit to an attempt to discover evidence that might be used to prosecute him for a criminal offense. He submitted only after the police officer rejected his objection and directed the physician to proceed. The officer's direction to the physician to administer the test over petitioner's objection constituted compulsion for the purposes of the privilege. The critical question, then, is whether petitioner was thus compelled "to be a witness against himself."

If the scope of the privilege coincided with the complex of values it helps to protect, we might be obliged to conclude that the privilege was violated. In *Miranda v. Arizona*, the Court said of the interests protected by the privilege: "All these policies point to one overriding thought: the constitutional foundation underlying the privilege is the respect a government—state or federal—must accord to the dignity and integrity of its citizens. To maintain a 'fair state-individual balance,' to require the government 'to shoulder the entire load,' . . . to respect the inviolability of the human personality, our accusatory system of criminal justice demands that the government seeking to punish an individual produce the evidence against him by its own independent labors, rather than by the cruel, simple expedient of compelling it from his own mouth." The withdrawal of blood necessarily involves puncturing the skin for extraction, and the percent by weight of alcohol in that blood, as established by chemical analysis, is evidence of criminal guilt. Compelled submission fails on one view to respect the "inviolability of the human personality." Moreover, since it enables the State to rely on evidence forced from the accused, the compulsion violates at least one meaning of the requirement that the State procure the evidence against an accused "by its own independent labors."

As the passage in *Miranda* implicitly recognizes, however, the privilege has never been given the full scope which the values it helps to protect suggest. History and a long line of authorities in lower courts have consistently limited its protection to situations in which the State seeks to submerge those values by obtaining the evidence against an accused through "the cruel, simple expedient of compelling it from his own mouth. . . . In sum, the privilege is fulfilled only when the person is guaranteed the right 'to remain silent unless he chooses to speak in the unfettered exercise of his own will.'" The leading case in this Court is *Holt v. United States*. There the question was whether evidence was admissible that the accused, prior to trial and over his protest, put on a blouse that fitted him. It was contended that compelling the accused to submit to the demand that he model the blouse violated the privilege. Mr. Justice Holmes, speaking for the Court, rejected the argument as "based upon an extravagant extension of the 5th Amendment," and went on to say: "(T)he prohibition of compelling a man in a criminal court to be witness against himself is a prohibition of the use of physical or moral compulsion to extort communications from him, not an exclusion of his body as evidence when it may be material. The objection in principle would forbid a jury to look at a prisoner and compare his features with a photograph in proof."

It is clear that the protection of the privilege reaches an accused's communications, whatever form they might take, and the compulsion of responses which are also communications, for example, compliance with a subpoena to produce one's papers. On the other hand, both federal and state courts have usually held that it offers no protection against compulsion to submit to fingerprinting, photographing, or measurements, to write or speak for identification, to appear in court, to stand, to assume a stance, to walk, or to make a particular gesture. The distinction which has emerged, often expressed in different ways, is that the privilege is a bar against compelling "communications" or "testimony," but that compulsion which makes a suspect or accused the source of "real or physical evidence" does not violate it.

Although we agree that this distinction is a helpful framework for analysis, we are not to be understood to agree with past applications in all instances. There will be many cases in which such a distinction is not readily drawn. Some tests seemingly directed to obtain "physical evidence," for example, lie detector tests measuring changes in body function during interrogation, may actually be directed to eliciting responses which are essentially testimonial. To compel a person to submit to testing in which an effort will be made to determine his guilt or innocence on the basis of physiological responses, whether willed or not, is to evoke the spirit and history of the Fifth Amendment. Such situations call to mind the principle that the protection of the privilege "is as broad as the mischief against which it seeks to guard."

In the present case, however, no such problem of application is presented. Not even a shadow of testimonial compulsion upon or enforced communication by the accused was involved either in the extraction or in the chemical analysis. Petitioner's testimonial capacities were in no way implicated; indeed, his participation, except as a donor, was irrelevant to the results of the test, which depend on chemical analysis and on that alone. Since the blood test evidence, although an incriminating product of compulsion, was neither petitioner's testimony nor evidence relating to some communicative act or writing by the petitioner, it was not inadmissible on privilege grounds.

• • •

We thus conclude that the present record shows no violation of petitioner's right under the Fourth and Fourteenth Amendments to be free of unreasonable searches and seizures. It bears repeating, however, that we reach this judgment only on the facts of the present record. The integrity of an individual's person is a cherished value of our society. That we today hold that the Constitution does not forbid the States minor intrusions into an individual's body under stringently limited conditions in no way indicates that it permits more substantial intrusions, or intrusions under other conditions.

Affirmed.

NOTES AND QUESTIONS

1. The Court uses a lengthy quote from *Miranda*, decided one week earlier, to describe the values protected by the Fifth Amendment:

> All these policies point to one overriding thought: the constitutional foundation underlying the privilege is the respect a government—state or federal—must accord to the dignity and integrity of its citizens. To maintain a "fair state-individual balance," to require the government "to shoulder the entire load, . . . to respect the inviolability of the human personality, our accusatory system of criminal justice demands that the government seeking to punish an individual produce the evidence against him by its own independent labors, rather than by the cruel, simple expedient of compelling it from his own mouth."

Miranda, 384 U.S. at 460. The Court acknowledges, however, that the Fifth Amendment's language is narrower than its values, and only forbids compelling a person "to be a witness against himself." Here, the government was plainly not content to prosecute Schmerber by "its own independent labors."

After *Schmerber* was argued, Justice Brennan was purportedly unsure how he would vote. He ultimately voted to affirm and, according to Bernard Schwartz, Super Chief: Earl Warren and His Supreme Court—A Judicial Biography 594 (1983), he said that "a comprehensive opinion should be written limiting the scope of the Fifth Amendment. That, he felt, would soften the impact of the *Miranda* decision."

2. How persuasive as a matter of language and logic, if not precedent, is the Court's view that being "a witness" requires action that is testimonial or communicative in nature? What would the result be here if the scope of the privilege were "as broad as the mischief against which it seeks to guard," as the Court had described it in 1892 in *Counselman v. Hitchcock*, 142 U.S. 547, 562 (1892)?

3. Is there nonetheless an argument based even on the precedents the Court cites that the blood sample evidence at issue is testimonial? What do you make of Justice Black's argument in dissent that the entire purpose of the extraction of the blood sample was so that its characteristics could be used in the testimony of a witness against Schmerber?

4. Is the result here surprising given the civil libertarian reputation of the Warren Court and the physically coercive nature of the "compulsion"—described by Justice Fortas in dissent as "a tort" —in this context? To reach a contrary result here would the Court's decision in *Holt* have to be overturned? How about the cases requiring submission to fingerprinting, photographing, etc.?

5. Justice Douglas dissents on his view that both the Fourth and Fifth Amendment are animated by a "a right of privacy":

> We are dealing with the right of privacy which we have held to be within the penumbra of some specific guarantees of the Bill of Rights. *Griswold v. State of Connecticut.* Thus, the Fifth Amendment marks "a zone of privacy" which the Government may not force a person to surrender. Likewise the Fourth Amendment recognizes that right when it guarantees the right of

> the people to be secure "in their persons." No clearer invasion of this right of privacy can be imagined than forcible bloodletting of the kind involved here.

Why don't the nature of the intrusion and the right of privacy provide a basis for persuasively distinguishing *Holt*? Would a different result in *Schmerber* have fortified the notion of a constitutional right to a "zone of privacy" thereby bolstering the constitutionality of *Roe v. Wade*, 410 U.S. 113 (1973), decided just seven years later?

In *California v. Byers*, 402 U.S. 424 (1971), the Court upheld against a Fifth Amendment challenge a "hit and run" statute that required a motorist involved in a car accident to stop at the scene and give his name and address. The Court reasoned that the statute's purpose was primarily regulatory, and that an "organized society" necessarily imposes demands on its citizens—filing tax returns, making SEC disclosures, etc.—that create some risk of prosecution. It noted that in *United States v. Sullivan*, 274 U.S. 424 (1927), one among many anti-defendant Supreme Court cases from the Prohibition era, the Court had rejected the Fifth Amendment claim of a "bootlegger" who argued that listing his source of income on his tax return would incriminate him for violating the Volstead Act.

The California Supreme Court had upheld the statute by imposing a judicially created "use" restriction in any criminal prosecution where the state sought to offer evidence of statutory disclosures. Why isn't that an adequate result? For analysis of a different variety of a self-identification statute under the Fifth Amendment *see* Chapter IV, *infra* (discussing *Hiibel v. Sixth Judicial District of Nevada*, 542 U.S. 177 (2004)).

In *Pennsylvania v. Muniz*, 496 U.S. 582 (1990), the Court considered *Schmerber*'s "testimonial" requirement in the context of the police's administration of sobriety tests to a DUI suspect who was under arrest but had not been read his *Miranda* warnings. The Court found that admission of the suspect's "slurred" responses to administrative questions (e.g., name, age, address) was nontestimonial as the statements were not being offered for their content but rather as something akin to physical evidence. *Id.* at 592. But the Court ruled otherwise regarding the suspect's inability to answer the question, "Do you know the date of your sixth birthday?" A response to this question, the Court held, was testimonial inasmuch as the answer by its content—and not simply by the manner of its delivery—incriminated the suspect. *Id.* at 594-98.

In the next case the Court considers the government's ability to circumvent the Fifth Amendment's requirements by granting immunity to a witness and thereby compelling the witness's testimony, a procedure that in theory should eliminate the possibility of the witness's prosecution based on the immunized testimony.

Kastigar v. United States

406 U.S. 441 (1972)

Mr. Justice Powell delivered the opinion of the Court.

This case presents the question whether the United States Government may compel testimony from an unwilling witness, who invokes the Fifth Amendment privilege against compulsory self-incrimination, by conferring on the witness immunity from use of the compelled testimony in subsequent criminal proceedings, as well as immunity from use of evidence derived from the testimony.

Petitioners were subpoenaed to appear before a United States grand jury in the Central District of California on February 4, 1971. The Government believed that petitioners were likely to assert their Fifth Amendment privilege. Prior to the scheduled appearances, the Government applied to the District Court for an order directing petitioners to answer questions and produce evidence before the grand jury under a grant of immunity conferred pursuant to 18 U.S.C. ss 6002, 6003. Petitioners opposed issuance of the order, contending primarily that the scope of the immunity provided by the statute was not coextensive with the scope of the privilege against self-incrimination, and therefore was not sufficient to supplant the privilege and compel their testimony. The District Court rejected this contention, and ordered petitioners to appear before the grand jury and answer its questions under the grant of immunity.

Petitioners appeared but refused to answer questions, asserting their privilege against compulsory self-incrimination. They were brought before the District Court, and each persisted in his refusal to answer the grand jury's questions, notwithstanding the grant of immunity. The court found both in contempt, and committed them to the custody of the Attorney General until either they answered the grand jury's questions or the term of the grand jury expired. The Court of Appeals for the Ninth Circuit affirmed. This Court granted certiorari to resolve the important question whether testimony may be compelled by granting immunity from the use of compelled testimony and evidence derived therefrom ("use and derivative use" immunity), or whether it is necessary to grant immunity from prosecution for offenses to which compelled testimony relates ("transactional" immunity).

I

The power of government to compel persons to testify in court or before grand juries and other governmental agencies is firmly established in Anglo-American jurisprudence. The power with respect to courts was established by statute in England as early as 1562, and Lord Bacon observed in 1612 that all subjects owed the King their "knowledge and discovery." While it is not clear when grand juries first resorted to compulsory process to secure the attendance and testimony of witnesses, the general common-law principle that "the public has a right to every man's evidence" was considered an "indubitable certainty" that "cannot be denied" by 1742. The power to compel testimony, and the corresponding duty to testify, are recognized in the Sixth Amendment requirements that an accused be confronted with the witnesses against him, and have compulsory process for obtaining witnesses in his favor. The first Congress recognized the testimonial duty in the Judiciary Act of 1789, which provided for compulsory attendance of witnesses in the federal courts. Mr. Justice White noted the importance of this essential power of government in his concurring opinion in *Murphy v. Waterfront Comm'n* (1964):

> Among the necessary and most important of the powers of the States as well as the Federal Government to assure the effective functioning of government in an ordered society is the broad power to compel residents to testify in court or before grand juries or agencies. Such testimony constitutes one of the Government's primary sources of information.

But the power to compel testimony is not absolute. There are a number of exemptions from the testimonial duty, the most important of which is the Fifth Amendment privilege against compulsory self-incrimination. The privilege reflects a complex of our fundamental values and aspirations, and marks an important advance in the development of our liberty. It can be asserted in any proceeding, civil or criminal, administrative or judicial, investigatory or adjudicatory; and it protects against any disclosures which the witness reasonably believes could be used in a criminal prosecution or could lead to other evidence that might be so used. This Court has been zealous to safeguard the values which underlie the privilege.

Immunity statutes, which have historical roots deep in Anglo-American jurisprudence, are not incompatible with these values. Rather, they seek a rational accommodation between the imperatives of the privilege and the legitimate demands of government to compel citizens to testify. The existence of these statutes reflects the importance of testimony, and the fact that many offenses are of such a character that the only persons capable of giving useful testimony are those implicated in the crime. Indeed, their origins were in the context of such offenses, and their primary use has been to investigate such offenses. Congress included immunity statutes in many of the regulatory measures adopted in the first half of this century. Indeed, prior to the enactment of the statute under consideration in this case, there were in force over 50 federal immunity statutes. In addition, every State in the Union, as well as the District of Columbia and Puerto Rico, has one or more such statutes. The commentators, and this Court on several occasions, have characterized immunity statutes as essential to the effective enforcement of various criminal statutes. As Mr. Justice Frankfurter observed, such statutes have "become part of our constitutional fabric."

II

Petitioners contend, first, that the Fifth Amendment's privilege against compulsory self-incrimination, which is that "(n)o person . . . shall be compelled in any criminal case to be a witness against himself," deprives Congress of power to enact laws that compel self-incrimination, even if complete immunity from prosecution is granted prior to the compulsion of the incriminatory testimony. In other words, petitioners assert that no immunity statute, however drawn, can afford a lawful basis for compelling incriminatory testimony. They ask us to reconsider and overrule *Brown v. Walker* (1896), and *Ullmann v. United States, supra,* decisions that uphold the constitutionality of immunity statutes.

We find no merit to this contention and reaffirm the decisions in *Brown* and *Ullmann.*

III

Petitioners' second contention is that the scope of immunity provided by the federal witness immunity statute, 18 U.S.C. s 6002, is not coextensive with the scope of the Fifth Amendment privilege against compulsory self-incrimination, and therefore is not sufficient to supplant the privilege and compel testimony over a claim of the privilege. The statute provides that when a witness is compelled by district court order to testify over a claim of the privilege:

> the witness may not refuse to comply with the order on the basis of his privilege against self-incrimination; but no testimony or other information compelled under the order (or any information directly or indirectly derived from such testimony or other information) may be used against the witness in any criminal case, except a prosecution for perjury, giving a false statement, or otherwise failing to comply with the order.

The constitutional inquiry, rooted in logic and history, as well as in the decisions of this Court, is whether the immunity granted under this statute is coextensive with the scope of the privilege. If so, petitioners' refusals to answer based on the privilege were unjustified, and the judgments of contempt were proper, for the grant of immunity has removed the dangers against which the privilege protects. If, on the other hand, the immunity granted is not as comprehensive as the protection afforded by the privilege, petitioners were justified in refusing to answer, and the judgments of contempt must be vacated.

Petitioners draw a distinction between statutes that provide transactional immunity and those that provide, as does the statute before us, immunity from use and derivative use. They contend that a statute must at a minimum grant full transactional immunity in order to be coextensive with the scope of the privilege. In support of this contention, they rely on

Counselman v. Hitchcock (1892), the first case in which this Court considered a constitutional challenge to an immunity statute. The statute, a reenactment of the Immunity Act of 1868, provided that no "evidence obtained from a party or witness by means of a judicial proceeding . . . shall be given in evidence, or in any manner used against him . . . in any court of the United States. . . ." Notwithstanding a grant of immunity and order to testify under the revised 1868 Act, the witness, asserting his privilege against compulsory self-incrimination, refused to testify before a federal grand jury. He was consequently adjudged in contempt of court. On appeal, this Court construed the statute as affording a witness protection only against the use of the specific testimony compelled from him under the grant of immunity. This construction meant that the statute "could not, and would not, prevent the use of his testimony to search out other testimony to be used in evidence against him." Since the revised 1868 Act, as construed by the Court, would permit the use against the immunized witness of evidence derived from his compelled testimony, it did not protect the witness to the same extent that a claim of the privilege would protect him. Accordingly, under the principle that a grant of immunity cannot supplant the privilege, and is not sufficient to compel testimony over a claim of the privilege, unless the scope of the grant of immunity is coextensive with the scope of the privilege, the witness' refusal to testify was held proper. In the course of its opinion, the Court made the following statement, on which petitioners heavily rely:

> We are clearly of opinion that no statute which leaves the party or witness subject to prosecution after he answers the criminating question put to him, can have the effect of supplanting the privilege conferred by the Constitution of the United States. (The immunity statute under consideration) does not supply a complete protection from all the perils against which the constitutional prohibition was designed to guard, and is not a full substitute for that prohibition. In view of the constitutional provision, a statutory enactment, to be valid, must afford absolute immunity against future prosecution for the offence to which the question relates.

Sixteen days after the *Counselman* decision, a new immunity bill was introduced by Senator Cullom, who urged that enforcement of the Interstate Commerce Act would be impossible in the absence of an effective immunity statute. The bill, which became the Compulsory Testimony Act of 1893, was drafted specifically to meet the broad language in *Counselman* set forth above. The new Act removed the privilege against self-incrimination in hearings before the Interstate Commerce Commission and provided that:

> no person shall be prosecuted or subjected to any penalty or forfeiture for or on account of any transaction, matter or thing, concerning which he may testify, or produce evidence, documentary or otherwise . . . .

This transactional immunity statute became the basic form for the numerous federal immunity statutes until 1970, when, after re-examining applicable constitutional principles and the adequacy of existing law, Congress enacted the statute here under consideration. The new statute, which does not "afford (the) absolute immunity against future prosecution" referred to in *Counselman*, was drafted to meet what Congress judged to be the conceptual basis of *Counselman*, as elaborated in subsequent decisions of the Court, namely, that immunity from the use of compelled testimony and evidence derived therefrom is coextensive with the scope of the privilege.

The statute's explicit proscription of the use in any criminal case of "testimony or other information compelled under the order (or any information directly or indirectly derived from such testimony or other information)" is consonant with Fifth Amendment standards. We hold that such immunity from use and derivative use is coextensive with the scope of the privilege against self-incrimination, and therefore is sufficient to compel testimony over a claim of the privilege. While a grant of immunity must afford protection commensurate with that afforded by the privilege, it need not be broader. Transactional immunity, which accords full immunity from prosecution for the offense to which the compelled testimony relates, affords the witness considerably broader protection than does the Fifth Amendment privilege. The privilege has never been construed to mean that one who invokes it cannot subsequently be prosecuted. Its sole concern is to afford protection against being "forced to give testimony leading to the infliction of 'penalties affixed to . . . criminal acts.'" Immunity from the use of compelled testimony, as well as evidence derived directly and indirectly therefrom, affords this protection. It prohibits the prosecutorial authorities from using the compelled testimony in any respect, and it therefore insures that the testimony cannot lead to the infliction of criminal penalties on the witness.

Our holding is consistent with the conceptual basis of *Counselman*. The *Counselman* statute, as construed by the Court, was plainly deficient in its failure to prohibit the use against the immunized witness of evidence derived from his compelled testimony. The Court repeatedly emphasized this deficiency, noting that the statute:

> could not, and would not, prevent the use of his testimony to search out other testimony to be used in evidence against him or his property, in a criminal proceeding . . . ;

that it:

> could not prevent the obtaining and the use of witnesses and evidence which should be attributable directly to the testimony he might give under compulsion and on which he might be convicted, when otherwise, and if he had refused to answer, he could not possibly have been convicted, ibid.;

and that it:

> affords no protection against that use of compelled testimony which consists in gaining therefrom a knowledge of the details of a crime, and of sources of information which may supply other means of convicting the witness or party.

The basis of the Court's decision was recognized in *Ullmann v. United States* (1956), in which the Court reiterated that the *Counselman* statute was insufficient:

> because the immunity granted was incomplete, in that it merely forbade the use of the testimony given and failed to protect a witness from future prosecution based on knowledge and sources of information obtained from the compelled testimony.

IV

Although an analysis of prior decisions and the purpose of the Fifth Amendment privilege indicates that use and derivative-use immunity is coextensive with the privilege, we must consider additional arguments advanced by petitioners against the sufficiency of such immunity. We start from the premise, repeatedly affirmed by this Court, that an appropriately broad immunity grant is compatible with the Constitution.

Petitioners argue that use and derivative-use immunity will not adequately protect a witness from various possible incriminating uses of the compelled testimony: for example, the prosecutor or other law enforcement officials may obtain leads, names of witnesses, or other information not otherwise available that might result in a prosecution. It will be difficult and perhaps impossible, the argument goes, to identify, by testimony or cross-examination, the subtle ways in which the compelled testimony may disadvantage a witness, especially in the jurisdiction granting the immunity.

This argument presupposes that the statute's prohibition will prove impossible to enforce. The statute provides a sweeping proscription of any use, direct or indirect, of the compelled testimony and any information derived therefrom:

> (N)o testimony or other information compelled under the order (or any information directly or indirectly derived from such testimony or other information) may be used against the witness in any criminal case. . . .

This total prohibition on use provides a comprehensive safeguard, barring the use of compelled testimony as an "investigatory lead," and also barring the use of any evidence obtained by focusing investigation on a witness as a result of his compelled disclosures.

A person accorded this immunity under 18 U.S.C. s 6002, and subsequently prosecuted, is not dependent for the preservation of his rights upon the integrity and good faith of the prosecuting authorities.

This burden of proof, which we reaffirm as appropriate, is not limited to a negation of taint; rather, it imposes on the prosecution the affirmative duty to prove that the evidence it proposes to use is derived from a legitimate source wholly independent of the compelled testimony.

This is very substantial protection, commensurate with that resulting from invoking the privilege itself. The privilege assures that a citizen is not compelled to incriminate himself by his own testimony. It usually operates to allow a citizen to remain silent when asked a question requiring an incriminatory answer. This statute, which operates after a witness has given incriminatory testimony, affords the same protection by assuring that the compelled testimony can in no way lead to the infliction of criminal penalties. The statute, like the Fifth Amendment, grants neither pardon nor amnesty. Both the statute and the Fifth Amendment allow the government to prosecute using evidence from legitimate independent sources.

The statutory proscription is analogous to the Fifth Amendment requirement in cases of coerced confessions. A coerced confession, as revealing of leads as testimony given in exchange for immunity, is inadmissible in a criminal trial, but it does not bar prosecution. Moreover, a defendant against whom incriminating evidence has been obtained through a grant of immunity may be in a stronger position at trial than a defendant who asserts a Fifth Amendment coerced-confession claim. One raising a claim under this statute need only show that he testified under a grant of immunity in order to shift to the government the heavy burden of proving that all of the evidence it proposes to use was derived from legitimate independent sources. On the other hand, a defendant raising a coerced-confession claim under the Fifth Amendment must first prevail in a voluntariness hearing before his confession and evidence derived from it become inadmissible.

There can be no justification in reason or policy for holding that the Constitution requires an amnesty grant where, acting pursuant to statute and accompanying safeguards, testimony is compelled in exchange for immunity from use and derivative use when no such amnesty is required where the government, acting without colorable right, coerces a defendant into incriminating himself.

We conclude that the immunity provided by 18 U.S.C. s 6002 leaves the witness and the prosecutorial authorities in substantially the same position as if the witness had claimed the Fifth Amendment privilege. The immunity therefore is coextensive with the privilege and suffices to supplant it. The judgment of the Court of Appeals for the Ninth Circuit accordingly is

Affirmed.

[Justice Douglas dissented.]

Mr. Justice MARSHALL, dissenting.

Today the Court holds that the United States may compel a witness to give incriminating testimony, and subsequently prosecute him for crimes to which that testimony relates. I cannot believe the Fifth Amendment permits that result.

The Fifth Amendment gives a witness an absolute right to resist interrogation, if the testimony sought would tend to incriminate him. A grant of immunity may strip the witness of the right to refuse to testify, but only if it is broad enough to eliminate all possibility that the testimony will in fact operate to incriminate him. It must put him in precisely the same position, vis-a-vis the government that has compelled his testimony, as he would have been in had he remained silent in reliance on the privilege.

The Court recognizes that an immunity statute must be tested by that standard, that the relevant inquiry is whether it "leaves the witness and the prosecutorial authorities in substantially the same position as if the witness had claimed the Fifth Amendment privilege." I assume, moreover, that in theory that test would be met by a complete ban on the use of the compelled testimony, including all derivative, use, however remote and indirect. But I cannot agree that a ban on use will in practice be total, if it remains open for the government to convict the witness on the basis of evidence derived from a legitimate independent source. The Court asserts that the witness is adequately protected by a rule imposing on the government a heavy burden of proof if it would establish the independent character of evidence to be used against the witness. But in light of the inevitable uncertainties of the fact-finding process, a greater margin of protection is required in order to provide a reliable guarantee that the witness is in exactly the same position as if he had not testified. That margin can be provided only by immunity from prosecution for the offenses to which the testimony relates, i.e., transactional immunity.

I do not see how it can suffice merely to put the burden of proof on the government. First, contrary to the Court's assertion, the Court's rule does leave the witness "dependent for the preservation of his rights upon the integrity and good faith of the prosecuting authorities." For the information relevant to the question of taint is uniquely within the knowledge of the prosecuting authorities. They alone are in a position to trace the chains of information and investigation that lead to the evidence to be used in a criminal prosecution. A witness who suspects that his compelled testimony was used to develop a lead will be hard pressed indeed to ferret out the evidence necessary to prove it. And of course it is no answer to say he need not prove it, for though the Court puts the burden of proof on the government, the government will have no difficulty in meeting its burden by mere assertion if the witness produces no contrary evidence. The good faith of the prosecuting authorities is thus the sole safeguard of the witness' rights. Second, even their good faith is not a sufficient safeguard. For the paths of information through the investigative bureaucracy may well be long and winding, and even a prosecutor acting in the best of faith cannot be certain that somewhere in the depths of his investigative apparatus, often including hundreds of employees, there was not some prohibited use of the compelled testimony. The Court today sets out a loose net to trap tainted evidence and prevent its use against the witness, but it accepts an intolerably great risk that tainted evidence will in fact slip through that net.

In my view the Court turns reason on its head when it compares a statutory grant of immunity to the "immunity" that is inadvertently conferred by an unconstitutional interrogation. The exclusionary rule of evidence that applies in that situation has nothing whatever to do with this case. Evidence obtained through a coercive interrogation, like evidence obtained through an illegal search, is excluded at trial because the Constitution prohibits such methods of gathering evidence. The exclusionary rules provide a partial and inadequate remedy to some victims of illegal police conduct, and a similarly partial and inadequate deterrent to police officers. An immunity statute, on the other hand, is much more ambitious than any exclusionary rule. It does not merely attempt to provide a remedy for past police misconduct, which never should have occurred. An immunity statute operates in advance of the event, and it authorizes—even encourages—interrogation that would otherwise be prohibited by the Fifth Amendment. An immunity statute thus differs from an exclusionary rule of evidence in at least two critical respects.

First, because an immunity statute gives constitutional approval to the resulting interrogation, the government is under an obligation here to remove the danger of incrimination completely and absolutely, whereas in the case of the exclusionary rules it may be sufficient to shield the witness from the fruits of the illegal search or interrogation in a partial and reasonably adequate manner. For when illegal police conduct has occurred, the exclusion of evidence does not purport to purge the conduct of its unconstitutional character. The constitutional violation remains, and may provide the basis for other relief, such as a civil action for or a criminal prosecution of the responsible officers (see 18 U.S.C. ss 241, 242). The Constitution does not authorize police officers to coerce confessions or to invade privacy without cause, so long as no use is made of the evidence they obtain. But this Court has held that the Constitution does authorize the government to compel a witness to give potentially incriminating testimony, so long as no incriminating use is made of the resulting evidence. Before the government puts its seal of approval on such an interrogation, it must provide an absolutely reliable guarantee that it will not use the testimony in any way at all in aid of prosecution of the witness. The only way to provide that guarantee is to give the witness immunity from prosecution for crimes to which his testimony relates.

Second, because an immunity statute operates in advance of the interrogation, there is room to require a broad grant of transactional immunity without imperiling large numbers of otherwise valid convictions. An exclusionary rule comes into play after the interrogation or search has occurred; and the decision to question or to search is often made in haste, under pressure, by an officer who is not a lawyer. If an unconstitutional interrogation or search were held to create transactional immunity, that might well be regarded as an excessively high price to pay for the "constable's blunder." An immunity statute, on the other hand, creates a framework in which the prosecuting attorney can make a calm and reasoned decision whether to compel testimony and suffer the resulting ban on prosecution, or to forgo the testimony.

For both these reasons it is clear to me that an immunity statute must be tested by a standard far more demanding than that appropriate for an exclusionary rule fashioned to deal with past constitutional violations. Measured by that standard, the statute approved today by the Court fails miserably. I respectfully dissent.

NOTES AND QUESTIONS

1. The Court describes the rule that "the public has a right to every man's evidence" as a "common law principle." What does this mean? Does the rule exist independently of statutory authority for a public body—a court, an agency, a legislative committee—to subpoena witnesses to testify? Is the rule of constitutional dimension?

2. The Court notes the longstanding history of immunity statutes and the rule established in *Counselman v. Hitchcock* that the Fifth Amendment requires an immunity statute to "afford absolute immunity against future prosecution for the offence to which the question relates." 142 U.S. at 585-86. Thus so-called transactional immunity became the normal price the government had to pay for compelling testimony from 1892 to 1970.

Is the *Counselman* formulation of a "transactional immunity" rule self-executing? Does it depend on the proceeding in which the testimony is given? Will it always be obvious, for example, in the sometimes freewheeling and sprawling arena of a grand jury investigation, *see* Chapter VII *infra*, what "offence" a question relates to?

Note also that one of the government's concerns about transactional immunity was that savvy and gutsy witnesses could, upon receiving immunity, attempt to take an "immunity bath" by testifying to crimes not directly related to the prosecutor's inquiry.

3. The Court concludes that the new 1970 federal immunity statute, 18 U.S.C. §§ 6002-6003, satisfies the Fifth Amendment even though it only prohibits the use and derivative use of immunized testimony. It describes transactional immunity as providing a witness with "considerably broader protection" than the Fifth Amendment. Do you agree? Wouldn't a textual interpretation of the Fifth Amendment prohibit immunity altogether in criminal cases, in that even where a witness is immunized he is still "providing evidence against himself"?

On the other hand, can you think of circumstances where a prohibition on the use and derivative use of immunized testimony might provide greater protection than transactional immunity? Consider an immunized gang member's testimony in a grand jury investigation of a gang murder where the gang member testifies about the structure and operations of the gang. Would transactional immunity necessarily prohibit the use of such testimony in a subsequent prosecution of the witness on drug charges arising out of his gang activities?

4. The Court doesn't mention the one-sided nature of the immunity statute, an asymmetry of which defense attorneys are keenly aware. Under 18 U.S.C. § 6003 only the Department of Justice is authorized to obtain an order immunizing a witness and compelling his testimony. This gives the government a powerful investigative tool to obtain testimony from witnesses who will help the government's case. The defense, on the other hand, can only in the rarest of circumstances prevail on a court to authorize immunity for a defense witness. *See* Leonard N. Sosnov, *Separation of Powers Shell Game: The Federal Witness Immunity Act,* 73 Temp. L. Rev. 171, 213-14 (2000) (discussing the extremely narrow circumstances where a defendant can obtain judicially ordered use immunity for a defense witness).

Consider a health care fraud investigation where sales representatives have engaged in illegal sales activity but disagree about whether the illegal practices were known to senior management. The government can immunize the witnesses who admit the practices were known to management and stealthily imply that the witnesses who dispute this view might be committing perjury—whether or not it truly believes they are lying—so that they will be afraid to testify. Accordingly, if senior executives are prosecuted, they will likely be unable to adduce favorable testimony from the nervous representatives, who will assert the Fifth Amendment to protect themselves.

5. In *New Jersey v. Portash,* 440 U.S. 450 (1979), the Court held that the Fifth Amendment prohibited the government from using immunized testimony to impeach a defendant. The government had relied on the Court's decision in *Harris v. New York,* 401 U.S. 222 (1971), *see infra,* that a defendant could be impeached by statements he had made in a confession that had been ruled inadmissible because he had not been given proper *Miranda* warnings. The Court in *Portash,* however, said that the "crucial distinction" between the two situations was the issue of coercion: "Testimony given in response to a grant of immunity is the essence of coerced testimony."

OLIVER'S ARMY

In *United States v. North,* 910 F.2d 843 (D.C. Cir. 1990), the D.C. Circuit grappled with the "heavy burden" the government would have to discharge under *Kastigar* in proving the absence of "taint" if it elects to prosecute someone who had given immunized testimony. This case illustrates the concerns expressed by Justice Marshall in his *Kastigar* dissent about the "good faith" of prosecutors and "the inevitable uncertainties of the fact-finding process."

In November of 1986, a Lebanese newspaper reported that the United States had secretly and illegally sold weapons to Iran. Congress immediately established two committees charged with investigating the sales of arms to Iran, the diversion of proceeds therefrom to rebels (or "Contras") fighting in Nicaragua, and the attempted cover-up of these activities.

The saga, which was in the news almost daily for almost two years, became popularly if unpoetically known as "the Iran/Contra affair."

At the center of things was Lieutenant Colonel Oliver L. North, a former member of the National Security Council (NSC) staff. *Id.* at 851. When North was subpoenaed to testify before the Iran/Contra congressional committees he asserted his Fifth Amendment rights, but the government compelled his testimony by a grant of use immunity pursuant to 18 U.S.C. § 6002. Thus immunized, North testified for six days. His testimony was carried live on national television and radio, replayed on news shows, and analyzed in the public media. *Id.*

Contemporaneously with the congressional investigation, and pursuant to the Independent Counsel statute, 28 U.S.C. §§ 591-599, the Special Division of the D.C. Circuit appointed Lawrence E. Walsh as Independent Counsel (IC) and charged him with the investigation and prosecution of any criminal wrongdoing by government officials in the Iran/Contra events. As a result of the efforts of the IC, North was indicted and tried on 12 counts arising from his role in the Iran/Contra affair. After extensive pretrial proceedings and a 12-week trial, North was convicted in May of 1989 on 3 counts: aiding and abetting an endeavor to obstruct Congress in violation of 18 U.S.C. §§ 1505 and 2 ("Count 6"); destroying, altering, or removing official NSC documents in violation of 18 U.S.C. § 2071 ("Count 9"); and accepting an illegal gratuity, consisting of a security system for his home, in violation of 18 U.S.C. § 201(c)(1)(B) ("Count 10").

North appealed his convictions on multiple grounds, including that his prosecution was tainted by the government's indirect use of his congressional testimony in violation of 18 U.S.C. § 6002 and *Kastigar*. The D.C. Circuit reversed the convictions. It found that the trial court insufficiently discharged its responsibilities under *Kastigar* to hold the government to its "heavy burden" of proving the absence of taint. Further, while the D.C. Circuit acknowledged that the prosecution team scrupulously avoided any exposure to the North testimony, it found that multiple government witnesses had their memories refreshed by North's testimony, which in itself was a fatal "indirect use" of the testimony. The Court also noted that the IC had warned Congress in advance not to immunize witnesses as any such grants of immunity "would create serious—and perhaps insurmountable—barriers to the prosecution of immunized witnesses." *Id.* at 863.

Do you think North was prosecuted, at least in part, due to the dynamic that the prosecutor was an appointed Independent Counsel who was specifically charged with "the investigation and prosecution of any criminal wrongdoing by government officials in the Iran/Contra Affair"?

Put differently, do you think the United States Attorney for the District of Columbia would have prosecuted North?

What level of deference, if any, should a prosecutor have afforded the congressional decision to immunize North?

On its terms the Fifth Amendment speaks not to "testimony" but to the act of being a "witness": "No person . . . shall be compelled to be a witness against himself." But does the Fifth Amendment apply to a court order or other compulsory process requiring the production of documents or other tangible items? For a long time the answer was yes. In *Boyd v. United States*, 116 U.S. 616 (1886), the Supreme Court held that a court order requiring a partnership to produce an incriminating invoice in connection with a civil forfeiture proceeding was a violation of the Fifth Amendment inasmuch as it compelled the owner of the papers to be a witness against himself. *Id.* at 634-35. (*Boyd* also held that the order worked a violation of the Fourth Amendment as the invoice was a private paper. *Id.*)

Boyd was eventually drained of all meaning, gradually then suddenly, beginning with a pair of Fourth Amendment cases. *Warden v. Hayden*, 387 U.S. 294 (1967), overruled *Gouled v. United States*, 255 U.S. 298 (1921), and allowed for searches for mere evidence of crime and not just fruits or instrumentalities. *Andresen v. Maryland*, 427 U.S. 463 (1976), subsequently held that a search warrant for potentially incriminating private papers did not independently offend the Fifth Amendment. On the Fifth Amendment front, two cases from the 1960s clarified that the Fifth Amendment protects against only compelled communications or testimony, but not obtaining incriminating evidence from the suspect. *See United States v. Wade*, 388 U.S. 218, 221-23 (1967) (holding that compelled participation in lineup did not violate Fifth Amendment); *Schmerber*, *supra*, 384 U.S. 757, 767 (1966) (holding withdrawal of defendant's blood sample is not violative of Fifth Amendment). On another Fifth Amendment front, the Court held that neither collective entities nor their individual representatives are shielded from the compelled production of records of the entity on Fifth Amendment grounds. *See Bellis v. United States*, 417 U.S. 85, 88 (1974) (ruling that artificial entities, such as corporations, do not have Fifth Amendment privilege); *Braswell v. United States*, 487 U.S. 99, 103-04 (1988) (reaffirming that the longstanding "collective entities doctrine" remained valid and unaffected by new analyses of document production in *Fisher* and *Doe I*).

The "suddenly" aspect of *Boyd*'s demise came in *Fisher v. United States*, 425 U.S. 391 (1976), where the Court explicitly renounced *Boyd* in considering the application of the Fifth Amendment to IRS summonses served on two attorneys directing them to produce accountants' workpapers relating to the attorneys' clients. *Id.* at 394-95. The Court found that the summonses did not violate the Fifth Amendment for multiple reasons: (1) no testimonial communications or authentication of the papers were required of the clients; (2) the documents were the accountants' papers, not the clients, and had been prepared by the accountants; (3) the papers were prepared voluntarily; and (4) the existence of the papers was known to the government. *Id.* at 409-14.

But the Court went beyond this holding and attempted to articulate a framework for what has become known as the "act of production" doctrine, based on the recognition that producing evidence does have certain "communicative aspects of its own." *Id.* at 410. These include the tacit admissions that the requested material exists, is in the possession or control of the order recipient, and is responsive to what the order requests. *Id.* The determination of whether, in light of these issues, the act of production is both "testimonial" and "incriminating," the Court stated, will depend on the facts and circumstances of individual cases. On the facts in *Fisher*, however, the Court found that production required no testimonial communication because (1) the existence of the documents was a foregone conclusion, (2) responding to the summons would not require the client to authenticate the documents, and (3) there was nothing incriminating in the client seeking accounting or legal assistance in connection with his tax returns. *Id.* at 411-13.

Fisher explicitly declined to rule whether the Fifth Amendment would protect a taxpayer from having to produce his own tax records. *Id.* at 414. That question was answered eight years later in *United States v. Doe*, 465 U.S. 605 (1984) (*Doe I*). *Doe I* held that the contents of voluntarily prepared business records had no Fifth Amendment protection from production in response to grand jury subpoenas. *Id.* at 610-11. Because the documents' creation was not compelled, there was no Fifth Amendment violation. *Id.* As to the "act of production" raised in *Fisher*, however, the Court deferred—without analysis or explanation—to the district court's finding, with which the court of appeals agreed, that producing the documents would have communicated the records' existence and authenticity, and that they were in the possession of the recipient. *Id.* at 614. The government had conceded, moreover, that the documents were potentially incriminating. *Id.* at 608. Accordingly, the Court held that production of the documents would be required only by a grant of act of production immunity under 18 U.S.C. §§ 6002 and 6003.

In sum, the contours of the "act of production" doctrine were substantially uncertain when Independent Counsel Kenneth Starr sought to press the matter in the D.C. Circuit and then the Supreme Court in response to an assertion of the Fifth Amendment by an Arkansas lawyer named Webster Hubbell.

United States v. Hubbell

530 U.S. 27 (2000)

Justice STEVENS delivered the opinion of the Court.

The two questions presented concern the scope of a witness' protection against compelled self-incrimination: (1) whether the Fifth Amendment privilege protects a witness from being compelled to disclose the existence of incriminating documents that the Government is unable to describe with reasonable particularity; and (2) if the witness produces such documents pursuant to a grant of immunity, whether 18 U.S.C. § 6002 prevents the Government from using them to prepare criminal charges against him.

I

This proceeding arises out of the second prosecution of respondent, Webster Hubbell, commenced by the Independent Counsel appointed in August 1994 to investigate possible violations of federal law relating to the Whitewater Development Corporation. The first prosecution was terminated pursuant to a plea bargain. In December 1994, respondent pleaded guilty to charges of mail fraud and tax evasion arising out of his billing practices as a member of an Arkansas law firm from 1989 to 1992, and was sentenced to 21 months in prison. In the plea agreement, respondent promised to provide the Independent Counsel with "full, complete, accurate, and truthful information" about matters relating to the Whitewater investigation.

The second prosecution resulted from the Independent Counsel's attempt to determine whether respondent had violated that promise. In October 1996, while respondent was incarcerated, the Independent Counsel served him with a subpoena duces tecum calling for the production of 11 categories of documents before a grand jury sitting in Little Rock, Arkansas. On November 19, he appeared before the grand jury and invoked his Fifth Amendment privilege against self-incrimination. In response to questioning by the prosecutor, respondent initially refused "to state whether there are documents within my possession, custody, or control responsive to the Subpoena." App. 62. Thereafter, the prosecutor produced an order, which had previously been obtained from the District Court pursuant to 18 U.S.C. § 6003(a), directing him to respond to the subpoena and granting him immunity "to the extent allowed by law." Respondent then produced 13,120 pages of documents and records and responded to a series of questions that established that those were all of the documents in his custody or control that were responsive to the commands in the subpoena, with the exception of a few documents he claimed were shielded by the attorney-client and attorney work-product privileges.

The contents of the documents produced by respondent provided the Independent Counsel with the information that led to this second prosecution. On April 30, 1998, a grand jury in the District of Columbia returned a 10-count indictment charging respondent with various tax-related crimes and mail and wire fraud. The District Court dismissed the indictment relying, in part, on the ground that the Independent Counsel's use of the subpoenaed documents violated § 6002 because all of the evidence he would offer against respondent at trial derived either directly or indirectly from the testimonial aspects of respondent's immunized act of producing those documents. Noting that the Independent Counsel had admitted that he was not investigating tax-related issues when he issued the subpoena, and that he had "'learned about the unreported income and other crimes from studying the records' contents,'" the District Court characterized the subpoena as "the quintessential fishing expedition."

The Court of Appeals vacated the judgment and remanded for further proceedings. The majority concluded that the District Court had incorrectly relied on the fact that the Independent Counsel did not have prior knowledge of the contents of the subpoenaed documents. The question the District Court should have addressed was the extent of the Government's independent knowledge of the documents' existence and authenticity, and of respondent's possession or control of them. It explained:

> On remand, the district court should hold a hearing in which it seeks to establish the extent and detail of the [G]overnment's knowledge of Hubbell's financial affairs (or of the paperwork documenting it) on the day the subpoena issued. It is only then that the court will be in a position to assess the testimonial value of Hubbell's response to the subpoena. Should the Independent Counsel prove capable of demonstrating with reasonable particularity a prior awareness that the exhaustive litany of documents sought in the subpoena existed and were in Hubbell's possession, then the wide distance evidently traveled from the subpoena to the substantive allegations contained in the indictment would be based upon legitimate intermediate steps. To the extent that the information conveyed through Hubbell's compelled act of production provides the necessary linkage, however, the indictment deriving therefrom is tainted.

In the opinion of the dissenting judge, the majority failed to give full effect to the distinction between the contents of the documents and the limited testimonial significance of the act of producing them. In his view, as long as the prosecutor could make use of information contained in the documents or derived therefrom without any reference to the fact that respondent had produced them in response to a subpoena, there would be no improper use of the testimonial aspect of the immunized act of production. In other words, the constitutional privilege and the statute conferring use immunity would only shield the witness from the use of any information resulting from his subpoena response "beyond what the prosecutor would receive if the documents appeared in the grand jury room or in his office unsolicited and unmarked, like manna from heaven."

On remand, the Independent Counsel acknowledged that he could not satisfy the "reasonable particularity" standard prescribed by the Court of Appeals and entered into a conditional plea agreement with respondent. In essence, the agreement provides for the dismissal of the charges unless this Court's disposition of the case makes it reasonably likely that respondent's "act [of] production immunity" would not pose a significant bar to his prosecution. The case is not moot, however, because the agreement also provides for the entry of a guilty plea and a sentence that will not include incarceration if we should reverse and issue an opinion that is sufficiently favorable to the Government to satisfy that condition. Despite that agreement, we granted the Independent Counsel's petition for a writ of certiorari in order to determine the precise scope of a grant of immunity with respect to the production of documents in response to a subpoena. We now affirm.

II

It is useful to preface our analysis of the constitutional issue with a restatement of certain propositions that are not in dispute. The term "privilege against self-incrimination" is not an entirely accurate description of a person's constitutional protection against being "compelled in any criminal case to be a witness against himself."

The word "witness" in the constitutional text limits the relevant category of compelled incriminating communications to those that are "testimonial" in character. As Justice Holmes observed, there is a significant difference between the use of compulsion to extort communications from a defendant and compelling a person to engage in conduct that may be incriminating. Thus, even though the act may provide incriminating evidence, a criminal suspect may be compelled to put on a shirt, to provide a blood sample or handwriting exemplar, or to make a recording of his voice. The act of exhibiting such physical characteristics is not the same as a sworn communication by a witness that relates either express or implied assertions of fact or belief. Similarly, the fact that incriminating evidence may be the byproduct of obedience to a regulatory requirement, such as filing an income tax return, maintaining required records, or reporting an accident, does not clothe such required conduct with the testimonial privilege.

More relevant to this case is the settled proposition that a person may be required to produce specific documents even though they contain incriminating assertions of fact or belief because the creation of those documents was not "compelled" within the meaning of the privilege. Our decision in *Fisher v. United States* (1976), dealt with summonses issued by the Internal Revenue Service (IRS) seeking working papers used in the preparation of tax returns. Because the papers had been voluntarily prepared prior to the issuance of the summonses, they could not be "said to contain compelled testimonial evidence, either of the taxpayers or of anyone else." Accordingly, the taxpayer could not "avoid compliance with the subpoena merely by asserting that the item of evidence which he is required to produce contains incriminating writing, whether his own or that of someone else." It is clear, therefore, that respondent Hubbell could not avoid compliance with the subpoena served on him merely because the demanded documents contained incriminating evidence, whether written by others or voluntarily prepared by himself.

On the other hand, we have also made it clear that the act of producing documents in response to a subpoena may have a compelled testimonial aspect. We have held that "the act of production" itself may implicitly communicate "statements of fact." By "producing documents in compliance with a subpoena, the witness would admit that the papers existed, were in his possession or control, and were authentic." Moreover, as was true in this case, when the custodian of documents responds to a subpoena, he may be compelled to take the witness stand and answer questions designed to determine whether he has produced everything demanded by the subpoena. The answers to those questions, as well as the act of production itself, may certainly communicate information about the existence, custody, and authenticity of the documents. Whether the constitutional privilege protects the answers to such questions, or protects the act of production itself, is a question that is distinct from the question whether the unprotected contents of the documents themselves are incriminating.

Finally, the phrase "in any criminal case" in the text of the Fifth Amendment might have been read to limit its coverage to compelled testimony that is used against the defendant in the trial itself. It has, however, long been settled that its protection encompasses compelled statements that lead to the discovery of incriminating evidence even though the statements themselves are not incriminating and are not introduced into evidence. Thus, a half century ago we held that a trial judge had erroneously rejected a defendant's claim of privilege on the ground that his answer to the pending question would not itself constitute evidence of the charged offense. As we explained:

> The privilege afforded not only extends to answers that would in themselves support a conviction under a federal criminal statute but likewise embraces those which would furnish a link in the chain of evidence needed to prosecute the claimant for a federal crime.

Compelled testimony that communicates information that may "lead to incriminating evidence" is privileged even if the information itself is not inculpatory. It is the Fifth

Amendment's protection against the prosecutor's use of incriminating information derived directly or indirectly from the compelled testimony of the respondent that is of primary relevance in this case.

III

Acting pursuant to 18 U.S.C. § 6002, the District Court entered an order compelling respondent to produce "any and all documents" described in the grand jury subpoena and granting him "immunity to the extent allowed by law." In *Kastigar v. United States* (1972), we upheld the constitutionality of § 6002 because the scope of the "use and derivative-use" immunity that it provides is coextensive with the scope of the constitutional privilege against self-incrimination.

The protection against the derivative use of compelled testimony distinguishes § 6002 from the 1868 statute that had been held invalid in *Counselman v. Hitchcock* (1892), because it merely provided "use" immunity, as well as from the more recent federal statutes that broadly provide "transactional" immunity. In *Kastigar* the petitioners argued that, under our reasoning in *Counselman*, nothing less than full transactional immunity from prosecution for any offense to which compelled testimony relates could suffice to supplant the privilege. In rejecting that argument, we stressed the importance of § 6002's "explicit proscription" of the use in any criminal case of "'testimony or other information compelled under the order (or any information directly or indirectly derived from such testimony or other information).'" We particularly emphasized the critical importance of protection against a future prosecution "'based on knowledge and sources of information obtained from the compelled testimony.'"

We also rejected the petitioners' argument that derivative-use immunity under § 6002 would not obviate the risk that the prosecutor or other law enforcement officials may use compelled testimony to obtain leads, names of witnesses, or other information not otherwise available to support a prosecution. That argument was predicated on the incorrect assumption that the derivative-use prohibition would prove impossible to enforce. But given that the statute contains a "comprehensive safeguard" in the form of a "sweeping proscription of any use, direct or indirect, of the compelled testimony and any information derived therefrom," we concluded that a person who is prosecuted for matters related to testimony he gave under a grant of immunity does not have the burden of proving that his testimony was improperly used. Instead, we held that the statute imposes an affirmative duty on the prosecution, not merely to show that its evidence is not tainted by the prior testimony, but "to prove that the evidence it proposes to use is derived from a legitimate source wholly independent of the compelled testimony." Requiring the prosecution to shoulder this burden ensures that the grant of immunity has "le[ft] the witness and the Federal Government in substantially the same position as if the witness had claimed his privilege in the absence of a grant of immunity."

The "compelled testimony" that is relevant in this case is not to be found in the contents of the documents produced in response to the subpoena. It is, rather, the testimony inherent in the act of producing those documents. The disagreement between the parties focuses entirely on the significance of that testimonial aspect.

IV

The Government correctly emphasizes that the testimonial aspect of a response to a subpoena duces tecum does nothing more than establish the existence, authenticity, and custody of items that are produced. We assume that the Government is also entirely correct in its submission that it would not have to advert to respondent's act of production in order to prove the existence, authenticity, or custody of any documents that it might offer in evidence at a criminal trial; indeed, the Government disclaims any need to introduce any of the documents produced by respondent into evidence in order to prove the charges against him. It follows, according to the Government, that it has no intention of making improper "use" of respondent's compelled testimony.

The question, however, is not whether the response to the subpoena may be introduced into evidence at his criminal trial. That would surely be a prohibited "use" of the immunized act of production. But the fact that the Government intends no such use of the act of production leaves open the separate question whether it has already made "derivative use" of the testimonial aspect of that act in obtaining the indictment against respondent and in preparing its case for trial. It clearly has.

It is apparent from the text of the subpoena itself that the prosecutor needed respondent's assistance both to identify potential sources of information and to produce those sources. See Appendix, infra. Given the breadth of the description of the 11 categories of documents called for by the subpoena, the collection and production of the materials demanded was tantamount to answering a series of interrogatories asking a witness to disclose the existence and location of particular documents fitting certain broad descriptions. The assembly of literally hundreds of pages of material in response to a request for "any and all documents reflecting, referring, or relating to any direct or indirect sources of money or other things of value received by or provided to" an individual or members of his family during a 3-year period, Appendix, infra, at 2048-2050, is the functional equivalent of the preparation of an answer to either a detailed written interrogatory or a series of oral questions at a discovery deposition. Entirely apart from the contents of the 13,120 pages of materials that respondent produced in this case, it is undeniable that providing a catalog of existing documents fitting within any of the 11 broadly worded subpoena categories could provide a prosecutor with a "lead to incriminating evidence," or "a link in the chain of evidence needed to prosecute."

Indeed, the record makes it clear that that is what happened in this case. The documents were produced before a grand jury sitting in the Eastern District of Arkansas in aid of the Independent Counsel's attempt to determine whether respondent had violated a commitment in his first plea agreement. The use of those sources of information eventually led to the return of an indictment by a grand jury sitting in the District of Columbia for offenses that apparently are unrelated to that plea agreement. What the District Court characterized as a "fishing expedition" did produce a fish, but not the one that the Independent Counsel expected to hook. It is abundantly clear that the testimonial aspect of respondent's act of producing subpoenaed documents was the first step in a chain of evidence that led to this prosecution. The documents did not magically appear in the prosecutor's office like "manna from heaven." They arrived there only after respondent asserted his constitutional privilege, received a grant of immunity, and — under the compulsion of the District Court's order — took the mental and physical steps necessary to provide the prosecutor with an accurate inventory of the many sources of potentially incriminating evidence sought by the subpoena. It was only through respondent's truthful reply to the subpoena that the Government received the incriminating documents of which it made "substantial use . . . in the investigation that led to the indictment."

For these reasons, we cannot accept the Government's submission that respondent's immunity did not preclude its derivative use of the produced documents because its "possession of the documents [was] the fruit only of a simple physical act — the act of producing the documents." It was unquestionably necessary for respondent to make extensive use of "the contents of his own mind" in identifying the hundreds of documents responsive to the requests in the subpoena. The assembly of those documents was like telling an inquisitor the combination to a wall safe, not like being forced to surrender the key to a strongbox. The Government's anemic view of respondent's act of production as a mere physical act that is principally nontestimonial in character and can be entirely divorced from its "implicit" testimonial aspect so as to constitute a "legitimate, wholly independent source" (as required by *Kastigar*) for the documents produced simply fails to account for these realities.

In sum, we have no doubt that the constitutional privilege against self-incrimination protects the target of a grand jury investigation from being compelled to answer questions designed to elicit information about the existence of sources of potentially incriminating evidence. That constitutional privilege has the same application to the testimonial aspect of a response to a subpoena seeking discovery of those sources. Before the District Court, the Government arguably conceded that respondent's act of production in this case had a testimonial aspect that entitled him to respond to the subpoena by asserting his privilege against self-incrimination. On appeal and again before this Court, however, the Government has argued that the communicative aspect of respondent's act of producing ordinary business records is insufficiently "testimonial" to support a claim of privilege because the existence and possession of such records by any businessman is a "foregone conclusion" under our decision in *Fisher*. This argument both misreads *Fisher* and ignores our subsequent decision in *United States v. Doe* (1984).

As noted in Part II, supra, *Fisher* involved summonses seeking production of working papers prepared by the taxpayers' accountants that the IRS knew were in the possession of the taxpayers' attorneys. In rejecting the taxpayers' claim that these documents were protected by the Fifth Amendment privilege, we stated:

> It is doubtful that implicitly admitting the existence and possession of the papers rises to the level of testimony within the protection of the Fifth Amendment. The papers belong to the accountant, were prepared by him, and are the kind usually prepared by an accountant working on the tax returns of his client. Surely the Government is in no way relying on the "truthtelling" of the taxpayer to prove the existence of or his access to the documents. . . . The existence and location of the papers are a foregone conclusion and the taxpayer adds little or nothing to the sum total of the Government's information by conceding that he in fact has the papers.

Whatever the scope of this "foregone conclusion" rationale, the facts of this case plainly fall outside of it. While in *Fisher* the Government already knew that the documents were in the attorneys' possession and could independently confirm their existence and authenticity through the accountants who created them, here the Government has not shown that it had any prior knowledge of either the existence or the whereabouts of the 13,120 pages of documents ultimately produced by respondent. The Government cannot cure this deficiency through the overbroad argument that a businessman such as respondent will always possess general business and tax records that fall within the broad categories described in this subpoena. The *Doe* subpoenas also sought several broad categories of general business records, yet we upheld the District Court's finding that the act of producing those records would involve testimonial self-incrimination.

Given our conclusion that respondent's act of production had a testimonial aspect, at least with respect to the existence and location of the documents sought by the Government's subpoena, respondent could not be compelled to produce those documents without first receiving a grant of immunity under § 6003. As we construed § 6002 in *Kastigar*, such immunity is coextensive with the constitutional privilege. *Kastigar* requires that respondent's motion to dismiss the indictment on immunity grounds be granted unless the Government proves that the evidence it used in obtaining the indictment and proposed to use at trial was derived from legitimate sources "wholly independent" of the testimonial aspect of respondent's immunized conduct in assembling and producing the documents described in the subpoena. The Government, however, does not claim that it could make such a showing. Rather, it contends that its prosecution of respondent must be considered proper unless someone—presumably respondent—shows that "there is some substantial relation between the compelled testimonial communications implicit in the act of production (as opposed to the act of production standing alone) and some aspect of the information used in the investigation or the evidence presented at trial." We could not accept this submission without repudiating the basis for our conclusion in *Kastigar* that the statutory guarantee of use and derivative-use immunity is as broad as the constitutional privilege itself. This we are not prepared to do.

Accordingly, the indictment against respondent must be dismissed. The judgment of the Court of Appeals is affirmed.

It is so ordered.

APPENDIX TO OPINION OF THE COURT

On October 31, 1996, upon application by the Independent Counsel, a subpoena was issued commanding respondent to appear and testify before the grand jury of the United States District Court for the Eastern District of Arkansas on November 19, 1996, and to bring with him various documents described in a "Subpoena Rider" as follows:

> A. Any and all documents reflecting, referring, or relating to any direct or indirect sources of money or other things of value received by or provided to Webster Hubbell, his wife, or children from January 1, 1993 to the present, including but not limited to the identity of employers or clients of legal or any other type of work.
>
> B. Any and all documents reflecting, referring, or relating to any direct or indirect sources of money of other things of value received by or provided to Webster Hubbell, his wife, or children from January 1, 1993 to the present, including but not limited to billing memoranda, draft statements, bills, final statements, and/or bills for work performed or time billed from January 1, 1993 to the present.
>
> C. Copies of all bank records of Webster Hubbell, his wife, or children for all accounts from January 1, 1993 to the present, including but not limited to all statements, registers and ledgers, cancelled checks, deposit items, and wire transfers.
>
> D. Any and all documents reflecting, referring, or relating to time worked or billed by Webster Hubbell from January 1, 1993 to the present, including but not limited to original time sheets, books, notes, papers, and/or computer records.
>
> E. Any and all documents reflecting, referring, or relating to expenses incurred by and/or disbursements of money by Webster Hubbell during the course of any work performed or to be performed by Mr. Hubbell from January 1, 1993 to the present.
>
> F. Any and all documents reflecting, referring, or relating to Webster Hubbell's schedule of activities, including but not limited to any and all calendars, day-timers, time books, appointment books, diaries, records of reverse telephone toll calls, credit card calls, telephone message slips, logs, other telephone records, minutes, databases, electronic mail messages, travel records, itineraries, tickets for transportation of any kind, payments, bills, expense backup documentation, schedules, and/or any other document or database that would disclose Webster Hubbell's activities from January 1, 1993 to the present.
>
> G. Any and all documents reflecting, referring, or relating to any retainer agreements or contracts for employment of Webster Hubbell, his wife, or his children from January 1, 1993 to the present.
>
> H. Any and all tax returns and tax return information, including but not limited to all W-2s, form 1099s, schedules, draft returns, work papers, and backup documents filed, created or held by or on behalf of Webster Hubbell, his wife, his children, and/or any business in which he, his wife, or his children holds or has held an interest, for the tax years 1993 to the present.
>
> I. Any and all documents reflecting, referring, or relating to work performed or to be performed or on behalf of the City of Los Angeles, California, the Los Angeles Department of Airports or any other Los Angeles municipal Governmental entity, Mary Leslie, and/or Alan S. Arkatov, including but not limited to correspondence, retainer agreements, contracts, time sheets, appointment calendars, activity calendars, diaries, billing statements, billing memoranda, telephone records, telephone message slips, telephone credit card statements, itineraries,

tickets for transportation, payment records, expense receipts, ledgers, check registers, notes, memoranda, electronic mail, bank deposit items, cashier's checks, traveler's checks, wire transfer records and/or other records of financial transactions.

J. Any and all documents reflecting, referring, or relating to work performed or to be performed by Webster Hubbell, his wife, or his children on the recommendation, counsel or other influence of Mary Leslie and/or Alan S. Arkatov, including but not limited to correspondence, retainer agreements, contracts, time sheets, appointment calendars, activity calendars, diaries, billing statements, billing memoranda, telephone records, telephone message slips, telephone credit card statements, itineraries, tickets for transportation, payment records, expense receipts, ledgers, check registers, notes, memoranda, electronic mail, bank deposit items, cashier's checks, traveler's checks, wire transfer records and/or other records of financial transactions.

K. Any and all documents related to work performed or to be performed for or on behalf of Lippo Ltd. (formerly Public Finance (H.K.) Ltd.), the Lippo Group, the Lippo Bank, Mochtar Riady, James Riady, Stephen Riady, John Luen Wai Lee, John Huang, Mark W. Grobmyer, C. Joseph Giroir, Jr., or any affiliate, subsidiary, or corporation owned or controlled by or related to the aforementioned entities or individuals, including but not limited to correspondence, retainer agreements, contracts, time sheets, appointment calendars, activity calendars, diaries, billing statements, billing memoranda, telephone records, telephone message slips, telephone credit card statements, itineraries, tickets for transportation, payment records, expense receipts, ledgers, check registers, notes, memoranda, electronic mail, bank deposit items, cashier's checks, traveler's checks, wire transfer records and/or other records of financial transactions.

NOTES AND QUESTIONS

Kenneth Starr, Independent Counsel in the Whitewater/Clinton investigations

1. Pursuant to the Ethics in Government Act of 1978, on August 5, 1994, upon the application of Attorney General Janet Reno, Kenneth Starr was appointed as Independent Counsel by a special three-judge division of the D.C. Circuit.

The appointing order gave him authority to investigate:

> whether any individuals or entities have committed a violation of any federal criminal law . . . relating in any way to James B. McDougal's, President William Jefferson Clinton's, or Mrs. Hillary Rodham Clinton's relationships with Madison Guaranty Savings & Loan Association, Whitewater Development Corporation, or Capital Management Services, Inc.

United States v. Hubbell, 11 F. Supp. 2d 25, 27 (D.D.C. 1998), *rev'd, vacated by* 167 F.3d 552 (1999), *aff'd*, 530 U.S. 27 (2000). That original grant of authority, expanded multiple times by the Special Division under the "related to" provision in the statute, lead to prosecutions of Webster Hubbell, a Clinton family friend and professional colleague of Hillary Rodham Clinton at the Rose law firm in Little Rock, Arkansas. *Id.* at 28. In December 1994 Hubbell pleaded guilty to tax and mail fraud charges arising out of overbilling of clients. *Id.*

2. It is unclear whether the Court is sensitive to the ironies of Hubbell's multiple prosecutions by the Independent Counsel. In the first paragraph of Part I of its decision it refers to the substance of the Independent Counsel's original grant of authority ("Whitewater

Development Corporation") and then, without comment on any relationship, describes the subject of Hubbell's previous conviction ("billing practices" at an Arkansas law firm). And while it describes the instant prosecution as based on an alleged failure to "cooperate" with the Whitewater investigation, the Court refers, again without comment, to the subpoena at issue—described by the district court as "the quintessential fishing expedition"—that sought from Hubbell nothing but personal financial information, that is, materials apparently unrelated to his "cooperation" with the investigation. The Court does note in a footnote that the district court dismissed the indictment of Hubbell not only on the immunity issue before it, but also on the ground that the Independent Counsel had exceeded his jurisdiction in bringing the case against Hubbell, although that decision was reversed by the D.C. Circuit.

3. Take a close look at the subpoena categories, located in the Appendix. While it is true that an individual subpoena is just one piece of an investigation, and the perspective of a defendant is inherently imperfect, there are exceptions. What do these subpoena topics have to do with Hubbell's "cooperation" with the Independent Counsel? Is it more likely that the Independent Counsel is simply trying—for the second time—to pressure Hubbell into serving up incriminating information on the Clintons?

4. As the Court notes, even the most damning of documents in a defendant's possession are not covered by the Fifth Amendment privilege because their creation was not compelled by the government. But because producing such documents in response to a subpoena or other compulsory process has a testimonial component, a witness can nonetheless assert the Fifth Amendment privilege, as Hubbell did here, in response to the subpoena. But once he received "act-of-production immunity" under 18 U.S.C. § 6002 that privilege is eliminated, and he can be compelled to answer questions about the production, but not the contents, of the documents.

5. The Independent Counsel claims it can prove its tax evasion case against Hubbell without using either the documents produced by Hubbell or his testimony about their production. How could this be accomplished? Why does this matter?

6. In what precise ways were Hubbell's act of producing the documents testimonial?

7. The government essentially conceded that it had used the documents produced by Hubbell in preparing the indictment, and that it could not satisfy the showing the Court of Appeals required it to make on remand. Is that concession fatal? Is this an application of *Kastigar*?

8. Professor Mosteller notes that while *Hubbell* says nothing about overruling *Fisher* on the "act of production" doctrine, it is clear that the significance of *Fisher* has been narrowed to the proposition that requiring the production of incriminating documents from a target does not violate the Fifth Amendment if the government can establish advance knowledge of the existence and location of the requested documents and if the production requires no selection by the target. Robert P. Mosteller, *Cowboy Prosecutors and Subpoenas for Incriminating Evidence: The Consequences and Correction of Excess*, 58 Wash. & Lee L. Rev. 487, 520 (2001). He also makes the point that the Department of Justice would have been much better off, institutionally, had the Independent Counsel not pursued this matter. *See id.* at 488 ("The [Independent Counsel's] recklessness severely impaired the value of use immunity applied to subpoenas for documents from the perspective of prosecutors.").

The core of the Fifth Amendment's protection is that a criminal defendant cannot be forced to testify in his own defense in a criminal trial. But is the prosecution permitted to comment on the defendant's decision not to testify in his defense? A federal statute had since 1878 prohibited such comment in federal prosecutions. Shortly after holding that the Fifth Amendment applied to the states in *Malloy v. Hogan*, 378 U.S. 1 (1965), the Court considered whether the Amendment prohibited such comment in state prosecutions.

Griffin v. California

380 U.S. 609 (1965)

Mr. Justice Douglas delivered the opinion of the Court.

Petitioner was convicted of murder in the first degree after a jury trial in a California court. He did not testify at the trial on the issue of guilt, though he did testify at the separate trial on the issue of penalty. The trial court instructed the jury on the issue of guilt, stating that a defendant has a constitutional right not to testify. But it told the jury:

> As to any evidence or facts against him which the defendant can reasonably be expected to deny or explain because of facts within his knowledge, if he does not testify or if, though he does testify, he fails to deny or explain such evidence, the jury may take that failure into consideration as tending to indicate the truth of such evidence and as indicating that among the inferences that may be reasonably drawn therefrom those unfavorable to the defendant are the more probable.

It added, however, that no such inference could be drawn as to evidence respecting which he had no knowledge. It stated that failure of a defendant to deny or explain the evidence of which he had knowledge does not create a presumption of guilt nor by itself warrant an inference of guilt nor relieve the prosecution of any of its burden of proof.

Petitioner had been seen with the deceased the evening of her death, the evidence placing him with her in the alley where her body was found. The prosecutor made much of the failure of petitioner to testify:

> The defendant certainly knows whether Essie Mae had this beat up appearance at the time he left her apartment and went down the alley with her.
>
> What kind of a man is it that would want to have sex with a woman that beat up if she was beat up at the time he left?
>
> He would know that. He would know how she got down the alley. He would know how the blood got on the bottom of the concrete steps. He would know how long he was with her in that box. He would know how her wig got off. He would know whether he beat her or mistreated her. He would know whether he walked away from that place cool as a cucumber when he saw Mr. Villasenor because he was conscious of his own guilt and wanted to get away from that damaged or injured woman.
>
> These things he has not seen fit to take the stand and deny or explain.
>
> And in the whole world, if anybody would know, this defendant would know.
>
> Essie Mae is dead, she can't tell you her side of the story. The defendant won't.

The death penalty was imposed and the California Supreme Court affirmed. The case is here on a writ of certiorari which we granted to consider whether comment on the failure to testify violated the Self-Incrimination Clause of the Fifth Amendment which we made applicable to the States by the Fourteenth in *Malloy v. Hogan*, decided after the Supreme Court of California had affirmed the present conviction.

If this were a federal trial, reversible error would have been committed. It is said, however, that the *Wilson* decision rested not on the Fifth Amendment, but on an Act of Congress. That indeed is the fact, as the opinion of the Court in the *Wilson* case states. But that is the beginning, not the end, of our inquiry. The question remains whether, statute or not, the comment rule, approved by California, violates the Fifth Amendment.

We think it does. It is in substance a rule of evidence that allows the State the privilege of tendering to the jury for its consideration the failure of the accused to testify. No formal offer of proof is made as in other situations; but the prosecutor's comment and the court's acquiescence are the equivalent of an offer of evidence and its acceptance. The Court in the *Wilson* case stated:

> . . . the act was framed with a due regard also to those who might prefer to rely upon the presumption of innocence which the law gives to every one, and not wish to be witnesses. It is not

> every one who can safely venture on the witness stand, though entirely innocent of the charge against him. Excessive timidity, nervousness when facing others and attempting to explain transactions of a suspicious character, and offenses charged against him, will often confuse and embarrass him to such a degree as to increase rather than remove prejudices against him. It is not every one, however honest, who would therefore willingly be placed on the witness stand. The statute, in tenderness to the weakness of those who from the causes mentioned might refuse to ask to be witnesses, particularly when they may have been in some degree compromised by their association with others, declares that the failure of a defendant in a criminal action to request to be a witness shall not create any presumption against him.

If the words "fifth Amendment" are substituted for "act" and for "statute" the spirit of the Self-Incrimination Clause is reflected. For comment on the refusal to testify is a remnant of the "inquisitorial system of criminal justice," which the Fifth Amendment outlaws. It is a penalty imposed by courts for exercising a constitutional privilege. It cuts down on the privilege by making its assertion costly. It is said, however, that the inference of guilt for failure to testify as to facts peculiarly within the accused's knowledge is in any event natural and irresistible, and that comment on the failure does not magnify that inference into a penalty for asserting a constitutional privilege. What the jury may infer, given no help from the court, is one thing. What it may infer when the court solemnizes the silence of the accused into evidence against him is quite another. That the inference of guilt is not always so natural or irresistible is brought out in the *Modesto* opinion itself:

> Defendant contends that the reason a defendant refuses to testify is that his prior convictions will be introduced in evidence to impeach him ((Cal.) Code Civ. Proc. s 2051) and not that he is unable to deny the accusations. It is true that the defendant might fear that his prior convictions will prejudice the jury, and therefore another possible inference can be drawn from his refusal to take the stand.

We said in *Malloy v. Hogan* that "the same standards must determine whether an accused's silence in either a federal or state proceeding is justified." We take that in its literal sense and hold that the Fifth Amendment, in its direct application to the Federal Government and in its bearing on the States by reason of the Fourteenth Amendment, forbids either comment by the prosecution on the accused's silence or instructions by the court that such silence is evidence of guilt.

Reversed.

[Justice Harlan concurred. Justices White and Stewart dissented.]

NOTES AND QUESTIONS

1. Consider closely the instruction the trial court gave the jury after informing it of the defendant's right not to testify:

> As to any evidence or facts against him which the defendant can reasonably be expected to deny or explain because of facts within his knowledge, if he does not testify or if, though he does testify, he fails to deny or explain such evidence, the jury may take that failure into consideration as tending to indicate the truth of such evidence and as indicating that among the inferences that may be reasonably drawn therefrom those unfavorable to the defendant are the more probable.

Putting aside whether this instruction impermissibly comments on the defendant's failure to testify, and also putting aside whether the instruction is comprehensible, is this instruction even consistent with the government's burden to prove its case beyond a reasonable doubt?

2. Note the Court's sensitive recognition in the 1893 *Wilson* case of the reasons for the federal statute prohibiting comment on a defendant's failure to testify in a federal criminal case, which the Court adopts as "the spirit" of the Fifth Amendment.

Would you say the "no comment" rule as applied to the states is a constitutional rule, driven by the Fifth Amendment itself, or rather a rule that simply reinforces a constitutional guarantee? Could you describe it as a "prophylactic rule," aimed to prevent Fifth Amendment violations?

3. The Court acknowledges that the jury may nonetheless draw its own inference of guilt from the defendant's refusal to testify, whether encouraged by the court or not. Do you agree that juries are likely draw such an inference?

4. The "no comment" rule is a continual source of prosecutorial misconduct cases, as there are innumerable ways in which prosecutors can intentionally, carelessly, or inadvertently comment on the witness's failure to testify, including in some circumstances by referring to the government's evidence as "undisputed" or "unopposed."

5. *Griffin* has been widely criticized since it was decided, and Justice Thomas has explicitly called for the case to be "reexamined." *Mitchell v. United States*, 526 U.S. 314, 342 (1999) (Thomas, J., dissenting). For references to criticism of *Griffin*, *see* Tracey Maclin, *Is Silence Golden?*, 65 Ariz. L. Rev. 43, 47-48 & nn.12-19 (2023). Professor Maclin defends *Griffin* because allowing the state to argue for an inference of guilt from a defendant's silence undermines the defendant's absolute right not to testify against himself. *Id.* at 49.

The Court in *Kastigar* made it clear that a witness can assert the Fifth Amendment privilege in any proceeding, including civil proceedings. The Fifth Amendment "not only protects the individual against being involuntarily called as a witness against himself in a criminal prosecution but also privileges him not to answer official questions put to him in any other proceeding, civil or criminal, formal or informal, where the answers might incriminate him in future criminal proceedings." *Lefkowitz v. Turley*, 414 U.S. 70, 77 (1973). Accordingly, although corporations and other "collective entities" do not have Fifth Amendment rights (e.g., *United States v. Braswell*, 487 U.S. 99 (1988)), individuals in all manner of civil litigation can assert the privilege in depositions, responses to interrogatories, or any other form of questioning or examination.

But there are important differences between the assertion of the Fifth Amendment in a civil as opposed to a criminal proceeding. Among other things, unlike in criminal cases after *Griffin*, in a civil case an adverse inference may be drawn from the assertion of the Fifth Amendment. *Baxter v. Palmigiano*, 425 U.S. 308 (1976). Typically, if a party takes the Fifth Amendment in a civil trial, the judge will instruct the jury that an adverse inference may—not shall—be drawn from the witness's assertion. The nature of the inference that will be permitted depends on the facts and circumstances of the case, and there is considerable variation among the states and even the federal circuits about the circumstances in which an adverse inference will be permitted.

Further, while the popular conception of the Fifth Amendment may be that it affords a right to remain silent (*but see Salinas v. Texas*, 570 U.S. 178 (2013); *infra* at Section E), in a civil proceeding the right must be asserted on a question-by-question basis. Part of this is so that a court will be able to determine what adverse inferences, if any, are permissible. But there also may be judicial scrutiny of Fifth Amendment assertions in civil proceedings to ensure that they are justified. The scope of the right extends not only to "answers that would in themselves support a conviction under a federal criminal statute," but also to answers "which would furnish a link in the chain of evidence needed to prosecute the claimant for a federal crime." *Hoffman v. United States*, 341 U.S. 479, 486 (1951). Courts typically will uphold assertions of the privilege unless the possibility of criminal exposure is extremely remote. *In re Folding Carton Antitrust Litigation*, 609 F.2d 867 (7th Cir. 1979).

B. POLICE INTERROGATION: VOLUNTARINESS AND THE ROAD TO *MIRANDA*

In an ideal world of criminal justice the government would prosecute based entirely on "its own independent labors," *Miranda*, 384 U.S. at 360, without resorting to interrogation at all. But the law has forever countenanced some forms of interrogation even as it recognized the danger of coerced and false confessions. That danger could no longer be considered speculative in the twenty-first century, as the evidence mounted that in a significant percentage of cases where defendants were exonerated by DNA evidence they had been convicted based at least in part on confessions.

In *Brown v. Mississippi*, *see* Chapter II *supra*, the Court found that the extortion of a confession by physical coercion was a violation of due process. After *Brown* the Court increasingly was confronted with confessions induced by more subtle means of coercion, and decided no fewer than 30 such cases between *Brown* and *Miranda*. *Dickerson v. United States*, 530 U.S. 428, 433 (2000). Referring to this period unsentimentally in 2004, the Court described "the old way of doing things" by "litigating the voluntariness of any statement in nearly every instance." *Missouri v. Seibert*, 542 U.S. 600, 609 (2004).

Two of those instances follow.

Ashcraft v. Tennessee

322 U.S. 143 (1944)

Mr. Justice Black delivered the opinion of the Court.

About three o'clock on the morning of Thursday, June 5, 1941, Mrs. Zelma Ida Ashcraft got in her automobile at her home in Memphis, Tennessee, and set out on a trip to visit her mother's home in Kentucky. Late in the afternoon of the same day her car was observed a few miles out of Memphis, standing on the wrong side of a road which she would likely have taken on her journey. Just off the road, in a slough, her lifeless body was found. On her head were cut places inflicted by blows sufficient to have caused her death. Petitioner Ware, age 20, a Negro, was indicted in a state court and found guilty of her murder. Petitioner Ashcraft, age 45, a white man, husband of the deceased, charged with having hired Ware to commit the murder, was tried jointly with Ware and convicted as an accessory before the fact. Both were sentenced to ninety-nine years in the state penitentiary. The Supreme Court of Tennessee affirmed the convictions.

In applying to us for certiorari, Ware and Ashcraft urged that alleged confessions were used at their trial which had been extorted from them by state law enforcement officers in violation of the Fourteenth Amendment, and that "solely and alone" on the basis of these confessions they had been convicted. Their contentions raised a federal question which the record showed to be substantial and we brought both cases here for review. Upon oral argument before this Court Tennessee's legal representatives conceded that the convictions could not be sustained without the confessions but defended their use upon the ground that they were not compelled but were "freely and voluntarily made."

The record discloses that neither the trial court nor the Tennessee Supreme Court actually held as a matter of fact that petitioners' confessions were "freely and voluntarily made." The trial court heard evidence on the issue out of the jury's hearing, but did not itself determine from that evidence that the confessions were voluntary. Instead it over-ruled Ashcraft's objection to the use of his alleged confession with the statement that, "This Court is not able to hold, as a matter of law, that reasonable minds might not differ on the question of whether or not that alleged confession was voluntarily obtained." And it likewise over-ruled Ware's objection to use of his alleged confession, stating that "the reasonable minds of twelve men might . . . differ as to . . . whether Ware's confession was voluntary, and . . . therefore, that is a question of fact for the jury to pass on." Nor did the State Supreme Court review the evidence pertaining to the confessions and affirmatively hold them voluntary. In sustaining the petitioners' convictions, one Justice dissenting, it went no further than to point out that, "The trial judge . . . held . . . he could not say that the confessions were not voluntarily made and, therefore, permitted them to go to the jury," and to declare that it, likewise, was "unable to say that the confessions were not freely and voluntarily made."

If, therefore, the question of the voluntariness of the two confessions was actually decided at all it was by the jury. And the jury was charged generally on the subject of the two confessions as follows:

> I further charge you that if verbal or written statements made by the defendants freely and voluntarily and without fear of punishment or hope of reward, have been proven to you in this case, you may take them into consideration with all of the other facts and circumstances in the case. . . . In statements made at the time of the arrest, you may take into consideration the condition of the minds of the prisoners owing to their arrest and whether they were influenced by motives of hope or fear, to make the statements. Such a statement is competent evidence against the defendant who makes it and is not competent evidence against the other defendant. . . . You cannot consider it for any purpose against the other defendant.

Concerning Ashcraft's alleged confession this general charge constituted the sole instruction to the jury. But with regard to Ware's alleged confession the jury further was instructed:

> It is his (Ware's) further theory that he was induced by the fear of violence at the hands of a mob and by fear of the officers of the law to confess his guilt of the crime charged against him, but that such confession was false and that he had nothing whatsoever to do with, and no knowledge of the alleged crime. If you believe the theory of the defendant, Ware, . . . it is your duty to acquit him.

Having submitted the two alleged confessions to the jury in this manner, the trial court instructed the jury that:

> what the proof may show you, if anything, that the defendants have said against themselves, the law presumes to be true, but anything the defendants have said in their own behalf, you are not obliged to believe. . . .

This treatment of the confessions by the two State courts, the manner of the confessions' submission to the jury, and the emphasis upon the great weight to be given confessions make all the more important the kind of "independent examination" of petitioners' claims which, in any event, we are bound to make. Our duty to make that examination could not have been "foreclosed by the finding of a court, or the verdict of a jury, or both." We proceed therefore to consider the evidence relating to the circumstances out of which the alleged confessions came.

First, as to Ashcraft. Ashcraft was born on an Arkansas farm. At the age of eleven he left the farm and became a farm hand working for others. Years later he gravitated into construction work, finally becoming a skilled dragline and steam shovel operator. Uncontradicted evidence in the record was that he had acquired for himself "an excellent reputation." In 1929 he married the deceased Zelma Ida Ashcraft. Childless, they accumulated, apparently through Ashcraft's earnings, a very modest amount of jointly held property including bank accounts and an equity in the home in which they lived. The Supreme Court of Tennessee found "nothing to show but what the home life of Ashcraft and the deceased was pleasant and happy." Several of Mrs. Ashcraft's friends who were guests at the Ashcraft home on the night before her tragic death testified that both husband and wife appeared to be in a happy frame of mind.

The officers first talked to Ashcraft about 6 p.m. on the day of his wife's murder as he was returning home from work. Informed by them of the tragedy, he was taken to an undertaking establishment to identify her body which previously had been identified only by a driver's license. From there he was taken to the county jail where he conferred with the officers until about 2 a.m. No clues of ultimate value came from this conference, though it did result in the officers' holding and interrogating the Ashcrafts' maid and several of her friends. During the following week the officers made extensive investigations in Ashcraft's neighborhood and elsewhere and further conferred with Ashcraft himself on several occasions, but none of these activities produced tangible evidence pointing to the identity of the murderer.

Then, early in the evening of Saturday, June 14, the officers came to Ashcraft's home and "took him into custody." In the words of the Tennessee Supreme Court,

> They took him to an office or room on the northwest corner of the fifth Floor of the Shelby County jail. This office is equipped with all sorts of crime and detective devices such as a fingerprint outfit, cameras, high-powered lights, and such other devices as might be found in a homicide investigating office. . . . It appears that the officers placed Ashcraft at a table in this room on the fifth floor of the county jail with a light over his head and began to quiz him. They questioned him in relays until the following Monday morning, June 16, 1941, around nine-thirty or ten o'clock. It appears that Ashcraft from Saturday evening at seven o'clock until Monday morning at approximately nine-thirty never left this homicide room of the fifth floor.

Testimony of the officers shows that the reason they questioned Ashcraft "in relays" was that they became so tired they were compelled to rest. But from 7:00 Saturday evening until 9:30 Monday morning Ashcraft had no rest. One officer did say that he gave the suspect a single five minutes respite, but except for this five minutes the procedure consisted of one continuous stream of questions.

As to what happened in the fifth-floor jail room during this thirty-six hour secret examination the testimony follows the usual pattern and is in hopeless conflict. Ashcraft swears that the first thing said to him when he was taken into custody was, "Why in hell did you kill your wife?"; that during the course of the examination he was threatened and abused in various ways; and that as the hours passed his eyes became blinded by a powerful electric light, his body became weary, and the strain on his nerves became unbearable. The officers, on the other hand, swear that throughout the questioning they were kind and considerate. They say that they did not accuse Ashcraft of the murder until four hours after he was brought to the jail building, though they freely admit that from that time on their barrage of questions was constantly directed at him on the assumption that he was the murderer. Together with other persons whom they brought in on Monday morning to witness the culmination of the thirty-six hour ordeal the officers declare that at that time Ashcraft was "cool," "calm," "collected," "normal"; that his vision was unimpaired and his eyes not bloodshot; and that he showed no outward signs of being tired or sleepy.

As to whether Ashcraft actually confessed there is a similar conflict of testimony. Ashcraft maintains that although the officers incessantly attempted by various tactics of intimidation to entrap him into a confession, not once did he admit knowledge concerning or participation in the crime. And he specifically denies the officers' statements that he accused Ware of the crime, insisting that in response to their questions he merely gave them the name of Ware as one of several men who occasionally had ridden with him to work. The officers' version of what happened, however, is that about 11 p.m. on Sunday night, after twenty-eight hours' constant questioning, Ashcraft made a statement that Ware had overpowered him at his home and abducted the deceased, and was probably the killer. About midnight the officers found Ware and took him into custody, and, according to their testimony, Ware made a self-incriminating statement as of early Monday morning, and at 5:40 a.m. signed by mark a written confession in which appeared the statement that Ashcraft had hired him to commit the murder. This alleged confession of Ware was read to Ashcraft about six o'clock Monday morning, whereupon Ashcraft is said substantially to have admitted its truth in a detailed statement taken down by a reporter. About 9:30 Monday morning a transcript of Ashcraft's purported statement was read to him. The State's position is that he affirmed its truth but refused to sign the transcript, saying that he first wanted to consult his lawyer. As to this latter 9:30 episode the officers' testimony is reinforced by testimony of the several persons whom they brought in to witness the end of the examination.

In reaching our conclusion as to the validity of Ashcraft's confession we do not resolve any of the disputed questions of fact relating to the details of what transpired within the confession chamber of the jail or whether Ashcraft actually did confess. Such disputes, we may say, are an inescapable consequence of secret inquisitorial practices. And always evidence concerning the inner details of secret inquisitions is weighted against an accused, particularly where, as here, he is charged with a brutal crime, or where, as in many other cases, his supposed offense bears relation to an unpopular economic, political, or religious cause.

Our conclusion is that if Ashcraft made a confession it was not voluntary but compelled. We reach this conclusion from facts which are not in dispute at all. Ashcraft, a citizen of excellent reputation, was taken into custody by police officers. Ten days' examination of the Ashcrafts' maid, and of several others, in jail where they were held, had revealed nothing whatever against Ashcraft. Inquiries among his neighbors and business associates likewise had failed to unearth one single tangible clue pointing to his guilt. For thirty-six hours after Ashcraft's seizure during which period he was held incommunicado, without sleep or rest, relays of officers, experienced investigators, and highly trained lawyers questioned him without respite. From the beginning of the questioning at 7 o'clock on Saturday evening until 6 o'clock on Monday morning Ashcraft denied that he had anything to do with the murder of his wife. And at a hearing before a magistrate about 8:30 Monday morning Ashcraft pleaded not guilty to the charge of murder which the officers had sought to make him confess during the previous thirty-six hours.

We think a situation such as that here shown by uncontradicted evidence is so inherently coercive that its very existence is irreconcilable with the possession of mental freedom by a lone suspect against whom its full coercive force is brought to bear. It is inconceivable that any court of justice in the land, conducted as our courts are, open to the public, would permit prosecutors serving in relays to keep a defendant witness under continuous cross examination for thirty-six hours without rest or sleep in an effort to extract a "voluntary" confession. Nor can we, consistently with Constitutional due process of law, hold voluntary a confession where prosecutors do the same thing away from the restraining influences of a public trial in an open court room.

The Constitution of the United States stands as a bar against the conviction of any individual in an American court by means of a coerced confession. There have been, and are now, certain foreign nations with governments dedicated to an opposite policy: governments which convict individuals with testimony obtained by police organizations possessed of an unrestrained power to seize persons suspected of crimes against the state, hold them in secret custody, and wring from them confessions by physical or mental torture. So long as the Constitution remains the basic law of our Republic, America will not have that kind of government.

Second, as to Ware. Ashcraft and Ware were jointly tried, and were convicted on the theory that Ashcraft hired Ware to perform the murder. Ware's conviction was sustained by the

Tennessee Supreme Court on the assumption that Ashcraft's confession was properly admitted and his conviction valid. Whether it would have been sustained had the court reached the conclusion we have reached as to Ashcraft we cannot know. Doubt as to what the State court would have done under the changed circumstances brought about by our reversal of its decision as to Ashcraft is emphasized by the position of the State's representatives in this Court. They have asked that if we reverse Ashcraft's conviction we also reverse Ware's.

In disposing of cases before us it is our responsibility to make such disposition as justice may require. "And in determining what justice does require, the Court is bound to consider any change, either in fact or in law, which has supervened since the judgment was entered." Application of this guiding principle to the case at hand requires that we send Ware's case back to the Tennessee Supreme Court. Should that Court in passing on Ware's conviction in the light of our ruling as to Ashcraft adopt the State Attorney General's view and reverse the conviction there then would be no occasion for our passing on the federal question here raised by Ware. Under these circumstances we vacate the judgment of the Tennessee Supreme Court affirming Ware's conviction, and remand his case to that court for further proceedings.

The judgment affirming Ashcraft's conviction is reversed and the cause is remanded to the Supreme Court of Tennessee for proceedings not inconsistent with this opinion. It is so ordered.

NOTES AND QUESTIONS

1. Note that the trial judge made no assessment of the confessions besides finding that reasonable jurors could disagree as to whether the confessions were "freely and voluntarily made." The Supreme Court makes no ruling as to this procedural practice, as it determines that it must do an "independent examination" of the confessions regardless.

Is there anything about the power of confessions as evidence that makes their voluntariness particularly ill-suited to consideration by a jury in the first instance? Consider that confession evidence will almost always come in through the testimony of a police officer who participated in the interrogation, and the circumstances of the questioning can usually only be rebutted if the defendant testifies.

2. The trial judge instructed the jury that the statements by the defendant were "competent evidence" against the defendant and, further, that statements by the defendants "against themselves, the law presumes to be true." While the Federal Rules of Evidence make admissions against interest an exception to the hearsay rule, Fed. R. Evid. 804(b)(3), and therefore admissible in evidence, such statements are not "presumed to be true."

3. Do the personal characteristics of Mr. E. E. Ashcraft matter to the result here? The Court describes his circumstances in detail and in its conclusion it calls him a "citizen of excellent reputation." Does the Court do this because it senses that Ashcraft did not really confess? Or because even the best citizens can have their will overborne by interrogation that is "inherently coercive"?

4. The Court wrings its hands at the "hopeless conflict" in the testimony surrounding what actually transpired in the interrogation itself. The conflict extends not only to the circumstances of the interrogation but also as to what Ashcraft actually said. It concludes that the undisputed evidence reveals an interrogation that was "inherently coercive."

Note that *Ashcraft* was decided on May 1, 1944, just five weeks before the D-Day invasion of Normandy, at a time when the ultimate fate of Western Europe was by no means assured. This may explain the Court's acknowledgment of "certain foreign nations" with an "opposite policy" to a prohibition of coerced confessions.

5. In footnotes the Court refers to findings of the "Wickersham Report," the memorialized findings of a national commission charged in 1929 by President Hoover to study the

The members of the Wickersham Commission

widespread failure of state and local police to enforce Prohibition. Its conclusion was that Prohibition laws were not rigorously enforced. The commission's most notable findings, ironically, were in the area of abusive and coercive police interrogation tactics. The Court cites some of the commission's findings relevant here: that the "third degree" interrogation tactics often take place in a "back room" selected for its privacy and that "persistent questioning continuing hour after hour, sometimes by relays of officers" causing a "deprivation of sleep is the most effective torture and certain to produce any confession desired."

Some but by no means all of the Court's coerced confessions came out of the South.

Spano v. New York

360 U.S. 215 (1959)

Mr. Chief Justice Warren delivered the opinion of the Court.

This is another in the long line of cases presenting the question whether a confession was properly admitted into evidence under the Fourteenth Amendment. As in all such cases, we are forced to resolve a conflict between two fundamental interests of society; its interest in prompt and efficient law enforcement, and its interest in preventing the rights of its individual members from being abridged by unconstitutional methods of law enforcement. Because of the delicate nature of the constitutional determination which we must make, we cannot escape the responsibility of making our own examination of the record. *Norris v. State of Alabama.*

The State's evidence reveals the following: Petitioner Vincent Joseph Spano is a derivative citizen of this country, having been born in Messina, Italy. He was 25 years old at the time of the shooting in question and had graduated from junior high school. He had a record of regular employment. The shooting took place on January 22, 1957.

On that day, petitioner was drinking in a bar. The decedent, a former professional boxer weighing almost 200 pounds who had fought in Madison Square Garden, took some of petitioner's money from the bar. Petitioner followed him out of the bar to recover it. A fight ensued, with the decedent knocking petitioner down and then kicking him in the head three or four times. Shock from the force of these blow caused petitioner to vomit. After the bartender applied some ice to his head, petitioner left the bar, walked to his apartment, secured a gun, and walked eight or nine blocks to a candy store where the decedent was frequently to be found. He entered the store in which decedent, three friends of decedent, at least two of whom were ex-convicts, and a boy who was supervising the store were present. He fired five shots, two of which entered the decedent's body, causing his death. The boy was the only eyewitness; the three friends of decedent did not see the person who fired the shot. Petitioner then disappeared for the next week or so.

On February 1, 1957, the Bronx County Grand Jury returned an indictment for first-degree murder against petitioner. Accordingly, a bench warrant was issued for his arrest, commanding that he be forthwith brought before the court to answer the indictment, or, if the court had adjourned for the term, that he be delivered into the custody of the Sheriff of Bronx County.

On February 3, 1957, petitioner called one Gaspar Bruno, a close friend of 8 or 10 years' standing who had attended school with him. Bruno was a fledgling police officer, having at that time not yet finished attending police academy. According to Bruno's testimony, petitioner told him "that he took a terrific beating, that the deceased hurt him real bad and he dropped him a couple of times and he was dazed; he didn't know what he was doing and that he went and shot at him." Petitioner told Bruno that he intended to get a lawyer and give himself up. Bruno relayed this information to his superiors.

The following day, February 4, at 7:10 p.m., petitioner, accompanied by counsel, surrendered himself to the authorities in front of the Bronx County Building, where both the office of the Assistant District Attorney who ultimately prosecuted his case and the court-room in which he was ultimately tried were located. His attorney had cautioned him to answer no questions, and left him in the custody of the officers. He was promptly taken to the office of the Assistant District Attorney and at 7:15 p.m. the questioning began, being conducted by Assistant District Attorney Goldsmith, Lt. Gannon, Detectives Farrell, Lehrer and Motta, and Sgt. Clarke. The record reveals that the questioning was both persistent and continuous. Petitioner, in accordance with his attorney's instructions, steadfastly refused to answer. Detective Motta testified: "He refused to talk to me." "He just looked up to the ceiling and refused to talk to me." Detective Farrell testified:

Q. And you started to interrogate him? A. That is right.

Q. What did he say? A. He said "you would have to see my attorney. I tell you nothing but my name."

Q. Did you continue to examine him? A. Verbally, yes, sir.

He asked one officer, Detective Ciccone, if he could speak to his attorney, but that request was denied. Detective Ciccone testified that he could not find the attorney's name in the telephone book. He was given two sandwiches, coffee and cake at 11 p.m.

At 12:15 a.m. on the morning of February 5, after five hours of questioning in which it became evident that petitioner was following his attorney's instructions, on the Assistant District Attorney's orders petitioner was transferred to the 46th Squad, Ryer Avenue Police Station. The Assistant District Attorney also went to the police station and to some extent continued to participate in the interrogation. Petitioner arrived at 12:30 and questioning was resumed at 12:40. The character of the questioning is revealed by the testimony of Detective Farrell:

> **Q.** Who did you leave him in the room with? A. With Detective Lehrer and Sergeant Clarke came in and Mr. Goldsmith came in or Inspector Halk came in. It was back and forth. People just came in, spoke a few words to the defendant or they listened a few minutes and they left.

But petitioner persisted in his refusal to answer, and again requested permission to see his attorney, this time from Detective Lehrer. His request was again denied.

It was then that those in charge of the investigation decided that petitioner's close friend, Bruno, could be of use. He had been called out on the case around 10 or 11 p.m., although he was not connected with the 46th Squad or Precinct in any way. Although, in fact, his job was in no way threatened, Bruno was told to tell petitioner that petitioner's telephone call had gotten him "in a lot of trouble," and that he should seek to extract sympathy from petitioner for Bruno's pregnant wife and three children. Bruno developed this theme with petitioner without success, and petitioner, also without success, again sought to see his attorney, a request which Bruno relayed unavailingly to his superiors. After this first session with petitioner, Bruno was again directed by Lt. Gannon to play on petitioner's sympathies, but again no confession was forthcoming. But the Lieutenant a third time ordered Bruno falsely to importune his friend to confess but again petitioner clung to his attorney's advice. Inevitably, in the fourth such session directed by the Lieutenant, lasting a full hour, petitioner succumbed to his friend's prevarications and agreed to make a statement. Accordingly, at 3:25 a.m. the Assistant District Attorney, a stenographer, and several other law enforcement officials entered the room where petitioner was being questioned, and took his statement in question and answer form with the Assistant District Attorney asking the questions. The statement was completed at 4:05 a.m.

But this was not the end. At 4:30 a.m. three detectives took petitioner to Police Headquarters in Manhattan. On the way they attempted to find the bridge from which petitioner said he had thrown the murder weapon. They crossed the Triborough Bridge into Manhattan, arriving at Police Headquarters at 5 a.m., and left Manhattan for the Bronx at 5:40 a.m. via the Willis Avenue Bridge. When petitioner recognized neither bridge as the one from which he had thrown the weapon, they re-entered Manhattan via the Third Avenue Bridge, which petitioner stated was the right one, and then returned to the Bronx well after 6 a.m. During that trip the officers also elicited a statement from petitioner that the deceased was always "on (his) back," "always pushing" him and that he was "not sorry" he had shot the deceased. All three detectives testified to that statement at the trial.

Court opened at 10 a.m. that morning, and petitioner was arraigned at 10:15.

At the trial, the confession was introduced in evidence over appropriate objections. The jury was instructed that it could rely on it only if it was found to be voluntary. The jury returned a guilty verdict and petitioner was sentenced to death. The New York Court of Appeals affirmed the conviction over three dissents, and we granted certiorari to resolve the serious problem presented under the Fourteenth Amendment.

Petitioner's first contention is that his absolute right to counsel in a capital case, became operative on the return of an indictment against him, for at that time he was in every sense a defendant in a criminal case, the grand jury having found sufficient cause to believe that he had committed the crime. He argues accordingly that following indictment no confession obtained in the absence of counsel can be used without violating the Fourteenth Amendment. We find it unnecessary to reach that contention, for we find use of the confession obtained here inconsistent with the Fourteenth Amendment under traditional principles.

The abhorrence of society to the use of involuntary confessions does not turn alone on their inherent untrustworthiness. It also turns on the deep-rooted feeling that the police must obey the law while enforcing the law; that in the end life and liberty can be as much endangered from illegal methods used to convict those thought to be criminals as from the actual criminals themselves. Accordingly, the actions of police in obtaining confessions have come under scrutiny in a long series of cases. Those cases suggest that in recent years law enforcement officials have become increasingly aware of the burden which they share, along with our courts, in protecting fundamental rights of our citizenry, including that portion of our citizenry suspected of crime. The facts of no case recently in this Court have quite approached the brutal beatings in *Brown v. State of Mississippi*, or the 36 consecutive hours of questioning present in *Ashcraft v. State of Tennessee.* But as law enforcement officers become more responsible, and the methods used to extract confessions more sophisticated, our duty to enforce federal constitutional protections does not cease. It only becomes more difficult because of the more delicate judgments to be made. Our judgment here is that, on all the facts, this conviction cannot stand.

Petitioner was a foreign-born young man of 25 with no past history of law violation or of subjection to official interrogation, at least insofar as the record shows. He had progressed only one-half year into high school and the record indicates that he had a history of emotional instability. He did not make a narrative statement, but was subject to the leading questions of a skillful prosecutor in a question and answer confession. He was subjected to questioning not by a few men, but by many. They included Assistant District Attorney Goldsmith, one Hyland of the District Attorney's Office, Deputy Inspector Halks, Lieutenant Gannon, Detective Ciccone, Detective Motta, Detective Lehrer, Detective Marshal, Detective Farrell, Detective Leira, Detective Murphy, Detective Murtha, Sergeant Clarke, Patrolman Bruno and Stenographer Baldwin. All played some part, and the effect of such massive official interrogation must have been felt. Petitioner was questioned for virtually eight straight hours before he confessed, with his only respite being a transfer to an arena presumably considered more appropriate by the police for the task at hand. Nor was the questioning conducted during normal business hours, but began in early evening, continued into the night, and did not bear fruition until the not-too-early morning. The drama was not played out, with the final admissions obtained, until almost sunrise. In such circumstances slowly mounting fatigue does, and is calculated to, play its part. The questioners persisted in the face of his repeated refusals to answer on the advice of his attorney, and they ignored his reasonable requests to contact the local attorney whom he had already retained and who had personally delivered him into the custody of these officers in obedience to the bench warrant.

The use of Bruno, characterized in this Court by counsel for the State as a "childhood friend" of petitioner's, is another factor which deserves mention in the totality of the situation. Bruno's was the one face visible to petitioner in which he could put some trust. There was a bond of friendship between them going back a decade into adolescence. It was with this material that the officers felt that they could overcome petitioner's will. They instructed Bruno falsely to state that petitioner's telephone call had gotten him into trouble, that his job was in jeopardy, and that loss of his job would be disastrous to his three children, his wife and his unborn child. And Bruno played this part of a worried father, harried by his superiors, in not one, but four different acts, the final one lasting an hour. Petitioner was apparently unaware of John Gay's famous couplet:

> An open foe may prove a curse, But a pretended friend is worse,

and he yielded to his false friend's entreaties.

We conclude that petitioner's will was overborne by official pressure, fatigue and sympathy falsely aroused after considering all the facts in their post-indictment setting. Here a grand jury had already found sufficient cause to require petitioner to face trial on a charge of first-degree murder, and the police had an eyewitness to the shooting. The police were not therefore merely trying to solve a crime, or even to absolve a suspect. They were rather concerned primarily with securing a statement from defendant on which they could convict him. The undeviating intent of the officers to extract a confession from petitioner is therefore patent. When such an intent is shown, this Court has held that the confession obtained must be examined with the most careful scrutiny, and has reversed a conviction on facts less compelling than these. Accordingly, we hold that petitioner's conviction cannot stand under the Fourteenth Amendment.

Reversed.

NOTES AND QUESTIONS

1. Chief Justice Warren describes the defendant, Joseph Spano, as a "derivative citizen," whatever that may mean. How if at all might Spano's personal characteristics—his age, his education, his employment status, his "citizenship"—be relevant?

2. How significant to the result here is it that, at the time of his confession, Spano was already under indictment? That he had already retained counsel? That the government had a witness to the alleged murder?

Four Justices concurred, noting that Spano had counsel and/or had been indicted, facts that were sufficient grounds themselves for reversal.

3. The Court distinguishes between police action aimed to "extract a confession" as opposed to action "merely to solve a crime." Should the circumstances and status of the investigation matter in a constitutional sense? Should the police get more leeway when a crime is unsolved or unwitnessed?

4. What is the significance to the result that the assistant district attorney who ultimately prosecuted the case, a "skillful" cross-examiner, participated in the interrogation, including relocating to the police station to continue the interrogation after five hours at the D.A.'s office? Would it have been ethical for the ADA to participate in the deception of the defendant by his friend Bruno?

5. Are there any limits on the deception a police officer can use in questioning a suspect? Note that the Court does not explicitly say that the deception of Spano was unconstitutionally coercive. Was the length of the questioning of Spano unconstitutionally coercive?

The Court's reference to a suspect's need for counsel in the Fifth Amendment interrogation context can sometimes be difficult to take seriously. In some instances, the Court seems to harbor the illusion that a criminal suspect is actually in need of advice about whether to submit to questioning by the police. But the Court knows better, and has known better since at least as long as Justice Robert Jackson had been on the Court, as this excerpt from his concurring opinion in *Watts v. Indiana*, 338 U.S. 49 (1949), makes clear:

> Amid much that is irrelevant or trivial one serious situation seems to me to stand out in these cases. The suspect neither had nor was advised of his right to get counsel. This presents a real dilemma in a free society. To subject one without counsel to questioning which may and is intended to convict him, is a real peril to individual freedom. To bring in a lawyer means a real peril to solution of the crime because, under our adversary system, he deems that his sole duty is to protect his client—guilty or innocent—and that in such a capacity he owes no duty whatever to help society solve its crime problem. Under this conception of criminal procedure, any

> lawyer worth his salt will tell the suspect in no uncertain terms to make no statement to police under any circumstances.
>
> If the State may arrest on suspicion and interrogate without counsel, there is no denying the fact that it largely negates the benefits of the constitutional guaranty of the right to assistance of counsel. Any lawyer who has ever been called into a case after his client has "told all" and turned any evidence he has over to the Government, knows how helpless he is to protect his client against the facts thus disclosed.

Id. at 59.

The Court further reflected on the meaning of the right to counsel in the interrogation context in the next case, where the defendant, like the defendant in *Spano*, was already under indictment and represented by counsel when the interrogation occurred.

Massiah v. United States

377 U.S. 201 (1964)

Mr. Justice Stewart delivered the opinion of the Court.

The petitioner was indicted for violating the federal narcotics laws. He retained a lawyer, pleaded not guilty, and was released on bail. While he was free on bail a federal agent succeeded by surreptitious means in listening to incriminating statements made by him. Evidence of these statements was introduced against the petitioner at his trial over his objection. He was convicted, and the Court of Appeals affirmed. We granted certiorari to consider whether, under the circumstances here presented, the prosecution's use at the trial of evidence of the petitioner's own incriminating statements deprived him of any right secured to him under the Federal Constitution.

The petitioner, a merchant seaman, was in 1958 a member of the crew of the S. S. Santa Maria. In April of that year federal customs officials in New York received information that he was going to transport a quantity of narcotics aboard that ship from South America to the United States. As a result of this and other information, the agents searched the Santa Maria upon its arrival in New York and found in the afterpeak of the vessel five packages containing about three and a half pounds of cocaine. They also learned of circumstances, not here relevant, tending to connect the petitioner with the cocaine. He was arrested, promptly arraigned, and subsequently indicted for possession of narcotics aboard a United States vessel. In July a superseding indictment was returned, charging the petitioner and a man named Colson with the same substantive offense, and in separate counts charging the petitioner, Colson, and others with having conspired to possess narcotics aboard a United States vessel, and to import, conceal, and facilitate the sale of narcotics. The petitioner, who had retained a lawyer, pleaded not guilty and was released on bail, along with Colson.

A few days later, and quite without the petitioner's knowledge, Colson decided to cooperate with the government agents in their continuing investigation of the narcotics activities in which the petitioner, Colson, and others had allegedly been engaged. Colson permitted an agent named Murphy to install a Schmidt radio transmitter under the front seat of Colson's automobile, by means of which Murphy, equipped with an appropriate receiving device, could overhear from some distance away conversations carried on in Colson's car.

On the evening of November 19, 1959, Colson and the petitioner held a lengthy conversation while sitting in Colson's automobile, parked on a New York street. By prearrangement with Colson, and totally unbeknown to the petitioner, the agent Murphy sat in a car parked out of sight down the street and listened over the radio to the entire conversation. The petitioner made several incriminating statements during the course of this conversation.

At the petitioner's trial these incriminating statements were brought before the jury through Murphy's testimony, despite the insistent objection of defense counsel. The jury convicted the petitioner of several related narcotics offenses, and the convictions were affirmed by the Court of Appeals.

The petitioner argues that it was an error of constitutional dimensions to permit the agent Murphy at the trial to testify to the petitioner's incriminating statements which Murphy had overheard under the circumstances disclosed by this record. This argument is based upon two distinct and independent grounds. First, we are told that Murphy's use of the radio equipment violated the petitioner's rights under the Fourth Amendment, and, consequently, that all evidence which Murphy thereby obtained was, under the rule of *Weeks v. United States*, inadmissible against the petitioner at the trial. Secondly, it is said that the petitioner's Fifth and Sixth Amendment rights were violated by the use in evidence against him of incriminating statements which government agents had deliberately elicited from him after he had been indicted and in the absence of his retained counsel. Because of the way we dispose of the case, we do not reach the Fourth Amendment issue.

In *Spano v. New York*, this Court reversed a state criminal conviction because a confession had been wrongly admitted into evidence against the defendant at his trial. In that case the defendant had already been indicted for first-degree murder at the time he confessed. The Court held that the defendant's conviction could not stand under the Fourteenth Amendment. While the Court's opinion relied upon the totality of the circumstances under which the confession had been obtained, four concurring Justices pointed out that the Constitution required reversal of the conviction upon the sole and specific ground that the confession had been deliberately elicited by the police after the defendant had been indicted, and therefore at a time when he was clearly entitled to a lawyer's help. It was pointed out that under our system of justice the most elemental concepts of due process of law contemplate that an indictment be followed by a trial, "in an orderly courtroom, presided over by a judge, open to the public, and protected by all the procedural safeguards of the law. It was said that a Constitution which guarantees a defendant the aid of counsel at such a trial could surely vouchsafe no less to an indicted defendant under interrogation by the police in a completely extrajudicial proceeding. Anything less, it was said, might deny a defendant 'effective representation by counsel at the only stage when legal aid and advice would help him.'"

Ever since this Court's decision in the *Spano* case, the New York courts have unequivocally followed this constitutional rule. "Any secret interrogation of the defendant, from and after the finding of the indictment, without the protection afforded by the presence of counsel, contravenes the basic dictates of fairness in the conduct of criminal causes and the fundamental rights of persons charged with crime."

This view no more than reflects a constitutional principle established as long ago as *Powell v. Alabama*, where the Court noted that ". . . during perhaps the most critical period of the proceedings . . . that is to say, from the time of their arraignment until the beginning of their trial, when consultation, thorough-going investigation and preparation (are) vitally important, the defendants . . . (are) as much entitled to such aid (of counsel) during that period as at the trial itself." And since the *Spano* decision the same basic constitutional principle has been broadly reaffirmed by this Court.

Here we deal not with a state court conviction, but with a federal case, where the specific guarantee of the Sixth Amendment directly applies. We hold that the petitioner was denied the basic protections of that guarantee when there was used against him at his trial evidence of his own incriminating words, which federal agents had deliberately elicited from him after he had been indicted and in the absence of his counsel. It is true that in the *Spano* case the defendant was interrogated in a police station, while here the damaging testimony was elicited from the defendant without his knowledge while he was free on bail. But, as Judge Hays pointed out in his dissent in the Court of Appeals, "if such a rule is to have any efficacy it must apply to indirect and surreptitious interrogations as well as those conducted in the jailhouse. In this case, Massiah was more seriously imposed upon . . . because he did not even know that he was under interrogation by a government agent."

The Solicitor General, in his brief and oral argument, has strenuously contended that the federal law enforcement agents had the right, if not indeed the duty, to continue their investigation of the petitioner and his alleged criminal associates even though the petitioner had been indicted. He points out that the Government was continuing its investigation in order to uncover not only the source of narcotics found on the S. S. Santa Maria, but also their intended buyer. He says that the quantity of narcotics involved was such as to suggest that the petitioner was part of a large and well-organized ring, and indeed that the continuing investigation confirmed this suspicion, since it resulted in criminal charges against many defendants. Under these circumstances the Solicitor General concludes that the Government agents were completely "justified in making use of Colson's cooperation by having Colson continue his normal associations and by surveilling them."

We may accept and, at least for present purposes, completely approve all that this argument implies, Fourth Amendment problems to one side. We do not question that in this case, as in many cases, it was entirely proper to continue an investigation of the suspected criminal activities of the defendant and his alleged confederates, even though the defendant had already been indicted. All that we hold is that the defendant's own incriminating statements, obtained by federal agents under the circumstances here disclosed, could not constitutionally be used by the prosecution as evidence against him at his trial.

Reversed.

[Justices White, Clark, and Harlan dissented.]

NOTES AND QUESTIONS

1. The Court states that "under our system of justice the most elemental concepts of due process contemplate that an indictment be followed by a trial, 'in an orderly courtroom, presided over by a judge, open to the public, and protected by all the procedural safeguards of the law'" (citing and quoting from) *Spano v. New York*, 360 U.S. 315, 327 (1959). What is the point of this observation? Is there tension between this observation and the Court's later statement that it may in some cases "be entirely proper to continue an investigation of the suspected activities of the defendant and his alleged confederates, even though the defendant had already been indicted"? In what category of cases is this sort of post-indictment investigation appropriate?

The Court quotes with apparent approval the line from the dissenting judge in the Second Circuit, who noted that Massiah was "more seriously imposed upon" than the defendant in *Spano*, who was openly, and not surreptitiously, interrogated. Do you agree with this sentiment? Is the Court nostalgic for some bygone norms of criminal justice, where the police observed recognized boundaries? Is it clear that the government's use of Colson to secretly record his conversations with Massiah would have been permissible prior to indictment? What if Massiah had hired an attorney prior to indictment because he had got wind of the government's investigation, and the government was aware of this representation?

2. Is it fair to read *Massiah* as recognizing what might be thought of as a "defensive" component of the right to counsel? If this understanding of *Massiah* is correct, what is the relevance of the Court's citation to and reliance on such right-to-counsel cases as *Powell*, *Gideon*, and *Johnson v. Zerbst*?

What might the contours of such a defensive right to counsel be? Is this view compatible with the language of the Sixth Amendment, which speaks in terms of the "assistance of counsel"? The dissent points out that this "new rule" rests on the likelihood that, if counsel were to participate in any attempt to interrogate a defendant post-indictment, counsel would advise defendant not to say anything. Is the dissent correct? Does such advice amount to "assistance of counsel"?

3. Unfortunately, the opinion does not include the recorded conversation between Colson (the cooperator) and Massiah. Does it seem likely that Colson's conversation with Massiah had the benefit of substantive input from Murphy, the agent? Suppose Colson had not been given the recording device but had been directed by Murphy on how to handle the conversation and had immediately reported the substance of the conversation to Murphy after it ended. What result? Consider further the situation where Colson is cooperating with Murphy but receives neither recording equipment nor instruction from Murphy on how to handle the conversation and, instead, has the conversation entirely of his own volition but then reports admissions by Massiah to Murphy?

The dissent makes several interesting points in addition to its general lament that the new rule will make it harder to convict criminals. First, it points out that Massiah's statements to Colson are suppressed without any showing of coercion, which at this point (pre-*Miranda*) was the standard used in confession cases. Second, the dissent argues that the rule exceeds the Fifth Amendment bar on self-incrimination, which does not bar voluntary pretrial admissions. Third, there is no suggestion that the government in any way interfered with Massiah's relationship with his counsel. What is the best response to these points, individually or collectively?

Miranda v. Arizona, 384 U.S. 436 (1966), decided seven years after *Spano* and two years after *Massiah*, was to fundamentally and forever change the landscape of police interrogation. But the concept of voluntariness—though eclipsed by the "warnings" required by *Miranda*—did not cease to be relevant. In *Colorado v. Connelly*, 479 U.S. 157 (1986), 20 years after *Miranda*, the Court held that an unprompted confession by a person with a history of mental illness was voluntary for due process purposes even though there was undisputed medical evidence that, at the moment of confession, the defendant was experiencing "command hallucinations" and thus lacked "the ability to make free and rational choices." *Id.* at 161. The Court held that coercive police activity was "a necessary predicate" to establishing a constitutional violation. Dissenting, Justice Brennan argued that due to the enormous power of a confession as a type of evidence, an involuntary confession should be admissible only where bulwarked by "substantial indicia of reliability" extrinsic to the confession itself, evidence that was totally lacking in *Connelly*. *Id.* at 184.

In *Arizona v. Fulminante*, 499 U.S. 279 (1991), defendant was incarcerated in federal prison on a felon-in-possession firearms charge. He had previously been a suspect in the murder of his stepdaughter but had not been charged. A fellow federal prisoner, who was also an FBI informant, heard rumors about the defendant's having been a suspect in a child murder. He offered to arrange for the defendant's protection in prison, but agreed to do so only if the defendant came clean about his involvement in the murder. The defendant's subsequent confession to the informant was found to be involuntary and hence inadmissible inasmuch as it was induced by "a credible threat of physical violence." *Id.* at 288.

C. *MIRANDA*

We turn now to the centerpiece of the Warren Court revolution, the best-known case name ever, the Supreme Court's 1966 decision in *Miranda v. Arizona*, 384 U.S. 436 (1966). The term "revolution" is not hyperbole. Consider that in a state court criminal prosecution in 1960 the Fourth, Fifth, and Sixth Amendments played no role. Just eight years later in such a prosecution, illegally obtained evidence could be suppressed, *Mapp v. Ohio*, 367 U.S. 643 (1961); indigent felony defendants had to be afforded counsel, *Gideon v. Wainwright*, 372 U.S. 335 (1963); a person could not be subpoenaed to give testimony that might incriminate him, *Malloy v. Hogan*, 378 U.S. 1 (1964); warnings were required for custodial interrogations, *Miranda*; and states were required to provide jury trials in serious criminal cases, *Duncan v. Louisiana*, 391 U.S. 145 (1968). *See* Stephen Schulhofer, Miranda v. Arizona*: A Modest But Important Legacy* 157, in Criminal Procedure Stories (Carol Steiker ed., 2006). The authors of these five opinions had not come to the Court ordained with civil libertarian credentials, moreover. Four of the five of them — Justices Clark (*Mapp*), White (*Duncan*), Black (*Gideon*) and Warren (*Miranda*) — had been state or federal prosecutors.

The immediate predicate to *Miranda* was what the Court calls in *Miranda* the "spirited debate" engendered by its decision just two years earlier in *Escobedo v. Illinois*, 378 U.S. 478 (1964). In *Escobedo*, the police interrogated a suspect in custody at the police station, all the while denying his requests for counsel and preventing his retained attorney, who had come to the police station, from consulting with him. The suspect eventually made incriminating statements that were admitted against him at trial. The Court overturned the conviction, holding the statements "constitutionally inadmissible."

Miranda v. Arizona

384 U.S. 436 (1966)

Mr. Chief Justice Warren delivered the opinion of the Court.

The cases before us raise questions which go to the roots of our concepts of American criminal jurisprudence: the restraints society must observe consistent with the Federal Constitution in prosecuting individuals for crime. More specifically, we deal with the admissibility of statements obtained from an individual who is subjected to custodial police interrogation and the necessity for procedures which assure that the individual is accorded his privilege under the Fifth Amendment to the Constitution not to be compelled to incriminate himself.

We dealt with certain phases of this problem recently in *Escobedo*. There, as in the four cases before us, law enforcement officials took the defendant into custody and interrogated him in a police station for the purpose of obtaining a confession. The police did not effectively advise him of his right to remain silent or of his right to consult with his attorney. Rather, they confronted him with an alleged accomplice who accused him of having perpetrated a murder. When the defendant denied the accusation and said "I didn't shoot Manuel, you did it," they handcuffed him and took him to an interrogation room. There, while handcuffed and standing, he was questioned for four hours until he confessed. During this interrogation, the police denied his request to speak to his attorney, and they prevented his retained attorney, who had come to the police station, from consulting with him. At his trial, the State, over his objection, introduced the confession against him. We held that the statements thus made were constitutionally inadmissible.

This case has been the subject of judicial interpretation and spirited legal debate since it was decided two years ago. Both state and federal courts, in assessing its implications, have arrived at varying conclusions. A wealth of scholarly material has been written tracing its ramifications and underpinnings. Police and prosecutor have speculated on its range and desirability. We granted certiorari in these cases in order further to explore some facets of the problems, thus exposed, of applying the privilege against self-incrimination to in-custody interrogation, and to give concrete constitutional guidelines for law enforcement agencies and courts to follow.

We start here, as we did in *Escobedo*, with the premise that our holding is not an innovation in our jurisprudence, but is an application of principles long recognized and applied in other settings. We have undertaken a thorough re-examination of the *Escobedo* decision and the principles it announced, and we reaffirm it. That case was but an explication of basic rights that are enshrined in our Constitution—that "No person . . . shall be compelled in any criminal case to be a witness against himself," and that "the accused shall . . . have the Assistance of Counsel"—rights which were put in jeopardy in that case through official overbearing. These precious rights were fixed in our Constitution only after centuries of persecution and struggle. And in the words of Chief Justice Marshall, they were secured "for ages to come, and . . . designed to approach immortality as nearly as human institutions can approach it."

Over 70 years ago, our predecessors on this Court eloquently stated:

> The maxim "Nemo tenetur seipsum accusare," had its origin in a protest against the inquisitorial and manifestly unjust methods of interrogating accused persons, which (have) long obtained in the continental system, and, until the expulsion of the Stuarts from the British throne in 1688, and the erection of additional barriers for the protection of the people against the exercise of arbitrary power, (were) not uncommon even in England. While the admissions or confessions of the prisoner, when voluntarily and freely made, have always ranked high in the scale of incriminating evidence, if an accused person be asked to explain his apparent connection with a crime under investigation, the ease with which the questions put to him may assume an inquisitorial character, the temptation to press the witness unduly, to browbeat him if he be timid or reluctant, to push him into a corner, and to entrap him into fatal contradictions, which is so painfully evident in many of the earlier state trials, notably in those of Sir Nicholas Throckmorton, and Udal, the Puritan minister, made the system so odious as to give rise to a demand for its total abolition. The change in the English criminal procedure in that particular seems to be founded upon no statute and no judicial opinion, but upon a general and silent acquiescence of the courts in a popular demand. But, however adopted, it has become firmly embedded in English, as well as in American jurisprudence. So deeply did the iniquities of the ancient system impress themselves upon the minds of the American colonists that the States, with one accord, made a denial of the right to question an accused person a part of their fundamental law, so that a maxim, which in England was a mere rule of evidence, became clothed in this country with the impregnability of a constitutional enactment.

In stating the obligation of the judiciary to apply these constitutional rights, this Court declared in *Weems v. United States* (1910):

> . . . our contemplation cannot be only of what has been, but of what may be. Under any other rule a constitution would indeed be as easy of application as it would be deficient in efficacy and power. Its general principles would have little value, and be converted by precedent into impotent and lifeless formulas. Rights declared in words might be lost in reality. And this has been recognized. The meaning and vitality of the Constitution have developed against narrow and restrictive construction.

This was the spirit in which we delineated, in meaningful language, the manner in which the constitutional rights of the individual could be enforced against overzealous police practices. It was necessary in *Escobedo*, as here, to insure that what was proclaimed in the Constitution had not become but a "form of words," in the hands of government officials. And it is in this spirit, consistent with our role as judges, that we adhere to the principles of *Escobedo* today.

Our holding will be spelled out with some specificity in the pages which follow but briefly stated it is this: the prosecution may not use statements, whether exculpatory or inculpatory, stemming from custodial interrogation of the defendant unless it demonstrates the use of procedural safeguards effective to secure the privilege against self-incrimination. By custodial interrogation, we mean questioning initiated by law enforcement officers after a person has been taken into custody or otherwise deprived of his freedom of action in any significant way. As for the procedural safeguards to be employed, unless other fully effective means are devised to inform accused persons of their right of silence and to assure a continuous opportunity to exercise it, the following measures are required. Prior to any questioning, the person must be warned that he has a right to remain silent, that any statement he does make may be used as evidence against him, and that he has a right to the presence of an attorney, either retained or appointed. The defendant may waive effectuation of these rights, provided the waiver is made voluntarily, knowingly and intelligently. If, however, he indicates in any manner and at any stage of the process that he wishes to consult with an attorney before speaking there can be no questioning. Likewise, if the individual is alone and indicates in any manner that he does not wish to be interrogated, the police may not question him. The mere fact that he may have answered some questions or volunteered some statements on his own does not deprive him of the right to refrain from answering any further inquiries until he has consulted with an attorney and thereafter consents to be questioned.

1

The constitutional issue we decide in each of these cases is the admissibility of statements obtained from a defendant questioned while in custody or otherwise deprived of his freedom of action in any significant way. In each, the defendant was questioned by police officers, detectives, or a prosecuting attorney in a room in which he was cut off from the outside world. In none of these cases was the defendant given a full and effective warning of his rights at the outset of the interrogation process. In all the cases, the questioning elicited oral admissions, and in three of them, signed statements as well which were admitted at their trials. They all thus share salient features — incommunicado interrogation of individuals in a police-dominated atmosphere, resulting in self-incriminating statements without full warnings of constitutional rights.

An understanding of the nature and setting of this in-custody interrogation is essential to our decisions today. The difficulty in depicting what transpires at such interrogations stems from the fact that in this country they have largely taken place incommunicado. From extensive factual studies undertaken in the early 1930's, including the famous Wickersham Report to Congress by a Presidential Commission, it is clear that police violence and the "third degree" flourished at that time. In a series of cases decided by this Court long after these studies, the police resorted to physical brutality — beatings, hanging, whipping — and to sustained and protracted questioning incommunicado in order to extort confessions. The Commission on Civil Rights in 1961 found much evidence to indicate that "some policemen still resort to physical force to obtain confessions." The use of physical brutality and violence is not, unfortunately, relegated to the past or to any part of the country. Only recently in Kings County, New York, the police brutally beat, kicked and placed lighted cigarette butts on the back of a potential witness under interrogation for the purpose of securing a statement incriminating a third party.

The examples given above are undoubtedly the exception now, but they are sufficiently widespread to be the object of concern. Unless a proper limitation upon custodial interrogation is achieved — such as these decisions will advance — there can be no assurance that practices of this nature will be eradicated in the foreseeable future. The conclusion of the Wickersham Commission Report, made over 30 years ago, is still pertinent:

> To the contention that the third degree is necessary to get the facts, the reporters aptly reply in the language of the present Lord Chancellor of England (Lord Sankey): "It is not admissible to do a great right by doing a little wrong. . . . It is not sufficient to do justice by obtaining a proper result by irregular or improper means." Not only does the use of the third degree involve a flagrant violation of law by the officers of the law, but it involves also the dangers of false confessions, and it tends to make police and prosecutors less zealous in the search for objective evidence. As the New York prosecutor quoted in the report said, "It is a short cut and makes the police lazy and unenterprising." Or, as another official quoted remarked: "If you use your fists, you are not so likely to use your wits." We agree with the conclusion expressed in the report, that "The third degree brutalizes the police, hardens the prisoner against society, and lowers the esteem in which the administration of justice is held by the public."

Again we stress that the modern practice of in-custody interrogation is psychologically rather than physically oriented. As we have stated before, "this Court has recognized that coercion can be mental as well as physical, and that the blood of the accused is not the only hallmark of an unconstitutional inquisition." Interrogation still takes place in privacy. Privacy results in secrecy and this in turn results in a gap in our knowledge as to what in fact goes on in the interrogation rooms. A valuable source of information about present police practices, however, may be found in various police manuals and texts which document procedures employed with success in the past, and which recommend various other effective tactics. These texts are used by law enforcement agencies themselves as guides. It should be noted that these texts professedly present the most enlightened and effective means presently used to obtain statements through custodial interrogation. By considering these texts and other data, it is possible to describe procedures observed and noted around the country.

• • •

II

We sometimes forget how long it has taken to establish the privilege against self-incrimination, the sources from which it came and the fervor with which it was defended. Its roots go back into ancient times. Perhaps the critical historical event shedding light on its origins and evolution was the trial of one John Lilburn, a vocal anti-Stuart Leveller, who was made to take the Star Chamber Oath in 1637. The oath would have bound him to answer to all questions posed to him on any subject. The Trial of John Lilburn and John Wharton. He resisted the oath and declaimed the proceedings, stating:

> Another fundamental right I then contended for, was, that no man's conscience ought to be racked by oaths imposed, to answer to questions concerning himself in matters criminal, or pretended to be so.

On account of the Lilburn Trial, Parliament abolished the inquisitorial Court of Star Chamber and went further in giving him generous reparation. The lofty principles to which Lilburn had appealed during his trial gained popular acceptance in England. These sentiments worked their way over to the Colonies and were implanted after great struggle into the Bill of Rights. Those who framed our Constitution and the Bill of Rights were ever aware of subtle encroachments on individual liberty. They knew that "illegitimate and unconstitutional practices get their first footing . . . by silent approaches and slight deviations from legal modes of procedure." The privilege was elevated to constitutional status and has always been "as broad as the mischief against which it seeks to guard." *Counselman*. We cannot depart from this noble heritage.

Thus we may view the historical development of the privilege as one which groped for the proper scope of governmental power over the citizen. As a "noble principle often transcends its origins," the privilege has come rightfully to be recognized in part as an individual's substantive right, a "right to a private enclave where he may lead a private life. That right is the hallmark of our democracy." We have recently noted that the privilege against self-incrimination — the essential mainstay of our adversary system — is founded on a complex of values. All these policies point to one overriding thought: the constitutional foundation underlying the privilege is the respect a government — state or federal — must accord to the dignity and integrity of its citizens. To maintain a "fair state-individual balance," to require the government "to shoulder the entire load," to respect the inviolability of the human personality, our accusatory system of criminal justice demands that the government seeking to punish an individual produce the evidence against him by its own independent labors, rather than by the cruel, simple expedient of compelling it from his own mouth. In sum, the privilege is fulfilled only when the person is guaranteed the right "to remain silent unless he chooses to speak in the unfettered exercise of his own will."

The question in these cases is whether the privilege is fully applicable during a period of custodial interrogation. We are satisfied that all the principles embodied in the privilege apply to informal compulsion exerted by law-enforcement officers during in-custody questioning. An individual swept from familiar surroundings into police custody, surrounded by antagonistic forces, and subjected to the techniques of persuasion described above cannot be otherwise than under compulsion to speak. As a practical matter, the compulsion to speak in the isolated setting of the police station may well be greater than in courts or other official investigations, where there are often impartial observers to guard against intimidation or trickery.

This question, in fact, could have been taken as settled in federal courts almost 70 years ago, when, in *Bram v. United States*, this Court held:

> In criminal trials, in the courts of the United States, wherever a question arises whether a confession is incompetent because not voluntary, the issue is controlled by that portion of the fifth amendment . . . commanding that no person "shall be compelled in any criminal case to be a witness against himself."

In *Bram*, the Court reviewed the British and American history and case law and set down the Fifth Amendment standard for compulsion which we implement today:

> Much of the confusion which has resulted from the effort to deduce from the adjudged cases what would be a sufficient quantum of proof to show that a confession was or was not voluntary has arisen from a misconception of the subject to which the proof must address itself. The rule is not that, in order to render a statement admissible, the proof must be adequate to establish that the particular communications contained in a statement were voluntarily made, but it must be sufficient to establish that the making of the statement was voluntary; that is to say, that, from the causes which the law treats as legally sufficient to engender in the mind of the accused hope or fear in respect to the crime charged, the accused was not involuntarily impelled to make a statement when but for the improper influences he would have remained silent.

The Court has adhered to this reasoning. In 1924, Mr. Justice Brandeis wrote for a unanimous Court in reversing a conviction resting on a compelled confession. He stated:

> In the federal courts, the requisite of voluntariness is not satisfied by establishing merely that the confession was not induced by a promise or a threat. A confession is voluntary in law if, and only if, it was, in fact, voluntarily made. A confession may have been given voluntarily, although

> it was made to police officers, while in custody, and in answer to an examination conducted by them. But a confession obtained by compulsion must be excluded whatever may have been the character of the compulsion, and whether the compulsion was applied in a judicial proceeding or otherwise.

In addition to the expansive historical development of the privilege and the sound policies which have nurtured its evolution, judicial precedent thus clearly establishes its application to incommunicado interrogation. In fact, the Government concedes this point as well established.

Because of the adoption by Congress of Rule 5(a) of the Federal Rules of Criminal Procedure, and the Court's effectuation of that Rule in *McNabb v. United States*, we have had little occasion in the past quarter century to reach the constitutional issues in dealing with federal interrogations.

Our decision in *Malloy v. Hogan* (1964) necessitates an examination of the scope of the privilege in state cases as well. In *Malloy*, we squarely held the privilege applicable to the States, and held that the substantive standards underlying the privilege applied with full force to state court proceedings. Aside from the holding itself, the reasoning in *Malloy* made clear what had already become apparent—that the substantive and procedural safeguards surrounding admissibility of confessions in state cases had become exceedingly exacting, reflecting all the policies embedded in the privilege. The voluntariness doctrine in the state cases, as *Malloy* indicates, encompasses all interrogation practices which are likely to exert such pressure upon an individual as to disable him from making a free and rational choice. The implications of this proposition were elaborated in our decision in *Escobedo*, decided one week after *Malloy* applied the privilege to the States.

Our holding there stressed the fact that the police had not advised the defendant of his constitutional privilege to remain silent at the outset of the interrogation, and we drew attention to that fact at several points in the decision. This was no isolated factor, but an essential ingredient in our decision. The entire thrust of police interrogation there, as in all the cases today, was to put the defendant in such an emotional state as to impair his capacity for rational judgment. The abdication of the constitutional privilege—the choice on his part to speak to the police—was not made knowingly or competently because of the failure to apprise him of his rights; the compelling atmosphere of the in-custody interrogation, and not an independent decision on his part, caused the defendant to speak.

A different phase of the *Escobedo* decision was significant in its attention to the absence of counsel during the questioning. There, as in the cases today, we sought a protective device to dispel the compelling atmosphere of the interrogation. In *Escobedo*, however, the police did not relieve the defendant of the anxieties which they had created in the interrogation rooms. Rather, they denied his request for the assistance of counsel. This heightened his dilemma, and made his later statements the product of this compulsion. The denial of the defendant's request for his attorney thus undermined his ability to exercise the privilege—to remain silent if he chose or to speak without any intimidation, blatant or subtle. The presence of counsel, in all the cases before us today, would be the adequate protective device necessary to make the process of police interrogation conform to the dictates of the privilege. His presence would insure that statements made in the government-established atmosphere are not the product of compulsion.

It was in this manner that *Escobedo* explicated another facet of the pre-trial privilege, noted in many of the Court's prior decisions: the protection of rights at trial. That counsel is present when statements are taken from an individual during interrogation obviously enhances the integrity of the fact-finding processes in court. The presence of an attorney, and the warnings delivered to the individual, enable the defendant under otherwise compelling circumstances to tell his story without fear, effectively, and in a way that eliminates the evils in the interrogation process. Without the protections flowing from adequate warning and the rights of counsel, "all the careful safeguards erected around the giving of testimony, whether by an accused or any other witness, would become empty formalities in a procedure where the most compelling possible evidence of guilt, a confession, would have already been obtained at the unsupervised pleasure of the police."

III

Today, then, there can be no doubt that the Fifth Amendment privilege is available outside of criminal court proceedings and serves to protect persons in all settings in which their freedom of action is curtailed in any significant way from being compelled to incriminate themselves. We have concluded that without proper safeguards the process of in-custody interrogation of persons suspected or accused of crime contains inherently compelling pressures which work to undermine the individual's will to resist and to compel him to speak where he would not otherwise do so freely. In order to combat these pressures and to permit a full opportunity to exercise the privilege against self-incrimination, the accused must be adequately and effectively apprised of his rights and the exercise of those rights must be fully honored.

It is impossible for us to foresee the potential alternatives for protecting the privilege which might be devised by Congress or the States in the exercise of their creative rule-making capacities. Therefore we cannot say that the Constitution necessarily requires adherence to any particular solution for the inherent compulsions of the interrogation process as it is presently conducted. Our decision in no way creates a constitutional straitjacket which will handicap sound efforts at reform, nor is it intended to have this effect. We encourage Congress and the States to continue their laudable search for increasingly effective ways of protecting the rights of the individual while promoting efficient enforcement of our criminal laws. However, unless we are shown other procedures which are at least as effective in apprising accused persons of their right of silence and in assuring a continuous opportunity to exercise it, the following safeguards must be observed.

At the outset, if a person in custody is to be subjected to interrogation, he must first be informed in clear and unequivocal terms that he has the right to remain silent. For those unaware of the privilege, the warning is needed simply to make them aware of it—the threshold requirement for an intelligent decision as to its exercise. More important, such a warning is an absolute prerequisite in overcoming the inherent pressures of the interrogation atmosphere. It is not just the subnormal or woefully ignorant who succumb to an interrogator's imprecations, whether implied or expressly stated, that the interrogation will continue until a confession is obtained or that silence in the face of accusation is itself damning and will bode ill when presented to a jury. Further, the warning will show the individual that his interrogators are prepared to recognize his privilege should he choose to exercise it.

The Fifth Amendment privilege is so fundamental to our system of constitutional rule and the expedient of giving an adequate warning as to the availability of the privilege so simple, we will not pause to inquire in individual cases whether the defendant was aware of his rights without a warning being given. Assessments of the knowledge the defendant possessed, based on information as to his age, education, intelligence, or prior contact with authorities, can never be more than speculation; a warning is a clearcut fact. More important, whatever the background of the person interrogated, a warning at the time of the interrogation is indispensable to overcome its pressures and to insure that the individual knows he is free to exercise the privilege at that point in time.

The warning of the right to remain silent must be accompanied by the explanation that anything said can and will be used against the individual in court. This warning is needed in order to make him aware not only of the privilege, but also of the consequences of forgoing it. It is only through an awareness of these consequences that there can be any assurance of real understanding and intelligent exercise of the privilege. Moreover, this warning may serve to make the individual more acutely aware that he is faced with a phase of the adversary system—that he is not in the presence of persons acting solely in his interest.

The circumstances surrounding in-custody interrogation can operate very quickly to overbear the will of one merely made aware of his privilege by his interrogators. Therefore, the right to have counsel present at the interrogation is indispensable to the protection of the Fifth Amendment privilege under the system we delineate today. Our aim is to assure that the individual's right to choose between silence and speech remains unfettered throughout the interrogation process. A once-stated warning, delivered by those who will conduct the interrogation, cannot itself suffice to that end among those who most require knowledge of their rights. A mere warning given by the interrogators is not alone sufficient to accomplish that end. Prosecutors themselves claim that the admonishment of the right to remain silent without more "will benefit only the recidivist and the professional." Even preliminary advice given to the accused by his own attorney can be swiftly overcome by the secret interrogation process. Thus, the need for counsel to protect the Fifth Amendment privilege comprehends not merely a right to consult with counsel prior to questioning, but also to have counsel present during any questioning if the defendant so desires.

The presence of counsel at the interrogation may serve several significant subsidiary functions as well. If the accused decides to talk to his interrogators, the assistance of counsel can mitigate the dangers of untrustworthiness. With a lawyer present the likelihood that the police will practice coercion is reduced, and if coercion is nevertheless exercised the lawyer can testify to it in court. The presence of a lawyer can also help to guarantee that the accused gives a fully accurate statement to the police and that the statement is rightly reported by the prosecution at trial.

An individual need not make a pre-interrogation request for a lawyer. While such request affirmatively secures his right to have one, his failure to ask for a lawyer does not constitute a waiver. No effective waiver of the right to counsel during interrogation can be recognized unless specifically made after the warnings we here delineate have been given. The accused who does not know his rights and therefore does not make a request may be the person who most needs counsel. As the California Supreme Court has aptly put it:

> Finally, we must recognize that the imposition of the requirement for the request would discriminate against the defendant who does not know his rights. The defendant who does not ask for counsel is the very defendant who most needs counsel. We cannot penalize a defendant who, not understanding his constitutional rights, does not make the formal request and by such failure demonstrates his helplessness. To require the request would be to favor the defendant whose sophistication or status had fortuitously prompted him to make it.

Accordingly we hold that an individual held for interrogation must be clearly informed that he has the right to consult with a lawyer and to have the lawyer with him during interrogation under the system for protecting the privilege we delineate today. As with the warnings of the right to remain silent and that anything stated can be used in evidence against him, this warning is an absolute prerequisite to interrogation. No amount of circumstantial evidence that the person may have been aware of this right will suffice to stand in its stead. Only through such a warning is there ascertainable assurance that the accused was aware of this right.

If an individual indicates that he wishes the assistance of counsel before any interrogation occurs, the authorities cannot rationally ignore or deny his request on the basis that the individual does not have or cannot afford a retained attorney. The financial ability of the individual has no relationship to the scope of the rights involved here. The privilege against self-incrimination secured by the Constitution applies to all individuals. The need for counsel in order to protect the privilege exists for the indigent as well as the affluent. In fact, were we to limit these constitutional rights to those who can retain an attorney, our decisions today would be of little significance. The cases before us as well as the vast majority of confession cases with which we have dealt in the past involve those unable to retain counsel. While authorities are not required to relieve the accused of his poverty, they have the obligation not to take advantage of indigence in the administration of justice. Denial of counsel to the indigent at the time of interrogation while allowing an attorney to those who can afford one would be no more supportable by reason or logic than the similar situation at trial and on appeal struck down in *Gideon.*

In order fully to apprise a person interrogated of the extent of his rights under this system then, it is necessary to warn him not only that he has the right to consult with an attorney, but also that if he is indigent a lawyer will be appointed to represent him. Without this additional warning, the admonition of the right to consult with counsel would often be understood as meaning only that he can consult with a lawyer if he has one or has the funds to obtain one. The warning of a right to counsel would be hollow if not couched in terms that would convey to the indigent—the person most often subjected to interrogation—the knowledge that he too has a right to have counsel present. As with the warnings of the right to remain silent and of the general right to counsel, only by effective and express explanation to the indigent of this right can there be assurance that he was truly in a position to exercise it.

Once warnings have been given, the subsequent procedure is clear. If the individual indicates in any manner, at any time prior to or during questioning, that he wishes to remain silent, the interrogation must cease. At this point he has shown that he intends to exercise his Fifth Amendment privilege; any statement taken after the person invokes his privilege cannot be other than the product of compulsion, subtle or otherwise. Without the right to cut off questioning, the setting of in-custody interrogation operates on the individual to overcome free choice in producing a statement after the privilege has been once invoked. If the individual states that he wants an attorney, the interrogation must cease until an attorney is present. At that time, the individual must have an opportunity to confer with the attorney and to have him present during any subsequent questioning. If the individual cannot obtain an attorney and he indicates that he wants one before speaking to police, they must respect his decision to remain silent.

This does not mean, as some have suggested, that each police station must have a "station house lawyer" present at all times to advise prisoners. It does mean, however, that if police propose to interrogate a person they must make known to him that he is entitled to a lawyer and that if he cannot afford one, a lawyer will be provided for him prior to any interrogation. If authorities conclude that they will not provide counsel during a reasonable period of time in which investigation in the field is carried out, they may refrain from doing so without violating the person's Fifth Amendment privilege so long as they do not question him during that time.

If the interrogation continues without the presence of an attorney and a statement is taken, a heavy burden rests on the government to demonstrate that the defendant knowingly and intelligently waived his privilege against self-incrimination and his right to retained or appointed counsel. This Court has always set high standards of proof for the waiver of constitutional rights, and we reassert these standards as applied to in custody interrogation. Since the State is responsible for establishing the isolated circumstances under which the interrogation takes place and has the only means of making available corroborated evidence of warnings given during incommunicado interrogation, the burden is rightly on its shoulders.

An express statement that the individual is willing to make a statement and does not want an attorney followed closely by a statement could constitute a waiver. But a valid waiver will not be presumed simply from the silence of the accused after warnings are given or simply from the fact that a confession was in fact eventually obtained.

Whatever the testimony of the authorities as to waiver of rights by an accused, the fact of lengthy interrogation or incommunicado incarceration before a statement is made is strong evidence that the accused did not validly waive his rights. In these circumstances the fact that the individual eventually made a statement is consistent with the conclusion that the compelling influence of the interrogation finally forced him to do so. It is inconsistent with any notion of a voluntary relinquishment of the privilege. Moreover, any evidence that the accused was threatened, tricked, or cajoled into a waiver will, of course, show that the defendant did not voluntarily waive his privilege. The requirement of warnings and waiver of rights is a fundamental with respect to the Fifth Amendment privilege and not simply a preliminary ritual to existing methods of interrogation.

The warnings required and the waiver necessary in accordance with our opinion today are, in the absence of a fully effective equivalent, prerequisites to the admissibility of any statement made by a defendant. No distinction can be drawn between statements which are direct confessions and statements which amount to "admissions" of part or all of an offense. The privilege against self-incrimination protects the individual from being compelled to incriminate himself in any manner; it does not distinguish degrees of incrimination. Similarly, or precisely the same reason, no distinction may be drawn between inculpatory statements and statements alleged to be merely "exculpatory." If a statement made were in fact truly exculpatory it would, of course, never be used by the prosecution. In fact, statements merely intended to be exculpatory by the defendant are often used to impeach his testimony at trial or to demonstrate untruths in the statement given under interrogation and thus to prove guilt by implication. These statements are incriminating in any meaningful sense of the word and may not be used without the full warnings and effective waiver required for any other statement. In *Escobedo* itself, the defendant fully intended his accusation of another as the slayer to be exculpatory as to himself.

The principles announced today deal with the protection which must be given to the privilege against self-incrimination when the individual is first subjected to police interrogation while in custody at the station or otherwise deprived of his freedom of action in any significant way. It is at this point that our adversary system of criminal proceedings commences, distinguishing itself at the outset from the inquisitorial system recognized in some countries. Under the system of warnings we delineate today or under any other system which may be devised and found effective, the safeguards to be erected about the privilege must come into play at this point.

Our decision is not intended to hamper the traditional function of police officers in investigating crime. When an individual is in custody on probable cause, the police may, of course, seek out evidence in the field to be used at trial against him. Such investigation may include inquiry of persons not under restraint. General on-the-scene questioning as to facts surrounding a crime or other general questioning of citizens in the fact-finding process is not affected by our holding. It is an act of responsible citizenship for individuals to give whatever information they may have to aid in law enforcement. In such situations the compelling atmosphere inherent in the process of in-custody interrogation is not necessarily present.

In dealing with statements obtained through interrogation, we do not purport to find all confessions inadmissible. Confessions remain a proper element in law enforcement. Any statement given freely and voluntarily without any compelling influences is, of course, admissible in evidence. The fundamental import of the privilege while an individual is in custody is not whether he is allowed to talk to the police without the benefit of warnings and counsel, but whether he can be interrogated. There is no requirement that police stop a person who enters a police station and states that he wishes to confess to a crime, or a person who calls the police to offer a confession or any other statement he desires to make. Volunteered statements of any kind are not barred by the Fifth Amendment and their admissibility is not affected by our holding today.

To summarize, we hold that when an individual is taken into custody or otherwise deprived of his freedom by the authorities in any significant way and is subjected to questioning, the privilege against self-incrimination is jeopardized. Procedural safeguards must be employed to protect the privilege and unless other fully effective means are adopted to notify the person of his right of silence and to assure that the exercise of the right will be scrupulously honored, the following measures are required. He must be warned prior to any questioning that he has the right to remain silent, that anything he says can be used against him in a court of law, that he has the right to the presence of an attorney, and that if he cannot afford an attorney one will be appointed for him prior to any questioning if he so desires. Opportunity to exercise these rights must be afforded to him throughout the interrogation. After such warnings have been given, and such opportunity afforded him, the individual may knowingly and intelligently waive these rights and agree to answer questions or make a statement. But unless and until such warnings and waiver are demonstrated by the prosecution at trial, no evidence obtained as a result of interrogation can be used against him.

IV

A recurrent argument made in these cases is that society's need for interrogation outweighs the privilege. This argument is not unfamiliar to this Court. The whole thrust of our foregoing discussion demonstrates that the Constitution has prescribed the rights of the individual when confronted with the power of government when it provided in the Fifth Amendment that an individual cannot be compelled to be a witness against himself. That right cannot be abridged. As Mr. Justice Brandeis once observed:

> Decency, security, and liberty alike demand that government officials shall be subjected to the same rules of conduct that are commands to the citizen. In a government of laws, existence of the government will be imperiled if it fails to observe the law scrupulously. Our government is the potent, the omnipresent teacher. For good or for ill, it teaches the whole people by its example. Crime is contagious. If the government becomes a lawbreaker, it breeds contempt for law; it invites every man to become a law unto himself; it invites anarchy. To declare that in the administration of the criminal law the end justifies the means . . . would bring terrible retribution. Against that pernicious doctrine this court should resolutely set its face. *Olmstead.*

In this connection, one of our country's distinguished jurists has pointed out: "The quality of a nation's civilization can be largely measured by the methods it uses in the enforcement of its criminal law."

If the individual desires to exercise his privilege, he has the right to do so. This is not for the authorities to decide. An attorney may advise his client not to talk to police until he has had an opportunity to investigate the case, or he may wish to be present with his client during any police questioning. In doing so an attorney is merely exercising the good professional judgment he has been taught. This is not cause for considering the attorney a menace to law enforcement. He is merely carrying out what he is sworn to do under his oath—to protect to the extent of his ability the rights of his client. In fulfilling this responsibility the attorney plays a vital role in the administration of criminal justice under our Constitution.

In announcing these principles, we are not unmindful of the burdens which law enforcement officials must bear, often under trying circumstances. We also fully recognize the obligation of all citizens to aid in enforcing the criminal laws. This Court, while protecting individual rights, has always given ample latitude to law enforcement agencies in the legitimate exercise of their duties. The limits we have placed on the interrogation process should not constitute an undue interference with a proper system of law enforcement. As we have noted, our decision does not in any way preclude police from carrying out their traditional investigatory functions. Although confessions may play an important role in some convictions, the cases before us present graphic examples of the overstatement of the "need" for confessions. In each case authorities conducted interrogations ranging up to five days in duration despite the presence, through standard investigating practices, of considerable evidence against each defendant.

It is also urged that an unfettered right to detention for interrogation should be allowed because it will often redound to the benefit of the person questioned. When police inquiry determines that there is no reason to believe that the person has committed any crime, it is said, he will be released without need for further formal procedures. The person who has committed no offense, however, will be better able to clear himself after warnings with counsel present than without. It can be assumed that in such circumstances a lawyer would advise his client to talk freely to police in order to clear himself.

Custodial interrogation, by contrast, does not necessarily afford the innocent an opportunity to clear themselves. A serious consequence of the present practice of the interrogation alleged to be beneficial for the innocent is that many arrests "for investigation" subject large numbers of innocent persons to detention and interrogation. In one of the cases before us, police held four persons, who were in the defendant's house at the time of the arrest, in jail for five days until defendant confessed. At that time they were finally released. Police stated that there was "no evidence to connect them with any crime." Available statistics on the extent of this practice where it is condoned indicate that these four are far from alone in being subjected to arrest, prolonged detention, and interrogation without the requisite probable cause.

Over the years the Federal Bureau of Investigation has compiled an exemplary record of effective law enforcement while advising any suspect or arrested person, at the outset of an interview, that he is not required to make a statement, that any statement may be used against him in court, that the individual may obtain the services of an attorney of his own choice and, more recently, that he has a right to free counsel if he is unable to pay. A letter received from the Solicitor General in response to a question from the Bench makes it clear that the present pattern of warnings and respect for the rights of the individual followed as a practice by the FBI is consistent with the procedure which we delineate today. It states:

> At the oral argument of the above cause, Mr. Justice Fortas asked whether I could provide certain information as to the practices followed by the Federal Bureau of Investigation. I have directed these questions to the attention of the Director of the Federal Bureau of Investigation and am submitting herewith a statement of the questions and of the answers which we have received.
>
> "(1) When an individual is interviewed by agents of the Bureau, what warning is given to him?
>
> "The standard warning long given by Special Agents of the FBI to both suspects and persons under arrest is that the person has a right to say nothing and a right to counsel, and that any statement he does make may be used against him in court.
>
> "After passage of the Criminal Justice Act of 1964, which provides free counsel for Federal defendants unable to pay, we added to our instructions to Special Agents the requirement that any person who is under arrest for an offense under FBI jurisdiction, or whose arrest is contemplated following the interview, must also be advised of his right to free counsel if he is unable to pay, and the fact that such counsel will be assigned by the Judge. At the same time, we broadened the right to counsel warning to read counsel of his own choice, or anyone else with whom he might wish to speak.
>
> "(2) When is the warning given?
>
> "The FBI warning is given to a suspect at the very outset of the interview. The warning may be given to a person arrested as soon as practicable after the arrest, but in any event it must precede the interview with the person for a confession or admission of his own guilt.

"(3) What is the Bureau's practice in the event that (a) the individual requests counsel and (b) counsel appears?

"When the person who has been warned of his right to counsel decides that he wishes to consult with counsel before making a statement, the interview is terminated at that point. It may be continued, however, as to all matters other than the person's own guilt or innocence. If he is indecisive in his request for counsel, there may be some question on whether he did or did not waive counsel. Situations of this kind must necessarily be left to the judgment of the interviewing Agent.

"A person being interviewed and desiring to consult counsel by telephone must be permitted to do so. When counsel appears in person, he is permitted to confer with his client in private.

"(4) What is the Bureau's practice if the individual requests counsel, but cannot afford to retain an attorney?

"If any person being interviewed after warning of counsel decides that he wishes to consult with counsel before proceeding further the interview is terminated, as shown above. FBI Agents do not pass judgment on the ability of the person to pay for counsel. They do, however, advise those who have been arrested for an offense under FBI jurisdiction, or whose arrest is contemplated following the interview, of a right to free counsel if they are unable to pay, and the availability of such counsel from the Judge."

The practice of the FBI can readily be emulated by state and local enforcement agencies. The argument that the FBI deals with different crimes than are dealt with by state authorities does not mitigate the significance of the FBI experience.

The experience in some other countries also suggests that the danger to law enforcement in curbs on interrogation is overplayed. The English procedure since 1912 under the Judges' Rules is significant. As recently strengthened, the Rules require that a cautionary warning be given an accused by a police officer as soon as he has evidence that affords reasonable grounds for suspicion; they also require that any statement made be given by the accused without questioning by police. The right of the individual to consult with an attorney during this period is expressly recognized.

The safeguards present under Scottish law may be even greater than in England. Scottish judicial decisions bar use in evidence of most confessions obtained through police interrogation. In India, confessions made to police not in the presence of a magistrate have been excluded by rule of evidence since 1872, at a time when it operated under British law. Identical provisions appear in the Evidence Ordinance of Ceylon, enacted in 1895. Similarly, in our country the Uniform Code of Military Justice has long provided that no suspect may be interrogated without first being warned of his right not to make a statement and that any statement he makes may be used against him. Denial of the right to consult counsel during interrogation has also been proscribed by military tribunals. There appears to have been no marked detrimental effect on criminal law enforcement in these jurisdictions as a result of these rules. Conditions of law enforcement in our country are sufficiently similar to permit reference to this experience as assurance that lawlessness will not result from warning an individual of his rights or allowing him to exercise them. Moreover, it is consistent with our legal system that we give at least as much protection to these rights as is given in the jurisdictions described. We deal in our country with rights grounded in a specific requirement of the Fifth Amendment of the Constitution, whereas other jurisdictions arrived at their conclusions on the basis of principles of justice not so specifically defined.

It is also urged upon us that we withhold decision on this issue until state legislative bodies and advisory groups have had an opportunity to deal with these problems by rule making. We have already pointed out that the Constitution does not require any specific code of procedures for protecting the privilege against self-incrimination during custodial interrogation. Congress and the States are free to develop their own safeguards for the privilege, so long as they are fully as effective as those described above in informing accused persons of their right of silence and in affording a continuous opportunity to exercise it. In any event, however, the issues presented are of constitutional dimensions and must be determined by the courts. The admissibility of a statement in the face of a claim that it was obtained in violation of the defendant's constitutional rights is an issue the resolution of which has long since been undertaken by this Court. Judicial solutions to problems of constitutional dimension have evolved decade by decade. As courts have been presented with the need to enforce constitutional rights, they have found means of doing so. That was our responsibility when *Escobedo* was before us and it is our responsibility today. Where rights secured by the Constitution are involved, there can be no rule making or legislation which would abrogate them.

V

Because of the nature of the problem and because of its recurrent significance in numerous cases, we have to this point discussed the relationship of the Fifth Amendment privilege to police interrogation without specific concentration on the facts of the cases before us. We turn now to these facts to consider the application to these cases of the constitutional principles discussed above. In each instance, we have concluded that statements were obtained from the defendant under circumstances that did not meet constitutional standards for protection of the privilege.

• • •

[Justices Harlan, Stewart, and White dissented.]

NOTES AND QUESTIONS

Ernesto Miranda

1. Is the premise of the Court's decision that custodial interrogation is inherently coercive? The Court defines "custodial" as when a person is "taken into custody or otherwise deprived of his freedom in any meaningful way." Is there a reason the Court does not equate "custody" with "under arrest"?

2. The Court devotes most of Part II of its opinion to examples of interrogation techniques from "police manuals," largely omitted here, most of which are at least manipulative if not rooted in outright deception. Why not regulate interrogation techniques rather than require warnings? Is the concern that the techniques themselves are essential to law enforcement?

The Court is mindful that, particularly in the wake of *Escobedo*, its audience is a large one. Accordingly it takes pains to note that "our decision does not in any way preclude police from carrying out their traditional investigatory functions." Doesn't this statement at least implicitly condone the interrogation techniques itemized in the opinion? *See* Christopher Slobogin, *Manipulation of Suspects and Unrecorded Questioning: After Fifty Years of* Miranda *Jurisprudence, Still Two (Or Maybe Three) Remaining Issues*, 97 B.U. L. Rev. 1157, 1158 (2017) (noting that the Court has rarely addressed the subject of manipulative interrogation techniques).

3. In describing *Escobedo* the Court notes that the interrogators' denial of the suspect's right to talk to his lawyer "undermined his ability to exercise the privilege to remain silent if he chose or to speak without any intimidation, blatant or subtle." In the same vein the Court notes how the presence of counsel at an interrogation can mitigate the dangers of untrustworthiness by deterring coercive tactics and by keeping an accurate record of events.

Does the Court really believe that a lawyer "worth his salt" would have permitted Escobedo to speak to his interrogators under those circumstances? Is the Court trying, albeit disingenuously, to avoid the inference that the presence of counsel means the end of interrogation?

4. The Court caveats its holding as follows:

> [T]he Constitution does not require any specific code of procedures for protecting the privilege against self-incrimination during custodial interrogation. Congress and the States are free to develop their own safeguards for the privilege, so long as they are fully as effective as those described above in informing accused persons of their right of silence and in affording a continuous opportunity to exercise it. In any event, however, the issues presented are of constitutional dimensions and must be determined by the courts.

What does it mean that the issues in *Miranda* are of a constitutional dimension? The idea for allowing the states a modicum of flexibility in service of the Fifth Amendment privilege was made to Chief Justice Warren by Justice Brennan as a measure to appease critics of the Court and make the opinion more acceptable to the general public. Letter from Justice William J. Brennan to Chief Justice Earl Warren 2-4 (May 11, 1966) (on file with the Library of Congress).

The extent to which *Miranda* is "constitutional" is an issue that will recur for decades. Read on.

5. In rejecting the view that unfettered interrogation is a law enforcement necessity, the Court lavishes praise on the standard warnings the FBI voluntarily chooses to give Gideon to suspects and arrestees, which closely resemble the warnings the Court requires in its holding. The Court states that the FBI's practices "can readily be emulated by state and local enforcement agencies."

The Court is dismissive of the argument that the FBI experience is not analogous to the situations of thousands of state and local agencies, as "the FBI deals with different crimes than are dealt with by state authorities." The Court's only real response is in a footnote, which states:

> Among the crimes within the enforcement jurisdiction of the FBI are kidnapping, 18 U.S.C. s 1201 (1964 ed.), white slavery, 18 U.S.C. ss 2421-2423 (1964 ed.), bank robbery, 18 U.S.C. s 2113 (1964 ed.), interstate transportation and sale of stolen property, 18 U.S.C. ss 2311-2317 (1964 ed.), all manner of conspiracies, 18 U.S.C. s 371 (1964 ed.), and violations of civil rights, 18 U.S.C. ss 241-242 (1964 ed.). *See also* 18 U.S.C. s 1114 (1964 ed.) (murder of officer or employee of the United States).

384 U.S. at 486 n.56. Is this an adequate response to the argument that the FBI experience is not analogous?

6. The Court's required four-part warning—actually three warnings and a "cutoff right"—was criticized as something that a legislature, and not a court, should impose. Do you agree? Does it matter that the Court did not mandate specific language to be used or insist that these were the only warnings that could make a custodial interrogation constitutional?

7. The first and most famous of the warnings is the right to remain silent. The Court refers to this right as if it were a preexisting bedrock constitutional principle, so well established as to need no elaboration or explanation. But was it? Is it? Did the right exist before *Miranda*? *See* Tracey Maclin, *The Right to Silence v. the Fifth Amendment*, 2016 U. Chi. Legal F. 255, 258 & n.15 (agreeing with Professor Kamisar that there was no general right to remain silent prior to *Miranda*, although whether a suspect was advised of such a right was a factor in determining the voluntariness of a confession). *See* Yale Kamisar, *A Rejoinder to Professor Schauer's Commentary*, 88 Wash. L. Rev. 171, 172-73 (2013).

8. *Miranda* says nothing at all about race, but one academic attributes it to concerns about racial injustice in the South:

> In retrospect, *Miranda* seems most understandable as an exaggerated response to the times rather than as an enunciation of a natural right mined at last from the Constitution. *Miranda* was a child of the racially troubled 1960's and our tragic legacy of slavery. It was decided when blood was actually being spilled in the streets. There were civil rights protests in the South and civil disorders in urban areas elsewhere. On national television, black protesters [and their supporters] were bullied and beaten, black rioters beaten and shot. *Miranda* itself was decided not only in the shadow of the police practices exposed in *Brown v. Mississippi* and *Chambers v. Florida* but also in the more recent past of the third degree applied particularly to southern blacks.

Gerald M. Caplan, *Questioning* Miranda, 38 Vand. L. Rev. 1417, 1470 (1985). *See* Chapter II *supra*.

9. After the Supreme Court's decision Miranda was retried without his confession being offered in evidence and was again convicted. In the wake of the *Miranda* decision, many police departments distributed to their officers printed *Miranda* warnings on cards. While out on parole in the mid-1970s, Miranda sold autographed "*Miranda* warnings" cards for $1.50 outside the courthouse in downtown Phoenix. Miranda was fatally stabbed in a bar fight in Phoenix in 1976. One of the murder suspects refused to talk to police, invoking his *Miranda* rights.

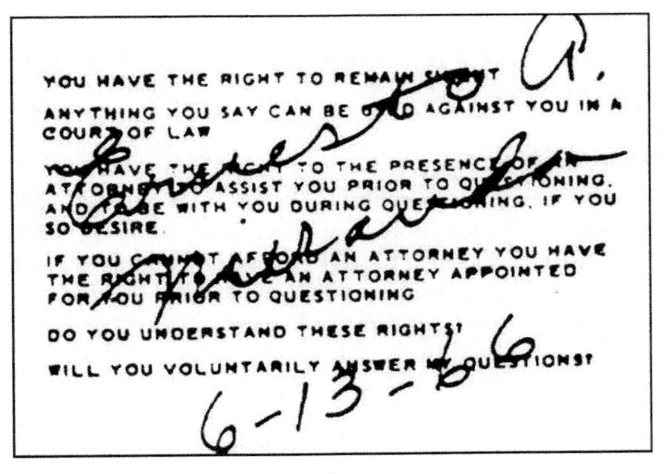

Autographed *Miranda* warnings card

Miranda drew heat from the outset. Law enforcement authorities complained loudly that the police had been "handcuffed" by the decision, echoing the concerns of the Court's dissenters. Congress piled on too, as the emergence of crime as a national issue was well underway by 1966. As part of the Omnibus Crime Control and Safe Streets Act of 1968, Congress claimed to "overrule" *Miranda* and declare that voluntariness was the only criterion for the admissibility of a confession in federal court. 18 U.S.C. § 3501. In furtherance of a national public focus on crime, Richard Nixon campaigned successfully for President in 1968 on the same message of law and order that Barry Goldwater had used (unsuccessfully) four years earlier, and ultimately was able to remake the Supreme Court as he had promised on the campaign trail. Stephen Schulhofer, Miranda v. Arizona*: A Modest But Important Legacy* 164, in Criminal Procedure Stories (Carol Steiker ed., 2006).

The resulting Burger Court demonized *Miranda*. It denigrated the *Miranda* decision in a snarky tone that was then unusual for Supreme Court opinions, found exceptions to the doctrine's applicability, degraded some of its core principles, and criticized its semi-constitutional foundation. Yet somehow *Miranda* survived. When Edwin Meese, attorney general under President Reagan in the 1980s, wanted to do *Miranda* in by invoking § 3501 in federal prosecutions he was talked out of it by his own solicitor general, Republican Charles Fried. *Id.* at 165. It had already turned out by the 1980s that police officials did not view *Miranda* as the law enforcement bogeyman they had feared it would be. *Id.* As Professor Schulhofer put it, *Miranda* had instead become for the police "a legitimating symbol of their own professionalism, a highly public affirmation of their respect for the rights of suspects and for the rule of law." In *Dickerson v. United States*, 530 U.S. 428 (2000), the Court refused to overrule *Miranda*, rejecting the claim that it could be displaced by § 3501, and observing that *Miranda* warnings "have become part of our national culture." *See infra*.

This is not to say that the *Miranda* doctrine was not materially weakened in the following decades. Exceptions were found. Central doctrinal terms like "interrogation" and "custody" were narrowly interpreted. Much of the weakening of the original conception of *Miranda* took place in connection with law enforcement conduct occurring before, during, and after indisputably appropriate warnings were given to suspects. The Court had stated in *Miranda* that "[o]nce warnings have been given the subsequent procedure is clear." It was not to be so simple.

D. *MIRANDA* IN PRACTICE I: EXCEPTIONS, INTERROGATION, AND CUSTODY

1. *Miranda* Exceptions

One of the earliest of the cases sometimes called *Miranda* "exceptions" held that a statement obtained in violation of *Miranda* could be used to cross-examine a testifying defendant. *Harris v. New York*, 401 U.S. 222 (1971). This case is fully considered in Chapter V *infra* in discussing the impeachment exception to the exclusionary rule.

The next case makes no bones about its status as an "exception" to *Miranda.*

New York v. Quarles

467 U.S. 649 (1984)

Justice Rehnquist delivered the opinion of the Court.

Respondent Benjamin Quarles was charged in the New York trial court with criminal possession of a weapon. The trial court suppressed the gun in question, and a statement made by respondent, because the statement was obtained by police before they read respondent his "Miranda rights." That ruling was affirmed on appeal through the New York Court of Appeals. We granted certiorari and we now reverse. We conclude that under the circumstances involved in this case, overriding considerations of public safety justify the officer's failure to provide *Miranda* warnings before he asked questions devoted to locating the abandoned weapon.

On September 11, 1980, at approximately 12:30 a.m., Officer Frank Kraft and Officer Sal Scarring were on road patrol in Queens, N.Y., when a young woman approached their car. She told them that she had just been raped by a black male, approximately six feet tall, who was wearing a black jacket with the name "Big Ben" printed in yellow letters on the back. She told the officers that the man had just entered an A & P supermarket located nearby and that the man was carrying a gun.

The officers drove the woman to the supermarket, and Officer Kraft entered the store while Officer Scarring radioed for assistance. Officer Kraft quickly spotted respondent, who matched the description given by the woman, approaching a checkout counter. Apparently upon seeing the officer, respondent turned and ran toward the rear of the store, and Officer Kraft pursued him with a drawn gun. When respondent turned the corner at the end of an aisle, Officer Kraft lost sight of him for several seconds, and upon regaining sight of respondent, ordered him to stop and put his hands over his head.

Although more than three other officers had arrived on the scene by that time, Officer Kraft was the first to reach respondent. He frisked him and discovered that he was wearing a shoulder holster which was then empty. After handcuffing him, Officer Kraft asked him where the gun was. Respondent nodded in the direction of some empty cartons and responded, "the gun is over there." Officer Kraft thereafter retrieved a loaded .38-caliber revolver from one of the cartons, formally placed respondent under arrest, and read him his *Miranda* rights from a printed card. Respondent indicated that he would be willing to answer questions without an attorney present. Officer Kraft then asked respondent if he owned the gun and where he had purchased it. Respondent answered that he did own it and that he had purchased it in Miami, Fla.

In the subsequent prosecution of respondent for criminal possession of a weapon, the judge excluded the statement, "the gun is over there," and the gun because the officer had not given respondent the warnings required by our decision in *Miranda* before asking him where the gun was located. The judge excluded the other statements about respondent's ownership of the gun and the place of purchase, as evidence tainted by the prior *Miranda* violation.

The Court of Appeals granted leave to appeal and affirmed by a 4-3 vote. It concluded that respondent was in "custody" within the meaning of *Miranda* during all questioning and rejected the State's argument that the exigencies of the situation justified Officer Kraft's failure to read respondent his *Miranda* rights until after he had located the gun. The court declined to recognize an exigency exception to the usual requirements of *Miranda* because it found no indication from Officer Kraft's testimony at the suppression hearing that his subjective motivation in asking the question was to protect his own safety or the safety of the public. For the reasons which follow, we believe that this case presents a situation where concern for public safety must be paramount to adherence to the literal language of the prophylactic rules enunciated in *Miranda*.

The Fifth Amendment guarantees that "[n]o person . . . shall be compelled in any criminal case to be a witness against himself." In *Miranda* this Court for the first time extended the Fifth Amendment privilege against compulsory self-incrimination to individuals subjected to custodial interrogation by the police. The Fifth Amendment itself does not prohibit all incriminating admissions; "[a]bsent some officially coerced self-accusation, the Fifth Amendment privilege is not violated by even the most damning admissions." The *Miranda* Court, however, presumed that interrogation in certain custodial circumstances is inherently coercive and held that statements made under those circumstances are inadmissible unless the suspect is specifically informed of his *Miranda* rights and freely decides to forgo those rights. The prophylactic *Miranda* warnings therefore are "not themselves rights protected by the Constitution but [are] instead measures to insure that the right against compulsory self-incrimination [is] protected." Requiring *Miranda* warnings before custodial interrogation provides "practical reinforcement" for the Fifth Amendment right.

In this case we have before us no claim that respondent's statements were actually compelled by police conduct which overcame his will to resist. Thus the only issue before us is whether Officer Kraft was justified in failing to make available to respondent the procedural safeguards associated with the privilege against compulsory self-incrimination since *Miranda*.

The New York Court of Appeals was undoubtedly correct in deciding that the facts of this case come within the ambit of the *Miranda* decision as we have subsequently interpreted it. We agree that respondent was in police custody because we have noted that "the ultimate inquiry is simply whether there is a 'formal arrest or restraint on freedom of movement' of the degree associated with a formal arrest." Here Quarles was surrounded by at least four police officers and was handcuffed when the questioning at issue took place. As the New York Court of Appeals observed, there was nothing to suggest that any of the officers were any longer concerned for their own physical safety. The New York Court of Appeals' majority declined to express an opinion as to whether there might be an exception to the *Miranda* rule if the police had been acting to protect the public, because the lower courts in New York had made no factual determination that the police had acted with that motive.

We hold that on these facts there is a "public safety" exception to the requirement that *Miranda* warnings be given before a suspect's answers may be admitted into evidence, and that the availability of that exception does not depend upon the motivation of the individual officers involved. In a kaleidoscopic situation such as the one confronting these officers, where spontaneity rather than adherence to a police manual is necessarily the order of the day, the application of the exception which we recognize today should not be made to depend on post hoc findings at a suppression hearing concerning the subjective motivation of the arresting officer. Undoubtedly most police officers, if placed in Officer Kraft's position, would act out of a host of different, instinctive, and largely unverifiable motives—their own safety, the safety of others, and perhaps as well the desire to obtain incriminating evidence from the suspect.

Whatever the motivation of individual officers in such a situation, we do not believe that the doctrinal underpinnings of *Miranda* require that it be applied in all its rigor to a situation in which police officers ask questions reasonably prompted by a concern for the public safety. The *Miranda* decision was based in large part on this Court's view that the warnings which it required police to give to suspects in custody would reduce the likelihood that the suspects would fall victim to constitutionally impermissible practices of police interrogation in the presumptively coercive environment of the station house. The dissenters warned that the requirement of *Miranda* warnings would have the effect of decreasing the number of suspects who respond to police questioning. The *Miranda* majority, however, apparently felt that whatever the cost to society in terms of fewer convictions of guilty suspects, that cost would simply have to be borne in the interest of enlarged protection for the Fifth Amendment privilege.

The police in this case, in the very act of apprehending a suspect, were confronted with the immediate necessity of ascertaining the whereabouts of a gun which they had every reason to believe the suspect had just removed from his empty holster and discarded in the supermarket. So long as the gun was concealed somewhere in the supermarket, with its actual whereabouts unknown, it obviously posed more than one danger to the public safety: an accomplice might make use of it, a customer or employee might later come upon it.

In such a situation, if the police are required to recite the familiar *Miranda* warnings before asking the whereabouts of the gun, suspects in Quarles' position might well be deterred from responding. Procedural safeguards which deter a suspect from responding were deemed acceptable in *Miranda* in order to protect the Fifth Amendment privilege; when the primary social cost of those added protections is the possibility of fewer convictions, the *Miranda* majority was willing to bear that cost. Here, had *Miranda* warnings deterred Quarles from responding to Officer Kraft's question about the whereabouts of the gun, the cost would have been something more than merely the failure to obtain evidence useful in convicting Quarles. Officer Kraft needed an answer to his question not simply to make his case against Quarles but to insure that further danger to the public did not result from the concealment of the gun in a public area.

We conclude that the need for answers to questions in a situation posing a threat to the public safety outweighs the need for the prophylactic rule protecting the Fifth Amendment's privilege against self-incrimination. We decline to place officers such as Officer Kraft in the untenable position of having to consider, often in a matter of seconds, whether it best serves society for them to ask the necessary questions without the *Miranda* warnings and render whatever probative evidence they uncover inadmissible, or for them to give the warnings in order to preserve the admissibility of evidence they might uncover but possibly damage or destroy their ability to obtain that evidence and neutralize the volatile situation confronting them.

In recognizing a narrow exception to the *Miranda* rule in this case, we acknowledge that to some degree we lessen the desirable clarity of that rule. At least in part in order to preserve its clarity, we have over the years refused to sanction attempts to expand our *Miranda* holding. As we have in other contexts, we recognize here the importance of a workable rule "to guide police officers, who have only limited time and expertise to reflect on and balance the social and individual interests involved in the specific circumstances they confront." But as we have pointed out, we believe that the exception which we recognize today lessens the necessity of that on-the-scene balancing process. The exception will not be difficult for police officers to apply because in each case it will be circumscribed by the exigency which justifies it. We think police officers can and will distinguish almost instinctively between questions necessary to secure their own safety or the safety of the public and questions designed solely to elicit testimonial evidence from a suspect.

The facts of this case clearly demonstrate that distinction and an officer's ability to recognize it. Officer Kraft asked only the question necessary to locate the missing gun before advising respondent of his rights. It was only after securing the loaded revolver and giving the warnings that he continued with investigatory questions about the ownership and place of purchase of the gun. The exception which we recognize today, far from complicating the thought processes and the on-the-scene judgments of police officers, will simply free them to follow their legitimate instincts when confronting situations presenting a danger to the public safety.

We hold that the Court of Appeals in this case erred in excluding the statement, "the gun is over there," and the gun because of the officer's failure to read respondent his *Miranda* rights before attempting to locate the weapon. Accordingly we hold that it also erred in excluding the subsequent statements as illegal fruits of a *Miranda* violation. We therefore reverse and remand for further proceedings not inconsistent with this opinion.

[Justice O'Connor wrote a concurring opinion. Justices Marshall, Brennan, and Stevens dissented.]

NOTES AND QUESTIONS

1. In *Quarles* the Court stated in no uncertain terms that it was finding a "public safety exception" to *Miranda.* A difficulty the Court elided was that the New York Court of Appeals, perhaps astutely reading the room in which its decision would ultimately be evaluated, had explicitly held that, in view of the arresting officer's testimony that the situation was "under control" at the time of the unwarned questioning of the defendant about the location of the gun, there was no record evidence of exigent circumstances posing a risk to public safety. *People v. Quarles*, 444 N.E.2d 984, 985 (N.Y. 1982).

Was the "objective evidence" of a risk to public safety sufficient to warrant an exception to *Miranda*?

2. In reaching this conclusion the Court described the *Miranda* warnings as "prophylactic" and cited its decision in *Michigan v. Tucker*, 417 U.S. 182 (1974), where it had stated that *Miranda* warnings were "not themselves rights protected by the Constitution." This drumbeat would continue through *Dickerson* and beyond.

3. The police officer who questioned Quarles as to the location of the gun had been living under *Miranda* for his whole career or at least the last 18 years of it. Yet he apparently recognized that under the circumstances a single unwarned question of the suspect was necessary. When that question was answered the officer administered *Miranda* warnings and further questioning followed after the suspect waived his rights.

If the lesson of *Quarles* is that this is how we want police officers to behave, is a "public safety" exception even necessary?

Is another part of the lesson that the state should not be penalized by the suppression of evidence when police act as we want them to? Was Quarles's unwarned statement necessary to his conviction? If you were the prosecutor at trial, operating in a world where *Miranda* had been the law for 18 years, how would you have made the decision whether to offer the unwarned statement in evidence?

4. The Court describes *Quarles* as a "narrow exception," and it has not addressed the exception's dimensions in any subsequent case. The exception's history in lower courts is another story. *See* Jim Weller, *The Legacy of* Quarles*: A Summary of the Public Safety Exception to* Miranda *in the Federal Courts*, 49 Baylor L. Rev. 1107, 1113 (1997) (summarizing expansions of the public safety exception by the federal circuit courts).

5. The *Quarles* exception has been heavily relied on by law enforcement in the twenty-first century in connection with the investigation of terrorist activities. The interrogation of the suspected perpetrator of the Boston Marathon bombing, Dzhokhar Tsarnaev, since convicted, is itself the focus of two law review articles. *See* Joanna Wright, *Applying* Miranda's *Public Safety Exception to Dzhokhar Tsarnaev: Restricting Criminal Procedure Rights by Expanding Judicial Exceptions*, 113 Colum. L. Rev. Sidebar 136 (2013); Brian Gallini, *The Unlikely Meeting Between Dzhokhar Tsarnaev and Benjamin Quarles*, 66 Case W. Rsrv. L. Rev. 393 (2015).

2. Interrogation

To precisely what kind of police communication does *Miranda* apply? Is all questioning "interrogation"? Do declarative statements that are not explicitly framed as questions count? The Court addressed these issues for the first time in the next case.

Rhode Island v. Innis

446 U.S. 291 (1980)

Mr. Justice STEWART delivered the opinion of the Court.

In *Miranda* the Court held that, once a defendant in custody asks to speak with a lawyer, all interrogation must cease until a lawyer is present. The issue in this case is whether the respondent was "interrogated" in violation of the standards promulgated in the *Miranda* opinion.

I

On the night of January 12, 1975, John Mulvaney, a Providence, R.I., taxicab driver, disappeared after being dispatched to pick up a customer. His body was discovered four days later buried in a shallow grave in Coventry, R.I. He had died from a shotgun blast aimed at the back of his head.

On January 17, 1975, shortly after midnight, the Providence police received a telephone call from Gerald Aubin, also a taxicab driver, who reported that he had just been robbed by a man wielding a sawed-off shotgun. Aubin further reported that he had dropped off his assailant near Rhode Island College in a section of Providence known as Mount Pleasant. While at the Providence police station waiting to give a statement, Aubin noticed a picture of his assailant on a bulletin board. Aubin so informed one of the police officers present. The officer prepared a photo array, and again Aubin identified a picture of the same person. That person was the respondent. Shortly thereafter, the Providence police began a search of the Mount Pleasant area.

At approximately 4:30 a.m. on the same date, Patrolman Lovell, while cruising the streets of Mount Pleasant in a patrol car, spotted the respondent standing in the street facing him. When Patrolman Lovell stopped his car, the respondent walked towards it. Patrolman Lovell then arrested the respondent, who was unarmed, and advised him of his so-called *Miranda* rights. While the two men waited in the patrol car for other police officers to arrive, Patrolman Lovell did not converse with the respondent other than to respond to the latter's request for a cigarette.

Within minutes, Sergeant Sears arrived at the scene of the arrest, and he also gave the respondent the *Miranda* warnings. Immediately thereafter, Captain Leyden and other police officers arrived. Captain Leyden advised the respondent of his *Miranda* rights. The respondent stated that he understood those rights and wanted to speak with a lawyer. Captain Leyden then directed that the respondent be placed in a "caged wagon," a four-door police car with a wire screen mesh between the front and rear seats, and be driven to the central police station. Three officers, Patrolmen Gleckman, Williams, and McKenna, were assigned to accompany the respondent to the central station. They placed the respondent in the vehicle and shut the doors. Captain Leyden then instructed the officers not to question the respondent or intimidate or coerce him in any way. The three officers then entered the vehicle, and it departed.

While en route to the central station, Patrolman Gleckman initiated a conversation with Patrolman McKenna concerning the missing shotgun. As Patrolman Gleckman later testified:

> A. At this point, I was talking back and forth with Patrolman McKenna stating that I frequent this area while on patrol and [that because a school for handicapped children is located nearby,] there's a lot of handicapped children running around in this area, and God forbid one of them might find a weapon with shells and they might hurt themselves.

Patrolman McKenna apparently shared his fellow officer's concern:

> A. I more or less concurred with him [Gleckman] that it was a safety factor and that we should, you know, continue to search for the weapon and try to find it.

Id., at 53.

While Patrolman Williams said nothing, he overheard the conversation between the two officers:

> A. He [Gleckman] said it would be too bad if the little—I believe he said a girl—would pick up the gun, maybe kill herself.

The respondent then interrupted the conversation, stating that the officers should turn the car around so he could show them where the gun was located. At this point, Patrolman McKenna radioed back to Captain Leyden that they were returning to the scene of the arrest and that the respondent would inform them of the location of the gun. At the time the respondent indicated that the officers should turn back, they had traveled no more than a mile, a trip encompassing only a few minutes.

The police vehicle then returned to the scene of the arrest where a search for the shotgun was in progress. There, Captain Leyden again advised the respondent of his *Miranda* rights.

The respondent replied that he understood those rights but that he "wanted to get the gun out of the way because of the kids in the area in the school." The respondent then led the police to a nearby field, where he pointed out the shotgun under some rocks by the side of the road.

On March 20, 1975, a grand jury returned an indictment charging the respondent with the kidnaping, robbery, and murder of John Mulvaney. Before trial, the respondent moved to suppress the shotgun and the statements he had made to the police regarding it. After an evidentiary hearing at which the respondent elected not to testify, the trial judge found that the respondent had been "repeatedly and completely advised of his *Miranda* rights." He further found that it was "entirely understandable that [the officers in the police vehicle] would voice their concern [for the safety of the handicapped children] to each other." The judge then concluded that the respondent's decision to inform the police of the location of the shotgun was "a waiver, clearly, and on the basis of the evidence that I have heard, and [sic] intelligent waiver, of his [*Miranda*] right to remain silent." Thus, without passing on whether the police officers had in fact "interrogated" the respondent, the trial court sustained the admissibility of the shotgun and testimony related to its discovery. That evidence was later introduced at the respondent's trial, and the jury returned a verdict of guilty on all counts.

On appeal, the Rhode Island Supreme Court, in a 3-2 decision, set aside the respondent's conviction. Relying at least in part on this Court's decision in *Brewer v. Williams*, the court concluded that the respondent had invoked his Miranda right to counsel and that, contrary to *Miranda*'s mandate that, in the absence of counsel, all custodial interrogation then cease, the police officers in the vehicle had "interrogated" the respondent without a valid waiver of his right to counsel. It was the view of the state appellate court that, even though the police officers may have been genuinely concerned about the public safety and even though the respondent had not been addressed personally by the police officers, the respondent nonetheless had been subjected to "subtle coercion" that was the equivalent of "interrogation" within the meaning of the *Miranda* opinion. Moreover, contrary to the holding of the trial court, the appellate court concluded that the evidence was insufficient to support a finding of waiver. Having concluded that both the shotgun and testimony relating to its discovery were obtained in violation of the *Miranda* standards and therefore should not have been admitted into evidence, the Rhode Island Supreme Court held that the respondent was entitled to a new trial.

We granted certiorari to address for the first time the meaning of "interrogation" under *Miranda*.

II

In its *Miranda* opinion, the Court concluded that in the context of "custodial interrogation" certain procedural safeguards are necessary to protect a defendant's Fifth and Fourteenth Amendment privilege against compulsory self-incrimination. More specifically, the Court held that "the prosecution may not use statements, whether exculpatory or inculpatory, stemming from custodial interrogation of the defendant unless it demonstrates the use of procedural safeguards effective to secure the privilege against self-incrimination." Those safeguards included the now familiar *Miranda* warnings—namely, that the defendant be informed "that he has the right to remain silent, that anything he says can be used against him in a court of law, that he has the right to the presence of an attorney, and that if he cannot afford an attorney one will be appointed for him prior to any questioning if he so desires"—or their equivalent.

The Court in the *Miranda* opinion also outlined in some detail the consequences that would result if a defendant sought to invoke those procedural safeguards. With regard to the right to the presence of counsel, the Court noted:

> Once warnings have been given, the subsequent procedure is clear. . . . If the individual states that he wants an attorney, the interrogation must cease until an attorney is present. At that time, the individual must have an opportunity to confer with the attorney and to have him present during

> any subsequent questioning. If the individual cannot obtain an attorney and he indicates that he wants one before speaking to police, they must respect his decision to remain silent.

In the present case, the parties are in agreement that the respondent was fully informed of his *Miranda* rights and that he invoked his *Miranda* right to counsel when he told Captain Leyden that he wished to consult with a lawyer. It is also uncontested that the respondent was "in custody" while being transported to the police station.

The issue, therefore, is whether the respondent was "interrogated" by the police officers in violation of the respondent's undisputed right under *Miranda* to remain silent until he had consulted with a lawyer. In resolving this issue, we first define the term "interrogation" under *Miranda* before turning to a consideration of the facts of this case.

A

The starting point for defining "interrogation" in this context is, of course, the Court's *Miranda* opinion. There the Court observed that "[b]y custodial interrogation, we mean questioning initiated by law enforcement officers after a person has been taken into custody or otherwise deprived of his freedom of action in any significant way." This passage and other references throughout the opinion to "questioning" might suggest that the *Miranda* rules were to apply only to those police interrogation practices that involve express questioning of a defendant while in custody.

We do not, however, construe the *Miranda* opinion so narrowly. The concern of the Court in *Miranda* was that the "interrogation environment" created by the interplay of interrogation and custody would "subjugate the individual to the will of his examiner" and thereby undermine the privilege against compulsory self-incrimination. The police practices that evoked this concern included several that did not involve express questioning. For example, one of the practices discussed in *Miranda* was the use of line-ups in which a coached witness would pick the defendant as the perpetrator. This was designed to establish that the defendant was in fact guilty as a predicate for further interrogation. A variation on this theme discussed in *Miranda* was the so-called "reverse line-up" in which a defendant would be identified by coached witnesses as the perpetrator of a fictitious crime, with the object of inducing him to confess to the actual crime of which he was suspected in order to escape the false prosecution. The Court in *Miranda* also included in its survey of interrogation practices the use of psychological ploys, such as to "posi[t]" "the guilt of the subject," to "minimize the moral seriousness of the offense," and "to cast blame on the victim or on society." It is clear that these techniques of persuasion, no less than express questioning, were thought, in a custodial setting, to amount to interrogation.

This is not to say, however, that all statements obtained by the police after a person has been taken into custody are to be considered the product of interrogation. As the Court in *Miranda* noted:

> Confessions remain a proper element in law enforcement. Any statement given freely and voluntarily without any compelling influences is, of course, admissible in evidence. The fundamental import of the privilege while an individual is in custody is not whether he is allowed to talk to the police without the benefit of warnings and counsel, but whether he can be interrogated. . . . Volunteered statements of any kind are not barred by the Fifth Amendment and their admissibility is not affected by our holding today.

It is clear therefore that the special procedural safeguards outlined in *Miranda* are required not where a suspect is simply taken into custody, but rather where a suspect in custody is subjected to interrogation. "Interrogation," as conceptualized in the *Miranda* opinion, must reflect a measure of compulsion above and beyond that inherent in custody itself.

We conclude that the *Miranda* safeguards come into play whenever a person in custody is subjected to either express questioning or its functional equivalent. That is to say, the term "interrogation" under *Miranda* refers not only to express questioning, but also to any words or actions on the part of the police (other than those normally attendant to arrest and custody) that the police should know are reasonably likely to elicit an incriminating response from the suspect. The latter portion of this definition focuses primarily upon the perceptions of the suspect, rather than the intent of the police. This focus reflects the fact that the *Miranda* safeguards were designed to vest a suspect in custody with an added measure of protection against coercive police practices, without regard to objective proof of the underlying intent of the police. A practice that the police should know is reasonably likely to evoke an incriminating response from a suspect thus amounts to interrogation. But, since the police surely cannot be held accountable for the unforeseeable results of their words or actions, the definition of interrogation can extend only to words or actions on the part of police officers that they should have known were reasonably likely to elicit an incriminating response.

B

Turning to the facts of the present case, we conclude that the respondent was not "interrogated" within the meaning of *Miranda*. It is undisputed that the first prong of the definition of "interrogation" was not satisfied, for the conversation between Patrolmen Gleckman and McKenna included no express questioning of the respondent. Rather, that conversation was, at least in form, nothing more than a dialogue between the two officers to which no response from the respondent was invited.

Moreover, it cannot be fairly concluded that the respondent was subjected to the "functional equivalent" of questioning. It cannot be said, in short, that Patrolmen Gleckman and McKenna should have known that their conversation was reasonably likely to elicit an incriminating response from the respondent. There is nothing in the record to suggest that the officers were aware that the respondent was peculiarly susceptible to an appeal to his conscience concerning the safety of handicapped children. Nor is there anything in the record to suggest that the police knew that the respondent was unusually disoriented or upset at the time of his arrest.

The case thus boils down to whether, in the context of a brief conversation, the officers should have known that the respondent would suddenly be moved to make a self-incriminating response. Given the fact that the entire conversation appears to have consisted of no more than a few off hand remarks, we cannot say that the officers should have known that it was reasonably likely that Innis would so respond. This is not a case where the police carried on a lengthy harangue in the presence of the suspect. Nor does the record support the respondent's contention that, under the circumstances, the officers' comments were particularly "evocative." It is our view, therefore, that the respondent was not subjected by the police to words or actions that the police should have known were reasonably likely to elicit an incriminating response from him.

The Rhode Island Supreme Court erred, in short, in equating "subtle compulsion" with interrogation. That the officers' comments struck a responsive chord is readily apparent. Thus, it may be said, as the Rhode Island Supreme Court did say, that the respondent was subjected to "subtle compulsion." But that is not the end of the inquiry. It must also be established that a suspect's incriminating response was the product of words or actions on the part of the police that they should have known were reasonably likely to elicit an incriminating response. This was not established in the present case.

For the reasons stated, the judgment of the Supreme Court of Rhode Island is vacated, and the case is remanded to that court for further proceedings not inconsistent with this opinion.

It is so ordered.

[Justices Stevens, Marshall, and Brennan dissented.]

NOTES AND QUESTIONS

1. Suppose the prosecution had decided to defend the police conduct not on the ground that it wasn't interrogation but rather on a "public safety" exception as the prosecution was to do a few years later in *Quarles*. Is this a stronger or weaker case for such an exception than *Quarles*?

2. In a footnote the Court states that "[t]he record in no way suggests that the officers' remarks were designed to elicit a response." Do you agree?

As support for this assertion the Court states that the trial judge, after hearing the officers' testimony, concluded that it was "entirely understandable that [the officers] would voice their concern [for the safety of the handicapped children] to each other." Is the trial judge's conclusion inconsistent with an intent to elicit a response from the defendant?

3. Should it matter—as the dissent points out, citing the leading authority on police interrogation tactics—that appealing to the defendant's sense of "decency" is a "classic interrogation technique"? Should that fact be relevant to whether the officers should have known their statements "were reasonably likely to elicit an incriminating response"?

Did the Court correctly apply the "reasonable likelihood" test here?

4. Why wasn't this case remanded so the trial court could apply the test the Court prescribes? If it had been remanded, and you had represented Innis, how would you try to prove the officers intended to elicit an incriminating response and reasonably believed they could get one? What information would you subpoena to use at the suppression hearing?

Consider whether each of the following statements made to a suspect in custody who had received *Miranda* warnings and invoked his rights amount to interrogation under *Innis*:

- You could really help yourself here, you know.
- Any cooperation will be brought to the attention of the assistant U.S. attorney.
- There could be immigration consequences here.
- We've got a warrant for your apartment too.

3. Custody

Prior to the next case, *Berkemer v. McCarty*, 468 U.S. 420 (1984), the Court had seldom dealt with any difficulty regarding the definition of "custody" for *Miranda* purposes. In two fairly straightforward cases where the defendants had voluntarily appeared for questioning, the Court had essentially just restated what it had held in *Miranda*, that custody is when "a person is taken into custody or otherwise deprived of his freedom in any significant way." 384 U.S. at 444. *See Oregon v. Mathiason*, 429 U.S. 492 (1977) (per curiam); *California v. Beheler*, 463 U.S. 112 (1983).

In *Berkemer* the Court considers whether the amount of detention associated with a "routine" traffic stop amounts to custody for *Miranda* purposes.

Berkemer v. McCarty

468 U.S. 420 (1984)

Justice Marshall delivered the opinion of the Court.

This case presents two related questions: First, does our decision in *Miranda* govern the admissibility of statements made during custodial interrogation by a suspect accused of a misdemeanor traffic offense? Second, does the roadside questioning of a motorist detained pursuant to a traffic stop constitute custodial interrogation for the purposes of the doctrine enunciated in *Miranda*?

I

A

The parties have stipulated to the essential facts. On the evening of March 31, 1980, Trooper Williams of the Ohio State Highway Patrol observed respondent's car weaving in and out of a lane on Interstate Highway 270. After following the car for two miles, Williams forced respondent to stop and asked him to get out of the vehicle. When respondent complied, Williams noticed that he was having difficulty standing. At that point, "Williams concluded that [respondent] would be charged with a traffic offense and, therefore, his freedom to leave the scene was terminated." However, respondent was not told that he would be taken into custody. Williams then asked respondent to perform a field sobriety test, commonly known as a "balancing test." Respondent could not do so without falling.

While still at the scene of the traffic stop, Williams asked respondent whether he had been using intoxicants. Respondent replied that "he had consumed two beers and had smoked several joints of marijuana a short time before." Respondent's speech was slurred, and Williams had difficulty understanding him. Williams thereupon formally placed respondent under arrest and transported him in the patrol car to the Franklin County Jail.

At the jail, respondent was given an intoxilyzer test to determine the concentration of alcohol in his blood. The test did not detect any alcohol whatsoever in respondent's system. Williams then resumed questioning respondent in order to obtain information for inclusion in the State Highway Patrol Alcohol Influence Report. Respondent answered affirmatively a question whether he had been drinking. When then asked if he was under the influence of alcohol, he said, "I guess, barely." Williams next asked respondent to indicate on the form whether the marijuana he had smoked had been treated with any chemicals. In the section of the report headed "Remarks," respondent wrote, "No ang[el] dust or PCP in the pot. Rick McCarty."

At no point in this sequence of events did Williams or anyone else tell respondent that he had a right to remain silent, to consult with an attorney, and to have an attorney appointed for him if he could not afford one.

B

Respondent was charged with operating a motor vehicle while under the influence of alcohol and/or drugs. Under Ohio law, that offense is a first-degree misdemeanor and is punishable by fine or imprisonment for up to six months. Incarceration for a minimum of three days is mandatory.

Respondent moved to exclude the various incriminating statements he had made to Trooper Williams on the ground that introduction into evidence of those statements would violate the Fifth Amendment insofar as he had not been informed of his constitutional rights prior to his interrogation. When the trial court denied the motion, respondent pleaded "no contest" and was found guilty. He was sentenced to 90 days in jail, 80 of which were suspended, and was fined $300, $100 of which were suspended.

On appeal to the Franklin County Court of Appeals, respondent renewed his constitutional claim. Relying on a prior decision by the Ohio Supreme Court, which held that the rule announced in *Miranda* "is not applicable to misdemeanors," the Court of Appeals rejected respondent's argument and affirmed his conviction. The Ohio Supreme Court dismissed respondent's appeal on the ground that it failed to present a "substantial constitutional question."

Respondent then filed an action for a writ of habeas corpus in the District Court for the Southern District of Ohio. The District Court dismissed the petition, holding that "*Miranda* warnings do not have to be given prior to in custody interrogation of a suspect arrested for a traffic offense."

A divided panel of the Court of Appeals for the Sixth Circuit reversed, holding that "*Miranda* warnings must be given to all individuals prior to custodial interrogation, whether the offense investigated be a felony or a misdemeanor traffic offense." In applying this principle to the facts of the case, the Court of Appeals distinguished between the statements made by respondent before and after his formal arrest. The postarrest statements, the court ruled, were plainly inadmissible; because respondent was not warned of his constitutional rights prior to or "[a]t the point that Trooper Williams took [him] to the police station," his ensuing admissions could not be used against him. The court's treatment of respondent's prearrest statements was less clear. It eschewed a holding that "the mere stopping of a motor vehicle triggers *Miranda*," but did not expressly rule that the statements made by respondent at the scene of the traffic stop could be used against him. In the penultimate paragraph of its opinion, the court asserted that "[t]he failure to advise [respondent] of his constitutional rights rendered at least some of his statements inadmissible," suggesting that the court was uncertain as to the status of the prearrest confessions. "Because [respondent] was convicted on inadmissible evidence," the court deemed it necessary to vacate his conviction and order the District Court to issue a writ of habeas corpus. Ibid. However, the Court of Appeals did not specify which statements, if any, could be used against respondent in a retrial.

We granted certiorari to resolve confusion in the federal and state courts regarding the applicability of our ruling in *Miranda* to interrogations involving minor offenses and to questioning of motorists detained pursuant to traffic stops.

II

• • •

III

To assess the admissibility of the self-incriminating statements made by respondent prior to his formal arrest, we are obliged to address a second issue concerning the scope of our decision in *Miranda*: whether the roadside questioning of a motorist detained pursuant to a routine traffic stop should be considered "custodial interrogation." Respondent urges that it should, on the ground that *Miranda* by its terms applies whenever "a person has been taken into custody or otherwise deprived of his freedom of action in any significant way." Petitioner contends that a holding that every detained motorist must be advised of his rights before being questioned would constitute an unwarranted extension of the *Miranda* doctrine.

It must be acknowledged at the outset that a traffic stop significantly curtails the "freedom of action" of the driver and the passengers, if any, of the detained vehicle. Under the law of most States, it is a crime either to ignore a policeman's signal to stop one's car or, once having stopped, to drive away without permission. Certainly few motorists would feel free either to disobey a directive to pull over or to leave the scene of a traffic stop without being told they might do so. Partly for these reasons, we have long acknowledged that "stopping an automobile and detaining its occupants constitute a 'seizure' within the meaning of [the Fourth] Amendmen[t], even though the purpose of the stop is limited and the resulting detention quite brief."

However, we decline to accord talismanic power to the phrase in the *Miranda* opinion emphasized by respondent. Fidelity to the doctrine announced in *Miranda* requires that it be enforced strictly, but only in those types of situations in which the concerns that powered the decision are implicated. Thus, we must decide whether a traffic stop exerts upon a detained person pressures that sufficiently impair his free exercise of his privilege against self-incrimination to require that he be warned of his constitutional rights.

Two features of an ordinary traffic stop mitigate the danger that a person questioned will be induced "to speak where he would not otherwise do so freely." First, detention of a motorist pursuant to a traffic stop is presumptively temporary and brief. The vast majority of roadside detentions last only a few minutes. A motorist's expectations, when he sees a policeman's light flashing behind him, are that he will be obliged to spend a short period of time answering questions and waiting while the officer checks his license and registration, that he may then be given a citation, but that in the end he most likely will be allowed to continue on his way. In this respect, questioning incident to an ordinary traffic stop is quite different from stationhouse interrogation, which frequently is prolonged, and in which the detainee often is aware that questioning will continue until he provides his interrogators the answers they seek.

Second, circumstances associated with the typical traffic stop are not such that the motorist feels completely at the mercy of the police. To be sure, the aura of authority surrounding an armed, uniformed officer and the knowledge that the officer has some discretion in deciding whether to issue a citation, in combination, exert some pressure on the detainee to respond to questions. But other aspects of the situation substantially offset these forces. Perhaps most importantly, the typical traffic stop is public, at least to some degree. Passersby, on foot or in other cars, witness the interaction of officer and motorist. This exposure to public view both reduces the ability of an unscrupulous policeman to use illegitimate means to elicit self-incriminating statements and diminishes the motorist's fear that, if he does not cooperate, he will be subjected to abuse. The fact that the detained motorist typically is confronted by only one or at most two policemen further mutes his sense of vulnerability. In short, the atmosphere surrounding an ordinary traffic stop is substantially less "police dominated" than that surrounding the kinds of interrogation at issue in *Miranda* itself, and in the subsequent cases in which we have applied *Miranda*.

In both of these respects, the usual traffic stop is more analogous to a so-called "Terry stop," see *Terry v. Ohio* (1968), than to a formal arrest. Under the Fourth Amendment, we have held, a policeman who lacks probable cause but whose "observations lead him reasonably to suspect" that a particular person has committed, is committing, or is about to commit a crime, may detain that person briefly in order to "investigate the circumstances that provoke suspicion." "[T]he stop and inquiry must be 'reasonably related in scope to the justification for their initiation.'" Typically, this means that the officer may ask the detainee a moderate number of questions to determine his identity and to try to obtain information confirming or dispelling the officer's suspicions. But the detainee is not obliged to respond. And, unless the detainee's answers provide the officer with probable cause to arrest him, he must then be released. The comparatively nonthreatening character of detentions of this sort explains the absence of any suggestion in our opinions that *Terry* stops are subject to the dictates of *Miranda*. The similarly noncoercive aspect of ordinary traffic stops prompts us to hold that persons temporarily detained pursuant to such stops are not "in custody" for the purposes of *Miranda*.

Respondent contends that to "exempt" traffic stops from the coverage of *Miranda* will open the way to widespread abuse. Policemen will simply delay formally arresting detained motorists, and will subject them to sustained and intimidating interrogation at the scene of their initial detention. The net result, respondent contends, will be a serious threat to the rights that the *Miranda* doctrine is designed to protect.

We are confident that the state of affairs projected by respondent will not come to pass. It is settled that the safeguards prescribed by *Miranda* become applicable as soon as a suspect's freedom of action is curtailed to a "degree associated with formal arrest." If a motorist who has been detained pursuant to a traffic stop thereafter is subjected to treatment that renders him "in custody" for practical purposes, he will be entitled to the full panoply of protections prescribed by *Miranda*.

Admittedly, our adherence to the doctrine just recounted will mean that the police and lower courts will continue occasionally to have difficulty deciding exactly when a suspect has been taken into custody. Either a rule that *Miranda* applies to all traffic stops or a rule that a suspect need not be advised of his rights until he is formally placed under arrest would provide a clearer, more easily administered line. However, each of these two alternatives has drawbacks that make it unacceptable. The first would substantially impede the enforcement of the Nation's traffic laws—by compelling the police either to take the time to warn all detained motorists of their constitutional rights or to forgo use of self-incriminating statements made by those motorists—while doing little to protect citizens' Fifth Amendment rights. The second would enable the police to circumvent the constraints on custodial interrogations established by *Miranda*.

Turning to the case before us, we find nothing in the record that indicates that respondent should have been given *Miranda* warnings at any point prior to the time Trooper Williams placed him under arrest. For the reasons indicated above, we reject the contention that the initial stop of respondent's car, by itself, rendered him "in custody." And respondent has failed to demonstrate that, at any time between the initial stop and the arrest, he was subjected to restraints comparable to those associated with a formal arrest. Only a short period of time elapsed between the stop and the arrest. At no point during that interval was respondent informed that his detention would not be temporary. Although Trooper Williams apparently decided as soon as respondent stepped out of his car that respondent would be taken into custody and charged with a traffic offense, Williams never communicated his intention to respondent. A policeman's unarticulated plan has no bearing on the question whether a suspect was "in custody" at a particular time; the only relevant inquiry is how a reasonable man in the suspect's position would have understood his situation. Nor do other aspects of the interaction of Williams and respondent support the contention that respondent was exposed to "custodial interrogation" at the scene of the stop. From aught that appears in the stipulation of facts, a single police officer asked respondent a modest number of questions and requested him to perform a simple balancing test at a location visible to passing motorists. Treatment of this sort cannot fairly be characterized as the functional equivalent of formal arrest.

We conclude, in short, that respondent was not taken into custody for the purposes of *Miranda* until Williams arrested him. Consequently, the statements respondent made prior to that point were admissible against him. . . .

NOTES AND QUESTIONS

1. While acknowledging that traffic stops undeniably involve a degree of "deprivation of freedom," the Court distinguishes questioning during traffic stops from custodial interrogation on several grounds: They are presumptively temporary and brief, take place in public view, usually involve fewer police, and are "comparatively nonthreatening." Which of these reasons do you find the most persuasive? Least persuasive?

In the almost 40 years since *Berkemer* was decided there has been an enormous increase in the criminal penalties for driving-under-the-influence violations. *See Birchfield v. North Dakota*, 579 U.S. 438, 448-49 (2016) (noting the toughening of drunk-driving laws). Are traffic stops, accordingly, still comparatively nonthreatening compared to custodial interrogation?

2. The Court analogizes the curtailment of freedom in traffic stops to *Terry* stops, *see* Chapter IV *infra*, both being presumptively brief detentions based on reasonable suspicion. Is that an apt analogy? In what ways are the two police interdictions different?

3. As the Court points out, in a *Terry* stop the detainee is not obliged to respond to the officer's inquiries and the detainee's silence cannot be used against him. Is the same true in a traffic stop?

4. Can an ordinary traffic stop escalate into a situation that would be more analogous to custodial detention such that *Miranda* warnings would be required before interrogation?

Stansbury v. California

511 U.S. 318 (1994)

Per Curiam.

This case concerns the rules for determining whether a person being questioned by law enforcement officers is held in custody, and thus entitled to the warnings required by *Miranda*. We hold, not for the first time, that an officer's subjective and undisclosed view concerning whether the person being interrogated is a suspect is irrelevant to the assessment whether the person is in custody.

I

Ten-year-old Robyn Jackson disappeared from a playground in Baldwin Park, California, at around 6:30 p.m. on September 28, 1982. Early the next morning, about 10 miles away in Pasadena, Andrew Zimmerman observed a large man emerge from a turquoise American sedan and throw something into a nearby flood control channel. Zimmerman called the police, who arrived at the scene and discovered the girl's body in the channel. There was evidence that she had been raped, and the cause of death was determined to be asphyxia complicated by blunt force trauma to the head.

Lieutenant Thomas Johnston, a detective with the Los Angeles County Sheriff's Department, investigated the homicide. From witnesses interviewed on the day the body was discovered, he learned that Robyn had talked to two ice cream truck drivers, one being petitioner Robert Edward Stansbury, in the hours before her disappearance. Given these contacts, Johnston thought Stansbury and the other driver might have some connection with the homicide or knowledge thereof, but for reasons unimportant here Johnston considered only the other driver to be a leading suspect. After the suspect driver was brought in for interrogation, Johnston asked Officer Lee of the Baldwin Park Police Department to contact Stansbury to see if he would come in for questioning as a potential witness.

Lee and three other plainclothes officers arrived at Stansbury's trailer home at about 11:00 that evening. The officers surrounded the door and Lee knocked. When Stansbury answered, Lee told him the officers were investigating a homicide to which Stansbury was a possible witness and asked if he would accompany them to the police station to answer some questions. Stansbury agreed to the interview and accepted a ride to the station in the front seat of Lee's police car.

At the station, Lieutenant Johnston, in the presence of another officer, questioned Stansbury about his whereabouts and activities during the afternoon and evening of September 28. Neither Johnston nor the other officer issued *Miranda* warnings. Stansbury told the officers (among other things) that on the evening of the 28th he spoke with the victim at about 6:00, returned to his trailer home after work at 9:00, and left the trailer at about midnight in his housemate's turquoise, American-made car. This last detail aroused Johnston's suspicions, as the turquoise car matched the description of the one Andrew Zimmerman had observed in Pasadena. When Stansbury, in response to a further question, admitted to prior convictions for rape, kidnaping, and child molestation, Johnston terminated the interview and another officer advised Stansbury of his *Miranda* rights. Stansbury declined to make further statements, requested an attorney, and was arrested. Respondent State of California charged Stansbury with first-degree murder and other crimes.

Stansbury filed a pretrial motion to suppress all statements made at the station, and the evidence discovered as a result of those statements. The trial court denied the motion in relevant part, ruling that Stansbury was not "in custody"—and thus not entitled to *Miranda* warnings—until he mentioned that he had taken his housemate's turquoise car for a midnight drive. Before that stage of the interview, the trial court reasoned, "the focus in [Lieutenant Johnston's] mind certainly was on the other ice cream [truck] driver"; only "after Mr. Stansbury made the comment . . . describing the . . . turquoise-colored automobile" did Johnston's suspicions "shif[t] to Mr. Stansbury." Based upon its conclusion that Stansbury was not in custody until Johnston's suspicions had focused on him, the trial court permitted the prosecution to introduce in its case in chief the statements Stansbury made before that time. At trial, the jury convicted Stansbury of first-degree murder, rape, kidnaping, and lewd act on a child under the age of 14, and fixed the penalty for the first-degree murder at death.

The California Supreme Court affirmed. Before determining whether Stansbury was in custody during the interview at the station, the court set out what it viewed as the applicable legal standard:

> In deciding the custody issue, the totality of the circumstances is relevant, and no one factor is dispositive. However, the most important considerations include (1) the site of the interrogation, (2) whether the investigation has focused on the subject, (3) whether the objective indicia of arrest are present, and (4) the length and form of questioning.

The court proceeded to analyze the second factor in detail, in the end accepting the trial court's factual determination "that suspicion focused on [Stansbury] only when he mentioned that he had driven a turquoise car on the night of the crime." The court "conclude[d] that [Stansbury] was not subject to custodial interrogation before he mentioned the turquoise car," and thus approved the trial court's ruling that *Miranda* did not bar the admission of statements Stansbury made before that point.

We granted certiorari.

II

We held in *Miranda* that a person questioned by law enforcement officers after being "taken into custody or otherwise deprived of his freedom of action in any significant way" must first "be warned that he has a right to remain silent, that any statement he does make may be used as evidence against him, and that he has a right to the presence of an attorney, either retained or appointed." . . .

Our decisions make clear that the initial determination of custody depends on the objective circumstances of the interrogation, not on the subjective views harbored by either the interrogating officers or the person being questioned.

Berkemer reaffirmed the conclusions reached in *Beckwith*. *Berkemer* concerned the roadside questioning of a motorist detained in a traffic stop. We decided that the motorist was not in custody for purposes of *Miranda* even though the traffic officer "apparently decided as soon as [the motorist] stepped out of his car that [the motorist] would be taken into custody and charged with a traffic offense." The reason, we explained, was that the officer "never communicated his intention to" the motorist during the relevant questioning. The lack of communication was crucial, for under *Miranda* "[a] policeman's unarticulated plan has no bearing on the question whether a suspect was 'in custody' at a particular time"; rather, "the only relevant inquiry is how a reasonable man in the suspect's position would have understood his situation." Other cases of ours have been consistent in adhering to this understanding of the custody element of *Miranda*.

It is well settled, then, that a police officer's subjective view that the individual under questioning is a suspect, if undisclosed, does not bear upon the question whether the individual is in custody for purposes of *Miranda*. The same principle obtains if an officer's undisclosed assessment is that the person being questioned is not a suspect. In either instance, one cannot expect the person under interrogation to probe the officer's innermost thoughts. Save as they are communicated or otherwise manifested to the person being questioned, an officer's evolving but unarticulated suspicions do not affect the objective circumstances of an interrogation or interview, and thus cannot affect the *Miranda* custody inquiry. "The threat to a citizen's Fifth Amendment rights that *Miranda* was designed to neutralize has little to do with the strength of an interrogating officer's suspicions."

An officer's knowledge or beliefs may bear upon the custody issue if they are conveyed, by word or deed, to the individual being questioned. Those beliefs are relevant only to the extent they would affect how a reasonable person in the position of the individual being questioned would gauge the breadth of his or her "'freedom of action.'" Even a clear statement from an officer that the person under interrogation is a prime suspect is not, in itself, dispositive of the custody issue, for some suspects are free to come and go until the police decide to make an arrest. The weight and pertinence of any communications regarding the officer's degree of suspicion will depend upon the facts and circumstances of the particular case. In sum, an officer's views concerning the nature of an interrogation, or beliefs concerning the potential culpability of the individual being questioned, may be one among many factors that bear upon the assessment whether that individual was in custody, but only if the officer's views or beliefs were somehow manifested to the individual under interrogation and would have affected how a reasonable person in that position would perceive his or her freedom to leave. (Of course, instances may arise in which the officer's undisclosed views are relevant in testing the credibility of his or her account of what happened during an interrogation; but it is the objective surroundings, and not any undisclosed views, that control the *Miranda* custody inquiry.)

We decide on this state of the record that the California Supreme Court's analysis of whether Stansbury was in custody is not consistent in all respects with the foregoing principles. Numerous statements in the court's opinion are open to the interpretation that the court regarded the officers' subjective beliefs regarding Stansbury's status as a suspect (or nonsuspect) as significant in and of themselves, rather than as relevant only to the extent they influenced the objective conditions surrounding his interrogation. So understood, the court's analysis conflicts with our precedents. The court's apparent conclusion that Stansbury's *Miranda* rights were triggered by virtue of the fact that he had become the focus of the officers' suspicions, is incorrect as well. Our cases make clear, in no uncertain terms, that any inquiry into whether the interrogating officers have focused their suspicions upon the individual being questioned (assuming those suspicions remain undisclosed) is not relevant for purposes of *Miranda*.

The State acknowledges that Lieutenant Johnston's and the other officers' subjective and undisclosed suspicions (or lack thereof) do not bear upon the question whether Stansbury was in custody, for purposes of *Miranda*, during the station house interview. It maintains, however, that the objective facts in the record support a finding that Stansbury was not in custody until his arrest. Stansbury, by contrast, asserts that the objective circumstances show that he was in custody during the entire interrogation. We think it appropriate for the California Supreme Court to consider this question in the first instance. We therefore reverse its judgment and remand the case for further proceedings not inconsistent with this opinion.

NOTES AND QUESTIONS

1. Note that Stansbury was interrupted in his "trailer home" at 11:00 p.m. by four police officers, who "asked" if he would come to the police station with them and answer some questions. From a reasonable person in Stansbury's position, does this feel like an invitation you can refuse? How does it cut that he "accepted a ride" to the station in the police car? That there were four officers who came to visit to extend this invitation?

2. What was the question that elicited Stansbury's response that he had prior convictions for rape, kidnapping, and child molestation? How could this question not "convey" the interrogator's belief that Stansbury was a suspect?

3. Does it matter that Stansbury was in all likelihood lured by deceptive means to go to the police station?

4. Why do the police officer's intentions not matter unless they are communicated to the individual who is questioned? Is it really because they are not relevant to the inquiry whether a reasonable person would feel he is free to leave? Or is it because the Court wants to avoid litigation over the police officer's state of mind in every *Miranda* case where custody is an issue?

This next case considers whether the interrogation of a minor presents special circumstances relevant to the application of *Miranda* requirements.

J.D.B. v. North Carolina

564 U.S. 261 (2011)

Justice Sotomayor delivered the opinion of the Court.

This case presents the question whether the age of a child subjected to police questioning is relevant to the custody analysis of *Miranda*. It is beyond dispute that children will often feel bound to submit to police questioning when an adult in the same circumstances would feel free to leave. Seeing no reason for police officers or courts to blind themselves to that commonsense reality, we hold that a child's age properly informs the *Miranda* custody analysis.

I

A

Petitioner J.D.B. was a 13-year-old, seventh-grade student attending class at Smith Middle School in Chapel Hill, North Carolina when he was removed from his classroom by a uniformed police officer, escorted to a closed-door conference room, and questioned by police for at least half an hour.

This was the second time that police questioned J.D.B. in the span of a week. Five days earlier, two home break-ins occurred, and various items were stolen. Police stopped and questioned J.D.B. after he was seen behind a residence in the neighborhood where the crimes occurred. That same day, police also spoke to J.D.B.'s grandmother — his legal guardian — as well as his aunt.

Police later learned that a digital camera matching the description of one of the stolen items had been found at J.D.B.'s middle school and seen in J.D.B.'s possession. Investigator DiCostanzo, the juvenile investigator with the local police force who had been assigned to the case, went to the school to question J.D.B. Upon arrival, DiCostanzo informed the uniformed police officer on detail to the school (a so-called school resource officer), the assistant principal, and an administrative intern that he was there to question J.D.B. about the break-ins.

Although DiCostanzo asked the school administrators to verify J.D.B.'s date of birth, address, and parent contact information from school records, neither the police officers nor the school administrators contacted J.D.B.'s grandmother.

The uniformed officer interrupted J.D.B.'s afternoon social studies class, removed J.D.B. from the classroom, and escorted him to a school conference room. There, J.D.B. was met by DiCostanzo, the assistant principal, and the administrative intern. The door to the conference room was closed. With the two police officers and the two administrators present, J.D.B. was questioned for the next 30 to 45 minutes. Prior to the commencement of questioning, J.D.B. was given neither *Miranda* warnings nor the opportunity to speak to his grandmother. Nor was he informed that he was free to leave the room.

Questioning began with small talk — discussion of sports and J.D.B.'s family life. DiCostanzo asked, and J.D.B. agreed, to discuss the events of the prior weekend. Denying any wrongdoing, J.D.B. explained that he had been in the neighborhood where the crimes occurred because he was seeking work mowing lawns. DiCostanzo pressed J.D.B. for additional detail about his efforts to obtain work; asked J.D.B. to explain a prior incident, when one of the victims returned home to find J.D.B. behind her house; and confronted J.D.B. with the stolen camera. The assistant principal urged J.D.B. to "do the right thing," warning J.D.B. that "the truth always comes out in the end."

Eventually, J.D.B. asked whether he would "still be in trouble" if he returned the "stuff." In response, DiCostanzo explained that return of the stolen items would be helpful, but "this thing is going to court" regardless. DiCostanzo then warned that he may need to seek a secure custody order if he believed that J.D.B. would continue to break into other homes. When J.D.B. asked what a secure custody order was, DiCostanzo explained that "it's where you get sent to juvenile detention before court."

After learning of the prospect of juvenile detention, J.D.B. confessed that he and a friend were responsible for the break-ins. DiCostanzo only then informed J.D.B. that he could refuse to answer the investigator's questions and that he was free to leave. Asked whether he understood, J.D.B. nodded and provided further detail, including information about the location of the stolen items. Eventually J.D.B. wrote a statement, at DiCostanzo's request. When the bell rang indicating the end of the schoolday, J.D.B. was allowed to leave to catch the bus home.

B

Two juvenile petitions were filed against J.D.B., each alleging one count of breaking and entering and one count of larceny. J.D.B.'s public defender moved to suppress his statements and the evidence derived therefrom, arguing that suppression was necessary because J.D.B. had been "interrogated by police in a custodial setting without being afforded *Miranda* warning[s]," and because his statements were involuntary under the totality of the circumstances test. After a suppression hearing at which DiCostanzo and J.D.B. testified, the trial court denied the motion, deciding that J.D.B. was not in custody at the time of the schoolhouse interrogation and that his statements were voluntary. As a result, J.D.B. entered a transcript of admission to all four counts, renewing his objection to the denial of his motion to suppress, and the court adjudicated J.D.B. delinquent.

We granted certiorari to determine whether the *Miranda* custody analysis includes consideration of a juvenile suspect's age.

II

A

Any police interview of an individual suspected of a crime has "coercive aspects to it." Only those interrogations that occur while a suspect is in police custody, however, "heighte[n] the risk" that statements obtained are not the product of the suspect's free choice.

By its very nature, custodial police interrogation entails "inherently compelling pressures." Even for an adult, the physical and psychological isolation of custodial interrogation can "undermine the individual's will to resist and . . . compel him to speak where he would not otherwise do so freely." Indeed, the pressure of custodial interrogation is so immense that it "can induce a frighteningly high percentage of people to confess to crimes they never committed." *Corley v. United States* (2009) (citing Drizin & Leo, The Problem of False Confessions in the Post-DNA World, 82 N.C. L. Rev. 891, 906-907 (2004)); see also *Miranda*, 384 U.S., at 455, n. 23. That risk is all the more troubling—and recent studies suggest, all the more acute—when the subject of custodial interrogation is a juvenile. See Brief for Center on Wrongful Convictions of Youth et al. as Amici Curiae 21-22 (collecting empirical studies that "illustrate the heightened risk of false confessions from youth").

Recognizing that the inherently coercive nature of custodial interrogation "blurs the line between voluntary and involuntary statements," this Court in *Miranda* adopted a set of prophylactic measures designed to safeguard the constitutional guarantee against self-incrimination. Prior to questioning, a suspect "must be warned that he has a right to remain silent, that any statement he does make may be used as evidence against him, and that he has a right to the presence of an attorney, either retained or appointed."

Because these measures protect the individual against the coercive nature of custodial interrogation, they are required "'only where there has been such a restriction on a person's freedom as to render him "in custody." ' " As we have repeatedly emphasized, whether a suspect is "in custody" is an objective inquiry.

"Two discrete inquiries are essential to the determination: first, what were the circumstances surrounding the interrogation; and second, given those circumstances, would a reasonable person have felt he or she was at liberty to terminate the interrogation and leave. Once the scene is set and the players' lines and actions are reconstructed, the court must apply an objective test to resolve the ultimate inquiry: was there a formal arrest or restraint on freedom of movement of the degree associated with formal arrest."

Rather than demarcate a limited set of relevant circumstances, we have required police officers and courts to "examine all of the circumstances surrounding the interrogation," including any circumstance that "would have affected how a reasonable person" in the suspect's position "would perceive his or her freedom to leave." On the other hand, the "subjective views harbored by either the interrogating officers or the person being questioned" are irrelevant. The test, in other words, involves no consideration of the "actual mindset" of the particular suspect subjected to police questioning.

The benefit of the objective custody analysis is that it is "designed to give clear guidance to the police." Police must make in-the-moment judgments as to when to administer *Miranda* warnings. By limiting analysis to the objective circumstances of the interrogation, and asking how a reasonable person in the suspect's position would understand his freedom to terminate questioning and leave, the objective test avoids burdening police with the task of anticipating the idiosyncrasies of every individual suspect and divining how those particular traits affect each person's subjective state of mind.

B

The State and its amici contend that a child's age has no place in the custody analysis, no matter how young the child subjected to police questioning. We cannot agree. In some circumstances, a child's age "would have affected how a reasonable person" in the suspect's position "would perceive his or her freedom to leave." That is, a reasonable child subjected to police questioning will sometimes feel pressured to submit when a reasonable adult would feel free to go. We think it clear that courts can account for that reality without doing any damage to the objective nature of the custody analysis.

A child's age is far "more than a chronological fact." Such conclusions apply broadly to children as a class. And, they are self-evident to anyone who was a child once himself, including any police officer or judge.

Time and again, this Court has drawn these commonsense conclusions for itself. We have observed that children "generally are less mature and responsible than adults"; that they "often lack the experience, perspective, and judgment to recognize and avoid choices that could be detrimental to them"; that they "are more vulnerable or susceptible to . . . outside pressures" than adults, and so on. Addressing the specific context of police interrogation, we have observed that events that "would leave a man cold and unimpressed can overawe and overwhelm a lad in his early teens." Describing no one child in particular, these observations restate what "any parent knows"—indeed, what any person knows—about children generally.

Our various statements to this effect are far from unique. The law has historically reflected the same assumption that children characteristically lack the capacity to exercise mature judgment and possess only an incomplete ability to understand the world around them. Like this Court's own generalizations, the legal disqualifications placed on children as a class—e.g., limitations on their ability to alienate property, enter a binding contract enforceable against them, and marry without parental consent—exhibit the settled understanding that the differentiating characteristics of youth are universal.

Indeed, even where a "reasonable person" standard otherwise applies, the common law has reflected the reality that children are not adults. In negligence suits, for instance, where liability turns on what an objectively reasonable person would do in the circumstances, "[a]ll American jurisdictions accept the idea that a person's childhood is a relevant circumstance" to be considered.

As this discussion establishes, "[o]ur history is replete with laws and judicial recognition" that children cannot be viewed simply as miniature adults. *Eddings*, 455 U.S., at 115-116, 102 S. Ct. 869. We see no justification for taking a different course here. So long as the child's age was known to the officer at the time of the interview, or would have been objectively apparent to any reasonable officer, including age as part of the custody analysis requires officers neither to consider circumstances "unknowable" to them, nor to "anticipat[e] the frailties or idiosyncrasies" of the particular suspect whom they question. The same "wide basis of community experience" that makes it possible, as an objective matter, "to determine what is to be expected" of children in other contexts, and likewise makes it possible to know what to expect of children subjected to police questioning.

In other words, a child's age differs from other personal characteristics that, even when known to police, have no objectively discernible relationship to a reasonable person's understanding of his freedom of action. *Alvarado*, holds, for instance, that a suspect's prior interrogation history with law enforcement has no role to play in the custody analysis because such experience could just as easily lead a reasonable person to feel free to walk away as to feel compelled to stay in place. Because the effect in any given case would be "contingent [on the] psycholog[y]" of the individual suspect, the Court explained, such experience cannot be considered without compromising the objective nature of the custody analysis. A child's age, however, is different. Precisely because childhood yields objective conclusions like those we have drawn ourselves—among others, that children are "most susceptible to influence" and "outside pressures"—considering age in the custody analysis in no way involves a determination of how youth "subjectively affect[s] the mindset" of any particular child."

In fact, in many cases involving juvenile suspects, the custody analysis would be nonsensical absent some consideration of the suspect's age. This case is a prime example. Were the court precluded from taking J.D.B.'s youth into account, it would be forced to evaluate the circumstances present here through the eyes of a reasonable person of average years. In other words, how would a reasonable adult understand his situation, after being removed from a seventh-grade social studies class by a uniformed school resource officer; being encouraged by his assistant principal to "do the right thing"; and being warned by a police investigator of the prospect of juvenile detention and separation from his guardian and primary caretaker? To describe such an inquiry is to demonstrate its absurdity. Neither officers nor courts can reasonably evaluate the effect of objective circumstances that, by their nature, are specific to children without accounting for the age of the child subjected to those circumstances.

Indeed, although the dissent suggests that concerns "regarding the application of the *Miranda* custody rule to minors can be accommodated by considering the unique circumstances present when minors are questioned in school," the effect of the schoolhouse setting cannot be disentangled from the identity of the person questioned. A student—whose presence at school is compulsory and whose disobedience at school is cause for disciplinary action—is in a far different position than, say, a parent volunteer on school grounds to chaperone an event, or an adult from the community on school grounds to attend a basketball game. Without asking whether the person "questioned in school" is a "minor" the coercive effect of the schoolhouse setting is unknowable.

• • •

Reviewing the question de novo today, we hold that so long as the child's age was known to the officer at the time of police questioning, or would have been objectively apparent to a reasonable officer, its inclusion in the custody analysis is consistent with the objective nature of that test. This is not to say that a child's age will be a determinative, or even a significant, factor in every case. It is, however, a reality that courts cannot simply ignore.

III

The State and its amici offer numerous reasons that courts must blind themselves to a juvenile defendant's age. None is persuasive.

To start, the State contends that a child's age must be excluded from the custody inquiry because age is a personal characteristic specific to the suspect himself rather than an "external" circumstance of the interrogation. Despite the supposed significance of this distinction, however, at oral argument counsel for the State suggested without hesitation that at least some undeniably personal characteristics—for instance, whether the individual being questioned is blind—are circumstances relevant to the custody analysis. Thus, the State's quarrel cannot be that age is a personal characteristic, without more.

The State further argues that age is irrelevant to the custody analysis because it "go[es] to how a suspect may internalize and perceive the circumstances of an interrogation." But the same can be said of every objective circumstance that the State agrees is relevant to the custody analysis: Each circumstance goes to how a reasonable person would "internalize and perceive" every other. Indeed, this is the very reason that we ask whether the objective circumstances "add up to custody" instead of evaluating the circumstances one by one.

In the same vein, the State and its amici protest that the "effect of . . . age on [the] perception of custody is internal." But the whole point of the custody analysis is to determine whether, given the circumstances, "a reasonable person [would] have felt he or she was . . . at liberty to terminate the interrogation and leave." Because the *Miranda* custody inquiry turns on the mindset of a reasonable person in the suspect's position, it cannot be the case that a circumstance is subjective simply because it has an "internal" or "psychological" impact on perception. Were that so, there would be no objective circumstances to consider at all.

Relying on our statements that the objective custody test is "designed to give clear guidance to the police," the State next argues that a child's age must be excluded from the analysis in order to preserve clarity. Similarly, the dissent insists that the clarity of the custody analysis will be destroyed unless a "one-size-fits-all reasonable-person test" applies. In reality, however, ignoring a juvenile defendant's age will often make the inquiry more artificial, and thus only add confusion. And in any event, a child's age, when known or apparent, is hardly an obscure factor to assess. Though the State and the dissent worry about gradations among children of different ages, that concern cannot justify ignoring a child's age altogether. Just as police officers are competent to account for other objective circumstances that are a matter of degree such as the length of questioning or the number of officers present, so too are they competent to evaluate the effect of relative age. Indeed, they are competent to do so even though an interrogation room lacks the "reflective atmosphere of a [jury] deliberation room." The same is true of judges, including those whose childhoods have long since passed. In short, officers and judges need no imaginative powers, knowledge of developmental psychology, training in cognitive science, or expertise in social and cultural anthropology to account for a child's age. They simply need the common sense to know that a 7-year-old is not a 13-year-old and neither is an adult.

There is, however, an even more fundamental flaw with the State's plea for clarity and the dissent's singular focus on simplifying the analysis: Not once have we excluded from the custody analysis a circumstance that we determined was relevant and objective, simply to make the fault line between custodial and noncustodial "brighter." Indeed, were the guiding concern clarity and nothing else, the custody test would presumably ask only whether the suspect had been placed under formal arrest. But we have rejected that "more easily administered line," recognizing that it would simply "enable the police to circumvent the constraints on custodial interrogations established by *Miranda*."

Finally, the State and the dissent suggest that excluding age from the custody analysis comes at no cost to juveniles' constitutional rights because the due process voluntariness test independently accounts for a child's youth. To be sure, that test permits consideration of a child's age, and it erects its own barrier to admission of a defendant's inculpatory statements at trial. But *Miranda*'s procedural safeguards exist precisely because the voluntariness test is an inadequate barrier when custodial interrogation is at stake. To hold, as the State requests, that a child's age is never relevant to whether a suspect has been taken into custody—and thus to ignore the very real differences between children and adults—would be to deny children the full scope of the procedural safeguards that *Miranda* guarantees to adults.

• • •

The question remains whether J.D.B. was in custody when police interrogated him. We remand for the state courts to address that question, this time taking account of all of the relevant circumstances of the interrogation, including J.D.B.'s age at the time. The judgment of the North Carolina Supreme Court is reversed, and the case is remanded for proceedings not inconsistent with this opinion.

NOTES AND QUESTIONS

1. This is one of the Supreme Court's first opinions in which it openly acknowledges not just the theoretical possibility of false confessions but data demonstrating the fact of false confessions. If anything, the Court understates the problem of false confessions by juveniles. By the time of this decision most of America was aware of the wrongful conviction of the "Central Park Five," in which five juveniles were convicted of assault and rape based on their confessions, only to have the real perpetrator surface years later and confess, leading to the convictions of the Central Park Five being vacated. *See generally* N. Jeremi Duru, *The Central Park Five, the Scottsboro Boys, and the Myth of the Bestial Black Man*, 25 Cardozo L. Rev. 1315, 1320 (2004). *See also The Central Park Five* (Sundance Selects 2012); *When They See Us* (Netflix 2019).

2. Did the presence of the school administrators likely add to or lessen the custodial nature of the interrogation?

3. On remand, how should the trial court go about taking into account the fact of J.D.B.'s youth in making the custody determination? Will this be purely the subject of expert testimony? Will the trial court have discretion not to take expert testimony on the issue? Will J.D.B. be allowed to testify as to whether he believed he was free to refuse the interview? What is the significance of the fact that J.D.B. was required to be in school?

4. What do you think of the dissent's slippery slope argument—that age is no different than intelligence, education, occupation, etc.—and that all such factors will inevitably become part of a fact-intensive custody standard?

E. *MIRANDA* IN PRACTICE II: WAIVER AND INVOCATION OF *MIRANDA* RIGHTS

Michigan v. Mosley

423 U.S. 96 (1975)

Mr. Justice Stewart delivered the opinion of the Court.

The respondent, Richard Bert Mosley, was arrested in Detroit, Mich., in the early afternoon of April 8, 1971, in connection with robberies that had recently occurred at the Blue Goose Bar and the White Tower Restaurant on that city's lower east side. The arresting officer, Detective James Cowie of the Armed Robbery Section of the Detroit Police Department, was acting on a tip implicating Mosley and three other men in the robberies. After effecting the arrest, Detective Cowie brought Mosley to the Robbery, Breaking and Entering Bureau of the Police Department, located on the fourth floor of the departmental headquarters building. The officer advised Mosley of his rights under this Court's decision in *Miranda* and had him read and sign the department's constitutional rights notification certificate. After filling out the necessary arrest papers, Cowie began questioning Mosley about the robbery of the White Tower Restaurant. When Mosley said he did not want to answer any questions about the robberies, Cowie promptly ceased the interrogation. The completion of the arrest papers and the questioning of Mosley together took approximately 20 minutes. At no time during the questioning did Mosley indicate a desire to consult with a lawyer, and there is no claim that the procedures followed to this point did not fully comply with the strictures of the *Miranda* opinion. Mosley was then taken to a ninth-floor cell block.

Shortly after 6 p.m., Detective Hill of the Detroit Police Department Homicide Bureau brought Mosley from the cell block to the fifth-floor office of the Homicide Bureau for questioning about the fatal shooting of a man named Leroy Williams. Williams had been killed on January 9, 1971, during a holdup attempt outside the 101 Ranch Bar in Detroit. Mosley had not been arrested on this charge or interrogated about it by Detective Cowie. Before questioning Mosley about this homicide, Detective Hill carefully advised him of his "*Miranda* rights." Mosley read the notification form both silently and aloud, and Detective Hill then read and explained the warnings to him and had him sign the form. Mosley at first denied any involvement in the Williams murder, but after the officer told him that Anthony Smith had confessed to participating in the slaying and had named him as the "shooter," Mosley made a statement implicating himself in the homicide. The interrogation by Detective Hill lasted approximately 15 minutes, and at no time during its course did Mosley ask to consult with a lawyer or indicate that he did not want to discuss the homicide. In short, there is no claim that the procedures followed during Detective Hill's interrogation of Mosley, standing alone, did not fully comply with the strictures of the *Miranda* opinion.

Mosley was subsequently charged in a one-count information with first-degree murder. Before the trial he moved to suppress his incriminating statement on a number of grounds, among them the claim that under the doctrine of the *Miranda* case it was constitutionally impermissible for Detective Hill to question him about the Williams murder after he had told Detective Cowie that he did not want to answer any questions about the robberies. The trial court denied the motion to suppress after an evidentiary hearing, and the incriminating statement was subsequently introduced in evidence against Mosley at his trial. The jury convicted Mosley of first-degree murder, and the court imposed a mandatory sentence of life imprisonment.

On appeal to the Michigan Court of Appeals, Mosley renewed his previous objections to the use of his incriminating statement in evidence. The appellate court reversed the judgment of conviction, holding that Detective Hill's interrogation of Mosley had been a per se violation of the *Miranda* doctrine. Accordingly, without reaching Mosley's other contentions, the Court remanded the case for a new trial with instructions that Mosley's statement be suppressed as evidence. After further appeal was denied by the Michigan Supreme Court, the State filed a petition for certiorari here. We granted the writ because of the important constitutional question presented.

In the *Miranda* case this Court promulgated a set of safeguards to protect the there-delineated constitutional rights of persons subjected to custodial police interrogation. In sum, the Court held in that case that unless law enforcement officers give certain specified warnings before questioning a person in custody, and follow certain specified procedures during the course of any subsequent interrogation, any statement made by the person in custody cannot over his objection be admitted in evidence against him as a defendant at trial, even though the statement may in fact be wholly voluntary.

Neither party in the present case challenges the continuing validity of the *Miranda* decision, or of any of the so-called guidelines it established to protect what the Court there said was a person's constitutional privilege against compulsory self-incrimination. The issue in this case, rather, is whether the conduct of the Detroit police that led to Mosley's incriminating statement did in fact violate the *Miranda* "guidelines," so as to render the statement inadmissible in evidence against Mosley at his trial. Resolution of the question turns almost entirely on the interpretation of a single passage in the *Miranda* opinion, upon which the Michigan appellate court relied in finding a per se violation of *Miranda*:

> Once warnings have been given, the subsequent procedure is clear. If the individual indicates in any manner, at any time prior to or during questioning, that he wishes to remain silent, the interrogation must cease. At this point he has shown that he intends to exercise his Fifth Amendment privilege; any statement taken after the person invokes his privilege cannot be other than the product of compulsion, subtle or otherwise. Without the right to cut off questioning, the setting of in-custody interrogation operates on the individual to overcome free choice in producing a statement after the privilege has been once invoked.

This passage states that "the interrogation must cease" when the person in custody indicates that "he wishes to remain silent." It does not state under what circumstances, if any, a resumption of questioning is permissible. The passage could be literally read to mean that a person who has invoked his "right to silence" can never again be subjected to custodial interrogation by any police officer at any time or place on any subject. Another possible construction of the passage would characterize "any statement taken after the person invokes his privilege" as "the product of compulsion" and would therefore mandate its exclusion from evidence, even if it were volunteered by the person in custody without any further interrogation whatever. Or the passage could be interpreted to require only the immediate cessation of questioning, and to permit a resumption of interrogation after a momentary respite.

It is evident that any of these possible literal interpretations would lead to absurd and unintended results. To permit the continuation of custodial interrogation after a momentary cessation would clearly frustrate the purposes of *Miranda* by allowing repeated rounds of questioning to undermine the will of the person being questioned. At the other extreme, a blanket prohibition against the taking of voluntary statements or a permanent immunity from further interrogation, regardless of the circumstances, would transform the *Miranda* safeguards into wholly irrational obstacles to legitimate police investigative activity, and deprive suspects of an opportunity to make informed and intelligent assessments of their interests. Clearly, therefore, neither this passage nor any other passage in the *Miranda* opinion can sensibly be read to create a per se proscription of indefinite duration upon any further questioning by any police officer on any subject, once the person in custody has indicated a desire to remain silent.

A reasonable and faithful interpretation of the *Miranda* opinion must rest on the intention of the Court in that case to adopt "fully effective means . . . to notify the person of his right of silence and to assure that the exercise of the right will be scrupulously honored. . . ." The critical safeguard identified in the passage at issue is a person's "right to cut off questioning." Through the exercise of his option to terminate questioning he can control the time at which questioning occurs, the subjects discussed, and the duration of the interrogation. The requirement that law enforcement authorities must respect a person's exercise of that option counteracts the coercive pressures of the custodial setting. We therefore conclude that the admissibility of statements obtained after the person in custody has decided to remain silent depends under *Miranda* on whether his "right to cut off questioning" was "scrupulously honored."

A review of the circumstances leading to Mosley's confession reveals that his "right to cut off questioning" was fully respected in this case. Before his initial interrogation, Mosley was carefully advised that he was under no obligation to answer any questions and could remain silent if he wished. He orally acknowledged that he understood the *Miranda* warnings and then signed a printed notification-of-rights form. When Mosley stated that he did not want to discuss the robberies, Detective Cowie immediately ceased the interrogation and did not try either to resume the questioning or in any way to persuade Mosley to reconsider his position. After an interval of more than two hours, Mosley was questioned by another police officer at another location about an unrelated holdup murder. He was given full and complete *Miranda* warnings at the outset of the second interrogation. He was thus reminded again that he could remain silent and could consult with a lawyer, and was carefully given a full and fair opportunity to exercise these options. The subsequent questioning did not undercut Mosley's previous decision not to answer Detective Cowie's inquiries. Detective Hill did not resume the interrogation about the White Tower Restaurant robbery or inquire about the Blue Goose Bar robbery, but instead focused exclusively on the Leroy Williams homicide, a crime different in nature and in time and place of occurrence from the robberies for which Mosley had been arrested and interrogated by Detective Cowie. Although it is not clear from the record how much Detective Hill knew about the earlier interrogation, his questioning of Mosley about an unrelated homicide was quite consistent with a reasonable interpretation of Mosley's earlier refusal to answer any questions about the robberies.

This is not a case, therefore, where the police failed to honor a decision of a person in custody to cut off questioning, either by refusing to discontinue the interrogation upon request or by persisting in repeated efforts to wear down his resistance and make him change his mind. In contrast to such practices, the police here immediately ceased the interrogation, resumed questioning only after the passage of a significant period of time and the provision of a fresh set of warnings, and restricted the second interrogation to a crime that had not been a subject of the earlier interrogation.

For these reasons, we conclude that the admission in evidence of Mosley's incriminating statement did not violate the principles of *Miranda*. Accordingly, the judgment of the Michigan Court of Appeals is vacated, and the case is remanded to that court for further proceedings not inconsistent with this opinion.

[Justices Marshall and Brennan dissented.]

NOTES AND QUESTIONS

1. The Court's references to *Miranda* could hardly be more grudging. Note the following examples of what can only be described as petulance: "In the *Miranda* case this Court," instead of "In *Miranda* we . . ."; the gratuitous reference to the inadmissibility of a statement "even though the statement may in fact be wholly voluntary"; the characterization of the decision's required warnings as "so-called guidelines"; and the apparent disappointment that "[n]either party in the present case challenges the continuing validity of the *Miranda* decision."

2. The Court states that Mosley was "arrested . . . in connection with" recent robberies based on a tip. What does "in connection with" mean in this context? Was there an arrest warrant issued? Was there probable cause for his arrest for the recent robberies?

Information relegated to a footnote supplies the answer to these questions: "The officer testified that information supplied by an anonymous caller was the sole basis for his arrest of Mosley."

In short, there was not probable cause for Mosley's arrest. What does this fact suggest to you about the lack of clarity in the record about "how much defendant Hill knew about the earlier interrogation"? Shouldn't this have been a focus of the defense attorney's cross-examination of the officers at the suppression hearing? How did Detective Hill learn that Mosley, a suspect in Hill's homicide investigation, was being held in the same building?

The dissent points out that, contrary to the Court's description of the subject of Detective Hill's questioning as an "unrelated holdup murder," the tip received by Detective Cowie included information about that murder.

3. Do you agree that it would be an "absurd and unintended result" for *Miranda* to be interpreted as "a permanent immunity from further interrogation"? The Court states that such a "blanket prohibition" has two evils: imposing "irrational obstacles to legitimate police investigative activity" and "depriv[ing] suspects of an opportunity to make informed and intelligent assessments of their interests." Are the police here engaged in "legitimate police activity"? Won't Mosley be able to make an informed decision if (and when) he is lawfully arrested and has the advice of counsel?

4. The Court notes that Mosley never indicated a desire to consult with a lawyer. Would this have made a difference? If Mosley had uttered those words, would he have been entitled to a "permanent immunity" as to further questioning?

If Mosley were resolute in his desire not to talk to the police—to exercise his right to remain silent—why would he have thought a lawyer necessary?

5. The Court seems to view it as material that the second interrogation was two hours later and in another location (in the same building) by a different police officer (from the same department) about a different (more serious) crime. Why do any of these factors matter?

6. Note that the Supreme Court had held just a few months earlier in *Gerstein v. Pugh*, 420 U.S. 103 (1975), that a person arrested without a warrant must "promptly" be brought before a magistrate to establish probable cause for continued detention. Many more years would pass before the Court, in *County of Riverside v. McLaughlin*, 500 U.S. 44 (1991), specified 48 hours as the time within which the police must comply with *Gerstein.*

Edwards v. Arizona

451 U.S. 477 (1981)

Justice White delivered the opinion of the Court.

We granted certiorari in this case limited to Q 1 presented in the petition, which in relevant part was "whether the Fifth, Sixth, and Fourteenth Amendments require suppression of a post-arrest confession, which was obtained after Edwards had invoked his right to consult counsel before further interrogation. . . ."

I

On January 19, 1976, a sworn complaint was filed against Edwards in Arizona state court charging him with robbery, burglary, and first-degree murder. An arrest warrant was issued pursuant to the complaint, and Edwards was arrested at his home later that same day. At the police station, he was informed of his rights as required by *Miranda*. Petitioner stated that he understood his rights, and was willing to submit to questioning. After being told that another suspect already in custody had implicated him in the crime, Edwards denied involvement and gave a taped statement presenting an alibi defense. He then sought to "make a deal." The interrogating officer told him that he wanted a statement, but that he did not have the authority to negotiate a deal. The officer provided Edwards with the telephone number of a county attorney. Petitioner made the call, but hung up after a few moments. Edwards then said: "I want an attorney before making a deal." At that point, questioning ceased and Edwards was taken to county jail.

At 9:15 the next morning, two detectives, colleagues of the officer who had interrogated Edwards the previous night, came to the jail and asked to see Edwards. When the detention officer informed Edwards that the detectives wished to speak with him, he replied that he did not want to talk to anyone. The guard told him that "he had" to talk and then took him to meet with the detectives. The officers identified themselves, stated they wanted to talk to him, and informed him of his *Miranda* rights. Edwards was willing to talk, but he first wanted to hear the taped statement of the alleged accomplice who had implicated him. After listening to the tape for several minutes, petitioner said that he would make a statement so long as it was not tape-recorded. The detectives informed him that the recording was irrelevant since they could testify in court concerning whatever he said. Edwards replied: "I'll tell you anything you want to know, but I don't want it on tape." He thereupon implicated himself in the crime.

Prior to trial, Edwards moved to suppress his confession on the ground that his *Miranda* rights had been violated when the officers returned to question him after he had invoked his right to counsel. The trial court initially granted the motion to suppress, but reversed its ruling when presented with a supposedly controlling decision of a higher Arizona court. The court stated without explanation that it found Edwards' statement to be voluntary. Edwards was tried twice and convicted. Evidence concerning his confession was admitted at both trials.

On appeal, the Arizona Supreme Court held that Edwards had invoked both his right to remain silent and his right to counsel during the interrogation conducted on the night of January 19. The court then went on to determine, however, that Edwards had waived both rights during the January 20 meeting when he voluntarily gave his statement to the detectives after again being informed that he need not answer questions and that he need not answer without the advice of counsel: "The trial court's finding that the waiver and confession were voluntarily and knowingly made is upheld."

Because the use of Edwards' confession against him at his trial violated his rights under the Fifth and Fourteenth Amendments as construed in *Miranda* we reverse the judgment of the Arizona Supreme Court.

II

In *Miranda* the Court determined that the Fifth and Fourteenth Amendments' prohibition against compelled self-incrimination required that custodial interrogation be preceded by advice to the putative defendant that he has the right to remain silent and also the right to the presence of an attorney. The Court also indicated the procedures to be followed subsequent to the warnings. If the accused indicates that he wishes to remain silent, "the interrogation must cease." If he requests counsel, "the interrogation must cease until an attorney is present."

Miranda thus declared that an accused has a Fifth and Fourteenth Amendment right to have counsel present during custodial interrogation. Here, the critical facts as found by the Arizona Supreme Court are that Edwards asserted his right to counsel and his right to remain silent on January 19, but that the police, without furnishing him counsel, returned the next morning to confront him and as a result of the meeting secured incriminating oral admissions. Contrary to the holdings of the state courts, Edwards insists that having exercised his right on the 19th to have counsel present during interrogation, he did not validly waive that right on the 20th. For the following reasons, we agree.

First, the Arizona Supreme Court applied an erroneous standard for determining waiver where the accused has specifically invoked his right to counsel. It is reasonably clear under our cases that waivers of counsel must not only be voluntary, but must also constitute a knowing and intelligent relinquishment or abandonment of a known right or privilege, a matter which depends in each case "upon the particular facts and circumstances surrounding that case, including the background, experience, and conduct of the accused."

Considering the proceedings in the state courts in the light of this standard, we note that in denying petitioner's motion to suppress, the trial court found the admission to have been "voluntary," without separately focusing on whether Edwards had knowingly and intelligently relinquished his right to counsel. The Arizona Supreme Court, in a section of its opinion entitled "Voluntariness of Waiver," stated that in Arizona, confessions are prima facie involuntary and that the State had the burden of showing by a preponderance of the evidence that the confession was freely and voluntarily made. The court stated that the issue of voluntariness should be determined based on the totality of the circumstances as it related to whether an accused's action was "knowing and intelligent and whether his will [was] overborne." Once the trial court determines that "the confession is voluntary, the finding will not be upset on appeal absent clear and manifest error." The court then upheld the trial court's finding that the "waiver and confession were voluntarily and knowingly made."

In referring to the necessity to find Edwards' confession knowing and intelligent the State Supreme Court cited *Schneckloth*. Yet, it is clear that *Schneckloth* does not control the issue presented in this case. The issue in *Schneckloth* was under what conditions an individual could be found to have consented to a search and thereby waived his Fourth Amendment rights. The Court declined to impose the "intentional relinquishment or abandonment of a known right or privilege" standard and required only that the consent be voluntary under the totality of the circumstances. The Court specifically noted that the right to counsel was a prime example of those rights requiring the special protection of the knowing and intelligent waiver standard, but held that "[t]he considerations that informed the Court's holding in *Miranda* are simply inapplicable in the present case." *Schneckloth* itself thus emphasized that the voluntariness of a consent or an admission on the one hand, and a knowing and intelligent waiver on the other, are discrete inquiries. Here, however sound the conclusion of the state courts as to the voluntariness of Edwards' admission may be, neither the trial court nor the Arizona Supreme Court undertook to focus on whether Edwards understood his right to counsel and intelligently and knowingly relinquished it. It is thus apparent that the decision below misunderstood the requirement for finding a valid waiver of the right to counsel, once invoked.

Second, although we have held that after initially being advised of his *Miranda* rights, the accused may himself validly waive his rights and respond to interrogation, the Court has strongly indicated that additional safeguards are necessary when the accused asks for counsel; and we now hold that when an accused has invoked his right to have counsel present during custodial interrogation, a valid waiver of that right cannot be established by showing only that he responded to further police-initiated custodial interrogation even if he has been advised of his rights. We further hold that an accused, such as Edwards, having expressed his desire to deal with the police only through counsel, is not subject to further interrogation by the authorities until counsel has been made available to him, unless the accused himself initiates further communication, exchanges, or conversations with the police.

Miranda itself indicated that the assertion of the right to counsel was a significant event and that once exercised by the accused, "the interrogation must cease until an attorney is present." Our later cases have not abandoned that view. In *Mosley*, the Court noted that *Miranda* had distinguished between the procedural safeguards triggered by a request to remain silent and a request for an attorney and had required that interrogation cease until an attorney was present only if the individual stated that he wanted counsel. In *Fare v. Michael C.*, the Court referred to *Miranda*'s "rigid rule that an accused's request for an attorney is per se an invocation of his Fifth Amendment rights, requiring that all interrogation cease." And just last Term, in a case where a suspect in custody had invoked his *Miranda* right to counsel, the Court again referred to the "undisputed right" under *Miranda* to remain silent and to be free of interrogation "until he had consulted with a lawyer." *Rhode Island v. Innis*. We reconfirm these views and, to lend them substance, emphasize that it is inconsistent with *Miranda* and its progeny for the authorities, at their instance, to reinterrogate an accused in custody if he has clearly asserted his right to counsel.

In concluding that the fruits of the interrogation initiated by the police on January 20 could not be used against Edwards, we do not hold or imply that Edwards was powerless to countermand his election or that the authorities could in no event use any incriminating statements made by Edwards prior to his having access to counsel. Had Edwards initiated the meeting on January 20, nothing in the Fifth and Fourteenth Amendments would prohibit the police from merely listening to his voluntary, volunteered statements and using them against him at the trial. The Fifth Amendment right identified in *Miranda* is the right to have counsel present at any custodial interrogation. Absent such interrogation, there would have been no infringement of the right that Edwards invoked and there would be no occasion to determine whether there had been a valid waiver.

But this is not what the facts of this case show. Here, the officers conducting the interrogation on the evening of January 19 ceased interrogation when Edwards requested counsel as he had been advised he had the right to do. The Arizona Supreme Court was of the opinion that this was a sufficient invocation of his *Miranda* rights, and we are in accord. It is also clear that without making counsel available to Edwards, the police returned to him the next day. This was not at his suggestion or request. Indeed, Edwards informed the detention officer that he did not want to talk to anyone. At the meeting, the detectives told Edwards that they wanted to talk to him and again advised him of his *Miranda* rights. Edwards stated that he would talk, but what prompted this action does not appear. He listened at his own request to part of the taped statement made by one of his alleged accomplices and then made an incriminating statement, which was used against him at his trial. We think it is clear that Edwards was subjected to custodial interrogation on January 20 within the meaning of *Rhode Island v. Innis*, and that this occurred at the instance of the authorities. His statement made without having had access to counsel, did not amount to a valid waiver and hence was inadmissible.

Accordingly, the holding of the Arizona Supreme Court that Edwards had waived his right to counsel was infirm, and the judgment of that court is reversed.

NOTES AND QUESTIONS

1. Unlike Mosley, Edwards was lawfully under arrest. So an arrest warrant had issued, based on a determination by a magistrate or judge that there was probable cause to believe that Edwards had committed the charged offenses. If this is the case, why the urgency on the part of the detectives? Did they fear a lawyer would be on the scene soon?

2. In his first interrogation, after being given *Miranda* warnings, Edwards was told that another suspect had implicated him in the crime. After hearing this, Edwards provided the detectives with an alibi defense and then stated that he "wanted to make a deal" after first consulting an attorney.

Why would Edwards want to "make a deal" if he had an alibi? Did the detectives really need to get an explicit confession after this exchange? Isn't it likely that a competent defense attorney, knowing about the first interrogation, would have advised Edwards to make a deal?

3. Judging by Edwards's behavior the next day it would seem that the detectives had been telling the truth when they told Edwards they had a taped statement of an accomplice that implicated Edwards. But they could have lied about that fact in the interrogation with virtual impunity. *See Frazier v. Cupp*, 394 U.S. 731 (1969) (false representation by interrogator that defendant's companion had confessed to the murder and implicated defendant does not render subsequent confession involuntary).

4. Why is the right to counsel, at issue here, treated so differently than the right to remain silent at issue in *Mosley*? The Court suggests that if Edwards had initiated the second meeting, there would have been no *Miranda* violation. Why shouldn't the same rule apply in a *Mosley* scenario where a suspect has asserted not his right to counsel but his right to remain silent?

5. In *Oregon v. Bradshaw*, 462 U.S. 1039 (1983), and *Davis v. United States*, 512 U.S. 452 (1994), the Court made it difficult for defendants to suppress statements they claimed resulted from violations of *Edwards*. In *Bradshaw*, the defendant was given *Miranda* warnings in connection with a murder investigation, denied any involvement, then asserted his right to counsel. *Id.* at 1041-42. Shortly thereafter, as he was about to be transported from the police station to a local jail, Bradshaw asked a police officer, "What is going to happen to me now?" *Id.* at 1042. This inquiry led to some colloquy and then to an unsuccessful polygraph, after which Bradshaw incriminated himself. *Id.* The Supreme Court ultimately found that Bradshaw had "initiated" a discussion under *Edwards*, and had thus withdrawn his previous assertion of the right to counsel, even though it acknowledged that his language was ambiguous. *Id.* at 1045-46. Per Justice Marshall, the four dissenters interpreted the defendant's question as more likely a question about where he was going than it was indicative of a desire to resume the interrogation. *Id.* at 1055 (Marshall, J., dissenting).

In *Davis*, after 90 minutes of interrogation the defendant said, "Maybe I should talk to a lawyer?" The interrogators asked him follow-up questions designed to enable him to clarify his request, which he did not, and then they re-Mirandized him and resumed questioning, eliciting incriminating information that was used to convict him. 512 U.S. at 455. The Supreme Court held that only an unambiguous request could trigger the protection of *Edwards*. Both *Bradshaw* and *Davis* have been sharply criticized by commentators. *See, e.g.*, Marcy Strauss, *Understanding* Davis v. United States, 40 Loy. L.A. L. Rev. 1011, 1012 (2006) (concluding that *Davis* will eviscerate the *Miranda* guarantees, particularly for women and minorities who may be less likely to speak in clear, declarative terms).

6. The Supreme Court eventually clarified that *Edwards* did not impose an "eternal" prohibition on a resumption of questioning once a suspect had invoked his right to counsel. In *Maryland v. Shatzer*, 559 U.S. 98 (2010), the Court held that a two-week "break in custody" is sufficient to dispel the coercive effects of custody, and defended the legislative feel of its announced ruling — the second interrogation in *Shatzer* of the defendant was more than two years after the first — on the ground that "law officers need to know" what is lawful. The Court could have cited *Miranda*, of course, as a justification for its giving such detailed guidance to the police. It did not, instead noting its decision in *County of Riverside v. McLaughlin*, 500 U.S. 44 (1991), which specified 48 hours as the time within which the police must comply with *Gerstein v. Pugh*.

The Court considered the significance of counsel to an arrestee again in *Moran v. Burbine*, 475 U.S. 412 (1986). Brian Burbine was arrested — as was Mosley — "in connection with" a burglary in Cranston, Rhode Island, after a confidential informant had implicated him in a notorious unsolved murder in neighboring Providence. In short, as with Mosley, there was no probable cause for his arrest. Burbine was given *Miranda* warnings but refused to answer questions by a Cranston police detective.

A few hours later he was questioned again, by Providence police, and after being given *Miranda* warnings, and explicitly stating that he did not want an attorney, confessed to the murder. So far, does *Mosley* control? But here's the wrinkle: Between the two interrogations Burbine's sister, having learned of her brother's arrest, arranged for him to have a lawyer. That lawyer called the Cranston police station, identified herself as Burbine's lawyer, and was told that Burbine would not be questioned. The factual record was unclear as to exactly what transpired in the police station with respect to the lawyer's phone call, but the Court held that "the state of mind of the police is irrelevant to the question of the intelligence and voluntariness of respondent's election to abandon his rights." *Id.* at 423. Three Justices dissented, noting a recurring pattern in state court cases of the police affirmatively deceiving attorneys who are seeking to consult with clients under arrest.

The Court had more directly dealt with the issue of a "waiver" of *Miranda* rights before *Edwards* and *Moran* in *North Carolina v. Butler*, 441 U.S. 369 (1979). In that case the defendant was provided with the FBI's standard "Advice of Rights" form, which he read and thereafter stated that he understood. *Id.* at 370-71. He agreed to talk but refused to sign the portion of the form indicating "waiver" and said, "I will talk to you but I am not signing any form." And then he began answering questions and inculpated himself. The Court found that although the burden of proving waiver was on the government, Butler's decision to speak to agents after refusing to sign the form was sufficient evidence of waiver and that nothing more "explicit" was required. In dissent, Justice Brennan argued that fidelity to *Miranda* required an express waiver requirement, and that "ambiguity be interpreted against the interrogator."

Revisiting the issue of *Miranda* waiver 30 years after *Butler*, the Court held that while a waiver need not be explicit an assertion of the right to remain silent must be unambiguous.

Berghuis v. Thompkins
560 U.S. 370 (2010)

Justice KENNEDY delivered the opinion of the Court.

The United States Court of Appeals for the Sixth Circuit, in a habeas corpus proceeding challenging a Michigan conviction for first-degree murder and certain other offenses, ruled that there had been two separate constitutional errors in the trial that led to the jury's guilty verdict. First, the Court of Appeals determined that a statement by the accused, relied on at trial by the prosecution, had been elicited in violation of *Miranda*. . . .

On January 10, 2000, a shooting occurred outside a mall in Southfield, Michigan. Among the victims was Samuel Morris, who died from multiple gunshot wounds. The other victim, Frederick France, recovered from his injuries and later testified. Thompkins, who was a suspect, fled. About one year later he was found in Ohio and arrested there.

Two Southfield police officers traveled to Ohio to interrogate Thompkins, then awaiting transfer to Michigan. The interrogation began around 1:30 p.m. and lasted about three hours. The interrogation was conducted in a room that was 8 by 10 feet, and Thompkins sat in a chair that resembled a school desk (it had an arm on it that swings around to provide a surface to write on). At the beginning of the interrogation, one of the officers, Detective Helgert, presented Thompkins with a form derived from the *Miranda* rule. It stated:

> "NOTIFICATION OF CONSTITUTIONAL RIGHTS AND STATEMENT
>
> "1. You have the right to remain silent.
>
> "2. Anything you say can and will be used against you in a court of law.
>
> "3. You have a right to talk to a lawyer before answering any questions and you have the right to have a lawyer present with you while you are answering any questions.
>
> "4. If you cannot afford to hire a lawyer, one will be appointed to represent you before any questioning, if you wish one.
>
> "5. You have the right to decide at any time before or during questioning to use your right to remain silent and your right to talk with a lawyer while you are being questioned."

Brief for Petitioner 60 (some capitalization omitted).

Helgert asked Thompkins to read the fifth warning out loud. Thompkins complied. Helgert later said this was to ensure that Thompkins could read, and Helgert concluded that Thompkins understood English. Helgert then read the other four *Miranda* warnings out loud and asked Thompkins to sign the form to demonstrate that he understood his rights. Thompkins declined to sign the form. The record contains conflicting evidence about whether Thompkins then verbally confirmed that he understood the rights listed on the form.

Officers began an interrogation. At no point during the interrogation did Thompkins say that he wanted to remain silent, that he did not want to talk with the police, or that he wanted an attorney. Thompkins was "[l]argely" silent during the interrogation, which lasted about three hours. He did give a few limited verbal responses, however, such as "yeah," "no," or "I don't know." And on occasion he communicated by nodding his head. Thompkins also said that he "didn't want a peppermint" that was offered to him by the police and that the chair he was "sitting in was hard."

About 2 hours and 45 minutes into the interrogation, Helgert asked Thompkins, "Do you believe in God?" Thompkins made eye contact with Helgert and said "Yes," as his eyes "well[ed] up with tears." Helgert asked, "Do you pray to God?" Thompkins said "Yes." Helgert asked, "Do you pray to God to forgive you for shooting that boy down?" Thompkins answered "Yes" and looked away. Thompkins refused to make a written confession, and the interrogation ended about 15 minutes later.

Thompkins was charged with first-degree murder, assault with intent to commit murder, and certain firearms-related offenses. He moved to suppress the statements made during the interrogation. He argued that he had invoked his Fifth Amendment right to remain silent, requiring police to end the interrogation at once, that he had not waived his right to remain silent, and that his inculpatory statements were involuntary. The trial court denied the motion.

• • •

The jury found Thompkins guilty on all counts. He was sentenced to life in prison without parole.

III

The *Miranda* Court formulated a warning that must be given to suspects before they can be subjected to custodial interrogation. The substance of the warning still must be given to suspects today. A suspect in custody must be advised as follows:

"He must be warned prior to any questioning that he has the right to remain silent, that anything he says can be used against him in a court of law, that he has the right to the presence of an attorney, and that if he cannot afford an attorney one will be appointed for him prior to any questioning if he so desires."

All concede that the warning given in this case was in full compliance with these requirements. The dispute centers on the response—or nonresponse—from the suspect.

A

Thompkins makes various arguments that his answers to questions from the detectives were inadmissible. He first contends that he "invoke[d] his privilege" to remain silent by not saying anything for a sufficient period of time, so the interrogation should have "cease[d]" before he made his inculpatory statements.

This argument is unpersuasive. In the context of invoking the *Miranda* right to counsel, the Court in *Davis* held that a suspect must do so "unambiguously." If an accused makes a statement concerning the right to counsel "that is ambiguous or equivocal" or makes no statement, the police are not required to end the interrogation, or ask questions to clarify whether the accused wants to invoke his or her *Miranda* rights.

The Court has not yet stated whether an invocation of the right to remain silent can be ambiguous or equivocal, but there is no principled reason to adopt different standards for determining when an accused has invoked the *Miranda* right to remain silent and the *Miranda* right to counsel.

There is good reason to require an accused who wants to invoke his or her right to remain silent to do so unambiguously. A requirement of an unambiguous invocation of *Miranda* rights results in an objective inquiry that "avoid[s] difficulties of proof and . . . provide[s] guidance to officers" on how to proceed in the face of ambiguity. If an ambiguous act, omission, or statement could require police to end the interrogation, police would be required to make difficult decisions about an accused's unclear intent and face the consequence of suppression "if they guess wrong." Suppression of a voluntary confession in these circumstances would place a significant burden on society's interest in prosecuting criminal activity. Treating an ambiguous or equivocal act, omission, or statement as an invocation of *Miranda* rights "might add marginally to *Miranda*'s goal of dispelling the compulsion inherent in custodial interrogation." But "as *Miranda* holds, full comprehension of the rights to remain silent and request an attorney are sufficient to dispel whatever coercion is inherent in the interrogation process."

Thompkins did not say that he wanted to remain silent or that he did not want to talk with the police. Had he made either of these simple, unambiguous statements, he would have invoked his "'right to cut off questioning.'" Here he did neither, so he did not invoke his right to remain silent.

B

We next consider whether Thompkins waived his right to remain silent. Even absent the accused's invocation of the right to remain silent, the accused's statement during a custodial interrogation is inadmissible at trial unless the prosecution can establish that the accused "in fact knowingly and voluntarily waived [*Miranda*] rights" when making the statement. The waiver inquiry "has two distinct dimensions": waiver must be "voluntary in the sense that it was the product of a free and deliberate choice rather than intimidation, coercion, or deception," and "made with a full awareness of both the nature of the right being abandoned and the consequences of the decision to abandon it."

Some language in *Miranda* could be read to indicate that waivers are difficult to establish absent an explicit written waiver or a formal, express oral statement. *Miranda* said "a valid waiver will not be presumed simply from the silence of the accused after warnings are given or simply from the fact that a confession was in fact eventually obtained." In addition, the *Miranda* Court stated that "a heavy burden rests on the government to demonstrate that the defendant knowingly and intelligently waived his privilege against self-incrimination and his right to retained or appointed counsel."

The course of decisions since *Miranda*, informed by the application of *Miranda* warnings in the whole course of law enforcement, demonstrates that waivers can be established even absent formal or express statements of waiver that would be expected in, say, a judicial hearing to determine if a guilty plea has been properly entered. Cf. Fed. Rule Crim. Proc. 11. The main purpose of *Miranda* is to ensure that an accused is advised of and understands the right to remain silent and the right to counsel. Thus, "[i]f anything, our subsequent cases have reduced the impact of the *Miranda* rule on legitimate law enforcement while reaffirming the decision's core ruling that unwarned statements may not be used as evidence in the prosecution's case in chief."

One of the first cases to decide the meaning and import of *Miranda* with respect to the question of waiver was *North Carolina v. Butler*. The *Butler* Court, after discussing some of the problems created by the language in *Miranda*, established certain important propositions. *Butler* interpreted the *Miranda* language concerning the "heavy burden" to show waiver, in accord with usual principles of determining waiver, which can include waiver implied from all the circumstances. And in a later case, the Court stated that this "heavy burden" is not more than the burden to establish waiver by a preponderance of the evidence.

The prosecution therefore does not need to show that a waiver of *Miranda* rights was express. An "implicit waiver" of the "right to remain silent" is sufficient to admit a suspect's statement into evidence. *Butler* made clear that a waiver of *Miranda* rights may be implied through "the defendant's silence, coupled with an understanding of his rights and a course of conduct indicating waiver." The Court in *Butler* therefore "retreated" from the "language and tenor of the *Miranda* opinion," which "suggested that the Court would require that a waiver . . . be 'specifically made.'"

If the State establishes that a *Miranda* warning was given and the accused made an uncoerced statement, this showing, standing alone, is insufficient to demonstrate "a valid waiver" of *Miranda* rights. Where the prosecution shows that a *Miranda* warning was given and that it was understood by the accused, an accused's uncoerced statement establishes an implied waiver of the right to remain silent.

Although *Miranda* imposes on the police a rule that is both formalistic and practical when it prevents them from interrogating suspects without first providing them with a *Miranda* warning, it does not impose a formalistic waiver procedure that a suspect must follow to relinquish those rights. As a general proposition, the law can presume that an individual who, with a full understanding of his or her rights, acts in a manner inconsistent with their exercise has made a deliberate choice to relinquish the protection those rights afford. As *Butler* recognized, *Miranda* rights can therefore be waived through means less formal than a typical waiver on the record in a courtroom, cf. Fed. Rule Crim. Proc. 11, given the practical constraints and necessities of interrogation and the fact that *Miranda*'s main protection lies in advising defendants of their rights.

The record in this case shows that Thompkins waived his right to remain silent. There is no basis in this case to conclude that he did not understand his rights; and on these facts it follows that he chose not to invoke or rely on those rights when he did speak. First, there is no contention that Thompkins did not understand his rights; and from this it follows that he knew what he gave up when he spoke. There was more than enough evidence in the record to conclude that Thompkins understood his *Miranda* rights. Thompkins received a written copy of the *Miranda* warnings; Detective Helgert determined that Thompkins could read and understand English; and Thompkins was given time to read the warnings. Thompkins, furthermore, read aloud the fifth warning, which stated that "you have the right to decide at any time before or during questioning to use your right to remain silent and your right to talk with a lawyer while you are being questioned." He was thus aware that his right to remain silent would not dissipate after a certain amount of time and that police would have to honor his right to be silent and his right to counsel during the whole course of interrogation. Those rights, the warning made clear, could be asserted at any time. Helgert, moreover, read the warnings aloud.

Second, Thompkins' answer to Detective Helgert's question about whether Thompkins prayed to God for forgiveness for shooting the victim is a "course of conduct indicating waiver" of the right to remain silent. If Thompkins wanted to remain silent, he could have said nothing in response to Helgert's questions, or he could have unambiguously invoked his *Miranda* rights and ended the interrogation. The fact that Thompkins made a statement about three hours after receiving a *Miranda* warning does not overcome the fact that he engaged in a course of conduct indicating waiver. Police are not required to rewarn suspects from time to time. Thompkins' answer to Helgert's question about praying to God for forgiveness for shooting the victim was sufficient to show a course of conduct indicating waiver. This is confirmed by the fact that before then Thompkins had given sporadic answers to questions throughout the interrogation.

Third, there is no evidence that Thompkins' statement was coerced. Thompkins does not claim that police threatened or injured him during the interrogation or that he was in any way fearful. The interrogation was conducted in a standard-sized room in the middle of the afternoon. It is true that apparently he was in a straight-backed chair for three hours, but there is no authority for the proposition that an interrogation of this length is inherently coercive. Indeed, even where interrogations of greater duration were held to be improper, they were accompanied, as this one was not, by other facts indicating coercion, such as an incapacitated and sedated suspect, sleep and food deprivation, and threats. The fact that Helgert's question referred to Thompkins' religious beliefs also did not render Thompkins' statement involuntary. "[T]he Fifth Amendment privilege is not concerned 'with moral and psychological pressures to confess emanating from sources other than official coercion.'" In these circumstances, Thompkins knowingly and voluntarily made a statement to police, so he waived his right to remain silent.

Thompkins next argues that, even if his answer to Detective Helgert could constitute a waiver of his right to remain silent, the police were not allowed to question him until they obtained a waiver first. *Butler* forecloses this argument. The *Butler* Court held that courts can infer a waiver of *Miranda* rights "from the actions and words of the person interrogated." This principle would be inconsistent with a rule that requires a waiver at the outset. The *Butler* Court thus rejected the rule proposed by the *Butler* dissent, which would have "requir[ed] the police to obtain an express waiver of [*Miranda* rights] before proceeding with interrogation." This holding also makes sense given that "the primary protection afforded suspects subject[ed] to custodial interrogation is the *Miranda* warnings themselves." The *Miranda* rule and its requirements are met if a suspect receives adequate *Miranda* warnings, understands them, and has an opportunity to invoke the rights before giving any answers or admissions. Any waiver, express or implied, may be contradicted by an invocation at any time. If the right to counsel or the right to remain silent is invoked at any point during questioning, further interrogation must cease.

Interrogation provides the suspect with additional information that can put his or her decision to waive, or not to invoke, into perspective. As questioning commences and then continues, the suspect has the opportunity to consider the choices he or she faces and to make a more informed decision, either to insist on silence or to cooperate. When the suspect knows that *Miranda* rights can be invoked at any time, he or she has the opportunity to reassess his or her immediate and long-term interests. Cooperation with the police may result in more favorable treatment for the suspect; the apprehension of accomplices; the prevention of continuing injury and fear; beginning steps toward relief or solace for the victims; and the beginning of the suspect's own return to the law and the social order it seeks to protect.

In order for an accused's statement to be admissible at trial, police must have given the accused a *Miranda* warning. If that condition is established, the court can proceed to consider whether there has been an express or implied waiver of *Miranda* rights. In making its ruling on the admissibility of a statement made during custodial questioning, the trial court, of course, considers whether there is evidence to support the conclusion that, from the whole course of questioning, an express or implied waiver has been established. Thus, after giving a *Miranda* warning, police may interrogate a suspect who has neither invoked nor waived his or her *Miranda* rights. On these premises, it follows the police were not required to obtain a waiver of Thompkins' *Miranda* rights before commencing the interrogation.

In sum, a suspect who has received and understood the *Miranda* warnings, and has not invoked his *Miranda* rights, waives the right to remain silent by making an uncoerced statement to the police. Thompkins did not invoke his right to remain silent and stop the questioning. Understanding his rights in full, he waived his right to remain silent by making a voluntary statement to the police. The police, moreover, were not required to obtain a waiver of Thompkins' right to remain silent before interrogating him.

[Justices Sotomayor, Stevens, Breyer, and Ginsburg dissented.]

NOTES AND QUESTIONS

1. Why would the police officers travel from Southfield, Michigan to Ohio to question the defendant given that he was awaiting transfer to Michigan? Why would they continue the interrogation after Thompkins refused to sign the form?

2. Consider carefully the description of the right to counsel in item 3 on the form:

> You have a right to talk to a lawyer before answering any questions and you have the right to have a lawyer present with you while you are answering any questions.

Is this warning accurate? Is it misleading? Does this description make clear that the right to have counsel does not mean that you lose the right to remain silent? In other words, does the language suggest that you only have the right to counsel if you agree to answer questions? What are the likely consequences of such a misunderstanding of the right to counsel?

The Court has been lax about the actual content of *Miranda* warnings. "[N]o talismanic incantation [is] required to satisfy [*Miranda*'s] strictures." *California v. Prysock*, 453 U.S. 355, 359 (1981) (per curiam). The inquiry is simply whether the warnings reasonably communicated to a suspect his rights. *Duckworth v. Eagan*, 492 U.S. 195 (1989).

3. The police officer appears to have admitted that Thompkins was "largely silent" during the three-hour interrogation, and that Thompkins only gave a handful of verbal responses. But why isn't the factual record better? What else happened in the interrogation room in the other 2 hours and 40 minutes of interrogation? Did either officer have notes reflecting Thompkins's verbal acknowledgment that he understood his rights?

4. The Court holds that since an invocation of the right to counsel must be done "unambiguously," so must an invocation of the right to remain silent. Is the analogy apt? Can you invoke the right to counsel without speaking?

5. Note the three reasons the Court gives for its finding that Thompkins waived his right to silence. Does the Court hold the prosecution to its burden of proving waiver? Is the fact of silence — itself — irrelevant to the waiver finding?

6. Would the case have come out differently if Thompkins had said literally nothing after he refused to sign the form? What would Thompkins have needed to say to "invoke" his right to remain silent? Would "I'm not talking" be sufficient? How about simply "silence" or "shut up"? Would those words have acted as the proverbial "cutoff" and precluded any further questioning?

Would simply saying "lawyer" or "lawyer!" be enough to invoke the right to counsel?

Salinas v. Texas

570 U.S. 178 (2013)

Justice ALITO announced the judgment of the Court and delivered an opinion in which THE CHIEF JUSTICE and Justice KENNEDY join.

Without being placed in custody or receiving *Miranda* warnings, petitioner voluntarily answered the questions of a police officer who was investigating a murder. But petitioner balked when the officer asked whether a ballistics test would show that the shell casings found at the crime scene would match petitioner's shotgun. Petitioner was subsequently charged with murder, and at trial prosecutors argued that his reaction to the officer's question suggested that he was guilty. Petitioner claims that this argument violated the Fifth Amendment, which guarantees that "[n]o person . . . shall be compelled in any criminal case to be a witness against himself."

Petitioner's Fifth Amendment claim fails because he did not expressly invoke the privilege against self-incrimination in response to the officer's question. It has long been settled that the privilege "generally is not self-executing" and that a witness who desires its protection "'must claim it.'" Although "no ritualistic formula is necessary in order to invoke the privilege," a witness does not do so by simply standing mute. Because petitioner was required to assert the privilege in order to benefit from it, the judgment of the Texas Court of Criminal Appeals rejecting petitioner's Fifth Amendment claim is affirmed.

I

On the morning of December 18, 1992, two brothers were shot and killed in their Houston home. There were no witnesses to the murders, but a neighbor who heard gunshots saw someone run out of the house and speed away in a dark-colored car. Police recovered six shotgun shell casings at the scene. The investigation led police to petitioner, who had been a guest at a party the victims hosted the night before they were killed. Police visited petitioner at his home, where they saw a dark blue car in the driveway. He agreed to hand over his shotgun for ballistics testing and to accompany police to the station for questioning.

Petitioner's interview with the police lasted approximately one hour. All agree that the interview was noncustodial, and the parties litigated this case on the assumption that he was not read *Miranda* warnings. For most of the interview, petitioner answered the officer's questions. But when asked whether his shotgun "would match the shells recovered at the scene of the murder," petitioner declined to answer. Instead, petitioner "[l]ooked down at the floor, shuffled his feet, bit his bottom lip, cl[e]nched his hands in his lap, [and] began to tighten up." After a few moments of silence, the officer asked additional questions, which petitioner answered.

Following the interview, police arrested petitioner on outstanding traffic warrants. Prosecutors soon concluded that there was insufficient evidence to charge him with the murders, and he was released. A few days later, police obtained a statement from a man who said he had heard petitioner confess to the killings. On the strength of that additional evidence, prosecutors decided to charge petitioner, but by this time he had absconded. In 2007, police discovered petitioner living in the Houston area under an assumed name.

Petitioner did not testify at trial. Over his objection, prosecutors used his reaction to the officer's question during the 1993 interview as evidence of his guilt. The jury found petitioner guilty, and he received a 20-year sentence. On direct appeal to the Court of Appeals of Texas, petitioner argued that prosecutors' use of his silence as part of their case in chief violated the Fifth Amendment. The Court of Appeals rejected that argument, reasoning that petitioner's prearrest, pre-Miranda silence was not "compelled" within the meaning of the Fifth Amendment. The Texas Court of Criminal Appeals took up this case and affirmed on the same ground.

We granted certiorari, to resolve a division of authority in the lower courts over whether the prosecution may use a defendant's assertion of the privilege against self-incrimination during a noncustodial police interview as part of its case in chief. But because petitioner did not invoke the privilege during his interview, we find it unnecessary to reach that question.

II

A

The privilege against self-incrimination "is an exception to the general principle that the Government has the right to everyone's testimony." To prevent the privilege from shielding information not properly within its scope, we have long held that a witness who "'desires the protection of the privilege . . . must claim it'" at the time he relies on it.

That requirement ensures that the Government is put on notice when a witness intends to rely on the privilege so that it may either argue that the testimony sought could not be self-incriminating, or cure any potential self-incrimination through a grant of immunity. The express invocation requirement also gives courts tasked with evaluating a Fifth Amendment claim a contemporaneous record establishing the witness' reasons for refusing to answer. In these ways, insisting that witnesses expressly invoke the privilege "assures that the Government obtains all the information to which it is entitled."

We have previously recognized two exceptions to the requirement that witnesses invoke the privilege, but neither applies here. First, we held in *Griffin v. California* that a criminal defendant need not take the stand and assert the privilege at his own trial. That exception reflects the fact that a criminal defendant has an "absolute right not to testify." Since a defendant's reasons for remaining silent at trial are irrelevant to his constitutional right to do so, requiring that he expressly invoke the privilege would serve no purpose; neither a showing that his testimony would not be self-incriminating nor a grant of immunity could force him to speak. Because petitioner had no comparable unqualified right during his interview with police, his silence falls outside the *Griffin* exception.

Second, we have held that a witness' failure to invoke the privilege must be excused where governmental coercion makes his forfeiture of the privilege involuntary. Thus, in *Miranda*, we said that a suspect who is subjected to the "inherently compelling pressures" of an unwarned custodial interrogation need not invoke the privilege. Due to the uniquely coercive nature of custodial interrogation, a suspect in custody cannot be said to have voluntarily forgone the privilege "unless [he] fails to claim [it] after being suitably warned."

For similar reasons, we have held that threats to withdraw a governmental benefit such as public employment sometimes make exercise of the privilege so costly that it need not be affirmatively asserted. And where assertion of the privilege would itself tend to incriminate, we have allowed witnesses to exercise the privilege through silence. The principle that unites all of those cases is that a witness need not expressly invoke the privilege where some form of official compulsion denies him "a 'free choice to admit, to deny, or to refuse to answer.'"

Petitioner cannot benefit from that principle because it is undisputed that his interview with police was voluntary. As petitioner himself acknowledges, he agreed to accompany the officers to the station and "was free to leave at any time during the interview." That places petitioner's situation outside the scope of *Miranda* and other cases in which we have held that various forms of governmental coercion prevented defendants from voluntarily invoking the privilege. The dissent elides this point when it cites our precedents in this area for the proposition that "[c]ircumstances, rather than explicit invocation, trigger the protection of the Fifth Amendment." The critical question is whether, under the "circumstances" of this case, petitioner was deprived of the ability to voluntarily invoke the Fifth Amendment. He was not. We have before us no allegation that petitioner's failure to assert the privilege was involuntary, and it would have been a simple matter for him to say that he was not answering the officer's question on Fifth Amendment grounds. Because he failed to do so, the prosecution's use of his noncustodial silence did not violate the Fifth Amendment.

B

Petitioner urges us to adopt a third exception to the invocation requirement for cases in which a witness stands mute and thereby declines to give an answer that officials suspect would be incriminating. Our cases all but foreclose such an exception, which would needlessly burden the Government's interests in obtaining testimony and prosecuting criminal activity. We therefore decline petitioner's invitation to craft a new exception to the "general rule" that a witness must assert the privilege to subsequently benefit from it.

Our cases establish that a defendant normally does not invoke the privilege by remaining silent. In *Roberts* for example, we rejected the Fifth Amendment claim of a defendant who remained silent throughout a police investigation and received a harsher sentence for his failure to cooperate. In so ruling, we explained that "if [the defendant] believed that his failure to cooperate was privileged, he should have said so at a time when the sentencing court could have determined whether his claim was legitimate." A witness does not expressly invoke the privilege by standing mute.

We have also repeatedly held that the express invocation requirement applies even when an official has reason to suspect that the answer to his question would incriminate the witness. Thus, in *Murphy* we held that the defendant's self-incriminating answers to his probation officer were properly admitted at trial because he failed to invoke the privilege. In reaching that conclusion, we rejected the notion "that a witness must 'put the Government on notice by formally availing himself of the privilege' only when he alone 'is reasonably aware of the incriminating tendency of the questions.'"

Petitioner does not dispute the vitality of either of those lines of precedent but instead argues that we should adopt an exception for cases at their intersection. Thus, petitioner would have us hold that although neither a witness' silence nor official suspicions are enough to excuse the express invocation requirement, the invocation requirement does not apply where a witness is silent in the face of official suspicions. For the same reasons that neither of those factors is sufficient by itself to relieve a witness of the obligation to expressly invoke the privilege, we conclude that they do not do so together. A contrary result would do little to protect those genuinely relying on the Fifth Amendment privilege while placing a needless new burden on society's interest in the admission of evidence that is probative of a criminal defendant's guilt.

Petitioner's proposed exception would also be very difficult to reconcile with *Berghuis v. Thompkins.* There, we held in the closely related context of post-*Miranda* silence that a defendant failed to invoke the privilege when he refused to respond to police questioning for 2 hours and 45 minutes. If the extended custodial silence in that case did not invoke the privilege, then surely the momentary silence in this case did not do so either.

Petitioner and the dissent attempt to distinguish *Berghuis* by observing that it did not concern the admissibility of the defendant's silence but instead involved the admissibility of his subsequent statements. But regardless of whether prosecutors seek to use silence or a confession that follows, the logic of *Berghuis* applies with equal force: A suspect who stands mute has not done enough to put police on notice that he is relying on his Fifth Amendment privilege.

In support of their proposed exception to the invocation requirement, petitioner and the dissent argue that reliance on the Fifth Amendment privilege is the most likely explanation for silence in a case such as this one. But whatever the most probable explanation, such silence is "insolubly ambiguous." To be sure, someone might decline to answer a police officer's question in reliance on his constitutional privilege. But he also might do so because he is trying to think of a good lie, because he is embarrassed, or because he is protecting someone else. Not every such possible explanation for silence is probative of guilt, but neither is every possible explanation protected by the Fifth Amendment. Petitioner alone knew why he did not answer the officer's question, and it was therefore his "burden . . . to make a timely assertion of the privilege."

At oral argument, counsel for petitioner suggested that it would be unfair to require a suspect unschooled in the particulars of legal doctrine to do anything more than remain silent in order to invoke his "right to remain silent." But popular misconceptions notwithstanding, the Fifth Amendment guarantees that no one may be "compelled in any criminal case to be a witness against himself"; it does not establish an unqualified "right to remain silent." A witness' constitutional right to refuse to answer questions depends on his reasons for doing so, and courts need to know those reasons to evaluate the merits of a Fifth Amendment claim.

In any event, it is settled that forfeiture of the privilege against self-incrimination need not be knowing. Statements against interest are regularly admitted into evidence at criminal trials, see Fed. Rule of Evid. 804(b)(3), and there is no good reason to approach a defendant's silence any differently.

C

Finally, we are not persuaded by petitioner's arguments that applying the usual express invocation requirement where a witness is silent during a noncustodial police interview will prove unworkable in practice. Petitioner and the dissent suggest that our approach will "unleash complicated and persistent litigation" over what a suspect must say to invoke the privilege, but our cases have long required that a witness assert the privilege to subsequently benefit from it.

That rule has not proved difficult to apply. Nor did the potential for close cases dissuade us from adopting similar invocation requirements for suspects who wish to assert their rights and cut off police questioning during custodial interviews.

Notably, petitioner's approach would produce its own line-drawing problems, as this case vividly illustrates. When the interviewing officer asked petitioner if his shotgun would match the shell casings found at the crime scene, petitioner did not merely remain silent; he made movements that suggested surprise and anxiety. At precisely what point such reactions transform "silence" into expressive conduct would be a difficult and recurring question that our decision allows us to avoid.

We also reject petitioner's argument that an express invocation requirement will encourage police officers to "'unfairly "tric[k]"'"suspects into cooperating. Petitioner worries that officers could unduly pressure suspects into talking by telling them that their silence could be used in a future prosecution. But as petitioner himself concedes, police officers "have done nothing wrong" when they "accurately stat[e] the law." We found no constitutional infirmity in government officials telling the defendant in *Murphy* that he was required to speak truthfully to his parole officer, and we see no greater danger in the interview tactics petitioner identifies. So long as police do not deprive a witness of the ability to voluntarily invoke the privilege, there is no Fifth Amendment violation.

• • •

Before petitioner could rely on the privilege against self-incrimination, he was required to invoke it. Because he failed to do so, the judgment of the Texas Court of Criminal Appeals is affirmed.

[Justices Breyer, Ginsburg, Sotomayor, and Kagan dissented.]

NOTES AND QUESTIONS

1. What do you think would have happened here if Salinas had refused to turn over the shotgun and accompany the officer to the station? Would the officer have arrested him and taken him in for a custodial interrogation where he would have had to give *Miranda* warnings? Do you think the officer was instead hoping to do a noncustodial interrogation so he could avoid his *Miranda* obligations? How would a police officer weigh the pros and cons of which approach to use? Why does the Court not say how many officers came to Salinas's house? Would that be relevant as to the intent of the officer(s)?

2. The plurality opinion conveniently omits any reference to the police officer's lie that seems to have induced Salinas to go to the police station (just to "clear him as a suspect"). Of course the fact of a police lie normally has no legal consequence. But why doesn't either the plurality or the dissent explain more about the substance of the hour of questioning other than the single exchange about the shotgun? The dissent suggests the shotgun question was a change of subject, implying that Salinas was lulled into a false sense of security before having the "money" question sprung on him. What about the questioning that occurred after the silence?

3. The plurality casually notes that "[f]ollowing the interview, police arrested petitioner on outstanding traffic warrants." Was the plan all along to arrest him on these warrants, either with or without his initial voluntary cooperation? Was this approach of Salinas originally on a track to be more like *Mosley* or *Burbine*, where a suspect is arrested on a semi-pretextual lesser crime, sometimes without probable cause, but then — once in custody and as the pressure mounts — to be questioned on a more serious crime? Note that it was explicitly settled by *Colorado v. Spring*, 479 U.S. 564, 574 (1987), that a suspect's waiver of his *Miranda* rights was not involuntary because the suspect was unaware of which crimes he might be questioned about.

4. Did defense counsel give up too easily on the custody issue? Is it dispositive that Salinas appears to have voluntarily gone to the police station? Does it matter that the officers had received the shotgun from Salinas's father in connection with the execution of a search warrant at Salinas's house that day (facts from the state appellate opinion)? Why did Salinas's counsel appear to allow him to testify at the suppression hearing that he felt he "was free to leave" during the interrogation? Did he still feel free to leave after being asked the question about the shotgun? Did the shotgun question "convey" to Salinas that he was a suspect and thereby make the interrogation from that point forward custodial? *See Stansbury v. California*, 511 U.S. 318, 325 (1994) (officer's views as to whether witness is a suspect not relevant unless "conveyed" to individual being questioned). What if at some point in the interrogation the officer had said "I think you're lying to me" or "I just might have to arrest you"? Would a reasonable person still feel "free to leave"?

Even if litigating custody for *Miranda* applicability purposes was a long shot, note that one of the "exceptions" the Court finds to the rule that the Fifth Amendment has to be asserted is where a witness has been subjected to "some form of official compulsion." It might have been worth trying to establish that even if the interrogation was not "custodial" for *Miranda* purposes it was "custodial-ish" and thus within that line of cases.

5. Once Salinas made the horrible decision to agree to be interviewed, what were his options when the shotgun question came up? What words did he need to say to invoke the Fifth Amendment, which everyone seems to assume — at least for the sake of argument — applies here? Would he have had to include the term "Fifth Amendment" as the Court suggests? What if he had simply said, "I'm not going to answer that"? Or, uneducated and/or confused, "I'm taking the Sixth" on that? Assuming those answers successfully invoked the right, could the interrogator have kept going with more questioning after the invocation? Would the prosecutor have been allowed to use the defendant's invocation of his right to silence against him at trial just as he was allowed to use his actual silence against him?

What if Salinas had responded to the shotgun question by wordlessly getting up and leaving, which he had every right to do? Could the officer testify about his exit at trial?

6. The Court says a witness must assert the privilege in order to provide "notice" to the government. Do any of the justifications the Court provides for the "notice" rationale even remotely apply in the context of an interrogation? In his dissenting opinion Justice Breyer establishes that all the cases the plurality relies on for the "invocation requirement" are readily distinguishable, as they were all situations where there were specific reasons the questioner needed to know whether the witness was taking the Fifth.

7. Is the fact that the *Miranda* warnings have become "part of our national culture," as the Court said in *Dickerson*, relevant here? In other words, is the widespread cultural understanding that Americans have a "right to remain silent" relevant to how a reasonable person in Salinas's position would have understood his options in dealing with the shotgun question? Note that the actual words "Fifth Amendment" are not normally part of the *Miranda* warnings that are heard in the movies or on television.

8. The Court brushes off the policy concern that after *Salinas* the police could pressure suspects into agreeing to be questioned by telling them, in effect, that their silence can be used against them in court. The Court says that there is nothing wrong with police officers accurately stating the law, and dismisses those concerns. What it could have added, as this case makes clear, is that there is also nothing wrong with police officers lying to a witness in order to get him to agree to being questioned.

But is it true that a witness's silence can be used against them in court? Doesn't it depend on whether the interrogation is voluntary (it can be used) or custodial (it can't)? And might it also depend on whether the witness sufficiently invoked the Fifth Amendment or not? Recall that the circuit split on which the Court granted cert—still undecided after *Salinas*—was over whether comments on assertions of the Fifth Amendment in a noncustodial interview were permissible.

9. Justice Thomas and Justice Scalia concur only in the judgment in *Salinas*. Justice Thomas renews his call for overturning *Griffin v. California* on the ground that the Fifth Amendment is only a "trial right," precluding a person from being compelled to testify against himself in court, and that Salinas had no Fifth Amendment rights during his interview.

Does Justice Thomas's textualist view of the Fifth Amendment also require overturning *Kastigar* and invalidating all immunity statutes?

10. One of the priceless things about *Salinas* is the plurality's description of the Fifth Amendment as "an exception to the general principle that the Government has the right to everyone's testimony." The ten amendments found in the Bill of Rights are not often described as "exceptions."

A separate and older line of cases deals with a defendant's "right to silence" in the context of a defendant's post-arrest silence.

Doyle v. Ohio

426 U.S. 610 (1976)

Mr. Justice Powell delivered the opinion of the Court.

The question in these consolidated cases is whether a state prosecutor may seek to impeach a defendant's exculpatory story, told for the first time at trial, by cross-examining the defendant about his failure to have told the story after receiving *Miranda* warnings at the time of his arrest. We conclude that use of the defendant's post-arrest silence in this manner violates due process, and therefore reverse the convictions of both petitioners.

I

Petitioners Doyle and Wood were arrested together and charged with selling 10 pounds of marihuana to a local narcotics bureau informant. They were convicted in the Common Pleas Court of Tuscarawas County, Ohio, in separate trials held about one week apart. The evidence at their trials was identical in all material respects.

The State's witnesses sketched a picture of a routine marihuana transaction. William Bonnell, a well-known "street person" with a long criminal record, offered to assist the local narcotics investigation unit in setting up drug "pushers" in return for support in his efforts to receive lenient treatment in his latest legal problems. The narcotics agents agreed. A short time later, Bonnell advised the unit that he and Doyle had arranged a "buy" of 10 pounds of marihuana and needed $1,750 to pay for it. Since the banks were closed and time was short, the agents were able to collect only $1,320. Bonnell took this money and left for the rendezvous, under surveillance by four narcotics agents in two cars. As planned, he met petitioners in a bar in Dover, Ohio. From there, he and petitioner Wood drove in Bonnell's pickup truck to the nearby town of New Philadelphia, Ohio, while petitioner Doyle drove off to obtain the marihuana and then meet them at a prearranged location in New Philadelphia. The narcotics agents followed the Bonnell truck. When Doyle arrived at Bonnell's waiting truck in New Philadelphia, the two vehicles proceeded to a parking lot where the transaction took place. Bonnell left in his truck, and Doyle and Wood departed in Doyle's car. They quickly discovered that they had been paid $430 less than the agreed-upon price, and began circling the neighborhood looking for Bonnell. They were stopped within minutes by New Philadelphia police acting on radioed instructions from the narcotics agents. One of those agents, Kenneth Beamer, arrived on the scene promptly, arrested petitioners, and gave them *Miranda* warnings. A search of the car, authorized by warrant, uncovered the $1,320.

At both trials, defense counsel's cross-examination of the participating narcotics agents was aimed primarily at establishing that due to a limited view of the parking lot, none of them had seen the actual transaction but had seen only Bonnell standing next to Doyle's car with a package under his arm, presumably after the transaction. Each petitioner took the stand at his trial and admitted practically everything about the State's case except the most crucial point: who was selling marihuana to whom. According to petitioners, Bonnell had framed them. The arrangement had been for Bonnell to sell Doyle 10 pounds of marihuana. Doyle had left the Dover bar for the purpose of borrowing the necessary money, but while driving by himself had decided that he only wanted one or two pounds instead of the agreed-upon 10 pounds. When Bonnell reached Doyle's car in the New Philadelphia parking lot, with the marihuana under his arm, Doyle tried to explain his change of mind. Bonnell grew angry, threw the $1,320 into Doyle's car, and took all 10 pounds of the marihuana back to his truck. The ensuing chase was the effort of Wood and Doyle to catch Bonnell to find out what the $1,320 was all about.

Petitioners' explanation of the events presented some difficulty for the prosecution, as it was not entirely implausible and there was little if any direct evidence to contradict it. As part of a wide-ranging cross-examination for impeachment purposes, and in an effort to undercut the explanation, the prosecutor asked each petitioner at his respective trial why he had not told the frameup story to Agent Beamer when he arrested petitioners. In the first trial, that of petitioner Wood, the following colloquy occurred:

Q. (By the prosecutor.) Mr. Beamer did arrive on the scene?
A. (by Wood.) Yes, he did.
Q. And I assume you told him all about what happened to you?
A. No.
Q. You didn't tell Mr. Beamer?
A. No.
Q. You didn't tell Mr. Beamer this guy put $1,300 in your car?
A. No, sir.
Q. And we can't understand any reason why anyone would put money in your car and you were chasing him around town and trying to give it back?
A. I didn't understand that.
Q. You mean you didn't tell him that?
A. Tell him what?
Q. Mr. Wood, if that is all you had to do with this and you are innocent, when Mr. Beamer arrived on the scene why didn't you tell him?
Q. But in any event you didn't bother to tell Mr. Beamer anything about this?
A. No, sir.

Defense counsel's timely objections to the above questions of the prosecutor were overruled. The cross-examination of petitioner Doyle at his trial contained a similar exchange, and again defense counsel's timely objections were overruled.

Each petitioner appealed to the Court of Appeals, Fifth District, Tuscarawas County, alleging, Inter alia, that the trial court erred in allowing the prosecutor to cross-examine the petitioner at his trial about his post-arrest silence. The Court of Appeals affirmed the convictions, stating as to the contentions about the post-arrest silence:

> This was not evidence offered by the state in its case in chief as confession by silence or as substantive evidence of guilt but rather cross examination of a witness as to why he had not told the same story earlier at his first opportunity.
>
> We find no error in this. It goes to credibility of the witness.

The Supreme Court of Ohio denied further review. We granted certiorari to decide whether impeachment use of a defendant's post-arrest silence violates any provision of the Constitution, a question left open last Term in *United States v. Hale* (1975), and on which the Federal Courts of Appeals are in conflict.

II

The State pleads necessity as justification for the prosecutor's action in these cases. It argues that the discrepancy between an exculpatory story at trial and silence at time of arrest gives rise to an inference that the story was fabricated somewhere along the way, perhaps to fit within the seams of the State's case as it was developed at pretrial hearings. Noting that the prosecution usually has little else with which to counter such an exculpatory story, the State seeks only the right to cross-examine a defendant as to post-arrest silence for the limited purpose of impeachment. In support of its position the State emphasizes the importance of cross-examination in general, and relies upon those cases in which this Court has permitted use for impeachment purposes of post-arrest statements that were inadmissible as evidence of guilt because of an officer's failure to follow *Miranda*'s dictates. Thus, although the State does not suggest petitioners' silence could be used as evidence of guilt, it contends that the need to present to the jury all information relevant to the truth of petitioners' exculpatory story fully justifies the cross-examination that is at issue.

Despite the importance of cross-examination, we have concluded that the *Miranda* decision compels rejection of the State's position. The warnings mandated by that case, as a prophylactic means of safeguarding Fifth Amendment rights, require that a person taken into custody be advised immediately that he has the right to remain silent, that anything he says may be used against him, and that he has a right to retained or appointed counsel before submitting to interrogation. Silence in the wake of these warnings may be nothing more than the arrestee's exercise of these *Miranda* rights. Thus, every post-arrest silence is insolubly ambiguous because of what the State is required to advise the person arrested. Moreover, while it is true that the *Miranda* warnings contain no express assurance that silence will carry no penalty, such assurance is implicit to any person who receives the warnings. In such circumstances, it would be fundamentally unfair and a deprivation of due process to allow the arrested person's silence to be used to impeach an explanation subsequently offered at trial. Mr. Justice White, concurring in the judgment in *United States v. Hale*, put it very well:

> (W)hen a person under arrest is informed, as *Miranda* requires, that he may remain silent, that anything he says may be used against him, and that he may have an attorney if he wishes, it seems to me that it does not comport with due process to permit the prosecution during the trial to call attention to his silence at the time of arrest and to insist that because he did not speak about the facts of the case at that time, as he was told he need not do, an unfavorable inference might be drawn as to the truth of his trial testimony. . . . Surely Hale was not informed here that his silence, as well as his words, could be used against him at trial. Indeed, anyone would reasonably conclude from *Miranda* warnings that this would not be the case.

We hold that the use for impeachment purposes of petitioners' silence, at the time of arrest and after receiving *Miranda* warnings, violated the Due Process Clause of the Fourteenth

Amendment. The State has not claimed that such use in the circumstances of this case might have been harmless error. Accordingly, petitioners' convictions are reversed and their causes remanded to the state courts for further proceedings not inconsistent with this opinion.

So ordered.

Mr. Justice STEVENS, with whom Mr. Justice BLACKMUN and Mr. Justice REHNQUIST join, dissenting.

Petitioners assert that the prosecutor's cross-examination about their failure to mention the purported "frame" until they testified at trial violated their constitutional right to due process and also their constitutional privilege against self-incrimination. I am not persuaded by the first argument; though there is merit in a portion of the second, I do not believe it warrants reversal of these state convictions.

I

The Court's due process rationale has some of the characteristics of an estoppel theory. If (a) the defendant is advised that he may remain silent, and (b) he does remain silent, then we (c) presume that his decision was made in reliance on the advice, and (d) conclude that it is unfair in certain cases, though not others, to use his silence to impeach his trial testimony. The key to the Court's analysis is apparently a concern that the *Miranda* warning, which is intended to increase the probability that a person's response to police questioning will be intelligent and voluntary, will actually be deceptive unless we require the State to honor an unstated promise not to use the accused's silence against him.

In my judgment there is nothing deceptive or prejudicial to the defendant in the *Miranda* warning. Nor do I believe that the fact that such advice was given to the defendant lessens the probative value of his silence, or makes the prosecutor's cross-examination about his silence any more unfair than if he had received no such warning.

This is a case in which the defendants' silence at the time of their arrest was graphically inconsistent with their trial testimony that they were the unwitting victims of a "frameup" in which the police did not participate. If defendants had been framed, their failure to mention that fact at the time of their arrest is almost inexplicable; for that reason, under accepted rules of evidence, their silence is tantamount to a prior inconsistent statement and admissible for purposes of impeachment.

Indeed, there is irony in the fact that the *Miranda* warning provides the only plausible explanation for their silence. If it were the true explanation, I should think that they would have responded to the questions on cross-examination about why they had remained silent by stating that they relied on their understanding of the advice given by the arresting officers. Instead, however, they gave quite a different jumble of responses. Those response negate the Court's presumption that their silence was induced by reliance on deceptive advice.

Since the record requires us to put to one side the Court's presumption that the defendants' silence was the product of reliance on the *Miranda* warning, the Court's entire due process rationale collapses. For without reliance on the waiver, the case is no different than if no warning had been given, and nothing in the Court's opinion suggests that there would be any unfairness in using petitioners' prior inconsistent silence for impeachment purposes in such a case.

Indeed, as a general proposition, if we assume the defendant's silence would be admissible for impeachment purposes if no *Miranda* warning had been given, I should think that the warning would have a tendency to salvage the defendant's credibility as a witness. If the defendant is a truthful witness, and if his silence is the consequence of his understanding of the *Miranda* warning, he may explain that fact when he is on the stand. Even if he is untruthful, the availability of that explanation puts him in a better position than if he had received no warning. In my judgment, the risk that a truthful defendant will be deceived by the *Miranda* warning and also will be unable to explain his honest misunderstanding is so much less than the risk that exclusion of the evidence will merely provide a shield for perjury that I cannot accept the Court's due process rationale.

Accordingly, if we assume that the use of a defendant's silence for impeachment purposes would be otherwise unobjectionable, I find no merit in the notion that he is denied due process of law because he received a *Miranda* warning.

II

Petitioners argue that the State violated their Fifth Amendment privilege against self-incrimination by asking the jury to draw an inference of guilt from their constitutionally protected silence. They challenge both the prosecutor's cross-examination and his closing argument.

A

Petitioners claim that the cross-examination was improper because it referred to their silence at the time of their arrest, to their failure to testify at the preliminary hearing, and to their failure to reveal the "frame" prior to trial. Their claim applies to the testimony of each defendant at his own trial, and also to the testimony each gave as a witness at the trial of the other. Since I think it quite clear that a defendant may not object to the violation of another person's privilege, I shall only discuss the argument that a defendant may not be cross-examined about his own prior inconsistent silence.

In support of their objections to the cross-examination about their silence at the time of arrest, petitioners primarily rely on the statement in *Miranda* that the prosecution may not use at trial the fact that the defendant stood mute or claimed the privilege in the face of accusations during custodial interrogation. There are two reasons why that statement does not adequately support petitioners' argument.

First, it is not accurate to say that the petitioners "stood mute or claimed the privilege in the face of accusations." Neither petitioner claimed the privilege and petitioner Doyle did not even remain silent. The case is not one in which a description of the actual conversation between the defendants and the police would give rise to any inference of guilt if it were not so flagrantly inconsistent with their trial testimony. Rather than a claim of privilege, we simply have a failure to advise the police of a "frame" at a time when it most surely would have been mentioned if petitioners' trial testimony were true. That failure gave rise to an inference of guilt only because it belied their trial testimony.

Second, the dictum in the footnote in *Miranda* relies primarily upon *Griffin v. California*, which held that the Fifth Amendment, as incorporated in the Fourteenth, prohibited the prosecution's use of the defendant's silence in its case in chief. But as long ago as *Raffel v. United States*, this Court recognized the distinction between the prosecution's affirmative use of the defendant's prior silence and the use of prior silence for impeachment purposes. *Raffel* expressly held that the defendant's silence at a prior trial was admissible for purposes of impeachment despite the application in federal prosecutions of the prohibition that Griffin found in the Fifth Amendment. *Raffel.*

Moreover, Mr. Chief Justice Warren, the author of the Court's opinion in *Miranda*, joined the opinion in *Walder v. United States*, which squarely held that a valid constitutional objection to the admissibility of evidence as part of the Government's case in chief did not bar the use of that evidence to impeach the defendant's trial testimony. The availability of an objection to the affirmative use of improper evidence does not provide the defendant "with a shield against contradiction of his untruths." The need to ensure the integrity of the truth-determining function of the adversary trial process has provided the predicate for an unbroken line of decisions so holding.

Although I have no doubt concerning the propriety of the cross-examination about petitioners' failure to mention the purported "frame" at the time of their arrest, a more difficult question is presented by their objection to the questioning about their failure to testify at the preliminary hearing and their failure generally to mention the "frame" before trial. Unlike the failure to make the kind of spontaneous comment that discovery of a "frame" would be expected to prompt, there is no significant inconsistency between petitioners' trial testimony and their adherence to counsel's advice not to take the stand at the preliminary hearing; moreover, the decision not to divulge their defense prior to trial is probably attributable to counsel rather than to petitioners. Nevertheless, unless and until this Court overrules *Raffel v. United States*, I think a state court is free to regard the defendant's decision to take the stand as a waiver of his objection to the use of his failure to testify at an earlier proceeding or his failure to offer his version of the events prior to trial.

B

In my judgment portions of the prosecutor's argument to the jury overstepped permissible bounds. In each trial, he commented upon the defendant's silence not only as inconsistent with his testimony that he had been "framed," but also as inconsistent with the defendant's innocence. Comment on the lack of credibility of the defendant is plainly proper; it is not proper, however, for the prosecutor to ask the jury to draw a direct inference of guilt from silence — to argue, in effect, that silence is inconsistent with innocence. But since the two inferences perjury and guilt are inextricably intertwined because they have a common source, it would be unrealistic to permit comment on the former but to find reversible error in the slightest reference to the latter. In the context of the entire argument and the entire trial, I am not persuaded that the rather sophisticated distinction between permissible comment on credibility and impermissible comment on an inference of guilt justifies a reversal of these state convictions.

Accordingly, although I have some doubt concerning the propriety of the cross-examination about the preliminary hearing and consider a portion of the closing argument improper, I would affirm these convictions.

NOTES AND QUESTIONS

1. The Court says that a defendant's silence in response to *Miranda* warnings is "insolubly ambiguous." The dissent rejects this view, claiming that the defendants' silence here is "almost inexplicable" and "tantamount to a prior inconsistent statement" and thus fair ground for impeachment. Which view do you find more persuasive?

Why do you think the defendants might not have shared with the arresting officers their "frame up" defense?

2. The dissent suggests that the presumption that the defendants' silence was the product of *Miranda* warnings is unwarranted because if that were in fact the reason, the defendants could have testified to that effect. Do you agree? Would it be unfair to require a defendant to so testify?

3. Do you agree that it is implicit in the *Miranda* warnings that a defendant's silence cannot be used against him? Put somewhat differently, how would it affect the character of *Miranda* warnings if they included a statement to the effect that "if you choose to remain silent that silence can be used against you"?

4. Why do you think the Court bases its holding on the Due Process Clause of the Fourteenth Amendment instead of the Fifth Amendment?

Four years later, in *Jenkins v. Anderson*, 447 U.S. 231 (1980), the Court revisited the issue of the government's use at trial of a defendant's silence, this time prior to his arrest. Defendant Dennis Seay Jenkins was charged with murder. The defense was self-defense. The defendant turned himself in two weeks after the killing. *Id.* at 232. The defendant testified, explained how he acted in self-defense, but admitted on cross-examination that he had waited two weeks before turning himself in, a fact the prosecutor emphasized in closing argument in arguing that the defense was fabricated. *Id.* at 233-34. The Court held the impeachment was permissible. It found *Doyle* distinguishable because there, unlike in *Jenkins*, government action (giving *Miranda* warnings) had induced the defendant's silence. *Id.* at 241.

In *Fletcher v. Weir*, 455 U.S. 603 (1982), the defendant was also accused of murder and also testified that he had acted in self-defense. He was impeached at trial on his silence during the time period (of unclear length) between his arrest and when he was given *Miranda* warnings. *Id.* at 603-04. The court of appeals found that *Doyle* was applicable inasmuch as the government's arrest of the defendant effectively induced his silence. *Id.* at 605-06. The Court reversed, finding the lack of "the sort of affirmative assurances embodied in the *Miranda* warnings" to be dispositive. *Id.* at 607.

In both of these post-*Doyle* cases the Court emphasized that the states were free to apply their own rules of evidence to govern the use of pre-arrest and post-arrest silence. What is the best evidentiary argument that the admission of pre-arrest and/or post-arrest silence for impeachment purposes is more prejudicial than probative? Does *Miranda*'s role in popular culture figure into either scenario?

Since the *Doyle/Jenkins/Weir* trilogy, several circuits have considered whether a defendant's pre-arrest or pre-*Miranda* silence can be used not just for impeachment but substantively, as part of the government's case-in-chief. The Fifth, Ninth, and Eleventh Circuits have all held that the government may use pre-arrest silence in its case-in-chief. *United States v. Oplinger*, 150 F.3d 1061, 1067 (9th Cir. 1998) (holding government may use pre-arrest silence in its case-in-chief); *United States v. Zanabria*, 74 F.3d 590 (5th Cir. 1996) (same); *United States v. Rivera*, 944 F.2d 1563, 1568 (11th Cir. 1991) (same). Four circuits have found such use prohibited by the Constitution. *See Coppola v. Powell*, 878 F.2d 1562, 1568 (1st Cir. 1989) (holding pre-arrest silence cannot be used in the government's case-in-chief); *United States ex rel. Savory v. Lane*, 832 F.2d 1011, 1018 (7th Cir. 1987) (holding government cannot use pre-arrest silence in its case-in-chief); *United States v. Caro*, 637 F.2d 869, 876 (2d Cir. 1981) (suggesting government cannot comment on a defendant's silence in its case-in-chief). *See* David S. Romantz, *"You Have the Right to Remain Silent": A Case for the Use of Silence as Substantive Proof of the Criminal Defendant's Guilt*, 38 Ind. L. Rev. 1, 28-29 (2005).

F. CONSEQUENCES OF *MIRANDA* VIOLATIONS

The next two cases feature a "successive interrogation" technique in which the police conduct an interrogation without *Miranda* warnings followed by a second interrogation after warnings are given.

Oregon v. Elstad

470 U.S. 298 (1985)

Justice O'Connor delivered the opinion of the Court.

This case requires us to decide whether an initial failure of law enforcement officers to administer the warnings required by *Miranda*, without more, "taints" subsequent admissions made after a suspect has been fully advised of and has waived his *Miranda* rights. Respondent, Michael James Elstad, was convicted of burglary by an Oregon trial court. The Oregon Court of Appeals reversed, holding that respondent's signed confession, although voluntary, was rendered inadmissible by a prior remark made in response to questioning without benefit of *Miranda* warnings. We granted certiorari and we now reverse.

I

In December 1981, the home of Mr. and Mrs. Gilbert Gross, in the town of Salem, Polk County, Ore., was burglarized. Missing were art objects and furnishings valued at $150,000. A witness to the burglary contacted the Polk County Sheriff's office, implicating respondent Michael Elstad, an 18-year-old neighbor and friend of the Grosses' teenage son. Thereupon, Officers Burke and McAllister went to the home of respondent Elstad, with a warrant for his arrest. Elstad's mother answered the door. She led the officers to her son's room where he lay on his bed, clad in shorts and listening to his stereo. The officers asked him to get dressed and to accompany them into the living room. Officer McAllister asked respondent's mother to step into the kitchen, where he explained that they had a warrant for her son's arrest for the burglary of a neighbor's residence. Officer Burke remained with Elstad in the living room. He later testified:

> I sat down with Mr. Elstad and I asked him if he was aware of why Detective McAllister and myself were there to talk with him. He stated no, he had no idea why we were there. I then asked him if he knew a person by the name of Gross, and he said yes, he did, and also added that he heard that there was a robbery at the Gross house. And at that point I told Mr. Elstad that I felt he was involved in that, and he looked at me and stated, "Yes, I was there."

The officers then escorted Elstad to the back of the patrol car. As they were about to leave for the Polk County Sheriff's office, Elstad's father arrived home and came to the rear of the patrol car. The officers advised him that his son was a suspect in the burglary. Officer Burke testified that Mr. Elstad became quite agitated, opened the rear door of the car and admonished his son: "I told you that you were going to get into trouble. You wouldn't listen to me. You never learn."

Elstad was transported to the Sheriff's headquarters and approximately one hour later, Officers Burke and McAllister joined him in McAllister's office. McAllister then advised respondent for the first time of his *Miranda* rights, reading from a standard card. Respondent indicated he understood his rights, and, having these rights in mind, wished to speak with the officers. Elstad gave a full statement, explaining that he had known that the Gross family was out of town and had been paid to lead several acquaintances to the Gross residence and show them how to gain entry through a defective sliding glass door. The statement was typed, reviewed by respondent, read back to him for correction, initialed and signed by Elstad and both officers. As an afterthought, Elstad added and initialed the sentence, "After leaving the house Robby & I went back to [the] van & Robby handed me a small bag of grass." Respondent concedes that the officers made no threats or promises either at his residence or at the Sheriff's office.

Respondent was charged with first-degree burglary. He was represented at trial by retained counsel. Elstad waived his right to a jury, and his case was tried by a Circuit Court Judge. Respondent moved at once to suppress his oral statement and signed confession. He contended that the statement he made in response to questioning at his house "let the cat out of the bag," citing *United States v. Bayer* (1947), and tainted the subsequent confession as "fruit of the poisonous tree," citing *Wong Sun v. United States* (1963). The judge ruled that the statement, "I was there," had to be excluded because the defendant had not been advised of his *Miranda* rights. The written confession taken after Elstad's arrival at the Sheriff's office, however, was admitted in evidence. The court found:

"[H]is written statement was given freely, voluntarily and knowingly by the defendant after he had waived his right to remain silent and have counsel present which waiver was evidenced by the card which the defendant had signed. [It] was not tainted in any way by the previous brief statement between the defendant and the Sheriff's Deputies that had arrested him."

Elstad was found guilty of burglary in the first degree. He received a 5-year sentence and was ordered to pay $18,000 in restitution.

Following his conviction, respondent appealed to the Oregon Court of Appeals, relying on *Wong Sun* and *Bayer*. The State conceded that Elstad had been in custody when he made his statement, "I was there," and accordingly agreed that this statement was inadmissible as having been given without the prescribed Miranda warnings. But the State maintained that any conceivable "taint" had been dissipated prior to the respondent's written confession by McAllister's careful administration of the requisite warnings. The Court of Appeals reversed respondent's conviction, identifying the crucial constitutional inquiry as "whether there was a sufficient break in the stream of events between [the] inadmissible statement and the written confession to insulate the latter statement from the effect of what went before." The Oregon court concluded:

> Regardless of the absence of actual compulsion, the coercive impact of the unconstitutionally obtained statement remains, because in a defendant's mind it has sealed his fate. It is this impact that must be dissipated in order to make a subsequent confession admissible. In determining whether it has been dissipated, lapse of time, and change of place from the original surroundings are the most important considerations.

Because of the brief period separating the two incidents, the "cat was sufficiently out of the bag to exert a coercive impact on [respondent's] later admissions."

The State of Oregon petitioned the Oregon Supreme Court for review, and review was declined. This Court granted certiorari to consider the question whether the Self-Incrimination Clause of the Fifth Amendment requires the suppression of a confession, made after proper *Miranda* warnings and a valid waiver of rights, solely because the police had obtained an earlier voluntary but unwarned admission from the defendant.

II

The arguments advanced in favor of suppression of respondent's written confession rely heavily on metaphor. One metaphor, familiar from the Fourth Amendment context, would require that respondent's confession, regardless of its integrity, voluntariness, and probative value, be suppressed as the "tainted fruit of the poisonous tree" of the *Miranda* violation. A second metaphor questions whether a confession can be truly voluntary once the "cat is out of the bag." Taken out of context, each of these metaphors can be misleading. They should not be used to obscure fundamental differences between the role of the Fourth Amendment exclusionary rule and the function of *Miranda* in guarding against the prosecutorial use of compelled statements as prohibited by the Fifth Amendment. The Oregon court assumed and respondent here contends that a failure to administer *Miranda* warnings necessarily breeds the same consequences as police infringement of a constitutional right, so that evidence uncovered following an unwarned statement must be suppressed as "fruit of the poisonous tree." We believe this view misconstrues the nature of the protections afforded by *Miranda* warnings and therefore misreads the consequences of police failure to supply them.

A

• • •

Respondent's contention that his confession was tainted by the earlier failure of the police to provide *Miranda* warnings and must be excluded as "fruit of the poisonous tree" assumes the existence of a constitutional violation. This figure of speech is drawn from *Wong Sun*, in which the Court held that evidence and witnesses discovered as a result of a search in violation of the Fourth Amendment must be excluded from evidence. The *Wong Sun* doctrine applies as well when the fruit of the Fourth Amendment violation is a confession. It is settled law that "a confession obtained through custodial interrogation after an illegal arrest should be excluded unless intervening events break the causal connection between the illegal arrest and the confession so that the confession is 'sufficiently an act of free will to purge the primary taint.'"

But as we explained in *Quarles* and *Tucker*, a procedural *Miranda* violation differs in significant respects from violations of the Fourth Amendment, which have traditionally mandated a broad application of the "fruits" doctrine. The purpose of the Fourth Amendment exclusionary rule is to deter unreasonable searches, no matter how probative their fruits. Where a Fourth Amendment violation "taints" the confession, a finding of voluntariness for the purposes of the Fifth Amendment is merely a threshold requirement in determining whether the confession may be admitted in evidence. Beyond this, the prosecution must show a sufficient break in events to undermine the inference that the confession was caused by the Fourth Amendment violation.

The *Miranda* exclusionary rule, however, serves the Fifth Amendment and sweeps more broadly than the Fifth Amendment itself. It may be triggered even in the absence of a Fifth Amendment violation. The Fifth Amendment prohibits use by the prosecution in its case in chief only of compelled testimony. Failure to administer *Miranda* warnings creates a presumption of compulsion. Consequently, unwarned statements that are otherwise voluntary within the meaning of the Fifth Amendment must nevertheless be excluded from evidence under *Miranda*. Thus, in the individual case, *Miranda*'s preventive medicine provides a remedy even to the defendant who has suffered no identifiable constitutional harm.

But the *Miranda* presumption, though irrebuttable for purposes of the prosecution's case in chief, does not require that the statements and their fruits be discarded as inherently tainted. Despite the fact that patently voluntary statements taken in violation of *Miranda* must be excluded from the prosecution's case, the presumption of coercion does not bar their use for impeachment purposes on cross-examination. *Harris v. New York* (1971). The Court in *Harris* rejected as an "extravagant extension of the Constitution," the theory that a defendant who had confessed under circumstances that made the confession inadmissible, could thereby enjoy the freedom to "deny every fact disclosed or discovered as a 'fruit' of his confession, free from confrontation with his prior statements" and that the voluntariness of his confession would be totally irrelevant. Where an unwarned statement is preserved for use in situations that fall outside the sweep of the *Miranda* presumption, "the primary criterion of admissibility [remains] the 'old' due process voluntariness test."

In *Michigan v. Tucker, supra*, the Court was asked to extend the *Wong Sun* fruits doctrine to suppress the testimony of a witness for the prosecution whose identity was discovered as the result of a statement taken from the accused without benefit of full *Miranda* warnings. As in respondent's case, the breach of the *Miranda* procedures in *Tucker* involved no actual compulsion. The Court concluded that the unwarned questioning "did not abridge respondent's constitutional privilege . . . but departed only from the prophylactic standards later laid down by this Court in *Miranda* to safeguard that privilege." Since there was no actual infringement of the suspect's constitutional rights, the case was not controlled by the doctrine expressed in that fruits of a constitutional violation must be suppressed. In deciding "how sweeping the judicially imposed consequences" of a failure to administer *Miranda* warnings should be, the *Tucker* Court noted that neither the general goal of deterring improper police conduct nor the Fifth Amendment goal of assuring trustworthy evidence would be served by suppression of the witness' testimony. The unwarned confession must, of course, be suppressed, but the Court ruled that introduction of the third-party witness' testimony did not violate Tucker's Fifth Amendment rights.

We believe that this reasoning applies with equal force when the alleged "fruit" of a noncoercive *Miranda* violation is neither a witness nor an article of evidence but the accused's own voluntary testimony. As in *Tucker*, the absence of any coercion or improper tactics undercuts the twin rationales—trustworthiness and deterrence—for a broader rule. Once warned, the suspect is free to exercise his own volition in deciding whether or not to make a statement to the authorities. The Court has often noted: "'[A] living witness is not to be mechanically equated with the proffer of inanimate evidentiary objects illegally seized. . . . [T]he living witness is an individual human personality whose attributes of will, perception, memory and volition interact to determine what testimony he will give.'"

Because *Miranda* warnings may inhibit persons from giving information, this Court has determined that they need be administered only after the person is taken into "custody" or his freedom has otherwise been significantly restrained. Unfortunately, the task of defining "custody" is a slippery one, and "policemen investigating serious crimes [cannot realistically be expected to] make no errors whatsoever." If errors are made by law enforcement officers in administering the prophylactic *Miranda* procedures, they should not breed the same irremediable consequences as police infringement of the Fifth Amendment itself. It is an unwarranted extension of *Miranda* to hold that a simple failure to administer the warnings, unaccompanied by any actual coercion or other circumstances calculated to undermine the suspect's ability to exercise his free will, so taints the investigatory process that a subsequent voluntary and informed waiver is ineffective for some indeterminate period. Though *Miranda* requires that the unwarned admission must be suppressed, the admissibility of any subsequent statement should turn in these circumstances solely on whether it is knowingly and voluntarily made.

B

The Oregon court, however, believed that the unwarned remark compromised the voluntariness of respondent's later confession. It was the court's view that the prior answer and not the unwarned questioning impaired respondent's ability to give a valid waiver and that only lapse of time and change of place could dissipate what it termed the "coercive impact" of the inadmissible statement. When a prior statement is actually coerced, the time that passes between confessions, the change in place of interrogations, and the change in identity of the interrogators all bear on whether that coercion has carried over into the second confession. The failure of police to administer *Miranda* warnings does not mean that the statements received have actually been coerced, but only that courts will presume the privilege against compulsory self-incrimination has not been intelligently exercised. Of the courts that have considered whether a properly warned confession must be suppressed because it was preceded by an unwarned but clearly voluntary admission, the majority have explicitly or implicitly recognized that *Westover*'s requirement of a break in the stream of events is inapposite. In these circumstances, a careful and thorough administration of *Miranda* warnings serves to cure the condition that rendered the unwarned statement inadmissible. The warning conveys the relevant information and thereafter the suspect's choice whether to exercise his privilege to remain silent should ordinarily be viewed as an "act of free will."

The Oregon court nevertheless identified a subtle form of lingering compulsion, the psychological impact of the suspect's conviction that he has let the cat out of the bag and, in so doing, has sealed his own fate. But endowing the psychological effects of voluntary unwarned admissions with constitutional implications would, practically speaking, disable the police from obtaining the suspect's informed cooperation even when the official coercion proscribed by the Fifth Amendment played no part in either his warned or unwarned confessions. As the Court remarked in *Bayer*:

> [A]fter an accused has once let the cat out of the bag by confessing, no matter what the inducement, he is never thereafter free of the psychological and practical disadvantages of having confessed. He can never get the cat back in the bag. The secret is out for good. In such a sense, a later confession may always be looked upon as fruit of the first. But this Court has never gone so far as to hold that making a confession under circumstances which preclude its use, perpetually disables the confessor from making a usable one after those conditions have been removed.

Even in such extreme cases as *Lyons v. Oklahoma* (1944), in which police forced a full confession from the accused through unconscionable methods of interrogation, the Court has assumed that the coercive effect of the confession could, with time, be dissipated.

This Court has never held that the psychological impact of voluntary disclosure of a guilty secret qualifies as state compulsion or compromises the voluntariness of a subsequent informed waiver. The Oregon court, by adopting this expansive view of Fifth Amendment compulsion, effectively immunizes a suspect who responds to pre-*Miranda* warning questions from the consequences of his subsequent informed waiver of the privilege of remaining silent. This immunity comes at a high cost to legitimate law enforcement activity, while adding little desirable protection to the individual's interest in not being compelled to testify against himself. When neither the initial nor the subsequent admission is coerced, little justification exists for permitting the highly probative evidence of a voluntary confession to be irretrievably lost to the factfinder.

There is a vast difference between the direct consequences flowing from coercion of a confession by physical violence or other deliberate means calculated to break the suspect's will and the uncertain consequences of disclosure of a "guilty secret" freely given in response to an unwarned but noncoercive question, as in this case. Justice Brennan's contention that it is impossible to perceive any causal distinction between this case and one involving a confession that is coerced by torture is wholly unpersuasive. Certainly, in respondent's case, the causal connection between any psychological disadvantage created by his admission and his ultimate decision to cooperate is speculative and attenuated best. It is difficult to tell with certainty what motivates a suspect to speak. A suspect's confession may be traced to factors as disparate as "a prearrest event such as a visit with a minister" or an intervening event such as the exchange of words respondent had with his father. We must conclude that, absent deliberately coercive or improper tactics in obtaining the initial statement, the mere fact that a suspect has made an unwarned admission does not warrant a presumption of compulsion. A subsequent administration of *Miranda* warnings to a suspect who has given a voluntary but unwarned statement ordinarily should suffice to remove the conditions that precluded admission of the earlier statement. In such circumstances, the finder of fact may reasonably conclude that the suspect made a rational and intelligent choice whether to waive or invoke his rights.

III

Though belated, the reading of respondent's rights was undeniably complete. McAllister testified that he read the *Miranda* warnings aloud from a printed card and recorded Elstad's responses. There is no question that respondent knowingly and voluntarily waived his right to remain silent before he described his participation in the burglary. It is also beyond dispute that respondent's earlier remark was voluntary, within the meaning of the Fifth Amendment. Neither the environment nor the manner of either "interrogation" was coercive. The initial conversation took place at midday, in the living room area of respondent's own home, with his mother in the kitchen area, a few steps away. Although in retrospect the officers testified that respondent was then in custody, at the time he made his statement he had not been informed that he was under arrest. The arresting officers' testimony indicates that the brief stop in the living room before proceeding to the station house was not to interrogate the suspect but to notify his mother of the reason for his arrest.

The State has conceded the issue of custody and thus we must assume that Burke breached *Miranda* procedures in failing to administer *Miranda* warnings before initiating the discussion in the living room. This breach may have been the result of confusion as to whether the brief exchange qualified as "custodial interrogation" or it may simply have reflected Burke's reluctance to initiate an alarming police procedure before McAllister had spoken with respondent's mother. Whatever the reason for Burke's oversight, the incident had none of the earmarks of coercion. Nor did the officers exploit the unwarned admission to pressure respondent into waiving his right to remain silent.

Respondent, however, has argued that he was unable to give a fully informed waiver of his rights because he was unaware that his prior statement could not be used against him. Respondent suggests that Officer McAllister, to cure this deficiency, should have added an additional warning to those given him at the Sheriff's office. Such a requirement is neither practicable nor constitutionally necessary. In many cases, a breach of *Miranda* procedures may not be identified as such until long after full *Miranda* warnings are administered and a valid confession obtained. The standard *Miranda* warnings explicitly inform the suspect of his right to consult a lawyer before speaking. Police officers are ill-equipped to pinch-hit for counsel, construing the murky and difficult questions of when "custody" begins or whether a given unwarned statement will ultimately be held admissible.

This Court has never embraced the theory that a defendant's ignorance of the full consequences of his decisions vitiates their voluntariness. If the prosecution has actually violated the defendant's Fifth Amendment rights by introducing an inadmissible confession at trial, compelling the defendant to testify in rebuttal, the rule announced in *Harrison* precludes use of that testimony on retrial. "Having 'released the spring' by using the petitioner's unlawfully obtained confessions against him, the Government must show that its illegal action did not induce his testimony." But the Court has refused to find that a defendant who confesses, after being falsely told that his codefendant has turned State's evidence, does so involuntarily. The Court has also rejected the argument that a defendant's ignorance that a prior coerced confession could not be admitted in evidence compromised the voluntariness of his guilty plea. Likewise, in *California v. Beheler, supra*, the Court declined to accept defendant's contention that, because he was unaware of the potential adverse consequences of statements he made to the police, his participation in the interview was involuntary. Thus we have not held that the sine qua non for a knowing and voluntary waiver of the right to remain silent is a full and complete appreciation of all of the consequences flowing from the nature and the quality of the evidence in the case.

IV

When police ask questions of a suspect in custody without administering the required warnings, *Miranda* dictates that the answers received be presumed compelled and that they be excluded from evidence at trial in the State's case in chief. The Court has carefully adhered to this principle, permitting a narrow exception only where pressing public safety concerns demanded. The Court today in no way retreats from the bright-line rule of *Miranda*. We do not imply that good faith excuses a failure to administer *Miranda* warnings; nor do we condone inherently coercive police tactics or methods offensive to due process that render the initial admission involuntary and undermine the suspect's will to invoke his rights once they are read to him. A handful of courts have, however, applied our precedents relating to confessions obtained under coercive circumstances to situations involving wholly voluntary admissions, requiring a passage of time or break in events before a second, fully warned statement can be deemed voluntary. Far from establishing a rigid rule, we direct courts to avoid one; there is no warrant for presuming coercive effect where the suspect's initial inculpatory statement, though technically in violation of *Miranda*, was voluntary. The relevant inquiry is whether, in fact, the second statement was also voluntarily made. As in any such inquiry, the finder of fact must examine the surrounding circumstances and the entire course of police conduct with respect to the suspect in evaluating the voluntariness of his statements. The fact that a suspect chooses to speak after being informed of his rights is, of course, highly probative. We find that the dictates of *Miranda* and the goals of the Fifth Amendment proscription against use of compelled testimony are fully satisfied in the circumstances of this case by barring use of the unwarned statement in the case in chief. No further purpose is served by imputing "taint" to subsequent statements obtained pursuant to a voluntary and knowing waiver. We hold today that a suspect who has once responded to unwarned yet uncoercive questioning is not thereby disabled from waiving his rights and confessing after he has been given the requisite *Miranda* warnings.

The judgment of the Court of Appeals of Oregon is reversed, and the case is remanded for further proceedings not inconsistent with this opinion.

[Justices Brennan, Marshall, and Stevens dissented.]

NOTES AND QUESTIONS

1. The selection of every fact for inclusion in an opinion is purposeful. And the Court here mentions some very random details about 18-year old defendant Michael Elstad that must be meant to affect our view of him. He was found by the police in his room "clad in shorts and listening to his stereo." Was he a slacker? He added a gratuitous note to his written statement that he acquired a "bag of grass" in connection with the burglary. A pothead? His dad yelled at the defendant as he was being escorted away, "I told you that you were going to get into trouble. You wouldn't listen to me. You never learn." A bad kid? Or maybe a rough home situation? He was represented at trial by "retained counsel." A rich kid?

Or was the detail about the "bag of grass" added to show the cathartic purification of the soul that attends confessions?

Would it be too much to expect the 18-year old son of a man who yells at his kid in front of police officers to invoke his right of silence when given *Miranda* warnings?

2. The State conceded that the questioning at the Elstads' home was custodial. Should it have? Did the officer's statement that "I feel you were involved" render it custodial? But the Court finds nonetheless that the initial interrogation was not "coercive." However the interrogation is described colloquially, isn't one of the points of *Miranda* that custodial interrogation is "inherently coercive"?

3. The Court uncritically accepts the officers' explanation for the purpose of their visit to the Elstads' home: that they had not stopped by to interrogate the defendant at all but rather to notify his mother of the reason for the arrest. Is this believable? And how could "retained counsel" have allowed that testimony to stand unquestioned? (Of course, it's possible the officers were superbly cross-examined and simply lied at the suppression hearing.)

If the officers were telling the truth, why did both officers approach Michael in his room *before* notifying his mother of the reason for their visit? (And why on earth would the mother let them in and show them to her son's room?) And why did the officers immediately separate the defendant from his mother once he came down the stairs? Note that all the police manuals encourage so-called incommunicado interrogation whereby the suspect is isolated and cannot receive support or advice from family members or counsel.

4. Is the brevity of the questioning of Michael in the house relevant, as the Court seems to find? Was it brief only because it was immediately successful, and Michael "let the cat out of the bag" without much resistance? Did the interrogation need to go much further once the defendant admitted — or as the Court has it, made a "remark" — that he "was there" and a longer, warned interrogation was in the offing?

5. Will police after *Elstad* be incentivized to use the successive-interrogation ploy in future cases? The dissent offers a litany of case law and police interrogation manuals demonstrating the widespread nature of the successive-interrogation ploy and multiple variations on the theme.

6. Do you agree with the Court that any "psychological impact" of defendant's admission at his home ("I was there") had on his subsequent waiver of his rights at the police station was "speculative and attenuated"? Would a reasonable person in Michael's position have believed he had "let the cat out of the bag" by saying "I was there"? Would you?

In 1998 Professor Charles Weisselberg wrote an article based on police training materials received through discovery in civil litigation against California police departments alleging systemic *Miranda* violations. Charles D. Weisselberg, *Saving* Miranda, 84 Cornell L. Rev. 109 (1998). The materials showed that officers were encouraged to ignore a person's *Miranda* rights when necessary to serve law enforcement goals such as developing impeachment material (should the person testify), obtaining physical evidence, locating a crime scene, and identifying other accomplices and witnesses. *Id.* at 134. One training bulletin advised that officers had "little to lose and perhaps something to gain" by questioning "outside *Miranda*." *Id.* at 133.

It turns out that police agencies and the lawyers that advise them pay attention to Supreme Court opinions on police tactics. The successive-interrogation technique validated by the Court in *Elstad* was not ignored in police training manuals, as the next case makes clear.

Missouri v. Seibert

542 U.S. 600 (2004)

Justice Souter announced the judgment of the Court and delivered an opinion in which Justice Stevens, Justice Ginsburg, and Justice Breyer join.

This case tests a police protocol for custodial interrogation that calls for giving no warnings of the rights to silence and counsel until interrogation has produced a confession. Although such a statement is generally inadmissible, since taken in violation of *Miranda*, the interrogating officer follows it with *Miranda* warnings and then leads the suspect to cover the same ground a second time. The question here is the admissibility of the repeated statement. Because this midstream recitation of warnings after interrogation and unwarned confession could not effectively comply with *Miranda*'s constitutional requirement, we hold that a statement repeated after a warning in such circumstances is inadmissible.

I

Respondent Patrice Seibert's 12-year-old son Jonathan had cerebral palsy, and when he died in his sleep she feared charges of neglect because of bedsores on his body. In her presence, two of her teenage sons and two of their friends devised a plan to conceal the facts surrounding Jonathan's death by incinerating his body in the course of burning the family's mobile home, in which they planned to leave Donald Rector, a mentally ill teenager living with the family, to avoid any appearance that Jonathan had been unattended. Seibert's son Darian and a friend set the fire, and Donald died.

Five days later, the police awakened Seibert at 3 a.m. at a hospital where Darian was being treated for burns. In arresting her, Officer Kevin Clinton followed instructions from Rolla, Missouri, Officer Richard Hanrahan that he refrain from giving *Miranda* warnings. After Seibert had been taken to the police station and left alone in an interview room for 15 to 20 minutes, Officer Hanrahan questioned her without *Miranda* warnings for 30 to 40 minutes, squeezing her arm and repeating "Donald was also to die in his sleep." After Seibert finally admitted she knew Donald was meant to die in the fire, she was given a 20-minute coffee and cigarette break. Officer Hanrahan then turned on a tape recorder, gave Seibert the *Miranda* warnings, and obtained a signed waiver of rights from her. He resumed the questioning with "Ok, 'Trice, we've been talking for a little while about what happened on Wednesday the twelfth, haven't we?" and confronted her with her prewarning statements:

Hanrahan: "Now, in discussion you told us, you told us that there was a[n] understanding about Donald."
Seibert: "Yes."
Hanrahan: "Did that take place earlier that morning?"
Seibert: "Yes."
Hanrahan: "And what was the understanding about Donald?"
Seibert: "If they could get him out of the trailer, to take him out of the trailer."
Hanrahan: "And if they couldn't?"
Seibert: "I, I never even thought about it. I just figured they would."
Hanrahan: "'Trice, didn't you tell me that he was supposed to die in his sleep?"
Seibert: "If that would happen, 'cause he was on that new medicine, you know. . . ."
Hanrahan: "The Prozac? And it makes him sleepy. So he was supposed to die in his sleep?"
Seibert: "Yes."

After being charged with first-degree murder for her role in Donald's death, Seibert sought to exclude both her prewarning and postwarning statements. At the suppression hearing, Officer Hanrahan testified that he made a "conscious decision" to withhold *Miranda* warnings, thus resorting to an interrogation technique he had been taught: question first, then give the warnings, and then repeat the question "until I get the answer that she's already provided once. He acknowledged that Seibert's ultimate statement was "largely a repeat of information . . . obtained" prior to the warning.

The trial court suppressed the prewarning statement but admitted the responses given after the *Miranda* recitation. A jury convicted Seibert of second-degree murder. On appeal, the Missouri Court of Appeals affirmed, treating this case as indistinguishable from *Oregon v. Elstad*.

The Supreme Court of Missouri reversed, holding that "[i]n the circumstances here, where the interrogation was nearly continuous, . . . the second statement, clearly the product of the invalid first statement, should have been suppressed." The court distinguished *Elstad* on the ground that warnings had not intentionally been withheld there, and reasoned that "Officer Hanrahan's intentional omission of a *Miranda* warning was intended to deprive Seibert of the opportunity knowingly and intelligently to waive her *Miranda* rights." Since there were "no circumstances that would seem to dispel the effect of the *Miranda* violation," the court held that the postwarning confession was involuntary and therefore inadmissible. To allow the police to achieve an "end run" around *Miranda*, the court explained, would encourage *Miranda* violations and diminish *Miranda*'s role in protecting the privilege against self-incrimination. Three judges dissented, taking the view that Elstad applied even though the police intentionally withheld *Miranda* warnings before the initial statement, and believing that "Seibert's unwarned responses to Officer Hanrahan's questioning did not prevent her from waiving her rights and confessing."

We granted certiorari to resolve a split in the Courts of Appeals. We now affirm.

II

• • •

III

There are those, of course, who preferred the old way of doing things, giving no warnings and litigating the voluntariness of any statement in nearly every instance. In the aftermath of *Miranda*, Congress even passed a statute seeking to restore that old regime, 18 U.S.C. § 3501, although the Act lay dormant for years until finally invoked and challenged in *Dickerson. Dickerson* reaffirmed *Miranda* and held that its constitutional character prevailed against the statute.

The technique of interrogating in successive, unwarned and warned phases raises a new challenge to *Miranda*. Although we have no statistics on the frequency of this practice, it is not confined to Rolla, Missouri. An officer of that police department testified that the strategy of withholding *Miranda* warnings until after interrogating and drawing out a confession was promoted not only by his own department, but by a national police training organization and other departments in which he had worked. Consistently with the officer's testimony, the Police Law Institute, for example, instructs that "officers may conduct a two-stage interrogation. . . . At any point during the pre-*Miranda* interrogation, usually after arrestees have confessed, officers may then read the *Miranda* warnings and ask for a waiver. If the arrestees waive their *Miranda* rights, officers will be able to repeat any subsequent incriminating statements later in court." The upshot of all this advice is a question-first practice of some popularity, as one can see from the reported cases describing its use, sometimes in obedience to departmental policy.

IV

When a confession so obtained is offered and challenged, attention must be paid to the conflicting objects of *Miranda* and question-first. *Miranda* addressed "interrogation practices . . . likely . . . to disable [an individual] from making a free and rational choice" about speaking, and held that a suspect must be "adequately and effectively" advised of the choice the Constitution guarantees." The object of question-first is to render *Miranda* warnings ineffective by waiting for a particularly opportune time to give them, after the suspect has already confessed.

Just as "no talismanic incantation [is] required to satisfy [*Miranda*'s] strictures," it would be absurd to think that mere recitation of the litany suffices to satisfy *Miranda* in every conceivable circumstance. "The inquiry is simply whether the warnings reasonably 'conve[y] to [a suspect] his rights as required by *Miranda*.'" The threshold issue when interrogators question first and warn later is thus whether it would be reasonable to find that in these circumstances the warnings could function "effectively" as *Miranda* requires. Could the warnings effectively advise the suspect that he had a real choice about giving an admissible statement at that juncture? Could they reasonably convey that he could choose to stop talking even if he had talked earlier? For unless the warnings could place a suspect who has just been interrogated in a position to make such an informed choice, there is no practical justification for accepting the formal warnings as compliance with *Miranda*, or for treating the second stage of interrogation as distinct from the first, unwarned and inadmissible segment.

There is no doubt about the answer that proponents of question-first give to this question about the effectiveness of warnings given only after successful interrogation, and we think their answer is correct. By any objective measure, applied to circumstances exemplified here, it is likely that if the interrogators employ the technique of withholding warnings until after interrogation succeeds in eliciting a confession, the warnings will be ineffective in preparing the suspect for successive interrogation, close in time and similar in content. After all, the reason that question-first is catching on is as obvious as its manifest purpose, which is to get a confession the suspect would not make if he understood his rights at the outset; the sensible underlying assumption is that with one confession in hand before the warnings, the interrogator can count on getting its duplicate, with trifling additional trouble. Upon hearing warnings only in the aftermath of interrogation and just after making a confession, a suspect would hardly think he had a genuine right to remain silent, let alone persist in so believing once the police began to lead him over the same ground again. A more likely reaction on a suspect's part would be perplexity about the reason for discussing rights at that point, bewilderment being an unpromising frame of mind for knowledgeable decision. What is worse, telling a suspect that "anything you say can and will be used against you," without expressly excepting the statement just given, could lead to an entirely reasonable inference that what he has just said will be used, with subsequent silence being of no avail. Thus, when *Miranda* warnings are inserted in the midst of coordinated and continuing interrogation, they are likely to mislead and "depriv[e] a defendant of knowledge essential to his ability to understand the nature of his rights and the consequences of abandoning them." By the same token, it would ordinarily be unrealistic to treat two spates of integrated and proximately conducted questioning as independent interrogations subject to independent evaluation simply because *Miranda* warnings formally punctuate them in the middle.

V

Missouri argues that a confession repeated at the end of an interrogation sequence envisioned in a question-first strategy is admissible on the authority of *Oregon v. Elstad*, but the argument disfigures that case. In *Elstad*, the police went to the young suspect's house to take him into custody on a charge of burglary. Before the arrest, one officer spoke with the suspect's mother, while the other one joined the suspect in a "brief stop in the living room," where the officer said he "felt" the young man was involved in a burglary. The suspect acknowledged he had been at the scene. This Court noted that the pause in the living room "was not to interrogate the suspect but to notify his mother of the reason for his arrest," and described the incident as having "none of the earmarks of coercion." The Court, indeed, took care to mention that the officer's initial failure to warn was an "oversight" that "may have been the result of confusion as to whether the brief exchange qualified as 'custodial interrogation' or . . . may simply have reflected . . . reluctance to initiate an alarming police procedure before [an officer] had spoken with respondent's mother." At the outset of a later and systematic station house interrogation going well beyond the scope of the laconic prior admission, the suspect was given *Miranda* warnings and made a full confession. In holding the second statement admissible and voluntary, *Elstad* rejected the "cat out of the bag" theory that any short, earlier admission, obtained in arguably innocent neglect of *Miranda*, determined the character of the later, warned confession, *Elstad*; on the facts of that case, the Court thought any causal connection between the first and second responses to the police was "speculative and attenuated." Although the *Elstad* Court expressed no explicit conclusion about either officer's state of mind, it is fair to read *Elstad* as treating the living room conversation as a good-faith *Miranda* mistake, not only open to correction by careful warnings before systematic questioning in that particular case, but posing no threat to warn-first practice generally.

The contrast between *Elstad* and this case reveals a series of relevant facts that bear on whether *Miranda* warnings delivered midstream could be effective enough to accomplish their object: the completeness and detail of the questions and answers in the first round of interrogation, the overlapping content of the two statements, the timing and setting of the first and the second, the continuity of police personnel, and the degree to which the interrogator's questions treated the second round as continuous with the first. In *Elstad*, it was not unreasonable to see the occasion for questioning at the station house as presenting a markedly different experience from the short conversation at home; since a reasonable person in the suspect's shoes could have seen the station house questioning as a new and distinct experience, the *Miranda* warnings could have made sense as presenting a genuine choice whether to follow up on the earlier admission.

At the opposite extreme are the facts here, which by any objective measure reveal a police strategy adapted to undermine the *Miranda* warnings. The unwarned interrogation was conducted in the station house, and the questioning was systematic, exhaustive, and managed with psychological skill. When the police were finished there was little, if anything, of incriminating potential left unsaid. The warned phase of questioning proceeded after a pause of only 15 to 20 minutes, in the same place as the unwarned segment. When the same officer who had conducted the first phase recited the *Miranda* warnings, he said nothing to counter the probable misimpression that the advice that anything Seibert said could be used against her also applied to the details of the inculpatory statement previously elicited. In particular, the police did not advise that her prior statement could not be used. Nothing was said or done to dispel the oddity of warning about legal rights to silence and counsel right after the police had led her through a systematic interrogation, and any uncertainty on her part about a right to stop talking about matters previously discussed would only have been aggravated by the way Officer Hanrahan set the scene by saying "we've been talking for a little while about what happened on Wednesday the twelfth, haven't we?" The impression that the further questioning was a mere continuation of the earlier questions and responses was fostered by references back to the confession already given. It would have been reasonable to regard the two sessions as parts of a continuum, in which it would have been unnatural to refuse to repeat at the second stage what had been said before. These circumstances must be seen as challenging the comprehensibility and efficacy of the *Miranda* warnings to the point that a reasonable person in the suspect's shoes would not have understood them to convey a message that she retained a choice about continuing to talk.

VI

Strategists dedicated to draining the substance out of *Miranda* cannot accomplish by training instructions what *Dickerson* held Congress could not do by statute. Because the question-first tactic effectively threatens to thwart *Miranda*'s purpose of reducing the risk that a coerced confession would be admitted, and because the facts here do not reasonably support a conclusion that the warnings given could have served their purpose, Seibert's postwarning statements are inadmissible. The judgment of the Supreme Court of Missouri is affirmed.

NOTES AND QUESTIONS

1. Officer Hanrahan is to be commended for his truthful testimony at the suppression hearing. He not only admitted to being trained to use the successive-interrogation technique but acknowledged that its purpose was to get a suspect to essentially ratify a previously unwarned confession. Would the case have come out differently if he had not been so forthcoming?

2. The Court finds that the successive-interrogation technique at issue here is "by any objective measure . . . a police strategy adapted to undermine the *Miranda* warnings," and in fact it rendered the *Miranda* warnings given before the second interrogation ineffective. But the Court ties its holding to the specific facts of Hanrahan's interrogations and not to his admission of its purpose.

Do you see any room for creative successive-interrogation proponents to get around *Seibert*? What if the suspect was questioned the second time after a much longer interval? By a different officer? In a different place? What if the second interrogation covered new subjects?

3. Justice Breyer in a concurring opinion grounds his vote in the fruits-of-the-poisonous-tree doctrine, which was rejected by the Court in a footnote in reliance on the precedent of *Elstad*, rather than the sufficiency of the *Miranda* warnings. Which approach is preferable?

4. The Court otherwise distinguishes *Elstad*, as "it is fair to read *Elstad* as treating the living room 'conversation' as a good faith *Miranda* mistake." That certainly is a fair reading of *Elstad*. But the Court then identifies a laundry list of factual differences between *Elstad* and *Seibert*. Do you see any of these differences as being material to whether the *Miranda* warnings before the second interrogation would have "made sense," as the Court puts it?

5. What if before the second interrogation the suspect was advised, in addition to receiving the *Miranda* warnings, that nothing she had said up until now could be "used against her"? Would this suffice to make the *Miranda* warnings effective?

6. The vigorous dissent by Justice O'Connor, who wrote for the Court in *Elstad*, criticizes Justice Kennedy's concurring opinion for injecting the interrogating officer's "state of mind" into the analysis, as it adds a third step of analysis into every "two stage interrogation case." Are the four dissenters suggesting that "two stage interrogation cases" are here to stay notwithstanding *Seibert*?

G. THE DURABILITY OF *MIRANDA*

As noted above, there was speculation about *Miranda*'s staying power from its inception. Just two years after the decision Congress passed a statute, 18 U.S.C. § 3501, purporting to overrule *Miranda* in federal cases and replace it with a "voluntariness" test. That test included among a list of factors to be considered whether the suspect had received the equivalent of the warnings that *Miranda* had required. Although the Supreme Court once referred to § 3501 as "the statute governing the admissibility of confessions in federal prosecutions," *United States v. Alvarez-Sanchez*, 511 U.S. 350, 351 (1994), the Court for over 30 years never considered whether the statute overruled *Miranda*. *Davis v. United States*, 512 U.S. 452, 457 n.* (1994). Several lower courts have found that § 3501, rather than *Miranda*, governs the admissibility of confessions in federal courts. *See United States v. Crocker*, 510 F.2d 1129, 1137 (10th Cir. 1975); *United States v. Rivas-Lopez*, 988 F. Supp. 1424, 1430-36 (D. Utah 1997).

Remarkably the Department of Justice—including under the "tough on crime" Republican administrations of Nixon, Reagan, and Bush and the "tough on crime" Democratic administration of Clinton—never pressed the point in court. Justice Scalia publicly complained about the department's refusal to invoke § 3501 in 1994. *See Davis*, 512 U.S. at 453-54 (Scalia, J., concurring) (noting that "the provision has been studiously avoided by every Administration . . . since its enactment more than 25 years ago"). He also stated that the department's passivity had "caused the federal judiciary to confront a host of '*Miranda*' issues that might be entirely irrelevant under federal law," and "may have produced—during an era of intense national concern about the problem of run-away crime—the acquittal and the nonprosecution of many dangerous felons." *Id.* at 457. In fact, after initially declining to take a position on the applicability of § 3501, the Clinton Administration eventually asserted that it believed the statute to be unconstitutional. Letter from Janet Reno, Attorney General, to Congress (Sept. 10, 1997).

Charles Thomas Dickerson was arrested in 1997 and charged with bank robbery. Dickerson had incriminated himself to the FBI, but there was a factual dispute over whether he had been given proper *Miranda* warnings. At an evidentiary hearing the trial judge found that the testifying FBI agent lacked credibility and suppressed the confession. *Dickerson v. United States*, 971 F. Supp. 1023 (E.D. Va. 1997). The government appealed to the Fourth Circuit, which sua sponte held that 18 U.S.C. § 3501 was applicable because *Miranda* was not a constitutional holding and, since the confession was voluntary, reversed the district court's suppression ruling. *Dickerson v. United States*, 166 F.3d 667 (4th Cir. 1999).

The Supreme Court granted certiorari.

Dickerson v. United States

530 U.S. 428 (2000)

Chief Justice Rehnquist delivered the opinion of the Court.

In *Miranda* we held that certain warnings must be given before a suspect's statement made during custodial interrogation could be admitted in evidence. In the wake of that decision, Congress enacted 18 U.S.C. § 3501, which in essence laid down a rule that the admissibility of such statements should turn only on whether or not they were voluntarily made. We hold that *Miranda*, being a constitutional decision of this Court, may not be in effect overruled by an Act of Congress, and we decline to overrule *Miranda* ourselves. We therefore hold that *Miranda* and its progeny in this Court govern the admissibility of statements made during custodial interrogation in both state and federal courts.

Petitioner Dickerson was indicted for bank robbery, conspiracy to commit bank robbery, and using a firearm in the course of committing a crime of violence, all in violation of the applicable provisions of Title 18 of the United States Code. Before trial, Dickerson moved to suppress a statement he had made at a Federal Bureau of Investigation field office, on the grounds that he had not received "*Miranda* warnings" before being interrogated. The District Court granted his motion to suppress, and the Government took an interlocutory appeal to the United States Court of Appeals for the Fourth Circuit. That court, by a divided vote, reversed the District Court's suppression order. It agreed with the District Court's conclusion that petitioner had not received *Miranda* warnings before making his statement. But it went on to hold that § 3501, which in effect makes the admissibility of statements such as Dickerson's turn solely on whether they were made voluntarily, was satisfied in this case. It then concluded that our decision in *Miranda* was not a constitutional holding, and that, therefore, Congress could by statute have the final say on the question of admissibility.

Because of the importance of the questions raised by the Court of Appeals' decision, we granted certiorari and now reverse.

We begin with a brief historical account of the law governing the admission of confessions. Prior to *Miranda*, we evaluated the admissibility of a suspect's confession under a voluntariness test. The roots of this test developed in the common law, as the courts of England and then the United States recognized that coerced confessions are inherently untrustworthy. Over time, our cases recognized two constitutional bases for the requirement that a confession be voluntary to be admitted into evidence: the Fifth Amendment right against self-incrimination and the Due Process Clause of the Fourteenth Amendment.

While *Bram* was decided before *Brown* and its progeny, for the middle third of the 20th century our cases based the rule against admitting coerced confessions primarily, if not exclusively, on notions of due process. We applied the due process voluntariness test in "some 30 different cases decided during the era that intervened between *Brown* and *Escobedo*." Those cases refined the test into an inquiry that examines "whether a defendant's will was overborne" by the circumstances surrounding the giving of a confession. The due process test takes into consideration "the totality of all the surrounding circumstances—both the characteristics of the accused and the details of the interrogation." The determination "depend[s] upon a weighing of the circumstances of pressure against the power of resistance of the person confessing."

We have never abandoned this due process jurisprudence, and thus continue to exclude confessions that were obtained involuntarily. But our decisions in *Malloy v. Hogan* (1964) and *Miranda* changed the focus of much of the inquiry in determining the admissibility of suspects' incriminating statements.

In *Miranda*, we noted that the advent of modern custodial police interrogation brought with it an increased concern about confessions obtained by coercion. Because custodial police interrogation, by its very nature, isolates and pressures the individual, we stated that "[e]ven without employing brutality, the 'third degree' or [other] specific stratagems, . . . custodial interrogation exacts a heavy toll on individual liberty and trades on the weakness of individuals." We concluded that the coercion inherent in custodial interrogation blurs the line between voluntary and involuntary statements, and thus heightens the risk that an individual will not be "accorded his privilege under the Fifth Amendment . . . not to be compelled to incriminate himself." Accordingly, we laid down "concrete constitutional guidelines for law enforcement agencies and courts to follow." Those guidelines established that the admissibility in evidence of any statement given during custodial interrogation of a suspect would depend on whether the police provided the suspect with four warnings. These warnings (which have come to be known colloquially as "*Miranda* rights") are: a suspect "has the right to remain silent, that anything he says can be used against him in a court of law, that he has the right to the presence of an attorney, and that if he cannot afford an attorney one will be appointed for him prior to any questioning if he so desires."

Two years after *Miranda* was decided, Congress enacted § 3501. That section provides, in relevant part:

> (a) In any criminal prosecution brought by the United States or by the District of Columbia, a confession . . . shall be admissible in evidence if it is voluntarily given. Before such confession is received in evidence, the trial judge shall, out of the presence of the jury, determine any issue as to voluntariness. If the trial judge determines that the confession was voluntarily made it shall be admitted in evidence and the trial judge shall permit the jury to hear relevant evidence on the issue of voluntariness and shall instruct the jury to give such weight to the confession as the jury feels it deserves under all the circumstances.
>
> (b) The trial judge in determining the issue of voluntariness shall take into consideration all the circumstances surrounding the giving of the confession, including (1) the time elapsing between arrest and arraignment of the defendant making the confession, if it was made after arrest and before arraignment, (2) whether such defendant knew the nature of the offense with which he was charged or of which he was suspected at the time of making the confession, (3) whether or not such defendant was advised or knew that he was not required to make any statement and that any such statement could be used against him, (4) whether or not such defendant had been advised prior to questioning of his right to the assistance of counsel; and

> (5) whether or not such defendant was without the assistance of counsel when questioned and when giving such confession.
>
> The presence or absence of any of the above-mentioned factors to be taken into consideration by the judge need not be conclusive on the issue of voluntariness of the confession.

Given § 3501's express designation of voluntariness as the touchstone of admissibility, its omission of any warning requirement, and the instruction for trial courts to consider a nonexclusive list of factors relevant to the circumstances of a confession, we agree with the Court of Appeals that Congress intended by its enactment to overrule *Miranda*. Because of the obvious conflict between our decision in *Miranda* and § 3501, we must address whether Congress has constitutional authority to thus supersede *Miranda*. If Congress has such authority, § 3501's totality-of-the-circumstances approach must prevail over *Miranda*'s requirement of warnings; if not, that section must yield to *Miranda*'s more specific requirements.

The law in this area is clear. This Court has supervisory authority over the federal courts, and we may use that authority to prescribe rules of evidence and procedure that are binding in those tribunals. Congress retains the ultimate authority to modify or set aside any judicially created rules of evidence and procedure that are not required by the Constitution.

But Congress may not legislatively supersede our decisions interpreting and applying the Constitution. This case therefore turns on whether the *Miranda* Court announced a constitutional rule or merely exercised its supervisory authority to regulate evidence in the absence of congressional direction. Recognizing this point, the Court of Appeals surveyed *Miranda* and its progeny to determine the constitutional status of the *Miranda* decision. Relying on the fact that we have created several exceptions to *Miranda*'s warnings requirement and that we have repeatedly referred to the *Miranda* warnings as "prophylactic," *New York v. Quarles*, and "not themselves rights protected by the Constitution," *Michigan v. Tucker*, the Court of Appeals concluded that the protections announced in *Miranda* are not constitutionally required.

We disagree with the Court of Appeals' conclusion, although we concede that there is language in some of our opinions that supports the view taken by that court. But first and foremost of the factors on the other side—that *Miranda* is a constitutional decision—is that both *Miranda* and two of its companion cases applied the rule to proceedings in state courts. Since that time, we have consistently applied *Miranda*'s rule to prosecutions arising in state courts. It is beyond dispute that we do not hold a supervisory power over the courts of the several States. With respect to proceedings in state courts, our "authority is limited to enforcing the commands of the United States Constitution."

The *Miranda* opinion itself begins by stating that the Court granted certiorari "to explore some facets of the problems . . . of applying the privilege against self-incrimination to in-custody interrogation, and to give concrete constitutional guidelines for law enforcement agencies and courts to follow." In fact, the majority opinion is replete with statements indicating that the majority thought it was announcing a constitutional rule. Indeed, the Court's ultimate conclusion was that the unwarned confessions obtained in the four cases before the Court in *Miranda* "were obtained from the defendant under circumstances that did not meet constitutional standards for protection of the privilege."

Additional support for our conclusion that *Miranda* is constitutionally based is found in the *Miranda* Court's invitation for legislative action to protect the constitutional right against coerced self-incrimination. After discussing the "compelling pressures" inherent in custodial police interrogation, the *Miranda* Court concluded that, "[i]n order to combat these pressures and to permit a full opportunity to exercise the privilege against self-incrimination, the accused must be adequately and effectively apprised of his rights and the exercise of those rights must be fully honored." However, the Court emphasized that it could not foresee "the potential alternatives for protecting the privilege which might be devised by Congress or the

States," and it accordingly opined that the Constitution would not preclude legislative solutions that differed from the prescribed *Miranda* warnings but which were "at least as effective in apprising accused persons of their right of silence and in assuring a continuous opportunity to exercise it."

The Court of Appeals also relied on the fact that we have, after our *Miranda* decision, made exceptions from its rule in cases such as *New York v. Quarles* and *Harris v. New York*. But we have also broadened the application of the *Miranda* doctrine in cases such as *Doyle v. Ohio* (1976), and *Arizona v. Roberson* (1988). These decisions illustrate the principle—not that *Miranda* is not a constitutional rule—but that no constitutional rule is immutable. No court laying down a general rule can possibly foresee the various circumstances in which counsel will seek to apply it, and the sort of modifications represented by these cases are as much a normal part of constitutional law as the original decision.

The Court of Appeals also noted that in *Oregon v. Elstad* we stated that "'[t]he *Miranda* exclusionary rule . . . serves the Fifth Amendment and sweeps more broadly than the Fifth Amendment itself.'" Our decision in that case—refusing to apply the traditional "fruits" doctrine developed in Fourth Amendment cases—does not prove that *Miranda* is a nonconstitutional decision, but simply recognizes the fact that unreasonable searches under the Fourth Amendment are different from unwarned interrogation under the Fifth Amendment.

As an alternative argument for sustaining the Court of Appeals' decision, the court-invited amicus curiae contends that the section complies with the requirement that a legislative alternative to *Miranda* be equally as effective in preventing coerced confessions. We agree with the amicus' contention that there are more remedies available for abusive police conduct than there were at the time *Miranda* was decided to hold that a suspect may bring a federal cause of action under the Due Process Clause for police misconduct during custodial interrogation. But we do not agree that these additional measures supplement § 3501's protections sufficiently to meet the constitutional minimum. *Miranda* requires procedures that will warn a suspect in custody of his right to remain silent and which will assure the suspect that the exercise of that right will be honored. As discussed above, § 3501 explicitly eschews a requirement of preinterrogation warnings in favor of an approach that looks to the administration of such warnings as only one factor in determining the voluntariness of a suspect's confession. The additional remedies cited by amicus do not, in our view, render them, together with § 3501, an adequate substitute for the warnings required by *Miranda*.

The dissent argues that it is judicial overreaching for this Court to hold § 3501 unconstitutional unless we hold that the *Miranda* warnings are required by the Constitution, in the sense that nothing else will suffice to satisfy constitutional requirements. But we need not go further than *Miranda* to decide this case. In *Miranda*, the Court noted that reliance on the traditional totality-of-the-circumstances test raised a risk of overlooking an involuntary custodial confession, a risk that the Court found unacceptably great when the confession is offered in the case in chief to prove guilt. The Court therefore concluded that something more than the totality test was necessary. As discussed above, § 3501 reinstates the totality test as sufficient. Section 3501 therefore cannot be sustained if *Miranda* is to remain the law.

Whether or not we would agree with *Miranda*'s reasoning and its resulting rule, were we addressing the issue in the first instance, the principles of stare decisis weigh heavily against overruling it now.

We do not think there is such justification for overruling *Miranda*. *Miranda* has become embedded in routine police practice to the point where the warnings have become part of our national culture. While we have overruled our precedents when subsequent cases have undermined their doctrinal underpinnings, we do not believe that this has happened to the *Miranda* decision. If anything, our subsequent cases have reduced the impact of the *Miranda* rule on legitimate law enforcement while reaffirming the decision's core ruling that unwarned statements may not be used as evidence in the prosecution's case in chief.

The disadvantage of the *Miranda* rule is that statements which may be by no means involuntary, made by a defendant who is aware of his "rights," may nonetheless be excluded and a guilty defendant go free as a result. But experience suggests that the totality-of-the-circumstances test which § 3501 seeks to revive is more difficult than *Miranda* for law enforcement officers to conform to, and for courts to apply in a consistent manner. The requirement that *Miranda* warnings be given does not, of course, dispense with the voluntariness inquiry. But as we said in *Berkemer*, "[c]ases in which a defendant can make a colorable argument that a self-incriminating statement was 'compelled' despite the fact that the law enforcement authorities adhered to the dictates of *Miranda* are rare."

In sum, we conclude that *Miranda* announced a constitutional rule that Congress may not supersede legislatively. Following the rule of stare decisis, we decline to overrule *Miranda* ourselves. The judgment of the Court of Appeals is therefore

Reversed.

NOTES AND QUESTIONS

1. The Court does not retreat from any of its previous decisions finding "exceptions" to *Miranda* or failing to treat the decision as if it were a full-blown constitutional right as opposed to a "prophylactic rule"—or even from its acknowledgment in *Elstad* that *Miranda* "sweeps more broadly than the Fifth Amendment itself." Do you understand how the Fourth Circuit could have concluded from these decisions that *Miranda* was not a "constitutional rule"?

The Supreme Court concludes that, notwithstanding these limits on the doctrine, *Miranda* is nonetheless a "constitutional decision." Is the Court's reasoning on this point persuasive?

2. Is the fact that *Miranda* has been held to apply in state court proceedings—that is, that the Court itself has treated *Miranda* as a constitutional rule—dispositive on this issue?

3. If § 3501 had displaced *Miranda*, how much would this have altered the behavior of federal law enforcement agents in the field, given that whether warnings were given is a factor in the statutory voluntariness test?

4. Do you think the outcome in *Dickerson* was attributable in part to the fact-intensive nature of the voluntariness test under § 3501? To the Court's previous experience with the voluntariness test prior to *Miranda*? To the comparative administrative ease of *Miranda* warnings?

5. Should the DOJ's nonenforcement of § 3501 have had any impact on the Court's decision in *Dickerson*? Was the DOJ a reliable proxy for law enforcement generally?

6. What do you make of the Court's comment that *Miranda* warnings "have become part of the national culture"? Does this mean that *Miranda* might have been more vulnerable to being overturned earlier, before it had been incorporated into the zeitgeist?

Indeed, confining *Miranda*'s impact to the "national" culture may be an understatement. Professor Frederick Schauer has observed that on Russian television shows Russian police officers administer *Miranda* warnings to arrestees even though Russian law has no such requirement. Frederick Schauer, *The* Miranda *Warning*, 88 Wash. L. Rev. 155, 155 (2013).

Dickerson seemed to have settled for good *Miranda*'s stability as a Supreme Court precedent. Or maybe not.

Just three years after *Dickerson*, in a civil action under 42 U.S.C. § 1983, a plurality of the Court in an opinion by Justice Thomas embraced a conception of the Fifth Amendment as purely a "trial right." (This view was in rough alignment with Justice Thomas's concurrence ten years later in *Salinas*, where he called for overturning *Griffin v. California*.) In *Chavez v. Martinez*, 538 U.S. 760 (2003), a badly injured man was questioned by police in the hospital without receiving *Miranda* warnings. He was never charged with a crime. The plurality held that he had no claim for a "deprivation of rights" under § 1983 because he was not charged and therefore his statements were not used against him at trial. The decision has been heavily criticized. *See* Tracey Maclin, *The Prophylactic Fifth Amendment*, 97 B.U. L. Rev. 1047, 1059-77 (2017) (arguing, inter alia, that *Chavez* ignores substantial precedent recognizing Fifth Amendment violations where statements were not used against a defendant at trial).

Chavez did not directly involve the constitutionality of *Miranda* but it did reflect a willingness by some members of the Court to think "creatively" about the Fifth Amendment.

A year later, in *United States v. Patane*, 542 U.S. 630 (2004), the implications of *Dickerson* were very much on the table. A DEA agent and a local police officer went to the home of Samuel Patane to investigate tips that he was harassing his ex-girlfriend, despite being under a no-contact restraining order, and that he illegally possessed a .40 Glock pistol. Patane invoked his *Miranda* rights, but the agent continued to question him about the gun and eventually Patane relented and directed the officer to it. Patane was charged with being a felon in possession under 18 U.S.C. § 922(g)(1); the district court granted a motion to suppress the gun; and the Tenth Circuit affirmed, reasoning that the gun was the fruit of the poisonous tree and that *Dickerson*'s holding that *Miranda* was a constitutional rule had essentially overruled *Elstad*'s earlier holding that the "fruits" doctrine was inapplicable to *Miranda* violations.

The Supreme Court, in another plurality opinion, reversed. It found that *Dickerson* did not warrant an extension of *Miranda* to the "fruits" context, and that *Miranda* only requires that a defendant's unwarned statements be inadmissible at trial, not derivative physical evidence. The opinion again invoked the conception of the Fifth Amendment as being only a "trial right," as it had done in *Chavez*.

Justice Souter, joined by Justices Stevens and Ginsburg, worried about the incentives *Patane* would provide to law enforcement. And the incentives that the Court's decisions provide were very much in mind—or at least should have been—given that *Patane* was decided the same day as *Missouri v. Seibert*. Justice Souter wrote: "There is no way to read this case except as an unjustifiable invitation to law enforcement officers to flout *Miranda* when there may be physical evidence to be gained. The incentive is an odd one, coming from the Court on the same day it decides *Missouri v. Seibert, ante*, 542 U.S. 600, 124 S. Ct. 2601. I respectfully dissent."

Although it may have seemed self-explanatory, the next case considers what *Dickerson* meant in holding that *Miranda* was a "constitutional rule." Not that much, it turns out, to a majority of the Court.

Vega v. Tekoh

597 U.S. 134 (2022)

Justice ALITO delivered the opinion of the Court.

This case presents the question whether a plaintiff may sue a police officer under Rev. Stat. § 1979, 42 U.S.C. § 1983, based on the allegedly improper admission of an "un-Mirandized" statement in a criminal prosecution. The case arose out of the interrogation of respondent, Terence Tekoh, by petitioner, Los Angeles County Sheriff's Deputy Carlos Vega. Deputy Vega questioned Tekoh at his place of employment and did not give him a *Miranda* warning. Tekoh was prosecuted, and his confession was admitted into evidence, but the jury returned a verdict of not guilty. Tekoh then sued Vega under § 1983, and the United States Court of Appeals for the Ninth Circuit held that the use of Tekoh's un-Mirandized statement provided a valid basis for a § 1983 claim against Vega. We now reject this extension of our *Miranda* case law.

I

In March 2014, Tekoh was working as a certified nursing assistant at a Los Angeles medical center. When a female patient accused him of sexually assaulting her, the hospital staff reported the accusation to the Los Angeles County Sheriff's Department, and Deputy Vega responded. Vega questioned Tekoh at length in the hospital, and Tekoh eventually provided a written statement apologizing for inappropriately touching the patient's genitals. The parties dispute whether Vega used coercive investigatory techniques to extract the statement, but it is undisputed that he never informed Tekoh of his rights under *Miranda* which held that during a custodial interrogation police officers must inform a suspect that "he has the right to remain silent, that anything he says can be used against him in a court of law, that he has the right to the presence of an attorney, and that if he cannot afford an attorney one will be appointed for him prior to any questioning."

Tekoh was arrested and charged in California state court with unlawful sexual penetration. At Tekoh's first trial, the judge held that *Miranda* had not been violated because Tekoh was not in custody when he provided the statement, but the trial resulted in a mistrial. When Tekoh was retried, a second judge again denied his request to exclude the confession. This trial resulted in acquittal, and Tekoh then brought this action under 42 U.S.C. § 1983 against Vega and several other defendants seeking damages for alleged violations of his constitutional rights, including his Fifth Amendment right against compelled self-incrimination.

When this § 1983 case was first tried, the jury returned a verdict in favor of Vega, but the judge concluded that he had given an improper jury instruction and thus granted a new trial. Before the second trial, Tekoh asked the court to instruct the jury that it was required to find that Vega violated the Fifth Amendment right against compelled self-incrimination if it determined that he took a statement from Tekoh in violation of *Miranda* and that the statement was then improperly used against Tekoh at his criminal trial. The District Court declined, reasoning that *Miranda* established a prophylactic rule and that such a rule could not alone provide a ground for § 1983 liability. Instead, the jury was asked to decide whether Tekoh's Fifth Amendment right had been violated. The court instructed the jury to determine, based on "the totality of all the surrounding circumstances," whether Tekoh's statement had been "improperly coerced or compelled," and the court explained that "[a] confession is improperly coerced or compelled . . . if a police officer uses physical or psychological force or threats not permitted by law to undermine a person's ability to exercise his or her free will." The jury found in Vega's favor, and Tekoh appealed.

A Ninth Circuit panel reversed, holding that the "use of an un-Mirandized statement against a defendant in a criminal proceeding violates the Fifth Amendment and may support a § 1983 claim" against the officer who obtained the statement. The panel acknowledged that this Court has repeatedly said that *Miranda* adopted prophylactic rules designed to protect against constitutional violations and that the decision did not hold that the contravention of those rules necessarily constitutes a constitutional violation. But the panel thought that our decision in *Dickerson* "made clear that the right of a criminal defendant against having an un-Mirandized statement introduced in the prosecution's case in chief is indeed a right secured by the Constitution." Therefore the panel concluded that Tekoh could establish a violation of his Fifth Amendment right against compelled self-incrimination simply by showing that *Miranda* had been violated. The panel thus remanded the case for a new trial.

II

Section 1983 provides a cause of action against any person acting under color of state law who "subjects" a person or "causes [a person] to be subjected . . . to the deprivation of any rights, privileges, or immunities secured by the Constitution and laws." The question we must decide is whether a violation of the *Miranda* rules provides a basis for a claim under § 1983. We hold that it does not.

A

If a *Miranda* violation were tantamount to a violation of the Fifth Amendment, our answer would of course be different. The Fifth Amendment, made applicable to the States by the Fourteenth Amendment, *Malloy v. Hogan* (1964), provides that "[n]o person . . . shall be compelled in any criminal case to be a witness against himself." This Clause "permits a person to refuse to testify against himself at a criminal trial in which he is a defendant" and "also 'privileges him not to answer official questions put to him in any other proceeding, civil or criminal, formal or informal, where the answers might incriminate him in future criminal proceedings.'" In addition, the right bars the introduction against a criminal defendant of out-of-court statements obtained by compulsion.

In *Miranda*, the Court concluded that additional procedural protections were necessary to prevent the violation of this important right when suspects who are in custody are interrogated by the police. To afford this protection, the Court required that custodial interrogation be preceded by the now-familiar warnings mentioned above, and it directed that statements obtained in violation of these new rules may not be used by the prosecution in its case-in-chief.

In this case, the Ninth Circuit held—and Tekoh now argues—that a violation of *Miranda* constitutes a violation of the Fifth Amendment right against compelled self-incrimination, but that is wrong. *Miranda* itself and our subsequent cases make clear that *Miranda* imposed a set of prophylactic rules. Those rules, to be sure, are "constitutionally based," *Dickerson*, but they are prophylactic rules nonetheless.

B

Miranda itself was clear on this point. *Miranda* did not hold that a violation of the rules it established necessarily constitute a Fifth Amendment violation, and it is difficult to see how it could have held otherwise. For one thing, it is easy to imagine many situations in which an un-Mirandized suspect in custody may make self-incriminating statements without any hint of compulsion. In addition, the warnings that the Court required included components, such as notification of the right to have retained or appointed counsel present during questioning, that do not concern self-incrimination per se but are instead plainly designed to safeguard that right. And the same is true of *Miranda*'s detailed rules about the waiver of the right to remain silent and the right to an attorney.

At no point in the opinion did the Court state that a violation of its new rules constituted a violation of the Fifth Amendment right against compelled self-incrimination. Instead, it claimed only that those rules were needed to safeguard that right during custodial interrogation.

In accordance with this understanding of the nature of the rules it imposed, the *Miranda* Court stated quite clearly that the Constitution did not itself require "adherence to any particular solution for the inherent compulsions of the interrogation process" and that its decision "in no way create[d] a constitutional straitjacket." The opinion added that its new rules might not be needed if Congress or the States adopted "other procedures which are at least as effective," and the opinion suggested that there might not have been any actual Fifth Amendment violations in the four cases that were before the Court. The Court could not have said any of these things if a violation of the *Miranda* rules necessarily constituted a violation of the Fifth Amendment.

Since *Miranda*, the Court has repeatedly described the rules it adopted as "prophylactic."

C

After *Miranda* was handed down, the Court engaged in the process of charting the dimensions of these new prophylactic rules. As we would later spell out, this process entailed a weighing of the benefits and costs of any clarification of the rules' scope.

Some post-*Miranda* decisions found that the balance of interests justified restrictions that would not have been possible if *Miranda* represented an explanation of the meaning of the Fifth Amendment right as opposed to a set of rules designed to protect that right. For example, in *Harris v. New York*, the Court held that a statement obtained in violation of *Miranda* could be used to impeach the testimony of a defendant, even though an involuntary statement obtained in violation of the Fifth Amendment could not have been employed in this way. Engaging in the process we described in *Shatzer*, the *Harris* Court considered the benefits of forbidding impeachment but dismissed "the speculative possibility" that this would discourage "impermissible police conduct," and on the other side of the scale, it feared that barring impeachment would turn *Miranda* into "a license to use perjury by way of a defense."

A similar analysis was used in *Michigan v. Tucker*, where the Court held that the "fruits" of an un-Mirandized statement can be admitted. The Court noted that "the 'fruits' of police conduct which actually infringe[s]" a defendant's constitutional rights must be suppressed. Because there had been only a *Miranda* violation in that case, the *Wong Sun* rule of automatic exclusion was found to be inapplicable. Instead, the Court asked whether the *Miranda* rules' prophylactic purposes justified the exclusion of the fruits of the violation, and after "balancing the interests involved," it held that exclusion was not required.

In *New York v. Quarles*, the Court held that statements obtained in violation of *Miranda* need not be suppressed when the questioning is conducted to address an ongoing "public safety" concern.

Finally, in *Elstad*, the Court again distinguished between a constitutional violation and a violation of *Miranda*. In that case, a suspect in custody was initially questioned without receiving a *Miranda* warning, and the statements made at that time were suppressed. But the suspect was later given *Miranda* warnings, chose to waive his *Miranda* rights, and signed a written confession. Asked to decide whether this confession was admissible, the Court followed the reasoning in *Tucker* and again held that the fruit-of-the-poisonous-tree rule that applies to constitutional violations does not apply to violations of *Miranda*. The Court refused to exclude the signed confession and emphasized that an officer's error "in administering the prophylactic *Miranda* procedures . . . should not breed the same irremediable consequences as police infringement of the Fifth Amendment itself."

It is hard to see how these decisions could stand if a violation of *Miranda* constituted a violation of the Fifth Amendment.

D

While these decisions imposed limits on *Miranda*'s prophylactic rules, other decisions found that the balance of interests called for expansion. . . .

• • •

Thus, all the post-*Miranda* cases we have discussed acknowledged the prophylactic nature of the *Miranda* rules and engaged in cost-benefit analysis to define the scope of these prophylactic rules.

E

Contrary to the decision below and Tekoh's argument here, our decision in *Dickerson* did not upset the firmly established prior understanding of *Miranda* as a prophylactic decision. *Dickerson* involved a federal statute, 18 U.S.C. § 3501, that effectively overruled *Miranda* by making the admissibility of a statement given during custodial interrogation turn solely on whether it was made voluntarily. The Court held that Congress could not abrogate *Miranda* by statute because *Miranda* was a "constitutional decision" that adopted a "constitutional rule," and the Court noted that these rules could not have been made applicable to the States if it did not have that status.

At the same time, however, the Court made it clear that it was not equating a violation of the *Miranda* rules with an outright Fifth Amendment violation. For one thing, it reiterated *Miranda*'s observation that "the Constitution would not preclude legislative solutions that differed from the prescribed *Miranda* warnings but which were 'at least as effective in apprising accused persons'" of their rights.

Even more to the point, the Court rejected the dissent's argument that § 3501 could not be held unconstitutional unless "*Miranda* warnings are required by the Constitution, in the sense that nothing else will suffice to satisfy constitutional requirements." The Court's answer, in substance, was that the *Miranda* rules, though not an explication of the meaning of the Fifth Amendment right, are rules that are necessary to protect that right (at least until a better alternative is found and adopted). Thus, in the words of the *Dickerson* Court, the *Miranda* rules are "constitutionally based" and have "constitutional underpinnings." But the obvious point of these formulations was to avoid saying that a *Miranda* violation is the same as a violation of the Fifth Amendment right.

What all this boils down to is basically as follows. The *Miranda* rules are prophylactic rules that the Court found to be necessary to protect the Fifth Amendment right against compelled self-incrimination. In that sense, *Miranda* was a "constitutional decision" and it adopted a "constitutional rule" because the decision was based on the Court's judgment about what is required to safeguard that constitutional right. And when the Court adopts a constitutional prophylactic rule of this nature, *Dickerson* concluded, the rule has the status of a "La[w] of the United States" that is binding on the States under the Supremacy Clause (as *Miranda* implicitly held, since three of the four decisions it reversed came from state court), and the rule cannot be altered by ordinary legislation.

This was a bold and controversial claim of authority, but we do not think that *Dickerson* can be understood any other way without (1) taking the insupportable position that a *Miranda* violation is tantamount to a violation of the Fifth Amendment, (2) calling into question the prior decisions that were predicated on the proposition that a *Miranda* violation is not the same as a constitutional violation, and (3) excising from the United States Reports a mountain of statements describing the *Miranda* rules as prophylactic.

Subsequent cases confirm that *Dickerson* did not upend the Court's understanding of the *Miranda* rules as prophylactic.

In sum, a violation of *Miranda* does not necessarily constitute a violation of the Constitution, and therefore such a violation does not constitute "the deprivation of [a] right . . . secured by the Constitution." 42 U.S.C. § 1983.

III

This conclusion does not necessarily dictate reversal because a § 1983 claim may also be based on "the deprivation of any rights, privileges, or immunities secured by the . . . *laws*." (Emphasis added.) It may thus be argued that the *Miranda* rules constitute federal "law" and that an abridgment of those rules can therefore provide the ground for a § 1983 claim. But whatever else may be said about this argument, it cannot succeed unless Tekoh can persuade us that this "law" should be expanded to include the right to sue for damages under § 1983.

As we have noted, "[a] judicially crafted" prophylactic rule should apply "only where its benefits outweigh its costs," and here, while the benefits of permitting the assertion of *Miranda* claims under § 1983 would be slight, the costs would be substantial.

Miranda rests on a pragmatic judgment about what is needed to stop the violation at trial of the Fifth Amendment right against compelled self-incrimination. That prophylactic purpose is served by the suppression at trial of statements obtained in violation of *Miranda* and by the application of that decision in other recognized contexts. Allowing the victim of a *Miranda* violation to sue a police officer for damages under § 1983 would have little additional deterrent value, and permitting such claims would cause many problems.

Allowing a claim like Tekoh's would disserve "judicial economy," by requiring a federal judge or jury to adjudicate a factual question (whether Tekoh was in custody when questioned) that had already been decided by a state court. This re-adjudication would not only be wasteful; it would undercut the "'strong judicial policy against the creation of two conflicting resolutions'" based on the same set of facts. And it could produce "unnecessary friction" between the federal and state court systems by requiring the federal court entertaining the § 1983 claim to pass judgment on legal and factual issues already settled in state court.

Allowing § 1983 suits based on *Miranda* claims could also present many procedural issues, such as whether a federal court considering a § 1983 claim would owe any deference to a trial court's factual findings; whether forfeiture and plain error rules carry over from the criminal trial; whether harmless-error rules apply; and whether civil damages are available in instances where the unwarned statement had no impact on the outcome of the criminal case.

We therefore refuse to extend *Miranda* in the way Tekoh requests. *Miranda*, *Dickerson*, and the other cases in that line provide sufficient protection for the Fifth Amendment right against compelled self-incrimination. "The identification of a *Miranda* violation and its consequences . . . ought to be determined at trial." *Chavez v. Martinez* (2003). And except in unusual circumstances, the "exclusion of unwarned statements" should be "a complete and sufficient remedy."

• • •

Because a violation of *Miranda* is not itself a violation of the Fifth Amendment, and because we see no justification for expanding *Miranda* to confer a right to sue under § 1983, the judgment of the Court of Appeals is reversed, and the case is remanded for further proceedings consistent with this opinion.

It is so ordered.

Justice KAGAN, with whom Justice BREYER and Justice SOTOMAYOR join, dissenting.

The Court's decision in *Miranda* affords well-known protections to suspects who are interrogated by police while in custody. Those protections derive from the Constitution: *Dickerson* tells us in no uncertain terms that *Miranda* is a "constitutional rule." And that rule grants a corresponding right: If police fail to provide the *Miranda* warnings to a suspect before interrogating him, then he is generally entitled to have any resulting confession excluded from his trial. From those facts, only one conclusion can follow—that *Miranda*'s protections are a "right[ ]" "secured by the Constitution" under the federal civil rights statute. 42 U.S.C. § 1983. Yet the Court today says otherwise. It holds that *Miranda* is not a constitutional right enforceable through a § 1983 suit. And so it prevents individuals from obtaining any redress when police violate their rights under *Miranda*. I respectfully dissent.

Miranda responded to problems stemming from the interrogation of suspects "incommunicado" and "in a police-dominated atmosphere." In such an environment, *Miranda* said, there are "pressures" which may "compel [a suspect] to speak where he would not otherwise do so freely." And so *Miranda* found a "necessity for procedures which assure that the individual is accorded his" Fifth Amendment privilege "not to be compelled to incriminate himself." *Miranda* set out protocols (including the now-familiar warnings) that would safeguard the constitutional privilege against self-incrimination. And *Miranda* held that if police failed to follow those requirements (without substituting equally effective ones), the prosecution could not use at trial a statement obtained from the interrogation.

The question in this case is whether *Miranda*'s protections are a "right[ ]" that is "secured by the Constitution" within the meaning of § 1983. If the answer is yes, then a person may sue a state actor who deprives him of the right. In past cases, the Court has given a broad construction to § 1983's broad language. Under § 1983 (as elsewhere), a "right[ ]" is anything that creates specific "obligations binding on [a] governmental unit" that an individual may ask the judiciary to enforce. And the phrase "secured by the Constitution" also has a capacious meaning. It refers to any right that is "protect[ed] or ma[de] certain" by the country's foundational charter.

Begin with whether *Miranda* is "secured by the Constitution." We know that it is, because the Court's decision in *Dickerson* says so. *Dickerson* tells us again and again that *Miranda* is a "constitutional rule." It is a "constitutional decision" that sets forth "'concrete constitutional guidelines.'" *Miranda* "is constitutionally based"; or again, it has a "constitutional basis." It is "of constitutional origin"; it has "constitutional underpinnings." And—one more—*Miranda* sets a "constitutional minimum." Over and over, *Dickerson* labels *Miranda* a rule stemming from the Constitution.

Dickerson also makes plain that *Miranda* has all the substance of a constitutional rule—including that it cannot be "abrogate[d]" by any "legislation. In *Dickerson*, the Court considered a federal statute whose obvious purpose was to override *Miranda*. *Dickerson* held that *Miranda* is a "constitutional decision" that cannot be "overruled by" any "Act of Congress." To be sure, Congress may devise "legislative solutions that differ[ ] from the prescribed *Miranda* warnings," but only if those solutions are "'at least as effective.'" *Dickerson* therefore instructs (as noted above) that *Miranda* sets a "constitutional minimum." No statute may provide lesser protection than that baseline.

And *Dickerson* makes clear that the constitutional substance of *Miranda* does not end there. Rules arising from "the United States Constitution" are applicable in state-court proceedings, but non-constitutional rules are not. Too, constitutional rules are enforceable in federal-court habeas proceedings, where a prisoner is entitled to claim he "is in custody in violation of the Constitution." 28 U.S.C. § 2254(a). *Miranda* checks both boxes. The Court has "consistently applied *Miranda*'s rule to prosecutions arising in state courts." And prisoners may claim *Miranda* violations in federal-court habeas proceedings. So *Dickerson* is unequivocal: *Miranda* is set in constitutional stone.

Miranda's constitutional rule gives suspects a correlative "right[ ]." § 1983. Under *Miranda*, a suspect typically has a right to be tried without the prosecutor using his un-Mirandized statement. And we know how that right operates in the real world. Suppose a defendant standing trial was able to show the court that he gave an un-Mirandized confession during a custodial interrogation. The court would have no choice but to exclude it from the prosecutor's case. As one judge below put it: "*Miranda* indisputably creates individual legal rights that are judicially enforceable."

The majority basically agrees with everything I've just explained. It concurs that, per *Dickerson*, *Miranda* "adopted a 'constitutional rule.'" How could it not? That *Miranda* is a constitutional rule is what *Dickerson* said (and said and said). The majority also agrees that *Miranda* "directed that statements obtained in violation of [its] rules may not be used by the prosecution in its case-in-chief"—which is simply another way of saying that *Miranda* grants suspects a right to the exclusion of those statements from the prosecutor's case.

So how does the majority hold that a violation of *Miranda* is not a "deprivation of [a] right[ ]" "secured by the Constitution"? § 1983. How does it agree with my premises, but not my conclusion? The majority's argument is that "a violation of *Miranda* does not necessarily constitute a violation of the Constitution," because *Miranda*'s rules are "prophylactic." The idea is that the Fifth Amendment prohibits the use only of statements obtained by compulsion, whereas *Miranda* excludes non-compelled statements too. That is why, the majority says, the Court has been able to recognize exceptions permitting certain uses of un-Mirandized statements at trial (when it could not do so for compelled statements).

But none of that helps the majority's case. Let's assume, as the majority says, that *Miranda* extends beyond—in order to safeguard—the Fifth Amendment's core guarantee. Still, *Miranda* is enforceable through § 1983. It remains a constitutional rule, as *Dickerson* held (and the majority agrees). And it grants the defendant a legally enforceable entitlement—in a word, a right—to have his confession excluded. So, to refer back to the language of § 1983, *Miranda* grants a "right[ ]" "secured by the Constitution." Whether that right to have evidence excluded safeguards a yet deeper constitutional commitment makes no difference to § 1983. The majority has no response to that point—except to repeat what our argument assumes already.

Compare the majority's holding today to a prior decision, in which the Court "rejected [an] attempt[ ] to limit the types of constitutional rights that are encompassed within" § 1983. There, the Court held that a plaintiff could sue under § 1983 for a violation of the so-called dormant Commerce Clause, which safeguards interstate commerce. To the Court, it did not matter that the Commerce Clause might be viewed as "merely allocat[ing] power between the Federal and State Governments" over interstate commerce, rather than as "confer[ring] 'rights.'" Nor did it matter that the dormant Commerce Clause's protection is only "implied" by the constitutional text. The dormant Commerce Clause, the Court said, still provides a "right"—in the "ordinary" sense of being "'[a] legally enforceable claim of one person against another.'" That describes *Miranda* to a tee. And if a right implied from Congress's constitutional authority over interstate commerce is enforceable under § 1983, how could it be that *Miranda*—which the Court has found necessary to safeguard the personal protections of the Fifth Amendment—is not also enforceable? The majority again has no answer.

• • •

Today, the Court strips individuals of the ability to seek a remedy for violations of the right recognized in *Miranda*. The majority observes that defendants may still seek "the suppression at trial of statements obtained" in violation of *Miranda*'s procedures. But sometimes, such a statement will not be suppressed. And sometimes, as a result, a defendant will be wrongly convicted and spend years in prison. He may succeed, on appeal or in habeas, in getting the conviction reversed. But then, what remedy does he have for all the harm he has suffered? The point of § 1983 is to provide such redress—because a remedy "is a vital component of any scheme for vindicating cherished constitutional guarantees." The majority here, as elsewhere, injures the right by denying the remedy. *See, e.g., Egbert v. Boule* (2022). I respectfully dissent.

NOTES AND QUESTIONS

1. For a closer look at 42 U.S.C. § 1983, and in particular its use in remedying police misconduct such as that alleged to have been committed by Officer Vega, *see* Chapter VI *infra.*

2. The Court labels as "a bold and controversial claim" the holding of a case that was 23 years old and decided by a vote of 7-2. As support for this point the Court cites in a footnote the dissenting opinion in *Dickerson* and the titles of three law review articles (from the 1970s and 1980s) that appear to represent a "debate" about the "authority" of the Supreme Court to make prophylactic rules. Didn't *Dickerson* settle this "debate"? Didn't *Miranda* itself settle this debate?

3. The language of § 1983 is simple. The pertinent part provides:

> Every person who, under color of any statute, ordinance, regulation, custom, or usage, of any State or Territory or the District of Columbia, subjects, or causes to be subjected, any citizen of the United States or other person within the jurisdiction thereof to the deprivation of any rights, privileges, or immunities secured by the *Constitution and laws*, shall be liable . . .

Note how the Court carves up its presentation of § 1983's language in order to advance its position that alleging a deprivation of a right secured by "law" as opposed to "the Constitution" is some sort of an exotic vehicle for recovery under § 1983.

Is there any doubt that *Miranda* is "law"? Why isn't that the end of the inquiry?

4. Even if *Miranda* was "merely a prophylactic rule," wasn't the cost-benefit analysis the Court proceeds to do in determining whether a violation would be redressable under § 1983 already done by Congress in including the word "law" without qualification in the statute?

5. A federal criminal statute, 18 U.S.C. § 242, enacted by the same Reconstruction-era Congress that passed the original version of § 1983, contains similar language:

> Whoever, under color of any law, statute, ordinance, regulation, or custom, willfully subjects any person in any State, Territory, Commonwealth, Possession, or District to the deprivation of any rights, privileges, or immunities secured or protected by the Constitution or laws of the United States . . . shall be [punished].

Might the current Court similarly interpret the term "law" in this criminal statute to not include *Miranda* violations based on its own cost-benefit analysis? Is the same cost-benefit analysis that was done in *Tekoh* equally applicable to § 242?

6. The Court says that "allowing a claim like Tekoh's would disserve "judicial economy . . . by requiring a federal judge or jury to adjudicate a factual question (whether Tekoh was in custody when questioned) that had already been decided by a state court." Isn't this true of many (or all) § 1983 actions? For example, in an action based on an allegedly illegal search, wouldn't the federal court have to independently determine whether the search was unconstitutional?

Recall that in *Chavez* the plurality held there was no § 1983 claim precisely because the plaintiff's statements had *not* been offered previously in court.

CHAPTER IV

THE FOURTH AMENDMENT

Section A of this chapter examines how the Supreme Court has determined what constitutes a search for Fourth Amendment purposes, a journey that is as much about technology—wiretaps, beepers, pen registers, thermal imaging, GPS devices, cellphones—as legal doctrine. Section B looks at the law regarding search's sister, seizure, with a particular focus on how race has been considered in this context. Section C examines the warrant "requirement" and its many exceptions: plain view, warrantless arrests, searches incident to arrest, consent searches, exigent circumstances, administrative or "special need" searches, and the automobile exception. Section D looks at another exception—the *Terry* doctrine and its elimination of a probable cause requirement for a search or seizure. Section E focuses on race and suspicion, with particular emphasis on the racial origin and impact of *Terry*, racial profiling, and traffic stops.

A. WHAT IS A SEARCH FOR FOURTH AMENDMENT PURPOSES?

Much of the Court's analysis of whether a particular government intrusion amounts to a "search" for Fourth Amendment purposes is, even today, governed at least in part by the "reasonable expectation of privacy" test that is attributable to *Katz v. United States*, 389 U.S. 347 (1967). But *Katz* must be understood against the backdrop of the decision it overruled, *Olmstead v. United* States, 277 U.S. 438, 455-56 (1928), and the government's investigative excesses of the Prohibition era.

Roy Olmstead was a Seattle policeman who dabbled in smuggling liquor into the country from Canada during Prohibition. After he was caught and fired from the police force, he became a full-time and hugely successful rum-runner. His bootlegging empire included fleets of cars, ships, motorboats, and dozens of employees and associates, not counting his former police force colleagues whom he bribed generously. Federal Prohibition agents in Seattle were atypically, let's say, aggressive. They not only cared about detecting and prosecuting violations of Prohibition laws, unlike many of their fellow agents, but were willing to be creative. Although the Treasury Department, the agents' employer, prohibited wiretapping, as did Washington state law and the FBI under Attorney General (later Justice) Harlan Fiske Stone, the agents nonetheless tapped into several phone lines used by Olmstead and his associates. They listened for months. Based on the evidence obtained from these wiretaps Olmstead and his codefendants were convicted in federal court of violations of the Volstead Act. *See* Daniel Okrent, Last Call: The Rise and Fall of Prohibition 284-86 (2010).

The Supreme Court rejected Olmstead's Fourth Amendment challenge for the simple reason that there was no violation of Olmstead's property rights and therefore no "search": "There was no entry of the houses or offices of the defendants." *Olmstead*, 277 U.S. at 464. Justice Brandeis famously dissented. He found the lack of a property right "immaterial." *Id.* at 479. The Founders, he claimed,

> conferred, as against the government, the right to be let alone—the most comprehensive of rights and the right most valued by civilized men. To protect, that right, every unjustifiable intrusion by the government upon the privacy of the individual, whatever the means employed, must be deemed a violation of the Fourth Amendment.

Id. at 478. Justice Brandeis also warned that "[t]he progress of science in furnishing the government with means of espionage is not likely to stop with wire tapping. Ways may some day be developed by which the government, without removing papers from secret drawers, can reproduce them in court. . . ." *Id.* at 473-74.

A less well-known aspect of the dissent was Justice Brandeis's denunciation of the Justice Department, which he asserted had assumed "moral responsibility" for the Prohibition agents' illegal wiretapping by using its fruits in a federal prosecution.

Elise and Roy Olmstead, Seattle, 1925

That is more or less where things stood doctrinally until the 1960s. On the one hand, the Court after *Olmstead* expressed criticism of the ethics of wiretapping in considering the government's use of intercepted communications in the prosecutions of another bootlegger, Frank Nardone, and reversed his convictions by interpreting a statute prohibiting "divulging" such communications as a bar to admissibility. *United States v. Nardone*, 302 U.S. 379, 382 (1937) (reversing conviction and finding intercepted statements inadmissible); *United States v. Nardone*, 308 U.S. 338, 340-43 (1939) (reversing retrial conviction for use of evidence derived from intercepted communications). On the other hand, the Court refused to find a Fourth Amendment violation where agents used a "detectaphone," a device that amplified sound waves, which agents used to eavesdrop from an adjacent room on statements made by the target on the telephone, relying on the "trespass" principle of *Olmstead. Goldman v. United States* 316 U.S. 129 (1942).

Two cases in the 1960s set the stage for *Katz*. In *Silverman v. United States*, 365 U.S. 505 (1961), the Court found a Fourth Amendment search where agents inserted a "spike mike" into a shared wall in the defendants' rowhouse in order to eavesdrop on conversations. *Id.* at 506-07. The Court found this "encroachment" to be a Fourth Amendment search even though there had been no "technical trespass under . . . local property law." *Id.* at 511. And shortly before *Katz* was decided, the Court issued its decision in *Berger v. New York*, 388 U.S. 41 (1967), striking down on Fourth Amendment grounds a New York statute that authorized judges to issue warrants to law enforcement agents for bugging or wiretapping. The opinion for the Court held that the warrants lacked probable cause to be issued, were insufficiently particular, had no time limit, and did not have a means for providing notice to the targets. *Id.* at 55-63. The many opinions in *Berger* left it unclear how many Justices believed that electronic eavesdropping could ever satisfy the Fourth Amendment warrant requirement.

In the next handful of cases the Court considers whether law enforcement use of some sort of technology, in the broadest sense of the term, constitutes a "search" under the Fourth Amendment. In none of these cases did the government have a search warrant, which it could have obtained if it had been able to persuade a magistrate or judge that it had probable cause to believe criminal activity was afoot and it could have drawn up a sufficiently particularized warrant describing what and where it wanted to search. Ask yourself as you read these cases, why did the police or agents not get a warrant? There are usually three possible explanations: They could not satisfy the warrant requirements. They didn't want to bother with a warrant. They had already tried to get a warrant and failed.

Consider also in these cases, as the Court roots the Fourth Amendment in the protection of "privacy," what privacy can mean in these varied contexts. Does privacy mean secrecy? Does privacy mean, if not absolute secrecy, at least control over who has access to personal information? Do people "assume the risk"—and reasonably so—of compromising their privacy by sharing information with some third parties?

Katz v. United States

389 U.S. 347 (1967)

Mr. Justice Stewart delivered the opinion of the Court.

The petitioner was convicted in the District Court for the Southern District of California under an eight-count indictment charging him with transmitting wagering information by telephone from Los Angeles to Miami and Boston in violation of a federal statute. At trial the Government was permitted, over the petitioner's objection, to introduce evidence of the petitioner's end of telephone conversation, overheard by FBI agents who had attached an electronic listening and recording device to the outside of the public telephone booth from which he had placed his calls. In affirming his conviction, the Court of Appeals rejected the contention that the recordings had been obtained in violation of the Fourth Amendment, because "(t)here was no physical entrance into the area occupied by (the petitioner)." We granted certiorari in order to consider the constitutional questions thus presented.

The petitioner had phrased those questions as follows:

> A. Whether a public telephone booth is a constitutionally protected area so that evidence obtained by attaching an electronic listening recording device to the top of such a booth is obtained in violation of the right to privacy of the user of the booth.
>
> B. Whether physical penetration of a constitutionally protected area is necessary before a search and seizure can be said to be violative of the Fourth Amendment to the United States Constitution.

We decline to adopt this formulation of the issues. In the first place the correct solution of Fourth Amendment problems is not necessarily promoted by incantation of the phrase "constitutionally protected area." Secondly, the Fourth Amendment cannot be translated into a general constitutional "right to privacy." That Amendment protects individual privacy against certain kinds of governmental intrusion, but its protections go further, and often have nothing to do with privacy at all. Other provisions of the Constitution protect personal privacy from other forms of governmental invasion. But the protection of a person's general right to privacy—his right to be let alone by other people—is, like the protection of his property and of his very life, left largely to the law of the individual States.

Because of the misleading way the issues have been formulated, the parties have attached great significance to the characterization of the telephone booth from which the petitioner placed his calls. The petitioner has strenuously argued that the booth was a "constitutionally protected area." The Government has maintained with equal vigor that it was not. But this effort to decide whether or not a given "area," viewed in the abstract, is "constitutionally protected" deflects attention from the problem presented by this case. For the Fourth Amendment protects people, not places. What a person knowingly exposes to the public, even in his own home or office, is not a subject of Fourth Amendment protection. But what he seeks to preserve as private, even in an area accessible to the public, may be constitutionally protected.

The Government stresses the fact that the telephone booth from which the petitioner made his calls was constructed partly of glass, so that he was as visible after he entered it as he would have been if he had remained outside. But what he sought to exclude when he entered the booth was not the intruding eye—it was the uninvited ear. He did not shed his right to do so simply because he made his calls from a place where he might be seen. No less than an individual in a business office, in a friend's apartment, or in a taxicab, a person in a telephone booth may rely upon the protection of the Fourth Amendment. One who occupies it, shuts the door behind him, and pays the toll that permits him to place a call is surely entitled to assume that the words he utters into the mouthpiece will not be broadcast to the world. To read the Constitution more narrowly is to ignore the vital role that the public telephone has come to play in private communication.

The Government contends, however, that the activities of its agents in this case should not be tested by Fourth Amendment requirements, for the surveillance technique they employed involved no physical penetration of the telephone booth from which the petitioner placed his calls. It is true that the absence of such penetration was at one time thought to foreclose further Fourth Amendment inquiry, for that Amendment was thought to limit only searches and seizures of tangible property. But "(t)he premise that property interests control the right of the Government to search and seize has been discredited." Thus, although a closely divided Court supposed in *Olmstead* that surveillance without any trespass and without the seizure of any material object fell outside the ambit of the Constitution, we have since departed from the narrow view on which that decision rested. Indeed, we have expressly held that the Fourth Amendment governs not only the seizure of tangible items, but extends as well to the recording of oral statements overheard without any "technical trespass under . . . local property law." Once this much is acknowledged, and once it is recognized that the Fourth Amendment protects people—and not simply "areas"—against unreasonable searches and seizures it becomes clear that the reach of that Amendment cannot turn upon the presence or absence of a physical intrusion into any given enclosure.

We conclude that the underpinnings of *Olmstead* and *Goldman* have been so eroded by our subsequent decisions that the "trespass" doctrine there enunciated can no longer be regarded as controlling. The Government's activities in electronically listening to and recording the petitioner's words violated the privacy upon which he justifiably relied while using the telephone booth and thus constituted a "search and seizure" within the meaning of the Fourth Amendment. The fact that the electronic device employed to achieve that end did not happen to penetrate the wall of the booth can have no constitutional significance.

The question remaining for decision, then, is whether the search and seizure conducted in this case complied with constitutional standards. In that regard, the Government's position is that its agents acted in an entirely defensible manner: They did not begin their electronic surveillance until investigation of the petitioner's activities had established a strong probability that he was using the telephone in question to transmit gambling information to persons in other States, in violation of federal law. Moreover, the surveillance was limited, both in scope and in duration, to the specific purpose of establishing the contents of the petitioner's unlawful telephonic communications. The agents confined their surveillance to the brief periods during which he used the telephone booth, and they took great care to overhear only the conversations of the petitioner himself.

Accepting this account of the Government's actions as accurate, it is clear that this surveillance was so narrowly circumscribed that a duly authorized magistrate, properly notified of the need for such investigation, specifically informed of the basis on which it was to proceed, and clearly apprised of the precise intrusion it would entail, could constitutionally have authorized, with appropriate safeguards, the very limited search and seizure that the Government asserts in fact took place. Only last Term we sustained the validity of such an authorization, holding that, under sufficiently "precise and discriminate circumstances," a federal court may empower government agents to employ a concealed electronic device "for the narrow and particularized purpose of ascertaining the truth of the . . . allegations" of a "detailed factual affidavit alleging the commission of a specific criminal offense." Discussing that holding, the Court in *Berger v. State of New York*, said that "the order authorizing the use of the electronic device" in *Osborn* "afforded similar protections to those . . . of conventional warrants authorizing the seizure of tangible evidence." Through those protections, "no greater invasion of privacy was permitted than was necessary under the circumstances." Here, too, a similar judicial order could have accommodated "the legitimate needs of law enforcement" by authorizing the carefully limited use of electronic surveillance.

The Government urges that, because its agents relied upon the decisions in *Olmstead* and *Goldman*, and because they did no more here than they might properly have done with prior judicial sanction, we should retroactively validate their conduct. That we cannot do. It is apparent that the agents in this case acted with restraint. Yet the inescapable fact is that this restraint was imposed by the agents themselves, not by a judicial officer. They were not required, before commencing the search, to present their estimate of probable cause for detached scrutiny by a neutral magistrate. They were not compelled, during the conduct of the search itself, to observe precise limits established in advance by a specific court order. Nor were they directed, after the search had been completed, to notify the authorizing magistrate in detail of all that had been seized. In the absence of such safeguards, this Court has never sustained a search upon the sole ground that officers reasonably expected to find evidence of a particular crime and voluntarily confined their activities to the least intrusive means consistent with that end. Searches conducted without warrants have been held unlawful "notwithstanding facts unquestionably showing probable cause," for the Constitution requires "that the deliberate, impartial judgment of a judicial officer . . . be interposed between the citizen and the police. . . ." "Over and over again this Court has emphasized that the mandate of the (Fourth) Amendment requires adherence to judicial processes," and that searches conducted outside the judicial process, without prior approval by judge or magistrate, are per se unreasonable under the Fourth Amendment—subject only to a few specifically established and well-delineated exceptions.

It is difficult to imagine how any of those exceptions could ever apply to the sort of search and seizure involved in this case. Even electronic surveillance substantially contemporaneous with an individual's arrest could hardly be deemed an "incident" of that arrest. Nor could the use of electronic surveillance without prior authorization be justified on grounds of "hot pursuit." And, of course, the very nature of electronic surveillance precludes its use pursuant to the suspect's consent.

The Government does not question these basic principles. Rather, it urges the creation of a new exception to cover this case. It argues that surveillance of a telephone booth should be exempted from the usual requirement of advance authorization by a magistrate upon a showing of probable cause. We cannot agree. Omission of such authorization

> bypasses the safeguards provided by an objective predetermination of probable cause, and substitutes instead the far less reliable procedure of an after-the-event justification for the . . . search, too likely to be subtly influenced by the familiar shortcomings of hindsight judgment.

And bypassing a neutral predetermination of the scope of a search leaves individuals secure from Fourth Amendment violations "only in the discretion of the police."

These considerations do not vanish when the search in question is transferred from the setting of a home, an office, or a hotel room to that of a telephone booth. Wherever a man may be, he is entitled to know that he will remain free from unreasonable searches and seizures. The government agents here ignored "the procedure of antecedent justification . . . that is central to the Fourth Amendment," a procedure that we hold to be a constitutional precondition of the kind of electronic surveillance involved in this case. Because the surveillance here failed to meet that condition, and because it led to the petitioner's conviction, the judgment must be reversed.

NOTES AND QUESTIONS

1. The Court firmly denounces the framing of the Fourth Amendment issue in terms of property interests. No more "trespass." No more "constitutionally protected area." Because, we are told, the Fourth Amendment "protects people not places." But doesn't where the people are, and what they are doing, bear on what protection the Fourth Amendment provides?

Even in *Katz* itself, weren't the physical characteristics of a phone booth relevant to the outcome?

2. In *Berger* it had been unclear how many of the Justices thought electronic eavesdropping could satisfy the Fourth Amendment warrant requirement. *Katz* answers this question unambiguously. But strangely the Court in *Katz* also says that in this case the government could have gotten a warrant given that its eavesdropping was "narrowly circumscribed." Even that is debatable—they appear to have intercepted 100 percent of Katz's calls from the phone booth for a week.

But what about probable cause? What facts in the opinion indicate the agents had probable cause to believe Katz was engaged in criminal activity? The record before the Court included information that Katz attracted the agents' attention after a tip from an informant. *See generally* David A. Sklansky, Katz v. United States: *The Limits of Aphorism*, in Criminal Procedure Stories 224 (Carol Steiker ed., 2007). But that doesn't establish probable cause without independent corroboration.

The agents observed Katz regularly walking to the phone booth to make telephone calls. Isn't that a purely innocuous activity? To paraphrase the Court, to infer illicit activity from using a pay phone "is to ignore the vital role that the public telephone has come to play in private communication."

3. Justice Harlan's concurring opinion puts a helpful gloss on the Court's pithy but useless "people not places" slogan:

> My understanding of the rule that has emerged from prior decisions is that there is a twofold requirement, first that a person have exhibited an actual (subjective) expectation of privacy and, second, that the expectation be one that society is prepared to recognize as "reasonable."

389 U.S. at 516. Although sometimes criticized for the circularity of the objective component of the standard, *see, e.g., Minnesota v. Carter*, 525 U.S. 83, 97 (1998) (Scalia, J., concurring), this was a standard that courts could and did apply in subsequent Fourth Amendment cases.

Why should a person's subjective view of what is private affect what protection the Fourth Amendment affords?

4. Though often praised for its vindication of privacy interests, *Katz* made explicit that the Fourth Amendment did not embody a generalized constitutional right to privacy. 389 U.S. at 510. Justice Brandeis's *Olmstead* dissent was not acknowledged in the opinion, although the Court in a footnote does make reference to his famous law review article on the protection of privacy rights through private tort actions. *See* Samuel D. Warren & Louis Brandeis, *The Right to Privacy*, 4 Harv. L. Rev. 193 (1890).

5. The most profound immediate response to *Katz* was not judicial but legislative. In 1968, Congress enacted comprehensive federal wiretapping legislation as part of the Omnibus Crime Control and Safe Streets Act. Title III of the act permitted wiretapping but imposed procedural requirements (probable cause, time limits, notice, minimization, etc.) flowing directly from *Berger* and *Katz*. To this day, the primary regulation of wiretapping is legislative not judicial. *See* Orin Kerr, *The Fourth Amendment and New Technologies: Constitutional Myths and the Case for Caution*, 102 Mich. L. Rev. 801, 805 (2004) (arguing that legislative rules are preferable to judicial interpretations of the Fourth Amendment in regulating new technologies).

Classic phone booth

Katz belongs in a museum. Its co-starring character, a public telephone booth, once such a common feature of public life, has largely disappeared. The activity for which Charlie Katz was charged, betting on sporting events, is now ubiquitous and wholly legal in many states. Crime rates were sufficiently low when Katz was under investigation that the FBI could devote several agents to the pursuit of one gambler, who was not even (as far as we are told) a bookie.

Katz is also a reminder that the doctrinal stakes involved in cases that reach the Supreme Court often exceed the stakes to the litigants. Katz's jury-waived trial lasted two days. The evidence included the telephone recordings, records seized from his hotel rooms, and a police officer who offered "expert testimony" about the gambling jargon on the recordings. Katz was found guilty and fined $300, the equivalent of about $2,700 today. *See generally* David A. Sklansky, Katz v. United States: *The Limits of Aphorism*, in Criminal Procedure Stories 223-33 (Carol Steiker ed., 2007).

The Court applied *Katz*'s "reasonable expectations of privacy" test to all manner of law enforcement techniques, some involving technology (aerial surveillance, beepers, pen registers) and some more old school (using informants, looking through trash), in the ensuing decades. In *United States v. White*, 401 U.S. 745 (1971), the Court found no search where an informant recorded his conversations with a defendant because a person has no reasonable expectation of privacy in what he says to another person. Similarly, in *Smith v. Maryland*, 442 U.S. 735 (1979), the government's use of a "pen register," a device that records the numbers dialed on a telephone, was not a search because the defendant shared such numbers with the phone company, a third party. That physical location still mattered to the "reasonable expectations of privacy" test, however, was seen in a pair of cases involving government use of beepers as an investigative tool. *United States v. Knotts*, 460 U.S. 276 (1983); *United States v. Karo*, 468 U.S. 705 (1984). The "home" as a physical structure as opposed to a metaphor also retained significance. In *Oliver v. United States*, 466 U.S. 170 (1984), a warrantless search of "open fields" on a defendant's property, but distant from his home, was not forbidden by the Fourth Amendment; neither was a warrantless search of garbage bags defendants left for curbside collection. *California v. Greenwood*, 486 U.S. 35 (1988).

Florida v. Riley

488 U.S. 445 (1989)

Justice White announced the judgment of the Court and delivered an opinion in which The Chief Justice, Justice Scalia, and Justice Kennedy join.

On certification to it by a lower state court, the Florida Supreme Court addressed the following question: "Whether surveillance of the interior of a partially covered greenhouse in a residential backyard from the vantage point of a helicopter located 400 feet above the greenhouse constitutes a 'search' for which a warrant is required under the Fourth Amendment and Article I, § 12 of the Florida Constitution." The court answered the question in the affirmative, and we granted the State's petition for certiorari challenging that conclusion.

Respondent Riley lived in a mobile home located on five acres of rural property. A greenhouse was located 10 to 20 feet behind the mobile home. Two sides of the greenhouse were enclosed. The other two sides were not enclosed but the contents of the greenhouse were obscured from view from surrounding property by trees, shrubs, and the mobile home. The greenhouse was covered by corrugated roofing panels, some translucent and some opaque. At the time relevant to this case, two of the panels, amounting to approximately 10% of the roof area, were missing. A wire fence surrounded the mobile home and the greenhouse, and the property was posted with a "DO NOT ENTER" sign.

This case originated with an anonymous tip to the Pasco County Sheriff's office that marijuana was being grown on respondent's property. When an investigating officer discovered that he could not see the contents of the greenhouse from the road, he circled twice over respondent's property in a helicopter at the height of 400 feet. With his naked eye, he was able to see through the openings in the roof and one or more of the open sides of the greenhouse and to identify what he thought was marijuana growing in the structure. A warrant was obtained based on these observations, and the ensuing search revealed marijuana growing in the greenhouse. Respondent was charged with possession of marijuana under Florida law. The trial court granted his motion to suppress; the Florida Court of Appeals reversed but certified the case to the Florida Supreme Court, which quashed the decision of the Court of Appeals and reinstated the trial court's suppression order.

We agree with the State's submission that our decision in *California v. Ciraolo* (1986), controls this case. There, acting on a tip, the police inspected the back-yard of a particular house while flying in a fixed-wing aircraft at 1,000 feet. With the naked eye the officers saw what they concluded was marijuana growing in the yard. A search warrant was obtained on the strength of this airborne inspection, and marijuana plants were found. The trial court refused to suppress this evidence, but a state appellate court held that the inspection violated the Fourth and Fourteenth Amendments to the United States Constitution, and that the warrant was therefore invalid. We in turn reversed, holding that the inspection was not a search subject to the Fourth Amendment. We recognized that the yard was within the curtilage of the house, that a fence shielded the yard from observation from the street, and that the occupant had a subjective expectation of privacy. We held, however, that such an expectation was not reasonable and not one "that society is prepared to honor." Our reasoning was that the home and its curtilage are not necessarily protected from inspection that involves no physical invasion. "'What a person knowingly exposes to the public, even in his own home or office, is not a subject of Fourth Amendment protection.'" As a general proposition, the police may see what may be seen "from a public vantage point where [they have] a right to be," Thus the police, like the public, would have been free to inspect the backyard garden from the street if their view had been unobstructed. They were likewise free to inspect the yard from the vantage point of an aircraft flying in the navigable airspace as this plane was. "In an age where private and commercial flight in the public airways is routine, it is unreasonable for respondent to expect that his marijuana plants were constitutionally protected from being observed with the naked eye from an altitude of 1,000 feet. The Fourth Amendment simply does not require the police traveling in the public airways at this altitude to obtain a warrant in order to observe what is visible to the naked eye."

We arrive at the same conclusion in the present case. In this case, as in *Ciraolo*, the property surveyed was within the curtilage of respondent's home. Riley no doubt intended and expected that his greenhouse would not be open to public inspection, and the precautions he took protected against ground-level observation. Because the sides and roof of his greenhouse were left partially open, however, what was growing in the greenhouse was subject to viewing from the air. Under the holding in Ciraolo, Riley could not reasonably have expected the contents of his greenhouse to be immune from examination by an officer seated in a fixed-wing aircraft flying in navigable airspace at an altitude of 1,000 feet or, as the Florida Supreme Court seemed to recognize, at an altitude of 500 feet, the lower limit of the navigable airspace for such an aircraft. Here, the inspection was made from a helicopter, but as is the case with fixed-wing planes, "private and commercial flight [by helicopter] in the public airways is routine" in this country, *Ciraolo*, and there is no indication that such flights are unheard of in Pasco County, Florida. Riley could not reasonably have expected that his greenhouse was protected from public or official observation from a helicopter had it been flying within the navigable airspace for fixed-wing aircraft.

Nor on the facts before us, does it make a difference for Fourth Amendment purposes that the helicopter was flying at 400 feet when the officer saw what was growing in the greenhouse through the partially open roof and sides of the structure. We would have a different case if flying at that altitude had been contrary to law or regulation. But helicopters are not bound by the lower limits of the navigable airspace allowed to other aircraft. Any member of the public could legally have been flying over Riley's property in a helicopter at the altitude of 400 feet and could have observed Riley's greenhouse. The police officer did no more. This is not to say that an inspection of the curtilage of a house from an aircraft will always pass muster under the Fourth Amendment simply because the plane is within the navigable airspace specified by law. But it is of obvious importance that the helicopter in this case was not violating the law, and there is nothing in the record or before us to suggest that helicopters flying at 400 feet are sufficiently rare in this country to lend substance to respondent's claim that he reasonably anticipated that his greenhouse would not be subject to observation from that altitude. Neither is there any intimation here that the helicopter interfered with respondent's normal use of the greenhouse or of other parts of the curtilage. As far as this record reveals, no intimate details connected with the use of the home or curtilage were observed, and there was no undue noise, and no wind, dust, or threat of injury. In these circumstances, there was no violation of the Fourth Amendment.

The judgment of the Florida Supreme Court is accordingly reversed.

[Justice O'Connor wrote an opinion concurring in the judgment. Justice Blackmun wrote a separate disappointing opinion.]

Justice BRENNAN, with whom Justice MARSHALL and Justice STEVENS join, dissenting.

The Court holds today that police officers need not obtain a warrant based on probable cause before circling in a helicopter 400 feet above a home in order to investigate what is taking place behind the walls of the curtilage. I cannot agree that the Fourth Amendment to the Constitution, which safeguards "[t]he right of the people to be secure in their persons, houses, papers, and effects, against unreasonable searches and seizures," tolerates such an intrusion on privacy and personal security.

I

The opinion for a plurality of the Court reads almost as if *Katz* had never been decided. Notwithstanding the disclaimers of its final paragraph, the opinion relies almost exclusively on the fact that the police officer conducted his surveillance from a vantage point where, under applicable Federal Aviation Administration regulations, he had a legal right to be. *Katz* teaches, however, that the relevant inquiry is whether the police surveillance "violated the privacy upon which [the defendant] justifiably relied" —or, as Justice Harlan put it, whether the police violated an "expectation of privacy . . . that society is prepared to recognize as 'reasonable.'" The result of that inquiry in any given case depends ultimately on the judgment "whether, if the particular form of surveillance practiced by the police is permitted to go unregulated by constitutional restraints, the amount of privacy and freedom remaining to citizens would be diminished to a compass inconsistent with the aims of a free and open society."

The plurality undertakes no inquiry into whether low-level helicopter surveillance by the police of activities in an enclosed backyard is consistent with the "aims of a free and open society." Instead, it summarily concludes that Riley's expectation of privacy was unreasonable because "[a]ny member of the public could legally have been flying over Riley's property in a helicopter at the altitude of 400 feet and could have observed Riley's greenhouse." This observation is, in turn, based solely on the fact that the police helicopter was within the airspace within which such craft are allowed by federal safety regulations to fly.

I agree, of course, that "[w]hat a person knowingly exposes to the public . . . is not a subject of Fourth Amendment protection." But I cannot agree that one "knowingly exposes [an area] to the public" solely because a helicopter may legally fly above it. Under the plurality's exceedingly grudging Fourth Amendment theory, the expectation of privacy is defeated if a single member of the public could conceivably position herself to see into the area in question without doing anything illegal. It is defeated whatever the difficulty a person would have in so positioning herself, and however infrequently anyone would in fact do so. In taking this view the plurality ignores the very essence of *Katz*. The reason why there is no reasonable expectation of privacy in an area that is exposed to the public is that little diminution in "the amount of privacy and freedom remaining to citizens" will result from police surveillance of something that any passerby readily sees. To pretend, as the plurality opinion does, that the same is true when the police use a helicopter to peer over high fences is, at best, disingenuous.

Notwithstanding the plurality's statistics about the number of helicopters registered in this country, can it seriously be questioned that Riley enjoyed virtually complete privacy in his backyard greenhouse, and that that privacy was invaded solely by police helicopter surveillance? Is the theoretical possibility that any member of the public (with sufficient means) could also have hired a helicopter and looked over Riley's fence of any relevance at all in determining whether Riley suffered a serious loss of privacy and personal security through the police action?

In *Ciraolo*, we held that whatever might be observed from the window of an airplane flying at 1,000 feet could be deemed unprotected by any reasonable expectation of privacy. That decision was based on the belief that airplane traffic at that altitude was sufficiently common that no expectation of privacy could inure in anything on the ground observable with the naked eye from so high. Indeed, we compared those airways to "public thoroughfares," and made the obvious point that police officers passing by a home on such thoroughfares were not required by the Fourth Amendment to "shield their eyes." Seizing on a reference in *Ciraolo* to the fact that the police officer was in a position "where he ha[d] a right to be," today's plurality professes to find this case indistinguishable because FAA regulations do not impose a minimum altitude requirement on helicopter traffic; thus, the officer in this case too made his observations from a vantage point where he had a right to be.

It is a curious notion that the reach of the Fourth Amendment can be so largely defined by administrative regulations issued for purposes of flight safety. It is more curious still that the plurality relies to such an extent on the legality of the officer's act, when we have consistently refused to equate police violation of the law with infringement of the Fourth Amendment. But the plurality's willingness to end its inquiry when it finds that the officer was in a position he had a right to be in is misguided for an even more fundamental reason. Finding determinative the fact that the officer was where he had a right to be is, at bottom, an attempt to analogize surveillance from a helicopter to surveillance by a police officer standing on a public road and viewing evidence of crime through an open window or a gap in a fence. In such a situation, the occupant of the home may be said to lack any reasonable expectation of privacy in what can be seen from that road — even if, in fact, people rarely pass that way.

The police officer positioned 400 feet above Riley's backyard was not, however, standing on a public road. The vantage point he enjoyed was not one any citizen could readily share. His ability to see over Riley's fence depended on his use of a very expensive and sophisticated piece of machinery to which few ordinary citizens have access. In such circumstances it makes no more sense to rely on the legality of the officer's position in the skies than it would to judge the constitutionality of the wiretap in Katz by the legality of the officer's position outside the telephone booth. The simple inquiry whether the police officer had the legal right to be in the position from which he made his observations cannot suffice, for we cannot assume that Riley's curtilage was so open to the observations of passersby in the skies that he retained little privacy or personal security to be lost to police surveillance. The question before us must be not whether the police were where they had a right to be, but whether public observation of Riley's curtilage was so commonplace that Riley's expectation of privacy in his backyard could not be considered reasonable. To say that an invasion of Riley's privacy from the skies was not impossible is most emphatically not the same as saying that his expectation of privacy within his enclosed curtilage was not "one that society is prepared to recognize as 'reasonable.'" While, as we held in *Ciraolo*, air traffic at elevations of 1,000 feet or more may be so common that whatever could be seen with the naked eye from that elevation is unprotected by the Fourth Amendment, it is a large step from there to say that the Amendment offers no protection against low-level helicopter surveillance of enclosed curtilage areas. To take this step is error enough. That the plurality does so with little analysis beyond its determination that the police complied with FAA regulations is particularly unfortunate.

II

Equally disconcerting is the lack of any meaningful limit to the plurality's holding. It is worth reiterating that the FAA regulations the plurality relies on as establishing that the officer was where he had a right to be set no minimum flight altitude for helicopters. It is difficult, therefore, to see what, if any, helicopter surveillance would run afoul of the plurality's rule that there exists no reasonable expectation of privacy as long as the helicopter is where it has a right to be.

Only in its final paragraph does the plurality opinion suggest that there might be some limits to police helicopter surveillance beyond those imposed by FAA regulations:

> Neither is there any intimation here that the helicopter interfered with respondent's normal use of the greenhouse or of other parts of the curtilage. As far as this record reveals, no intimate details connected with the use of the home or curtilage were observed, and there was no undue noise, and no wind, dust, or threat of injury. In these circumstances, there was no violation of the Fourth Amendment.

I will deal with the "intimate details" below. For the rest, one wonders what the plurality believes the purpose of the Fourth Amendment to be. If through noise, wind, dust, and threat of injury from helicopters the State "interfered with respondent's normal use of the greenhouse or of other parts of the curtilage," Riley might have a cause of action in inverse condemnation, but that is not what the Fourth Amendment is all about. Nowhere is this better stated than in Justice White's opinion for the Court in *Camara*: "The basic purpose of this Amendment, as recognized in countless decisions of this Court, is to safeguard the privacy and security of individuals against arbitrary invasions by governmental officials."

If indeed the purpose of the restraints imposed by the Fourth Amendment is to "safeguard the privacy and security of individuals," then it is puzzling why it should be the helicopter's noise, wind, and dust that provides the measure of whether this constitutional safeguard has been infringed. Imagine a helicopter capable of hovering just above an enclosed courtyard or patio without generating any noise, wind, or dust at all—and, for good measure, without posing any threat of injury. Suppose the police employed this miraculous tool to discover not only what crops people were growing in their greenhouses, but also what books they were reading and who their dinner guests were. Suppose, finally, that the FAA regulations remained unchanged, so that the police were undeniably "where they had a right to be." Would today's plurality continue to assert that "[t]he right of the people to be secure in their persons, houses, papers, and effects, against unreasonable searches and seizures" was not infringed by such surveillance? Yet that is the logical consequence of the plurality's rule that, so long as the police are where they have a right to be under air traffic regulations, the Fourth Amendment is offended only if the aerial surveillance interferes with the use of the backyard as a garden spot. Nor is there anything in the plurality's opinion to suggest that any different rule would apply were the police looking from their helicopter, not into the open curtilage, but through an open window into a room viewable only from the air.

III

Perhaps the most remarkable passage in the plurality opinion is its suggestion that the case might be a different one had any "intimate details connected with the use of the home or curtilage [been] observed." What, one wonders, is meant by "intimate details"? If the police had observed Riley embracing his wife in the backyard greenhouse, would we then say that his reasonable expectation of privacy had been infringed? Where in the Fourth Amendment or in our cases is there any warrant for imposing a requirement that the activity observed must be "intimate" in order to be protected by the Constitution?

It is difficult to avoid the conclusion that the plurality has allowed its analysis of Riley's expectation of privacy to be colored by its distaste for the activity in which he was engaged. It is indeed easy to forget, especially in view of current concern over drug trafficking, that the scope of the Fourth Amendment's protection does not turn on whether the activity disclosed by a search is illegal or innocuous. But we dismiss this as a "drug case" only at the peril of our own liberties. Justice Frankfurter once noted that "[i]t is a fair summary of history to say that the safeguards of liberty have frequently been forged in controversies involving not very nice people," and nowhere is this observation more apt than in the area of the Fourth Amendment, whose words have necessarily been given meaning largely through decisions suppressing evidence of criminal activity. The principle enunciated in this case determines what limits the Fourth Amendment imposes on aerial surveillance of any person, for any reason. If the Constitution does not protect Riley's marijuana garden against such surveillance, it is hard to see how it will prohibit the government from aerial spying on the activities of a law-abiding citizen on her fully enclosed outdoor patio. As Professor Amsterdam has eloquently written: "The question is not whether you or I must draw the blinds before we commit a crime. It is whether you and I must discipline ourselves to draw the blinds every time we enter a room, under pain of surveillance if we do not."

IV

I find little to disagree with Justice O'Connor's concurrence, apart from its closing paragraphs. A majority of the Court thus agrees that the fundamental inquiry is not whether the police were where they had a right to be under FAA regulations, but rather whether Riley's expectation of privacy was rendered illusory by the extent of public observation of his backyard from aerial traffic at 400 feet.

What separates me from Justice O'Connor is essentially an empirical matter concerning the extent of public use of the airspace at that altitude, together with the question of how to resolve that issue. I do not think the constitutional claim should fail simply because "there is reason to believe" that there is "considerable" public flying this close to earth or because Riley "introduced no evidence to the contrary before the Florida courts." I should think that this might be an apt occasion for the application of Professor Davis' distinction between "adjudicative" and "legislative" facts. If so, I think we could take judicial notice that, while there may be an occasional privately owned helicopter that flies over populated areas at an altitude of 400 feet, such flights are a rarity and are almost entirely limited to approaching or leaving airports or to reporting traffic congestion near major roadways. And, as the concurrence agrees, at 699, the extent of police surveillance traffic cannot serve as a bootstrap to demonstrate public use of the airspace.

If, however, we are to resolve the issue by considering whether the appropriate party carried its burden of proof, I again think that Riley must prevail. Because the State has greater access to information concerning customary flight patterns and because the coercive power of the State ought not be brought to bear in cases in which it is unclear whether the prosecution is a product of an unconstitutional, warrantless search, the burden of proof properly rests with the State and not with the individual defendant. The State quite clearly has not carried this burden.

V

The issue in this case is, ultimately, "how tightly the Fourth Amendment permits people to be driven back into the recesses of their lives by the risk of surveillance." The Court today approves warrantless helicopter surveillance from an altitude of 400 feet. While Justice O'Connor's opinion gives reason to hope that this altitude may constitute a lower limit, I find considerable cause for concern in the fact that a plurality of four Justices would remove virtually all constitutional barriers to police surveillance from the vantage point of helicopters. The Fourth Amendment demands that we temper our efforts to apprehend criminals with a concern for the impact on our fundamental liberties of the methods we use. I hope it will be a matter of concern to my colleagues that the police surveillance methods they would sanction were among those described 40 years ago in George Orwell's dread vision of life in the 1980s:

> The black-mustachio'd face gazed down from every commanding corner. There was one on the house front immediately opposite. BIG BROTHER IS WATCHING YOU, the caption said. . . . In the far distance a helicopter skimmed down between the roofs, hovered for an instant like a bluebottle, and darted away again with a curving flight. It was the Police Patrol, snooping into people's windows.

Nineteen Eighty-Four 4 (1949).

Who can read this passage without a shudder, and without the instinctive reaction that it depicts life in some country other than ours? I respectfully dissent.

NOTES AND QUESTIONS

1. All of the opinions here seem to ignore the elephant in the room: the credibility of the police officer's testimony at the suppression hearing that he was able to identify with his naked eye from a distance of 400'—1.3 times the length of a football field—what he "thought" were marijuana plants in a greenhouse defendant's backyard. Bad defense lawyering? A credulous judge? Or maybe just a bad record due to the fact that the suppression motion was granted on the ground that the surveillance constituted a warrantless search? *See* Adam M. Gershowitz & Caroline E. Lewis, *Laundering Police Lies*, 2023 Wis. L. Rev. 1187, 1229-30 (2023) (describing *Florida v. Riley* as a leading example of the Supreme Court countenancing farfetched police testimony). *See generally* Bennett Capers, *Crime, Legitimacy and Testilying*, 83 Ind. L.J. 835 (2008).

2. Note that Michael Riley came to the attention of police only by the way of an anonymous tip. And the police went airborne only after they were unable to see the contents of the greenhouse from the road, a detail that makes mighty curious the plurality opinion's reference to the line from *Ciraolo* that officers need not "shield their eyes" when on public streets. In short, the only basis for finding probable cause for the ultimate search of the property was the officer's "naked eye" observation.

What does *Riley* teach about the role of the "subject expectation of privacy" aspect of the *Katz* test? That it doesn't matter? That it's a one-way factor, only relevant if a person does *not* manifest such an expectation?

3. Riley's expectation of privacy was unreasonable, we are told, because "there is reason to believe that there is considerable public use of airspace at altitudes of 400' and above."

What is the basis for this conclusion, other than the FAA regulations that are discussed? And don't the regulations only mean the location of the helicopter was legal, not that it was common? And why does the legality of the helicopter's location matter one way or the other? Recall that in *Olmstead* the fact that the agents' wiretapping was illegal was irrelevant.

4. Is the extent of the use of the airspace a purely factual issue? In her concurring opinion Justice O'Connor suggests that it is, and says the burden of proof is defendant's, which was not met here. How would a defendant meet such a burden? Would a defendant's testimony that she had never before seen a helicopter anywhere near her home be relevant? Would data—countywide, statewide, national—on the incidence and elevation of helicopter travel be required?

What do you make of the dissent's point that a court should be able to take "judicial notice" of the fact that helicopter flights over homes at an elevation of 400' are a rarity?

5. Is the result in *Riley* required by the Court's previous decision in *Ciraolo*? If so, is it because the facts of the case are sufficiently close that *Ciraolo* is controlling precedent? Or is it because after *Ciraolo* it was no longer reasonable to have an expectation of privacy in curtilage that was visible from airspace? Does the "objective reasonableness" of an expectation of privacy turn to any degree on what the Supreme Court has held in previous cases?

6. What is the constitutional significance of "curtilage" after *Riley*?

7. Should the cultural association of helicopters with intrusive police investigative activity—note Justice Brennan's quote from *1984*, or the terrifying helicopter scene from *Goodfellas* (1990)—have any bearing on reasonable expectations of privacy? Should the nature of the technology used by the police be part of the mix?

Classic paperback edition of George Orwell's *1984*

Ray Liotta as Henry Hill near the end of *Goodfellas* as police helicopters appear to be closing in on him.

Law enforcement's use of modern technology was very much the issue in the next few cases.

Kyllo v. United States

533 U.S. 27 (2000)

Justice Scalia delivered the opinion of the Court.

This case presents the question whether the use of a thermal-imaging device aimed at a private home from a public street to detect relative amounts of heat within the home constitutes a "search" within the meaning of the Fourth Amendment.

I

In 1991 Agent William Elliott of the United States Department of the Interior came to suspect that marijuana was being grown in the home belonging to petitioner Danny Kyllo, part of a triplex on Rhododendron Drive in Florence, Oregon. Indoor marijuana growth typically requires high-intensity lamps. In order to determine whether an amount of heat was emanating from petitioner's home consistent with the use of such lamps, at 3:20 a.m. on January 16, 1992, Agent Elliott and Dan Haas used an Agema Thermovision 210 thermal imager to scan the triplex. Thermal imagers detect infrared radiation, which virtually all objects emit but which is not visible to the naked eye. The imager converts radiation into images based on relative warmth—black is cool, white is hot, shades of gray connote relative differences; in that respect, it operates somewhat like a video camera showing heat images. The scan of Kyllo's home took only a few minutes and was performed from the passenger seat of Agent Elliott's vehicle across the street from the front of the house and also from the street in back of the house. The scan showed that the roof over the garage and a side wall of petitioner's home were relatively hot compared to the rest of the home and substantially warmer than neighboring homes in the triplex. Agent Elliott concluded that petitioner was using halide lights to grow marijuana in his house, which indeed he was. Based on tips from informants, utility bills, and the thermal imaging, a Federal Magistrate Judge issued a warrant authorizing a search of petitioner's home, and the agents found an indoor growing operation involving more than 100 plants. Petitioner was indicted on one count of manufacturing marijuana, in violation of 21 U.S.C. § 841(a)(1). He unsuccessfully moved to suppress the evidence seized from his home and then entered a conditional guilty plea.

The Court of Appeals for the Ninth Circuit remanded the case for an evidentiary hearing regarding the intrusiveness of thermal imaging. On remand the District Court found that the Agema 210 "is a non-intrusive device which emits no rays or beams and shows a crude visual image of the heat being radiated from the outside of the house"; it "did not show any people or activity within the walls of the structure"; "[t]he device used cannot penetrate walls or windows to reveal conversations or human activities"; and "[n]o intimate details of the home were observed." Based on these findings, the District Court upheld the validity of the warrant that relied in part upon the thermal imaging, and reaffirmed its denial of the motion to suppress. The [Ninth Circuit] held that petitioner had shown no subjective expectation of privacy because he had made no attempt to conceal the heat escaping from his home, and even if he had, there was no objectively reasonable expectation of privacy because the imagery "did not expose any intimate details of Kyllo's life," only "amorphous 'hot spots' on the roof and exterior wall." We granted certiorari.

II

The Fourth Amendment provides that "[t]he right of the people to be secure in their persons, houses, papers, and effects, against unreasonable searches and seizures, shall not be violated." "At the very core" of the Fourth Amendment "stands the right of a man to retreat into his own home and there be free from unreasonable governmental intrusion." With few exceptions, the question whether a warrantless search of a home is reasonable and hence constitutional must be answered no.

On the other hand, the antecedent question whether or not a Fourth Amendment "search" has occurred is not so simple under our precedent. The permissibility of ordinary visual surveillance of a home used to be clear because, well into the 20th century, our Fourth Amendment jurisprudence was tied to common-law trespass. Visual surveillance was unquestionably lawful because "'the eye cannot by the laws of England be guilty of a trespass.'" We have since decoupled violation of a person's Fourth Amendment rights from trespassory violation of his property, but the lawfulness of warrantless visual surveillance of a home has still been preserved. As we observed in *Ciraolo*, "[t]he Fourth Amendment protection of the home has never been extended to require law enforcement officers to shield their eyes when passing by a home on public thoroughfares."

One might think that the new validating rationale would be that examining the portion of a house that is in plain public view, while it is a "search" despite the absence of trespass, is not an "unreasonable" one under the Fourth Amendment. But in fact we have held that visual observation is no "search" at all—perhaps in order to preserve somewhat more intact our doctrine that warrantless searches are presumptively unconstitutional. In assessing when a search is not a search, we have applied somewhat in reverse the principle first enunciated in *Katz. Katz* involved eavesdropping by means of an electronic listening device placed on the outside of a telephone booth—a location not within the catalog ("persons, houses, papers, and effects") that the Fourth Amendment protects against unreasonable searches. We held that the Fourth Amendment nonetheless protected Katz from the warrantless eavesdropping because he "justifiably relied" upon the privacy of the telephone booth. As Justice Harlan's oft-quoted concurrence described it, a Fourth Amendment search occurs when the government violates a subjective expectation of privacy that society recognizes as reasonable. We have subsequently applied this principle to hold that a Fourth Amendment search does not occur—even when the explicitly protected location of a house is concerned—unless "the individual manifested a subjective expectation of privacy in the object of the challenged search," and "society [is] willing to recognize that expectation as reasonable." We have applied this test in holding that it is not a search for the police to use a pen register at the phone company to determine what numbers were dialed in a private home, and we have applied the test on two different occasions in holding that aerial surveillance of private homes and surrounding areas does not constitute a search.

The present case involves officers on a public street engaged in more than naked-eye surveillance of a home. We have previously reserved judgment as to how much technological enhancement of ordinary perception from such a vantage point, if any, is too much. While we upheld enhanced aerial photography of an industrial complex in *Dow Chemical*, we noted that we found "it important that this is not an area immediately adjacent to a private home, where privacy expectations are most heightened."

III

It would be foolish to contend that the degree of privacy secured to citizens by the Fourth Amendment has been entirely unaffected by the advance of technology. For example, as the cases discussed above make clear, the technology enabling human flight has exposed to public view (and hence, we have said, to official observation) uncovered portions of the house and its curtilage that once were private. The question we confront today is what limits there are upon this power of technology to shrink the realm of guaranteed privacy.

The *Katz* test—whether the individual has an expectation of privacy that society is prepared to recognize as reasonable—has often been criticized as circular, and hence subjective and unpredictable. While it may be difficult to refine *Katz* when the search of areas such as telephone booths, automobiles, or even the curtilage and uncovered portions of residences is at issue, in the case of the search of the interior of homes—the prototypical and hence most commonly litigated area of protected privacy—there is a ready criterion, with roots deep in the common law, of the minimal expectation of privacy that exists, and that is acknowledged to be reasonable. To withdraw protection of this minimum expectation would be to permit police technology to erode the privacy guaranteed by the Fourth Amendment. We think that obtaining by sense-enhancing technology any information regarding the interior of the home that could not otherwise have been obtained without physical "intrusion into a constitutionally protected area," constitutes a search—at least where (as here) the technology in question is not in general public use. This assures preservation of that degree of privacy against government that existed when the Fourth Amendment was adopted. On the basis of this criterion, the information obtained by the thermal imager in this case was the product of a search.

The Government maintains, however, that the thermal imaging must be upheld because it detected "only heat radiating from the external surface of the house." The dissent makes this its leading point, contending that there is a fundamental difference between what it calls "off-the-wall" observations and "through-the-wall surveillance." But just as a thermal imager captures only heat emanating from a house, so also a powerful directional microphone picks up only sound emanating from a house-and a satellite capable of scanning from many miles away would pick up only visible light emanating from a house. We rejected such a mechanical interpretation of the Fourth Amendment in *Katz*, where the eavesdropping device picked up only sound waves that reached the exterior of the phone booth. Reversing that approach would leave the homeowner at the mercy of advancing technology—including imaging technology that could discern all human activity in the home. While the technology used in the present case was relatively crude, the rule we adopt must take account of more sophisticated systems that are already in use or in development. The dissent's reliance on the distinction between "off-the-wall" and "through-the-wall" observation is entirely incompatible with the dissent's belief, which we discuss below, that thermal-imaging observations of the intimate details of a home are impermissible. The most sophisticated thermal-imaging devices continue to measure heat "off-the-wall" rather than "through-the-wall"; the dissent's disapproval of these more sophisticated thermal-imaging devices, is an acknowledgement that there is no substance to this distinction. As for the dissent's extraordinary assertion that anything learned through "an inference" cannot be a search, that would validate even the "through-the-wall" technologies that the dissent purports to disapprove. Surely the dissent does not believe that the through-the-wall radar or ultrasound technology produces an 8-by-10 Kodak glossy that needs no analysis (i.e., the making of inferences). And, of course, the novel proposition that inference insulates a search is blatantly contrary to *Karo*, where the police "inferred" from the activation of a beeper that a certain can of ether was in the home. The police activity was held to be a search, and the search was held unlawful.

The Government also contends that the thermal imaging was constitutional because it did not "detect private activities occurring in private areas." It points out that in *Dow Chemical* we observed that the enhanced aerial photography did not reveal any "intimate details." *Dow Chemical*, however, involved enhanced aerial photography of an industrial complex, which does not share the Fourth Amendment sanctity of the home. The Fourth Amendment's protection of the home has never been tied to measurement of the quality or quantity of information obtained. In *Silverman*, for example, we made clear that any physical invasion of the structure of the home, "by even a fraction of an inch," was too much, and there is certainly no exception to the warrant requirement for the officer who barely cracks open the front door and sees nothing but the nonintimate rug on the vestibule floor. In the home, our cases show, all details are intimate details, because the entire area is held safe from prying government eyes. Thus, in *Karo, supra*, the only thing detected was a can of ether in the home; and in *Arizona v. Hicks* (1987), the only thing detected by a physical search that went beyond what officers lawfully present could observe in "plain view" was the registration number of a phonograph turntable. These were intimate details because they were details of the home, just as was the detail of how warm—or even how relatively warm—Kyllo was heating his residence.

Limiting the prohibition of thermal imaging to "intimate details" would not only be wrong in principle; it would be impractical in application, failing to provide "a workable accommodation between the needs of law enforcement and the interests protected by the Fourth Amendment." To begin with, there is no necessary connection between the sophistication of the surveillance equipment and the "intimacy" of the details that it observes—which means that one cannot say (and the police cannot be assured) that use of the relatively crude equipment at issue here will always be lawful. The Agema Thermovision 210 might disclose, for example, at what hour each night the lady of the house takes her daily sauna and bath—a detail that many would consider "intimate"; and a much more sophisticated system might detect nothing more intimate than the fact that someone left a closet light on. We could not, in other words, develop a rule approving only that through-the-wall surveillance which identifies objects no smaller than 36 by 36 inches, but would have to develop a jurisprudence specifying which home activities are "intimate" and which are not. And even when (if ever) that jurisprudence were fully developed, no police officer would be able to know in advance whether his through-the-wall surveillance picks up "intimate" details—and thus would be unable to know in advance whether it is constitutional.

The dissent's proposed standard—whether the technology offers the "functional equivalent of actual presence in the area being searched"—would seem quite similar to our own at first blush. The dissent concludes that *Katz* was such a case, but then inexplicably asserts that if the same listening device only revealed the volume of the conversation, the surveillance would be permissible. Yet if, without technology, the police could not discern volume without being actually present in the phone booth, Justice Stevens should conclude a search has occurred. The same should hold for the interior heat of the home if only a person present in the home could discern the heat. Thus the driving force of the dissent, despite its recitation of the above standard, appears to be a distinction among different types of information—whether the "homeowner would even care if anybody noticed." The dissent offers no practical guidance for the application of this standard, and for reasons already discussed, we believe there can be none. The people in their houses, as well as the police, deserve more precision.

We have said that the Fourth Amendment draws "a firm line at the entrance to the house." That line, we think, must be not only firm but also bright—which requires clear specification of those methods of surveillance that require a warrant. While it is certainly possible to conclude from the videotape of the thermal imaging that occurred in this case that no "significant" compromise of the homeowner's privacy has occurred, we must take the long view, from the original meaning of the Fourth Amendment forward.

The Fourth Amendment is to be construed in the light of what was deemed an unreasonable search and seizure when it was adopted, and in a manner which will conserve public interests as well as the interests and rights of individual citizens." *Carroll v. United States* (1925).

Where, as here, the Government uses a device that is not in general public use, to explore details of the home that would previously have been unknowable without physical intrusion, the surveillance is a "search" and is presumptively unreasonable without a warrant.

Since we hold the Thermovision imaging to have been an unlawful search, it will remain for the District Court to determine whether, without the evidence it provided, the search warrant issued in this case was supported by probable cause—and if not, whether there is any other basis for supporting admission of the evidence that the search pursuant to the warrant produced.

The judgment of the Court of Appeals is reversed; the case is remanded for further proceedings consistent with this opinion.

NOTES AND QUESTIONS

1. Does the result here reveal itself in the first paragraph of the Court's analysis, with the Court's reminder that the home is at the "very core" of the Fourth Amendment's protection? Does the Court's recitation of the Fourth Amendment's language—"persons, houses, papers, and effects"—portend revitalized interest in a textualist approach to the Amendment?

2. The Court finds it material that thermal imaging is "sense enhancing" technology. The point seems to be that the technology permits police officers who are situated in perfectly legitimate investigative locations — across the street from Kyllo's home — to improve on what they could discern with their own eyes and ears and thereby defeat reasonable expectations of privacy. Don't devices such as binoculars confer a similar sensory "enhancement"?

3. Why does the Court limit its holding to "sense enhancing" technology that is "not in general public use"? What if at some point every police department in the country gets an Agema Thermovision 210 or its equivalent and uses it routinely but only after getting a search warrant? General public use? Does "public use" mean that the use has to spread to include uses for purposes other than law enforcement? In 2024, just 24 years after *Kyllo*, dozens of different types of thermal imaging devices could be purchased on Amazon for under $500.

Handheld thermal imaging device

4. "With few exceptions, the question whether a warrantless search of a home is reasonable and hence constitutional must be answered no," says the Court in *Kyllo*. Is the use of thermal imagery only found to be a search here because it was directed at a home? What if it was directed at Kyllo's garage? Or a greenhouse in his backyard?

5. The Court says that it has "decoupled" Fourth Amendment violations from notions of trespass. Is that how you read *Katz*, as a decoupling?

United States v. Jones

565 U.S. 400 (2012)

Justice Scalia delivered the opinion of the Court.

We decide whether the attachment of a Global-Positioning-System (GPS) tracking device to an individual's vehicle, and subsequent use of that device to monitor the vehicle's movements on public streets, constitutes a search or seizure within the meaning of the Fourth Amendment.

I

In 2004 respondent Antoine Jones, owner and operator of a nightclub in the District of Columbia, came under suspicion of trafficking in narcotics and was made the target of an investigation by a joint Federal Bureau of Investigation and Metropolitan Police Department task force. Officers employed various investigative techniques, including visual surveillance of the nightclub, installation of a camera focused on the front door of the club, and a pen register and wiretap covering Jones's cellular phone.

Based in part on information gathered from these sources, in 2005 the Government applied to the United States District Court for the District of Columbia for a warrant authorizing the use of an electronic tracking device on the Jeep Grand Cherokee registered to Jones's wife. A warrant issued, authorizing installation of the device in the District of Columbia and within 10 days.

On the 11th day, and not in the District of Columbia but in Maryland, agents installed a GPS tracking device on the undercarriage of the Jeep while it was parked in a public parking lot. Over the next 28 days, the Government used the device to track the vehicle's movements, and once had to replace the device's battery when the vehicle was parked in a different public lot in Maryland. By means of signals from multiple satellites, the device established the vehicle's location within 50 to 100 feet, and communicated that location by cellular phone to a Government computer. It relayed more than 2,000 pages of data over the 4-week period.

The Government ultimately obtained a multiple-count indictment charging Jones and several alleged co-conspirators with, as relevant here, conspiracy to distribute and possess with intent to distribute five kilograms or more of cocaine and 50 grams or more of cocaine base, in violation of 21 U.S.C. §§ 841 and 846. Before trial, Jones filed a motion to suppress evidence obtained through the GPS device. The District Court granted the motion only in part, suppressing the data obtained while the vehicle was parked in the garage adjoining Jones's residence. It held the remaining data admissible, because "'[a] person traveling in an automobile on public thoroughfares has no reasonable expectation of privacy in his movements from one place to another.'" Jones's trial in October 2006 produced a hung jury on the conspiracy count.

In March 2007, a grand jury returned another indictment, charging Jones and others with the same conspiracy. The Government introduced at trial the same GPS-derived locational data admitted in the first trial, which connected Jones to the alleged conspirators' stash house that contained $850,000 in cash, 97 kilograms of cocaine, and 1 kilogram of cocaine base. The jury returned a guilty verdict, and the District Court sentenced Jones to life imprisonment.

The United States Court of Appeals for the District of Columbia Circuit reversed the conviction because of admission of the evidence obtained by warrantless use of the GPS device which, it said, violated the Fourth Amendment. The D.C. Circuit denied the Government's petition for rehearing en banc, with four judges dissenting. We granted certiorari.

II

A

The Fourth Amendment provides in relevant part that "[t]he right of the people to be secure in their persons, houses, papers, and effects, against unreasonable searches and seizures, shall not be violated." It is beyond dispute that a vehicle is an "effect" as that term is used in the Amendment. We hold that the Government's installation of a GPS device on a target's vehicle, and its use of that device to monitor the vehicle's movements, constitutes a "search."

It is important to be clear about what occurred in this case: The Government physically occupied private property for the purpose of obtaining information. We have no doubt that such a physical intrusion would have been considered a "search" within the meaning of the Fourth Amendment when it was adopted.

The text of the Fourth Amendment reflects its close connection to property, since otherwise it would have referred simply to "the right of the people to be secure against unreasonable searches and seizures"; the phrase "in their persons, houses, papers, and effects" would have been superfluous.

Consistent with this understanding, our Fourth Amendment jurisprudence was tied to common-law trespass, at least until the latter half of the 20th century.

Our later cases, of course, have deviated from that exclusively property-based approach. In *Katz* we said that "the Fourth Amendment protects people, not places," and found a violation in attachment of an eavesdropping device to a public telephone booth. Our later cases have applied the analysis of Justice Harlan's concurrence in that case, which said that a violation occurs when government officers violate a person's "reasonable expectation of privacy."

The Government contends that the Harlan standard shows that no search occurred here, since Jones had no "reasonable expectation of privacy" in the area of the Jeep accessed by Government agents (its underbody) and in the locations of the Jeep on the public roads, which were visible to all. But we need not address the Government's contentions, because Jones's Fourth Amendment rights do not rise or fall with the *Katz* formulation. At bottom, we must "assur[e] preservation of that degree of privacy against government that existed when the Fourth Amendment was adopted." As explained, for most of our history the Fourth Amendment was understood to embody a particular concern for government trespass upon the areas ("persons, houses, papers, and effects") it enumerates. *Katz* did not repudiate that understanding. Less than two years later the Court upheld defendants' contention that the Government could not introduce against them conversations between other people obtained by warrantless placement of electronic surveillance devices in their homes. The opinion rejected the dissent's contention that there was no Fourth Amendment violation "unless the conversational privacy of the homeowner himself is invaded."

More recently, the Court unanimously rejected the argument that although a "seizure" had occurred "in a 'technical' sense" when a trailer home was forcibly removed, no Fourth Amendment violation occurred because law enforcement had not "invade[d] the [individuals'] privacy." *Katz*, the Court explained, established that "property rights are not the sole measure of Fourth Amendment violations," but did not "snuf[f] out the previously recognized protection for property." As Justice Brennan explained in his concurrence in *Knotts*, *Katz* did not erode the principle "that, when the Government does engage in physical intrusion of a constitutionally protected area in order to obtain information, that intrusion may constitute a violation of the Fourth Amendment." We have embodied that preservation of past rights in our very definition of "reasonable expectation of privacy" which we have said to be an expectation "that has a source outside of the Fourth Amendment, either by reference to concepts of real or personal property law or to understandings that are recognized and permitted by society."

The Government contends that several of our post-*Katz* cases foreclose the conclusion that what occurred here constituted a search. It relies principally on two cases in which we rejected Fourth Amendment challenges to "beepers," electronic tracking devices that represent another form of electronic monitoring. The first case, *Knotts*, upheld against Fourth Amendment challenge the use of a "beeper" that had been placed in a container of chloroform, allowing law enforcement to monitor the location of the container. We said that there had been no infringement of Knotts' reasonable expectation of privacy since the information obtained—the location of the automobile carrying the container on public roads, and the location of the off-loaded container in open fields near Knotts' cabin—had been voluntarily conveyed to the public. But as we have discussed, the *Katz* reasonable-expectation-of-privacy test has been added to, not substituted for, the common-law trespassory test. The holding in *Knotts* addressed only the former, since the latter was not at issue. The beeper had been placed in the container before it came into Knotts' possession, with the consent of the then-owner. Knotts did not challenge that installation, and we specifically declined to consider its effect on the Fourth Amendment analysis. *Knotts* would be relevant, perhaps, if the Government were making the argument that what would otherwise be an unconstitutional search is not such where it produces only public information. The Government does not make that argument, and we know of no case that would support it.

The second "beeper" case, *United States v. Karo* (1984), does not suggest a different conclusion. There we addressed the question left open by *Knotts*, whether the installation of a beeper in a container amounted to a search or seizure. As in *Knotts*, at the time the beeper was installed the container belonged to a third party, and it did not come into possession of the defendant until later. Thus, the specific question we considered was whether the installation "with the consent of the original owner constitute[d] a search or seizure . . . when the container is delivered to a buyer having no knowledge of the presence of the beeper." We held not. The Government, we said, came into physical contact with the container only before it belonged to the defendant Karo; and the transfer of the container with the unmonitored beeper inside did not convey any information and thus did not invade Karo's privacy. That conclusion is perfectly consistent with the one we reach here. Karo accepted the container as it came to him, beeper and all, and was therefore not entitled to object to the beeper's presence, even though it was used to monitor the container's location. Jones, who possessed the Jeep at the time the Government trespassorily inserted the information-gathering device, is on much different footing.

The Government also points to our exposition in *New York v. Class* (1986), that "[t]he exterior of a car . . . is thrust into the public eye, and thus to examine it does not constitute a 'search.'" That statement is of marginal relevance here since, as the Government acknowledges, "the officers in this case did more than conduct a visual inspection of respondent's vehicle." By attaching the device to the Jeep, officers encroached on a protected area. In *Class* itself we suggested that this would make a difference, for we concluded that an officer's momentary reaching into the interior of a vehicle did constitute a search.

Finally, the Government's position gains little support from our conclusion in *Oliver v. United States* (1984), that officers' information-gathering intrusion on an "open field" did not constitute a Fourth Amendment search even though it was a trespass at common law. Quite simply, an open field, unlike the curtilage of a home, is not one of those protected areas enumerated in the Fourth Amendment. The Government's physical intrusion on such an area — unlike its intrusion on the "effect" at issue here — is of no Fourth Amendment significance.

B

The concurrence begins by accusing us of applying "18th-century tort law." That is a distortion. What we apply is an 18th-century guarantee against unreasonable searches, which we believe must provide at a minimum the degree of protection it afforded when it was adopted. The concurrence does not share that belief. It would apply exclusively *Katz*'s reasonable-expectation-of-privacy test, even when that eliminates rights that previously existed.

The concurrence faults our approach for "present[ing] particularly vexing problems" in cases that do not involve physical contact, such as those that involve the transmission of electronic signals. We entirely fail to understand that point. For unlike the concurrence, which would make *Katz* the exclusive test, we do not make trespass the exclusive test. Situations involving merely the transmission of electronic signals without trespass would remain subject to *Katz* analysis.

In fact, it is the concurrence's insistence on the exclusivity of the *Katz* test that needlessly leads us into "particularly vexing problems" in the present case. This Court has to date not deviated from the understanding that mere visual observation does not constitute a search. We accordingly held in *Knotts* that "[a] person traveling in an automobile on public thoroughfares has no reasonable expectation of privacy in his movements from one place to another." Thus, even assuming that the concurrence is correct to say that "[t]raditional surveillance" of Jones for a 4-week period "would have required a large team of agents, multiple vehicles, and perhaps aerial assistance," our cases suggest that such visual observation is constitutionally permissible. It may be that achieving the same result through electronic means, without an accompanying trespass, is an unconstitutional invasion of privacy, but the present case does not require us to answer that question.

And answering it affirmatively leads us needlessly into additional thorny problems. The concurrence posits that "relatively short-term monitoring of a person's movements on public streets" is okay, but that "the use of longer term GPS monitoring in investigations of *most offenses*" is no good (emphasis added). That introduces yet another novelty into our jurisprudence. There is no precedent for the proposition that whether a search has occurred depends on the nature of the crime being investigated. And even accepting that novelty, it remains unexplained why a 4-week investigation is "surely" too long and why a drug-trafficking conspiracy involving substantial amounts of cash and narcotics is not an "extraordinary offens[e]" which may permit longer observation. What of a 2-day monitoring of a suspected purveyor of stolen electronics? Or of a 6-month monitoring of a suspected terrorist? We may have to grapple with these "vexing problems" in some future case where a classic trespassory search is not involved and resort must be had to *Katz* analysis; but there is no reason for rushing forward to resolve them here.

• • •

Justice ALITO, with whom Justice GINSBURG, Justice BREYER, and Justice KAGAN join, concurring in the judgment.

This case requires us to apply the Fourth Amendment's prohibition of unreasonable searches and seizures to a 21st-century surveillance technique, the use of a Global Positioning System (GPS) device to monitor a vehicle's movements for an extended period of time. Ironically, the Court has chosen to decide this case based on 18th-century tort law. By attaching a small GPS device to the underside of the vehicle that respondent drove, the law enforcement officers in this case engaged in conduct that might have provided grounds in 1791 for a suit for trespass to chattels. And for this reason, the Court concludes, the installation and use of the GPS device constituted a search.

This holding, in my judgment, is unwise. It strains the language of the Fourth Amendment; it has little if any support in current Fourth Amendment case law; and it is highly artificial.

I would analyze the question presented in this case by asking whether respondent's reasonable expectations of privacy were violated by the long-term monitoring of the movements of the vehicle he drove.

I

A

The Fourth Amendment prohibits "unreasonable searches and seizures," and the Court makes very little effort to explain how the attachment or use of the GPS device fits within these terms. The Court does not contend that there was a seizure. A seizure of property occurs when there is "some meaningful interference with an individual's possessory interests in that property," *United States v. Jacobsen* (1984), and here there was none. Indeed, the success of the surveillance technique that the officers employed was dependent on the fact that the GPS did not interfere in any way with the operation of the vehicle, for if any such interference had been detected, the device might have been discovered.

The Court does claim that the installation and use of the GPS constituted a search, but this conclusion is dependent on the questionable proposition that these two procedures cannot be separated for purposes of Fourth Amendment analysis. If these two procedures are analyzed separately, it is not at all clear from the Court's opinion why either should be regarded as a search. It is clear that the attachment of the GPS device was not itself a search; if the device had not functioned or if the officers had not used it, no information would have been obtained. And the Court does not contend that the use of the device constituted a search either. On the contrary, the Court accepts the holding in *Knotts* that the use of a surreptitiously planted electronic device to monitor a vehicle's movements on public roads did not amount to a search.

The Court argues — and I agree — that "we must 'assur[e] preservation of that degree of privacy against government that existed when the Fourth Amendment was adopted.'" But it is almost impossible to think of late-18th-century situations that are analogous to what took place in this case. (Is it possible to imagine a case in which a constable secreted himself somewhere in a coach and remained there for a period of time in order to monitor the movements of the coach's owner?) The Court's theory seems to be that the concept of a search, as originally understood, comprehended any technical trespass that led to the gathering of evidence, but we know that this is incorrect. At common law, any unauthorized intrusion on private property was actionable, but a trespass on open fields, as opposed to the "curtilage" of a home, does not fall within the scope of the Fourth Amendment because private property outside the curtilage is not part of a "hous[e]" within the meaning of the Fourth Amendment.

B

'The Court's reasoning in this case is very similar to that in the Court's early decisions involving wiretapping and electronic eavesdropping, namely, that a technical trespass followed by the gathering of evidence constitutes a search. In the early electronic surveillance cases, the Court concluded that a Fourth Amendment search occurred when private conversations were monitored as a result of an "unauthorized physical penetration into the premises occupied" by the defendant. *Silverman v. United States*. In *Silverman*, police officers listened to conversations in an attached home by inserting a "spike mike" through the wall that this house shared with the vacant house next door. This procedure was held to be a search because the mike made contact with a heating duct on the other side of the wall and thus "usurp[ed] . . . an integral part of the premises."

By contrast, in cases in which there was no trespass, it was held that there was no search. Thus, in *Olmstead*, the Court found that the Fourth Amendment did not apply because "[t] he taps from house lines were made in the streets near the houses." Similarly, the Court concluded that no search occurred in *Goldman*, where a "detectaphone" was placed on the outer wall of defendant's office for the purpose of overhearing conversations held within the room.

This trespass-based rule was repeatedly criticized. In *Olmstead*, Justice Brandeis wrote that it was "immaterial where the physical connection with the telephone wires . . . was made. Although a private conversation transmitted by wire did not fall within the literal words of the Fourth Amendment, he argued, the Amendment should be understood as prohibiting "every unjustifiable intrusion by the Government upon the privacy of the individual."

Katz finally did away with the old approach, holding that a trespass was not required for a Fourth Amendment violation. *Katz* involved the use of a listening device that was attached to the outside of a public telephone booth and that allowed police officers to eavesdrop on one end of the target's phone conversation. This procedure did not physically intrude on the area occupied by the target, but the *Katz* Court "repudiate[ed]" the old doctrine, and held that "[t]he fact that the electronic device employed . . . did not happen to penetrate the wall of the booth can have no constitutional significance." What mattered, the Court now held, was whether the conduct at issue "violated the privacy upon which [the defendant] justifiably relied while using the telephone booth." *Katz.*

Under this approach, as the Court later put it when addressing the relevance of a technical trespass, "an actual trespass is neither necessary nor sufficient to establish a constitutional violation." In *Oliver*, the Court wrote:

> The existence of a property right is but one element in determining whether expectations of privacy are legitimate. "The premise that property interests control the right of the Government to search and seize has been discredited." *Katz.*

II

The majority suggests that two post-*Katz* decisions—*Soldal v. Cook County* (1992), and *Alderman v. United States* (1969)—show that a technical trespass is sufficient to establish the existence of a search, but they provide little support.

In *Soldal*, the Court held that towing away a trailer home without the owner's consent constituted a seizure even if this did not invade the occupants' personal privacy. But in the present case, the Court does not find that there was a seizure, and it is clear that none occurred.

In *Alderman*, the Court held that the Fourth Amendment rights of homeowners were implicated by the use of a surreptitiously planted listening device to monitor third-party conversations that occurred within their home. *Alderman* is best understood to mean that the homeowners had a legitimate expectation of privacy in all conversations that took place under their roof.

In sum, the majority is hard pressed to find support in post-*Katz* cases for its trespass-based theory.

III

Disharmony with a substantial body of existing case law is only one of the problems with the Court's approach in this case.

I will briefly note four others. First, the Court's reasoning largely disregards what is really important (the use of a GPS for the purpose of long-term tracking) and instead attaches great significance to something that most would view as relatively minor (attaching to the bottom of a car a small, light object that does not interfere in any way with the car's operation). Attaching such an object is generally regarded as so trivial that it does not provide a basis for recovery under modern tort law. *See* Prosser & Keeton § 14, at 87 (harmless or trivial contact with personal property not actionable); D. Dobbs, Law of Torts 124 (2000) (same). But under the Court's reasoning, this conduct may violate the Fourth Amendment. By contrast, if long-term monitoring can be accomplished without committing a technical trespass—suppose, for example, that the Federal Government required or persuaded auto manufacturers to include a GPS tracking device in every car—the Court's theory would provide no protection.

Second, the Court's approach leads to incongruous results. If the police attach a GPS device to a car and use the device to follow the car for even a brief time, under the Court's theory, the Fourth Amendment applies. But if the police follow the same car for a much longer period using unmarked cars and aerial assistance, this tracking is not subject to any Fourth Amendment constraints.

In the present case, the Fourth Amendment applies, the Court concludes, because the officers installed the GPS device after respondent's wife, to whom the car was registered, turned it over to respondent for his exclusive use. But if the GPS had been attached prior to that time, the Court's theory would lead to a different result. The Court proceeds on the assumption that respondent "had at least the property rights of a bailee," but a bailee may sue for a trespass to chattel only if the injury occurs during the term of the bailment. So if the GPS device had been installed before respondent's wife gave him the keys, respondent would have no claim for trespass—and, presumably, no Fourth Amendment claim either.

Third, under the Court's theory, the coverage of the Fourth Amendment may vary from State to State. If the events at issue here had occurred in a community-property State or a State that has adopted the Uniform Marital Property Act, respondent would likely be an owner of the vehicle, and it would not matter whether the GPS was installed before or after his wife turned over the keys. In non-community-property States, on the other hand, the registration of the vehicle in the name of respondent's wife would generally be regarded as presumptive evidence that she was the sole owner.

Fourth, the Court's reliance on the law of trespass will present particularly vexing problems in cases involving surveillance that is carried out by making electronic, as opposed to physical, contact with the item to be tracked. For example, suppose that the officers in the present case had followed respondent by surreptitiously activating a stolen vehicle detection system that came with the car when it was purchased. Would the sending of a radio signal to activate this system constitute a trespass to chattels? Trespass to chattels has traditionally required a physical touching of the property. In recent years, courts have wrestled with the application of this old tort in cases involving unwanted electronic contact with computer systems, and some have held that even the transmission of electrons that occurs when a communication is sent from one computer to another is enough. But may such decisions be followed in applying the Court's trespass theory? Assuming that what matters under the Court's theory is the law of trespass as it existed at the time of the adoption of the Fourth Amendment, do these recent decisions represent a change in the law or simply the application of the old tort to new situations?

IV

A

The *Katz* expectation-of-privacy test avoids the problems and complications noted above, but it is not without its own difficulties. It involves a degree of circularity, and judges are apt to confuse their own expectations of privacy with those of the hypothetical reasonable person to which the *Katz* test looks. In addition, the *Katz* test rests on the assumption that this hypothetical reasonable person has a well-developed and stable set of privacy expectations. But technology can change those expectations. Dramatic technological change may lead to periods in which popular expectations are in flux and may ultimately produce significant changes in popular attitudes. New technology may provide increased convenience or security at the expense of privacy, and many people may find the tradeoff worthwhile. And even if the public does not welcome the diminution of privacy that new technology entails, they may eventually reconcile themselves to this development as inevitable.

On the other hand, concern about new intrusions on privacy may spur the enactment of legislation to protect against these intrusions. This is what ultimately happened with respect to wiretapping. After *Katz*, Congress did not leave it to the courts to develop a body of Fourth Amendment case law governing that complex subject. Instead, Congress promptly enacted a comprehensive statute, and since that time, the regulation of wiretapping has been governed primarily by statute and not by case law. In an ironic sense, although *Katz* overruled *Olmstead*,

Chief Justice Taft's suggestion in the latter case that the regulation of wiretapping was a matter better left for Congress, has been borne out.

B

Recent years have seen the emergence of many new devices that permit the monitoring of a person's movements. In some locales, closed-circuit television video monitoring is becoming ubiquitous. On toll roads, automatic toll collection systems create a precise record of the movements of motorists who choose to make use of that convenience. Many motorists purchase cars that are equipped with devices that permit a central station to ascertain the car's location at any time so that roadside assistance may be provided if needed and the car may be found if it is stolen.

Perhaps most significant, cell phones and other wireless devices now permit wireless carriers to track and record the location of users—and as of June 2011, it has been reported, there were more than 322 million wireless devices in use in the United States. For older phones, the accuracy of the location information depends on the density of the tower network, but new "smart phones," which are equipped with a GPS device, permit more precise tracking. For example, when a user activates the GPS on such a phone, a provider is able to monitor the phone's location and speed of movement and can then report back real-time traffic conditions after combining ("crowdsourcing") the speed of all such phones on any particular road. Similarly, phone-location-tracking services are offered as "social" tools, allowing consumers to find (or to avoid) others who enroll in these services. The availability and use of these and other new devices will continue to shape the average person's expectations about the privacy of his or her daily movements.

V

In the precomputer age, the greatest protections of privacy were neither constitutional nor statutory, but practical. Traditional surveillance for any extended period of time was difficult and costly and therefore rarely undertaken. The surveillance at issue in this case—constant monitoring of the location of a vehicle for four weeks—would have required a large team of agents, multiple vehicles, and perhaps aerial assistance. Only an investigation of unusual importance could have justified such an expenditure of law enforcement resources. Devices like the one used in the present case, however, make long-term monitoring relatively easy and cheap. In circumstances involving dramatic technological change, the best solution to privacy concerns may be legislative. A legislative body is well situated to gauge changing public attitudes, to draw detailed lines, and to balance privacy and public safety in a comprehensive way.

To date, however, Congress and most States have not enacted statutes regulating the use of GPS tracking technology for law enforcement purposes. The best that we can do in this case is to apply existing Fourth Amendment doctrine and to ask whether the use of GPS tracking in a particular case involved a degree of intrusion that a reasonable person would not have anticipated.

Under this approach, relatively short-term monitoring of a person's movements on public streets accords with expectations of privacy that our society has recognized as reasonable. But the use of longer term GPS monitoring in investigations of most offenses impinges on expectations of privacy. For such offenses, society's expectation has been that law enforcement agents and others would not—and indeed, in the main, simply could not—secretly monitor and catalogue every single movement of an individual's car for a very long period. In this case, for four weeks, law enforcement agents tracked every movement that respondent made in the vehicle he was driving. We need not identify with precision the point at which the tracking of this vehicle became a search, for the line was surely crossed before the 4-week mark. Other cases may present more difficult questions. But where uncertainty exists with respect to whether a certain period of GPS surveillance is long enough to constitute a Fourth Amendment search, the police may always seek a warrant. We also need not consider whether prolonged GPS monitoring in the context of investigations involving extraordinary offenses would similarly intrude on a constitutionally protected sphere of privacy. In such cases, long-term tracking might have been mounted using previously available techniques.

For these reasons, I conclude that the lengthy monitoring that occurred in this case constituted a search under the Fourth Amendment. I therefore agree with the majority that the decision of the Court of Appeals must be affirmed. . . .

NOTES AND QUESTIONS

1. What is the relationship between the "trespass" test and the "reasonable expectation of privacy" test after *Jones*? Is a trespass a sufficient condition for a Fourth Amendment violation even if not a necessary condition? Is the Court correct that the latter test has "added to not substituted for" the former test?

2. The government contends, in what appears to be something of an eleventh-hour Hail Mary pass, that even if the use of the GPS monitoring device was a search, it was supported by "reasonable suspicion" and thus constitutional. What is your reaction to this argument? How does the government's use of GPS monitoring here compare to a permissible *Terry* stop?

3. In her concurring opinion Justice Sotomayor questions the continuing validity of the Court's third-party cases, pointing out Justice Marshall's observation in dissent in *Smith v. Maryland*, 442 U.S. 735, 749 (1979) (Marshall, J., dissenting): "Privacy is not a discrete commodity, possessed absolutely or not at all. Those who disclose certain facts to a bank or phone company for a limited business purpose need not assume that this information will be released to other persons for other purposes."

Should the issue be reframed as a reasonable expectation of privacy with respect to the government?

4. Justice Alito's concurrence suggests that some shorter period of surveillance than the 28 days here might not constitute a search. What is the relevance of the duration of the monitoring?

5. What are the pros and cons of legislative solutions to government use of technology for investigative purposes?

With respect to living "technology," the Court rejected the notion that police use of drug-sniffing dogs was a search given the limited nature of both the intrusion and the information derived. *United States v. Place*, 462 U.S. 696 (1983). *See also Illinois v. Caballes*, 543 U.S. 205 (2005) (subjecting vehicle pulled over for traffic stop to canine sniff does not violate Fourth Amendment where duration of stop not unreasonably extended; no legitimate expectation of privacy inasmuch as dog only able to detect illegal substances).

But traditional notions of property and home can still be trump cards.

Florida v. Jardines

569 U.S. 1 (2013)

Justice Scalia delivered the opinion of the Court.

We consider whether using a drug-sniffing dog on a homeowner's porch to investigate the contents of the home is a "search" within the meaning of the Fourth Amendment.

I

In 2006, Detective William Pedraja of the Miami-Dade Police Department received an unverified tip that marijuana was being grown in the home of respondent Joelis Jardines. One month later, the Department and the Drug Enforcement Administration sent a joint surveillance team to Jardines' home. Detective Pedraja was part of that team. He watched the home for fifteen minutes and saw no vehicles in the driveway or activity around the home, and could not see inside because the blinds were drawn. Detective Pedraja then approached Jardines' home accompanied by Detective Douglas Bartelt, a trained canine handler who had just arrived at the scene with his drug-sniffing dog. The dog was trained to detect the scent of marijuana, cocaine, heroin, and several other drugs, indicating the presence of any of these substances through particular behavioral changes recognizable by his handler.

Detective Bartelt had the dog on a six-foot leash, owing in part to the dog's "wild" nature, and tendency to dart around erratically while searching. As the dog approached Jardines' front porch, he apparently sensed one of the odors he had been trained to detect, and began energetically exploring the area for the strongest point source of that odor. As Detective Bartelt explained, the dog "began tracking that airborne odor by . . . tracking back and forth," engaging in what is called "bracketing," "back and forth, back and forth." Detective Bartelt gave the dog "the full six feet of the leash plus whatever safe distance [he could] give him" to do this—he testified that he needed to give the dog "as much distance as I can." And Detective Pedraja stood back while this was occurring, so that he would not "get knocked over" when the dog was "spinning around trying to find" the source.

After sniffing the base of the front door, the dog sat, which is the trained behavior upon discovering the odor's strongest point. Detective Bartelt then pulled the dog away from the door and returned to his vehicle. He left the scene after informing Detective Pedraja that there had been a positive alert for narcotics.

On the basis of what he had learned at the home, Detective Pedraja applied for and received a warrant to search the residence. When the warrant was executed later that day, Jardines attempted to flee and was arrested; the search revealed marijuana plants, and he was charged with trafficking in cannabis.

At trial, Jardines moved to suppress the marijuana plants on the ground that the canine investigation was an unreasonable search. The trial court granted the motion, and the Florida Third District Court of Appeal reversed. On a petition for discretionary review, the Florida Supreme Court quashed the decision of the Third District Court of Appeal and approved the trial court's decision to suppress, holding (as relevant here) that the use of the trained narcotics dog to investigate Jardines' home was a Fourth Amendment search unsupported by probable cause, rendering invalid the warrant based upon information gathered in that search.

We granted certiorari, limited to the question of whether the officers' behavior was a search within the meaning of the Fourth Amendment.

II

The Fourth Amendment provides in relevant part that the "right of the people to be secure in their persons, houses, papers, and effects, against unreasonable searches and seizures, shall not be violated." The Amendment establishes a simple baseline, one that for much of our history formed the exclusive basis for its protections: When "the Government obtains information by physically intruding" on persons, houses, papers, or effects, "a 'search' within the original meaning of the Fourth Amendment" has "undoubtedly occurred."

That principle renders this case a straightforward one. The officers were gathering information in an area belonging to Jardines and immediately surrounding his house—in the curtilage of the house, which we have held enjoys protection as part of the home itself. And they gathered that information by physically entering and occupying the area to engage in conduct not explicitly or implicitly permitted by the homeowner.

A

The Fourth Amendment "indicates with some precision the places and things encompassed by its protections": persons, houses, papers, and effects. The Fourth Amendment does not, therefore, prevent all investigations conducted on private property; for example, an officer may (subject to *Katz*) gather information in what we have called "open fields"—even if those fields are privately owned—because such fields are not enumerated in the Amendment's text.

But when it comes to the Fourth Amendment, the home is first among equals. At the Amendment's "very core" stands "the right of a man to retreat into his own home and there be free from unreasonable governmental intrusion." This right would be of little practical value if the State's agents could stand in a home's porch or side garden and trawl for evidence with impunity; the right to retreat would be significantly diminished if the police could enter a man's property to observe his repose from just outside the front window.

We therefore regard the area "immediately surrounding and associated with the home"—what our cases call the curtilage—as "part of the home itself for Fourth Amendment purposes." That principle has ancient and durable roots. Just as the distinction between the home and the open fields is "as old as the common law," so too is the identity of home and what Blackstone called the "curtilage or homestall," for the "house protects and privileges all its branches and appurtenants." This area around the home is "intimately linked to the home, both physically and psychologically," and is where "privacy expectations are most heightened."

While the boundaries of the curtilage are generally "clearly marked," the "conception defining the curtilage" is at any rate familiar enough that it is "easily understood from our daily experience." Here there is no doubt that the officers entered it: The front porch is the classic exemplar of an area adjacent to the home and "to which the activity of home life extends."

B

Since the officers' investigation took place in a constitutionally protected area, we turn to the question of whether it was accomplished through an unlicensed physical intrusion. While law enforcement officers need not "shield their eyes" when passing by the home "on public thoroughfares," an officer's leave to gather information is sharply circumscribed when he steps off those thoroughfares and enters the Fourth Amendment's protected areas. In permitting, for example, visual observation of the home from "public navigable airspace," we were careful to note that it was done "in a physically nonintrusive manner." "[O]ur law holds the property of every man so sacred, that no man can set his foot upon his neighbour's close without his leave." As it is undisputed that the detectives had all four of their feet and all four of their companion's firmly planted on the constitutionally protected extension of Jardines' home, the only question is whether he had given his leave (even implicitly) for them to do so. He had not.

"A license may be implied from the habits of the country," notwithstanding the "strict rule of the English common law as to entry upon a close." We have accordingly recognized that "the knocker on the front door is treated as an invitation or license to attempt an entry, justifying ingress to the home by solicitors, hawkers and peddlers of all kinds." This implicit license typically permits the visitor to approach the home by the front path, knock promptly, wait briefly to be received, and then (absent invitation to linger longer) leave. Complying with the terms of that traditional invitation does not require fine-grained legal knowledge; it is generally managed without incident by the Nation's Girl Scouts and trick-or-treaters. Thus, a police officer not armed with a warrant may approach a home and knock, precisely because that is "no more than any private citizen might do."

But introducing a trained police dog to explore the area around the home in hopes of discovering incriminating evidence is something else. There is no customary invitation to do that. An invitation to engage in canine forensic investigation assuredly does not inhere in the very act of hanging a knocker. To find a visitor knocking on the door is routine (even if sometimes unwelcome); to spot that same visitor exploring the front path with a metal detector, or marching his bloodhound into the garden before saying hello and asking permission, would inspire most of us to — well, call the police. The scope of a license — express or implied — is limited not only to a particular area but also to a specific purpose. Consent at a traffic stop to an officer's checking out an anonymous tip that there is a body in the trunk does not permit the officer to rummage through the trunk for narcotics. Here, the background social norms that invite a visitor to the front door do not invite him there to conduct a search.

The State points to our decisions holding that the subjective intent of the officer is irrelevant. See *Ashcroft v. al-Kidd* (2011); *Whren v. United States* (1996). But those cases merely hold that a stop or search that is objectively reasonable is not vitiated by the fact that the officer's real reason for making the stop or search has nothing to do with the validating reason. Thus, the defendant will not be heard to complain that although he was speeding the officer's real reason for the stop was racial harassment. Here, however, the question before the court is precisely whether the officer's conduct was an objectively reasonable search. As we have described, that depends upon whether the officers had an implied license to enter the porch, which in turn depends upon the purpose for which they entered. Here, their behavior objectively reveals a purpose to conduct a search, which is not what anyone would think he had license to do.

III

The State argues that investigation by a forensic narcotics dog by definition cannot implicate any legitimate privacy interest. The State cites for authority our decisions in *United States v. Place*, (1983), *United States v. Jacobsen* (1984), and *Illinois v. Caballes* (2005), which held, respectively, that canine inspection of luggage in an airport, chemical testing of a substance that had fallen from a parcel in transit, and canine inspection of an automobile during a lawful traffic stop, do not violate the "reasonable expectation of privacy" described in *Katz.*

Just last Term, we considered an argument much like this. *Jones* held that tracking an automobile's whereabouts using a physically-mounted GPS receiver is a Fourth Amendment search. The Government argued that the *Katz* standard "show[ed] that no search occurred," as the defendant had "no 'reasonable expectation of privacy'" in his whereabouts on the public roads — a proposition with at least as much support in our case law as the one the State marshals here. But because the GPS receiver had been physically mounted on the defendant's automobile (thus intruding on his "effects"), we held that tracking the vehicle's movements was a search: a person's "Fourth Amendment rights do not rise or fall with the *Katz* formulation." The *Katz* reasonable-expectations test "has been added to, not substituted for," the traditional property-based understanding of the Fourth Amendment, and so is unnecessary to consider when the government gains evidence by physically intruding on constitutionally protected areas.

Thus, we need not decide whether the officers' investigation of Jardines' home violated his expectation of privacy under *Katz*. One virtue of the Fourth Amendment's property-rights baseline is that it keeps easy cases easy. That the officers learned what they learned only by physically intruding on Jardines' property to gather evidence is enough to establish that a search occurred.

For a related reason we find irrelevant the State's argument (echoed by the dissent) that forensic dogs have been commonly used by police for centuries. This argument is apparently directed to our holding in *Kyllo* that surveillance of the home is a search where "the Government uses a device that is not in general public use" to "explore details of the home that would previously have been unknowable without physical intrusion." But the implication of that statement (inclusio unius est exclusio alterius) is that when the government uses a physical intrusion to explore details of the home (including its curtilage), the antiquity of the tools that they bring along is irrelevant.

• • •

The government's use of trained police dogs to investigate the home and its immediate surroundings is a "search" within the meaning of the Fourth Amendment. The judgment of the Supreme Court of Florida is therefore affirmed.

[Justices Alito, Kennedy, and Breyer and Chief Justice Roberts dissented.]

NOTES AND QUESTIONS

1. Do you agree that this is a "straightforward" case? Because of *Kyllo*? Because of *Jones*?

2. Consider the first use of drug-sniffing dogs. Is such "technology" similar to the thermal imaging in *Kyllo* in that it is "sense enhancing"? Does the use of drug-sniffing dogs ever come into "general public use" within the meaning of *Kyllo*?

3. Did the defendant have a reasonable expectation of privacy in his porch area, even though it was accessible to trick-or-treaters and the like? Should the answer depend on common law notions of "license"?

4. In her concurring opinion Justice Kagan analogizes *Jardines* to a stranger (or a policeman) standing on a porch with "super high-powered binoculars" with which he can see into every nook and cranny of the home. Based on this analogy she concludes that *Jardines* involves a search under both a property theory and a *Katz* theory. Do you agree?

5. "But when it comes to the Fourth Amendment, the home is first among equals," the Court says, and *Kyllo* and *Jardines* certainly seem to be examples of this. For a contrary view, see Ric Simmons, Lange, Caniglia, *and the Myth of Home Exceptionalism*, 54 Ariz. St. L.J. 145 (2022).

Carpenter v. United States

585 U.S. 296 (2018)

Chief Justice Roberts delivered the opinion of the Court.

This case presents the question whether the Government conducts a search under the Fourth Amendment when it accesses historical cell phone records that provide a comprehensive chronicle of the user's past movements.

I

A

There are 396 million cell phone service accounts in the United States—for a Nation of 326 million people. Cell phones perform their wide and growing variety of functions by connecting to a set of radio antennas called "cell sites." Although cell sites are usually mounted on a tower, they can also be found on light posts, flagpoles, church steeples, or the sides of buildings. Cell sites typically have several directional antennas that divide the covered area into sectors.

Cell phones continuously scan their environment looking for the best signal, which generally comes from the closest cell site. Most modern devices, such as smartphones, tap into the wireless network several times a minute whenever their signal is on, even if the owner is not using one of the phone's features. Each time the phone connects to a cell site, it generates a time-stamped record known as cell-site location information (CSLI). The precision of this information depends on the size of the geographic area covered by the cell site. The greater the concentration of cell sites, the smaller the coverage area. As data usage from cell phones has increased, wireless carriers have installed more cell sites to handle the traffic. That has led to increasingly compact coverage areas, especially in urban areas.

Wireless carriers collect and store CSLI for their own business purposes, including finding weak spots in their network and applying "roaming" charges when another carrier routes data through their cell sites. In addition, wireless carriers often sell aggregated location records to data brokers, without individual identifying information of the sort at issue here. While carriers have long retained CSLI for the start and end of incoming calls, in recent years phone companies have also collected location information from the transmission of text messages and routine data connections. Accordingly, modern cell phones generate increasingly vast amounts of increasingly precise CSLI.

B

In 2011, police officers arrested four men suspected of robbing a series of Radio Shack and (ironically enough) T-Mobile stores in Detroit. One of the men confessed that, over the previous four months, the group (along with a rotating cast of getaway drivers and lookouts) had robbed nine different stores in Michigan and Ohio. The suspect identified 15 accomplices who had participated in the heists and gave the FBI some of their cell phone numbers; the FBI then reviewed his call records to identify additional numbers that he had called around the time of the robberies.

Based on that information, the prosecutors applied for court orders under the Stored Communications Act to obtain cell phone records for petitioner Timothy Carpenter and several other suspects. That statute, as amended in 1994, permits the Government to compel the disclosure of certain telecommunications records when it "offers specific and articulable facts showing that there are reasonable grounds to believe" that the records sought "are relevant and material to an ongoing criminal investigation." 18 U.S.C. § 2703(d). Federal Magistrate Judges issued two orders directing Carpenter's wireless carriers—MetroPCS and Sprint—to disclose "cell/site sector [information] for [Carpenter's] telephone[ ] at call origination and at call termination for incoming and outgoing calls" during the four-month period when the string of robberies occurred. The first order sought 152 days of cell-site records from MetroPCS, which produced records spanning 127 days. The second order requested seven days of CSLI from Sprint, which produced two days of records covering the period when Carpenter's phone was "roaming" in northeastern Ohio. Altogether the Government obtained 12,898 location points cataloging Carpenter's movements—an average of 101 data points per day.

Carpenter was charged with six counts of robbery and an additional six counts of carrying a firearm during a federal crime of violence. See 18 U.S.C. §§ 924(c), 1951(a). Prior to trial, Carpenter moved to suppress the cell-site data provided by the wireless carriers. He argued that the Government's seizure of the records violated the Fourth Amendment because they had been obtained without a warrant supported by probable cause. The District Court denied the motion.

At trial, seven of Carpenter's confederates pegged him as the leader of the operation. In addition, FBI agent Christopher Hess offered expert testimony about the cell-site data. Hess explained that each time a cell phone taps into the wireless network, the carrier logs a time-stamped record of the cell site and particular sector that were used. With this information, Hess produced maps that placed Carpenter's phone near four of the charged robberies. In the Government's view, the location records clinched the case: They confirmed that Carpenter was "right where the . . . robbery was at the exact time of the robbery." App. 131 (closing argument). Carpenter was convicted on all but one of the firearm counts and sentenced to more than 100 years in prison.

The Court of Appeals for the Sixth Circuit affirmed. The court held that Carpenter lacked a reasonable expectation of privacy in the location information collected by the FBI because he had shared that information with his wireless carriers. Given that cell phone users voluntarily convey cell-site data to their carriers as "a means of establishing communication," the court concluded that the resulting business records are not entitled to Fourth Amendment protection.

We granted certiorari.

II

A

• • •

B

The case before us involves the Government's acquisition of wireless carrier cell-site records revealing the location of Carpenter's cell phone whenever it made or received calls. This sort of digital data — personal location information maintained by a third party — does not fit neatly under existing precedents. Instead, requests for cell-site records lie at the intersection of two lines of cases, both of which inform our understanding of the privacy interests at stake.

The first set of cases addresses a person's expectation of privacy in his physical location and movements. In *Knotts* we considered the Government's use of a "beeper" to aid in tracking a vehicle through traffic. Police officers in that case planted a beeper in a container of chloroform before it was purchased by one of Knotts's co-conspirators. The officers (with intermittent aerial assistance) then followed the automobile carrying the container from Minneapolis to Knotts's cabin in Wisconsin, relying on the beeper's signal to help keep the vehicle in view. The Court concluded that the "augment[ed]" visual surveillance did not constitute a search because "[a] person traveling in an automobile on public thoroughfares has no reasonable expectation of privacy in his movements from one place to another." Since the movements of the vehicle and its final destination had been "voluntarily conveyed to anyone who wanted to look."

This Court in *Knotts*, however, was careful to distinguish between the rudimentary tracking facilitated by the beeper and more sweeping modes of surveillance. The Court emphasized the "limited use which the government made of the signals from this particular beeper" during a discrete "automotive journey." Significantly, the Court reserved the question whether "different constitutional principles may be applicable" if "twenty-four hour surveillance of any citizen of this country [were] possible."

Three decades later, the Court considered more sophisticated surveillance of the sort envisioned in Knotts and found that different principles did indeed apply. In *Jones*, FBI agents installed a GPS tracking device on Jones's vehicle and remotely monitored the vehicle's movements for 28 days. The Court decided the case based on the Government's physical trespass of the vehicle. At the same time, five Justices agreed that related privacy concerns would be raised by, for example, "surreptitiously activating a stolen vehicle detection system" in Jones's car to track Jones himself, or conducting GPS tracking of his cell phone. Since GPS monitoring of a vehicle tracks "every movement" a person makes in that vehicle, the concurring Justices concluded that "longer term GPS monitoring in investigations of most offenses impinges on expectations of privacy" — regardless whether those movements were disclosed to the public at large.

In a second set of decisions, the Court has drawn a line between what a person keeps to himself and what he shares with others. We have previously held that "a person has no legitimate expectation of privacy in information he voluntarily turns over to third parties." That remains true "even if the information is revealed on the assumption that it will be used only for a limited purpose." As a result, the Government is typically free to obtain such information from the recipient without triggering Fourth Amendment protections.

This third-party doctrine largely traces its roots to *Miller*. While investigating Miller for tax evasion, the Government subpoenaed his banks, seeking several months of canceled checks, deposit slips, and monthly statements. The Court rejected a Fourth Amendment challenge to the records collection. For one, Miller could "assert neither ownership nor possession" of the documents; they were "business records of the banks." For another, the nature of those records confirmed Miller's limited expectation of privacy, because the checks were "not confidential communications but negotiable instruments to be used in commercial transactions," and the bank statements contained information "exposed to [bank] employees in the ordinary course of business." The Court thus concluded that Miller had "take[n] the risk, in revealing his affairs to another, that the information [would] be conveyed by that person to the Government."

Three years later, *Smith* applied the same principles in the context of information conveyed to a telephone company. The Court ruled that the Government's use of a pen register — a device that recorded the outgoing phone numbers dialed on a landline telephone — was not a search. Noting the pen register's "limited capabilities," the Court "doubt[ed] that people in general entertain any actual expectation of privacy in the numbers they dial." Telephone subscribers know, after all, that the numbers are used by the telephone company "for a variety of legitimate business purposes," including routing calls. And at any rate, the Court explained, such an expectation "is not one that society is prepared to recognize as reasonable." When Smith placed a call, he "voluntarily conveyed" the dialed numbers to the phone company by "expos[ing] that information to its equipment in the ordinary course of business." Once again, we held that the defendant "assumed the risk" that the company's records "would be divulged to police."

III

The question we confront today is how to apply the Fourth Amendment to a new phenomenon: the ability to chronicle a person's past movements through the record of his cell phone signals. Such tracking partakes of many of the qualities of the GPS monitoring we considered in *Jones*. Much like GPS tracking of a vehicle, cell phone location information is detailed, encyclopedic, and effortlessly compiled.

At the same time, the fact that the individual continuously reveals his location to his wireless carrier implicates the third-party principle of *Smith* and *Miller*. But while the third-party doctrine applies to telephone numbers and bank records, it is not clear whether its logic extends to the qualitatively different category of cell-site records. After all, when *Smith* was decided in 1979, few could have imagined a society in which a phone goes wherever its owner goes, conveying to the wireless carrier not just dialed digits, but a detailed and comprehensive record of the person's movements.

We decline to extend *Smith* and *Mille*r to cover these novel circumstances. Given the unique nature of cell phone location records, the fact that the information is held by a third party does not by itself overcome the user's claim to Fourth Amendment protection. Whether the Government employs its own surveillance technology as in Jones or leverages the technology of a wireless carrier, we hold that an individual maintains a legitimate expectation of privacy in the record of his physical movements as captured through CSLI. The location information obtained from Carpenter's wireless carriers was the product of a search.

A

A person does not surrender all Fourth Amendment protection by venturing into the public sphere. To the contrary, "what [one] seeks to preserve as private, even in an area accessible to the public, may be constitutionally protected." A majority of this Court has already recognized that individuals have a reasonable expectation of privacy in the whole of their physical movements. Prior to the digital age, law enforcement might have pursued a suspect for a brief stretch, but doing so "for any extended period of time was difficult and costly and therefore rarely undertaken." For that reason, "society's expectation has been that law enforcement agents and others would not—and indeed, in the main, simply could not—secretly monitor and catalogue every single movement of an individual's car for a very long period."

Allowing government access to cell-site records contravenes that expectation. Although such records are generated for commercial purposes, that distinction does not negate Carpenter's anticipation of privacy in his physical location. Mapping a cell phone's location over the course of 127 days provides an all-encompassing record of the holder's whereabouts. As with GPS information, the time-stamped data provides an intimate window into a person's life, revealing not only his particular movements, but through them his "familial, political, professional, religious, and sexual associations." These location records "hold for many Americans the 'privacies of life.'" And like GPS monitoring, cell phone tracking is remarkably easy, cheap, and efficient compared to traditional investigative tools. With just the click of a button, the Government can access each carrier's deep repository of historical location information at practically no expense.

In fact, historical cell-site records present even greater privacy concerns than the GPS monitoring of a vehicle we considered in *Jones*. Unlike the bugged container in *Knotts* or the car in *Jones*, a cell phone—almost a "feature of human anatomy," tracks nearly exactly the movements of its owner. While individuals regularly leave their vehicles, they compulsively carry cell phones with them all the time. A cell phone faithfully follows its owner beyond public thoroughfares and into private residences, doctor's offices, political headquarters, and other potentially revealing locales.

Moreover, the retrospective quality of the data here gives police access to a category of information otherwise unknowable. In the past, attempts to reconstruct a person's movements were limited by a dearth of records and the frailties of recollection. With access to CSLI, the Government can now travel back in time to retrace a person's whereabouts, subject only to the retention polices of the wireless carriers, which currently maintain records for up to five years. Critically, because location information is continually logged for all of the 400 million devices in the United States—not just those belonging to persons who might happen to come under investigation—this newfound tracking capacity runs against everyone. Unlike with the GPS device in *Jones*, police need not even know in advance whether they want to follow a particular individual, or when.

Whoever the suspect turns out to be, he has effectively been tailed every moment of every day for five years, and the police may—in the Government's view—call upon the results of that surveillance without regard to the constraints of the Fourth Amendment. Only the few without cell phones could escape this tireless and absolute surveillance.

The Government and Justice Kennedy contend, however, that the collection of CSLI should be permitted because the data is less precise than GPS information. Not to worry, they maintain, because the location records did "not on their own suffice to place [Carpenter] at the crime scene"; they placed him within a wedge-shaped sector ranging from one-eighth to four square miles. Yet the Court has already rejected the proposition that "inference insulates a search." From the 127 days of location data it received, the Government could, in combination with other information, deduce a detailed log of Carpenter's movements, including when he was at the site of the robberies. And the Government thought the CSLI accurate enough to highlight it during the closing argument of his trial.

At any rate, the rule the Court adopts "must take account of more sophisticated systems that are already in use or in development." While the records in this case reflect the state of technology at the start of the decade, the accuracy of CSLI is rapidly approaching GPS-level precision. As the number of cell sites has proliferated, the geographic area covered by each cell sector has shrunk, particularly in urban areas. In addition, with new technology measuring the time and angle of signals hitting their towers, wireless carriers already have the capability to pinpoint a phone's location within 50 meters.

Accordingly, when the Government accessed CSLI from the wireless carriers, it invaded Carpenter's reasonable expectation of privacy in the whole of his physical movements.

B

The Government's primary contention to the contrary is that the third-party doctrine governs this case. In its view, cell-site records are fair game because they are "business records" created and maintained by the wireless carriers. The Government (along with Justice Kennedy) recognizes that this case features new technology, but asserts that the legal question nonetheless turns on a garden-variety request for information from a third-party witness.

The Government's position fails to contend with the seismic shifts in digital technology that made possible the tracking of not only Carpenter's location but also everyone else's, not for a short period but for years and years. Sprint Corporation and its competitors are not your typical witnesses. Unlike the nosy neighbor who keeps an eye on comings and goings, they are ever alert, and their memory is nearly infallible. There is a world of difference between the limited types of personal information addressed in *Smith* and *Miller* and the exhaustive chronicle of location information casually collected by wireless carriers today. The Government thus is not asking for a straightforward application of the third-party doctrine, but instead a significant extension of it to a distinct category of information.

The third-party doctrine partly stems from the notion that an individual has a reduced expectation of privacy in information knowingly shared with another. But the fact of "diminished privacy interests does not mean that the Fourth Amendment falls out of the picture entirely." *Smith* and *Mille*r, after all, did not rely solely on the act of sharing. Instead, they considered "the nature of the particular documents sought" to determine whether "there is a legitimate 'expectation of privacy' concerning their contents." *Smith* pointed out the limited capabilities of a pen register; as explained in *Riley*, telephone call logs reveal little in the way of "identifying information." *Miller* likewise noted that checks were "not confidential communications but negotiable instruments to be used in commercial transactions." In mechanically applying the third-party doctrine to this case, the Government fails to appreciate that there are no comparable limitations on the revealing nature of CSLI.

The Court has in fact already shown special solicitude for location information in the third-party context. In *Knotts*, the Court relied on *Smith* to hold that an individual has no reasonable expectation of privacy in public movements that he "voluntarily conveyed to anyone who wanted to look." But when confronted with more pervasive tracking, five Justices agreed that longer term GPS monitoring of even a vehicle traveling on public streets constitutes a search. Justice Gorsuch wonders why "someone's location when using a phone" is sensitive, and Justice Kennedy assumes that a person's discrete movements "are not particularly private." Yet this case is not about "using a phone" or a person's movement at a particular time. It is about a detailed chronicle of a person's physical presence compiled every day, every moment, over several years. Such a chronicle implicates privacy concerns far beyond those considered in *Smith* and *Miller.*

Neither does the second rationale underlying the third-party doctrine—voluntary exposure—hold up when it comes to CSLI. Cell phone location information is not truly "shared" as one normally understands the term. In the first place, cell phones and the services they provide are "such a pervasive and insistent part of daily life" that carrying one is indispensable to participation in modern society. Second, a cell phone logs a cell-site record by dint of its operation, without any affirmative act on the part of the user beyond powering up. Virtually any activity on the phone generates CSLI, including incoming calls, texts, or e-mails and countless other data connections that a phone automatically makes when checking for news, weather, or social media updates. Apart from disconnecting the phone from the network, there is no way to avoid leaving behind a trail of location data. As a result, in no meaningful sense does the user voluntarily "assume[ ] the risk" of turning over a comprehensive dossier of his physical movements.

We therefore decline to extend *Smith* and *Miller* to the collection of CSLI. Given the unique nature of cell phone location information, the fact that the Government obtained the information from a third party does not overcome Carpenter's claim to Fourth Amendment protection. The Government's acquisition of the cell-site records was a search within the meaning of the Fourth Amendment.

• • •

Our decision today is a narrow one. We do not express a view on matters not before us: real-time CSLI or "tower dumps" (a download of information on all the devices that connected to a particular cell site during a particular interval). We do not disturb the application of *Smith* and *Miller* or call into question conventional surveillance techniques and tools, such as security cameras. Nor do we address other business records that might incidentally reveal location information. Further, our opinion does not consider other collection techniques involving foreign affairs or national security. As Justice Frankfurter noted when considering new innovations in airplanes and radios, the Court must tread carefully in such cases, to ensure that we do not "embarrass the future."

IV

Having found that the acquisition of Carpenter's CSLI was a search, we also conclude that the Government must generally obtain a warrant supported by probable cause before acquiring such records. Although the "ultimate measure of the constitutionality of a governmental search is 'reasonableness,'" our cases establish that warrantless searches are typically unreasonable where "a search is undertaken by law enforcement officials to discover evidence of criminal wrongdoing." Thus, "[i]n the absence of a warrant, a search is reasonable only if it falls within a specific exception to the warrant requirement."

The Government acquired the cell-site records pursuant to a court order issued under the Stored Communications Act, which required the Government to show "reasonable grounds" for believing that the records were "relevant and material to an ongoing investigation." 18 U.S.C. § 2703(d). That showing falls well short of the probable cause required for a warrant. The Court usually requires "some quantum of individualized suspicion" before a search or seizure may take place. Under the standard in the Stored Communications Act, however, law enforcement need only show that the cell-site evidence might be pertinent to an ongoing investigation—a "gigantic" departure from the probable cause rule, as the Government explained below. Consequently, an order issued under Section 2703(d) of the Act is not a permissible mechanism for accessing historical cell-site records. Before compelling a wireless carrier to turn over a subscriber's CSLI, the Government's obligation is a familiar one—get a warrant.

Justice Alito contends that the warrant requirement simply does not apply when the Government acquires records using compulsory process. Unlike an actual search, he says, subpoenas for documents do not involve the direct taking of evidence; they are at most a "constructive search" conducted by the target of the subpoena. Given this lesser intrusion on personal privacy, Justice Alito argues that the compulsory production of records is not held to the same probable cause standard. In his view, this Court's precedents set forth a categorical rule—separate and distinct from the third-party doctrine—subjecting subpoenas to lenient scrutiny without regard to the suspect's expectation of privacy in the records.

But this Court has never held that the Government may subpoena third parties for records in which the suspect has a reasonable expectation of privacy. Almost all of the examples Justice Alito cites, contemplated requests for evidence implicating diminished privacy interests or for a corporation's own books. The lone exception, of course, is *Miller*, where the Court's analysis of the third-party subpoena merged with the application of the third-party doctrine.

Justice Alito overlooks the critical issue. At some point, the dissent should recognize that CSLI is an entirely different species of business record—something that implicates basic Fourth Amendment concerns about arbitrary government power much more directly than corporate tax or payroll ledgers. When confronting new concerns wrought by digital technology, this Court has been careful not to uncritically extend existing precedents.

If the choice to proceed by subpoena provided a categorical limitation on Fourth Amendment protection, no type of record would ever be protected by the warrant requirement. Under Justice Alito's view, private letters, digital contents of a cell phone—any personal information reduced to document form, in fact—may be collected by subpoena for no reason other than "official curiosity." Justice Kennedy declines to adopt the radical implications of this theory, leaving open the question whether the warrant requirement applies "when the Government obtains the modern-day equivalents of an individual's own 'papers' or 'effects,' even when those papers or effects are held by a third party." That would be a sensible exception, because it would prevent the subpoena doctrine from overcoming any reasonable expectation of privacy. If the third-party doctrine does not apply to the "modern-day equivalents of an individual's own 'papers' or 'effects,'" then the clear implication is that the documents should receive full Fourth Amendment protection. We simply think that such protection should extend as well to a detailed log of a person's movements over several years.

This is certainly not to say that all orders compelling the production of documents will require a showing of probable cause. The Government will be able to use subpoenas to acquire records in the overwhelming majority of investigations. We hold only that a warrant is required in the rare case where the suspect has a legitimate privacy interest in records held by a third party.

Further, even though the Government will generally need a warrant to access CSLI, case-specific exceptions may support a warrantless search of an individual's cell-site records under certain circumstances. "One well-recognized exception applies when ' "the exigencies of the situation" make the needs of law enforcement so compelling that [a] warrantless search is objectively reasonable under the Fourth Amendment.'" Such exigencies include the need to pursue a fleeing suspect, protect individuals who are threatened with imminent harm, or prevent the imminent destruction of evidence.

As a result, if law enforcement is confronted with an urgent situation, such fact-specific threats will likely justify the warrantless collection of CSLI. Lower courts, for instance, have approved warrantless searches related to bomb threats, active shootings, and child abductions. Our decision today does not call into doubt warrantless access to CSLI in such circumstances. While police must get a warrant when collecting CSLI to assist in the mine-run criminal investigation, the rule we set forth does not limit their ability to respond to an ongoing emergency.

• • •

As Justice Brandeis explained in his famous dissent, the Court is obligated — as "[s]ubtler and more far-reaching means of invading privacy have become available to the Government" — to ensure that the "progress of science" does not erode Fourth Amendment protections. Here the progress of science has afforded law enforcement a powerful new tool to carry out its important responsibilities. At the same time, this tool risks Government encroachment of the sort the Framers, "after consulting the lessons of history," drafted the Fourth Amendment to prevent.

We decline to grant the state unrestricted access to a wireless carrier's database of physical location information. In light of the deeply revealing nature of CSLI, its depth, breadth, and comprehensive reach, and the inescapable and automatic nature of its collection, the fact that such information is gathered by a third party does not make it any less deserving of Fourth Amendment protection. The Government's acquisition of the cell-site records here was a search under that Amendment.

The judgment of the Court of Appeals is reversed, and the case is remanded for further proceedings consistent with this opinion.

[Justices Kennedy, Thomas, Gorsuch, and Alito dissented.]

Justice GORSUCH, dissenting.

In the late 1960s this Court suggested for the first time that a search triggering the Fourth Amendment occurs when the government violates an "expectation of privacy" that "society is prepared to recognize as 'reasonable.'" *Katz.* Then, in a pair of decisions in the 1970s applying the *Katz* test, the Court held that a "reasonable expectation of privacy" doesn't attach to information shared with "third parties." *Smith v. Maryland*; *United States v. Miller*. By these steps, the Court came to conclude, the Constitution does nothing to limit investigators from searching records you've entrusted to your bank, accountant, and maybe even your doctor.

What's left of the Fourth Amendment? Today we use the Internet to do most everything. Smartphones make it easy to keep a calendar, correspond with friends, make calls, conduct banking, and even watch the game. Countless Internet companies maintain records about us and, increasingly, for us. Even our most private documents — those that, in other eras, we would have locked safely in a desk drawer or destroyed — now reside on third party servers. *Smith* and *Miller* teach that the police can review all of this material, on the theory that no one reasonably expects any of it will be kept private. But no one believes that, if they ever did.

What to do? It seems to me we could respond in at least three ways. The first is to ignore the problem, maintain *Smith* and *Miller*, and live with the consequences. If the confluence of these decisions and modern technology means our Fourth Amendment rights are reduced to nearly nothing, so be it. The second choice is to set *Smith* and *Miller* aside and try again using the *Katz* "reasonable expectation of privacy" jurisprudence that produced them. The third is to look for answers elsewhere.

• • •

Start with the first option. *Smith* held that the government's use of a pen register to record the numbers people dial on their phones doesn't infringe a reasonable expectation of privacy because that information is freely disclosed to the third party phone company. *Miller* held that a bank account holder enjoys no reasonable expectation of privacy in the bank's records of his account activity. That's true, the Court reasoned, "even if the information is revealed on the assumption that it will be used only for a limited purpose and the confidence placed in the third party will not be betrayed." Today the Court suggests that *Smith* and *Miller* distinguish between kinds of information disclosed to third parties and require courts to decide whether to "extend" those decisions to particular classes of information, depending on their sensitivity. But as the Sixth Circuit recognized and Justice Kennedy explains, no balancing test of this kind can be found in *Smith* and *Miller*. Those cases announced a categorical rule: Once you disclose information to third parties, you forfeit any reasonable expectation of privacy you might have had in it. And even if *Smith* and *Miller* did permit courts to conduct a balancing contest of the kind the Court now suggests, it's still hard to see how that would help the petitioner in this case. Why is someone's location when using a phone so much more sensitive than who he was talking to (*Smith*) or what financial transactions he engaged in (*Miller*)? I do not know and the Court does not say.

The problem isn't with the Sixth Circuit's application of *Smith* and *Miller* but with the cases themselves. Can the government demand a copy of all your e-mails from Google or Microsoft without implicating your Fourth Amendment rights? Can it secure your DNA from 23 and Me without a warrant or probable cause? *Smith* and *Miller* say yes it can—at least without running afoul of *Katz*. But that result strikes most lawyers and judges today—me included—as pretty unlikely. In the years since its adoption, countless scholars, too, have come to conclude that the "third-party doctrine is not only wrong, but horribly wrong." Kerr, The Case for the Third-Party Doctrine, 107 Mich. L. Rev. 561, 563, n. 5, 564 (2009) (collecting criticisms but defending the doctrine (footnotes omitted)). The reasons are obvious. "As an empirical statement about subjective expectations of privacy," the doctrine is "quite dubious." Baude & Stern, The Positive Law Model of the Fourth Amendment, 129 Harv. L. Rev. 1821, 1872 (2016). People often do reasonably expect that information they entrust to third parties, especially information subject to confidentiality agreements, will be kept private. Meanwhile, if the third party doctrine is supposed to represent a normative assessment of when a person should expect privacy, the notion that the answer might be "never" seems a pretty unattractive societal prescription.

What, then, is the explanation for our third party doctrine? The truth is, the Court has never offered a persuasive justification. The Court has said that by conveying information to a third party you "'assum[e] the risk'" it will be revealed to the police and therefore lack a reasonable expectation of privacy in it. But assumption of risk doctrine developed in tort law. It generally applies when "by contract or otherwise [one] expressly agrees to accept a risk of harm" or impliedly does so by "manifest[ing] his willingness to accept" that risk and thereby "take[s] his chances as to harm which may result from it. That rationale has little play in this context. Suppose I entrust a friend with a letter and he promises to keep it secret until he delivers it to an intended recipient. In what sense have I agreed to bear the risk that he will turn around, break his promise, and spill its contents to someone else? More confusing still, what have I done to "manifest my willingness to accept" the risk that the government will pry the document from my friend and read it without his consent?

One possible answer concerns knowledge. I know that my friend might break his promise, or that the government might have some reason to search the papers in his possession. But knowing about a risk doesn't mean you assume responsibility for it. Whenever you walk down the sidewalk you know a car may negligently or recklessly veer off and hit you, but that hardly means you accept the consequences and absolve the driver of any damage he may do to you.

Some have suggested the third party doctrine is better understood to rest on consent than assumption of risk. "So long as a person knows that they are disclosing information to a third party," the argument goes, "their choice to do so is voluntary and the consent valid." I confess I still don't see it. Consenting to give a third party access to private papers that remain my property is not the same thing as consenting to a search of those papers by the government. Perhaps there are exceptions, like when the third party is an undercover government agent. But otherwise this conception of consent appears to be just assumption of risk relabeled—you've "consented" to whatever risks are foreseeable.

Another justification sometimes offered for third party doctrine is clarity. You (and the police) know exactly how much protection you have in information confided to others: none. As rules go, "the king always wins" is admirably clear. But the opposite rule would be clear too: Third party disclosures never diminish Fourth Amendment protection (call it "the king always loses"). So clarity alone cannot justify the third party doctrine.

In the end, what do *Smith* and *Miller* add up to? A doubtful application of *Katz* that lets the government search almost whatever it wants whenever it wants. The Sixth Circuit had to follow that rule and faithfully did just that, but it's not clear why we should.

• • •

There's a second option. What if we dropped *Smith* and *Miller*'s third party doctrine and retreated to the root *Katz* question whether there is a "reasonable expectation of privacy" in data held by third parties? Rather than solve the problem with the third party doctrine, I worry this option only risks returning us to its source: After all, it was *Katz* that produced *Smith* and *Miller* in the first place.

Katz's problems start with the text and original understanding of the Fourth Amendment, as Justice Thomas thoughtfully explains today. The Amendment's protections do not depend on the breach of some abstract "expectation of privacy" whose contours are left to the judicial imagination. Much more concretely, it protects your "person," and your "houses, papers, and effects." Nor does your right to bring a Fourth Amendment claim depend on whether a judge happens to agree that your subjective expectation to privacy is a "reasonable" one. Under its plain terms, the Amendment grants you the right to invoke its guarantees whenever one of your protected things (your person, your house, your papers, or your effects) is unreasonably searched or seized. Period.

History too holds problems for *Katz*. Little like it can be found in the law that led to the adoption of the Fourth Amendment or in this Court's jurisprudence until the late 1960s. The Fourth Amendment came about in response to a trio of 18th century cases "well known to the men who wrote and ratified the Bill of Rights, [and] famous throughout the colonial population." Stuntz, The Substantive Origins of Criminal Procedure, 105 Yale L.J. 393, 397 (1995). The first two were English cases invalidating the Crown's use of general warrants to enter homes and search papers. *Entick v. Carrington*; *Wilkes v. Wood*; *Boyd v. United States.* The third was American: the Boston Writs of Assistance Case, which sparked colonial outrage at the use of writs permitting government agents to enter houses and business, breaking open doors and chests along the way, to conduct searches and seizures—and to force third parties to help them. No doubt the colonial outrage engendered by these cases rested in part on the government's intrusion upon privacy. But the framers chose not to protect privacy in some ethereal way dependent on judicial intuitions. They chose instead to protect privacy in particular places and things—"persons, houses, papers, and effects"—and against particular threats—"unreasonable" governmental "searches and seizures."

Even taken on its own terms, *Katz* has never been sufficiently justified. In fact, we still don't even know what its "reasonable expectation of privacy" test is. Is it supposed to pose an empirical question (what privacy expectations do people actually have) or a normative one (what expectations should they have)? Either way brings problems. If the test is supposed to be an empirical one, it's unclear why judges rather than legislators should conduct it. Legislators are responsive to their constituents and have institutional resources designed to help them discern and enact majoritarian preferences. Politically insulated judges come armed with only the attorneys' briefs, a few law clerks, and their own idiosyncratic experiences. They are hardly the representative group you'd expect (or want) to be making empirical judgments for hundreds of millions of people. Unsurprisingly, too, judicial judgments often fail to reflect public views. Consider just one example. Our cases insist that the seriousness of the offense being investigated does not reduce Fourth Amendment protection. Yet scholars suggest that most people are more tolerant of police intrusions when they investigate more serious crimes. And I very much doubt that this Court would be willing to adjust its *Katz* cases to reflect these findings even if it believed them.

Maybe, then, the *Katz* test should be conceived as a normative question. But if that's the case, why (again) do judges, rather than legislators, get to determine whether society should be prepared to recognize an expectation of privacy as legitimate? Deciding what privacy interests should be recognized often calls for a pure policy choice, many times between incommensurable goods—between the value of privacy in a particular setting and society's interest in combating crime. Answering questions like that calls for the exercise of raw political will belonging to legislatures, not the legal judgment proper to courts. When judges abandon legal judgment for political will we not only risk decisions where "reasonable expectations of privacy" come to bear "an uncanny resemblance to those expectations of privacy" shared by Members of this Court. We also risk undermining public confidence in the courts themselves.

My concerns about *Katz* come with a caveat. Sometimes, I accept, judges may be able to discern and describe existing societal norms. That is particularly true when the judge looks to positive law rather than intuition for guidance on social norms. So there may be some occasions where *Katz* is capable of principled application—though it may simply wind up approximating the more traditional option I will discuss in a moment. Sometimes it may also be possible to apply *Katz* by analogizing from precedent when the line between an existing case and a new fact pattern is short and direct. But so far this Court has declined to tie itself to any significant restraints like these.

As a result, *Katz* has yielded an often unpredictable—and sometimes unbelievable—jurisprudence. *Smith* and *Miller* are only two examples; there are many others. Take *Florida v. Riley*, which says that a police helicopter hovering 400 feet above a person's property invades no reasonable expectation of privacy. Try that one out on your neighbors. Or *California v. Greenwood*, which holds that a person has no reasonable expectation of privacy in the garbage he puts out for collection. In that case, the Court said that the homeowners forfeited their privacy interests because "[i]t is common knowledge that plastic garbage bags left on or at the side of a public street are readily accessible to animals, children, scavengers, snoops, and other members of the public." But the habits of raccoons don't prove much about the habits of the country. I doubt, too, that most people spotting a neighbor rummaging through their garbage would think they lacked reasonable grounds to confront the rummager. Making the decision all the stranger, California state law expressly protected a homeowner's property rights in discarded trash. Yet rather than defer to that as evidence of the people's habits and reasonable expectations of privacy, the Court substituted its own curious judgment.

Resorting to *Katz* in data privacy cases threatens more of the same. Just consider. The Court today says that judges should use *Katz*'s reasonable expectation of privacy test to decide what Fourth Amendment rights people have in cell-site location information, explaining that "no single rubric definitively resolves which expectations of privacy are entitled to protection." But then it offers a twist. Lower courts should be sure to add two special principles to their *Katz* calculus: the need to avoid "arbitrary power" and the importance of "plac[ing] obstacles in the way of a too permeating police surveillance." While surely laudable, these principles don't offer lower courts much guidance. The Court does not tell us, for example, how far to carry either principle or how to weigh them against the legitimate needs of law enforcement. At what point does access to electronic data amount to "arbitrary" authority? When does police surveillance become "too permeating"? And what sort of "obstacles" should judges "place" in law enforcement's path when it does? We simply do not know.

The Court's application of these principles supplies little more direction. The Court declines to say whether there is any sufficiently limited period of time "for which the Government may obtain an individual's historical [location information] free from Fourth Amendment scrutiny." But then it tells us that access to seven days' worth of information does trigger Fourth Amendment scrutiny—even though here the carrier "produced only two days of records." Why is the relevant fact the seven days of information the government asked for instead of the two days of information the government actually saw? Why seven days instead of ten or three or one? And in what possible sense did the government "search" five days' worth of location information it was never even sent? We do not know.

Later still, the Court adds that it can't say whether the Fourth Amendment is triggered when the government collects "real-time CSLI or 'tower dumps' (a download of information on all the devices that connected to a particular cell site during a particular interval)." But what distinguishes historical data from real-time data, or seven days of a single person's data from a download of everyone's data over some indefinite period of time? Why isn't a tower dump the paradigmatic example of "too permeating police surveillance" and a dangerous tool of "arbitrary" authority—the touchstones of the majority's modified *Katz* analysis? On what possible basis could such mass data collection survive the Court's test while collecting a single person's data does not? Here again we are left to guess. At the same time, though, the Court offers some firm assurances. It tells us its decision does not "call into question conventional surveillance techniques and tools, such as security cameras." That, however, just raises more questions for lower courts to sort out about what techniques qualify as "conventional" and why those techniques would be okay even if they lead to "permeating police surveillance" or "arbitrary police power."

Nor is this the end of it. After finding a reasonable expectation of privacy, the Court says there's still more work to do. Courts must determine whether to "extend" *Smith* and *Miller* to the circumstances before them. So apparently *Smith* and *Miller* aren't quite left for dead; they just no longer have the clear reach they once did. How do we measure their new reach? The Court says courts now must conduct a second *Katz*-like balancing inquiry, asking whether the fact of disclosure to a third party outweighs privacy interests in the "category of information" so disclosed. But how are lower courts supposed to weigh these radically different interests? Or assign values to different categories of information? All we know is that historical cell-site location information (for seven days, anyway) escapes *Smith* and *Miller*'s shorn grasp, while a lifetime of bank or phone records does not. As to any other kind of information, lower courts will have to stay tuned.

In the end, our lower court colleagues are left with two amorphous balancing tests, a series of weighty and incommensurable principles to consider in them, and a few illustrative examples that seem little more than the product of judicial intuition. In the Court's defense, though, we have arrived at this strange place not because the Court has misunderstood *Katz*. Far from it. We have arrived here because this is where *Katz* inevitably leads.

• • •

There is another way. From the founding until the 1960s, the right to assert a Fourth Amendment claim didn't depend on your ability to appeal to a judge's personal sensibilities about the "reasonableness" of your expectations or privacy. It was tied to the law. The Fourth

Amendment protects "the right of the people to be secure in their persons, houses, papers and effects, against unreasonable searches and seizures." True to those words and their original understanding, the traditional approach asked if a house, paper or effect was yours under law. No more was needed to trigger the Fourth Amendment. Though now often lost in *Katz*'s shadow, this traditional understanding persists. *Katz* only "supplements, rather than displaces the traditional property-based understanding of the Fourth Amendment."

Beyond its provenance in the text and original understanding of the Amendment, this traditional approach comes with other advantages. Judges are supposed to decide cases based on "democratically legitimate sources of law"—like positive law or analogies to items protected by the enacted Constitution—rather than "their own biases or personal policy preferences." A Fourth Amendment model based on positive legal rights "carves out significant room for legislative participation in the Fourth Amendment context," too, by asking judges to consult what the people's representatives have to say about their rights. Nor is this approach hobbled by *Smith* and *Miller*, for those cases are just limitations on *Katz*, addressing only the question whether individuals have a reasonable expectation of privacy in materials they share with third parties. Under this more traditional approach, Fourth Amendment protections for your papers and effects do not automatically disappear just because you share them with third parties.

Given the prominence *Katz* has claimed in our doctrine, American courts are pretty rusty at applying the traditional approach to the Fourth Amendment. We know that if a house, paper, or effect is yours, you have a Fourth Amendment interest in its protection. But what kind of legal interest is sufficient to make something yours? And what source of law determines that? Current positive law? The common law at 1791, extended by analogy to modern times? Both? Much work is needed to revitalize this area and answer these questions. I do not begin to claim all the answers today, but (unlike with *Katz*) at least I have a pretty good idea what the questions are. And it seems to me a few things can be said.

First, the fact that a third party has access to or possession of your papers and effects does not necessarily eliminate your interest in them. Ever hand a private document to a friend to be returned? Toss your keys to a valet at a restaurant? Ask your neighbor to look after your dog while you travel? You would not expect the friend to share the document with others; the valet to lend your car to his buddy; or the neighbor to put Fido up for adoption. Entrusting your stuff to others is a bailment. A bailment is the "delivery of personal property by one person (the bailor) to another (the bailee) who holds the property for a certain purpose." A bailee normally owes a legal duty to keep the item safe, according to the terms of the parties' contract if they have one, and according to the "implication[s] from their conduct" if they don't. A bailee who uses the item in a different way than he's supposed to, or against the bailor's instructions, is liable for conversion. This approach is quite different from *Smith* and *Miller*'s (counter)-intuitive approach to reasonable expectations of privacy; where those cases extinguish Fourth Amendment interests once records are given to a third party, property law may preserve them.

Our Fourth Amendment jurisprudence already reflects this truth. In *Ex parte Jackson* (1878), this Court held that sealed letters placed in the mail are "as fully guarded from examination and inspection, except as to their outward form and weight, as if they were retained by the parties forwarding them in their own domiciles." The reason, drawn from the Fourth Amendment's text, was that "[t]he constitutional guaranty of the right of the people to be secure in their papers against unreasonable searches and seizures extends to *their* papers, thus closed against inspection, wherever they may be." Ibid. (emphasis added). It did not matter that letters were bailed to a third party (the government, no less). The sender enjoyed the same Fourth Amendment protection as he does "when papers are subjected to search in one's own household." Ibid.

These ancient principles may help us address modern data cases too. Just because you entrust your data—in some cases, your modern-day papers and effects—to a third party may not mean you lose any Fourth Amendment interest in its contents. Whatever may be left of *Smith* and *Miller*, few doubt that e-mail should be treated much like the traditional mail it has largely supplanted—as a bailment in which the owner retains a vital and protected legal interest.

Second, I doubt that complete ownership or exclusive control of property is always a necessary condition to the assertion of a Fourth Amendment right. Where houses are concerned, for example, individuals can enjoy Fourth Amendment protection without fee simple title. Both the text of the Amendment and the common law rule support that conclusion. "People call a house 'their' home when legal title is in the bank, when they rent it, and even when they merely occupy it rent free." That rule derives from the common law. That is why tenants and resident family members—though they have no legal title—have standing to complain about searches of the houses in which they live.

Another point seems equally true: just because you have to entrust a third party with your data doesn't necessarily mean you should lose all Fourth Amendment protections in it. Not infrequently one person comes into possession of someone else's property without the owner's consent. Think of the finder of lost goods or the policeman who impounds a car. The law recognizes that the goods and the car still belong to their true owners, for "where a person comes into lawful possession of the personal property of another, even though there is no formal agreement between the property's owner and its possessor, the possessor will become a constructive bailee when justice so requires." At least some of this Court's decisions have already suggested that use of technology is functionally compelled by the demands of modern life, and in that way the fact that we store data with third parties may amount to a sort of involuntary bailment too.

Third, positive law may help provide detailed guidance on evolving technologies without resort to judicial intuition. State (or sometimes federal) law often creates rights in both tangible and intangible things. In the context of the Takings Clause we often ask whether those state-created rights are sufficient to make something someone's property for constitutional purposes. A similar inquiry may be appropriate for the Fourth Amendment. Both the States and federal government are actively legislating in the area of third party data storage and the rights users enjoy. State courts are busy expounding common law property principles in this area as well. If state legislators or state courts say that a digital record has the attributes that normally make something property, that may supply a sounder basis for judicial decisionmaking than judicial guesswork about societal expectations.

Fourth, while positive law may help establish a person's Fourth Amendment interest there may be some circumstances where positive law cannot be used to defeat it. *Ex parte Jackson* reflects that understanding. There this Court said that "[n]o law of Congress" could authorize letter carriers "to invade the secrecy of letters." 96 U.S., at 733. So the post office couldn't impose a regulation dictating that those mailing letters surrender all legal interests in them once they're deposited in a mailbox. If that is right, *Jackson* suggests the existence of a constitutional floor below which Fourth Amendment rights may not descend. Legislatures cannot pass laws declaring your house or papers to be your property except to the extent the police wish to search them without cause. As the Court has previously explained, "we must 'assur[e] preservation of that degree of privacy against government that existed when the Fourth Amendment was adopted.'" Nor does this mean protecting only the specific rights known at the founding; it means protecting their modern analogues too. So, for example, while thermal imaging was unknown in 1791, this Court has recognized that using that technology to look inside a home constitutes a Fourth Amendment "search" of that "home" no less than a physical inspection might.

Fifth, this constitutional floor may, in some instances, bar efforts to circumvent the Fourth Amendment's protection through the use of subpoenas. No one thinks the government can evade *Jackson*'s prohibition on opening sealed letters without a warrant simply by issuing a subpoena to a postmaster for "all letters sent by John Smith" or, worse, "all letters sent by John Smith concerning a particular transaction." So the question courts will confront will be this: What other kinds of records are sufficiently similar to letters in the mail that the same rule should apply?

It may be that, as an original matter, a subpoena requiring the recipient to produce records wasn't thought of as a "search or seizure" by the government implicating the Fourth Amendment, but instead as an act of compelled self-incrimination implicating the Fifth Amendment. But the common law of searches and seizures does not appear to have confronted a case where private documents equivalent to a mailed letter were entrusted to a bailee and then subpoenaed. As a result, "[t]he common-law rule regarding subpoenas for documents held by third parties entrusted with information from the target is . . . unknown and perhaps unknowable." Given that (perhaps insoluble) uncertainty, I am content to adhere to *Jackson* and its implications for now.

To be sure, we must be wary of returning to the doctrine of *Boyd v. United States*. *Boyd* invoked the Fourth Amendment to restrict the use of subpoenas even for ordinary business records and, as Justice Alito notes, eventually proved unworkable. But if we were to overthrow *Jackson* too and deny Fourth Amendment protection to any subpoenaed materials, we would do well to reconsider the scope of the Fifth Amendment while we're at it. Our precedents treat the right against self-incrimination as applicable only to testimony, not the production of incriminating evidence. But there is substantial evidence that the privilege against self-incrimination was also originally understood to protect a person from being forced to turn over potentially incriminating evidence.

What does all this mean for the case before us? To start, I cannot fault the Sixth Circuit for holding that *Smith* and *Miller* extinguish any *Katz*-based Fourth Amendment interest in third party cell-site data. That is the plain effect of their categorical holdings. Nor can I fault the Court today for its implicit but unmistakable conclusion that the rationale of *Smith* and *Miller* is wrong; indeed, I agree with that. The Sixth Circuit was powerless to say so, but this Court can and should. At the same time, I do not agree with the Court's decision today to keep *Smith* and *Miller* on life support and supplement them with a new and multilayered inquiry that seems to be only *Katz*-squared. Returning there, I worry, promises more trouble than help. Instead, I would look to a more traditional Fourth Amendment approach. Even if *Katz* may still supply one way to prove a Fourth Amendment interest, it has never been the only way. Neglecting more traditional approaches may mean failing to vindicate the full protections of the Fourth Amendment.

Our case offers a cautionary example. It seems to me entirely possible a person's cell-site data could qualify as his papers or effects under existing law. Yes, the telephone carrier holds the information. But 47 U.S.C. § 222 designates a customer's cell-site location information as "customer proprietary network information," and gives customers certain rights to control use of and access to CPNI about themselves. The statute generally forbids a carrier to "use, disclose, or permit access to individually identifiable" CPNI without the customer's consent, except as needed to provide the customer's telecommunications services. It also requires the carrier to disclose CPNI "upon affirmative written request by the customer, to any person designated by the customer." § 222(c)(2). Congress even afforded customers a private cause of action for damages against carriers who violate the Act's terms. § 207. Plainly, customers have substantial legal interests in this information, including at least some right to include, exclude, and control its use. Those interests might even rise to the level of a property right.

The problem is that we do not know anything more. Before the district court and court of appeals, Mr. Carpenter pursued only a *Katz* "reasonable expectations" argument. He did not invoke the law of property or any analogies to the common law, either there or in his petition for certiorari. Even in his merits brief before this Court, Mr. Carpenter's discussion of his positive law rights in cell-site data was cursory. He offered no analysis, for example, of what rights state law might provide him in addition to those supplied by § 222. In these circumstances, I cannot help but conclude — reluctantly — that Mr. Carpenter forfeited perhaps his most promising line of argument.

Unfortunately, too, this case marks the second time this Term that individuals have forfeited Fourth Amendment arguments based on positive law by failing to preserve them. Litigants have had fair notice since at least *United States v. Jones* (2012) and *Florida v. Jardines* (2013) that arguments like these may vindicate Fourth Amendment interests even where *Katz* arguments do not. Yet the arguments have gone unmade, leaving courts to the usual *Katz* handwaving. These omissions do not serve the development of a sound or fully protective Fourth Amendment jurisprudence.

NOTES AND QUESTIONS

1. The FBI and the prosecutors probably thought that the fact that they received a court order under a federal statute protected their acquisition of the CSLI. But why didn't they get a search warrant just to be sure? Do you see any reason why they could not have gotten a search warrant?

2. Why does it matter that the use of CSLI is easy and cheap? Is the point simply that the use of such technology is likely to be frequent and commonplace?

3. Does the comparative lack of precision of CSLI provide a basis for distinguishing *Jones*? Given the lack of precision, does the use of CSLI really permit the government to retrospectively "tail" someone?

4. Justice Alito in dissent claims that two aspects of the Court's decision are "revolutionary" (a) treating a judicial production order as a "search" under the Fourth Amendment and (b) allowing a defendant to object to the "search" of a third party's property. Are both of these criticisms a function of the reality that the CSLI is in the possession of a third party?

5. Justice Alito also expresses a preference for legislative solutions over Fourth Amendment case law in dealing with problems of "rapidly changing technology." Here, there was just such a legislative resolution, the Stored Communications Act, which permitted a court order to issue based on the government's mere showing that information was "relevant and material" to an "ongoing investigation." Is this a meaningful layer of judicial scrutiny?

B. WHAT IS A SEIZURE FOR FOURTH AMENDMENT PURPOSES? RACE, SEIZURE, AND FORCE

There are three essential categories of seizure for Fourth Amendment purposes. The most extreme form of seizure is an arrest, a clear manifestation or exertion of force by a police officer that constitutionally requires probable cause to believe the restrained individual has committed a crime. The least extreme is a temporary detention of an individual for questioning and sometimes frisking that constitutionally only requires "reasonable suspicion." *See infra*. In this category the person approached normally may have the right to ignore the questioner and walk away. In between is a mushier category where a reasonable person would not feel free to leave but has not been arrested.

The next case considers the circumstances of a woman being approached in the Detroit airport by DEA agents using a "drug courier profile." Do not lose focus on the consequences of the determination whether a law enforcement encounter rises to the level of a seizure. If it does, the encounter would have to have been justified by "reasonable suspicion" on the officers' part, a concept that will be explored in more depth *infra*.

1. Police Encounters and Seizures

United States v. Mendenhall

446 U.S. 544 (1980)

Mr. Justice STEWART announced the judgment of the Court and delivered an opinion in which Mr. Justice REHNQUIST joined.

The respondent was brought to trial in the United States District Court for the Eastern District of Michigan on a charge of possessing heroin with intent to distribute it. She moved to suppress the introduction at trial of the heroin as evidence against her on the ground that it had been acquired from her through an unconstitutional search and seizure by agents of the Drug Enforcement Administration (DEA). The District Court denied the respondent's motion, and she was convicted after a trial upon stipulated facts. The Court of Appeals reversed, finding the search of the respondent's person to have been unlawful. We granted certiorari to consider whether any right of the respondent guaranteed by the Fourth Amendment was violated in the circumstances presented by this case.

I

At the hearing in the trial court on the respondent's motion to suppress, it was established how the heroin she was charged with possessing had been obtained from her. The respondent arrived at the Detroit Metropolitan Airport on a commercial airline flight from Los Angeles early in the morning on February 10, 1976. As she disembarked from the airplane, she was observed by two agents of the DEA, who were present at the airport for the purpose of detecting unlawful traffic in narcotics. After observing the respondent's conduct, which appeared to the agents to be characteristic of persons unlawfully carrying narcotics, the agents approached her as she was walking through the concourse, identified themselves as federal agents, and asked to see her identification and airline ticket. The respondent produced her driver's license, which was in the name of Sylvia Mendenhall, and, in answer to a question of one of the agents, stated that she resided at the address appearing on the license. The airline ticket was issued in the name of "Annette Ford." When asked why the ticket bore a name different from her own, the respondent stated that she "just felt like using that name." In response to a further question, the respondent indicated that she had been in California only two days. Agent Anderson then specifically identified himself as a federal narcotics agent and, according to his testimony, the respondent "became quite shaken, extremely nervous. She had a hard time speaking."

After returning the airline ticket and driver's license to her, Agent Anderson asked the respondent if she would accompany him to the airport DEA office for further questions. She did so, although the record does not indicate a verbal response to the request. The office, which was located up one flight of stairs about 50 feet from where the respondent had first been approached, consisted of a reception area adjoined by three other rooms. At the office the agent asked the respondent if she would allow a search of her person and handbag and told her that she had the right to decline the search if she desired. She responded: "Go ahead." She then handed Agent Anderson her purse, which contained a receipt for an airline ticket that had been issued to "F. Bush" three days earlier for a flight from Pittsburgh through Chicago to Los Angeles. The agent asked whether this was the ticket that she had used for her flight to California, and the respondent stated that it was.

A female police officer then arrived to conduct the search of the respondent's person. She asked the agents if the respondent had consented to be searched. The agents said that she had, and the respondent followed the policewoman into a private room. There the policewoman again asked the respondent if she consented to the search, and the respondent replied that she did. The policewoman explained that the search would require that the respondent remove her clothing. The respondent stated that she had a plane to catch and was assured by the policewoman that if she were carrying no narcotics, there would be no problem. The respondent then began to disrobe without further comment. As the respondent removed her clothing, she took from her undergarments two small packages, one of which appeared to contain heroin, and handed both to the policewoman. The agents then arrested the respondent for possessing heroin.

It was on the basis of this evidence that the District Court denied the respondent's motion to suppress. The court concluded that the agents' conduct in initially approaching the respondent and asking to see her ticket and identification was a permissible investigative stop under the standards of *Terry v. Ohio*, finding that this conduct was based on specific and articulable facts that justified a suspicion of criminal activity. The court also found that the respondent had not been placed under arrest or otherwise detained when she was asked to accompany the agents to the DEA office, but had accompanied the agents "'voluntarily in a spirit of apparent cooperation.'" It was the court's view that no arrest occurred until after the heroin had been found. Finally, the trial court found that the respondent "gave her consent to the search [in the DEA office] and . . . such consent was freely and voluntarily given."

The Court of Appeals reversed the respondent's subsequent conviction.

II

The Fourth Amendment provides that "the right of the people to be secure in their persons, houses, papers, and effects, against unreasonable searches and seizures, shall not be violated. . . ." There is no question in this case that the respondent possessed this constitutional right of personal security as she walked through the Detroit Airport, for "the Fourth Amendment protects people, not places." Here the Government concedes that its agents had neither a warrant nor probable cause to believe that the respondent was carrying narcotics when the agents conducted a search of the respondent's person. It is the Government's position, however, that the search was conducted pursuant to the respondent's consent, and thus was excepted from the requirements of both a warrant and probable cause. Evidently, the Court of Appeals concluded that the respondent's apparent consent to the search was in fact not voluntarily given and was in any event the product of earlier official conduct violative of the Fourth Amendment. We must first consider, therefore, whether such conduct occurred, either on the concourse or in the DEA office at the airport.

A

The Fourth Amendment's requirement that searches and seizures be founded upon an objective justification, governs all seizures of the person, "including seizures that involve only a brief detention short of traditional arrest. Accordingly, if the respondent was "seized" when the DEA agents approached her on the concourse and asked questions of her, the agents' conduct in doing so was constitutional only if they reasonably suspected the respondent of wrongdoing. But "[o]bviously, not all personal intercourse between policemen and citizens involves 'seizures' of persons. Only when the officer, by means of physical force or show of authority, has in some way restrained the liberty of a citizen may we conclude that a 'seizure' has occurred."

The distinction between an intrusion amounting to a "seizure" of the person and an encounter that intrudes upon no constitutionally protected interest is illustrated by the facts of *Terry v. Ohio*, which the Court recounted as follows: "Officer McFadden approached the three men, identified himself as a police officer and asked for their names. . . . When the men 'mumbled something' in response to his inquiries, Officer McFadden grabbed petitioner Terry, spun him around so that they were facing the other two, with Terry between McFadden and the others, and patted down the outside of his clothing." Obviously the officer "seized" Terry and subjected him to a "search" when he took hold of him, spun him around, and patted down the outer surfaces of his clothing. What was not determined in that case, however, was that a seizure had taken place before the officer physically restrained Terry for purposes of searching his person for weapons. The court "assume[d] that up to that point no intrusion upon constitutionally protected rights had occurred." The Court's assumption appears entirely correct in view of the fact, noted in the concurring opinion of Mr. Justice White, that "[t]here is nothing in the Constitution which prevents a policeman from addressing questions to anyone on the streets." Police officers enjoy "the liberty (again, possessed by every citizen) to address questions to other persons," although "ordinarily the person addressed has an equal right to ignore his interrogator and walk away."

We adhere to the view that a person is "seized" only when, by means of physical force or a show of authority, his freedom of movement is restrained. Only when such restraint is imposed is there any foundation whatever for invoking constitutional safeguards. The purpose of the Fourth Amendment is not to eliminate all contact between the police and the citizenry, but "to prevent arbitrary and oppressive interference by enforcement officials with the privacy and personal security of individuals." As long as the person to whom questions are put remains free to disregard the questions and walk away, there has been no intrusion upon that person's liberty or privacy as would under the Constitution require some particularized and objective justification.

Moreover, characterizing every street encounter between a citizen and the police as a "seizure," while not enhancing any interest secured by the Fourth Amendment, would impose wholly unrealistic restrictions upon a wide variety of legitimate law enforcement practices. The Court has on other occasions referred to the acknowledged need for police questioning as a tool in the effective enforcement of the criminal laws. "Without such investigation, those who were innocent might be falsely accused, those who were guilty might wholly escape prosecution, and many crimes would go unsolved. In short, the security of all would be diminished.

We conclude that a person has been "seized" within the meaning of the Fourth Amendment only if, in view of all of the circumstances surrounding the incident, a reasonable person would have believed that he was not free to leave. Examples of circumstances that might indicate a seizure, even where the person did not attempt to leave, would be the threatening presence of several officers, the display of a weapon by an officer, some physical touching of the person of the citizen, or the use of language or tone of voice indicating that compliance with the officer's request might be compelled. In the absence of some such evidence, otherwise inoffensive contact between a member of the public and the police cannot, as a matter of law, amount to a seizure of that person.

On the facts of this case, no "seizure" of the respondent occurred. The events took place in the public concourse. The agents wore no uniforms and displayed no weapons. They did not summon the respondent to their presence, but instead approached her and identified themselves as federal agents. They requested, but did not demand to see the respondent's identification and ticket. Such conduct without more, did not amount to an intrusion upon any constitutionally protected interest. The respondent was not seized simply by reason of the fact that the agents approached her, asked her if she would show them her ticket and identification, and posed to her a few questions. Nor was it enough to establish a seizure that the person asking the questions was a law enforcement official. In short, nothing in the record suggests that the respondent had any objective reason to believe that she was not free to end the conversation in the concourse and proceed on her way, and for that reason we conclude that the agents' initial approach to her was not a seizure.

Our conclusion that no seizure occurred is not affected by the fact that the respondent was not expressly told by the agents that she was free to decline to cooperate with their inquiry, for the voluntariness of her responses does not depend upon her having been so informed. We also reject the argument that the only inference to be drawn from the fact that the respondent acted in a manner so contrary to her self-interest is that she was compelled to answer the agents' questions. It may happen that a person makes statements to law enforcement officials that he later regrets, but the issue in such cases is not whether the statement was self-protective, but rather whether it was made voluntarily.

• • •

B

Although we have concluded that the initial encounter between the DEA agents and the respondent on the concourse at the Detroit Airport did not constitute an unlawful seizure, it is still arguable that the respondent's Fourth Amendment protections were violated when she went from the concourse to the DEA office. Such a violation might in turn infect the subsequent search of the respondent's person.

The District Court specifically found that the respondent accompanied the agents to the office "'voluntarily in a spirit of apparent cooperation.'" Notwithstanding this determination by the trial court, the Court of Appeals evidently concluded that the agents' request that the respondent accompany them converted the situation into an arrest requiring probable cause in order to be found lawful. But because the trial court's finding was sustained by the record, the Court of Appeals was mistaken in substituting for that finding its view of the evidence.

The question whether the respondent's consent to accompany the agents was in fact voluntary or was the product of duress or coercion, express or implied, is to be determined by the totality of all the circumstances, and is a matter which the Government has the burden of proving. The respondent herself did not testify at the hearing. The Government's evidence showed that the respondent was not told that she had to go to the office, but was simply asked if she would accompany the officers. There were neither threats nor any show of force. The respondent had been questioned only briefly, and her ticket and identification were returned to her before she was asked to accompany the officers.

On the other hand, it is argued that the incident would reasonably have appeared coercive to the respondent, who was 22 years old and had not been graduated from high school. It is additionally suggested that the respondent, a female and a Negro, may have felt unusually threatened by the officers, who were white males. While these factors were not irrelevant, neither were they decisive, and the totality of the evidence in this case was plainly adequate to support the District Court's finding that the respondent voluntarily consented to accompany the officers to the DEA office.

C

Because the search of the respondent's person was not preceded by an impermissible seizure of her person, it cannot be contended that her apparent consent to the subsequent search was infected by an unlawful detention. There remains to be considered whether the respondent's consent to the search was for any other reason invalid. The District Court explicitly credited the officers' testimony and found that the "consent was freely and voluntarily given." There was more than enough evidence in this case to sustain that view. First, we note that the respondent, who was 22 years old and had an 11th-grade education, was plainly capable of a knowing consent. Second, it is especially significant that the respondent was twice expressly told that she was free to decline to consent to the search, and only thereafter explicitly consented to it. Although the Constitution does not require "proof of knowledge of a right to refuse as the sine qua non of an effective consent to a search," such knowledge was highly relevant to the determination that there had been consent. And, perhaps more important for present purposes, the fact that the officers themselves informed the respondent that she was free to withhold her consent substantially lessened the probability that their conduct could reasonably have appeared to her to be coercive.

Counsel for the respondent has argued that she did in fact resist the search, relying principally on the testimony that when she was told that the search would require the removal of her clothing, she stated to the female police officer that "she had a plane to catch." But the trial court was entitled to view the statement as simply an expression of concern that the search be conducted quickly. The respondent had twice unequivocally indicated her consent to the search, and when assured by the police officer that there would be no problem if nothing were turned up by the search, she began to undress without further comment.

Counsel for the respondent has also argued that because she was within the DEA office when she consented to the search, her consent may have resulted from the inherently coercive nature of those surroundings. But in view of the District Court's finding that the respondent's presence in the office was voluntary, the fact that she was there is little or no evidence that she was in any way coerced. And in response to the argument that the respondent would not voluntarily have consented to a search that was likely to disclose the narcotics that she carried, we repeat that the question is not whether the respondent acted in her ultimate self-interest, but whether she acted voluntarily.

III

We conclude that the District Court's determination that the respondent consented to the search of her person "freely and voluntarily" was sustained by the evidence and that the Court of Appeals was, therefore, in error in setting it aside. Accordingly, the judgment of the Court of Appeals is reversed, and the case is remanded to that court for further proceedings.

[Justices White, Marshall, Brennan, and Stevens dissented.]

NOTES AND QUESTIONS

1. This is a case about the meaning of "seizure" under the Fourth Amendment. But in working toward a definition of that term the Court also underscores the legitimate authority of police officers to engage in what might be called "consensual encounters," as recognized in *Terry v. Ohio*, 328 U.S. 1, 8, 10-11 (1968). *See* Aliza Hochman Bloom, *Long Overdue: Confronting Race in the Fourth Amendment's Free-to-Leave Analysis*, 65 Howard L.J. 1, 8-18 (2021) (discussing the significance of the consensual encounter category of police interaction).

2. The Court defines a "seizure" under the Fourth Amendment as a law enforcement interaction where, under the totality of the circumstances, "a reasonable person would have believed that he was not free to leave." Does "free to leave" mean a belief that one could leave combined with the belief that the officer would abandon any further investigative effort, including asking questions of, or following, a person?

3. The Court provides examples of law enforcement "force or a show of authority" that likely would constitute a seizure: display of a weapon, physical contact, the use of an aggressive tone. How might the nature of the questioning by the officer affect the seizure analysis?

The Court also acknowledges that the person's individual characteristics, including race (Sylvia Mendenhall was a Black woman) age, and gender, may be relevant to the totality of the circumstances insofar as they bear on whether the individual felt free to leave. Would it even be relevant whether the individual subjectively believed she was not free to leave?

If the agent had not returned her identification before continuing to question Mendenhall, would that have turned the interaction into a seizure? What if the officer had asked her to accompany him to the office before returning the identification?

4. Three Justices, concurring, would have found reasonable suspicion justifying a seizure based to some unspecified degree on the DEA's drug courier profile, and cited statistics from an unrelated district court case on the efficacy of that profile. To the extent those statistics were relevant to a reasonable suspicion, shouldn't they have been subject to cross-examination at the suppression hearing?

5. Why do you think Sylvia Mendenhall did not testify at her suppression hearing? Note that the factual record established at the hearing was entirely the result of law enforcement testimony. Isn't it likely she would have been able to provide additional details about her interaction with the agents that would have been relevant as to the officers' manifestations of authority, or to her own assessment of the situation?

If she had testified at the hearing, could she have been questioned about whether she had been in possession of heroin? The Supreme Court in 1968 held that a defendant's testimony at a suppression hearing—sometimes necessary to establish standing to contest an illegal search—cannot be used against the defendant on the question of guilt or innocence although it can be used to impeach the credibility of a testifying defendant at trial. *Simmons v. United States*, 390 U.S. 27 (1968). *See* Chapter V *infra.*

If the DEA had opposed the motion solely on the basis of the drug courier profile, would her testimony have been necessary?

The Court applied the *Mendenhall* standard in several cases over the next decade, each time concluding that a reasonable person in the defendant's position would have felt "free to leave." The defendants in these cases were Black people or other minorities, although the defendant's race was never mentioned, raising the possibility that the observations about race in *Mendenhall* were only a cruel head fake. In *Florida v. Royer*, 460 U.S. 491 (1983), plainclothes DEA agents singled out and approached Royer pursuant to their drug courier profile inasmuch as he was nervous, young, had paid cash for his ticket, and had checked heavy luggage. The Court held that the DEA's approach and questioning of Royer about his identification and travel intentions did not rise to the level of a seizure until the moment when they identified themselves as agents and asked him to accompany them to another room, while retaining his ticket, as before that particular point a reasonable person would have felt free to leave. *Id.* at 502. *See infra* Section E.

In *INS v. Delgado*, 466 U.S. 210 (1984), the Court held that raids of two factories by INS agents, and systematic questioning of the entire work forces at both factories regarding potential immigration offenses, was not a seizure under *Mendenhall.* The Court noted that the mere questioning about their identification issues (despite the subject's sensitivity in this particular context) did not amount to a seizure, as it had previously held to similar effect in *Royer*, and that reasonable persons in the workers' position would have felt free to leave. It reached this conclusion even though some of the INS agents—all of whom were badged, armed, and carried handcuffs—had been strategically situated at the factories' exits, as if to inhibit that very feeling. *Id.* at 218.

The Court noted that the workers' freedom of movement had already been curtailed by their conditions of employment, suggesting that similar investigative activity in a different environment—say, a law firm?—might have different consequences. None of the opinions do justice to the facts "on the ground" in *Delgado*, which included that several workers who attempted to exit the factory during the raid were arrested by the agents. Brief for Respondents at 30, *INS v. Delgado*, 466 U.S. 210 (1984) (No. 82-1271). In a dissenting opinion, Justice Brennan stated that the Court's opinion had a "studied air of unreality." *Id.* at 226 (Brennan, J., dissenting).

Finally, in *Michigan v. Chesternut*, 486 U.S. 567 (1988), a police car pursued Chesternut as he began running away after observing the police car. After following him around a corner and catching up with him, the police drive alongside him for a "short distance." Although one of the officers described the action as "a chase," and the Court agreed the police actions may have been "somewhat intimidating," the Court held that a reasonable person would have felt free to leave. The Court did not acknowledge that "leaving" is exactly what Chesternut was trying to do all along.

Not satisfied with so much police success on the seizure front, the Court in the next case changed the *Mendenhall* test to make seizures even more difficult to establish.

California v. Hodari D.

499 U.S. 621 (1991)

Justice Scalia delivered the opinion of the Court.

Late one evening in April 1988, Officers Brian McColgin and Jerry Pertoso were on patrol in a high-crime area of Oakland, California. They were dressed in street clothes but wearing jackets with "Police" embossed on both front and back. Their unmarked car proceeded west on Foothill Boulevard, and turned south onto 63rd Avenue. As they rounded the corner, they saw four or five youths huddled around a small red car parked at the curb. When the youths saw the officers' car approaching they apparently panicked, and took flight. The respondent here, Hodari D., and one companion ran west through an alley; the others fled south. The red car also headed south, at a high rate of speed.

The officers were suspicious and gave chase. McColgin remained in the car and continued south on 63rd Avenue; Pertoso left the car, ran back north along 63rd, then west on Foothill Boulevard, and turned south on 62nd Avenue. Hodari, meanwhile, emerged from the alley onto 62nd and ran north. Looking behind as he ran, he did not turn and see Pertoso until the officer was almost upon him, whereupon he tossed away what appeared to be a small rock. A moment later, Pertoso tackled Hodari, handcuffed him, and radioed for assistance. Hodari was found to be carrying $130 in cash and a pager; and the rock he had discarded was found to be crack cocaine.

In the juvenile proceeding brought against him, Hodari moved to suppress the evidence relating to the cocaine. The court denied the motion without opinion. The California Court of Appeal reversed, holding that Hodari had been "seized" when he saw Officer Pertoso running towards him, that this seizure was unreasonable under the Fourth Amendment, and that the evidence of cocaine had to be suppressed as the fruit of that illegal seizure. The California Supreme Court denied the State's application for review. We granted certiorari.

As this case comes to us, the only issue presented is whether, at the time he dropped the drugs, Hodari had been "seized" within the meaning of the Fourth Amendment. If so, respondent argues, the drugs were the fruit of that seizure and the evidence concerning them was properly excluded. If not, the drugs were abandoned by Hodari and lawfully recovered by the police, and the evidence should have been admitted. (In addition, of course, Pertoso's seeing the rock of cocaine, at least if he recognized it as such, would provide reasonable suspicion for the unquestioned seizure that occurred when he tackled Hodari.)

We have long understood that the Fourth Amendment's protection against "unreasonable . . . seizures" includes seizure of the person. From the time of the founding to the present, the word "seizure" has meant a "taking possession." For most purposes at common law, the word connoted not merely grasping, or applying physical force to, the animate or inanimate object in question, but actually bringing it within physical control.

"There can be constructive detention, which will constitute an arrest, although the party is never actually brought within the physical control of the party making an arrest. This is accomplished by merely touching, however slightly, the body of the accused, by the party making the arrest and for that purpose, although he does not succeed in stopping or holding him even for an instant; as where the bailiff had tried to arrest one who fought him off by a fork, the court said, 'If the bailiff had touched him, that had been an arrest. . . .'"

To say that an arrest is effected by the slightest application of physical force, despite the arrestee's escape, is not to say that for Fourth Amendment purposes there is a continuing arrest during the period of fugitivity. If, for example, Pertoso had laid his hands upon Hodari to arrest him, but Hodari had broken away and had then cast away the cocaine, it would hardly be realistic to say that that disclosure had been made during the course of an arrest. The present case, however, is even one step further removed. It does not involve the application of any physical force; Hodari was untouched by Officer Pertoso at the time he discarded the cocaine. His defense relies instead upon the proposition that a seizure occurs "when the officer, by means of physical force or show of authority, has in some way restrained the liberty of a citizen." Hodari contends (and we accept as true for purposes of this decision) that Pertoso's pursuit qualified as a "show of authority" calling upon Hodari to halt. The narrow question before us is whether, with respect to a show of authority as with respect to application of physical force, a seizure occurs even though the subject does not yield. We hold that it does not.

The language of the Fourth Amendment, of course, cannot sustain respondent's contention. The word "seizure" readily bears the meaning of a laying on of hands or application of physical force to restrain movement, even when it is ultimately unsuccessful. ("She seized the purse-snatcher, but he broke out of her grasp.") It does not remotely apply, however, to the prospect of a policeman yelling "Stop, in the name of the law!" at a fleeing form that continues to flee. That is no seizure. Nor can the result respondent wishes to achieve be produced—indirectly, as it were—by suggesting that Pertoso's uncomplied-with show of authority was a common-law arrest, and then appealing to the principle that all common-law arrests are seizures. An arrest requires either physical force (as described above) or, where that is absent, submission to the assertion of authority.

"Mere words will not constitute an arrest, while, on the other hand, no actual, physical touching is essential. The apparent inconsistency in the two parts of this statement is explained by the fact that an assertion of authority and purpose to arrest followed by submission of the arrestee constitutes an arrest. There can be no arrest without either touching or submission."

We do not think it desirable, even as a policy matter, to stretch the Fourth Amendment beyond its words and beyond the meaning of arrest, as respondent urges. Street pursuits always place the public at some risk, and compliance with police orders to stop should therefore be encouraged. Only a few of those orders, we must presume, will be without adequate basis, and since the addressee has no ready means of identifying the deficient ones it almost invariably is the responsible course to comply. Unlawful orders will not be deterred, moreover, by sanctioning through the exclusionary rule those of them that are not obeyed. Since policemen do not command "Stop!" expecting to be ignored, or give chase hoping to be outrun, it fully suffices to apply the deterrent to their genuine, successful seizures.

Respondent contends that his position is sustained by the so-called *Mendenhall* test. In seeking to rely upon that test here, respondent fails to read it carefully. It says that a person has been seized "only if," not that he has been seized "whenever"; it states a necessary, but not a sufficient, condition for seizure—or, more precisely, for seizure effected through a "show of authority." *Mendenhall* establishes that the test for existence of a "show of authority" is an objective one: not whether the citizen perceived that he was being ordered to restrict his movement, but whether the officer's words and actions would have conveyed that to a reasonable person. Application of this objective test was the basis for our decision in the other case principally relied upon by respondent, *Chesternut, supra*, where we concluded that the police cruiser's slow following of the defendant did not convey the message that he was not free to disregard the police and go about his business. We did not address in *Chesternut*, however, the question whether, if the *Mendenhall* test was met—if the message that the defendant was not free to leave had been conveyed—a Fourth Amendment seizure would have occurred.

Quite relevant to the present case, however, was our decision in *Brower v. Inyo County* (1989). In that case, police cars with flashing lights had chased the decedent for 20 miles—surely an adequate "show of authority"—but he did not stop until his fatal crash into a police-erected blockade. The issue was whether his death could be held to be the consequence of an unreasonable seizure in violation of the Fourth Amendment. We did not even consider the possibility that a seizure could have occurred during the course of the chase because, as we explained, that "show of authority" did not produce his stop. And we discussed an opinion of Justice Holmes, involving a situation not much different from the present case, where revenue agents had picked up containers dropped by moonshiners whom they were pursuing without adequate warrant. The containers were not excluded as the product of an unlawful seizure because "[t]he defendant's own acts, and those of his associates, disclosed the jug, the jar and the bottle—and there was no seizure in the sense of the law when the officers examined the contents of each after they had been abandoned." The same is true here.

In sum, assuming that Pertoso's pursuit in the present case constituted a "show of authority" enjoining Hodari to halt, since Hodari did not comply with that injunction he was not seized until he was tackled. The cocaine abandoned while he was running was in this case not the fruit of a seizure, and his motion to exclude evidence of it was properly denied. We reverse the decision of the California Court of Appeal, and remand for further proceedings not inconsistent with this opinion.

[Justices Stevens and Marshall dissented.]

NOTES AND QUESTIONS

1. Is *Hodari D.* based on a fair reading of *Mendenhall*? Put differently, is it reasonable to interpret *Mendenhall* as establishing only a necessary condition of a seizure and not also a sufficient condition of a seizure?

2. Does the Court in *Hodari D.* equate seizure with arrest?

3. If Hodari had yielded to the police officer's pursuit (and hung on to the cocaine) he may have thereby been under "arrest." Was there probable cause for his arrest? Was there "reasonable suspicion" to temporarily detain him? The Court makes this observation in footnote 1:

> California conceded below that Officer Pertoso did not have the "reasonable suspicion" required to justify stopping Hodari, *see Terry v. Ohio*, 392 U.S. 1 (1968). That it would be unreasonable to stop, for brief inquiry, young men who scatter in panic upon the mere sighting of the police is not self-evident, and arguably contradicts proverbial common sense. *See* Proverbs 28:1 ("The wicked flee when no man pursueth"). We do not decide that point here, but rely entirely upon the State's concession.

Do you agree with Justice Scalia's point about a connection between flight and suspicion? Does Proverbs 28:1 consider the possibility that to some persons, especially Black people and other minorities, the pursuers themselves may reasonably be regarded as wicked? *See infra* Section E.

4. The Court doubled down on the common law of arrests in *Torres v. Madrid*, 592 U.S. 306 (2021), where a police officer shot and hit a car driven by a woman trying to escape the officers, whom she had mistakenly believed were car jackers, and had accordingly rebuffed their approach to her vehicle. In a 5-4 decision featuring a dispute over competing originalist interpretations of "arrest," the majority found an "arrest" and therefore a "seizure" even though the woman was not successfully apprehended.

5. According to the 2023 survey in the *Mississippi Law Journal* referenced in Chapter I, 16 states have refused to follow *Hodari D*, the second most states (after *Leon)* than any other Supreme Court criminal procedure decision. Christopher R. Green et. al., *State-Court Departures from the Supreme Court: A Comprehensive Survey*, 92 Miss. L.J. 329, 330 (2023).

United States v. Drayton

536 U.S. 194 (2002)

Justice Kennedy delivered the opinion of the Court.

The Fourth Amendment permits police officers to approach bus passengers at random to ask questions and to request their consent to searches, provided a reasonable person would understand that he or she is free to refuse. *Florida v. Bostick*. his case requires us to determine whether officers must advise bus passengers during these encounters of their right not to cooperate.

I

On February 4, 1999, respondents Christopher Drayton and Clifton Brown, Jr., were traveling on a Greyhound bus en route from Ft. Lauderdale, Florida, to Detroit, Michigan. The bus made a scheduled stop in Tallahassee, Florida. The passengers were required to disembark so the bus could be refueled and cleaned. As the passengers reboarded, the driver checked their tickets and then left to complete paperwork inside the terminal. As he left, the driver allowed three members of the Tallahassee Police Department to board the bus as part of a routine drug and weapons interdiction effort. The officers were dressed in plain clothes and carried concealed weapons and visible badges.

Once onboard Officer Hoover knelt on the driver's seat and faced the rear of the bus. He could observe the passengers and ensure the safety of the two other officers without blocking the aisle or otherwise obstructing the bus exit. Officers Lang and Blackburn went to the rear of the bus. Blackburn remained stationed there, facing forward. Lang worked his way toward the front of the bus, speaking with individual passengers as he went. He asked the passengers about their travel plans and sought to match passengers with luggage in the overhead racks. To avoid blocking the aisle, Lang stood next to or just behind each passenger with whom he spoke.

According to Lang's testimony, passengers who declined to cooperate with him or who chose to exit the bus at any time would have been allowed to do so without argument. In Lang's experience, however, most people are willing to cooperate. Some passengers go so far as to commend the police for their efforts to ensure the safety of their travel. Lang could recall five to six instances in the previous year in which passengers had declined to have their luggage searched. It also was common for passengers to leave the bus for a cigarette or a snack while the officers were on board. Lang sometimes informed passengers of their right to refuse to cooperate. On the day in question, however, he did not.

Respondents were seated next to each other on the bus. Drayton was in the aisle seat, Brown in the seat next to the window. Lang approached respondents from the rear and leaned over Drayton's shoulder. He held up his badge long enough for respondents to identify him as a police officer. With his face 12-to-18 inches away from Drayton's, Lang spoke in a voice just loud enough for respondents to hear:

> I'm Investigator Lang with the Tallahassee Police Department. We're conducting bus interdiction [sic], attempting to deter drugs and illegal weapons being transported on the bus. Do you have any bags on the bus?

Both respondents pointed to a single green bag in the overhead luggage rack. Lang asked, "Do you mind if I check it?," and Brown responded, "Go ahead." Lang handed the bag to Officer Blackburn to check. The bag contained no contraband.

Officer Lang noticed that both respondents were wearing heavy jackets and baggy pants despite the warm weather. In Lang's experience drug traffickers often use baggy clothing to conceal weapons or narcotics. The officer thus asked Brown if he had any weapons or drugs in his possession. And he asked Brown: "Do you mind if I check your person?" Brown answered, "Sure," and cooperated by leaning up in his seat, pulling a cell phone out of his pocket, and opening up his jacket. Lang reached across Drayton and patted down Brown's jacket and pockets, including his waist area, sides, and upper thighs. In both thigh areas, Lang detected hard objects similar to drug packages detected on other occasions. Lang arrested and handcuffed Brown. Officer Hoover escorted Brown from the bus.

Lang then asked Drayton, "Mind if I check you?" Drayton responded by lifting his hands about eight inches from his legs. Lang conducted a patdown of Drayton's thighs and detected hard objects similar to those found on Brown. He arrested Drayton and escorted him from the bus. A further search revealed that respondents had duct-taped plastic bundles of powder cocaine between several pairs of their boxer shorts. Brown possessed three bundles containing 483 grams of cocaine. Drayton possessed two bundles containing 295 grams of cocaine.

Respondents were charged with conspiring to distribute cocaine, in violation of 21 U.S.C. §§ 841(a)(1) and 846, and with possessing cocaine with intent to distribute it, in violation of § 841(a)(1). They moved to suppress the cocaine, arguing that the consent to the patdown search was invalid. Following a hearing at which only Officer Lang testified, the United States District Court for the Northern District of Florida denied their motions to suppress. The District Court determined that the police conduct was not coercive and respondents' consent to the search was voluntary. The District Court pointed to the fact that the officers were dressed in plain clothes, did not brandish their badges in an authoritative manner, did not make a general announcement to the entire bus, and did not address anyone in a menacing tone of voice. It noted that the officers did not block the aisle or the exit, and stated that it was "obvious that [respondents] can get up and leave, as can the people ahead of them." The District Court concluded: "[E]verything that took place between Officer Lang and Mr. Drayton and

Mr. Brown suggests that it was cooperative. There was nothing coercive, there was nothing confrontational about it."

The Court of Appeals for the Eleventh Circuit reversed and remanded with instructions to grant respondents' motions to suppress.

We granted certiorari. The respondents, we conclude, were not seized and their consent to the search was voluntary; and we reverse.

II

Law enforcement officers do not violate the Fourth Amendment's prohibition of unreasonable seizures merely by approaching individuals on the street or in other public places and putting questions to them if they are willing to listen. Even when law enforcement officers have no basis for suspecting a particular individual, they may pose questions, ask for identification, and request consent to search luggage—provided they do not induce cooperation by coercive means. If a reasonable person would feel free to terminate the encounter, then he or she has not been seized.

The Court has addressed on a previous occasion the specific question of drug interdiction efforts on buses. In *Bostick*, two police officers requested a bus passenger's consent to a search of his luggage. The passenger agreed, and the resulting search revealed cocaine in his suitcase. The Florida Supreme Court suppressed the cocaine. In doing so it adopted a per se rule that due to the cramped confines onboard a bus the act of questioning would deprive a person of his or her freedom of movement and so constitute a seizure under the Fourth Amendment.

This Court reversed. *Bostick* first made it clear that for the most part per se rules are inappropriate in the Fourth Amendment context. The proper inquiry necessitates a consideration of "all the circumstances surrounding the encounter." The Court noted next that the traditional rule, which states that a seizure does not occur so long as a reasonable person would feel free "to disregard the police and go about his business," is not an accurate measure of the coercive effect of a bus encounter. A passenger may not want to get off a bus if there is a risk it will depart before the opportunity to reboard. A bus rider's movements are confined in this sense, but this is the natural result of choosing to take the bus; it says nothing about whether the police conduct is coercive. The proper inquiry "is whether a reasonable person would feel free to decline the officers' requests or otherwise terminate the encounter." Finally, the Court rejected Bostick's argument that he must have been seized because no reasonable person would consent to a search of luggage containing drugs. The reasonable person test, the Court explained, is objective and "presupposes an innocent person."

In light of the limited record, *Bostick* refrained from deciding whether a seizure occurred. The Court, however, identified two factors "particularly worth noting" on remand. First, although it was obvious that an officer was armed, he did not remove the gun from its pouch or use it in a threatening way. Second, the officer advised the passenger that he could refuse consent to the search.

• • •

Applying the *Bostick* framework to the facts of this particular case, we conclude that the police did not seize respondents when they boarded the bus and began questioning passengers. The officers gave the passengers no reason to believe that they were required to answer the officers' questions. When Officer Lang approached respondents, he did not brandish a weapon or make any intimidating movements. He left the aisle free so that respondents could exit. He spoke to passengers one by one and in a polite, quiet voice. Nothing he said would suggest to a reasonable person that he or she was barred from leaving the bus or otherwise terminating the encounter.

There were ample grounds for the District Court to conclude that "everything that took place between Officer Lang and [respondents] suggests that it was cooperative" and that there "was nothing coercive [or] confrontational" about the encounter. There was no application of force, no intimidating movement, no overwhelming show of force, no brandishing of weapons, no blocking of exits, no threat, no command, not even an authoritative tone of voice. It is beyond question that had this encounter occurred on the street, it would be constitutional. The fact that an encounter takes place on a bus does not on its own transform standard police questioning of citizens into an illegal seizure. Indeed, because many fellow passengers are present to witness officers' conduct, a reasonable person may feel even more secure in his or her decision not to cooperate with police on a bus than in other circumstances.

Respondents make much of the fact that Officer Lang displayed his badge. And while neither Lang nor his colleagues were in uniform or visibly armed, those factors should have little weight in the analysis. Officers are often required to wear uniforms and in many circumstances this is cause for assurance, not discomfort. Much the same can be said for wearing sidearms. That most law enforcement officers are armed is a fact well known to the public. The presence of a holstered firearm thus is unlikely to contribute to the coerciveness of the encounter absent active brandishing of the weapon.

Officer Hoover's position at the front of the bus also does not tip the scale in respondents' favor. Hoover did nothing to intimidate passengers, and he said nothing to suggest that people could not exit and indeed he left the aisle clear. In *Delgado*, the Court determined there was no seizure even though several uniformed INS officers were stationed near the exits of the factory. The Court noted: "The presence of agents by the exits posed no reasonable threat of detention to these workers, . . . the mere possibility that they would be questioned if they sought to leave the buildings should not have resulted in any reasonable apprehension by any of them that they would be seized or detained in any meaningful way."

Finally, the fact that in Officer Lang's experience only a few passengers have refused to cooperate does not suggest that a reasonable person would not feel free to terminate the bus encounter. In Lang's experience it was common for passengers to leave the bus for a cigarette or a snack while the officers were questioning passengers. And of more importance, bus passengers answer officers' questions and otherwise cooperate not because of coercion but because the passengers know that their participation enhances their own safety and the safety of those around them. "While most citizens will respond to a police request, the fact that people do so, and do so without being told they are free not to respond, hardly eliminates the consensual nature of the response."

Drayton contends that even if Brown's cooperation with the officers was consensual, Drayton was seized because no reasonable person would feel free to terminate the encounter with the officers after Brown had been arrested. The Court of Appeals did not address this claim; and in any event the argument fails. The arrest of one person does not mean that everyone around him has been seized by police. If anything, Brown's arrest should have put Drayton on notice of the consequences of continuing the encounter by answering the officers' questions. Even after arresting Brown, Lang addressed Drayton in a polite manner and provided him with no indication that he was required to answer Lang's questions.

We turn now from the question whether respondents were seized to whether they were subjected to an unreasonable search, i.e., whether their consent to the suspicionless search was involuntary. In circumstances such as these, where the question of voluntariness pervades both the search and seizure inquiries, the respective analyses turn on very similar facts. And, as the facts above suggest, respondents' consent to the search of their luggage and their persons was voluntary. Nothing Officer Lang said indicated a command to consent to the search. Rather, when respondents informed Lang that they had a bag on the bus, he asked for their permission to check it. And when Lang requested to search Brown and Drayton's persons, he asked first if they objected, thus indicating to a reasonable person that he or she was free to refuse. Even after arresting Brown, Lang provided Drayton with no indication that he was required to consent to a search. To the contrary, Lang asked for Drayton's permission to search him ("Mind if I check you?"), and Drayton agreed.

The Court has rejected in specific terms the suggestion that police officers must always inform citizens of their right to refuse when seeking permission to conduct a warrantless consent search. "While knowledge of the right to refuse consent is one factor to be taken into account, the government need not establish such knowledge as the sine qua non of an effective consent." Nor do this Court's decisions suggest that even though there are no per se rules, a presumption of invalidity attaches if a citizen consented without explicit notification that he or she was free to refuse to cooperate. Instead, the Court has repeated that the totality of the circumstances must control, without giving extra weight to the absence of this type of warning. Although Officer Lang did not inform respondents of their right to refuse the search, he did request permission to search, and the totality of the circumstances indicates that their consent was voluntary, so the searches were reasonable.

In a society based on law, the concept of agreement and consent should be given a weight and dignity of its own. Police officers act in full accord with the law when they ask citizens for consent. It reinforces the rule of law for the citizen to advise the police of his or her wishes and for the police to act in reliance on that understanding. When this exchange takes place, it dispels inferences of coercion.

• • •

The judgment of the Court of Appeals is reversed, and the case is remanded for further proceedings consistent with this opinion.

Justice SOUTER, with whom Justice STEVENS and Justice GINSBURG join, dissenting.

Anyone who travels by air today submits to searches of the person and luggage as a condition of boarding the aircraft. It is universally accepted that such intrusions are necessary to hedge against risks that, nowadays, even small children understand. The commonplace precautions of air travel have not, thus far, been justified for ground transportation, however, and no such conditions have been placed on passengers getting on trains or buses. There is therefore an air of unreality about the Court's explanation that bus passengers consent to searches of their luggage to "enhanc[e] their own safety and the safety of those around them." Nor are the other factual assessments underlying the Court's conclusion in favor of the Government more convincing.

The issue we took to review is whether the police's examination of the bus passengers, including respondents, amounted to a suspicionless seizure under the Fourth Amendment. If it did, any consent to search was plainly invalid as a product of the illegal seizure.

Florida v. Bostick (1991), established the framework for determining whether the bus passengers were seized in the constitutional sense. In that case, we rejected the position that police questioning of bus passengers was a per se seizure, and held instead that the issue of seizure was to be resolved under an objective test considering all circumstances: whether a reasonable passenger would have felt "free to decline the officers' requests or otherwise terminate the encounter." We thus applied to a bus passenger the more general criterion, whether the person questioned was free "to ignore the police presence and go about his business."

Before applying the standard in this case, it may be worth getting some perspective from different sets of facts. A perfect example of police conduct that supports no colorable claim of seizure is the act of an officer who simply goes up to a pedestrian on the street and asks him a question. A pair of officers questioning a pedestrian, without more, would presumably support the same conclusion. Now consider three officers, one of whom stands behind the pedestrian, another at his side toward the open sidewalk, with the third addressing questions to the pedestrian a foot or two from his face. Finally, consider the same scene in a narrow alley. On such barebones facts, one may not be able to say a seizure occurred, even in the last case, but one can say without qualification that the atmosphere of the encounters differed significantly from the first to the last examples. In the final instance there is every reason to believe that the pedestrian would have understood, to his considerable discomfort, what Justice Stewart described as the "threatening presence of several officers." The police not only carry legitimate authority but also exercise power free from immediate check, and when the attention of several officers is brought to bear on one civilian the imbalance of immediate power is unmistakable. We all understand this, as well as we understand that a display of power rising to Justice Stewart's "threatening" level may overbear a normal person's ability to act freely, even in the absence of explicit commands or the formalities of detention. As common as this understanding is, however, there is little sign of it in the Court's opinion. My own understanding of the relevant facts and their significance follows.

When the bus in question made its scheduled stop in Tallahassee, the passengers were required to disembark while the vehicle was cleaned and refueled. When the passengers returned, they gave their tickets to the driver, who kept them and then left himself, after giving three police officers permission to board the bus in his absence. Although they were not in uniform, the officers displayed badges and identified themselves as police. One stationed himself in the driver's seat by the door at the front, facing back to observe the passengers. The two others went to the rear, from which they worked their way forward, with one of them speaking to passengers, the other backing him up. They necessarily addressed the passengers at very close range; the aisle was only 15 inches wide, and each seat only 18. The quarters were cramped further by the overhead rack, 19 inches above the top of the passenger seats. The passenger by the window could not have stood up straight, and the face of the nearest officer was only a foot or 18 inches from the face of the nearest passenger being addressed. During the exchanges, the officers looked down, and the passengers had to look up if they were to face the police. The officer asking the questions spoke quietly. He prefaced his requests for permission to search luggage and do a body patdown by identifying himself by name as a police investigator "conducting bus interdiction" and saying, "'We would like for your cooperation. Do you have any luggage on the bus?'"

Thus, for reasons unexplained, the driver with the tickets entitling the passengers to travel had yielded his custody of the bus and its seated travelers to three police officers, whose authority apparently superseded the driver's own. The officers took control of the entire passenger compartment, one stationed at the door keeping surveillance of all the occupants, the others working forward from the back. With one officer right behind him and the other one forward, a third officer accosted each passenger at quarters extremely close and so cramped that as many as half the passengers could not even have stood to face the speaker. None was asked whether he was willing to converse with the police or to take part in the enquiry. Instead the officer said the police were "conducting bus interdiction," in the course of which they "would like . . . cooperation." The reasonable inference was that the "interdiction" was not a consensual exercise, but one the police would carry out whatever the circumstances; that they would prefer "cooperation" but would not let the lack of it stand in their way. There was no contrary indication that day, since no passenger had refused the cooperation requested, and there was no reason for any passenger to believe that the driver would return and the trip resume until the police were satisfied. The scene was set and an atmosphere of obligatory participation was established by this introduction. Later requests to search prefaced with "Do you mind . . ." would naturally have been understood in the terms with which the encounter began.

It is very hard to imagine that either Brown or Drayton would have believed that he stood to lose nothing if he refused to cooperate with the police, or that he had any free choice to ignore the police altogether. No reasonable passenger could have believed that, only an uncomprehending one. It is neither here nor there that the interdiction was conducted by three officers, not one, as a safety precaution. The fact was that there were three, and when Brown and Drayton were called upon to respond, each one was presumably conscious of an officer in front watching, one at his side questioning him, and one behind for cover, in case he became unruly, perhaps, or "cooperation" was not forthcoming. The situation is much like the one in the alley, with civilians in close quarters, unable to move effectively, being told their cooperation is expected. While I am not prepared to say that no bus interrogation and search can pass the *Bostick* test without a warning that passengers are free to say no, the facts here surely required more from the officers than a quiet tone of voice. A police officer who is certain to get his way has no need to shout.

It is true of course that the police testified that a bus passenger sometimes says no, but that evidence does nothing to cast the facts here in a different light. We have no way of knowing the circumstances in which a passenger elsewhere refused a request; maybe that has happened only when the police have told passengers they had a right to refuse (as the officers sometimes advised them). Nor is it fairly possible to see the facts of this case differently by recalling *Delgado* as precedent. In that case, a majority of this Court found no seizure when a factory force was questioned by immigration officers, with an officer posted at every door leading from the workplace. Whether that opinion was well reasoned or not, the facts as the Court viewed them differed from the case here. *Delgado* considered an order granting summary judgment in favor of respondents, with the consequence that the Court was required to construe the record and all issues of fact favorably to the Immigration and Naturalization Service. The Court therefore emphasized that even after "th[e] surveys were initiated, the employees were about their ordinary business, operating machinery and performing other job assignments." In this case, however, Brown and Drayton were seemingly pinned-in by the officers and the customary course of events was stopped flat. The bus was going nowhere, and with one officer in the driver's seat, it was reasonable to suppose no passenger would tend to his own business until the officers were ready to let him.

In any event, I am less concerned to parse this case against *Delgado* than to apply *Bostick*'s totality of circumstances test, and to ask whether a passenger would reasonably have felt free to end his encounter with the three officers by saying no and ignoring them thereafter. In my view the answer is clear. The Court's contrary conclusion tells me that the majority cannot see what Justice Stewart saw, and I respectfully dissent.

NOTES AND QUESTIONS

1. The Court revisits the seizure question it had deferred in *Florida v. Bostick*, 501 U.S. 429 (1991), due to a limited record on the issue in that case. In *Bostick*, notably, the officers had informed the passenger that he could refuse consent to the search.

2. Drayton argues that the dynamic of his interaction with the police changed once his traveling companion and virtual seatmate was handcuffed and arrested before his eyes. The Court responds to this argument by stating that the arrest "should have put Drayton on notice of the consequences of continuing the encounter by answering the officers' questions."

But what is the relevance of this "notice" to the "coerciveness" of the altercation, which the Court seems to think is a proxy for whether cooperation could be refused?

3. In connection with acknowledging the officer's testimony that it was common for passengers to step off the bus for a cigarette or a snack — presumably after being questioned, although the Court doesn't clarify and maybe the record didn't either — the Court offers this observation:

And of more importance, bus passengers answer officers' questions and otherwise cooperate not because of coercion but because the passengers know that their participation enhances their own safety and the safety of those around them.

This sentiment does not appear to be either directly or even indirectly based on any evidence from the suppression hearing. The sentiment reflects yet another example of "a studied air of unreality." It is also rank supposition that no police officer would be permitted to testify to in court.

Professor Bennett Capers collects and discusses these little civics tutorials that the Court so often imparts—mostly in cases with minority defendants—in Bennett Capers, Essay, *Criminal Procedure and the Good Citizen*, 118 Colum. L. Rev. 653, 670 (2018).

4. The dissent points to three factual circumstances that in its view the Court fails to acknowledge: the location of the officers at the bus's exits, which it reinforces by the "narrow alley" analogy; the cramped, almost claustrophobic quarters of the bus, including not just its narrowness but the physical location of the interrogating officers; and the bus driver's apparent abandonment of authority to the police officers, for at least the indefinite future. Which of these factors is most supportive of the dissent's conclusion that an "atmosphere of obligatory participation was established"?

What do you make of the Court's point that the lack of freedom of movement was largely a function of the "choice" to travel by bus as opposed to any action by law enforcement? *See ACLU Amicus Brief, Florida v. Bostick*, 501 U.S. 429 (1991) at 8 n.19 (noting that drug raids on buses disproportionally affect minorities). Are Fourth Amendment seizure rules different for people who work in factories (as in *Delgado*) and take buses?

5. There appears to be substantial case law on drug interdiction bus searches. Any wonder why police officers continue to use this tactic?

All of the Court's seizure case law has an "air of unreality" about it. Most reasonable people would not "feel free to leave" almost any encounter with police. Some courts have acknowledged that this is the actual "reality" of such interactions. "[A]s a practical matter, citizens almost never feel free to end an encounter initiated by the police." *State v. Jones*, 172 N.H. 774, 777 (2020) (quoting *State v. Rodriguez*, 172 N.J. 117, 796 A.2d 857, 863 (2002)); *United States v. Tanguay*, 918 F.3d 1, 5-6 (1st Cir. 2019) ("few people . . . would ever feel free to walk away from any police questioning"); *United States v. Thompson*, 546 F.3d 1223, 1226 n.1 (10th Cir. 2008) (describing the notion that a reasonable person would feel free to disregard the police as potentially "unrealistic"). Academics unanimously agree. *See* Tracey Maclin, *The Decline of the Right of Locomotion: The Fourth Amendment on the Streets*, 75 Cornell L. Rev. 1258, 1301 n.205 (1990) (listing sources).

2. Should Race Matter?

Professor Maclin suggested over 30 years ago that the Court should discard the notion of using a hypothesized reasonable person to judge the constitutionality of police encounters. Instead, taking *Mendenhall* seriously, in assessing the coercive nature of an interaction the Court should take the citizen's race into account, and how race might have influenced the person's perception of the encounter. *See* Tracey Maclin, *Black and Blue Encounters—Some Preliminary Thoughts About Fourth Amendment Seizures: Should Race Matter?*, 26 Val. L. Rev. 243, 250 (1991). Because of widespread fear of police violence in the Black community, Black people have "internalized racial obedience toward, and fear of, the police." Devon W. Carbado, *(E)racing the Fourth Amendment*, 100 Mich. L. Rev. 946, 966 (2002).

A handful of state and federal courts have discussed whether race should matter in the seizure context. The most unequivocal affirmative answer to Professor Maclin's question—Should race matter?—has come from the Supreme Court of Washington, which held in *State v. Sum*, 199 Wash. 2d 627, 656 (2022) (en banc) that courts "must" consider the race and ethnicity of the allegedly seized person in assessing an encounter.

State v. Sum

199 Wash. 2d 627 (2022) (en banc)

Yu, J.

This case concerns the analysis that courts must apply to determine whether a person has been seized by law enforcement for purposes of article I, section 7 of the Washington Constitution. It is well established that an encounter with law enforcement rises to the level of a seizure if "considering all the circumstances, an individual's freedom of movement is restrained and the individual would not believe [they are] free to leave or decline a request due to an officer's use of force or display of authority." Today, we are asked whether "all the circumstances" of the encounter includes the race and ethnicity of the allegedly seized person.

As the parties correctly agree, the answer is yes. Our precedent has always required that the seizure inquiry be made in light of the totality of the circumstances, and we have never stated that race and ethnicity cannot be relevant circumstances. However, we have not explicitly held that in interactions with law enforcement, race and ethnicity matter. We do so today. Furthermore, to ensure that all the circumstances of a law enforcement encounter are properly considered, including race and ethnicity, we take this opportunity to clarify the seizure inquiry as a matter of independent state law, taking guidance from GR 37.

As set forth in this court's precedent, the seizure inquiry is an objective test in which the allegedly seized person has the burden to show that a seizure occurred. To aid courts in the application of this test, we now clarify that a person is seized for purposes of article I, section 7 if, based on the totality of the circumstances, an objective observer could conclude that the person was not free to leave, to refuse a request, or to otherwise terminate the encounter due to law enforcement's display of authority or use of physical force. For purposes of this analysis, an objective observer is aware that implicit, institutional, and unconscious biases, in addition to purposeful discrimination, have resulted in disproportionate police contacts, investigative seizures, and uses of force against Black, Indigenous, and other People of Color (BIPOC) in Washington. Finally, in accordance with our precedent, if the person shows there was a seizure, then the burden shifts to the State to prove that the seizure was lawfully justified by a warrant or an applicable exception to the warrant requirement.

Based on the totality of the circumstances presented in this case, we hold that petitioner Palla Sum was seized when a sheriff's deputy requested Sum's identification while implying that Sum was under investigation for car theft. As the State properly concedes, at that time, the deputy did not have a warrant, reasonable suspicion, or any other lawful authority to seize Sum. As a result, Sum was unlawfully seized, and the false name and birth date he gave to the deputy must be suppressed. We therefore reverse the Court of Appeals and remand to the trial court for further proceedings.

FACTUAL BACKGROUND AND PROCEDURAL HISTORY

On April 9, 2019, Pierce County Sheriff's Deputy Mark Rickerson was on patrol, driving an unmarked police vehicle through an area where there were "some problem houses" that Deputy Rickerson liked to "keep an eye on." At 9:15 a.m., the deputy noticed a Honda Civic parked near the entry gate to a church parking lot.

The Honda was not blocking the entry gate, and there is no indication that it was parked illegally. Nevertheless, the car attracted the deputy's attention because "it was parked there."

The location was significant to Deputy Rickerson because "four or five months before . . . another deputy in [his] unit arrested another subject there in a stolen vehicle." Within that same four- to five-month time frame, an unnamed person approached Deputy Rickerson in a nearby grocery store parking lot to tell the deputy that they were "concerned about all the vehicles that were parking there that didn't belong in the area."

As Deputy Rickerson observed the Honda, he saw Sum, who "was slumped over and appeared to be unconscious in the driver's seat." At that point, the deputy decided to conduct "a social contact" and parked nearby, "making sure to leave enough room so as not to block the Honda Civic or prevent it from leaving." Before getting out of his police vehicle, Deputy Rickerson conducted a records check of the Honda's license plate and discovered a report of sale, although it was not clear when the sale had occurred. The records check also showed that the car had not been reported stolen, but the records did not state the name of the current owner. Deputy Rickerson noted the last four digits of the vehicle identification number (VIN) associated with the Honda's license plate, then approached the driver's side of the car on foot, wearing his full uniform.

As he approached, Deputy Rickerson noticed another man in the car, who was in the front passenger seat. Both Sum and the passenger "appeared to be unconscious and did not notice Rickerson approach." Before attempting to wake them, Deputy Rickerson checked the Honda's public VIN to confirm that it matched the license plates. The deputy then knocked on the driver's side window. After "seven to eight seconds," Sum "slowly woke up" and "rolled the window down slightly."

Deputy Rickerson asked Sum what he and his passenger were doing there, and Sum responded that they "were waiting for a friend." The deputy then asked Sum who owned the Honda. Sum said the Honda was not his, and he identified the owner "with the given name, but not the surname, of an individual." At the suppression hearing, Deputy Rickerson could not recall the name Sum provided.

Deputy Rickerson next asked Sum and his passenger for identification, and Sum "asked him why he wanted it." The deputy responded "that the two men were sitting in an area known for stolen vehicles and that [Sum] did not appear to know to whom the vehicle he was sitting in belonged." Sum provided a false name and date of birth. The passenger gave his true name and birth date.

Deputy Rickerson walked back to his patrol vehicle to check the names Sum and his passenger provided. While the deputy was in his vehicle, Sum started the Honda's engine, "backed up quickly, and then took off," driving partially on the sidewalk and over some grass. Deputy Rickerson activated his emergency lights and started pursuing the Honda, soon joined by another deputy in a separate vehicle. Sum drove at a high rate of speed through a stop sign and multiple red lights before ultimately crashing in someone's front yard. Deputy Rickerson handcuffed Sum and read him the *Miranda* warnings.

A search of Sum's person incident to arrest turned up the Honda's title and registration, which showed that the car did, in fact, belong to Palla Sum. He had purchased it two weeks earlier. The search of Sum's person also uncovered a small holster in his pants, and when the Honda was later searched pursuant to a warrant, police discovered a pistol.

Sum was charged by amended information with unlawful possession of a firearm in the first degree, attempting to elude a pursuing police vehicle, and making a false or misleading statement to a public servant. The original and amended charging documents both specify that Sum's race is "ASIAN/PACIFIC ISLAND[ER]."

Sum filed a pretrial motion to suppress pursuant to CrR 3.6, contending that he was unlawfully seized without reasonable suspicion when Deputy Rickerson requested Sum's identification while implying that Sum was under investigation for car theft. The court denied Sum's motion to suppress, ruling that "[b]ecause Rickerson did not retain [Sum]'s physical identification to conduct his records check, [Sum] was not seized when Rickerson asked him to identify himself." Sum was convicted of all three charges by a jury. Like the charging documents, Sum's felony judgment and sentence states that his race is "Asian/Pacific Islander." His ethnicity is listed as "Non-Hispanic."

Sum appealed, and the Court of Appeals affirmed in an unpublished opinion, holding that Sum was not seized by the deputy's request for identification because "merely asking for identification is properly characterized as a social contact." Sum petitioned for review, reiterating his previous arguments and further contending for the first time that "there is no justification — aside from unacceptably ignoring the issue of race altogether — for courts considering the totality of the circumstances to disregard the effect of race as one of the circumstances affecting evaluation of police contact."

We granted Sum's petition for review and accepted for filing a joint amici brief by the King County Department of Public Defense, the American Civil Liberties Union of Washington, the Fred T. Korematsu Center for Law and Equality, and the Washington Defender Association. We now reverse.

• • •

As discussed above, the parties correctly agree that race and ethnicity can be relevant to the seizure inquiry, and we further hold that Sum's race is relevant to the seizure inquiry in this case. Although this decision flows directly from our precedent, Washington case law provides no guidance as to how a court is to consider the allegedly seized person's race or ethnicity because we have never done so before. Moreover, some of the analysis offered in this case indicates there is a need to reiterate that the seizure inquiry depends on the totality of the circumstances, rather than a list of factors. We therefore clarify the seizure inquiry, taking guidance from GR 37. In doing so, we do not disavow our precedent, and we do not suggest that any particular case would have had a different outcome pursuant to the clarification we announce today.

1. The seizure analysis must properly account for all the circumstances of Sum's encounter with Deputy Rickerson

On the ultimate question of when Sum was seized, the State contends that "Sum was not seized until he drove off at a high rate of speed, over grass and the sidewalk, and Deputy Rickerson activated his lights in pursuit." To reach this conclusion, the State focuses on the circumstances that were not present in Sum's encounter with Deputy Rickerson. For instance, as the State correctly notes, there were not multiple officers, Deputy Rickerson did not physically block Sum's car from leaving, the deputy did not "activate[ ] his lights or siren," and he did not "display[ ] his weapon, physically touch[ ] Sum, or use[ ] language or tone indicating mandatory compliance." The Court of Appeals took a similar approach in its seizure analysis. Likewise, the trial court appears to have placed dispositive weight on the fact that Deputy "Rickerson did not retain [Sum]'s physical identification to conduct his records check"; that was the only reason the court identified in its written ruling concluding that Sum was not seized.

Without question, each of those circumstances, if present, would weigh in favor of holding that Sum was seized. However, the lack of those particular circumstances fails to show that Sum was not seized. To the contrary, because the seizure inquiry depends on "all the circumstances," there will always be factual distinctions between cases. As a result, our precedent requires courts to carefully assess "all surrounding circumstances" that are presented in each encounter, rather than focusing on the circumstances that are not presented, or considering each encounter against a predetermined set of factors. Nevertheless, we recognize that this requirement can be difficult to apply with consistency and objectivity. We therefore take this opportunity to clarify the article I, section 7 seizure analysis as a matter of independent state law.

2. GR 37 appropriately guides our clarification of the seizure inquiry

In order to provide courts and parties with a clearer framework for conducting an article I, section 7 seizure analysis, we take guidance from GR 37. GR 37 was adopted to bring increased clarity, consistency, and justice to jury selection, an area of law where all three qualities have long proved elusive. Many of the same concerns arise in the context of warrantless seizures.

This court adopted GR 37 in an effort "to eliminate the unfair exclusion of potential jurors based on race or ethnicity." GR 37 replaces the *Batson* test, which "has done very little to make juries more diverse or to prevent prosecutors from exercising race-based challenges." The differences between GR 37 and *Batson* are informative in contexts beyond jury selection, including the seizure analysis required by article I, section 7.

For instance, in order to bring a successful *Batson* challenge, a defendant must show that a peremptory challenge was motivated by "purposeful discrimination." GR 37, by contrast, provides that a "court need not find purposeful discrimination" and, instead, must deny the peremptory challenge if "an objective observer could view race or ethnicity as a factor." GR 37(e). This shift away from purposeful discrimination "take[s] the focus off of the credibility and integrity of the attorneys and ease[s] the accusatory strain of sustaining a *Batson* challenge," which "simplif[ies] the task of reducing racial bias in our criminal justice system, both conscious and unconscious."

Similar concerns are presented in the warrantless seizure context, where it is well known that BIPOC are wrongfully subject to excessive police scrutiny. Nevertheless, purposeful, explicit discrimination may be absent or impossible to prove in individual cases because "identifying the influence of racial bias generally, and implicit racial bias specifically, presents unique challenges." Beyond the problem of proof, GR 37's rejection of the need to show purposeful discrimination also better aligns with the objective seizure inquiry required by our precedent, which holds that the "subjective intent of police is irrelevant to the question [of] whether a seizure occurred unless it is conveyed to the defendant."

Another relevant difference between *Batson* and GR 37 is that *Batson* permits a party to exercise their peremptory challenges on an apparently discriminatory basis, so long as the party can "articulate a neutral explanation" to justify their actions. The list of potential "neutral explanations" is limitless, and "[p]roffered reasons sometimes involve subtle observations about a prospective juror's appearance or demeanor, which are easily alleged but often extremely difficult to scrutinize." GR 37 addresses this concern by specifying that "allegations that the prospective juror was sleeping, inattentive, or staring or failing to make eye contact; exhibited a problematic attitude, body language, or demeanor; or provided unintelligent or confused answers" cannot be a valid basis for a peremptory challenge without "corroboration by the judge or opposing counsel verifying the behavior" because such allegations "have historically been associated with improper discrimination in jury selection in Washington State." GR 37(i). Moreover, as noted above, GR 37 also provides a list of presumptively invalid reasons for exercising peremptory challenges, such as prior contacts with, and distrust of, law enforcement, which "have been associated with improper discrimination in jury selection in Washington State."

These presumptively invalid reasons for exercising peremptory challenges reflect that unless carefully drawn, facially neutral standards can have a disproportionate impact in jury selection. The same is true in the seizure context. As discussed above, BIPOC are subject to excessive police contacts, investigative seizures, and uses of force by law enforcement. Moreover, the BIPOC community, as a whole, is generally well aware of such patterns of excessive police scrutiny. As a result, "generations of children have had to grow up with 'the Talk,'" in which parents must educate their children "about how to interact with law enforcement so no officer will have any reason to misperceive them as a threat and take harmful or fatal action against them." "Against that awareness," an encounter with law enforcement would certainly feel "more pointed and coercive." Thus, "[t]he fear of harm and resulting protective conditioning to submit to avoid harm at the hands of police is relevant to whether there was a seizure because feeling 'free' to leave or terminate an encounter with police officers is rooted in an assessment of the consequences of doing so."

A final relevant point of comparison between *Batson* and GR 37 is the perspective from which the ultimate determination is made. A successful *Batson* challenge requires the trial judge to "decide[ ] that the facts establish, prima facie, purposeful discrimination," and that the State failed to "come forward with a neutral explanation for [its] action." However, *Batson* does not specify from whose perspective "purposeful discrimination" and "neutral explanations" are to be evaluated. As a result, "[g]iven the inevitably clumsy fit between any objectively measurable standard and the subjective decisionmaking at issue, [we should not be] surprised to find studies and anecdotal reports suggesting that, despite *Batson*, the discriminatory use of peremptory challenges remains a problem."

GR 37 seeks to address this problem by explicitly providing that (1) the analysis must be made from the perspective of "an objective observer," (2) the necessary showing is made if the objective observer "could view race or ethnicity as a factor in the use of the peremptory challenge," and (3) an objective observer "is aware that implicit, institutional, and unconscious biases, in addition to purposeful discrimination, have resulted in the unfair exclusion of potential jurors in Washington State." Thus, "GR 37 was written in terms of possibilities, not actualities," and the rule "teaches that peremptory strikes exercised against prospective jurors who appear to be members of racial or ethnic minority groups must be treated with skepticism and considerable caution."

The seizure context presents similar issues. Washington's seizure test is intended to be "'a purely objective one'" based on what a hypothetical "reasonable person" in the defendant's position would have believed under the same circumstances. However, without more specific guidance, the perspective of a "reasonable person" is measured from the perspective of the judicial decision-maker. Judicial officers are especially well situated to know their legal rights and may also be unusually likely to expect that their rights, if asserted, will be respected by law enforcement. This commonsense observation is not to suggest that judicial perspectives are unreasonable; we merely acknowledge that it is unrealistic to equate the perspective of a judicial officer with the perspective of a "reasonable person" in this context. Therefore, following GR 37's example and reframing the seizure inquiry to focus on what an objective observer could believe about a person's encounter with law enforcement provides a valuable safeguard.

Thus, there are relevant parallels between the contexts of jury selection and warrantless seizures, showing that GR 37 should guide our clarification of the seizure inquiry.

3. We now clarify the analysis that courts must apply when determining whether a person has been seized by law enforcement

As provided by our precedent, the article I, section 7 seizure inquiry is an objective test in which the allegedly seized person has the burden of showing that a seizure occurred. To properly apply this test, we now clarify that a person has been seized as a matter of independent state law if, based on the totality of the circumstances, an objective observer could conclude that the person was not free to leave, to refuse a request, or to otherwise terminate a police encounter due to law enforcement's display of authority or use of physical force. For purposes of this analysis, an objective observer is aware that implicit, institutional, and unconscious biases, in addition to purposeful discrimination, have resulted in disproportionate police contacts, investigative seizures, and uses of force against BIPOC in Washington.

Moreover, in determining whether there has been a seizure in light of all the circumstances of the encounter, courts may take guidance from some of the circumstances specified in GR 37, in addition to case law and the contentions of the parties. For instance, "the number and types of questions posed" or requests made of the allegedly seized person, and the extent to which similar law enforcement encounters are "disproportionately associated with a race or ethnicity" may be relevant considerations, among others.

Finally, in accordance with our precedent, if the person shows that there was a seizure, then the burden shifts to the State to prove that the seizure was supported by a warrant or "was justified by an exception to the warrant requirement." Our opinion today is not intended to modify or clarify the warrant requirement or any of its exceptions.

D. Given the totality of the circumstances, we hold that Deputy Rickerson seized Sum before Sum identified himself with a false name and birth date

As discussed above, although Sum's race is relevant to the seizure inquiry, it is certainly not dispositive. We must instead consider all of the circumstances to determine whether an objective observer could conclude that Sum was not free to refuse Deputy Rickerson's request for identification based on the deputy's display of authority. The answer is yes.

The circumstances, as found by the trial court, were as follows. Sum, a person of color, was asleep in his car, which was parked on a public street in a "high-crime area." At 9:15 in the morning, Sum was awoken by a sheriff's deputy in full uniform knocking on the car window next to where Sum was sleeping. Deputy Rickerson did not ask about Sum's health or safety, and he did not ask if Sum and his passenger required assistance. Instead, the deputy asked what Sum and his passenger were doing, clearly implying that they did not belong there.

Sum answered that "they were visiting a friend across the street." This answer proved insufficient to satisfy the deputy's interest in Sum and his passenger because Deputy Rickerson next asked "to whom the Honda Civic belonged." Sum provided a name, but this also failed to satisfy the deputy because he then requested Sum's identification. When Sum "asked him why he wanted" identification, the deputy "explained that the two men were sitting in an area known for stolen vehicles and that [Sum] did not appear to know to whom the vehicle he was sitting in belonged."

Assuming, without deciding, that Sum was not already seized, then Deputy Rickerson's explanation was certainly "the tipping point at which the weight of the circumstances transformed a simple encounter into a seizure." At that point, it would have been clear to any reasonable person that Deputy Rickerson wanted Sum's identification because he suspected Sum of car theft. Indeed, the deputy stated as much, and we have recognized that law enforcement's subjective intent is relevant if "it is conveyed to the defendant." "[T]he number and types" of Deputy Rickerson's questions and requests further indicated his investigative purpose, despite the lack of reasonable suspicion. It is also "no secret" that "suspicionless stop[s]" are "disproportionately associated" with people of color.

Thus, this case is not like others in which we have held that a seizure does not occur "merely because a police officer engages [a person] in conversation in a public place and asks for identification." There were far more circumstances at play here.

Based on the totality of the circumstances, an objective observer could easily conclude that if Sum had refused to identify himself and requested to be left alone, Deputy Rickerson would have failed to honor Sum's request because the deputy was investigating Sum for car theft. In other words, an objective observer could conclude that Sum was not free to refuse Deputy Rickerson's request due to the deputy's display of authority. At that point, Sum was seized. As the State correctly concedes, this seizure was not supported by a warrant, reasonable suspicion, or any other authority of law.

Thus, the false name and birth date that Sum gave to Deputy Rickerson was the product of an unlawful seizure. Sum's false statement must be suppressed because "[o]ur state exclusionary rule requires the suppression of evidence obtained in violation of article I, section 7."

CONCLUSION

Today, we formally recognize what has always been true: in interactions with law enforcement, race and ethnicity matter. Therefore, courts must consider the race and ethnicity of the allegedly seized person as part of the totality of the circumstances when deciding whether there was a seizure for purposes of article I, section 7. Here, in light of all the circumstances of Sum's encounter with Deputy Rickerson, we hold that Sum was unlawfully seized before he provided a false name and birth date to the deputy, so his false statement must be suppressed. We reverse the Court of Appeals and remand to the trial court for further proceedings consistent with this opinion.

NOTES AND QUESTIONS

Fred Korematsu

1. The court insists that the question of whether a seizure occurred is "a purely objective one" under Washington law. How is it possible to account for race or ethnicity in applying an objective test?

2. The court also relies on the fact that under Washington law the seizure inquiry requires consideration of the totality of the circumstances. Is there tension between this requirement and the "objective" nature of the test?

3. Washington's GR 37 rejected the federal framework derived from *Batson v. Kentucky*, 476 U.S. 79 (1986), for determining whether a party has improperly discriminated in exercising peremptory challenges. In short, the rule supplants *Batson*'s requirement of proof of "purposeful discrimination" with an "objective observer" test. How does the court import this aspect of GR 37 into its seizure analysis? Does this aspect of the decision seem forced?

4. How does the court use Sum's ethnicity in determining that a seizure occurred here prior to Sum's false statements? Was the fact of his ethnicity necessary to the court's conclusion?

5. For a discussion of *Sum*, *see* Aliza Hochman Bloom, *"What Has Always Been True": The Washington Supreme Court Decides That Seizure Law Must Account for Racial Disparity in Policing*, 107 Minn. L. Rev. Headnotes 1 (2022).

6. An amicus brief in *Sum* was filed by the Fred T. Korematsu Center for Law and Equality, a public interest organization named for pioneering civil rights hero Fred Korematsu that has the mission to use legal research, litigation advocacy, and clinical education to achieve durable social change related to racial equality and social justice.

Sum was not the first case to acknowledge the use of race as a factor in seizure analysis but it is the most emphatic. In *United States v. Washington*, 490 F.3d 765, 773-74 (9th Cir. 2007), the Ninth Circuit found that one factor tipping the balance in favor of finding a seizure in a white police officer's encounter with a Black man was the recently publicized shootings of Black men by white Portland police officers. Similar reasoning prevailed in *Dozier v. United States*, 220 A.3d 933 (D.C. 2019). In evaluating whether a consensual encounter had escalated into a seizure, the D.C. Circuit found that race surely bore on whether a reasonable person in the defendant's position would have believed he was free to leave. "As is known from well-publicized and documented examples, an African-American man facing armed policemen would reasonably be especially apprehensive" in defendant's situation, having been "perceived by hyper vigilant police officers expecting to find criminal activity in a particular area." *Id.* at 944. In *United States v. Smith*, 794 F.3d 681 (7th Cir. 2015), citing the observation about the potential relevance of race in *Mendenhall*, the Seventh Circuit found that it did not need to consider race in finding a seizure in the case at hand, but observed: "We do not deny the relevance of race in everyday police encounters with citizens in Milwaukee and around the country. Nor do we ignore empirical data demonstrating the existence of racial profiling, police brutality, and other racial disparities in the criminal justice system." *Id.* at 688. *See also State v. Jones*, 172 N.H. 774, 780-81 (2020) ("race is an appropriate circumstance to consider in conducting the totality of the circumstances seizure analysis").

Two federal circuits have explicitly rejected the use of race in evaluating police encounters. In *United States v. Easley*, 911 F.3d 1074 (10th Cir. 2018), the Tenth Circuit stated: "There is no uniform life experience for persons of color, and there are surely divergent attitudes toward law enforcement officers among members of the population. Thus, there is no uniform way to apply a reasonable person test that adequately accounts for racial differences consistent with an objective standard for Fourth Amendment seizures." *Id.* at 1082.

The Eleventh Circuit echoed *Easley*'s concerns in *United States v. Knights*, 989 F.3d 1281 (11th Cir. 2021), and also noted that consideration of race as a factor might run afoul of the Equal Protection Clause. *Id.* at 1287-89. In a concurring opinion in *Knights*, Judge Rosenbaum acknowledged the equal protection issue and advocated for the adoption of a rule requiring police officers to inform persons being questioned of their right to end the encounter. Professor Carbado argues that *not* taking race into account in seizure analysis is tantamount to imposing a racial preference for whites. Devon W. Carbado, Unreasonable: Black Lives, Police Power, and the Fourth Amendment 62 (2022).

In the debate over whether seizure analysis should account for race, both sides have enlisted *J.D.B v. North Carolina*, 564 U.S. 261 (2011), *see* Chapter III *supra*, where the Supreme Court held that a child's age must be considered in determining whether a valid waiver of *Miranda* rights occurred. Professor Carbado, for example, suggests that "reasonable children" and "reasonable black persons"—for very different reasons, obviously—might view their "freedom to leave" differently than white adults. *See also Sum*, 199 Wash. 2d at 642 (discussing *J.D.B.*). On the other hand, in *Knights* the Eleventh Circuit cited *J.D.B.* as a basis for distinguishing between age, a chronological fact that has an "objectively discernible relationship to a reasonable person's understanding of his freedom of action," and other personal characteristics such as race that do not.

3. Seizures and Police Use of Force

Prior to 1985, the Supreme Court had not clarified the constitutional source, if any, of claims that police used excessive force in connection with arrests or other citizen encounters. In the two cases that follow it held that such claims flow from the Fourth Amendment's requirement that "seizures" must be "reasonable." Because a successful allegation of an unreasonable seizure is not a defense to an otherwise valid criminal charge, and does not require the exclusion of evidence, these claims—as in the next two cases—are typically brought as civil damages actions under 42 U.S.C. § 1983. *See* Chapter VI *infra*.

Tennessee v. Garner

471 U.S. 1 (1985)

Justice White delivered the opinion of the Court.

This case requires us to determine the constitutionality of the use of deadly force to prevent the escape of an apparently unarmed suspected felon. We conclude that such force may not be used unless it is necessary to prevent the escape and the officer has probable cause to believe that the suspect poses a significant threat of death or serious physical injury to the officer or others.

I

At about 10:45 p.m. on October 3, 1974, Memphis Police Officers Elton Hymon and Leslie Wright were dispatched to answer a "prowler inside call." Upon arriving at the scene they saw a woman standing on her porch and gesturing toward the adjacent house. She told them she had heard glass breaking and that "they" or "someone" was breaking in next door. While Wright radioed the dispatcher to say that they were on the scene, Hymon went behind the house. He heard a door slam and saw someone run across the backyard. The fleeing suspect, who was appellee-respondent's decedent, Edward Garner, stopped at a 6-feet-high chain link fence at the edge of the yard. With the aid of a flashlight, Hymon was able to see Garner's face and hands. He saw no sign of a weapon, and, though not certain, was "reasonably sure" and "figured" that Garner was unarmed. He thought Garner was 17 or 18 years old and about 5'5" or 5'7" tall. While Garner was crouched at the base of the fence, Hymon called out "police, halt" and took a few steps toward him. Garner then began to climb over the fence. Convinced that if Garner made it over the fence he would elude capture, Hymon shot him. The bullet hit Garner in the back of the head. Garner was taken by ambulance to a hospital, where he died on the operating table. Ten dollars and a purse taken from the house were found on his body.

In using deadly force to prevent the escape, Hymon was acting under the authority of a Tennessee statute and pursuant to Police Department policy. The statute provides that "[i]f, after notice of the intention to arrest the defendant, he either flee or forcibly resist, the officer may use all the necessary means to effect the arrest." The Department policy was slightly more restrictive than the statute, but still allowed the use of deadly force in cases of burglar. The incident was reviewed by the Memphis Police Firearm's Review Board and presented to a grand jury. Neither took any action.

Garner's father then brought this action in the Federal District Court for the Western District of Tennessee, seeking damages under 42 U.S.C. § 1983 for asserted violations of Garner's constitutional rights. The complaint alleged that the shooting violated the Fourth, Fifth, Sixth, Eighth, and Fourteenth Amendments of the United States Constitution. It named as defendants Officer Hymon, the Police Department, its Director, and the Mayor and city of Memphis. After a 3-day bench trial, the District Court entered judgment for all defendants. It dismissed the claims against the Mayor and the Director for lack of evidence. It then concluded that Hymon's actions were authorized by the Tennessee statute, which in turn was constitutional. Hymon had employed the only reasonable and practicable means of preventing Garner's escape. Garner had "recklessly and heedlessly attempted to vault over the fence to escape, thereby assuming the risk of being fired upon."

• • •

II

Whenever an officer restrains the freedom of a person to walk away, he has seized that person. While it is not always clear just when minimal police interference becomes a seizure, there can be no question that apprehension by the use of deadly force is a seizure subject to the reasonableness requirement of the Fourth Amendment.

A

A police officer may arrest a person if he has probable cause to believe that person committed a crime. Petitioners and appellant argue that if this requirement is satisfied the Fourth Amendment has nothing to say about how that seizure is made. This submission ignores the many cases in which this Court, by balancing the extent of the intrusion against the need for it, has examined the reasonableness of the manner in which a search or seizure is conducted. To determine the constitutionality of a seizure "[w]e must balance the nature and quality of the intrusion on the individual's Fourth Amendment interests against the importance of the governmental interests alleged to justify the intrusion." We have described "the balancing of competing interests" as "the key principle of the Fourth Amendment." Because one of the factors is the extent of the intrusion, it is plain that reasonableness depends on not only when a seizure is made, but also how it is carried out.

• • •

In each of these cases, the question was whether the totality of the circumstances justified a particular sort of search or seizure.

B

The same balancing process applied in the cases cited above demonstrates that, notwithstanding probable cause to seize a suspect, an officer may not always do so by killing him. The intrusiveness of a seizure by means of deadly force is unmatched. The suspect's fundamental interest in his own life need not be elaborated upon. The use of deadly force also frustrates the interest of the individual, and of society, in judicial determination of guilt and punishment. Against these interests are ranged governmental interests in effective law enforcement. It is argued that overall violence will be reduced by encouraging the peaceful submission of suspects who know that they may be shot if they flee. Effectiveness in making arrests requires the resort to deadly force, or at least the meaningful threat thereof. "Being able to arrest such individuals is a condition precedent to the state's entire system of law enforcement."

Without in any way disparaging the importance of these goals, we are not convinced that the use of deadly force is a sufficiently productive means of accomplishing them to justify the killing of nonviolent suspects. The use of deadly force is a self-defeating way of apprehending a suspect and so setting the criminal justice mechanism in motion. If successful, it guarantees that that mechanism will not be set in motion. And while the meaningful threat of deadly force might be thought to lead to the arrest of more live suspects by discouraging escape attempts, the presently available evidence does not support this thesis. The fact is that a majority of police departments in this country have forbidden the use of deadly force against nonviolent suspects. If those charged with the enforcement of the criminal law have abjured the use of deadly force in arresting nondangerous felons, there is a substantial basis for doubting that the use of such force is an essential attribute of the arrest power in all felony cases. Petitioners and appellant have not persuaded us that shooting nondangerous fleeing suspects is so vital as to outweigh the suspect's interest in his own life.

The use of deadly force to prevent the escape of all felony suspects, whatever the circumstances, is constitutionally unreasonable. It is not better that all felony suspects die than that they escape. Where the suspect poses no immediate threat to the officer and no threat to others, the harm resulting from failing to apprehend him does not justify the use of deadly force to do so. It is no doubt unfortunate when a suspect who is in sight escapes, but the fact that the police arrive a little late or are a little slower afoot does not always justify killing the suspect. A police officer may not seize an unarmed, nondangerous suspect by shooting him dead. The Tennessee statute is unconstitutional insofar as it authorizes the use of deadly force against such fleeing suspects.

It is not, however, unconstitutional on its face. Where the officer has probable cause to believe that the suspect poses a threat of serious physical harm, either to the officer or to others, it is not constitutionally unreasonable to prevent escape by using deadly force. Thus, if the suspect threatens the officer with a weapon or there is probable cause to believe that he has committed a crime involving the infliction or threatened infliction of serious physical harm, deadly force may be used if necessary to prevent escape, and if, where feasible, some warning has been given. As applied in such circumstances, the Tennessee statute would pass constitutional muster.

III

A

It is insisted that the Fourth Amendment must be construed in light of the common-law rule, which allowed the use of whatever force was necessary to effect the arrest of a fleeing felon, though not a misdemeanant.

The State and city argue that because this was the prevailing rule at the time of the adoption of the Fourth Amendment and for some time thereafter, and is still in force in some States, use of deadly force against a fleeing felon must be "reasonable." It is true that this Court has often looked to the common law in evaluating the reasonableness, for Fourth Amendment purposes, of police activity. On the other hand, it "has not simply frozen into constitutional law those law enforcement practices that existed at the time of the Fourth Amendment's passage." Because of sweeping change in the legal and technological context, reliance on the common-law rule in this case would be a mistaken literalism that ignores the purposes of a historical inquiry.

B

It has been pointed out many times that the common-law rule is best understood in light of the fact that it arose at a time when virtually all felonies were punishable by death. "Though effected without the protections and formalities of an orderly trial and conviction, the killing of a resisting or fleeing felon resulted in no greater consequences than those authorized for punishment of the felony of which the individual was charged or suspected." Courts have also justified the common-law rule by emphasizing the relative dangerousness of felons.

Neither of these justifications makes sense today. Almost all crimes formerly punishable by death no longer are or can be. And while in earlier times "the gulf between the felonies and the minor offences was broad and deep," today the distinction is minor and often arbitrary. Many crimes classified as misdemeanors, or nonexistent, at common law are now felonies. These changes have undermined the concept, which was questionable to begin with, that use of deadly force against a fleeing felon is merely a speedier execution of someone who has already forfeited his life. They have also made the assumption that a "felon" is more dangerous than a misdemeanant untenable. Indeed, numerous misdemeanors involve conduct more dangerous than many felonies.

There is an additional reason why the common-law rule cannot be directly translated to the present day. The common-law rule developed at a time when weapons were rudimentary.

Deadly force could be inflicted almost solely in a hand-to-hand struggle during which, necessarily, the safety of the arresting officer was at risk. Handguns were not carried by police officers until the latter half of the last century. Only then did it become possible to use deadly force from a distance as a means of apprehension. As a practical matter, the use of deadly force under the standard articulation of the common-law rule has an altogether different meaning—and harsher consequences—now than in past centuries.

One other aspect of the common-law rule bears emphasis. It forbids the use of deadly force to apprehend a misdemeanant, condemning such action as disproportionately severe.

In short, though the common-law pedigree of Tennessee's rule is pure on its face, changes in the legal and technological context mean the rule is distorted almost beyond recognition when literally applied.

C

In evaluating the reasonableness of police procedures under the Fourth Amendment, we have also looked to prevailing rules in individual jurisdictions. Some 19 States have codified the common-law rule, though in two of these the courts have significantly limited the statute. Four States, though without a relevant statute, apparently retain the common-law rule. Two States have adopted the Model Penal Code's provision verbatim. Eighteen others allow, in slightly varying language, the use of deadly force only if the suspect has committed a felony involving the use or threat of physical or deadly force, or is escaping with a deadly weapon, or is likely to endanger life or inflict serious physical injury if not arrested. Louisiana and Vermont, though without statutes or case law on point, do forbid the use of deadly force to prevent any but violent felonies. The remaining States either have no relevant statute or case law, or have positions that are unclear.

It cannot be said that there is a constant or overwhelming trend away from the common-law rule. In recent years, some States have reviewed their laws and expressly rejected abandonment of the common-law rule. Nonetheless, the long-term movement has been away from the rule that deadly force may be used against any fleeing felon, and that remains the rule in less than half the States.

This trend is more evident and impressive when viewed in light of the policies adopted by the police departments themselves. Overwhelmingly, these are more restrictive than the common-law rule. The Federal Bureau of Investigation and the New York City Police Department, for example, both forbid the use of firearms except when necessary to prevent death or grievous bodily harm. For accreditation by the Commission on Accreditation for Law Enforcement Agencies, a department must restrict the use of deadly force to situations where "the officer reasonably believes that the action is in defense of human life . . . or in defense of any person in immediate danger of serious physical injury." A 1974 study reported that the police department regulations in a majority of the large cities of the United States allowed the firing of a weapon only when a felon presented a threat of death or serious bodily harm. Overall, only 7.5% of departmental and municipal policies explicitly permit the use of deadly force against any felon; 86.8% explicitly do not. In light of the rules adopted by those who must actually administer them, the older and fading common-law view is a dubious indicium of the constitutionality of the Tennessee statute now before us.

D

Actual departmental policies are important for an additional reason. We would hesitate to declare a police practice of long standing "unreasonable" if doing so would severely hamper effective law enforcement. But the indications are to the contrary. There has been no suggestion that crime has worsened in any way in jurisdictions that have adopted, by legislation or departmental policy, rules similar to that announced today. Amici noted that "[a] fter extensive research and consideration, [they] have concluded that laws permitting police officers to use deadly force to apprehend unarmed, non-violent fleeing felony suspects actually do not protect citizens or law enforcement officers, do not deter crime or alleviate problems caused by crime, and do not improve the crime-fighting ability of law enforcement agencies." The submission is that the obvious state interests in apprehension are not sufficiently served to warrant the use of lethal weapons against all fleeing felons.

Nor do we agree with petitioners and appellant that the rule we have adopted requires the police to make impossible, split-second evaluations of unknowable facts. We do not deny the practical difficulties of attempting to assess the suspect's dangerousness. However, similarly difficult judgments must be made by the police in equally uncertain circumstances. Nor is there any indication that in States that allow the use of deadly force only against dangerous suspects, the standard has been difficult to apply or has led to a rash of litigation involving inappropriate second-guessing of police officers' split-second decisions. Moreover, the highly technical felony/misdemeanor distinction is equally, if not more, difficult to apply in the field. An officer is in no position to know, for example, the precise value of property stolen, or whether the crime was a first or second offense. Finally, as noted above, this claim must be viewed with suspicion in light of the similar self-imposed limitations of so many police departments.

IV

The District Court concluded that Hymon was justified in shooting Garner because state law allows, and the Federal Constitution does not forbid, the use of deadly force to prevent the escape of a fleeing felony suspect if no alternative means of apprehension is available. This conclusion made a determination of Garner's apparent dangerousness unnecessary. The court did find, however, that Garner appeared to be unarmed, though Hymon could not be certain that was the case. Restated in Fourth Amendment terms, this means Hymon had no articulable basis to think Garner was armed.

In reversing, the Court of Appeals accepted the District Court's factual conclusions and held that "the facts, as found, did not justify the use of deadly force." We agree. Officer Hymon could not reasonably have believed that Garner—young, slight, and unarmed—posed any threat. Indeed, Hymon never attempted to justify his actions on any basis other than the need to prevent an escape. The District Court stated in passing that "[t]he facts of this case did not indicate to Officer Hymon that Garner was 'non-dangerous.'" This conclusion is not explained, and seems to be based solely on the fact that Garner had broken into a house at night. However, the fact that Garner was a suspected burglar could not, without regard to the other circumstances, automatically justify the use of deadly force. Hymon did not have probable cause to believe that Garner, whom he correctly believed to be unarmed, posed any physical danger to himself or others.

The dissent argues that the shooting was justified by the fact that Officer Hymon had probable cause to believe that Garner had committed a nighttime burglary. While we agree that burglary is a serious crime, we cannot agree that it is so dangerous as automatically to justify the use of deadly force. The FBI classifies burglary as a "property" rather than a "violent" crime. Although the armed burglar would present a different situation, the fact that an unarmed suspect has broken into a dwelling at night does not automatically mean he is physically dangerous. This case demonstrates as much. In fact, the available statistics demonstrate that burglaries only rarely involve physical violence. During the 10-year period from 1973-1982, only 3.8% of all burglaries involved violent crime.

• • •

The judgment of the Court of Appeals is affirmed, and the case is remanded for further proceedings consistent with this opinion.

[Justices O'Connor and Rehnquist and Chief Justice Burger dissented.]

NOTES AND QUESTIONS

Memphis police officer Elton Hymon

1. Note that the predicate for the Tennessee statute and the common law "fleeing felon" rule is that the officer has probable cause to arrest. Is it obvious that Officer Hymon had probable cause to arrest Edward Garner when he observed him going over the fence?

Does the Court do a convincing job explaining why the common law rule should not carry over to the present day, given the differences in criminal penalties and police and firearms practices?

If *Garner* were to be reconsidered today from a purely originalist perspective, would the result be different?

2. In balancing the relevant interests in determining the appropriate situations justifying the use of deadly force, the Court considers not only the state of state law on the subject but also actual police practices in weighing the law enforcement interests at stake. Is this a sensible approach? Do you see any downsides to using this factor?

3. Would this case have come out differently if Officer Hymon observed a gun in Garner's hand as he was making his way over the fence? What if Garner had a gun in his hand and, upon seeing Hymon, turned and ran back into the house?

4. The Court does not mention race. Both Officer Hymon and Edward Garner were Black. The Garner family's lawyer, famed Memphis civil rights activist and defense attorney Walter Bailey, argued in his brief to the Supreme Court that the discretion afforded police in using deadly force against nondangerous fleeing property crime suspects violated the Equal Protection Clause. He pointed to statistics showing that, as compared to similarly situated white suspects, Black suspects were twice as likely to be shot at, four times as likely to be wounded, and 40 percent more likely to be killed. (Interestingly Bailey's statistics revealed no racial disparity in police shooting of fleeing violent crime suspects.) *Tennessee v. Garner*, Brief for Appellee-Respondent, 1984 WL 566020, at *99-100.

5. Consider how easy it would have been for Officer Hymon to testify that "he thought" Garner had a gun. And there was a more insidious alternative to that "embellishment." Interviewed in 2019 by a reporter for the *New Tri-State Defender*, retired Officer Elton Hymon gave context for the case that became *Tennessee v. Garner*. Hymon had only been on the force for five months and was still getting acclimated to police culture. "The N word was used often without hesitation and several white officers proudly notched their revolvers for every African-American they had killed," he said. Hymon also disclosed the widespread practice of officers carrying with them a "drop gun," which could be placed on or near a shot or killed suspect in order to manufacture a justifiable use of force.

6. In the same article, Attorney Bailey credited Officer Hymon's truthful testimony (and failure to use a drop gun) with the Garners' litigation success. Officer Hymon probably deserves even more credit than that, as the number of persons shot and killed by police decreased dramatically after *Garner*, as many police departments abandoned the common law rule to comply with the decision. Cynthia Lee, *Reforming the Law on Police Use of Deadly Force: De-Escalation, Preseizure Conduct, and Imperfect Self-Defense*, 2018 U. Ill. L. Rev. 629, 641 (citing Abraham N. Tennenbaum, *The Influence of the* Garner *Decision on Police Use of Deadly Force*, 85 J. Crim. L. & Criminology 241, 255-56 (1994) (finding that overall police shootings declined by 16 percent following the *Garner* decision)).

Bailey, a longtime Memphis civil rights lawyer, had earlier represented Dr. Martin Luther King Jr. in connection with the 1968 sanitation workers' strike. His portrait was unveiled at the National Civil Rights Museum in Memphis in December 2022.

The Court applied *Garner* over two decades later in a case involving a different sort of deadly force. In *Scott v. Harris*, 550 U.S. 372 (2007), the Court reversed a denial of summary judgment for a defendant police officer alleged to have unreasonably used deadly force by ramming his police car into the plaintiff's car in a high-speed chase. Finding that a videotape of the encounter so clearly showed that the officer's use of force was not excessive, the Court—substituting itself for a "reasonable jury"—entered judgment for the police officer. Justice Stevens, who dissented, the district judge, and three members of the court of appeals panel all reached a different conclusion.

Three academics used the videotape of the high-speed chase in *Harris* to do a study to test the Court's conclusion as to what a "reasonable jury" could have found. They found that 75 percent of the 1,350 participants in the study found that the use of deadly force was justified, although the results varied significantly depending on the demographics, politics, and values of the participants. Dan M. Kahan et al., *Whose Eyes Are You Going to Believe?* Scott v. Harris *and the Perils of Cognitive Illiberalism*, 122 Harv. L. Rev. 837, 838 (2009).

In the next case the Court considered how to evaluate allegations of improper uses of force by police that are not deadly but only "excessive."

Graham v. Connor

490 U.S. 386 (1989)

Chief Justice Rehnquist delivered the opinion of the Court.

This case requires us to decide what constitutional standard governs a free citizen's claim that law enforcement officials used excessive force in the course of making an arrest, investigatory stop, or other "seizure" of his person. We hold that such claims are properly analyzed under the Fourth Amendment's "objective reasonableness" standard, rather than under a substantive due process standard.

In this action under 42 U.S.C. § 1983, petitioner Dethorne Graham seeks to recover damages for injuries allegedly sustained when law enforcement officers used physical force against him during the course of an investigatory stop. Because the case comes to us from a decision of the Court of Appeals affirming the entry of a directed verdict for respondents, we take the evidence hereafter noted in the light most favorable to petitioner. On November 12, 1984, Graham, a diabetic, felt the onset of an insulin reaction. He asked a friend, William Berry, to drive him to a nearby convenience store so he could purchase some orange juice to counteract the reaction. Berry agreed, but when Graham entered the store, he saw a number of people ahead of him in the check outline. Concerned about the delay, he hurried out of the store and asked Berry to drive him to a friend's house instead.

Respondent Connor, an officer of the Charlotte, North Carolina, Police Department, saw Graham hastily enter and leave the store. The officer became suspicious that something was amiss and followed Berry's car. About one-half mile from the store, he made an investigative stop. Although Berry told Connor that Graham was simply suffering from a "sugar reaction," the officer ordered Berry and Graham to wait while he found out what, if anything, had happened at the convenience store. When Officer Connor returned to his patrol car to call for backup assistance, Graham got out of the car, ran around it twice, and finally sat down on the curb, where he passed out briefly.

In the ensuing confusion, a number of other Charlotte police officers arrived on the scene in response to Officer Connor's request for backup. One of the officers rolled Graham over on the sidewalk and cuffed his hands tightly behind his back, ignoring Berry's pleas to get him some sugar. Another officer said: "I've seen a lot of people with sugar diabetes that never acted like this. Ain't nothing wrong with the M.F. but drunk. Lock the S.B. up." Several officers then lifted Graham up from behind, carried him over to Berry's car, and placed him face down on its hood. Regaining consciousness, Graham asked the officers to check in his wallet for a diabetic decal that he carried. In response, one of the officers told him to "shut up" and shoved his face down against the hood of the car. Four officers grabbed Graham and threw him headfirst into the police car. A friend of Graham's brought some orange juice to the car, but the officers refused to let him have it. Finally, Officer Connor received a report that Graham had done nothing wrong at the convenience store, and the officers drove him home and released him.

At some point during his encounter with the police, Graham sustained a broken foot, cuts on his wrists, a bruised forehead, and an injured shoulder; he also claims to have developed a loud ringing in his right ear that continues to this day. He commenced this action under 42 U.S.C. § 1983 against the individual officers involved in the incident, all of whom are respondents here, alleging that they had used excessive force in making the investigatory stop, in violation of "rights secured to him under the Fourteenth Amendment to the United States Constitution and 42 U.S.C. § 1983." The case was tried before a jury. At the close of petitioner's evidence, respondents moved for a directed verdict. In ruling on that motion, the District Court considered the following four factors, which it identified as "[t]he factors to be considered in determining when the excessive use of force gives rise to a cause of action under § 1983": (1) the need for the application of force; (2) the relationship between that need and the amount of force that was used; (3) the extent of the injury inflicted; and (4) "[w]hether the force was applied in a good faith effort to maintain and restore discipline or maliciously and sadistically for the very purpose of causing harm." Finding that the amount of force used by the officers was "appropriate under the circumstances," that "[t]here was no discernable injury inflicted," and that the force used "was not applied maliciously or sadistically for the very purpose of causing harm," but in "a good faith effort to maintain or restore order in the face of a potentially explosive situation," the District Court granted respondents' motion for a directed verdict.

A divided panel of the Court of Appeals for the Fourth Circuit affirmed. . . . We granted certiorari and now reverse.

• • •

We reject this notion that all excessive force claims brought under § 1983 are governed by a single generic standard. As we have said many times, § 1983 "is not itself a source of substantive rights," but merely provides "a method for vindicating federal rights elsewhere conferred." In addressing an excessive force claim brought under § 1983, analysis begins by identifying the specific constitutional right allegedly infringed by the challenged application of force. In most instances, that will be either the Fourth Amendment's prohibition against unreasonable seizures of the person, or the Eighth Amendment's ban on cruel and unusual punishments, which are the two primary sources of constitutional protection against physically abusive governmental conduct. The validity of the claim must then be judged by reference to the specific constitutional standard which governs that right, rather than to some generalized "excessive force" standard.

Where, as here, the excessive force claim arises in the context of an arrest or investigatory stop of a free citizen, it is most properly characterized as one invoking the protections of the Fourth Amendment, which guarantees citizens the right "to be secure in their persons . . . against unreasonable . . . seizures" of the person. This much is clear from our decision in *Garner.* In *Garner*, we addressed a claim that the use of deadly force to apprehend a fleeing suspect who did not appear to be armed or otherwise dangerous violated the suspect's constitutional rights, notwithstanding the existence of probable cause to arrest. Though the complaint alleged violations of both the Fourth Amendment and the Due Process Clause, we analyzed the constitutionality of the challenged application of force solely by reference to the Fourth Amendment's prohibition against unreasonable seizures of the person, holding that the "reasonableness" of a particular seizure depends not only on when it is made, but also on how it is carried out. Today we make explicit what was implicit in *Garner's* analysis, and hold that all claims that law enforcement officers have used excessive force—deadly or not—in the course of an arrest, investigatory stop, or other "seizure" of a free citizen should be analyzed under the Fourth Amendment and its "reasonableness" standard, rather than under a "substantive due process" approach. Because the Fourth Amendment provides an explicit textual source of constitutional protection against this sort of physically intrusive governmental conduct, that Amendment, not the more generalized notion of "substantive due process," must be the guide for analyzing these claims.

Determining whether the force used to effect a particular seizure is "reasonable" under the Fourth Amendment requires a careful balancing of "'the nature and quality of the intrusion on the individual's Fourth Amendment interests'" against the countervailing governmental interests at stake. Our Fourth Amendment jurisprudence has long recognized that the right to make an arrest or investigatory stop necessarily carries with it the right to use some degree of physical coercion or threat thereof to effect it. Because "[t]he test of reasonableness under the Fourth Amendment is not capable of precise definition or mechanical application," however, its proper application requires careful attention to the facts and circumstances of each particular case, including the severity of the crime at issue, whether the suspect poses an immediate threat to the safety of the officers or others, and whether he is actively resisting arrest or attempting to evade arrest by flight.

The "reasonableness" of a particular use of force must be judged from the perspective of a reasonable officer on the scene, rather than with the 20/20 vision of hindsight. The Fourth Amendment is not violated by an arrest based on probable cause, even though the wrong person is arrested, nor by the mistaken execution of a valid search warrant on the wrong premises. With respect to a claim of excessive force, the same standard of reasonableness at the moment applies: "Not every push or shove, even if it may later seem unnecessary in the peace of a judge's chambers," violates the Fourth Amendment. The calculus of reasonableness must embody allowance for the fact that police officers are often forced to make split-second judgments — in circumstances that are tense, uncertain, and rapidly evolving — about the amount of force that is necessary in a particular situation.

As in other Fourth Amendment contexts, however, the "reasonableness" inquiry in an excessive force case is an objective one: the question is whether the officers' actions are "objectively reasonable" in light of the facts and circumstances confronting them, without regard to their underlying intent or motivation. An officer's evil intentions will not make a Fourth Amendment violation out of an objectively reasonable use of force; nor will an officer's good intentions make an objectively unreasonable use of force constitutional.

Because petitioner's excessive force claim is one arising under the Fourth Amendment, the Court of Appeals erred in analyzing it under the four-part *Johnson v. Glick* test. That test, which requires consideration of whether the individual officers acted in "good faith" or "maliciously and sadistically for the very purpose of causing harm," is incompatible with a proper Fourth Amendment analysis. We do not agree with the Court of Appeals' suggestion that the "malicious and sadistic" inquiry is merely another way of describing conduct that is objectively unreasonable under the circumstances. Whatever the empirical correlations between "malicious and sadistic" behavior and objective unreasonableness may be, the fact remains that the "malicious and sadistic" factor puts in issue the subjective motivations of the individual officers, which our prior cases make clear has no bearing on whether a particular seizure is "unreasonable" under the Fourth Amendment. Nor do we agree with the Court of Appeals' conclusion, that because the subjective motivations of the individual officers are of central importance in deciding whether force used against a convicted prisoner violates the Eighth Amendment, it cannot be reversible error to inquire into them in deciding whether force used against a suspect or arrestee violates the Fourth Amendment. Differing standards under the Fourth and Eighth Amendments are hardly surprising: the terms "cruel" and "punishments" clearly suggest some inquiry into subjective state of mind, whereas the term "unreasonable" does not. Moreover, the less protective Eighth Amendment standard applies "only after the State has complied with the constitutional guarantees traditionally associated with criminal prosecutions." The Fourth Amendment inquiry is one of "objective reasonableness" under the circumstances, and subjective concepts like "malice" and "sadism" have no proper place in that inquiry.

Because the Court of Appeals reviewed the District Court's ruling on the motion for directed verdict under an erroneous view of the governing substantive law, its judgment must be vacated and the case remanded to that court for reconsideration of that issue under the proper Fourth Amendment standard.

NOTES AND QUESTIONS

1. Compare the four-factor test that some courts had been applying in excessive force claims to the test announced by the Court in *Graham*. What are the most important differences between the two tests?

2. Does the Court's conclusion that excessive force claims should be analyzed as unreasonable seizures under the Fourth Amendment follow inevitably from the decision in *Garner*?

3. The test announced in *Graham* has been widely criticized as being, among other things, overly deferential to police. Do you agree? The Court cautions that the test must account for the "tense, uncertain, and rapidly evolving" circumstances in which police must make "split-second judgments." Is this layer of deference baked into every evaluation of police use of force or only where such circumstances are present?

4. A leading scholar on police misconduct, Professor Rachel Harmon, has offered this critique of the *Graham v. Connor* test:

> *Graham* permits courts to consider any circumstance in determining whether force is reasonable without providing a standard for measuring relevance, it gives little instruction on how to weigh relevant factors, and it apparently requires courts to consider the severity of the underlying crime in all cases, a circumstance that is sometimes irrelevant and misleading in determining whether force is reasonable. Thus, *Graham* has largely left judges and juries to their intuitions, and what direction it does give sometimes steers them off course.

Rachel A. Harmon, *When Is Police Violence Justified?*, 102 Nw. U. L. Rev. 1119, 1130-31 (2008). Fair criticism? Do you agree that the severity of the crime should not always be relevant? Does the open-ended nature of the test leave the jury with too much discretion to decide the issue? Does that discretion cut for or against police officer defendants in civil damages actions?

5. Does the irrelevance of the police officer's subjective intentions to the reasonableness of the seizure mean that statements made by the officer in connection with the application of force will be relevant only as they may bear on the objective considerations? Consider, for example, the statements made by the officer questioning the legitimacy of Graham's sugar reaction. Are they relevant? Consider the following hypothetical statements made by an officer in subduing a suspect who is resisting arrest:

> "Stay cool, I'm not going to hurt you."
> "Let's do this the easy way, not the hard way."
> "I'm going to have to mess you up."

Relevant to the objective test? Admissible regardless?

6. As in *Garner*, the Court in *Graham* does not mention race. Officer Connor was Black; the race of his codefendant officers does not appear to be publicly available. Graham was Black. Cynthia Lee, *Reforming the Law on Police Use of Deadly Force: De-Escalation, Pre-Seizure Conduct, and Imperfect Self-Defense*, 2018 U. Ill. L. Rev. 629, 643 (citation omitted).

7. Seven years prior to *Graham*, in *Harlow v. Fitzgerald*, 457 U.S. 800 (1982), the Court had held that police officers enjoyed qualified immunity from suits for damages unless they violated "clearly established law," and that officers' subjective intentions were not relevant to the inquiry. *See* Chapter VI *infra*. Does the open-ended, totality-of-the-circumstances nature of the *Graham* test make it unlikely that an excessive force plaintiff will be able to prove that the conduct at issue violated precedent that was "clearly established" at any meaningful level of detail? *Id.*

8. Litigation of Fourth Amendment excessive force claims often involves "use of force" expert witnesses. Indeed, one of the important advantages in the federal (compared to the state) prosecution of the Los Angeles Police Department officers in the Rodney King trials was the prosecution's presentation of such a "use of force" expert. Such litigation also often focuses on internal police department "use of force" policies. For an argument that courts too often rely on such internal policies to shape what constitutes excessive force as a constitutional matter, *see generally* Osagie K. Obasogie & Zachary Newman, *The Endogenous Fourth Amendment: An Empirical Assessment of How Police Understandings of Excessive Force Become Constitutional Law*, 104 Cornell L. Rev. 1281 (2019).

C. THE WARRANT REQUIREMENT AND ITS EXCEPTIONS

The next few subsections focus on special issues that arise in connection with search warrants. Arrest warrants are less often the subject of litigation, although the proliferation of so-called bench warrants, which can authorize the arrest of a person for comparatively trivial reasons (e.g., failure to appear in court or to pay a traffic ticket), raise enormous problems. *See* Chapter V *infra.*

1. Warrant Requirements: Search Warrants

The Fourth Amendment provides: "no Warrants shall issue, but upon probable cause, supported by Oath or affirmation, and particularly describing the place to be searched, and the persons or things to be seized." U.S. Const. amend. IV. "The chief evil that prompted the framing and adoption of the Fourth Amendment was the 'indiscriminate searches and seizures' conducted by the British 'under the authority of general warrants.'" *Payton v. New York*, 445 U.S. 573, 583 (1980). Thus the particularity and probable cause requirements aim to prevent a "general, exploratory rummaging in a person's belongings." *Coolidge v. New Hampshire*, 403 U.S. 443, 467 (1971). The two requirements are related: Together they limit the officer's authority to a search only of "the specific areas and things for which there is probable cause to search." *Maryland v. Garrison*, 480 U.S. 79, 84 (1987).

The warrant requirement is a microcosm of the separation of powers, a check of the judiciary upon the executive. As the Supreme Court has put it:

> The point of the Fourth Amendment, which often is not grasped by zealous officers, is not that it denies law enforcement the support of the usual inferences that reasonable men draw from evidence. Its protection consists in requiring that those inferences be drawn by a neutral and detached magistrate instead of being judged by the officer engaged in the often competitive enterprise of ferreting out crime.

Johnson v. United States, 333 U.S. 10, 13-14 (1948).

The Supreme Court was once fond of saying that searches without warrants are "per se unreasonable." *Katz v. United States*, 389 U.S. 347, 357 (1967). But in the intervening decades the number and breadth of the exceptions to the warrant "requirement," *see infra*, have expanded. For a strong argument that the warrant requirement should be, well, taken more seriously, *see generally* Oren Bar-Gill & Barry Friedman, *Taking Warrants Seriously*, 106 Nw. U. L. Rev. 1609 (2012) (arguing that a serious ex ante warrant requirement will be much clearer and more effective than a deterrence model focused on the exclusionary rule).

It must not be lost in the doctrinal shuffle that a search warrant is not an abstraction but a document. The theory is that the searching officer is guided by the language of the warrant—by its words—when executing a search.

a. Particularity

As to particularity, the idea is that the scope of discretion of the searching officer must be as small as possible. *Marron v. United States*, 275 U.S. 192 (1927) ("As to what is to be taken, nothing is left to the discretion of the officer executing the warrant"). Some courts break the requirement into three necessary criteria. *United States v. Galpin*, 720 F.3d 436, 445 (2d Cir. 2013). First, the warrant must identify the specific offense for which the police or agents have established probable cause. *Id.* Second, the warrant must, as the plain language of the Amendment commands, "describe the place to be searched." *Id.* at 445-46. And third, it must "specify the items to be seized by their relation to designated crimes." *Id.* at 446. In most contexts, a warrant must also require the specification of a time frame that would limit the scope of a search. Overbreadth is a fatal warrant flaw at the intersection of particularity and probable cause. A warrant is overbroad where its "description of the objects to be seized . . . is broader than can be justified by the probable cause upon which the warrant is based." *Galpin*, 720 F.3d at 446.

The particularity must be supplied by the text of the warrant itself, along with any documents attached to and incorporated in the warrant. *Groh v. Ramirez*, 540 U.S. 551, 557, (2004). That some other document, such as the application for the warrant, provides further specificity will not save an insufficiently particularized warrant. The purpose of this requirement, loftier than the technicality it appears to be, is twofold: first, any document adding particularity must actually in theory serve to guide the searching officer during the search, and therefore must be present at the search location with, and part of, the warrant; second, the owner of the property being searched has the right to inspect any document that functions as part of the warrant. *See* Fed. R. Crim. P. 41(f)(B) (requiring officer to provide a copy of the warrant to the person whose property was searched).

Special caution is necessary when warrants target electronically stored information, as many do now. As the Second Circuit has recognized, where the property to be searched is a computer hard drive, "the particularity requirement assumes even greater importance." *Galpin*, 720 F.3d at 446. That is because the seizure of a computer hard drive, and its subsequent retention by the government, can give the government possession of a vast trove of personal information about the person to whom the drive belongs, much of which may be entirely irrelevant to the criminal investigation that led to the seizure. *United States v. Ganias*, 824 F.3d 199, 217 (2d Cir. 2016) (en banc). *See supra Carpenter v. United States*, 585 U.S. 296 (2018). "The potential for privacy violations in such a context is compounded by the nature of digital storage." *Galpin*, 720 F.3d at 447. Indeed, the government, once it has obtained authorization to search a hard drive, may in theory claim that the contents of every file it chose to open were in plain view and thereby available to it regardless of the scope of the warrant, rendering the Fourth Amendment irrelevant. *United States v. Comprehensive Drug Testing, Inc., (BALCO)*, 621 F.3d 1162, 1176 (9th Cir. 2010) (en banc) (per curiam). Accordingly, a "heightened sensitivity to the particularity requirement in the context of digital searches" is necessary. *Galpin*, 720 F.3d at 447.

b. Probable Cause

Illinois v. Gates

462 U.S. 213 (1983)

Justice Rehnquist delivered the opinion of the Court.

Respondents Lance and Susan Gates were indicted for violation of state drug laws after police officers, executing a search warrant, discovered marijuana and other contraband in their automobile and home. Prior to trial the Gates moved to suppress evidence seized during this search. The Illinois Supreme Court affirmed the decisions of lower state courts granting the motion. It held that the affidavit submitted in support of the State's application for a warrant to search the Gates' property was inadequate under this Court's decisions in *Aguilar v. Texas* (1964) and *Spinelli v. United States* (1969).

We granted certiorari to consider the application of the Fourth Amendment to a magistrate's issuance of a search warrant on the basis of a partially corroborated anonymous informant's tip. After receiving briefs and hearing oral argument on this question, however, we requested the parties to address an additional question:

> Whether the rule requiring the exclusion at a criminal trial of evidence obtained in violation of the Fourth Amendment, *Mapp v. Ohio* (1961); *Weeks v. United States* (1914), should to any extent be modified, so as, for example, not to require the exclusion of evidence obtained in the reasonable belief that the search and seizure at issue was consistent with the Fourth Amendment.

We decide today, with apologies to all, that the issue we framed for the parties was not presented to the Illinois courts and, accordingly, do not address it. Rather, we consider the question originally presented in the petition for certiorari, and conclude that the Illinois Supreme Court read the requirements of our Fourth Amendment decisions too restrictively. Initially, however, we set forth our reasons for not addressing the question regarding modification of the exclusionary rule framed in our order.

• • •

II

We now turn to the question presented in the State's original petition for certiorari, which requires us to decide whether respondents' rights under the Fourth and Fourteenth Amendments were violated by the search of their car and house. A chronological statement of events usefully introduces the issues at stake. Bloomingdale, Ill., is a suburb of Chicago located in DuPage County. On May 3, 1978, the Bloomingdale Police Department received by mail an anonymous handwritten letter which read as follows:

> This letter is to inform you that you have a couple in your town who strictly make their living on selling drugs. They are Sue and Lance Gates, they live on Greenway, off Bloomingdale Rd. in the condominiums. Most of their buys are done in Florida. Sue his wife drives their car to Florida, where she leaves it to be loaded up with drugs, then Lance flys down and drives it back. Sue flys back after she drops the car off in Florida. May 3 she is driving down there again and Lance will be flying down in a few days to drive it back. At the time Lance drives the car back he has the trunk loaded with over $100,000.00 in drugs. Presently they have over $100,000.00 worth of drugs in their basement.
>
> They brag about the fact they never have to work, and make their entire living on pushers.
>
> I guarantee if you watch them carefully you will make a big catch. They are friends with some big drugs dealers, who visit their house often.
>
> Lance & Susan Gates
>
> Greenway
>
> in Condominiums

The letter was referred by the Chief of Police of the Bloomingdale Police Department to Detective Mader, who decided to pursue the tip. Mader learned, from the office of the Illinois Secretary of State, that an Illinois driver's license had been issued to one Lance Gates, residing at a stated address in Bloomingdale. He contacted a confidential informant, whose examination of certain financial records revealed a more recent address for the Gates, and he also learned from a police officer assigned to O'Hare Airport that "L. Gates" had made a reservation on Eastern Airlines flight 245 to West Palm Beach, Fla., scheduled to depart from Chicago on May 5 at 4:15 p.m.

Mader then made arrangements with an agent of the Drug Enforcement Administration for surveillance of the May 5 Eastern Airlines flight. The agent later reported to Mader that Gates had boarded the flight, and that federal agents in Florida had observed him arrive in West Palm Beach and take a taxi to the nearby Holiday Inn. They also reported that Gates went to a room registered to one Susan Gates and that, at 7:00 a.m. the next morning, Gates and an unidentified woman left the motel in a Mercury bearing Illinois license plates and drove northbound on an interstate frequently used by travelers to the Chicago area. In addition, the DEA agent informed Mader that the license plate number on the Mercury registered to a Hornet station wagon owned by Gates. The agent also advised Mader that the driving time between West Palm Beach and Bloomingdale was approximately 22 to 24 hours.

Mader signed an affidavit setting forth the foregoing facts, and submitted it to a judge of the Circuit Court of DuPage County, together with a copy of the anonymous letter. The judge of that court thereupon issued a search warrant for the Gates' residence and for their automobile. The judge, in deciding to issue the warrant, could have determined that the modus operandi of the Gates had been substantially corroborated. As the anonymous letter predicted, Lance Gates had flown from Chicago to West Palm Beach late in the afternoon of May 5th, had checked into a hotel room registered in the name of his wife, and, at 7:00 a.m. the following morning, had headed north, accompanied by an unidentified woman, out of West Palm Beach on an interstate highway used by travelers from South Florida to Chicago in an automobile bearing a license plate issued to him.

At 5:15 a.m. on March 7th, only 36 hours after he had flown out of Chicago, Lance Gates, and his wife, returned to their home in Bloomingdale, driving the car in which they had left West Palm Beach some 22 hours earlier. The Bloomingdale police were awaiting them, searched the trunk of the Mercury, and uncovered approximately 350 pounds of marijuana. A search of the Gates' home revealed marijuana, weapons, and other contraband. The Illinois Circuit Court ordered suppression of all these items, on the ground that the affidavit submitted to the Circuit Judge failed to support the necessary determination of probable cause to believe that the Gates' automobile and home contained the contraband in question. This decision was affirmed in turn by the Illinois Appellate Court and by a divided vote of the Supreme Court of Illinois.

The Illinois Supreme Court concluded—and we are inclined to agree—that, standing alone, the anonymous letter sent to the Bloomingdale Police Department would not provide the basis for a magistrate's determination that there was probable cause to believe contraband would be found in the Gates' car and home. The letter provides virtually nothing from which one might conclude that its author is either honest or his information reliable; likewise, the letter gives absolutely no indication of the basis for the writer's predictions regarding the Gates' criminal activities. Something more was required, then, before a magistrate could conclude that there was probable cause to believe that contraband would be found in the Gates' home and car.

The Illinois Supreme Court also properly recognized that Detective Mader's affidavit might be capable of supplementing the anonymous letter with information sufficient to permit a determination of probable cause. In holding that the affidavit in fact did not contain sufficient additional information to sustain a determination of probable cause, the Illinois court applied a "two-pronged test," derived from our decision in *Spinelli*. The Illinois Supreme Court, like some others, apparently understood *Spinelli* as requiring that the anonymous letter satisfy each of two independent requirements before it could be relied on. According to this view, the letter, as supplemented by Mader's affidavit, first had to adequately reveal the "basis of knowledge" of the letter writer—the particular means by which he came by the information given in his report. Second, it had to provide facts sufficiently establishing either the "veracity" of the affiant's informant, or, alternatively, the "reliability" of the informant's report in this particular case.

The Illinois court, alluding to an elaborate set of legal rules that have developed among various lower courts to enforce the "two-pronged test," found that the test had not been satisfied. First, the "veracity" prong was not satisfied because, "there was simply no basis [for] . . . conclud[ing] that the anonymous person [who wrote the letter to the Bloomingdale Police Department] was credible." The court indicated that corroboration by police of details contained in the letter might never satisfy the "veracity" prong, and in any event, could not do so if, as in the present case, only "innocent" details are corroborated. In addition, the letter gave no indication of the basis of its writer's knowledge of the Gates' activities. The Illinois court understood *Spinelli* as permitting the detail contained in a tip to be used to infer that the informant had a reliable basis for his statements, but it thought that the anonymous letter failed to provide sufficient detail to permit such an inference. Thus, it concluded that no showing of probable cause had been made.

We agree with the Illinois Supreme Court that an informant's "veracity," "reliability" and "basis of knowledge" are all highly relevant in determining the value of his report. We do not agree, however, that these elements should be understood as entirely separate and independent requirements to be rigidly exacted in every case, which the opinion of the Supreme Court of Illinois would imply. Rather, as detailed below, they should be understood simply as closely intertwined issues that may usefully illuminate the commonsense, practical question whether there is "probable cause" to believe that contraband or evidence is located in a particular place.

III

This totality-of-the-circumstances approach is far more consistent with our prior treatment of probable cause than is any rigid demand that specific "tests" be satisfied by every informant's tip. Perhaps the central teaching of our decisions bearing on the probable cause standard is that it is a "practical, nontechnical conception." *Brinegar* (1949). "In dealing with probable cause, . . . as the very name implies, we deal with probabilities. These are not technical; they are the factual and practical considerations of everyday life on which reasonable and prudent men, not legal technicians, act." Our observation in *United States v. Cortez* (1981), regarding "particularized suspicion," is also applicable to the probable cause standard:

> The process does not deal with hard certainties, but with probabilities. Long before the law of probabilities was articulated as such, practical people formulated certain common-sense conclusions about human behavior; jurors as factfinders are permitted to do the same—and so are law enforcement officers. Finally, the evidence thus collected must be seen and weighed not in terms of library analysis by scholars, but as understood by those versed in the field of law enforcement.

As these comments illustrate, probable cause is a fluid concept—turning on the assessment of probabilities in particular factual contexts—not readily, or even usefully, reduced to a neat set of legal rules. Informants' tips doubtless come in many shapes and sizes from many different types of persons. As we said in *Adams v. Williams*, "Informants' tips, like all other clues and evidence coming to a policeman on the scene may vary greatly in their value and reliability." Rigid legal rules are ill-suited to an area of such diversity. "One simple rule will not cover every situation."

Moreover, the "two-pronged test" directs analysis into two largely independent channels—the informant's "veracity" or "reliability" and his "basis of knowledge." There are persuasive arguments against according these two elements such independent status. Instead, they are better understood as relevant considerations in the totality-of-the-circumstances analysis that traditionally has guided probable cause determinations: a deficiency in one may be compensated for, in determining the overall reliability of a tip, by a strong showing as to the other, or by some other indicia of reliability.

If, for example, a particular informant is known for the unusual reliability of his predictions of certain types of criminal activities in a locality, his failure, in a particular case, to thoroughly set forth the basis of his knowledge surely should not serve as an absolute bar to a finding of probable cause based on his tip. Likewise, if an unquestionably honest citizen comes forward with a report of criminal activity—which if fabricated would subject him to criminal liability—we have found rigorous scrutiny of the basis of his knowledge unnecessary. *Adams v. Williams, supra*. Conversely, even if we entertain some doubt as to an informant's motives, his explicit and detailed description of alleged wrongdoing, along with a statement that the event was observed first-hand, entitles his tip to greater weight than might otherwise be the case. Unlike a totality-of-the-circumstances analysis, which permits a balanced assessment of the relative weights of all the various indicia of reliability (and unreliability) attending an informant's tip, the "two-pronged test" has encouraged an excessively technical dissection of informants' tips, with undue attention being focused on isolated issues that cannot sensibly be divorced from the other facts presented to the magistrate.

As early as *Locke v. United States* (1813), Chief Justice Marshall observed, in a closely related context, that "the term 'probable cause,' according to its usual acceptation, means less than evidence which would justify condemnation. . . . It imports a seizure made under circumstances which warrant suspicion." More recently, we said that "the quanta . . . of proof" appropriate in ordinary judicial proceedings are inapplicable to the decision to issue a warrant. Finely-tuned standards such as proof beyond a reasonable doubt or by a preponderance of the evidence, useful in formal trials, have no place in the magistrate's decision. While an effort to fix some general, numerically precise degree of certainty corresponding to "probable cause" may not be helpful, it is clear that "only the probability, and not a prima facie showing, of criminal activity is the standard of probable cause."

We also have recognized that affidavits "are normally drafted by nonlawyers in the midst and haste of a criminal investigation. Technical requirements of elaborate specificity once exacted under common law pleading have no proper place in this area." Likewise, search and arrest warrants long have been issued by persons who are neither lawyers nor judges, and who certainly do not remain abreast of each judicial refinement of the nature of "probable cause." The rigorous inquiry into the *Spinelli* prongs and the complex superstructure of evidentiary and analytical rules that some have seen implicit in our *Spinelli* decision, cannot be reconciled with the fact that many warrants are—quite properly, ibid.—issued on the basis of nontechnical, common-sense judgments of laymen applying a standard less demanding than those used in more formal legal proceedings. Likewise, given the informal, often hurried context in which it must be applied, the "built-in subtleties," of the "two-pronged test" are particularly unlikely to assist magistrates in determining probable cause.

Similarly, we have repeatedly said that after-the-fact scrutiny by courts of the sufficiency of an affidavit should not take the form of de novo review. A magistrate's "determination of probable cause should be paid great deference by reviewing courts." "A grudging or negative attitude by reviewing courts toward warrants," is inconsistent with the Fourth Amendment's strong preference for searches conducted pursuant to a warrant "courts should not invalidate . . . warrant[s] by interpreting affidavit[s] in a hypertechnical, rather than a commonsense, manner." [sic]

If the affidavits submitted by police officers are subjected to the type of scrutiny some courts have deemed appropriate, police might well resort to warrantless searches, with the hope of relying on consent or some other exception to the warrant clause that might develop at the time of the search. In addition, the possession of a warrant by officers conducting an arrest or search greatly reduces the perception of unlawful or intrusive police conduct, by assuring "the individual whose property is searched or seized of the lawful authority of the executing officer, his need to search, and the limits of his power to search." Reflecting this preference for the warrant process, the traditional standard for review of an issuing magistrate's probable cause determination has been that so long as the magistrate had a "substantial basis for . . . conclud[ing]" that a search would uncover evidence of wrongdoing, the Fourth Amendment requires no more. We think reaffirmation of this standard better serves the purpose of encouraging recourse to the warrant procedure and is more consistent with our traditional deference to the probable cause determinations of magistrates than is the "two-pronged test."

Finally, the direction taken by decisions following *Spinelli* poorly serves "the most basic function of any government": "to provide for the security of the individual and of his property." The strictures that inevitably accompany the "two-pronged test" cannot avoid seriously impeding the task of law enforcement. If, as the Illinois Supreme Court apparently thought, that test must be rigorously applied in every case, anonymous tips seldom would be of greatly diminished value in police work. Ordinary citizens, like ordinary witnesses, see Federal Rules of Evidence 701, Advisory Committee Note (1976), generally do not provide extensive recitations of the basis of their everyday observations. Likewise, as the Illinois Supreme Court observed in this case, the veracity of persons supplying anonymous tips is by hypothesis largely unknown, and unknowable. As a result, anonymous tips seldom could survive a rigorous application of either of the *Spinelli* prongs. Yet, such tips, particularly when supplemented by independent police investigation, frequently contribute to the solution of otherwise "perfect crimes." While a conscientious assessment of the basis for crediting such tips is required by the Fourth Amendment, a standard that leaves virtually no place for anonymous citizen informants is not.

For all these reasons, we conclude that it is wiser to abandon the "two-pronged test" established by our decisions in *Aguilar* and *Spinelli*. In its place we reaffirm the totality-of-the-circumstances analysis that traditionally has informed probable cause determinations. The task of the issuing magistrate is simply to make a practical, common-sense decision whether, given all the circumstances set forth in the affidavit before him, including the "veracity" and "basis of knowledge" of persons supplying hearsay information, there is a fair probability that contraband or evidence of a crime will be found in a particular place. And the duty of a reviewing court is simply to ensure that the magistrate had a "substantial basis for . . . conclud[ing]" that probable cause existed. We are convinced that this flexible, easily applied standard will better achieve the accommodation of public and private interests that the Fourth Amendment requires than does the approach that has developed from *Aguilar* and *Spinelli*.

Our earlier cases illustrate the limits beyond which a magistrate may not venture in issuing a warrant. A sworn statement of an affiant that "he has cause to suspect and does believe that" liquor illegally brought into the United States is located on certain premises will not do. An affidavit must provide the magistrate with a substantial basis for determining the existence of probable cause, and the wholly conclusory statement at issue in *Nathanson* failed to meet this requirement. An officer's statement that "affiants have received reliable information from a credible person and believe" that heroin is stored in a home, is likewise inadequate. As in *Nathanson*, this is a mere conclusory statement that gives the magistrate virtually no basis at all for making a judgment regarding probable cause. Sufficient information must be presented to the magistrate to allow that official to determine probable cause; his action cannot be a mere ratification of the bare conclusions of others. In order to ensure that such an abdication of the magistrate's duty does not occur, courts must continue to conscientiously review the sufficiency of affidavits on which warrants are issued. But when we move beyond the "bare bones" affidavits present in cases such as *Nathanson* and *Aguilar*, this area simply does not lend itself to a prescribed set of rules, like that which had developed from *Spinelli*. Instead, the flexible, common-sense standard articulated in *Jones*, *Ventresca*, and *Brinegar* better serves the purposes of the Fourth Amendment's probable cause requirement.

Justice Brennan's dissent suggests in several places that the approach we take today somehow downgrades the role of the neutral magistrate, because *Aguilar* and *Spinelli* "preserve the role of magistrates as independent arbiters of probable cause. . . ." Quite the contrary, we believe, is the case. The essential protection of the warrant requirement of the Fourth Amendment is in "requiring that [the usual inferences which reasonable men draw from evidence] be drawn by a neutral and detached magistrate instead of being judged by the officer engaged in the often competitive enterprise of ferreting out crime." *Johnson*. Nothing in our opinion in any way lessens the authority of the magistrate to draw such reasonable inferences as he will from the material supplied to him by applicants for a warrant; indeed, he is freer than under the regime of *Aguilar* and *Spinelli* to draw such inferences, or to refuse to draw them if he is so minded.

The real gist of Justice Brennan's criticism seems to be a second argument, somewhat at odds with the first, that magistrates should be restricted in their authority to make probable cause determinations by the standards laid down in *Aguilar* and *Spinelli*, and that such findings "should not be authorized unless there is some assurance that the information on which they are based has been obtained in a reliable way by an honest or credible person." However, under our opinion magistrates remain perfectly free to exact such assurances as they deem necessary, as well as those required by this opinion, in making probable cause determinations. Justice Brennan would apparently prefer that magistrates be restricted in their findings of probable cause by the development of an elaborate body of case law dealing with the "veracity" prong of the *Spinelli* test, which in turn is broken down into two "spurs"—the informant's "credibility" and the "reliability" of his information, together with the "basis of knowledge" prong of the *Spinelli* test. That such a labyrinthine body of judicial refinement bears any relationship to familiar definitions of probable cause is hard to imagine. Probable cause deals "with probabilities. These are not technical; they are the factual and practical considerations of everyday life on which reasonable and prudent men, not legal technicians, act." *Brinegar.*

Justice Brennan's dissent also suggests that "words such as 'practical,' 'nontechnical,' and 'common sense,' as used in the Court's opinion, are but code words for an overly-permissive attitude towards police practices in derogation of the rights secured by the Fourth Amendment." An easy, but not a complete, answer to this rather florid statement would be that nothing we know about Justice Rutledge suggests that he would have used the words he chose in *Brinegar* in such a manner. More fundamentally, no one doubts that "under our Constitution only measures consistent with the Fourth Amendment may be employed by government to cure [the horrors of drug trafficking]"; but this agreement does not advance the inquiry as to which measures are, and which measures are not, consistent with the Fourth Amendment. "Fidelity" to the commands of the Constitution suggests balanced judgment rather than exhortation. The highest "fidelity" is achieved neither by the judge who instinctively goes furthest in upholding even the most bizarre claim of individual constitutional rights, any more than it is achieved by a judge who instinctively goes furthest in accepting the most restrictive claims of governmental authorities. The task of this Court, as of other courts, is to "hold the balance true," and we think we have done that in this case.

IV

Our decisions applying the totality-of-the-circumstances analysis outlined above have consistently recognized the value of corroboration of details of an informant's tip by independent police work. In *Jones v. United States*, we held that an affidavit relying on hearsay "is not to be deemed insufficient on that score, so long as a substantial basis for crediting the hearsay is presented." We went on to say that even in making a warrantless arrest an officer "may rely upon information received through an informant, rather than upon his direct observations, so long as the informant's statement is reasonably corroborated by other matters within the officer's knowledge." Likewise, we recognized the probative value of corroborative efforts of police officials in *Aguilar*—the source of the "two-pronged test"—by observing that if the police had made some effort to corroborate the informant's report at issue, "an entirely different case" would have been presented.

Our decision in *Draper v. United States* (1959), however, is the classic case on the value of corroborative efforts of police officials. There, an informant named Hereford reported that Draper would arrive in Denver on a train from Chicago on one of two days, and that he would be carrying a quantity of heroin. The informant also supplied a fairly detailed physical description of Draper, and predicted that he would be wearing a light colored raincoat, brown slacks and black shoes, and would be walking "real fast." Hereford gave no indication of the basis for his information.

On one of the stated dates police officers observed a man matching this description exit a train arriving from Chicago; his attire and luggage matched Hereford's report and he was walking rapidly. We explained in *Draper* that, by this point in his investigation, the arresting officer "had personally verified every facet of the information given him by Hereford except whether petitioner had accomplished his mission and had the three ounces of heroin on his person or in his bag. And surely, with every other bit of Hereford's information being thus personally verified, [the officer] had 'reasonable grounds' to believe that the remaining unverified bit of Hereford's information—that Draper would have the heroin with him—was likewise true."

The showing of probable cause in the present case was fully as compelling as that in *Draper*. Even standing alone, the facts obtained through the independent investigation of Mader and the DEA at least suggested that the Gates were involved in drug trafficking. In addition to being a popular vacation site, Florida is well-known as a source of narcotics and other illegal drugs. Lance Gates' flight to Palm Beach, his brief, overnight stay in a motel, and apparent immediate return north to Chicago in the family car, conveniently awaiting him in West Palm Beach, is as suggestive of a pre-arranged drug run, as it is of an ordinary vacation trip.

In addition, the magistrate could rely on the anonymous letter, which had been corroborated in major part by Mader's efforts—just as had occurred in *Draper*. The Supreme Court of Illinois reasoned that *Draper* involved an informant who had given reliable information on previous occasions, while the honesty and reliability of the anonymous informant in this case were unknown to the Bloomingdale police. While this distinction might be an apt one at the time the police department received the anonymous letter, it became far less significant after Mader's independent investigative work occurred. The corroboration of the letter's predictions that the Gates' car would be in Florida, that Lance Gates would fly to Florida in the next day or so, and that he would drive the car north toward Bloomingdale all indicated, albeit not with certainty, that the informant's other assertions also were true. "Because an informant is right about some things, he is more probably right about other facts"—including the claim regarding the Gates' illegal activity. This may well not be the type of "reliability" or "veracity" necessary to satisfy some views of the "veracity prong" of *Spinelli*, but we think it suffices for the practical, common-sense judgment called for in making a probable cause determination. It is enough, for purposes of assessing probable cause, that "corroboration through other sources of information reduced the chances of a reckless or prevaricating tale," thus providing "a substantial basis for crediting the hearsay."

Finally, the anonymous letter contained a range of details relating not just to easily obtained facts and conditions existing at the time of the tip, but to future actions of third parties ordinarily not easily predicted. The letter writer's accurate information as to the travel plans of each of the Gates was of a character likely obtained only from the Gates themselves, or from someone familiar with their not entirely ordinary travel plans. If the informant had access to accurate information of this type a magistrate could properly conclude that it was not unlikely that he also had access to reliable information of the Gates' alleged illegal activities. Of course, the Gates' travel plans might have been learned from a talkative neighbor or travel agent; under the "two-pronged test" developed from *Spinelli*, the character of the details in the anonymous letter might well not permit a sufficiently clear inference regarding the letter writer's "basis of knowledge." But, as discussed previously, probable cause does not demand the certainty we associate with formal trials. It is enough that there was a fair probability that the writer of the anonymous letter had obtained his entire story either from the

Gates or someone they trusted. And corroboration of major portions of the letter's predictions provides just this probability. It is apparent, therefore, that the judge issuing the warrant had a "substantial basis for . . . conclud[ing]" that probable cause to search the Gates' home and car existed. The judgment of the Supreme Court of Illinois therefore must be

Reversed.

[Justices Brennan, Marshall, and Stevens dissented.]

NOTES AND QUESTIONS

1. The Court repeatedly refers to the *Aguilar-Spinelli* test as if it were some indecipherable object of interpretation by Talmudic scholars. It is "an elaborate set of legal rules." The inquiry it demands turns on a "complex superstructure" of evidentiary and analytical rules. This is overstated. *Aguilar* required that for an informant's tip to establish probable cause there must be some basis provided for both the informant's source of knowledge and the reliability of the information provided. *Aguilar v. Texas*, 378 U.S. 108, 114-15 (1964). *Spinelli v. United States*, 393 U.S. 410, 413 (1969), added that corroboration of the details of the tip could satisfy the "reliability" prong.

2. How did the tip at issue in *Gates* fail under the traditional *Aguilar-Spinelli* test? Justice Stevens dissents, joined by Justice Brennan, and argues that the affidavit failed to establish probable cause under even the new "totality of the circumstances" test, inasmuch as the tipster was mistaken about Susan Gates's return travel to Chicago and that the fact of the Gateses' 22-hour nonstop car trip from West Palm Beach to Chicago was unknown to the magistrate when he issued the warrant. Do you agree?

3. Note that after accepting certiorari in *Gates* the government asked the parties for additional briefing on whether the Court should consider a "good faith" exception to the exclusionary rule under which exclusion would not be required where the government had a reasonable belief that the search and seizure at issue was constitutional. The Court did not reach the issue in *Gates*, but adopted such a rule the following year in *United States v. Leon*, 468 U.S. 897 (1984). *See* Chapter V *infra*. Would the existence of such an exception have precluded the exclusion of evidence in *Gates*?

The Supreme Court really doesn't like being pinned down on the meaning of probable cause. It says things like "probable cause is a fluid concept—turning on the assessment of probabilities in particular factual contexts—not readily, or even usefully, reduced to a neat set of legal rules." *Gates*, 462 U.S. at 232. And this: "In evaluating probable cause in any given case, a judge must make a practical common-sense decision whether, given all the circumstances set forth in the affidavit before him, there is a fair probability that contraband or evidence of a crime will be found in a particular place." *Id.* at 238. Although the magistrate judge issuing a warrant is normally entitled to some degree of deference, a reviewing court "may properly conclude that . . . a warrant was invalid because the [magistrate judge's] probable-cause determination reflected an improper analysis of the totality of circumstances." *Leon*, 468 U.S. at 915.

c. *Warrant Execution Issues*

Police officers' lawful presence at a location where a search has been judicially authorized confers on the officers some ancillary authority consistent with the authority to conduct the search. Accordingly, officers may take reasonable steps to prevent the flight of property occupants, minimize the risk of harm to the officers, and facilitate the orderly completion of the search. *See Muehler v. Mena*, 544 U.S. 93 (2005) (detention of house occupants in handcuffs during two- to three-hour search of home does not violate Fourth Amendment). On the other hand, a warrant to search a bar and a bartender did not authorize pat-downs of bar patrons. *Ybarra v. Illinois*, 444 U.S. 85, 91 (1979).

The Supreme Court has held that the common law included a general "knock and announce" requirement on officers executing a search warrant, subject to exception for competing law enforcement interests. *Wilson v. Arkansas*, 514 U.S. 927 (1995) (common law knock-and-announce requirement rule applies absent circumstances suggesting a risk of violence to officers or reason to believe evidence will be destroyed). In *Richards v. Wisconsin*, 520 U.S. 385 (1997), the Court considered the constitutionality of a Wisconsin rule that categorically approved no-knock warrants in all felony drug investigations. The Court held that while drug investigations do tend to involve the type of risks identified in *Wilson*, the rule was overly broad in that not all executions of search warrants in drug investigations run such risks, and that other broad categories of investigations could be similarly characterized.

2. Plain View Exception

The plain view doctrine is about leverage. The rationale for the exception is that where police are lawfully in a private location by virtue of a warrant or an exception to the warrant requirement they may leverage that lawful position to take notice of patently incriminating evidence they observe that may not be related to the basis for their lawful presence. Officers need not avert their eyes to incriminating material, in other words.

In *Coolidge v. New Hampshire*, 403 U.S. 443 (1971), a plurality of the Court suppressed the government's evidentiary use of two automobiles that it had seized from defendant's driveway—in "plain view"—in connection with the defendant's arrest, as the incriminating character of the cars only became apparent after their interiors were searched. The Court held that the incriminating character of the evidence in plain view must be "immediately apparent" and a search cannot be artificially prolonged in the hopes of stumbling upon incriminating evidence. Among the questions that remained open after *Coolidge* were (1) what level of suspicion or cause did an officer need to justify a seizure of the incriminating item, and (2) did the discovery of the incriminating evidence have to be, as the *Coolidge* plurality stated, "inadvertent."

In *Arizona v. Hicks*, 480 U.S. 321 (1987), a police officer entered the defendant's apartment under exigent circumstances to investigate a gunshot fired from defendant's apartment into the apartment below it. Upon seeing high-end stereo equipment in the otherwise "squalid" apartment, and suspecting the equipment might be stolen, the officer took a closer look and turned the turntable over to obtain its serial number. It ultimately turned out that the turntable was stolen, a determination made possible by knowledge of the serial number. The Court found the plain view doctrine inapplicable because the officer had lacked probable cause for the search that his moving of the turntable entailed.

In the next case the Court considers whether the plain view doctrine only applies where the discovery of the incriminating evidence was "inadvertent."

Horton v. California

496 U.S. 128 (1990)

Justice STEVENS delivered the opinion of the Court.

In this case we revisit an issue that was considered, but not conclusively resolved, in *Coolidge v. New Hampshire* (1971): Whether the warrantless seizure of evidence of crime in plain view is prohibited by the Fourth Amendment if the discovery of the evidence was not inadvertent. We conclude that even though inadvertence is a characteristic of most legitimate "plain-view" seizures, it is not a necessary condition.

I

Petitioner was convicted of the armed robbery of Erwin Wallaker, the treasurer of the San Jose Coin Club. When Wallaker returned to his home after the Club's annual show, he entered his garage and was accosted by two masked men, one armed with a machine gun and the other with an electrical shocking device, sometimes referred to as a "stun gun." The two men shocked Wallaker, bound and handcuffed him, and robbed him of jewelry and cash. During the encounter sufficient conversation took place to enable Wallaker subsequently to identify petitioner's distinctive voice. His identification was partially corroborated by a witness who saw the robbers leaving the scene and by evidence that petitioner had attended the coin show.

Sergeant LaRault, an experienced police officer, investigated the crime and determined that there was probable cause to search petitioner's home for the proceeds of the robbery and for the weapons used by the robbers. His affidavit for a search warrant referred to police reports that described the weapons as well as the proceeds, but the warrant issued by the Magistrate only authorized a search for the proceeds, including three specifically described rings.

Pursuant to the warrant, LaRault searched petitioner's residence, but he did not find the stolen property. During the course of the search, however, he discovered the weapons in plain view and seized them. Specifically, he seized an Uzi machine gun, a .38-caliber revolver, two stun guns, a handcuff key, a San Jose Coin Club advertising brochure, and a few items of clothing identified by the victim. LaRault testified that while he was searching for the rings, he also was interested in finding other evidence connecting petitioner to the robbery. Thus, the seized evidence was not discovered "inadvertently."

The trial court refused to suppress the evidence found in petitioner's home and, after a jury trial, petitioner was found guilty and sentenced to prison. The California Court of Appeal affirmed. It rejected petitioner's argument that our decision in *Coolidge* required suppression of the seized evidence that had not been listed in the warrant because its discovery was not inadvertent. The court relied on the California Supreme Court's decision in *North v. Superior Court*. In that case the court noted that the discussion of the inadvertence limitation on the "plain-view" doctrine in Justice Stewart's opinion in *Coolidge* had been joined by only three other Members of this Court and therefore was not binding on it. The California Supreme Court denied petitioner's request for review.

Because the California courts' interpretation of the "plain-view" doctrine conflicts with the view of other courts and because the unresolved issue is important, we granted certiorari.

II

• • •

The criteria that generally guide "plain-view" seizures were set forth in *Coolidge v. New Hampshire* (1971). The Court held that the police, in seizing two automobiles parked in plain view on the defendant's driveway in the course of arresting the defendant, violated the Fourth Amendment. Accordingly, particles of gunpowder that had been subsequently found in vacuum sweepings from one of the cars could not be introduced in evidence against the defendant. The State endeavored to justify the seizure of the automobiles, and their subsequent search at the police station, on four different grounds, including the "plain-view" doctrine. The scope of that doctrine as it had developed in earlier cases was fairly summarized in these three paragraphs from Justice Stewart's opinion:

> It is well established that under certain circumstances the police may seize evidence in plain view without a warrant. But it is important to keep in mind that, in the vast majority of cases, any

> evidence seized by the police will be in plain view, at least at the moment of seizure. The problem with the "plain view" doctrine has been to identify the circumstances in which plain view has legal significance rather than being simply the normal concomitant of any search, legal or illegal.
>
> An example of the applicability of the "plain view" doctrine is the situation in which the police have a warrant to search a given area for specified objects, and in the course of the search come across some other article of incriminating character. Where the initial intrusion that brings the police within plain view of such an article is supported, not by a warrant, but by one of the recognized exceptions to the warrant requirement, the seizure is also legitimate. Thus the police may inadvertently come across evidence while in "hot pursuit" of a fleeing suspect. And an object that comes into view during a search incident to arrest that is appropriately limited in scope under existing law may be seized without a warrant. Finally, the "plain view" doctrine has been applied where a police officer is not searching for evidence against the accused, but nonetheless inadvertently comes across an incriminating object.
>
> What the "plain view" cases have in common is that the police officer in each of them had a prior justification for an intrusion in the course of which he came inadvertently across a piece of evidence incriminating the accused. The doctrine serves to supplement the prior justification—whether it be a warrant for another object, hot pursuit, search incident to lawful arrest, or some other legitimate reason for being present unconnected with a search directed against the accused—and permits the warrantless seizure. Of course, the extension of the original justification is legitimate only where it is immediately apparent to the police that they have evidence before them; the "plain view" doctrine may not be used to extend a general exploratory search from one object to another until something incriminating at last emerges.

Justice Stewart then described the two limitations on the doctrine that he found implicit in its rationale: First, that "plain view alone is never enough to justify the warrantless seizure of evidence," and second, that "the discovery of evidence in plain view must be inadvertent." Id., at 469.

Justice Stewart's analysis of the "plain-view" doctrine did not command a majority, and a plurality of the Court has since made clear that the discussion is "not a binding precedent." Justice Harlan, who concurred in the Court's judgment and in its response to the dissenting opinions, did not join the plurality's discussion of the "plain-view" doctrine. The decision nonetheless is a binding precedent. Before discussing the second limitation, which is implicated in this case, it is therefore necessary to explain why the first adequately supports the Court's judgment.

It is, of course, an essential predicate to any valid warrantless seizure of incriminating evidence that the officer did not violate the Fourth Amendment in arriving at the place from which the evidence could be plainly viewed. There are, moreover, two additional conditions that must be satisfied to justify the warrantless seizure. First, not only must the item be in plain view; its incriminating character must also be "immediately apparent." Thus, in *Coolidge*, the cars were obviously in plain view, but their probative value remained uncertain until after the interiors were swept and examined microscopically. Second, not only must the officer be lawfully located in a place from which the object can be plainly seen, but he or she must also have a lawful right of access to the object itself. As the United States has suggested, Justice Harlan's vote in *Coolidge* may have rested on the fact that the seizure of the cars was accomplished by means of a warrantless trespass on the defendant's property. In all events, we are satisfied that the absence of inadvertence was not essential to the Court's rejection of the State's "plain-view" argument in *Coolidge.*

III

Justice Stewart concluded that the inadvertence requirement was necessary to avoid a violation of the express constitutional requirement that a valid warrant must particularly describe the things to be seized. He explained:

> The rationale of the exception to the warrant requirement, as just stated, is that a plain-view seizure will not turn an initially valid (and therefore limited) search into a "general" one, while

> the inconvenience of procuring a warrant to cover an inadvertent discovery is great. But where the discovery is anticipated, where the police know in advance the location of the evidence and intend to seize it, the situation is altogether different. The requirement of a warrant to seize imposes no inconvenience whatever, or at least none which is constitutionally cognizable in a legal system that regards warrantless searches as "per se unreasonable" in the absence of "exigent circumstances."
>
> If the initial intrusion is bottomed upon a warrant that fails to mention a particular object, though the police know its location and intend to seize it, then there is a violation of the express constitutional requirement of "Warrants . . . particularly describing . . . [the] things to be seized.

We find two flaws in this reasoning. First, evenhanded law enforcement is best achieved by the application of objective standards of conduct, rather than standards that depend upon the subjective state of mind of the officer. The fact that an officer is interested in an item of evidence and fully expects to find it in the course of a search should not invalidate its seizure if the search is confined in area and duration by the terms of a warrant or a valid exception to the warrant requirement. If the officer has knowledge approaching certainty that the item will be found, we see no reason why he or she would deliberately omit a particular description of the item to be seized from the application for a search warrant. Specification of the additional item could only permit the officer to expand the scope of the search. On the other hand, if he or she has a valid warrant to search for one item and merely a suspicion concerning the second, whether or not it amounts to probable cause, we fail to see why that suspicion should immunize the second item from seizure if it is found during a lawful search for the first. The hypothetical case put by Justice White in his concurring and dissenting opinion in *Coolidge* is instructive:

> Let us suppose officers secure a warrant to search a house for a rifle. While staying well within the range of a rifle search, they discover two photographs of the murder victim, both in plain sight in the bedroom. Assume also that the discovery of the one photograph was inadvertent but finding the other was anticipated. The Court would permit the seizure of only one of the photographs. But in terms of the "minor" peril to Fourth Amendment values there is surely no difference between these two photographs: the interference with possession is the same in each case and the officers' appraisal of the photograph they expected to see is no less reliable than their judgment about the other. And in both situations the actual inconvenience and danger to evidence remain identical if the officers must depart and secure a warrant.

Second, the suggestion that the inadvertence requirement is necessary to prevent the police from conducting general searches, or from converting specific warrants into general warrants, is not persuasive because that interest is already served by the requirements that no warrant issue unless it "particularly describ[es] the place to be searched and the persons or things to be seized." Scrupulous adherence to these requirements serves the interests in limiting the area and duration of the search that the inadvertence requirement inadequately protects. Once those commands have been satisfied and the officer has a lawful right of access, however, no additional Fourth Amendment interest is furthered by requiring that the discovery of evidence be inadvertent. If the scope of the search exceeds that permitted by the terms of a validly issued warrant or the character of the relevant exception from the warrant requirement, the subsequent seizure is unconstitutional without more. Thus, in the case of a search incident to a lawful arrest, "[i]f the police stray outside the scope of an authorized *Chimel* search they are already in violation of the Fourth Amendment, and evidence so seized will be excluded; adding a second reason for excluding evidence hardly seems worth the candle." Similarly, the object of a warrantless search of an automobile also defines its scope:

> The scope of a warrantless search of an automobile thus is not defined by the nature of the container in which the contraband is secreted. Rather, it is defined by the object of the search and the places in which there is probable cause to believe that it may be found. Just as probable

> cause to believe that a stolen lawnmower may be found in a garage will not support a warrant to search an upstairs bedroom, probable cause to believe that undocumented aliens are being transported in a van will not justify a warrantless search of a suitcase. Probable cause to believe that a container placed in the trunk of a taxi contains contraband or evidence does not justify a search of the entire cab.

In this case, the scope of the search was not enlarged in the slightest by the omission of any reference to the weapons in the warrant. Indeed, if the three rings and other items named in the warrant had been found at the outset—or if petitioner had them in his possession and had responded to the warrant by producing them immediately—no search for weapons could have taken place. Again, Justice White's concurring and dissenting opinion in *Coolidge* is instructive:

> Police with a warrant for a rifle may search only places where rifles might be and must terminate the search once the rifle is found; the inadvertence rule will in no way reduce the number of places into which they may lawfully look.

As we have already suggested, by hypothesis the seizure of an object in plain view does not involve an intrusion on privacy. If the interest in privacy has been invaded, the violation must have occurred before the object came into plain view and there is no need for an inadvertence limitation on seizures to condemn it. The prohibition against general searches and general warrants serves primarily as a protection against unjustified intrusions on privacy. But reliance on privacy concerns that support that prohibition is misplaced when the inquiry concerns the scope of an exception that merely authorizes an officer with a lawful right of access to an item to seize it without a warrant.

In this case the items seized from petitioner's home were discovered during a lawful search authorized by a valid warrant. When they were discovered, it was immediately apparent to the officer that they constituted incriminating evidence. He had probable cause, not only to obtain a warrant to search for the stolen property, but also to believe that the weapons and handguns had been used in the crime he was investigating. The search was authorized by the warrant; the seizure was authorized by the "plain-view" doctrine. The judgment is affirmed.

NOTES AND QUESTIONS

1. Are you curious as to why Sergeant LaRault was able to obtain a search warrant only for the "proceeds" of the robbery and not for the weapons used in the robbery, not even the comparatively rare (and thus specific) "stun gun"? Do you think the robbery victim was probably better able to particularly describe the items he was dispossessed of than the weapons used in the robbery?

2. The officer honestly testified at the suppression hearing that in executing the search warrant he was looking not just for what the warrant authorized but also for other evidence pertaining to the robbery. Suppose you were the assistant district attorney in charge of this prosecution and that you had been involved not only in the suppression hearing but also the obtaining of the warrant. How would you have advised Sergeant LaRault about his execution of the warrant (if he had asked) bearing in mind (a) the "half a loaf" nature of the warrant and (b) the uncertainty of *Coolidge*'s "inadvertence" requirement? How would you have prepared him for the suppression hearing on this issue?

3. What is the relevance of the fact that Officer LaRault did not seize other guns that were also in plain view?

4. Do you believe the incriminating character of the handcuff key was immediately apparent? Do you think it was immediately apparent that it was a handcuff key?

5. What if Officer LaRault had observed a clear baggie containing a white powdery substance on the kitchen table? In the bathroom on the sink?

6. What do you think of the dissent's argument that eliminating the "inadvertence" requirement gives the police an incentive to hold back information in applying for a warrant?

3. Warrantless Arrests

An arrest is the quintessential seizure under the Fourth Amendment. An arrest is not only a substantial curtailment of freedom in itself—an arrestee does not have to be brought before a judicial officer for consideration of bail for 48 hours, *County of Riverside v. McLaughlin*, 500 U.S. 44 (1991)—but it is the first step in a prosecution that may result in a further and substantially more extreme deprivation of liberty. Even more consequential to the arrestee in many cases are the further invasions of freedom that are occasioned and legitimated by an arrest: searches of the arrestee's person and immediate surroundings, sometimes including the arrestee's vehicle, as "incident" to the arrest.

Yet warrantless arrests are not really an "exception" to the warrant requirement inasmuch as there has never been any such uniform requirement. *Carroll v. United States*, 267 U.S. 132 (1925), described the common law: "The usual rule is that a police officer may arrest without warrant one believed by the officer upon reasonable cause to have been guilty of a felony. . . ." This was confirmed to still be good law 50 years later in *United States v. Watson*, 423 U.S. 41 (1976), where the Court held that where probable cause exists a warrantless arrest of a suspect in a public place on a felony charge was constitutional, despite the lack of exigency, at least where—as in *Watson*—such an arrest was authorized by a federal statute. The probable cause requirement for an arrest was absolute, however. A person could not be detained for questioning—even if given *Miranda* warnings—under circumstances similar to an arrest without probable cause. *Dunaway v. New York*, 442 U.S. 200, 208 (1979).

Statutory authority for an arrest is not a silver bullet, though. In the next case, *Payton v. New York*, 445 U.S. 573 (1980), the Court held that probable cause to arrest did not justify the warrantless entry of the suspect's home absent exigent circumstances, notwithstanding a New York statute authorizing such an arrest. Another case of "home exceptionalism"?

Payton v. New York

445 U.S. 573 (1980)

Mr. Justice Stevens delivered the opinion of the Court.

These appeals challenge the constitutionality of New York statutes that authorize police officers to enter a private residence without a warrant and with force, if necessary, to make a routine felony arrest.

The important constitutional question presented by this challenge has been expressly left open in a number of our prior opinions. In *United States v. Watson*, we upheld a warrantless "midday public arrest," expressly noting that the case did not pose "the still unsettled question . . . 'whether and under what circumstances an officer may enter a suspect's home to make a warrantless arrest.'" The question has been answered in different ways by other appellate courts. The Supreme Court of Florida rejected the constitutional attack, as did the New York Court of Appeals in this case. The courts of last resort in 10 other States, however, have held that unless special circumstances are present, warrantless arrests in the home are unconstitutional. Of the seven United States Courts of Appeals that have considered the question, five have expressed the opinion that such arrests are unconstitutional.

Last Term we noted probable jurisdiction of these appeals in order to address that question. After hearing oral argument, we set the case for reargument this Term. We now reverse the New York Court of Appeals and hold that the Fourth Amendment to the United States Constitution, made applicable to the States by the Fourteenth Amendment, prohibits the police from making a warrantless and nonconsensual entry into a suspect's home in order to make a routine felony arrest.

We first state the facts of both cases in some detail and put to one side certain related questions that are not presented by these records. We then explain why the New York statutes are not consistent with the Fourth Amendment and why the reasons for upholding warrantless arrests in a public place do not apply to warrantless invasions of the privacy of the home.

I

On January 14, 1970, after two days of intensive investigation, New York detectives had assembled evidence sufficient to establish probable cause to believe that Theodore Payton had murdered the manager of a gas station two days earlier. At about 7:30 a. m. on January 15, six officers went to Payton's apartment in the Bronx, intending to arrest him. They had not obtained a warrant. Although light and music emanated from the apartment, there was no response to their knock on the metal door. They summoned emergency assistance and, about 30 minutes later, used crowbars to break open the door and enter the apartment. No one was there. In plain view, however, was a .30-caliber shell casing that was seized and later admitted into evidence at Payton's murder trial.

In due course Payton surrendered to the police, was indicted for murder, and moved to suppress the evidence taken from his apartment. The trial judge held that the warrantless and forcible entry was authorized by the New York Code of Criminal Procedure, and that the evidence in plain view was properly seized. He found that exigent circumstances justified the officers' failure to announce their purpose before entering the apartment as required by the statute. He had no occasion, however, to decide whether those circumstances also would have justified the failure to obtain a warrant, because he concluded that the warrantless entry was adequately supported by the statute without regard to the circumstances. The Appellate Division, First Department, summarily affirmed.

On March 14, 1974, Obie Riddick was arrested for the commission of two armed robberies that had occurred in 1971. He had been identified by the victims in June 1973, and in January 1974 the police had learned his address. They did not obtain a warrant for his arrest. At about noon on March 14, a detective, accompanied by three other officers, knocked on the door of the Queens house where Riddick was living. When his young son opened the door, they could see Riddick sitting in bed covered by a sheet. They entered the house and placed him under arrest. Before permitting him to dress, they opened a chest of drawers two feet from the bed in search of weapons and found narcotics and related paraphernalia. Riddick was subsequently indicted on narcotics charges. At a suppression hearing, the trial judge held that the warrantless entry into his home was authorized by the revised New York statute, and that the search of the immediate area was reasonable under *Chimel v. California*. The Appellate Division, Second Department, affirmed the denial of the suppression motion.

The New York Court of Appeals, in a single opinion, affirmed the convictions of both Payton and Riddick. The court recognized that the question whether and under what circumstances an officer may enter a suspect's home to make a warrantless arrest had not been settled either by that court or by this Court. In answering that question, the majority of four judges relied primarily on its perception that there is a

> . . . substantial difference between the intrusion which attends an entry for the purpose of searching the premises and that which results from an entry for the purpose of making an

> arrest, and [a] significant difference in the governmental interest in achieving the objective of the intrusion in the two instances.

The majority supported its holding by noting the "apparent historical acceptance" of warrantless entries to make felony arrests, both in the English common law and in the practice of many American States.

Three members of the New York Court of Appeals dissented on this issue because they believed that the Constitution requires the police to obtain a "warrant to enter a home in order to arrest or seize a person, unless there are exigent circumstances." Starting from the premise that, except in carefully circumscribed instances, "the Fourth Amendment forbids police entry into a private home to search for and seize an object without a warrant," the dissenters reasoned that an arrest of the person involves an even greater invasion of privacy and should therefore be attended with at least as great a measure of constitutional protection. The dissenters noted "the existence of statutes and the American Law Institute imprimatur codifying the common-law rule authorizing warrantless arrests in private homes" and acknowledged that "the statutory authority of a police officer to make a warrantless arrest in this State has been in effect for almost 100 years," but concluded that "neither antiquity nor legislative unanimity can be determinative of the grave constitutional question presented" and "can never be a substitute for reasoned analysis."

Before addressing the narrow question presented by these appeals, we put to one side other related problems that are not presented today. Although it is arguable that the warrantless entry to effect Payton's arrest might have been justified by exigent circumstances, none of the New York courts relied on any such justification. The Court of Appeals majority treated both Payton's and Riddick's cases as involving routine arrests in which there was ample time to obtain a warrant, and we will do the same. Accordingly, we have no occasion to consider the sort of emergency or dangerous situation, described in our cases as "exigent circumstances," that would justify a warrantless entry into a home for the purpose of either arrest or search.

Nor do these cases raise any question concerning the authority of the police, without either a search or arrest warrant, to enter a third party's home to arrest a suspect. The police broke into Payton's apartment intending to arrest Payton, and they arrested Riddick in his own dwelling. We also note that in neither case is it argued that the police lacked probable cause to believe that the suspect was at home when they entered. Finally, in both cases we are dealing with entries into homes made without the consent of any occupant. In *Payton*, the police used crowbars to break down the door and in *Riddick*, although his 3-year-old son answered the door, the police entered before Riddick had an opportunity either to object or to consent.

II

It is familiar history that indiscriminate searches and seizures conducted under the authority of "general warrants" were the immediate evils that motivated the framing and adoption of the Fourth Amendment. Indeed, as originally proposed in the House of Representatives, the draft contained only one clause, which directly imposed limitations on the issuance of warrants, but imposed no express restrictions on warrantless searches or seizures. As it was ultimately adopted, however, the Amendment contained two separate clauses, the first protecting the basic right to be free from unreasonable searches and seizures and the second requiring that warrants be particular and supported by probable cause. The Amendment provides:

> The right of the people to be secure in their persons, houses, papers, and effects, against unreasonable searches and seizures, shall not be violated, and no Warrants shall issue, but upon probable cause, supported by Oath or affirmation, and particularly describing the place to be searched, and the persons or things to be seized.

It is thus perfectly clear that the evil the Amendment was designed to prevent was broader than the abuse of a general warrant. Unreasonable searches or seizures conducted without any warrant at all are condemned by the plain language of the first clause of the Amendment. Almost a century ago the Court stated in resounding terms that the principles reflected in the Amendment "reached farther than the concrete form" of the specific cases that gave it birth, and "apply to all invasions on the part of the government and its employees of the sanctity of a man's home and the privacies of life." Without pausing to consider whether that broad language may require some qualification, it is sufficient to note that the warrantless arrest of a person is a species of seizure required by the Amendment to be reasonable. Indeed, as Mr. Justice Powell noted in his concurrence in *United States v. Watson*, the arrest of a person is "quintessentially a seizure."

The simple language of the Amendment applies equally to seizures of persons and to seizures of property. Our analysis in this case may therefore properly commence with rules that have been well established in Fourth Amendment litigation involving tangible items. As the Court reiterated just a few years ago, the "physical entry of the home is the chief evil against which the wording of the Fourth Amendment is directed. And we have long adhered to the view that the warrant procedure minimizes the danger of needless intrusions of that sort.

It is a "basic principle of Fourth Amendment law" that searches and seizures inside a home without a warrant are presumptively unreasonable. Yet it is also well settled that objects such as weapons or contraband found in a public place may be seized by the police without a warrant. The seizure of property in plain view involves no invasion of privacy and is presumptively reasonable, assuming that there is probable cause to associate the property with criminal activity. The distinction between a warrantless seizure in an open area and such a seizure on private premises was plainly stated in *G. M. Leasing Corp. v. United States*:

> It is one thing to seize without a warrant property resting in an open area or seizable by levy without an intrusion into privacy, and it is quite another thing to effect a warrantless seizure of property, even that owned by a corporation, situated on private premises to which access is not otherwise available for the seizing officer.

As the late Judge Leventhal recognized, this distinction has equal force when the seizure of a person is involved. Writing on the constitutional issue now before us for the United States Court of Appeals for the District of Columbia Circuit sitting en banc, Judge Leventhal first noted the settled rule that warrantless arrests in public places are valid. He immediately recognized, however, that

> [a] greater burden is placed . . . on officials who enter a home or dwelling without consent. Freedom from intrusion into the home or dwelling is the archetype of the privacy protection secured by the Fourth Amendment.

His analysis of this question then focused on the long-settled premise that, absent exigent circumstances, a warrantless entry to search for weapons or contraband is unconstitutional even when a felony has been committed and there is probable cause to believe that incriminating evidence will be found within. He reasoned that the constitutional protection afforded to the individual's interest in the privacy of his own home is equally applicable to a warrantless entry for the purpose of arresting a resident of the house; for it is inherent in such an entry that a search for the suspect may be required before he can be apprehended. Judge Leventhal concluded that an entry to arrest and an entry to search for and to seize property implicate the same interest in preserving the privacy and the sanctity of the home, and justify the same level of constitutional protection.

This reasoning has been followed in other Circuits. Thus, the Second Circuit recently summarized its position:

> To be arrested in the home involves not only the invasion attendant to all arrests but also an invasion of the sanctity of the home. This is simply too substantial an invasion to allow without a warrant, at least in the absence of exigent circumstances, even when it is accomplished under statutory authority and when probable cause is clearly present.

We find this reasoning to be persuasive and in accord with this Court's Fourth Amendment decisions.

The majority of the New York Court of Appeals, however, suggested that there is a substantial difference in the relative intrusiveness of an entry to search for property and an entry to search for a person. It is true that the area that may legally be searched is broader when executing a search warrant than when executing an arrest warrant in the home. This difference may be more theoretical than real, however, because the police may need to check the entire premises for safety reasons, and sometimes they ignore the restrictions on searches incident to arrest.

But the critical point is that any differences in the intrusiveness of entries to search and entries to arrest are merely ones of degree rather than kind. The two intrusions share this fundamental characteristic: the breach of the entrance to an individual's home. The Fourth Amendment protects the individual's privacy in a variety of settings. In none is the zone of privacy more clearly defined than when bounded by the unambiguous physical dimensions of an individual's home—a zone that finds its roots in clear and specific constitutional terms: "The right of the people to be secure in their . . . houses . . . shall not be violated." That language unequivocally establishes the proposition that "[a]t the very core [of the Fourth Amendment] stands the right of a man to retreat into his own home and there be free from unreasonable governmental intrusion." In terms that apply equally to seizures of property and to seizures of persons, the Fourth Amendment has drawn a firm line at the entrance to the house. Absent exigent circumstances, that threshold may not reasonably be crossed without a warrant.

III

Without contending that *United States v. Watson* decided the question presented by these appeals, New York argues that the reasons that support the *Watson* holding require a similar result here. In *Watson* the Court relied on (a) the well-settled common-law rule that a warrantless arrest in a public place is valid if the arresting officer had probable cause to believe the suspect is a felon; (b) the clear consensus among the States adhering to that well-settled common-law rule; and (c) the expression of the judgment of Congress that such an arrest is "reasonable." We consider each of these reasons as it applies to a warrantless entry into a home for the purpose of making a routine felony arrest.

A

An examination of the common-law understanding of an officer's authority to arrest sheds light on the obviously relevant, if not entirely dispositive, consideration of what the Framers of the Amendment might have thought to be reasonable. Initially, it should be noted that the common-law rules of arrest developed in legal contexts that substantially differ from the cases now before us. In these cases, which involve application of the exclusionary rule, the issue is whether certain evidence is admissible at trial. At common law, the question whether an arrest was authorized typically arose in civil damages actions for trespass or false arrest, in which a constable's authority to make the arrest was a defense. Additionally, if an officer was killed while attempting to effect an arrest, the question whether the person resisting the arrest was guilty of murder or manslaughter turned on whether the officer was acting within the bounds of his authority.

A study of the common law on the question whether a constable had the authority to make warrantless arrests in the home on mere suspicion of a felony—as distinguished from an officer's right to arrest for a crime committed in his presence—reveals a surprising lack of judicial decisions and a deep divergence among scholars.

The most cited evidence of the common-law rule consists of an equivocal dictum in a case actually involving the sheriff's authority to enter a home to effect service of civil process. In *Semayne's Case*, the Court stated:

> In all cases when the King is party, the Sheriff (if the doors be not open) may break the party's house, either to arrest him, or to do other execution of the K.'s process, if otherwise he cannot enter. But before he breaks it, he ought to signify the cause of his coming, and to make request to open doors; and that appears well by the stat. of Westm. 1. c. 17. (which it but an affirmance of the common law) as hereafter appears, for the law without a default in the owner abhors the destruction or breaking of any house (which is for the habitation and safety of man) by which great damage and inconvenience might ensue to the party, when no default is in him; for perhaps he did not know of the process, of which, if he had notice, it is to be presumed that he would obey it, and that appears by the book in 18 E. 2. Execut. 252. where it is said, that the K.'s officer who comes to do execution, &c. may open the doors which are shut, and break them, if he cannot have the keys; which proves, that he ought first to demand them, 7 E. 3.16. (Footnotes omitted.)

This passage has been read by some as describing an entry without a warrant. The context strongly implies, however, that the court was describing the extent of authority in executing the King's writ. This reading is confirmed by the phrase "either to arrest him, or to do other execution of the K.'s process" and by the further point that notice was necessary because the owner may "not know of the process." In any event, the passage surely cannot be said unambiguously to endorse warrantless entries.

The common-law commentators disagreed sharply on the subject. Three distinct views were expressed. Lord Coke, widely recognized by the American colonists "as the greatest authority of his time on the laws of England," clearly viewed a warrantless entry for the purpose of arrest to be illegal. Burn, Foster, and Hawkins agreed, as did East and Russell, though the latter two qualified their opinions by stating that if an entry to arrest was made without a warrant, the officer was perhaps immune from liability for the trespass if the suspect was actually guilty. Blackstone, Chitty, and Stephen took the opposite view, that entry to arrest without a warrant was legal, though Stephen relied on Blackstone who, along with Chitty, in turn relied exclusively on Hale. But Hale's view was not quite so unequivocally expressed. Further, Hale appears to rely solely on a statement in an early Yearbook, quoted in *Burdett v. Abbot*:

> that for felony, or suspicion of felony, a man may break open the house to take the felon; for it is for the commonweal to take them.

Considering the diversity of views just described, however, it is clear that the statement was never deemed authoritative. Indeed, in *Burdett*, the statement was described as an "extrajudicial opinion."

It is obvious that the common-law rule on warrantless home arrests was not as clear as the rule on arrests in public places. Indeed, particularly considering the prominence of Lord Coke, the weight of authority as it appeared to the Framers was to the effect that a warrant was required, or at the minimum that there were substantial risks in proceeding without one. The common-law sources display a sensitivity to privacy interests that could not have been lost on the Framers. The zealous and frequent repetition of the adage that a "man's house is his castle," made it abundantly clear that both in England and in the Colonies "the freedom of one's house" was one of the most vital elements of English liberty.

Thus, our study of the relevant common law does not provide the same guidance that was present in *Watson*. Whereas the rule concerning the validity of an arrest in a public place was supported by cases directly in point and by the unanimous views of the commentators, we have found no direct authority supporting forcible entries into a home to make a routine arrest and the weight of the scholarly opinion is somewhat to the contrary. Indeed, the absence of any 17th- or 18th-century English cases directly in point, together with the unequivocal endorsement of the tenet that "a man's house is his castle," strongly suggests that the prevailing practice was not to make such arrests except in hot pursuit or when authorized by a warrant. In all events, the issue is not one that can be said to have been definitively settled by the common law at the time the Fourth Amendment was adopted.

B

A majority of the States that have taken a position on the question permit warrantless entry into the home to arrest even in the absence of exigent circumstances. At this time, 24 States permit such warrantless entries; 15 States clearly prohibit them, though 3 States do so on federal constitutional grounds alone; and 11 States have apparently taken no position on the question.

But these current figures reflect a significant decline during the last decade in the number of States permitting warrantless entries for arrest. Recent dicta in this Court raising questions about the practice, and Federal Courts of Appeals' decisions on point, have led state courts to focus on the issue. Virtually all of the state courts that have had to confront the constitutional issue directly have held warrantless entries into the home to arrest to be invalid in the absence of exigent circumstances. Three state courts have relied on Fourth Amendment grounds alone, while seven have squarely placed their decisions on both federal and state constitutional grounds. A number of other state courts, though not having had to confront the issue directly, have recognized the serious nature of the constitutional question. Apparently, only the Supreme Court of Florida and the New York Court of Appeals in this case have expressly upheld warrantless entries to arrest in the face of a constitutional challenge.

A longstanding, widespread practice is not immune from constitutional scrutiny. But neither is it to be lightly brushed aside. This is particularly so when the constitutional standard is as amorphous as the word "reasonable," and when custom and contemporary norms necessarily play such a large role in the constitutional analysis. In this case, although the weight of state-law authority is clear, there is by no means the kind of virtual unanimity on this question that was present in *United States v. Watson*, with regard to warrantless arrests in public places. Only 24 of the 50 States currently sanction warrantless entries into the home to arrest, and there is an obvious declining trend. Further, the strength of the trend is greater than the numbers alone indicate. Seven state courts have recently held that warrantless home arrests violate their respective State Constitutions. That is significant because by invoking a state constitutional provision, a state court immunizes its decision from review by this Court. This heightened degree of immutability underscores the depth of the principle underlying the result.

C

No congressional determination that warrantless entries into the home are "reasonable" has been called to our attention. None of the federal statutes cited in the Watson opinion reflects any such legislative judgment. Thus, that support for the *Watson* holding finds no counterpart in this case.

Mr. Justice Powell, concurring in *United States v. Watson*, stated:

> But logic sometimes must defer to history and experience. The Court's opinion emphasizes the historical sanction accorded warrantless felony arrests [in public places].

In this case, however, neither history nor this Nation's experience requires us to disregard the overriding respect for the sanctity of the home that has been embedded in our traditions since the origins of the Republic.

IV

The parties have argued at some length about the practical consequences of a warrant requirement as a precondition to a felony arrest in the home. In the absence of any evidence that effective law enforcement has suffered in those States that already have such a requirement, we are inclined to view such arguments with skepticism. More fundamentally, however, such arguments of policy must give way to a constitutional command that we consider to be unequivocal.

Finally, we note the State's suggestion that only a search warrant based on probable cause to believe the suspect is at home at a given time can adequately protect the privacy interests at stake, and since such a warrant requirement is manifestly impractical, there need be no warrant of any kind. We find this ingenious argument unpersuasive. It is true that an arrest warrant requirement may afford less protection than a search warrant requirement, but it will suffice to interpose the magistrate's determination of probable cause between the zealous officer and the citizen. If there is sufficient evidence of a citizen's participation in a felony to persuade a judicial officer that his arrest is justified, it is constitutionally reason able to require him to open his doors to the officers of the law. Thus, for Fourth Amendment purposes, an arrest warrant founded on probable cause implicitly carries with it the limited authority to enter a dwelling in which the suspect lives when there is reason to believe the suspect is within.

Because no arrest warrant was obtained in either of these cases, the judgments must be reversed and the cases remanded to the New York Court of Appeals for further proceedings not inconsistent with this opinion.

It is so ordered.

NOTES AND QUESTIONS

1. The police officers who arrested Payton and Reddick did not bother to get arrest warrants, presumably because they were relying on the New York statute that authorized officers to enter a private residence, without a warrant, to effectuate an arrest. Were there any obstacles to them getting a warrant on these facts? Could they demonstrate probable cause?

2. The Court notes that no congressional legislation appears to authorize a warrantless entry into a home to effectuate an arrest. What difference would such legislation make? Is the result in *Payton* not required by the Constitution? Could Congress statutorily override *Payton*?

3. The New York Court of Appeals found a substantial difference between the intrusiveness of the entry of a home to search for property and an entry to make an arrest. Is the Court's response to this point—that the difference is more theoretical than real because police may ignore the constitutional limits on searches incident to arrest—satisfactory?

4. It is clear from *Payton* that an arrest warrant authorizes police to enter, by force if necessary, the home of the subject of the warrant to effectuate an arrest. What about the home of a third party, where police have probable cause to believe the subject is in that home? The Supreme Court confronted this question the year after *Payton* in *Steagald v. United States*, 451 U.S. 204 (1981), where DEA agents, armed with an arrest warrant for one Lyons, believed him to be in Steagald's home. Without obtaining a search warrant or consent, and in the absence of exigent circumstances, the agents entered the home and discovered cocaine belonging to Steagald but not Lyons. *Id.* at 206. The Court reversed the conviction because the arrest warrant for a third party was insufficient to protect Steagald's Fourth Amendment privacy interests. *Id.* at 212.

The next case — on extreme facts — considers whether the Fourth Amendment prohibits a warrantless arrest on a misdemeanor charge.

Atwater v. City of Lago Vista

532 U.S. 318 (2001)

Justice Souter delivered the opinion of the Court.

The question is whether the Fourth Amendment forbids a warrantless arrest for a minor criminal offense, such as a misdemeanor seatbelt violation punishable only by a fine. We hold that it does not.

I

A

In Texas, if a car is equipped with safety belts, a front-seat passenger must wear one, and the driver must secure any small child riding in front. Violation of either provision is "a misdemeanor punishable by a fine not less than $25 or more than $50." Texas law expressly authorizes "[a]ny peace officer [to] arrest without warrant a person found committing a violation" of these seatbelt laws, although it permits police to issue citations in lieu of arrest.

In March 1997, petitioner Gail Atwater was driving her pickup truck in Lago Vista, Texas, with her 3-year-old son and 5-year-old daughter in the front seat. None of them was wearing a seatbelt. Respondent Bart Turek, a Lago Vista police officer at the time, observed the seatbelt violations and pulled Atwater over. According to Atwater's complaint (the allegations of which we assume to be true for present purposes), Turek approached the truck and "yell[ed]" something to the effect of "[w]e've met before" and "[y]ou're going to jail." He then called for backup and asked to see Atwater's driver's license and insurance documentation, which state law required her to carry. When Atwater told Turek that she did not have the papers because her purse had been stolen the day before, Turek said that he had "heard that story two-hundred times."

Atwater asked to take her "frightened, upset, and crying" children to a friend's house nearby, but Turek told her, "[y]ou're not going anywhere." As it turned out, Atwater's friend learned what was going on and soon arrived to take charge of the children. Turek then handcuffed Atwater, placed her in his squad car, and drove her to the local police station, where booking officers had her remove her shoes, jewelry, and eyeglasses, and empty her pockets. Officers took Atwater's "mug shot" and placed her, alone, in a jail cell for about one hour, after which she was taken before a magistrate and released on $310 bond.

Atwater was charged with driving without her seatbelt fastened, failing to secure her children in seatbelts, driving without a license, and failing to provide proof of insurance. She ultimately pleaded no contest to the misdemeanor seatbelt offenses and paid a $50 fine; the other charges were dismissed.

B

Atwater and her husband, petitioner Michael Haas, filed suit in a Texas state court under 42 U.S.C. § 1983 against Turek and respondents City of Lago Vista and Chief of Police Frank Miller. So far as concerns us, petitioners (whom we will simply call Atwater) alleged that respondents (for simplicity, the City) had violated Atwater's Fourth Amendment "right to be free from unreasonable seizure," and sought compensatory and punitive damages.

• • •

We granted certiorari to consider whether the Fourth Amendment, either by incorporating common-law restrictions on misdemeanor arrests or otherwise, limits police officers' authority to arrest without warrant for minor criminal offenses. We now affirm.

• • •

III

While it is true here that history, if not unequivocal, has expressed a decided, majority view that the police need not obtain an arrest warrant merely because a misdemeanor stopped short of violence or a threat of it, Atwater does not wager all on history. Instead, she asks us to mint a new rule of constitutional law on the understanding that when historical practice fails to speak conclusively to a claim grounded on the Fourth Amendment, courts are left to strike a current balance between individual and societal interests by subjecting particular contemporary circumstances to traditional standards of reasonableness. Atwater accordingly argues for a modern arrest rule, one not necessarily requiring violent breach of the peace, but nonetheless forbidding custodial arrest, even upon probable cause, when conviction could not ultimately carry any jail time and when the government shows no compelling need for immediate detention.

If we were to derive a rule exclusively to address the uncontested facts of this case, Atwater might well prevail. She was a known and established resident of Lago Vista with no place to hide and no incentive to flee, and common sense says she would almost certainly have buckled up as a condition of driving off with a citation. In her case, the physical incidents of arrest were merely gratuitous humiliations imposed by a police officer who was (at best) exercising extremely poor judgment. Atwater's claim to live free of pointless indignity and confinement clearly outweighs anything the City can raise against it specific to her case.

But we have traditionally recognized that a responsible Fourth Amendment balance is not well served by standards requiring sensitive, case-by-case determinations of government need, lest every discretionary judgment in the field be converted into an occasion for constitutional review. Often enough, the Fourth Amendment has to be applied on the spur (and in the heat) of the moment, and the object in implementing its command of reasonableness is to draw standards sufficiently clear and simple to be applied with a fair prospect of surviving judicial second-guessing months and years after an arrest or search is made. Courts attempting to strike a reasonable Fourth Amendment balance thus credit the government's side with an essential interest in readily administrable rules.

At first glance, Atwater's argument may seem to respect the values of clarity and simplicity, so far as she claims that the Fourth Amendment generally forbids warrantless arrests for minor crimes not accompanied by violence or some demonstrable threat of it (whether "minor crime" be defined as a fine-only traffic offense, a fine-only offense more generally, or a misdemeanor.) But the claim is not ultimately so simple, nor could it be, for complications arise the moment we begin to think about the possible applications of the several criteria Atwater proposes for drawing a line between minor crimes with limited arrest authority and others not so restricted.

One line, she suggests, might be between "jailable" and "fine-only" offenses, between those for which conviction could result in commitment and those for which it could not. The trouble with this distinction, of course, is that an officer on the street might not be able to tell. It is not merely that we cannot expect every police officer to know the details of frequently complex penalty schemes, but that penalties for ostensibly identical conduct can vary on account of facts difficult (if not impossible) to know at the scene of an arrest. Is this the first offense or is the suspect a repeat offender? Is the weight of the marijuana a gram above or a gram below the fine-only line? Where conduct could implicate more than one criminal prohibition, which one will the district attorney ultimately decide to charge? And so on.

But Atwater's refinements would not end there. She represents that if the line were drawn at nonjailable traffic offenses, her proposed limitation should be qualified by a proviso authorizing warrantless arrests where "necessary for enforcement of the traffic laws or when [an] offense would otherwise continue and pose a danger to others on the road." The proviso only compounds the difficulties. Would, for instance, either exception apply to speeding? At oral argument, Atwater's counsel said that "it would not be reasonable to arrest a driver for speeding unless the speeding rose to the level of reckless driving." But is it not fair to expect that the chronic speeder will speed again despite a citation in his pocket, and should that not qualify as showing that the "offense would . . . continue" under Atwater's rule? And why, as a constitutional matter, should we assume that only reckless driving will "pose a danger to others on the road" while speeding will not?

There is no need for more examples to show that Atwater's general rule and limiting proviso promise very little in the way of administrability. It is no answer that the police routinely make judgments on grounds like risk of immediate repetition; they surely do and should. But there is a world of difference between making that judgment in choosing between the discretionary leniency of a summons in place of a clearly lawful arrest, and making the same judgment when the question is the lawfulness of the warrantless arrest itself. It is the difference between no basis for legal action challenging the discretionary judgment, on the one hand, and the prospect of evidentiary exclusion or (as here) personal § 1983 liability for the misapplication of a constitutional standard, on the other. Atwater's rule therefore would not only place police in an almost impossible spot but would guarantee increased litigation over many of the arrests that would occur. For all these reasons, Atwater's various distinctions between permissible and impermissible arrests for minor crimes strike us as "very unsatisfactory line[s]" to require police officers to draw on a moment's notice.

One may ask, of course, why these difficulties may not be answered by a simple tie breaker for the police to follow in the field: if in doubt, do not arrest. The first answer is that in practice the tie breaker would boil down to something akin to a least-restrictive-alternative limitation, which is itself one of those "ifs, ands, and buts" rules, generally thought inappropriate in working out Fourth Amendment protection. Beyond that, whatever help the tie breaker might give would come at the price of a systematic disincentive to arrest in situations where even Atwater concedes that arresting would serve an important societal interest. An officer not quite sure that the drugs weighed enough to warrant jail time or not quite certain about a suspect's risk of flight would not arrest, even though it could perfectly well turn out that, in fact, the offense called for incarceration and the defendant was long gone on the day of trial. Multiplied many times over, the costs to society of such underenforcement could easily outweigh the costs to defendants of being needlessly arrested and booked, as Atwater herself acknowledges.

Just how easily the costs could outweigh the benefits may be shown by asking, as one Member of this Court did at oral argument, "how bad the problem is out there." The very fact that the law has never jelled the way Atwater would have it leads one to wonder whether warrantless misdemeanor arrests need constitutional attention, and there is cause to think the answer is no. So far as such arrests might be thought to pose a threat to the probable-cause requirement, anyone arrested for a crime without formal process, whether for felony or misdemeanor, is entitled to a magistrate's review of probable cause within 48 hours, and there is no reason to think the procedure in this case atypical in giving the suspect a prompt opportunity to request release. Many jurisdictions, moreover, have chosen to impose more restrictive safeguards through statutes limiting warrantless arrests for minor offenses. It is of course easier to devise a minor-offense limitation by statute than to derive one through the Constitution, simply because the statute can let the arrest power turn on any sort of practical consideration without having to subsume it under a broader principle. It is, in fact, only natural that States should resort to this sort of legislative regulation, for, as Atwater's own amici emphasize, it is in the interest of the police to limit petty-offense arrests, which carry costs that are simply too great to incur without good reason. Finally, and significantly, under current doctrine the preference for categorical treatment of Fourth Amendment claims gives way to individualized review when a defendant makes a colorable argument that an arrest, with or without a warrant, was "conducted in an extraordinary manner, unusually harmful to [his] privacy or even physical interests."

The upshot of all these influences, combined with the good sense (and, failing that, the political accountability) of most local lawmakers and law-enforcement officials, is a dearth of horribles demanding redress. Indeed, when Atwater's counsel was asked at oral argument for any indications of comparably foolish, warrantless misdemeanor arrests, he could offer only one. We are sure that there are others, but just as surely the country is not confronting anything like an epidemic of unnecessary minor-offense arrests. That fact caps the reasons for rejecting Atwater's request for the development of a new and distinct body of constitutional law.

Accordingly, we confirm today what our prior cases have intimated: the standard of probable cause "applie[s] to all arrests, without the need to 'balance' the interests and circumstances involved in particular situations." If an officer has probable cause to believe that an individual has committed even a very minor criminal offense in his presence, he may, without violating the Fourth Amendment, arrest the offender.

IV

Atwater's arrest satisfied constitutional requirements. There is no dispute that Officer Turek had probable cause to believe that Atwater had committed a crime in his presence. She admits that neither she nor her children were wearing seatbelts, as required by Tex. Transp. Code Ann. § 545.413 (1999). Turek was accordingly authorized (not required, but authorized) to make a custodial arrest without balancing costs and benefits or determining whether or not Atwater's arrest was in some sense necessary.

Nor was the arrest made in an "extraordinary manner, unusually harmful to [her] privacy or . . . physical interests." Atwater's arrest was surely "humiliating," as she says in her brief, but it was no more "harmful to . . . privacy or . . . physical interests" than the normal custodial arrest. She was handcuffed, placed in a squad car, and taken to the local police station, where officers asked her to remove her shoes, jewelry, and glasses, and to empty her pockets. They then took her photograph and placed her in a cell, alone, for about an hour, after which she was taken before a magistrate, and released on $310 bond. The arrest and booking were inconvenient and embarrassing to Atwater, but not so extraordinary as to violate the Fourth Amendment.

• • •

Justice O'Connor, with whom Justice Stevens, Justice Ginsburg, and Justice Breyer join, dissenting.

The Fourth Amendment guarantees the right to be free from "unreasonable searches and seizures." The Court recognizes that the arrest of Gail Atwater was a "pointless indignity" that served no discernible state interest, ante, and yet holds that her arrest was constitutionally permissible. Because the Court's position is inconsistent with the explicit guarantee of the Fourth Amendment, I dissent.

I

A full custodial arrest, such as the one to which Ms. Atwater was subjected, is the quintessential seizure. When a full custodial arrest is effected without a warrant, the plain language of the Fourth Amendment requires that the arrest be reasonable. It is beyond cavil that "[t] he touchstone of our analysis under the Fourth Amendment is always 'the reasonableness in all the circumstances of the particular governmental invasion of a citizen's personal security.'"

We have "often looked to the common law in evaluating the reasonableness, for Fourth Amendment purposes, of police activity." But history is just one of the tools we use in conducting the reasonableness inquiry. And when history is inconclusive, as the majority amply demonstrates it is in this case, see ante, we will "evaluate the search or seizure under traditional standards of reasonableness by assessing, on the one hand, the degree to which it intrudes upon an individual's privacy and, on the other, the degree to which it is needed for the promotion of legitimate governmental interests."

The majority gives a brief nod to this bedrock principle of our Fourth Amendment jurisprudence, and even acknowledges that "Atwater's claim to live free of pointless indignity and confinement clearly outweighs anything the City can raise against it specific to her case." But instead of remedying this imbalance, the majority allows itself to be swayed by the worry that "every discretionary judgment in the field [will] be converted into an occasion for constitutional review." It therefore mints a new rule that "[i]f an officer has probable cause to believe that an individual has committed even a very minor criminal offense in his presence, he may, without violating the Fourth Amendment, arrest the offender." This rule is not only unsupported by our precedent, but runs contrary to the principles that lie at the core of the Fourth Amendment.

As the majority tacitly acknowledges, we have never considered the precise question presented here, namely, the constitutionality of a warrantless arrest for an offense punishable only by fine. Indeed, on the rare occasions that Members of this Court have contemplated such an arrest, they have indicated disapproval.

To be sure, we have held that the existence of probable cause is a necessary condition for an arrest. And in the case of felonies punishable by a term of imprisonment, we have held that the existence of probable cause is also a sufficient condition for an arrest. In *Watson*, however, there was a clear and consistently applied common law rule permitting warrantless felony arrests. Accordingly, our inquiry ended there and we had no need to assess the reasonableness of such arrests by weighing individual liberty interests against state interests.

Here, however, we have no such luxury. The Court's thorough exegesis makes it abundantly clear that warrantless misdemeanor arrests were not the subject of a clear and consistently applied rule at common law. We therefore must engage in the balancing test required by the Fourth Amendment. While probable cause is surely a necessary condition for warrantless arrests for fine-only offenses, any realistic assessment of the interests implicated by such arrests demonstrates that probable cause alone is not a sufficient condition.

Our decision in *Whren v. United States* (1996), is not to the contrary. The specific question presented there was whether, in evaluating the Fourth Amendment reasonableness of a traffic stop, the subjective intent of the police officer is a relevant consideration. We held that it is not, and stated that "[t]he making of a traffic stop . . . is governed by the usual rule that probable cause to believe the law has been broken 'outbalances' private interest in avoiding police contact."

We of course did not have occasion in *Whren* to consider the constitutional preconditions for warrantless arrests for fine-only offenses. Nor should our words be taken beyond their context. There are significant qualitative differences between a traffic stop and a full custodial arrest. While both are seizures that fall within the ambit of the Fourth Amendment, the latter entails a much greater intrusion on an individual's liberty and privacy interests. As we have said, "[a] motorist's expectations, when he sees a policeman's light flashing behind him, are that he will be obliged to spend a short period of time answering questions and waiting while the officer checks his license and registration, that he may be given a citation, but that in the end he most likely will be allowed to continue on his way." Thus, when there is probable cause to believe that a person has violated a minor traffic law, there can be little question that the state interest in law enforcement will justify the relatively limited intrusion of a traffic stop. It is by no means certain, however, that where the offense is punishable only by fine, "probable cause to believe the law has been broken [will] 'outbalanc[e]' private interest in avoiding" a full custodial arrest. Justifying a full arrest by the same quantum of evidence that justifies a traffic stop—even though the offender cannot ultimately be imprisoned for her conduct—defies any sense of proportionality and is in serious tension with the Fourth Amendment's proscription of unreasonable seizures.

A custodial arrest exacts an obvious toll on an individual's liberty and privacy, even when the period of custody is relatively brief. The arrestee is subject to a full search of her person and confiscation of her possessions. If the arrestee is the occupant of a car, the entire passenger compartment of the car, including packages therein, is subject to search as well. The arrestee may be detained for up to 48 hours without having a magistrate determine whether there in fact was probable cause for the arrest. Because people arrested for all types of violent and non-violent offenses may be housed together awaiting such review, this detention period is potentially dangerous. And once the period of custody is over, the fact of the arrest is a permanent part of the public record.

We have said that "the penalty that may attach to any particular offense seems to provide the clearest and most consistent indication of the State's interest in arresting individuals suspected of committing that offense." If the State has decided that a fine, and not imprisonment, is the appropriate punishment for an offense, the State's interest in taking a person suspected of committing that offense into custody is surely limited, at best. This is not to say that the State will never have such an interest. A full custodial arrest may on occasion vindicate legitimate state interests, even if the crime is punishable only by fine. Arrest is the surest way to abate criminal conduct. It may also allow the police to verify the offender's identity and, if the offender poses a flight risk, to ensure her appearance at trial. But when such considerations are not present, a citation or summons may serve the State's remaining law enforcement interests every bit as effectively as an arrest.

Because a full custodial arrest is such a severe intrusion on an individual's liberty, its reasonableness hinges on "the degree to which it is needed for the promotion of legitimate governmental interests." In light of the availability of citations to promote a State's interests when a fine-only offense has been committed, I cannot concur in a rule which deems a full custodial arrest to be reasonable in every circumstance. Giving police officers constitutional carte blanche to effect an arrest whenever there is probable cause to believe a fine-only misdemeanor has been committed is irreconcilable with the Fourth Amendment's command that seizures be reasonable. Instead, I would require that when there is probable cause to believe that a fine-only offense has been committed, the police officer should issue a citation unless the officer is "able to point to specific and articulable facts which, taken together with rational inferences from those facts, reasonably warrant [the additional] intrusion" of a full custodial arrest.

The majority insists that a bright-line rule focused on probable cause is necessary to vindicate the State's interest in easily administrable law enforcement rules. Probable cause itself, however, is not a model of precision. "The quantum of information which constitutes probable cause — evidence which would 'warrant a man of reasonable caution in the belief' that a [crime] has been committed — must be measured by the facts of the particular case." The rule I propose — which merely requires a legitimate reason for the decision to escalate the seizure into a full custodial arrest — thus does not undermine an otherwise "clear and simple" rule.

While clarity is certainly a value worthy of consideration in our Fourth Amendment jurisprudence, it by no means trumps the values of liberty and privacy at the heart of the Amendment's protections. What the *Terry* rule lacks in precision it makes up for in fidelity to the Fourth Amendment's command of reasonableness and sensitivity to the competing values protected by that Amendment. Over the past 30 years, it appears that the *Terry* rule has been workable and easily applied by officers on the street.

At bottom, the majority offers two related reasons why a bright-line rule is necessary: the fear that officers who arrest for fine-only offenses will be subject to "personal [42 U.S.C.] § 1983 liability for the misapplication of a constitutional standard," and the resulting "systematic disincentive to arrest . . . where . . . arresting would serve an important societal interest." These concerns are certainly valid, but they are more than adequately resolved by the doctrine of qualified immunity.

Qualified immunity was created to shield government officials from civil liability for the performance of discretionary functions so long as their conduct does not violate clearly established statutory or constitutional rights of which a reasonable person would have known. This doctrine is "the best attainable accommodation of competing values," namely, the obligation to enforce constitutional guarantees and the need to protect officials who are required to exercise their discretion.

In *Anderson v. Creighton* (1987), we made clear that the standard of reasonableness for a search or seizure under the Fourth Amendment is distinct from the standard of reasonableness for qualified immunity purposes. If a law enforcement officer "reasonably but mistakenly conclude[s]" that the constitutional predicate for a search or seizure is present, he "should not be held personally liable."

This doctrine thus allays any concerns about liability or disincentives to arrest. If, for example, an officer reasonably thinks that a suspect poses a flight risk or might be a danger to the community if released, he may arrest without fear of the legal consequences. Similarly, if an officer reasonably concludes that a suspect may possess more than four ounces of marijuana and thus might be guilty of a felony, the officer will be insulated from liability for arresting the suspect even if the initial assessment turns out to be factually incorrect. As we have said, "officials will not be liable for mere mistakes in judgment." Of course, even the specter of liability can entail substantial social costs, such as inhibiting public officials in the discharge of their duties. We may not ignore the central command of the Fourth Amendment, however, to avoid these costs.

II

The record in this case makes it abundantly clear that Ms. Atwater's arrest was constitutionally unreasonable. Atwater readily admits — as she did when Officer Turek pulled her over — that she violated Texas' seatbelt law. While Turek was justified in stopping Atwater, neither law nor reason supports his decision to arrest her instead of simply giving her a citation. The officer's actions cannot sensibly be viewed as a permissible means of balancing Atwater's Fourth Amendment interests with the State's own legitimate interests.

There is no question that Officer Turek's actions severely infringed Atwater's liberty and privacy. Turek was loud and accusatory from the moment he approached Atwater's car. Atwater's young children were terrified and hysterical. Yet when Atwater asked Turek to lower his voice because he was scaring the children, he responded by jabbing his finger in Atwater's face and saying, "You're going to jail." Having made the decision to arrest, Turek did not inform Atwater of her right to remain silent. He instead asked for her license and insurance information.

Atwater asked if she could at least take her children to a friend's house down the street before going to the police station. But Turek—who had just castigated Atwater for not caring for her children—refused and said he would take the children into custody as well. Only the intervention of neighborhood children who had witnessed the scene and summoned one of Atwater's friends saved the children from being hauled to jail with their mother.

With the children gone, Officer Turek handcuffed Ms. Atwater with her hands behind her back, placed her in the police car, and drove her to the police station. Ironically, Turek did not secure Atwater in a seatbelt for the drive. At the station, Atwater was forced to remove her shoes, relinquish her possessions, and wait in a holding cell for about an hour. A judge finally informed Atwater of her rights and the charges against her, and released her when she posted bond. Atwater returned to the scene of the arrest, only to find that her car had been towed.

Ms. Atwater ultimately pleaded no contest to violating the seatbelt law and was fined $50. Even though that fine was the maximum penalty for her crime, and even though Officer Turek has never articulated any justification for his actions, the city contends that arresting Atwater was constitutionally reasonable because it advanced two legitimate interests: "the enforcement of child safety laws and encouraging [Atwater] to appear for trial."

It is difficult to see how arresting Atwater served either of these goals any more effectively than the issuance of a citation. With respect to the goal of law enforcement generally, Atwater did not pose a great danger to the community. She had been driving very slowly—approximately 15 miles per hour—in broad daylight on a residential street that had no other traffic. Record 380. Nor was she a repeat offender; until that day, she had received one traffic citation in her life—a ticket, more than 10 years earlier, for failure to signal a lane change. Although Officer Turek had stopped Atwater approximately three months earlier because he thought that Atwater's son was not wearing a seatbelt, Turek had been mistaken. Moreover, Atwater immediately accepted responsibility and apologized for her conduct. Thus, there was every indication that Atwater would have buckled herself and her children in had she been cited and allowed to leave.

With respect to the related goal of child welfare, the decision to arrest Atwater was nothing short of counterproductive. Atwater's children witnessed Officer Turek yell at their mother and threaten to take them all into custody. Ultimately, they were forced to leave her behind with Turek, knowing that she was being taken to jail. Understandably, the 3-year-old boy was "very, very, very traumatized." After the incident, he had to see a child psychologist regularly, who reported that the boy "felt very guilty that he couldn't stop this horrible thing . . . he was powerless to help his mother or sister." Both of Atwater's children are now terrified at the sight of any police car. According to Atwater, the arrest "just never leaves us. It's a conversation we have every other day, once a week, and it's—it raises its head constantly in our lives."

Citing Atwater surely would have served the children's interests well. It would have taught Atwater to ensure that her children were buckled up in the future. It also would have taught the children an important lesson in accepting responsibility and obeying the law. Arresting Atwater, though, taught the children an entirely different lesson: that "the bad person could just as easily be the policeman as it could be the most horrible person they could imagine."

Respondents also contend that the arrest was necessary to ensure Atwater's appearance in court. Atwater, however, was far from a flight risk. A 16-year resident of Lago Vista, population 2,486, Atwater was not likely to abscond. Although she was unable to produce her driver's license because it had been stolen, she gave Officer Turek her license number and address. In addition, Officer Turek knew from their previous encounter that Atwater was a local resident.

The city's justifications fall far short of rationalizing the extraordinary intrusion on Gail Atwater and her children. Measuring "the degree to which [Atwater's custodial arrest was] needed for the promotion of legitimate governmental interests," against "the degree to which it intrud[ed] upon [her] privacy," it can hardly be doubted that Turek's actions were disproportionate to Atwater's crime. The majority's assessment that "Atwater's claim to live free of pointless indignity and confinement clearly outweighs anything the City can raise against it specific to her case," is quite correct. In my view, the Fourth Amendment inquiry ends there.

III

The Court's error, however, does not merely affect the disposition of this case. The per se rule that the Court creates has potentially serious consequences for the everyday lives of Americans. A broad range of conduct falls into the category of fine-only misdemeanors. In Texas alone, for example, disobeying any sort of traffic warning sign is a misdemeanor punishable only by fine, as is failing to pay a highway toll, and driving with expired license plates. Nor are fine-only crimes limited to the traffic context. In several States, for example, littering is a criminal offense punishable only by fine.

To be sure, such laws are valid and wise exercises of the States' power to protect the public health and welfare. My concern lies not with the decision to enact or enforce these laws, but rather with the manner in which they may be enforced. Under today's holding, when a police officer has probable cause to believe that a fine-only misdemeanor offense has occurred, that officer may stop the suspect, issue a citation, and let the person continue on her way. Or, if a traffic violation, the officer may stop the car, arrest the driver, see ante, at 1557, search the driver, search the entire passenger compartment of the car including any purse or package inside, and impound the car and inventory all of its contents. Although the Fourth Amendment expressly requires that the latter course be a reasonable and proportional response to the circumstances of the offense, the majority gives officers unfettered discretion to choose that course without articulating a single reason why such action is appropriate.

Such unbounded discretion carries with it grave potential for abuse. The majority takes comfort in the lack of evidence of "an epidemic of unnecessary minor-offense arrests." But the relatively small number of published cases dealing with such arrests proves little and should provide little solace. Indeed, as the recent debate over racial profiling demonstrates all too clearly, a relatively minor traffic infraction may often serve as an excuse for stopping and harassing an individual. After today, the arsenal available to any officer extends to a full arrest and the searches permissible concomitant to that arrest. An officer's subjective motivations for making a traffic stop are not relevant considerations in determining the reasonableness of the stop. But it is precisely because these motivations are beyond our purview that we must vigilantly ensure that officers' poststop actions—which are properly within our reach—comport with the Fourth Amendment's guarantee of reasonableness.

The Court neglects the Fourth Amendment's express command in the name of administrative ease. In so doing, it cloaks the pointless indignity that Gail Atwater suffered with the mantle of reasonableness. I respectfully dissent.

NOTES AND QUESTIONS

1. The upshot of the exhaustive Part II of the Court's opinion (not included here) is that unlike the common law rule with respect to felonies, there is no historical consensus on whether warrants were required for arrests for minor criminal offenses. Accordingly, as the

Gail Atwater

dissent notes, this typically leads to a balancing test: a weighing of the severity of the intrusion against the needs of law enforcement.

The Court does not conduct the usual balancing test it would do in such cases. As a matter of the devil's advocacy, what is the best argument to be made for the government under a balancing test?

2. Instead of engaging in balancing analysis, the Court criticizes possible versions of any "rule" that would result from a decision in Atwater's favor, noting the complexity of traffic codes and the difficulties of "administrability" of any rule. None of this, of course, is Atwater's fault. At some level, shouldn't the state of Texas—and its law enforcement agents—have to pay some price for a motor vehicle code that criminalizes a first-offense failure to wear a seatbelt?

Further, how can police officers, who feast on traffic code violations for pretextual vehicle stops, *see infra*, and thus as gateways to more serious criminal matters, be heard to complain about the complexity of the state's regulation of motor vehicles? Shouldn't they be required to take the bitter with the sweet?

3. The dissent unflinchingly catalogues the seriousness of the intrusion on personal liberty that an arrest entails. It also notes the potential for racial bias to affect the exercise of the enormous discretion *Atwater* affords to police officers. It would have been nice if the metes and bounds of a search incident to an arrest had first arisen in a case like Gail Atwater's, and not drug cases in the 1970s and 1980s. *See infra.*

4. The dissent notes that "the rule" of *Atwater* has pernicious effects on a larger societal scale given the lack of any constitutional limits on the ability of state and federal government to criminalize conduct. Does *Whren* necessarily mean, as the dissent suggests, that the subjective motivation of a police officer's decision to arrest someone on a misdemeanor charge is irrelevant? *See* Part V *infra*

5. Two years before *Atwater*, in *Knowles v. Iowa*, 525 U.S. 113 (1998), the Court had rejected the concept of a "search-incident-to-citation," holding that only custodial arrests justified incidental searches. Does Atwater incentivize police officers to do pretextual traffic-violation custodial arrests of persons they suspect of more serious wrongdoing in order to conduct searches of their person and inventory searches of their vehicle? Note that they may be able to execute such a plan regardless of whether state law permits a warrantless arrest for the violation chosen by the officer. *See Virginia v. Moore*, 553 U.S. 164 (2008) (search incident to arrest that was supported by probable cause, though unlawful under Virginia law, does not violate Fourth Amendment).

It should not surprise that *Atwater* has been harshly criticized. *See* Richard S. Fraser, *What Were They Thinking: Fourth Amendment Unreasonableness in* Atwater v. City of Lago Vista, 71 Fordham L. Rev. 329, 331 n.4 (2002) (citing criticism); *id.* at 407-15 (proposing a reasonable and workable arrest limitation rule that could easily have been adopted by the Court in *Atwater*: "arrest for a fine-only traffic violation should only be permitted if the officer has a reasonable, articulable basis to believe that custodial arrest is needed to verify identity, ensure payment of the fine, prevent imminent bodily harm, or prevent immediate repetition of the violation"); Thomas Y. Davies, *The Fictional Character of Law-and-Order Originalism: A Case Study of the Distortions and Evasions of Framing-Era Arrest Doctrine in* Atwater v. Lago Vista, 37 Wake Forest L. Rev. 239, 246 (2002) (contrary to the Court's conclusion, "[t]he historical authorities regarding arrest authority actually show that warrantless misdemeanor arrests for minor offenses were usually unlawful, except in some categories of minor offenses that gave rise to an unusual need for a prompt arrest—the position advocated by Gail Atwater's counsel and endorsed by the four dissenting justices in *Atwater*").

Stepping back from it all, Professor Rachel Harmon asks "Why Arrest"? Rachel Harmon, *Why Arrest?,* 115 Mich. L. Rev. 307 (2016). Professor Harmon points out that the Fourth Amendment does not generally regulate arrests other than by the warrant (sometimes) and probable cause requirements, which overlooks the substantial costs of arrests to society (potentially violent confrontations with police; collateral consequences to arrestees, e.g., loss of income/job). *Id.*at 313-15. For many misdemeanors and other nonviolent offenses, she argues, arrests are unnecessary and the costs of proceeding by way of summonses to appear (a marginally increased incidence of failures to appear) are significantly lower than the costs of arrests. *Id.* at 334-36.

4. Search Incident to Arrest

The search-incident-to-arrest exception to the warrant requirement was first recognized by the Court in dictum in *Weeks v. United States*, 232 U.S. 383, 392 (1914), a case better known for mandating the exclusionary rule in federal prosecutions. The modern scope of the search-incident-to-arrest exception came into shape in *Chimel v. California*, 395 U.S. 752 (1969).

Chimel v. California

395 U.S. 752 (1969)

Mr. Justice Stewart delivered the opinion of the Court.

This case raises basic questions concerning the permissible scope under the Fourth Amendment of a search incident to a lawful arrest.

The relevant facts are essentially undisputed. Late in the afternoon of September 13, 1965, three police officers arrived at the Santa Ana, California, home of the petitioner with a warrant authorizing his arrest for the burglary of a coin shop. The officers knocked on the door, identified themselves to the petitioner's wife, and asked if they might come inside. She ushered them into the house, where they waited 10 or 15 minutes until the petitioner returned home from work. When the petitioner entered the house, one of the officers handed him the arrest warrant and asked for permission to "look around." The petitioner objected, but was advised that "on the basis of the lawful arrest," the officers would nonetheless conduct a search. No search warrant had been issued.

Accompanied by the petitioner's wife, the officers then looked through the entire three-bedroom house, including the attic, the garage, and a small workshop. In some rooms the search was relatively cursory. In the master bedroom and sewing room, however, the officers directed the petitioner's wife to open drawers and "to physically move contents of the drawers from side to side so that (they) might view any items that would have come from (the) burglary." After completing the search, they seized numerous items—primarily coins, but also several medals, tokens, and a few other objects. The entire search took between 45 minutes and an hour.

At the petitioner's subsequent state trial on two charges of burglary, the items taken from his house were admitted into evidence against him, over his objection that they had been unconstitutionally seized. He was convicted, and the judgments of conviction were affirmed by both the California Court of Appeal, and the California Supreme Court. Both courts accepted the petitioner's contention that the arrest warrant was invalid because the supporting affidavit was set out in conclusory terms, but held that since the arresting officers had procured the warrant "in good faith," and since in any event they had had sufficient information to constitute probable cause for the petitioner's arrest, that arrest had been lawful. From this conclusion the appellate courts went on to hold that the search of the petitioner's home had been justified, despite the absence of a search warrant, on the ground that it had been incident to a valid arrest. We granted certiorari in order to consider the petitioner's substantial constitutional claims.

Without deciding the question, we proceed on the hypothesis that the California courts were correct in holding that the arrest of the petitioner was valid under the Constitution. This brings us directly to the question whether the warrantless search of the petitioner's entire house can be constitutionally justified as incident to that arrest. The decisions of this Court bearing upon that question have been far from consistent, as even the most cursory review makes evident.

Approval of a warrantless search incident to a lawful arrest seems first to have been articulated by the Court in 1914 as dictum in *Weeks v. United States*, in which the Court stated:

> What then is the present case? Before answering that inquiry specifically, it may be well by a process of exclusion to state what it is not. It is not an assertion of the right on the part of the Government, always recognized under English and American law, to search the person of the accused when legally arrested to discover and seize the fruits or evidences of crime.

That statement made no reference to any right to search the place where an arrest occurs, but was limited to a right to search the "person." Eleven years later the case of *Carroll v. United States*, brought the following embellishment of the Weeks statement:

> When a man is legally arrested for an offense, whatever is found upon his person or in his control which it is unlawful for him to have and which may be used to prove the offense may be seized and held as evidence in the prosecution.

• • •

Only last Term in *Terry v. Ohio*, we emphasized that "the police must, whenever practicable, obtain advance judicial approval of searches and seizures through the warrant procedure," and that "(t)he scope of (a) search must be 'strictly tied to and justified by' the circumstances which rendered its initiation permissible." The search undertaken by the officer in that "stop and frisk" case was sustained under that test, because it was no more than a "protective . . . search for weapons." But in a companion case, *Sibron v. New York*, we applied the same standard to another set of facts and reached a contrary result, holding that a policeman's action in thrusting his hand into a suspect's pocket had been neither motivated by nor limited to the objective of protection. Rather, the search had been made in order to find narcotics, which were in fact found.

A similar analysis underlies the "search incident to arrest" principle, and marks its proper extent. When an arrest is made, it is reasonable for the arresting officer to search the person arrested in order to remove any weapons that the latter might seek to use in order to resist arrest or effect his escape. Otherwise, the officer's safety might well be endangered, and the arrest itself frustrated. In addition, it is entirely reasonable for the arresting officer to search for and seize any evidence on the arrestee's person in order to prevent its concealment or destruction. And the area into which an arrestee might reach in order to grab a weapon or evidentiary items must, of course, be governed by a like rule. A gun on a table or in a drawer in front of one who is arrested can be as dangerous to the arresting officer as one concealed in the clothing of the person arrested. There is ample justification, therefore, for a search of the arrestee's person and the area "within his immediate control"—construing that phrase to mean the area from within which he might gain possession of a weapon or destructible evidence.

There is no comparable justification, however, for routinely searching any room other than that in which an arrest occurs—or, for that matter, for searching through all the desk drawers or other closed or concealed areas in that room itself. Such searches, in the absence of well-recognized exceptions, may be made only under the authority of a search warrant. The "adherence to judicial processes" mandated by the Fourth Amendment requires no less.

This is the principle that underlay our decision in *Preston v. United States*. In that case three men had been arrested in a parked car, which had later been towed to a garage and searched by police. We held that search to have been unlawful under the Fourth Amendment, despite the contention that it had been incidental to a valid arrest. Our reasoning was straightforward:

> The rule allowing contemporaneous searches is justified, for example, by the need to seize weapons and other things which might be used to assault an officer or effect an escape, as well as by the need to prevent the destruction of evidence of the crime—things which might easily happen where the weapon or evidence is on the accused's person or under his immediate control. But these justifications are absent where a search is remote in time or place from the arrest.

The same basic principle was reflected in our opinion last Term in *Sibron*. That opinion dealt with *Peters v. New York*, as well as with Sibron's case, and *Peters* involved a search that we upheld as incident to a proper arrest. We sustained the search, however, only because its scope had been "reasonably limited" by the "need to seize weapons" and "to prevent the destruction of evidence," to which *Preston* had referred. We emphasized that the arresting officer "did not engage in an unrestrained and thorough going examination of Peters and his personal effects. He seized him to cut short his flight, and he searched him primarily for weapons."

It is argued in the present case that it is "reasonable" to search a man's house when he is arrested in it. But that argument is founded on little more than a subjective view regarding the acceptability of certain sorts of police conduct, and not on consideration relevant to Fourth Amendment interests. Under such an unconfined analysis, Fourth Amendment protection in this area would approach the evaporation point. It is not easy to explain why, for instance, it is less subjectively "reasonable" to search a man's house when he is arrested on his front lawn—or just down the street—than it is when he happens to be in the house at the time of arrest. As Mr. Justice Frankfurter put it:

> To say that the search must be reasonable is to require some criterion of reason. It is no guide at all either for a jury or for district judges or the police to say that an "unreasonable search" is forbidden—that the search must be reasonable. What is the test of reason which makes a search reasonable? The test is the reason underlying and expressed by the Fourth Amendment: the history and experience which it embodies and the safeguards afforded by it against the evils to which it was a response.

Thus, although "(t)he recurring questions of the reasonableness of searches" depend upon "the facts and circumstances—the total atmosphere of the case," those facts and circumstances must be viewed in the light of established Fourth Amendment principles.

It would be possible, of course, to draw a line between *Rabinowitz* and *Harris* on the one hand, and this case on the other. For *Rabinowitz* involved a single room, and *Harris* a four-room apartment, while in the case before us an entire house was searched. But such a distinction would be highly artificial. The rationale that allowed the searches and seizures in *Rabinowitz* and *Harris* would allow the searches and seizures in this case. No consideration relevant to the Fourth Amendment suggests any point of rational limitation, once the search is allowed to go beyond the area from which the person arrested might obtain weapons or evidentiary items. The only reasoned distinction is one between a search of the person arrested and the area within his reach on the one hand, and more extensive searches on the other.

The petitioner correctly points out that one result of decisions such as *Rabinowitz* and *Harris* is to give law enforcement officials the opportunity to engage in searches not justified by probable cause, by the simple expedient of arranging to arrest suspects at home rather than elsewhere. We do not suggest that the petitioner is necessarily correct in his assertion that such a strategy was utilized here, but the fact remains that had he been arrested earlier in the day, at his place of employment rather than at home, no search of his house could have been made without a search warrant. In any event, even apart from the possibility of such police tactics, the general point so forcefully made by Judge Learned Hand in *United States v. Kirschenblatt*, remains:

> After arresting a man in his house, to rummage at will among his papers in search of whatever will convict him, appears to us to be indistinguishable from what might be done under a general warrant; indeed, the warrant would give more protection, for presumably it must be issued by a magistrate. True, by hypothesis the power would not exist, if the supposed offender were not found on the premises; but it is small consolation to know that one's papers are safe only so long as one is not at home.

Rabinowitz and *Harris* have been the subject of critical commentary for many years, and have been relied upon less and less in our own decisions. It is time, for the reasons we have stated, to hold that on their own facts, and insofar as the principles they stand for are inconsistent with those that we have endorsed today, they are no longer to be followed.

Application of sound Fourth Amendment principles to the facts of this case produces a clear result. The search here went far beyond the petitioner's person and the area from within which he might have obtained either a weapon or something that could have been used as evidence against him. There was no constitutional justification, in the absence of a search warrant, for extending the search beyond that area. The scope of the search was, therefore, "unreasonable" under the Fourth and Fourteenth Amendments and the petitioner's conviction cannot stand.

Reversed.

NOTES AND QUESTIONS

1. The Court accepts *Weeks*'s negative definition of the valid purpose of a search incident to arrest, namely, that it is not "to discover and seize the fruits or evidences of crime." Why this strange locution? And why should a search for "fruits or evidence" be an impermissible purpose of a search incident to arrest?

2. The Court ultimately holds—after a lengthy discussion of 50 years of inconsistent precedents on this subject that is omitted here—that the scope of a search incident to an arrest must be limited to a search of the person of the arrestee and the area subject to his immediate control, for the narrow purposes of removing weapons that could be used to effect an escape or evidence that might be concealed or destroyed. To what extent is the permissible scope issue a function of the presumption in favor of warrants? Is the scope issue also driven by the fear that agents could game the timing and place of arrests to get around the warrant requirement?

3. Did Chimel's wife impliedly consent to the search by showing the officers around the house and guiding them in their search? Did she have authority to consent even after Chimel refused to give them their permission? Does it matter in what form the Chimels owned or occupied the property?

4. How important was it to the result here that the search the Court found to exceed the proper scope was of Chimel's home? Suppose that instead he had been arrested at his place of business, in—let's say—a large private office in an office building, and that the officers had searched the entire office?

Just four years later the Court dramatically expanded the permissible scope of a search incident to arrest.

United States v. Robinson

414 U.S. 218 (1973)

Mr. Justice Rehnquist delivered the opinion of the Court.

Respondent Robinson was convicted in United States District Court for the District of Columbia of the possession and facilitation of concealment of heroin in violation of 26 U.S.C. s 4704(a) (1964 ed.), and 21 U.S.C. s 174 (1964 ed.). He was sentenced to concurrent terms of imprisonment for these offenses. On his appeal to the Court of Appeals for the District of Columbia Circuit, that court first remanded the case to the District Court for an evidentiary hearing concerning the scope of the search of respondent's person which had occurred at the time of his arrest. The District Court made findings of fact and conclusions of law adverse to respondent, and he again appealed. This time the Court of Appeals en banc reversed the judgment of conviction, holding that the heroin introduced in evidence against respondent had been obtained as a result of a search which violated the Fourth Amendment to the United States Constitution. We granted certiorari.

On April 23, 1968, at approximately 11 p.m., Officer Richard Jenks, a 15-year veteran of the District of Columbia Metropolitan Police Department, observed the respondent driving a 1965 Cadillac near the intersection of 8th and C Streets, N.E., in the District of Columbia. Jenks, as a result of previous investigation following a check of respondent's operator's permit four days earlier, determined there was reason to believe that respondent was operating a motor vehicle after the revocation of his operator's permit. This is an offense defined by statute in the District of Columbia which carries a mandatory minimum jail term, a mandatory minimum fine, or both. D.C. Code Ann. s 40-302(d) (1967).

Jenks signaled respondent to stop the automobile, which respondent did, and all three of the occupants emerged from the car. At that point Jenks informed respondent that he was under arrest for "operating after revocation and obtaining a permit by misrepresentation." It was assumed by the Court of Appeals, and is conceded by the respondent here, that Jenks had probable cause to arrest respondent, and that he effected a full custody arrest.

In accordance with procedures prescribed in police department instructions, Jenks then began to search respondent. He explained at a subsequent hearing that he was "face-to-face" with the respondent, and "placed (his) hands on (the respondent), my right-hand to his left breast like this (demonstrating) and proceeded to pat him down thus (with the right hand)." During this patdown, Jenks felt an object in the left breast pocket of the heavy coat respondent was wearing, but testified that he "couldn't tell what it was" and also that he "couldn't actually tell the size of it." Jenks then reached into the pocket and pulled out the object, which turned out to be a "crumpled up cigarette package." Jenks testified that at this point he still did not know what was in the package:

> As I felt the package I could feel objects in the package but I couldn't tell what they were. . . . I knew they weren't cigarettes.

The officer then opened the cigarette pack and found 14 gelatin capsules of white powder which he thought to be, and which later analysis proved to be, heroin. Jenks then continued his search of respondent to completion, feeling around his waist and trouser legs, and examining the remaining pockets. The heroin seized from the respondent was admitted into evidence at the trial which resulted in his conviction in the District Court.

The opinion for the plurality judges of the Court of Appeals, written by Judge Wright, the concurring opinion of Chief Judge Bazelon, and the dissenting opinion of Judge Wilkey, concurred in by three judges, gave careful and comprehensive treatment to the authority of a police officer to search the person of one who has been validly arrested and taken into custody. We conclude that the search conducted by Jenks in this case did not offend the limits imposed by the Fourth Amendment, and we therefore reverse the judgment of the Court of Appeals.

I

It is well settled that a search incident to a lawful arrest is a traditional exception to the warrant requirement of the Fourth Amendment. This general exception has historically been formulated into two distinct propositions. The first is that a search may be made of the person of the arrestee by virtue of the lawful arrest. The second is that a search may be made of the area within the control of the arrestee.

Examination of this Court's decisions shows that these two propositions have been treated quite differently. The validity of the search of a person incident to a lawful arrest has been regarded as settled from its first enunciation, and has remained virtually unchallenged until the present case. The validity of the second proposition, while likewise conceded in principle, has been subject to differing interpretations as to the extent of the area which may be searched.

Because the rule requiring exclusion of evidence obtained in violation of the Fourth Amendment was first enunciated in *Weeks v. United States* (1914), it is understandable that virtually all of this Court's search-and-seizure law has been developed since that time. In *Weeks*, the Court made clear its recognition of the validity of a search incident to a lawful arrest:

> What then is the present case? Before answering that inquiry specifically, it may be well by a process of exclusion to state what it is not. It is not an assertion of the right on the part of the Government, always recognized under English and American law, to search the person of the accused when legally arrested to discover and seize the fruits or evidences of crime. This right has been uniformly maintained in many cases.

Agnello v. United States (1925), decided 11 years after *Weeks*, repeats the categorical recognition of the validity of a search incident to lawful arrest:

> The right without a search warrant contemporaneously to search persons lawfully arrested while committing crime and to search the place where the arrest is made in order to find and seize things connected with the crime as its fruits or as the means by which it was committed, as well as weapons and other things to effect an escape from custody, is not to be doubted.

Throughout the series of cases in which the Court has addressed the second proposition relating to a search incident to a lawful arrest — the permissible area beyond the person of the arrestee which such a search may cover — no doubt has been expressed as to the unqualified authority of the arresting authority to search the person of the arrestee. In *Chimel*, where the Court overruled *Rabinowitz* and *Harris* as to the area of permissible search incident to a lawful arrest, full recognition was again given to the authority to search the person of the arrestee:

> When an arrest is made, it is reasonable for the arresting officer to search the person arrested in order to remove any weapons that the latter might seek to use in order to resist arrest or effect his escape. Otherwise, the officer's safety might well be endangered, and the arrest itself frustrated. In addition, it is entirely reasonable for the arresting officer to search for and seize any evidence on the arrestee's person in order to prevent its concealment or destruction.

Three years after the decision in *Chimel, supra*, we upheld the validity of a search in which heroin had been taken from the person of the defendant after his arrest on a weapons charge, in *Adams v. Williams* (1972), saying:

> Under the circumstances surrounding Williams' possession of the gun seized by Sgt. Connolly, the arrest on the weapons charge was supported by probable cause, and the search of his person and of the car incident to that arrest was lawful.

Last Term, we again reaffirmed the traditional statement of the authority to search incident to a valid arrest.

Thus the broadly stated rule, and the reasons for it, have been repeatedly affirmed in the decisions of this Court since *Weeks v. United States*, supra, nearly 60 years ago. Since the statements in the cases speak not simply in terms of an exception to the warrant requirement, but in terms of an affirmative authority to search, they clearly imply that such searches also meet the Fourth Amendment's requirement of reasonableness.

II

In its decision of this case, the Court of Appeals decided that even after a police officer lawfully places a suspect under arrest for the purpose of taking him into custody, he may not ordinarily proceed to fully search the prisoner. He must, instead, conduct a limited frisk of the outer clothing and remove such weapons that he may, as a result of that limited frisk, reasonably believe and ascertain that the suspect has in his possession. While recognizing that *Terry v. Ohio* (1968), dealt with a permissible "frisk" incident to an investigative stop based on less than probable cause to arrest, the Court of Appeals felt that the principles of that case should be carried over to this probable-cause arrest for driving while one's license is revoked. Since there would be no further evidence of such a crime to be obtained in a search of the arrestee, the court held that only a search for weapons could be justified.

Terry v. Ohio, supra, did not involve an arrest for probable cause, and it made quite clear that the "protective frisk" for weapons which it approved might be conducted without probable cause. Id., at 21-22, 24-25, 88 S. Ct. at 1879-1880, 1881-1882. This Court's opinion explicitly recognized that there is a "distinction in purpose, character, and extent between a search incident to an arrest and a limited search for weapons."

> The former, although justified in part by the acknowledged necessity to protect the arresting officer from assault with a concealed weapon, *Preston v. United State* (1964), is also justified on other grounds, ibid., and can therefore involve a relatively extensive exploration of the person. A search for weapons in the absence of probable cause to arrest, however, must, like any other search, be strictly circumscribed by the exigencies which justify its initiation. *Warden v. Hayden* (1967) (Mr. Justice Fortas, concurring). Thus it must be limited to that which is necessary for the discovery of weapons which might be used to harm the officer or others nearby, and may realistically be characterized as something less than a "full" search, even though it remains a serious intrusion.
>
> . . . An arrest is a wholly different kind of intrusion upon individual freedom from a limited search for weapons, and the interests each is designed to serve are likewise quite different. An arrest is the initial stage of a criminal prosecution. It is intended to vindicate society's interest in having its laws obeyed, and it is inevitably accompanied by future interference with the individual's freedom of movement, whether or not trial or conviction ultimately follows. The protective search for weapons, on the other hand, constitutes brief, though far from inconsiderable, intrusion upon the sanctity of the person.

Terry, therefore, affords no basis to carry over to a probable-cause arrest the limitations this Court placed on a stop-and-frisk search permissible without probable cause.

The Court of Appeals also relied on language in *Peters v. New York* (1968), a companion case to *Terry*. There the Court held that the police officer had authority to search Peters because he had probable cause to arrest him, and went on to say:

> (T)he incident search was obviously justified "by the need to seize weapons and other things which might be used to assault an officer or effect an escape, as well as by the need to prevent the destruction of evidence of the crime." *Preston v. United States* (1964). Moreover, it was reasonably limited in scope by these purposes. Officer Lasky did not engage in an unrestrained and thorough-going examination of Peters and his personal effects.

It is, of course, possible to read the second sentence from this quotation as imposing a novel limitation on the established doctrine set forth in the first sentence. It is also possible to read it as did Mr. Justice Harlan in his opinion concurring in the result:

> The second possible source of confusion is the Court's statement that "Officer Lasky did not engage in an unrestrained and thorough-going examination of Peters and his personal effects." Since the Court found probable cause to arrest Peters, and since an officer arresting on probable cause is entitled to make a very full incident search, I assume that this is merely a factual observation. As a factual matter, I agree with it.

We do not believe that the Court in *Peters* intended in one unexplained and unelaborated sentence to impose a novel and far-reaching limitation on the authority to search the person of an arrestee incident to his lawful arrest. While the language from *Peters* was quoted with approval in *Chimel*, it is preceded by a full exposition of the traditional and unqualified authority of the arresting officer to search the arrestee's person. We do not believe that either *Terry* or *Peters*, when considered in the light of the previously discussed statements of this Court, justified the sort of limitation upon that authority which the Court of Appeals fashioned in this case.

III

Virtually all of the statements of this Court affirming the existence of an unqualified authority to search incident to a lawful arrest are dicta. We would not, therefore, be foreclosed by principles of stare decisis from further examination into history and practice in order to see whether the sort of qualifications imposed by the Court of Appeals in this case were in fact intended by the Framers of the Fourth Amendment or recognized in cases decided prior to *Weeks*. Unfortunately such authorities as exist are sparse. Such common-law treatises as Blackstone's Commentaries and Holmes' Common Law are simply silent on the subject. Pollock and Maitland, in their History of English Law, describe the law of arrest as "rough and rude" before the time of Edward I, but do not address the authority to search incident to arrest.

The issue was apparently litigated in the English courts in *Dillon v. O'Brien*, 16 Cox C.C. 245 (Exch. Ireland, 1887), cited in *Weeks v. United States*, supra, There Baron Palles said:

> But the interest of the State in the person charged being brought to trial in due course necessarily extends, as well to the preservation of material evidence of his guilt or innocence, as to his custody for the purpose of trial. His custody is of no value if the law is powerless to prevent the abstraction or destruction of this evidence, without which a trial would be no more than an empty form. But if there be a right to production or preservation of this evidence, I cannot see how it can be enforced otherwise than by capture.

Spalding v. Preston (1848), represents an early holding in this country that evidence may be seized from one who is lawfully arrested. in *Closson v. Morrison* (1867), the Court made the following statement:

> (W)e think that an officer would also be justified in taking from a person whom he had arrested for crime, any deadly weapon he might find upon him, such as a revolver, a dirk, a knife, a sword cane, a slung shot, or a club, though it had not been used or intended to be used in the

> commission of the offence for which the prisoner had been arrested, and even though no threats of violence towards the officer had been made. A due regard for his own safety on the part of the officer, and also for the public safety, would justify a sufficient search to ascertain if such weapons were carried about the person of the prisoner, or were in his possession, and if found, to seize and hold them until the prisoner should be discharged, or until they could be otherwise properly disposed of.
>
> So we think it might be with money or other articles of value, found upon the prisoner, by means of which, if left in his possession, he might procure his escape, or obtain tools, or implements, or weapons with which to effect his escape. We think the officer arresting a man for crime, not only may, but frequently should, make such searches and seizures; that in many cases they might be reasonable and proper, and courts would hold him harmless for so doing, when he acts in good faith, and from a regard to his own or the public safety, or the security of his prisoner.

Similarly, in *Holker v. Hennessey* (1897), the Supreme Court of Missouri said:

> Generally speaking, in the absence of a statute, an officer has no right to take any property from the person of the prisoner except such as may afford evidence of the crime charged, or means of identifying the criminal, or may be helpful in making an escape.

Then Associate Judge Cardozo of the New York Court of Appeals summarized his understanding of the historical basis for the authority to search incident to arrest in these words:

> The basic principle is this: Search of the person is unlawful when the seizure of the body is a trespass, and the purpose of the search is to discover grounds as yet unknown for arrest or accusation (citation omitted). Search of the person becomes lawful when grounds for arrest and accusation have been discovered, and the law is in the act of subjecting the body of the accused to its physical dominion.
>
> The distinction may seem subtle, but in truth it is founded in shrewd appreciation of the necessities of government. We are not to strain an immunity to the point at which human nature rebels against honoring it in conduct. The peace officer empowered to arrest must be empowered to disarm. If he many disarm, he may search, lest a weapon be concealed. The search being lawful, he retains what he finds if connected with the crime.

People v. Chiagles (1923).

While these earlier authorities are sketchy, they tend to support the broad statement of the authority to search incident to arrest found in the successive decisions of this Court, rather than the restrictive one which was applied by the Court of Appeals in this case. The scarcity of case law before *Weeks* is doubtless due in part to the fact that the exclusionary rule there enunciated had been first adopted only 11 years earlier in Iowa; but it would seem to be also due in part to the fact that the issue was regarded as well settled.

The Court of Appeals in effect determined that the only reason supporting the authority for a full search incident to lawful arrest was the possibility of discovery of evidence or fruits. Concluding that there could be no evidence or fruits in the case of an offense such as that with which respondent was charged, it held that any protective search would have to be limited by the conditions laid down in *Terry* for a search upon less than probable cause to arrest. Quite apart from the fact that *Terry* clearly recognized the distinction between the two types of searches, and that a different rule governed one than governed the other, we find additional reason to disagree with the Court of Appeals.

The justification or reason for the authority to search incident to a lawful arrest rests quite as much on the need to disarm the suspect in order to take him into custody as it does on the need to preserve evidence on his person for later use at trial. The standards traditionally governing a search incident to lawful arrest are not, therefore, commuted to the stricter *Terry* standards by the absence of probable fruits or further evidence of the particular crime for which the arrest is made.

Nor are we inclined, on the basis of what seems to us to be a rather speculative judgment, to qualify the breadth of the general authority to search incident to a lawful custodial arrest on an assumption that persons arrested for the offense of driving while their licenses have been revoked are less likely to possess dangerous weapons than are those arrested for other crimes. It is scarcely open to doubt that the danger to an officer is far greater in the case of the extended exposure which follows the taking of a suspect into custody and transporting him to the police station than in the case of the relatively fleeting contact resulting from the typical *Terry*-type stop. This is an adequate basis for treating all custodial arrests alike for purposes of search justification.

But quite apart from these distinctions, our more fundamental disagreement with the Court of Appeals arises from its suggestion that there must be litigated in each case the issue of whether or not there was present one of the reasons supporting the authority for a search of the person incident to a lawful arrest. We do not think the long line of authorities of this Court dating back to *Weeks*, or what we can glean from the history of practice in this country and in England, requires such a case-by-case adjudication. A police officer's determination as to how and where to search the person of a suspect whom he has arrested is necessarily a quick ad hoc judgment which the Fourth Amendment does not require to be broken down in each instance into an analysis of each step in the search. The authority to search the person incident to a lawful custodial arrest, while based upon the need to disarm and to discover evidence, does not depend on what a court may later decide was the probability in a particular arrest situation that weapons or evidence would in fact be found upon the person of the suspect. A custodial arrest of a suspect based on probable cause is a reasonable intrusion under the Fourth Amendment; that intrusion being lawful, a search incident to the arrest requires no additional justification. It is the fact of the lawful arrest which establishes the authority to search, and we hold that in the case of a lawful custodial arrest a full search of the person is not only an exception to the warrant requirement of the Fourth Amendment, but is also a "reasonable" search under that Amendment.

IV

The search of respondent's person conducted by Officer Jenks in this case and the seizure from him of the heroin, were permissible under established Fourth Amendment law. While thorough, the search partook of none of the extreme or patently abusive characteristics which were held to violate the Due Process Clause of the Fourteenth Amendment in *Rochin v. California* (1952). Since it is the fact of custodial arrest which gives rise to the authority to search, it is of no moment that Jenks did not indicate any subjective fear of the respondent or that he did not himself suspect that respondent was armed. Having in the course of a lawful search come upon the crumpled package of cigarettes, he was entitled to inspect it; and when his inspection revealed the heroin capsules, he was entitled to seize them as "fruits, instrumentalities, or contraband" probative of criminal conduct. The judgment of the Court of Appeals holding otherwise is reversed.

Reversed.

NOTES AND QUESTIONS

1. Is this a pretextual arrest? Was Robinson really arrested simply because he was driving with a revoked driver's license? Officer Jenks plainly had his eye on Robinson — he had been monitoring his driving records — and it couldn't have been only for driving with a revoked driver's license.

2. The court of appeals analogizes the scope of a search incident to arrest to a *Terry* stop and frisk, as both involve a search for weapons. What is wrong with that analogy? Why does the Supreme Court reject it? If the analogy were controlling, what should the officer have done when he felt the "crumpled up cigarette pack"?

3. The crime at issue here, driving with a revoked license, is unusual in that it is almost impossible to contend that the defendant would be in possession of evidence or fruits of the commission of the crime. So the permissible purpose and scope of the search should be limited to a search for weapons. The Court rejects the argument that the need for a weapons search should be determined on a case-by-case basis, and holds that such a search is always justified. Does this make sense? Is the potential for violent confrontation inherent in any arrest, regardless of the underlying charge? If so, what does this say about whether arrests for nonviolent, minor offenses such as this one should be the norm? Did the scope of the permissible scope of the search extend to Washington's car?

4. Does the Court's conclusion that Officer Jenks was entitled to "inspect" the cigarette pack once he felt it seem like a non sequitur in view of the opinion's emphasis on officer safety up to that point? Are there any limits to the scope of the search of the person incident to arrest after *Robinson*?

Robinson is an early example of the ominous power that the police wield by virtue of their traffic law enforcement responsibilities. Here, a routine traffic violation ultimately justified an arrest, which justified an all-encompassing search of the person, which in turn eventually leads to a drug conviction. For discussion of how law enforcement weaponized its traffic regulatory powers in investigating drug crimes, *see infra* Section E. The Court used a similar bright-line approach to searches incident to arrest in *New York v. Belton*, 453 U.S. 454 (1981), holding—under a broad reading—that the arrest of the recent occupant of a vehicle justified a search incident to that arrest of the entire passenger compartment of the vehicle and any containers therein.

Recall at this juncture Justice O'Connor's warning in her *Atwater* dissent about the risk of racial profiling where police are given broad discretionary power. In that dissent she also notes the holding in *Whren v. United States*, 517 U.S. 806 (1996), which will be addressed fully *infra*. In short, *Whren* held that the Fourth Amendment doesn't prohibit pretextual vehicle stops where there is probable cause for the traffic violation supporting the stop. So the upshot of the combination of *Robinson, Belton, Whren*, and *Atwater* is that a motorist can be stopped for a traffic violation, even if the stop is pretextual (*Whren*), can be arrested for that violation (*Atwater*), and can have his person (*Robinson*) and car (*Belton*) searched incident to that arrest. In short, in the discretionary regime in which even a conservative member of the Supreme Court admits is fraught with potential for racial profiling, the police can with impunity effectively select a motorist virtually at random and have their person and car searched. *See* Donald A. Dripps, *The Fourth Amendment and the Fallacy of Composition: Determinacy versus Legitimacy in a Regime of Bright-Line Rules*, 74 Miss. L.J. 341, 392-92 (2004) (describing the "Iron Triangle" of *Belton, Whren*, and *Atwater*, which "means in practice that police have general search power over anyone traveling by automobile"). *See* Frank Rudy Cooper, *Post-Racialism and Searches Incident to Arrest*, 44 Ariz. St. L.J. 113, 147 (2012) ("Police officers racially profile all the time. The point of racial profiling is to catch them 'dirty.' The search incident to arrest is the primary means of potentially catching the prey.").

In *Arizona v. Gant*, 556 U.S. 332 (2009), the Court clarified—or overruled—*Belton*, at least in part, holding that the passenger area of a vehicle cannot be searched incident to an arrest after the arrestee has been secured and cannot access the interior of the vehicle. The Court may have realized *Belton* was ripe for reconsideration when it learned that at the suppression hearing in *Gant* the arresting officer, when asked why he searched the passenger area of the car, could only respond: "Because the law says we can." The Court did find that the passenger area could nonetheless be searched if it was reasonable to believe that evidence relevant to the crime of arrest might be found, but no such reasonable belief was available here as Gant was charged only with driving with a suspended license. Four Justices dissented on stare decisis grounds.

Gant does not, however, mean that the police cannot search a car after the car's driver has been arrested. The vehicle of an arrestee under some circumstances can be impounded by the police and searched under the administrative exception for "inventory searches." *Florida v. Wells*, 495 U.S. 1 (1990). Such searches serve to protect an owner's property while it is in the custody of the police, to insure against claims of lost, stolen, or vandalized property, and to guard the police from danger. *Id.* at 4. They are permissible where performed pursuant to standardized criteria or established routine—for the purpose of producing an inventory—and must not be a ruse for a general rummaging in order to discover incriminating evidence. *Id.*

Being afoot, rather than in a vehicle, hardly insulates one from the powers wielded by police "search-incident-to-arrest" powers. Individuals in public areas can be approached by police for no reason at all and questioned. If their freedom to leave the interaction has not been curtailed, they have not been "seized," *see supra*, and no level of suspicion for the encounter is required. A wholesale practice of precisely such interactions was infamously described as "pedestrian checks" by the police department in Ferguson, Missouri. *See* U.S. Dept. of Justice, Civil Rights Division, Investigation of the Ferguson Police Department (2015) (hereinafter DOJ Ferguson Report) at 16-20. *See* Devon W. Carbado, Unreasonable: Black Lives, Police Power, and the Fourth Amendment 41-44 (2022) (discussing Ferguson Police Department's "ped checks"). In these interactions the police are almost always able to acquire the names of the persons they approach, which enables the police to remotely determine if the individuals have any outstanding warrants. The existence of such warrants—including bench warrants for comparably minor civil violations such as traffic violations or failures to appear in court—justifies an arrest that in turn justifies a search incident to that arrest. Justice O'Connor's concerns about the potential for racial profiling, of course, are at least as applicable in this context as in the traffic stop context.

Indeed, this was precisely the fact pattern in *Utah v. Strieff*, 579 U.S. 232, 235-36 (2016): An individual was stopped and questioned by police, showed identification, was subsequently arrested when the police were able to learn remotely of an outstanding warrant for an unpaid traffic ticket, and was convicted of drug possession when the search incident to his arrest turned up methamphetamine in a pocket. (*Strieff* is discussed more thoroughly in the chapter on the exclusionary rule, *see* Chapter V, *infra*.) Bench warrants of this type are commonplace, as is their use as a method of policing. The DOJ Ferguson Report found that of the 21,000 persons living in Ferguson, 16,000 people had outstanding warrants against them. DOJ Ferguson Report, at 6, 55. Ferguson may be an extreme example but there is no reason to think it is an outlier, as other DOJ investigations have shown. For example, in a single year in New Orleans, officers "made nearly 60,000 arrests, of which about 20,000 were of people with outstanding traffic or misdemeanor warrants from neighboring parishes for such infractions as unpaid tickets." Dept. of Justice, Civil Rights Div., Investigation of the New Orleans Police Department 29 (2011).

The Court turned down an opportunity to further expand search-incident-to-arrest powers in 2014. In *Riley v. California*, 573 U.S. 373 (2014), the Court considered whether the police may without a warrant search digital information on a cell phone seized from an arrestee as an incident to that arrest. The Court rejected a categorical application of *Robinson* in this context, as a search of the type of information a person has on his cell phone "bears little resemblance" to the type of physical search at issue in *Robinson*. Ultimately the Court found that neither of the twin *Chimel* rationales justified the search while, on the other hand, the intrusion on an individual's privacy was extreme, employing reasoning similar to that in *Carpenter v. United Carpenter States*, 585 U.S. 296 (2018), *supra*.

In *Birchfield v. North Dakota*, 579 U.S. 438 (2016), the Court considered statutory schemes under which motorists arrested on drunk-driving charges are required, under an "implied consent" theory, to undergo warrantless blood alcohol tests. Refusal of the tests was itself a crime. Analyzing these schemes under the "search incident to arrest" framework, the Court found that breath tests were permissible but the more invasive blood tests—involving a physical piercing of the skin, and generating information beyond blood alcohol content—were not. The Court dismissed almost out of hand the suggestion that such tests should require a warrant:

> In order to persuade a magistrate that there is probable cause for a search warrant, the officer would typically recite the same facts that led the officer to find that there was probable cause for arrest, namely, that there is probable cause to believe that a BAC breath test will reveal that the motorist's blood alcohol level is over the limit. . . . [T]he facts that establish probable cause are largely the same from one drunk-driving stop to the next and consist largely of the officer's own characterization of his or her observations—for example, that there was a strong odor of alcohol, that the motorist wobbled when attempting to stand, that the motorist paused when reciting the alphabet or counting backwards, and so on. A magistrate would be in a poor position to challenge such characterizations.

Is the Court trying to say that police officers simply recite boilerplate language to justify probable cause for drunk-driving arrests?

Wouldn't the possibility of judicial scrutiny cause police to take more care in preparing their police reports knowing they needed a factual basis for their arrest that would be put into an affidavit? Might the possibility of judicial scrutiny also cause them to be more thorough and disciplined in reaching the probable cause conclusion in the first place?

5. Consent Searches

Schneckloth v. Bustamonte

412 U.S. 218 (1973)

Mr. Justice Stewart delivered the opinion of the Court.

It is well settled under the Fourth and Fourteenth Amendments that a search conducted without a warrant issued upon probable cause is "per se unreasonable . . . subject only to a few specifically established and well-delineated exceptions." It is equally well settled that one of the specifically established exceptions to the requirements of both a warrant and probable cause is a search that is conducted pursuant to consent. The constitutional question in the present case concerns the definition of "consent" in this Fourth and Fourteenth Amendment context.

I

The respondent was brought to trial in a California court upon a charge of possessing a check with intent to defraud. He moved to suppress the introduction of certain material as evidence against him on the ground that the material had been acquired through an unconstitutional search and seizure. In response to the motion, the trial judge conducted an evidentiary hearing where it was established that the material in question had been acquired by the State under the following circumstances:

While on routine patrol in Sunnyvale, California, at approximately 2:40 in the morning, Police Officer James Rand stopped an automobile when he observed that one headlight and its license plate light were burned out. Six men were in the vehicle. Joe Alcala and the respondent, Robert Bustamonte, were in the front seat with Joe Gonzales, the driver. Three older men were seated in the rear. When, in response to the policeman's question, Gonzales could not produce a driver's license, Officer Rand asked if any of the other five had any evidence of identification. Only Alcala produced a license, and he explained that the car was his brother's. After the six occupants had stepped out of the car at the officer's request and after two additional policemen had arrived, Officer Rand asked Alcala if he could search the car. Alcala replied, "Sure, go ahead." Prior to the search no one was threatened with arrest and, according to Officer Rand's uncontradicted testimony, it "was all very congenial at this time." Gonzales testified that Alcala actually helped in the search of the car, by opening the trunk and glove compartment. In Gonzales' words: "(T)he police officer asked Joe (Alcala), he goes, 'Does the trunk open?' And Joe said, 'Yes.' He went to the car and got the keys and opened up the trunk." Wadded up under the left rear seat, the police officers found three checks that had previously been stolen from a car wash.

The trial judge denied the motion to suppress, and the checks in question were admitted in evidence at Bustamonte's trial. On the basis of this and other evidence he was convicted, and the California Court of Appeal for the First Appellate District affirmed the conviction.

• • •

II

It is important to make it clear at the outset what is not involved in this case. The respondent concedes that a search conducted pursuant to a valid consent is constitutionally permissible.

The precise question in this case, then, is what must the prosecution prove to demonstrate that a consent was "voluntarily" given. And upon that question there is a square conflict of views between the state and federal courts that have reviewed the search involved in the case before us. The Court of Appeals for the Ninth Circuit concluded that it is an essential part of the State's initial burden to prove that a person knows he has a right to refuse consent. The California courts have followed the rule that voluntariness is a question of fact to be determined from the totality of all the circumstances, and that the state of a defendant's knowledge is only one factor to be taken into account in assessing the voluntariness of a consent.

A

The most extensive judicial exposition of the meaning of "voluntariness" has been developed in those cases in which the Court has had to determine the "voluntariness" of a defendant's confession for purposes of the Fourteenth Amendment.

• • •

Similar considerations lead us to agree with the courts of California that the question whether a consent to a search was in fact "voluntary" or was the product of duress or coercion, express or implied, is a question of fact to be determined from the totality of all the circumstances. While knowledge of the right to refuse consent is one factor to be taken into account, the government need not establish such knowledge as the sine qua non of an effective consent. As with police questioning, two competing concerns must be accommodated in determining the meaning of a "voluntary" consent—the legitimate need for such searches and the equally important requirement of assuring the absence of coercion.

In situations where the police have some evidence of illicit activity, but lack probable cause to arrest or search, a search authorized by a valid consent may be the only means of obtaining important and reliable evidence. In the present case for example, while the police had reason to stop the car for traffic violations, the State does not contend that there was probable cause to search the vehicle or that the search was incident to a valid arrest of any of the occupants. Yet, the search yielded tangible evidence that served as a basis for a prosecution, and provided some assurance that others, wholly innocent of the crime, were not mistakenly brought to trial. And in those cases where there is probable cause to arrest or search, but where the police lack a warrant, a consent search may still be valuable. If the search is conducted and proves fruitless, that in itself may convince the police that an arrest with its possible stigma and embarrassment is unnecessary, or that a far more extensive search pursuant to a warrant is not justified. In short, a search pursuant to consent may result in considerably less inconvenience for the subject of the search, and, properly conducted, is a constitutionally permissible and wholly legitimate aspect of effective police activity.

But the Fourth and Fourteenth Amendments require that a consent not be coerced, by explicit or implicit means, by implied threat or covert force. For, no matter how subtly the coercion was applied, the resulting "consent" would be no more than a pretext for the unjustified police intrusion against which the Fourth Amendment is directed. In the words of the classic admonition in *Boyd v. United States*:

> It may be that it is the obnoxious thing in its mildest and least repulsive form; but illegitimate and unconstitutional practices get their first footing in that way, namely, by silent approaches and slight deviations from legal modes of procedure. This can only be obviated by adhering to the rule that constitutional provisions for the security of person and property should be liberally construed. A close and literal construction deprives them of half their efficacy, and leads to gradual depreciation of the right, as if it consisted more in sound than in substance. It is the duty of courts to be watchful for the constitutional rights of the citizen, and against any stealthy encroachments thereon.

The problem of reconciling the recognized legitimacy of consent searches with the requirement that they be free from any aspect of official coercion cannot be resolved by any infallible touchstone. To approve such searches without the most careful scrutiny would sanction the possibility of official coercion; to place artificial restrictions upon such searches would jeopardize their basic validity. Just as was true with confessions, the requirement of a "voluntary" consent reflects a fair accommodation of the constitutional requirements involved. In examining all the surrounding circumstances to determine if in fact the consent to search was coerced, account must be taken of subtly coercive police questions, as well as the possibly vulnerable subjective state of the person who consents. Those searches that are the product of police coercion can thus be filtered out without undermining the continuing validity of consent searches. In sum, there is no reason for us to depart in the area of consent searches, from the traditional definition of "voluntariness."

The approach of the Court of Appeals for the Ninth Circuit finds no support in any of our decisions that have attempted to define the meaning of "voluntariness." Its ruling, that the State must affirmatively prove that the subject of the search knew that he had a right to refuse consent, would, in practice, create serious doubt whether consent searches could continue to be conducted. There might be rare cases where it could be proved from the record that a person in fact affirmatively knew of his right to refuse—such as a case where he announced to the police that if he didn't sign the consent form, "you (police) are going to get a search warrant"; or a case where by prior experience and training a person had clearly and convincingly demonstrated such knowledge. But more commonly where there was no evidence of any coercion, explicit or implicit, the prosecution would nevertheless be unable to demonstrate that the subject of the search in fact had known of his right to refuse consent.

The very object of the inquiry—the nature of a person's subjective understanding—underlines the difficulty of the prosecution's burden under the rule applied by the Court of Appeals in this case. Any defendant who was the subject of a search authorized solely by his consent could effectively frustrate the introduction into evidence of the fruits of that search by simply failing to testify that he in fact knew he could refuse to consent. And the near impossibility of meeting this prosecutorial burden suggests why this Court has never accepted any such litmus-paper test of voluntariness. It is instructive to recall the fears of then Justice Traynor of the California Supreme Court:

> (I)t is not unreasonable for officers to seek interviews with suspects or witnesses or to call upon them at their homes for such purposes. Such inquiries, although courteously made and not accompanied with any assertion of a right to enter or search or secure answers, would permit the criminal to defeat his prosecution by voluntarily revealing all of the evidence against him and then contending that he acted only in response to an implied assertion of unlawful authority.

One alternative that would go far toward proving that the subject of a search did know he had a right to refuse consent would be to advise him of that right before eliciting his consent. That, however, is a suggestion that has been almost universally repudiated by both federal and state courts, and, we think, rightly so. For it would be thoroughly impractical to impose on the normal consent search the detailed requirements of an effective warning. Consent searches are part of the standard investigatory techniques of law enforcement agencies. They normally occur on the highway, or in a person's home or office, and under informal and unstructured conditions. The circumstances that prompt the initial request to search may develop quickly or be a logical extension of investigative police questioning. The police may seek to investigate further suspicious circumstances or to follow up leads developed in questioning persons at the scene of a crime. These situations are a far cry from the structured atmosphere of a trial where, assisted by counsel if he chooses, a defendant is informed of his trial rights. And, while surely a closer question, these situations are still immeasurably, far removed from "custodial interrogation" where, in *Miranda* we found that the Constitution required certain now familiar warnings as a prerequisite to police interrogation. Indeed, in language applicable to the typical consent search, we refused to extend the need for warnings:

> Our decision is not intended to hamper the traditional function of police officers in investigating crime. . . . When an individual is in custody on probable cause, the police may, of course, seek out evidence in the field to be used at trial against him. Such investigation may include inquiry of persons not under restraint. General on-the-scene questioning as to facts surrounding a crime or other general questioning of citizens in the fact-finding process is not affected by our holding. It is an act of responsible citizenship for individuals to give whatever information they may have to aid in law enforcement.

Consequently, we cannot accept the position of the Court of Appeals in this case that proof of knowledge of the right to refuse consent is a necessary prerequisite to demonstrating a "voluntary" consent. Rather it is only by analyzing all the circumstances of an individual consent that it can be ascertained whether in fact it was voluntary or coerced. It is this careful sifting of the unique facts and circumstances of each case that is evidenced in our prior decisions involving consent searches.

• • •

In short, neither this Court's prior cases, nor the traditional definition of "voluntariness" requires proof of knowledge of a right to refuse as the sine qua non of an effective consent to a search.

It is said, however, that a "consent" is a "waiver" of a person's rights under the Fourth and Fourteenth Amendments. The argument is that by allowing the police to conduct a search, a person "waives" whatever right he had to prevent the police from searching. It is argued that under the doctrine of *Johnson v. Zerbst*, to establish such a "waiver" the State must demonstrate "an intentional relinquishment or abandonment of a known right or privilege."

But these standards were enunciated in *Johnson* in the context of the safeguards of a fair criminal trial. Our cases do not reflect an uncritical demand for a knowing and intelligent waiver in every situation where a person has failed to invoke a constitutional protection. As Mr. Justice Black once observed for the Court: "Waiver is a vague term used for a great variety of purposes, good and bad, in the law." With respect to procedural due process, for example, the Court has acknowledged that waiver is possible, while explicitly leaving open the question whether a "knowing and intelligent" waiver need be shown.

The requirement of a "knowing" and "intelligent" waiver was articulated in a case involving the validity of a defendant's decision to forego a right constitutionally guaranteed to protect a fair trial and the reliability of the truth-determining process. *Johnson v. Zerbst* dealt with the denial of counsel in a federal criminal trial. There the Court held that under the Sixth Amendment a criminal defendant is entitled to the assistance of counsel, and that if he lacks sufficient funds to retain counsel, it is the Government's obligation to furnish him with a lawyer. As Mr. Justice Black wrote for the Court: "The Sixth Amendment stands as a constant admonition that if the constitutional safeguards it provides be lost, justice will not 'still be done.' It embodies a realistic recognition of the obvious truth that the average defendant does not have the professional legal skill to protect himself when brought before a tribunal with power to take his life or liberty, wherein the prosecution is presented by experienced and learned counsel. That which is simple, orderly, and necessary to the lawyer—to the untrained layman may appear intricate, complex and mysterious." To preserve the fairness of the trial process the Court established an appropriately heavy burden on the Government before waiver could be found—"an intentional relinquishment or abandonment of a known right or privilege."

Almost without exception, the requirement of a knowing and intelligent waiver has been applied only to those rights which the Constitution guarantees to a criminal defendant in order to preserve a fair trial. Hence, and hardly surprisingly in view of the facts of *Johnson* itself, the standard of a knowing and intelligent waiver has most often been applied to test the validity of a waiver of counsel, either at trial, or upon a guilty plea. And the Court has also applied the *Johnson* criteria to assess the effectiveness of a waiver of other trial rights such as the right to confrontation, to a jury trial, and to a speedy trial, and the right to be free from twice being placed in jeopardy. Guilty pleas have been carefully scrutinized to determine whether the accused knew and understood all the rights to which he would be entitled at trial, and that he had intentionally chosen to forgo them. And the Court has evaluated the knowing and intelligent nature of the waiver of trial rights in trial-type situations, such as the waiver of the privilege against compulsory self-incrimination before an administrative agency or a congressional committee, or the waiver of counsel in a juvenile proceeding.

The guarantees afforded a criminal defendant at trial also protect him at certain stages before the actual trial, and any alleged waiver must meet the strict standard of an intentional relinquishment of a "known" right. But the "trial" guarantees that have been applied to the "pretrial" stage of the criminal process are similarly designed to protect the fairness of the trial itself.

• • •

Hence, in *Wade* and *Gilbert* the Court held "that a post-indictment pretrial lineup at which the accused is exhibited to identifying witnesses is a critical stage of the criminal prosecution; that police conduct of such a lineup without notice to and in the absence of his counsel denies the accused his Sixth (and Fourteenth) Amendment right to counsel. . . ." Accordingly, the

Court indicated that the standard of a knowing and intelligent waiver must be applied to test the waiver of counsel at such a lineup. The Court stressed the necessary interrelationship between the presence of counsel at a post-indictment lineup before trial and the protection of the trial process itself:

> Insofar as the accused's conviction may rest on a courtroom identification in fact the fruit of a suspect pretrial identification which the accused is helpless the subject to effective scrutiny at trial, the accused is deprived of that right of cross-examination which is an essential safeguard to his right to confront the witnesses against him. And even though cross-examination is a precious safeguard to a fair trial, it cannot be viewed as an absolute assurance of accuracy and reliability. Thus in the present context, where so many variables and pitfalls exist, the first line of defense must be the prevention of unfairness and the lessening of the hazards of eyewitness identification at the lineup itself. The trial which might determine the accused's fate may well not be that in the courtroom but that at the pretrial confrontation, with the State aligned against the accused, the witness the sole jury, and the accused unprotected against the overreaching, intentional or unintentional, and with little or no effective appeal from the judgment there rendered by the witness—"that's the man."

And in *Miranda* the Court found that custodial interrogation by the police was inherently coercive, and consequently held that detailed warnings were required to protect the privilege against compulsory self-incrimination. The Court made it clear that the basis for decision was the need to protect the fairness of the trial itself:

> That counsel is present when statements are taken from an individual during interrogation obviously enhances the integrity of the fact-finding processes in court. The presence of an attorney, and the warnings delivered to the individual, enable the defendant under otherwise compelling circumstances to tell his story without fear, effectively, and in a way that eliminates the evils in the interrogation process. Without the protections flowing from adequate warnings and the rights of counsel, "all the careful safeguards erected around the giving of testimony, whether by an accused or any other witness, would become empty formalities in a procedure where the most compelling possible evidence of guilt, a confession, would have already been obtained at the unsupervised pleasure of the police."

The standards of *Johnson* were, therefore, found to be a necessary prerequisite to a finding of a valid waiver.

There is a vast difference between those rights that protect a fair criminal trial and the rights guaranteed under the Fourth Amendment. Nothing, either in the purposes behind requiring a "knowing" and "intelligent" waiver of trial rights, or in the practical application of such a requirement suggests that it ought to be extended to the constitutional guarantee against unreasonable searches and seizures.

A strict standard of waiver has been applied to those rights guaranteed to a criminal defendant to insure that he will be accorded the greatest possible opportunity to utilize every facet of the constitutional model of a fair criminal trial. Any trial conducted in derogation of that model leaves open the possibility that the trial reached an unfair result precisely because all the protections specified in the Constitution were not provided. A prime example is the right to counsel. For without that right, a wholly innocent accused faces the real and substantial danger that simply because of his lack of legal expertise he may be convicted. As Mr. Justice Harlan once wrote: "The sound reason why (the right to counsel) is so freely extended for a criminal trial is the severe injustice risked by confronting an untrained defendant with a range of technical points of law, evidence, and tactics familiar to the prosecutor but not to himself." The Constitution requires that every effort be made to see to it that a defendant in a criminal case has not unknowingly relinquished the basic protections that the Framers thought indispensable to a fair trial.

The protections of the Fourth Amendment are of a wholly different order, and have nothing whatever to do with promoting the fair ascertainment of truth at a criminal trial. Rather, as Mr. Justice Frankfurter's opinion for the Court put it in *Wolf v. Colorado*, the Fourth Amendment protects the "security of one's privacy against arbitrary intrusion by the police. . . ." In declining to apply the exclusionary rule of *Mapp v. Ohio* to convictions that had become final before rendition of that decision, the Court emphasized that "there is no likelihood of unreliability or coercion present in a search-and-seizure case." The Fourth Amendment "is not an adjunct to the ascertainment of truth." The guarantees of the Fourth Amendment stand "as a protection of quite different constitutional values—values reflecting the concern of our society for the right of each individual to be let alone. To recognize this is no more than to accord those values undiluted respect."

Nor can it even be said that a search, as opposed to an eventual trial, is somehow "unfair" if a person consents to a search. While the Fourth and Fourteenth Amendments limit the circumstances under which the police can conduct a search, there is nothing constitutionally suspect in a person's voluntarily allowing a search. The actual conduct of the search may be precisely the same as if the police had obtained a warrant. And, unlike those constitutional guarantees that protect a defendant at trial, it cannot be said every reasonable presumption ought to be indulged against voluntary relinquishment. We have only recently stated: "(I) t is no part of the policy underlying the Fourth and Fourteenth Amendments to discourage citizens from aiding to the utmost of their ability in the apprehension of criminals." Rather, the community has a real interest in encouraging consent, for the resulting search may yield necessary evidence for the solution and prosecution of crime, evidence that may insure that a wholly innocent person is not wrongly charged with a criminal offense.

Those cases that have dealt with the application of the *Johnson v. Zerbst* rule make clear that it would be next to impossible to apply to a consent search the standard of "an intentional relinquishment or abandonment of a known right or privilege." To be true to *Johnson* and its progeny, there must be examination into the knowing and understanding nature of the waiver, an examination that was designed for a trial judge in the structured atmosphere of a courtroom. As the Court expressed it in *Johnson*:

> The constitutional right of an accused to be represented by counsel invokes, of itself, the protection of a trial court, in which the accused—whose life or liberty is at stake—is without counsel. This protecting duty imposes the serious and weighty responsibility upon the trial judge of determining whether there is an intelligent and competent waiver by the accused. While an accused may waive the right to counsel, whether there is a proper waiver should be clearly determined by the trial court, and it would be fitting and appropriate for that determination to appear upon the record.

It would be unrealistic to expect that in the informal, unstructured context of a consent search, a policeman, upon pain of tainting the evidence obtained, could make the detailed type of examination demanded by *Johnson*. And, if for this reason a diluted form of "waiver" were found acceptable, that would itself be ample recognition of the fact that there is no universal standard that must be applied in every situation where a person foregoes a constitutional right.

Similarly, a "waiver" approach to consent searches would be thoroughly inconsistent with our decisions that have approved "third party consents." . . .

In short, there is nothing in the purposes or application of the waiver requirements of *Johnson v. Zerbst* that justifies, much less compels, the easy equation of a knowing waiver with a consent search. To make such an equation is to generalize from the broad rhetoric of some of our decisions, and to ignore the substance of the differing constitutional guarantees. We decline to follow what one judicial scholar has termed "the domino method of constitutional adjudication . . . wherein every explanatory statement in a previous opinion is made the basis for extension to a wholly different situation."

D

Much of what has already been said disposes of the argument that the Court's decision in the *Miranda* case requires the conclusion that knowledge of a right to refuse is an indispensable element of a valid consent. The considerations that informed the Court's holding in *Miranda* are simply inapplicable in the present case. In *Miranda* the Court found that the techniques of police questioning and the nature of custodial surroundings produce an inherently coercive situation. The Court concluded that "(u)nless adequate protective devices are employed to dispel the compulsion inherent in custodial surroundings, no statement obtained from the defendant can truly be the product of his free choice." And at another point the Court noted that "without proper safeguards the process of in-custody interrogation of persons suspected or accused of crime contains inherently compelling pressures which work to undermine the individual's will to resist and to compel him to speak where he would not otherwise do so freely."

In this case, there is no evidence of any inherently coercive tactics—either from the nature of the police questioning or the environment in which it took place. Indeed, since consent searches will normally occur on a person's own familiar territory, the specter of incommunicado police interrogation in some remote station house is simply inapposite. There is no reason to believe, under circumstances such as are present here, that the response to a policeman's question is presumptively coerced; and there is, therefore, no reason to reject the traditional test for determining the voluntariness of a person's response. *Miranda*, of course, did not reach investigative questioning of a person not in custody, which is most directly analogous to the situation of a consent search, and it assuredly did not indicate that such questioning ought to be deemed inherently coercive.

It is also argued that the failure to require the Government to establish knowledge as a prerequisite to a valid consent, will relegate the Fourth Amendment to the special province of "the sophisticated, v. knowledgeable and the privileged." We cannot agree. The traditional definition of voluntariness we accept today has always taken into account evidence of minimal schooling, low intelligence, and the lack of any effective warnings to a person of his rights; and the voluntariness of any statement taken under those conditions has been carefully scrutinized to determine whether it was in fact voluntarily given.

E

Our decision today is a narrow one. We hold only that when the subject of a search is not in custody and the State attempts to justify a search on the basis of his consent, the Fourth and Fourteenth Amendments require that it demonstrate that the consent was in fact voluntarily given, and not the result of duress or coercion, express or implied. Voluntariness is a question of fact to be determined from all the circumstances, and while the subject's knowledge of a right to refuse is a factor to be taken into account, the prosecution is not required to demonstrate such knowledge as a prerequisite to establishing a voluntary consent. Because the California court followed these principles in affirming the respondent's conviction, and because the Court of Appeals for the Ninth Circuit in remanding for an evidentiary hearing required more, its judgment must be reversed.

[Justices Douglas, Brennan, and Marshall dissented.]

NOTES AND QUESTIONS

1. The case could not begin with a more quintessential traffic stop: a burned-out headlight and license plate light. The Court notes that the testimony of Officer Rand that the mood of the stop was "all very congenial" was uncontradicted. Maybe it really was congenial.

But what risks do you think Bustamonte would have run by taking the stand and offering a different account of the mood?

2. Do you think most people understand that they have a right to refuse to consent to a vehicle search? Do you think that, even if they do understand that they have such a right in the abstract, they think that they can exercise it without penalty (e.g., further questioning, a ticket instead of a citation, arrest, etc.)? Do you think people understand that their consent to a vehicle search includes consent to a search the scope of which, as here, extends to areas underneath the seats? To removal of door panels in some cases? To a search that can last over an hour?

3. As you saw in Chapter III *supra*, the Court seven years earlier in *Miranda* had rejected the due process "voluntariness" test (the Court's discussion of which is omitted here) for analyzing allegedly coercive confessions, in part due to its lack of administrative ease. Why employ it here?

4. In doing "balancing" here the Court offers about as unapologetic, ends-justifying-means appraisal of the law enforcement interests as can be imagined:

> In situations where the police have some evidence of illicit activity, but lack probable cause to arrest or search, a search authorized by a valid consent may be the only means of obtaining important and reliable evidence. In the present case for example, while the police had reason to stop the car for traffic violations, the State does not contend that there was probable cause to search the vehicle or that the search was incident to a valid arrest of any of the occupants. Yet, the search yielded tangible evidence that served as a basis for a prosecution, and provided some assurance that others, wholly innocent of the crime, were not mistakenly brought to trial. And in those cases where there is probable cause to arrest or search, but where the police lack a warrant, a consent search may still be valuable. If the search is conducted and proves fruitless, that in itself may convince the police that an arrest with its possible stigma and embarrassment is unnecessary, or that a far more extensive search pursuant to a warrant is not justified. In short, a search pursuant to consent may result in considerably less inconvenience for the subject of the search, and, properly conducted, is a constitutionally permissible and wholly legitimate aspect of effective police activity.

Id. at 227-28. Of course, depending on California law, after *Atwater* it may be constitutionally permissible to arrest at least the driver for the traffic code violations.

This spirit is also reflected in the Court's civics lesson on the virtue of consent: "the community has a real interest in encouraging consent, for the resulting search may yield necessary evidence for the solution and prosecution of crime, evidence that may insure that a wholly innocent person is not wrongly charged with a criminal offense." As a rule of thumb, you can always tell that the defendant is losing when the Court justifies a police practice by invoking the exoneration of innocent people.

5. The Court seems to genuinely resist conceptualizing a consent to a car search as a "waiver" of Fourth Amendment rights. It even cites gratuitously from a case saying that waiver can be for both "good and bad" purposes, and also cites two civil cases — civil cases! — for the proposition that waiver need not always be "knowing and intelligent." What possible explanation is there for such resistance to the well-established concept of waiver?

6. Is there any basis for the Court's distinction in this context between Fourth Amendment rights and rights that ensure a fair trial? How does the guilty plea — a waiver of the right to a jury trial, among other things — figure into this construct?

7. The Court contends it would be "next to impossible" to import into a traffic stop the full-blown colloquy required for determining whether a waiver was knowing and intelligent in other contexts. Is such a colloquy required? How about something like *Miranda* but shorter?

8. Very few people refuse to consent to a search of their car. *See* Kathryne M. Young & Christin L. Munsch, *Fact and Fiction in Constitutional Criminal Procedure*, 66 S.C. L. Rev. 445 (2014). Moreover, as Professors Young and Munsch find, rights assertion in police-citizen encounters differs based on social class and other background factors: lower socioeconomic status is associated with a greater reluctance to assert constitutional rights in interactions with the police. *Id.* at 476. Professor Carbado confirms that race may often be at play in the dynamic of the consent search inquiry:

> If Black Americans believe that police officers are likely to perceive Black people as criminally suspect, they may feel extra pressure to consent to say yes to consent to searches to disconfirm that stereotype. Black Americans might also feel pressured to say yes to consent searches on the view that saying no carries the risk of both prolonging the encounter and escalating the situation.

Devon W. Carbado, Unreasonable: Black Lives, Police Power, and the Fourth Amendment 51 (2022).

Schneckloth is still good law 50 years later, even as traffic stops have morphed into a critical and relentless law enforcement weapon that may not have been fully anticipated in 1973. If anything, the Court has extended its reach. In *Ohio v. Robinette*, 519 U.S. 33 (1996), the driver of the car, Robert Robinette, was stopped for speeding. The police officer wrote up a warning and handed it Robinette. The purpose of the stop had ended. Rather than return to his cruiser, however, the officer began to ask Robinette questions about whether there was any contraband in the car. Robinette responded in the negative. The officer then asked Robinette—"just one more thing"—if he could search the car. Robinette consented and drugs were found. The Court rejected the bright-line Ohio traffic-stop rule that once the purpose of the stop was over the driver had to be advised he was free to leave. Echoing the reasoning of *Schneckloth* the Court said such a requirement would be "unrealistic." Dissenting, Justice Stevens stated what would appear to most people to be obvious: "Repeated decisions by ordinary citizens to surrender [their self-interest] cannot satisfactorily be explained on any hypothesis other than an assumption that they believed they had had a legal duty to do so." *Id.* at 48.

Consent issues have reached the Supreme Court in other contexts, such as a third party's consent to the search of shared living space. In *United States v. Matlock*, 415 U.S. 164 (1974), the Court held that a warrantless entry and search is permissible if consent to the search were given by a third party with common authority over the premises. Quaintly, the Court noted in *Matlock* that a woman's statement authorizing consent to search the bedroom in the premises she shared with her boyfriend was admissible at the boyfriend's trial as an admission-against-interest because "cohabitation" was a crime under state law.

It's unclear when and whether law enforcement determined that *Matlock* gave it the ability to leverage domestic acrimony into an extra exception to the warrant requirement. Fourteen years after *Matlock*, in *Illinois v. Rodriguez*, 497 U.S. 177 (1990), police were able to leverage a woman's alleged physical abuse by her boyfriend into the latter's arrest on drug charges.

Illinois v. Rodriguez

497 U.S. 177 (1990)

Justice Scalia delivered the opinion of the Court.

In *United States v. Matlock*, this Court reaffirmed that a warrantless entry and search by law enforcement officers does not violate the Fourth Amendment's proscription of "unreasonable searches Illinois and seizures" if the officers have obtained the consent of a third party who possesses common authority over the premises. The present case presents an issue we expressly reserved in *Matlock*: Whether a warrantless entry is valid when based upon the consent of a third party whom the police, at the time of the entry, reasonably believe to possess common authority over the premises, but who in fact does not do so.

I

Respondent Edward Rodriguez was arrested in his apartment by law enforcement officers and charged with possession of illegal drugs. The police gained entry to the apartment with the consent and assistance of Gail Fischer, who had lived there with respondent for several months. The relevant facts leading to the arrest are as follows.

On July 26, 1985, police were summoned to the residence of Dorothy Jackson on South Wolcott in Chicago. They were met by Ms. Jackson's daughter, Gail Fischer, who showed signs of a severe beating. She told the officers that she had been assaulted by respondent Edward Rodriguez earlier that day in an apartment on South California. Fischer stated that Rodriguez was then asleep in the apartment, and she consented to travel there with the police in order to unlock the door with her key so that the officers could enter and arrest him. During this conversation, Fischer several times referred to the apartment on South California as "our" apartment, and said that she had clothes and furniture there. It is unclear whether she indicated that she currently lived at the apartment, or only that she used to live there.

The police officers drove to the apartment on South California, accompanied by Fischer. They did not obtain an arrest warrant for Rodriguez, nor did they seek a search warrant for the apartment. At the apartment, Fischer unlocked the door with her key and gave the officers permission to enter. They moved through the door into the living room, where they observed in plain view drug paraphernalia and containers filled with white powder that they believed (correctly, as later analysis showed) to be cocaine. They proceeded to the bedroom, where they found Rodriguez asleep and discovered additional containers of white powder in two open attaché cases. The officers arrested Rodriguez and seized the drugs and related paraphernalia.

Rodriguez was charged with possession of a controlled substance with intent to deliver. He moved to suppress all evidence seized at the time of his arrest, claiming that Fischer had vacated the apartment several weeks earlier and had no authority to consent to the entry. The Cook County Circuit Court granted the motion, holding that at the time she consented to the entry Fischer did not have common authority over the apartment. The Court concluded that Fischer was not a "usual resident" but rather an "infrequent visitor" at the apartment on South California, based upon its findings that Fischer's name was not on the lease, that she did not contribute to the rent, that she was not allowed to invite others to the apartment on her own, that she did not have access to the apartment when respondent was away, and that she had moved some of her possessions from the apartment. The Circuit Court also rejected the State's contention that, even if Fischer did not possess common authority over the premises, there was no Fourth Amendment violation if the police reasonably believed at the time of their entry that Fischer possessed the authority to consent.

The Appellate Court of Illinois affirmed the Circuit Court in all respects. The Illinois Supreme Court denied the State's petition for leave to appeal, and we granted certiorari.

II

The Fourth Amendment generally prohibits the warrantless entry of a person's home, whether to make an arrest or to search for specific objects. *Payton v. New York* (1980); *Johnson v. United States* (1948). The prohibition does not apply, however, to situations in which voluntary consent has been obtained, either from the individual whose property is searched, see *Schneckloth v. Bustamonte* (1973), or from a third party who possesses common authority over the premises, see *United States v. Matlock*. The State of Illinois contends that that exception applies in the present case.

As we stated in *Matlock*, "[c]ommon authority" rests "on mutual use of the property by persons generally having joint access or control for most purposes. . . ." The burden of establishing that common authority rests upon the State. On the basis of this record, it is clear that burden was not sustained. The evidence showed that although Fischer, with her two small children, had lived with Rodriguez beginning in December 1984, she had moved out on July 1, 1985, almost a month before the search at issue here, and had gone to live with her mother. She took her and her children's clothing with her, though leaving behind some furniture and household effects. During the period after July 1 she sometimes spent the night at Rodriguez's apartment, but never invited her friends there, and never went there herself when he was not home. Her name was not on the lease nor did she contribute to the rent. She had a key to the apartment, which she said at trial she had taken without Rodriguez's knowledge (though she testified at the preliminary hearing that Rodriguez had given her the key). On these facts the State has not established that, with respect to the South California apartment, Fischer had "joint access or control for most purposes." To the contrary, the Appellate Court's determination of no common authority over the apartment was obviously correct.

III

A

The State contends that, even if Fischer did not in fact have authority to give consent, it suffices to validate the entry that the law enforcement officers reasonably believed she did. Before reaching the merits of that contention, we must consider a jurisdictional objection: that the decision below rests on an adequate and independent state ground. Respondent asserts that the Illinois Constitution provides greater protection than is afforded under the Fourth Amendment, and that the Appellate Court relied upon this when it determined that a reasonable belief by the police officers was insufficient.

When a state-court decision is clearly based on state law that is both adequate and independent, we will not review the decision. *Michigan v. Long* (1983). But when "a state court decision fairly appears to rest primarily on federal law, or to be interwoven with the federal law," we require that it contain a "'plain statement' that [it] rests upon adequate and independent state grounds"; otherwise, "we will accept as the most reasonable explanation that the state court decided the case the way it did because it believed that federal law required it to do so." Here, the Appellate Court's opinion contains no "plain statement" that its decision rests on state law. The opinion does not rely on (or even mention) any specific provision of the Illinois Constitution, nor even the Illinois Constitution generally. Even the Illinois cases cited by the opinion rely upon no constitutional provisions other than the Fourth and Fourteenth Amendments of the United States Constitution. We conclude that the Appellate Court of Illinois rested its decision on federal law.

B

On the merits of the issue, respondent asserts that permitting a reasonable belief of common authority to validate an entry would cause a defendant's Fourth Amendment rights to be "vicariously waived." We disagree.

We have been unyielding in our insistence that a defendant's waiver of his trial rights cannot be given effect unless it is "knowing" and "intelligent." We would assuredly not permit, therefore, evidence seized in violation of the Fourth Amendment to be introduced on the basis of a trial court's mere "reasonable belief"—derived from statements by unauthorized persons—that the defendant has waived his objection. But one must make a distinction between, on the one hand, trial rights that derive from the violation of constitutional guarantees and, on the other hand, the nature of those constitutional guarantees themselves. As we said in *Schneckloth*:

> There is a vast difference between those rights that protect a fair criminal trial and the rights guaranteed under the Fourth Amendment. Nothing, either in the purposes behind requiring a "knowing" and "intelligent" waiver of trial rights, or in the practical application of such a requirement suggests that it ought to be extended to the constitutional guarantee against unreasonable searches and seizures.

What Rodriguez is assured by the trial right of the exclusionary rule, where it applies, is that no evidence seized in violation of the Fourth Amendment will be introduced at his trial unless he consents. What he is assured by the Fourth Amendment itself, however, is not that no government search of his house will occur unless he consents; but that no such search will occur that is "unreasonable." There are various elements, of course, that can make a search of a person's house "reasonable"—one of which is the consent of the person or his cotenant. The essence of respondent's argument is that we should impose upon this element a requirement that we have not imposed upon other elements that regularly compel government officers to exercise judgment regarding the facts: namely, the requirement that their judgment be not only responsible but correct.

The fundamental objective that alone validates all unconsented government searches is, of course, the seizure of persons who have committed or are about to commit crimes, or of evidence related to crimes. But "reasonableness," with respect to this necessary element, does not demand that the government be factually correct in its assessment that that is what a search will produce. Warrants need only be supported by "probable cause," which demands no more than a proper "assessment of probabilities in particular factual contexts. . . ." If a magistrate, based upon seemingly reliable but factually inaccurate information, issues a warrant for the search of a house in which the sought-after felon is not present, has never been present, and was never likely to have been present, the owner of that house suffers one of the inconveniences we all expose ourselves to as the cost of living in a safe society; he does not suffer a violation of the Fourth Amendment.

Another element often, though not invariably, required in order to render an unconsented search "reasonable" is, of course, that the officer be authorized by a valid warrant. Here also we have not held that "reasonableness" precludes error with respect to those factual judgments that law enforcement officials are expected to make. In *Maryland v. Garrison* (1987), a warrant supported by probable cause with respect to one apartment was erroneously issued for an entire floor that was divided (though not clearly) into two apartments. We upheld the search of the apartment not properly covered by the warrant. We said:

> [T]he validity of the search of respondent's apartment pursuant to a warrant authorizing the search of the entire third floor depends on whether the officers' failure to realize the overbreadth of the warrant was objectively understandable and reasonable. Here it unquestionably was. The objective facts available to the officers at the time suggested no distinction between [the suspect's] apartment and the third-floor premises.

The ordinary requirement of a warrant is sometimes supplanted by other elements that render the unconsented search "reasonable." Here also we have not held that the Fourth Amendment requires factual accuracy. A warrant is not needed, for example, where the search is incident to an arrest. In *Hill v. California* (1971), we upheld a search incident to an arrest, even though the arrest was made of the wrong person. We said:

> The upshot was that the officers in good faith believed Miller was Hill and arrested him. They were quite wrong as it turned out, and subjective good-faith belief would not in itself justify either the arrest or the subsequent search. But sufficient probability, not certainty, is the

> touchstone of reasonableness under the Fourth Amendment and on the record before us the officers' mistake was understandable and the arrest a reasonable response to the situation facing them at the time.

It would be superfluous to multiply these examples. It is apparent that in order to satisfy the "reasonableness" requirement of the Fourth Amendment, what is generally demanded of the many factual determinations that must regularly be made by agents of the government—whether the magistrate issuing a warrant, the police officer executing a warrant, or the police officer conducting a search or seizure under one of the exceptions to the warrant requirement—is not that they always be correct, but that they always be reasonable. As we put it in *Brinegar v. United States* (1949):

> Because many situations which confront officers in the course of executing their duties are more or less ambiguous, room must be allowed for some mistakes on their part. But the mistakes must be those of reasonable men, acting on facts leading sensibly to their conclusions of probability.

We see no reason to depart from this general rule with respect to facts bearing upon the authority to consent to a search. Whether the basis for such authority exists is the sort of recurring factual question to which law enforcement officials must be expected to apply their judgment; and all the Fourth Amendment requires is that they answer it reasonably. The Constitution is no more violated when officers enter without a warrant because they reasonably (though erroneously) believe that the person who has consented to their entry is a resident of the premises, than it is violated when they enter without a warrant because they reasonably (though erroneously) believe they are in pursuit of a violent felon who is about to escape.

Stoner v. California (1964) is in our view not to the contrary. There, in holding that police had improperly entered the defendant's hotel room based on the consent of a hotel clerk, we stated that "the rights protected by the Fourth Amendment are not to be eroded . . . by unrealistic doctrines of 'apparent authority.'" It is ambiguous, of course, whether the word "unrealistic" is descriptive or limiting—that is, whether we were condemning as unrealistic all reliance upon apparent authority, or whether we were condemning only such reliance upon apparent authority as is unrealistic. Similarly ambiguous is the opinion's earlier statement that "there [is no] substance to the claim that the search was reasonable because the police, relying upon the night clerk's expressions of consent, had a reasonable basis for the belief that the clerk had authority to consent to the search." Was there no substance to it because it failed as a matter of law, or because the facts could not possibly support it? At one point the opinion does seem to speak clearly:

> It is important to bear in mind that it was the petitioner's constitutional right which was at stake here, and not the night clerk's nor the hotel's. It was a right, therefore, which only the petitioner could waive by word or deed, either directly or through an agent.

But as we have discussed, what is at issue when a claim of apparent consent is raised is not whether the right to be free of searches has been waived, but whether the right to be free of unreasonable searches has been violated. Even if one does not think the *Stoner* opinion had this subtlety in mind, the supposed clarity of its foregoing statement is immediately compromised, as follows:

> It is true that the night clerk clearly and unambiguously consented to the search. But there is nothing in the record to indicate that the *police had any basis whatsoever to believe that* the night clerk had been authorized by the petitioner to permit the police to search the petitioner's room.

The italicized language should have been deleted, of course, if the statement two sentences earlier meant that an appearance of authority could never validate a search. In the last analysis, one must admit that the rationale of *Stoner* was ambiguous—and perhaps deliberately so. It is at least a reasonable reading of the case, and perhaps a preferable one, that the police could not rely upon the obtained consent because they knew it came from a hotel clerk, knew that the room was rented and exclusively occupied by the defendant, and could not reasonably have believed that the former had general access to or control over the latter. Similarly ambiguous in its implications (the Court's opinion does not even allude to, much less discuss the effects of, "reasonable belief") is *Chapman v. United States*. In sum, we were correct in *Matlock*, when we regarded the present issue as unresolved.

As *Stoner* demonstrates, what we hold today does not suggest that law enforcement officers may always accept a person's invitation to enter premises. Even when the invitation is accompanied by an explicit assertion that the person lives there, the surrounding circumstances could conceivably be such that a reasonable person would doubt its truth and not act upon it without further inquiry. As with other factual determinations bearing upon search and seizure, determination of consent to enter must "be judged against an objective standard: would the facts available to the officer at the moment . . . 'warrant a man of reasonable caution in the belief'" that the consenting party had authority over the premises? If not, then warrantless entry without further inquiry is unlawful unless authority actually exists. But if so, the search is valid.

• • •

In the present case, the Appellate Court found it unnecessary to determine whether the officers reasonably believed that Fischer had the authority to consent, because it ruled as a matter of law that a reasonable belief could not validate the entry. Since we find that ruling to be in error, we remand for consideration of that question. The judgment of the Illinois Appellate Court is reversed, and the case is remanded for further proceedings not inconsistent with this opinion.

So ordered.

NOTES AND QUESTIONS

1. Note the issue as to whether the Appellate Court of Illinois rested its decision that the search was legal on an adequate and independent state law ground. Why should the Court need to require such unmistakable clarity that a decision was grounded in state law? Why didn't the Appellate Court make its decision clear if that was its intention?

2. What do you think of the police officers' questioning of Fischer as to whether Rodriguez dealt in narcotics, a question to which she did not respond, a fact pointed out by the dissent but not the majority? Were the police really going to Rodriguez's house in order to arrest him for battery?

3. Why is this case not considered under the good faith exception to the exclusionary rule instead of as a third-party consent to search case?

4. The dissent accuses the majority of failing to analyze the consent issue in terms of the defendant's reasonable expectations of privacy, as it had done in *Matlock*, where it had held that a joint tenant assumes the risk that her cotenant might permit a common area to be searched. Did Rodriguez have a reasonable expectation of privacy here? Should a joint tenant really be seen as assuming the risk that his or her cotenant will consent to a search of the premises by law enforcement?

In *Georgia v. Randolph*, 547 U.S. 103 (2006), events led police to the exterior of a house where a bitterly feuding and separated husband and wife had lived together until a few weeks earlier. Janet Randolph told police that her husband was a drug user and that the house contained evidence of that usage. *Id.* Her husband, Scott Randolph, refused to give the police permission to search the house; Janet Randolph enthusiastically gave it to them. *Id.* The police entered the house with Janet, who led them to drug paraphernalia and cocaine. *Id.* The Court held that the *Matlock* rule does not apply where a person who also has common authority over the premises is physically present and refuses to give consent. *Id.* at 108, 123.

In *Fernandez v. California*, 571 U.S. 292 (2014), the Court again considered the issue of the authority of a joint tenant to consent to a search in the face of an objecting cotenant. In the course of investigating a robbery, the police came to the home of a woman who appeared to have been injured in a fight. A man who turned out to be the woman's cotenant appeared at the door and refused to let the police enter the apartment. The man was arrested and ultimately taken to the police station, where he was identified as the perpetrator of the robbery. *Id.* at 295-96. The police later returned to the apartment and received the woman's consent to search the home, where they found evidence inculpating the defendant in the robbery. *Id.* at 296. The Court refused to "extend" *Randolph* to this situation given that the defendant was not present when his cotenant gave permission for the search. The Court refused to consider the intent of the officers in removing the objecting cotenant from the scene, even though it was not clear that they had probable cause to arrest him. *Id.* at 295-96.

6. Exigent Circumstances

The Supreme Court has long recognized that sometimes "exigent circumstances" justify a warrantless entry and search as an urgent investigative need that would go unmet if a warrant were required. As the term suggests, both the exigency and the circumstances are case-specific, but some general categories recur. *See Ker v. California*, 374 U.S. 23 (1963) (plurality opinion) (to prevent the imminent destruction of evidence); *United States v. Santana*, 427 U.S. 38 (1976) (to engage in hot pursuit of a fleeing suspect). In *Welsh v. Wisconsin*, 466 U.S. 740 (1984), the Court found that a warrantless entry of a home to arrest a drunk-driving suspect was not justified where the only exigency was the preservation of the suspect's blood alcohol level. The Court frequently states that "searches and seizures inside a home without a warrant are presumptively unreasonable." *Groh v. Ramirez*, 540 U.S. 551, 559 (2004).

Brigham City v. Stuart

547 U.S. 398 (2006)

Chief Justice Roberts delivered the opinion of the Court.

In this case we consider whether police may enter a home without a warrant when they have an objectively reasonable basis for believing that an occupant is seriously injured or imminently threatened with such injury. We conclude that they may.

I

This case arises out of a melee that occurred in a Brigham City, Utah, home in the early morning hours of July 23, 2000. At about 3 a.m., four police officers responded to a call regarding a loud party at a residence. Upon arriving at the house, they heard shouting from inside, and proceeded down the driveway to investigate. There, they observed two juveniles drinking beer in the backyard. They entered the backyard, and saw—through a screen door and windows—an altercation taking place in the kitchen of the home. According to the testimony of one of the officers, four adults were attempting, with some difficulty, to restrain a juvenile. The juvenile eventually "broke free, swung a fist and struck one of the adults in the face." The officer testified that he observed the victim of the blow spitting blood into a nearby sink. The other adults continued to try to restrain the juvenile, pressing him up against a refrigerator with such force that the refrigerator began moving across the floor. At this point, an officer opened the screen door and announced the officers' presence. Amid the tumult, nobody noticed. The officer entered the kitchen and again cried out, and as the occupants slowly became aware that the police were on the scene, the altercation ceased.

The officers subsequently arrested respondents and charged them with contributing to the delinquency of a minor, disorderly conduct, and intoxication. In the trial court, respondents filed a motion to suppress all evidence obtained after the officers entered the home, arguing that the warrantless entry violated the Fourth Amendment. The court granted the motion, and the Utah Court of Appeals affirmed.

Before the Supreme Court of Utah, Brigham City argued that although the officers lacked a warrant, their entry was nevertheless reasonable on either of two grounds. The court rejected both contentions and, over two dissenters, affirmed. First, the court held that the injury caused by the juvenile's punch was insufficient to trigger the so-called "emergency aid doctrine" because it did not give rise to an "objectively reasonable belief that an unconscious, semi-conscious, or missing person feared injured or dead [was] in the home." Furthermore, the court suggested that the doctrine was inapplicable because the officers had not sought to assist the injured adult, but instead had acted "exclusively in their law enforcement capacity."

The court also held that the entry did not fall within the exigent circumstances exception to the warrant requirement. This exception applies, the court explained, where police have probable cause and where "a reasonable person [would] believe that the entry was necessary to prevent physical harm to the officers or other persons." Under this standard, the court stated, the potential harm need not be as serious as that required to invoke the emergency aid exception. Although it found the case "a close and difficult call," the court nevertheless concluded that the officers' entry was not justified by exigent circumstances.

We granted certiorari in light of differences among state courts and the Courts of Appeals concerning the appropriate Fourth Amendment standard governing warrantless entry by law enforcement in an emergency situation.

II

It is a "'basic principle of Fourth Amendment law that searches and seizures inside a home without a warrant are presumptively unreasonable.'"

One exigency obviating the requirement of a warrant is the need to assist persons who are seriously injured or threatened with such injury. "'The need to protect or preserve life or avoid serious injury is justification for what would be otherwise illegal absent an exigency or emergency.'" Accordingly, law enforcement officers may enter a home without a warrant to render emergency assistance to an injured occupant or to protect an occupant from imminent injury.

Respondents do not take issue with these principles, but instead advance two reasons why the officers' entry here was unreasonable. First, they argue that the officers were more interested in making arrests than quelling violence. They urge us to consider, in assessing the reasonableness of the entry, whether the officers were "indeed motivated primarily by a desire to save lives and property." The Utah Supreme Court also considered the officers' subjective motivations relevant.

Our cases have repeatedly rejected this approach. An action is "reasonable" under the Fourth Amendment, regardless of the individual officer's state of mind, "as long as the circumstances, viewed objectively, justify [the] action." The officer's subjective motivation is irrelevant. It therefore does not matter here—even if their subjective motives could be so neatly unraveled—whether the officers entered the kitchen to arrest respondents and gather evidence against them or to assist the injured and prevent further violence.

As respondents note, we have held in the context of programmatic searches conducted without individualized suspicion — such as checkpoints to combat drunk driving or drug trafficking — that "an inquiry into programmatic purpose" is sometimes appropriate. But this inquiry is directed at ensuring that the purpose behind the program is not "ultimately indistinguishable from the general interest in crime control." It has nothing to do with discerning what is in the mind of the individual officer conducting the search.

Respondents further contend that their conduct was not serious enough to justify the officers' intrusion into the home. They rely on *Welsh v. Wisconsin* (1984), in which we held that "an important factor to be considered when determining whether any exigency exists is the gravity of the underlying offense for which the arrest is being made." This contention, too, is misplaced. *Welsh* involved a warrantless entry by officers to arrest a suspect for driving while intoxicated. There, the "only potential emergency" confronting the officers was the need to preserve evidence (i.e., the suspect's blood-alcohol level) — an exigency that we held insufficient under the circumstances to justify entry into the suspect's home. Here, the officers were confronted with ongoing violence occurring within the home. Welsh did not address such a situation.

We think the officers' entry here was plainly reasonable under the circumstances. The officers were responding, at 3 o'clock in the morning, to complaints about a loud party. As they approached the house, they could hear from within "an altercation occurring, some kind of a fight." "It was loud and it was tumultuous." The officers heard "thumping and crashing" and people yelling "stop, stop" and "get off me." As the trial court found, "it was obvious that . . . knocking on the front door" would have been futile. The noise seemed to be coming from the back of the house; after looking in the front window and seeing nothing, the officers proceeded around back to investigate further. They found two juveniles drinking beer in the backyard. From there, they could see that a fracas was taking place inside the kitchen. A juvenile, fists clenched, was being held back by several adults. As the officers watch, he breaks free and strikes one of the adults in the face, sending the adult to the sink spitting blood.

In these circumstances, the officers had an objectively reasonable basis for believing both that the injured adult might need help and that the violence in the kitchen was just beginning. Nothing in the Fourth Amendment required them to wait until another blow rendered someone "unconscious" or "semi-conscious" or worse before entering. The role of a peace officer includes preventing violence and restoring order, not simply rendering first aid to casualties; an officer is not like a boxing (or hockey) referee, poised to stop a bout only if it becomes too one-sided.

The manner of the officers' entry was also reasonable. After witnessing the punch, one of the officers opened the screen door and "yelled in police." When nobody heard him, he stepped into the kitchen and announced himself again. Only then did the tumult subside. The officer's announcement of his presence was at least equivalent to a knock on the screen door. Indeed, it was probably the only option that had even a chance of rising above the din. Under these circumstances, there was no violation of the Fourth Amendment's knock-and-announce rule. Furthermore, once the announcement was made, the officers were free to enter; it would serve no purpose to require them to stand dumbly at the door awaiting a response while those within brawled on, oblivious to their presence.

Accordingly, we reverse the judgment of the Supreme Court of Utah, and remand the case for further proceedings not inconsistent with this opinion.

NOTES AND QUESTIONS

1. Does the nature of the "exigent circumstances" exception justify an exception to the Court's general Fourth Amendment rule that police officers' subjective motivation is irrelevant? Aren't inquiries under this exception always going to be fact-specific regardless?

2. Does the Court persuasively distinguish *Welsh*? What if all the persons scuffling had been—or appeared to be—juveniles? What if the officers had not observed any exchange of blows but had overheard threats of violence amid the tumult?

3. In *Kentucky v. King*, 563 U.S. 452 (2011), the Court considered an exception that many lower courts had carved out of the exigent circumstances doctrine where the exigency had been created by the conduct of the police. The rationale for the exception was that the police should not be able to exploit an exigency of their own making—such as by approaching a person or property that was under surveillance—to get around the warrant requirement. The Court essentially rejected the lower courts' exception, holding that as long as the police did not violate the Fourth Amendment by their conduct the fact that the conduct may have induced the exigency—such as the imminent destruction of evidence due to police in the vicinity—the exigent circumstances doctrine applied in full force.

4. The Court returned to the significance of the severity of the crime under investigation in *Lange v. California*, 141 S. Ct. 2011 (2021). A police officer on patrol in his vehicle followed defendant Arthur Lange after Lange attracted attention by playing loud music with his windows down and honking his horn. By the time the officer turned on his overhead lights to signal that Lange should pull over they were a hundred feet from Lange's home. Lange pulled into his driveway and entered the garage. The officer followed him into the garage and administered field sobriety tests that Lange failed. Lange was charged with misdemeanor drink driving.

The Court held that the result was not automatically determined by *Santana*, the Court's "hot pursuit" precedent, inasmuch as *Santana* was a felony drug case. Emphasizing the sanctity of the home, the Court rejected a categorical "hot pursuit" exigency for misdemeanants, and held that all circumstances must be considered:

> The flight of a suspected misdemeanant does not always justify a warrantless entry into a home. An officer must consider all the circumstances in a pursuit case to determine whether there is a law enforcement emergency. On many occasions, the officer will have good reason to enter—to prevent imminent harms of violence, destruction of evidence, or escape from the home. But when the officer has time to get a warrant, he must do so—even though the misdemeanant fled.

Id. at 2025. The case was remanded for application of this newly announced test. How do you think Lange will fare under it? Should the dissipation in the body of one's blood alcohol content be considered "destruction of evidence" for purposes of the exigent circumstances exception? Do fleeing suspects almost always—by virtue of the presence of police and their flight therefrom—create a risk of destruction of evidence?

7. Administrative or "Special Needs" Searches

An enormous and varied category of government searches lives largely outside the strictures of the Fourth Amendment. These searches often don't require warrants, probable cause, or even individualized suspicion. They fall into none of the above exceptions to the warrant requirement. As a category, they are sometimes called "administrative" or "suspicionless" or "special needs" searches. They are often justified by the fact that the regulatory authority under which they occur does not have criminal investigation and prosecution as its purpose, or at least not its primary purpose. Sometimes these searches are considered "special" just because they target high school kids.

An early example of such an administrative search was blessed in *Camara v. Municipal Court of City and County of San Francisco*, 387 U.S. 523 (1967), where the Court sanctioned city officials' inspection of buildings in a specified location for compliance with health-and-safety housing codes pursuant to an "area warrant" but without any individualized cause or suspicion as to particular buildings. The Court did not dismiss entirely the interests of the private citizens whose residences were searched but under the circumstances found them to be outweighed by the government's interests. *See also Michigan v. Tyler*, 436 U.S. 499 (1978) (allowing warrantless entry for purposes of fighting fire and for reasonable inspection of premises to determine cause of blaze).

In *New York v. Burger*, 482 U.S. 691 (1987), the Court upheld the constitutionality of a warrantless inspection of an automobile "junkyard" on the ground that the business was "closely regulated" and therefore any exalted expectation of privacy was unrealistic. This was a classic example of the circularity of the reasonable expectation of privacy doctrine: Because a state statute authorizes warrantless inspections of the business the proprietor's expectation of privacy was unreasonable. The Court was clearly thinking "chop shop," not junkyard, as was the New York legislature. The Court upheld the warrantless intrusion even though the regulatory framework was plainly law enforcement adjacent, at a minimum: The stated purpose of the regulatory scheme was to "deter motor vehicle theft," the inspections were done by police officers, and one of the records required to be maintained by the statute was called a "police book."

A warrantless search of a home was even upheld in *Griffin v. Wisconsin*, 483 U.S. 868 (1987). Joseph Griffin had been sentenced to probation after being convicted of disorderly conduct. The probation department got a tip that Griffin had a gun at his home, which—for a probationer—would have required approval by his probation officer, which had not been given. Under a statute authorizing a warrantless search of a probationer's home based on "reasonable grounds" to believe "contraband" would be found there, a probation officer (with three police officers) searched Griffin's home and found a gun. The Court found the warrantless search among the "exceptions when special needs, beyond the normal need for law enforcement, make the warrant and probable-cause requirement impracticable." *Id.* at 873. Observing, correctly, that probation is a form of punishment, the Court found that the regulatory regime for supervision of probationers justified the intrusion, in particular as it pertained to Griffin's "rehabilitation." (Ironically the federal Sentencing Reform Act of 1986—a year earlier than *Griffin* was decided—had explicitly renounced rehabilitation as a goal of federal sentencing.)

a. Vehicle Checkpoints

Sometimes the government isn't satisfied with its ability to stop and search cars without warrants, or to pull them over for trivial traffic code violations. Sometimes the government just passes a law that requires vehicles to pull themselves over for inspection at a checkpoint. Sometimes it works.

In *United States v. Martinez-Fuerte*, 428 U.S. 543 (1976), discussed further below in the section on racial profiling, the Court considered the constitutionality of immigration checkpoints designed to intercept illegal "aliens" that were located less than 100 miles from the Mexican border. Balancing the interests—the permitted intrusion was comparatively minor; stopping illegal immigration is hard—the Court found the checkpoints passed Fourth Amendment scrutiny. Just two years later, in *Delaware v. Prouse*, 440 U.S. 648, 663 (1979), in invalidating a suspicionless stop of a motorist, the Court—in a truly remarkable "write your congressperson" manner—suggested that a similar type of vehicle checkpoint for the regulatory purpose of verifying drivers' licenses and vehicle registrations might be permissible:

> This holding does not preclude the State of Delaware or other States from developing methods for spot checks that involve less intrusion or that do not involve the unconstrained exercise of discretion. Questioning of all oncoming traffic at roadblock-type stops is one possible alternative.

Id. at 663. Yikes. Could you imagine how such discretion would be exercised in practice?

The first case involving a vehicle checkpoint—Michigan cleverly called it a "sobriety checkpoint program," as if it were a therapeutic modality—reached the Court 11 years later. In *Michigan Dep't of State Police v. Sitz*, 496 U.S. 444 (1990), the Court upheld the checkpoint program due to its aim of combating the dangers of drunk driving notwithstanding the obvious overlap between safety and law enforcement interests in that context. *Id.* at 451.

In the next case the Court considered a less crafty attempt to use checkpoints.

City of Indianapolis v. Edmond

531 U.S. 32 (2000)

Justice O'Connor delivered the opinion of the Court.

In *Michigan Dept. of State Police v. Sitz* and *United States v. Martinez-Fuerte* we held that brief, suspicionless seizures at highway checkpoints for the purposes of combating drunk driving and intercepting illegal immigrants were constitutional. We now consider the constitutionality of a highway checkpoint program whose primary purpose is the discovery and interdiction of illegal narcotics.

I

In August 1998, the city of Indianapolis began to operate vehicle checkpoints on Indianapolis roads in an effort to interdict unlawful drugs. The city conducted six such roadblocks between August and November that year, stopping vehicles and arresting 104 motorists. Fifty-five arrests were for drug-related crimes, while 49 were for offenses unrelated to drugs. The overall "hit rate" of the program was thus approximately nine percent.

The parties stipulated to the facts concerning the operation of the checkpoints by the Indianapolis Police Department (IPD) for purposes of the preliminary injunction proceedings instituted below. At each checkpoint location, the police stop a predetermined number of vehicles. Approximately 30 officers are stationed at the checkpoint. Pursuant to written directives issued by the chief of police, at least one officer approaches the vehicle, advises the driver that he or she is being stopped briefly at a drug checkpoint, and asks the driver to produce a license and registration. The officer also looks for signs of impairment and conducts an open-view examination of the vehicle from the outside. A narcotics-detection dog walks around the outside of each stopped vehicle.

The directives instruct the officers that they may conduct a search only by consent or based on the appropriate quantum of particularized suspicion. The officers must conduct each stop in the same manner until particularized suspicion develops, and the officers have no discretion to stop any vehicle out of sequence. The city agreed in the stipulation to operate the checkpoints in such a way as to ensure that the total duration of each stop, absent reasonable suspicion or probable cause, would be five minutes or less.

The affidavit of Indianapolis Police Sergeant Marshall DePew, although it is technically outside the parties' stipulation, provides further insight concerning the operation of the checkpoints. According to Sergeant DePew, checkpoint locations are selected weeks in advance based on such considerations as area crime statistics and traffic flow. The checkpoints are generally operated during daylight hours and are identified with lighted signs reading, "'NARCOTICS CHECKPOINT—MILE AHEAD, NARCOTICS K-9 IN USE, BE PREPARED TO STOP.'" Once a group of cars has been stopped, other traffic proceeds without interruption until all the stopped cars have been processed or diverted for further processing. Sergeant DePew also stated that the average stop for a vehicle not subject to further processing lasts two to three minutes or less.

Respondents James Edmond and Joell Palmer were each stopped at a narcotics checkpoint in late September 1998. Respondents then filed a lawsuit on behalf of themselves and the class of all motorists who had been stopped or were subject to being stopped in the future at the Indianapolis drug checkpoints. Respondents claimed that the roadblocks violated the Fourth Amendment of the United States Constitution and the search and seizure provision of the Indiana Constitution. Respondents requested declaratory and injunctive relief for the class, as well as damages and attorney's fees for themselves.

Respondents then moved for a preliminary injunction. Although respondents alleged that the officers who stopped them did not follow the written directives, they agreed to the stipulation concerning the operation of the checkpoints for purposes of the preliminary injunction proceedings. The parties also stipulated to certification of the plaintiff class. The United States District Court for the Southern District of Indiana agreed to class certification and denied the motion for a preliminary injunction, holding that the checkpoint program did not violate the Fourth Amendment. A divided panel of the United States Court of Appeals for the Seventh Circuit reversed, holding that the checkpoints contravened the Fourth Amendment. The panel denied rehearing. We granted certiorari, and now affirm.

II

The Fourth Amendment requires that searches and seizures be reasonable. A search or seizure is ordinarily unreasonable in the absence of individualized suspicion of wrongdoing. While such suspicion is not an "irreducible" component of reasonableness, we have recognized only limited circumstances in which the usual rule does not apply. For example, we have upheld certain regimes of suspicionless searches where the program was designed to serve "special needs, beyond the normal need for law enforcement." We have also allowed searches for certain administrative purposes without particularized suspicion of misconduct, provided that those searches are appropriately limited.

We have also upheld brief, suspicionless seizures of motorists at a fixed Border Patrol checkpoint designed to intercept illegal aliens, and at a sobriety checkpoint aimed at removing drunk drivers from the road. In addition, in *Delaware v. Prouse*, we suggested that a similar type of roadblock with the purpose of verifying drivers' licenses and vehicle registrations would be permissible. In none of these cases, however, did we indicate approval of a checkpoint program whose primary purpose was to detect evidence of ordinary criminal wrongdoing.

In *Martinez-Fuerte*, we entertained Fourth Amendment challenges to stops at two permanent immigration checkpoints located on major United States highways less than 100 miles from the Mexican border. We noted at the outset the particular context in which the constitutional question arose, describing in some detail the "formidable law enforcement problems" posed by the northbound tide of illegal entrants into the United States. These problems had also been the focus of several earlier cases addressing the constitutionality of other Border Patrol traffic-checking operations. In *Martinez-Fuerte*, we found that the balance tipped in favor of the Government's interests in policing the Nation's borders. In so finding, we emphasized the difficulty of effectively containing illegal immigration at the border itself. We also stressed the impracticality of the particularized study of a given car to discern whether it was transporting illegal aliens, as well as the relatively modest degree of intrusion entailed by the stops.

Our subsequent cases have confirmed that considerations specifically related to the need to police the border were a significant factor in our *Martinez-Fuerte* decision.

In *Sitz*, we evaluated the constitutionality of a Michigan highway sobriety checkpoint program. The *Sitz* checkpoint involved brief, suspicionless stops of motorists so that police officers could detect signs of intoxication and remove impaired drivers from the road. Motorists who exhibited signs of intoxication were diverted for a license and registration check and, if warranted, further sobriety tests. This checkpoint program was clearly aimed at reducing the immediate hazard posed by the presence of drunk drivers on the highways, and there was an obvious connection between the imperative of highway safety and the law enforcement practice at issue. The gravity of the drunk driving problem and the magnitude of the State's interest in getting drunk drivers off the road weighed heavily in our determination that the program was constitutional.

In *Prouse*, we invalidated a discretionary, suspicionless stop for a spot check of a motorist's driver's license and vehicle registration. The officer's conduct in that case was unconstitutional primarily on account of his exercise of "standardless and unconstrained discretion." We nonetheless acknowledged the States' "vital interest in ensuring that only those qualified to do so are permitted to operate motor vehicles, that these vehicles are fit for safe operation, and hence that licensing, registration, and vehicle inspection requirements are being observed." Accordingly, we suggested that "[q]uestioning of all oncoming traffic at roadblock-type stops" would be a lawful means of serving this interest in highway safety.

We further indicated in *Prouse* that we considered the purposes of such a hypothetical roadblock to be distinct from a general purpose of investigating crime. The State proffered the additional interests of "the apprehension of stolen motor vehicles and of drivers under the influence of alcohol or narcotics" in its effort to justify the discretionary spot check. We attributed the entirety of the latter interest to the State's interest in roadway safety. Ibid. We also noted that the interest in apprehending stolen vehicles may be partly subsumed by the interest in roadway safety. Ibid. We observed, however, that "[t]he remaining governmental interest in controlling automobile thefts is not distinguishable from the general interest in crime control." Not only does the common thread of highway safety thus run through *Sitz* and *Prouse*, but *Prouse* itself reveals a difference in the Fourth Amendment significance of highway safety interests and the general interest in crime control.

III

It is well established that a vehicle stop at a highway checkpoint effectuates a seizure within the meaning of the Fourth Amendment. The fact that officers walk a narcotics-detection dog around the exterior of each car at the Indianapolis checkpoints does not transform the seizure into a search. Just as in *Place*, an exterior sniff of an automobile does not require entry into the car and is not designed to disclose any information other than the presence or absence of narcotics. Like the dog sniff in *Place*, a sniff by a dog that simply walks around a car is "much less intrusive than a typical search." Rather, what principally distinguishes these checkpoints from those we have previously approved is their primary purpose.

As petitioners concede, the Indianapolis checkpoint program unquestionably has the primary purpose of interdicting illegal narcotics. In their stipulation of facts, the parties repeatedly refer to the checkpoints as "drug checkpoints" and describe them as "being operated by the City of Indianapolis in an effort to interdict unlawful drugs in Indianapolis." In addition, the first document attached to the parties' stipulation is entitled "DRUG CHECKPOINT CONTACT OFFICER DIRECTIVES BY ORDER OF THE CHIEF OF POLICE." These directives instruct officers to "[a]dvise the citizen that they are being stopped briefly at a drug checkpoint." The second document attached to the stipulation is entitled "1998 Drug Road Blocks" and contains a statistical breakdown of information relating to the checkpoints conducted. Further, according to Sergeant DePew, the checkpoints are identified with lighted signs reading, "'NARCOTICS CHECKPOINT ___ MILE AHEAD, NARCOTICS K-9 IN USE, BE PREPARED TO STOP.'" Finally, both the District Court and the Court of Appeals recognized that the primary purpose of the roadblocks is the interdiction of narcotics.

We have never approved a checkpoint program whose primary purpose was to detect evidence of ordinary criminal wrongdoing. Rather, our checkpoint cases have recognized only limited exceptions to the general rule that a seizure must be accompanied by some measure of individualized suspicion. We suggested in *Prouse* that we would not credit the "general interest in crime control" as justification for a regime of suspicionless stops. Consistent with this suggestion, each of the checkpoint programs that we have approved was designed primarily to serve purposes closely related to the problems of policing the border or the necessity of ensuring roadway safety. Because the primary purpose of the Indianapolis narcotics checkpoint program is to uncover evidence of ordinary criminal wrongdoing, the program contravenes the Fourth Amendment.

Petitioners propose several ways in which the narcotics-detection purpose of the instant checkpoint program may instead resemble the primary purposes of the checkpoints in *Sitz* and *Martinez-Fuerte*. Petitioners state that the checkpoints in those cases had the same ultimate purpose of arresting those suspected of committing crimes. Brief for Petitioners. Securing the border and apprehending drunk drivers are, of course, law enforcement activities, and law enforcement officers employ arrests and criminal prosecutions in pursuit of these goals. If we were to rest the case at this high level of generality, there would be little check on the ability of the authorities to construct roadblocks for almost any conceivable law enforcement purpose. Without drawing the line at roadblocks designed primarily to serve the general interest in crime control, the Fourth Amendment would do little to prevent such intrusions from becoming a routine part of American life.

Petitioners also emphasize the severe and intractable nature of the drug problem as justification for the checkpoint program. There is no doubt that traffic in illegal narcotics creates social harms of the first magnitude. The law enforcement problems that the drug trade creates likewise remain daunting and complex, particularly in light of the myriad forms of spin-off crime that it spawns. The same can be said of various other illegal activities, if only to a lesser degree. But the gravity of the threat alone cannot be dispositive of questions concerning what means law enforcement officers may employ to pursue a given purpose. Rather, in determining whether individualized suspicion is required, we must consider the nature of the interests threatened and their connection to the particular law enforcement practices at issue. We are particularly reluctant to recognize exceptions to the general rule of individualized suspicion where governmental authorities primarily pursue their general crime control ends.

Nor can the narcotics-interdiction purpose of the checkpoints be rationalized in terms of a highway safety concern similar to that present in *Sitz*. The detection and punishment of almost any criminal offense serves broadly the safety of the community, and our streets would no doubt be safer but for the scourge of illegal drugs. Only with respect to a smaller class of offenses, however, is society confronted with the type of immediate, vehicle-bound threat to life and limb that the sobriety checkpoint in *Sitz* was designed to eliminate.

Petitioners also liken the anticontraband agenda of the Indianapolis checkpoints to the antismuggling purpose of the checkpoints in *Martinez-Fuerte*. Petitioners cite this Court's conclusion in *Martinez-Fuerte* that the flow of traffic was too heavy to permit "particularized study of a given car that would enable it to be identified as a possible carrier of illegal aliens," and claim that this logic has even more force here. The problem with this argument is that the same logic prevails any time a vehicle is employed to conceal contraband or other evidence of a crime. This type of connection to the roadway is very different from the close connection to roadway safety that was present in *Sitz* and *Prouse*. Further, the Indianapolis checkpoints are far removed from the border context that was crucial in *Martinez-Fuerte*. While the difficulty of examining each passing car was an important factor in validating the law enforcement technique employed in *Martinez-Fuerte*, this factor alone cannot justify a regime of suspicionless searches or seizures. Rather, we must look more closely at the nature of the public interests that such a regime is designed principally to serve.

The primary purpose of the Indianapolis narcotics checkpoints is in the end to advance "the general interest in crime control." We decline to suspend the usual requirement of individualized suspicion where the police seek to employ a checkpoint primarily for the ordinary enterprise of investigating crimes. We cannot sanction stops justified only by the generalized and ever-present possibility that interrogation and inspection may reveal that any given motorist has committed some crime.

Of course, there are circumstances that may justify a law enforcement checkpoint where the primary purpose would otherwise, but for some emergency, relate to ordinary crime control. For example, as the Court of Appeals noted, the Fourth Amendment would almost certainly permit an appropriately tailored roadblock set up to thwart an imminent terrorist attack or to catch a dangerous criminal who is likely to flee by way of a particular route. The exigencies created by these scenarios are far removed from the circumstances under which authorities might simply stop cars as a matter of course to see if there just happens to be a felon leaving the jurisdiction. While we do not limit the purposes that may justify a checkpoint program to any rigid set of categories, we decline to approve a program whose primary purpose is ultimately indistinguishable from the general interest in crime control.

Petitioners argue that our prior cases preclude an inquiry into the purposes of the checkpoint program. For example, they cite *Whren v. United States* (1996), and *Bond v. United States*, 529 (2000) to support the proposition that "where the government articulates and pursues a legitimate interest for a suspicionless stop, courts should not look behind that interest to determine whether the government's 'primary purpose' is valid." These cases, however, do not control the instant situation.

In *Whren*, we held that an individual officer's subjective intentions are irrelevant to the Fourth Amendment validity of a traffic stop that is justified objectively by probable cause to believe that a traffic violation has occurred. We observed that our prior cases "foreclose any argument that the constitutional reasonableness of traffic stops depends on the actual motivations of the individual officers involved." In so holding, we expressly distinguished cases where we had addressed the validity of searches conducted in the absence of probable cause.

Whren therefore reinforces the principle that, while "[s]ubjective intentions play no role in ordinary, probable-cause Fourth Amendment analysis," programmatic purposes may be relevant to the validity of Fourth Amendment intrusions undertaken pursuant to a general scheme without individualized suspicion. Accordingly, *Whren* does not preclude an inquiry into programmatic purpose in such contexts. It likewise does not preclude an inquiry into programmatic purpose here.

Last Term in *Bond*, we addressed the question whether a law enforcement officer violated a reasonable expectation of privacy in conducting a tactile examination of carry-on luggage in the overhead compartment of a bus. In doing so, we simply noted that the principle of *Whren* rendered the subjective intent of an officer irrelevant to this analysis. While, as petitioners correctly observe, the analytical rubric of *Bond* was not "ordinary, probable-cause Fourth Amendment analysis," nothing in *Bond* suggests that we would extend the principle of *Whren* to all situations where individualized suspicion was lacking. Rather, subjective intent was irrelevant in *Bond* because the inquiry that our precedents required focused on the objective effects of the actions of an individual officer. By contrast, our cases dealing with intrusions that occur pursuant to a general scheme absent individualized suspicion have often required an inquiry into purpose at the programmatic level.

Petitioners argue that the Indianapolis checkpoint program is justified by its lawful secondary purposes of keeping impaired motorists off the road and verifying licenses and registrations. If this were the case, however, law enforcement authorities would be able to establish checkpoints for virtually any purpose so long as they also included a license or sobriety check. For this reason, we examine the available evidence to determine the primary purpose of the checkpoint program. While we recognize the challenges inherent in a purpose inquiry, courts routinely engage in this enterprise in many areas of constitutional jurisprudence as a means of sifting abusive governmental conduct from that which is lawful. As a result, a program driven by an impermissible purpose may be proscribed while a program impelled by licit purposes is permitted, even though the challenged conduct may be outwardly similar. While reasonableness under the Fourth Amendment is predominantly an objective inquiry, our special needs and administrative search cases demonstrate that purpose is often relevant when suspicionless intrusions pursuant to a general scheme are at issue.

It goes without saying that our holding today does nothing to alter the constitutional status of the sobriety and border checkpoints that we approved in *Sitz* and *Martinez-Fuerte*, or of the type of traffic checkpoint that we suggested would be lawful in *Prouse*. The constitutionality of such checkpoint programs still depends on a balancing of the competing interests at stake and the effectiveness of the program. When law enforcement authorities pursue primarily general crime control purposes at checkpoints such as here, however, stops can only be justified by some quantum of individualized suspicion.

Our holding also does not affect the validity of border searches or searches at places like airports and government buildings, where the need for such measures to ensure public safety can be particularly acute. Nor does our opinion speak to other intrusions aimed primarily at purposes beyond the general interest in crime control. Our holding also does not impair the ability of police officers to act appropriately upon information that they properly learn during a checkpoint stop justified by a lawful primary purpose, even where such action may result in the arrest of a motorist for an offense unrelated to that purpose. Finally, we caution that the purpose inquiry in this context is to be conducted only at the programmatic level and is not an invitation to probe the minds of individual officers acting at the scene. Because the primary purpose of the Indianapolis checkpoint program is ultimately indistinguishable from the general interest in crime control, the checkpoints violate the Fourth Amendment. The judgment of the Court of Appeals is, accordingly, affirmed.

NOTES AND QUESTIONS

1. The Court discusses the checkpoint program in a fair amount of detail but is cryptic about how the checkpoint locations are determined, saying only that they are "based on such considerations as area crime statistics and traffic flow." What else would you like to know about the selection of locations? Would there be any legal issues if all the locations were located in areas with predominantly minority populations? At a more general level, do you see any legal issues if police disproportionately patrol areas with predominantly minority populations?

2. The Court concludes that "the Indianapolis checkpoint program has the primary purpose of interdicting illegal narcotics." Should it matter that the trial court, which denied a motion to preliminarily enjoin the program, found that another purpose of the program was checking licenses and registrations?

3. Could better lawyering have saved the city's checkpoint program? Large urban cities and their police departments sometimes have excellent lawyers, fully capable of reading Supreme Court precedent—such as *Sitz*—and advising accordingly. Couldn't the city's lawyers have created a self-serving document outlining the program—there doesn't seem to have been one here—that explicitly announces the program's dual purposes? Why in the world did the city's lawyers enter into a stipulation that calls the very intrusions at issue—the checkpoints—"drug checkpoints"?

Admittedly, the use of a canine drug-sniff at each and every stop might have given the game away regardless.

4. Does the Court persuasively distinguish the forbidden inquiry into purpose required by *Whren* from the permitted inquiry into "programmatic" purpose here? If the program had been better dressed up in "dual purpose" clothing, would *Whren* have precluded consideration of whether the regulatory part of the clothing was pretextual?

5. Do these statistics — 104 arrests (55 for drugs; 49 for other) out of 1,161 vehicles stopped — suggest to you the program was successful or unsuccessful? Would you need to know more about the other 49 arrests? More about whether charges were brought based on the arrests and, if so, to what end (prior to the Seventh Circuit decision reversing the denial of the injunction)? More about how many vehicles were stopped for "further processing"? Demographic information about the occupants of the vehicles subjected to "further processing"?

b. High School Students

As seen in the next case, the Supreme Court is fond of duly noting — right before it denies them their rights — that high school students do not "shed their constitutional rights . . . at the schoolhouse gate." *Tinker v. Des Moines Independent Community School Dist.*, 393 U.S. 503 (1969) (school district could not discipline students for protesting Vietnam War by wearing black armbands absent reasonable prospect of disruption of school activities). In *New Jersey v. T.L.O.*, 469 U.S. 325 (1985), the Court held that a search of a high school student's purse would be governed by a flexible "reasonableness" standard and did not require a showing of probable cause, given the different interests and responsibilities in the school environment.

In the next case, the Court considers a suspicionless drug-testing program directed at all students in a school district who participate in interscholastic athletics.

Vernonia School District 47J v. Acton

515 U.S. 646 (1995)

Justice Scalia delivered the opinion of the Court.

The Student Athlete Drug Policy adopted by School District 47J in the town of Vernonia, Oregon, authorizes random urinalysis drug testing of students who participate in the District's school athletics programs. We granted certiorari to decide whether this violates the Fourth and Fourteenth Amendments to the United States Constitution.

I

A

Petitioner Vernonia School District 47J (District) operates one high school and three grade schools in the logging community of Vernonia, Oregon. As elsewhere in small-town America, school sports play a prominent role in the town's life, and student athletes are admired in their schools and in the community.

Drugs had not been a major problem in Vernonia schools. In the mid-to-late 1980's, however, teachers and administrators observed a sharp increase in drug use. Students began to speak out about their attraction to the drug culture, and to boast that there was nothing the school could do about it. Along with more drugs came more disciplinary problems. Between 1988 and 1989 the number of disciplinary referrals in Vernonia schools rose to more than twice the number reported in the early 1980's, and several students were suspended. Students became increasingly rude during class; outbursts of profane language became common.

Not only were student athletes included among the drug users but, as the District Court found, athletes were the leaders of the drug culture. This caused the District's administrators particular concern, since drug use increases the risk of sports-related injury. Expert testimony at the trial confirmed the deleterious effects of drugs on motivation, memory, judgment, reaction, coordination, and performance. The high school football and wrestling coach witnessed a severe sternum injury suffered by a wrestler, and various omissions of safety procedures and misexecutions by football players, all attributable in his belief to the effects of drug use.

Initially, the District responded to the drug problem by offering special classes, speakers, and presentations designed to deter drug use. It even brought in a specially trained dog to detect drugs, but the drug problem persisted. According to the District Court:

> [T]he administration was at its wits end and . . . a large segment of the student body, particularly those involved in interscholastic athletics, was in a state of rebellion. Disciplinary actions had reached "epidemic proportions." The coincidence of an almost three-fold increase in classroom disruptions and disciplinary reports along with the staff's direct observations of students using drugs or glamorizing drug and alcohol use led the administration to the inescapable conclusion that the rebellion was being fueled by alcohol and drug abuse as well as the student's misperceptions about the drug culture.

At that point, District officials began considering a drug-testing program. They held a parent "input night" to discuss the proposed Student Athlete Drug Policy (Policy), and the parents in attendance gave their unanimous approval. The school board approved the Policy for implementation in the fall of 1989. Its expressed purpose is to prevent student athletes from using drugs, to protect their health and safety, and to provide drug users with assistance programs.

B

The Policy applies to all students participating in interscholastic athletics. Students wishing to play sports must sign a form consenting to the testing and must obtain the written consent of their parents. Athletes are tested at the beginning of the season for their sport. In addition, once each week of the season the names of the athletes are placed in a "pool" from which a student, with the supervision of two adults, blindly draws the names of 10% of the athletes for random testing. Those selected are notified and tested that same day, if possible.

The student to be tested completes a specimen control form which bears an assigned number. Prescription medications that the student is taking must be identified by providing a copy of the prescription or a doctor's authorization. The student then enters an empty locker room accompanied by an adult monitor of the same sex. Each boy selected produces a sample at a urinal, remaining fully clothed with his back to the monitor, who stands approximately 12 to 15 feet behind the student. Monitors may (though do not always) watch the student while he produces the sample, and they listen for normal sounds of urination. Girls produce samples in an enclosed bathroom stall, so that they can be heard but not observed. After the sample is produced, it is given to the monitor, who checks it for temperature and tampering and then transfers it to a vial.

The samples are sent to an independent laboratory, which routinely tests them for amphetamines, cocaine, and marijuana. Other drugs, such as LSD, may be screened at the request of the District, but the identity of a particular student does not determine which drugs will be tested. The laboratory's procedures are 99.94% accurate. The District follows strict procedures regarding the chain of custody and access to test results. The laboratory does not know the identity of the students whose samples it tests. It is authorized to mail written test reports only to the superintendent and to provide test results to District personnel by telephone only after the requesting official recites a code confirming his authority. Only the superintendent, principals, vice-principals, and athletic directors have access to test results, and the results are not kept for more than one year.

If a sample tests positive, a second test is administered as soon as possible to confirm the result. If the second test is negative, no further action is taken. If the second test is positive, the athlete's parents are notified, and the school principal convenes a meeting with the student and his parents, at which the student is given the option of (1) participating for six weeks in an assistance program that includes weekly urinalysis, or (2) suffering suspension from athletics for the remainder of the current season and the next athletic season. The student is then retested prior to the start of the next athletic season for which he or she is eligible. The Policy states that a second offense results in automatic imposition of option (2); a third offense in suspension for the remainder of the current season and the next two athletic seasons.

C

In the fall of 1991, respondent James Acton, then a seventh grader, signed up to play football at one of the District's grade schools. He was denied participation, however, because he and his parents refused to sign the testing consent forms. The Actons filed suit, seeking declaratory and injunctive relief from enforcement of the Policy on the grounds that it violated the Fourth and Fourteenth Amendments to the United States Constitution and Article I, § 9, of the Oregon Constitution. After a bench trial, the District Court entered an order denying the claims on the merits and dismissing the action. The United States Court of Appeals for the Ninth Circuit reversed, holding that the Policy violated both the Fourth and Fourteenth Amendments and Article I, § 9, of the Oregon Constitution. We granted certiorari.

II

The Fourth Amendment to the United States Constitution provides that the Federal Government shall not violate "[t]he right of the people to be secure in their persons, houses, papers, and effects, against unreasonable searches and seizures. . . ." We have held that the Fourteenth Amendment extends this constitutional guarantee to searches and seizures by state officers, including public school officials. In *Skinner v. Railway Labor Executives' Assn.* (1989), we held that state-compelled collection and testing of urine, such as that required by the Policy, constitutes a "search" subject to the demands of the Fourth Amendment.

As the text of the Fourth Amendment indicates, the ultimate measure of the constitutionality of a governmental search is "reasonableness." At least in a case such as this, where there was no clear practice, either approving or disapproving the type of search at issue, at the time the constitutional provision was enacted, whether a particular search meets the reasonableness standard "'is judged by balancing its intrusion on the individual's Fourth Amendment interests against its promotion of legitimate governmental interests.'" Where a search is undertaken by law enforcement officials to discover evidence of criminal wrongdoing, this Court has said that reasonableness generally requires the obtaining of a judicial warrant. Warrants cannot be issued, of course, without the showing of probable cause required by the Warrant Clause. But a warrant is not required to establish the reasonableness of all government searches; and when a warrant is not required (and the Warrant Clause therefore not applicable), probable cause is not invariably required either. A search unsupported by probable cause can be constitutional, we have said, "when special needs, beyond the normal need for law enforcement, make the warrant and probable-cause requirement impracticable." *Griffin v. Wisconsin* (1987).

We have found such "special needs" to exist in the public school context. There, the warrant requirement "would unduly interfere with the maintenance of the swift and informal disciplinary procedures [that are] needed," and "strict adherence to the requirement that searches be based upon probable cause" would undercut "the substantial need of teachers and administrators for freedom to maintain order in the schools." The school search we approved in *T.L.O.*, while not based on probable cause, was based on individualized suspicion of wrongdoing. As we explicitly acknowledged, however, "'the Fourth Amendment imposes no irreducible requirement of such suspicion.'" We have upheld suspicionless searches and seizures to conduct drug testing of railroad personnel involved in train accidents; to conduct random drug testing of federal customs officers who carry arms or are involved in drug interdiction; and to maintain automobile checkpoints looking for illegal immigrants and contraband.

III

The first factor to be considered is the nature of the privacy interest upon which the search here at issue intrudes. The Fourth Amendment does not protect all subjective expectations of privacy, but only those that society recognizes as "legitimate." What expectations are legitimate varies, of course, with context, depending, for example, upon whether the individual asserting the privacy interest is at home, at work, in a car, or in a public park. In addition, the legitimacy of certain privacy expectations vis-à-vis the State may depend upon the individual's legal relationship with the State. For example, in *Griffin*, we held that, although a "probationer's home, like anyone else's, is protected by the Fourth Amendmen[t]," the supervisory relationship between probationer and State justifies "a degree of impingement upon [a probationer's] privacy that would not be constitutional if applied to the public at large." Central, in our view, to the present case is the fact that the subjects of the Policy are (1) children, who (2) have been committed to the temporary custody of the State as schoolmaster.

Traditionally at common law, and still today, unemancipated minors lack some of the most fundamental rights of self-determination—including even the right of liberty in its narrow sense, i.e., the right to come and go at will. They are subject, even as to their physical freedom, to the control of their parents or guardians. When parents place minor children in private schools for their education, the teachers and administrators of those schools stand in loco parentis over the children entrusted to them. In fact, the tutor or schoolmaster is the very prototype of that status. As Blackstone describes it, a parent "may . . . delegate part of his parental authority, during his life, to the tutor or schoolmaster of his child; who is then in loco parentis, and has such a portion of the power of the parent committed to his charge, viz. that of restraint and correction, as may be necessary to answer the purposes for which he is employed."

In *T.L.O.* we rejected the notion that public schools, like private schools, exercise only parental power over their students, which of course is not subject to constitutional constraints. Such a view of things, we said, "is not entirely 'consonant with compulsory education laws,' and is inconsistent with our prior decisions treating school officials as state actors for purposes of the Due Process and Free Speech Clauses." But while denying that the State's power over schoolchildren is formally no more than the delegated power of their parents, *T.L.O.* did not deny, but indeed emphasized, that the nature of that power is custodial and tutelary, permitting a degree of supervision and control that could not be exercised over free adults. "[A] proper educational environment requires close supervision of schoolchildren, as well as the enforcement of rules against conduct that would be perfectly permissible if undertaken by an adult." While we do not, of course, suggest that public schools as a general matter have such a degree of control over children as to give rise to a constitutional "duty to protect," we have acknowledged that for many purposes "school authorities ac[t] in loco parentis," with the power and indeed the duty to "inculcate the habits and manners of civility." Thus, while children assuredly do not "shed their constitutional rights . . . at the schoolhouse gate," the nature of those rights is what is appropriate for children in school.

Fourth Amendment rights, no less than First and Fourteenth Amendment rights, are different in public schools than elsewhere; the "reasonableness" inquiry cannot disregard the schools' custodial and tutelary responsibility for children. For their own good and that of their classmates, public school children are routinely required to submit to various physical examinations, and to be vaccinated against various diseases. According to the American Academy of Pediatrics, most public schools "provide vision and hearing screening and dental and dermatological checks. . . . Others also mandate scoliosis screening at appropriate grade levels." In the 1991-1992 school year, all 50 States required public school students to be vaccinated against diphtheria, measles, rubella, and polio. Particularly with regard to medical examinations and procedures, therefore, "students within the school environment have a lesser expectation of privacy than members of the population generally."

Legitimate privacy expectations are even less with regard to student athletes. School sports are not for the bashful. They require "suiting up" before each practice or event, and showering and changing afterwards. Public school locker rooms, the usual sites for these activities, are not notable for the privacy they afford. The locker rooms in Vernonia are typical: No individual dressing rooms are provided; shower heads are lined up along a wall, unseparated by any sort of partition or curtain; not even all the toilet stalls have doors. As the United States Court of Appeals for the Seventh Circuit has noted, there is "an element of 'communal undress' inherent in athletic participation."

There is an additional respect in which school athletes have a reduced expectation of privacy. By choosing to "go out for the team," they voluntarily subject themselves to a degree of regulation even higher than that imposed on students generally. In Vernonia's public schools, they must submit to a preseason physical exam (James testified that his included the giving of a urine sample), they must acquire adequate insurance coverage or sign an insurance waiver, maintain a minimum grade point average, and comply with any "rules of conduct, dress, training hours and related matters as may be established for each sport by the head coach and athletic director with the principal's approval." Somewhat like adults who choose to participate in a "closely regulated industry," students who voluntarily participate in school athletics have reason to expect intrusions upon normal rights and privileges, including privacy.

IV

Having considered the scope of the legitimate expectation of privacy at issue here, we turn next to the character of the intrusion that is complained of. We recognized in *Skinner* that collecting the samples for urinalysis intrudes upon "an excretory function traditionally shielded by great privacy." We noted, however, that the degree of intrusion depends upon the manner in which production of the urine sample is monitored. Under the District's Policy, male students produce samples at a urinal along a wall. They remain fully clothed and are only observed from behind, if at all. Female students produce samples in an enclosed stall, with a female monitor standing outside listening only for sounds of tampering. These conditions are nearly identical to those typically encountered in public restrooms, which men, women, and especially schoolchildren use daily. Under such conditions, the privacy interests compromised by the process of obtaining the urine sample are in our view negligible.

The other privacy-invasive aspect of urinalysis is, of course, the information it discloses concerning the state of the subject's body, and the materials he has ingested. In this regard it is significant that the tests at issue here look only for drugs, and not for whether the student is, for example, epileptic, pregnant, or diabetic. Moreover, the drugs for which the samples are screened are standard, and do not vary according to the identity of the student. And finally, the results of the tests are disclosed only to a limited class of school personnel who have a need to know; and they are not turned over to law enforcement authorities or used for any internal disciplinary function.

Respondents argue, however, that the District's Policy is in fact more intrusive than this suggests, because it requires the students, if they are to avoid sanctions for a falsely positive test, to identify in advance prescription medications they are taking. We agree that this raises some cause for concern. In *Von Raab*, we flagged as one of the salutary features of the Customs Service drug-testing program the fact that employees were not required to disclose medical information unless they tested positive, and, even then, the information was supplied to a licensed physician rather than to the Government employer. On the other hand, we have never indicated that requiring advance disclosure of medications is per se unreasonable. Indeed, in *Skinner* we held that it was not "a significant invasion of privacy." It can be argued that, in *Skinner*, the disclosure went only to the medical personnel taking the sample, and the Government personnel analyzing it; and that disclosure to teachers and coaches — to persons who personally know the student — is a greater invasion of privacy. Assuming for the sake of argument that both those propositions are true, we do not believe they establish a difference that respondents are entitled to rely on here.

The General Authorization Form that respondents refused to sign, which refusal was the basis for James's exclusion from the sports program, said only (in relevant part): "I . . . authorize the Vernonia School District to conduct a test on a urine specimen which I provide to test for drugs and/or alcohol use. I also authorize the release of information concerning the results of such a test to the Vernonia School District and to the parents and/or guardians of the student." While the practice of the District seems to have been to have a school official take medication information from the student at the time of the test, that practice is not set forth in, or required by, the Policy, which says simply: "Student athletes who . . . are or have been taking prescription medication must provide verification (either by a copy of the prescription or by doctor's authorization) prior to being tested." It may well be that, if and when James was selected for random testing at a time that he was taking medication, the School District would have permitted him to provide the requested information in a confidential manner — for example, in a sealed envelope delivered to the testing lab. Nothing in the Policy contradicts that, and when respondents choose, in effect, to challenge the Policy on its face, we will not assume the worst. Accordingly, we reach the same conclusion as in *Skinner*: that the invasion of privacy was not significant.

V

Finally, we turn to consider the nature and immediacy of the governmental concern at issue here, and the efficacy of this means for meeting it. In both *Skinner* and *Von Raab*, we characterized the government interest motivating the search as "compelling." Relying on these cases, the District Court held that because the District's program also called for drug testing in the absence of individualized suspicion, the District "must demonstrate a 'compelling need' for the program." The Court of Appeals appears to have agreed with this view. It is a mistake, however, to think that the phrase "compelling state interest," in the Fourth Amendment context, describes a fixed, minimum quantum of governmental concern, so that one can dispose of a case by answering in isolation the question: Is there a compelling state interest here? Rather, the phrase describes an interest that appears important enough to justify the particular search at hand, in light of other factors that show the search to be relatively intrusive upon a genuine expectation of privacy. Whether that relatively high degree of government concern is necessary in this case or not, we think it is met.

That the nature of the concern is important — indeed, perhaps compelling — can hardly be doubted. Deterring drug use by our Nation's schoolchildren is at least as important as enhancing efficient enforcement of the Nation's laws against the importation of drugs, which was the governmental concern in *Von Raab*, or deterring drug use by engineers and trainmen, which was the governmental concern in *Skinner*. School years are the time when the physical, psychological, and addictive effects of drugs are most severe. "Maturing nervous systems are more critically impaired by intoxicants than mature ones are; childhood losses in learning are lifelong and profound"; "children grow chemically dependent more quickly than adults, and their record of recovery is depressingly poor." And of course the effects of a drug-infested school are visited not just upon the users, but upon the entire student body and faculty, as the educational process is disrupted. In the present case, moreover, the necessity for the State to act is magnified by the fact that this evil is being visited not just upon individuals at large, but upon children for whom it has undertaken a special responsibility of care and direction. Finally, it must not be lost sight of that this program is directed more narrowly to drug use by school athletes, where the risk of immediate physical harm to the drug user or those with whom he is playing his sport is particularly high. Apart from psychological effects, which include impairment of judgment, slow reaction time, and a lessening of the perception of pain, the particular drugs screened by the District's Policy have been demonstrated to pose substantial physical risks to athletes. Amphetamines produce an "artificially induced heart rate increase, [p]eripheral vasoconstriction, [b]lood pressure increase, and [m]asking of the normal fatigue response," making them a "very dangerous drug when used during exercise of any type." Marijuana causes "[i]rregular blood pressure responses during changes in body position," "[r]eduction in the oxygen-carrying capacity of the blood," and "[i]nhibition of the normal sweating responses resulting in increased body temperature." Cocaine produces "[v]asoconstriction[,] [e]levated blood pressure," and "[p]ossible coronary artery spasms and myocardial infarction."

As for the immediacy of the District's concerns: We are not inclined to question—indeed, we could not possibly find clearly erroneous—the District Court's conclusion that "a large segment of the student body, particularly those involved in interscholastic athletics, was in a state of rebellion," that "[d]isciplinary actions had reached 'epidemic proportions,'" and that "the rebellion was being fueled by alcohol and drug abuse as well as by the student's misperceptions about the drug culture." That is an immediate crisis of greater proportions than existed in *Skinner*, where we upheld the Government's drug-testing program based on findings of drug use by railroad employees nationwide, without proof that a problem existed on the particular railroads whose employees were subject to the test. And of much greater proportions than existed in *Von Raab*, where there was no documented history of drug use by any customs officials.

As to the efficacy of this means for addressing the problem: It seems to us self-evident that a drug problem largely fueled by the "role model" effect of athletes' drug use, and of particular danger to athletes, is effectively addressed by making sure that athletes do not use drugs. Respondents argue that a "less intrusive means to the same end" was available, namely, "drug testing on suspicion of drug use." We have repeatedly refused to declare that only the "least intrusive" search practicable can be reasonable under the Fourth Amendment. Respondents' alternative entails substantial difficulties—if it is indeed practicable at all. It may be impracticable, for one thing, simply because the parents who are willing to accept random drug testing for athletes are not willing to accept accusatory drug testing for all students, which transforms the process into a badge of shame. Respondents' proposal brings the risk that teachers will impose testing arbitrarily upon troublesome but not drug-likely students. It generates the expense of defending lawsuits that charge such arbitrary imposition, or that simply demand greater process before accusatory drug testing is imposed. And not least of all, it adds to the ever-expanding diversionary duties of schoolteachers the new function of spotting and bringing to account drug abuse, a task for which they are ill prepared, and which is not readily compatible with their vocation. In many respects, we think, testing based on "suspicion" of drug use would not be better, but worse.

VI

Taking into account all the factors we have considered above—the decreased expectation of privacy, the relative unobtrusiveness of the search, and the severity of the need met by the search—we conclude Vernonia's Policy is reasonable and hence constitutional.

We caution against the assumption that suspicionless drug testing will readily pass constitutional muster in other contexts. The most significant element in this case is the first we discussed: that the Policy was undertaken in furtherance of the government's responsibilities, under a public school system, as guardian and tutor of children entrusted to its care. Just as when the government conducts a search in its capacity as employer (a warrantless search of an absent employee's desk to obtain an urgently needed file, for example), the relevant question is whether that intrusion upon privacy is one that a reasonable employer might engage in; so also when the government acts as guardian and tutor the relevant question is whether the search is one that a reasonable guardian and tutor might undertake. Given the findings of need made by the District Court, we conclude that in the present case it is.

We may note that the primary guardians of Vernonia's schoolchildren appear to agree. The record shows no objection to this districtwide program by any parents other than the couple before us here—even though, as we have described, a public meeting was held to obtain parents' views. We find insufficient basis to contradict the judgment of Vernonia's parents, its school board, and the District Court, as to what was reasonably in the interest of these children under the circumstances.

The Ninth Circuit held that Vernonia's Policy not only violated the Fourth Amendment, but also, by reason of that violation, contravened Article I, § 9, of the Oregon Constitution. Our conclusion that the former holding was in error means that the latter holding rested on a flawed premise. We therefore vacate the judgment, and remand the case to the Court of Appeals for further proceedings consistent with this opinion.

[Justices Souter, Stevens, and O'Connor dissented.]

NOTES AND QUESTIONS

1. What inferences can you draw from the opening line of the opinion:

> As elsewhere in small-town America, school sports play a prominent role in the town's life, and student athletes are admired in their schools and in the community.

Id. at 648. Any doubt that Justice Scalia was from a city? And did not play sports in high school?

2. Note the meticulous attention to detail in the four-paragraph description of the school district's drug-testing program. Is there any doubt at this point in the opinion who is going to win?

3. The Court relies, as it did in *T.L.O.*, on the notion that the state's power over schoolchildren is both "custodial and tutelary," which permits "a degree of supervision and control that could not be exercised over free adults." Do you accept this premise? If so, is the greater degree of control permitted more a function of the compulsory nature of public education or the educational mission of public education?

4. Do you agree with the Court that high school athletes have reduced legitimate expectations in their urine because they may shower in locker rooms and to some extent experience "communal undress"? Because they have to comply with other requirements (a physical, GPA, etc.) not imposed on the student body at large?

Are these two points necessary to the Court's conclusion, or could this drug-testing regime be applied to the entire student body?

Is the school's purported concern for sports-related injury to members of the Loggers (including the football and wrestling coach's testimony) plausible?

Vernonia High, home of the Loggers

5. Is there anything preventing the local district attorney from serving a grand jury subpoena for the high school's drug-testing records and prosecuting those students who tested positive?

6. Just five years later, in *Bd. of Educ. v. Earls*, 536 U.S. 822 (2002), the Court upheld on virtually identical reasoning a school district's drug-testing regime for all students participating in "competitive extracurricular activities." The Court did not find it necessary to revisit the sports-related implications of *Vernonia*. In dissent, however, Justice Ginsburg distinguished *Vernonia* in part on the basis of her view of the superiority of non-athletic extracurricular activities over the interscholastic sports at issue in *Vernonia*.

As noted in *Vernonia*, the Court has upheld drug-testing regimens in other contexts under the special needs/administrative exception. *See, e.g., Skinner v. Railway Labor Executives' Assn.*, 489 U.S. 602 (1989); *Treasury Employees v. Von Raab*, 489 U.S. 656 (1989). It has rejected as too broad, however, a Georgia law requiring every candidate for state office to take and pass a drug test. *Chandler v. Miller*, 520 U.S. 305 (1997).

8. The Automobile Exception

Carroll v. United States

267 U.S. 132 (1925)

Mr. Chief Justice Taft, after stating the case as above, delivered the opinion of the Court.

The constitutional and statutory provisions involved in this case include the Fourth Amendment and the National Prohibition Act.

The Fourth Amendment is in part as follows:

> The right of the people to be secure in their persons, houses, papers and effects against unreasonable searches and seizures shall not be violated, and no warrants shall issue but upon probable cause, supported by oath or affirmation, and particularly describing the place to be searched, and the persons or things to be seized.

Section 25, title 2, of the National Prohibition Act, passed to enforce the Eighteenth Amendment, makes it unlawful to have or possess any liquor intended for use in violating the act, or which has been so used, and provides that no property rights shall exist in such liquor. A search warrant may issue and such liquor, with the containers thereof, may be seized under the warrant and be ultimately destroyed. The section further provides:

> No search warrant shall issue to search any private dwelling occupied as such unless it is being used for the unlawful sale of intoxicating liquor, or unless it is in part used for some business purpose such as a store, shop, saloon, restaurant, hotel, or boarding house. The term "private dwelling" shall be construed to include the room or rooms used and occupied not transiently but solely as a residence in an apartment house, hotel, or boarding house.

Section 26, title 2, under which the seizure herein was made, provides in part as follows:

> When the commissioner, his assistants, inspectors, or any officer of the law shall discover any person in the act of transporting in violation of the law, intoxicating liquors in any wagon, buggy, automobile, water or air craft, or other vehicle, it shall be his duty to seize any and all intoxicating liquors found therein being transported contrary to law. Whenever intoxicating liquors transported or possessed illegally shall be seized by an officer he shall take possession of the vehicle and team or automobile, boat, air or water craft, or any other conveyance, and shall arrest any person in charge thereof.

The section then provides that the court upon conviction of the person so arrested shall order the liquor destroyed, and except for good cause shown shall order a sale by public auction of the other property seized, and that the proceeds shall be paid into the Treasury of the United States.

By section 6 of an act supplemental to the National Prohibition it is provided that if any officer or agent or employee of the United States engaged in the enforcement of the Prohibition Act or this Amendment, "shall search any private dwelling," as defined in that act, "without a warrant directing such search," or "shall without a search warrant maliciously and without reasonable cause search any other building or property," he shall be guilty of a misdemeanor and subject to fine or imprisonment or both.

In the passage of the supplemental act through the Senate, amendment No. 32, known as the Stanley Amendment, was adopted, the relevant part of which was as follows:

> Sec. 6. That any officer, agent or employee of the United States engaged in the enforcement of this act or the National Prohibition Act, or any other law of the United States, who shall search or attempt to search the property or premises of any person without previously securing a search warrant, as provided by law, shall be guilty of a misdemeanor and upon conviction thereof shall be fined not to exceed $1,000, or imprisoned not to exceed one year, or both so fined and imprisoned in the discretion of the court.

This amendment was objected to in the House, and the judiciary committee, to whom it was referred, reported to the House of Representatives the following as a substitute:

> Sec. 6. That no officer, agent or employee of the United States, while engaged in the enforcement of this act, the National Prohibition Act, or any law in reference to the manufacture or taxation of, or traffic in, intoxicating liquor, shall search any private dwelling without a warrant directing such search, and no such warrant shall issue unless there is reason to believe

> such dwelling is used as a place in which liquor is manufactured for sale or sold. The term "private dwelling" shall be construed to include the room or rooms occupied not transiently, but solely as a residence in an apartment house, hotel, or boarding house. Any violation of any provision of this paragraph shall be punished by a fine of not to exceed $1,000 or imprisonment not to exceed one year, or both such fine and imprisonment, in the discretion of the court.

In its report the committee spoke in part as follows:

> It appeared to the committee that the effect of the Senate amendment No. 32, if agreed to by the House, would greatly cripple the enforcement of the National Prohibition Act and would otherwise seriously interfere with the government in the enforcement of many other laws, as its scope is not limited to the prohibition law, but applies equally to all laws where prompt action is necessary. There are on the statute books of the United States a number of laws authorizing search without a search warrant. Under the common law and agreeable to the Constitution search may in many cases be legally made without a warrant. The Constitution does not forbid search, as some parties contend, but it does forbid unreasonable search. This provision in regard to search is as a rule contained in the various state Constitutions, but notwithstanding that fact search without a warrant is permitted in many cases, and especially is that true in the enforcement of liquor legislation.
>
> The Senate amendment prohibits all search or attempt to search any property or premises without a search warrant. The effect of that would necessarily be to prohibit all search, as no search can take place if it is not on some property or premises.
>
> Not only does this amendment prohibit search of any lands but it prohibits the search of all property. It will prevent the search of the common bootlegger and his stock in trade, though caught and arrested in the act of violating the law. But what is perhaps more serious, it will make it impossible to stop the rum-running automobiles engaged in like illegal traffic. It would take from the officers the power that they absolutely must have to be of any service, for if they cannot search for liquor without a warrant they might as well be discharged. It is impossible to get a warrant to stop an automobile. Before a warrant could be secured the automobile would be beyond the reach of the officer with its load of illegal liquor disposed of.

The conference report resulted, so far as the difference between the two houses was concerned, in providing for the punishment of any officer, agent, or employee of the government who searches a "private dwelling" without a warrant, and for the punishment of any such officer, etc., who searches any "other building or property" where, and only where, he makes the search without a warrant "maliciously and without probable cause." In other words, it left the way open for searching an automobile or vehicle of transportation without a warrant, if the search was not malicious or without probable cause.

The intent of Congress to make a distinction between the necessity for a search warrant in the searching of private dwellings and in that of automobiles and other road vehicles in the enforcement of the Prohibition Act is thus clearly established by the legislative history of the Stanley Amendment. Is such a distinction consistent with the Fourth Amendment? We think that it is. The Fourth Amendment does not denounce all searches or seizures, but only such as are unreasonable.

The leading case on the subject of search and seizure is *Boyd v. United States*, 116 U.S. 616. An Act of Congress authorized a court of the United States in revenue cases, on motion of the government attorney, to require the defendant to produce in court his private books, invoices, and papers on pain in case of refusal of having the allegations of the attorney in his motion taken as confessed. This was held to be unconstitutional and void as applied to suits for penalties or to establish a forfeiture of goods, on the ground that under the Fourth Amendment the compulsory production of invoices to furnish evidence for forfeiture of goods constituted an unreasonable search even where made upon a search warrant, and was also a violation of the

Fifth Amendment, in that it compelled the defendant in a criminal case to produce evidence against himself or be in the attitude of confessing his guilt.

In *Weeks v. United States*, it was held that a court in a criminal prosecution could not retain letters of the accused seized in his house, in his absence and without his authority, by a United States marshal holding no warrant for his arrest and none for the search of his premises, to be used as evidence against him, the accused having made timely application to the court for an order for the return of the letters.

In *Silverthorne Lumber Co. v. United States* a writ of error was brought to reverse a judgment of contempt of the District Court, fining the company and imprisoning one Silverthorne, its president, until he should purge himself of contempt in not producing books and documents of the company before the grand jury to prove violation of the statutes of the United States by the company and Silverthorne. Silverthorne had been arrested, and while under arrest the marshal had gone to the office of the company without a warrant and made a clean sweep of all books, papers, and documents found there and had taken copies and photographs of the papers. The District Court ordered the return of the originals, but impounded the photographs and copies. This was held to be an unreasonable search of the property and possessions of the corporation and a violation of the Fourth Amendment and the judgment for contempt was reversed.

In *Gouled v. United States*, the obtaining through stealth by a representative of the government from the office of one suspected of defrauding the government of a paper which had no pecuniary value in itself, but was only to be used as evidence against its owner, was held to be a violation of the Fourth Amendment. It was further held that when the paper was offered in evidence and duly objected to it must be ruled inadmissible because obtained through an unreasonable search and seizure and also in violation of the Fifth Amendment because working compulsory incrimination.

In *Amos v. United States*, it was held that where concealed liquor was found by government officers without a search warrant in the home of the defendant, in his absence, and after a demand made upon his wife, it was inadmissible as evidence against the defendant, because acquired by an unreasonable seizure.

In none of the cases cited is there any ruling as to the validity under the Fourth Amendment of a seizure without a warrant of contraband goods in the course of transportation and subject to forfeiture or destruction.

On reason and authority the true rule is that if the search and seizure without a warrant are made upon probable cause, that is, upon a belief, reasonably arising out of circumstances known to the seizing officer, that an automobile or other vehicle contains that which by law is subject to seizure and destruction, the search and seizure are valid. The Fourth Amendment is to be construed in the light of what was deemed an unreasonable search and seizure when it was adopted, and in a manner which will conserve public interests as well as the interests and rights of individual citizens.

In *Boyd v. United States* as already said, the decision did not turn on whether a reasonable search might be made without a warrant; but for the purpose of showing the principle on which the Fourth Amendment proceeds, and to avoid any misapprehension of what was decided, the court, speaking through Mr. Justice Bradley, used language which is of particular significance and applicability here. It was there said:

> The search for and seizure of stolen or forfeited goods, or goods liable to duties and concealed to avoid the payment thereof, are totally different things from a search for and seizure of a man's private books and papers for the purpose of obtaining information therein contained, or of using them as evidence against him. The two things differ *toto coelo*. In the one case, the government is entitled to the possession of the property; in the other it is not. The seizure of stolen goods is authorized by the common law; and the seizure of goods forfeited for a breach of the

> revenue laws, or concealed to avoid the duties payable on them, has been authorized by English statutes for at least two centuries past; and the like seizures have been authorized by our own revenue acts from the commencement of the government.

• • •

We have made a somewhat extended reference to these statutes to show that the guaranty of freedom from unreasonable searches and seizures by the Fourth Amendment has been construed, practically since the beginning of the government, as recognizing a necessary difference between a search of a store, dwelling house, or other structure in respect of which a proper official warrant readily may be obtained and a search of a ship, motor boat, wagon, or automobile for contraband goods, where it is not practicable to secure a warrant, because the vehicle can be quickly moved out of the locality or jurisdiction in which the warrant must be sought.

Having thus established that contraband goods concealed and illegally transported in an automobile or other vehicle may be searched for without a warrant, we come now to consider under what circumstances such search may be made. It would be intolerable and unreasonable if a prohibition agent were authorized to stop every automobile on the chance of finding liquor, and thus subject all persons lawfully using the highways to the inconvenience and indignity of such a search. Travelers may be so stopped in crossing an international boundary because of national self-protection reasonably requiring one entering the country to identify himself as entitled to come in, and his belongings as effects which may be lawfully brought in. But those lawfully within the country, entitled to use the public highways, have a right to free passage without interruption or search unless there is known to a competent official, authorized to search, probable cause for believing that their vehicles are carrying contraband or illegal merchandise. Section 26, title 2, of the National Prohibition Act, like the second section of the act of 1789, for the searching of vessels, like the provisions of the act of 1815, and section 3601, Revised Statutes, for searching vehicles for smuggled goods, and like the act of 1822, and that of 1834 and section 2140, R. S., and the act of 1917 for the search of vehicles and automobiles for liquor smuggled into the Indian country, was enacted primarily to accomplish the seizure and destruction of contraband goods; secondly, the automobile was to be forfeited; and, thirdly, the driver was to be arrested. Under section 29, title 2, of the act the latter might be punished by not more than $500 fine for the first offense, not more than $1,000 fine and 90 days' imprisonment for the second offense, and by a fine of $500 or more and by not more than 2 years' imprisonment for the third offense. Thus he is to be arrested for a misdemeanor for his first and second offenses, and for a felony if he offends the third time.

The main purpose of the act obviously was to deal with the liquor and its transportation, and to destroy it. The mere manufacture of liquor can do little to defeat the policy of the Eighteenth Amendment and the Prohibition Act, unless the for bidden product can be distributed for illegal sale and use. Section 26 was intended to reach and destroy the forbidden liquor in transportation and the provisions for forfeiture of the vehicle and the arrest of the transporter were incidental. The rule for determining what may be required before a seizure may be made by a competent seizing official is not to be determined by the character of the penalty to which the transporter may be subjected. Under section 28, title 2, of the Prohibition Act, the Commissioner of Internal Revenue, his assistants, agents and inspectors are to have the power and protection in the enforcement of the act conferred by the existing laws relating to the manufacture or sale of intoxicating liquors. Officers who seize under section 26 of the Prohibition Act are therefore protected by section 970 of the Revised Statutes, providing that:

> When, in any prosecution commenced on account of the seizure of any vessel, goods, wares, or merchandise, made by any collector or other officer, under any act of Congress authorizing such seizure, judgment is rendered for the claimant, but it appears to the court that there was

> reasonable cause of seizure, the court shall cause a proper certificate thereof to be entered, and the claimant shall not, in such case, be entitled to costs, nor shall the person who made the seizure, nor the prosecutor, be liable to suit or judgment on account of such suit or prosecution: Provided, that the vessel, goods, wares, or merchandise be, after judgment, forthwith returned to such claimant or his agent.

It follows from this that, if an officer seizes an automobile or the liquor in it without a warrant, and the facts as subsequently developed do not justify a judgment of condemnation and forfeiture, the officer may escape costs or a suit for damages by a showing that he had reasonable or probable cause for the seizure. The measure of legality of such a seizure is, therefore, that the seizing officer shall have reasonable or probable cause for believing that the automobile which he stops and seizes has contraband liquor therein which is being illegally transported.

We here find the line of distinction between legal and illegal seizures of liquor in transport in vehicles. It is certainly a reasonable distinction. It gives the owner of an automobile or other vehicle seized under section 26, in absence of probable cause, a right to have restored to him the automobile, it protects him under the *Weeks* and *Amos* cases from use of the liquor as evidence against him, and it subjects the officer making the seizures to damages. On the other hand, in a case showing probable cause, the government and its officials are given the opportunity which they should have, to make the investigation necessary to trace reasonably suspected contraband goods and to seize them.

Such a rule fulfills the guaranty of the Fourth Amendment. In cases where the securing of a warrant is reasonably practicable, it must be used and when properly supported by affidavit and issued after judicial approval protects the seizing officer against a suit for damages. In cases where seizure is impossible except without warrant, the seizing officer acts unlawfully and at his peril unless he can show the court probable cause.

But we are pressed with the argument that if the search of the automobile discloses the presence of liquor and leads under the statue to the arrest of the person in charge of the automobile, the right of seizure should be limited by the common-law rule as to the circumstances justifying an arrest without a warrant for a misdemeanor. The usual rule is that a police officer may arrest without warrant one believed by the officer upon reasonable cause to have been guilty of a felony, and that he may only arrest without a warrant one guilty of a misdemeanor if committed in his presence. The rule is sometimes expressed as follows:

> In cases of misdemeanor, a peace officer like a private person has at common law no power of arresting without a warrant except when a breach of the peace has been committed in his presence or there is reasonable ground for supposing that a breach of peace is about to be committed or renewed in his presence.

The reason for arrest for misdemeanors without warrant at common law was promptly to suppress breaches of the peace, while the reason for arrest without warrant on a reliable report of a felony was because the public safety and the due apprehension of criminals charged with heinous offenses required that such arrests should be made at once without warrant. The argument for defendants is that, as the misdemeanor to justify arrest without warrant must be committed in the presence of the police officer, the offense is not committed in his presence unless he can by his senses detect that the liquor is being transported, no matter how reliable his previous information by which he can identify the automobile as loaded with it.

So it is that under the rule contended for by defendants the liquor if carried by one who has been already twice convicted of the same offense may be seized on information other than the senses, while if he has been only once convicted it may not be seized unless the presence of the liquor is detected by the senses as the automobile concealing it rushes by. This is certainly a very unsatisfactory line of difference when the main object of the section is to forfeit and suppress the liquor, the arrest of the individual being only incidental as shown by the lightness of the penalty. In England at the common law the difference in punishment between felonies and misdemeanors was very great. Under our present federal statutes, it is much less important and Congress may exercise a relatively wide discretion in classing particular offenses as felonies or misdemeanors. As the main purpose of section 26 was seizure and forfeiture, it is not so much the owner as the property that offends. The language of the section provides for seizure when the officer of the law "discovers" any one in the act of transporting the liquor by automobile or other vehicle. Certainly it is a very narrow and technical construction of this word which would limit it to what the officer sees, hears or smells as the automobile rolls by and excludes therefrom when he identifies the car the convincing information that he may previously have received as to the use being made of it.

We do not think such a nice distinction is applicable in the present case. When a man is legally arrested for an offense, whatever is found upon his person or in his control which it is unlawful for him to have and which may be used to prove the offense may be seized and held as evidence in the prosecution. The argument of defendants is based on the theory that the seizure in this case can only be thus justified. If their theory were sound, their conclusion would be. The validity of the seizure then would turn wholly on the validity of the arrest without a seizure. But the theory is unsound. The right to search and the validity of the seizure are not dependent on the right to arrest. They are dependent on the reasonable cause the seizing officer has for belief that the contents of the automobile offend against the law. The seizure in such a proceeding comes before the arrest as section 26 indicates. It is true that section 26, title 2, provides for immediate proceedings against the person arrested and that upon conviction the liquor is to be destroyed and the automobile or other vehicle is to be sold, with the saving of the interest of a lienor who does not know of its unlawful use; but it is evident that if the person arrested is ignorant of the contents of the vehicle, or if he escapes, proceedings can be had against the liquor for destruction or other disposition under section 25 of the same title. The character of the offense for which, after the contraband liquor is found and seized, the driver can be prosecuted does not affect the validity of the seizure.

This conclusion is in keeping with the requirements of the Fourth Amendment and the principles of search and seizure of contraband forfeitable property; and it is a wise one because it leaves the rule one which is easily applied and understood and is uniform.

Finally, was there probable cause?

• • •

In *The Apollon*, the question was whether the seizure of a French vessel at a particular place was upon probable cause that she was there for the purpose of smuggling. In this discussion Mr. Justice Story, who delivered the judgment of the court, said:

> It has been very justly observed at the bar that the court is bound to take notice of public facts and geographical positions, and that this remote part of the country has been infested, at different periods, by smugglers, is matter of general notoriety, and may be gathered from the public documents of the government.

We know in this way that Grand Rapids is about 152 miles from Detroit, and that Detroit and its neighborhood along the Detroit river, which is the international boundary, is one of the most active centers for introducing illegally into this country spirituous liquors for distribution into the interior. It is obvious from the evidence that the prohibition agents were engaged in a regular patrol along the important highways from Detroit to Grand Rapids to stop and seize liquor carried in automobiles. They knew or had convincing evidence to make them believe that the Carroll boys, as they called them, were so-called "bootleggers" in Grand Rapids; i.e., that they were engaged in plying the unlawful trade of selling such liquor in that city. The officers had soon after noted their going from Grand Rapids half way to Detroit, and attempted to follow them to that city to see where they went, but they escaped observation. Two months later these officers suddenly met the same men on their way westward presumably from Detroit. The partners in the original combination to sell liquor in Grand Rapids were together in the same automobile they had been in the night when they tried to furnish the whisky to the officers, which was thus identified as part of the firm equipment. They were coming from the direction of the great source of supply for their stock to Grand Rapids, where they plied their trade. That the officers, when they saw the defendants, believed that they were carrying liquor, we can have no doubt, and we think it is equally clear that they had reasonable cause for thinking so. Emphasis is put by defendants' counsel on the statement made by one of the officers that they were not looking for defendants at the particular time when they appeared. We do not perceive that it has any weight. As soon as they did appear, the officers were entitled to use their reasoning faculties upon all the facts of which they had previous knowledge in respect to the defendants.

The necessity for probable cause in justifying seizures on land or sea, in making arrests without warrant for past felonies, and in malicious prosecution and false imprisonment cases has led to frequent definition of the phrase. In *Stacey v. Emery*, a suit for damages for seizure by a collector, this court defined probable cause as follows:

> If the facts and circumstances before the officer are such as to warrant a man of prudence and caution in believing that the offense has been committed, it is sufficient.

• • •

In the light of these authorities, and what is shown by this record, it is clear the officers here had justification for the search and seizure. This is to say that the facts and circumstances within their knowledge and of which they had reasonably trustworthy information were sufficient in themselves to warrant a man of reasonable caution in the belief that intoxicating liquor was being transported in the automobile which they stopped and searched.

Counsel finally argue that the defendants should be permitted to escape the effect of the conviction because the court refused on motion to deliver them the liquor when, as they say, the evidence adduced on the motion was much less than that shown on the trial, and did not show probable cause. The record does not make it clear what evidence was produced in support of or against the motion. But, apart from this, we think the point is without substance here. If the evidence given on the trial was sufficient, as we think it was, to sustain the introduction of the liquor as evidence, it is immaterial that there was an inadequacy of evidence when application was made for its return. A conviction on adequate and admissible evidence should not be set aside on such a ground. The whole matter was gone into at the trial, so no right of the defendants was infringed.

Counsel for the government contend that Kiro, the defendant who did not own the automobile, could not complain of the violation of the Fourth Amendment in the use of the liquor as evidence against him, whatever the view taken as to Carroll's rights. Our conclusion as to the whole case makes it unnecessary for us to discuss this aspect of it.

NOTES AND QUESTIONS

1. In parts of the opinion mostly omitted here, the Court goes into some detail about congressional legislation regarding search and seizure, both in connection with Prohibition — a movement with not only its own constitutional amendment but multiple implementing statutes — and otherwise. The Court notes that the Volstead Act established a dichotomy between automobiles and dwellings, explicitly requiring warrants for searches for the latter but not the former. The Court also notes that other legislation over the previous century more generally permitted warrantless searches of ships and other vessels.

Why would the Court look to such congressional "precedent" in applying the Fourth Amendment? Part of the answer may be due to the fact that federal case law on the subject was scanty—prior to Prohibition federal law enforcement agents were few and far between and there was not much federal criminal law for them to enforce. Federal customs officials—the investigators in *Boyd v. United States* (*see* Chapter III *supra*)—were an exception.

2. *Carroll* nonetheless established new Fourth Amendment law by dispensing with the warrant requirement, and the corresponding judicial oversight of police action, for a "reasonable or probable cause" standard that would be applied by law enforcement agents in the field. Chief Justice Taft, though an avowed opponent of Prohibition as a matter of policy, was an equally forceful proponent of what he viewed as the rule of law. Daniel Okrent, Last Call: The Rise and Fall of Prohibition 282-83 (2010). Despite the matter-of-fact tone of the opinion, Taft was well aware that the Court was making brand new law, as he privately confided in letters to his son and fellow Justice Van Devanter. Sarah A. Seo, Policing the Open Road: How Cars Transformed American Freedom 138 (2019).

3. Another novel aspect of *Carroll* was its abrogation of the common law of arrests. Prior to *Carroll* a warrantless arrest on a misdemeanor charge—first and second violations of the Volstead Act were misdemeanors—required that the arresting officer personally witness the crime. The Court shrugged off this requirement as a concession to law enforcement necessity, noting that the difference between felonies and misdemeanors was more important under English common law than today. This is a classic example of the Court confronting new technology and concluding that the impact of that technology on law enforcement requires ignoring or modifying existing precedent. Not all such clashes are resolved in favor of the government, but most are.

4. Ironically Justice Brandeis, the passionate spokesperson for the interests of privacy in his *Olmstead* dissent just three years later, and in the *Harvard Law Review* 35 years earlier, joined the Court's opinion. The explanation, according to Professor Seo and others, may lie in the fact that Brandeis was something of a Luddite or what we would now call a technophobe, who never owned a car and viewed cars as an urban menace. Seo, Policing the Open Road, *supra* at 131-32. Brandeis may have in some way seen automobiles as of a piece with the new and evolving forms of privacy-reducing technology that animated his *Olmstead* dissent.

5. Does the *Carroll* exception apply only to automobiles that are actually in motion, or is it a categorical rule, owing to the inherent mobility of an automobile? Consider a car parked on a street or in a driveway, for two days, a week, a month. Is a warrant required for a search?

6. Do you agree with the Court that the officers had "probable cause" for the search and seizure of "the Carroll boys'" car? Note that the ultraconservative Justice McReynolds says the stop was made "on mere suspicion." To what extent does it appear that the Court defers to the officers' "expertise"?

7. Can *Carroll* be read as a compromise insofar as it imposes a "reasonableness" requirement even as it abandons the "warrant" requirement?

Carroll was controversial from its inception yet its reach was somewhat unclear. Arguably, perhaps hopefully, it could be read to authorize warrantless automobile searches only where Congress had authorized them by statute, as it had done in the Volstead Act. *See* Tracey Maclin, *Cops and Cars: How the Automobile Drove Fourth Amendment Law*, 99 B.U. L. Rev. 2317, 2342-43 (2019) (reviewing Seo, Policing the Open Road, *supra*). *See United States v. Di Re*, 332 U.S. 581, 585 (1948) (noting that the Court had never held that *Carroll* applied in the absence of federal legislation).

The answer came in 1949, in another illegal liquor case, even though federal Prohibition had long since been repealed. In *Brinegar v. United States*, 338 U.S. 160 (1949), on facts remarkably similar to those in *Carroll*, the Court upheld a warrantless search of a car in the absence of legislation even as it acknowledged that the facts of both *Carroll* and *Brinegar* hovered somewhere "between mere suspicion and probable cause." *Id.* at 176. Even more explicitly than in *Carroll*, the Court articulated its deference to a police officer's "act of judgment," and noted that officers in the field must be given "leeway." *Id.*

Professor Seo reports that the Court in *Brinegar* was in genuine conflict about whether *Carroll* should be overturned, and that Justice Jackson's dissent—which follows—started off as the majority opinion. Seo, Policing the Open Road, *supra* at 164.

Brinegar v. United States

338 U.S. 160 (1949) (Jackson, J., dissenting)

Mr. Justice JACKSON, dissenting.

When this Court recently has promulgated a philosophy that some rights derived from the Constitution are entitled to "a preferred position," I have not agreed. We cannot give some constitutional rights a preferred position without relegating others to a deferred position; we can establish no firsts without thereby establishing seconds. Indications are not wanting that Fourth Amendment freedoms are tacitly marked as secondary rights, to be relegated to a deferred position.

The Fourth Amendment states:

> The right of the people to be secure in their persons, houses, papers, and effects, against unreasonable searches and seizures, shall not be violated, and no Warrants shall issue, but upon probable cause, supported by Oath or affirmation, and particularly describing the place to be searched, and the persons or things to be seized.

These, I protest, are not mere second-class rights but belong in the catalog of indispensable freedoms. Among deprivations of rights, none is so effective in cowing a population, crushing the spirit of the individual and putting terror in every heart. Uncontrolled search and seizure is one of the first and most effective weapons in the arsenal of every arbitrary government. And one need only briefly to have dwelt and worked among a people possessed of many admirable qualities but deprived of these rights to know that the human personality deteriorates and dignity and self-reliance disappear where homes, persons and possessions are subject at any hour to unheralded search and seizure by the police.

But the right to be secure against searches and seizures is one of the most difficult to protect. Since the officers are themselves the chief invaders, there is no enforcement outside of court.

Only occasional and more flagrant abuses come to the attention of the courts, and then only those where the search and seizure yields incriminating evidence and the defendant is at least sufficiently compromised to be indicted. If the officers raid a home, an office, or stop and search an automobile but find nothing incriminating, this invasion of the personal liberty of the innocent too often finds no practical redress. There may be, and I am convinced that there are, many unlawful searches of homes and automobiles of innocent people which turn up nothing incriminating, in which no arrest is made, about which courts do nothing, and about which we never hear.

Courts can protect the innocent against such invasions indirectly and through the medium of excluding evidence obtained against those who frequently are guilty. Federal courts have used this method of enforcement of the Amendment, in spite of its unfortunate consequences on law enforcement, although many state courts do not. This inconsistency does not disturb me, for local excesses or invasions of liberty are more amenable to political correction, the

Amendment was directed only against the new and centralized government, and any really dangerous threat to the general liberties of the people can come only from this source. We must therefore look upon the exclusion of evidence in federal prosecutions if obtained in violation of the Amendment as a means of extending protection against the central government's agencies. So a search against Brinegar's car must be regarded as a search of the car of Everyman.

We must remember that the extent of any privilege of search and seizure without warrant which we sustain, the officers interpret and apply themselves and will push to the limit. We must remember, too, that freedom from unreasonable search differs from some of the other rights of the Constitution in that there is no way the innocent citizen can invoke advance protection. For example, any effective interference with freedom of the press, or free speech, or religion, usually requires a course of suppressions against which the citizen can and often does go to the court and obtain an injunction. Other rights, such as that to an impartial jury or the aid of counsel, are within the supervisory power of the courts themselves. Such a right as just compensation for the taking of private property may be vindicated after the act in terms of money.

But an illegal search and seizure usually is a single incident, perpetrated by surprise, conducted in haste, kept purposely beyond the court's supervision and limited only by the judgment and moderation of officers whose own interests and records are often at stake in the search. There is no opportunity for injunction or appeal to disinterested intervention. The citizen's choice is quietly to submit to whatever the officers undertake or to resist at risk of arrest or immediate violence.

And we must remember that the authority which we concede to conduct searches and seizures without warrant may be exercised by the most unfit and ruthless officers as well as by the fit and responsible, and resorted to in case of petty misdemeanors as well as in the case of the gravest felonies.

• • •

I do not, of course, contend that officials may never stop a car on the highway without the halting being considered an arrest or a search. Regulations of traffic, identifications where proper, traffic census, quarantine regulations, and many other causes give occasion to stop cars in circumstances which do not imply arrest or charge of crime. And to trail or pursue a suspected car to its destination, to observe it and keep it under surveillance, is not in itself an arrest nor a search. But when a car is forced off the road, summoned to stop by a siren, and brought to a halt under such circumstances as are here disclosed, we think the officers are then in the position of one who has entered a home: the search at its commencement must be valid and cannot be saved by what it turns up.

The findings of the two courts below make it clear that this search began and proceeded through critical and coercive phases without the justification of probable cause. What it yielded cannot save it. I would reverse the judgment.

NOTES

1. All criminal procedure cases should be read from the perspective of Justice Jackson's Everyman.

2. Justice Jackson spoke with uncommon authority on the Court on the realities of law enforcement proclivities, having previous experience as a general practitioner for 15 years, a Department of Justice prosecutor for 5 years, and, ultimately, Attorney General of the United

States. Thus, his warning that the powers accorded to law enforcement "may be exercised by the most unfit and ruthless officers as well as by the fit and responsible" carry a special ring of truth. Recall also his reference in *Johnson v. United States, supra*, to the "competitive enterprise" of law enforcement. 333 U.S. 10, 13-14.

In the decades following *Brinegar*, the automobile exceptionalism of *Carroll* was layered into all cases where cars touched the Fourth Amendment. And cars touched the Fourth Amendment everywhere, especially as both the general population and police forces became increasingly mobile. The Court upheld warrantless searches of cars even in situations where it was indisputable that the rationale for the exception—"automobility," to use Professor Seo's term—was inapplicable. In *Chambers v. Mahoney*, 399 U.S. 42 (1970), a car's occupants were arrested for armed robbery and the vehicle was impounded by police and taken to the police station. It was searched at the station without a warrant—even though it was immobilized and the officers had all the time in the world—and incriminating evidence was found and used at the defendants' trial. The Court upheld the search because it was supported by probable cause.

The *Carroll* principle was further extended by the Court—ultimately—through a line of cases that began in 1977. *See* Maclin, *Cops and Cars*, *supra* at 2355-61; Seo, Policing the Open Road, *supra* at 247-53. In *United States v. Chadwick*, 433 U.S. 1 (1977), federal narcotics agents in Boston had probable cause to search for drugs in a footlocker that was on a train heading their way. When the train arrived at South Station and the footlocker was placed in the trunk of a waiting car by its transporters, the agents pounced: They arrested the individuals and seized the footlocker, which they later opened at their office, finding marijuana. The Court held that while the agents had been permitted to seize the footlocker from the trunk, they could not open it without a warrant, since a person has a heightened privacy expectation in luggage. In *Arkansas v. Sanders*, 442 U.S. 753 (1979), a similar result was reached with respect to a suitcase in the trunk of a moving taxi. Then in *United States v. Ross*, 456 U.S. 798 (1982), the Court held that probable cause to search an entire car—the police had information that the defendant was selling drugs "out of his car" and kept the drugs in the car's trunk—included authority to search containers in the trunk. So, to review the bidding: A warrant was required for the search of a container in a car under *Chadwick* and *Sanders* unless there was probable cause to search the entire car, as there was in *Ross*.

A majority of the Court was to find this state of affairs untenable, even though probable cause determinations were always circumstances-dependent. Nine years after *Ross*, in a case with a factual resemblance to *Sanders*—officers observed a man place a bag likely containing marijuana in a car trunk—the Court seized on and exaggerated the confusion engendered by the *Ross* dichotomy to overrule *Chadwick* and *Sanders*. In *California v. Acevedo*, 500 U.S. 565 (1991), the automobile exception of *Carroll* was extended to containers simply by virtue of their placement in an automobile. Maclin, *Cops and Cars*, *supra* at 2359 ("*Acevedo* is an extension of *Carroll*"). Confusion remained, however. As Justice Stevens observed in dissent, "it is anomalous to prohibit a search of a briefcase while the owner is carrying it exposed on a public street yet to permit a search once the owner has placed the briefcase in the locked trunk of his car." Justice Stevens also famously noted in his *Acevedo* dissent that "decisions like the one today will support the conclusion that this Court has become a loyal foot soldier in the Executive's fight against crime." While some see *Acevedo* as the apotheosis of automobile exceptionalism, others have recognized it as emblematic of a different Fourth Amendment trend. *See* Erik Luna, *Drug Exceptionalism*, 47 Vill. L. Rev. 753, 755-56 (2002) ("Legal commentators have likewise identified a 'drug exception' to the Bill of Rights created through judicial acquiescence to the activities of narcotics agents.").

A subsidiary yet equally important legacy of *Carroll* that traveled into the future along with the automobility exception was the notion of judicial deference to police officer expertise. Such deference was explicitly relied on by the Court in upholding the police officers' judgments in *Carroll* and *Brinegar*, and was part of the *Carroll* playbook that the Court relied on in embracing a "reasonable suspicion" Fourth Amendment standard in *Terry v. Ohio, see infra*, and continues to be relied on today. In 1996 this notion of law enforcement deference was enshrined in, of all places, the appellate review standard for probable cause and reasonable suspicion determinations, as the Court held that appellate courts should give due weight not only to trial judges' factual findings but also to the conclusions of "local law enforcement officers." *Ornelas v. United States*, 517 U.S. 690 (1996).

It was only a matter of time before the Court considered a case involving the ultimate Fourth Amendment hybrid—a mobile home.

California v. Carney

471 U.S. 386 (1985)

Chief Justice Burger delivered the opinion of the Court.

We granted certiorari to decide whether law enforcement agents violated the Fourth Amendment when they conducted a warrantless search, based on probable cause, of a fully mobile "motor home" located in a public place.

I

On May 31, 1979, Drug Enforcement Agency Agent Robert Williams watched respondent, Charles Carney, approach a youth in downtown San Diego. The youth accompanied Carney to a Dodge Mini Motor Home parked in a nearby lot. Carney and the youth closed the window shades in the motor home, including one across the front window. Agent Williams had previously received uncorroborated information that the same motor home was used by another person who was exchanging marihuana for sex. Williams, with assistance from other agents, kept the motor home under surveillance for the entire one and one-quarter hours that Carney and the youth remained inside. When the youth left the motor home, the agents followed and stopped him. The youth told the agents that he had received marijuana in return for allowing Carney sexual contacts.

At the agents' request, the youth returned to the motor home and knocked on its door; Carney stepped out. The agents identified themselves as law enforcement officers. Without a warrant or consent, one agent entered the motor home and observed marihuana, plastic bags, and a scale of the kind used in weighing drugs on a table. Agent Williams took Carney into custody and took possession of the motor home. A subsequent search of the motor home at the police station revealed additional marihuana in the cupboards and refrigerator.

Respondent was charged with possession of marihuana for sale. At a preliminary hearing, he moved to suppress the evidence discovered in the motor home. The Magistrate denied the motion, upholding the initial search as a justifiable search for other persons, and the subsequent search as a routine inventory search.

Respondent renewed his suppression motion in the Superior Court. The Superior Court also rejected the claim, holding that there was probable cause to arrest respondent, that the search of the motor home was authorized under the automobile exception to the Fourth Amendment's warrant requirement, and that the motor home itself could be seized without a warrant as an instrumentality of the crime. Respondent then pleaded nolo contendere to the charges against him, and was placed on probation for three years.

Respondent appealed from the order placing him on probation. The California Court of Appeal affirmed, reasoning that the vehicle exception applied to respondent's motor home.

The California Supreme Court reversed the conviction. The Supreme Court did not disagree with the conclusion of the trial court that the agents had probable cause to arrest respondent and to believe that the vehicle contained evidence of a crime; however, the court held that the search was unreasonable because no warrant was obtained, rejecting the State's argument that the vehicle exception to the warrant requirement should apply. That court reached its decision by concluding that the mobility of a vehicle "is no longer the prime justification for the automobile exception; rather, 'the answer lies in the diminished expectation of privacy which surrounds the automobile.'" The California Supreme Court held that the expectations of privacy in a motor home are more like those in a dwelling than in an automobile because the primary function of motor homes is not to provide transportation but to "provide the occupant with living quarters."

We granted certiorari. We reverse.

II

The Fourth Amendment protects the "right of the people to be secure in their persons, houses, papers, and effects, against unreasonable searches and seizures." This fundamental right is preserved by a requirement that searches be conducted pursuant to a warrant issued by an independent judicial officer. There are, of course, exceptions to the general rule that a warrant must be secured before a search is undertaken; one is the so-called "automobile exception" at issue in this case. This exception to the warrant requirement was first set forth by the Court 60 years ago in *Carroll.* There, the Court recognized that the privacy interests in an automobile are constitutionally protected; however, it held that the ready mobility of the automobile justifies a lesser degree of protection of those interests. The Court rested this exception on a long-recognized distinction between stationary structures and vehicles:

> [T]he guaranty of freedom from unreasonable searches and seizures by the Fourth Amendment has been construed, practically since the beginning of Government, as recognizing a necessary difference between a search of a store, dwelling house or other structure in respect of which a proper official warrant readily may be obtained, and a search of a ship, motor boat, wagon or automobile, for contraband goods, where it is not practicable to secure a warrant because the vehicle can be quickly moved out of the locality or jurisdiction in which the warrant must be sought.

The capacity to be "quickly moved" was clearly the basis of the holding in *Carroll,* and our cases have consistently recognized ready mobility as one of the principal bases of the automobile exception. In *Chambers*, for example, commenting on the rationale for the vehicle exception, we noted that "the opportunity to search is fleeting since a car is readily movable." More recently, in *United States v. Ross* (1982), we once again emphasized that "an immediate intrusion is necessary" because of "the nature of an automobile in transit. . . ." The mobility of automobiles, we have observed, "creates circumstances of such exigency that, as a practical necessity, rigorous enforcement of the warrant requirement is impossible."

However, although ready mobility alone was perhaps the original justification for the vehicle exception, our later cases have made clear that ready mobility is not the only basis for the exception. The reasons for the vehicle exception, we have said, are twofold. "Besides the element of mobility, less rigorous warrant requirements govern because the expectation of privacy with respect to one's automobile is significantly less than that relating to one's home or office."

Even in cases where an automobile was not immediately mobile, the lesser expectation of privacy resulting from its use as a readily mobile vehicle justified application of the vehicular exception. In some cases, the configuration of the vehicle contributed to the lower expectations of privacy; for example, we held in *Cardwell v. Lewis* that, because the passenger compartment of a standard automobile is relatively open to plain view, there are lesser expectations of privacy. But even when enclosed "repository" areas have been involved, we have concluded that the lesser expectations of privacy warrant application of the exception. We have applied the exception in the context of a locked car trunk, a sealed package in a car trunk, a closed compartment under the dashboard, the interior of a vehicle's upholstery, or sealed packages inside a covered pickup truck.

These reduced expectations of privacy derive not from the fact that the area to be searched is in plain view, but from the pervasive regulation of vehicles capable of traveling on the public highways. As we explained in *South Dakota v. Opperman*, an inventory search case:

> Automobiles, unlike homes, are subjected to pervasive and continuing governmental regulation and controls, including periodic inspection and licensing requirements. As an everyday occurrence, police stop and examine vehicles when license plates or inspection stickers have expired, or if other violations, such as exhaust fumes or excessive noise, are noted, or if headlights or other safety equipment are not in proper working order.

The public is fully aware that it is accorded less privacy in its automobiles because of this compelling governmental need for regulation. Historically, "individuals always [have] been on notice that movable vessels may be stopped and searched on facts giving rise to probable cause that the vehicle contains contraband, without the protection afforded by a magistrate's prior evaluation of those facts." In short, the pervasive schemes of regulation, which necessarily lead to reduced expectations of privacy, and the exigencies attendant to ready mobility justify searches without prior recourse to the authority of a magistrate so long as the overriding standard of probable cause is met.

When a vehicle is being used on the highways, or if it is readily capable of such use and is found stationary in a place not regularly used for residential purposes—temporary or otherwise—the two justifications for the vehicle exception come into play. First, the vehicle is obviously readily mobile by the turn of an ignition key, if not actually moving. Second, there is a reduced expectation of privacy stemming from its use as a licensed motor vehicle subject to a range of police regulation inapplicable to a fixed dwelling. At least in these circumstances, the overriding societal interests in effective law enforcement justify an immediate search before the vehicle and its occupants become unavailable.

While it is true that respondent's vehicle possessed some, if not many of the attributes of a home, it is equally clear that the vehicle falls clearly within the scope of the exception laid down in *Carroll* and applied in succeeding cases. Like the automobile in *Carroll*, respondent's motor home was readily mobile. Absent the prompt search and seizure, it could readily have been moved beyond the reach of the police. Furthermore, the vehicle was licensed to "operate on public streets; [was] serviced in public places; . . . and [was] subject to extensive regulation and inspection." And the vehicle was so situated that an objective observer would conclude that it was being used not as a residence, but as a vehicle.

Respondent urges us to distinguish his vehicle from other vehicles within the exception because it was capable of functioning as a home. In our increasingly mobile society, many vehicles used for transportation can be and are being used not only for transportation but for shelter, i.e., as a "home" or "residence." To distinguish between respondent's motor home and an ordinary sedan for purposes of the vehicle exception would require that we apply the exception depending upon the size of the vehicle and the quality of its appointments. Moreover, to fail to apply the exception to vehicles such as a motor home ignores the fact that a motor home lends itself easily to use as an instrument of illicit drug traffic and other illegal activity. In *United States v. Ross*, we declined to distinguish between "worthy" and "unworthy" containers, noting that "the central purpose of the Fourth Amendment forecloses such a distinction." We decline today to distinguish between "worthy" and "unworthy" vehicles which are either on the public roads and highways, or situated such that it is reasonable to conclude that the vehicle is not being used as a residence.

Our application of the vehicle exception has never turned on the other uses to which a vehicle might be put. The exception has historically turned on the ready mobility of the vehicle, and on the presence of the vehicle in a setting that objectively indicates that the vehicle is being used for transportation. These two requirements for application of the exception ensure that law enforcement officials are not unnecessarily hamstrung in their efforts to detect and prosecute criminal activity, and that the legitimate privacy interests of the public are protected. Applying the vehicle exception in these circumstances allows the essential purposes served by the exception to be fulfilled, while assuring that the exception will acknowledge legitimate privacy interests.

III

The question remains whether, apart from the lack of a warrant, this search was unreasonable. Under the vehicle exception to the warrant requirement, "[o]nly the prior approval of the magistrate is waived; the search otherwise [must be such] as the magistrate could authorize."

This search was not unreasonable; it was plainly one that the magistrate could authorize if presented with these facts. The DEA agents had fresh, direct, uncontradicted evidence that the respondent was distributing a controlled substance from the vehicle, apart from evidence of other possible offenses. The agents thus had abundant probable cause to enter and search the vehicle for evidence of a crime notwithstanding its possible use as a dwelling place.

The judgment of the California Supreme Court is reversed, and the case is remanded for further proceedings not inconsistent with this opinion.

NOTES AND QUESTIONS

1. The Court acknowledges that the Dodge Mini Motor Home carries many indicia of domesticity: curtains, cupboards, a refrigerator, etc.

But why is the record so bad here? The lawyers on both sides must have known what was at stake in this suppression hearing, as the case presented the classic hybrid between an automobile and a home. Even its name—Motor Home—embraced this duality.

Why are we only told that the vehicle was located "in a nearby lot." What kind of lot? A parking lot? Was the lot public or private property?

Where was the vehicle when the agents observed it recently?

2. The dissent does not make the point that the DEA agents could have avoided any risk involved in getting a warrant simply by continuing to keep the vehicle under surveillance while one agent got a warrant. If the vehicle were to try to take off in the meantime, the surveilling agents could have stopped it and executed a warrantless arrest, as it would seem clear that if the vehicle were actually moving the automobile exception would come into play.

3. Perhaps defensive about relying too heavily on the automobile's mobility on the facts of this case, and after the shame of *Chambers*, the Court in the 1970s and 1980s and especially in *Carney* began to lean hard into the "closely regulated" trope that it would rely on two years later in upholding a warrantless search of a junkyard in *New York v. Burger*, 482 U.S. 691 (1987), and the correlative notion that people have a lessened expectation of privacy in their cars.

Is this persuasive? Consider the regulation of your car. You have to have a license to drive it. You have to have insurance. When driving it, you have to comply with numerous safety regulations: wearing seatbelts, signaling for turns, stopping at stop signs, observing speed limits. You have to take the car to a garage for an annual or biannual inspection. If you get stopped while impaired, depending on the state, you may have to take a blood alcohol test or risk significant collateral consequences, for example, suspension of license or a criminal offense. Do any of these regulatory tentacles reach into and compromise the private space within the four (or two or three) doors of the car? Recall that in *Burger* the regulatory regime at issue explicitly authorized warrantless searches of junkyards.

4. The reliance on a reduced expectation of privacy in automobiles did not fade away with time, or yield to a more nuanced and disciplined view of people's relationship with their cars. This reduced expectation of privacy was explicitly relied on, reflexively it would seem, in *Wyoming v. Houghton*, 526 U.S. 295 (1999), where the Court found that the scope of a car search justified by probable cause to believe the car contained contraband extended to a purse in the backseat.

Are people who are driven to work by chauffeurs driving government vehicles capable of adequately assessing people's reasonable expectations of privacy in their cars?

Do people's actual expectations of privacy in their cars sometimes, and under some circumstances, exceed those in their homes? *See* Elizabeth Merritt, Note, *VanLife: An Argument to Reconsider the Automobile Exception and Ensure Fourth Amendment Protections for All Citizens,* 56 Ind. L. Rev. 599, 599-600 (2023) (acknowledging the increasingly widespread of people living in their vans (vanlife) and arguing that the automobile exception should not apply in such cases). What are the Fourth Amendment consequences, if any, of the answer to that question?

5. Concepts of "home" may sometimes still trump the automobile exception, however. *See Collins v. Virginia*, 584 U.S. 586 (2018) (search of motorcycle parked in a covered portion of driveway abutting the house requires a warrant, notwithstanding the automobile exception, inasmuch as that area is "curtilage" under cases such as *Florida v. Jardines*, 569 U.S. 1, 6 (2013)).

We now turn from exceptions to the warrant requirement to what will prove to be a gaping exception to the probable cause requirement.

D. EXCEPTION TO THE PROBABLE CAUSE REQUIREMENT: THE *TERRY* DOCTRINE

By the time the constitutionality of police "stop and frisk" encounters reached the Supreme Court in 1968 both the term and the practice were familiar to the Court. Police had been stopping people on the streets and questioning and frisking them without probable cause for decades. *See* Sam B. Warner, *The Uniform Arrest Act*, 28 Va. L. Rev. 315, 320 (1942) ("Every day large numbers of persons are questioned by police officers. This questioning, without immediate arrest, is essential to proper policing."). Because these encounters, sometimes called "field interrogation" or "patrol," often did not result in prosecutions—in which resultant statements or physical evidence might be challenged—they usually stayed below the legal radar. People who were the "victims" of such arguably unconstitutional encounters, moreover, may quite reasonably have seen little upside in "pressing charges" against a police officer given their small damages, the uncertainty of any remedial vehicles (§ 1983 was not resuscitated until 1960), and a not unrealistic risk of retaliation.

This state of affairs began to change in the 1960s, as crime rates began to rise. New York enacted a statute that affirmatively authorized stop and frisk, N.Y. Code Crim. Proc. § 180-a (1964), and the incidence of field interrogation was otherwise increasing. Lawrence P. Tiffany,

Field Interrogation: Administrative, Judicial and Legislative Approaches, 43 Denv. L.J. 389, 389 (1966) ("A common police practice, probably in all localities, is to stop and question suspects on the street when there are insufficient grounds to arrest."). Police officers, however, were unsure of the legality of such stops. Loren G. Stern, *Stop and Frisk: An Historical Answer to a Modern Problem*, 58 J. Crim. L. Criminology & Police Sci. 532, 533 (1967). Lower courts were increasingly being confronted with constitutional challenges to the practice in the wake of *Mapp* and *Gideon*. And a commission created by President Johnson recommended that states define the authority for such police encounters. President's Commission on Law Enforcement and Administration of Justice, Task Force Report: The Police 183 (1967). *See generally* John Q. Barrett, Terry v. Ohio*: The Fourth Amendment Reasonableness of Police Stops and Frisks Based on Less Than Probable Cause*, in Criminal Procedure Stories 299-300 (Carol Steiker ed., 2005).

Terry v. Ohio

392 U.S. 1 (1968)

Mr. Chief Justice Warren delivered the opinion of the Court.

This case presents serious questions concerning the role of the Fourth Amendment in the confrontation on the street between the citizen and the policeman investigating suspicious circumstances.

Petitioner Terry was convicted of carrying a concealed weapon and sentenced to the statutorily prescribed term of one to three years in the penitentiary. Following the denial of a pretrial motion to suppress, the prosecution introduced in evidence two revolvers and a number of bullets seized from Terry and a codefendant, Richard Chilton, by Cleveland Police Detective Martin McFadden. At the hearing on the motion to suppress this evidence, Officer McFadden testified that while he was patrolling in plain clothes in downtown Cleveland at approximately 2:30 in the afternoon of October 31, 1963, his attention was attracted by two men, Chilton and Terry, standing on the corner of Huron Road and Euclid Avenue. He had never seen the two men before, and he was unable to say precisely what first drew his eye to them. However, he testified that he had been a policeman for 39 years and a detective for 35 and that he had been assigned to patrol this vicinity of downtown Cleveland for shoplifters and pickpockets for 30 years. He explained that he had developed routine habits of observation over the years and that he would "stand and watch people or walk and watch people at many intervals of the day." He added: "Now, in this case when I looked over they didn't look right to me at the time."

His interest aroused, Officer McFadden took up a post of observation in the entrance to a store 300 to 400 feet away from the two men. "I get more purpose to watch them when I seen their movements," he testified. He saw one of the men leave the other one and walk southwest on Huron Road, past some stores. The man paused for a moment and looked in a store window, then walked on a short distance, turned around and walked back toward the corner, pausing once again to look in the same store window. He rejoined his companion at the corner, and the two conferred briefly. Then the second man went through the same series of motions, strolling down Huron Road, looking in the same window, walking on a short distance, turning back, peering in the store window again, and returning to confer with the first man at the corner. The two men repeated this ritual alternately between five and six times apiece—in all, roughly a dozen trips. At one point, while the two were standing together on the corner, a third man approached them and engaged them briefly in conversation. This man then left the two others and walked west on Euclid Avenue. Chilton and Terry resumed their measured pacing, peering and conferring. After this had gone on for 10 to 12 minutes, the two men walked off together, heading west on Euclid Avenue, following the path taken earlier by the third man.

By this time Officer McFadden had become thoroughly suspicious. He testified that after observing their elaborately casual and oft-repeated reconnaissance of the store window on Huron Road, he suspected the two men of "casing a job, a stick-up," and that he considered it his duty as a police officer to investigate further. He added that he feared "they may have a gun." Thus, Officer McFadden followed Chilton and Terry and saw them stop in front of Zucker's store to talk to the same man who had conferred with them earlier on the street corner. Deciding that the situation was ripe for direct action, Officer McFadden approached the three men, identified himself as a police officer and asked for their names. At this point his knowledge was confined to what he had observed. He was not acquainted with any of the three men by name or by sight, and he had received no information concerning them from any other source. When the men "mumbled something" in response to his inquiries, Officer McFadden grabbed petitioner Terry, spun him around so that they were facing the other two, with Terry between McFadden and the others, and patted down the outside of his clothing. In the left breast pocket of Terry's overcoat Officer McFadden felt a pistol. He reached inside the overcoat pocket, but was unable to remove the gun. At this point, keeping Terry between himself and the others, the officer ordered all three men to enter Zucker's store. As they went in, he removed Terry's overcoat completely, removed a .38-caliber revolver from the pocket and ordered all three men to face the wall with their hands raised. Officer McFadden proceeded to pat down the outer clothing of Chilton and the third man, Katz. He discovered another revolver in the outer pocket of Chilton's overcoat, but no weapons were found on Katz. The officer testified that he only patted the men down to see whether they had weapons, and that he did not put his hands beneath the outer garments of either Terry or Chilton until he felt their guns. So far as appears from the record, he never placed his hands beneath Katz' outer garments. Officer McFadden seized Chilton's gun, asked the proprietor of the store to call a police wagon, and took all three men to the station, where Chilton and Terry were formally charged with carrying concealed weapons.

On the motion to suppress the guns the prosecution took the position that they had been seized following a search incident to a lawful arrest. The trial court rejected this theory, stating that it "would be stretching the facts beyond reasonable comprehension" to find that Officer McFadden had had probable cause to arrest the men before he patted them down for weapons. However, the court denied the defendants' motion on the ground that Officer McFadden, on the basis of his experience, "had reasonable cause to believe . . . that the defendants were conducting themselves suspiciously, and some interrogation should be made of their action." Purely for his own protection, the court held, the officer had the right to pat down the outer clothing of these men, who he had reasonable cause to believe might be armed. The court distinguished between an investigatory "stop" and an arrest, and between a "frisk" of the outer clothing for weapons and a full-blown search for evidence of crime. The frisk, it held, was essential to the proper performance of the officer's investigatory duties, for without it "the answer to the police officer may be a bullet, and a loaded pistol discovered during the frisk is admissible."

After the court denied their motion to suppress, Chilton and Terry waived jury trial and pleaded not guilty. The court adjudged them guilty, and the Court of Appeals for the Eighth Judicial District, Cuyahoga County, affirmed. The Supreme Court of Ohio dismissed their appeal on the ground that no "substantial constitutional question" was involved. We granted certiorari, to determine whether the admission of the revolvers in evidence violated petitioner's rights under the Fourth Amendment, made applicable to the States by the Fourteenth. We affirm the conviction.

I.

The Fourth Amendment provides that "the right of the people to be secure in their persons, houses, papers, and effects, against unreasonable searches and seizures, shall not be violated. . . ." This inestimable right of personal security belongs as much to the citizen on the streets of our cities as to the homeowner closeted in his study to dispose of his secret affairs. For, as this Court has always recognized:

> No right is held more sacred, or is more carefully guarded, by the common law, than the right of every individual to the possession and control of his own person, free from all restraint or interference of others, unless by clear and unquestionable authority of law.

We have recently held that "the Fourth Amendment protects people, not places," *Katz v. United States* (1967), and wherever an individual may harbor a reasonable "expectation of privacy," he is entitled to be free from unreasonable governmental intrusion. Of course, the specific content and incidents of this right must be shaped by the context in which it is asserted. For "what the Constitution forbids is not all searches and seizures, but unreasonable searches and seizures." The question is whether in all the circumstances of this on-the-street encounter, his right to personal security was violated by an unreasonable search and seizure.

We would be less than candid if we did not acknowledge that this question thrusts to the fore difficult and troublesome issues regarding a sensitive area of police activity—issues which have never before been squarely presented to this Court. Reflective of the tensions involved are the practical and constitutional arguments pressed with great vigor on both sides of the public debate over the power of the police to "stop and frisk"—as it is sometimes euphemistically termed—suspicious persons.

On the one hand, it is frequently argued that in dealing with the rapidly unfolding and often dangerous situations on city streets the police are in need of an escalating set of flexible responses, graduated in relation to the amount of information they possess. For this purpose it is urged that distinctions should be made between a "stop" and an "arrest" (or a "seizure" of a person), and between a "frisk" and a "search." Thus, it is argued, the police should be allowed to "stop" a person and detain him briefly for questioning upon suspicion that he may be connected with criminal activity. Upon suspicion that the person may be armed, the police should have the power to "frisk" him for weapons. If the "stop" and the "frisk" give rise to probable cause to believe that the suspect has committed a crime, then the police should be empowered to make a formal "arrest," and a full incident "search" of the person. This scheme is justified in part upon the notion that a "stop" and a "frisk" amount to a mere "minor inconvenience and petty indignity," which can properly be imposed upon the citizen in the interest of effective law enforcement on the basis of a police officer's suspicion.

On the other side the argument is made that the authority of the police must be strictly circumscribed by the law of arrest and search as it has developed to date in the traditional jurisprudence of the Fourth Amendment. It is contended with some force that there is not—and cannot be—a variety of police activity which does not depend solely upon the voluntary cooperation of the citizen and yet which stops short of an arrest based upon probable cause to make such an arrest. The heart of the Fourth Amendment, the argument runs, is a severe requirement of specific justification for any intrusion upon protected personal security, coupled with a highly developed system of judicial controls to enforce upon the agents of the State the commands of the Constitution. Acquiescence by the courts in the compulsion inherent in the field interrogation practices at issue here, it is urged, would constitute an abdication of judicial control over, and indeed an encouragement of, substantial interference with liberty and personal security by police officers whose judgment is necessarily colored by their primary involvement in "the often competitive enterprise of ferreting out crime." This, it is argued, can only serve to exacerbate police-community tensions in the crowded centers of our Nation's cities.

In this context we approach the issues in this case mindful of the limitations of the judicial function in controlling the myriad daily situations in which policemen and citizens confront each other on the street. The State has characterized the issue here as "the right of a police officer . . . to make an on-the-street stop, interrogate and pat down for weapons (known in street vernacular as 'stop and frisk')." But this is only partly accurate. For the issue is not the abstract propriety of the police conduct, but the admissibility against petitioner of the evidence uncovered by the search and seizure. Ever since its inception, the rule excluding evidence seized in violation of the Fourth Amendment has been recognized as a principal mode of discouraging lawless police conduct. Thus its major thrust is a deterrent one, and experience has taught that it is the only effective deterrent to police misconduct in the criminal context, and that without it the constitutional guarantee against unreasonable searches and seizures would be a mere "form of words." Courts which sit under our Constitution cannot and will not be made party to lawless invasions of the constitutional rights of citizens by permitting unhindered governmental use of the fruits of such invasions. Thus in our system evidentiary rulings provide the context in which the judicial process of inclusion and exclusion approves some conduct as comporting with constitutional guarantees and disapproves other actions by state agents. A ruling admitting evidence in a criminal trial, we recognize, has the necessary effect of legitimizing the conduct which produced the evidence, while an application of the exclusionary rule withholds the constitutional imprimatur.

The exclusionary rule has its limitations, however, as a tool of judicial control. It cannot properly be invoked to exclude the products of legitimate police investigative techniques on the ground that much conduct which is closely similar involves unwarranted intrusions upon constitutional protections. Moreover, in some contexts the rule is ineffective as a deterrent. Street encounters between citizens and police officers are incredibly rich in diversity. They range from wholly friendly exchanges of pleasantries or mutually useful information to hostile confrontations of armed men involving arrests, or injuries, or loss of life. Moreover, hostile confrontations are not all of a piece. Some of them begin in a friendly enough manner, only to take a different turn upon the injection of some unexpected element into the conversation. Encounters are initiated by the police for a wide variety of purposes, some of which are wholly unrelated to a desire to prosecute for crime. Doubtless some police "field interrogation" conduct violates the Fourth Amendment. But a stern refusal by this Court to condone such activity does not necessarily render it responsive to the exclusionary rule. Regardless of how effective the rule may be where obtaining convictions is an important objective of the police, it is powerless to deter invasions of constitutionally guaranteed rights where the police either have no interest in prosecuting or are willing to forgo successful prosecution in the interest of serving some other goal.

Proper adjudication of cases in which the exclusionary rule is invoked demands a constant awareness of these limitations. The wholesale harassment by certain elements of the police community, of which minority groups, particularly Negroes, frequently complain, will not be stopped by the exclusion of any evidence from any criminal trial. Yet a rigid and unthinking application of the exclusionary rule, in futile protest against practices which it can never be used effectively to control, may exact a high toll in human injury and frustration of efforts to prevent crime. No judicial opinion can comprehend the protean variety of the street encounter, and we can only judge the facts of the case before us. Nothing we say today is to be taken as indicating approval of police conduct outside the legitimate investigative sphere. Under our decision, courts still retain their traditional responsibility to guard against police conduct which is over-bearing or harassing, or which trenches upon personal security without the objective evidentiary justification which the Constitution requires. When such conduct is identified, it must be condemned by the judiciary and its fruits must be excluded from evidence in criminal trials. And, of course, our approval of legitimate and restrained investigative conduct undertaken on the basis of ample factual justification should in no way discourage the employment of other remedies than the exclusionary rule to curtail abuses for which that sanction may prove inappropriate.

Having thus roughly sketched the perimeters of the constitutional debate over the limits on police investigative conduct in general and the background against which this case presents itself, we turn our attention to the quite narrow question posed by the facts before us: whether it is always unreasonable for a policeman to seize a person and subject him to a limited search for weapons unless there is probable cause for an arrest. Given the narrowness of this question, we have no occasion to canvass in detail the constitutional limitations upon the scope of a policeman's power when he confronts a citizen without probable cause to arrest him.

II

Our first task is to establish at what point in this encounter the Fourth Amendment becomes relevant. That is, we must decide whether and when Officer McFadden "seized" Terry and whether and when he conducted a "search." There is some suggestion in the use of such terms as "stop" and "frisk" that such police conduct is outside the purview of the Fourth Amendment because neither action rises to the level of a "search" or "seizure" within the meaning of the Constitution. We emphatically reject this notion. It is quite plain that the Fourth Amendment governs "seizures" of the person which do not eventuate in a trip to the station house and prosecution for crime—"arrests" in traditional terminology. It must be recognized that whenever a police officer accosts an individual and restrains his freedom to walk away, he has "seized" that person. And it is nothing less than sheer torture of the English language to suggest that a careful exploration of the outer surfaces of a person's clothing all over his or her body in an attempt to find weapons is not a "search," Moreover, it is simply fantastic to urge that such a procedure performed in public by a policeman while the citizen stands helpless, perhaps facing a wall with his hands raised, is a "petty indignity." It is a serious intrusion upon the sanctity of the person, which may inflict great indignity and arouse strong resentment, and it is not to be undertaken lightly.

The danger in the logic which proceeds upon distinctions between a "stop" and an "arrest," or "seizure" of the person, and between a "frisk" and a "search" is twofold. It seeks to isolate from constitutional scrutiny the initial stages of the contact between the policeman and the citizen. And by suggesting a rigid all-or-nothing model of justification and regulation under the Amendment, it obscures the utility of limitations upon the scope, as well as the initiation, of police action as a means of constitutional regulation. This Court has held in the past that a search which is reasonable at its inception may violate the Fourth Amendment by virtue of its intolerable intensity and scope. The scope of the search must be "strictly tied to and justified by" the circumstances which rendered its initiation permissible.

The distinctions of classical "stop-and-frisk" theory thus serve to divert attention from the central inquiry under the Fourth Amendment—the reasonableness in all the circumstances of the particular governmental invasion of a citizen's personal security. "Search" and "seizure" are not talismans. We therefore reject the notions that the Fourth Amendment does not come into play at all as a limitation upon police conduct if the officers stop short of something called a "technical arrest" or a "full-blown search."

In this case there can be no question, then, that Officer McFadden "seized" petitioner and subjected him to a "search" when he took hold of him and patted down the outer surfaces of his clothing. We must decide whether at that point it was reasonable for Officer McFadden to have interfered with petitioner's personal security as he did. And in determining whether the seizure and search were "unreasonable" our inquiry is a dual one—whether the officer's action was justified at its inception, and whether it was reasonably related in scope to the circumstances which justified the interference in the first place.

III

If this case involved police conduct subject to the Warrant Clause of the Fourth Amendment, we would have to ascertain whether "probable cause" existed to justify the search and seizure which took place. However, that is not the case. We do not retreat from our holdings that the police must, whenever practicable, obtain advance judicial approval of searches and seizures through the warrant procedure, or that in most instances failure to comply with the warrant requirement can only be excused by exigent circumstances. But we deal here with an entire rubric of police conduct—necessarily swift action predicated upon the on-the-spot observations of the officer on the beat—which historically has not been, and as a practical matter could not be, subjected to the warrant procedure. Instead, the conduct involved in this case must be tested by the Fourth Amendment's general proscription against unreasonable searches and seizures.

Nonetheless, the notions which underlie both the warrant procedure and the requirement of probable cause remain fully relevant in this context. In order to assess the reasonableness of Officer McFadden's conduct as a general proposition, it is necessary "first to focus upon the governmental interest which allegedly justifies official intrusion upon the constitutionally protected interests of the private citizen," for there is "no ready test for determining reasonableness other than by balancing the need to search (or seize) against the invasion which the search (or seizure) entails." And in justifying the particular intrusion the police officer must be able to point to specific and articulable facts which, taken together with rational inferences from those facts, reasonably warrant that intrusion. The scheme of the Fourth Amendment becomes meaningful only when it is assured that at some point the conduct of those charged with enforcing the laws can be subjected to the more detached, neutral scrutiny of a judge who must evaluate the reasonableness of a particular search or seizure in light of the particular circumstances. And in making that assessment it is imperative that the facts be judged against an objective standard: would the facts available to the officer at the moment of the seizure or the search "warrant a man of reasonable caution in the belief" that the action taken was appropriate? Anything less would invite intrusions upon constitutionally guaranteed rights based on nothing more substantial than inarticulate hunches, a result this Court has consistently refused to sanction. And simple "good faith on the part of the arresting officer is not enough. . . . If subjective good faith alone were the test, the protections of the Fourth Amendment would evaporate, and the people would be 'secure in their persons, houses, papers and effects,' only in the discretion of the police."

Applying these principles to this case, we consider first the nature and extent of the governmental interests involved. One general interest is of course that of effective crime prevention and detection; it is this interest which underlies the recognition that a police officer may in appropriate circumstances and in an appropriate manner approach a person for purposes of investigating possibly criminal behavior even though there is no probable cause to make an arrest. It was this legitimate investigative function Officer McFadden was discharging when he decided to approach petitioner and his companions. He had observed Terry, Chilton, and Katz go through a series of acts, each of them perhaps innocent in itself, but which taken together warranted further investigation. There is nothing unusual in two men standing together on a street corner, perhaps waiting for someone. Nor is there anything suspicious about people in such circumstances strolling up and down the street, singly or in pairs. Store windows, moreover, are made to be looked in. But the story is quite different where, as here, two men hover about a street corner for an extended period of time, at the end of which it becomes apparent that they are not waiting for anyone or anything; where these men pace alternately along an identical route, pausing to stare in the same store window roughly 24 times; where each completion of this route is followed immediately by a conference between the two men on the corner; where they are joined in one of these conferences by a third man who leaves swiftly; and where the two men finally follow the third and rejoin him a couple of blocks away. It would have been poor police work indeed for an officer of 30 years' experience in the detection of thievery from stores in this same neighborhood to have failed to investigate this behavior further.

The crux of this case, however, is not the propriety of Officer McFadden's taking steps to investigate petitioner's suspicious behavior, but rather, whether there was justification for McFadden's invasion of Terry's personal security by searching him for weapons in the course of that investigation. We are now concerned with more than the governmental interest in investigating crime; in addition, there is the more immediate interest of the police officer in taking steps to assure himself that the person with whom he is dealing is not armed with a weapon that could unexpectedly and fatally be used against him. Certainly it would be unreasonable to require that police officers take unnecessary risks in the performance of their duties. American criminals have a long tradition of armed violence, and every year in this country many law enforcement officers are killed in the line of duty, and thousands more are wounded. Virtually all of these deaths and a substantial portion of the injuries are inflicted with guns and knives.

In view of these facts, we cannot blind ourselves to the need for law enforcement officers to protect themselves and other prospective victims of violence in situations where they may lack probable cause for an arrest. When an officer is justified in believing that the individual whose suspicious behavior he is investigating at close range is armed and presently dangerous to the officer or to others, it would appear to be clearly unreasonable to deny the officer the power to take necessary measures to determine whether the person is in fact carrying a weapon and to neutralize the threat of physical harm.

We must still consider, however, the nature and quality of the intrusion on individual rights which must be accepted if police officers are to be conceded the right to search for weapons in situations where probable cause to arrest for crime is lacking. Even a limited search of the outer clothing for weapons constitutes a severe, though brief, intrusion upon cherished personal security, and it must surely be an annoying, frightening, and perhaps humiliating experience. Petitioner contends that such an intrusion is permissible only incident to a lawful arrest, either for a crime involving the possession of weapons or for a crime the commission of which led the officer to investigate in the first place. However, this argument must be closely examined.

Petitioner does not argue that a police officer should refrain from making any investigation of suspicious circumstances until such time as he has probable cause to make an arrest; nor does he deny that police officers in properly discharging their investigative function may find themselves confronting persons who might well be armed and dangerous. Moreover, he does not say that an officer is always unjustified in searching a suspect to discover weapons. Rather, he says it is unreasonable for the policeman to take that step until such time as the situation evolves to a point where there is probable cause to make an arrest. When that point has been reached, petitioner would concede the officer's right to conduct a search of the suspect for weapons, fruits or instrumentalities of the crime, or "mere" evidence, incident to the arrest.

There are two weaknesses in this line of reasoning however. First, it fails to take account of traditional limitations upon the scope of searches, and thus recognizes no distinction in purpose, character, and extent between a search incident to an arrest and a limited search for weapons. The former, although justified in part by the acknowledged necessity to protect the arresting officer from assault with a concealed weapon, is also justified on other grounds, and can therefore involve a relatively extensive exploration of the person. A search for weapons in the absence of probable cause to arrest, however, must, like any other search, be strictly circumscribed by the exigencies which justify its initiation. Thus it must be limited to that which is necessary for the discovery of weapons which might be used to harm the officer or others nearby, and may realistically be characterized as something less than a "full" search, even though it remains a serious intrusion.

A second, and related, objection to petitioner's argument is that it assumes that the law of arrest has already worked out the balance between the particular interests involved here—the neutralization of danger to the policeman in the investigative circumstance and the sanctity of the individual. But this is not so. An arrest is a wholly different kind of intrusion upon individual freedom from a limited search for weapons, and the interests each is designed to serve are likewise quite different. An arrest is the initial stage of a criminal prosecution. It is intended to vindicate society's interest in having its laws obeyed, and it is inevitably accompanied by future interference with the individual's freedom of movement, whether or not trial or conviction ultimately follows. The protective search for weapons, on the other hand, constitutes a brief, though far from inconsiderable, intrusion upon the sanctity of the person. It does not follow that because an officer may lawfully arrest a person only when he is apprised of facts sufficient to warrant a belief that the person has committed or is committing a crime, the officer is equally unjustified, absent that kind of evidence, in making any intrusions short of an arrest. Moreover, a perfectly reasonable apprehension of danger may arise long before the officer is possessed of adequate information to justify taking a person into custody for the purpose of prosecuting him for a crime. Petitioner's reliance on cases which have worked out standards of reasonableness with regard to "seizures" constituting arrests and searches incident thereto is thus misplaced. It assumes that the interests sought to be vindicated and the invasions of personal security may be equated in the two cases, and thereby ignores a vital aspect of the analysis of the reasonableness of particular types of conduct under the Fourth Amendment.

Our evaluation of the proper balance that has to be struck in this type of case leads us to conclude that there must be a narrowly drawn authority to permit a reasonable search for weapons for the protection of the police officer, where he has reason to believe that he is dealing with an armed and dangerous individual, regardless of whether he has probable cause to arrest the individual for a crime. The officer need not be absolutely certain that the individual is armed; the issue is whether a reasonably prudent man in the circumstances would be warranted in the belief that his safety or that of others was in danger. And in determining whether the officer acted reasonably in such circumstances, due weight must be given, not to his inchoate and unparticularized suspicion or "hunch," but to the specific reasonable inferences which he is entitled to draw from the facts in light of his experience. *Cf. Brinegar v. United States.*

IV

We must now examine the conduct of Officer McFadden in this case to determine whether his search and seizure of petitioner were reasonable, both at their inception and as conducted. He had observed Terry, together with Chilton and another man, acting in a manner he took to be preface to a "stick-up." We think on the facts and circumstances Officer McFadden detailed before the trial judge a reasonably prudent man would have been warranted in believing petitioner was armed and thus presented a threat to the officer's safety while he was investigating his suspicious behavior. The actions of Terry and Chilton were consistent with McFadden's hypothesis that these men were contemplating a daylight robbery—which, it is reasonable to assume, would be likely to involve the use of weapons—and nothing in their conduct from the time he first noticed them until the time he confronted them and identified himself as a police officer gave him sufficient reason to negate that hypothesis. Although the trio had departed the original scene, there was nothing to indicate abandonment of an intent to commit a robbery at some point. Thus, when Officer McFadden approached the three men gathered before the display window at Zucker's store he had observed enough to make it quite reasonable to fear that they were armed; and nothing in their response to his hailing them, identifying himself as a police officer, and asking their names served to dispel that reasonable belief. We cannot say his decision at that point to seize Terry and pat his clothing for weapons was the product of a volatile or inventive imagination, or was undertaken simply as an act of harassment; the record evidences the tempered act of a policeman who in the course of an investigation had to make a quick decision as to how to protect himself and others from possible danger, and took limited steps to do so.

The manner in which the seizure and search were conducted is, of course, as vital a part of the inquiry as whether they were warranted at all. The Fourth Amendment proceeds as much by limitations upon the scope of governmental action as by imposing preconditions upon its initiation. The entire deterrent purpose of the rule excluding evidence seized in violation of the Fourth Amendment rests on the assumption that "limitations upon the fruit to be gathered tend to limit the quest itself." Thus, evidence may not be introduced if it was discovered by means of a seizure and search which were not reasonably related in scope to the justification for their initiation.

We need not develop at length in this case, however, the limitations which the Fourth Amendment places upon a protective seizure and search for weapons. These limitations will have to be developed in the concrete factual circumstances of individual cases. Suffice it to note that such a search, unlike a search without a warrant incident to a lawful arrest, is not justified by any need to prevent the disappearance or destruction of evidence of crime. The sole justification of the search in the present situation is the protection of the police officer and others nearby, and it must therefore be confined in scope to an intrusion reasonably designed to discover guns, knives, clubs, or other hidden instruments for the assault of the police officer.

The scope of the search in this case presents no serious problem in light of these standards. Officer McFadden patted down the outer clothing of petitioner and his two companions. He did not place his hands in their pockets or under the outer surface of their garments until he had felt weapons, and then he merely reached for and removed the guns. He never did invade Katz' person beyond the outer surfaces of his clothes, since he discovered nothing in his patdown which might have been a weapon. Officer McFadden confined his search strictly to what was minimally necessary to learn whether the men were armed and to disarm them once he discovered the weapons. He did not conduct a general exploratory search for whatever evidence of criminal activity he might find.

V

We conclude that the revolver seized from Terry was properly admitted in evidence against him. At the time he seized petitioner and searched him for weapons, Officer McFadden had reasonable grounds to believe that petitioner was armed and dangerous, and it was necessary for the protection of himself and others to take swift measures to discover the true facts and neutralize the threat of harm if it materialized. The policeman carefully restricted his search to what was appropriate to the discovery of the particular items which he sought. Each case of this sort will, of course, have to be decided on its own facts. We merely hold today that where a police officer observes unusual conduct which leads him reasonably to conclude in light of his experience that criminal activity may be afoot and that the persons with whom he is dealing may be armed and presently dangerous, where in the course of investigating this behavior he identifies himself as a policeman and makes reasonable inquiries, and where nothing in the initial stages of the encounter serves to dispel his reasonable fear for his own or others' safety, he is entitled for the protection of himself and others in the area to conduct a carefully limited search of the outer clothing of such persons in an attempt to discover weapons which might be used to assault him. Such a search is a reasonable search under the Fourth Amendment, and any weapons seized may properly be introduced in evidence against the person from whom they were taken

Affirmed.

• • •

Mr. Justice WHITE, concurring.

I join the opinion of the Court, reserving judgment, however, on some of the Court's general remarks about the scope and purpose of the exclusionary rule which the Court has fashioned in the process of enforcing the Fourth Amendment.

Also, although the Court puts the matter aside in the context of this case, I think an additional word is in order concerning the matter of interrogation during an investigative stop. There is nothing in the Constitution which prevents a policeman from addressing questions to anyone on the streets. Absent special circumstances, the person approached may not be detained or frisked but may refuse to cooperate and go on his way. However, given the proper circumstances, such as those in this case, it seems to me the person may be briefly detained against his will while pertinent questions are directed to him. Of course, the person stopped is not obliged to answer, answers may not be compelled, and refusal to answer furnishes no basis for an arrest, although it may alert the officer to the need for continued observation. In my view, it is temporary detention, warranted by the circumstances, which chiefly justifies the protective frisk for weapons. Perhaps the frisk itself, where proper, will have beneficial results whether questions are asked or not. If weapons are found, an arrest will follow. If none are found, the frisk may nevertheless serve preventive ends because of its unmistakable message that suspicion has been aroused. But if the investigative stop is sustainable at all, constitutional rights are not necessarily violated if pertinent questions are asked and the person is restrained briefly in the process.

Mr. Justice DOUGLAS, dissenting.

I agree that petitioner was "seized" within the meaning of the Fourth Amendment. I also agree that frisking petitioner and his companions for guns was a "search." But it is a mystery how that "search" and that "seizure" can be constitutional by Fourth Amendment standards, unless there was "probable cause" to believe that (1) a crime had been committed or (2) a crime was in the process of being committed or (3) a crime was about to be committed.

The opinion of the Court disclaims the existence of "probable cause." If loitering were in issue and that was the offense charged, there would be "probable cause" shown. But the crime here is carrying concealed weapons; and there is no basis for concluding that the officer had "probable cause" for believing that that crime was being committed. Had a warrant been sought, a magistrate would, therefore, have been unauthorized to issue one, for he can act only if there is a showing of "probable cause." We hold today that the police have greater authority to make a "seizure" and conduct a "search" than a judge has to authorize such action. We have said precisely the opposite over and over again.

In other words, police officers up to today have been permitted to effect arrests or searches without warrants only when the facts within their personal knowledge would satisfy the constitutional standard of probable cause. At the time of their "seizure" without a warrant they must possess facts concerning the person arrested that would have satisfied a magistrate that "probable cause" was indeed present. The term "probable cause" rings a bell of certainty that is not sounded by phrases such as "reasonable suspicion." Moreover, the meaning of "probable cause" is deeply imbedded in our constitutional history. As we stated in *Henry v. United States*:

> The requirement of probable cause has roots that are deep in our history. The general warrant, in which the name of the person to be arrested was left blank, and the writs of assistance, against which James Otis inveighed, both perpetuated the oppressive practice of allowing the police to arrest and search on suspicion. Police control took the place of judicial control, since no showing of "probable cause" before a magistrate was required.
>
> That philosophy (rebelling against these practices) later was reflected in the Fourth Amendment. And as the early American decisions both before and immediately after its adoption show, common rumor or report, suspicion, or even "strong reason to suspect" was not adequate to support a warrant for arrest. And that principle has survived to this day. . . .
>
> . . . It is important, we think, that this requirement (of probable cause) be strictly enforced, for the standard set by the Constitution protects both the officer and the citizen. If the officer acts with probable cause, he is protected even though it turns out that the citizen is innocent. . . . And while a search without a warrant is, within limits, permissible if incident to a lawful arrest, if an arrest without a warrant is to support an incidental search, it must be made with probable cause. . . . This immunity of officers cannot fairly be enlarged without jeopardizing the privacy or security of the citizen.

The infringement on personal liberty of any "seizure" of a person can only be "reasonable" under the Fourth Amendment if we require the police to possess "probable cause" before they seize him. Only that line draws a meaningful distinction between an officer's mere inkling and the presence of facts within the officer's personal knowledge which would convince a reasonable man that the person seized has committed, is committing, or is about to commit a particular crime. "In dealing with probable cause, . . . as the very name implies, we deal with probabilities. These are not technical; they are the factual and practical considerations of everyday life on which reasonable and prudent men, not legal technicians, act."

To give the police greater power than a magistrate is to take a long step down the totalitarian path. Perhaps such a step is desirable to cope with modern forms of lawlessness. But if it is taken, it should be the deliberate choice of the people through a constitutional amendment. Until the Fourth Amendment, which is closely allied with the Fifth, is rewritten, the person and the effects of the individual are beyond the reach of all government agencies until there are reasonable grounds to believe (probable cause) that a criminal venture has been launched or is about to be launched.

There have been powerful hydraulic pressures throughout our history that bear heavily on the Court to water down constitutional guarantees and give the police the upper hand. That hydraulic pressure has probably never been greater than it is today.

Yet if the individual is no longer to be sovereign, if the police can pick him up whenever they do not like the cut of his jib, if they can "seize" and "search" him in their discretion, we enter a new regime. The decision to enter it should be made only after a full debate by the people of this country.

NOTES AND QUESTIONS

1. *Terry* tries very hard not to be a case about race, even as it acknowledges the "harassment" about which "Negroes frequently complain" and in a footnote references the report of the President's Commission on Law Enforcement and Administration of Justice cited above, and its finding that "stop and frisk" practices are a "major source of friction between the police and minority groups." But *Terry* of course is all about race. The racial implications of *Terry* will be explored more fully in the next section.

2. The legal proposition for which *Terry* became known is that the limited type of search and seizure reflected in a "stop and frisk"—also known eventually as a *Terry* stop—satisfies the Fourth Amendment based on a showing not of probable cause but only of "reasonable suspicion." Yet the term "reasonable suspicion" is nowhere in the opinion. Did the Court not want to make explicit the standard it was substituting for probable cause in this context? Did it believe a vaguer concept of untethered reasonableness was more palatable?

3. In its conclusion the Court connects Detective McFadden's actions to his reasonable conclusion that "criminal activity may be afoot." But do the facts of the case suggest that a temporal limitation to ongoing or imminent criminal activity is warranted? What were the two men doing when they were apprehended?

4. Does the rule in *Terry* actually make police officers safer? Aren't police officers always going to do what they believe they need to do to protect themselves during an encounter with civilians? Is the only real-world consequence of *Terry* that the evidence officers come upon in frisks will not be subject to the exclusionary rule?

As to officer safety: Officer McFadden said nothing at all in the suppression hearing about safety, protection, or even why he frisked the three men. When asked if he knew the men had guns, he replied "[a]bsolutely not." Transcript of Suppression Hearing, reprinted in State of Ohio v. Richard D. Chilton *and* State of Ohio v. John W. Terry*: The Suppression Hearing and Trial Transcripts*, 72 St. John's L. Rev. 1387, Appendix B at 1419 (John Q. Barrett ed., 1998) (hereinafter Suppression Hearing Transcript).

5. *Terry* is sometimes described as a compromise because the Court found that a stop and frisk was a "search and seizure" within the meaning of the Fourth Amendment. Is that really a compromise? Is there any serious argument that the "stop" half is anything but a seizure, at least insofar as a reasonable person would not feel free to leave? Any serious argument that the "frisk" half is not a search?

6. The Court assumes that a classic "stop" has the requisite curtailment of freedom to amount to a seizure: "It must be recognized that whenever a police officer accosts an individual and restrains his freedom to walk away, he has 'seized' that person." But does the stopped person also have an obligation to respond to the officer's questioning? Justice White concurs for the sole purpose of answering this question in the negative:

> Of course, the person stopped is not obliged to answer, answers may not be compelled, and refusal to answer furnishes no basis for an arrest, although it may alert the officer to the need for continued observation.

Do you agree that this follows from the rest of *Terry*? On what basis? Fifth Amendment? Justice White's observation would not hold the day when the Court began to consider the constitutionality of so-called stop-and-identify statutes. *See infra.*

7. Professor Seo has observed that the Court used the same playbook in *Terry* as it had earlier used in *Carroll.* It dispensed with the Fourth Amendment's probable cause requirement in *Terry* just as it had dispensed with the Fourth Amendment's warrant requirement in *Carroll*, and in both instances the Court ushered in an era of police discretion, based only on "reasonableness," to be filtered through the policeman's expertise. Seo, Policing the Open Road, *supra* at 151-55. In both cases, moreover, the Court appeared to be reaching a "compromise," a view some academics have accepted. *Id. See, e.g.*, Stephen A. Saltzburg, Terry v. Ohio: *A Practically Perfect Doctrine*, 72 St. John's L. Rev. 911 (1998).

Others have not. Professor Carbado sees the decision as Solomonic in the more accurate historical sense: "Like Solomon, [Chief Justice] Warren only feigned compromise, but in reality he handed the entire baby to the government, wrapped in the blanket of *reasonable suspicion.*" Carbado, Unreasonable, *supra* at 126.

8. Officer safety is of course a laudable goal. But note that in *Terry* the frisk of Terry results not only in preserving the safety of the encounter but also in yielding all the evidence needed to convict Terry of a firearms offense, an all too common result. What if the *Terry* rule had a proviso that any evidence yielded as a result of a frisk was inadmissible? Sort of a reverse good faith exception? For one thing, this would reduce the collateral consequences of an arguably subconstitutional encounter. For another, it would ensure that *Terry* frisks were only done where there were legitimate officer safety concerns and not as pretextual searches for evidence.

The reverse good faith exception would be conceptually similar to the tradeoff in the federal immunity statute. *See* 18 U.S.C. § 6001 (conditioning the compulsion of immunized testimony on the requirement that the government may not make any direct or indirect use of the testimony).

9. Do you see any foreshadowing of Justice Douglas's opinion for the Court in *Papachristou (see* Chapter II, *supra*), striking down a Florida vagrancy statute, in his *Terry* dissent here, just four years earlier? Do you think the decision in *Papachristou*—by an already more conservative Court than in *Terry*—was easier for the Court to reach inasmuch as it had already enabled police by endorsing the "reasonable suspicion" standard for an investigative stop. In other words, after *Terry* did the police even need the power conferred by vagrancy statutes?

The Court did specify in *Terry* that the "justification" for the intrusion could not simply be an "inarticulate hunch." "[T]he police officer must be able to point to specific and articulable facts which, taken together with rational inferences from those facts, reasonably warrant that intrusion." The Court later in the opinion put a deadly gloss on the term "rational inferences," restating it as "the specific reasonable inferences which he is entitled to draw from the facts in light of his experience."

Refreshingly candid in this regard, the Court doesn't try to sugarcoat Detective McFadden's experience. He had been on the lookout in downtown Cleveland for "shoplifters and pickpockets for 30 years." Despite the narrowness of his beat, McFadden nonetheless deduces that an "armed robbery" is afoot. What do armed robberies have in common with pickpocketing and shoplifting, besides being illegal? Nothing in the opinion suggests that McFadden has any experience investigating armed robbery.

John W. Terry

Martin McFadden

And as to his specific interpretation of the men's odd behavior as "casing the place," as a predicate to an "armed robbery," consider this exchange in the suppression hearing when the judge—unforgivably—jumped into the examination and got an answer from McFadden that he probably wasn't expecting:

> **Q.** Have you ever had any experience in observing the activities of individuals in casing a place?
> **A.** To be truthful with you, no.
> **Q.** You never observed anybody casing a place?
> **A.** No.
> **Q.** But you have had the experience of a detective in apprehending, and doing your police job as assigned?
> **A:** Yes.

Suppression Hearing Transcript at 1420.

The Court nonetheless saw fit to bless Detective McFadden's expertise and experience, assuming it uncritically, as courts have often unthoughtfully done and will probably continue to do. *See generally* Anna Lvovsky, *The Judicial Presumption of Police Expertise*, 130 Harv. L. Rev. 1995 (2017).

Terry is sometimes seen as inconsistent with the legacy of the Warren Court. But as Professor Maclin and others have observed, by 1968, having taken a public beating over its 1966 *Miranda* decision, the Warren Court had lost some of its civil libertarian mojo. *See* Tracey Maclin, Terry v. Ohio*'s Fourth Amendment Legacy: Black Men and Police Discretion*, 72 St. John's L. Rev. 1271, 1277-78 (1998). *See also* Yale Kamisar, *The Warren Court (Was It Really So Defense-Minded?), The Burger Court (Is it Really So Prosecution-Oriented?), and Police Investigatory Practices*, in The Burger Court: The Counter Revolution That Wasn't 67 (Vincent Blasi ed., 1983) ("In its final years, 'the Warren Court,' I think it may be argued, was not the same Court that had produced *Miranda* or *Mapp*.").

This plaque honoring Detective McFadden, sponsored by the Cleveland Police Historical Society and the Ohio Historical Society, was erected in 2003 on Euclid Avenue in downtown Cleveland.

There were also cultural and political realities that of course influenced the Court. In the 12 months between the grant of certiorari and the decision in *Terry*, there had been what were then inaptly called "race riots" in 13 cities, most notably in Newark and Detroit, during the "long hot summer" of 1967; the assassination by gun of Martin Luther King Jr. on April 4, 1968, precipitating "race riots" in 100 cities, and of presidential candidate Robert Kennedy, on June 5, five days before the decision in *Terry*. During this same period Richard Nixon was hard on the campaign trail for the 1968 presidential election with his anti-crime message, vowing to make over the Supreme Court with "strict constructionists." And crime rates were, in fact, soaring. Not only Congress but President Johnson was chomping at the bit for tough-on-crime legislation. Perhaps poetically, the Omnibus Crime Control and Safe Streets Act of 1968, the most significant general criminal legislation passed perhaps ever by Congress, became effective on June 10, 1968, the same day the decision in *Terry* was handed down. This, of course, was precisely what Justice Douglas was referring to in his dissent in *Terry*:

> There have been powerful hydraulic pressures throughout our history that bear heavily on the Court to water down constitutional guarantees and give the police the upper hand. That hydraulic pressure has probably never been greater than it is today.

398 U.S. at 38 (Douglas, J., dissenting).

Chief Justice Warren's law clerk at the time stated later that *Terry* was the product of perceived political necessity. The Court was unwilling to be seen as the body that had "tied the hands of the police" in an age of escalating street violence. Earl C. Dudley Jr., Terry v. Ohio, *the Warren Court and the Fourth Amendment: A Law Clerk's Perspective*, 72 St. John's L. Rev. 891, 893 (1998). *See also* Bennett Capers, *Crime, Legitimacy and Testilying*, 83 Ind. L.J. 835, 862-65 (2008).

President Johnson announced he would not run for reelection on March 31, 1968. Chief Justice Warren retired effective June 30, 1968. An era was over.

The street-level impact of *Terry* was enormous, especially after the 1982 publication in *The Atlantic* of the influential "Broken Windows" article by criminologists George Kelling and James Q. Wilson, which advocated for prompt police attention to low-grade criminality as a deterrent to more serious crime. Ben Grunwald & Jeffrey Fagan, *The End of Intuition-Based High-Crime Areas*, 107 Cal. L. Rev. 345, 357 (2019). Almost overnight, field interrogation was everywhere and no level of urban hijinks was too innocuous for police inquiry. *Id. See also* Debra Livingston, *Police Discretion and the Quality of Life in Public Places: Courts, Communities, and the New Policing*, 97 Colum. L. Rev. 551 (1997). As occasions for *Terry* stops spread with the popularization of broken windows policing, police officers quickly discovered that when and if they wanted to it was fairly simple to escalate—even unilaterally—a *Terry* stop into a situation where there was probable cause to arrest, especially for such "contempt of cop" misdemeanors as obstruction, disorderly conduct, and the like. *See* Alexandra Napatoff, *A Stop Is Just a Stop:* Terry*'s Formalism*, 15 Ohio St. J. Crim. L. 113, 121 (2017).

Terry, while cast originally as a narrow exception to the probable cause requirement, was read generously by the reconstituted Burger Court in the 1970s and 1980s. In *Pennsylvania v. Mimms*, 434 U.S. 106 (1977), for example, the Court held that police may order persons out of a car during a routine traffic stop as a matter of routine, without any quantum of suspicion, purely as a means to protect the safety of the officers. *Id.* at 111. Further, if the police officers have reasonable suspicion that the passengers may be armed—an observed "bulge" under a passenger's sport coat satisfied that test in *Mimms*—the officers may frisk them for weapons. In *Michigan v. Long*, 463 U.S. 1032 (1983), the Court upheld the frisk of an apparently drunk driver and search of the front compartment area of the vehicle where officers saw a hunting knife on front floor board. And in *Maryland v. Buie*, 494 U.S. 325 (1990), the Court found that *Terry* justified a "protective sweep" of the premises in connection with the execution of an arrest warrant in a home to protect the safety of the officers and others, where the officers reasonably believed other dangerous persons might be present.

In the next case the Court considers the extent to which the "frisk" warranted under *Terry* can serve as a gateway to investigation unrelated to securing the safety of the questioning officers. The frisker here, an unnamed Minneapolis officer, purports to have a superhero's sense of touch rivaled only by Tommy, the mythical "deaf, dumb, and blind kid" of The Who's eponymous rock opera.

Minnesota v. Dickerson

508 U.S. 366 (1993)

Justice WHITE delivered the opinion of the Court.

In this case, we consider whether the Fourth Amendment permits the seizure of contraband detected through a police officer's sense of touch during a protective patdown search.

I

On the evening of November 9, 1989, two Minneapolis police officers were patrolling an area on the city's north side in a marked squad car. At about 8:15 p.m., one of the officers observed respondent leaving a 12-unit apartment building on Morgan Avenue North. The officer, having previously responded to complaints of drug sales in the building's hallways and having executed several search warrants on the premises, considered the building to be a notorious "crack house." According to testimony credited by the trial court, respondent began walking toward the police but, upon spotting the squad car and making eye contact with one of the officers, abruptly halted and began walking in the opposite direction. His suspicion aroused, this officer watched as respondent turned and entered an alley on the other side of the apartment building. Based upon respondent's seemingly evasive actions and the fact that he had just left a building known for cocaine traffic, the officers decided to stop respondent and investigate further.

The officers pulled their squad car into the alley and ordered respondent to stop and submit to a patdown search. The search revealed no weapons, but the officer conducting the search did take an interest in a small lump in respondent's nylon jacket. The officer later testified:

> [A]s I pat-searched the front of his body, I felt a lump, a small lump, in the front pocket. I examined it with my fingers and it slid and it felt to be a lump of crack cocaine in cellophane.

The officer then reached into respondent's pocket and retrieved a small plastic bag containing one fifth of one gram of crack cocaine. Respondent was arrested and charged in Hennepin County District Court with possession of a controlled substance.

Before trial, respondent moved to suppress the cocaine. The trial court first concluded that the officers were justified under *Terry* in stopping respondent to investigate whether he might be engaged in criminal activity. The court further found that the officers were justified in frisking respondent to ensure that he was not carrying a weapon. Finally, analogizing to the "plain-view" doctrine, under which officers may make a warrantless seizure of contraband found in plain view during a lawful search for other items, the trial court ruled that the officers' seizure of the cocaine did not violate the Fourth Amendment:

> To this Court there is no distinction as to which sensory perception the officer uses to conclude that the material is contraband. An experienced officer may rely upon his sense of smell in DWI stops or in recognizing the smell of burning marijuana in an automobile. The sound of a shotgun being racked would clearly support certain reactions by an officer. The sense of touch, grounded in experience and training, is as reliable as perceptions drawn from other senses. "Plain feel," therefore, is no different than plain view and will equally support the seizure here.

His suppression motion having failed, respondent proceeded to trial and was found guilty.

On appeal, the Minnesota Court of Appeals reversed. The court agreed with the trial court that the investigative stop and protective patdown search of respondent were lawful under *Terry* because the officers had a reasonable belief based on specific and articulable facts that respondent was engaged in criminal behavior and that he might be armed and dangerous. The court concluded, however, that the officers had overstepped the bounds allowed by *Terry* in seizing the cocaine. In doing so, the Court of Appeals "decline [d] to adopt the plain feel exception" to the warrant requirement.

The Minnesota Supreme Court affirmed. Like the Court of Appeals, the State Supreme Court held that both the stop and the frisk of respondent were valid under *Terry*, but found the seizure of the cocaine to be unconstitutional. The court expressly refused "to extend the plain view doctrine to the sense of touch" on the grounds that "the sense of touch is inherently less immediate and less reliable than the sense of sight" and that "the sense of touch is far more intrusive into the personal privacy that is at the core of the [F]ourth [A]mendment." The court thus appeared to adopt a categorical rule barring the seizure of any contraband detected by an officer through the sense of touch during a patdown search for weapons. The court further noted that "[e]ven if we recognized a 'plain feel' exception, the search in this case would not qualify" because "[t]he pat search of the defendant went far beyond what is permissible under *Terry*." Id., As the State Supreme Court read the record, the officer conducting the search ascertained that the lump in respondent's jacket was contraband only after probing and investigating what he certainly knew was not a weapon.

We granted certiorari to resolve a conflict among the state and federal courts over whether contraband detected through the sense of touch during a patdown search may be admitted into evidence. We now affirm.

II

A

The Fourth Amendment, made applicable to the States by way of the Fourteenth Amendment, guarantees "[t]he right of the people to be secure in their persons, houses, papers, and effects, against unreasonable searches and seizures." Time and again, this Court has observed that searches and seizures "'conducted outside the judicial process, without prior approval by judge or magistrate, are per se unreasonable under the Fourth Amendment—subject only to a few specifically established and well delineated exceptions.'" One such exception was recognized in *Terry*, which held that "where a police officer observes unusual conduct which leads him reasonably to conclude in light of his experience that criminal activity may be afoot . . .," the officer may briefly stop the suspicious person and make "reasonable inquiries" aimed at confirming or dispelling his suspicions.

Terry further held that "[w]hen an officer is justified in believing that the individual whose suspicious behavior he is investigating at close range is armed and presently dangerous to the officer or to others," the officer may conduct a patdown search "to determine whether the person is in fact carrying a weapon." "The purpose of this limited search is not to discover evidence of crime, but to allow the officer to pursue his investigation without fear of violence. . . ." Rather, a protective search—permitted without a warrant and on the basis of reasonable suspicion less than probable cause—must be strictly "limited to that which is necessary for the discovery of weapons which might be used to harm the officer or others nearby." If the protective search goes beyond what is necessary to determine if the suspect is armed, it is no longer valid under *Terry* and its fruits will be suppressed.

These principles were settled 25 years ago when, on the same day, the Court announced its decisions in *Terry* and *Sibron*. The question presented today is whether police officers may seize nonthreatening contraband detected during a protective patdown search of the sort permitted by *Terry*. We think the answer is clearly that they may, so long as the officers' search stays within the bounds marked by *Terry*.

B

We have already held that police officers, at least under certain circumstances, may seize contraband detected during the lawful execution of a *Terry* search. In *Michigan v. Long*, for example, police approached a man who had driven his car into a ditch and who appeared to be under the influence of some intoxicant. As the man moved to reenter the car from the roadside, police spotted a knife on the floorboard. The officers stopped the man, subjected him to a patdown search, and then inspected the interior of the vehicle for other weapons. During the search of the passenger compartment, the police discovered an open pouch containing marijuana and seized it. This Court upheld the validity of the search and seizure under *Terry*. The Court held first that, in the context of a roadside encounter, where police have reasonable suspicion based on specific and articulable facts to believe that a driver may be armed and dangerous, they may conduct a protective search for weapons not only of the driver's person but also of the passenger compartment of the automobile. Of course, the protective search of the vehicle, being justified solely by the danger that weapons stored there could be used against the officers or bystanders, must be "limited to those areas in which a weapon may be placed or hidden." The Court then held: "If, while conducting a legitimate *Terry* search of the interior of the automobile, the officer should, as here, discover contraband other than weapons, he clearly cannot be required to ignore the contraband, and the Fourth Amendment does not require its suppression in such circumstances."

The Court in *Long* justified this latter holding by reference to our cases under the "plain-view" doctrine. Under that doctrine, if police are lawfully in a position from which they view an object, if its incriminating character is immediately apparent, and if the officers have a lawful right of access to the object, they may seize it without a warrant. If, however, the police lack probable cause to believe that an object in plain view is contraband without conducting some further search of the object—i.e., if "its incriminating character [is not] 'immediately apparent,'"—the plain-view doctrine cannot justify its seizure.

We think that this doctrine has an obvious application by analogy to cases in which an officer discovers contraband through the sense of touch during an otherwise lawful search. The rationale of the plain-view doctrine is that if contraband is left in open view and is observed by a police officer from a lawful vantage point, there has been no invasion of a legitimate expectation of privacy and thus no "search" within the meaning of the Fourth Amendment—or at least no search independent of the initial intrusion that gave the officers their vantage point. The warrantless seizure of contraband that presents itself in this manner is deemed justified by the realization that resort to a neutral magistrate under such circumstances would often be impracticable and would do little to promote the objectives of the Fourth Amendment. The same can be said of tactile discoveries of contraband. If a police officer lawfully pats down a suspect's outer clothing and feels an object whose contour or mass makes its identity immediately apparent, there has been no invasion of the suspect's privacy beyond that already authorized by the officer's search for weapons; if the object is contraband, its warrantless seizure would be justified by the same practical considerations that inhere in the plain-view context.

The Minnesota Supreme Court rejected an analogy to the plain-view doctrine on two grounds: first, its belief that "the sense of touch is inherently less immediate and less reliable than the sense of sight," and second, that "the sense of touch is far more intrusive into the personal privacy that is at the core of the [F]ourth [A]mendment." We have a somewhat different view. First, *Terry* itself demonstrates that the sense of touch is capable of revealing the nature of an object with sufficient reliability to support a seizure. The very premise of *Terry*, after all, is that officers will be able to detect the presence of weapons through the sense of touch and *Terry* upheld precisely such a seizure. Even if it were true that the sense of touch is generally less reliable than the sense of sight, that only suggests that officers will less often be able to justify seizures of unseen contraband. Regardless of whether the officer detects the contraband by sight or by touch, however, the Fourth Amendment's requirement that the officer have probable cause to believe that the item is contraband before seizing it ensures against excessively speculative seizures. The court's second concern—that touch is more intrusive into privacy than is sight—is inapposite in light of the fact that the intrusion the court fears has already been authorized by the lawful search for weapons. The seizure of an item whose identity is already known occasions no further invasion of privacy. Accordingly, the suspect's privacy interests are not advanced by a categorical rule barring the seizure of contraband plainly detected through the sense of touch.

III

It remains to apply these principles to the facts of this case. Respondent has not challenged the finding made by the trial court and affirmed by both the Court of Appeals and the State Supreme Court that the police were justified under *Terry* in stopping him and frisking him for weapons. Thus, the dispositive question before this Court is whether the officer who conducted the search was acting within the lawful bounds marked by *Terry* at the time he gained probable cause to believe that the lump in respondent's jacket was contraband. The State District Court did not make precise findings on this point, instead finding simply that the officer, after feeling "a small, hard object wrapped in plastic" in respondent's pocket, "formed the opinion that the object . . . was crack . . . cocaine." The District Court also noted that the officer made "no claim that he suspected this object to be a weapon," a finding affirmed on appeal. The Minnesota Supreme Court, after "a close examination of the record," held that the officer's own testimony "belies any notion that he 'immediately'" recognized the lump as crack cocaine. Rather, the court concluded, the officer determined that the lump was contraband only after "squeezing, sliding and otherwise manipulating the contents of the defendant's pocket"—a pocket which the officer already knew contained no weapon.

Under the State Supreme Court's interpretation of the record before it, it is clear that the court was correct in holding that the police officer in this case overstepped the bounds of the "strictly circumscribed" search for weapons allowed under *Terry*. Where, as here, "an officer who is executing a valid search for one item seizes a different item," this Court rightly "has been sensitive to the danger . . . that officers will enlarge a specific authorization, furnished by a warrant or an exigency, into the equivalent of a general warrant to rummage and seize at will." Here, the officer's continued exploration of respondent's pocket after having concluded that it contained no weapon was unrelated to "[t]he sole justification of the search [under *Terry*:] . . . the protection of the police officer and others nearby." It therefore amounted to the sort of evidentiary search that *Terry* expressly refused to authorize and that we have condemned in subsequent cases.

Once again, the analogy to the plain-view doctrine is apt. In *Arizona v. Hicks*, this Court held invalid the seizure of stolen stereo equipment found by police while executing a valid search for other evidence. Although the police were lawfully on the premises, they obtained probable cause to believe that the stereo equipment was contraband only after moving the equipment to permit officers to read its serial numbers. The subsequent seizure of the equipment could not be justified by the plain-view doctrine, this Court explained, because the incriminating character of the stereo equipment was not immediately apparent; rather, probable cause to believe that the equipment was stolen arose only as a result of a further search—the moving of the equipment—that was not authorized by a search warrant or by any exception to the warrant requirement. The facts of this case are very similar. Although the officer was lawfully in a position to feel the lump in respondent's pocket, because *Terry* entitled him to place his hands upon respondent's jacket, the court below determined that the incriminating character of the object was not immediately apparent to him. Rather, the officer determined that the item was contraband only after conducting a further search, one not authorized by *Terry* or by any other exception to the warrant requirement. Because this further search of respondent's pocket was constitutionally invalid, the seizure of the cocaine that followed is likewise unconstitutional.

IV

For these reasons, the judgment of the Minnesota Supreme Court is
Affirmed.

NOTES AND QUESTIONS

1. Is the case for reasonable suspicion ironclad here? Is criminal activity "afoot"? What is the probative value of "walking away"? Do you see irony in the notion that "walking away" can contribute to the basis for reasonable suspicion for a *Terry* stop, while at the same time a reasonable belief in the ability to "walk away" signifies the absence of a seizure?

2. The Court notes the police officer's "interest" in a "lump" in a jacket pocket. The Court seemingly legitimates this interest even though the only constitutional basis for the officer's hands on the defendant is to search for weapons. Isn't the officer just supposed to ignore the "lump" because it isn't a weapon?

Is the officer's testimony that "by feel" he had determined that he had felt "a lump of cocaine wrapped in cellophane" even remotely credible? Wasn't he cross-examined on this conclusion? What's in the record? Why does the Court just seem to accept this?

3. The Court recognizes the theoretical possibility of a "plain feel" exception but finds it inapplicable here, apparently because the officer continued his search even after its original and legitimate purpose of looking for weapons was over. Can you imagine a scenario where the exception would be applicable?

In the next case the Court considers what happens when a *Terry* stop doesn't go as planned, as well as whether Justice White's concurring opinion in *Terry* on "the right to remain" silent still has legs.

Hiibel v. Sixth Judicial District Court of Nevada

542 U.S. 177 (2004)

Justice Kennedy delivered the opinion of the Court.

The petitioner was arrested and convicted for refusing to identify himself during a stop allowed by *Terry*. He challenges his conviction under the Fourth and Fifth Amendments to the United States Constitution, applicable to the States through the Fourteenth Amendment.

I

The sheriff's department in Humboldt County, Nevada, received an afternoon telephone call reporting an assault. The caller reported seeing a man assault a woman in a red and silver GMC truck on Grass Valley Road. Deputy Sheriff Lee Dove was dispatched to investigate. When the officer arrived at the scene, he found the truck parked on the side of the road. A man was standing by the truck, and a young woman was sitting inside it. The officer observed skid marks in the gravel behind the vehicle, leading him to believe it had come to a sudden stop.

The officer approached the man and explained that he was investigating a report of a fight. The man appeared to be intoxicated. The officer asked him if he had "any identification on [him]," which we understand as a request to produce a driver's license or some other form of written identification. The man refused and asked why the officer wanted to see identification. The officer responded that he was conducting an investigation and needed to see some identification. The unidentified man became agitated and insisted he had done nothing wrong. The officer explained that he wanted to find out who the man was and what he was doing there. After continued refusals to comply with the officer's request for identification, the man began to taunt the officer by placing his hands behind his back and telling the officer to arrest him and take him to jail. This routine kept up for several minutes: The officer asked for identification 11 times and was refused each time. After warning the man that he would be arrested if he continued to refuse to comply, the officer placed him under arrest.

We now know that the man arrested on Grass Valley Road is Larry Dudley Hiibel. Hiibel was charged with "willfully resist[ing], delay[ing] or obstruct[ing] a public officer in discharging or attempting to discharge any legal duty of his office" in violation of Nev. Rev. Stat. (NRS) § 199.280 (2003). The government reasoned that Hiibel had obstructed the officer in carrying out his duties under § 171.123, a Nevada statute that defines the legal rights and duties of a police officer in the context of an investigative stop. Section 171.123 provides in relevant part:

> 1. Any peace officer may detain any person whom the officer encounters under circumstances which reasonably indicate that the person has committed, is committing or is about to commit a crime. . . .
>
> 3. The officer may detain the person pursuant to this section only to ascertain his identity and the suspicious circumstances surrounding his presence abroad. Any person so detained shall identify himself, but may not be compelled to answer any other inquiry of any peace officer.

Hiibel was tried in the Justice Court of Union Township. The court agreed that Hiibel's refusal to identify himself as required by § 171.123 "obstructed and delayed Dove as a public officer in attempting to discharge his duty" in violation of § 199.280. Hiibel was convicted and fined $250. The Sixth Judicial District Court affirmed, rejecting Hiibel's argument that the application of § 171.123 to his case violated the Fourth and Fifth Amendments. On review the Supreme Court of Nevada rejected the Fourth Amendment challenge in a divided opinion. Hiibel petitioned for rehearing, seeking explicit resolution of his Fifth Amendment challenge. The petition was denied without opinion. We granted certiorari.

II

NRS § 171.123(3) is an enactment sometimes referred to as a "stop and identify" statute. . . .

Stop and identify statutes often combine elements of traditional vagrancy laws with provisions intended to regulate police behavior in the course of investigatory stops. The statutes vary from State to State, but all permit an officer to ask or require a suspect to disclose his identity. A few States model their statutes on the Uniform Arrest Act, a model code that permits an officer to stop a person reasonably suspected of committing a crime and "demand of him his name, address, business abroad and whither he is going." Other statutes are based on the text proposed by the American Law Institute as part of the Institute's Model Penal Code. The provision, originally designated § 250.12, provides that a person who is loitering "under circumstances which justify suspicion that he may be engaged or about to engage in crime commits a violation if he refuses the request of a peace officer that he identify himself and give a reasonably credible account of the lawfulness of his conduct and purposes." In some States, a suspect's refusal to identify himself is a misdemeanor offense or civil violation; in others, it is a factor to be considered in whether the suspect has violated loitering laws. In other States, a suspect may decline to identify himself without penalty.

Stop and identify statutes have their roots in early English vagrancy laws that required suspected vagrants to face arrest unless they gave "a good Account of themselves," a power that itself reflected common-law rights of private persons to "arrest any suspicious night-walker, and detain him till he give a good account of himself . . . ." In recent decades, the Court has found constitutional infirmity in traditional vagrancy laws. In *Papachristou v. Jacksonville* (1972), the Court held that a traditional vagrancy law was void for vagueness. Its broad scope and imprecise terms denied proper notice to potential offenders and permitted police officers to exercise unfettered discretion in the enforcement of the law.

The Court has recognized similar constitutional limitations on the scope and operation of stop and identify statutes. In *Brown v. Texas* (1979), the Court invalidated a conviction for violating a Texas stop and identify statute on Fourth Amendment grounds. The Court ruled that the initial stop was not based on specific, objective facts establishing reasonable suspicion to believe the suspect was involved in criminal activity. Absent that factual basis for detaining the defendant, the Court held, the risk of "arbitrary and abusive police practices" was too great and the stop was impermissible. Four Terms later, the Court invalidated a modified stop and identify statute on vagueness grounds. The California law in *Kolender* required a suspect to give an officer "'credible and reliable'" identification when asked to identify himself. The Court held that the statute was void because it provided no standard for determining what a suspect must do to comply with it, resulting in "'virtually unrestrained power to arrest and charge persons with a violation.'"

The present case begins where our prior cases left off. Here there is no question that the initial stop was based on reasonable suspicion, satisfying the Fourth Amendment requirements noted in *Brown*. Further, the petitioner has not alleged that the statute is unconstitutionally vague, as in *Kolender*. Here the Nevada statute is narrower and more precise. The statute in *Kolender* had been interpreted to require a suspect to give the officer "credible and reliable" identification. In contrast, the Nevada Supreme Court has interpreted NRS § 171.123(3) to require only that a suspect disclose his name. As we understand it, the statute does not require a suspect to give the officer a driver's license or any other document. Provided that the suspect either states his name or communicates it to the officer by other means—a choice, we assume, that the suspect may make—the statute is satisfied and no violation occurs.

III

Hiibel argues that his conviction cannot stand because the officer's conduct violated his Fourth Amendment rights. We disagree.

Asking questions is an essential part of police investigations. In the ordinary course a police officer is free to ask a person for identification without implicating the Fourth Amendment. "[I]nterrogation relating to one's identity or a request for identification by the police does not, by itself, constitute a Fourth Amendment seizure." Beginning with *Terry*, the Court has recognized that a law enforcement officer's reasonable suspicion that a person may be involved in criminal activity permits the officer to stop the person for a brief time and take additional steps to investigate further. To ensure that the resulting seizure is constitutionally reasonable, a *Terry* stop must be limited. The officer's action must be "'justified at its inception, and . . . reasonably related in scope to the circumstances which justified the interference in the first place.'" For example, the seizure can not continue for an excessive period of time, or resemble a traditional arrest.

Our decisions make clear that questions concerning a suspect's identity are a routine and accepted part of many *Terry* stops.

Obtaining a suspect's name in the course of a *Terry* stop serves important government interests. Knowledge of identity may inform an officer that a suspect is wanted for another offense, or has a record of violence or mental disorder. On the other hand, knowing identity may help clear a suspect and allow the police to concentrate their efforts elsewhere. Identity may prove particularly important in cases such as this, where the police are investigating what appears to be a domestic assault. Officers called to investigate domestic disputes need to know whom they are dealing with in order to assess the situation, the threat to their own safety, and possible danger to the potential victim.

Although it is well established that an officer may ask a suspect to identify himself in the course of a *Terry* stop, it has been an open question whether the suspect can be arrested and prosecuted for refusal to answer. Petitioner draws our attention to statements in prior opinions that, according to him, answer the question in his favor. In *Terry*, Justice White stated in a concurring opinion that a person detained in an investigative stop can be questioned but is "not obliged to answer, answers may not be compelled, and refusal to answer furnishes no basis for an arrest." The Court cited this opinion in dicta in *Berkemer v. McCarty*, (1984), a decision holding that a routine traffic stop is not a custodial stop requiring the protections of *Miranda*. In the course of explaining why *Terry* stops have not been subject to *Miranda*, the Court suggested reasons why *Terry* stops have a "nonthreatening character," among them the fact that a suspect detained during a *Terry* stop "is not obliged to respond" to questions. According to petitioner, these statements establish a right to refuse to answer questions during a *Terry* stop.

We do not read these statements as controlling. The passages recognize that the Fourth Amendment does not impose obligations on the citizen but instead provides rights against the government. As a result, the Fourth Amendment itself cannot require a suspect to answer questions. This case concerns a different issue, however. Here, the source of the legal obligation arises from Nevada state law, not the Fourth Amendment. Further, the statutory obligation does not go beyond answering an officer's request to disclose a name. As a result, we cannot view the dicta in *Berkemer* or Justice White's concurrence in *Terry* as answering the question whether a State can compel a suspect to disclose his name during a *Terry* stop.

The principles of *Terry* permit a State to require a suspect to disclose his name in the course of a *Terry* stop. The reasonableness of a seizure under the Fourth Amendment is determined "by balancing its intrusion on the individual's Fourth Amendment interests against its promotion of legitimate government interests." The Nevada statute satisfies that standard. The request for identity has an immediate relation to the purpose, rationale, and practical demands of a *Terry* stop. The threat of criminal sanction helps ensure that the request for identity does not become a legal nullity. On the other hand, the Nevada statute does not alter the nature of the stop itself: it does not change its duration or its location. A state law requiring a suspect to disclose his name in the course of a valid *Terry* stop is consistent with Fourth Amendment prohibitions against unreasonable searches and seizures.

Petitioner argues that the Nevada statute circumvents the probable-cause requirement, in effect allowing an officer to arrest a person for being suspicious. According to petitioner, this creates a risk of arbitrary police conduct that the Fourth Amendment does not permit.

These are familiar concerns; they were central to the opinion in *Papachristou*, and also to the decisions limiting the operation of stop and identify statutes in *Kolender* and *Brown*. Petitioner's concerns are met by the requirement that a *Terry* stop must be justified at its inception and "reasonably related in scope to the circumstances which justified" the initial stop. Under these principles, an officer may not arrest a suspect for failure to identify himself if the request for identification is not reasonably related to the circumstances justifying the stop. The Court noted a similar limitation in *Hayes*, where it suggested that Terry may permit an officer to determine a suspect's identity by compelling the suspect to submit to fingerprinting only if there is "a reasonable basis for believing that fingerprinting will establish or negate the suspect's connection with that crime." It is clear in this case that the request for identification was "reasonably related in scope to the circumstances which justified" the stop. The officer's request was a commonsense inquiry, not an effort to obtain an arrest for failure to identify after a *Terry* stop yielded insufficient evidence. The stop, the request, and the State's requirement of a response did not contravene the guarantees of the Fourth Amendment.

• • •

The judgment of the Nevada Supreme Court is
Affirmed.

NOTES AND QUESTIONS

1. Every fact selected for inclusion in a case is purposeful. The skid marks in the gravel? Why? And why defendant's middle name?

2. Is the Court's description of Sheriff Dove's encounter with Larry Dudley Hiibel slanted? Sure, Larry Dudley is being a pain in the ass, but why does the Court not acknowledge Dove's harassment of him? Asking for identification once might have been "a commonsense inquiry" as the Court describes it. But 11 times? It wasn't like there were no other investigation avenues available to Dove. For one thing, the alleged victim, per the tip, is just sitting in the truck, apparently being ignored, while Dove goes *mano a mano* with Hiibel. Might she have relevant information? Are there other witnesses in the neighborhood? How about running the plate on the truck? Does Dove actually care about finding out what happened, or does he just want to win his showdown with Larry Dudley?

3. The Court states that "stop and identify" statutes like the Nevada statute at issue here contain provisions "intended to regulate police behavior." Do you agree? What provisions in the Nevada statute appear to have this purpose?

4. The Court also states that there is "no question" that Dove's "stop" of Hiibel was supported by reasonable suspicion. Do you agree? Under what circumstances should an anonymous tip be able to serve as the basis for reasonable suspicion? Isn't the original justification for *Terry* the purported expertise and experience that police officers bring to bear on situations they observe?

5. The Court sings a love song to the importance of questioning, as if the point were debatable. But it never acknowledges the peril that answering may bring. For example, if a person being questioned has an outstanding warrant, and gives his name to a police officer, the officer can easily learn of the warrant and the person will immediately become arrestable—and searchable incident to that arrest. These are essentially the facts of *Utah v. Strieff*, 579 U.S. 232 (2016), *see infra*, where questioning of the defendant—*without* reasonable suspicion—leads to the production of identification, discovery of a warrant for traffic violation, arrest, search incident to arrest, discovery of drugs, then prosecution, then conviction and jail.

Larry Dudley Hiibel

6. None of this was presumably on Justice White's mind when he wrote his concurrence in *Terry* 36 years prior to *Hiibel.* But does anything in *Terry* itself compel the conclusion the Court reaches here?

7. Does the Court satisfactorily address its explicit reliance on Justice White's *Terry* concurrence in *Berkemer v. McCarty*, 468 U.S. 420 (1984). What is the relevance of the fact that a state statute purports to compel a person to speak? Isn't this tantamount to saying that a state law could abrogate *Terry* by, say, permitting a frisk for contraband as well as weapons?

8. The Court notes that an important interest served by learning a suspect's name is that it "may inform an officer that a suspect is wanted for another offense." Acquiring such knowledge, of course, requires the intermediate step of the officer remotely consulting a criminal records database, which the officer can easily do. But is that intermediate step consistent with *Terry*, which requires that the search and seizure be "reasonably related in scope to the circumstances which justified the interference in the first place"? 392 U.S. at 20.

The next case deals with a police officer's "reasonable suspicion" as to whether automobile passengers in a traffic stop might be "armed and dangerous" such that they can be frisked for the protection of the officers.

Arizona v. Johnson

555 U.S. 323 (2009)

Justice Ginsburg delivered the opinion of the Court.

This case concerns the authority of police officers to "stop and frisk" a passenger in a motor vehicle temporarily seized upon police detection of a traffic infraction. In a pathmarking decision, *Terry*, the Court considered whether an investigatory stop (temporary detention) and frisk (patdown for weapons) may be conducted without violating the Fourth Amendment's ban on unreasonable searches and seizures. The Court upheld "stop and frisk" as constitutionally permissible if two conditions are met. First, the investigatory stop must be lawful.

That requirement is met in an on-the-street encounter, *Terry* determined, when the police officer reasonably suspects that the person apprehended is committing or has committed a criminal offense. Second, to proceed from a stop to a frisk, the police officer must reasonably suspect that the person stopped is armed and dangerous.

For the duration of a traffic stop, we recently confirmed, a police officer effectively seizes "everyone in the vehicle," the driver and all passengers. *Brendlin v. California* (2007). Accordingly, we hold that, in a traffic-stop setting, the first *Terry* condition—a lawful investigatory stop—is met whenever it is lawful for police to detain an automobile and its occupants pending inquiry into a vehicular violation. The police need not have, in addition, cause to believe any occupant of the vehicle is involved in criminal activity. To justify a patdown of the driver or a passenger during a traffic stop, however, just as in the case of a pedestrian reasonably suspected of criminal activity, the police must harbor reasonable suspicion that the person subjected to the frisk is armed and dangerous.

I

On April 19, 2002, Officer Maria Trevizo and Detectives Machado and Gittings, all members of Arizona's gang task force, were on patrol in Tucson near a neighborhood associated with the Crips gang. At approximately 9 p.m., the officers pulled over an automobile after a license plate check revealed that the vehicle's registration had been suspended for an insurance-related violation. Under Arizona law, the violation for which the vehicle was stopped constituted a civil infraction warranting a citation. At the time of the stop, the vehicle had three occupants—the driver, a front-seat passenger, and a passenger in the back seat, Lemon Montrea Johnson, the respondent here. In making the stop the officers had no reason to suspect anyone in the vehicle of criminal activity.

The three officers left their patrol car and approached the stopped vehicle. Machado instructed all of the occupants to keep their hands visible. He asked whether there were any weapons in the vehicle; all responded no. Machado then directed the driver to get out of the car. Gittings dealt with the front-seat passenger, who stayed in the vehicle throughout the stop. While Machado was getting the driver's license and information about the vehicle's registration and insurance, Trevizo attended to Johnson.

Trevizo noticed that, as the police approached, Johnson looked back and kept his eyes on the officers. When she drew near, she observed that Johnson was wearing clothing, including a blue bandana, that she considered consistent with Crips membership. She also noticed a scanner in Johnson's jacket pocket, which "struck [her] as highly unusual and cause [for] concern," because "most people" would not carry around a scanner that way "unless they're going to be involved in some kind of criminal activity or [are] going to try to evade the police by listening to the scanner." In response to Trevizo's questions, Johnson provided his name and date of birth but said he had no identification with him. He volunteered that he was from Eloy, Arizona, a place Trevizo knew was home to a Crips gang. Johnson further told Trevizo that he had served time in prison for burglary and had been out for about a year.

Trevizo wanted to question Johnson away from the front-seat passenger to gain "intelligence about the gang [Johnson] might be in." For that reason, she asked him to get out of the car. Johnson complied. Based on Trevizo's observations and Johnson's answers to her questions while he was still seated in the car, Trevizo suspected that "he might have a weapon on him." When he exited the vehicle, she therefore "patted him down for officer safety." During the patdown, Trevizo felt the butt of a gun near Johnson's waist. At that point Johnson began to struggle, and Trevizo placed him in handcuffs.

Johnson was charged in state court with, inter alia, possession of a weapon by a prohibited possessor. He moved to suppress the evidence as the fruit of an unlawful search. The trial court denied the motion, concluding that the stop was lawful and that Trevizo had cause to suspect Johnson was armed and dangerous. A jury convicted Johnson of the gun-possession charge.

A divided panel of the Arizona Court of Appeals reversed Johnson's conviction. Recognizing that "Johnson was [lawfully] seized when the officers stopped the car," the court nevertheless concluded that prior to the frisk the detention had "evolved into a separate, consensual encounter stemming from an unrelated investigation by Trevizo of Johnson's possible gang affiliation." Absent "reason to believe Johnson was involved in criminal activity," the Arizona appeals court held, Trevizo "had no right to pat him down for weapons, even if she had reason to suspect he was armed and dangerous."

II

A

We begin our consideration of the constitutionality of Officer Trevizo's patdown of Johnson by looking back to the Court's leading decision in *Terry. Terry* involved a stop for interrogation of men whose conduct had attracted the attention of a patrolling police officer. The officer's observation led him reasonably to suspect that the men were casing a jewelry shop in preparation for a robbery. He conducted a patdown, which disclosed weapons concealed in the men's overcoat pockets. This Court upheld the lower courts' determinations that the interrogation was warranted and the patdown, permissible.

Terry established the legitimacy of an investigatory stop "in situations where [the police] may lack probable cause for an arrest." When the stop is justified by suspicion (reasonably grounded, but short of probable cause) that criminal activity is afoot, the Court explained, the police officer must be positioned to act instantly on reasonable suspicion that the persons temporarily detained are armed and dangerous. Recognizing that a limited search of outer clothing for weapons serves to protect both the officer and the public, the Court held the patdown reasonable under the Fourth Amendment.

"[M]ost traffic stops," this Court has observed, "resemble, in duration and atmosphere, the kind of brief detention authorized in *Terry*." Furthermore, the Court has recognized that traffic stops are "especially fraught with danger to police officers." "'The risk of harm to both the police and the occupants [of a stopped vehicle] is minimized,'" we have stressed, "'if the officers routinely exercise unquestioned command of the situation.'" Three decisions cumulatively portray *Terry*'s application in a traffic-stop setting: *Pennsylvania v. Mimms*; *Maryland v. Wilson*; and *Brendlin v. California*.

In *Mimms*, the Court held that "once a motor vehicle has been lawfully detained for a traffic violation, the police officers may order the driver to get out of the vehicle without violating the Fourth Amendment's proscription of unreasonable searches and seizures." The government's "legitimate and weighty" interest in officer safety, the Court said, outweighs the "de minimis" additional intrusion of requiring a driver, already lawfully stopped, to exit the vehicle. Citing *Terry* as controlling, the Court further held that a driver, once outside the stopped vehicle, may be patted down for weapons if the officer reasonably concludes that the driver "might be armed and presently dangerous."

Wilson held that the *Mimms* rule applied to passengers as well as to drivers. Specifically, the Court instructed that "an officer making a traffic stop may order passengers to get out of the car pending completion of the stop." "[T]he same weighty interest in officer safety," the Court observed, "is present regardless of whether the occupant of the stopped car is a driver or passenger."

It is true, the Court acknowledged, that in a lawful traffic stop, "[t]here is probable cause to believe that the driver has committed a minor vehicular offense," but "there is no such reason to stop or detain the passengers." On the other hand, the Court emphasized, the risk of a violent encounter in a traffic-stop setting "stems not from the ordinary reaction of a motorist stopped for a speeding violation, but from the fact that evidence of a more serious crime might be uncovered during the stop." "[T]he motivation of a passenger to employ violence to prevent apprehension of such a crime," the Court stated, "is every bit as great as that of the driver." Moreover, the Court noted, "as a practical matter, the passengers are already stopped by virtue of the stop of the vehicle," so "the additional intrusion on the passenger is minimal."

Completing the picture, *Brendlin* held that a passenger is seized, just as the driver is, "from the moment [a car stopped by the police comes] to a halt on the side of the road." A passenger therefore has standing to challenge a stop's constitutionality.

After *Wilson*, but before *Brendlin*, the Court had stated, in dictum, that officers who conduct "routine traffic stop[s]" may "perform a 'patdown' of a driver and any passengers upon reasonable suspicion that they may be armed and dangerous." That forecast, we now confirm, accurately captures the combined thrust of the Court's decisions in *Mimms*, *Wilson*, and *Brendlin*.

B

The Arizona Court of Appeals recognized that, initially, Johnson was lawfully detained incident to the legitimate stop of the vehicle in which he was a passenger. But, that court concluded, once Officer Trevizo undertook to question Johnson on a matter unrelated to the traffic stop, i.e., Johnson's gang affiliation, patdown authority ceased to exist, absent reasonable suspicion that Johnson had engaged, or was about to engage, in criminal activity. In support of the Arizona court's portrayal of Trevizo's interrogation of Johnson as "consensual," Johnson emphasizes Trevizo's testimony at the suppression hearing. Responding to the prosecutor's questions, Trevizo affirmed her belief that Johnson could have "refused to get out of the car" and "to turn around for the pat down."

It is not clear why the prosecutor, in opposing the suppression motion, sought to portray the episode as consensual. In any event, Trevizo also testified that she never advised Johnson he did not have to answer her questions or otherwise cooperate with her. And during cross-examination, Trevizo did not disagree when defense counsel asked "in fact, you weren't seeking [Johnson's] permission . . . ?" As the dissenting judge observed, "consensual" is an "unrealistic" characterization of the Trevizo–Johnson interaction. "[T]he encounter . . . took place within minutes of the stop"; the patdown followed "within mere moments" of Johnson's exit from the vehicle; beyond genuine debate, the point at which Johnson could have felt free to leave had not yet occurred.

A lawful roadside stop begins when a vehicle is pulled over for investigation of a traffic violation. The temporary seizure of driver and passengers ordinarily continues, and remains reasonable, for the duration of the stop. Normally, the stop ends when the police have no further need to control the scene, and inform the driver and passengers they are free to leave. An officer's inquiries into matters unrelated to the justification for the traffic stop, this Court has made plain, do not convert the encounter into something other than a lawful seizure, so long as those inquiries do not measurably extend the duration of the stop.

In sum, as stated in *Brendlin*, a traffic stop of a car communicates to a reasonable passenger that he or she is not free to terminate the encounter with the police and move about at will. Nothing occurred in this case that would have conveyed to Johnson that, prior to the frisk, the traffic stop had ended or that he was otherwise free "to depart without police permission." Officer Trevizo surely was not constitutionally required to give Johnson an opportunity to depart the scene after he exited the vehicle without first ensuring that, in so doing, she was not permitting a dangerous person to get behind her.

• • •

For the reasons stated, the judgment of the Arizona Court of Appeals is reversed, and the case is remanded for further proceedings not inconsistent with this opinion.

NOTES AND QUESTIONS

1. Automobile insurance is important. Accidents happen, and when they do it is important that persons who are hurt or whose cars are damaged have recourse to recover. But note here how a civil infraction based on an insurance violation leads directly to a passenger's incarceration.

Should police be able to pull people over for civil infractions?

The Court doesn't say whether the driver was given a "citation," the penalty for the civil infraction. Do you think the officers, members of Arizona's "gang task force," even carried blank citation forms to issue?

2. How do you think the police officers discovered the existence of the vehicle's suspended registration while they were "on patrol" in a "neighborhood associated with the Crips gang"? Were they just driving around running plate checks on any car they thought was sketchy? Are the police required to have any quantum of suspicion before running a plate? Should they be?

3. The Court suggests that the result in *Johnson* is the inevitable culmination of its prior precedents: *Pennsylvania v. Mimms*, 434 U.S. 106 (1977) (police can order driver to get out of car in the interests of officer safety); *Maryland v. Wilson*, 519 U.S. 408 (1997) (same for passengers); *Brendlin v. California*, 551 U.S. 249 (2007) (passenger ordered out of car is "seized."

Why should the traffic stop be allowed to extend even 30 seconds longer than necessary to address the purpose of the stop?

4. But note that the police officers' power, without any basis for suspicion, to order the occupants out of the car does not necessarily also entitle them to frisk for weapons. Reasonable suspicion is needed for that step. Was that established here? The Arizona appellate court did not appear to reach that issue, relying instead on the interrogation's detour into another area.

What was the officer's basis for suspecting Johnson was armed and dangerous? We know this: he had no identification; he was wearing a blue bandana (consistent with Crips membership); he had a scanner; he was from Eloy, Arizona (a town of 15,000 50 miles from Tucson); and he had done time in prison. Is that enough?

5. In *Rodriguez v. United States*, 575 U.S. 348 (2015), the police officer extended a traffic stop by seven to eight minutes after issuing the driver a written warning in order to conduct a canine sniff. The Court found that extension of the stop transformed it into an unreasonable seizure, distinguishing de minimis temporal extensions such as the one in *Johnson*.

Between 1990 and 2014 the Court considered three cases about the relationship between an anonymous tip and reasonable suspicion for Fourth Amendment purposes. These cases bear on situations like the encounter between Officer Dove and Larry Dudley Hiibel, above, and less directly on the use of anonymous informants and tipsters in establishing the probable cause needed for search warrant.

In *Alabama v. White*, 496 U.S. 325 (1990), police received an anonymous tip that a woman was in possession of cocaine and might shortly be leaving a specified apartment building at a specified time in a car the tipster described, bound for a motel the tipster named. Police followed up on the tip and were able to confirm that the tipster had accurately described the woman's movements. At that point—upon confirmation of the details of the tip—the officers' suspicion became reasonable. The Court acknowledged that *White* was a close case inasmuch as the tipster's knowledge of the woman's anticipated movements did not necessarily include any knowledge about whether the woman would be bringing the cocaine with her on her journey.

Florida v. JL, 529 U.S. 266 (2000), involved an anonymous tip that a young Black male at a specified bus stop wearing a plaid shirt was in possession of a gun. Officers approached the bus stop and saw three black males hanging out at the bus stop, doing nothing to arouse suspicion. One, who turned out to be JL, was wearing a plaid shirt. The officers approached JL and one of them frisked him, finding a gun. The Court affirmed the suppression of the gun. It found that an anonymous tip, without more and with only weak corroboration, does not establish reasonable suspicion for a *Terry* stop.

Finally, in *Navarette v. California*, 572 U.S. 393 (2014), police received an anonymous tip in a 911 call from a motorist saying that a truck—for which the tipster provided the make and model and plate number—had just run the motorist off the road at a specified mile marker on U.S. 1 in Mendocino, California. Police were able to locate the truck within 13 minutes at a location consistent with the information the tipster had supplied earlier. The police pulled the truck over a few minutes later and during an investigatory stop discovered 30 pounds of marijuana. The Court found that although this was another "close case," there was sufficient indicia of reliability attending the tip to justify a traffic stop based on reasonable suspicion of reckless driving.

The Court's most recent case evaluating a police officer's claim of reasonable suspicion is *Kansas v. Glover*, 589 U.S. 376 (2020). In *Glover*, an officer initiated an investigative traffic stop of an automobile on the ground that the car's owner—not the driver—had a revoked driver's license, inferring that the driver and the owner were one and the same despite the revocation. The Kansas Supreme Court found that the stop was based not on "reasonable suspicion" but only on the sort of "hunch" condemned in *Terry*. The Court reversed, finding that the degree of suspicion here was a matter of common sense and well within the *Terry* standard, which was below a "preponderance" standard or even a "probable cause" standard. The Court quoted from its 2004 decision in *United States v. Arvizu*, 534 U.S. 266 (2004), to the effect that the reasonable suspicion standard does not require officers to "rule out the possibility of innocent conduct."

E. RACE AND SUSPICION

1. *Terry* and Race

As noted above, the Court in *Terry* acknowledges race to some extent. It notes the "wholesale harassment" of which the "Negroes complain," and references in this regard the findings of the President's Commission on Law Enforcement and Administration of Justice, Task Force Report: The Police 183 (1967). But in virtually the same breath the Court both minimizes the "harassment," attributing it to only "certain elements" of the police, and also throws its hands in the air, noting the "limitations of the judicial function in controlling the myriad daily situations in which policemen and citizens confront each other in the street." The Court is equally "equivocal," to use Professor Maclin's word, in footnote 14, noting that the "friction" between the police and Black people "is not susceptible of control by means of the exclusionary rule" while at the same time stating that "the degree of community resentment aroused by particular practices is clearly relevant to assessment of the quality of the intrusion upon reasonable expectations of personal security caused by those practices." Tracey Maclin, Terry v. Ohio*'s Fourth Amendment Legacy: Black Men and Police Discretion*, 72 St. John's L. Rev. 1271, 1284 (1998).

The Court also fails to acknowledge the explicit prediction and warning in the amicus brief of the NAACP Legal Defense and Educational Fund, Inc. In that brief, the LDF cited statistics showing that Black people were more prone to being stopped and frisked than white people. Observing that "many thousands of our citizens who have been or may be stopped and interrogated yearly, only to be released when the police find them innocent of any crime," the LDF explicitly warned that the police would exploit a diluted probable cause standard to engage in exploratory searches under the guise of protecting themselves. *See* Brief for the NAACP Legal Defense and Educational Fund, Inc., as Amicus Curiae at 4-5, *Sibron v. New York*, 392 U.S. 40 (1967) (No. 63) and *Terry v. Ohio*, 392 U.S. 1 (1967) (No. 67), reprinted in 66 Landmark Briefs and Arguments of the Supreme Court of the United States 577, 580-81 (Philip B. Kurland & Gerhard Casper eds., 1975). The NAACP's amicus brief was no outlier, either. By 1968 "objective evidence of police bias against Blacks had been well documented by scholars and observers of the police." Maclin, *Black Men and Police Discretion*, *supra* at 1311 (citations omitted).

But *Terry*'s silence on race runs even deeper. The Court fails to acknowledge that two of the three men that were stopped and frisked by Detective McFadden were Black. The trial court record reveals that the first two men observed by Detective McFadden, John Terry and Richard Chilton, were Black, and the third man, Katz, was white. *See* State of Ohio v. Richard D. Chilton *and* State of Ohio v. John W. Terry*: The Suppression Hearing and Trial Transcripts*, 72 St. John's L. Rev. app. at 1408 (1998) (John Q. Barrett ed.) [transcript] (reprinting suppression hearing testimony of Detective McFadden). *See generally* Anthony C. Thompson, *Stopping the Usual Suspects: Race and the Fourth Amendment*, 74 N.Y.U. L. Rev. 956, 962-74 (1999) (discussing the "constructed reality" of the Supreme Court's Fourth Amendment decisions, including *Terry*, where race is ignored). Even Justice Douglas's impassioned and prescient dissent, in which he remarked that "'probable cause' rings a bell of certainty that 'reasonable suspicion' does not," and bemoaned the impending era where a policeman can stop someone just because he doesn't like "the cut of his jib"—precisely as the NAACP was predicting—says nothing about race. *Id.* at 965-66.

So what? The Supreme Court fails to acknowledge race all the time. In *Terry*, however, the omission of race seems to have been more deliberate than usual. For one thing, the race of the

Louis Stokes. Less than six months after the decision in *Terry*, Stokes became the first Black person from Ohio to be elected to Congress.

two Black men was openly discussed at the suppression hearing. In describing Chilton and Terry's interaction with the "third man," Detective McFadden says the "white man came over and talked to these two colored men." Suppression Hearing Transcript at 1408. And at oral argument before the Supreme Court the lawyers for both the defendants and the state, both of whom were themselves Black, referred to the race of Terry and Chilton. Defense counsel Louis Stokes described his clients as "two Negro males." Barrett, *Terry v. Ohio, supra* at 302.

But in *Terry*, moreover, race indisputably mattered. It mattered in the implications of the Court's new rule in Black communities, as predicted by the NAACP. But it also mattered on the ground in Cleveland, on the street, that day in October 1963 when Detective McFadden's suspicions first became "aroused." Race was "afoot" on the streets of Cleveland.

Chief Justice Warren acknowledges in the case's second paragraph that Officer McFadden was "unable to say precisely what drew his eye to" the two Black men standing on a street corner that afternoon. The Court then describes Officer McFadden's experience, and his people-watching habits, and then presents to the reader—voilà—with McFadden's expert conclusion: "they didn't look right to me." The testimony is presented as if the men's actions didn't "look right." The more likely interpretation is that they didn't "look right" because they were Black. The Court studiously constrains this implication by omitting what McFadden had said in response to the previous question, which asked at what point he considered the men's actions unusual: "Well, to be truthful with you, I didn't like them. I was just attracted to them. . . ." Trial Transcript at 1456.

Further, the Court incorrectly states the source of McFadden's testimony. The quoted testimony that "they didn't look right to me" is not from the suppression hearing but from McFadden's trial testimony. Does that matter? Well, yes, because the issue before the Court is whether the gun found in the frisk of Terry should have been suppressed. The suppression hearing testimony was very different. Detective McFadden appears to have become emboldened at trial by the trial court's earlier denial of the defendants' suppression motion. At the suppression hearing he was much more cautious and circumspect, to the point where the prosecutor, Reuben Payne, must have been worried whether the trial court would be able to find any level of suspicion or expertise whatsoever. For one thing, as noted above, McFadden conceded that his expertise ran only to pickpocketing and shoplifting, and he further conceded that he had never observed a suspect "casing" a place. He was just as blunt when the court examined him about the reason for his suspicion:

> **Q.** What caused you specifically to be attracted to those two individuals at the location that you have mentioned, or let me put it to you this way:
>
> Supposing those two defendants here that are now in court were standing across the street from here, and doing the same activities that you observed them on Huron and Euclid, would you have had any cause for suspicion?
>
> **A.** I really don't know.

Suppression Hearing Transcript at 1421. That answer was the last thing McFadden said at the suppression hearing. This answer may have been the basis for the Court's acknowledgment that McFadden couldn't say what "drew his eye" to the two Black men, but it could just as easily have been the basis for a conclusion that McFadden lacked any reasonable suspicion whatsoever to stop and frisk them.

It is difficult to resist the conclusion that Detective McFadden had his eye on Terry and Chilton because they were Black. If the attorneys or the trial court were sensitive to this fact there is no suggestion of any such awareness in the transcripts. Indeed, at oral argument before the Supreme Court the prosecutor, Reuben Payne, who like Louis Stokes handled the case from indictment all the way to the Supreme Court, characterized McFadden's testimony as "he didn't like their looks." This remark prompted an exchange with Justice Marshall—who had been on the Court for just two months—in which Payne clarified that McFadden had not "meant by that any reference to pigmentation or anything else."

Even if the lawyers and trial judge had perceived a racial dynamic at work, it certainly wasn't clear in 1964—or even today—how race discrimination maps on to the Fourth Amendment. On the one hand, the Supreme Court had held just one year before Terry's arrest, in *Oyler v. Boles*, 368 U.S. 448, 546 (1962), that prosecutors could not bring criminal charges based on unconstitutional considerations such as race. But *Oyler* had also stated that "the conscious exercise of some selectivity in enforcement is not in itself a federal constitutional violation," which gave some courts pause, and it certainly wasn't clear that *Oyler* applied in a Fourth Amendment context.

Professor Thompson has observed that the *Terry* Court's silence on race was part of a pattern: The Court was silent on race when it ostensibly may have played a role or risked playing a role in reasonable suspicion or probable cause determinations, yet openly acknowledged race and approved of its usage as a factor when the Court deemed it necessary to a particular police practice. Thompson, *Stopping the Usual Suspects*, *supra* at 977-78. The next subsection will explore this further.

To Professor Carbado, one of the most profound legacies of *Terry* is what he calls "prophylactic racial profiling." On this view, the regime of wholesale and pervasive police encounters with urban residents that are legally *permissible* under *Terry*, not even to mention the ones that are contrived or manufactured, have dangerously increased the level of police-civilian interaction in Black communities and thereby expose Black people to a heightened risk of police violence. Devon W. Carbado, *From Stop and Frisk to Shoot and Kill:* Terry v. Ohio*'s Pathway to Police Violence*, 64 UCLA L. Rev. 1508, 1513, 1537 (2017).

One specific manifestation of the racial implications of *Terry* is in the specific factors that became regularly invoked to establish reasonable suspicion. The next case addresses two of them: "flight" and "high crime area." Of course, equally baked into the "reasonable suspicion" standard is the implicit racial bias police officers have in evaluating whether observed behaviors are "suspicious." *See* L. Song Richardson, *Cognitive Bias, Police Character, and the Fourth Amendment*, 44 Ariz. St. L.J. 267 (2012); L. Song Richardson, *Police Efficiency and the Fourth Amendment*, 87 Ind. L.J. 1143, 1145 (2012) (arguing that "[i]mplicit social cognition research demonstrates that implicit biases can affect whether police interpret an individual's ambiguous behaviors as suspicious").

Illinois v. Wardlow

528 U.S. 119 (2000)

Chief Justice Rehnquist delivered the opinion of the Court.

Respondent Wardlow fled upon seeing police officers patrolling an area known for heavy narcotics trafficking. Two of the officers caught up with him, stopped him and conducted a protective patdown search for weapons. Discovering a .38-caliber handgun, the officers arrested Wardlow. We hold that the officers' stop did not violate the Fourth Amendment to the United States Constitution.

On September 9, 1995, Officers Nolan and Harvey were working as uniformed officers in the special operations section of the Chicago Police Department. The officers were driving the last car of a four car caravan converging on an area known for heavy narcotics trafficking in order to investigate drug transactions. The officers were traveling together because they expected to find a crowd of people in the area, including lookouts and customers.

As the caravan passed 4035 West Van Buren, Officer Nolan observed respondent Wardlow standing next to the building holding an opaque bag. Respondent looked in the direction of the officers and fled. Nolan and Harvey turned their car southbound, watched him as he ran through the gangway and an alley, and eventually cornered him on the street. Nolan then exited his car and stopped respondent. He immediately conducted a protective pat-down search for weapons because in his experience it was common for there to be weapons in the near vicinity of narcotics transactions. During the frisk, Officer Nolan squeezed the bag respondent was carrying and felt a heavy, hard object similar to the shape of a gun. The officer then opened the bag and discovered a .38-caliber handgun with five live rounds of ammunition. The officers arrested Wardlow.

The Illinois trial court denied respondent's motion to suppress, finding the gun was recovered during a lawful stop and frisk. Following a stipulated bench trial, Wardlow was convicted of unlawful use of a weapon by a felon. The Illinois Appellate Court reversed Wardlow's conviction, concluding that the gun should have been suppressed because Officer Nolan did not have reasonable suspicion sufficient to justify an investigative stop pursuant to *Terry*.

The Illinois Supreme Court agreed. While rejecting the Appellate Court's conclusion that Wardlow was not in a high crime area, the Illinois Supreme Court determined that sudden flight in such an area does not create a reasonable suspicion justifying a *Terry* stop. Relying on *Florida v. Royer*, the court explained that although police have the right to approach individuals and ask questions, the individual has no obligation to respond.

The Illinois Supreme Court also rejected the argument that flight combined with the fact that it occurred in a high crime area supported a finding of reasonable suspicion because the "high crime area" factor was not sufficient standing alone to justify a *Terry* stop.

This case, involving a brief encounter between a citizen and a police officer on a public street, is governed by the analysis we first applied in *Terry*. In *Terry*, we held that an officer may, consistent with the Fourth Amendment, conduct a brief, investigatory stop when the officer has a reasonable, articulable suspicion that criminal activity is afoot. While "reasonable suspicion" is a less demanding standard than probable cause and requires a showing considerably less than preponderance of the evidence, the Fourth Amendment requires at least a minimal level of objective justification for making the stop. The officer must be able to articulate more than an "inchoate and unparticularized suspicion or 'hunch'" of criminal activity.

Nolan and Harvey were among eight officers in a four-car caravan that was converging on an area known for heavy narcotics trafficking, and the officers anticipated encountering a large number of people in the area, including drug customers and individuals serving as lookouts. It was in this context that Officer Nolan decided to investigate Wardlow after observing him flee. An individual's presence in an area of expected criminal activity, standing alone, is not enough to support a reasonable, particularized suspicion that the person is committing a crime. But officers are not required to ignore the relevant characteristics of a location in determining whether the circumstances are sufficiently suspicious to warrant further investigation. Accordingly, we have previously noted the fact that the stop occurred in a "high crime area" among the relevant contextual considerations in a *Terry* analysis.

In this case, moreover, it was not merely respondent's presence in an area of heavy narcotics trafficking that aroused the officers' suspicion, but his unprovoked flight upon noticing the police. Our cases have also recognized that nervous, evasive behavior is a pertinent factor in determining reasonable suspicion. Headlong flight—wherever it occurs—is the consummate act of evasion: It is not necessarily indicative of wrongdoing, but it is certainly suggestive of such. In reviewing the propriety of an officer's conduct, courts do not have available empirical studies dealing with inferences drawn from suspicious behavior, and we cannot reasonably demand scientific certainty from judges or law enforcement officers where none exists. Thus, the determination of reasonable suspicion must be based on commonsense judgments and inferences about human behavior. We conclude Officer Nolan was justified in suspecting that Wardlow was involved in criminal activity, and, therefore, in investigating further.

Such a holding is entirely consistent with our decision in *Florida v. Royer* (1983), where we held that when an officer, without reasonable suspicion or probable cause, approaches an individual, the individual has a right to ignore the police and go about his business. And any "refusal to cooperate, without more, does not furnish the minimal level of objective justification needed for a detention or seizure." But unprovoked flight is simply not a mere refusal to cooperate. Flight, by its very nature, is not "going about one's business"; in fact, it is just the opposite. Allowing officers confronted with such flight to stop the fugitive and investigate further is quite consistent with the individual's right to go about his business or to stay put and remain silent in the face of police questioning.

Respondent and amici also argue that there are innocent reasons for flight from police and that, therefore, flight is not necessarily indicative of ongoing criminal activity. This fact is undoubtedly true, but does not establish a violation of the Fourth Amendment. Even in *Terry*, the conduct justifying the stop was ambiguous and susceptible of an innocent explanation. The officer observed two individuals pacing back and forth in front of a store, peering into the window and periodically conferring. All of this conduct was by itself lawful, but it also suggested that the individuals were casing the store for a planned robbery. *Terry* recognized that the officers could detain the individuals to resolve the ambiguity.

In allowing such detentions, *Terry* accepts the risk that officers may stop innocent people. Indeed, the Fourth Amendment accepts that risk in connection with more drastic police action; persons arrested and detained on probable cause to believe they have committed a crime may turn out to be innocent. The *Terry* stop is a far more minimal intrusion, simply allowing the officer to briefly investigate further. If the officer does not learn facts rising to the level of probable cause, the individual must be allowed to go on his way. But in this case the officers found respondent in possession of a handgun, and arrested him for violation of an Illinois firearms statute. No question of the propriety of the arrest itself is before us.

The judgment of the Supreme Court of Illinois is reversed, and the cause is remanded for further proceedings not inconsistent with this opinion.

NOTES AND QUESTIONS

1. Whether a location is a "high crime area" is, or at least should be, an empirical fact — despite the term's imprecision — yet the Court appears to permit it to be established as a basis for reasonable suspicion by the say-so of police officers. Here, the Court says only that the area in which Wardlow was observed was "known for heavy narcotics trafficking." To be more precise, they observed Wardlow as they were "converging" on that area. The dissent notes that the record was silent on whether the police cars were marked, how fast they were going, and whether the police had arrived in their "high crime area" destination when they saw Wardlow. It also appears defense counsel failed to cross-examine on how this drug-investigation juggernaut of a caravan was utterly derailed by the sight of one guy with an "opaque bag" who was running away from it.

Despite its apparently empirical nature, in most jurisdictions courts have generally relied on an officer's testimony that an area is a "high crime area" without much analysis as to the basis of that conclusion. *See* Andrew Guthrie Ferguson & Damien Bernache, *The "High*

Crime Area" Question: Requiring Verifiable and Quantifiable Evidence for Fourth Amendment Reasonable Suspicion Analysis, 57 Am. U. L. Rev. 1587, 1607 (2008).

Shouldn't police departments—at least large urban ones, like Chicago's—have reliable data on the rates of criminality in various portions of their city? If not in 2000, at least now? Wouldn't such information be important for officer safety, if nothing else?

2. Lower federal and state courts and police departments after *Terry* had seized on "high crime area" as a reasonable suspicion factor. Even the 1972 case the Court cites in *Wardlow* as precedent on this point, *Adams v. Williams*, 407 U.S. 143 (1972), was actually a case where a "high crime area" was part of the justification for a seizure during a *Terry* stop. *Wardlow* seems to have been influential, however. Between 2000 and 2019 over 4,500 federal and state cases cited it. Ben Grunwald & Jeffrey Fagan, *The End of Intuition-Based High-Crime Areas*, 107 Cal. L. Rev. 345, 363 & n.83 (2019). Westlaw's "citing references" feature on May 20, 2023, puts the tally at an even 6,000.

The increase in "citing references" could mean one of at least two things. One, since *Wardlow*, courts are increasingly recognizing that a "high crime area" is a factor in analyzing reasonable suspicion. Two, since *Wardlow*, police officers are increasingly trying to justify reasonable suspicion conclusions by referring to "high crime areas."

3. It is likely that the people who live in and are present on the streets of "high crime areas" will disproportionately be ethnic and racial minorities. Accordingly, just by going about their normal daily lives such persons are already 0-1, with one reasonable suspicion strike against them. For this reason, the Ninth Circuit has cautioned that "the citing of an area as 'high-crime' requires careful examination by the court, because such a description, unless properly limited and factually based, can easily serve as a proxy for race or ethnicity." *United States v. Montero-Camargo*, 208 F.3d 1122, 1138 (9th Cir. 2000).

Is the "high crime area" factor's disproportionate effect on minorities reason enough to preclude its use in establishing reasonable suspicion? Would police work really be hampered if *Terry* factors had to be about the person police want to stop and question and not just the neighborhood?

This aspect of reasonable suspicion effects a double whammy on minorities, who generate suspicion where they live as well as when they venture into areas where they do not. *See, e.g.*, Sheri Lynn Johnson, *Race and the Decision to Detain a Suspect*, 93 Yale L.J. 214, 226 (1983) (reviewing Arizona Supreme Court decision from 1975 in which court approved racial profiling of Hispanic man and stated: "That a person is observed in a neighborhood not frequented by persons of his ethnic background is quite often a basis for an officer's initial suspicion. To attempt by judicial fiat to say he may not do this ignores the practical aspects of good law enforcement") (citation omitted); Lawrence P. Tiffany et al., Detection of Crime 20 (Frank J. Remington ed., 1967) (stating, one year before *Terry*, that "[a] person of one race observed in an area which is largely inhabited by a different racial group may be stopped and questioned").

4. In *Montero-Camargo* the Court upheld a finding of reasonable suspicion based in part on a finding that a particular spot just before an immigration checkpoint in El Centro, California, where the defendant had apparently made a U-turn to avoid the checkpoint, was a "high crime area." Concurring, Judge Kozinski was skeptical about the court's conclusion as well as officers' "high crime area" characterizations generally:

> The [court's] opinion recognizes the danger in allowing the police to characterize an area as "high-crime" to establish a basis for reasonable suspicion, but then proceeds to do just that, based on nothing more than the personal experiences of two arresting agents. As I discuss above, the agents didn't even claim this was a high crime area, but let's say they had. What in this record would support their conclusion? Both agents testified only that they had detected criminal violations after stopping people in the area. How often? One agent said he'd been involved in 15-20 stops over eight and a half years, and "[could]n't recall any . . . where we

> didn't have a violation of some sort." The other agent testified to "about a dozen" stops in the same period, all but one of which led to an arrest.
>
> Without hesitation, the majority treats this as a crime wave, but is it really? Does an arrest every four months or so make for a high crime area? Can we rely on the vague and undocumented recollections of the officers here? Do the two officers' figures of "15-20" and "about a dozen" reflect separate pools of incidents, or do they include some where, as here, both officers were involved? Are such estimates sufficiently precise to tell us anything useful about the area? I wouldn't have thought so, although I could be persuaded otherwise. But my colleagues don't even pause to ask the questions. To them, it's a high crime area, because the officers say it's a high crime area.
>
> Just as a man with a hammer sees every problem as a nail, so a man with a badge may see every corner of his beat as a high crime area. Police are trained to detect criminal activity and they look at the world with suspicious eyes. This is a good thing, because we rely on this suspicion to keep us safe from those who would harm us. But to rely on every cop's repertoire of war stories to determine what is a "high crime area"—and on that basis to treat otherwise innocuous behavior as grounds for reasonable suspicion—strikes me as an invitation to trouble. If the testimony of two officers that they made, at most, 32 arrests during the course of a decade is sufficient to turn the road here into a high crime area, then what area under police surveillance wouldn't qualify as one? There are street corners in our inner cities that see as much crime within a month—even a week. I would be most reluctant to give police the power to turn any area into a high crime area based on their unadorned personal experiences. . . .

Id. at 1143.

5. Professors Grunwald and Fagan note that *Wardlow* rests on three tacit empirical assumptions: first, that police officers are using the correct geographic scope when they characterize areas as "high crime"; second, that the officers' assessments of high crime areas are accurate; and third, that an assessment of a "high crime area" is predictive—that is, that persons' presence in a "high crime area" is probative of whether they are engaged in crime. Grunwald & Fagan, *End of Intuition-Based High-Crime Areas*, *supra* at 348-49.

The professors then tested these assumptions on the dataset of over 200 million police stops conducted by the NYPD between 2007 and 2012, where all police stops were required to be coded for reasonable suspicion in connection with the settlement of a lawsuit against the department. *Daniels v. New York*, 138 F. Supp. 2d 562 (S.D.N.Y. 2001). Professor Fagan was an expert statistical witness for the plaintiffs in *Floyd et al. v. City of New York*, 959 F. Supp. 2d 540 (S.D.N.Y. 2013), a follow-on action to *Daniels*. *See* Chapter VII *infra*.

Professors Grunwald and Fagan found that none of *Wardlow*'s assumptions were satisfied in practice. Grunwald & Fagan, *End of Intuition-Based High-Crime Areas*, *supra* at 370-96. They concluded:

> Our empirical investigation raises serious questions about whether *Wardlow*'s empirical assumptions are satisfied in practice. Indeed, at least based on administrative data from the NYPD during an era of intensive use of stop and frisk policing, implementation of the high-crime area standard appears haphazard at best, and discriminatory at worst. Officers call nearly every block in the city high crime. Their assessments of high-crime areas are only weakly correlated with actual crime rates. The suspect's race predicts whether an officer deems an area high crime as well as the actual crime rate itself. The racial composition of the area and the identity of the officer are stronger predictors of whether an officer deems an area high crime than the crime rate. And officers may even be using high-crime area as cover to bolster the appearance of constitutional validity in their weakest stops.

Id. at 396.

6. *Wardlow* is as much about "flight" as about high crime areas. Why do the Justices and the parties insist on using the term "unprovoked flight"? Isn't the type of flight we are talking about here always "provoked"—by the arrival of the police?

7. The Court places flight on one end of a continuum of evasive behavior, with "nervousness" at one end and "headlong flight" at the other. As a defense attorney at a suppression hearing, how would you go about cross-examining a police officer who testified about the defendant's behavior at either end of the spectrum?

8. The Court's seizure analysis emphasizes whether a reasonable person would "feel free to leave." And *Florida v. Royer*, 460 U.S. 491 (1983), *supra*, establishes that a person approached by police has every right to ignore the police and go about his business. Isn't "headlong flight" among the purest manifestations of a feeling of the freedom to leave? Put differently, isn't flight also a manifestation of a "refusal to cooperate"? Why should the police be able to draw a legally cognizable inference of suspicion from the pace at which a person expresses his freedom to leave or his refusal to cooperate?

9. The dissent notes that minorities may flee from the police, innocent or not, because they reasonably or unreasonably believe contact with the police may be dangerous. How can defense attorneys establish such a belief as a fact in litigating a motion to suppress? Judicial notice? Testimony from the defendant? Would a local history of police violence be required? Would an expert witness be needed?

10. In *Commonwealth v. Warren*, 58 N.E.3d 333 (Mass. 2016), the Massachusetts Supreme Judicial Court concluded that flight could not in itself support reasonable suspicion, especially the flight of a Black male. In relevant part the Court stated:

> *d. Flight.* We recognize that the defendant's evasive conduct during his successive encounters with police is a factor properly considered in the reasonable suspicion analysis. But evasive conduct in the absence of any other information tending toward an individualized suspicion that the defendant was involved in the crime is insufficient to support reasonable suspicion. "Were the rule otherwise, the police could turn a hunch into a reasonable suspicion by inducing the [flight] justifying the suspicion." Although flight is relevant to the reasonable suspicion analysis in appropriate circumstances, we add two cautionary notes regarding the weight to be given this factor.
>
> First, we perceive a factual irony in the consideration of flight as a factor in the reasonable suspicion calculus. Unless reasonable suspicion for a threshold inquiry already exists, our law guards a person's freedom to speak or not to speak to a police officer. A person also may choose to walk away, avoiding altogether any contact with police. Yet, because flight is viewed as inculpatory, we have endorsed it as a factor in the reasonable suspicion analysis. Where a suspect is under no obligation to respond to a police officer's inquiry, we are of the view that flight to avoid that contact should be given little, if any, weight as a factor probative of reasonable suspicion. Otherwise, our long-standing jurisprudence establishing the boundary between consensual and obligatory police encounters will be seriously undermined. Thus, in the circumstances of this case, the flight from [police officer] Anjos during the initial encounter added nothing to the reasonable suspicion calculus.
>
> Second, as set out by one of the dissenting Justices in the Appeals court opinion, where the suspect is a black male stopped by the police on the streets of Boston, the analysis of flight as a factor in the reasonable suspicion calculus cannot be divorced from the findings in a recent Boston Police Department (department) report documenting a pattern of racial profiling of black males in the city of Boston. According to the study, based on FIO data collected by the department, black men in the city of Boston were more likely to be targeted for police-civilian encounters such as stops, frisks, searches, observations, and interrogations. Black men were also disproportionally targeted for repeat police encounters. We do not eliminate flight as a factor in the reasonable suspicion analysis whenever a black male is the subject of an investigatory stop. However, in such circumstances, flight is not necessarily probative of a suspect's state of mind or consciousness of guilt. Rather, the finding that black males in Boston are disproportionately and repeatedly targeted for FIO encounters suggests a reason for flight totally unrelated to consciousness of guilt. Such an individual, when approached by the police, might just as easily be motivated by the desire to avoid the recurring indignity of being racially profiled as by the desire to hide criminal activity. Given this reality for black males in the city of Boston, a judge should, in appropriate cases, consider the report's findings in weighing flight as a factor in the reasonable suspicion calculus.

2. Border Searches and Racial Profiling

United States v. Brignoni-Ponce

422 U.S. 873 (1975)

Mr. Justice Powell delivered the opinion of the Court.

This case raises questions as to the United States Border Patrol's authority to stop automobiles in areas near the Mexican border. It differs from our decision in in that the Border Patrol does not claim authority to search cars, but only to question the occupants about their citizenship and immigration status.

I

As a part of its regular traffic-checking operations in southern California, the Border Patrol operates a fixed checkpoint on Interstate Highway 5 south of San Clemente. On the evening of March 11, 1973, the checkpoint was closed because of inclement weather, but two officers were observing northbound traffic from a patrol car parked at the side of the highway. The road was dark, and they were using the patrol car's headlights to illuminate passing cars. They pursued respondent's car and stopped it, saying later that their only reason for doing so was that its three occupants appeared to be of Mexican descent. The officers questioned respondent and his two passengers about their citizenship and learned that the passengers were aliens who had entered the country illegally. All three were then arrested, and respondent was charged with two counts of knowingly transporting illegal immigrants, a violation of s 274(a)(2) of the Immigration and Nationality Act, 66 Stat. 228, 8 U.S.C. s 1324(a)(2). At trial respondent moved to suppress the testimony of and about the two passengers, claiming that this evidence was the fruit of an illegal seizure. The trial court denied the motion, the aliens testified at trial, and respondent was convicted on both counts.

Respondent's appeal was pending in the Court of Appeals for the Ninth Circuit when we announced our decision in *Almeida-Sanchez*, holding that the Fourth Amendment prohibits the use of roving patrols to search vehicles, without a warrant or probable cause, at points removed from the border and its functional equivalents. The Court of Appeals, sitting en banc, held that the stop in this case more closely resembled a roving-patrol stop than a stop at a traffic checkpoint, and applied the principles of *Almeida-Sanchez*. The court held that the Fourth Amendment, as interpreted in *Almeida-Sanchez*, forbids stopping a vehicle, even for the limited purpose of questioning its occupants, unless the officers have a "founded suspicion" that the occupants are aliens illegally in the country. The court refused to find that Mexican ancestry alone supported such a "founded suspicion" and held that respondent's motion to suppress should have been granted. We granted certiorari.

The Government does not challenge the Court of Appeals' factual conclusion that the stop of respondent's car was a roving-patrol stop rather than a checkpoint stop. Nor does it challenge the retroactive application of *Almeida-Sanchez*, or contend that the San Clemente checkpoint is the functional equivalent of the border. The only issue presented for decision is whether a roving patrol may stop a vehicle in an area near the border and question its occupants when the only ground for suspicion is that the occupants appear to be of Mexican ancestry. For the reasons that follow, we affirm the decision of the Court of Appeals.

II

The Government claims two sources of statutory authority for stopping cars without warrants in the border areas. Section 287(a)(1) of the Immigration and Nationality Act, 8 U.S.C. s 1357(a)(1), authorizes any officer or employee of the Immigration and Naturalization Service (INS) without a warrant, "to interrogate any alien or person believed to be an alien as to his right to be or to remain in the United States." There is no geographical limitation on this authority. The Government contends that, at least in the areas adjacent to the Mexican border, a person's apparent Mexican ancestry alone justifies belief that he or she is an alien and satisfies the requirement of this statute. Section 287(a)(3) of the Act, 8 U.S.C. s 1357(a)(3), authorizes agents, without a warrant,

> within a reasonable distance from any external boundary of the United States, to board and search for aliens any vessel within the territorial waters of the United States and any railway car, aircraft, conveyance, or vehicle. . . .

Under current regulations, this authority may be exercised anywhere within 100 miles of the border. 8 CFR s 287.1(a) (1975). The Border Patrol interprets the statute as granting authority to stop moving vehicles and question the occupants about their citizenship, even when its officers have no reason to believe that the occupants are aliens or that other aliens may be concealed in the vehicle. But "no Act of Congress can authorize a violation of the Constitution," and we must decide whether the Fourth Amendment allows such random vehicle stops in the border areas.

III

The Fourth Amendment applies to all seizures of the person, including seizures that involve only a brief detention short of traditional arrest. As with other categories of police action subject to Fourth Amendment constraints, the reasonableness of such seizures depends on a balance between the public interest and the individual's right to personal security free from arbitrary interference by law officers.

The Government makes a convincing demonstration that the public interest demands effective measures to prevent the illegal entry of aliens at the Mexican border. Estimates of the number of illegal immigrants in the United States vary widely. A conservative estimate in 1972 produced a figure of about one million, but the INS now suggests there may be as many as 10 or 12 million aliens illegally in the country. Whatever the number, these aliens create significant economic and social problems, competing with citizens and legal resident aliens for jobs, and generating extra demand for social services. The aliens themselves are vulnerable to exploitation because they cannot complain of substandard working conditions without risking deportation.

The Government has estimated that 85% of the aliens illegally in the country are from Mexico. The Mexican border is almost 2,000 miles long, and even a vastly reinforced Border Patrol would find it impossible to prevent illegal border crossings. Many aliens cross the Mexican border on foot, miles away from patrolled areas, and then purchase transportation from the border area to inland cities, where they find jobs and elude the immigration authorities. Others gain entry on valid temporary border-crossing permits, but then violate the conditions of their entry. Most of these aliens leave the border area in private vehicles, often assisted by professional "alien smugglers." The Border Patrol's traffic-checking operations are designed to prevent this inland movement. They succeed in apprehending some illegal entrants and smugglers, and they deter the movement of others by threatening apprehension and increasing the cost of illegal transportation.

Against this valid public interest we must weigh the interference with individual liberty that results when an officer stops an automobile and questions its occupants. The intrusion is modest. The Government tells us that a stop by a roving patrol "usually consumes no more than a minute." There is no search of the vehicle or its occupants, and the visual inspection is limited to those parts of the vehicle that can be seen by anyone standing alongside. According to the Government, "(a)ll that is required of the vehicle's occupants is a response to a brief question or two and possibly the production of a document evidencing a right to be in the United States."

Because of the limited nature of the intrusion, stops of this sort may be justified on facts that do not amount to the probable cause required for an arrest. In *Terry*, the Court declined expressly to decide whether facts not amounting to probable cause could justify an "investigative 'seizure'" short of an arrest, but it approved a limited search—a pat-down for weapons—for the protection of an officer investigating suspicious behavior of persons he reasonably believed to be armed and dangerous. The Court approved such a search on facts that did not constitute probable cause to believe the suspects guilty of a crime, requiring only that "the police officer . . . be able to point to specific and articulable facts which, taken together with rational inferences from those facts, reasonably warrant" a belief that his safety or that of others is in danger.

We elaborated on Terry in *Adams v. Williams* (1972), holding that a policeman was justified in approaching the respondent to investigate a tip that he was carrying narcotics and a gun.

> The Fourth Amendment does not require a policeman who lacks the precise level of information necessary for probable cause to arrest to simply shrug his shoulders and allow a crime to occur or a criminal to escape. On the contrary, *Terry* recognizes that it may be the essence of good police work to adopt an intermediate response. . . . A brief stop of a suspicious individual, in order to determine his identity or to maintain the status quo momentarily while obtaining more information, may be most reasonable in light of the facts known to the officer at the time.

These cases together establish that in appropriate circumstances the Fourth Amendment allows a properly limited "search" or "seizure" on facts that do not constitute probable cause to arrest or to search for contraband or evidence of crime. In both *Terry* and *Adams v. Williams* the investigating officers had reasonable grounds to believe that the suspects were armed and that they might be dangerous. The limited searches and seizures in those cases were a valid method of protecting the public and preventing crime. In this case as well, because of the importance of the governmental interest at stake, the minimal intrusion of a brief stop, and the absence of practical alternatives for policing the border, we hold that when an officer's observations lead him reasonably to suspect that a particular vehicle may contain aliens who are illegally in the country, he may stop the car briefly and investigate the circumstances that provoke suspicion. As in *Terry*, the stop and inquiry must be "reasonably related in scope to the justification for their initiation." The officer may question the driver and passengers about their citizenship and immigration status, and he may ask them to explain suspicious circumstances, but any further detention or search must be based on consent or probable cause.

We are unwilling to let the Border Patrol dispense entirely with the requirement that officers must have a reasonable suspicion to justify roving-patrol stops. In the context of border area stops, the reasonableness requirement of the Fourth Amendment demands something more than the broad and unlimited discretion sought by the Government. Roads near the border carry not only aliens seeking to enter the country illegally, but a large volume of legitimate traffic as well. San Diego, with a metropolitan population of 1.4 million, is located on the border. Texas has two fairly large metropolitan areas directly on the border: El Paso, with a population of 360,000, and the Brownsville-McAllen area, with a combined population of 320,000. We are confident that substantially all of the traffic in these cities is lawful and that relatively few of their residents have any connection with the illegal entry and transportation of aliens. To approve roving-patrol stops of all vehicles in the border area, without any suspicion that a particular vehicle is carrying illegal immigrants, would subject the residents of these and other areas to potentially unlimited interference with their use of the highways, solely at the discretion of Border Patrol officers. The only formal limitation on that discretion appears to be the administrative regulation defining the term "reasonable distance" in s 287(a)(3) to mean within 100 air miles from the border. 8 CFR s 287.1(a) (1975). Thus, if we approved the Government's position in this case, Border Patrol officers could stop motorists at random for questioning, day or night, anywhere within 100 air miles of the 2,000-mile border, on a city street, a busy highway, or a desert road, without any reason to suspect that they have violated any law.

We are not convinced that the legitimate needs of law enforcement require this degree of interference with lawful traffic. As we discuss in Part IV, infra, the nature of illegal alien traffic and the characteristics of smuggling operations tend to generate articulable grounds for identifying violators. Consequently, a requirement of reasonable suspicion for stops allows the Government adequate means of guarding the public interest and also protects residents of the border areas from indiscriminate official interference. Under the circumstances, and even though the intrusion incident to a stop is modest, we conclude that it is not "reasonable" under the Fourth Amendment to make such stops on a random basis.

The Government also contends that the public interest in enforcing conditions on legal alien entry justifies stopping persons who may be aliens for questioning about their citizenship and immigration status. Although we may assume for purposes of this case that the broad congressional power over immigration, authorizes Congress to admit aliens on condition that they will submit to reasonable questioning about their right to be and remain in the country, this power cannot diminish the Fourth Amendment rights of citizens who may be mistaken for aliens. For the same reasons that the Fourth Amendment forbids stopping vehicles at random to inquire if they are carrying aliens who are illegally in the country, it also forbids stopping or detaining persons for questioning about their citizenship on less than a reasonable suspicion that they may be aliens.

IV

The effect of our decision is to limit exercise of the authority granted by both s 287(a)(1) and s 287(a)(3). Except at the border and its functional equivalents, officers on roving patrol may stop vehicles only if they are aware of specific articulable facts, together with rational inferences from those facts, that reasonably warrant suspicion that the vehicles contain aliens who may be illegally in the country.

Any number of factors may be taken into account in deciding whether there is reasonable suspicion to stop a car in the border area. Officers may consider the characteristics of the area in which they encounter a vehicle. Its proximity to the border, the usual patterns of traffic on the particular road, and previous experience with alien traffic are all relevant. They also may consider information about recent illegal border crossings in the area. The driver's behavior may be relevant, as erratic driving or obvious attempts to evade officers can support a reasonable suspicion. Aspects of the vehicle itself may justify suspicion. For instance, officers say that certain station wagons, with large compartments for fold-down seats or spare tires, are frequently used for transporting concealed aliens. The vehicle may appear to be heavily loaded, it may have an extraordinary number of passengers, or the officers may observe persons trying to hide. The Government also points out that trained officers can recognize the characteristic appearance of persons who live in Mexico, relying on such factors as the mode of dress and haircut. In all situations the officer is entitled to assess the facts in light of his experience in detecting illegal entry and smuggling.

In this case the officers relied on a single factor to justify stopping respondent's car: the apparent Mexican ancestry of the occupants. We cannot conclude that this furnished reasonable grounds to believe that the three occupants were aliens. At best the officers had only a fleeting glimpse of the persons in the moving car, illuminated by headlights. Even if they saw enough to think that the occupants were of Mexican descent, this factor alone would justify neither a reasonable belief that they were aliens, nor a reasonable belief that the car concealed other aliens who were illegally in the country. Large numbers of native-born and naturalized citizens have the physical characteristics identified with Mexican ancestry, and even in the border area a relatively small proportion of them are aliens. The likelihood that any given person of Mexican ancestry is an alien is high enough to make Mexican appearance a relevant factor, but standing alone it does not justify stopping all Mexican-Americans to ask if they are aliens.

The judgment of the Court of Appeals is affirmed.

NOTES AND QUESTIONS

1. The Court actually seems skeptical of the agent's testimony at the suppression hearing that the individuals he saw and stopped — based on a fleeting glance in only the light of the cruiser's headlights — "appeared to be of Mexican descent." It states: "Even if they saw enough to think that the occupants were of Mexican descent this factor alone would justify neither a reasonable belief that they were aliens nor a reasonable belief that the car concealed other aliens who were illegally in the country. Such skepticism is unusual. Typically the conservative members of the Court accept police officer testimony uncritically.

If it is truly concerned about the ease with which an "appearance of Mexican descent" factor can be contrived, why does the Court permit it to be used at all, even as one of many factors?

Under the reasonable suspicion standard the Court requires for such stops, what percentage level of confidence would an agent need to have to conclude the occupants of a car "appeared to be of Mexican descent"?" 10 percent? 30 percent? More?

2. The Court also recognizes that "[l]arge numbers of native-born and naturalized citizens have the physical characteristics identified with Mexican ancestry, and even in the border area a relatively small proportion of them are aliens." In fact, as the attorney for Brignoni-Ponce pointed out at oral argument before the Supreme Court, only two of the three occupants of the car were Mexican: The driver was a Spanish-speaking Puerto Rican-American citizen and the other passenger was from Guatemala. Transcript of Oral Argument at 47, *Brignoni-Ponce*, 422 U.S. 873 (1975) (No. 74-114).

3. The lawyer for Brignoni-Ponce argued throughout his briefing that the use of race or ethnicity in determining suspicion was unconstitutional, citing among other authorities *Yick Wo v. Hopkins*, 118 U.S. 356 (1886), but conceded at oral argument that, at a minimum, it could not be the only factor.

Professor Kevin Johnson is critical of the attorney on this point:

> [T]he conventional — and overly narrow, client-centered — representation by Brignoni-Ponce's counsel has resulted in deep damage, with many thousands, if not millions, of Latina/os adversely affected.
>
> This history demonstrates the challenges of truly rebellious lawyering by lawyers committed to social justice. Such creative lawyering requires a long-term view of litigation and the impacts of the law on communities of people, not just individual clients. A broad vision is what Thurgood Marshall and a team of civil rights attorneys pursued for a generation before realizing the milestone victory in *Brown v. Board of Education.* Such a vision requires careful

> evaluation of compromises, strategies, long-term goals, and the human impacts of legal rules. In the end, the attorneys' short-term strategy in *Brignoni-Ponce,* although successful for the individual defendant, set back the rights of Latina/os for decades.

Kevin R. Johnson, *How Racial Profiling in America Became the Law of the Land:* United States v. Brignoni-Ponce *and* Whren v. United States *and the Need for Truly Rebellious Lawyering,* 98 Geo. L.J. 1005, 1044-45 (2010). Fair criticism? What does Professor Johnson mean by "overly narrow, client-centered" representation?

4. Why does the Court feel obligated to enshrine in the U.S. Reports a laundry list of factors the Border Patrol can use as a basis for reasonable suspicion? Is the Court blessing these factors in advance so that the agents can rely on them with impunity, confident that their reasonable suspicion conclusions will be bullet-proof in suppression hearings? Note that the bookend anchors in the long paragraph supplying these factors are *Carroll* and *Terry,* the textbook opinions on deference to police "expertise."

5. Just a year later, in *United States v. Martinez-Fuerte,* 428 U.S. 543 (1976), the Court addressed the constitutionality of fixed immigration checkpoints located between 50 and 100 miles from the Mexican border. At one of the three checkpoints at issue, a point agent would visually screen all incoming northbound traffic, which would have come to almost a complete halt at the checkpoint, and based on that cursory inspection would direct a subset of motorists to a secondary inspection site where they would be questioned about citizenship and immigration status. The Court concluded that the intrusion was sufficiently minimal that even a reasonable suspicion standard was unnecessary, and reached this conclusion even under the assumption that the referrals by the point agent to the secondary inspection site would be based on nothing more than "apparent Mexican ancestry."

In a heated dissent, Justice Brennan, joined only by Justice Marshall, accused the Court of continuing its "evisceration" of the Fourth Amendment and undermining its one-year old decision in *Brignoni-Ponce.*

Brignoni-Ponce and *Martinez-Fuerte* had a significant and long-lasting effect on the Border Patrol's ability to use ethnicity in immigration enforcement. Johnson, *Racial Profiling in America, supra* at 1027-30. Lower courts sometimes referred to the "*Brignoni-Ponce* factors" in analyzing reasonable suspicion, as if they had actually been the facts of a case rather than an advisory bulletin from the Supreme Court. The Court further assisted this effort by holding, in *INS v. Lopez-Mendoza,* 468 U.S. 1032, 1050-51 (1984), that the exclusionary rule did not apply in deportation proceedings unless the Fourth Amendment violation was "egregious."

But on the other hand, the factors on which an agent could base reasonable suspicion near the border were so numerous and varied it is a fair question whether the Court's blessing of "apparent Mexican ancestry" as a factor was even necessary. One Fifth Circuit judge, lamenting a "border exception" to the Fourth Amendment, observed that courts accept as justiciable suspicion in border searches "virtually everything and anything":

> The vehicle was suspiciously dirty and muddy, or the vehicle was suspiciously squeaky-clean; the driver was suspiciously dirty, shabbily dressed and unkept, or the driver was too clean; the vehicle was suspiciously traveling fast, or was traveling suspiciously slow (or even was traveling suspiciously at precisely the legal speed limit); the [old car, new car, big car, station wagon, camper, oilfield service truck, SUV, van] is the kind of vehicle typically used for smuggling aliens or drugs; the driver would not make eye contact with the agent, or the driver made eye contact too readily; the driver appeared nervous (or the driver even appeared too cool, calm, and collected); the time of day [early morning, mid-morning, late afternoon, early evening, late evening, middle of the night] is when "they" tend to smuggle contraband or aliens; the

> vehicle was riding suspiciously low (overloaded), or suspiciously high (equipped with heavy duty shocks and springs); the passengers were slumped suspiciously in their seats, presumably to avoid detection, or the passengers were sitting suspiciously ramrod-erect; the vehicle suspiciously slowed when being overtaken by the patrol car traveling at a high rate of speed with its high-beam lights on, or the vehicle suspiciously maintained its same speed and direction despite being overtaken by a patrol car traveling at a high speed with its high-beam lights on; and on and on ad nauseam.

United States v. Zapata-Ibarra, 223 F.3d 281 (5th Cir. 2000) (Weiner, J., dissenting) (citations to 16 cases identifying these factors omitted).

Brignoni-Ponce and *Martinez-Fuerte* also provided a green light for profiling in other contexts. Bernard Harcourt, United States v. Brignoni-Ponce *and* United States v. Martinez-Fuerte*: The Road to Racial Profiling*, 323-24, 337-40, in Criminal Procedure Stories (Carol Steiker ed., 2006). The DEA had begun building a drug courier profile in the early 1970s, and had implemented an experimental pilot program at the Detroit Airport in the 1970s, even before Sylvia Mendenhall was apprehended there. *United States v. Mendenhall*, 446 U.S. 544 (1980). *See also Florida v. Royer*, 460 U.S. 491, 507 (1981) (describing the DEA's profile). The profile was implemented nationwide after *Brignoni-Ponce* and *Martinez-Fuerte*, and between 1976 and 1980 over 140 reported decisions involved DEA stops at airports based on the drug courier profile. Harcourt, *The Road to Racial Profiling, supra* at 337.

For obvious reasons, the DEA has never publicized or published a definitive drug courier profile. Nor is there necessarily a single profile, as much as DEA agents like to dress up what are sometimes little more than hunches in the clothing of "agencywide expertise." Professor David Cole has catalogued over 50 factors that DEA agents have offered in court as contributing to the basis for reasonable suspicion, including many—like those on Judge Wiener's list—that are mutually exclusive. *See* David Cole, No Equal Justice: Race and Class in the American Criminal Justice System 48-49 (1999) (e.g., "arrived late at night; arrived early in the morning; arrived in the afternoon").

DEA agents only infrequently acknowledge that race or ethnicity is part of their profile. In *United States v. Weaver*, 966 F.2d 391 (8th Cir. 1992), the DEA agent testified that one of the factors he relied on in doing a *Terry* stop of the defendant at the Kansas City airport was that he "was a roughly dressed young black male who might be a member of a Los Angeles street gang who had been bringing narcotics into the Kansas City area." The Court found that while the factor of race alone could not justify the stop, it could be used as one factor among others where the agent was in possession of "intelligence" that Black persons from Los Angeles were "flooding the Kansas City area with cocaine." David Cole is able to identify only five federal cases where agents openly admitted in court that race or ethnicity were among the factors in their suspicion conclusion. Cole, No Equal Justice, *supra* at 49 & nn.104-08.

There was a point in the 1990s that something of a consensus had emerged that "racial profiling"—undefined and in the abstract—was fundamentally wrong. Harcourt, *The Road to Racial Profiling, supra* at 346-47. Public opinion polls found widespread opposition to the practice. It was condemned by tough-on-crime Presidents George W. Bush and Bill Clinton. But any consensus collapsed in the wake of the 2001 terrorist attacks on the World Trade Center. *Id.* And the Supreme Court has subsequently eliminated any lingering doubt of its position on the subject, at least in the context of the Fourth Amendment. In 2011, the Court stated that its 1995 decision in *Whren v. United States*, 517 U.S. 806 (1996), meant that the Court "would not look behind an objectively reasonable traffic stop to determine whether racial profiling . . . was the real motive." *Ashcroft v. al-Kidd*, 563 U.S. 731, 739 (2011).

3. Traffic Stops: Pretext, Policing, and Race

The Supreme Court has historically been ambivalent about the intrusiveness of traffic stops. In 1979, in *Delaware v. Prouse*, 440 U.S. 648 (1979), the Court acknowledged the "substantial anxiety" such stops cause, and conceded that they curtail "freedom of movement, are inconvenient, and consume time." Just five years later, as traffic stops began to be increasingly weaponized in the war on drugs, the Court's leading civil libertarian, Justice Marshall, described traffic stops as benign—a "presumptively temporary and brief" form of detention. *Berkemer v. McCarty*, 468 U.S. 420, 437-38 (1984). *See* Chapter III, *supra*.

The Court has never considered the increased "anxiety," not to mention other increased emotions, experienced disproportionately by Black people and other minorities during traffic stops. *See* C. Epp et al., Pulled Over: How Police Stops Define Race and Citizenship 47, 124-33 (2014). *See, e.g.*, Angela J. Davis, *Race, Cops, and Traffic Stops*, 51 U. Miami L. Rev. 425, 425, 438-40 (1997); David Harris, *Factors for Reasonable Suspicion: When Black and Poor Means Stopped and Frisked*, 69 Ind. L.J. 659, 679-81 (1994); Tracey Maclin, *"Black and Blue Encounters"—Some Preliminary Thoughts About Fourth Amendment Seizures: Should Race Matter?*, 26 Val. U. L. Rev. 243, 251-53 (1991).

Law enforcement did not just stumble upon the utility of the traffic stop as an instrument of crime detection writ large, specifically, drug interdiction. A pioneer of the movement was a journalist and academic named Charles Remsberg, whose police academy textbook, *Tactics for Criminal Patrol: Vehicle Stops, Drug Discovery, and Officer Survival*, was used to train police throughout the country. Seo, Policing the Open Road, *supra* at 255-57. Remsberg's essential message was that police officers should leverage the ubiquitous traffic violations motorists commit as a matter of course into vehicle stops. And then those stops, in turn, can be leveraged into full-blown vehicle searches based on probable cause or, more likely, consent. *Id.* Among Remsberg's lessons was that most drivers are not aware they can refuse to consent to a search and will therefore consent. *Id. See generally* Epp et al., Pulled Over, *supra* at 8 (describing increased police attention on citizen encounters to enable further investigation).

Remsberg's views were evident in the DEA's Operation Pipeline, created in 1984 and still operating today, which was also used to train state and local law enforcement officers to use traffic stops as pretexts for drug interdiction. Officers learned how to lengthen a routine traffic stop and leverage it into a search for drugs by obtaining (or extorting) consent or obtaining (or manufacturing) probable cause. As of 2000, the DEA had trained more than 25,000 officers in 48 states in Pipeline tactics.

Operation Pipeline specifically teaches that the officers should have drivers exit their cars and ask them a series of questions about their origin, travel plans, and destination while looking for signs of nervousness or inconsistencies. After that line of questioning is apparently completed, the script—apparently deployed effectively in *Ohio v. Robinette*, *supra*—calls for officers to use the Columbo trope (from the humble detective in the eponymous 1970s television show) to cap off the inquiry—"just one more thing, sir"—and then to ask whether there are any drugs or guns in the car. And after receiving a "no" the officer says, "You don't mind if I search your car then, do you?" *See* Ricardo J. Bascuas, *Fourth Amendment Lessons from the Highway and the Subway: A Principled Approach to Suspicionless Searches*, 38 Rutgers L.J. 719, 761-66 (2007) (discussing Operation Pipeline).

The next case has it all: great judge, great facts, heroic lawyering—and, in a telling detail, a total repudiation of *Schneckloth*'s argument that requiring motorists' consent to a car search was unrealistic. This could have been the law.

United States v. Laymon

730 F. Supp. 332 (D. Colo. 1990)

ORDER GRANTING MOTION TO SUPPRESS EVIDENCE

CARRIGAN, District Judge.

Defendant Louis Laymon, Jr. has filed a motion to suppress evidence obtained by the government during a March 8, 1989 search of his automobile after a traffic stop on Interstate 70 in Eagle County, Colorado. Laymon is charged with violating Title 21 U.S.C. § 841(a)(1) and (b) (possession with intent to distribute cocaine) and Title 21 U.S.C. § 846 and Title 18 U.S.C. § 2 (conspiracy to possess cocaine with intent to distribute.) He is a 21-year-old Black resident of California.

Defendant contends: (1) that the search of his automobile was made following a pretextual traffic stop and therefore violated his Fourth Amendment right to be free from unreasonable searches and seizures, and (2) that the consent to search, given by him on a printed form he signed during the traffic stop, was the product of trickery, coercion or both, and not freely and voluntarily given. Plaintiff, the government, contends that the search was carried out pursuant to a voluntary consent following a valid traffic stop.

During extensive hearings both parties introduced evidence, including exhibits and the testimony of numerous witnesses. Briefs have been filed and the issues are ripe for decision. Jurisdiction is not questioned. This memorandum constitutes my findings of fact pursuant to Rule 12(e), Fed. R. Crim. P.

I. FINDINGS OF FACT

A. Pretextual Stop

On March 8, 1989, at about 2:10 p.m., the defendant Louis Laymon, Jr. was riding as a passenger in a vehicle titled or registered in the name of his sister, Edjunia Laymon, but actually owned by him. The vehicle, bearing California license plates, was being driven East toward Denver by Alvin Riley. Both Laymon and Riley are Black. Sergeant James Perry ("Perry"), of the Eagle County Sheriff's Department, who is White, observed the Laymon vehicle traveling eastbound well within the 65 mile per hour speed limit on Interstate 70 ("I-70"). Perry, although employed by the Eagle County Sheriff's Department, was assigned to the High Country Drug Task Force. At the time of the traffic stop here involved he was driving a sheriff's department vehicle that was unmarked except for decals on its sides. It had no overhead lights or other characteristics to distinguish or identify it as a police car when viewed from the front.

Perry testified that while following the Laymon vehicle he observed it gradually moving or edging toward the right shoulder of the road until the right front tire ultimately contacted the white line separating the travelled portion of the highway from the shoulder. He described this motion as "weaving." Perry did not assert, however, that the "weaving" he allegedly observed included any gross movement such as swerving. Both Riley and Laymon denied that Riley ever allowed the vehicle to come into contact with or cross the white shoulder stripe. Testimony and a videotape indicated that the highway through the area in question curves through mountainous terrain.

Perry stated that he became concerned by the car's "weaving" and he briefly signaled with his siren for the vehicle to stop. He testified that the car's occupants appeared not to notice the siren because they failed to stop. Perry also testified that he attempted to flash the red light or lights installed in or behind his car's grill. Again this effort elicited no apparent response from the vehicle.

Riley and Laymon testified that Perry never activated either his siren or his lights to signal Riley to stop the vehicle. Eagle County Sheriff A.J. Johnson testified that he recalled Perry having informed him at a later date that an electrical problem had prevented the red lights on Perry's vehicle from functioning properly. As stated, the patrol car had no overhead lights. I find that Sheriff Johnson was a credible witness and thus find that the car driven by Sergeant Perry had non-functioning red lights under its front grill, and therefore even if Perry did attempt to activate those lights, as he testified, they did not come on.

Finally, Perry testified, he pulled alongside the California vehicle and motioned the driver to pull over. Riley immediately complied. Riley and Laymon testified that neither had any idea who Perry was or what he wanted until he pulled alongside and motioned for Riley to pull over. They testified that they did not realize until Perry pulled alongside that the car behind them was a police car.

Perry, Riley and the defendant Laymon all testified that after pulling the Laymon vehicle over, Perry took Riley's driver's license and the vehicle registration and returned to his patrol car for five to ten minutes. While waiting for Perry to return, Riley got out and stood by the rear of the car. When Perry returned, he issued a written warning to Riley for weaving.

At this point, Perry's, Riley's and Laymon's testimony diverges drastically. Perry testified that after he issued the warning to Riley he approached Laymon, who was still in the front passenger seat, and asked him to step out of the car. He stated that he informed Laymon that the Eagle County Sheriff's Department had been having problems with people carrying narcotics, large amounts of cash and firearms through the county. Perry stated that he then asked Laymon for consent to search the vehicle, and Laymon voluntarily agreed. Perry testified that he returned to his vehicle to obtain a consent to search form, and that Laymon signed that consent form after fully reviewing it.

Riley testified that after Perry issued him the warning for weaving, Perry informed him that the Eagle County Sheriff's Department had been having problems with people transporting drugs and weapons. According to Riley, Perry then said that Laymon would also have to sign a warning for weaving. Riley stated that Perry then approached Laymon, who was seated in the front passenger seat, and that he (Riley) could not hear the verbal exchange between Perry and Laymon.

Laymon testified that Perry approached the passenger side of the car and told him to step out of the car. Laymon stated that he complied and Perry then told him that he would have to sign a warning for weaving. He stated that Perry put a piece of paper on the hood of the car for Laymon to sign, and that he (Laymon) signed it without examining or reading it to see what the document actually stated. Next, Laymon stated that Perry mentioned the drug trafficking problems and asked Laymon if he could search the vehicle.

Riley and Laymon both testified that Laymon had refused to allow Perry to search the car but that Perry then had declared forcefully that Laymon had already signed a consent to search form. Laymon testified that he thought he had only signed a warning for weaving and not a consent to search form.

At this point Perry's, Riley's and Laymon's testimony again becomes consistent. At about the time Perry commenced searching the vehicle, a second white uniformed officer drove up to the scene and told Riley and Laymon to step away from the vehicle and face away while Perry searched the vehicle.

Upon opening the vehicle's hatchback, Perry observed what appeared to be a glove compartment type door on an inside wall panel. Perry testified that he either forced open the compartment or simply turned the knob. Riley and Laymon testified that they heard a loud "popping" sound that they believed to be Perry breaking the compartment door. Upon opening the door Perry observed a box of Kleenex in front of a cardboard inside wall that appeared to be dislodged or out of place. When he removed the cardboard wall separating the glove box from the car's metal shell, Perry discovered plastic bags filled with what appeared to be cocaine. Riley and Laymon were immediately arrested.

Perry's credibility was seriously undermined by cross examination. Perry admitted that he had a history of stopping vehicles based upon a "drug courier profile." He testified that he had received training from the Drug Enforcement Administration and the Eagle County Sheriff's office regarding drug courier profiles.

Further, Officer Lee Roybal, formerly of the Eagle County Sheriff's Department and the chief training officer of the Drug Task Force, testified that the primary assignment of the Drug Task Force is drug interdiction, not traffic enforcement. He stated that it is the Colorado Highway Patrol's responsibility to enforce traffic laws on I-70, whereas the Drug Task Force investigates and attempts to curtail the transportation of illicit drugs on that highway. Clearly, at the time Perry stopped Laymon's car his primary responsibilities concerned narcotics laws and not traffic control.

Perry testified that in performing his Drug Task Force duties, he evaluates many factors to determine whether a particular person fits a drug courier profile. For example, Perry claimed that he considered whether the vehicle contained fast food wrappers, a map with cities marked, a radar detector, luggage in the passenger compartment rather than the trunk, and numerous other seemingly innocuous factors. Perry admitted, however, that during the period when he was stopping cars and seeking consents to search based solely upon the "profile," he could not have discerned these factors during his first observation of a vehicle because it would have been impossible for him to really examine a car's contents without first stopping it. These factors obviously could not have played a part in Perry's decision to stop a vehicle.

Perry was therefore forced to admit that his initial observation of a vehicle would give him only very limited information, including its make and model, whether its plates indicated that it was a rental vehicle, and the state of its registration as indicated by the license plates.

In evaluating Perry's credibility and the weight to be accorded his testimony, I have considered among other factors, his testimony that physical limitations on his vision make it difficult or impossible for him to discern whether a person is Black, Hispanic or Anglo. He testified that he suffers from both astigmatism and color blindness. His astigmatism requires him to wear glasses. With regard to his asserted color blindness, Perry swore that it is nearly impossible for him to distinguish among Black, Hispanic and White people. There was no hint of any medical opinion or other evidence to support that assertion.

Perry testified that the louvers on the back of Laymon's vehicle, rendered it impossible for him to identify the race of its occupants. Indeed, he went so far as to testify that even when he pulled alongside the defendant's vehicle, a few feet from it in broad daylight, his color blindness prevented him from determining that the driver and passenger were Black. On cross examination, however, he testified that in looking around the courtroom, he was able to distinguish Blacks, Whites and Hispanics, but that he could not always do so while on duty as a law officer. Laymon's and Riley's complexions are very dark and they are obviously Black. I find to be incredible Perry's testimony that he could not distinguish Black from non-Black drivers in broad daylight.

Additional evidence to support that finding as to credibility is found in prior testimony from an unrelated Eagle County case, *People v. Jose Fernando Encines*. Perry's testimony there contradicts his claim of vision restricting his ability to tell Blacks from Whites limitations by sight. He testified in that case that he had been able to identify by sight an Hispanic male who fit a description on a "wanted" poster in his office. He only observed that man in a car travelling toward him at approximately 65 m.p.h. while he was walking on I-70. After giving a motorist a ticket, he was walking back to his car on Interstate 70, when he observed the car coming. Perry chased Encines in his patrol car and discovered that Encines, although an Hispanic male, was not the same Hispanic male described on the "wanted" poster. Because

Perry was able to make an identification based upon race under those circumstances and based upon my evaluation of Perry's credibility, I find that he was able to and did determine the sex, approximate age and race of the occupants of the defendant's vehicle before stopping it. This conclusion is also supported by Riley's and Laymon's testimony that they had no knowledge that Perry was a police officer who wanted them to stop until Perry drove alongside their vehicle and signaled them to pull over.

Perry's daily activity logs, admitted into evidence, provided additional damage to his credibility. The logs were recorded from August 10, 1988 to May 8, 1989. The logs reflect that during this period, Perry made approximately 200 highway stops. Of that 200, 188 were stops of out of state vehicles. These logs also confirm that Perry's duties were primarily narcotics enforcement because he did not issue any traffic tickets during any of the recorded stops, but at most issued only traffic warnings.

Despite these entries in his own activity log, Perry testified that his pattern and practice of stopping individuals has nothing to do with a vehicle's state of registration. He testified that he stops all vehicles that violate traffic laws in his presence regardless of their place of origin.

In an apparent attempt to salvage lost credibility, Perry testified that if statistics prove that he overwhelmingly stops out of state vehicles, it is because during the ski season, most of the vehicles on I-70 in Eagle County are from out of state. Even a cursory examination of Perry's activity logs, however, belies this testimony. Officer Roybal testified that the ski season begins on Thanksgiving and ends in early April. Perry's daily logs show no change in the pattern of stopping out of state vehicles, regardless of the season, from August to May. Nor is there any claim by Perry that a disproportionately higher number of out of state skiers are Black or Hispanic than White.

More troubling than the evidence demonstrating that out of state travelers are at far greater risk of being subjected to highway stops in Eagle County, with all the implications that situation has in light of the Fourteenth Amendment's equal protection and privileges and immunities clauses, is the irrefutable evidence that Blacks and Hispanics were far more likely to be stopped by Perry than White, non-Hispanic motorists. This was proven by several items of evidence.

Perry testified that of all the stops he made from August 10, 1988 to May 8, 1989, only ten to fifteen percent involved Hispanic drivers. When confronted with the fact that approximately fifty percent of all of his consent to search forms obtained during that time period had been signed by motorists with Spanish surnames, Perry could only conclude that this alarming statistical disparity was coincidental. Of the remaining half, those not Spanish surnamed, at least some were Blacks who testified in this court about their encounters with Perry.

Jhenita and Janice Whitfield, two young Black women testified that they were stopped, while driving a car with California plates, for the alleged offense of failing to signal a sufficient distance prior to changing lanes on I-70, a four-lane highway. Along with their four infant children they testified that they were forced to stand alongside the highway in cold mountain weather for more than forty-five minutes while Perry searched their car, unpacking their luggage and rummaging through all their personal clothing and belongings. No contraband was found, and the only product of this exercise was the anger of these citizens who felt that they had been pressured to submit to the search because of their race. Perhaps ironically, one of them had served for years in the military service of the United States and had elected that service as her career.

Byron Boudreaux, a young black male, testified that he was stopped by Perry while driving a car with Oklahoma plates through Eagle County on I-70. Perry and two other officers informed him that they had received an anonymous tip that a man fitting his description was carrying drugs. Boudreaux testified that he was detained for approximately forty-five minutes while Perry and the other officers searched his car.

Aguinaldo Ferreria, a young Black male, was stopped by Perry while driving a car with California plates through Eagle County on I-70. Perry told him that he fit a description of someone suspected of carrying drugs. Ferreria was detained for about forty-five minutes while Perry conducted his search.

These Black drivers indicated that Perry gave them the impression the searches would be of the vehicle and would delay them only a few minutes, but the actual searches involved going through all their luggage and personal effects and took far longer.

Michael Misukanis, a young white male with hair longer than shoulder length, testified that he had been stopped by Perry while driving an old car with a loud engine and blotched body paint through Eagle County on I-70. His car carried California license plates. Perry told him that he fit a drug dealer description. Unlike the other victims who testified, Misukanis declined to give Perry consent to search his car. Perry persistently tried to pressure Misukanis to consent by stating that his refusal to consent indicated that he was transporting drugs. After an exchange lasting fifteen to twenty minutes, Misukanis asked Perry if he was going to be arrested for failing to sign the consent to search form. Finally, Perry allowed him to leave. There was no indication that Perry customarily informed those stopped that they were free to leave if they did not consent to a vehicle search. While not dispositive, the absence of such notice is a factor to be considered in determining whether a consent is voluntary.

The fact that Blacks and Hispanics are frequently targeted by the Eagle County Drug Task Force was further highlighted during the hearings on this matter, when Perry, Officer Roybal and Sheriff A.J. Johnson all testified that being Black or Hispanic was and is a factor in their drug courier profile on which they decide who to stop and search. Perry and Sheriff Johnson reluctantly made this admission, while Officer Roybal candidly admitted that race is part of the profile. Officer Roybal's admission is noteworthy and entitled to substantial weight because he was in charge of training for the Drug Task Force. This evidence was not contradicted.

Further evidence of a pattern, practice and habit of racist law enforcement is Perry's admission that in December of 1988 he had stopped three young Blacks with California license plates because he thought they might be gang members carrying drugs or weapons. Upon obtaining a "consent" to search, he found twenty pounds of cocaine. No charges were ever filed, however, because the Eagle County District Attorney concluded that Perry had violated the suspects' Fourth Amendment rights.

Perry testified that the arrest of the young blacks from Los Angeles taught him that "profiling" based on race was unconstitutional as a sole justification for stopping a vehicle. As a result of the District Attorney's refusing to file charges in that case, he asserted that he began to use traffic stops, rather than profiles, as his means of stopping vehicles. He claimed that his entire practice as a Drug Task Force officer changed and that he would no longer simply stop people because they were Black or Hispanic with out-of-state plates. However, the irrefutable evidence shows, and I find, that his practice was to stop disproportionately larger numbers of Blacks and Hispanics with out-of-state license plates on the pretext that they were committing some trivial traffic violation for which he would not have stopped Anglo drivers with Colorado license plates.

After the District Attorney refused to file the case involving the twenty pound cocaine seizure, Perry's activity logs markedly changed. His logs for the period prior to the December 1988 arrest, are filled with the notation "CI" meaning "criminal investigation" as the reason for the stop. Perry testified that the "CI" stops had been based solely on profiles.

After the December 1988 arrest, Perry entered "TE" as his reason for the stops, explaining that this stood for "traffic enforcement."

If Perry's own records are to be construed literally, Perry went from being a Drug Task Force officer who went for days at a time without ever concerning himself with any traffic violations, to a drug enforcement officer obsessed with traffic enforcement. The logs, however, reflect that Perry's routine was unaffected by his sudden passion for traffic enforcement. He still stopped approximately the same number of vehicles as he had stopped when he was admittedly unlawfully "profiling," and his primary focus remained on out of state vehicles. His consent forms continued to be signed by a disproportionately high percentage of Spanish surnamed people. In fact, from February to May 1989, Perry made 106 stops and obtained consents to search from twenty-eight persons. Fourteen, or one-half, of these individuals had Hispanic surnames. I reject as incredible the proffered explanation that this is explainable on the ground that Eagle County has a large number of Hispanic residents. The government presented no census or other statistics to support that contention, and even if true, it would not justify the disproportionately high number of stops and consents to search signed by Hispanic named travellers whose vehicles had out-of-state license plates. Surely most of them were not Eagle county residents.

The sworn testimony of Riley and Laymon provides further evidence of Perry's habit, practice and modus operandi to engage in pretextual stops. Their testimony, even when discounted by obvious factors likely to affect their credibility, is still more credible than Perry's after the other witnesses described his practices. Both unequivocally testified that Riley was not weaving at any time prior to being pulled over by Perry.

Further, there is no evidence that a reasonable officer would have made a stop under the circumstances of this case. Colorado Highway Patrolman Rogozik, testifying on behalf of the government, attempted to address this issue by stating what he personally would have done under the circumstances faced by Perry on March 8, 1989. This officer's testimony regarding his own practices, is irrelevant because it assumes that the Laymon vehicle was in fact weaving, and I find as a fact that it was not. Moreover Patrolman Rogozik gave no opinion as to what a reasonable, prudent officer would have done in Perry's situation even if the Laymon car had been weaving. Rather he testified only as to what he personally would have done. That falls short of meeting the standard set for the Tenth Circuit in *United States v. Guzman* (10th Cir. 1988).

I have considered Riley's and Laymon's testimony, Perry's testimony and his lack of credibility, the Highway Patrolman Rogozik's testimony and all the other evidence. I find as stated that the defendant's car did not weave or swerve in a manner that would have caused a reasonable, prudent police officer to pull it over for a traffic stop.

The inescapable conclusion from all the evidence is that Sergeant Perry engaged in a pattern and practice of making traffic stops based primarily on the most readily observable aspects of the vehicle that drew his attention as a Drug Task Force officer, i.e. out-of-state license plates and the driver's race or ethnicity. His failure to issue any traffic violation citations is further evidence that the traffic stops were merely subterfuges. I find as a fact that the alleged traffic stop in the instant case was pretextual.

B. Consent to Search

The period of time between the actual traffic stop and the issuance of the written warning for weaving was very brief. Perry claims that he returned the vehicle registration and the driver's licenses of both occupants before he asked Laymon for a consent to search the car. Riley and Laymon on the other hand, testified that Perry never asked Laymon for a consent to search, but instead deceived him into signing a consent to search by telling him that it was a warning for weaving. Riley's testimony before me is somewhat inconsistent with his testimony before the grand jury. Riley, testifying before the grand jury on this issue, stated:

Q. Did the officer force him to sign the form?
A. No. He did not tell him he had to or anything like that.

Q. In other words, Mr. Laymon freely signed it?

A. Yes.

Q. Mr. Laymon ever tell you what was going through his mind as to why he freely signed the form?

A. No.

Q. Did he ever tell you that he felt that he wouldn't be able to find the cocaine in the back of the car?

A. It was more or less we were just trying to be cool. (Transcript of Federal Grand Jury 88-1 (Denver), on April 12, 1989, at 33 and 34).

Therefore, it is somewhat suspicious, and casts serious doubt on Riley's and Laymon's credibility, that Riley deviated from his grand jury testimony when he testified before me that Perry had asked Laymon to sign a warning for weaving. Additionally, neither Riley nor Laymon testified that Perry coerced Laymon to sign the consent to search through the use of force or the threat of force. Further, Laymon testified that he had completed high school and is fully capable of reading and writing. Therefore, from all the evidence and circumstances surrounding Perry's acquisition of Laymon's signature on the search consent form, I find that Sergeant Perry's testimony on this point is more credible than that of Laymon and Riley and therefore I find that Laymon probably knew that he was signing a consent to search form and did not sign under the misapprehension that he was signing a warning for weaving.

II. CONCLUSIONS OF LAW

A. The Pretextual Stop Issue

Defendant contends that Perry conducted an unconstitutional pretextual stop of the defendant's vehicle that justifies suppressing the cocaine thereafter discovered. The Tenth Circuit has adopted an objective test for determining whether an investigatory stop is pretextual and therefore unconstitutional. The Court of Appeals has stated that:

> a court should ask "not whether the officer could validly have made the stop, but whether under the same circumstances a reasonable officer would have made the stop in the absence of the invalid purpose." "That an officer theoretically could validly have stopped the car for a possible traffic infraction [i]s not determinative. Similarly immaterial [i]s the actual subjective intent of the deputy. [A] stop [i]s unreasonable not because the officer secretly hope[s] to find evidence of a greater offence, but because it [i]s clear that an officer would have been uninterested in pursuing the lesser offence absent that hope." *United States v. Guzman* (10th Cir. 1988).

From my interpretation of the evidence, specifically Perry's demeanor and credibility, I already have determined that the alleged weaving of the defendant's car was a pretext for the invalid purpose of stopping it based on its California license plates and the race of its occupants. I find as a fact that Perry did not decide to stop the defendant's car until he pulled alongside and determined that Riley and Laymon were Black. The government has not carried its burden of proof to provide sufficient credible evidence that a reasonable, prudent officer would have made the stop absent the invalid purpose. Further, Perry's past habit and pattern of stopping vehicles based on a "profile" provides persuasive circumstantial evidence supporting a finding that he was uninterested in the alleged weaving as a traffic offense.

Lastly, Perry's lack of real interest in traffic law enforcement is strongly evidenced by his overall and consistent practice of not issuing traffic citations or "tickets," but merely warnings, and by his specific failure to follow-up by checking Riley's sobriety or competency to drive, a normal procedure for a police officer who observes a driver weaving.

Perry appeared to act in concert with and on instructions from the Eagle County Sheriff's Department and the Drug Task Force. He carried out policies that systematically violated the constitutionally protected rights of Blacks and Hispanics to travel and be free from unreasonable seizures on an equal basis with other persons travelling the highways of this nation. For these reasons, I conclude as a matter of law that on March 8, 1989 when Perry stopped his vehicle, the defendant suffered an unconstitutional pretextual stop amounting to a seizure that violated the Fourth Amendment.

This opinion does not hold that all "profile" investigatory stops are improper or unconstitutional. Higher courts have established guidelines for determining the validity of profile stops in the broad context. This case holds only that profile stops may not be predicated on unconstitutional discrimination based on race, ethnicity or state of residence.

Here the stop was tainted by violations of Laymon's rights guaranteed by the United States Constitution Amendment IV (freedom from unlawful seizures); Amendment I (freedom to travel); and Amendment XIV (right to equal protection of the law and freedom from discriminatory law enforcement based on race; equal access of citizens of other states to privileges and immunities accorded to citizens of Colorado, including travel without harassment on Colorado highways). Amendment XIV applies the First and Fourth Amendments to restrict state action such as that here involved. *Mapp v. Ohio* (1961) and its progeny require this court to suppress evidence obtained in violation of a defendant's Fourth Amendments rights.

B. Consent to Search

The question remains whether Laymon's consent to the search of his car was valid despite the constitutional violation. The government argues that the defendant's consent was free and voluntary and therefore it legitimized Perry's search.

The Tenth Circuit has stated that:

> When attempting to establish that there was voluntary consent after an illegal stop, however, the Government has a heavier burden to carry than when the consent is given after a permissible stop. . . .
>
> Moreover, when consent is obtained after an illegal arrest, the Government must establish a break in the causal connection between the illegality and the evidence thereby obtained.

In determining the voluntariness of the consent, Guzman stated:

> In *Brown v. Illinois* (1975), the Supreme Court held that where a confession is preceded by a Fourth Amendment violation, in determining the voluntariness of the confession the examining court must decide whether it was "'sufficiently an act of free will to purge the primary taint' [of the illegal arrest]." . . . Although the Court acknowledged that a determination of this issue is necessarily a complex one in which "no single fact is dispositive," . . . it placed special emphasis on three factors: "[t]he temporal proximity of the arrest and the confession, the presence of intervening circumstances, and particularly, the purpose and flagrancy of the official misconduct are all relevant."

These three elements of voluntariness clearly apply in this Circuit when evaluating consents to search following a Fourth Amendment violation.

The issue of consent is a question of fact. *Schneckloth v. Bustamonte* (1973). *Guzman* stated that:

> This Circuit has held that when a consent to search is preceded by a Fourth Amendment violation, the consent is valid only if it is voluntary in fact.

Ballard, interpreting prior Fifth Circuit case law, stated:

> The most significant factor relied upon by the court was a warning informing defendant of his right to refuse to permit the search. . . . The court reasoned: "While warnings prior to a consensual search may not have the same indispensability as those required prior to a confession . . . they do help insure that the consent is free, voluntary, and untainted by the arrest's possible illegality.

> In the instant case the presence of these warnings leads us to conclude that any coercion flowing from the possible illegality of appellant's arrest was dissipated." . . . Similarly . . . this court held that advising a defendant of his right to refuse to permit a search was a sufficient intervening occurrence to remove the influence of a prior fourth amendment violation.

Here the defendant signed the consent to search form after Perry had violated his Fourth Amendment rights by committing a pretextual stop. I find as a fact that the government has not met its burden to establish that Laymon's consent was "sufficiently an act of free will to purge the primary taint" of the illegal stop, and therefore I find and conclude that the alleged consent was not free or voluntary. The government has presented no evidence that Perry informed Laymon that he could refuse consent. Although the government is not required to make such a showing and its lack, standing alone, is not dispositive, this factor may be considered when evaluating the totality of the circumstances.

I find that the evidence demonstrates that Perry, in the past, conducted, and at least in this case, continued to conduct, stops on I-70 in a manner creating a coercive and intimidating atmosphere that most people, especially young minority citizens, would find coercive and impossible to resist. The testimony of Jhenita and Janice Whitfield, Byron Boudreaux, Aguinaldo Ferreria and Michael Misukanis, although not dispositive as to the totality of the circumstances present here, persuades me that Perry probably followed his normal habit, routine or practice to create a coercive atmosphere when he stopped Laymon. All of these individuals, with the exception of Misukanis, testified that they gave Perry consent to search because they felt intimidated and that they had no real alternative. Misukanis refused consent and was allowed to leave only after enduring Perry's unfounded accusations and pressure to consent for fifteen to twenty minutes.

If this nation were to win its "War on Drugs" at the cost of sacrificing its citizens' constitutional rights, it would be a Pyrrhic victory indeed. It ill behooves a great nation to compromise or sacrifice the freedoms of its citizens as the price of more efficient law enforcement. Many countries have written constitutions similar to ours that define the rights of their people in words as forceful and inspiring as those of the United States constitution. But for most people living under those other constitutions the rights so emphatically guaranteed them are hollow, because there is no practical means to enforce them. The rights they define are illusory and disappear like vapor in the face of governmental pressure. Our tradition is different. It requires judges and police officers, who are equally sworn to uphold the same Constitution, to enforce constitutionally guaranteed rights, even when their enforcement is unpopular and even when those rights are asserted on behalf of persons whose activities are considered despicable. If the rule of law—rather than the rule of man—is to prevail, there cannot be one set of search and seizure rules applicable to some and a different set applicable to others. We deal here with rights, not privileges. There must be one guarantee of rights for all. As a practical matter if we are not all free, none of us is really free, for exceptions which deny constitutional rights to some erode them for all. While we deal today only with denial of Mr. Laymon's rights, who knows which of us may be next.

A society cannot remain free or strong if it undermines its own principles. Law enforcement officials are not licensed to disregard the law—especially not the law enshrined in the Constitution. It is utter hypocrisy to celebrate as a national holiday the birthday of Martin Luther King, Jr. while applying to Blacks a practice of selective law enforcement in disregard of their constitutionally guaranteed status as equal citizens.

The Florida Supreme Court recently declared:

> Without doubt the inherently transient nature of drug courier activity presents difficult law enforcement problems. Roving patrols, random sweeps, and arbitrary searches or seizures would go far to eliminate such crime in this state [and nation]. Nazi Germany, Soviet Russia, and

Communist Cuba have demonstrated all too tellingly the effectiveness of such methods. Yet we are not a state that subscribes to the notion that ends justify means. History demonstrates that the adoption of repressive measures, even to eliminate a clear evil, usually results only in repression more mindless and terrifying than the evil that prompted them. Means have a disturbing tendency to become the end result. And as Judge Glickstein noted in his dissent in (Fla. App. 1986):

> "Occasionally the price we must pay to make innocent persons secure from unreasonable search and seizure of their persons or property is to let an offender go. Those who suffered harassment from King George III's forces would say that is not a great price to pay. So would residents of the numerous totalitarian and authoritarian states of our day." *Bostick v. State of Florida*, 554 So. 2d 1153 (Fla. 1989).

Considering Florida's past history in race relations and that it is probably the state most heavily impacted by drug trafficking, it would be ironic indeed if rights guaranteed by the Federal Constitution should be accorded greater protection in drug cases by the elected Florida state courts than by federal courts.

Although I have found that Laymon knew that he was signing a consent to search form, I further find as a fact that, under the circumstances existing at the time of his stop, any reasonable traveller, and especially two out-of-state young Black men in the company of two uniformed and armed white law officers on a roadside in rural Colorado, would not have felt that he could do anything other than sign the consent to search. In other words, I find as a fact that Laymon was coerced or intimidated into signing the consent to search. For this reason, I conclude that the government has not sustained its burden to demonstrate that his consent was "sufficiently an act of free will to purge the primary taint" of the illegal stop. Therefore, I conclude that the defendant is entitled to prevail on his motion to suppress.

Accordingly It Is Ordered that the defendant Laymon's motion to suppress is granted.

NOTES AND QUESTIONS

1. The Eagle County Police Department does not appear to be in the vanguard of progressive policing. But note its use of a simple standardized "consent form" to memorialize consents to searches. Recall how in *Schneckloth* and *Robinette* the Court said it would be "impractical" and "unrealistic" to require police to inform motorists of their right to refuse to consent to a search. Such printed *Miranda* warning cards and forms were in use shortly after the *Miranda* decision to memorialize an arrestee's consent to be interviewed; here a police department has implemented a similar system without any legal requirement to do so. Kudos Eagle County!

2. What great lawyering here by defense counsel. But note what made it all possible: an order from the court requiring the county to turn over the logs of Sergeant Perry's stops for a nine-month period, which probably required a threshold showing of pretext. For this to become dispositive evidence several other things were required: attendance at the suppression hearing of other "victims"—uncharged—of Perry's tactics; the court's willingness to view the matter through the perspective of Justice Jackson's Everyman in his *Brinegar* dissent; and, ultimately, candid (if criminal) testimony from Perry that he switched from relying solely on race for traffic stops to a system where he instead relied on trivial traffic violations.

(Note that the searches many of these Everyman witnesses consented to took almost an hour, almost surely longer than what they thought they were agreeing to.)

3. Judge Carrigan finds that the stop was unconstitutionally pretextual under the Tenth Circuit's rule in *Guzman*, which required an inquiry into whether a reasonable officer would have made the stop in the absence of the pretextual purpose. What difficulties do you see in courts' application of that test in contexts such as these? How do those difficulties compare to other Fourth Amendment tests, such as, for example, whether a person has a reasonable expectation of privacy?

4. Judge Carrigan makes an impassioned plea that civil rights cannot be sacrificed on the altar of the war on drugs, and notes the example of the Florida Supreme Court—"the state most heavily impacted by drug trafficking"—in recognizing individual rights.

In two years the Florida Supreme Court decision Judge Carrigan noted would be overturned by the United States Supreme Court. *Florida v. Bostick*, 501 U.S. 429 (1991). In five years, the United States Supreme Court would reject the Tenth Circuit's rule in *Guzman* relied on by Judge Carrigan, blessing traffic stops supported by probable cause regardless of a pretextual purpose. *Whren v. United States*, 517 U.S. 806 (1996).

We now turn to *Whren*.

Whren v. United States

517 U.S. 806 (1996)

Justice Scalia delivered the opinion of the Court.

In this case we decide whether the temporary detention of a motorist who the police have probable cause to believe has committed a civil traffic violation is inconsistent with the Fourth Amendment's prohibition against unreasonable seizures unless a reasonable officer would have been motivated to stop the car by a desire to enforce the traffic laws.

I

On the evening of June 10, 1993, plainclothes vice-squad officers of the District of Columbia Metropolitan Police Department were patrolling a "high drug area" of the city in an unmarked car. Their suspicions were aroused when they passed a dark Pathfinder truck with temporary license plates and youthful occupants waiting at a stop sign, the driver looking down into the lap of the passenger at his right. The truck remained stopped at the intersection for what seemed an unusually long time—more than 20 seconds. When the police car executed a U-turn in order to head back toward the truck, the Pathfinder turned suddenly to its right, without signaling, and sped off at an "unreasonable" speed. The policemen followed, and in a short while overtook the Pathfinder when it stopped behind other traffic at a red light. They pulled up alongside, and Officer Ephraim Soto stepped out and approached the driver's door, identifying himself as a police officer and directing the driver, petitioner Brown, to put the vehicle in park. When Soto drew up to the driver's window, he immediately observed two large plastic bags of what appeared to be crack cocaine in petitioner Whren's hands. Petitioners were arrested, and quantities of several types of illegal drugs were retrieved from the vehicle.

Petitioners were charged in a four-count indictment with violating various federal drug laws, including 21 U.S.C. §§ 844(a) and 860(a). At a pretrial suppression hearing, they challenged the legality of the stop and the resulting seizure of the drugs. They argued that the stop had not been justified by probable cause to believe, or even reasonable suspicion, that petitioners were engaged in illegal drug-dealing activity; and that Officer Soto's asserted ground for approaching the vehicle—to give the driver a warning concerning traffic violations—was pretextual. The District Court denied the suppression motion, concluding that "the facts of the stop were not controverted," and "[t]here was nothing to really demonstrate that the actions of the officers were contrary to a normal traffic stop."

Petitioners were convicted of the counts at issue here. The Court of Appeals affirmed the convictions, holding with respect to the suppression issue that, "regardless of whether a police officer subjectively believes that the occupants of an automobile may be engaging in some other illegal behavior, a traffic stop is permissible as long as a reasonable officer in the same circumstances could have stopped the car for the suspected traffic violation." We granted certiorari.

II

The Fourth Amendment guarantees "[t]he right of the people to be secure in their persons, houses, papers, and effects, against unreasonable searches and seizures." Temporary detention of individuals during the stop of an automobile by the police, even if only for a brief period and for a limited purpose, constitutes a "seizure" of "persons" within the meaning of this provision. An automobile stop is thus subject to the constitutional imperative that it not be "unreasonable" under the circumstances. As a general matter, the decision to stop an automobile is reasonable where the police have probable cause to believe that a traffic violation has occurred.

Petitioners accept that Officer Soto had probable cause to believe that various provisions of the District of Columbia traffic code had been violated. See 18 D.C. Mun. Regs. §§ 2213.4 (1995) ("An operator shall . . . give full time and attention to the operation of the vehicle"); 2204.3 ("No person shall turn any vehicle . . . without giving an appropriate signal"); 2200.3 ("No person shall drive a vehicle . . . at a speed greater than is reasonable and prudent under the conditions"). They argue, however, that "in the unique context of civil traffic regulations" probable cause is not enough. Since, they contend, the use of automobiles is so heavily and minutely regulated that total compliance with traffic and safety rules is nearly impossible, a police officer will almost invariably be able to catch any given motorist in a technical violation. This creates the temptation to use traffic stops as a means of investigating other law violations, as to which no probable cause or even articulable suspicion exists. Petitioners, who are both black, further contend that police officers might decide which motorists to stop based on decidedly impermissible factors, such as the race of the car's occupants. To avoid this danger, they say, the Fourth Amendment test for traffic stops should be, not the normal one (applied by the Court of Appeals) of whether probable cause existed to justify the stop; but rather, whether a police officer, acting reasonably, would have made the stop for the reason given.

A

Petitioners contend that the standard they propose is consistent with our past cases' disapproval of police attempts to use valid bases of action against citizens as pretexts for pursuing other investigatory agendas. We are reminded that in *Florida v. Wells* (1990), we stated that "an inventory search" must not be a ruse for a general rummaging in order to discover incriminating evidence"; that in *Colorado v. Bertine* (1987), in approving an inventory search, we apparently thought it significant that there had been "no showing that the police, who were following standardized procedures, acted in bad faith or for the sole purpose of investigation"; and that in *New York v. Burger* (1987), we observed, in upholding the constitutionality of a warrantless administrative inspection, that the search did not appear to be "a 'pretext' for obtaining evidence of . . . violation of . . . penal laws." But only an undiscerning reader would regard these cases as endorsing the principle that ulterior motives can invalidate police conduct that is justifiable on the basis of probable cause to believe that a violation of law has occurred. In each case we were addressing the validity of a search conducted in the absence of probable cause. Our quoted statements simply explain that the exemption from the need for probable cause (and warrant), which is accorded to searches made for the purpose of inventory or administrative regulation, is not accorded to searches that are not made for those purposes.

Petitioners also rely upon *Colorado v. Bannister* (1980) (per curiam), a case which, like this one, involved a traffic stop as the prelude to a plain-view sighting and arrest on charges wholly unrelated to the basis for the stop. Petitioners point to our statement that "[t]here was no evidence whatsoever that the officer's presence to issue a traffic citation was a pretext to confirm any other previous suspicion about the occupants" of the car. That dictum at most demonstrates that the Court in *Bannister* found no need to inquire into the question now under discussion; not that it was certain of the answer. And it may demonstrate even less than that: If by "pretext" the Court meant that the officer really had not seen the car speeding, the statement would mean only that there was no reason to doubt probable cause for the traffic stop.

It would, moreover, be anomalous, to say the least, to treat a statement in a footnote in the per curiam *Bannister* opinion as indicating a reversal of our prior law. Petitioners' difficulty is not simply a lack of affirmative support for their position. Not only have we never held, outside the context of inventory search or administrative inspection (discussed above), that an officer's motive invalidates objectively justifiable behavior under the Fourth Amendment; but we have repeatedly held and asserted the contrary. In *United States v. Villamonte-Marquez* (1983), we held that an otherwise valid warrantless boarding of a vessel by customs officials was not rendered invalid "because the customs officers were accompanied by a Louisiana state policeman, and were following an informant's tip that a vessel in the ship channel was thought to be carrying marihuana." We flatly dismissed the idea that an ulterior motive might serve to strip the agents of their legal justification. In *United States v. Robinson* (1973), we held that a traffic-violation arrest (of the sort here) would not be rendered invalid by the fact that it was "a mere pretext for a narcotics search," and that a lawful postarrest search of the person would not be rendered invalid by the fact that it was not motivated by the officer-safety concern that justifies such searches. And in *Scott v. United States* (1978), in rejecting the contention that wiretap evidence was subject to exclusion because the agents conducting the tap had failed to make any effort to comply with the statutory requirement that unauthorized acquisitions be minimized, we said that "[s]ubjective intent alone . . . does not make otherwise lawful conduct illegal or unconstitutional." We described *Robinson* as having established that "the fact that the officer does not have the state of mind which is hypothecated by the reasons which provide the legal justification for the officer's action does not invalidate the action taken as long as the circumstances, viewed objectively, justify that action."

We think these cases foreclose any argument that the constitutional reasonableness of traffic stops depends on the actual motivations of the individual officers involved. We of course agree with petitioners that the Constitution prohibits selective enforcement of the law based on considerations such as race. But the constitutional basis for objecting to intentionally discriminatory application of laws is the Equal Protection Clause, not the Fourth Amendment. Subjective intentions play no role in ordinary, probable-cause Fourth Amendment analysis.

B

Recognizing that we have been unwilling to entertain Fourth Amendment challenges based on the actual motivations of individual officers, petitioners disavow any intention to make the individual officer's subjective good faith the touchstone of "reasonableness." They insist that the standard they have put forward—whether the officer's conduct deviated materially from usual police practices, so that a reasonable officer in the same circumstances would not have made the stop for the reasons given—is an "objective" one.

But although framed in empirical terms, this approach is plainly and indisputably driven by subjective considerations. Its whole purpose is to prevent the police from doing under the guise of enforcing the traffic code what they would like to do for different reasons. Petitioners' proposed standard may not use the word "pretext," but it is designed to combat nothing other than the perceived "danger" of the pretextual stop, albeit only indirectly and over the run of cases. Instead of asking whether the individual officer had the proper state of mind, the petitioners would have us ask, in effect, whether (based on general police practices) it is plausible to believe that the officer had the proper state of mind.

Why one would frame a test designed to combat pretext in such fashion that the court cannot take into account actual and admitted pretext is a curiosity that can only be explained by the fact that our cases have foreclosed the more sensible option. If those cases were based only upon the evidentiary difficulty of establishing subjective intent, petitioners' attempt to root out subjective vices through objective means might make sense. But they were not based only upon that, or indeed even principally upon that. Their principal basis — which applies equally to attempts to reach subjective intent through ostensibly objective means — is simply that the Fourth Amendment's concern with "reasonableness" allows certain actions to be taken in certain circumstances, whatever the subjective intent. But even if our concern had been only an evidentiary one, petitioners' proposal would by no means assuage it. Indeed, it seems to us somewhat easier to figure out the intent of an individual officer than to plumb the collective consciousness of law enforcement in order to determine whether a "reasonable officer" would have been moved to act upon the traffic violation. While police manuals and standard procedures may sometimes provide objective assistance, ordinarily one would be reduced to speculating about the hypothetical reaction of a hypothetical constable — an exercise that might be called virtual subjectivity.

Moreover, police enforcement practices, even if they could be practicably assessed by a judge, vary from place to place and from time to time. We cannot accept that the search and seizure protections of the Fourth Amendment are so variable and can be made to turn upon such trivialities. The difficulty is illustrated by petitioners' arguments in this case. Their claim that a reasonable officer would not have made this stop is based largely on District of Columbia police regulations which permit plainclothes officers in unmarked vehicles to enforce traffic laws "only in the case of a violation that is so grave as to pose an immediate threat to the safety of others." This basis of invalidation would not apply in jurisdictions that had a different practice. And it would not have applied even in the District of Columbia, if Officer Soto had been wearing a uniform or patrolling in a marked police cruiser.

Petitioners argue that our cases support insistence upon police adherence to standard practices as an objective means of rooting out pretext. They cite no holding to that effect, and dicta in only two cases. In *Abel v. United States* (1960), the petitioner had been arrested by the Immigration and Naturalization Service (INS), on the basis of an administrative warrant that, he claimed, had been issued on pretextual grounds in order to enable the Federal Bureau of Investigation (FBI) to search his room after his arrest. We regarded this as an allegation of "serious misconduct," but rejected Abel's claims on the ground that "[a] finding of bad faith is . . . not open to us on th[e] record" in light of the findings below, including the finding that "'the proceedings taken by the [INS] differed in no respect from what would have been done in the case of an individual concerning whom [there was no pending FBI investigation].'" But it is a long leap from the proposition that following regular procedures is some evidence of lack of pretext to the proposition that failure to follow regular procedures proves (or is an operational substitute for) pretext. *Abel*, moreover, did not involve the assertion that pretext could invalidate a search or seizure for which there was probable cause — and even what it said about pretext in other contexts is plainly inconsistent with the views we later stated in *Robinson*, *Gustafson*, *Scott*, and *Villamonte-Marquez*. In the other case claimed to contain supportive dicta, *United States v. Robinson* (1973), in approving a search incident to an arrest for driving without a license, we noted that the arrest was "not a departure from established police department practice." That was followed, however, by the statement that "[w]e leave for another day questions which would arise on facts different from these." This is not even a dictum that purports to provide an answer, but merely one that leaves the question open.

III

In what would appear to be an elaboration on the "reasonable officer" test, petitioners argue that the balancing inherent in any Fourth Amendment inquiry requires us to weigh the governmental and individual interests implicated in a traffic stop such as we have here. That balancing, petitioners claim, does not support investigation of minor traffic infractions by plainclothes police in unmarked vehicles; such investigation only minimally advances the government's interest in traffic safety, and may indeed retard it by producing motorist confusion and alarm—a view said to be supported by the Metropolitan Police Department's own regulations generally prohibiting this practice. And as for the Fourth Amendment interests of the individuals concerned, petitioners point out that our cases acknowledge that even ordinary traffic stops entail "a possibly unsettling show of authority"; that they at best "interfere with freedom of movement, are inconvenient, and consume time" and at worst "may create substantial anxiety." That anxiety is likely to be even more pronounced when the stop is conducted by plainclothes officers in unmarked cars.

It is of course true that in principle every Fourth Amendment case, since it turns upon a "reasonableness" determination, involves a balancing of all relevant factors. With rare exceptions not applicable here, however, the result of that balancing is not in doubt where the search or seizure is based upon probable cause. That is why petitioners must rely upon cases like *Prouse* to provide examples of actual "balancing" analysis. There, the police action in question was a random traffic stop for the purpose of checking a motorist's license and vehicle registration, a practice that—like the practices at issue in the inventory search and administrative inspection cases upon which petitioners rely in making their "pretext" claim—involves police intrusion without the probable cause that is its traditional justification. Our opinion in *Prouse* expressly distinguished the case from a stop based on precisely what is at issue here: "probable cause to believe that a driver is violating any one of the multitude of applicable traffic and equipment regulations." It noted approvingly that "[t]he foremost method of enforcing traffic and vehicle safety regulations . . . is acting upon observed violations," which afford the "'quantum of individualized suspicion'" necessary to ensure that police discretion is sufficiently constrained. What is true of *Prouse* is also true of other cases that engaged in detailed "balancing" to decide the constitutionality of automobile stops, such as *Martinez-Fuerte*, which upheld checkpoint stops, and *Brignoni-Ponce*, which disallowed so-called "roving patrol" stops. The detailed "balancing" analysis was necessary because they involved seizures without probable cause.

Where probable cause has existed, the only cases in which we have found it necessary actually to perform the "balancing" analysis involved searches or seizures conducted in an extraordinary manner, unusually harmful to an individual's privacy or even physical interests—such as, for example, seizure by means of deadly force, see *Tennessee v. Garner* (1985), unannounced entry into a home, *see Wilson v. Arkansas* (1995), entry into a home without a warrant, *see Welsh v. Wisconsin* (1984), or physical penetration of the body. The making of a traffic stop out of uniform does not remotely qualify as such an extreme practice, and so is governed by the usual rule that probable cause to believe the law has been broken "outbalances" private interest in avoiding police contact.

Petitioners urge as an extraordinary factor in this case that the "multitude of applicable traffic and equipment regulations" is so large and so difficult to obey perfectly that virtually everyone is guilty of violation, permitting the police to single out almost whomever they wish for a stop. But we are aware of no principle that would allow us to decide at what point a code of law becomes so expansive and so commonly violated that infraction itself can no longer be the ordinary measure of the lawfulness of enforcement. And even if we could identify such exorbitant codes, we do not know by what standard (or what right) we would decide, as petitioners would have us do, which particular provisions are sufficiently important to merit enforcement.

For the run-of-the-mine case, which this surely is, we think there is no realistic alternative to the traditional common-law rule that probable cause justifies a search and seizure.

• • •

Here the District Court found that the officers had probable cause to believe that petitioners had violated the traffic code. That rendered the stop reasonable under the Fourth Amendment, the evidence thereby discovered admissible, and the upholding of the convictions by the Court of Appeals for the District of Columbia Circuit correct. The judgment is affirmed.

NOTES AND QUESTIONS

1. Note carefully how the police first had their suspicions "aroused" here. It had nothing to do with traffic. It was what most would think was an entirely benign observation: "a dark Pathfinder truck with temporary license plates and youthful occupants waiting at a stop sign, the driver looking down into the lap of the passenger at his right." Why would this arouse suspicion? In the 1990s motorists often consulted roadmaps, or printed out Mapquest directions for navigational guidance. Maybe the "youthful occupants" of the car were lost.

What if at the suppression hearing the police officers had admitted that they began observing the defendants and then followed the Pathfinder because its occupants were Black. Does *Whren* tell us that this would not be a Fourth Amendment violation? Would it be an Equal Protection Clause violation?

Would such an admission by the police bring the facts within the rule of *Oyler v. Boles*, 368 U.S. 448, 546 (1962) (prosecutors cannot bring criminal charges based on unconstitutional considerations such as race)? For an affirmative answer to this question, *see* Gabriel J. Chin & Charles J. Vernon, *Reasonable but Unconstitutional: Racial Profiling and the Radical Objectivity of* Whren v. United States, 83 Geo. Wash. L. Rev. 882, 932-34 (2015) (arguing that in such a scenario the resulting arrest would be a fruit of the poisonous tree).

2. We are often aghast at the notion that a police officer who observes a motorist commit a traffic violation will—depending on state law—often have the power to pull the motorist over, arrest him, perform a search incident to that arrest, and impound the vehicle (which will then be searched). And of course a police officer can embellish or flat out lie about a perceived violation. But can we take at least some comfort in the fact that traffic violations—speeding, wearing a seatbelt, using a turn signal, etc.—are usually marked by bright lines?

Certainly not in Washington, D.C. The Court notes that Officer Soto had probable cause—his actual beliefs and testimony at the suppression hearing are irrelevant, of course—to believe the following terms of the D.C. traffic code had been violated: D.C. Mun. Regs. §§ 2213.4 (1995) ("An operator shall . . . give full time and attention to the operation of the vehicle"); 2204.3 ("No person shall turn any vehicle . . . without giving an appropriate signal"); 2200.3 ("No person shall drive a vehicle . . . at a speed greater than is reasonable and prudent under the conditions").

Each of these requirements has a layer of discretion baked into it, just adding additional layers of discretion to the powers of the police.

3. Officer Soto did actually testify at the suppression hearing. And it's a shame that not one Justice on the Supreme Court or one judge on the D.C. Circuit panel dissented, or at least concurred, in order to discuss his testimony. Officer Soto testified that he did not intend to issue a ticket to the driver for stopping too long at the stop sign—he lacked authority to do so—but that he wished to stop the Pathfinder to inquire why it sped off without signaling in a school area. *United States v. Whren*, 53 F.3d 371, 373 (D.C. Cir. 1995). There is no suggestion there was cross-examination on whether school was in session that "evening."

4. Why does the Court go out of its way to decide the Fourth Amendment racial bias issue? Note that defendants had not argued they were stopped because they were Black. They argued, rather, that allowing the police to have the discretion to pull over anyone who has committed a civil traffic violation creates a risk that decisions will be made for impermissible reasons, such as race. Note that this type of argument has had some success in death penalty challenges.

Relatedly, how is it possible that *Whren* is a 9-0 decision?

5. Is *Whren* unusual in that the issue of pretext can be resolved on a purely objective basis in that (a) the traffic offenses were only civil violations and (b) the officers lacked authority to enforce the traffic laws under municipal regulations?

6. In two states, courts have interpreted state law to prohibit in at least some circumstances the sort of pretextual stop blessed in *Whren*. *See State v. Ladson*, 979 P.2d 833, 842 (Wash. 1999) (holding that while "police may enforce the traffic code . . . [t]hey may not, however, use that authority as a pretext or justification to avoid the warrant requirement for an unrelated criminal investigation"); *State v. Arreola*, 290 P.3d 983, 991 (Wash. 2012) (retreating from *Ladson* in a case involving a "mixed-motive" traffic stop). *See State v. Ochoa*, 206 P.3d 143, 148 (N.M. Ct. App. 2008) (refusing to follow *Whren* and finding its "analysis unpersuasive and incompatible with our state's distinctively protective standards for searches and seizures of automobiles").

For a discussion of how these and other courts have grappled with *Whren*, *see* Margaret Lawton, *State Responses to the* Whren *Decision*, 66 Case W. Rsrv. L. Rev. 1039 (2016).

For a "rewriting" of *Whren* in the voice of the late Justice Thurgood Marshall, see Devon W. Carbado & Jonathan Feingold, *Rewriting* Whren v. United States, 68 UCLA L. Rev. 1678 (2022).

7. A dataset of over 8 million traffic stops generated in the state of Washington in the period after the ban on pretext stops was essentially lifted in the *Arreola* case, *supra*, has confirmed what many have long suspected: that pretext stops disproportionately target drivers of color. *See* Stephen Rushin & Griffin Edwards, *An Empirical Assessment of Pretextual Stops and Racial Profiling*, 73 Stan. L. Rev. 637, 697 (2021) ("The data from Washington suggest that legal rules giving police officers increased discretion to conduct pretextual or mixed-motive traffic stops may contribute to inequality by facilitating racial profiling.").

Contemporaneous with *Whren* was a New Jersey case featuring data on racial profiling in traffic stops on the New Jersey Turnpike.

State v. Soto

734 A.2d 350 (N.J. 1996)

Robert E. Francis, J.S.C.

These are consolidated motions to suppress under the equal protection and due process clauses of the Fourteenth Amendment. Seventeen defendants of African ancestry claim that their arrests on the New Jersey Turnpike south of exit 3 between 1988 and 1991 result from discriminatory enforcement of the traffic laws by the New Jersey State Police. After a lengthy hearing, I find defendants have established a prima facie case of selective enforcement which the State has failed to rebut requiring suppression of all contraband and evidence seized.

Defendants base their claim of institutional racism primarily on statistics. During discovery, each side created a database of all stops and arrests by State Police members patrolling the Turnpike between exits 1 and 7A out of the Moorestown Station for thirty-five randomly selected days between April 1988 and May 1991 from arrest reports, patrol charts, radio logs and traffic tickets. The databases are essentially the same. Both sides counted 3060 stops which the State found to include 1212 race identified stops (39.6%), the defense 1146 (37.4%).

To establish a standard against which to compare the stop data, the defense conducted a traffic survey and a violator survey. Dr. John Lamberth, Chairman of the Psychology Department at Temple University who I found is qualified as an expert in statistics and social psychology, designed both surveys.

The traffic survey was conducted over twenty-one randomly selected two and one-half hour sessions between June 11 and June 24, 1993 and between 8:00 a.m. and 8:00 p.m. at four sites, two northbound and two southbound, between exits 1 and 3 of the Turnpike. Teams supervised by Fred Last, Esq., of the Office of the Public Defender observed and recorded the number of vehicles that passed them except for large trucks, tractor-trailers, buses and government vehicles, how many contained a "black" occupant and the state of origin of each vehicle. Of the 42,706 vehicles counted, 13.5% had a black occupant. Dr. Lamberth testified that this percentage is consistent with the 1990 Census figures for the eleven states from where almost 90% of the observed vehicles were registered. He said it is also consistent with a study done by the Triangle Group for the U.S. Department of Transportation with which he was familiar.

The violator survey was conducted over ten sessions in four days in July 1993 by Mr. Last traveling between exits 1 and 3 in his vehicle at sixty miles per hour on cruise control after the speedometer had been calibrated and observing and recording the number of vehicles that passed him, the number of vehicles he passed and how many had a black occupant. Mr. Last counted a total of 2096 vehicles other than large trucks, tractor-trailers, buses and government vehicles of which 2062 or 98.1% passed him going in excess of sixty miles per hour including 306 with a black occupant equaling about 15% of those vehicles clearly speeding. Multiple violators, that is those violating the speed limit and committing some other moving violation like tailgating, also equaled about 15% black. Dr. Lamberth testified that the difference between the percentage of black violators and the percentage of black travelers from the surveys is statistically insignificant and that there is no evidence traffic patterns changed between the period April 1988 to May 1991 in the databases and June-July 1993 when the surveys were done.

Using 13.5% as the standard or benchmark against which to compare the stop data, Dr. Lamberth found that 127 or 46.2% of the race identified stops between exits 1 and 3 were of blacks constituting an absolute disparity of 32.7%, a comparative disparity of 242% (32.7% divided by 13.5%) and 16.35 standard deviations. By convention, something is considered statistically significant if it would occur by chance fewer than five times in a hundred (over two standard deviations). In case I were to determine that the appropriate stop data for comparison with the standard is the stop data for the entire portion of the Turnpike patrolled by the Moorestown Station in recognition of the fact that the same troopers patrol between exits 3 and 7A as patrol between exits 1 and 3, Dr. Lamberth found that 408 or 35.6% of the race identified stops between exits 1 and 7A were of blacks constituting an absolute disparity of 22.1%, a comparative disparity of 164% and 22.1 standard deviations.3 He opined it is highly unlikely such statistics could have occurred randomly or by chance.

Defendants also presented the testimony of Dr. Joseph B. Kadane, an eminently qualified statistician. Among his many credentials, Dr. Kadane is a full professor of statistics and social sciences at Carnegie Mellon University, headed the Department of Statistics there between 1972 and 1981 and is a Fellow of the American Statistical Association, having served on its board of directors and a number of its committees and held various editorships on its

Journal. Dr. Kadane testified that in his opinion both the traffic and violator surveys were well designed, carefully performed and statistically reliable for analysis. From the surveys and the defense database, he calculated that a black was 4.85 times as likely as a white to be stopped between exits 1 and 3. This calculation led him to "suspect" a racially non-neutral stopping policy. While he noted that the surveys were done in 1993 and compared to data from 1988 to 1991, he was nevertheless satisfied that the comparisons were useable and accurate within a few percent. He was not concerned that the violator survey failed to count cars going less than sixty miles per hour and travelling behind Mr. Last when he started a session. He was concerned, however, with the fact that only 37.4% of the stops in the defense database were race identified. In order to determine if the comparisons were sensitive to the missing racial data, he did calculations performed on the log odds of being stopped. Whether he assumed the probability of having one's race recorded if black and stopped is the same as if white and stopped or two or three times as likely, the log odds were still greater than .99 that blacks were stopped at higher rates than whites on the Turnpike between exits 1 and 3 during the period April 1988 to May 1991. He therefore concluded that the comparisons were not sensitive to the missing racial data.

Supposing that the disproportionate stopping of blacks was related to police discretion, the defense studied the traffic tickets issued by State Police members between exits 1 and 7A on the thirty-five randomly selected days broken down by State Police unit. There are 533 racially identified tickets in the databases issued by either the now disbanded Radar Unit, the Tactical Patrol Unit or general road troopers ("Patrol Unit"). The testimony indicates that the Radar Unit focused mainly on speeders using a radar van and chase cars and exercised limited discretion regarding which vehicles to stop. The Tac-Pac concentrates on traffic problems at specific locations and exercises somewhat more discretion as regards which vehicles to stop. Responsible to provide general law enforcement, the Patrol Unit exercises by far the most discretion among the three units. From Mr. Last's count, Dr. Lamberth computed that 18% of the tickets issued by the Radar Unit were to blacks, 23.8% of the tickets issued by the Tac-Pac were to blacks while 34.2% of the tickets issued by the Patrol Unit were to blacks. South of exit 3, Dr. Lamberth computed that 19.4% of the tickets issued by the Radar Unit were to blacks, 0.0% of the tickets issued by the Tac-Pac were to blacks while 43.8% of the tickets issued by the Patrol Unit were to blacks. In his opinion, the Radar Unit percentages are statistically consistent with the standard established by the violator survey, but the differences between the Radar Unit and the Patrol Unit between both exits 1 and 3 and 1 and 7A are statistically significant or well in excess of two standard deviations.

The State presented the testimony of Dr. Leonard Cupingood to challenge or refute the statistical evidence offered by the defense. I found Dr. Cupingood is qualified to give expert testimony in the field of statistics based on his Ph.D in statistics from Temple and his work experience with the Center for Forensic Economic Studies, a for profit corporation headquartered in Philadelphia. Dr. Cupingood collaborated with Dr. Bernard Siskin, his superior at the Center for Forensic Economic Studies and a former chairman of the Department of Statistics at Temple.

Dr. Cupingood had no genuine criticism of the defense traffic survey. Rather, he centered his criticism of the defense statistical evidence on the violator survey. Throughout his testimony he maintained that the violator survey failed to capture the relevant data which he opined was the racial mix of those speeders most likely to be stopped or the "tail of the distribution." He even recommended the State authorize him to design a study to collect this data, but the State declined. He was unclear, though, how he would design a study to ascertain in a safe way the vehicle going the fastest above the speed limit at a given time at a given location and the race of its occupants without involving the credibility of State Police members. In any event, his supposition that maybe blacks drive faster than whites above the speed limit was repudiated by all State Police members called by the State who were questioned about it.

Colonel Clinton Pagano, Trooper Donald Nemeth, Trooper Stephen Baumann and Detective Timothy Grant each testified that blacks drive indistinguishably from whites. Moreover, Dr. Cupingood acknowledged that he knew of no study indicating that blacks drive worse than whites. Nor could he reconcile the notion with the evidence that 37% of the unticketed stops between exits 1 and 7A in his database were black and 63% of those between exits 1 and 3. Dr. James Fyfe, a criminal justice professor at Temple who the defense called in its rebuttal case and who I found is qualified as an expert in police science and police procedures, also testified that there is nothing in the literature or in his personal experience to support the theory that blacks drive differently from whites.

Convinced in his belief that the defense 15% standard or benchmark was open to question, Dr. Cupingood attempted to find the appropriate benchmark to compare with the databases. He did three studies of presumedly race-blind stops: night stops versus day stops; radar stops versus non-radar stops and drinking driving arrests triggered by calls for service.

In his study of night stops versus day stops, he compared the percentage of stops of blacks at night between exits 1 and 7A in the databases with the percentage of stops of blacks during daytime and found that night stops were 37.3% black versus 30.2% for daytime stops. Since he presumed the State Police generally cannot tell race at night, he concluded the higher percentage for night stops of blacks supported a standard well above 15%. His premise that the State Police generally cannot recognize race at night, however, is belied by the evidence. On July 16, 1994 between 9:40 p.m. and 11:00 p.m. Ahmad S. Corbitt, now an assistant deputy public defender, together with Investigator Minor of the Office of the Public Defender drove on the Turnpike at 55 miles per hour for a while and parked perpendicular to the Turnpike at a rest stop for a while to see if they could make out the races of the occupants of the vehicles they observed. Mr. Corbitt testified that the two could identify blacks versus whites about 80% of the time in the moving mode and close to 100% in the stationary mode. Over and above this proof is the fact the databases establish that the State Police only stopped an average of eight black occupied vehicles per night between exits 1 and 7A. Dr. Cupingood conceded a trooper could probably identify one or two black motorists per night.

Next, in his study of radar stops versus non-radar stops, Dr. Cupingood focused on the race identified tickets where radar was used in the databases and found that 28.5% of them were issued to blacks. Since he assumed that radar is race neutral, he suggested 28.5% might be the correct standard. As Dr. Kadane said in rebuttal, this study is fundamentally flawed because it assumes what is in question or that the people stopped are the best measure of who is eligible to be stopped. If racial prejudice were afoot, the standard would be tainted. In addition, although a radar device is race-blind, the operator may not be. Of far more significance is the defense study comparing the traffic tickets issued by the Radar, Tac-Pac and Patrol Units which shows again that where radar is used by a unit concerned primarily with speeders and acting with little or no discretion like the Radar Unit, the percentage of tickets issued to blacks is consistent with their percentage on the highway.

And lastly in his effort to find the correct standard, Dr. Cupingood considered a DUI study done by Lieutenant Fred Madden, Administrative Officer of the Records and Identification Section of the State Police. Lt. Madden tabulated DUI arrests between July 1988 and June 1991 statewide, statewide excluding the State Police, for Troop D of the State Police which patrols the entire length of the Turnpike, for Moorestown Station of Troop D and for Moorestown Station south of exit 3 broken down by race and between patrol related versus calls for service (i.e. accidents, motorist aids and other—the arrested motorist coming to the attention of the State Police by a toll-taker or civilian). Since Dr. Cupingood believed DUI arrests from calls for service were race neutral, he adopted the percentage of DUI arrests of blacks for the Moorestown Station from calls for service of 23% as a possible standard. Like his radar versus non-radar stop study, his use of the DUI arrest study is fundamentally flawed because he assumed what is in question. Further, he erred in assuming that DUI arrests from calls for service involve no discretion. While the encounters involve no discretion, the arrests surely do. He admitted that race/discretion may explain the following widespread statistics in the DUI arrest study:

Statewide (all departments)	12% black
Statewide (excluding State Police)	10.4% black
State Police	16% black
Troop D	23% black
Moorestown Station	34% black
Moorestown Station patrol related	41% black
Moorestown Station patrol related south of exit 3	50% black

After hearing the testimony of Kenneth Ruff and Kenneth Wilson, two former troopers called by the defense who were not reappointed at the end of their terms and who said they were trained and coached to make race based "profile" stops to increase their criminal arrests, the State asked Dr. Cupingood to study the race identified stops in his database and see how many possessed the profile characteristics cited by Ruff and Wilson, particularly how many were young (30 or under), black and male. Dr. Cupingood found that only 11.6% of the race identified stops were of young black males and only 6.6% of all stops were of young black males.

The defense then conducted a profile study of its own. It concentrated on the race identified stops of just blacks issued tickets and found that an adult black male was present in 88% of the cases where the gender of all occupants could be determined and that where gender and age could be determined, a black male 30 or younger was present in 63% of the cases. The defense study is more probative because it does concentrate on just stops of blacks issued tickets eliminating misleading comparisons with totals including whites or whites and a 62.6% group of race unknowns. Neither side, of course, could consider whether the blacks stopped and not issued tickets possessed profile characteristics since the databases contain no information about them.

Dr. Cupingood's so-called Mantel-Haentzel analysis ended the statistical evidence. He put forward this calculation of "expected black tickets" in an attempt to disprove the defense study showing the Patrol Unit, the unit with the most discretion, ticketed blacks at a rate not only well above the Radar and Tac-Pac Units, but also well above the standard fixed by the violator survey. The calculation insinuates that the Patrol Unit issued merely 5 excess tickets to blacks beyond what would have been expected. The calculation is worthless. First and foremost, Dr. Cupingood deleted the non-radar tickets which presumably involved a greater exercise of discretion. The role police discretion played in the issuance of tickets to blacks was the object of the defense study. Under the guise of comparing only things similarly situated, he thereupon deleted any radar tickets not issued in one of the four time periods he divided each of the thirty-five randomly selected days into for which there was not at least one race identified radar ticket issued by the Patrol Unit and at least one by the combined Radar, Tac-Pac Unit. He provided no justification for either creating the 140 time periods or combining the tickets of the Radar and Tac-Pac Units. To compound his defective analysis, he pooled the data in each time period into a single number and employed the resultant weighted average of the two units to compute the expected and excess, if any, tickets issued to blacks. By using weighted averages, he once again assumed the answer to the question he purported to address. He assumed the Patrol Unit gave the same number of tickets to blacks as did the Radar, Tac-Pac Unit, rather than test to see if it did. Even after "winnowing" the data, the comparison between the Patrol Unit and the Radar, Tac-Pac Unit is marginally statistically significant. Without winnowing, Dr. Kadane found the comparison of the radar tickets issued by the Patrol Unit to blacks with the radar tickets issued by the Radar, Tac-Pac Unit to blacks constituted 3.78 standard deviations which is distinctly above the 5% standard of statistical significance.

The defense did not rest on its statistical evidence alone. Along with the testimony of former troopers Kenneth Ruff and Kenneth Wilson about having been trained and coached to make race based profile stops but whose testimony is weakened by bias related to their not having been reappointed at the end of their terms, the defense elicited evidence through cross-examination of State witnesses and a rebuttal witness, Dr. James Fyfe, that the State Police hierarchy allowed, condoned, cultivated and tolerated discrimination between 1988 and 1991 in its crusade to rid New Jersey of the scourge of drugs.

Conjointly with the passage of the Comprehensive Drug Reform Act of 1987 and to advance the Attorney General's Statewide Action Plan for Narcotics Enforcement issued in January 1988 which "directed that the enforcement of our criminal drug laws shall be the highest priority law enforcement activity," Colonel Pagano formed the Drug Interdiction Training Unit (DITU) in late 1987 consisting of two supervisors and ten other members, two from each Troop selected for their successful seizure statistics, ". . . to actually patrol with junior road personnel and provide critical on-the-job training in recognizing potential violators." State Police Plan For Action dated July 7, 1987, at p. 14. According to Colonel Pagano, the DITU program was intended to be one step beyond the existing coach program to impart to newer troopers insight into drug enforcement and the "criminal program" (patrol related arrests) in general. DITU was disbanded in or around July 1992.

No training materials remain regarding the training DITU members themselves received, and few training materials remain regarding the training DITU members provided the newer troopers except for a batch of checklists. Just one impact study was ever prepared regarding the effectiveness of the DITU program rather than periodic impact evaluations and studies as required by S.O.P. F4 dated January 12, 1989, but this one undated report marked D-62 in evidence only provided statistics about the number of investigations conducted, the number of persons involved and the quantity and value of drugs seized without indicating the race of those involved or the number of fruitless investigations broken down by race. In the opinion of Dr. Fyfe, retention of training materials is important for review of the propriety of the training and to discern agency policy, and preparation of periodic impact evaluations and studies is important not only to determine the effectiveness of the program from a numbers standpoint, but more than that to enable administration to monitor and control the quality of the program and its impact on the public, especially a crackdown program like DITU which placed so much emphasis on stopping drug transportation by the use of "consents" to search following traffic stops in order to prevent constitutional excesses.

Despite the paucity of training materials and lack of periodic and complete impact evaluations and studies, a glimpse of the work of DITU emerges from the preserved checklists and the testimony of Sergeants Brian Caffrey and David Cobb. Sergeant Caffrey was the original assistant supervisor of DITU and became the supervisor in 1989. Sergeant Cobb was an original member of DITU and became the assistant supervisor in 1989. Sergeant Caffrey left DITU sometime in 1992, Sergeant Cobb sometime in 1991. Both testified that a major purpose of DITU was to teach trainees tip-offs and techniques about what to look for and do to talk or "dig" their way into a vehicle after, not before, a motor vehicle stop to effectuate patrol related arrests. Both denied teaching or using race as a tip-off either before or after a stop. Nevertheless, Sergeant Caffrey condoned a comment by a DITU trainer during the time he was the supervisor of DITU stating:

> Trooper Fash previously had DITU training, and it showed in the way he worked. He has become a little reluctant to stop cars in lieu [sic] of the Channel 9 News Report. He was told as long as he uses Title 39 he can stop any car he wants. He enjoys DITU and would like to ride again.

As the defense observes in its closing brief, "Why would a trooper who is acting in a racially neutral fashion become reluctant to stop cars as a result of a news story charging that racial minorities were being targeted [by the New Jersey State Police]?" Even A.A.G. Ronald Susswein, Deputy Director of the Division of Criminal Justice, acknowledged that this comment is incomplete because it fails to add the caveat, "as long as he doesn't also use race or ethnicity." Further, Sergeant Caffrey testified that "ethnicity is something to keep in mind" albeit not a tip-off and that he taught attendees at both the annual State Police in-service training session in March 1987 and the special State Police in-service training sessions in July and August 1987 that Hispanics are mainly involved in drug trafficking and showed them the film Operation Pipeline wherein the ethnicity of those arrested, mostly Hispanics, is prominently depicted. Dr. Fyfe criticized Sergeant Caffrey's teaching Hispanics are mainly involved and his showing Operation Pipeline as well as the showing of the Jamaican Posse film wherein only blacks are depicted as drug traffickers at the 1989 annual State Police in-service training session saying trainers should not teach what they do not intend their trainees to act upon. At a minimum, teaching Hispanics are mainly involved in drug trafficking and showing films depicting mostly Hispanics and blacks trafficking in drugs at training sessions worked at cross-purposes with concomitant instruction pointing out that neither race nor ethnicity may be considered in making traffic stops.

Key corroboration for finding the State Police hierarchy allowed and tolerated discrimination came from Colonel Pagano. Colonel Pagano was Superintendent of the State Police from 1975 to February 1990. He testified there was a noisy demand in the 1980s to get drugs off the streets. In accord, Attorney General Cary Edwards and he made drug interdiction the number one priority of law enforcement. He helped formulate the Attorney General's Statewide Action Plan for Narcotics Enforcement and established DITU within the State Police. He kept an eye on DITU through conversations with staff officers and Sergeants Mastella and Caffrey and review of reports generated under the traditional reporting system and D-62 in evidence. He had no thought DITU would engage in constitutional violations. He knew all State Police members were taught that they were guardians of the Constitution and that targeting any race was unconstitutional and poor police practice to boot. He recognized it was his responsibility to see that race was not a factor in who was stopped, searched and arrested. When he became Superintendent, he formed the Internal Affairs Bureau to investigate citizen complaints against State Police members to maintain the integrity of the Division. Substantiated deviations from regulations resulted in sanctions, additional training or counseling.

More telling, however, is what Colonel Pagano said and did, or did not do, in response to the Channel 9 exposé entitled "Without Just Cause" which aired in 1989 and which troubled Trooper Fash and what he did not do in response to complaints of profiling from the NAACP and ACLU and these consolidated motions to suppress and similar motions in Warren and Middlesex Counties. He said to Joe Collum of Channel 9 that "[violating rights of motorists was] of serious concern [to him], but no where near the concern that I think we have got to look to in trying to correct some of the problems we find with the criminal element in this State" and "the bottom line is that those stops were not made on the basis of *race alone*" (emphasis added). Since perhaps these isolated comments were said inadvertently or edited out of context, a truer reflection of his attitude about claims of racism would appear to be his videotaped remarks shown all members of the State Police at roll call in conjunction with the WOR series. Thereon he clearly said that he did not want targeting or discriminatory enforcement and that "[w]hen you put on this uniform, you leave your biases and your prejudices behind." But he also said as regarded the charge of a Trenton school principal named Jones that he had been stopped on the Turnpike and threatened, intimidated and assaulted by a trooper, "We know that the teacher assaulted the trooper. He didn't have a driver's license or a registration *for his fancy new Mercedes*" (emphasis added). And he called Paul McLemore, the first African-American trooper in New Jersey and now a practicing attorney and who spoke of discrimination within the ranks of the State Police, "an ingrate." And he told the members to "keep the heat on" and then assured them:

> . . . [H]ere at Division Headquarters we'll make sure that when the wheels start to squeak, we'll do whatever we can to make sure that you're supported out in the field. . . . Anything that goes toward implementing the Drug Reform Act is important. And, we'll handle the squeaky wheels here.

He admitted the Internal Affairs Bureau was not designed to investigate general complaints, so he could not refer the general complaints of discrimination to it for scrutiny. Yet he never requested the Analytical Unit to investigate stop data from radio logs, patrol charts and tickets or search and seizure data from arrest reports, operations reports, investigation reports and consent to search forms, not even after the Analytical Unit informed him in a report on arrests by region, race and crime that he had requested from it for his use in the WOR series that ". . . arrests are not a valid reflection of stops (data relative to stops with respect to race is not compiled)." The databases compiled for these motions attest, of course, to the fact that race identified stop data could have been compiled. He testified he could not launch an investigation into every general complaint because of limited resources and that there was insufficient evidence of discrimination in the Channel 9 series, the NAACP and ACLU complaints and the various motions to suppress for him to spend his "precious" resources. In short, he left the issue of discrimination up to the courts and months of testimony in this and other counties at State expense.

The right to be free from discrimination is firmly supported by the Fourteenth Amendment to the United States Constitution and the protections of Article I, paragraphs 1 and 5 of the New Jersey Constitution of 1947. To be sure, "[t]he eradication of the 'cancer of discrimination' has long been one of our State's highest priorities." It is indisputable, therefore, that the police may not stop a motorist based on race or any other invidious classification.

Generally, however, the inquiry for determining the constitutionality of a stop or a search and seizure is limited to "whether the conduct of the law enforcement officer who undertook the [stop or] search was objectively reasonable, without regard to his or her underlying motives or intent." Thus, it has been said that the courts will not inquire into the motivation of a police officer whose stop of a vehicle was based upon a traffic violation committed in his presence. But where objective evidence establishes "that a police agency has embarked upon an officially sanctioned or de facto policy of targeting minorities for investigation and arrest," any evidence seized will be suppressed to deter future insolence in office by those charged with enforcement of the law and to maintain judicial integrity.

Statistics may be used to make out a case of targeting minorities for prosecution of traffic offenses provided the comparison is between the racial composition of the motorist population violating the traffic laws and the racial composition of those arrested for traffic infractions on the relevant roadway patrolled by the police agency. While defendants have the burden of proving "the existence of purposeful discrimination," discriminatory intent may be inferred from statistical proof presenting a stark pattern or an even less extreme pattern in certain limited contexts. *Kennedy, supra*, implies that discriminatory intent may be inferred from statistical proof in a traffic stop context probably because only uniform variables (Title 39 violations) are relevant to the challenged stops and the State has an opportunity to explain the statistical disparity. "[A] selection procedure that is susceptible of abuse . . . supports the presumption of discrimination raised by the statistical showing." *Castaneda v. Partida* (1977).

Once defendants expose a prima facie case of selective enforcement, the State generally cannot rebut it by merely calling attention to possible flaws or unmeasured variables in defendants' statistics. Rather, the State must introduce specific evidence showing that either there actually are defects which bias the results or the missing factors, when properly organized and accounted for, eliminate or explain the disparity. Nor will mere denials or reliance on the good faith of the officers suffice.

Here, defendants have proven at least a de facto policy on the part of the State Police out of the Moorestown Station of targeting blacks for investigation and arrest between April 1988 and May 1991 both south of exit 3 and between exits 1 and 7A of the Turnpike. Their surveys satisfy *Wards Cove* [*Packing Co. v. Atonio*, 490 U.S. 642, (1989)], *supra*. The statistical disparities and standard deviations revealed are indeed stark. The discretion devolved upon general road troopers to stop any car they want as long as Title 39 is used evinces a selection process that is susceptible of abuse. The utter failure of the State Police hierarchy to monitor and control a crackdown program like DITU or investigate the many claims of institutional discrimination manifests its indifference if not acceptance. Against all this, the State submits only denials and the conjecture and flawed studies of Dr. Cupingood.

The eradication of illegal drugs from our State is an obviously worthy goal, but not at the expense of individual rights. As Justice Brandeis so wisely said dissenting in *Olmstead v. United States* (1928):

> Experience should teach us to be most on our guard to protect liberty when the government's purposes are beneficent. Men born to freedom are naturally alert to repel invasion of their liberty by evil-minded rulers. The greatest dangers to liberty lurk in insidious encroachment by men of zeal, well-meaning but without understanding.

Motions granted.

NOTES AND QUESTIONS

1. The data here are shocking but perhaps not surprising. But note the other powerful aspects of the defense case even in the absence of the existence of complete State Police training materials.

2. Note the central importance in the Drug Interdiction Training Unit, established 1987, of teaching trainees to "dig their way into a vehicle" after a traffic stop. This is consistent with the teachings of Remsberg and Operation Pipeline, *supra*.

New Jersey Turnpike, Exit 3

3. Note the court's use of federal equal protection case law to conclude that defendants established a prima facie case (at least) of purposeful discrimination that the state was able to rebut. The decision in *Soto* pre-dated *Whren* by just three months.

If a car is parked and not moving, can there be a pretextual "traffic" stop? Do the government's interests in enforcing traffic codes apply equally to parking regulations? Are there any violations of law that are beyond the reach of *Terry* and *Whren*?

United States v. Johnson

874 F.3d 571 (7th Cir. 2017)

Easterbrook, Circuit Judge.

Police in Milwaukee saw a car stopped within 15 feet of a crosswalk, which is unlawful unless the car is "actually engaged in loading or unloading or in receiving or discharging passengers." Wis. Stat. § 346.53. One police car drew up parallel to the stopped car, while another drew up behind. Shining lights through the car's windows (it was after 7 p.m. in January), police saw a passenger in the back seat try to hide a firearm. Randy Johnson, the passenger, was prosecuted for possessing a weapon that, as a felon, he was forbidden to have. 18 U.S.C. § 922(g)(1). After the district court denied his motion to suppress the gun, Johnson entered a conditional guilty plea and was sentenced to 46 months' imprisonment. A panel of this court affirmed the conviction, but that decision was vacated when the full court decided to hear the appeal en banc.

Johnson concedes that the car was stopped 7 or 8 feet from a crosswalk. The district court held that this gave the police probable cause to issue a ticket, a process that entails a brief seizure of the car and its occupants. As Officer Conway approached he saw Johnson make movements that led him to infer that Johnson was hiding something such as alcohol, drugs, or a gun. Concerned for his safety, Conway ordered Johnson to get out of the car. Once the car's door was open, Conway saw a gun on the floor. This led to Johnson's arrest.

Johnson says that the judge should have suppressed the gun, because the statutory exception for receiving or discharging cargo or passengers means that the police did not have adequate reason to issue a ticket or even to approach the car until they had observed long enough to know that the car was not within the scope of the exception. The district court rejected that contention, as do we.

First, the district court found that, when the police approached, all four doors of the car were shut and no one was standing nearby, so that the exception was inapplicable. That finding is not clearly erroneous. Indeed, Johnson does not contest it.

Second, although Johnson contends that Wisconsin's judiciary would treat a driver's stop to buy something from a nearby store as within the "loading or unloading or . . . receiving or discharging passengers" exception, we need not address that issue of state law. Officers who had probable cause — recall that it has been stipulated that the car was within 15 feet of the crosswalk — were entitled to approach the car before resolving statutory exceptions. Police possessed of probable cause can hand out tickets (or make arrests) and leave to the judicial process the question whether a defense, exception, proviso, or other limitation applies. Parking-enforcement patrols approach stopped cars countless times every day. Depending on what they find, sometimes they write tickets and sometimes they don't. If the car is occupied, the difference may turn on what the driver says. The Fourth Amendment requires searches and seizures to be reasonable; it does not demand that police and other public officials resolve all possible exceptions before approaching a stopped car and asking the first question.

When denying Johnson's motion to suppress, the district court relied on *Whren v. United States*, (1996), which holds that probable cause to believe that a car's driver is engaged in speeding or another motor-vehicle violation supports a stop and arrest—and that the possibility of an ulterior motive, such as a desire to investigate drugs, does not matter, because analysis under the Fourth Amendment is objective. Johnson, who believes that the police had an ulterior motive for approaching his car, contends that *Whren* does not apply to infractions by stopped cars, which he labels parking violations rather than moving violations.

Yet *Whren* did not create a special rule for moving offenses. The two doctrines that underlie *Whren*'s holding—(1) that probable cause justifies stops and arrests, even for fine-only offenses, and (2) that analysis of search-and-seizure issues disregards the officers' thoughts—are of general application.

We assumed in *United States v. Shields* (7th Cir. 2015), that *Whren* applies to parked as well as moving vehicles, and to parking violations as well as moving violations. Every other circuit that has addressed the issue expressly has so held. If there were to be a difference, it would be easier to deem "reasonable" (the constitutional standard) an officer's approach to a car already stopped than the halting of a car in motion. "[I]f police may pull over a vehicle if there is probable cause that a civil traffic violation has been committed, then [the police] surely did not violate the Fourth Amendment by walking up to [a suspect], who was sitting in a car that rested in a spot where it was violating one of [a city's] parking regulations."

The stop of a moving vehicle is more intrusive than approaching a parked car. Because the police approached Johnson's car with probable cause to believe that the driver was violating a traffic law, and the car was not moving, it is unnecessary to consider today how *Terry* applies when cars are in motion. It is enough to conclude that *Whren* applies to both parking and moving offenses.

We grant that the police did more than just stroll up: two squad cars, which bathed the parked car in bright light, implied that the occupants were not free to drive away. The district judge treated this as a seizure; so do we. But issuing a ticket always entails a brief seizure. Johnson concedes that the driver of a car approached with probable cause to investigate a parking offense is not entitled to leave. What is more, when the officers approached this parked car, no one was in the driver's seat. (The driver was inside a liquor store making a purchase.) So both as a matter of the suspects' legal entitlements and as a matter of brute fact, it did not make any difference whether the police approached with two cars rather than one, or whether the cars' spotlights were on. Johnson's car was not going anywhere.

The district court concluded that the way in which the stop was conducted was not responsible for the gun's discovery. That finding is not clearly erroneous. We therefore do not consider whether the officers' show of force was excessive under the circumstances. The United States contends that the use of two cars and searchlights was reasonable to reduce the risk the officers faced in making a nighttime stop in a high-crime area, circumstances in which a city will not rely on foot patrols to enforce traffic laws. The district court did not address that subject; we do not either.

Finally, it is worth noting that Johnson has never contended that the police considered the race of the car's occupants when deciding to approach it, or when deciding to use two cruisers rather than one. Indeed, Johnson has not contended that the police even observed the race of the car's occupants until after they approached it; recall that Johnson's principal contention is that police had the car in view for only an instant before deciding to approach. We therefore do not consider whether, and if so when, using racial criteria to select among potential targets of investigation would require the suppression of evidence.

Affirmed.

HAMILTON, Circuit Judge, joined by ROVNER and WILLIAMS, Circuit Judges, dissenting.

Five officers in two police cars seized the passengers of a stopped car. The officers swooped in on the car, suddenly parking close beside and behind it with bright lights shining in from both directions, opening the doors, pulling all the passengers out and handcuffing them. The district court found, and the majority and I agree, that the passengers were seized as the officers swarmed them, before the officers had any sign that one passenger had a firearm. The sole basis for this intrusive and even terrifying "investigatory stop"? A suspected parking violation . . . for parking too close to an unmarked crosswalk.

The majority errs by extending *Terry v. Ohio* (1968), and *Whren v. United States* (1996), to allow this pretextual seizure based on the suspected parking violation. This extension is not supported by existing law. It also runs contrary to the core Fourth Amendment standard of reasonableness. No other appellate court has tolerated such police tactics to address a suspected parking violation. Nor should we, at least absent extraordinary circumstances not present here. We should find a Fourth Amendment violation in this seizure of the passengers in the car idling outside a store.

As applied to moving traffic violations, Fourth Amendment doctrine has evolved in recent decades to give police officers so much discretion, including the power to conduct pretextual traffic stops, that some scholars have described this power as the "the twentieth-century version of the general warrant." Sarah A. Seo, The New Public, 125 Yale L.J. 1616, 1669 (2016); see also Barbara C. Salken, The General Warrant of the Twentieth Century? A Fourth Amendment Solution to Unchecked Discretion to Arrest for Traffic Offenses, 62 Temp. L. Rev. 221 (1989) (written before the most dramatic expansions of this discretion). The doctrinal evolution has enabled stops for what is often called "driving while black." See generally, e.g., David A. Harris, "Driving While Black" and All Other Traffic Offenses: The Supreme Court and Pretextual Traffic Stops, 87 J. Crim. L. & Criminology 544 (1997). Unless the target of such a seizure can offer evidence of racial motivation in the particular case, which is rarely available, such seizures are difficult to limit.

By extending *Terry* and *Whren* to the suspected parking violation in this case, the majority errs by taking the further step of enabling seizures that can be used for "parking while black." The majority's extension of doctrine is arguably defensible. But defensible does not mean correct. The police tactics here would never be tolerated in more affluent neighborhoods. This extension will further erode the Fourth Amendment, trading away privacy rights of some for the hope of more security for others, and stripping those targeted in searches of both security and privacy. We should find that the tactics in this case violated the Fourth Amendment. I respectfully dissent.

I

The Fourth Amendment provides: "The right of the people to be secure in their persons, houses, papers, and effects, against unreasonable searches and seizures, shall not be violated. . . ." "This inestimable right of personal security belongs as much to the citizen on the streets of our cities as to the homeowner closeted in his study to dispose of his secret affairs." In *Terry*, the Supreme Court struck a practical and necessary balance between protecting privacy and allowing effective law enforcement. *Terry* did so by allowing a brief investigatory stop in response to signs of an imminent armed robbery.

In applying *Terry*, "which is grounded in the standard of reasonableness embodied in the Fourth Amendment," the court "balances the nature and quality of the intrusion on personal security against the importance of the governmental interests alleged to justify the intrusion." When the governmental interest is based on a car parked too close to a crosswalk, the balance looks very different from the balance in *Terry*. The alleged governmental interests pale in comparison to the intrusion on personal security in this seizure.

Before digging into the doctrinal issues, consider the circumstances of this seizure. It was just after 7:30 p.m. on January 8, 2014 in Milwaukee. It was dark and very cold, during the memorable "Polar Vortex" of that winter. The air temperature was eight degrees Fahrenheit, with a wind-chill of twenty degrees below zero and eight inches of snow on the ground. The streets were quiet.

In a tough neighborhood in Milwaukee, five police officers were patrolling together in two squad cars. They were part of the Milwaukee Police Department's Neighborhood Task Force Street Crimes Unit assigned to patrol so-called "hot spots." As one officer testified, "part of our initiative is to look for smaller infractions and hope that possibly they may lead to bigger and better things," posing the danger of police overreach that was realized here.

In this search for "bigger and better things," the officers saw a car parked on a side street in front of a liquor store. The motor was running. The officer in charge saw an opportunity. The car was within fifteen feet of a crosswalk. That meant it might have been parked illegally.

The officer in charge made a split-second decision. The police cars quickly turned onto the side street and closed in on the parked car—one police car pulled up next to and a little in front of the parked car, and the other pulled up right behind it. From both directions, the police lit up the parked car with headlights and spotlights. The five officers got out of their cars and immediately opened the doors of the parked car, shined a flashlight at the passengers, and ordered the passengers out of the car and handcuffed them. One, defendant Johnson, was unlawfully in possession of a firearm that he had placed on the floor of the car.

The district court found, and the majority agrees, that the car's passengers were seized the moment the police cars pulled up next to and behind the parked car. From that moment, the passengers could not have felt free to walk away.

II

This was not a reasonable seizure. It cannot be justified as the constitutional equivalent of an officer strolling up to a parked car to see if the driver or passengers are willing to chat. The passengers in the car were seized, and in a sudden, terrifying, and unjustified way. Absent the most extraordinary circumstances, these intrusions on privacy and restraints on liberty—by police officers looking for "bigger and better things"—simply are not justifiable to write a parking ticket. And the government has not argued for any other ground to justify this seizure.

There are two distinct grounds for reversal here. The first is that the doctrines allowing pretextual traffic stops under the combination of *Terry* and *Whren* should not be extended to mere parking violations. The second and narrower ground is that even if such an extension might be available in theory, the police did not have a reasonable basis for this particular seizure.

On the first ground for reversal, the Supreme Court itself has not gone so far as to allow seizure of a person to investigate a possible parking violation. The core Fourth Amendment standard of reasonableness is what drove the balance between privacy and law enforcement in *Terry*. Extending *Terry* and *Whren* to allow police to use a mere parking violation as a pretext for seizing a car's passengers, and then using the occasion to remove them and handcuff them, loses sight of reasonableness and proportion.

Terry authorizes investigatory stops without a warrant when a police officer has a reasonable suspicion that a person is engaged or is about to engage in crime. The logic of *Terry* has been understood to authorize traffic stops for moving violations. Since *Whren*, Fourth Amendment law allows the police to carry out intrusive traffic stops based on the pretext of investigating a moving traffic violation.

This combination of constitutional decisions already enables a host of aggressive and intrusive police tactics. Police officers are trained to exploit those powers, as the officers tried to do here in their search for "bigger and better things." Officers who have probable cause for a trivial traffic violation can stop the car under *Whren* and then order all occupants out of the car, often question them in an intimidating way, visually inspect the interior of the car, often search at least portions of the vehicle's interior, and hold the driver and passengers while a drug-detection dog inspects the vehicle.

In these encounters, the danger of further escalation is always present. With authority to stop comes the authority to require the subject to submit to the stop, and to use reasonable force in doing so. The Fourth Amendment also allows police to arrest suspects for minor traffic infractions even if a court could impose only a fine, and arrested persons can be strip-searched, fingerprinted, photographed, and perhaps even subjected to a DNA test. Moreover, a *Terry* stop can even be justified by an officer's mistake of either law or fact.

Adding these doctrines together gives the police broad discretion to impose severe intrusions on the privacy and freedom of civilians going about their business. This potential is not entirely new. In 1940, the future Justice Jackson said: "We know that no local police force can strictly enforce the traffic laws, or it would arrest half the driving population on any given morning." R. Jackson, The Federal Prosecutor, Address Delivered at the Second Annual Conference of United States Attorneys, April 1, 1940, quoted in *Morrison v. Olson* (1988) (Scalia, J., dissenting); *see also, e.g.*, David A. Sklansky, Traffic Stops, Minority Motorists, and the Future of the Fourth Amendment, 1997 Sup. Ct. Rev. 271, 273 ("Since virtually everyone violates traffic laws at least occasionally, the upshot of these decisions is that police officers, if they are patient, can eventually pull over almost anyone they choose, order the driver and all passengers out of the car, and then ask for permission to search the vehicle without first making clear the detention is over.").

Courts usually examine these aspects of Fourth Amendment doctrine piecemeal, focusing on the one or two aspects most salient for the particular case. But when we consider a significant extension of Fourth Amendment authority, such as extending *Terry* and *Whren* to suspected parking violations, we must consider the cumulative effects of the doctrine. Those effects mean that authority to conduct an investigatory stop can trigger sweeping intrusions and even dangers. See Devon W. Carbado, From Stopping Black People to Killing Black People: The Fourth Amendment Pathways to Police Violence, 105 Calif. L. Rev. 125 (2017) (reviewing cumulative effects); Gabriel J. Chin & Charles J. Vernon, Reasonable but Unconstitutional: Racial Profiling and the Radical Objectivity of *Whren v. United States*, 83 Geo. Wash. L. Rev. 882, 884 n.2 (2015) (collecting literature on consequences of *Whren*).

The government's theory here is that the suspected parking violation justified the seizure of the passengers. The government sees no difference between parking violations and suspected traffic violations, so that all the police tactics permitted in a pretextual traffic stop under *Whren* can be used when a car might be parked illegally.

Relevant case law is both sparse and divided, perhaps because the notion of using such aggressive police tactics in response to parking violations seems so audacious. As noted, the Supreme Court has not extended these powers to the parking context. It should not do so, particularly with an eye toward practical consequences, including whether the cumulative effects of Fourth Amendment doctrine are reasonable and whether such intrusions may become "a routine part of American life."

In *United States v. Thornton* (7th Cir. 1999), two officers in a "high crime" neighborhood walked toward a car parked in a no-parking zone. They saw the driver get out of the car with what looked like a police-radio scanner. The officers patted down the driver and spotted what looked like a package of cocaine on the floor of the back seat. We said that whether "an illegally parked car, a crime-ridden neighborhood, the driver's sudden exit, and the driver's possession of a device that was monitoring police radio traffic adds up to sufficient suspicion to justify a *Terry* stop is a close call." In this case, by contrast, the police had much less to go on than the police had with that "close call" in *Thornton*. And the police tactics here were much more intrusive than walking up to the car, as in *Thornton*.

In *United States v. Shields* (7th Cir. 2015), the panel treated a parking violation as enough to support an investigatory *Terry* stop, though the real action in *Shields* concerned the driver's decision to flee from the officers.

These extensions of *Terry* to suspected parking violations remain few in number and are mistaken when there is no additional basis for the seizure. And at least two state supreme courts have taken a different view of the Fourth Amendment. See *State v. Duncan* (2002) (*Terry* did not extend to seizure to investigate suspected civil infractions such as possession of open container of alcohol in public); *State v. Holmes* (Minn. 1997) (*Terry* did not authorize seizure to investigate suspected parking violation). An illegally parked car is a far cry from the would-be robbers casing their target in *Terry v. Ohio*.

Extending *Terry* stops and the further intrusions they entail to pretextual parking violations loses sight of the core test of reasonableness and the balance at the core of *Terry* and the Fourth Amendment itself. "The makers of our Constitution . . . conferred, as against the Government, the right to be let alone—the most comprehensive of rights and the right most valued by civilized men. To protect that right, every unjustifiable intrusion by the Government upon the privacy of the individual, whatever the means employed, must be deemed a violation of the Fourth Amendment." We should find a violation of the Fourth Amendment in the unreasonable and intrusive seizure of the passengers in this case for the supposed purpose of investigating this parking violation.

III

Extending *Terry* and *Whren* to real parking violations is bad enough. The seizure here had even less foundation because the police did not have a reasonable basis for suspecting a parking violation. That is the second and narrower ground for reversal here.

The police relied on a Wisconsin statute that provides:

> No person shall stop or leave any vehicle standing in any of the following places except temporarily for the purpose of and while actually engaged in loading or unloading or in receiving or discharging passengers and while the vehicle is attended by a licensed operator so that it may promptly be moved in case of an emergency or to avoid obstruction of traffic:
>
> (1) In a loading zone.
> (2) In an alley in a business district.
> (3) Within 10 feet of a fire hydrant, unless a greater distance is indicated by an official traffic sign.
> (4) Within 4 feet of the entrance to an alley or a private road or driveway.
> (5) Closer than 15 feet to the near limits of a cross-walk.
> (6) Upon any portion of a highway where and at the time when parking is prohibited, limited or restricted by official traffic signs.

Wis. Stat. § 346.53.

The seized car and passengers could stand lawfully where they were if the car was there "temporarily for the purpose of and while actually engaged in loading or unloading or in receiving or discharging passengers and while the vehicle is attended by a licensed operator." That was all the police saw here: the driver had gone into a store, and the motor was running.

A car stopped in front of a store with its motor running is not itself suspicious. Given the sensible statutory proviso for cars that are loading and unloading, the police here could not reasonably decide, in the few seconds it took them to swoop in to seize this car and its passengers, that this seizure was justified.

Yet the majority treats what the police saw as suspicious enough to justify the seizure. That rationale overlooks the statute itself, which of course does not require the driver to "occupy" the car while loading or unloading. It requires only that the car be "attended" so it can be moved if needed. At the risk of stating the obvious, a driver making deliveries and pick-ups will not always occupy the vehicle, but he or she may "attend" it for these purposes.

To avoid the logic of the provision for loading and unloading, the majority cites cases from quite different contexts where police officers who receive conflicting information can make arrests and "leave to the judicial process the question whether a defense applies."

The majority's treatment of the loading-and-unloading proviso bears no practical relationship to reality or to what happened here on the streets of Milwaukee. Imagine that the police tried these tactics in Milwaukee's affluent east side. Citizens would be up in arms, and rightly so. No police officer could expect to keep his job if he treated a car standing in front of a store as worthy of such an intrusive *Terry* stop. The government's theory—that the seizure of a stopped car by the police would be justified because the occupants could always explain in court that they had merely stopped the car to make a purchase—invites intolerable intrusions on people just going about their business.

We have rejected similar efforts to authorize stops on grounds that would apply to a high proportion of people engaged in lawful behavior.

What made the officers decide so fast to swoop in to seize this car? On this record, the only explanation is the neighborhood, and the correlation with race is obvious. It is true that Johnson has not made an issue of race, but we should not close our eyes to the fact that this seizure and these tactics would never be tolerated in other communities and neighborhoods. If we tolerate these heavy-handed tactics here, we enable tactics that breed anger and resentment, and perhaps worse, toward the police.

Defendant Johnson is not a sympathetic champion of the Fourth Amendment, of course. That is not unusual in Fourth Amendment litigation. But the practical dangers of the majority's extension of *Terry* and *Whren* to suspected parking violations will sweep broadly. Who among us can say we have never overstayed a parking meter or parked a little too close to a crosswalk? We enforce the Fourth Amendment not for the sake of criminals but for the sake of everyone else who might be swept up by such intrusive and unjustified police tactics. I respectfully dissent.

NOTES AND QUESTIONS

1. Is there any doubt that the police had already figured out who was in, or at least who owned, the car before they pulled up and blocked it?

2. Why does the Court address the race of the car's occupants?

3. Is there a meaningful distinction between *Johnson* and *Whren*? What is the best argument as to why this sort of parking violation should be treated differently for *Terry* purposes than the sort of D.C. traffic code violations at issue on *Whren*? What is the best counter-argument?

4. The Court says the district court's finding that "the way in which the stop was conducted was not responsible for the gun's discovery" was not clearly erroneous. Do you agree?

5. Recall the limitation in *Terry* itself that both the search and seizure must be "reasonably related in scope to the circumstances which justified the interference in the first place." 392 U.S. at 20. Was the seizure here reasonably related to the parking violation that "justified it in the first place?" Was the search?

Professor Seo points out that automobile travel is the ultimate paradox of American culture. On the one hand, the car and the road — the "open road" — are icons of American freedom and imagination. On the other hand, an American in a car on the road is subject to a level of police scrutiny associated with repressive states. Seo, Policing the Open Road, *supra* at 159. For Black people and other minorities the term "paradox" here is misleading, as they have never been allowed to be full participants in the "American dream" half of the equation. As Nancy Leong describes it:

> American culture is steeped in the mythology of the open road. In our collective imagination, the road represents freedom, escape, friendship, romance, and above all, the possibility for a better life. But our shared dream of the open road comes to a halt in the mundane reality of the traffic stop — a judicially authorized policing procedure in which an officer may pull over a vehicle if she has cause to believe the driver has committed even the most minor traffic violation. . . . The traffic stop, I conclude, interrupts the open road narrative closely associated with the American dream. Those stopped most frequently — in particular, racial minorities — are consequently denied full participation in an abiding national fantasy.

Nancy Leong, *The Open Road and the Traffic Stop: Narratives and Counter Narratives of the American Dream*, 64 Fla. L. Rev. 305, 305 (2012).

Traffic stop reform may finally be afoot. Perhaps due to publicized shootings and other casualties of Black persons in connection with traffic stops (Philando Castile, Sandra Bland, Tyre Nichols, and others) many states and other jurisdictions are questioning whether the nation's 20 million traffic stops a year are worth the candle. Two states (Virginia and Oregon), four cities (Seattle, Philadelphia, Los Angeles, and Berkeley), and one county (Mecklenburg County, North Carolina) have adopted policies limiting traffic stops for minor infractions. A systematic study of stops in Fayetteville, North Carolina, found what would undoubtedly be true across the board. Traffic stops do not advance their ulterior law enforcement agenda (or at most do so inefficiently): just 3 percent of stops lead to search, only 20 percent of searches lead to the discovery of contraband, and only 50 percent of contraband discoveries result in an arrest — in short, just .3 percent of stops lead to an arrest. The same study also showed that Black drivers were three times more likely than white drivers to be searched after a stop. *See* Low-Level Traffic Stops Are Ineffective — And Sometimes Deadly. Why Are They Still Happening?, Vera Institute (Mar. 29, 2023).

Alternatively, would policing collapse if a warrant were required for a vehicle search after a traffic stop? The technology exists in many jurisdictions whereby an officer could apply for a warrant electronically from his vehicle and receive an answer within minutes. Oren Bar-Gill & Barry Friedman, *Taking Warrants Seriously*, 106 Nw. U. L. Rev. 1609, 1658-59 (2012). The obvious benefits to such a requirement would be that officers would go to the trouble only when they believed it truly necessary, and not as a matter of course or as a fishing expedition; that factual disputes about probable cause would be decreased; and that motorists would not be bullied into consenting to searches because they thought they had to.

Would this work? And at what cost to law enforcement? Professors Friedman and Bar-Gill make the following observations, comparing traffic stop data between Los Angeles and Pittsburgh while the latter was operating under a Department of Justice consent decree (*see* Chapter VI *infra*) that imposed quasi-warrant requirements for traffic stops:

> Comparing two jurisdictions in which traffic-stop data exists, there is evidence that a stringent ex ante warrant model can have a strong self-screening effect. While the total search rate in L.A. was 0.053 per capita, in Pittsburgh it was only 0.006 per capita. Why does the LAPD search almost ten times as often? One possible answer is that the Pittsburgh consent decree imposed a near-warrant level requirement on searches and seizures. Pittsburgh police officers were required to record every search and seizure in elaborate detail, including the location, basis

of the search, type of search conducted (warrantless, consent, etc.), demographic information about the search subject, and a description of what was searched. Subjects could only consent to searches after signing an officer's written form explaining their right to refuse.

Pittsburgh's decree monitors understood the impact of the consent decree, writing, "[S] upervisors and officers told us that officers were hesitant to conduct searches and to use force since the consent decree was signed. Of course, care in conducting searches and in the use of force was one of the goals of the decree." Our comparative data affirm these assessments: Pittsburgh's policing reforms resulted in fewer searches, as compared to other jurisdictions. Pittsburgh was performing about half as many total (auto and pedestrian) searches per capita than other jurisdictions were conducting per capita in the traffic-stop setting alone.What Part [this] suggests in theory seems to be borne out in practice: requiring officers to make a written justification makes a massive empirical difference. When the justification needs to be submitted to a magistrate, the difference might be even greater.

Although there may be reason to doubt the sharp difference between Los Angeles and Pittsburgh, if this difference is at all correct, then excluding arrests, the number of additional warrants required would be one-tenth, or roughly one million warrants. The two cities may be extremes on a continuum. Los Angeles officials may search more often than in most places. Pittsburgh officers may not have recorded all of their searches. Still, the data suggest a sharp decrease from our original estimate in the number of warrants needed under the permission model.

It also is interesting to note that despite the decrease in searches, police performance in Pittsburgh did not substantially deteriorate during the consent decree. Police morale was unaffected and crime rates, including homicides, either stayed the same or continued to steadily decrease. Officer activity on traffic-related matters remained relatively unchanged, and while felony clearance rates initially decreased, the rates bounced back to pre-decree levels towards the end of the decree. There is insufficient evidence to assess whether the Pittsburgh consent decree resulted in an overall increase or decrease in social welfare. But clearly the criminal justice system did not collapse or even suffer in any notable way.

Id. at 1667-68.

CHAPTER V

THE EXCLUSIONARY RULE, ITS EXCEPTIONS, AND SUPPRESSION HEARINGS

This chapter considers the exclusionary rule, once the glory of the Warren Court criminal procedure revolution, and its gradual erosion over the ensuing decades. Section A briefly introduces the rule itself, and the subsequent sections take on the most important exceptions: the good faith exception (Section B), the attenuation doctrine (Section C), standing (Section D), and impeachment (Section E). Section F looks at suppression hearings, the judicial proceedings in which motions to suppress evidence are litigated—that is, the court hearings in which defense counsel seeks to exclude evidence. This section pays particular attention to the problem of police perjury, or "testilying," a phenomenon that some judges and commentators have attributed to the advent of *Mapp v. Ohio* and its requirement that state courts exclude illegally obtained evidence.

A. THE EXCLUSIONARY RULE

As originally conceived as a matter of federal constitutional law, the exclusionary rule was seen as an inherent part of the Fourth Amendment, without which the constitutional guarantee would be a nullity. *See Weeks v. United States*, 232 U.S. 383, 393 (1914) ("If [illegally acquired materials can be] used in evidence against a citizen accused of an offense, the protection of the Fourth Amendment declaring his right to be secure against such searches and seizures is of no value, and, so far as those thus placed are concerned, might as well be stricken from the Constitution."); *Silverthorne Lumber Co. v. United States*, 251 U.S. 385, 392 (1920) ("The essence of a provision forbidding the acquisition of evidence in a certain way is that not merely evidence so acquired shall not be used before the Court but that it shall not be used at all.").

That premise went unquestioned in federal criminal prosecutions for decades. When the Court first applied the Fourth Amendment to the states, however, it decoupled the right from the remedy. In *Wolf v. Colorado*, 338 U.S. 25 (1949), the Court held that while the Fourth Amendment's substance applied to the states—via its incorporation—the Court declined to also apply the exclusionary rule remedy. The Court overruled that aspect of *Wolf* 12 years later in *Mapp v. Ohio*, 367 U.S. 643 (1961). The Court noted, among other things, that alternative state law remedies for enforcing the Fourth Amendment had proven ineffective and that the "imperative of judicial integrity" required the result. Echoing *Weeks*, it held that without the exclusionary rule the Fourth Amendment would only be a "valueless" "form of words."

Mapp v. Ohio

367 U.S. 643 (1961)

Mr. Justice Clark delivered the opinion of the Court.

Appellant stands convicted of knowingly having had in her possession and under her control certain lewd and lascivious books, pictures, and photographs in violation of § 2905.34 of Ohio's Revised Code. As officially stated in the syllabus to its opinion, the Supreme Court of Ohio found that her conviction was valid though "based primarily upon the introduction in evidence of lewd and lascivious books and pictures unlawfully seized during an unlawful search of defendant's home. . . ."

On May 23, 1957, three Cleveland police officers arrived at appellant's residence in that city pursuant to information that "a person (was) hiding out in the home, who was wanted for questioning in connection with a recent bombing, and that there was a large amount of policy paraphernalia being hidden in the home." Miss Mapp and her daughter by a former marriage lived on the top floor of the two-family dwelling. Upon their arrival at that house, the officers knocked on the door and demanded entrance but appellant, after telephoning her attorney, refused to admit them without a search warrant. They advised their headquarters of the situation and undertook a surveillance of the house.

The officers again sought entrance some three hours later when four or more additional officers arrived on the scene. When Miss Mapp did not come to the door immediately, at least one of the several doors to the house was forcibly opened and the policemen gained admittance. Meanwhile Miss Mapp's attorney arrived, but the officers, having secured their own entry, and continuing in their defiance of the law, would permit him neither to see Miss Mapp nor to enter the house. It appears that Miss Mapp was halfway down the stairs from the upper floor to the front door when the officers, in this highhanded manner, broke into the hall. She demanded to see the search warrant. A paper, claimed to be a warrant, was held up by one of the officers. She grabbed the "warrant" and placed it in her bosom. A struggle ensued in which the officers recovered the piece of paper and as a result of which they handcuffed appellant because she had been "belligerent" in resisting their official rescue of the "warrant" from her person. Running roughshod over appellant, a policeman "grabbed" her, "twisted (her) hand," and she "yelled (and) pleaded with him" because "it was hurting." Appellant, in handcuffs, was then forcibly taken upstairs to her bedroom where the officers searched a dresser, a chest of drawers, a closet and some suitcases. They also looked into a photo album and through personal papers belonging to the appellant. The search spread to the rest of the second floor including the child's bedroom, the living room, the kitchen and a dinette. The basement of the building and a trunk found therein were also searched. The obscene materials for possession of which she was ultimately convicted were discovered in the course of that widespread search.

At the trial no search warrant was produced by the prosecution, nor was the failure to produce one explained or accounted for. At best, "There is, in the record, considerable doubt as to whether there ever was any warrant for the search of defendant's home." The Ohio Supreme Court believed a "reasonable argument" could be made that the conviction should be reversed "because the methods employed to obtain the (evidence) were such as to 'offend "a sense of justice,"'" but the court found determinative the fact that the evidence had not been taken "from defendant's person by the use of brutal or offensive physical force against defendant."

The State says that even if the search were made without authority, or otherwise unreasonably, it is not prevented from using the unconstitutionally seized evidence at trial, citing *Wolf*, in which this Court did indeed hold "that in a prosecution in a State court for a State crime the Fourteenth Amendment does not forbid the admission of evidence obtained by an unreasonable search and seizure." On this appeal, of which we have noted probable jurisdiction, it is urged once again that we review that holding.

I

Seventy-five years ago, in *Boyd v. United States,* considering the Fourth and Fifth Amendments as running "almost into each other" on the facts before it, this Court held that the doctrines of those Amendments

> apply to all invasions on the part of the government and its employees of the sanctity of a man's home and the privacies of life. It is not the breaking of his doors, and the rummaging of his drawers, that constitutes the essence of the offence; but it is the invasion of his indefeasible right of personal security, personal liberty and private property. . . . Breaking into a house and opening boxes and drawers are circumstances of aggravation; but any forcible and compulsory extortion of a man's own testimony or of his private papers to be used as evidence to convict him of crime or to forfeit his goods, is within the condemnation . . . (of those Amendments).

The Court noted that

> constitutional provisions for the security of person and property should be liberally construed. . . . It is the duty of courts to be watchful for the constitutional rights of the citizen, and against any stealthy encroachments thereon.

In this jealous regard for maintaining the integrity of individual rights, the Court gave life to Madison's prediction that "independent tribunals of justice . . . will be naturally led to resist every encroachment upon rights expressly stipulated for in the Constitution by the declaration of rights." Concluding, the Court specifically referred to the use of the evidence there seized as "unconstitutional."

Less than 30 years after *Boyd,* this Court, in *Weeks v. United States,* stated that

> the 4th Amendment . . . put the courts of the United States and Federal officials, in the exercise of their power and authority, under limitations and restraints (and) . . . forever secure(d) the people, their persons, houses, papers, and effects, against all unreasonable searches and seizures under the guise of law . . . and the duty of giving to it force and effect is obligatory upon all entrusted under our Federal system with the enforcement of the laws.

Specifically dealing with the use of the evidence unconstitutionally seized, the Court concluded:

> If letters and private documents can thus be seized and held and used in evidence against a citizen accused of an offense, the protection of the Fourth Amendment declaring his right to be secure against such searches and seizures is of no value, and, so far as those thus placed are concerned, might as well be stricken from the Constitution. The efforts of the courts and their officials to bring the guilty to punishment, praiseworthy as they are, are not to be aided by the sacrifice of those great principles established by years of endeavor and suffering which have resulted in their embodiment in the fundamental law of the land.

Finally, the Court in that case clearly stated that use of the seized evidence involved "a denial of the constitutional rights of the accused." Thus, in the year 1914, in the *Weeks* case, this Court "for the first time" held that "in a federal prosecution the Fourth Amendment barred the use of evidence secured through an illegal search and seizure." This Court has ever since required of federal law officers a strict adherence to that command which this Court has held to be a clear, specific, and constitutionally required—even if judicially implied—deterrent safeguard without insistence upon which the Fourth Amendment would have been reduced to "a form of words." It meant, quite simply, that "conviction by means of unlawful seizures and enforced confessions . . . should find no sanction in the judgments of the courts . . .," *Weeks v. United States, supra*, and that such evidence "shall not be used at all."

There are in the cases of this Court some passing references to the *Weeks* rule as being one of evidence. But the plain and unequivocal language of *Weeks*—and its later paraphrase in *Wolf*—to the effect that the *Weeks* rule is of constitutional origin, remains entirely undisturbed. In *Byars v. United States*, a unanimous Court declared that "the doctrine (cannot) . . . be tolerated under our constitutional system, that evidences of crime discovered by a federal officer in making a search without lawful warrant may be used against the victim of the unlawful search where a timely challenge has been interposed." The Court, in *Olmstead v. United States*, in unmistakable language restated the *Weeks* rule:

> The striking outcome of the *Weeks* case and those which followed it was the sweeping declaration that the Fourth Amendment, although not referring to or limiting the use of evidence in court, really forbade its introduction if obtained by government officers through a violation of the amendment.

In *McNabb v. United States*, we note this statement:

> (A) conviction in the federal courts, the foundation of which is evidence obtained in disregard of liberties deemed fundamental by the Constitution, cannot stand. *Boyd v. United States* . . . *Weeks v. United States*. . . . And this Court has, on Constitutional grounds, set aside convictions, both in the federal and state courts, which were based upon confessions "secured by protracted and repeated questioning of ignorant and untutored persons, in whose minds the power of officers was greatly magnified" or "who have been unlawfully held incommunicado without advice of friends or counsel". . . .

Significantly, in *McNabb*, the Court did then pass on to formulate a rule of evidence, saying, "(i)n the view we take of the case, however, it becomes unnecessary to reach the Constitutional issue (for) . . . (t)he principles governing the admissibility of evidence in federal criminal trials have not been restricted . . . to those derived solely from the Constitution."

II

In 1949, 35 years after *Weeks* was announced, this Court, in *Wolf* again for the first time, discussed the effect of the Fourth Amendment upon the States through the operation of the Due Process Clause of the Fourteenth Amendment. It said:

> (W)e have no hesitation in saying that were a State affirmatively to sanction such police incursion into privacy it would run counter to the guaranty of the Fourteenth Amendment.

Nevertheless, after declaring that the "security of one's privacy against arbitrary intrusion by the police" is "implicit in 'the concept of ordered liberty' and as such enforceable against the States through the Due Process Clause," and announcing that it "stoutly adhere(d)" to the *Weeks* decision, the Court decided that the *Weeks* exclusionary rule would not then be imposed upon the States as "an essential ingredient of the right." The Court's reasons for not considering essential to the right to privacy, as a curb imposed upon the States by the Due Process Clause, that which decades before had been posited as part and parcel of the Fourth Amendment's limitations upon federal encroachment of individual privacy, were bottomed on factual considerations.

While they are not basically relevant to a decision that the exclusionary rule is an essential ingredient of the Fourth Amendment as the right it embodies is vouchsafed against the States by the Due Process Clause, we will consider the current validity of the factual grounds upon which *Wolf* was based.

The Court in *Wolf* first stated that "(t)he contrariety of views of the States" on the adoption of the exclusionary rule of *Weeks* was "particularly impressive" and, in this connection that it could not "brush aside the experience of States which deem the incidence of such conduct by the police too slight to call for a deterrent remedy . . . by overriding the (States') relevant rules of evidence." While in 1949, prior to the *Wolf* case, almost two-thirds of the States were opposed to the use of the exclusionary rule, now, despite the *Wolf* case, more than half of those since passing upon it, by their own legislative or judicial decision, have wholly or partly adopted or adhered to the *Weeks* rule. Significantly, among those now following the rule is California, which, according to its highest court, was "compelled to reach that conclusion because other remedies have completely failed to secure compliance with the constitutional provisions. . . ." In connection with this California case, we note that the second basis elaborated in *Wolf* in support of its failure to enforce the exclusionary doctrine against the States was that "other means of protection" have been afforded "the right to privacy." The experience of California that such other remedies have been worthless and futile is buttressed by the experience of other States. The obvious futility of relegating the Fourth Amendment of the protection of other remedies has, moreover, been recognized by this Court since *Wolf*.

Likewise, time has set its face against what *Wolf* called the "weighty testimony" of *People v. Defore*. There Justice (then Judge) Cardozo, rejecting adoption of the *Weeks* exclusionary rule in New York, had said that "(t)he Federal rule as it stands is either too strict or too lax." However, the force of that reasoning has been largely vitiated by later decisions of this Court. These include the recent discarding of the "silver platter" doctrine which allowed federal judicial use of evidence seized in violation of the Constitution by state agents, *Elkins v. United States, supra*; the relaxation of the formerly strict requirements as to standing to challenge the use of evidence thus seized, so that now the procedure of exclusion, "ultimately referable to constitutional safeguards," is available to anyone even "legitimately on (the) premises" unlawfully searched, *Jones v. United States*; and finally, the formulation of a method to prevent state use of evidence unconstitutionally seized by federal agents, *Rea v. United States*. Because there can be no fixed formula, we are admittedly met with "recurring questions of the reasonableness of searches," but less is not to be expected when dealing with a Constitution, and, at any rate, "(r)easonableness is in the first instance for the (trial court) to determine."

It, therefore, plainly appears that the factual considerations supporting the failure of the *Wolf* Court to include the *Weeks* exclusionary rule when it recognized the enforceability of the right to privacy against the States in 1949, while not basically relevant to the constitutional consideration, could not, in any analysis, now be deemed controlling.

III

Some five years after *Wolf*, in answer to a plea made here Term after Term that we overturn its doctrine on applicability of the *Weeks* exclusionary rule, this Court indicated that such should not be done until the States had "adequate opportunity to adopt or reject the (*Weeks*) rule." *Irvine v. People of State of California*, supra. There again it was said:

> Never until June of 1949 did this Court hold the basic search-and-seizure prohibition in any way applicable to the states under the Fourteenth Amendment.

And only last Term, after again carefully re-examining the *Wolf* doctrine in *Elkins* the Court pointed out that "the controlling principles" as to search and seizure and the problem of admissibility "seemed clear" until the announcement in *Wolf* "that the Due Process Clause of the Fourteenth Amendment does not itself require state courts to adopt the exclusionary rule" of the *Weeks* case. At the same time, the Court pointed out, "the underlying constitutional doctrine which *Wolf* established . . . that the Federal Constitution . . . prohibits unreasonable searches and seizures by state officers" had undermined the "foundation upon which the admissibility of state seized evidence in a federal trial originally rested. . . ." The Court concluded that it was therefore obliged to hold, although it chose the narrower ground on which to do so, that all evidence obtained by an unconstitutional search and seizure was inadmissible in a federal court regardless of its source. Today we once again examine *Wolf's* constitutional documentation of the right to privacy free from unreasonable state intrusion, and, after its dozen years on our books, are led by it to close the only courtroom door remaining open to evidence secured by official lawlessness in flagrant abuse of that basic right, reserved to all persons as a specific guarantee against that very same unlawful conduct. We hold that all evidence obtained by searches and seizures in violation of the Constitution is, by that same authority, inadmissible in a state court.

IV

Since the Fourth Amendment's right of privacy has been declared enforceable against the States through the Due Process Clause of the Fourteenth, it is enforceable against them by the same sanction of exclusion as is used against the Federal Government. Were it otherwise, then just as without the Weeks rule the assurance against unreasonable federal searches and seizures would be "a form of words" valueless and undeserving of mention in a perpetual charter of inestimable human liberties, so too, without that rule the freedom from state invasions of privacy would be so ephemeral and so neatly severed from its conceptual nexus with the freedom from all brutish means of coercing evidence as not to merit this Court's high regard as a freedom "implicit in the concept of ordered liberty." At the time that the Court held in *Wolf* that the Amendment was applicable to the States through the Due Process Clause, the cases of this Court, as we have seen, had steadfastly held that as to federal officers the Fourth Amendment included the exclusion of the evidence seized in violation of its provisions. Even *Wolf* "stoutly adhered" to that proposition. The right to privacy, when conceded operatively enforceable against the States, was not susceptible of destruction by avulsion of the sanction upon which its protection and enjoyment had always been deemed dependent under the *Boyd*, *Weeks* and *Silverthorne* cases. Therefore, in extending the substantive protections of due process to all constitutionally unreasonable searches — state or federal — it was logically and constitutionally necessary that the exclusion doctrine — an essential part of the right to privacy — be also insisted upon as an essential ingredient of the right newly recognized by the *Wolf* case. In short, the admission of the new constitutional right by *Wolf* could not consistently tolerate denial of its most important constitutional privilege, namely, the exclusion of the evidence which an accused had been forced to give by reason of the unlawful seizure. To hold otherwise is to grant the right but in reality to withhold its privilege and enjoyment. Only last year the Court itself recognized that the purpose of the exclusionary rule "is to deter — to compel respect for the constitutional guaranty in the only effectively available way — by removing the incentive to disregard it."

Indeed, we are aware of no restraint, similar to that rejected today, conditioning the enforcement of any other basic constitutional right. The right to privacy, no less important than any other right carefully and particularly reserved to the people, would stand in marked contrast to all other rights declared as "basic to a free society." This Court has not hesitated to enforce as strictly against the States as it does against the Federal Government the rights of free speech and of a free press, the rights to notice and to a fair, public trial, including, as it does, the right not to be convicted by use of a coerced confession, however logically relevant it be, and without regard to its reliability. And nothing could be more certain that that when a coerced confession is involved, "the relevant rules of evidence" are overridden without regard to "the incidence of such conduct by the police," slight or frequent. Why should not the same rule apply to what is tantamount to coerced testimony by way of unconstitutional seizure of goods, papers, effect, documents, etc.? We find that, as to the Federal Government, the Fourth and Fifth Amendments and, as to the States, the freedom from unconscionable invasions of privacy and the freedom from convictions based upon coerced confessions do enjoy an "intimate relation" in their perpetuation of "principles of humanity and civil liberty (secured) . . . only after years of struggle." They express "supplementing phases of the same constitutional purpose—to maintain inviolate large areas of personal privacy." The philosophy of each Amendment and of each freedom is complementary to, although not dependent upon, that of the other in its sphere of influence—the very least that together they assure in either sphere is that no man is to be convicted on unconstitutional evidence.

V

Moreover, our holding that the exclusionary rule is an essential part of both the Fourth and Fourteenth Amendments is not only the logical dictate of prior cases, but it also makes very good sense. There is no war between the Constitution and common sense. Presently, a federal prosecutor may make no use of evidence illegally seized, but a State's attorney across the street may, although he supposedly is operating under the enforceable prohibitions of the same Amendment. Thus the State, by admitting evidence unlawfully seized, serves to encourage disobedience to the Federal Constitution which it is bound to uphold. Moreover, as was said in *Elkins*, "(t)he very essence of a healthy federalism depends upon the avoidance of needless conflict between state and federal courts." Such a conflict, hereafter needless, arose this very Term, in *Wilson v. Schnettler*, in which, and in spite of the promise made by *Rea*, we gave full recognition to our practice in this regard by refusing to restrain a federal officer from testifying in a state court as to evidence unconstitutionally seized by him in the performance of his duties. Yet the double standard recognized until today hardly put such a thesis into practice. In non-exclusionary States, federal officers, being human, were by it invited to and did, as our cases indicate, step across the street to the State's attorney with their unconstitutionally seized evidence. Prosecution on the basis of that evidence was then had in a state court in utter disregard of the enforceable Fourth Amendment. If the fruits of an unconstitutional search had been inadmissible in both state and federal courts, this inducement to evasion would have been sooner eliminated. There would be no need to reconcile such cases as *Rea* and *Schnettler*, each pointing up the hazardous uncertainties of our heretofore ambivalent approach.

Federal-state cooperation in the solution of crime under constitutional standards will be promoted, if only by recognition of their now mutual obligation to respect the same fundamental criteria in their approaches. "However much in a particular case insistence upon such rules may appear as a technicality that inures to the benefit of a guilty person, the history of the criminal law proves that tolerance of shortcut methods in law enforcement impairs its enduring effectiveness." Denying shortcuts to only one of two cooperating law enforcement agencies tends naturally to breed legitimate suspicion of "working arrangements" whose results are equally tainted.

There are those who say, as did Justice (then Judge) Cardozo, that under our constitutional exclusionary doctrine "(t)he criminal is to go free because the constable has blundered." In some cases this will undoubtedly be the result. But, as was said in *Elkins*, "there is another consideration—the imperative of judicial integrity." The criminal goes free, if he must, but it is the law that sets him free. Nothing can destroy a government more quickly than its failure to observe its own laws, or worse, its disregard of the charter of its own existence. As Mr. Justice Brandeis, dissenting, said in *Olmstead v. United States*: "Our government is the potent, the omnipresent teacher. For good or for ill, it teaches the whole people by its example. . . . If the government becomes a lawbreaker, it breeds contempt for law; it invites every man to become a law unto himself; it invites anarchy." Nor can it lightly be assumed that, as a practical matter, adoption of the exclusionary rule fetters law enforcement. Only last year this Court expressly considered that contention and found that "pragmatic evidence of a sort" to the contrary was not wanting. The Court noted that

> The federal courts themselves have operated under the exclusionary rule of *Weeks* for almost half a century; yet it has not been suggested either that the Federal Bureau of Investigation has thereby been rendered ineffective, or that the administration of criminal justice in the federal courts has thereby been disrupted. Moreover, the experience of the states is impressive. . . . The movement towards the rule of exclusion has been halting but seemingly inexorable.

The ignoble shortcut to conviction left open to the State tends to destroy the entire system of constitutional restraints on which the liberties of the people rest. Having once recognized that the right to privacy embodied in the Fourth Amendment is enforceable against the States, and that the right to be secure against rude invasions of privacy by state officers is, therefore, constitutional in origin, we can no longer permit that right to remain an empty promise. Because it is enforceable in the same manner and to like effect as other basic rights secured by the Due Process Clause, we can no longer permit it to be revocable at the whim of any police officer who, in the name of law enforcement itself, chooses to suspend its enjoyment. Our decision, founded on reason and truth, gives to the individual no more than that which the Constitution guarantees him, to the police officer no less than that to which honest law enforcement is entitled, and, to the courts, that judicial integrity so necessary in the true administration of justice.

The judgment of the Supreme Court of Ohio is reversed and the cause remanded for further proceedings not inconsistent with this opinion.

NOTES AND QUESTIONS

Dollree Mapp

1. The Fourth Amendment violation here was particularly egregious. Cleveland police officers essentially broke into Dollree Mapp's home, lied to her about whether they had a search warrant, and arrested her when she demanded to see the warrant. Yet the Ohio Supreme Court, relying on *Wolf*, affirmed the conviction. The facts, of course, always matter. But does anything in the Supreme Court's opinion suggest that the invocation of the exclusionary rule depends on the egregiousness of the facts?

2. The Court notes Justice Cardozo's famous quip in opposition to the exclusionary rule, the logic of which he characterized as "the criminal is to go free because the constable has blundered." *People v. Defore*, 242 N.Y. 13, 21 (1926) (rejecting the exclusionary rule as a requirement in New York courts). The Court responds to this sentiment, a mainstay of exclusionary rule opponents, by making two related points: (a) it is the law that lets the criminal "go free," not the court; and (b) exclusion is required for the sake of "judicial integrity." In making this second point the Court relies on Justice Brandeis's dissent in *Olmstead v. United* States, 277 U.S. 438, 485 (1928), where he had dissented on the ground that the government's evidence was the product of illegal wiretapping.

Which of these two points is the more effective response to Justice Cardozo's quip?

3. The Court is sensitive to the fact that the decision in *Wolf*, which it overruled, was only 12 years old. It notes that whereas before *Wolf* two-thirds of the states were opposed to the exclusionary rule, by 1961 more than half of the states had wholly or partially adopted the rule by case law or legislation. It also singles out the experience of California, which had found that other, nonexclusionary remedies for Fourth Amendment violations had proven "worthless and futile." The leading role of two important state courts in *Mapp* is interesting: California, as an example for others to follow, and New York (through Justice Cardozo), as a relic to be left behind.

4. *Mapp* famously says that without the exclusionary rule the Fourth Amendment would be "valueless," and only "a form of words." The truth of the Court's statements about the centrality of the exclusionary rule to the Fourth Amendment was quickly proven. State police officials throughout the nation complained about the sea change inaugurated by *Mapp*, as if it had announced a new rule against illegal seizures and not simply a remedy. The New York City police commissioner described *Mapp* as a "tidal wave" and worried how his department could "implement" the decision.

The truth was, of course, that prior to *Mapp* state law enforcement had largely disregarded the requirements of the Fourth Amendment. *See* Yale Kamisar, Mapp v. Ohio*: The First Shot Fired in the Warren Court's Criminal Procedure Revolution*, in Criminal Procedure Stories 76-78 (Carol Steiker ed., 2006). In New York City the number of warrant applications increased from a handful before *Mapp* to 5,000 two years later. The theme was consistent nationwide. Warrants in Massachusetts were almost unknown before *Mapp*. They had also fallen into disuse in Philadelphia. *See* Sarah A. Seo, Policing the Open Road: How Cars Transformed American Freedom 197-98 (2019).

B. THE GOOD FAITH EXCEPTION

Hostility to *Mapp* eventually lead to erosion of the exclusionary rule, beginning with the "good faith exception" first established in the next case, *United States v. Leon*.

United States v. Leon

468 U.S. 897 (1984)

Justice White delivered the opinion of the Court.

This case presents the question whether the Fourth Amendment exclusionary rule should be modified so as not to bar the use in the prosecution's case in chief of evidence obtained by officers acting in reasonable reliance on a search warrant issued by a detached and neutral magistrate but ultimately found to be unsupported by probable cause. To resolve this question, we must consider once again the tension between the sometimes competing goals of, on the one hand, deterring official misconduct and removing inducements to unreasonable invasions of privacy and, on the other, establishing procedures under which criminal defendants are "acquitted or convicted on the basis of all the evidence which exposes the truth."

I

In August 1981, a confidential informant of unproven reliability informed an officer of the Burbank Police Department that two persons known to him as "Armando" and "Patsy" were selling large quantities of cocaine and methaqualone from their residence at 620 Price Drive in Burbank, Cal. The informant also indicated that he had witnessed a sale of methaqualone by "Patsy" at the residence approximately five months earlier and had observed at that time a shoebox containing a large amount of cash that belonged to "Patsy." He further declared that "Armando" and "Patsy" generally kept only small quantities of drugs at their residence and stored the remainder at another location in Burbank.

On the basis of this information, the Burbank police initiated an extensive investigation focusing first on the Price Drive residence and later on two other residences as well. Cars parked at the Price Drive residence were determined to belong to respondents Armando Sanchez, who had previously been arrested for possession of marihuana, and Patsy Stewart, who had no criminal record. During the course of the investigation, officers observed an automobile belonging to respondent Ricardo Del Castillo, who had previously been arrested for possession of 50 pounds of marihuana, arrive at the Price Drive residence. The driver of that car entered the house, exited shortly thereafter carrying a small paper sack, and drove away. A check of Del Castillo's probation records led the officers to respondent Alberto Leon, whose telephone number Del Castillo had listed as his employer's. Leon had been arrested in 1980 on drug charges, and a companion had informed the police at that time that Leon was heavily involved in the importation of drugs into this country. Before the current investigation began, the Burbank officers had learned that an informant had told a Glendale police officer that Leon stored a large quantity of methaqualone at his residence in Glendale. During the course of this investigation, the Burbank officers learned that Leon was living at 716 South Sunset Canyon in Burbank.

Subsequently, the officers observed several persons, at least one of whom had prior drug involvement, arriving at the Price Drive residence and leaving with small packages; observed a variety of other material activity at the two residences as well as at a condominium at 7902 Via Magdalena; and witnessed a variety of relevant activity involving respondents' automobiles. The officers also observed respondents Sanchez and Stewart board separate flights for Miami. The pair later returned to Los Angeles together, consented to a search of their luggage that revealed only a small amount of marihuana, and left the airport. Based on these and other observations summarized in the affidavit, Officer Cyril Rombach of the Burbank Police Department, an experienced and well-trained narcotics investigator, prepared an application for a warrant to search 620 Price Drive, 716 South Sunset Canyon, 7902 Via Magdalena, and automobiles registered to each of the respondents for an extensive list of items believed to be related to respondents' drug-trafficking activities. Officer Rombach's extensive application was reviewed by several Deputy District Attorneys.

A facially valid search warrant was issued in September 1981 by a State Superior Court Judge. The ensuing searches produced large quantities of drugs at the Via Magdalena and Sunset Canyon addresses and a small quantity at the Price Drive residence. Other evidence was discovered at each of the residences and in Stewart's and Del Castillo's automobiles. Respondents were indicted by a grand jury in the District Court for the Central District of California and charged with conspiracy to possess and distribute cocaine and a variety of substantive counts.

The respondents then filed motions to suppress the evidence seized pursuant to the warrant. The District Court held an evidentiary hearing and, while recognizing that the case was a close one, granted the motions to suppress in part. It concluded that the affidavit was insufficient to establish probable cause, but did not suppress all of the evidence as to all of the respondents because none of the respondents had standing to challenge all of the searches. In response to a request from the Government, the court made clear that Officer Rombach had acted in good faith, but it rejected the Government's suggestion that the Fourth Amendment exclusionary rule should not apply where evidence is seized in reasonable, good-faith reliance on a search warrant.

The District Court denied the Government's motion for reconsideration, and a divided panel of the Court of Appeals for the Ninth Circuit affirmed. The Court of Appeals first concluded that Officer Rombach's affidavit could not establish probable cause to search the Price Drive residence. To the extent that the affidavit set forth facts demonstrating the basis of the informant's knowledge of criminal activity, the information included was fatally stale. The affidavit, moreover, failed to establish the informant's credibility. Accordingly, the Court of Appeals concluded that the information provided by the informant was inadequate under both prongs of the two-part test established in *Aguilar v. Texas* (1964), and *Spinelli v. United States* (1969). The officers' independent investigation neither cured the staleness nor corroborated the details of the informant's declarations. The Court of Appeals then considered whether the affidavit formed a proper basis for the search of the Sunset Canyon residence. In its view, the affidavit included no facts indicating the basis for the informants' statements concerning respondent Leon's criminal activities and was devoid of information establishing the informants' reliability. Because these deficiencies had not been cured by the police investigation, the District Court properly suppressed the fruits of the search. The Court of Appeals refused the Government's invitation to recognize a good-faith exception to the Fourth Amendment exclusionary rule.

The Government's petition for certiorari expressly declined to seek review of the lower courts' determinations that the search warrant was unsupported by probable cause and presented only the question "[w]hether the Fourth Amendment exclusionary rule should be modified so as not to bar the admission of evidence seized in reasonable, good-faith reliance on a search warrant that is subsequently held to be defective." We granted certiorari to consider the propriety of such a modification. Although it undoubtedly is within our power to consider the question whether probable cause existed under the "totality of the circumstances" test announced last Term in *Illinois v. Gates* (1983), that question has not been briefed or argued; and it is also within our authority, which we choose to exercise, to take the case as it comes to us, accepting the Court of Appeals' conclusion that probable cause was lacking under the prevailing legal standards.

We have concluded that, in the Fourth Amendment context, the exclusionary rule can be modified somewhat without jeopardizing its ability to perform its intended functions. Accordingly, we reverse the judgment of the Court of Appeals.

II

Language in opinions of this Court and of individual Justices has sometimes implied that the exclusionary rule is a necessary corollary of the Fourth Amendment, or that the rule is required by the conjunction of the Fourth and Fifth Amendments. These implications need not detain us long. The Fifth Amendment theory has not withstood critical analysis or the test of time, and the Fourth Amendment "has never been interpreted to proscribe the introduction of illegally seized evidence in all proceedings or against all persons."

A

The Fourth Amendment contains no provision expressly precluding the use of evidence obtained in violation of its commands, and an examination of its origin and purposes makes clear that the use of fruits of a past unlawful search or seizure "work[s] no new Fourth Amendment wrong." The wrong condemned by the Amendment is "fully accomplished" by the unlawful search or seizure itself, and the exclusionary rule is neither intended nor able to "cure the invasion of the defendant's rights which he has already suffered." The rule thus operates as "a judicially created remedy designed to safeguard Fourth Amendment rights generally through its deterrent effect, rather than a personal constitutional right of the party aggrieved."

Whether the exclusionary sanction is appropriately imposed in a particular case, our decisions make clear, is "an issue separate from the question whether the Fourth Amendment rights of the party seeking to invoke the rule were violated by police conduct." Only the former question is currently before us, and it must be resolved by weighing the costs and benefits of preventing the use in the prosecution's case in chief of inherently trustworthy tangible evidence obtained in reliance on a search warrant issued by a detached and neutral magistrate that ultimately is found to be defective.

The substantial social costs exacted by the exclusionary rule for the vindication of Fourth Amendment rights have long been a source of concern. "Our cases have consistently recognized that unbending application of the exclusionary sanction to enforce ideals of governmental rectitude would impede unacceptably the truth-finding functions of judge and jury. An objectionable collateral consequence of this interference with the criminal justice system's truth-finding function is that some guilty defendants may go free or receive reduced sentences as a result of favorable plea bargains. Particularly when law enforcement officers have acted in objective good faith or their transgressions have been minor, the magnitude of the benefit conferred on such guilty defendants offends basic concepts of the criminal justice system. Indiscriminate application of the exclusionary rule, therefore, may well "generat[e] disrespect for the law and administration of justice." Accordingly, "[a]s with any remedial device, the application of the rule has been restricted to those areas where its remedial objectives are thought most efficaciously served."

B

Close attention to those remedial objectives has characterized our recent decisions concerning the scope of the Fourth Amendment exclusionary rule. The Court has, to be sure, not seriously questioned, "in the absence of a more efficacious sanction, the continued application of the rule to suppress evidence from the [prosecution's] case where a Fourth Amendment violation has been substantial and deliberate. . . ." Nevertheless, the balancing approach that has evolved in various contexts—including criminal trials—"forcefully suggest[s] that the exclusionary rule be more generally modified to permit the introduction of evidence obtained in the reasonable good-faith belief that a search or seizure was in accord with the Fourth Amendment."

In *Stone v. Powell, supra*, the Court emphasized the costs of the exclusionary rule, expressed its view that limiting the circumstances under which Fourth Amendment claims could be raised in federal habeas corpus proceedings would not reduce the rule's deterrent effect, and held that a state prisoner who has been afforded a full and fair opportunity to litigate a Fourth Amendment claim may not obtain federal habeas relief on the ground that unlawfully obtained evidence had been introduced at his trial. Proposed extensions of the exclusionary rule to proceedings other than the criminal trial itself have been evaluated and rejected under the same analytic approach. In *United States v. Calandra*, for example, we declined to allow grand jury witnesses to refuse to answer questions based on evidence obtained from an unlawful search or seizure since "[a]ny incremental deterrent effect which might be achieved by extending the rule to grand jury proceedings is uncertain at best." Similarly, in *United States v. Janis*, supra, we permitted the use in federal civil proceedings of evidence illegally seized by state officials since the likelihood of deterring police misconduct through such an extension of the exclusionary rule was insufficient to outweigh its substantial social costs. In so doing, we declared that, "[i]f . . . the exclusionary rule does not result in appreciable deterrence, then, clearly, its use in the instant situation is unwarranted."

As cases considering the use of unlawfully obtained evidence in criminal trials themselves make clear, it does not follow from the emphasis on the exclusionary rule's deterrent value that "anything which deters illegal searches is thereby commanded by the Fourth Amendment." In determining whether persons aggrieved solely by the introduction of damaging evidence unlawfully obtained from their co-conspirators or co-defendants could seek suppression, for example, we found that the additional benefits of such an extension of the exclusionary rule would not outweigh its costs. Standing to invoke the rule has thus been limited to cases in which the prosecution seeks to use the fruits of an illegal search or seizure against the victim of police misconduct.

Even defendants with standing to challenge the introduction in their criminal trials of unlawfully obtained evidence cannot prevent every conceivable use of such evidence. Evidence obtained in violation of the Fourth Amendment and inadmissible in the prosecution's case in chief may be used to impeach a defendant's direct testimony. A similar assessment of the "incremental furthering" of the ends of the exclusionary rule led us to conclude in *United States v. Havens* (1980), that evidence inadmissible in the prosecution's case in chief or otherwise as substantive evidence of guilt may be used to impeach statements made by a defendant in response to "proper cross-examination reasonably suggested by the defendant's direct examination."

When considering the use of evidence obtained in violation of the Fourth Amendment in the prosecution's case in chief, moreover, we have declined to adopt a per se or "but for" rule that would render inadmissible any evidence that came to light through a chain of causation that began with an illegal arrest. We also have held that a witness' testimony may be admitted even when his identity was discovered in an unconstitutional search. The perception underlying these decisions—that the connection between police misconduct and evidence of crime may be sufficiently attenuated to permit the use of that evidence at trial—is a product of considerations relating to the exclusionary rule and the constitutional principles it is designed to protect. In short, the "dissipation of the taint" concept that the Court has applied in deciding whether exclusion is appropriate in a particular case "attempts to mark the point at which the detrimental consequences of illegal police action become so attenuated that the deterrent effect of the exclusionary rule no longer justifies its cost." Not surprisingly in view of this purpose, an assessment of the flagrancy of the police misconduct constitutes an important step in the calculus.

The same attention to the purposes underlying the exclusionary rule also has characterized decisions not involving the scope of the rule itself. We have not required suppression of the fruits of a search incident to an arrest made in good-faith reliance on a substantive criminal statute that subsequently is declared unconstitutional. Similarly, although the Court has been unwilling to conclude that new Fourth Amendment principles are always to have only prospective effect, no Fourth Amendment decision marking a "clear break with the past" has been applied retroactively. The propriety of retroactive application of a newly announced Fourth Amendment principle, moreover, has been assessed largely in terms of the contribution retroactivity might make to the deterrence of police misconduct.

As yet, we have not recognized any form of good-faith exception to the Fourth Amendment exclusionary rule. But the balancing approach that has evolved during the years of experience with the rule provides strong support for the modification currently urged upon us. As we discuss below, our evaluation of the costs and benefits of suppressing reliable physical evidence seized by officers reasonably relying on a warrant issued by a detached and neutral magistrate leads to the conclusion that such evidence should be admissible in the prosecution's case in chief.

III

A

Because a search warrant "provides the detached scrutiny of a neutral magistrate, which is a more reliable safeguard against improper searches than the hurried judgment of a law enforcement officer 'engaged in the often competitive enterprise of ferreting out crime,'" we have expressed a strong preference for warrants and declared that "in a doubtful or marginal case a search under a warrant may be sustainable where without one it would fall." Reasonable minds frequently may differ on the question whether a particular affidavit establishes probable cause, and we have thus concluded that the preference for warrants is most appropriately effectuated by according "great deference" to a magistrate's determination.

Deference to the magistrate, however, is not boundless. It is clear, first, that the deference accorded to a magistrate's finding of probable cause does not preclude inquiry into the knowing or reckless falsity of the affidavit on which that determination was based. Second, the courts must also insist that the magistrate purport to "perform his 'neutral and detached' function and not serve merely as a rubber stamp for the police." A magistrate failing to "manifest that neutrality and detachment demanded of a judicial officer when presented with a warrant application" and who acts instead as "an adjunct law enforcement officer" cannot provide valid authorization for an otherwise unconstitutional search.

Third, reviewing courts will not defer to a warrant based on an affidavit that does not "provide the magistrate with a substantial basis for determining the existence of probable cause." "Sufficient information must be presented to the magistrate to allow that official to determine probable cause; his action cannot be a mere ratification of the bare conclusions of others." Even if the warrant application was supported by more than a "bare bones" affidavit, a reviewing court may properly conclude that, notwithstanding the deference that magistrates deserve, the warrant was invalid because the magistrate's probable-cause determination reflected an improper analysis of the totality of the circumstances, or because the form of the warrant was improper in some respect.

Only in the first of these three situations, however, has the Court set forth a rationale for suppressing evidence obtained pursuant to a search warrant; in the other areas, it has simply excluded such evidence without considering whether Fourth Amendment interests will be advanced. To the extent that proponents of exclusion rely on its behavioral effects on judges and magistrates in these areas, their reliance is misplaced. First, the exclusionary rule is designed to deter police misconduct rather than to punish the errors of judges and magistrates. Second, there exists no evidence suggesting that judges and magistrates are inclined to ignore or subvert the Fourth Amendment or that lawlessness among these actors requires application of the extreme sanction of exclusion.

Third, and most important, we discern no basis, and are offered none, for believing that exclusion of evidence seized pursuant to a warrant will have a significant deterrent effect on the issuing judge or magistrate. Many of the factors that indicate that the exclusionary rule cannot provide an effective "special" or "general" deterrent for individual offending law enforcement officers apply as well to judges or magistrates. And, to the extent that the rule is thought to operate as a "systemic" deterrent on a wider audience, it clearly can have no such effect on individuals empowered to issue search warrants. Judges and magistrates are not adjuncts to the law enforcement team; as neutral judicial officers, they have no stake in the outcome of particular criminal prosecutions. The threat of exclusion thus cannot be expected significantly to deter them. Imposition of the exclusionary sanction is not necessary meaningfully to inform judicial officers of their errors, and we cannot conclude that admitting evidence obtained pursuant to a warrant while at the same time declaring that the warrant was somehow defective will in any way reduce judicial officers' professional incentives to comply with the Fourth Amendment, encourage them to repeat their mistakes, or lead to the granting of all colorable warrant requests.

B

If exclusion of evidence obtained pursuant to a subsequently invalidated warrant is to have any deterrent effect, therefore, it must alter the behavior of individual law enforcement officers or the policies of their departments. One could argue that applying the exclusionary rule in cases where the police failed to demonstrate probable cause in the warrant application deters future inadequate presentations or "magistrate shopping" and thus promotes the ends of the Fourth Amendment. Suppressing evidence obtained pursuant to a technically defective warrant supported by probable cause also might encourage officers to scrutinize more closely the form of the warrant and to point out suspected judicial errors. We find such arguments speculative and conclude that suppression of evidence obtained pursuant to a warrant should be ordered only on a case-by-case basis and only in those unusual cases in which exclusion will further the purposes of the exclusionary rule.

We have frequently questioned whether the exclusionary rule can have any deterrent effect when the offending officers acted in the objectively reasonable belief that their conduct did not violate the Fourth Amendment. "No empirical researcher, proponent or opponent of the rule, has yet been able to establish with any assurance whether the rule has a deterrent effect. . . ." But even assuming that the rule effectively deters some police misconduct and provides incentives for the law enforcement profession as a whole to conduct itself in accord with the Fourth Amendment, it cannot be expected, and should not be applied, to deter objectively reasonable law enforcement activity.

As we observed in *Michigan v. Tucker*, and reiterated in *United States v. Peltier*:

> The deterrent purpose of the exclusionary rule necessarily assumes that the police have engaged in willful, or at the very least negligent, conduct which has deprived the defendant of some right. By refusing to admit evidence gained as a result of such conduct, the courts hope to instill in those particular investigating officers, or in their future counterparts, a greater degree of care toward the rights of an accused. Where the official action was pursued in complete good faith, however, the deterrence rationale loses much of its force.
>
> If the purpose of the exclusionary rule is to deter unlawful police conduct, then evidence obtained from a search should be suppressed only if it can be said that the law enforcement officer had knowledge, or may properly be charged with knowledge, that the search was unconstitutional under the Fourth Amendment.

In short, where the officer's conduct is objectively reasonable,

> excluding the evidence will not further the ends of the exclusionary rule in any appreciable way; for it is painfully apparent that . . . the officer is acting as a reasonable officer would and should act in similar circumstances. Excluding the evidence can in no way affect his future conduct unless it is to make him less willing to do his duty.

This is particularly true, we believe, when an officer acting with objective good faith has obtained a search warrant from a judge or magistrate and acted within its scope. In most such cases, there is no police illegality and thus nothing to deter. It is the magistrate's responsibility to determine whether the officer's allegations establish probable cause and, if so, to issue a warrant comporting in form with the requirements of the Fourth Amendment. In the ordinary case, an officer cannot be expected to question the magistrate's probable-cause determination or his judgment that the form of the warrant is technically sufficient. "[O]nce the warrant issues, there is literally nothing more the policeman can do in seeking to comply with the law." Penalizing the officer for the magistrate's error, rather than his own, cannot logically contribute to the deterrence of Fourth Amendment violations.

C

We conclude that the marginal or nonexistent benefits produced by suppressing evidence obtained in objectively reasonable reliance on a subsequently invalidated search warrant cannot justify the substantial costs of exclusion. We do not suggest, however, that exclusion is always inappropriate in cases where an officer has obtained a warrant and abided by its terms. "[S]earches pursuant to a warrant will rarely require any deep inquiry into reasonableness," for "a warrant issued by a magistrate normally suffices to establish" that a law enforcement officer has "acted in good faith in conducting the search." Nevertheless, the officer's reliance on the magistrate's probable-cause determination and on the technical sufficiency of the warrant he issues must be objectively reasonable, and it is clear that in some circumstances the officer will have no reasonable grounds for believing that the warrant was properly issued.

Suppression therefore remains an appropriate remedy if the magistrate or judge in issuing a warrant was misled by information in an affidavit that the affiant knew was false or would have known was false except for his reckless disregard of the truth. The exception we recognize today will also not apply in cases where the issuing magistrate wholly abandoned his judicial role in the manner condemned in *Lo-Ji Sales, Inc. v. New York* (1979); in such circumstances, no reasonably well trained officer should rely on the warrant. Nor would an officer manifest objective good faith in relying on a warrant based on an affidavit "so lacking in indicia of probable cause as to render official belief in its existence entirely unreasonable." Finally, depending on the circumstances of the particular case, a warrant may be so facially deficient — i.e., in failing to particularize the place to be searched or the things to be seized — that the executing officers cannot reasonably presume it to be valid.

In so limiting the suppression remedy, we leave untouched the probable-cause standard and the various requirements for a valid warrant. Other objections to the modification of the Fourth Amendment exclusionary rule we consider to be insubstantial. The good-faith exception for searches conducted pursuant to warrants is not intended to signal our unwillingness strictly to enforce the requirements of the Fourth Amendment, and we do not believe that it will have this effect. As we have already suggested, the good-faith exception, turning as it does on objective reasonableness, should not be difficult to apply in practice. When officers have acted pursuant to a warrant, the prosecution should ordinarily be able to establish objective good faith without a substantial expenditure of judicial time.

Nor are we persuaded that application of a good-faith exception to searches conducted pursuant to warrants will preclude review of the constitutionality of the search or seizure, deny needed guidance from the courts, or freeze Fourth Amendment law in its present state. There is no need for courts to adopt the inflexible practice of always deciding whether the officers' conduct manifested objective good faith before turning to the question whether the Fourth Amendment has been violated. Defendants seeking suppression of the fruits of allegedly unconstitutional searches or seizures undoubtedly raise live controversies which Art. III empowers federal courts to adjudicate. As cases addressing questions of good-faith immunity under 42 U.S.C. § 1983, and cases involving the harmless-error doctrine, make clear, courts have considerable discretion in conforming their decisionmaking processes to the exigencies of particular cases.

If the resolution of a particular Fourth Amendment question is necessary to guide future action by law enforcement officers and magistrates, nothing will prevent reviewing courts from deciding that question before turning to the good-faith issue. Indeed, it frequently will be difficult to determine whether the officers acted reasonably without resolving the Fourth Amendment issue. Even if the Fourth Amendment question is not one of broad import, reviewing courts could decide in particular cases that magistrates under their supervision need to be informed of their errors and so evaluate the officers' good faith only after finding a violation. In other circumstances, those courts could reject suppression motions posing no important Fourth Amendment questions by turning immediately to a consideration of the officers' good faith. We have no reason to believe that our Fourth Amendment jurisprudence would suffer by allowing reviewing courts to exercise an informed discretion in making this choice.

IV

When the principles we have enunciated today are applied to the facts of this case, it is apparent that the judgment of the Court of Appeals cannot stand. The Court of Appeals applied the prevailing legal standards to Officer Rombach's warrant application and concluded that the application could not support the magistrate's probable-cause determination. In so doing, the court clearly informed the magistrate that he had erred in issuing the challenged warrant. This aspect of the court's judgment is not under attack in this proceeding.

Having determined that the warrant should not have issued, the Court of Appeals understandably declined to adopt a modification of the Fourth Amendment exclusionary rule that this Court had not previously sanctioned. Although the modification finds strong support in our previous cases, the Court of Appeals' commendable self-restraint is not to be criticized. We have now reexamined the purposes of the exclusionary rule and the propriety of its application in cases where officers have relied on a subsequently invalidated search warrant. Our conclusion is that the rule's purposes will only rarely be served by applying it in such circumstances.

In the absence of an allegation that the magistrate abandoned his detached and neutral role, suppression is appropriate only if the officers were dishonest or reckless in preparing their affidavit or could not have harbored an objectively reasonable belief in the existence of probable cause. Only respondent Leon has contended that no reasonably well trained police officer could have believed that there existed probable cause to search his house; significantly, the other respondents advance no comparable argument. Officer Rombach's application for a warrant clearly was supported by much more than a "bare bones" affidavit. The affidavit related the results of an extensive investigation and, as the opinions of the divided panel of the Court of Appeals make clear, provided evidence sufficient to create disagreement among thoughtful and competent judges as to the existence of probable cause. Under these circumstances, the officers' reliance on the magistrate's determination of probable cause was objectively reasonable, and application of the extreme sanction of exclusion is inappropriate.

Accordingly, the judgment of the Court of Appeals is

Reversed.

NOTES AND QUESTIONS

1. Is the good faith exception fashioned by the Court dependent on the existence of a search warrant that had been approved by a detached and neutral magistrate? There is certainly much discussion of the importance of a warrant, but are there hints that the majority views the exception as broader?

2. Note the way the Department of Justice strategically litigated the case. First, DOJ asked the district court, which had granted defendants' motions to suppress in part, to make a finding that the officers had acted in good faith, which the district court did even though the officers' good faith was totally irrelevant under existing law. Second, it appealed from the district court's partial denial of the motion to suppress, even though much of the evidence obtained from the search was admissible. Third, the government petitioned for certiorari only on the issue of whether there should be a good faith exception, and not on whether the warrants were supported by probable cause.

The DOJ was not, however, just trying a Hail Mary pass here. There had been hints in at least two previous cases that the Court might be willing to recognize a good faith exception to the exclusionary rule. First, in his dissenting opinion in *Stone v. Powell*, 428 U.S. 465, 536 (1976), Justice White had proposed establishing a good faith exception to the exclusionary rule. And more recently, in *Illinois v. Gates*, 462 U.S. 213 (1983), the Court had asked for briefing on whether it should adopt the good faith exception, although it ultimately declined to reach the issue. *Id.* at 216-24.

3. Note that the Court relies entirely on the district court's finding—wholly gratuitous—that the police officer had acted in good faith. It doesn't reproduce, summarize, or in any way describe the affidavit filed in support of the search warrant applications, and does not explain how the affidavit fell short of establishing probable cause. The court of appeals, on the other hand, found that the informant's information was "fatally stale" and that the affidavit "failed to establish the informant's reliability," and thus the application failed under both prongs of the *Aguilar-Spinelli* test.

How could a warrant application resting on information that was "fatally stale" and that failed under both aspects of the applicable legal test have been made "in good faith."?

Is it significant that the police officer testified that the affidavit had been reviewed by several deputy district attorneys?

4. In a companion case to *Leon, Massachusetts v. Sheppard*, 468 U.S. 981 (1984), the Court found that a police officer had reasonably relied on a warrant issued by a judge even though the judge failed to conform the ultimately issued warrant to reflect edits the officer had made to the warrant form he had submitted. Relying on *Leon*, the Court held that the exclusionary rule did not apply because the officer had an "objectively reasonable belief" that the warrant was valid.

5. As the next cases will show, the scope of *Leon*'s good faith exception to the exclusionary rule has been repeatedly extended by the Court. At least 20 state courts, however, interpreting state constitutions, have rejected *Leon*. *See* Joseph Blocher, *Reverse Incorporation of State Constitutional Law*, 84 S. Cal. L. Rev. 323, 373 (2011) ("Perhaps the Court will revisit *Leon*'s reasoning and rule if that number reaches the fifty percent figure that seemed so significant in *Mapp*.").

It appeared to some that the "good faith exception" was limited to situations where search warrants had been issued by a "detached and neutral magistrate." That notion was dispelled in *Illinois v. Krull*, 480 U.S. 340 (1987), where the Court applied the exception in a case involving a warrantless administrative inspection of an automobile wrecking yard. In a prosecution based on the fruits of that inspection, the evidence was suppressed by the trial court because the statute authorizing the inspection had been found to be unconstitutional in that it conferred unbridled discretion on the searching officers. *Id.* at 344. The Supreme Court found the search to be within the good faith exception. Because the statute had not been found unconstitutional at the time of the search, and was not patently illegal, the officers were entitled to rely on it and no deterrent purpose would be served by suppressing the evidence the search yielded. *Id.* at 349-50. The Court dismissed any concerns that state legislatures needed incentives to deter them from passing unconstitutional statutes, and noted that the exclusionary rule focused only on police misconduct. *Id.* at 350. The Court also ignored that the effect of its ruling left no incentive for challenges to such potentially unconstitutional statutes because even successful actions would be remediless. *Id.* at 354. Justice O'Connor, the only Justice on the Court with any legislative experience (she had been an Arizona state senator), wrote a dissenting opinion in which Justices Brennan, Marshall, and Stevens joined. She reasoned, among other things, that legislatures did in fact need disincentives against passing unconstitutional statutes. *Id.* at 361, 366 (O'Connor, J., dissenting).

The Court's next significant good faith case was *Arizona v. Evans*, 514 U.S. 1 (1995). A police officer stopped Isaac Evans for driving the wrong way on a one-way street—right in front of apolice station—and upon entering Evans's name into a computerized criminal record database terminal in his car learned that Evans had an outstanding misdemeanor warrant for his arrest, based on his failure to appear in court to respond to alleged traffic violations. *Id.* at 4-5. Evans was arrested and in the search incident to that arrest, and subsequent search of his car, marijuana was discovered. *Id.* at 4.

It turned out the misdemeanor arrest warrant had been quashed 17 days earlier and was thus no longer effective. *Id.* Due to an error in the clerk's office, however, the judicial action quashing the warrant had not been communicated to the sheriff's office. *Id.* The Court found that excluding the evidence would not have any deterrent effect on police conduct, as the officer had acted objectively reasonably in reliance upon the police computer records. *Id.*

at 15-16. It also noted that the exclusionary rule's purpose was not aimed at deterring the conduct of judicial branch employees—the officials who had made the error here—and also that the error here was rare. *Id.*

The Court revisited the subject of a computer database error leading to an illegal arrest 12 years later.

Herring v. United States

555 U.S. 135 (2009)

Chief Justice ROBERTS delivered the opinion of the Court.

The Fourth Amendment forbids "unreasonable searches and seizures," and this usually requires the police to have probable cause or a warrant before making an arrest. What if an officer reasonably believes there is an outstanding arrest warrant, but that belief turns out to be wrong because of a negligent bookkeeping error by another police employee? The parties here agree that the ensuing arrest is still a violation of the Fourth Amendment, but dispute whether contraband found during a search incident to that arrest must be excluded in a later prosecution.

Our cases establish that such suppression is not an automatic consequence of a Fourth Amendment violation. Instead, the question turns on the culpability of the police and the potential of exclusion to deter wrongful police conduct. Here the error was the result of isolated negligence attenuated from the arrest. We hold that in these circumstances the jury should not be barred from considering all the evidence.

I

On July 7, 2004, Investigator Mark Anderson learned that Bennie Dean Herring had driven to the Coffee County Sheriff's Department to retrieve something from his impounded truck. Herring was no stranger to law enforcement, and Anderson asked the county's warrant clerk, Sandy Pope, to check for any outstanding warrants for Herring's arrest. When she found none, Anderson asked Pope to check with Sharon Morgan, her counterpart in neighboring Dale County. After checking Dale County's computer database, Morgan replied that there was an active arrest warrant for Herring's failure to appear on a felony charge. Pope relayed the information to Anderson and asked Morgan to fax over a copy of the warrant as confirmation. Anderson and a deputy followed Herring as he left the impound lot, pulled him over, and arrested him. A search incident to the arrest revealed methamphetamine in Herring's pocket, and a pistol (which as a felon he could not possess) in his vehicle.

There had, however, been a mistake about the warrant. The Dale County sheriff's computer records are supposed to correspond to actual arrest warrants, which the office also maintains. But when Morgan went to the files to retrieve the actual warrant to fax to Pope, Morgan was unable to find it. She called a court clerk and learned that the warrant had been recalled five months earlier. Normally when a warrant is recalled the court clerk's office or a judge's chambers calls Morgan, who enters the information in the sheriff's computer database and disposes of the physical copy. For whatever reason, the information about the recall of the warrant for Herring did not appear in the database. Morgan immediately called Pope to alert her to the mixup, and Pope contacted Anderson over a secure radio. This all unfolded in 10 to 15 minutes, but Herring had already been arrested and found with the gun and drugs, just a few hundred yards from the sheriff's office.

Herring was indicted in the District Court for the Middle District of Alabama for illegally possessing the gun and drugs, violations of 18 U.S.C. § 922(g)(1) and 21 U.S.C. § 844(a). He moved to suppress the evidence on the ground that his initial arrest had been illegal because the warrant had been rescinded. The Magistrate Judge recommended denying the motion because the arresting officers had acted in a good-faith belief that the warrant was still outstanding. Thus, even if there were a Fourth Amendment violation, there was "no reason to believe that application of the exclusionary rule here would deter the occurrence of any future mistakes." The District Court adopted the Magistrate Judge's recommendation, and the Court of Appeals for the Eleventh Circuit affirmed.

The Eleventh Circuit found that the arresting officers in Coffee County "were entirely innocent of any wrongdoing or carelessness." The court assumed that whoever failed to update the Dale County sheriff's records was also a law enforcement official, but noted that "the conduct in question [wa]s a negligent failure to act, not a deliberate or tactical choice to act." Ibid. Because the error was merely negligent and attenuated from the arrest, the Eleventh Circuit concluded that the benefit of suppressing the evidence "would be marginal or nonexistent), and the evidence was therefore admissible under the good-faith rule of *United States v. Leon* (1984).

Other courts have required exclusion of evidence obtained through similar police errors, so we granted Herring's petition for certiorari to resolve the conflict. We now affirm the Eleventh Circuit's judgment.

II

When a probable-cause determination was based on reasonable but mistaken assumptions, the person subjected to a search or seizure has not necessarily been the victim of a constitutional violation. The very phrase "probable cause" confirms that the Fourth Amendment does not demand all possible precision. And whether the error can be traced to a mistake by a state actor or some other source may bear on the analysis. For purposes of deciding this case, however, we accept the parties' assumption that there was a Fourth Amendment violation. The issue is whether the exclusionary rule should be applied.

A

The Fourth Amendment protects "[t]he right of the people to be secure in their persons, houses, papers, and effects, against unreasonable searches and seizures," but "contains no provision expressly precluding the use of evidence obtained in violation of its commands." Nonetheless, our decisions establish an exclusionary rule that, when applicable, forbids the use of improperly obtained evidence at trial. We have stated that this judicially created rule is "designed to safeguard Fourth Amendment rights generally through its deterrent effect."

In analyzing the applicability of the rule, *Leon* admonished that we must consider the actions of all the police officers involved. The Coffee County officers did nothing improper. Indeed, the error was noticed so quickly because Coffee County requested a faxed confirmation of the warrant.

The Eleventh Circuit concluded, however, that somebody in Dale County should have updated the computer database to reflect the recall of the arrest warrant. The court also concluded that this error was negligent, but did not find it to be reckless or deliberate. That fact is crucial to our holding that this error is not enough by itself to require "the extreme sanction of exclusion."

B

The fact that a Fourth Amendment violation occurred—i.e., that a search or arrest was unreasonable—does not necessarily mean that the exclusionary rule applies. Indeed, exclusion "has always been our last resort, not our first impulse," and our precedents establish important principles that constrain application of the exclusionary rule.

First, the exclusionary rule is not an individual right and applies only where it "'result[s] in appreciable deterrence.'" We have repeatedly rejected the argument that exclusion is a necessary consequence of a Fourth Amendment violation. Instead we have focused on the efficacy of the rule in deterring Fourth Amendment violations in the future.

In addition, the benefits of deterrence must outweigh the costs. "We have never suggested that the exclusionary rule must apply in every circumstance in which it might provide marginal deterrence." "[T]o the extent that application of the exclusionary rule could provide some incremental deterrent, that possible benefit must be weighed against [its] substantial social costs." The principal cost of applying the rule is, of course, letting guilty and possibly dangerous defendants go free—something that "offends basic concepts of the criminal justice system." "[T]he rule's costly toll upon truth-seeking and law enforcement objectives presents a high obstacle for those urging [its] application."

These principles are reflected in the holding of *Leon*: When police act under a warrant that is invalid for lack of probable cause, the exclusionary rule does not apply if the police acted "in objectively reasonable reliance" on the subsequently invalidated search warrant. We (perhaps confusingly) called this objectively reasonable reliance "good faith." Ibid., n. 23, 104 S. Ct. 3405. In a companion case, *Massachusetts v. Sheppard* (1984), we held that the exclusionary rule did not apply when a warrant was invalid because a judge forgot to make "clerical corrections" to it.

Shortly thereafter we extended these holdings to warrantless administrative searches performed in good-faith reliance on a statute later declared unconstitutional. Finally, in *Evans*, we applied this good-faith rule to police who reasonably relied on mistaken information in a court's database that an arrest warrant was outstanding. We held that a mistake made by a judicial employee could not give rise to exclusion for three reasons: The exclusionary rule was crafted to curb police rather than judicial misconduct; court employees were unlikely to try to subvert the Fourth Amendment; and "most important, there [was] no basis for believing that application of the exclusionary rule in [those] circumstances" would have any significant effect in deterring the errors. *Evans* left unresolved "whether the evidence should be suppressed if police personnel were responsible for the error," an issue not argued by the State in that case, but one that we now confront.

The extent to which the exclusionary rule is justified by these deterrence principles varies with the culpability of the law enforcement conduct. As we said in *Leon*, "an assessment of the flagrancy of the police misconduct constitutes an important step in the calculus" of applying the exclusionary rule. Similarly, in *Krull* we elaborated that "evidence should be suppressed 'only if it can be said that the law enforcement officer had knowledge, or may properly be charged with knowledge, that the search was unconstitutional under the Fourth Amendment.'"

Anticipating the good-faith exception to the exclusionary rule, Judge Friendly wrote that "[t]he beneficent aim of the exclusionary rule to deter police misconduct can be sufficiently accomplished by a practice . . . outlawing evidence obtained by flagrant or deliberate violation of rights."

Indeed, the abuses that gave rise to the exclusionary rule featured intentional conduct that was patently unconstitutional. In *Weeks*, a foundational exclusionary rule case, the officers had broken into the defendant's home (using a key shown to them by a neighbor), confiscated incriminating papers, then returned again with a U.S. Marshal to confiscate even more. Not only did they have no search warrant, which the Court held was required, but they could not have gotten one had they tried. They were so lacking in sworn and particularized information that "not even an order of court would have justified such procedure." *Silverthorne Lumber Co. v. United States* (1920), on which petitioner repeatedly relies, was similar; federal officials "without a shadow of authority" went to the defendants' office and "made a clean sweep" of every paper they could find. Even the Government seemed to acknowledge that the "seizure was an outrage."

Equally flagrant conduct was at issue in *Mapp v. Ohio* (1961), which overruled *Wolf v. Colorado* (1949), and extended the exclusionary rule to the States. Officers forced open a door to Ms. Mapp's house, kept her lawyer from entering, brandished what the court concluded was a false warrant, then forced her into handcuffs and canvassed the house for obscenity. An error that arises from nonrecurring and attenuated negligence is thus far removed from the core concerns that led us to adopt the rule in the first place. And in fact since *Leon*, we have never applied the rule to exclude evidence obtained in violation of the Fourth Amendment, where the police conduct was no more intentional or culpable than this.

To trigger the exclusionary rule, police conduct must be sufficiently deliberate that exclusion can meaningfully deter it, and sufficiently culpable that such deterrence is worth the price paid by the justice system. As laid out in our cases, the exclusionary rule serves to deter deliberate, reckless, or grossly negligent conduct, or in some circumstances recurring or systemic negligence. The error in this case does not rise to that level.

Our decision in *Franks v. Delaware* (1978), provides an analogy. In *Franks*, we held that police negligence in obtaining a warrant did not even rise to the level of a Fourth Amendment violation, let alone meet the more stringent test for triggering the exclusionary rule. We held that the Constitution allowed defendants, in some circumstances, "to challenge the truthfulness of factual statements made in an affidavit supporting the warrant," even after the warrant had issued. If those false statements were necessary to the Magistrate Judge's probable-cause determination, the warrant would be "voided." But we did not find all false statements relevant: "There must be allegations of deliberate falsehood or of reckless disregard for the truth," and "[a]llegations of negligence or innocent mistake are insufficient."

Both this case and *Franks* concern false information provided by police. Under *Franks*, negligent police miscommunications in the course of acquiring a warrant do not provide a basis to rescind a warrant and render a search or arrest invalid. Here, the miscommunications occurred in a different context—after the warrant had been issued and recalled—but that fact should not require excluding the evidence obtained.

The pertinent analysis of deterrence and culpability is objective, not an "inquiry into the subjective awareness of arresting officers." We have already held that "our good-faith inquiry is confined to the objectively ascertainable question whether a reasonably well trained officer would have known that the search was illegal" in light of "all of the circumstances." These circumstances frequently include a particular officer's knowledge and experience, but that does not make the test any more subjective than the one for probable cause, which looks to an officer's knowledge and experience, but not his subjective intent, *Whren v. United States* (1996).

We do not suggest that all recordkeeping errors by the police are immune from the exclusionary rule. In this case, however, the conduct at issue was not so objectively culpable as to require exclusion. In *Leon*, we held that "the marginal or nonexistent benefits produced by suppressing evidence obtained in objectively reasonable reliance on a subsequently invalidated search warrant cannot justify the substantial costs of exclusion." The same is true when evidence is obtained in objectively reasonable reliance on a subsequently recalled warrant.

If the police have been shown to be reckless in maintaining a warrant system, or to have knowingly made false entries to lay the groundwork for future false arrests, exclusion would certainly be justified under our cases should such misconduct cause a Fourth Amendment violation. We said as much in *Leon*, explaining that an officer could not "obtain a warrant on the basis of a 'bare bones' affidavit and then rely on colleagues who are ignorant of the circumstances under which the warrant was obtained to conduct the search." Petitioner's fears that our decision will cause police departments to deliberately keep their officers ignorant, are thus unfounded.

Justice Ginsburg's dissent also adverts to the possible unreliability of a number of databases not relevant to this case. In a case where systemic errors were demonstrated, it might be reckless for officers to rely on an unreliable warrant system. But there is no evidence that errors in Dale County's system are routine or widespread. Officer Anderson testified that he had never had reason to question information about a Dale County warrant, and both Sandy Pope and Sharon Morgan testified that they could remember no similar miscommunication ever happening on their watch. That is even less error than in the database at issue in *Evans*, where we also found reliance on the database to be objectively reasonable. Because no such showings were made here, the Eleventh Circuit was correct to affirm the denial of the motion to suppress.

• • •

Petitioner's claim that police negligence automatically triggers suppression cannot be squared with the principles underlying the exclusionary rule, as they have been explained in our cases. In light of our repeated holdings that the deterrent effect of suppression must be substantial and outweigh any harm to the justice system, we conclude that when police mistakes are the result of negligence such as that described here, rather than systemic error or reckless disregard of constitutional requirements, any marginal deterrence does not "pay its way." In such a case, the criminal should not "go free because the constable has blundered."

The judgment of the Court of Appeals for the Eleventh Circuit is affirmed.

NOTES AND QUESTIONS

1. The Court makes several observations about the type of "culpability" that will be required for exclusion. It notes that the exclusionary rule only serves "to deter deliberate, reckless, or grossly negligent conduct, or in some circumstances recurring or systemic negligence." How often do you think police violations fall in to these categories? Is a rogue police officer who commits the sort of flagrant constitutional violations the Court posits a better or worse candidate for deterrence that an officer who makes a mistake?

2. What do you understand the Court to mean in describing the "error" as "isolated negligence attenuated from the arrest"? How can the database error be seen as "attenuated" from the arrest where the existence of the warrant was in itself both the necessary and sufficient condition for the arrest? Would negligence in determining, say, reasonable suspicion for a *Terry* stop that led to an arrest be similarly "attenuated"?

3. Justice Ginsburg, dissenting along with Justices Stevens and Breyer, points out the inconsistency between the Court's exclusionary jurisprudence and the basic principles of tort law, which impose liability for negligence as an incentive for defendants to act with greater care. Fair analogy? Is there anything special about the deterrence rationale as applied to law enforcement that warrants a different approach?

What are the costs of overdeterrence in tort law? What are the costs of overdeterrence in the law enforcement context? Is it fair to think of the latter costs in terms of crimes going undetected or unprosecuted because police officers will take fewer risks? Or, alternatively, should those costs be viewed more broadly in terms of fewer violations of constitutional rights, even in those situations where there is not a prosecution and the exclusionary rule does not come into play?

4. Justice Ginsburg also stresses the enormous expansion of law enforcement databases, and how they can be called on instantly — as they were here — to find out if a person has an outstanding warrant, a state of affairs that can result in an immediate arrest and a search incident to that arrest. Shouldn't this terrifying power be subjected to a heightened degree of scrutiny? Should a police officer be permitted to embark on a database fishing expedition without probable cause or even reasonable suspicion? *See* Wayne A. Logan, *Policing Police Access to Criminal Justice Data,* 104 Iowa L. Rev. 619. 673-76 (2019) (discussing legislative restrictions on police access to certain database information).

5. The Court doesn't deem it worthy of inclusion in its opinion that Bennie Dean Herring had a target on his back. As the dissenting opinion notes:

> Investigator Mark Anderson . . . knew Herring from prior interactions: Herring had told the District Attorney, among others, of his suspicion that Anderson had been involved in the killing of a local teenager, and Anderson had pursued Herring to get him to drop the accusations. Informed that Herring was in the impoundment lot, Anderson asked the Coffee County warrant clerk whether there was an outstanding warrant for Herring's arrest.

Bennie Dean Herring

The Court presumably would have attached no legal relevance to this because of its fetish with ignoring police officers' "subjective motivations." But doesn't it hurt the Court's credibility when it fails to even acknowledge such information?

6. Commentators have debated the significance of *Herring* in that, on the one hand, it arguably involved only a "negligent bookkeeping error," as the Court framed the issue in the first paragraph of the opinion. Others disagree and focus on its statement that the exclusionary rule aims only "to deter deliberate, reckless, or grossly negligent conduct," and its references to the sort of "flagrant misconduct" at issue in *Weeks* and *Mapp*. *See* Albert W. Alschuler, Herring v. United States*: A Minnow or a Shark?*, 7 Ohio St. J. Crim. L. 463, 488-89 (2009) ("No decision prior to *Herring*, however, had suggested or implied that the exclusionary rule should be limited in the way the Court proposed.").

In *Davis v. United States*, 554 U.S. 229 (2011), the Court applied the exclusionary rule where a police officer searched the vehicle of a driver arrested for giving a false name. At the time the search was conducted it was in compliance with existing law (*New York v. Belton*), but while the defendant's appeal was pending *Arizona v. Gant* overruled *Belton*. *See* Chapter IV *supra*. The Court found the good faith exception applicable even though there was no evidence that the officer had actually relied on the authority of *Belton*. Dissenting, Justice Breyer openly wondered about the future of the exclusionary rule:

> If the Court means what it says, what will happen to the exclusionary rule, a rule that the Court adopted nearly a century ago for federal courts, and made applicable to state courts a half century ago through the Fourteenth Amendment? The Court has thought of that rule not as punishment for the individual officer or as reparation for the individual defendant but more generally as an effective way to secure enforcement of the Fourth Amendment's commands. This Court has deviated from the "suppression" norm in the name of "good faith" only a handful of times and in limited, atypical circumstances: where a magistrate has erroneously issued a warrant; where a database has erroneously informed police that they have a warrant; and where an unconstitutional statute purported to authorize the search.

Id. at 252, 257 (Breyer, J., dissenting). Professors Maclin and Rader argue that *Davis* represents an extension of *Herring* in that it applies the good faith exception to ordinary

Fourth Amendment violations, and not just situations — as in *Evans* and *Herring* — where the connection between the error and the violation is "attenuated." *See* Tracey Maclin & Jennifer Rader, *No More Chipping Away: The Roberts Court Uses an Axe to Take Out the Fourth Amendment Exclusionary Rule*, 81 Miss. L.J. 1183, 1206-07 (2011).

C. ATTENUATION

Attenuation of a different sort than at issue in *Herring* is its own categorical exception to the exclusionary rule. The attenuation doctrine applies in situations where the connection between police misconduct and illegally obtained evidence — the "fruit of the poisonous tree" — is indirect or "attenuated." Under this exception, evidence may be admissible where the misconduct is so distant or remote from the acquisition of the evidence that the original violation is effectively nullified. Usually the doctrine applies where there are intervening circumstances between the misconduct and the acquisition of the evidence sought to be suppressed. Related causation-based exceptions to the exclusionary rule are the "independent source" doctrine, which allows trial courts to admit evidence obtained in an unlawful search if officers acquired it from a separate, independent source, *Murray v. United States*, 487 U.S. 533 (1988), and the "inevitable discovery" doctrine, which permits the admission of evidence that would have been discovered even without the unconstitutional misconduct, *Nix v. Williams*, 467 U.S. 431 (1984).

The Court adopted a three-factor balancing test for application of the attenuation doctrine in *Brown v. Illinois*, 422 U.S. 590 (1975). This test requires analyzing (1) the temporal proximity of the unlawful police action and the seizure of evidence, (2) the presence of intervening circumstances, and (3) the existence of any purposeful or flagrant misconduct by a police officer. In *Brown*, the Court found that where the defendant had been illegally arrested without either probable cause or a warrant, and subsequently made admissions after being given *Miranda* warnings, that the *Miranda* warnings did not necessarily remove the taint of the illegal conduct.

The Court has applied the attenuation doctrine in numerous contexts before and after *Brown*, largely adhering to its general principles.

The next two cases, from 2006 and 2016 respectively, suggest this may no longer be the case.

Hudson v. Michigan

547 U.S. 586 (2006)

Justice Scalia delivered the opinion of the Court, except as to Part IV.

We decide whether violation of the "knock-and-announce" rule requires the suppression of all evidence found in the search.

I

Police obtained a warrant authorizing a search for drugs and firearms at the home of petitioner Booker Hudson. They discovered both. Large quantities of drugs were found, including cocaine rocks in Hudson's pocket. A loaded gun was lodged between the cushion and armrest of the chair in which he was sitting. Hudson was charged under Michigan law with unlawful drug and firearm possession.

This case is before us only because of the method of entry into the house. When the police arrived to execute the warrant, they announced their presence, but waited only a short time — perhaps "three to five seconds" — before turning the knob of the unlocked front door and entering Hudson's home. Hudson moved to suppress all the inculpatory evidence, arguing that the premature entry violated his Fourth Amendment rights.

II

The common-law principle that law enforcement officers must announce their presence and provide residents an opportunity to open the door is an ancient one. Since 1917, when Congress passed the Espionage Act, this traditional protection has been part of federal statutory law and is currently codified at 18 U.S.C. § 3109. We applied that statute in *Miller v. United States* (1958), and again in *Sabbath v. United States* (1968). Finally, in *Wilson*, we were asked whether the rule was also a command of the Fourth Amendment. Tracing its origins in our English legal heritage, we concluded that it was.

We recognized that the new constitutional rule we had announced is not easily applied. *Wilson* and cases following it have noted the many situations in which it is not necessary to knock and announce. It is not necessary when "circumstances presen[t] a threat of physical violence," or if there is "reason to believe that evidence would likely be destroyed if advance notice were given," or if knocking and announcing would be "futile," *Richards v. Wisconsin* (1997). We require only that police "have a reasonable suspicion . . . under the particular circumstances" that one of these grounds for failing to knock and announce exists, and we have acknowledged that "[t]his showing is not high."

When the knock-and-announce rule does apply, it is not easy to determine precisely what officers must do. How many seconds' wait are too few? Our "reasonable wait time" standard, is necessarily vague. *Banks* (a drug case, like this one) held that the proper measure was not how long it would take the resident to reach the door, but how long it would take to dispose of the suspected drugs — but that such a time (15 to 20 seconds in that case) would necessarily be extended when, for instance, the suspected contraband was not easily concealed. If our ex post evaluation is subject to such calculations, it is unsurprising that, ex ante, police officers about to encounter someone who may try to harm them will be uncertain how long to wait.

Happily, these issues do not confront us here. From the trial level onward, Michigan has conceded that the entry was a knock-and-announce violation. The issue here is remedy. *Wilson* specifically declined to decide whether the exclusionary rule is appropriate for violation of the knock-and-announce requirement. That question is squarely before us now.

III

A

In *Weeks v. United States* we adopted the federal exclusionary rule for evidence that was unlawfully seized from a home without a warrant in violation of the Fourth Amendment. We began applying the same rule to the States, through the Fourteenth Amendment, in *Mapp v. Ohio* (1961).

Suppression of evidence, however, has always been our last resort, not our first impulse. The exclusionary rule generates "substantial social costs," which sometimes include setting the guilty free and the dangerous at large. We have therefore been "cautio[us] against expanding" it, and "have repeatedly emphasized that the rule's 'costly toll' upon truth-seeking and law enforcement objectives presents a high obstacle for those urging [its] application." We have rejected "[i]ndiscriminate application" of the rule, and have held it to be applicable only "where its remedial objectives are thought most efficaciously served" — that is, "where its deterrence benefits outweigh its 'substantial social costs.'"

We did not always speak so guardedly. Expansive dicta in *Mapp*, for example, suggested wide scope for the exclusionary rule. But we have long since rejected that approach. As explained in *Arizona v. Evans* (1995): "In *Whiteley*, the Court treated identification of a Fourth Amendment violation as synonymous with application of the exclusionary rule to evidence secured incident to that violation. Subsequent case law has rejected this reflexive application of the exclusionary rule." We had said as much in *Leon*, a decade earlier, when we explained that "[w]hether the exclusionary sanction is appropriately imposed in a particular case . . . is 'an issue separate from the question whether the Fourth Amendment rights of the party seeking to invoke the rule were violated by police conduct.'"

In other words, exclusion may not be premised on the mere fact that a constitutional violation was a "but-for" cause of obtaining evidence. Our cases show that but-for causality is only a necessary, not a sufficient, condition for suppression. In this case, of course, the constitutional violation of an illegal manner of entry was not a but-for cause of obtaining the evidence. Whether that preliminary misstep had occurred or not, the police would have executed the warrant they had obtained, and would have discovered the gun and drugs inside the house. But even if the illegal entry here could be characterized as a but-for cause of discovering what was inside, we have "never held that evidence is 'fruit of the poisonous tree' simply because 'it would not have come to light but for the illegal actions of the police.'" Rather, but-for cause, or "causation in the logical sense alone," can be too attenuated to justify exclusion. Even in the early days of the exclusionary rule, we declined to

> hold that all evidence is "fruit of the poisonous tree" simply because it would not have come to light but for the illegal actions of the police. Rather, the more apt question in such a case is "whether, granting establishment of the primary illegality, the evidence to which instant objection is made has been come at by exploitation of that illegality or instead by means sufficiently distinguishable to be purged of the primary taint."

Attenuation can occur, of course, when the causal connection is remote. Attenuation also occurs when, even given a direct causal connection, the interest protected by the constitutional guarantee that has been violated would not be served by suppression of the evidence obtained. "The penalties visited upon the Government, and in turn upon the public, because its officers have violated the law must bear some relation to the purposes which the law is to serve." Thus, in *New York v. Harris* (1990), where an illegal warrantless arrest was made in Harris's house, we held:

> [S]uppressing [Harris's] statement taken outside the house would not serve the purpose of the rule that made Harris' in-house arrest illegal. The warrant requirement for an arrest in the home is imposed to protect the home, and anything incriminating the police gathered from arresting Harris in his home, rather than elsewhere, has been excluded, as it should have been; the purpose of the rule has thereby been vindicated.

For this reason, cases excluding the fruits of unlawful warrantless searches, say nothing about the appropriateness of exclusion to vindicate the interests protected by the knock-and-announce requirement. Until a valid warrant has issued, citizens are entitled to shield "their persons, houses, papers, and effects," from the government's scrutiny. Exclusion of the evidence obtained by a warrantless search vindicates that entitlement. The interests protected by the knock-and-announce requirement are quite different—and do not include the shielding of potential evidence from the government's eyes.

One of those interests is the protection of human life and limb, because an unannounced entry may provoke violence in supposed self-defense by the surprised resident. Another interest is the protection of property. Breaking a house (as the old cases typically put it) absent an announcement would penalize someone who "'did not know of the process, of which, if he had notice, it is to be presumed that he would obey it. . . .'" The knock-and-announce rule gives individuals "the opportunity to comply with the law and to avoid the destruction of property occasioned by a forcible entry." And thirdly, the knock-and-announce rule protects those elements of privacy and dignity that can be destroyed by a sudden entrance. It gives residents the "opportunity to prepare themselves for" the entry of the police. "The brief interlude between announcement and entry with a warrant may be the opportunity that an individual has to pull on clothes or get out of bed." In other words, it assures the opportunity to collect oneself before answering the door.

What the knock-and-announce rule has never protected, however, is one's interest in preventing the government from seeing or taking evidence described in a warrant. Since the interests that were violated in this case have nothing to do with the seizure of the evidence, the exclusionary rule is inapplicable.

B

Quite apart from the requirement of unattenuated causation, the exclusionary rule has never been applied except "where its deterrence benefits outweigh its 'substantial social costs.'" The costs here are considerable. In addition to the grave adverse consequence that exclusion of relevant incriminating evidence always entails (viz., the risk of releasing dangerous criminals into society), imposing that massive remedy for a knock-and-announce violation would generate a constant flood of alleged failures to observe the rule, and claims that any asserted *Richards* justification for a no-knock entry, had inadequate support. The cost of entering this lottery would be small, but the jackpot enormous: suppression of all evidence, amounting in many cases to a get-out-of-jail-free card. Courts would experience as never before the reality that "[t]he exclusionary rule frequently requires extensive litigation to determine whether particular evidence must be excluded." Unlike the warrant or *Miranda* requirements, compliance with which is readily determined (either there was or was not a warrant; either the *Miranda* warning was given, or it was not), what constituted a "reasonable wait time" in a particular case, or whether there was "reasonable suspicion" of the sort that would invoke the *Richards* exceptions, is difficult for the trial court to determine and even more difficult for an appellate court to review.

Another consequence of the incongruent remedy Hudson proposes would be police officers' refraining from timely entry after knocking and announcing. As we have observed, the amount of time they must wait is necessarily uncertain. If the consequences of running afoul of the rule were so massive, officers would be inclined to wait longer than the law requires — producing preventable violence against officers in some cases, and the destruction of evidence in many others. We deemed these consequences severe enough to produce our unanimous agreement that a mere "reasonable suspicion" that knocking and announcing "under the particular circumstances, would be dangerous or futile, or that it would inhibit the effective investigation of the crime," will cause the requirement to yield.

Next to these "substantial social costs" we must consider the deterrence benefits, existence of which is a necessary condition for exclusion. (It is not, of course, a sufficient condition: "[I]t does not follow that the Fourth Amendment requires adoption of every proposal that might deter police misconduct.") To begin with, the value of deterrence depends upon the strength of the incentive to commit the forbidden act. Viewed from this perspective, deterrence of knock-and-announce violations is not worth a lot. Violation of the warrant requirement sometimes produces incriminating evidence that could not otherwise be obtained. But ignoring knock-and-announce can realistically be expected to achieve absolutely nothing except the prevention of destruction of evidence and the avoidance of life-threatening resistance by occupants of the premises — dangers which, if there is even "reasonable suspicion" of their existence, suspend the knock-and-announce requirement anyway. Massive deterrence is hardly required.

It seems to us not even true, as Hudson contends, that without suppression there will be no deterrence of knock-and-announce violations at all. Of course even if this assertion were accurate, it would not necessarily justify suppression. Assuming (as the assertion must) that civil suit is not an effective deterrent, one can think of many forms of police misconduct that are similarly "undeterred." When, for example, a confessed suspect in the killing of a police officer, arrested (along with incriminating evidence) in a lawful warranted search, is subjected to physical abuse at the station house, would it seriously be suggested that the evidence must be excluded, since that is the only "effective deterrent"? And what, other than civil suit, is the "effective deterrent" of police violation of an already-confessed suspect's Sixth Amendment rights by denying him prompt access to counsel? Many would regard these violated rights as more significant than the right not to be intruded upon in one's nightclothes—and yet nothing but "ineffective" civil suit is available as a deterrent. And the police incentive for those violations is arguably greater than the incentive for disregarding the knock-and-announce rule.

We cannot assume that exclusion in this context is necessary deterrence simply because we found that it was necessary deterrence in different contexts and long ago. That would be forcing the public today to pay for the sins and inadequacies of a legal regime that existed almost half a century ago. Dollree Mapp could not turn to 42 U.S.C. § 1983, for meaningful relief; *Monroe v. Pape* (1961), which began the slow but steady expansion of that remedy, was decided the same Term as *Mapp*. It would be another 17 years before the § 1983 remedy was extended to reach the deep pocket of municipalities, *Monell v. New York City Dept. of Social Servs.* (1978). Citizens whose Fourth Amendment rights were violated by federal officers could not bring suit until 10 years after *Mapp*, with this Court's decision in *Bivens v. Six Unknown Fed. Narcotics Agents* (1971).

Hudson complains that "it would be very hard to find a lawyer to take a case such as this," but 42 U.S.C. § 1988(b) answers this objection. Since some civil-rights violations would yield damages too small to justify the expense of litigation, Congress has authorized attorney's fees for civil-rights plaintiffs. This remedy was unavailable in the heydays of our exclusionary-rule jurisprudence, because it is tied to the availability of a cause of action. For years after *Mapp*, "very few lawyers would even consider representation of persons who had civil rights claims against the police," but now "much has changed. Citizens and lawyers are much more willing to seek relief in the courts for police misconduct." The number of public-interest law firms and lawyers who specialize in civil-rights grievances has greatly expanded.

Hudson points out that few published decisions to date announce huge awards for knock-and-announce violations. But this is an unhelpful statistic. Even if we thought that only large damages would deter police misconduct (and that police somehow are deterred by "damages" but indifferent to the prospect of large § 1988 attorney's fees), we do not know how many claims have been settled, or indeed how many violations have occurred that produced anything more than nominal injury. It is clear, at least, that the lower courts are allowing colorable knock-and-announce suits to go forward, unimpeded by assertions of qualified immunity. As far as we know, civil liability is an effective deterrent here, as we have assumed it is in other contexts.

Another development over the past half-century that deters civil-rights violations is the increasing professionalism of police forces, including a new emphasis on internal police discipline. Even as long ago as 1980 we felt it proper to "assume" that unlawful police behavior would "be dealt with appropriately" by the authorities, but we now have increasing evidence that police forces across the United States take the constitutional rights of citizens seriously. There have been "wide-ranging reforms in the education, training, and supervision of police officers." Numerous sources are now available to teach officers and their supervisors what is required of them under this Court's cases, how to respect constitutional guarantees in various situations, and how to craft an effective regime for internal discipline. Failure to teach and enforce constitutional requirements exposes municipalities to financial liability. Moreover, modern police forces are staffed with professionals; it is not credible to assert that internal discipline, which can limit successful careers, will not have a deterrent effect. There is also evidence that the increasing use of various forms of citizen review can enhance police accountability.

In sum, the social costs of applying the exclusionary rule to knock-and-announce violations are considerable; the incentive to such violations is minimal to begin with, and the extant deterrences against them are substantial—incomparably greater than the factors deterring warrantless entries when *Mapp* was decided. Resort to the massive remedy of suppressing evidence of guilt is unjustified.

IV

A trio of cases—confirms our conclusion that suppression is unwarranted in this case.

Like today's case, *Segura* involved a concededly illegal entry. Police conducting a drug crime investigation waited for Segura outside an apartment building; when he arrived, he denied living there. The police arrested him and brought him to the apartment where they suspected illegal activity. An officer knocked. When someone inside opened the door, the police entered, taking Segura with them. They had neither a warrant nor consent to enter, and they did not announce themselves as police—an entry as illegal as can be. Officers then stayed in the apartment for 19 hours awaiting a search warrant. Once alerted that the search warrant had been obtained, the police—still inside, having secured the premises so that no evidence could be removed—conducted a search. We refused to exclude the resulting evidence. We recognized that only the evidence gained from the particular violation could be excluded, and therefore distinguished the effects of the illegal entry from the effects of the legal search: "None of the information on which the warrant was secured was derived from or related in any way to the initial entry into petitioners' apartment. . . ." It was therefore "beyond dispute that the information possessed by the agents before they entered the apartment constituted an independent source for the discovery and seizure of the evidence now challenged." Ibid.

If the search in *Segura* could be "wholly unrelated to the prior entry," when the only entry was warrantless, it would be bizarre to treat more harshly the actions in this case, where the only entry was with a warrant. If the probable cause backing a warrant that was issued later in time could be an "independent source" for a search that proceeded after the officers illegally entered and waited, a search warrant obtained before going in must have at least this much effect.

In the second case, *Harris*, the police violated the defendant's Fourth Amendment rights by arresting him at home without a warrant, contrary to *Payton v. New York* (1980). Once taken to the station house, he gave an incriminating statement. We refused to exclude it. Like the illegal entry which led to discovery of the evidence in today's case, the illegal arrest in *Harris* began a process that culminated in acquisition of the evidence sought to be excluded. While Harris's statement was "the product of an arrest and being in custody," it "was not the fruit of the fact that the arrest was made in the house rather than someplace else." Likewise here: While acquisition of the gun and drugs was the product of a search pursuant to warrant, it was not the fruit of the fact that the entry was not preceded by knock-and-announce.

United States v. Ramirez, supra, involved a claim that police entry violated the Fourth Amendment because it was effected by breaking a window. We ultimately concluded that the property destruction was, under all the circumstances, reasonable, but in the course of our discussion we unanimously said the following: "[D]estruction of property in the course of a search may violate the Fourth Amendment, even though the entry itself is lawful and the fruits of the search are not subject to suppression." Had the breaking of the window been unreasonable, the Court said, it would have been necessary to determine whether there had been a "sufficient causal relationship between the breaking of the window and the discovery of the guns to warrant suppression of the evidence." What clearer expression could there be of the proposition that an impermissible manner of entry does not necessarily trigger the exclusionary rule?

• • •

For the foregoing reasons we affirm the judgment of the Michigan Court of Appeals.

[Justice Kennedy filed an opinion concurring in part and concurring in the judgment. Justice Breyer filed an opinion dissenting, in which Justices Stevens, Souter, and Ginsburg joined.]

NOTES AND QUESTIONS

1. Does *Hudson* mean that suppression can never be a remedy for violation of a knock-and-announce requirement?

2. The Court suggests that because 42 U.S.C § 1983 provides a civil remedy for persons aggrieved by Fourth Amendment violations the deterrence afforded by the exclusionary rule is less necessary than it once was. The Court makes this point without irony, failing to acknowledge how it over the previous years has largely gutted that civil remedy by conferring an expansive, judicially created, qualified immunity on defendant police officers in § 1983 actions.

3. Note that the Court deviates from the general principles of *Brown*, to say nothing of its three-factor test, in finding that the interests that were violated in *Hudson* "have nothing to do with the seizure of the evidence," and — therefore, the Court implies — the exclusionary rule is inapplicable. Professors Maclin and Rader and others point out that this novel approach to attenuation makes vulnerable many cases finding Fourth Amendment violations based on the manner in which a search was executed. *See* Maclin & Rader, *No More Chipping Away*, *supra* at 1183, 1219-26.

The next case uses a more traditional application of the *Brown v. Illinois* test to justify a harsh result. Once again, computerized police criminal record databases figure prominently.

Utah v. Strieff

579 U.S. 232 (2016)

Justice Thomas delivered the opinion of the Court.

To enforce the Fourth Amendment's prohibition against "unreasonable searches and seizures," this Court has at times required courts to exclude evidence obtained by unconstitutional police conduct. But the Court has also held that, even when there is a Fourth Amendment violation, this exclusionary rule does not apply when the costs of exclusion outweigh its deterrent benefits. In some cases, for example, the link between the unconstitutional conduct and the discovery of the evidence is too attenuated to justify suppression. The question in this case is whether this attenuation doctrine applies when an officer makes an unconstitutional investigatory stop; learns during that stop that the suspect is subject to a valid arrest warrant; and proceeds to arrest the suspect and seize incriminating evidence during a search incident to that arrest. We hold that the evidence the officer seized as part of the search incident to arrest is admissible because the officer's discovery of the arrest warrant attenuated the connection between the unlawful stop and the evidence seized incident to arrest.

I

This case began with an anonymous tip. In December 2006, someone called the South Salt Lake City police's drug-tip line to report "narcotics activity" at a particular residence.

Narcotics detective Douglas Fackrell investigated the tip. Over the course of about a week, Officer Fackrell conducted intermittent surveillance of the home. He observed visitors who left a few minutes after arriving at the house. These visits were sufficiently frequent to raise his suspicion that the occupants were dealing drugs.

One of those visitors was respondent Edward Strieff. Officer Fackrell observed Strieff exit the house and walk toward a nearby convenience store. In the store's parking lot, Officer Fackrell detained Strieff, identified himself, and asked Strieff what he was doing at the residence.

As part of the stop, Officer Fackrell requested Strieff's identification, and Strieff produced his Utah identification card. Officer Fackrell relayed Strieff's information to a police dispatcher, who reported that Strieff had an outstanding arrest warrant for a traffic violation. Officer Fackrell then arrested Strieff pursuant to that warrant. When Officer Fackrell searched Strieff incident to the arrest, he discovered a baggie of methamphetamine and drug paraphernalia.

The State charged Strieff with unlawful possession of methamphetamine and drug paraphernalia. Strieff moved to suppress the evidence, arguing that the evidence was inadmissible because it was derived from an unlawful investigatory stop. At the suppression hearing, the prosecutor conceded that Officer Fackrell lacked reasonable suspicion for the stop but argued that the evidence should not be suppressed because the existence of a valid arrest warrant attenuated the connection between the unlawful stop and the discovery of the contraband.

• • •

II

A

The Fourth Amendment protects "[t]he right of the people to be secure in their persons, houses, papers, and effects, against unreasonable searches and seizures." Because officers who violated the Fourth Amendment were traditionally considered trespassers, individuals subject to unconstitutional searches or seizures historically enforced their rights through tort suits or self-help. Thomas Y. Davies, *Recovering the Original Fourth Amendment*, 98 Mich. L. Rev. 547, 625 (1999). In the 20th century, however, the exclusionary rule—the rule that often requires trial courts to exclude unlawfully seized evidence in a criminal trial—became the principal judicial remedy to deter Fourth Amendment violations.

Under the Court's precedents, the exclusionary rule encompasses both the "primary evidence obtained as a direct result of an illegal search or seizure" and, relevant here, "evidence later discovered and found to be derivative of an illegality," the so-called "'fruit of the poisonous tree.'" But the significant costs of this rule have led us to deem it "applicable only . . . where its deterrence benefits outweigh its substantial social costs." "Suppression of evidence . . . has always been our last resort, not our first impulse."

We have accordingly recognized several exceptions to the rule. Three of these exceptions involve the causal relationship between the unconstitutional act and the discovery of evidence. First, the independent source doctrine allows trial courts to admit evidence obtained in an unlawful search if officers independently acquired it from a separate, independent source. *See Murray v. United States* (1988). Second, the inevitable discovery doctrine allows for the admission of evidence that would have been discovered even without the unconstitutional source. *See Nix v. Williams* (1984). Third, and at issue here, is the attenuation doctrine: Evidence is admissible when the connection between unconstitutional police conduct and the evidence is remote or has been interrupted by some intervening circumstance, so that "the interest protected by the constitutional guarantee that has been violated would not be served by suppression of the evidence obtained."

B

Turning to the application of the attenuation doctrine to this case, we first address a threshold question: whether this doctrine applies at all to a case like this, where the intervening circumstance that the State relies on is the discovery of a valid, pre-existing, and untainted arrest warrant. The Utah Supreme Court declined to apply the attenuation doctrine because it read our precedents as applying the doctrine only "to circumstances involving an independent act of a defendant's 'free will' in confessing to a crime or consenting to a search." In this Court, Strieff has not defended this argument, and we disagree with it, as well. The attenuation doctrine evaluates the causal link between the government's unlawful act and the discovery of evidence, which often has nothing to do with a defendant's actions. And the logic of our prior attenuation cases is not limited to independent acts by the defendant.

It remains for us to address whether the discovery of a valid arrest warrant was a sufficient intervening event to break the causal chain between the unlawful stop and the discovery of drug-related evidence on Strieff's person. The three factors articulated in *Brown v. Illinois* (1975) guide our analysis. First, we look to the "temporal proximity" between the unconstitutional conduct and the discovery of evidence to determine how closely the discovery of evidence followed the unconstitutional search. Second, we consider "the presence of intervening circumstances." Third, and "particularly" significant, we examine "the purpose and flagrancy of the official misconduct." In evaluating these factors, we assume without deciding (because the State conceded the point) that Officer Fackrell lacked reasonable suspicion to initially stop Strieff. And, because we ultimately conclude that the warrant breaks the causal chain, we also have no need to decide whether the warrant's existence alone would make the initial stop constitutional even if Officer Fackrell was unaware of its existence.

1

The first factor, temporal proximity between the initially unlawful stop and the search, favors suppressing the evidence. Our precedents have declined to find that this factor favors attenuation unless "substantial time" elapses between an unlawful act and when the evidence is obtained. Here, however, Officer Fackrell discovered drug contraband on Strieff's person only minutes after the illegal stop. As the Court explained in *Brown*, such a short time interval counsels in favor of suppression; there, we found that the confession should be suppressed, relying in part on the "less than two hours" that separated the unconstitutional arrest and the confession.

In contrast, the second factor, the presence of intervening circumstances, strongly favors the State. In *Segura*, the Court addressed similar facts to those here and found sufficient intervening circumstances to allow the admission of evidence. There, agents had probable cause to believe that apartment occupants were dealing cocaine. They sought a warrant. In the meantime, they entered the apartment, arrested an occupant, and discovered evidence of drug activity during a limited search for security reasons. The next evening, the Magistrate Judge issued the search warrant. This Court deemed the evidence admissible notwithstanding the illegal search because the information supporting the warrant was "wholly unconnected with the [arguably illegal] entry and was known to the agents well before the initial entry."

Segura, of course, applied the independent source doctrine because the unlawful entry "did not contribute in any way to discovery of the evidence seized under the warrant." But the *Segura* Court suggested that the existence of a valid warrant favors finding that the connection between unlawful conduct and the discovery of evidence is "sufficiently attenuated to dissipate the taint." That principle applies here.

In this case, the warrant was valid, it predated Officer Fackrell's investigation, and it was entirely unconnected with the stop. And once Officer Fackrell discovered the warrant, he had an obligation to arrest Strieff. "A warrant is a judicial mandate to an officer to conduct a search or make an arrest, and the officer has a sworn duty to carry out its provisions." Officer Fackrell's arrest of Strieff thus was a ministerial act that was independently compelled by the pre-existing warrant. And once Officer Fackrell was authorized to arrest Strieff, it was undisputedly lawful to search Strieff as an incident of his arrest to protect Officer Fackrell's safety.

Finally, the third factor, "the purpose and flagrancy of the official misconduct," also strongly favors the State. The exclusionary rule exists to deter police misconduct. The third factor of the attenuation doctrine reflects that rationale by favoring exclusion only when the police misconduct is most in need of deterrence—that is, when it is purposeful or flagrant.

Officer Fackrell was at most negligent. In stopping Strieff, Officer Fackrell made two good-faith mistakes. First, he had not observed what time Strieff entered the suspected drug house, so he did not know how long Strieff had been there. Officer Fackrell thus lacked a sufficient basis to conclude that Strieff was a short-term visitor who may have been consummating a drug transaction. Second, because he lacked confirmation that Strieff was a short-term visitor, Officer Fackrell should have asked Strieff whether he would speak with him, instead of demanding that Strieff do so. Officer Fackrell's stated purpose was to "find out what was going on [in] the house." Nothing prevented him from approaching Strieff simply to ask. But these errors in judgment hardly rise to a purposeful or flagrant violation of Strieff's Fourth Amendment rights.

While Officer Fackrell's decision to initiate the stop was mistaken, his conduct thereafter was lawful. The officer's decision to run the warrant check was a "negligibly burdensome precautio[n]" for officer safety. And Officer Fackrell's actual search of Strieff was a lawful search incident to arrest.

Moreover, there is no indication that this unlawful stop was part of any systemic or recurrent police misconduct. To the contrary, all the evidence suggests that the stop was an isolated instance of negligence that occurred in connection with a bona fide investigation of a suspected drug house. Officer Fackrell saw Strieff leave a suspected drug house. And his suspicion about the house was based on an anonymous tip and his personal observations.

Applying these factors, we hold that the evidence discovered on Strieff's person was admissible because the unlawful stop was sufficiently attenuated by the pre-existing arrest warrant. Although the illegal stop was close in time to Strieff's arrest, that consideration is outweighed by two factors supporting the State. The outstanding arrest warrant for Strieff's arrest is a critical intervening circumstance that is wholly independent of the illegal stop. The discovery of that warrant broke the causal chain between the unconstitutional stop and the discovery of evidence by compelling Officer Fackrell to arrest Strieff. And, it is especially significant that there is no evidence that Officer Fackrell's illegal stop reflected flagrantly unlawful police misconduct.

We find Strieff's counterarguments unpersuasive.

First, he argues that the attenuation doctrine should not apply because the officer's stop was purposeful and flagrant. He asserts that Officer Fackrell stopped him solely to fish for evidence of suspected wrongdoing. But Officer Fackrell sought information from Strieff to find out what was happening inside a house whose occupants were legitimately suspected of dealing drugs. This was not a suspicionless fishing expedition "in the hope that something would turn up."

Strieff argues, moreover, that Officer Fackrell's conduct was flagrant because he detained Strieff without the necessary level of cause (here, reasonable suspicion). But that conflates the standard for an illegal stop with the standard for flagrancy. For the violation to be flagrant, more severe police misconduct is required than the mere absence of proper cause for the seizure. Neither the officer's alleged purpose nor the flagrancy of the violation rise to a level of misconduct to warrant suppression.

Second, Strieff argues that, because of the prevalence of outstanding arrest warrants in many jurisdictions, police will engage in dragnet searches if the exclusionary rule is not applied. We think that this outcome is unlikely. Such wanton conduct would expose police to civil liability. And in any event, the *Brown* factors take account of the purpose and flagrancy of police misconduct. Were evidence of a dragnet search presented here, the application of the *Brown* factors could be different. But there is no evidence that the concerns that Strieff raises with the criminal justice system are present in South Salt Lake City, Utah.

• • •

We hold that the evidence Officer Fackrell seized as part of his search incident to arrest is admissible because his discovery of the arrest warrant attenuated the connection between the unlawful stop and the evidence seized from Strieff incident to arrest. The judgment of the Utah Supreme Court, accordingly, is reversed.

It is so ordered.

Justice SOTOMAYOR, with whom Justice GINSBURG joins as to Parts I, II, and III, dissenting.

The Court today holds that the discovery of a warrant for an unpaid parking ticket will forgive a police officer's violation of your Fourth Amendment rights. Do not be soothed by the opinion's technical language: This case allows the police to stop you on the street, demand your identification, and check it for outstanding traffic warrants—even if you are doing nothing wrong. If the officer discovers a warrant for a fine you forgot to pay, courts will now excuse his illegal stop and will admit into evidence anything he happens to find by searching you after arresting you on the warrant. Because the Fourth Amendment should prohibit, not permit, such misconduct, I dissent.

I

Minutes after Edward Strieff walked out of a South Salt Lake City home, an officer stopped him, questioned him, and took his identification to run it through a police database. The officer did not suspect that Strieff had done anything wrong. Strieff just happened to be the first person to leave a house that the officer thought might contain "drug activity."

As the State of Utah concedes, this stop was illegal. The Fourth Amendment protects people from "unreasonable searches and seizures." An officer breaches that protection when he detains a pedestrian to check his license without any evidence that the person is engaged in a crime. The officer deepens the breach when he prolongs the detention just to fish further for evidence of wrongdoing. In his search for lawbreaking, the officer in this case himself broke the law.

The officer learned that Strieff had a "small traffic warrant." Pursuant to that warrant, he arrested Strieff and, conducting a search incident to the arrest, discovered methamphetamine in Strieff's pockets.

Utah charged Strieff with illegal drug possession. Before trial, Strieff argued that admitting the drugs into evidence would condone the officer's misbehavior. The methamphetamine, he reasoned, was the product of the officer's illegal stop. Admitting it would tell officers that unlawfully discovering even a "small traffic warrant" would give them license to search for evidence of unrelated offenses. The Utah Supreme Court unanimously agreed with Strieff. A majority of this Court now reverses.

II

It is tempting in a case like this, where illegal conduct by an officer uncovers illegal conduct by a civilian, to forgive the officer. After all, his instincts, although unconstitutional, were correct. But a basic principle lies at the heart of the Fourth Amendment: Two wrongs don't make a right. When "lawless police conduct" uncovers evidence of lawless civilian conduct, this Court has long required later criminal trials to exclude the illegally obtained evidence. For example, if an officer breaks into a home and finds a forged check lying around, that check may not be used to prosecute the homeowner for bank fraud. We would describe the check as "'fruit of the poisonous tree.'" Fruit that must be cast aside includes not only evidence directly found by an illegal search but also evidence "come at by exploitation of that illegality."

This "exclusionary rule" removes an incentive for officers to search us without proper justification. It also keeps courts from being "made party to lawless invasions of the constitutional rights of citizens by permitting unhindered governmental use of the fruits of such invasions." When courts admit only lawfully obtained evidence, they encourage "those who formulate law enforcement polices, and the officers who implement them, to incorporate Fourth Amendment ideals into their value system." But when courts admit illegally obtained evidence as well, they reward "manifest neglect if not an open defiance of the prohibitions of the Constitution."

Applying the exclusionary rule, the Utah Supreme Court correctly decided that Strieff's drugs must be excluded because the officer exploited his illegal stop to discover them. The officer found the drugs only after learning of Strieff's traffic violation; and he learned of Strieff's traffic violation only because he unlawfully stopped Strieff to check his driver's license.

The court also correctly rejected the State's argument that the officer's discovery of a traffic warrant unspoiled the poisonous fruit. The State analogizes finding the warrant to one of our earlier decisions, *Wong Sun v. United States*. There, an officer illegally arrested a person who, days later, voluntarily returned to the station to confess to committing a crime. Even though the person would not have confessed "but for the illegal actions of the police," we noted that the police did not exploit their illegal arrest to obtain the confession. Because the confession was obtained by "means sufficiently distinguishable" from the constitutional violation, we held that it could be admitted into evidence. The State contends that the search incident to the warrant-arrest here is similarly distinguishable from the illegal stop.

But *Wong Sun* explains why Strieff's drugs must be excluded. We reasoned that a Fourth Amendment violation may not color every investigation that follows but it certainly stains the actions of officers who exploit the infraction. We distinguished evidence obtained by innocuous means from evidence obtained by exploiting misconduct after considering a variety of factors: whether a long time passed, whether there were "intervening circumstances," and whether the purpose or flagrancy of the misconduct was "calculated" to procure the evidence. *Brown v. Illinois* (1975).

These factors confirm that the officer in this case discovered Strieff's drugs by exploiting his own illegal conduct. The officer did not ask Strieff to volunteer his name only to find out, days later, that Strieff had a warrant against him. The officer illegally stopped Strieff and immediately ran a warrant check. The officer's discovery of a warrant was not some intervening surprise that he could not have anticipated. Utah lists over 180,000 misdemeanor warrants in its database, and at the time of the arrest, Salt Lake County had a "backlog of outstanding warrants" so large that it faced the "potential for civil liability." The officer's violation was also calculated to procure evidence. His sole reason for stopping Strieff, he acknowledged, was investigative—he wanted to discover whether drug activity was going on in the house Strieff had just exited.

The warrant check, in other words, was not an "intervening circumstance" separating the stop from the search for drugs. It was part and parcel of the officer's illegal "expedition for evidence in the hope that something might turn up." Under our precedents, because the officer found Strieff's drugs by exploiting his own constitutional violation, the drugs should be excluded.

III

A

The Court sees things differently. To the Court, the fact that a warrant gives an officer cause to arrest a person severs the connection between illegal policing and the resulting discovery of evidence. This is a remarkable proposition: The mere existence of a warrant not only gives an officer legal cause to arrest and search a person, it also forgives an officer who, with no knowledge of the warrant at all, unlawfully stops that person on a whim or hunch.

To explain its reasoning, the Court relies on *Segura*. There, federal agents applied for a warrant to search an apartment but illegally entered the apartment to secure it before the judge issued the warrant. After receiving the warrant, the agents then searched the apartment for drugs. The question before us was what to do with the evidence the agents then discovered. We declined to suppress it because "[t]he illegal entry into petitioners' apartment did not contribute in any way to discovery of the evidence seized under the warrant."

According to the majority, *Segura* involves facts "similar" to this case and "suggest[s]" that a valid warrant will clean up whatever illegal conduct uncovered it. It is difficult to understand this interpretation. In *Segura*, the agents' illegal conduct in entering the apartment had nothing to do with their procurement of a search warrant. Here, the officer's illegal conduct in stopping Strieff was essential to his discovery of an arrest warrant. Segura would be similar only if the agents used information they illegally obtained from the apartment to procure a search warrant or discover an arrest warrant. Precisely because that was not the case, the Court admitted the untainted evidence.

The majority likewise misses the point when it calls the warrant check here a "'negligibly burdensome precautio[n]'" taken for the officer's "safety." Remember, the officer stopped Strieff without suspecting him of committing any crime. By his own account, the officer did not fear Strieff. Moreover, the safety rationale we discussed in *Rodriguez*, an opinion about highway patrols, is conspicuously absent here. A warrant check on a highway "ensur[es] that vehicles on the road are operated safely and responsibly." We allow such checks during legal traffic stops because the legitimacy of a person's driver's license has a "close connection to roadway safety." A warrant check of a pedestrian on a sidewalk, "by contrast, is a measure aimed at 'detect[ing] evidence of ordinary criminal wrongdoing.'" Surely we would not allow officers to warrant-check random joggers, dog walkers, and lemonade vendors just to ensure they pose no threat to anyone else.

The majority also posits that the officer could not have exploited his illegal conduct because he did not violate the Fourth Amendment on purpose. Rather, he made "good-faith mistakes." Never mind that the officer's sole purpose was to fish for evidence. The majority casts his unconstitutional actions as "negligent" and therefore incapable of being deterred by the exclusionary rule. Ibid.

But the Fourth Amendment does not tolerate an officer's unreasonable searches and seizures just because he did not know any better. Even officers prone to negligence can learn from courts that exclude illegally obtained evidence. Indeed, they are perhaps the most in need of the education, whether by the judge's opinion, the prosecutor's future guidance, or an updated manual on criminal procedure. If the officers are in doubt about what the law requires, exclusion gives them an "incentive to err on the side of constitutional behavior."

B

Most striking about the Court's opinion is its insistence that the event here was "isolated," with "no indication that this unlawful stop was part of any systemic or recurrent police misconduct." Respectfully, nothing about this case is isolated.

Outstanding warrants are surprisingly common. When a person with a traffic ticket misses a fine payment or court appearance, a court will issue a warrant. When a person on probation drinks alcohol or breaks curfew, a court will issue a warrant. The States and Federal Government maintain databases with over 7.8 million outstanding warrants, the vast majority of which appear to be for minor offenses. Even these sources may not track the "staggering" numbers of warrants, "'drawers and drawers'" full, that many cities issue for traffic violations and ordinance infractions. The county in this case has had a "backlog" of such warrants. The Department of Justice recently reported that in the town of Ferguson, Missouri, with a population of 21,000, 16,000 people had outstanding warrants against them.

Justice Department investigations across the country have illustrated how these astounding numbers of warrants can be used by police to stop people without cause. In a single year in New Orleans, officers "made nearly 60,000 arrests, of which about 20,000 were of people with outstanding traffic or misdemeanor warrants from neighboring parishes for such infractions as unpaid tickets." In the St. Louis metropolitan area, officers "routinely" stop people—on the street, at bus stops, or even in court—for no reason other than "an officer's desire to check whether the subject had a municipal arrest warrant pending." In Newark, New Jersey, officers stopped 52,235 pedestrians within a 4-year period and ran warrant checks on 39,308 of them. The Justice Department analyzed these warrant-checked stops and reported that "approximately 93% of the stops would have been considered unsupported by articulated reasonable suspicion."

I do not doubt that most officers act in "good faith" and do not set out to break the law. That does not mean these stops are "isolated instance[s] of negligence," however. Many are the product of institutionalized training procedures. The New York City Police Department long trained officers to, in the words of a District Judge, "stop and question first, develop reasonable suspicion later." The Utah Supreme Court described as "'routine procedure' or 'common practice'" the decision of Salt Lake City police officers to run warrant checks on pedestrians they detained without reasonable suspicion. In the related context of traffic stops, one widely followed police manual instructs officers looking for drugs to "run at least a warrants check on all drivers you stop. Statistically, narcotics offenders are . . . more likely to fail to appear on simple citations, such as traffic or trespass violations, leading to the issuance of bench warrants. Discovery of an outstanding warrant gives you cause for an immediate custodial arrest and search of the suspect." C. Remsberg, Tactics for Criminal Patrol 205-206 (1995); C. Epp et al., Pulled Over 23, 33-36 (2014).

The majority does not suggest what makes this case "isolated" from these and countless other examples. Nor does it offer guidance for how a defendant can prove that his arrest was the result of "widespread" misconduct. Surely it should not take a federal investigation of Salt Lake County before the Court would protect someone in Strieff's position.

IV

Writing only for myself, and drawing on my professional experiences, I would add that unlawful "stops" have severe consequences much greater than the inconvenience suggested by the name. This Court has given officers an array of instruments to probe and examine you. When we condone officers' use of these devices without adequate cause, we give them reason to target pedestrians in an arbitrary manner. We also risk treating members of our communities as second-class citizens.

Although many Americans have been stopped for speeding or jaywalking, few may realize how degrading a stop can be when the officer is looking for more. This Court has allowed an officer to stop you for whatever reason he wants—so long as he can point to a pretextual justification after the fact. That justification must provide specific reasons why the officer suspected you were breaking the law, but it may factor in your ethnicity, where you live, what you were wearing, and how you behaved. The officer does not even need to know which law you might have broken so long as he can later point to any possible infraction—even one that is minor, unrelated, or ambiguous.

The indignity of the stop is not limited to an officer telling you that you look like a criminal. The officer may next ask for your "consent" to inspect your bag or purse without telling you that you can decline. Regardless of your answer, he may order you to stand "helpless, perhaps facing a wall with [your] hands raised." If the officer thinks you might be dangerous, he may then "frisk" you for weapons. This involves more than just a pat down. As onlookers pass by, the officer may "'feel with sensitive fingers every portion of [your] body. A thorough search [may] be made of [your] arms and armpits, waistline and back, the groin and area about the testicles, and entire surface of the legs down to the feet.'"

The officer's control over you does not end with the stop. If the officer chooses, he may handcuff you and take you to jail for doing nothing more than speeding, jaywalking, or "driving [your] pickup truck . . . with [your] 3-year-old son and 5-year-old daughter . . . without [your] seatbelt fastened." At the jail, he can fingerprint you, swab DNA from the inside of your mouth, and force you to "shower with a delousing agent" while you "lift [your] tongue, hold out [your] arms, turn around, and lift [your] genitals." Even if you are innocent, you will now join the 65 million Americans with an arrest record and experience the "civil death" of discrimination by employers, landlords, and whoever else conducts a background check. And, of course, if you fail to pay bail or appear for court, a judge will issue a warrant to render you "arrestable on sight" in the future.

This case involves a suspicionless stop, one in which the officer initiated this chain of events without justification. As the Justice Department notes, supra, at 2068-2069, many innocent people are subjected to the humiliations of these unconstitutional searches. The white defendant in this case shows that anyone's dignity can be violated in this manner. But it is no secret that people of color are disproportionate victims of this type of scrutiny. For generations, black and brown parents have given their children "the talk"—instructing them never to run down the street; always keep your hands where they can be seen; do not even think of talking back to a stranger—all out of fear of how an officer with a gun will react to them.

By legitimizing the conduct that produces this double consciousness, this case tells everyone, white and black, guilty and innocent, that an officer can verify your legal status at any time. It says that your body is subject to invasion while courts excuse the violation of your rights. It implies that you are not a citizen of a democracy but the subject of a carceral state, just waiting to be cataloged.

We must not pretend that the countless people who are routinely targeted by police are "isolated." They are the canaries in the coal mine whose deaths, civil and literal, warn us that no one can breathe in this atmosphere. They are the ones who recognize that unlawful police stops corrode all our civil liberties and threaten all our lives. Until their voices matter too, our justice system will continue to be anything but.

I dissent.

NOTES AND QUESTIONS

1. Edward Strieff probably did not know that there was a warrant out for his arrest on a traffic violation, and that he could be searched incident to that arrest. But still, why didn't he just walk away when approached by the police officer? Did they not have a course on Street Law in his high school?

2. Even Justice Sotomayor seems to concede that the police officer's conduct was only negligent. Do you agree? Was there anything close to reasonable suspicion? Was the officer's purpose in approaching Strieff—"to find out what was going on in the house"—truly

Edward J. Strieff Jr.

benign? Wasn't the officer interested in whether Strieff was implicated in whatever was going on in the house?

3. Did the officer truly have an "obligation" to arrest Strieff because of the existence of an outstanding bench warrant for a traffic violation? Does it seem suspicious that the only support cited for this proposition is *Leon*, which involved a search warrant? *See* Nirej Sekhon, *Dangerous Warrants*, 93 Wash. L. Rev. 967, 998-1000 (2018) (observing that whether to arrest someone based solely on the existence of a warrant is an act of enforcement discretion similar to many other police functions).

4. Doesn't the *Strieff* decision provide exactly the perverse incentive *Strieff* warns of—that police will be free to do "drag-net" searches in the hopes of discovering people with outstanding warrants who can be arrested? Although those incentives may exist regardless of *Strieff* based on the data from the DOJ investigations noted by Justice Sotomayor.

5. For an interesting look into the varying uses of narrative in *Strieff*, *see* Danielle Hayes, *He Say, She Say:* Utah v. Strieff *and the Role of Narrative in Judicial Decisions*, 61 Howard L.J. 511 (2018).

D. STANDING

Who has the right to file a motion to suppress evidence? Anyone against whom illegally acquired evidence might be admitted at trial? The next cases explore this issue.

Jones v. United States

362 U.S. 257 (1960)

Mr. Justice Frankfurter delivered the opinion of the Court.

This is a prosecution for violation of federal narcotics laws. In the first count of a two-count indictment petitioner was charged with having "purchased, sold, dispensed and distributed" narcotics in violation of 26 U.S.C. § 4704(a), 26 U.S.C.A. § 4704(a), that is, not in or from the "original stamped package." In the second count petitioner was charged under 21 U.S.C. § 174, 21 U.S.C.A. § 174, with having "facilitated the concealment and sale of" the same narcotics, knowing them to have been imported illegally into the United States. Petitioner was found guilty on both counts and sentenced to seven years' imprisonment. The Court of Appeals, one judge dissenting, affirmed the conviction. Since the case presented important questions in the administration of criminal justice, more particularly a defendant's standing to challenge the legality of a search in the circumstances of this case, as well as the legality of the particular search should standing be established, we granted certiorari.

Both statutory provisions under which petitioner was prosecuted permit conviction upon proof of the defendant's possession of narcotics, and in the case of 26 U.S.C. § 4704(a), 26

U.S.C.A. § 4704(a), of the absence of the appropriate stamps. Possession was the basis of the Government's case against petitioner. The evidence against him may be briefly summarized. He was arrested in an apartment in the District of Columbia by federal narcotics officers, who were executing warrant to search for narcotics. Those officers found narcotics, without appropriate stamps, and narcotics paraphernalia in a bird's nest in an awning just outside a window in the apartment. Another officer, stationed outside the building, had a short time before seen petitioner put his hand on the awning. Upon the discovery of the narcotics and the paraphernalia petitioner had admitted to the officers that some of these were his and that he was living in the apartment.

Prior to trial petitioner duly moved to suppress the evidence obtained through the execution of the search warrant on the ground that the warrant had been issued without a showing of probable cause. The Government challenged petitioner's standing to make this motion because petitioner alleged neither ownership of the seized articles nor an interest in the apartment greater than that of an "invitee or guest." The District Court agreed to take evidence on the issue of petitioner's standing. Only petitioner gave evidence. On direct examination he testified that the apartment belonged to a friend, Evans, who had given him the use of it, and a key, with which petitioner had admitted himself on the day of the arrest. On cross-examination petitioner testified that he had a suit and shirt at the apartment, that his home was elsewhere, that he paid nothing for the use of the apartment, that Evans had let him use it "as a friend," that he had slept there "maybe a night," and that at the time of the search Evans had been away in Philadelphia for about five days.

Solely on the basis of petitioner's lack of standing to make it, the district judge denied petitioner's motion to suppress. When the case came on for trial before a different judge, the motion to suppress was renewed and was denied on the basis of the prior ruling. An unsuccessful objection was made when the seized items were offered in evidence at the trial.

In affirming petitioner's conviction the Court of Appeals agreed with the District Court that petitioner lacked standing, but proceeded to rule that even if it were to find that petitioner had standing, it would hold the evidence to have been lawfully received. A challenge to the search which petitioner had not made in the District Court, namely, that the method of executing the warrant had been illegal, was considered by the Court of Appeals and rejected, while the contention petitioner had made below, that there had been insufficient cause to issue the warrant, was rejected without discussion.

The issue of petitioner's standing is to be decided with reference to Rule 41(e) of the Federal Rules of Criminal Procedure, 18 U.S.C.A. This is a statutory direction governing the suppression of evidence acquired in violation of the conditions validating a search. It is desirable to set forth the Rule.

> A person aggrieved by an unlawful search and seizure may move the district court for the district in which the property was seized for the return of the property and to suppress for use as evidence anything so obtained on the ground that (1) the property was illegally seized without warrant, or (2) the warrant is insufficient on its face, or (3) property seized is not that described in the warrant, or (4) there was not probable cause for believing the existence of the grounds on which the warrant was issued, or (5) the warrant was illegally executed. The judge shall receive evidence on any issue of fact necessary to the decision of the motion. If the motion is granted the property shall be restored unless otherwise subject to lawful detention and it shall not be admissible in evidence at any hearing or trial. The motion to suppress evidence may also be made in the district where the trial is to be had. The motion shall be made before trial or hearing unless opportunity therefor did not exist or the defendant was not aware of the grounds for the motion, but the court in its discretion may entertain the motion at the trial or hearing.

In order to qualify as a "person aggrieved by an unlawful search and seizure" one must have been a victim of a search or seizure, one against whom the search was directed, as distinguished from one who claims prejudice only through the use of evidence gathered as a consequence of a search or seizure directed at someone else. Rule 41(e) applies the general principle that a party will not be heard to claim a constitutional protection unless he "belongs to the class for whose sake the constitutional protection is given." The restrictions upon searches and seizures were obviously designed for protection against official invasion of privacy and the security of property. They are not exclusionary provisions against the admission of kinds of evidence deemed inherently unreliable or prejudicial. The exclusion in federal trials of evidence otherwise competent but gathered by federal officials in violation of the Fourth Amendment is a means for making effective the protection of privacy.

Ordinarily, then, it is entirely proper to require of one who seeks to challenge the legality of a search as the basis for suppressing relevant evidence that he allege, and if the allegation be disputed that he establish, that he himself was the victim of an invasion of privacy. But prosecutions like this one have presented a special problem. To establish "standing," Courts of Appeals have generally required that the movant claim either to have owned or possessed the seized property or to have had a substantial possessory interest in the premises searched. Since narcotics charges like those in the present indictment may be established through proof solely of possession of narcotics, a defendant seeking to comply with what has been the conventional standing requirement has been forced to allege facts the proof of which would tend, if indeed not be sufficient, to convict him. At the least, such a defendant has been placed in the criminally tendentious position of explaining his possession of the premises. He has been faced, not only with the chance that the allegations made on the motion to suppress may be used against him at the trial, although that they may is by no means an inevitable holding, but also with the encouragement that he perjure himself if he seeks to establish "standing" while maintaining a defense to the charge of possession.

The dilemma that has thus been created for defendants in cases like this has been pointedly put by Judge Learned Hand:

> Men may wince at admitting that they were the owners, or in possession, of contraband property; may wish at one to secure the remedies of a possessor, and avoid the perils of the part; but equivocation will not serve. If they come as victims, they must take on that role, with enough detail to cast them without question. The petitioners at bar shrank from that predicament; but they were obliged to choose one horn of the dilemma.

Following this holding, several Courts of Appeals have pinioned a defendant within this dilemma. A District Court has held otherwise. The Government urges us to follow the body of Court of Appeals' decisions and to rule that the lower courts, including the courts below, have been right in barring a defendant in a case like this from challenging a search because of his failure, when making his motion to suppress, to allege either that he owned or possessed the property seized or that he had a possessory interest in the premises searched greater than the interest of an "invitee or guest."

Judge Hand's dilemma is not inescapable. It presupposes requirements of "standing" which we do not find compelling. Two separate lines of thought effectively sustain defendant's standing in this case. (1) The same element in this prosecution which has caused a dilemma, i.e., that possession both convicts and confers standing, eliminates any necessity for a preliminary showing of an interest in the premises searched or the property seized, which ordinarily is required when standing is challenged. (2) Even were this not a prosecution turning on illicit possession, the legally requisite interest in the premises was here satisfied, for it need not be as extensive a property interest as was required by the courts below.

As to the first ground, we are persuaded by this consideration: to hold to the contrary, that is, to hold that petitioner's failure to acknowledge interest in the narcotics or the premises prevented his attack upon the search, would be to permit the Government to have the advantage of contradictory positions as a basis for conviction. Petitioner's conviction flows from his possession of the narcotics at the time of the search. Yet the fruits of that search, upon which the conviction depends, were admitted into evidence on the ground that petitioner did not have possession of the narcotics at that time. The prosecution here thus subjected the defendant to the penalties meted out to one in lawless possession while refusing him the remedies designed for one in that situation. It is not consonant with the amenities, to put it mildly, of the administration of criminal justice to sanction such squarely contradictory assertions of power by the Government. The possession on the basis of which petitioner is to be and was convicted suffices to give him standing under any fair and rational conception of the requirements of Rule 41(e).

The Government's argument to the contrary essentially invokes elegantia juris. In the interest of normal procedural orderliness, a motion to suppress, under Rule 41(e), must be made prior to trial, if the defendant then has knowledge of the grounds on which to base the motion. The Government argues that the defendant therefore must establish his standing to suppress the evidence at that time through affirmative allegations and may not wait to rest standing upon the Government's case at the trial. This provision of Rule 41(e), requiring the motion to suppress to be made before trial, is a crystallization of decisions of this Court requiring that procedure, and is designed to eliminate from the trial disputes over police conduct not immediately relevant to the question of guilt. As codified, the rule is not a rigid one, for under Rule 41(e) "the court in its discretion may entertain the motion (to suppress) at the trial or hearing." This qualification proves that we are dealing with carrying out an important social policy and not a narrow, finicky procedural requirement. This underlying policy likewise precludes application of the Rule so as to compel the injustice of an internally inconsistent conviction. In cases where the indictment itself charges possession, the defendant in a very real sense is revealed as a "person aggrieved by an unlawful search and seizure" upon a motion to suppress evidence prior to trial. Rule 41(e) should not be applied to allow the Government to deprive the defendant of standing to bring a motion to suppress by framing the indictment in general terms, while prosecuting for possession.

As a second ground sustaining "standing" here we hold that petitioner's testimony on the motion to suppress made out a sufficient interest in the premises to establish him as a "person aggrieved" by their search. That testimony established that at the time of the search petitioner was present in the apartment with the permission of Evans, whose apartment it was. The Government asserts that such an interest is insufficient to give standing. The Government does not contend that only ownership of the premises may confer standing. It would draw distinctions among various classes of possessors, deeming some, such as "guests" and "invitees" with only the "use" of the premises, to have too "tenuous" an interest although concededly having "some measure of control" through their "temporary presence," while conceding that others, who in a "realistic sense, have dominion of the apartment" or who are "domiciled" there, have standing. Petitioner, it is insisted, by his own testimony falls in the former class.

While this Court has never passed upon the interest in the searched premises necessary to maintain a motion to suppress, the Government's argument closely follows the prevailing view in the lower courts. They have denied standing to "guests" and "invitees" and employees, who though in "control" or "occupancy" lacked possession. The necessary quantum of interest has been distinguished as being, variously, "ownership in or right to possession of the premises," the interest of a "lessee or licensee," or of one with "dominion." We do not lightly depart from this course of decisions by the lower courts. We are persuaded, however, that it is unnecessary and ill-advised to import into the law surrounding the constitutional right to be free from unreasonable searches and seizures subtle distinctions, developed and refined by the common law in evolving the body of private properly law which, more than almost any other branch of law, has been shaped by distinctions whose validity is largely historical. Even in the area from which they derive, due consideration has led to the discarding of these distinctions in the homeland of the common law. Distinctions such as those between "lessee," "licensee," "invitee" and "guest," often only of gossamer strength, ought not to be determinative in fashioning procedures ultimately referable to constitutional safeguards.

We rejected such distinctions as inappropriate to the law of maritime torts. We found there to be a duty of ordinary care to one rightfully on the ship, regardless of whether he was a "licensee" rather than an "invitee." "For the admiralty law at this late date to import such conceptual distinctions would be foreign to its traditions of simplicity and practicality." A fortiori we ought not to bow to them in the fair administration of the criminal law. To do so would not comport with our justly proud claim of the procedural protections accorded to those charged with crime. No just interest of the Government in the effective and rigorous enforcement of the criminal law will be hampered by recognizing that anyone legitimately on premises where a search occurs may challenge its legality by way of a motion to suppress, when its fruits are proposed to be used against him. This would of course not avail those who, by virtue of their wrongful presence, cannot invoke the privacy of the premises searched. As petitioner's testimony established Evans' consent to his presence in the apartment, he was entitled to have the merits of his motion to suppress adjudicated. . . .

NOTES AND QUESTIONS

1. Note the Court's reliance on Rule 41(e) of the Federal Rules of Criminal Procedure, which by statute gave a right to challenge a search and seizure to any person "aggrieved by" the intrusion. What is the range of possible interpretations of the quoted language?

2. Note that *Jones* was decided one year before *Mapp v. Ohio*, and is thus establishing a standing rule for federal courts only. Is it surprising that the Supreme Court, 46 years after *Weeks*, had never previously addressed the issue?

3. Here is the entirety of the probable cause showing that led to the issuance of the warrant. Under the general rule that an informant tip can only establish probable cause if the tip is corroborated, should this warrant have even been authorized?

> Affidavit in Support of a U.S. Commissioners Search Warrant for Premises 1436 Meridian Place, N.W., Washington, D.C., apartment including window spaces of said apartment. Occupied by Cecil Jones and Earline Richardson.
>
> In the late afternoon of Tuesday, August 20, 1957, I, Detective Thomas Didone, Jr. received information that Cecil Jones and Earline Richardson were involved in the illicit narcotic traffic and that they kept a ready supply of heroin on hand in the above mentioned apartment. The source of information also relates that the two aforementioned persons kept these same narcotics either on their person, under a pillow, on a dresser or on a window ledge in said apartment. The source of information goes on to relate that on many occasions the source of information has gone to said apartment and purchased narcotic drugs from the abovementioned persons and that the narcotics were secreated (sic) in the above mentioned places. The last time being August 20, 1957.
>
> Both the aforementioned persons are familiar to the undersigned and other members of the Narcotic Squad. Both have admitted to the use of narcotic drugs and display needle marks as evidence of same.
>
> This same information, regarding the illicit narcotic traffic, conducted by Cecil Jones and Earline Richardson, has been given to the undersigned and to other officers of the narcotic squad by other sources of information.
>
> Because the source of information mentioned in the opening paragraph has given information to the undersigned on previous occasion and which was correct, and because this same

> information is given by other sources does believe that there is now illicit narcotic drugs being secreted (sic) in the above apartment by Cecil Jones and Earline Richardson.
>
> Det. Thomas Didone, Jr.,
> Narcotic Squad, MPDC.

Given the D.C. Circuit precedent—denying standing to guests and invitees—if the agents knew Jones did not live in the apartment, would they have needed to get a warrant in the first place?

4. How much of an improvement over the "subtle distinctions" of the common law is the "legitimately on premises" test?

The *Jones* standard was explicitly repudiated by the Supreme Court in *Rakas v. Illinois*, 439 U.S. 128 (1978). A police officer on routine patrol received word of the robbery of a clothing store, including a description of the getaway car—we are not told anything about the level of detail in the description—and had stopped a car that "he thought might be the getaway car." The stop and subsequent search yielded a gun and shells. The Court found that none of the car's passengers had standing to contest the search as they had no "possessory" interest in the car and thus lacked a legitimate expectation of privacy. Dissenting, along with Justices Brennan, Marshall, and Stevens, Justice White pointed out, among other things, that the Court's decision "invites police to engage in unreasonable searches every time an automobile has more than one occupant." *Id.* at 169.

What are the implications of *Rakas* where multiple people occupy not an automobile but an apartment?

Minnesota v. Carter

523 U.S. 83 (1998)

Chief Justice Rehnquist delivered the opinion of the Court.

Respondents and the lessee of an apartment were sitting in one of its rooms, bagging cocaine. While so engaged they were observed by a police officer, who looked through a drawn window blind. The Supreme Court of Minnesota held that the officer's viewing was a search that violated respondents' Fourth Amendment rights. We hold that no such violation occurred.

James Thielen, a police officer in the Twin Cities' suburb of Eagan, Minnesota, went to an apartment building to investigate a tip from a confidential informant. The informant said that he had walked by the window of a ground-floor apartment and had seen people putting a white powder into bags. The officer looked in the same window through a gap in the closed blind and observed the bagging operation for several minutes. He then notified headquarters, which began preparing affidavits for a search warrant while he returned to the apartment building. When two men left the building in a previously identified Cadillac, the police stopped the car. Inside were respondents Carter and Johns. As the police opened the door of the car to let Johns out, they observed a black, zippered pouch and a handgun, later determined to be loaded, on the vehicle's floor. Carter and Johns were arrested, and a later police search of the vehicle the next day discovered pagers, a scale, and 47 grams of cocaine in plastic sandwich bags.

After seizing the car, the police returned to Apartment 103 and arrested the occupant, Kimberly Thompson, who is not a party to this appeal. A search of the apartment pursuant to a warrant revealed cocaine residue on the kitchen table and plastic baggies similar to those found in the Cadillac. Thielen identified Carter, Johns, and Thompson as the three people he had observed placing the powder into baggies. The police later learned that while Thompson was the lessee of the apartment, Carter and Johns lived in Chicago and had come to the apartment for the sole purpose of packaging the cocaine. Carter and Johns had never been to the apartment before and were only in the apartment for approximately 2½ hours. In return for the use of the apartment, Carter and Johns had given Thompson one-eighth of an ounce of the cocaine.

Carter and Johns were charged with conspiracy to commit a controlled substance crime in the first degree and aiding and abetting in a controlled substance crime in the first degree, in violation of Minn. Stat. §§ 152.021, subds. 1(1), 3(a), 609.05 (1996). They moved to suppress all evidence obtained from the apartment and the Cadillac, as well as to suppress several postarrest incriminating statements they had made. They argued that Thielen's initial observation of their drug packaging activities was an unreasonable search in violation of the Fourth Amendment and that all evidence obtained as a result of this unreasonable search was inadmissible as fruit of the poisonous tree. The Minnesota trial court held that since, unlike the defendant in *Minnesota v. Olson* (1990), Carter and Johns were not overnight social guests but temporary out-of-state visitors, they were not entitled to claim the protection of the Fourth Amendment against the government intrusion into the apartment. The trial court also concluded that Thielen's observation was not a search within the meaning of the Fourth Amendment. After a trial, Carter and Johns were each convicted of both offenses. The Minnesota Court of Appeals held that respondent Carter did not have "standing" to object to Thielen's actions because his claim that he was predominantly a social guest was "inconsistent with the only evidence concerning his stay in the apartment, which indicates that he used it for a business purpose-to package drugs." In a separate appeal, the Court of Appeals also affirmed Johns' conviction, without addressing what it termed the "standing" issue.

A divided Minnesota Supreme Court reversed, holding that respondents had "standing" to claim the protection of the Fourth Amendment because they had "'a legitimate expectation of privacy in the invaded place.'" We granted certiorari, and now reverse.

The Minnesota courts analyzed whether respondents had a legitimate expectation of privacy under the rubric of "standing" doctrine, an analysis that this Court expressly rejected 20 years ago in *Rakas*. In that case, we held that automobile passengers could not assert the protection of the Fourth Amendment against the seizure of incriminating evidence from a vehicle where they owned neither the vehicle nor the evidence. Central to our analysis was the idea that in determining whether a defendant is able to show the violation of his (and not someone else's) Fourth Amendment rights, the "definition of those rights is more properly placed within the purview of substantive Fourth Amendment law than within that of standing." Thus, we held that in order to claim the protection of the Fourth Amendment, a defendant must demonstrate that he personally has an expectation of privacy in the place searched, and that his expectation is reasonable; i.e., one that has "a source outside of the Fourth Amendment, either by reference to concepts of real or personal property law or to understandings that are recognized and permitted by society."

The Fourth Amendment guarantees: "The right of the people to be secure in their persons, houses, papers, and effects, against unreasonable searches and seizures, shall not be violated, and no Warrants shall issue, but upon probable cause, supported by Oath or affirmation, and particularly describing the place to be searched, and the persons or things to be seized." The Amendment protects persons against unreasonable searches of "their persons [and] houses" and thus indicates that the Fourth Amendment is a personal right that must be invoked by an individual. But the extent to which the Fourth Amendment protects people may depend upon where those people are. We have held that "capacity to claim the protection of the Fourth Amendment depends . . . upon whether the person who claims the protection of the Amendment has a legitimate expectation of privacy in the invaded place."

The text of the Amendment suggests that its protections extend only to people in "their" houses. But we have held that in some circumstances a person may have a legitimate expectation of privacy in the house of someone else. In *Minnesota v. Olson* (1990), for example, we decided that an overnight guest in a house had the sort of expectation of privacy that the Fourth Amendment protects. We said:

> To hold that an overnight guest has a legitimate expectation of privacy in his host's home merely recognizes the every day expectations of privacy that we all share. Staying overnight in another's home is a longstanding social custom that serves functions recognized as valuable by society. We stay in others' homes when we travel to a strange city for business or pleasure, when we visit our parents, children, or more distant relatives out of town, when we are in between jobs or homes, or when we house-sit for a friend. . . .
>
> From the overnight guest's perspective, he seeks shelter in another's home precisely because it provides him with privacy, a place where he and his possessions will not be disturbed by anyone but his host and those his host allows inside. We are at our most vulnerable when we are asleep because we cannot monitor our own safety or the security of our belongings. It is for this reason that, although we may spend all day in public places, when we cannot sleep in our own home we seek out another private place to sleep, whether it be a hotel room, or the home of a friend.

In *Jones v. United States* (1960), the defendant seeking to exclude evidence resulting from a search of an apartment had been given the use of the apartment by a friend. He had clothing in the apartment, had slept there "'maybe a night,'" and at the time was the sole occupant of the apartment. But while the holding of *Jones*—that a search of the apartment violated the defendant's Fourth Amendment rights—is still valid, its statement that "anyone legitimately on the premises where a search occurs may challenge its legality," was expressly repudiated in *Rakas*. Thus, an overnight guest in a home may claim the protection of the Fourth Amendment, but one who is merely present with the consent of the householder may not.

Respondents here were obviously not overnight guests, but were essentially present for a business transaction and were only in the home a matter of hours. There is no suggestion that they had a previous relationship with Thompson, or that there was any other purpose to their visit. Nor was there anything similar to the overnight guest relationship in *Olson* to suggest a degree of acceptance into the household. While the apartment was a dwelling place for Thompson, it was for these respondents simply a place to do business.

Property used for commercial purposes is treated differently for Fourth Amendment purposes from residential property. "An expectation of privacy in commercial premises, however, is different from, and indeed less than, a similar expectation in an individual's home." And while it was a "home" in which respondents were present, it was not their home. Similarly, the Court has held that in some circumstances a worker can claim Fourth Amendment protection over his own workplace. But there is no indication that respondents in this case had nearly as significant a connection to Thompson's apartment as the worker in O'Connor had to his own private office.

If we regard the overnight guest in *Minnesota v. Olson* as typifying those who may claim the protection of the Fourth Amendment in the home of another, and one merely "legitimately on the premises" as typifying those who may not do so, the present case is obviously somewhere in between. But the purely commercial nature of the transaction engaged in here, the relatively short period of time on the premises, and the lack of any previous connection between respondents and the householder, all lead us to conclude that respondents' situation is closer to that of one simply permitted on the premises. We therefore hold that any search which may have occurred did not violate their Fourth Amendment rights.

Because we conclude that respondents had no legitimate expectation of privacy in the apartment, we need not decide whether the police officer's observation constituted a "search." The judgments of the Supreme Court of Minnesota are accordingly reversed, and the cause is remanded for proceedings not inconsistent with this opinion.

It is so ordered.

Justice GINSBURG, with whom Justice STEVENS and Justice SOUTER join, dissenting.

The Court's decision undermines not only the security of short-term guests, but also the security of the home resident herself. In my view, when a homeowner or lessee personally invites a guest into her home to share in a common endeavor, whether it be for conversation, to engage in leisure activities, or for business purposes licit or illicit, that guest should share his host's shelter against unreasonable searches and seizures.

I do not here propose restoration of the "legitimately on the premises" criterion stated in *Jones v. United States*, for the Court rejected that formulation in *Rakas* as it did the "automatic standing rule" in *United States v. Salvucci* (1980). First, the disposition I would reach in this case responds to the unique importance of the home — the most essential bastion of privacy recognized by the law. Second, even within the home itself, the position to which I would adhere would not permit "a casual visitor who has never seen, or been permitted to visit, the basement of another's house to object to a search of the basement if the visitor happened to be in the kitchen of the house at the time of the search." Further, I would here decide only the case of the homeowner who chooses to share the privacy of her home and her company with a guest, and would not reach classroom hypotheticals like the milkman or pizza deliverer.

My concern centers on an individual's choice to share her home and her associations there with persons she selects. Our decisions indicate that people have a reasonable expectation of privacy in their homes in part because they have the prerogative to exclude others.

A homedweller places her own privacy at risk, the Court's approach indicates, when she opens her home to others, uncertain whether the duration of their stay, their purpose, and their "acceptance into the household" will earn protection. It remains textbook law that "[s]earches and seizures inside a home without a warrant are presumptively unreasonable absent exigent circumstances." The law in practice is less secure. Human frailty suggests that today's decision will tempt police to pry into private dwellings without warrant, to find evidence incriminating guests who do not rest there through the night. *Rakas* tolerates that temptation with respect to automobile searches. As I see it, people are not genuinely "secure in their . . . houses . . . against unreasonable searches and seizures," if their invitations to others increase the risk of unwarranted governmental peering and prying into their dwelling places.

Through the host's invitation, the guest gains a reasonable expectation of privacy in the home. *Minnesota v. Olson* (1990) so held with respect to an overnight guest. The logic of that decision extends to shorter term guests as well. Visiting the home of a friend, relative, or business associate, whatever the time of day, "serves functions recognized as valuable by society." One need not remain overnight to anticipate privacy in another's home, "a place where [the guest] and his possessions will not be disturbed by anyone but his host and those his host allows inside." In sum, when a homeowner chooses to share the privacy of her home and her company with a short-term guest, the twofold requirement "emerg[ing] from prior decisions" has been satisfied: Both host and guest "have exhibited an actual (subjective) expectation of privacy"; that "expectation [is] one [our] society is prepared to recognize as 'reasonable.'"

NOTES AND QUESTIONS

1. What about Kimberly Thompson? It appears she cooperated against Carter and Johns. Is that why the record is so murky? There is no suggestion that Carter and Johns disputed that they were solely in the apartment in connection with drug dealing and had no real relationship with Thompson. Is this the result of bad lawyering? Certainly after *Olson* there was no guaranty that mere presence would confer standing.

2. Officer Thielen tried to do the right thing here and get a warrant after corroborating the informant's tip. Will he even bother next time?

3. Justice Ginsburg's dissent notes that an aspect of the privacy in the home is that the owner or occupant can receive guests and be confident in the guests' security. Should this notion confer an associated protectable privacy interest in the guest?

Byrd v. United States

584 U.S. 395 (2018)

Justice Kennedy delivered the opinion of the Court.

In September 2014, Pennsylvania State Troopers pulled over a car driven by petitioner Terrence Byrd. Byrd was the only person in the car. In the course of the traffic stop the troopers learned that the car was rented and that Byrd was not listed on the rental agreement as an authorized driver. For this reason, the troopers told Byrd they did not need his consent to search the car, including its trunk where he had stored personal effects. A search of the trunk uncovered body armor and 49 bricks of heroin.

The evidence was turned over to federal authorities, who charged Byrd with distribution and possession of heroin with the intent to distribute in violation of 21 U.S.C. § 841(a)(1) and possession of body armor by a prohibited person in violation of 18 U.S.C. § 931(a)(1). Byrd moved to suppress the evidence as the fruit of an unlawful search. The United States District Court for the Middle District of Pennsylvania denied the motion, and the Court of Appeals for the Third Circuit affirmed. Both courts concluded that, because Byrd was not listed on the rental agreement, he lacked a reasonable expectation of privacy in the car. Based on this conclusion, it appears that both the District Court and Court of Appeals deemed it unnecessary to consider whether the troopers had probable cause to search the car.

This Court granted certiorari to address the question whether a driver has a reasonable expectation of privacy in a rental car when he or she is not listed as an authorized driver on the rental agreement. The Court now holds that, as a general rule, someone in otherwise lawful possession and control of a rental car has a reasonable expectation of privacy in it even if the rental agreement does not list him or her as an authorized driver.

The Court concludes a remand is necessary to address in the first instance the Government's argument that this general rule is inapplicable because, in the circumstances here, Byrd had no greater expectation of privacy than a car thief. If that is so, our cases make clear he would lack a legitimate expectation of privacy. It is necessary to remand as well to determine whether, even if Byrd had a right to object to the search, probable cause justified it in any event.

I

On September 17, 2014, petitioner Terrence Byrd and Latasha Reed drove in Byrd's Honda Accord to a Budget car-rental facility in Wayne, New Jersey. Byrd stayed in the parking lot in the Honda while Reed went to the Budget desk and rented a Ford Fusion. The agreement Reed signed required her to certify that she had a valid driver's license and had not committed certain vehicle-related offenses within the previous three years. An addendum to the agreement, which Reed initialed, provides the following restriction on who may drive the rental car:

> I understand that the only ones permitted to drive the vehicle other than the renter are the renter's spouse, the renter's co-employee (with the renter's permission, while on company business),

or a person who appears at the time of the rental and signs an Additional Driver Form. These other drivers must also be at least 25 years old and validly licensed.

PERMITTING AN UNAUTHORIZED DRIVER TO OPERATE THE VEHICLE IS A VIOLATION OF THE RENTAL AGREEMENT. THIS MAY RESULT IN ANY AND ALL COVERAGE OTHERWISE PROVIDED BY THE RENTAL AGREEMENT BEING VOID AND MY BEING FULLY RESPONSIBLE FOR ALL LOSS OR DAMAGE, INCLUDING LIABILITY TO THIRD PARTIES.

In filling out the paperwork for the rental agreement, Reed did not list an additional driver.

With the rental keys in hand, Reed returned to the parking lot and gave them to Byrd. The two then left the facility in separate cars—she in his Honda, he in the rental car. Byrd returned to his home in Patterson, New Jersey, and put his personal belongings in the trunk of the rental car. Later that afternoon, he departed in the car alone and headed toward Pittsburgh, Pennsylvania.

After driving nearly three hours, or roughly half the distance to Pittsburgh, Byrd passed State Trooper David Long, who was parked in the median of Interstate 81 near Harrisburg, Pennsylvania. Long was suspicious of Byrd because he was driving with his hands at the "10 and 2" position on the steering wheel, sitting far back from the steering wheel, and driving a rental car. Long knew the Ford Fusion was a rental car because one of its windows contained a barcode. Based on these observations, he decided to follow Byrd and, a short time later, stopped him for a possible traffic infraction.

When Long approached the passenger window of Byrd's car to explain the basis for the stop and to ask for identification, Byrd was "visibly nervous" and "was shaking and had a hard time obtaining his driver's license." He handed an interim license and the rental agreement to Long, stating that a friend had rented the car. Long returned to his vehicle to verify Byrd's license and noticed Byrd was not listed as an additional driver on the rental agreement. Around this time another trooper, Travis Martin, arrived at the scene. While Long processed Byrd's license, Martin conversed with Byrd, who again stated that a friend had rented the vehicle. After Martin walked back to Long's patrol car, Long commented to Martin that Byrd was "not on the renter agreement," to which Martin replied, "yeah, he has no expectation of privacy."

A computer search based on Byrd's identification returned two different names. Further inquiry suggested the other name might be an alias and also revealed that Byrd had prior convictions for weapons and drug charges as well as an outstanding warrant in New Jersey for a probation violation. After learning that New Jersey did not want Byrd arrested for extradition, the troopers asked Byrd to step out of the vehicle and patted him down.

Long asked Byrd if he had anything illegal in the car. When Byrd said he did not, the troopers asked for his consent to search the car. At that point Byrd said he had a "blunt" in the car and offered to retrieve it for them. The officers understood "blunt" to mean a marijuana cigarette. They declined to let him retrieve it and continued to seek his consent to search the car, though they stated they did not need consent because he was not listed on the rental agreement. The troopers then opened the passenger and driver doors and began a thorough search of the passenger compartment.

Martin proceeded from there to search the car's trunk, including by opening up and taking things out of a large cardboard box, where he found a laundry bag containing body armor. At this point, the troopers decided to detain Byrd. As Martin walked toward Byrd and said he would be placing him in handcuffs, Byrd began to run away. A third trooper who had arrived on the scene joined Long and Martin in pursuit. When the troopers caught up to Byrd, he surrendered and admitted there was heroin in the car. Back at the car, the troopers resumed their search of the laundry bag and found 49 bricks of heroin.

In pretrial proceedings Byrd moved to suppress the evidence found in the trunk of the rental car, arguing that the search violated his Fourth Amendment rights. Although Long contended at a suppression hearing that the troopers had probable cause to search the car after Byrd stated it contained marijuana, the District Court denied Byrd's motion on the ground that Byrd lacked "standing" to contest the search as an initial matter. Byrd later entered a conditional guilty plea, reserving the right to appeal the suppression ruling.

The Court of Appeals affirmed in a brief summary opinion. As relevant here, the Court of Appeals recognized that a "circuit split exists as to whether the sole occupant of a rental vehicle has a Fourth Amendment expectation of privacy when that occupant is not named in the rental agreement"; but it noted that Circuit precedent already had "spoken as to this issue . . . and determined such a person has no expectation of privacy and therefore no standing to challenge a search of the vehicle." The Court of Appeals did not reach the probable-cause question.

This Court granted Byrd's petition for a writ of certiorari to address the conflict among the Courts of Appeals over whether an unauthorized driver has a reasonable expectation of privacy in a rental car.

II

Few protections are as essential to individual liberty as the right to be free from unreasonable searches and seizures. The Framers made that right explicit in the Bill of Rights following their experience with the indignities and invasions of privacy wrought by "general warrants and warrantless searches that had so alienated the colonists and had helped speed the movement for independence." Ever mindful of the Fourth Amendment and its history, the Court has viewed with disfavor practices that permit "police officers unbridled discretion to rummage at will among a person's private effects."

This concern attends the search of an automobile. The Court has acknowledged, however, that there is a diminished expectation of privacy in automobiles, which often permits officers to dispense with obtaining a warrant before conducting a lawful search.

Whether a warrant is required is a separate question from the one the Court addresses here, which is whether the person claiming a constitutional violation "has had his own Fourth Amendment rights infringed by the search and seizure which he seeks to challenge." *Rakas v. Illinois* (1978). Answering that question requires examination of whether the person claiming the constitutional violation had a "legitimate expectation of privacy in the premises" searched. "Expectations of privacy protected by the Fourth Amendment, of course, need not be based on a common-law interest in real or personal property, or on the invasion of such an interest." Still, "property concepts" are instructive in "determining the presence or absence of the privacy interests protected by that Amendment."

Indeed, more recent Fourth Amendment cases have clarified that the test most often associated with legitimate expectations of privacy, which was derived from the second Justice Harlan's concurrence in *Katz v. United States* (1967), supplements, rather than displaces, "the traditional property-based understanding of the Fourth Amendment." *Florida v. Jardines* (2013). Perhaps in light of this clarification, Byrd now argues in the alternative that he had a common-law property interest in the rental car as a second bailee that would have provided him with a cognizable Fourth Amendment interest in the vehicle. But he did not raise this argument before the District Court or Court of Appeals, and those courts did not have occasion to address whether Byrd was a second bailee or what consequences might follow from that determination. In those courts he framed the question solely in terms of the *Katz* test noted above. Because this is "a court of review, not of first view," *Cutter v. Wilkinson*, it is generally unwise to consider arguments in the first instance, and the Court declines to reach Byrd's contention that he was a second bailee.

Reference to property concepts, however, aids the Court in assessing the precise question here: Does a driver of a rental car have a reasonable expectation of privacy in the car when he or she is not listed as an authorized driver on the rental agreement?

III

A

One who owns and possesses a car, like one who owns and possesses a house, almost always has a reasonable expectation of privacy in it. More difficult to define and delineate are the legitimate expectations of privacy of others.

On the one hand, as noted above, it is by now well established that a person need not always have a recognized common-law property interest in the place searched to be able to claim a reasonable expectation of privacy in it.

On the other hand, it is also clear that legitimate presence on the premises of the place searched, standing alone, is not enough to accord a reasonable expectation of privacy, because it "creates too broad a gauge for measurement of Fourth Amendment rights."

Although the Court has not set forth a single metric or exhaustive list of considerations to resolve the circumstances in which a person can be said to have a reasonable expectation of privacy, it has explained that "[l]egitimation of expectations of privacy by law must have a source outside of the Fourth Amendment, either by reference to concepts of real or personal property law or to understandings that are recognized and permitted by society." The two concepts in cases like this one are often linked. "One of the main rights attaching to property is the right to exclude others," and, in the main, "one who owns or lawfully possesses or controls property will in all likelihood have a legitimate expectation of privacy by virtue of the right to exclude." This general property-based concept guides resolution of this case.

B

Here, the Government contends that drivers who are not listed on rental agreements always lack an expectation of privacy in the automobile based on the rental company's lack of authorization alone. This per se rule rests on too restrictive a view of the Fourth Amendment's protections. Byrd, by contrast, contends that the sole occupant of a rental car always has an expectation of privacy in it based on mere possession and control. There is more to recommend Byrd's proposed rule than the Government's; but, without qualification, it would include within its ambit thieves and others who, not least because of their lack of any property-based justification, would not have a reasonable expectation of privacy.

1

Stripped to its essentials, the Government's position is that only authorized drivers of rental cars have expectations of privacy in those vehicles. This position is based on the following syllogism: Under *Rakas*, passengers do not have an expectation of privacy in an automobile glove compartment or like places; an unauthorized driver like Byrd would have been the passenger had the renter been driving; and the unauthorized driver cannot obtain greater protection when he takes the wheel and leaves the renter behind. The flaw in this syllogism is its major premise, for it is a misreading of *Rakas*.

The Court in *Rakas* did not hold that passengers cannot have an expectation of privacy in automobiles. To the contrary, the Court disclaimed any intent to hold "that a passenger lawfully in an automobile may not invoke the exclusionary rule and challenge a search of that vehicle unless he happens to own or have a possessory interest in it." The Court instead rejected the argument that legitimate presence alone was sufficient to assert a Fourth Amendment interest, which was fatal to the petitioners' case there because they had "claimed only that they were 'legitimately on [the] premises' and did not claim that they had any legitimate expectation of privacy in the areas of the car which were searched."

What is more, the Government's syllogism is beside the point, because this case does not involve a passenger at all but instead the driver and sole occupant of a rental car. As Justice Powell observed in his concurring opinion in *Rakas*, a "distinction . . . may be made in some circumstances between the Fourth Amendment rights of passengers and the rights of an individual who has exclusive control of an automobile or of its locked compartments." This situation would be similar to the defendant in *Jones*, supra, who, as *Rakas* notes, had a reasonable expectation of privacy in his friend's apartment because he "had complete dominion and control over the apartment and could exclude others from it." Justice Powell's observation was also consistent with the majority's explanation that "one who owns or lawfully possesses or controls property will in all likelihood have a legitimate expectation of privacy by virtue of [the] right to exclude," an explanation tied to the majority's discussion of *Jones*.

The Court sees no reason why the expectation of privacy that comes from lawful possession and control and the attendant right to exclude would differ depending on whether the car in question is rented or privately owned by someone other than the person in current possession of it, much as it did not seem to matter whether the friend of the defendant in Jones owned or leased the apartment he permitted the defendant to use in his absence. Both would have the expectation of privacy that comes with the right to exclude. Indeed, the Government conceded at oral argument that an unauthorized driver in sole possession of a rental car would be permitted to exclude third parties from it, such as a carjacker.

2

The Government further stresses that Byrd's driving the rental car violated the rental agreement that Reed signed, and it contends this violation meant Byrd could not have had any basis for claiming an expectation of privacy in the rental car at the time of the search. As anyone who has rented a car knows, car-rental agreements are filled with long lists of restrictions. Examples include prohibitions on driving the car on unpaved roads or driving while using a handheld cellphone. Few would contend that violating provisions like these has anything to do with a driver's reasonable expectation of privacy in the rental car—as even the Government agrees.

Despite this concession, the Government argues that permitting an unauthorized driver to take the wheel of a rental car is a breach different in kind from these others, so serious that the rental company would consider the agreement "void" the moment an unauthorized driver takes the wheel. To begin with, that is not what the contract says. It states: "Permitting an unauthorized driver to operate the vehicle is a violation of the rental agreement. This may result in any and all coverage otherwise provided by the rental agreement being void and my being fully responsible for all loss or damage, including liability to third parties."

Putting the Government's misreading of the contract aside, there may be countless innocuous reasons why an unauthorized driver might get behind the wheel of a rental car and drive it—perhaps the renter is drowsy or inebriated and the two think it safer for the friend to drive them to their destination. True, this constitutes a breach of the rental agreement, and perhaps a serious one, but the Government fails to explain what bearing this breach of contract, standing alone, has on expectations of privacy in the car. Stated in different terms, for Fourth Amendment purposes there is no meaningful difference between the authorized-driver provision and the other provisions the Government agrees do not eliminate an expectation of privacy, all of which concern risk allocation between private parties—violators might pay additional fees, lose insurance coverage, or assume liability for damage resulting from the breach. But that risk allocation has little to do with whether one would have a reasonable expectation of privacy in the rental car if, for example, he or she otherwise has lawful possession of and control over the car.

3

The central inquiry at this point turns on the concept of lawful possession, and this is where an important qualification of Byrd's proposed rule comes into play. *Rakas* makes clear that "'wrongful' presence at the scene of a search would not enable a defendant to object to the legality of the search." "A burglar plying his trade in a summer cabin during the off season," for example, "may have a thoroughly justified subjective expectation of privacy, but it is not one which the law recognizes as 'legitimate.'" Likewise, "a person present in a stolen automobile at the time of the search may [not] object to the lawfulness of the search of the automobile." No matter the degree of possession and control, the car thief would not have a reasonable expectation of privacy in a stolen car.

On this point, in its merits brief, the Government asserts that, on the facts here, Byrd should have no greater expectation of privacy than a car thief because he intentionally used a third party as a strawman in a calculated plan to mislead the rental company from the very outset, all to aid him in committing a crime. This argument is premised on the Government's inference that Byrd knew he would not have been able to rent the car on his own, because he would not have satisfied the rental company's requirements based on his criminal record, and that he used Reed, who had no intention of using the car for her own purposes, to procure the car for him to transport heroin to Pittsburgh.

It is unclear whether the Government's allegations, if true, would constitute a criminal offense in the acquisition of the rental car under applicable law. And it may be that there is no reason that the law should distinguish between one who obtains a vehicle through subterfuge of the type the Government alleges occurred here and one who steals the car outright.

The Government did not raise this argument in the District Court or the Court of Appeals, however. It relied instead on the sole fact that Byrd lacked authorization to drive the car. And it is unclear from the record whether the Government's inferences paint an accurate picture of what occurred. Because it was not addressed in the District Court or Court of Appeals, the Court declines to reach this question. The proper course is to remand for the argument and potentially further factual development to be considered in the first instance by the Court of Appeals or by the District Court.

IV

The Government argued in its brief in opposition to certiorari that, even if Byrd had a Fourth Amendment interest in the rental car, the troopers had probable cause to believe it contained evidence of a crime when they initiated their search. If that were true, the troopers may have been permitted to conduct a warrantless search of the car in line with the Court's cases concerning the automobile exception to the warrant requirement. The Court of Appeals did not reach this question because it concluded, as an initial matter, that Byrd lacked a reasonable expectation of privacy in the rental car.

It is worth noting that most courts analyzing the question presented in this case, including the Court of Appeals here, have described it as one of Fourth Amendment "standing," a concept the Court has explained is not distinct from the merits and "is more properly subsumed under substantive Fourth Amendment doctrine."

The concept of standing in Fourth Amendment cases can be a useful shorthand for capturing the idea that a person must have a cognizable Fourth Amendment interest in the place searched before seeking relief for an unconstitutional search; but it should not be confused with Article III standing, which is jurisdictional and must be assessed before reaching the merits. Because Fourth Amendment standing is subsumed under substantive Fourth Amendment doctrine, it is not a jurisdictional question and hence need not be addressed before addressing other aspects of the merits of a Fourth Amendment claim. On remand, then, the Court of Appeals is not required to assess Byrd's reasonable expectation of privacy in the rental car before, in its discretion, first addressing whether there was probable cause for the search, if it finds the latter argument has been preserved.

V

Though new, the fact pattern here continues a well-traveled path in this Court's Fourth Amendment jurisprudence. Those cases support the proposition, and the Court now holds, that the mere fact that a driver in lawful possession or control of a rental car is not listed on the rental agreement will not defeat his or her otherwise reasonable expectation of privacy. The Court leaves for remand two of the Government's arguments: that one who intentionally uses a third party to procure a rental car by a fraudulent scheme for the purpose of committing a crime is no better situated than a car thief; and that probable cause justified the search in any event. The Court of Appeals has discretion as to the order in which these questions are best addressed.

• • •

The judgment of the Court of Appeals is vacated, and the case is remanded for further proceedings consistent with this opinion.

It is so ordered.

NOTES AND QUESTIONS

1. The Court criticizes the government's argument about the significance of the language in the rental agreement as well as its factual argument about Byrd's alleged use of a straw person to rent the car because he was ineligible to do so because of his criminal record. Do you think the fact that the government overplayed its hand might have contributed to the result here?

2. On remand, Byrd will have to deal with the argument that his admission that there was marijuana in the car gave the police probable cause to search the entire car. Is there also a case for the good faith exception to the exclusionary rule? Is the police officer's comment about Byrd's "reasonable expectation of privacy" relevant to this inquiry?

3. Does the result here depend on the fact that Byrd was the only occupant and the driver of the rental car? What if he had been a passenger at the time of the stop, and a listed driver on the rental agreement, but the renter was driving? What if he had been driving but the renter was a passenger with him?

4. Is Trooper Long's explanation of the reasons why he began following Byrd believable? Did he have reasonable suspicion to stop Byrd prior to identifying "a possible traffic infraction"? Isn't this obviously a pretextual stop? The Court, needless to say, glosses over the basis for the stop and makes no mention of the fact that Byrd was Black. *See* Tracey Maclin, Byrd v. United States*: Unauthorized Drivers of Rental Cars Have Fourth Amendment Rights? Not as Evident as It Seems*, 2018 Sup. Ct. Rev. 81, 91 n.55 (2019).

5. The Ford Fusion Terrence Byrd was driving when he was stopped by police was rented from a Budget facility in Wayne, New Jersey. Wayne is best known as the location of the lawn ornament store Fountains of Wayne (closed in 2009), from which the eponymous rock band took its name in 1995. In episode 5 of season 3 of *The Sopranos*, "Another Toothpick," Tony visits Fountains of Wayne and interacts with a Black police officer, Leon Wilmore, who had recently given him a speeding ticket.

Fountains of Wayne

Tony Soprano at Fountains of Wayne

E. IMPEACHMENT

Can the government use information obtained illegally to impeach a testifying defendant even if it cannot use the evidence directly against the defendant in its case-in-chief? Would this allow the government to profit from its constitutional violation? Should the answer depend on the nature of the constitutional violation? The cases below explore this issue.

Walder v. United States

347 U.S. 62 (1954)

Mr. Justice Frankfurter delivered the opinion of the Court.

In May 1950, petitioner was indicted in the United States District Court for the Western District of Missouri for purchasing and possessing one grain of heroin. Claiming that the heroin capsule had been obtained through an unlawful search and seizure, petitioner moved to suppress it. The motion was granted, and shortly thereafter, on the Government's motion, the case against petitioner was dismissed.

In January of 1952, petitioner was again indicted, this time for four other illicit transactions in narcotics. The Government's case consisted principally of the testimony of two drug addicts who claimed to have procured the illicit stuff from petitioner under the direction of federal agents. The only witness for the defense was the defendant himself, petitioner here. He denied any narcotics dealings with the two Government informers and attributed the testimony against him to personal hostility.

Early on his direct examination petitioner testified as follows:

Q. Now, first, Mr. Walder, before we go further in your testimony, I want to you (sic) tell the Court and jury whether, not referring to these informers in this case, but whether you have ever sold any narcotics to anyone. A. I have never sold any narcotics to anyone in my life.

Q. Have you ever had any narcotics in your possession, other than what may have been given to you by a physician for an ailment? A. No.

Q. Now, I will ask you one more thing. Have you ever handed or given any narcotics to anyone as a gift or in any other manner without the receipt of any money or any other compensation? A. I have not.

Q. Have you ever even acted as, say, have you acted as a conduit for the purpose of handling what you knew to be a narcotic from one person to another? A. No, Sir.

On cross-examination, in response to a question by Government counsel making reference to this direct testimony, petitioner reiterated his assertion that he had never purchased, sold or possessed any narcotics. Over the defendant's objection, the Government then questioned him about the heroin capsule unlawfully seized from his home in his presence back in February 1950. The defendant stoutly denied that any narcotics were taken from him at that time. The Government then put on the stand one of the officers who had participated in the unlawful search and seizure and also the chemist who had analyzed the heroin capsule there seized. The trial judge admitted this evidence, but carefully charged the jury that it was not to be used to determine whether the defendant had committed the crimes here charged, but solely for the purpose of impeaching the defendant's credibility. The defendant was convicted and the Court of Appeals for the Eighth Circuit affirmed, one judge dissenting. The question which divided that court, and the sole issue here, is whether the defendant's assertion on direct examination that he had never possessed any narcotics opened the door, solely for the purpose of attacking the defendant's credibility, to evidence of the heroin unlawfully seized in connection with the earlier proceeding. Because this question presents a novel aspect of the scope of the doctrine of *Weeks v. United States*, we granted certiorari.

The Government cannot violate the Fourth Amendment—in the only way in which the Government can do anything, namely through its agents—and use the fruits of such unlawful conduct to secure a conviction. *Weeks v. United States, supra.* Nor can the Government make indirect use of such evidence for its case, or support a conviction on evidence obtained through leads from the unlawfully obtained evidence. All these methods are outlawed, and convictions obtained by means of them are invalidated, because they encourage the kind of society that is obnoxious to free men.

It is one thing to say that the Government cannot make an affirmative use of evidence unlawfully obtained. It is quite another to say that the defendant can turn the illegal method by which evidence in the Government's possession was obtained to his own advantage, and provide himself with a shield against contradiction of his untruths. Such an extension of the *Weeks* doctrine would be a perversion of the Fourth Amendment.

Take the present situation. Of his own accord, the defendant went beyond a mere denial of complicity in the crimes of which he was charged and made the sweeping claim that he had never dealt in or possessed any narcotics. Of course, the Constitution guarantees a defendant the fullest opportunity to meet the accusation against him. He must be free to deny all the elements of the case against him without thereby giving leave to the Government to introduce by way of rebuttal evidence illegally secured by it, and therefore not available for its case in chief. Beyond that, however, there is hardly justification for letting the defendant affirmatively resort to perjurious testimony in reliance on the Government's disability to challenge his credibility.

The situation here involved is to be sharply contrasted with that presented by *Agnello v. United States.* There the Government, after having failed in its efforts to introduce the tainted evidence in its case in chief, tried to smuggle it in on cross-examination by asking the accused the broad question "Did you ever see narcotics before?" After eliciting the expected denial, it sought to introduce evidence of narcotics located in the defendant's home by means of an unlawful search and seizure, in order to discredit the defendant. In holding that the Government could no more work in this evidence on cross-examination than it could in its case in chief, the Court foreshadowed, perhaps unwittingly, the result we reach today:

> And the contention that the evidence of the search and seizure was admissible in rebuttal is without merit. In his direct examination, Agnello was not asked and did not testify concerning

the can of cocaine. In cross-examination, in answer to a question permitted over his objection, he said he had never seen it. He did nothing to waive his constitutional protection or to justify cross-examination in respect of the evidence claimed to have been obtained by the search.

The judgment is affirmed.

NOTES AND QUESTIONS

1. Are you curious about the relationship between the 1950 and the 1952 prosecutions of Walder? It would appear that the government agents within a year or so of Walder's successful motion to suppress in the 1950 indictment were sending informants after Walder. Should that affect the result here? Was there anything Walder could have done otherwise?

2. The result here had to have been the result of reckless lawyering. Could defense counsel really have been confident that he could get away with having Walder make a blanket denial of involvement in narcotics? Would reading *Agnello* have helped? Was the sought-after testimony even necessary?

3. Is it essential to the result here that Walder "opened the door"? Would these questions have also opened the door:

- Mr. Walder, do you deny all the allegations against you?
- Mr. Walder, are you opposed to those who use and sell narcotics?
- Mr. Walder, do you deny that you are a narcotics dealer?

The next case considers whether information obtained from a *Miranda* violation can be used to impeach a testifying defendant. It is generally regarded as one of the first of many instances where the Court found exceptions to the *Miranda* doctrine.

Harris v. New York

401 U.S. 222 (1971)

Mr. Chief Justice Burger delivered the opinion of the Court.

We granted the writ in this case to consider petitioner's claim that a statement made by him to police under circumstances rendering it inadmissible to establish the prosecution's case in chief under *Miranda* may not be used to impeach his credibility.

The State of New York charged petitioner in a two-count indictment with twice selling heroin to an undercover police officer. At a subsequent jury trial the officer was the State's chief witness, and he testified as to details of the two sales. A second officer verified collateral details of the sales, and a third offered testimony about the chemical analysis of the heroin.

Petitioner took the stand in his own defense. He admitted knowing the undercover police officer but denied a sale on January 4, 1966. He admitted making a sale of contents of a glassine bag to the officer on January 6 but claimed it was baking powder and part of a scheme to defraud the purchaser.

On cross-examination petitioner was asked seriatim whether he had made specified statements to the police immediately following his arrest on January 7—statements that partially contradicted petitioner's direct testimony at trial. In response to the cross-examination, petitioner testified that he could not remember virtually any of the questions or answers recited by the prosecutor. At the request of petitioner's counsel the written statement from which the prosecutor had read questions and answers in his impeaching process was placed in the record for possible use on appeal; the statement was not shown to the jury.

The trial judge instructed the jury that the statements attributed to petitioner by the prosecution could be considered only in passing on petitioner's credibility and not as evidence of guilt. In closing summations both counsel argued the substance of the impeaching statements. The jury then found petitioner guilty on the second count of the indictment.

At trial the prosecution made no effort in its case in chief to use the statements allegedly made by petitioner, conceding that they were inadmissible under *Miranda*. The transcript of the interrogation used in the impeachment, but not given to the jury, shows that no warning of a right to appointed counsel was given before questions were put to petitioner when he was taken into custody. Petitioner makes no claim that the statements made to the police were coerced or involuntary.

Some comments in the *Miranda* opinion can indeed be read as indicating a bar to use of an uncounseled statement for any purpose, but discussion of that issue was not at all necessary to the Court's holding and cannot be regarded as controlling. *Miranda* barred the prosecution from making its case with statements of an accused made while in custody prior to having or effectively waiving counsel. It does not follow from *Miranda* that evidence inadmissible against an accused in the prosecution's case in chief is barred for all purposes, provided of course that the trustworthiness of the evidence satisfies legal standards.

In *Walder v. United States* (1954), the Court permitted physical evidence, inadmissible in the case in chief, to be used for impeachment purposes.

> It is one thing to say that the Government cannot make an affirmative use of evidence unlawfully obtained. It is quite another to say that the defendant can turn the illegal method by which evidence in the Government's possession was obtained to his own advantage, and provide himself with a shield against contradiction of his untruths. Such an extension of the *Weeks* doctrine would be a perversion of the Fourth Amendment.
>
> (T)here is hardly justification for letting the defendant affirmatively resort to perjurious testimony in reliance on the Government's disability to challenge his credibility.

It is true that Walder was impeached as to collateral matters included in his direct examination, whereas petitioner here was impeached as to testimony bearing more directly on the crimes charged. We are not persuaded that there is a difference in principle that warrants a result different from that reached by the Court in *Walder*. Petitioner's testimony in his own behalf concerning the events of January 7 contrasted sharply with what he told the police shortly after his arrest. The impeachment process here undoubtedly provided valuable aid to the jury in assessing petitioner's credibility, and the benefits of this process should not be lost, in our view, because of the speculative possibility that impermissible police conduct will be encouraged thereby. Assuming that the exclusionary rule has a deterrent effect on proscribed police conduct, sufficient deterrence flows when the evidence in question is made unavailable to the prosecution in its case in chief.

Every criminal defendant is privileged to testify in his own defense, or to refuse to do so. But that privilege cannot be construed to include the right to commit perjury. Having voluntarily taken the stand, petitioner was under an obligation to speak truthfully and accurately, and the prosecution here did no more than utilize the traditional truth-testing devices of the adversary process. Had inconsistent statements been made by the accused to some third person, it could hardly be contended that the conflict could not be laid before the jury by way of cross-examination and impeachment.

The shield provided by *Miranda* cannot be perverted into a license to use perjury by way of a defense, free from the risk of confrontation with prior inconsistent utterances. We hold, therefore, that petitioner's credibility was appropriately impeached by use of his earlier conflicting statements.

Affirmed.

[Justices Brennan, Marshall, and Douglas dissented.]

NOTES AND QUESTIONS

1. Why is the opinion so opaque? Was the trial testimony not transcribed? What was the defendant's testimony and what was the statement he made upon being arrested? How is the reader of this opinion to determine how much this case resembles *Walder*?

2. So the trial judge gave a limiting instruction to the effect that the cross-examination of the defendant—which the Court conceded bore "more directly [than the cross in *Walder*] on the crimes charged"—was to be considered only in evaluating the defendant's credibility. And, remarkably, the Court doubled down on this instruction as a palliative, stating without any sign of irony that "the impeachment process here undoubtedly provided valuable aid to the jury in assessing petitioner's credibility."

Can this be taken seriously? The futility of limiting instructions was not a novel concept in 1972. As Justice Jackson had observed decades previously: "The naive assumption that prejudicial effects can be overcome by instructions to the jury, all practicing lawyers know to be unmitigated fiction." *Krulewitch v. United States*, 336 U.S. 440, 453 (1949) (Jackson, J., concurring).

3. The Court dismisses the possibility that "impermissible police conduct will be encouraged" by its decision as "a speculative possibility." Maybe that notion was purely speculative in 1972. But what if it were to turn out that police officers would in fact be encouraged to violate *Miranda* in order to generate impeachment material? *See* Chapter III *supra*.

4. The dissent distinguishes the cross-examination in *Walder* as "completely unrelated" to the charges at issue in the case. Is this a legitimate distinction?

5. Was it necessary to the result in *Harris* that the statement made by the defendant appears to have been made voluntarily? Recall that in *New Jersey v. Portash*, 440 U.S. 450 (1979), the Court would hold that a defendant could not be impeached based on immunized testimony he had given in the grand jury as that testimony was the result of a state compulsion order and was therefore not voluntary.

United States v. Havens

466 U.S. 620 (1980)

Mr. Justice White delivered the opinion of the Court.

The petition for certiorari filed by the United States in this criminal case presented a single question: whether evidence suppressed as the fruit of an unlawful search and seizure may nevertheless be used to impeach a defendant's false trial testimony, given in response to proper cross-examination, where the evidence does not squarely contradict the defendant's testimony on direct examination. We issued the writ.

I

Respondent was convicted of importing, conspiring to import, and intentionally possessing a controlled substance, cocaine. According to the evidence at his trial, Havens and John McLeroth, both attorneys from Ft. Wayne, Ind., boarded a flight from Lima, Peru, to Miami, Fla. In Miami, a customs officer searched McLeroth and found cocaine sewed into makeshift pockets in a T-shirt he was wearing under his outer clothing. McLeroth implicated respondent, who had previously cleared customs and who was then arrested. His luggage was seized and searched without a warrant. The officers found no drugs but seized a T-shirt from which pieces had been cut that matched the pieces that had been sewn to McLeroth's T-shirt. The T-shirt and other evidence seized in the course of the search were suppressed on motion prior to trial.

Both men were charged in a three-count indictment, but McLeroth pleaded guilty to one count and testified against Havens. Among other things, he asserted that Havens had supplied him with the altered T-shirt and had sewed the makeshift pockets shut. Havens took the stand in his own defense and denied involvement in smuggling cocaine. His direct testimony included the following:

> **Q.** And you heard Mr. McLeroth testify earlier as to something to the effect that this material was taped or draped around his body and so on, you heard that testimony?
> **A.** Yes, I did.
> **Q.** Did you ever engage in that kind of activity with Mr. McLeroth and Augusto or Mr. McLeroth and anyone else on that fourth visit to Lima, Peru?
> **A.** I did not.

On cross-examination, Havens testified as follows:

> **Q.** Now, on direct examination, sir, you testified that on the fourth trip you had absolutely nothing to do with the wrapping of any bandages or tee shirts or anything involving Mr. McLeroth; is that correct?
> **A.** I don't—I said I had nothing to do with any wrapping or bandages or anything, yes. I had nothing to do with anything with McLeroth in connection with this cocaine matter.
> **Q.** And your testimony is that you had nothing to do with the sewing of the cotton swatches to make pockets on that tee shirt?
> **A.** Absolutely not.
> **Q.** Sir, when you came through Customs, the Miami International Airport, on October 2, 1977, did you have in your suitcase Size 38-40 medium tee shirts? Id., at 35.

An objection to the latter question was overruled and questioning continued:

> **Q.** On that day, sir, did you have in your luggage a Size 38-40 medium man's tee shirt with swatches of clothing missing from the tail of that tee shirt?
> **A.** Not to my knowledge.
> **Q.** Mr. Havens, I'm going to hand you what is Government's Exhibit 9 for identification and ask you if this tee shirt was in your luggage on October 2nd, 1975 [sic]?
> **A.** Not to my knowledge. No.

Respondent Havens also denied having told a Government agent that the T-shirts found in his luggage belonged to McLeroth.

On rebuttal, a Government agent testified that Exhibit 9 had been found in respondent's suitcase and that Havens claimed the T-shirts found in his bag, including Exhibit 9, belonged to McLeroth. Over objection, the T-shirt was then admitted into evidence, the jury being instructed that the rebuttal evidence should be considered only for impeaching Havens' credibility.

The Court of Appeals reversed, relying on *Agnello v. United States* (1925), and *Walder v. United States* (1954). The court held that illegally seized evidence may be used for impeachment only if the evidence contradicts a particular statement made by a defendant in the course of his direct examination. We reverse.

II

In *Agnello v. United States*, supra, a defendant charged with conspiracy to sell a package of cocaine testified on direct examination that he had possessed the packages involved but did not know what was in them. On cross-examination, he denied ever having seen narcotics and ever having seen a can of cocaine which was exhibited to him and which had been illegally seized from his apartment. The can of cocaine was permitted into evidence on rebuttal. Agnello was convicted and his conviction was affirmed by the Court of Appeals. This Court reversed, holding that the Fourth Amendment required exclusion of the evidence. The Court pointed out that "[i]n his direct examination, Agnello was not asked and did not testify concerning the can of cocaine" and "did nothing to waive his constitutional protection or to justify cross-examination in respect of the evidence claimed to have been obtained by the search." The Court also said, that the exclusionary rule not only commands that illegally seized evidence "shall not be used before the Court but that it shall not be used at all."

The latter statement has been rejected in our later cases, however, and *Agnello* otherwise limited. In *Walder*, the use of evidence obtained in an illegal search and inadmissible in the Government's case in chief was admitted to impeach the direct testimony of the defendant.

These cases were understood by the Court of Appeals to hold that tainted evidence, inadmissible when offered as part of the Government's main case, may not be used as rebuttal evidence to impeach a defendant's credibility unless the evidence is offered to contradict a particular statement made by a defendant during his direct examination; a statement made for the first time on cross-examination may not be so impeached. This approach required the exclusion of the T-shirt taken from Havens' luggage because, as the Court of Appeals read the record, Havens was asked nothing on his direct testimony about the incriminating T-shirt or about the contents of his luggage; the testimony about the T-shirt, which the Government desired to impeach first appeared on cross-examination, not on direct.

In reversing the District Court in the case before us, the Court of Appeals did not stop to consider how closely the cross-examination about the T-shirt and the luggage was connected with matters gone into in direct examination. If these questions would have been suggested to a reasonably competent cross-examiner by Havens' direct testimony, they were not "smuggled in"; and forbidding the Government to impeach the answers to these questions by using contrary and reliable evidence in its possession fails to take account of our cases, particularly *Harris* and *Hass*. In both cases, the Court stressed the importance of arriving at the truth in criminal trials, as well as the defendant's obligation to speak the truth in response to proper questions. We rejected the notion that the defendant's constitutional shield against having illegally seized evidence used against him could be "perverted into a license to use perjury by way of a defense, free from the risk of confrontation with prior inconsistent utterances." Both cases also held that the deterrent function of the rules excluding unconstitutionally obtained evidence is sufficiently served by denying its use to the government on its direct case. It was only a "speculative possibility" that also making it unavailable to the government for otherwise proper impeachment would contribute substantially in this respect.

Neither *Harris* nor *Hass* involved the impeachment of assertedly false testimony first given on cross-examination, but the reasoning of those cases controls this one. There is no gainsaying that arriving at the truth is a fundamental goal of our legal system. We have repeatedly insisted that when defendants testify, they must testify truthfully or suffer the consequences. This is true even though a defendant is compelled to testify against his will. It is essential, therefore, to the proper functioning of the adversary system that when a defendant takes the stand, the government be permitted proper and effective cross-examination in an attempt to elicit the truth. The defendant's obligation to testify truthfully is fully binding on him when he is cross-examined. His privilege against self-incrimination does not shield him from proper questioning. He would unquestionably be subject to a perjury prosecution if he knowingly lies on cross-examination. In terms of impeaching a defendant's seemingly false statements with his prior inconsistent utterances or with other reliable evidence available to the government, we see no difference of constitutional magnitude between the defendant's statements on direct examination and his answers to questions put to him on cross-examination that are plainly within the scope of the defendant's direct examination. Without this opportunity, the normal function of cross-examination would be severely impeded.

We also think that the policies of the exclusionary rule no more bar impeachment here than they did in *Walder, Harris*, and *Hass*. In those cases, the ends of the exclusionary rules were thought adequately implemented by denying the government the use of the challenged evidence to make out its case in chief. The incremental furthering of those ends by forbidding impeachment of the defendant who testifies was deemed insufficient to permit or require that false testimony go unchallenged, with the resulting impairment of the integrity of the factfinding goals of the criminal trial. We reaffirm this assessment of the competing interests, and hold that a defendant's statements made in response to proper cross-examination reasonably suggested by the defendant's direct examination are subject to otherwise proper impeachment by the government, albeit by evidence that has been illegally obtained and that is inadmissible on the government's direct case, or otherwise, as substantive evidence of guilt.

In arriving at its judgment, the Court of Appeals noted that in response to defense counsel's objection to the impeaching evidence on the ground that the matter had not been "covered on direct," the trial court had remarked that "[i]t does not have to be covered on direct." The Court of Appeals thought this was error since in its view illegally seized evidence could be used only to impeach a statement made on direct examination. As we have indicated, we hold a contrary view; and we do not understand the District Court to have indicated that the Government's question, the answer to which is sought to be impeached, need not be proper cross-examination in the first instance. The Court of Appeals did not suggest that either the cross-examination or the impeachment of Havens would have been improper absent the use of illegally seized evidence, and we cannot accept respondent's suggestions that because of the illegal search and seizure, the Government's questions about the T-shirt were improper cross-examination. McLeroth testified that Havens had assisted him in preparing the T-shirt for smuggling. Havens, in his direct testimony, acknowledged McLeroth's prior testimony that the cocaine "was taped or draped around his body and so on" but denied that he had "ever engage[d] in that kind of activity with Mr. McLeroth. . . . " This testimony could easily be understood as a denial of any connection with McLeroth's T-shirt and as a contradiction of McLeroth's testimony. Quite reasonably, it seems to us, the Government on cross-examination called attention to his answers on direct and then asked whether he had anything to do with sewing the cotton swatches on McLeroth's T-shirt. This was cross-examination growing out of Havens' direct testimony; and, as we hold above, the ensuing impeachment did not violate Havens' constitutional rights.

We reverse the judgment of the Court of Appeals and remand the case to that court for further proceedings consistent with this opinion.

NOTES AND QUESTIONS

1. Defense counsel here was playing with fire. Plus he asked a really bad question. Consider the full exchange:

> **Q.** And you heard Mr. McLeroth testify earlier as to something to the effect that this material was taped or draped around his body and so on, you heard that testimony?
>
> **A.** Yes, I did.
>
> **Q.** Did you ever engage in that kind of activity with Mr. McLeroth and Augusto or Mr. McLeroth and anyone else on that fourth visit to Lima, Peru?
>
> **A.** I did not.

The "engage in that kind of activity" formulation is just too loose. Could a more precise question have neutralized the cooperator's testimony more narrowly and not exposed Havens to cross-examination? How about: "You didn't have anything taped or draped on your body in the airport, did you?"

2. Having this important a rule turn on the allowable scope of cross-examination seems unwise. Wouldn't the cleanest and most understandable rule be one that simply prohibits the government from any use of illegally obtained evidence at trial in any way? Do you think the ambiguity in *Havens* could deter defendants from testifying?

3. In any event, was Havens's denial of "engaging in that kind of activity" false?

4. Note: Whenever the description of a trial is described, as here, as a "search for the truth," the defendant is likely to lose.

The next case considers the government's attempt to exploit a particularly egregious constitutional violation under the impeachment exception.

James v. Illinois

493 U.S. 307 (1990)

Justice Brennan delivered the opinion of the Court.

The impeachment exception to the exclusionary rule permits the prosecution in a criminal proceeding to introduce illegally obtained evidence to impeach the defendant's own testimony. The Illinois Supreme Court extended this exception to permit the prosecution to impeach the testimony of all defense witnesses with illegally obtained evidence. Finding this extension inconsistent with the balance of values underlying our previous applications of the exclusionary rule, we reverse.

I

On the night of August 30, 1982, eight young boys returning home from a party were confronted by a trio of other boys who demanded money. When the eight boys refused to comply, one member of the trio produced a gun and fired into the larger group, killing one boy and seriously injuring another. When the police arrived, the remaining members of the larger group provided eyewitness accounts of the event and descriptions of the perpetrators.

The next evening, two detectives of the Chicago Police Department took 15-year-old Darryl James into custody as a suspect in the shooting. James was found at his mother's beauty parlor sitting under a hair dryer; when he emerged, his hair was black and curly. After placing James in their car, the detectives questioned him about his prior hair color. He responded that the previous day his hair had been reddish brown, long, and combed straight back. The detectives questioned James again later at the police station, and he further stated that he had gone to the beauty parlor in order to have his hair "dyed black and curled in order to change his appearance."

The State subsequently indicted James for murder and attempted murder. Prior to trial, James moved to suppress the statements regarding his hair, contending that they were the fruit of a Fourth Amendment violation because the detectives lacked probable cause for his warrantless arrest. After an evidentiary hearing, the trial court sustained this motion and ruled that the statements would be inadmissible at trial.

At trial, five members of the larger group of boys testified for the State, and each made an in-court identification of the defendant. Each testified that the person responsible for the shooting had "reddish" hair, worn shoulder length in a slicked-back "butter" style. Each also recalled having seen James several weeks earlier at a parade, at which time James had the aforementioned hair color and style. At trial, however, his hair was black and worn in a "natural" style. Despite the discrepancy between the witnesses' description and his present appearance, the witnesses stood firm in their conviction that James had been present and had fired the shots.

James did not testify in his own defense. He called as a witness Jewel Henderson, a friend of his family. Henderson testified that on the day of the shooting she had taken James to register for high school and that, at that time, his hair was black. The State then sought, over James' objection, to introduce his illegally obtained statements as a means of impeaching the credibility of Henderson's testimony. After determining that the suppressed statements had been made voluntarily, the trial court overruled James' objection. One of the interrogating detectives then reported James' prior admissions that he had reddish hair the night of the shooting and he dyed and curled his hair the next day in order to change his appearance. James ultimately was convicted of both murder and attempted murder and sentenced to 30 years' imprisonment.

On appeal, the Illinois Appellate Court reversed James' convictions and ordered a new trial. The appellate court held that the exclusionary rule barred admission of James' illegally obtained statements for the purpose of impeaching a defense witness' testimony and that the resulting constitutional error was not harmless. However, the Illinois Supreme Court reversed. The court reasoned that, in order to deter the defendant from engaging in perjury "by proxy," the impeachment exception to the exclusionary rule ought to be expanded to allow the State to introduce illegally obtained evidence to impeach the testimony of defense witnesses other than the defendant himself. The court therefore ordered James' convictions reinstated. We granted certiorari.

II

"There is no gainsaying that arriving at the truth is a fundamental goal of our legal system." *United States v. Havens* (1980). But various constitutional rules limit the means by which government may conduct this search for truth in order to promote other values embraced by the Framers and cherished throughout our Nation's history. "Ever since its inception, the rule excluding evidence seized in violation of the Fourth Amendment has been recognized as a principal mode of discouraging lawless police conduct. . . . [W]ithout it the constitutional guarantee against unreasonable searches and seizures would be a mere 'form of words.'" The occasional suppression of illegally obtained yet probative evidence has long been considered a necessary cost of preserving overriding constitutional values: "[T]here is nothing new in the realization that the Constitution sometimes insulates the criminality of a few in order to protect the privacy of us all."

This Court has carved out exceptions to the exclusionary rule, however, where the introduction of reliable and probative evidence would significantly further the truthseeking function of a criminal trial and the likelihood that admissibility of such evidence would encourage police misconduct is but a "speculative possibility." One exception to the rule permits prosecutors to introduce illegally obtained evidence for the limited purpose of impeaching the credibility of the defendant's own testimony. This Court first recognized this exception in *Walder v. United States*, (1954), permitting the prosecutor to introduce into evidence heroin obtained through an illegal search to undermine the credibility of the defendant's claim that he had never possessed narcotics. The Court explained that a defendant

must be free to deny all the elements of the case against him without thereby giving leave to the Government to introduce by way of rebuttal evidence illegally secured by it, and therefore not available for its case in chief. Beyond that, however, there is hardly justification for letting the defendant affirmatively resort to perjurious testimony in reliance on the Government's disability to challenge his credibility.

In *Harris* and *Hass*, the Court applied the exception to permit prosecutors to impeach defendants using incriminating yet voluntary and reliable statements elicited in violation of *Miranda* requirements. Finally, in *Havens* the Court expanded the exception to permit prosecutors to introduce illegally obtained evidence in order to impeach a defendant's "answers to questions put to him on cross-examination that are plainly within the scope of the defendant's direct examination."

This Court insisted throughout this line of cases that "evidence that has been illegally obtained . . . is inadmissible on the government's direct case, or otherwise, as substantive evidence of guilt." However, because the Court believed that permitting the use of such evidence to impeach defendants' testimony would further the goal of truth-seeking by preventing defendants from perverting the exclusionary rule "'into a license to use perjury by way of a defense,'" and because the Court further believed that permitting such use would create only a "speculative possibility that impermissible police conduct will be encouraged thereby," the Court concluded that the balance of values underlying the exclusionary rule justified an exception covering impeachment of defendants' testimony.

III

In this case, the Illinois Supreme Court held that our balancing approach in *Walder* and its progeny justifies expanding the scope of the impeachment exception to permit prosecutors to use illegally obtained evidence to impeach the credibility of defense witnesses. We disagree. Expanding the class of impeachable witnesses from the defendant alone to all defense witnesses would create different incentives affecting the behavior of both defendants and law enforcement officers. As a result, this expansion would not promote the truthseeking function to the same extent as did creation of the original exception, and yet it would significantly undermine the deterrent effect of the general exclusionary rule. Hence, we believe that this proposed expansion would frustrate rather than further the purposes underlying the exclusionary rule.

The previously recognized exception penalizes defendants for committing perjury by allowing the prosecution to expose their perjury through impeachment using illegally obtained evidence. Thus defendants are discouraged in the first instance from "affirmatively resort[ing] to perjurious testimony." But the exception leaves defendants free to testify truthfully on their own behalf; they can offer probative and exculpatory evidence to the jury without opening the door to impeachment by carefully avoiding any statements that directly contradict the suppressed evidence. The exception thus generally discourages perjured testimony without discouraging truthful testimony.

In contrast, expanding the impeachment exception to encompass the testimony of all defense witnesses would not have the same beneficial effects. First, the mere threat of a subsequent criminal prosecution for perjury is far more likely to deter a witness from intentionally lying on a defendant's behalf than to deter a defendant, already facing conviction for the underlying offense, from lying on his own behalf. Hence the Illinois Supreme Court's underlying premise that a defendant frustrated by our previous impeachment exception can easily find a witness to engage in "perjury by proxy" is suspect.

More significantly, expanding the impeachment exception to encompass the testimony of all defense witnesses likely would chill some defendants from presenting their best defense and sometimes any defense at all—through the testimony of others. Whenever police obtained evidence illegally, defendants would have to assess prior to trial the likelihood that the evidence would be admitted to impeach the otherwise favorable testimony of any witness they call. Defendants might reasonably fear that one or more of their witnesses, in a position to offer truthful and favorable testimony, would also make some statement in sufficient tension with the tainted evidence to allow the prosecutor to introduce that evidence for impeachment. First, defendants sometimes need to call "reluctant" or "hostile" witnesses to provide reliable and probative exculpatory testimony, and such witnesses likely will not share the defendants' concern for avoiding statements that invite impeachment through contradictory evidence. Moreover, defendants often cannot trust even "friendly" witnesses to testify without subjecting themselves to impeachment, simply due to insufficient care or attentiveness. This concern is magnified in those occasional situations when defendants must call witnesses to testify despite having had only a limited opportunity to consult with or prepare them in advance. For these reasons, we have recognized in a variety of contexts that a party "cannot be absolutely certain that his witnesses will testify as expected." As a result, an expanded impeachment exception likely would chill some defendants from calling witnesses who would otherwise offer probative evidence.

This realization alters the balance of values underlying the current impeachment exception governing defendants' testimony. Our prior cases make clear that defendants ought not be able to "pervert" the exclusion of illegally obtained evidence into a shield for perjury, but it seems no more appropriate for the State to brandish such evidence as a sword with which to dissuade defendants from presenting a meaningful defense through other witnesses. Given the potential chill created by expanding the impeachment exception, the conceded gains to the truth-seeking process from discouraging or disclosing perjured testimony would be offset to some extent by the concomitant loss of probative witness testimony. Thus, the truth-seeking rationale supporting the impeachment of defendants in *Walder* and its progeny does not apply to other witnesses with equal force.

Moreover, the proposed expansion of the current impeachment exception would significantly weaken the exclusionary rule's deterrent effect on police misconduct. This Court has characterized as a mere "speculative possibility," the likelihood that permitting prosecutors to impeach defendants with illegally obtained evidence would encourage police misconduct. Law enforcement officers will think it unlikely that the defendant will first decide to testify at trial and will also open the door inadvertently to admission of any illegally obtained evidence. Hence, the officers' incentive to acquire evidence through illegal means is quite weak.

In contrast, expanding the impeachment exception to all defense witnesses would significantly enhance the expected value to the prosecution of illegally obtained evidence. First, this expansion would vastly increase the number of occasions on which such evidence could be used. Defense witnesses easily outnumber testifying defendants, both because many defendants do not testify themselves and because many if not most defendants call multiple witnesses on their behalf. Moreover, due to the chilling effect identified above, illegally obtained evidence holds even greater value to the prosecution for each individual witness than for each defendant. The prosecutor's access to impeachment evidence would not just deter perjury; it would also deter defendants from calling witnesses in the first place, thereby keeping from the jury much probative exculpatory evidence. For both of these reasons, police officers and their superiors would recognize that obtaining evidence through illegal means stacks the deck heavily in the prosecution's favor. It is thus far more than a "speculative possibility" that police misconduct will be encouraged by permitting such use of illegally obtained evidence.

The United States argues that this result is constitutionally acceptable because excluding illegally obtained evidence solely from the prosecution's case in chief would still provide a quantum of deterrence sufficient to protect the privacy interests underlying the exclusionary rule. We disagree. Of course, a police officer might in certain situations believe that obtaining particular evidence through illegal means, resulting in its suppression from the case in chief, would prevent the prosecution from establishing a prima facie case to take to a jury. In such situations, the officer likely would be deterred from obtaining the evidence illegally for fear of jeopardizing the entire case. But much if not most of the time, police officers confront opportunities to obtain evidence illegally after they have already legally obtained (or know that they have other means of legally obtaining) sufficient evidence to sustain a prima facie case. In these situations, a rule requiring exclusion of illegally obtained evidence from only the government's case in chief would leave officers with little to lose and much to gain by overstepping constitutional limits on evidence gathering. Narrowing the exclusionary rule in this manner, therefore, would significantly undermine the rule's ability "to compel respect for the constitutional guaranty in the only effectively available way — by removing the incentive to disregard it." So long as we are committed to protecting the people from the disregard of their constitutional rights during the course of criminal investigations, inadmissibility of illegally obtained evidence must remain the rule, not the exception.

IV

The cost to the truth-seeking process of evidentiary exclusion invariably is perceived more tangibly in discrete prosecutions than is the protection of privacy values through deterrence of future police misconduct. When defining the precise scope of the exclusionary rule, however, we must focus on systemic effects of proposed exceptions to ensure that individual liberty from arbitrary or oppressive police conduct does not succumb to the inexorable pressure to introduce all incriminating evidence, no matter how obtained, in each and every criminal case. Our previous recognition of an impeachment exception limited to the testimony of defendants reflects a careful weighing of the competing values. Because expanding the exception to encompass the testimony of all defense witnesses would not further the truth-seeking value with equal force but would appreciably undermine the deterrent effect of the exclusionary rule, we adhere to the line drawn in our previous cases.

Accordingly, we hold that the Illinois Supreme Court erred in affirming James' convictions despite the prosecutor's use of illegally obtained statements to impeach a defense witness' testimony. The court's judgment is reversed, and the case is remanded for further proceedings not inconsistent with this opinion.

NOTES AND QUESTIONS

1. Note the egregiousness of the misconduct here: The police essentially seized a 15-year old boy and absconded with him without probable cause or a warrant. Even if the nature of the misconduct does not affect the impeachment issue, it undoubtedly contributed to the result.

2. Why was the prosecutor here so greedy? How badly did the prosecutor need the rebuttal testimony from the police officer? He had five eyewitnesses who were able to identify the defendant as the shooter. And the prosecutor must have had some way to get into evidence — through Jewel Henderson, the family friend, perhaps — that James's mother had a beauty parlor.

F. SUPPRESSION HEARINGS

Suppression hearings are the vehicles for defendants to attempt to vindicate their constitutional rights before a judge and attempt to have illegally obtained evidence excluded in advance of their trial. In many cases the result of the suppression hearing will determine whether there will be a trial — success might mean the case is dropped while failure might lead to the conclusion that a guilty plea is in order. Suppression hearings often turn on competing versions of the facts leading up to a search, seizure, or other police encounter. And it is sometimes necessary for defendants to testify at suppression hearings.

Although the Supreme Court has held that a defendant's testimony at a suppression hearing cannot be used against the defendant on the question of guilt or innocence, *Simmons v. United States*, 390 U.S. 27 (1968), it can be used to impeach the credibility of a testifying defendant. *See supra.*

There are other risks as well, especially since the introduction of the United States Sentencing Guidelines, as the next case shows.

United States v. Matos

907 F.2d 274 (2d Cir. 1990)

Meskill, Circuit Judge:

This is an appeal from a judgment of conviction entered in the United States District Court for the Southern District of New York, Haight, J. Defendant-appellant was found guilty after a bench trial on stipulated facts of falsely making, forging and counterfeiting United States Federal Reserve Notes in violation of 18 U.S.C. §§ 471 and 2. He was subsequently sentenced under the Sentencing Guidelines (Guidelines) to twenty-four months imprisonment, two years supervised release and a $50 special assessment. On appeal, he contends that the district court erred in increasing his offense level by two points for obstruction of justice under Guidelines § 3C1.1 on the basis of his false testimony at a suppression hearing.

The facts relevant to the resolution of this appeal may be summarized as follows. On February 26, 1988, Secret Service Agents arrested appellant at his print shop on counterfeiting charges. After being advised of his constitutional rights, appellant admitted printing counterfeit currency and stated that he had given the counterfeit money along with the plates and negatives to someone named "Carmello." He was again advised of his rights and consented to a search of his print shop and his apartment.

After the searches, the agents took appellant to the Secret Service's New York Field Office. Special Agent James Figliuolo advised appellant of his constitutional rights, this time using a one page printed waiver form. Figliuolo wrote the date and time on the form, and appellant signed it. In response to questions that followed, appellant restated that he had printed the counterfeit money but had given the money, plates and negatives to "Carmello." Appellant thereafter agreed to take a polygraph test. Before the test, Figliuolo again advised appellant of his rights, using a two page printed waiver form on which appellant marked his initials and wrote the time and date. The results of the polygraph examination showed evidence of deception. After additional questioning, appellant finally admitted that he had given the counterfeit money to his girlfriend. He then signed and dated a three page statement detailing his counterfeiting activities.

At a pretrial suppression hearing, appellant testified, in contradiction to the testimony of the agents involved, that he had not been advised of his constitutional rights until after he had made his various oral and written statements, that he had been forced to sign the waiver forms with the times and dates left blank, and that the agents backdated the time on the forms. He also testified that he asked to consult a lawyer at the print shop and that his request was ignored. The district court discredited appellant's testimony, finding that his rendition of the events was "inherently implausible" and that his claim that his request for an attorney was ignored was nothing more than "an effort to shore up his motion."

Appellant was found guilty after a bench trial on stipulated facts. At sentencing, the district court added two points to the calculation of appellant's offense level for obstruction of justice under Guidelines § 3C1.1 on the ground that he had testified falsely at the suppression hearing.

Guidelines § 3C1.1 provides:

> If the defendant willfully impeded or obstructed, or attempted to impede or obstruct the administration of justice during the investigation or prosecution of the instant offense, increase the offense level by 2 levels.

Application Note 1(c) to this section specifically identifies "testifying untruthfully . . . concerning a material fact" during any judicial proceeding as within the scope of section 3C1.1. Appellant nevertheless argues that the district court erred in increasing his offense level by two points absent a finding that his testimony was motivated by an intent to deceive. In support of his position, appellant relies on Application Note 2 to section 3C1.1, which provides that "[i]n applying [section 3C1.1], suspect testimony and statements should be evaluated in a light most favorable to the defendant." Viewed in this light, appellant contends, his testimony can be seen as the product of confusion rather than an intent to deceive. He further argues that, if such testimony is not viewed in the light most favorable to the defendant, section 3C1.1 will have a chilling effect on a defendant's decision to testify.

We find these claims to be meritless. The district court specifically found that appellant's testimony contained a "basic and bald untruth on an important aspect of the [suppression] motion" and that his false testimony constituted willful obstruction. Application Note 2 "simply instructs the sentencing judge to resolve in favor of the defendant those conflicts about which the judge, after weighing the evidence, has no firm conviction." The district court without question found that appellant testified falsely with the purpose of affecting the outcome of the suppression hearing. This finding is not clearly erroneous.

This result does not, as appellant contends, unconstitutionally chill the exercise of the right to testify. A defendant has no protected right to testify falsely. When, as here, the district court comes away with the firm conviction that the defendant testified falsely with the intent of impeding the disposition of the criminal charges, there is no constitutional bar to an enhanced sentence.

The judgment of the district court is therefore affirmed.

NOTES AND QUESTIONS

1. Does Matos's version of the police interrogation suggest the officers might have been using the successive interrogation technique that was blessed by the Supreme Court in *Oregon v. Elstad*? Why would the district court—presumably well aware of *Elstad*—have found Matos's testimony "inherently implausible"?

2. A two-level guideline increase would probably have added six months to Matos's sentence. Do you agree with his argument about this adjustment having a "chilling effect" on defendants considering testifying at suppression hearings?

3. A trial judge's conclusion on the credibility of a witness is always going to be viewed deferentially on appeal. Given the high stakes in a context such as this one, would it serve any purpose to require the trial judge to make specific findings as to credibility?

4. It seems as if the judge's credibility comments were made at the hearing denying the suppression motion. Why in the world, then, did the defendant waive his right to a jury trial?

Testilying. The credibility of the defendant is hardly the only credibility issue relevant to suppression motions. A substantial body of literature exists on the subject of police perjury, much of it originating in the findings of the Mollen Commission, named after Judge Milton

Mollen, who led an investigation into corruption in the New York City Police Department in the 1990s. The Commission found the following:

> Officers reported a litany of manufactured tales. For example, when officers unlawfully stop and search a vehicle because they believe it contains drugs or guns, officers will falsely claim in police reports and under oath that the car ran a red light (or committed some other traffic violation) and that they subsequently saw contraband in the car in plain view. To conceal an unlawful search of an individual who officers believe is carrying drugs or a gun, they will falsely assert that they saw a bulge in the person's pocket or saw drugs and money changing hands. To justify unlawfully entering an apartment where officers believe narcotics or cash can be found, they pretend to have information from an unidentified civilian informant or claim they saw the drugs in plain view after responding to the premises on a radio run. To arrest people they suspect are guilty of dealing drugs, they falsely assert that the defendants had drugs in their possession when, in fact, the drugs were found elsewhere where the officers had no lawful right to be.

Commission to Investigate Allegations of Police Corruption and the Anti-Corruption Procedures of the Police Dept., City of New York, Commission Report 36 (1994) (Milton Mollen, Chair) (hereinafter Mollen Report). The phenomenon of police perjury was so widespread in some places that the police themselves came up with a name for it—"testilying." *Id.*

The problem of police perjury is most prevalent in suppression hearings, perhaps because in this context police officers see themselves as the righteous defenders of the fight against crime in a theater populated by factually guilty defendants, sleazy defense attorneys, permissive judges, and legal technicalities. *See* Carl B. Klockars, *Blue Lies and Police Placebos*, 27 Am. Behav. Sci. 529, 540 (1984) (Police lie at suppression hearings because they see search-and-seizure rules, and other evidentiary rules, as procedural rules "the violation of which does not affect a perpetrator's factual guilt."). Myron W. Orfield Jr., *Deterrence, Perjury, and the Heater Factor: An Exclusionary Rule in the Chicago Criminal Courts*, 63 U. Colo. L. Rev. 75, 107 (1992) (survey of prosecutors, defense attorneys, and judges indicates a belief that, on average, perjury occurs 20 percent of the time, with defense attorneys estimating it occurs 53 percent of the time in connection with Fourth Amendment issues; only 8 percent believe that police never, or almost never, lie in court).

The problem of police perjury had been in existence for decades when the Mollen Commission did its work, as the next case shows.

People v. McMurty

64 Misc. 2d 63 (1970)

Irving Younger, J.

For several years now, lawyers concerned with the administration of criminal justice have been troubled by the problem of "dropsy" testimony. This case shows why.

The facts are simple. On July 23, 1970, Patrolman Charles Frisina arrested defendant James McMurty on a charge of possession of marijuana. McMurty moved to suppress the marijuana for use as evidence, and, in due course, a hearing was held. Frisina took the stand. In condensed but substantially verbatim form, he testified as follows:

> At 8:30 p.m. on July 23, 1970, I was on duty driving a patrol car. While stopped for a light at West 3rd Street and Broadway, I observed two men in a doorway of the building at 677 Broadway. One of these men—James McMurty, as I later learned—saw the patrol car and stepped out of the doorway. From his right hand he let drop a small plastic container. I got out of the patrol car and retrieved it. In my opinion, based upon a fair amount of experience, its contents were marijuana. I approached McMurty, who had begun to walk away, and asked him if the container was his. He said no. I said that I had seen him drop it and placed him under arrest.

Then McMurty took the stand. In condensed but substantially verbatim form, he testified as follows:

> On July 23, 1970, at 8:30 p.m., I was walking on Broadway near West 3rd Street when I saw Patrolman Frisina coming toward me. I knew that I had a container of marijuana in my pocket. I also knew, after twelve years of involvement with drugs and four or five prior convictions, that illegal-search-and-seizure was my only defense. The last thing I would do is drop the marijuana to the ground. I simply left it in my pocket. Frisina told me to get into a doorway. I obeyed, hoping that he would search me. He did just that, found the marijuana, and arrested me.

The prosecutor stands on Frisina's testimony. Since the marijuana had been abandoned, he argues, its seizure was lawful. Defense counsel stands on McMurty's testimony. The arrest occurred when McMurty was ordered into the doorway, he argues, and since the officer then had no probable cause to arrest, the search which followed was unlawful.

Were this the first time a policeman had testified that a defendant dropped a packet of drugs to the ground, the matter would be unremarkable. The extraordinary thing is that each year in our criminal courts policemen give such testimony in hundreds, perhaps thousands, of cases—and that, in a nutshell, is the problem of "dropsy" testimony. It disturbs me now, and it disturbed me when I was at the Bar.

Policemen see themselves as fighting a two-front war—against criminals in the street and against "liberal" rules of law in court. All's fair in this war, including the use of perjury to subvert "liberal" rules of law that might free those who "ought" to be jailed. . . . It is a peculiarity of our legal system that the police have unique opportunities (and unique temptations) to give false testimony. When the Supreme Court lays down a rule to govern the conduct of the police, the rule does not enforce itself. Some further proceeding . . . is almost always necessary to determine what actually happened. In *Mapp v. Ohio*, for example, the Supreme Court laid down the rule that evidence obtained by the police through an unreasonable search and seizure may not be used in a state criminal prosecution. But before applying the rule to any particular case, a hearing must be held to establish the facts. Then the judge decides whether those facts constitute an unreasonable search and seizure. . . . The difficulty arises when one stands back from the particular case and looks at a series of cases. It then becomes apparent that policemen are committing perjury at least in some of them, and perhaps in nearly all of them.

Narcotics prosecutions in New York City can be so viewed. Before *Mapp*, the policeman typically testified that he stopped the defendant for little or no reason, searched him, and found narcotics on his person. This had the ring of truth. It was an illegal search (not based upon "probable cause"), but the evidence was admissible because *Mapp* had not yet been decided. Since it made no difference, the policeman testified truthfully. After the decision in *Mapp*, it made a great deal of difference. For the first few months, New York policemen continued to tell the truth about the circumstances of their searches, with the result that evidence was suppressed. Then the police made the great discovery that if the defendant drops the narcotics on the ground, after which the policeman arrests him, the search is reasonable and the evidence is admissible.

Spend a few hours in the New York City Criminal Court nowadays, and you will hear case after case in which a policeman testifies that the defendant dropped the narcotics on the ground, whereupon the policeman arrested him. Usually the very language of the testimony is identical from one case to another. This is now known among defense lawyers and prosecutors as "dropsy" testimony. The judge has no reason to disbelieve it in any particular case, and of course the judge must decide each case on its own evidence, without regard to the testimony in other cases. Surely, though, not in every case was the defendant unlucky enough to drop his narcotics at the feet of a policeman. It follows that at least in some of these cases the police are lying.

So far as I know, there has been only one statistical study of "dropsy" complaints. It confirms my impressions (pp. 556-557): "In the period after *Mapp*, the number of complaints alleging that the suspect dropped the contraband increased for all groups of officers. The Narcotics Squad showed the smallest percentages increase (45.3 per cent), although the rise in the number of their "dropsies" (93, from 205 to 298) was the largest. The plainclothesmen recorded a 71.8 per cent rise in complaints based on this circumstance, an increase from 32 to 55; while the uniformed officers showed the highest percentage increase (79.6 per cent), with the number of complaints alleging drops rising from 69 to 128."

Beyond any doubt, then, the problem exists. Its solution, I suppose, is prosecutors' work. The courts can only deplore. They are ill-equipped to persuade the police to change their practices or alter their philosophy. In Judge Wright's words, "the time is ripe for some soul searching in the prosecutor's office before it offers any more ['dropsy' testimony]."

Withal, Judges must decide the cases that come before them. In this case, my reasoning has taken four steps.

First. "Dropsy" testimony should be scrutinized with especial caution.

I am aware that Judge (as he then was) Burger wrote, with respect to narcotics policemen: "But it would be a dismal reflection on society to say that when the guardians of its security are called to testify in court under oath, their testimony must be viewed with suspicion."

With all possible deference, I disagree. When there are grounds for believing that "the guardians of its security" sometimes give deliberately false testimony, it is no "dismal reflection on society" for Judges to acknowledge what all can see. If courage is the secret of liberty, the first task of free men is to call things by their right name.

Second. Should the policeman's testimony seem inherently unreal, it will forthwith be rejected. This is a consequence of the first consideration.

Here, the evidence given by neither witness strikes me as against the grain of human experience. If Frisina's testimony stood alone, I could believe it. If McMurty's testimony stood alone, I could believe it.

Third. The slightest independent contradiction of the policeman's testimony or corroboration of the defendant's testimony will warrant suppression of the evidence. This too is a consequence of the first consideration.

Here, there was no independent contradiction of Frisina and no independent corroboration of McMurty. The testimony of each remains poised in the balance.

Fourth. Determine whether the burden of proof has been carried.

Had the issue been open, I would hold that the People must prove beyond a reasonable doubt that the seizure was lawful. But the issue is closed. The Court of Appeals declares the burden of proof to be the defendant's. Where the testimony on one side balances the testimony on the other, as here, it is the People who prevail. Defendant's motion to suppress is therefore denied.

I come to this decision reluctantly. Our refusal to face up to the "dropsy" problem soils the rectitude of the administration of justice. One is tempted to deal with it now by suppressing "dropsy" evidence out of hand; yet I cannot. Reason and settled rules of law lead the other way, and Judge serve the integrity of the means, not the attractiveness of the end.

Somehow, policemen must be made to understand that their duty is no different.

NOTES AND QUESTIONS

1. Why are prosecutors largely getting off the hook here? Their most fundamental ethical obligation is to not present perjured testimony.

2. Does this case come out the right way? Is this really a perfect credibility tie, with the government winning the tiebreaker because the burden of proof is on the defendant?

Irving Younger

3. Judge Irving Younger, a former assistant U.S. attorney in the Southern District of New York, was a practicing lawyer and law professor before and after being a judge, and was widely known for his writings and lectures on trial practice. Most trial lawyers to this day regard his "The Ten Commandments of Cross-Examination" as gospel.

Judge Younger attributes dropsy testimony to *Mapp*. This is a standard account, although there are variations on the theme. Professor Bennett Capers, for example, notes that police perjury has an ancient pedigree but that, echoing Judge Younger, the police had little reason to lie and began doing so once the exclusionary rule became applicable. I. Bennett Capers, *Crime, Legitimacy, and Testilying*, 83 Ind. L.J. 835, 868 (2008). Professor Morgan Cloud notes longstanding evidence of police corruption uncovered by the Wickersham Commission in the 1930s, and links testilying to the decisions of the Warren Court. *See* Morgan Cloud, *Judges, "Testilying," and the Constitution*, 69 S. Cal. L. Rev. 1341, 1342-43, 1350-53 (1996); Morgan Cloud, *The Dirty Little Secret*, 43 Emory L.J. 1311, 1314-21 (1994) ("The change in police testimony about investigative practices can be traced to the Supreme Court's decisions constitutionalizing criminal procedure.").

United States v. Restrepo

890 F. Supp. 180 (E.D.N.Y. 1995)

WEINSTEIN, Senior District Judge.

I. INTRODUCTION

Alberto Caro, Jose Francisco Guevara and Christian John Restrepo seek to suppress statements and other evidence of a drug conspiracy. They are charged with conspiring to distribute and to possess with intent to distribute, and with possessing with intent to distribute, cocaine. 21 U.S.C. §§ 841(a)(1) & 841(b)(1)(A)(ii)(II). They move to suppress the following statements and other evidence: Guevara: evidence and statements obtained by law enforcement officials following a traffic stop, on grounds of a series of alleged Fourth Amendment violations; Caro: tapes of conversations between himself and Guevara on the ground that the statutorily required consents to the recordings were not obtained; and Restrepo: evidence obtained as a result of a "security sweep" of his house.

Guevara's motion is granted: law enforcement officials violated his constitutional rights, starting with an illegal stop and search of his car.

• • •

II. GUEVARA'S MOTION TO SUPPRESS

A. Facts

An officer of the Memphis Police Department stopped Guevara, a swarthy Hispanic-appearing male driving a Cadillac with California license plates on an interstate highway in Tennessee. Guevara's eleven-year-old son, Rodolfo, was in the front passenger seat and his wife and two younger children were in the rear.

At a full evidentiary hearing in the Eastern District of New York, the officer testified that Guevara was speeding—driving 65 miles per hour in a 55 miles per hour zone. Guevara and Rodolfo both testified that Guevara was driving slowly because the family was seeking a place to stop for breakfast. Guevara also stated that he was driving at less than 55 miles per hour because he did not want to be intercepted while he was carrying drugs. Rodolfo testified that as they passed the police car he noticed that the car's speedometer read 47-50 miles per hour and that his mother had just chided his father for driving too slowly.

Because Guevara does not speak English, the officer used Rodolfo as an interpreter for communicating with Guevara during the stop.

Rodolfo testified that the officer stated that the reason for the stop was that Guevara was driving too closely behind a tractor trailer. Guevara testified that the officer never told him, through Rodolfo, the reason for the stop. He did, however, acknowledge driving within five or six meters of a tractor trailer. He also believes that at some point during the stop, Rodolfo told him that the officer had mentioned tailgating. The "traffic courtesy warning" issued by the officer states that Guevara was "speeding 65 MPH in a 55 MPH zone."

The officer sought and received Guevara's driver's license which he used to fill out a "courtesy warning." Guevara did not ask his son to translate the courtesy warning, believing that it was not important and that after signing it, he would be permitted to depart.

As the officer filled out the courtesy warning, he questioned Guevara and Rodolfo about their trip. According to Guevara, the officer was "burning time while he filled out the courtesy ticket, he was continuing to ask me questions." Guevara explained that the family was headed to Queens, New York for three days' vacation. Rodolfo testified that the officer also asked Guevara if he is "Mexican."

The officer testified that during this conversation, he noticed that Guevara was growing "more and more nervous," that "[h]is hands were quivering," and that Mrs. Guevara "kept looking back like, you know, nervously every time I would talk to [Guevara,] . . . a real nervous type reaction to me." Under cross examination he explained that general conversation is used to elicit signs of possible criminal activity independent of a traffic violation.

As or immediately after the officer issued the courtesy warning, a second officer arrived. According to the first officer, the second officer happened upon the scene. The second testified, however, that he had been radioed by the first, and Guevara testified that the first used the radio in his patrol car after taking Guevara's license and registration. The second officer asked Guevara many of the same questions that the first had already asked, and received consistent answers.

After Guevara signed the courtesy warning, the second officer asked if he could speak with Mrs. Guevara, and Guevara agreed. The second officer stayed with Guevara while the first went to open the driver's side door. As he opened it, he "observed that the door was overly heavy for a regular door. Felt like it was heavy to me." Then, according to the first officer, he realized that traffic was coming and that it would be better for Mrs. Guevara to exit from the other side; he shut the door and walked back to the squad car, while the second officer walked over to the passenger side door.

Through the open window of the car, the second officer attempted to communicate with Mrs. Guevara in Spanish. In response to his questions, Mrs. Guevara explained that the family was headed to New York, that they were to be gone a week, and that the trip's purpose was to visit relatives.

Based on the observed nervousness of Mr. and Mrs. Guevara, the fact of the heavy door, and what they felt were discrepancies in the Guevaras' replies to questions about the length and purpose of the trip, the officers decided to request permission to search the car. According to the first officer, it "[a]ppeared like it was more than just a speeding violation at that time. We didn't know what it was."

The second officer asked Guevara in Spanish if he had any guns or illegal drugs in the car and if he would consent to a search. According to the first, Guevara denied that there was anything illegal in the car but agreed to the search.

The second officer asked Guevara to sign a written consent-to-search form. He testified that he first explained the form in English. When Guevara looked confused, this officer flipped the form over to the Spanish side whereupon Guevara "scann[ed] the form with his eyes it looked to me like line-by-line." According to the first officer, Guevara "signed the English side first and then the Spanish side I believe." Both officers testified that the blanks on both sides of the form had already been filled in when it was presented to Guevara.

The first officer testified that the officers did not specify in their request a particular part of the car for the search, such as the trunk or glove compartment. The pre-typed portion of the consent form authorizes "a complete search" of the car.

According to the officers' account, after Mrs. Guevara and the remaining children exited the car, the search of the car commenced. While the second officer stayed with the family, the first opened the driver's side door, "popped" the panel and some additional plastic covering, and observed "a bundle of possibly some type of narcotic."

Guevara's and Rodolfo's testimony contradicted that of the officers. Guevara denied that he was asked whether there was anything illegal in the car. He testified that the blanks on the consent-to-search form were not filled in when it was handed to him to sign and that the officers asked only to search the trunk. He testified that he could not read the English-language consent-to-search form, and that he did not ask his son to translate because he believed it merely authorized a search of the trunk, after which he would be permitted to leave. Guevara's signature appears on both sides of the form. Guevara testified that he signed where the officer pointed, without ever holding the form in his hands. He recognized his signature on the Spanish-language side of the form but did not recall signing that side, noting that the process happened "very fast." He claimed that he did not feel free to leave, but he hoped he would be allowed to if he consented to the search of the trunk.

Rodolfo also testified that the officers stated only that they were going to search the trunk. He denied that the officers asked for or received permission to search the inside of the car. He testified that in response to the officers' request, Guevara agreed to open the trunk, and did so, whereupon it was searched by both officers. One of the officers then went on to search the glove compartment, and then pulled apart the plastic paneling on the driver's door.

After discovering a bundle in the door panel, the officer pointed his gun at Guevara and told him to drop to his knees and put his hands behind his back. Guevara complied and was handcuffed. The children and Mrs. Guevara were directed to the back of a squad car. One of the officers retrieved the package. It tested positive for cocaine.

The first officer then informed Guevara that he was under arrest for possession of cocaine. According to the officers' testimony, both of them recited *Miranda* rights to Guevara—the first in English from memory, and the second in English and then Spanish from a card when Guevara appeared confused. The second officer testified that Guevara shook his head in the affirmative when asked whether he would answer questions. Neither officer made a record that the *Miranda* warnings were given. Guevara denied receiving *Miranda* warnings at his arrest.

The second officer then asked Guevara how much cocaine was in the car. Guevara responded "sixty" in English. Ultimately 60 1-kilogram bricks of cocaine were found secreted within the side panels of the car.

Two additional officers, one a Lieutenant, joined the scene. Upon learning at this time that Mrs. Guevara was a Colombian, Rodolfo testified that the second officer responded, "No wonder." The family and their car were taken to the Memphis Police Department.

• • •

The court finds the defendant, Guevara, his son, Rodolfo, and the attorney, April Ferguson, credible. It finds that the first and second officer at the scene of the stop lied. Where there are material inconsistencies between the three defense witnesses' testimony and that of the government's witnesses, the court credits the defense version. The court also finds that Guevara truthfully described his language ability; the government's argument that he understands English is unsupported. These assessments of credibility are based upon the court's observations of the witnesses and all other factors normally utilized in assessing credibility. See, e.g., 1 Leonard B. Sand, John S. Siffert, Walter P. Loughlin & Steven A. Reiss, Modern Federal Jury Instructions: Criminal ¶ 7.01 (1994) ("Witness Credibility").

NOTES AND QUESTIONS

1. This is an outlier case. Judges are notoriously reluctant to openly question the credibility of a testifying police officer. Cloud, *The Dirty Little Secret*, *supra* at 1311, 1321-24. Crediting police testimony is almost another aspect of the deference that the Supreme Court has told federal judges over and over again that they should give to police expertise. *See generally* Anna Lvovsky, *The Judicial Presumption of Police Expertise*, 130 Harv. L. Rev. 1995 (2017) (describing the historical arc of police reform efforts).

2. Was there probable cause to stop Guevara for tailgating? Does it matter that the police identified the stop as based on speeding? Would the stop of Guevara's car have been legal after *Whren*?

For an argument that the remarkable thing about police lying is not that it happens but that the Supreme Court shows little skepticism about it, *see* Adam M. Gershowitz & Caroline E. Lewis, *Laundering Police Lies*, 2023 Wis. L. Rev. 1187, 1189-90 (2023). For creative proposals for solutions to the police perjury problem, *see generally* Vida B. Johnson, *Bias in Blue: Instructing Jurors to Consider the Testimony of Police Officer Witnesses with Caution*, 44 Pepp. L. Rev. 245 (2017) (proposing jury instruction on the biases and interests of testifying police officers); David N. Dorfman, *Proving the Lie: Litigating Police Credibility*, 26 Am. J. Crim. L. 455 (1998) (proposing expanded discovery into materials regarding police credibility).

[illegible]

NOTES AND QUESTIONS

[illegible]

CHAPTER VI

ADDRESSING POLICE MISCONDUCT

What to do about police misconduct? It is generally accepted that most police officers discharge their difficult responsibilities honestly and without resort to undue force, yet some police officers — be they rogues or otherwise — all too often beat or kill civilians. *See, e.g.*, Paul Chevigny, Edge of the Knife: Police Violence in the Americas 97 (1995) (stating that generally, a small number of officers appear to be responsible for most of the misconduct). Yet the problem of police misconduct persists, and is apparently impervious to reform from within on any broad basis.

There would appear to be a federal statute that aims to address this problem, 42 U.S.C. § 1983, originally part of the Ku Klux Klan Act of 1871. It provides:

> Every person who, under color of any statute, ordinance, regulation, custom or usage, of any State or Territory, subjects, or causes to be subjected, any citizen of the United States or other person within the jurisdiction thereof to the deprivation of any rights, privileges, or immunities secured by the Constitution and laws, shall be liable to the party injured in an action at law, suit in equity, or other proper proceeding for redress.

Police misconduct sure seems to be "under color" of law. When police use unreasonable force or conduct illegal searches or impermissibly interrogate persons, they "deprive" persons of federal rights. And the statute promises not only money damages but also equitable relief.

But the Supreme Court has hamstrung § 1983 in several ways that have rendered the statute, despite its apparent textual fit, a poor remedial device for addressing police misconduct. Those barriers will be explored below. Two other potential avenues for deterring police misconduct, each with challenges of its own, are specifically addressed elsewhere in this book. Chapter V *supra* examines the exclusionary rule, which aims to deter police misconduct by preventing the admissibility of evidence derived from illegal police activity, and Chapter X *infra* explores the Department of Justice's use of criminal civil rights statutes to prosecute police officers for deprivations of constitutional rights. Neither of these avenues provides for the compensation of victims, however.

Section A below focuses on the reawakening of § 1983 from a long period of dormancy. *Monroe v. Pape*, 365 U.S. 167 (1961), recognized a damages cause of action against defendant police officers under § 1983, but held that their municipality employers were not proper defendants under the statute. Just 17 years later, in *Monell v. Dept. of Social Services of the City of New York*, 436 U.S. 658 (1978), the Court reversed *Monroe*'s holding shielding municipalities from suit, but at the same time rejected municipal liability under a theory of respondeat superior. Section B addresses what remains of municipal liability under § 1983 after *Monell*, including the cases and doctrine that make not only damages but also injunctive relief against police department defendants generally so unobtainable. Section C looks at § 1983 litigation directed at individual police officers, and how the judicially created doctrine of "qualified immunity" undermines that potential avenue of redress. Section D looks at an entirely different federal remedy, 42 U.S.C. § 14141, which authorizes the Department of Justice to bring actions against police departments that engage in a "pattern or practice" of police misconduct.

A. AWAKENING OF § 1983

Prior to *Monroe*, § 1983 was rarely used. Between 1871 and 1920, only 21 cases were brought under § 1983, and the statute was still rarely used into the 1950s. *See Developments in the Law—Section 1983 and Federalism*, 90 Harv. L. Rev. 1137, 1161 & n.39 (1977). At least some of this impotence was because most of the expansion of constitutional rights (via incorporation of the Bill of Rights into the Fourteenth Amendment) occurred beginning in the 1950s. *See* Jack Beermann, *The History of Civil Rights Legislation, Fifty Years Later*, 34 Conn. L. Rev. 98, 1003-04 (2002). For example, the Fourth Amendment, the violation of which is the basis for James Monroe's claim below, was not held applicable to the states until 1949. *Wolf v. Colorado*, 338 U.S. 25 (1949). The Harvard Law Review editors were not being hyperbolic when they declared that "*Monroe v. Pape* resurrected section 1983 from ninety years of obscurity." *Developments in the Law*, *supra* at 1137, 1169.

Monroe v. Pape

365 U.S. 167 (1961)

Mr. Justice Douglas delivered the opinion of the Court.

This case presents important questions concerning the construction of [42 U.S.C. s 1983], which reads as follows:

> Every person who, under color of any statute, ordinance, regulation, custom or usage, of any State or Territory, subjects, or causes to be subjected, any citizen of the United States or other person within the jurisdiction thereof to the deprivation of any rights, privileges, or immunities secured by the Constitution and laws, shall be liable to the party injured in an action at law, suit in equity, or other proper proceeding for redress.

The complaint alleges that 13 Chicago police officers broke into petitioners' home in the early morning, routed them from bed, made them stand naked in the living room, and ransacked every room, emptying drawers and ripping mattress covers. It further alleges that Mr. Monroe was then taken to the police station and detained on "open" charges for 10 hours, while he was interrogated about a two-day-old murder, that he was not taken before a magistrate, though one was accessible, that he was not permitted to call his family or attorney, that he was subsequently released without criminal charges being preferred against him. It is alleged that the officers had no search warrant and no arrest warrant and that they acted "under color of the statutes, ordinances, regulations, customs and usages" of Illinois and of the City of Chicago. Federal jurisdiction was asserted under, which we have set out above.

The City of Chicago moved to dismiss the complaint on the ground that it is not liable under the Civil Rights Acts nor for acts committed in performance of its governmental functions. All defendants moved to dismiss, alleging that the complaint alleged no cause of action under those Acts or under the Federal Constitution. The District Court dismissed the complaint. The Court of Appeals affirmed. The case is here on a writ of certiorari which we granted because of a seeming conflict of that ruling with our prior cases.

Petitioners claim that the invasion of their home and the subsequent search without a warrant and the arrest and detention of Mr. Monroe without a warrant and without arraignment constituted a deprivation of their "rights, privileges, or immunities secured by the

Constitution" within the meaning of [§ 1983]. It has been said that when 18 U.S.C. s 241, 18 U.S.C.A. s 241, made criminal a conspiracy "to injure, oppress, threaten, or intimidate any citizen in the free exercise or enjoyment of any right or privilege secured to him by the Constitution," it embraced only rights that an individual has by reason of his relation to the central government, not to state governments. But the history of the section of the Civil Rights Act presently involved does not permit such a narrow interpretation.

Section [1983] came onto the books as s 1 of the Ku Klux Act of April 20, 1871. 17 Stat. 13. It was one of the means whereby Congress exercised the power vested in it by s 5 of the Fourteenth Amendment to enforce the provisions of that Amendment.

Its purpose is plain from the title of the legislation, "An Act to enforce the Provisions of the Fourteenth Amendment to the Constitution of the United States, and for other Purposes." Allegation of facts constituting a deprivation under color of state authority of a right guaranteed by the Fourteenth Amendment satisfies to that extent the requirement of the statute. So far petitioners are on solid ground. For the guarantee against unreasonable searches and seizures contained in the Fourth Amendment has been made applicable to the States by reason of the Due Process Clause of the Fourteenth Amendment. *Wolf v. People of State of Colorado.*

• • •

There can be no doubt at least since *Ex parte Virginia* that Congress has the power to enforce provisions of the Fourteenth Amendment against those who carry a badge of authority of a State and represent it in some capacity, whether they act in accordance with their authority or misuse it. The question with which we now deal is the narrower one of whether Congress meant to give a remedy to parties deprived of constitutional rights, privileges and immunities by an official's abuse of his position. *Williams*; *Screws*; *Classic*. We conclude that it did so intend.

It is argued that "under color of" enumerated state authority excludes acts of an official or policeman who can show no authority under state law, state custom, or state usage to do what he did. In this case it is said that these policemen, in breaking into petitioners' apartment, violated the Constitution and laws of Illinois. It is pointed out that under Illinois law a simple remedy is offered for that violation and that, so far as it appears, the courts of Illinois are available to give petitioners that full redress which the common law affords for violence done to a person; and it is earnestly argued that no "statute, ordinance, regulation, custom or usage" of Illinois bars that redress.

The Ku Klux Act grew out of a message sent to Congress by President Grant on March 23, 1871, reading:

> A condition of affairs now exists in some States of the Union rendering life and property insecure and the carrying of the mails and the collection of the revenue dangerous. The proof that such a condition of affairs exists in some localities is now before the Senate. That the power to correct these evils is beyond the control of State authorities I do not doubt; that the power of the Executive of the United States, acting within the limits of existing laws, is sufficient for present emergencies is not clear. Therefore, I urgently recommend such legislation as in the judgment of Congress shall effectually secure life, liberty, and property, and the enforcement of law in all parts of the United States.
>
> The legislation—in particular the section with which we are now concerned—had several purposes. There are threads of many thoughts running through the debates. One who reads them in their entirety sees that the present section had three main aims.
>
> First, it might, of course, override certain kinds of state laws. . . .
>
> Second, it provided a remedy where state law was inadequate.

But the purposes were much broader. The third aim was to provide a federal remedy where the state remedy, though adequate in theory, was not available in practice. The opposition to the measure complained that "It overrides the reserved powers of the States," just as they argued that the second section of the bill "absorb(ed) the entire jurisdiction of the State over their local and domestic affairs."

This Act of April 20, 1871, sometimes called "the third force bill," was passed by a Congress that had the Klan "particularly in mind."

The debates are replete with references to the lawless conditions existing in the South in 1871. There was available to the Congress during these debates a report, nearly 600 pages in length, dealing with the activities of the Klan and the inability of the state governments to cope with it. This report was drawn on by many of the speakers. It was not the unavailability of state remedies but the failure of certain States to enforce the laws with an equal hand that furnished the powerful momentum behind this "force bill.". . .

• • •

Although the legislation was enacted because of the conditions that existed in the South at that time, it is cast in general language and is as applicable to Illinois as it is to the States whose names were mentioned over and again in the debates. It is no answer that the State has a law which if enforced would give relief. The federal remedy is supplementary to the state remedy, and the latter need not be first sought and refused before the federal one is invoked. Hence the fact that Illinois by its constitution and laws outlaws unreasonable searches and seizures is no barrier to the present suit in the federal court.

We had before us in *Classic* 18 U.S.C. s 242, which provides a criminal punishment for anyone who "under color of any law, statute, ordinance, regulation, or custom" subjects any inhabitant of a State to the deprivation of "any rights, privileges, or immunities secured or protected by the Constitution or laws of the United States." The right involved in the *Classic* case was the right of voters in a primary to have their votes counted. The laws of Louisiana required the defendants "to count the ballots, to record the result of the count, and to certify the result of the election." But according to the indictment they did not perform their duty. In an opinion written by Mr. Justice (later Chief Justice) Stone, in which Mr. Justice Roberts, Mr. Justice Reed, and Mr. Justice Frankfurter joined, the Court ruled, "Misuse of power, possessed by virtue of state law and made possible only because the wrongdoer is clothed with the authority of state law, is action taken 'under color of' state law."

That view of the meaning of the words "under color of" state law, 18 U.S.C. s 242, was reaffirmed in *Screws*. The acts there complained of were committed by state officers in performance of their duties, viz., making an arrest effective. It was urged there, as it is here, that "under color of" state law should not be construed to duplicate in federal law what was an offense under state law. It was said there, as it is here, that the ruling in the *Classic* case as to the meaning of "under color of" state law was not in focus and was ill-advised. It was argued there, as it is here, that "under color of" state law included only action taken by officials pursuant to state law. We rejected that view.

We adhered to that view in *Williams*.

• • •

Thus, it is beyond doubt that this phrase should be accorded the same construction in both statutes—in [§ 1983] and in 18 U.S.C. s 242.

Since the *Screws* and *Williams* decisions, Congress has had several pieces of civil rights legislation before it. [Though vigorously debated there was no criticism of the phrase "under color of" state law as previously construed by the Court.] If the results of our construction of "under color of" law were as horrendous as now claimed, if they were as disruptive of our federal scheme as now urged, if they were such an unwarranted invasion of States' rights as pretended, surely the voice of the opposition would have been heard in those Committee reports. Their silence and the new uses to which "under color of" law have recently been given reinforce our conclusion that our prior decisions were correct on this matter of construction.

We conclude that the meaning given "under color of" law in the *Classic* case and in the *Screws* and Williams cases was the correct one; and we adhere to it.

In the *Screws* case we dealt with a statute that imposed criminal penalties for acts "wilfully" done. We construed that word in its setting to mean the doing of an act with "a specific intent to deprive a person of a federal right." We do not think that gloss should be placed on [§ 1983] which we have here. The word "wilfully" does not appear in [§ 1983]. Moreover, [§ 1983]. provides a civil remedy, while in the *Screws* case we dealt with a criminal law challenged on the ground of vagueness. Section [1983] should be read against the background of tort liability that makes a man responsible for the natural consequences of his actions.

So far, then, the complaint states a cause of action. There remains to consider only a defense peculiar to the City of Chicago.

• • •

The City of Chicago asserts that it is not liable under [§ 1983]. We do not stop to explore the whole range of questions tendered us on this issue at oral argument and in the briefs. For we are of the opinion that Congress did not undertake to bring municipal corporations within the ambit of [§ 1983].

• • •

The response of the Congress to the proposal to make municipalities liable for certain actions being brought within federal purview by the Act of April 20, 1871, was so antagonistic that we cannot believe that the word "person" was used in this particular Act to include them. Accordingly we hold that the motion to dismiss the complaint against the City of Chicago was properly granted. But since the complaint should not have been dismissed against the officials the judgment must be and is reversed.

Reversed.

[Justices Harlan and Stewart concurred; Justice Frankfurter dissented.]

NOTES AND QUESTIONS

1. The methodology of *Monroe* is odd. There is almost no discussion of any precedent discussing or applying § 1983. The Court acknowledges that the Seventh Circuit affirmed the district court's dismissal of the complaint but says nothing whatsoever about the court's reasoning or whether other circuits are in agreement. As to why it granted certiorari, the Court states only that the Seventh Circuit's decision conflicted "with our prior cases."

2. Those "prior cases" appear to be two criminal cases: *Screws v. United States*, 325 U.S. 91 (1945), and *United States v. Classic*, 313 U.S. 299 (1941), both of which interpreted related Reconstruction era statutes containing the same "under color of law" language as in § 1983.

Is it obvious that the language in § 1983 should be interpreted the same as it was in *Screws* and *Classic*?

Is it relevant to the interpretation question that *Screws* and *Classic* were criminal cases?

Is the failure of congressional opponents of then-recent civil rights legislation to object to the "under color of law" language in those bills persuasive?

Why does the Court even address the issue of the requirement in 18 U.S.C. § 242 that a violation must be done "willfully," inasmuch as that adverb is not in § 1983?

3. The Court rejects the view that § 1983 should only apply where the state has no remedy for the misconduct at issue, which is part of the basis for Justice Frankfurter's dissenting opinion. "The federal remedy is supplementary to the state remedy." 365 U.S. at 184.

William A. Dunning

This is not surprising, as the Court may have had the question of the adequacy of state law remedies on its radar. Four months after *Monroe* was decided the Court would issue its decision in *Mapp v. Ohio*, 367 U.S. 643 (1961), *see supra*, overruling *Wolf v. Colorado*, 338 U.S. 25 (1949), and holding the federal exclusionary rule applicable to the states. A key reason for the decision in *Mapp* was the conclusion that the state remedies for Fourth Amendment violations that the Court had previously relied on for its decision in *Wolf* were largely ineffective. *Id.* at 653.

4. The Court devotes a substantial amount of attention to the legislative history of the Ku Klux Klan Act, which is mostly omitted here. By contrast the decisions in *Screws* and *Classic* paid almost no attention to that same legislative history. The dissenters in *Screws*, moreover, vilified Reconstruction era legislation: "It is familiar history that much of this legislation was born of that vengeful spirit which to no small degree envenomed the Reconstruction era." This history is apparently so familiar that the dissenters felt no obligation to cite any authority for it.

They could have, though. The *Screws* dissenters were not inaccurately reflecting the conventional, white supremacist view of the "Dunning School" of Reconstruction historiography, which was predominant into the 1960s. On this view, named after Columbia professor William Dunning and his students, the Reconstruction era was condemned as producing corrupt rule by "uncivilized Negroes" in the South and radical Republicans at the national level. *See* Eric Foner, The Second Founding: How the Civil War and Reconstruction Remade the Constitution xxi-xxiv (2019). Professor Foner has observed that the portrait of Reconstruction advanced by the Dunning School provided "an intellectual foundation for Jim Crow, the racial system of the South and in many ways the United States as a whole, from the 1890s until the civil rights era of the 1960s." *Id.* at xxii. One notable exception to the view of the Dunning School was W.E.B. DuBois's *Black Reconstruction in America 1860-1880* (1935). Although largely ignored by contemporary historians, the message of DuBois's work was largely embraced by Eric Foner's seminal *Reconstruction: America's Unfinished Revolution, 1863-1877* (1988).

W.E.B. DuBois

Professor Eric Foner

The Dunning School still held sway in 1961 when *Monroe* was decided. It is to the Court's credit that it relied on the legislative history directly, unmediated by the then prevailing academic perspective.

5. In deciding that municipalities do not fall under the term "person" in the statute, the Court acknowledges the policy considerations favoring municipal liability: "It is said that doubts should be resolved in favor of municipal liability because private remedies against officers for illegal searches and seizures are conspicuously ineffective, and because municipal liability will not only afford plaintiffs responsible defendants but cause those defendants to eradicate abuses that exist at the police level."

What other policy considerations favor municipal liability?

What about constitutional violations by federal law enforcement officers? Section 1983 does not apply to them.

Just a few years after James Monroe's mistreatment by Chicago police a similar fate befell a man named Webster Bivens in New York City. Agents of the now defunct Federal Bureau of Narcotics entered his home with weapons drawn, searched his apartment, threatened his family, arrested him on narcotics charges, and subjected him to a strip search upon booking at the federal courthouse in Brooklyn. After the criminal complaint against him was dismissed, Bivens filed a pro se complaint in the Eastern District of New York, seeking $15,000 in damages against each of the six officers for allegedly violating his Fourth Amendment right to be free of unreasonable search and seizure. Bivens did not know the officers' names, hence the case's wonderful title—*Bivens v. Six Unknown Named Agents of Federal Bureau of Narcotics*. 403 U.S. 388 (1971). In *Bivens*, the Supreme Court held for the first time that federal officials could be sued individually for damages for violations of the Fourth Amendment. In finding an implied private right of action under the Fourth Amendment, the Court reasoned that damages are the "ordinary remedy for an invasion of personal interests in liberty," that nothing warranted hesitation in the absence of affirmative action by Congress, and that the alternative of a patchwork of varying and less effective state remedies was undesirable. *Id.* at 397.

The Court relied on *Bivens* in recognizing a right of action for two other federal rights in the subsequent decade. *See Davis v. Passman*, 442 U.S. 228 (1979) (former congressional staffer's Fifth Amendment sex-discrimination claim); *Carlson v. Green*, 446 U.S. 14 (1980) (federal prisoner's inadequate-care claim under the Eighth Amendment). But it's been downhill ever since. Since *Carlson* the Court has refused to infer a private right of action for other constitutional violations at least a dozen times, most recently in *Egbert v. Boule*, 596 U.S. 482, 486 (2022). In *Egbert*, the Court refused to recognize a *Bivens* action for a First Amendment retaliation claim where a U.S. Border Patrol agent in a remote part of Washington state near the Canadian border retaliated against the plaintiff, who complained about the agent's use of excessive force against him. The agent retaliated by persuading the IRS, the Social Security Administration, and state authorities to investigate the plaintiff's business. The Court also refused to recognize the original *Bivens* right of action under the Fourth Amendment in the context of an excessive force case with "national security" implications. *Id.* at 494-97. The Court frankly acknowledged that it did not overrule *Bivens* in *Egbert* only because it didn't need to. *Id.* at 502.

The current Court has limited the § 1983 remedy primarily through application of the qualified immunity doctrine, discussed in Section C below. But it has also narrowly interpreted the term "law" in the statute, finding that a *Miranda* violation did not amount to a deprivation of a right secured by "the Constitution and laws" under § 1983. *Vega v. Tekoh*, 142 S. Ct. 2095 (2022). The plaintiff in *Vega* was investigated for sexual assault and was interrogated without being given *Miranda* warnings. After being tried twice (the jury hung in the first trial) and found not guilty, he brought suit against the interrogating officer under § 1983. By a 6-3 vote, in an opinion that purported to cast doubt on the legitimacy of *Miranda* itself, *see* Chapter III *supra*, the Court held that inasmuch as *Miranda* was only a constitutionally derived "prophylactic" rule it was not part of the "law" referred to in § 1983. Recall that the Court had earlier held that § 1983 afforded no remedy where an illegally obtained confession was not used against a defendant at trial because the Fifth Amendment was only a "trial right." *Chavez v. Martinez*, 528 U.S. 760 (2003).

B. SECTION 1983 ACTIONS AGAINST MUNICIPALITIES

Monell v. Department of Social Services of the City of New York

436 U.S. 658 (1978)

Mr. Justice Brennan delivered the opinion of the Court.

Petitioners, a class of female employees of the Department of Social Services and of the Board of Education of the city of New York, commenced this action under 42 U.S.C. § 1983 in July 1971. The gravamen of the complaint was that the Board and the Department had as a matter of official policy compelled pregnant employees to take unpaid leaves of absence before such leaves were required for medical reasons. The suit sought injunctive relief and backpay for periods of unlawful forced leave. Named as defendants in the action were the Department and its Commissioner, the Board and its Chancellor, and the city of New York and its Mayor. In each case, the individual defendants were sued solely in their official capacities.

On cross-motions for summary judgment, the District Court for the Southern District of New York held moot petitioners' claims for injunctive and declaratory relief since the City of New York and the Board, after the filing of the complaint, had changed their policies relating to maternity leaves so that no pregnant employee would have to take leave unless she was medically unable to continue to perform her job. No one now challenges this conclusion. The court did conclude, however, that the acts complained of were unconstitutional under *LaFleur*, supra. Nonetheless plaintiffs' prayers for backpay were denied because any such damages would come ultimately from the City of New York and, therefore, to hold otherwise would be to "circumven[t]" the immunity conferred on municipalities by *Monroe v. Pape*.

On appeal, petitioners renewed their arguments that the Board of Education was not a "municipality" within the meaning of *Monroe v. Pape* and that, in any event, the District Court had erred in barring a damages award against the individual defendants. The Court of Appeals for the Second Circuit rejected both contentions. The court first held that the Board of Education was not a "person" under § 1983 because "it performs a vital governmental function . . ., and, significantly, while it has the right to determine how the funds appropriated to it shall be spent . . ., it has no final say in deciding what its appropriations shall be." The individual defendants, however, were "persons" under § 1983, even when sued solely in their official capacities. Yet, because a damages award would "have to be paid by a city that was held not to be amenable to such an action in *Monroe v. Pape*," a damages action against officials sued in their official capacities could not proceed.

We granted certiorari in this case to consider:

> Whether local governmental officials and/or local independent school boards are "persons" within the meaning of 42 U.S.C. § 1983 when equitable relief in the nature of back pay is sought against them in their official capacities?

Although, after plenary consideration, we have decided the merits of over a score of cases brought under § 1983 in which the principal defendant was a school board —and, indeed, in some of which § 1983 and its jurisdictional counterpart, 28 U.S.C. § 1343, provided the only basis for jurisdiction—we indicated last Term that the question presented here was open and would be decided "another day." That other day has come and we now overrule *Monroe v. Pape*, insofar as it holds that local governments are wholly immune from suit under § 1983.

• • •

Our analysis of the legislative history of the Civil Rights Act of 1871 compels the conclusion that Congress did intend municipalities and other local government units to be included among those persons to whom § 1983 applies. Local governing bodies, therefore, can be sued directly under § 1983 for monetary, declaratory, or injunctive relief where, as here, the action that is alleged to be unconstitutional implements or executes a policy statement, ordinance, regulation, or decision officially adopted and promulgated by that body's officers. Moreover, although the touchstone of the § 1983 action against a government body is an allegation that official policy is responsible for a deprivation of rights protected by the Constitution, local governments, like every other § 1983 "person," by the very terms of the statute, may be sued for constitutional deprivations visited pursuant to governmental "custom" even though such a custom has not received formal approval through the body's official decisionmaking channels. As Mr. Justice Harlan, writing for the Court, said in *Adickes v. S. H. Kress & Co.*: "Congress included customs and usages [in § 1983] because of the persistent and widespread discriminatory practices of state officials. . . . Although not authorized by written law, such practices of state officials could well be so permanent and well settled as to constitute a 'custom or usage' with the force of law."

On the other hand, the language of § 1983, read against the background of the same legislative history, compels the conclusion that Congress did not intend municipalities to be held liable unless action pursuant to official municipal policy of some nature caused a constitutional tort. In particular, we conclude that a municipality cannot be held liable solely because it employs a tortfeasor—or, in other words, a municipality cannot be held liable under § 1983 on a respondeat superior theory.

We begin with the language of § 1983 as originally passed:

> [*A*]*ny person who*, under color of any law, statute, ordinance, regulation, custom, or usage of any State, *shall subject, or cause to be subjected*, any person . . . to the deprivation of any rights, privileges, or immunities secured by the Constitution of the United States, shall, any such law, statute, ordinance, regulation, custom, or usage of the State to the contrary notwithstanding, be liable to the party injured in any action at law, suit in equity, or other proper proceeding for redress. . . .

The italicized language plainly imposes liability on a government that, under color of some official policy, "causes" an employee to violate another's constitutional rights. At the same time, that language cannot be easily read to impose liability vicariously on governing bodies solely on the basis of the existence of an employer-employee relationship with a tortfeasor. Indeed, the fact that Congress did specifically provide that A's tort became B's liability if B "caused" A to subject another to a tort suggests that Congress did not intend § 1983 liability to attach where such causation was absent.

Equally important, creation of a federal law of respondeat superior would have raised all the constitutional problems associated with the obligation to keep the peace, an obligation Congress chose not to impose because it thought imposition of such an obligation unconstitutional. To this day, there is disagreement about the basis for imposing liability on an employer for the torts of an employee when the sole nexus between the employer and the tort is the fact of the employer-employee relationship. See W. Prosser, Law of Torts § 69, p. 459 (4th ed. 1971). Nonetheless, two justifications tend to stand out. First is the common-sense notion that no matter how blameless an employer appears to be in an individual case, accidents might nonetheless be reduced if employers had to bear the cost of accidents. See, e.g., ibid.; 2 F. Harper & F. James, Law of Torts, § 26.3, pp. 1368-1369 (1956). Second is the argument that the cost of accidents should be spread to the community as a whole on an insurance theory. See, e.g., id., § 26.5; Prosser, supra, at 459.

The first justification is of the same sort that was offered for statutes like the Sherman amendment: "The obligation to make compensation for injury resulting from riot is, by arbitrary enactment of statutes, affirmatory law, and the reason of passing the statute is to secure a more perfect police regulation." This justification was obviously insufficient to sustain the amendment against perceived constitutional difficulties and there is no reason to suppose that a more general liability imposed for a similar reason would have been thought less constitutionally objectionable. The second justification was similarly put forward as a justification for the Sherman amendment: "we do not look upon [the Sherman amendment] as a punishment. . . . It is a mutual insurance." Again, this justification was insufficient to sustain the amendment.

We conclude, therefore, that a local government may not be sued under § 1983 for an injury inflicted solely by its employees or agents. Instead, it is when execution of a government's policy or custom, whether made by its lawmakers or by those whose edicts or acts may fairly be said to represent official policy, inflicts the injury that the government as an entity is responsible under § 1983. Since this case unquestionably involves official policy as the moving force of the constitutional violation found by the District Court, we must reverse the judgment below. In so doing, we have no occasion to address, and do not address, what the full contours of municipal liability under § 1983 may be. We have attempted only to sketch so much of the § 1983 cause of action against a local government as is apparent from the history of the 1871 Act and our prior cases, and we expressly leave further development of this action to another day.

[Justices Stevens and Powell concurred; Chief Justice Burger and Justice Rehnquist dissented.]

NOTES AND QUESTIONS

1. *Monell* is not a Fifth Amendment case but at its heart are two notable confessions. First, the Court confesses that it misinterpreted the legislative history of § 1983 in holding in *Monroe* that municipalities were not "persons" under the statute. Second, the Court confesses that despite what it said in *Monroe* it had been routinely deciding school desegregation lawsuits that had been brought against school districts (many of them municipalities) under § 1983. One of these decisions was issued the same year *Monroe* was decided; another one, which you will have heard of, *Brown v. Board of Education*, 347 U.S. 483 (1954), was decided seven years before *Monroe.*

2. In rejecting its previous interpretation of legislative history in *Monroe*, the Court does an exhaustive canvassing of the legislative history of § 1983, even more exhaustive than in *Monroe,* which is not reproduced here. Two dissenters disagree with the Court's analysis of that legislative history. And a noted law professor and Reconstruction scholar disagrees with both the majority and the dissent. *See* Robert J. Kaczorowski, *Reflections on* Monell's *Analysis of the Legislative History of § 1983*, 31 Urb. Law. 407, 408 (1999) (the evidence that Congress intended municipalities to be sued under § 1983 is "far from compelling" but, if they were amenable to suit the evidence is that they would have been "vicariously liable" for the actions of their agents).

3. In rejecting a respondeat superior basis for municipal liability, the Court looks at the language of the statute and the legislative history. The Court does not look at the extent to which the principle of respondeat superior liability—a doctrine that is at least old enough to have a Latin name—was part of the common law in 1871, when the statute was enacted. One commentator argues that common law principles of respondeat superior liability would have been well known to the members of Congress, and that those members would have expected those principles to be operative in litigation under § 1983. *See* David Jacks Achtenberg, *Taking History Seriously: Municipal Liability Under § 1983 and the Debate over Respondeat Superior*, 73 Fordham L. Rev. 2183, 2196-97 (2005).

This oversight by the Supreme Court may have been the result of the fact that the full scope of municipal liability was not even at issue in *Monell*, as the leave policy challenged by the plaintiff class was an official municipal policy, and there was no need to delve into whether liability could be "vicarious." *See* 436 U.S. at 714 (Stevens, J., concurring in part) (not joining the parts of the opinion on respondeat superior liability as they are "merely advisory"). Justice Stevens later pointed out in dissenting from an opinion that applied the respondeat superior aspect of *Monell* as precedent, that "the commentary on respondeat superior in *Monell* was not responsive to any argument advanced by either party and was not even relevant to the Court's actual holding." *City of Oklahoma City v. Tuttle*, 471 U.S. 808, 842 (1985).

4. The Court notes a contemporary "disagreement" about the wisdom of respondeat superior liability. Is any such disagreement reflected in your understanding of contemporary tort law principles? Did you learn that such a disagreement existed 45 years ago?

Although the Court in *Monell* gratuitously rejected a respondeat superior theory of liability, it did not address "the full contours of municipal liability" under § 1983. 436 U.S. at 695. In *Monell*'s wake, four narrow paths to municipal liability have emerged: liability based on a formal municipal policy (as in *Monell* itself); liability based on a custom (the word is in the statute and cannot be avoided), a settled practice that amounts to the force of law even if not officially adopted; liability based on a failure to train or supervise municipal employees that amounts to a "deliberate indifference" to the rights of the citizens the employees will interact with; and a very limited liability for hiring an employee where an adequate screening or interview process would have shown the hiree's subsequent violation of rights was likely. Achtenberg, *Taking History Seriously*, *supra* at 2183, 2187-90.

The narrowness of these pathways cannot be overemphasized. The standards for municipal liability under § 1983 are not only stricter than the standards for private employer liability, they are stricter than the standards for awarding *punitive damages* against private employers. *Id.* at 2191. "*Monell* confines entity liability in a manner that is unique to § 1983 and exists in no other area of the law." *Id.*

The next two cases consider these narrow pathways.

Canton v. Harris

489 U.S. 378 (1989)

Justice White delivered the opinion of the Court.

In this case, we are asked to determine if a municipality can ever be liable under 42 U.S.C. § 1983 for constitutional violations resulting from its failure to train municipal employees. We hold that, under certain circumstances, such liability is permitted by the statute.

In April 1978, respondent Geraldine Harris was arrested by officers of the Canton Police Department. Mrs. Harris was brought to the police station in a patrol wagon.

When she arrived at the station, Mrs. Harris was found sitting on the floor of the wagon. She was asked if she needed medical attention, and responded with an incoherent remark.

After she was brought inside the station for processing, Mrs. Harris slumped to the floor on two occasions. Eventually, the police officers left Mrs. Harris lying on the floor to prevent her from falling again. No medical attention was ever summoned for Mrs. Harris. After about an hour, Mrs. Harris was released from custody, and taken by an ambulance (provided by her family) to a nearby hospital. There, Mrs. Harris was diagnosed as suffering from several emotional ailments; she was hospitalized for one week and received subsequent outpatient treatment for an additional year.

Some time later, Mrs. Harris commenced this action alleging many state-law and constitutional claims against the city of Canton and its officials. Among these claims was one seeking to hold the city liable under 42 U.S.C. § 1983 for its violation of Mrs. Harris' right, under the Due Process Clause of the Fourteenth Amendment, to receive necessary medical attention while in police custody.

A jury trial was held on Mrs. Harris' claims. Evidence was presented that indicated that, pursuant to a municipal regulation, shift commanders were authorized to determine, in their sole discretion, whether a detainee required medical care. In addition, testimony also suggested that Canton shift commanders were not provided with any special training (beyond first-aid training) to make a determination as to when to summon medical care for an injured detainee.

At the close of the evidence, the District Court submitted the case to the jury, which rejected all of Mrs. Harris' claims except one: her § 1983 claim against the city resulting from its failure to provide her with medical treatment while in custody. In rejecting the city's subsequent motion for judgment notwithstanding the verdict, the District Court explained the theory of liability as follows:

> The evidence construed in a manner most favorable to Mrs. Harris could be found by a jury to demonstrate that the City of Canton had a custom or policy of vesting complete authority with the police supervisor of when medical treatment would be administered to prisoners. Further, the jury could find from the evidence that the vesting of such carte blanche authority with the police supervisor without adequate training to recognize when medical treatment is needed was grossly negligent or so reckless that future police misconduct was almost inevitable or substantially certain to result.

On appeal, the Sixth Circuit affirmed this aspect of the District Court's analysis, holding that "a municipality is liable for failure to train its police force, [where] the plaintiff . . . prove[s] that the municipality acted recklessly, intentionally, or with gross negligence." The Court of Appeals also stated that an additional prerequisite of this theory of liability was that the plaintiff must prove "that the lack of training was so reckless or grossly negligent that deprivations of persons' constitutional rights were substantially certain to result." Thus, the Court of Appeals found that there had been no error in submitting Mrs. Harris' "failure to train" claim to the jury. However, the Court of Appeals reversed the judgment for respondent, and remanded this case for a new trial, because it found that certain aspects of the District Court's jury instructions might have led the jury to believe that it could find against the city on a mere respondeat superior theory. Because the jury's verdict did not state the basis on which it had ruled for Mrs. Harris on her § 1983 claim, a new trial was ordered.

The city petitioned for certiorari, arguing that the Sixth Circuit's holding represented an impermissible broadening of municipal liability under § 1983. We granted the petition.

• • •

In *Monell* we decided that a municipality can be found liable under § 1983 only where the municipality itself causes the constitutional violation at issue. Respondeat superior or vicarious liability will not attach under § 1983. "It is only when the 'execution of the government's policy or custom . . . inflicts the injury' that the municipality may be held liable under § 1983."

Thus, our first inquiry in any case alleging municipal liability under § 1983 is the question whether there is a direct causal link between a municipal policy or custom and the alleged constitutional deprivation. The inquiry is a difficult one; one that has left this Court deeply divided in a series of cases that have followed *Monell*; one that is the principal focus of our decision again today.

Based on the difficulty that this Court has had defining the contours of municipal liability in these circumstances, petitioner urges us to adopt the rule that a municipality can be found liable under § 1983 only where "the policy in question [is] itself unconstitutional." Whether such a rule is a valid construction of § 1983 is a question the Court has left unresolved. Under such an approach, the outcome here would be rather clear: we would have to reverse and remand the case with instructions that judgment be entered for petitioner. There can be little doubt that on its face the city's policy regarding medical treatment for detainees is constitutional. The policy states that the city jailer "shall . . . have [a person needing medical care] taken to a hospital for medical treatment, with permission of his supervisor. . . ." It is difficult to see what constitutional guarantees are violated by such a policy.

Nor, without more, would a city automatically be liable under § 1983 if one of its employees happened to apply the policy in an unconstitutional manner, for liability would then rest on respondeat superior. The claim in this case, however, is that if a concededly valid policy is unconstitutionally applied by a municipal employee, the city is liable if the employee has not been adequately trained and the constitutional wrong has been caused by that failure to train. For reasons explained below, we conclude, as have all the Courts of Appeals that have addressed this issue, that there are limited circumstances in which an allegation of a "failure to train" can be the basis for liability under § 1983. Thus, we reject petitioner's contention that only unconstitutional policies are actionable under the statute.

Though we agree with the court below that a city can be liable under § 1983 for inadequate training of its employees, we cannot agree that the District Court's jury instructions on this issue were proper, for we conclude that the Court of Appeals provided an overly broad rule for when a municipality can be held liable under the "failure to train" theory. Unlike the question whether a municipality's failure to train employees can ever be a basis for § 1983 liability—on which the Courts of Appeals have all agreed—there is substantial division among the lower courts as to what degree of fault must be evidenced by the municipality's inaction before liability will be permitted. We hold today that the inadequacy of police training may serve as the basis for § 1983 liability only where the failure to train amounts to deliberate indifference to the rights of persons with whom the police come into contact. This rule is most consistent with our admonition in *Monell* that a municipality can be liable under § 1983 only where its policies are the "moving force [behind] the constitutional violation." Only where a municipality's failure to train its employees in a relevant respect evidences a "deliberate indifference" to the rights of its inhabitants can such a shortcoming be properly thought of as a city "policy or custom" that is actionable under § 1983. "[M]unicipal liability under § 1983 attaches where—and only where—a deliberate choice to follow a course of action is made from among various alternatives" by city policymakers. Only where a failure to train reflects a "deliberate" or "conscious" choice by a municipality—a "policy" as defined by our prior cases—can a city be liable for such a failure under § 1983.

Monell's rule that a city is not liable under § 1983 unless a municipal policy causes a constitutional deprivation will not be satisfied by merely alleging that the existing training program for a class of employees, such as police officers, represents a policy for which the city is responsible. That much may be true. The issue in a case like this one, however, is whether that training program is adequate; and if it is not, the question becomes whether such inadequate training can justifiably be said to represent "city policy." It may seem contrary to common sense to assert that a municipality will actually have a policy of not taking reasonable steps to train its employees. But it may happen that in light of the duties assigned to specific officers or employees the need for more or different training is so obvious, and the inadequacy so likely to result in the violation of constitutional rights, that the policymakers of the city can reasonably be said to have been deliberately indifferent to the need. In that event, the failure to provide proper training may fairly be said to represent a policy for which the city is responsible, and for which the city may be held liable if it actually causes injury.

In resolving the issue of a city's liability, the focus must be on adequacy of the training program in relation to the tasks the particular officers must perform. That a particular officer may be unsatisfactorily trained will not alone suffice to fasten liability on the city, for the officer's shortcomings may have resulted from factors other than a faulty training program. It may be, for example, that an otherwise sound program has occasionally been negligently administered. Neither will it suffice to prove that an injury or accident could have been avoided if an officer had had better or more training, sufficient to equip him to avoid the particular injury-causing conduct. Such a claim could be made about almost any encounter resulting in injury, yet not condemn the adequacy of the program to enable officers to respond properly to the usual and recurring situations with which they must deal. And plainly, adequately trained officers occasionally make mistakes; the fact that they do says little about the training program or the legal basis for holding the city liable.

Moreover, for liability to attach in this circumstance the identified deficiency in a city's training program must be closely related to the ultimate injury. Thus in the case at hand, respondent must still prove that the deficiency in training actually caused the police officers' indifference to her medical needs. Would the injury have been avoided had the employee been trained under a program that was not deficient in the identified respect? Predicting how a hypothetically well-trained officer would have acted under the circumstances may not be an easy task for the factfinder, particularly since matters of judgment may be involved, and since officers who are well trained are not free from error and perhaps might react very much like the untrained officer in similar circumstances. But judge and jury, doing their respective jobs, will be adequate to the task.

To adopt lesser standards of fault and causation would open municipalities to unprecedented liability under § 1983. In virtually every instance where a person has had his or her constitutional rights violated by a city employee, a § 1983 plaintiff will be able to point to something the city "could have done" to prevent the unfortunate incident. Thus, permitting cases against cities for their "failure to train" employees to go forward under § 1983 on a lesser standard of fault would result in de facto respondeat superior liability on municipalities — a result we rejected in *Monell*, It would also engage the federal courts in an endless exercise of second-guessing municipal employee-training programs. This is an exercise we believe the federal courts are ill suited to undertake, as well as one that would implicate serious questions of federalism.

Consequently, while claims such as respondent's — alleging that the city's failure to provide training to municipal employees resulted in the constitutional deprivation she suffered — are cognizable under § 1983, they can only yield liability against a municipality where that city's failure to train reflects deliberate indifference to the constitutional rights of its inhabitants.

IV

The final question here is whether this case should be remanded for a new trial, or whether, as petitioner suggests, we should conclude that there are no possible grounds on which respondent can prevail. It is true that the evidence in the record now does not meet the standard of § 1983 liability we have set forth above. But, the standard of proof the District Court ultimately imposed on respondent (which was consistent with Sixth Circuit precedent) was a lesser one than the one we adopt today. Whether respondent should have an opportunity to prove her case under the "deliberate indifference" rule we have adopted is a matter for the Court of Appeals to deal with on remand.

Consequently, for the reasons given above, we vacate the judgment of the Court of Appeals and remand this case for further proceedings consistent with this opinion.

NOTES AND QUESTIONS

1. Do these seem like strong or weak facts for establishing a failure-to-train violation? Consider in your analysis the nature of the injuries suffered, the existence of any municipal policy, the nature of any training that would be necessary to prevent the injury, and the likelihood of harm from the lack of training. As a plaintiff's lawyer, how would you attempt to develop evidence of deliberate indifference? As a lawyer for the city, how would you try to disprove deliberate indifference?

2. This case was tried to a jury. The court of appeals reversed because the jury instruction "might have led the jury to believe that it could find against the city on a mere respondeat superior theory." *Id.* at 383. How could the court have made such an error so many years after *Monell*? Weak lawyering by the city? Weak law clerks? Assuming the city had filed a motion for summary judgment, as typically happens in a civil case, does the trial court's jury instruction explain why that motion may have been denied?

3. How much different is the "deliberate indifference" standard announced by the Court than the standard applied by the Sixth Circuit, which held that liability requires that in failing to train a municipality must have "acted recklessly, intentionally, or with gross negligence" and "that the lack of training was so reckless or grossly negligent that deprivations of persons' constitutional rights were substantially certain to result"? *Id.* at 382. Can you imagine a set of facts where a jury could find all of the elements required by the Sixth Circuit formulation yet ultimately conclude that the city was not deliberately indifferent to the potential harms?

4. The Court emphasizes that whether inadequate training rises to the level of a city "policy" relates to the duties of the city officials involved. It gives the following hypothetical example in footnote 10:

> For example, city policymakers know to a moral certainty that their police officers will be required to arrest fleeing felons. The city has armed its officers with firearms, in part to allow them to accomplish this task. Thus, the need to train officers in the constitutional limitations on the use of deadly force, see *Tennessee v. Garner*, 471 U.S. 1, 105 S. Ct. 1694, 85 L. Ed. 2d 1 (1985), can be said to be "so obvious," that failure to do so could properly be characterized as "deliberate indifference" to constitutional rights.

Does the need to train police station employees on how to determine whether an arrestee needs medical attention meet this standard?

5. The Court goes into full hyperbole mode at the end of its opinion, claiming that "permitting cases against cities for their 'failure to train' employees to go forward under § 1983 on a lesser standard of fault would result in de facto respondeat superior liability on municipalities—a result we rejected in *Monell*." Do you agree? Consider the facts of *Harris* with this variation: The police department supervisor in charge of the station when Harris was arrested had been properly trained on when to seek medical attention for arrestees but had misinterpreted Harris's symptoms and failed to get her medical attention. Result under respondeat superior? Result under a lower standard of "reckless failure to train"?

Note that the jury rejected all of Harris's state law claims but found for her on her § 1983 claim. Might this be responsible for the Court's closing observation, where it decries federal courts engaging "in an endless exercise of second-guessing employee-training programs"? Were the congressmen who voted in favor of the Ku Klux Klan Act concerned about federal courts second-guessing state administrators?

Please ignore the fact that the next case is not about "police misconduct" but rather "prosecutor misconduct" and so arguably doesn't belong in this chapter.

Connick v. Thompson

563 U.S. 51 (2011)

Justice THOMAS delivered the opinion of the Court.

The Orleans Parish District Attorney's Office now concedes that, in prosecuting respondent John Thompson for attempted armed robbery, prosecutors failed to disclose evidence that should have been turned over to the defense under *Brady v. Maryland* (1963). Thompson was convicted. Because of that conviction Thompson elected not to testify in his own defense in his later trial for murder, and he was again convicted. Thompson spent 18 years in prison, including 14 years on death row. One month before Thompson's scheduled execution, his investigator discovered the undisclosed evidence from his armed robbery trial. The reviewing court determined that the evidence was exculpatory, and both of Thompson's convictions were vacated.

After his release from prison, Thompson sued petitioner Harry Connick, in his official capacity as the Orleans Parish district attorney, for damages under 42 U.S.C. § 1983. Thompson alleged that Connick had failed to train his prosecutors adequately about their duty to produce exculpatory evidence and that the lack of training had caused the nondisclosure in Thompson's robbery case. The jury awarded Thompson $14 million, and the Court of Appeals for the Fifth Circuit affirmed by an evenly divided en banc court. We granted certiorari to decide whether a district attorney's office may be held liable under § 1983 for failure to train based on a single *Brady* violation. We hold that it cannot.

• • •

In early 1985, John Thompson was charged with the murder of Raymond T. Liuzza, Jr., in New Orleans. Publicity following the murder charge led the victims of an unrelated armed robbery to identify Thompson as their attacker. The district attorney charged Thompson with attempted armed robbery.

As part of the robbery investigation, a crime scene technician took from one of the victims' pants a swatch of fabric stained with the robber's blood. Approximately one week before Thompson's armed robbery trial, the swatch was sent to the crime laboratory. Two days before the trial, Assistant District Attorney Bruce Whittaker received the crime lab's report, which stated that the perpetrator had blood type B. There is no evidence that the prosecutors ever had Thompson's blood tested or that they knew what his blood type was. Whittaker claimed he placed the report on Assistant District Attorney James Williams' desk, but Williams denied seeing it. The report was never disclosed to Thompson's counsel.

Williams tried the armed robbery case with Assistant District Attorney Gerry Deegan. On the first day of trial, Deegan checked all of the physical evidence in the case out of the police property room, including the bloodstained swatch. Deegan then checked all of the evidence but the swatch into the courthouse property room. The prosecutors did not mention the swatch or the crime lab report at trial, and the jury convicted Thompson of attempted armed robbery.

A few weeks later, Williams and Special Prosecutor Eric Dubelier tried Thompson for the Liuzza murder. Because of the armed robbery conviction, Thompson chose not to testify in his own defense. He was convicted and sentenced to death. In the 14 years following Thompson's murder conviction, state and federal courts reviewed and denied his challenges to the conviction and sentence. The State scheduled Thompson's execution for May 20, 1999.

In late April 1999, Thompson's private investigator discovered the crime lab report from the armed robbery investigation in the files of the New Orleans Police Crime Laboratory. Thompson was tested and found to have blood type O, proving that the blood on the swatch was not his. Thompson's attorneys presented this evidence to the district attorney's office, which, in turn, moved to stay the execution and vacate Thompson's armed robbery conviction. The Louisiana Court of Appeal then reversed Thompson's murder conviction, concluding that the armed robbery conviction unconstitutionally deprived Thompson of his right to testify in his own defense at the murder trial. In 2003, the district attorney's office retried Thompson for Liuzza's murder. The jury found him not guilty.

Thompson then brought this action against the district attorney's office, Connick, Williams, and others, alleging that their conduct caused him to be wrongfully convicted, incarcerated for 18 years, and nearly executed. The only claim that proceeded to trial was Thompson's claim under § 1983 that the district attorney's office had violated *Brady* by failing to disclose the crime lab report in his armed robbery trial. Thompson alleged liability under two theories: (1) The *Brady* violation was caused by an unconstitutional policy of the district attorney's office; and (2) the violation was caused by Connick's deliberate indifference to an obvious need to train the prosecutors in his office in order to avoid such constitutional violations.

Before trial, Connick conceded that the failure to produce the crime lab report constituted a *Brady* violation. Accordingly, the District Court instructed the jury that the "only issue" was whether the nondisclosure was caused by either a policy, practice, or custom of the district attorney's office or a deliberately indifferent failure to train the office's prosecutors.

Although no prosecutor remembered any specific training session regarding *Brady* prior to 1985, it was undisputed at trial that the prosecutors were familiar with the general *Brady* requirement that the State disclose to the defense evidence in its possession that is favorable to the accused. Prosecutors testified that office policy was to turn crime lab reports and other scientific evidence over to the defense. They also testified that, after the discovery of the undisclosed crime lab report in 1999, prosecutors disagreed about whether it had to be disclosed under *Brady* absent knowledge of Thompson's blood type.

The jury rejected Thompson's claim that an unconstitutional office policy caused the *Brady* violation, but found the district attorney's office liable for failing to train the prosecutors. The jury awarded Thompson $14 million in damages, and the District Court added more than $1 million in attorney's fees and costs.

After the verdict, Connick renewed his objection—which he had raised on summary judgment—that he could not have been deliberately indifferent to an obvious need for more or different Brady training because there was no evidence that he was aware of a pattern of similar *Brady* violations. The District Court rejected this argument for the reasons that it had given in the summary judgment order. In that order, the court had concluded that a pattern of violations is not necessary to prove deliberate indifference when the need for training is "so obvious." Relying on *Canton v. Harris*, the court had held that Thompson could demonstrate deliberate indifference by proving that "the DA's office knew to a moral certainty that assistan[t] [district attorneys] would acquire *Brady* material, that without training it is not always obvious what *Brady* requires, and that withholding *Brady* material will virtually always lead to a substantial violation of constitutional rights."

A panel of the Court of Appeals for the Fifth Circuit affirmed. The panel acknowledged that Thompson did not present evidence of a pattern of similar *Brady* violations, but held that Thompson did not need to prove a pattern. According to the panel, Thompson demonstrated that Connick was on notice of an obvious need for *Brady* training by presenting evidence "that attorneys, often fresh out of law school, would undoubtedly be required to confront *Brady* issues while at the DA's Office, that erroneous decisions regarding *Brady* evidence would result in serious constitutional violations, that resolution of *Brady* issues was often unclear, and that training in *Brady* would have been helpful."

The Court of Appeals sitting en banc vacated the panel opinion, granted rehearing, and divided evenly, thereby affirming the District Court. We granted certiorari.

The *Brady* violation conceded in this case occurred when one or more of the four prosecutors involved with Thompson's armed robbery prosecution failed to disclose the crime lab report to Thompson's counsel. Under Thompson's failure-to-train theory, he bore the burden of proving both (1) that Connick, the policymaker for the district attorney's office, was deliberately indifferent to the need to train the prosecutors about their *Brady* disclosure obligation with respect to evidence of this type and (2) that the lack of training actually caused the *Brady* violation in this case. Connick argues that he was entitled to judgment as a matter of law because Thompson did not prove that he was on actual or constructive notice of, and therefore deliberately indifferent to, a need for more or different *Brady* training. We agree.

• • •

In limited circumstances, a local government's decision not to train certain employees about their legal duty to avoid violating citizens' rights may rise to the level of an official government policy for purposes of § 1983. A municipality's culpability for a deprivation of rights is at its most tenuous where a claim turns on a failure to train. To satisfy the statute, a municipality's failure to train its employees in a relevant respect must amount to "deliberate indifference to the rights of persons with whom the [untrained employees] come into contact."

"'[D]eliberate indifference' is a stringent standard of fault, requiring proof that a municipal actor disregarded a known or obvious consequence of his action." Thus, when city policymakers are on actual or constructive notice that a particular omission in their training program causes city employees to violate citizens' constitutional rights, the city may be deemed deliberately indifferent if the policymakers choose to retain that program.

A pattern of similar constitutional violations by untrained employees is "ordinarily necessary" to demonstrate deliberate indifference for purposes of failure to train. Policymakers' "continued adherence to an approach that they know or should know has failed to prevent tortious conduct by employees may establish the conscious disregard for the consequences of their action—the 'deliberate indifference'—necessary to trigger municipal liability." Without notice that a course of training is deficient in a particular respect, decisionmakers can hardly be said to have deliberately chosen a training program that will cause violations of constitutional rights.

Although Thompson does not contend that he proved a pattern of similar *Brady* violations, he points out that, during the 10 years preceding his armed robbery trial, Louisiana courts had overturned four convictions because of *Brady* violations by prosecutors in Connick's office. Those four reversals could not have put Connick on notice that the office's *Brady* training was inadequate with respect to the sort of *Brady* violation at issue here. None of those cases involved failure to disclose blood evidence, a crime lab report, or physical or scientific evidence of any kind. Because those incidents are not similar to the violation at issue here, they could not have put Connick on notice that specific training was necessary to avoid this constitutional violation.

Instead of relying on a pattern of similar *Brady* violations, Thompson relies on the "single-incident" liability that this Court hypothesized in *Canton*. He contends that the

Brady violation in his case was the "obvious" consequence of failing to provide specific *Brady* training, and that this showing of "obviousness" can substitute for the pattern of violations ordinarily necessary to establish municipal culpability.

In *Canton*, the Court left open the possibility that, "in a narrow range of circumstances," a pattern of similar violations might not be necessary to show deliberate indifference. The Court posed the hypothetical example of a city that arms its police force with firearms and deploys the armed officers into the public to capture fleeing felons without training the officers in the constitutional limitation on the use of deadly force. Given the known frequency with which police attempt to arrest fleeing felons and the "predictability that an officer lacking specific tools to handle that situation will violate citizens' rights," the Court theorized that a city's decision not to train the officers about constitutional limits on the use of deadly force could reflect the city's deliberate indifference to the "highly predictable consequence," namely, violations of constitutional rights. The Court sought not to foreclose the possibility, however rare, that the unconstitutional consequences of failing to train could be so patently obvious that a city could be liable under § 1983 without proof of a pre-existing pattern of violations.

Failure to train prosecutors in their *Brady* obligations does not fall within the narrow range of *Canton*'s hypothesized single-incident liability. The obvious need for specific legal training that was present in the *Canton* scenario is absent here. Armed police must sometimes make split-second decisions with life-or-death consequences. There is no reason to assume that police academy applicants are familiar with the constitutional constraints on the use of deadly force. And, in the absence of training, there is no way for novice officers to obtain the legal knowledge they require. Under those circumstances there is an obvious need for some form of training. In stark contrast, legal "[t]raining is what differentiates attorneys from average public employees."

Attorneys are trained in the law and equipped with the tools to interpret and apply legal principles, understand constitutional limits, and exercise legal judgment. Before they may enter the profession and receive a law license, all attorneys must graduate from law school or pass a substantive examination; attorneys in the vast majority of jurisdictions must do both. These threshold requirements are designed to ensure that all new attorneys have learned how to find, understand, and apply legal rules.

Nor does professional training end at graduation. Most jurisdictions require attorneys to satisfy continuing-education requirements. Even those few jurisdictions that do not impose mandatory continuing-education requirements mandate that attorneys represent their clients competently and encourage attorneys to engage in continuing study and education. Before Louisiana adopted continuing-education requirements, it imposed similar general competency requirements on its state bar.

Attorneys who practice with other attorneys, such as in district attorney's offices, also train on the job as they learn from more experienced attorneys. For instance, here in the Orleans Parish District Attorney's Office, junior prosecutors were trained by senior prosecutors who supervised them as they worked together to prepare cases for trial, and trial chiefs oversaw the preparation of the cases. Senior attorneys also circulated court decisions and instructional memoranda to keep the prosecutors abreast of relevant legal developments.

In addition, attorneys in all jurisdictions must satisfy character and fitness standards to receive a law license and are personally subject to an ethical regime designed to reinforce the profession's standards. Trial lawyers have a "duty to bring to bear such skill and knowledge as will render the trial a reliable adversarial testing process." Prosecutors have a special "duty to seek justice, not merely to convict. Among prosecutors' unique ethical obligations is the duty to produce *Brady* evidence to the defense. An attorney who violates his or her ethical obligations is subject to professional discipline, including sanctions, suspension, and disbarment.

In light of this regime of legal training and professional responsibility, recurring constitutional violations are not the "obvious consequence" of failing to provide prosecutors with formal in-house training about how to obey the law. Prosecutors are not only equipped but are also ethically bound to know what *Brady* entails and to perform legal research when they are uncertain. A district attorney is entitled to rely on prosecutors' professional training and ethical obligations in the absence of specific reason, such as a pattern of violations, to believe that those tools are insufficient to prevent future constitutional violations in "the usual and recurring situations with which [the prosecutors] must deal." A licensed attorney making legal judgments, in his capacity as a prosecutor, about *Brady* material simply does not present the same "highly predictable" constitutional danger as *Canton*'s untrained officer.

A second significant difference between this case and the example in *Canton* is the nuance of the allegedly necessary training. The *Canton* hypothetical assumes that the armed police officers have no knowledge at all of the constitutional limits on the use of deadly force. But it is undisputed here that the prosecutors in Connick's office were familiar with the general *Brady* rule. Thompson's complaint therefore cannot rely on the utter lack of an ability to cope with constitutional situations that underlies the *Canton* hypothetical, but rather must assert that prosecutors were not trained about particular *Brady* evidence or the specific scenario related to the violation in his case. That sort of nuance simply cannot support an inference of deliberate indifference here. As the Court said in *Canton*, "[i]n virtually every instance where a person has had his or her constitutional rights violated by a city employee, a § 1983 plaintiff will be able to point to something the city 'could have done' to prevent the unfortunate incident."

Thompson suggests that the absence of any formal training sessions about *Brady* is equivalent to the complete absence of legal training that the Court imagined in Canton. But failure-to-train liability is concerned with the substance of the training, not the particular instructional format. The statute does not provide plaintiffs or courts carte blanche to micromanage local governments throughout the United States.

We do not assume that prosecutors will always make correct *Brady* decisions or that guidance regarding specific *Brady* questions would not assist prosecutors. But showing merely that additional training would have been helpful in making difficult decisions does not establish municipal liability. "[P]rov[ing] that an injury or accident could have been avoided if an [employee] had had better or more training, sufficient to equip him to avoid the particular injury-causing conduct" will not suffice. The possibility of single-incident liability that the Court left open in *Canton* is not this case.

The dissent rejects our holding that *Canton*'s hypothesized single-incident liability does not, as a legal matter, encompass failure to train prosecutors in their *Brady* obligation. It would instead apply the *Canton* hypothetical to this case, and thus devotes almost all of its opinion to explaining why the evidence supports liability under that theory. But the dissent's attempt to address our holding—by pointing out that not all prosecutors will necessarily have enrolled in criminal procedure class—misses the point. The reason why the *Canton* hypothetical is inapplicable is that attorneys, unlike police officers, are equipped with the tools to find, interpret, and apply legal principles.

By the end of its opinion, however, the dissent finally reveals that its real disagreement is not with our holding today, but with this Court's precedent. The dissent does not see "any reason," post, for the Court's conclusion in *Bryan County* that a pattern of violations is "ordinarily necessary" to demonstrate deliberate indifference for purposes of failure to train. As our precedent makes clear, proving that a municipality itself actually caused a constitutional violation by failing to train the offending employee presents "difficult problems of proof," and we must adhere to a "stringent standard of fault," lest municipal liability under § 1983 collapse into respondeat superior.

The role of a prosecutor is to see that justice is done. *Berger v. United States* (1935). "It is as much [a prosecutor's] duty to refrain from improper methods calculated to produce a wrongful conviction as it is to use every legitimate means to bring about a just one." By their own admission, the prosecutors who tried Thompson's armed robbery case failed to carry out that responsibility. But the only issue before us is whether Connick, as the policymaker for the district attorney's office, was deliberately indifferent to the need to train the attorneys under his authority.

We conclude that this case does not fall within the narrow range of "single-incident" liability hypothesized in *Canton* as a possible exception to the pattern of violations necessary to prove deliberate indifference in § 1983 actions alleging failure to train. The District Court should have granted Connick judgment as a matter of law on the failure-to-train claim because Thompson did not prove a pattern of similar violations that would "establish that the 'policy of inaction' [was] the functional equivalent of a decision by the city itself to violate the Constitution."

The judgment of the United States Court of Appeals for the Fifth Circuit is reversed.

It is so ordered.

NOTES AND QUESTIONS

1. Do not let the impact of the *Brady* violation here get lost in the shuffle. Thompson was convicted of armed robbery in a trial where the prosecution never turned over to the defense a swatch of fabric stained with the robber's blood, which a crime lab report determined was blood type B. Thompson had blood type O. Because of that conviction Thompson did not take the stand in his murder trial, and was convicted and sentenced to death.

When he was retried on the murder case after the exculpatory evidence was disclosed and both convictions vacated, he took the stand in his own defense. He was found not guilty.

2. Note how the Court attempts to add ever more burdensome glosses onto the "deliberate indifference" proof standard it set forth in *Harris*. The failure-to-train theory is only available "in limited circumstances." A municipality's liability "is at its most tenuous" in a failure-to-train case.

None of these quoted phrases are quotes from *Harris* or other cases, but they are plainly being framed so that they can be used as quotes in subsequent cases, e.g., "As we held in *Connick*, municipality liability 'is at its most tenuous'. . . ."

3. Why should it be necessary that Thompson prove a pattern of "similar" *Brady* violations? Isn't Thompson's allegation that Connick failed to train his prosecutors adequately about their *Brady* obligations generally, and that as a result the exculpatory evidence was not disclosed in Thompson's armed robbery case? Shouldn't the four reversals of convictions for *Brady* violations by Connick's prosecutors have put Connick on notice of the need for *Brady* training as a general matter?

Brady violations resulting in reversals of convictions are rare. A particular nondisclosure is only "material" for *Brady* purposes "if there is a reasonable probability that, had the evidence been disclosed to the defense, the result of the proceeding would have been different." *United States v. Bagley*, 473 U.S. 667, 682 (1985). When this standard is applied after a conviction, and a full evidentiary record has been established that supports that conviction, courts rarely find that the *Bagley* materiality standard has been met.

In other words, the four reversals by Connick's prosecutors were likely the result of very serious *Brady* violations.

4. The hypothetical from footnote 10 in *Harris*—about the need for training police officers about the use of deadly force in pursuing fleeing felons—gets a surprising amount of attention in *Connick*. How analogous do you find the need to provide prosecutors with training on their *Brady* obligations? Are the consequences of a misuse of deadly force and a failure to observe *Brady* requirements equally likely to result in a deprivation of constitutional rights?

5. What do you make of the Court's point that Connick was entitled to rely on the fact that the prosecutors in his office, by virtue of their legal education, training, and professional responsibilities, would have been aware of their *Brady* obligations? Was the jury entitled to reach a different conclusion based on the abundant evidence that Connick and other prosecutors misunderstood their *Brady* obligations?

6. Connick's reaction to the Supreme Court's decision in *Kyles v. Whitley*, 514 U.S. 419 (1995)—a seminal case on *Brady* violations made in a capital prosecution by Connick's own office, *see infra*—is especially shocking. As pointed out by Justice Ginsburg in her dissent, when he was questioned about *Kyles* at trial Connick told the jury he was satisfied with his office's practices and saw no need to make any changes as a result of the decision. Not only should the case have warranted some level of soul-searching or at least introspection by any reasonable prosecutor, *Kyles* clarified two aspects of *Brady* obligations that every prosecutor needed to understand going forward: (a) *Brady* is violated where the cumulative effect of non-disclosures is material, that is, pieces of exculpatory information cannot be viewed in isolation, and (b) a prosecutor's *Brady* obligations extend to "agents" of the prosecution, that is, the prosecutor is responsible for information contained in police files.

7. Defendant Harry F. Connick, the father of American musician Harry Connick Jr., was the district attorney in New Orleans from 1973 to 2003. He won two cases in the Supreme Court on entirely unrelated issues. In addition to *Connick v. Thompson*, he was also the prevailing party in *Connick v. Myers*, 461 U.S. 138 (1983), where the Supreme Court upheld his decision to fire a prosecutor for internally circulating a questionnaire on office morale, finding no First Amendment violation because the questionnaire was not primarily focused on matters of "public concern." Connick was indicted on federal racketeering charges in 1989 but found not guilty at trial.

The deliberate indifference standard is not the only barrier to liability under § 1983. Additional hurdles confront § 1983 plaintiffs who seek injunctive relief against allegedly unconstitutional action by law enforcement. In *O'Shea v. Littleton*, 414 U.S. 488 (1974), Black residents sought class certification and injunctive relief against several different local law enforcement defendants, including a judge and magistrate, alleging a litany of discriminatory practices in setting bail conditions, sentencing, and charging fees for jury trials. *Id.* at 491-92. The Supreme Court held that the case should have been dismissed because, inasmuch as none of the 19 named plaintiffs had been injured by the allegedly discriminatory practices, there was no "case or controversy." *Id.* at 495-96. The Court also implied that equitable relief might be inappropriate for the independent reasons that the injunction sought was "intrusive and unworkable" and offensive to concerns of "equity, comity, and federalism." *Id.* at 499-500.

Two years later, in *Rizzo v. Goode*, 423 U.S. 362 (1976), the Supreme Court reversed a district court's award of injunctive relief against Philadelphia city officials that mandated procedures for improving the handling of complaints of police misconduct. The Court found, as it had in *O'Shea*, the lack of a "case or controversy" and also found § 1983 did not provide for liability under a "failure to act" theory. *Id.* at 372-76. The Court also found that "important considerations of federalism are additional factors weighing against" injunctive relief, and that federal courts must be constantly mindful of the "special delicacy of the adjustment to be preserved between federal equitable power and State administration of its own law." *Id.* at 378.

O'Shea and *Rizzo* paved the way for the following even sharper curtailment of § 1983's utility as a vehicle for obtaining injunctive relief against a municipality.

City of Los Angeles v. Lyons

461 U.S. 95 (1983)

Justice White delivered the opinion of the Court.

The issue here is whether respondent Lyons satisfied the prerequisites for seeking injunctive relief in the federal district court.

I

This case began on February 7, 1977, when respondent, Adolph Lyons, filed a complaint for damages, injunction, and declaratory relief in the United States District Court for the Central District of California. The defendants were the City of Los Angeles and four of its police officers. The complaint alleged that on October 6, 1976, at 2 a.m., Lyons was stopped by the defendant officers for a traffic or vehicle code violation and that although Lyons offered no resistance or threat whatsoever, the officers, without provocation or justification, seized Lyons and applied a "chokehold"—either the "bar arm control" hold or the "carotid-artery control" hold or both—rendering him unconscious and causing damage to his larynx. Counts I through IV of the complaint sought damages against the officers and the City. Count V, with which we are principally concerned here, sought a preliminary and permanent injunction against the City barring the use of the control holds. That count alleged that the city's police officers, "pursuant to the authorization, instruction and encouragement of defendant City of Los Angeles, regularly and routinely apply these choke holds in innumerable situations where they are not threatened by the use of any deadly force whatsoever," that numerous persons have been injured as the result of the application of the chokeholds, that Lyons and others similarly situated are threatened with irreparable injury in the form of bodily injury and loss of life, and that Lyons "justifiably fears that any contact he has with Los Angeles police officers may result in his being choked and strangled to death without provocation, justification or other legal excuse." Lyons alleged the threatened impairment of rights protected by the First, Fourth, Eighth and Fourteenth Amendments. Injunctive relief was sought against the use of the control holds "except in situations where the proposed victim of said control reasonably appears to be threatening the immediate use of deadly force." Count VI sought declaratory relief against the City, i.e., a judgment that use of the chokeholds absent the threat of immediate use of deadly force is a per se violation of various constitutional rights.

The District Court, by order, granted the City's motion for partial judgment on the pleadings and entered judgment for the City on Count V and VI. The Court of Appeals reversed the judgment for the City on Count V and VI, holding Lyons had standing to seek relief against the application of the chokeholds. The Court of Appeals held that there was a sufficient likelihood that Lyons would again be stopped and subjected to the unlawful use of force to constitute a case or controversy and to warrant the issuance of an injunction, if the injunction was otherwise authorized. We denied certiorari.

On remand, Lyons applied for a preliminary injunction. Lyons pressed only the Count V claim at this point. The motion was heard on affidavits, depositions and government records. The District Court found that Lyons had been stopped for a traffic infringement and that without provocation or legal justification the officers involved had applied a "department-authorized chokehold which resulted in injuries to the plaintiff." The court further found that the department authorizes the use of the holds in situations where no one is threatened by death or grievous bodily harm, that officers are insufficiently trained, that the use of the holds involves a high risk of injury or death as then employed, and that their continued use in situations where neither death nor serious bodily injury is threatened "is unconscionable in a civilized society." The court concluded that such use violated Lyons' substantive due process rights under the Fourteenth Amendment. A preliminary injunction was entered enjoining "the use of both the carotid-artery and bar arm holds under circumstances which do not threaten death or serious bodily injury." An improved training program and regular reporting and record keeping were also ordered. The Court of Appeals affirmed in a brief per curiam opinion stating that the District Court had not abused its discretion in entering a preliminary injunction. We granted certiorari, and now reverse.

II

Since our grant of certiorari, circumstances pertinent to the case have changed. Originally, Lyons' complaint alleged that at least two deaths had occurred as a result of the application of chokeholds by the police. His first amended complaint alleged that 10 chokehold-related deaths had occurred. By May, 1982, there had been five more such deaths. On May 6, 1982, the Chief of Police in Los Angeles prohibited the use of the bar-arm chokehold in any circumstances. A few days later, on May 12, 1982, the Board of Police Commissioners imposed a six-month moratorium on the use of the carotid-artery chokehold except under circumstances where deadly force is authorized.

Based on these events, on June 3, 1982, the City filed in this Court a Memorandum Suggesting a Question of Mootness, reciting the facts but arguing that the case was not moot. Lyons in turn filed a motion to dismiss the writ of certiorari as improvidently granted. We denied that motion but reserved the question of mootness for later consideration.

In his brief and at oral argument, Lyons has reasserted his position that in light of changed conditions, an injunctive decree is now unnecessary because he is no longer subject to a threat of injury. He urges that the preliminary injunction should be vacated. The City, on the other hand, while acknowledging that subsequent events have significantly changed the posture of this case, again asserts that the case is not moot because the moratorium is not permanent and may be lifted at any time.

We agree with the City that the case is not moot, since the moratorium by its terms is not permanent. Intervening events have not "irrevocably eradicated the effects of the alleged violation." We nevertheless hold, for another reason, that the federal courts are without jurisdiction to entertain Lyons' claim for injunctive relief.

III

It goes without saying that those who seek to invoke the jurisdiction of the federal courts must satisfy the threshold requirement imposed by Article III of the Constitution by alleging an actual case or controversy.

In *O'Shea v. Littleton* we dealt with a case brought by a class of plaintiffs claiming that they had been subjected to discriminatory enforcement of the criminal law. Among other things, a county magistrate and judge were accused of discriminatory conduct in various respects, such as sentencing members of plaintiff's class more harshly than other defendants. The Court of Appeals reversed the dismissal of the suit by the District Court, ruling that if the allegations were proved, an appropriate injunction could be entered.

We reversed for failure of the complaint to allege a case or controversy. Although it was claimed in that case that particular members of the plaintiff class had actually suffered from the alleged unconstitutional practices, we observed that "[p]ast exposure to illegal conduct does not in itself show a present case or controversy regarding injunctive relief . . .

if unaccompanied by any continuing, present adverse effects." Past wrongs were evidence bearing on "whether there is a real and immediate threat of repeated injury." But the prospect of future injury rested "on the likelihood that [plaintiffs] will again be arrested for and charged with violations of the criminal law and will again be subjected to bond proceedings, trial, or sentencing before petitioners." The most that could be said for plaintiffs' standing was "that if [plaintiffs] proceed to violate an unchallenged law and if they are charged, held to answer, and tried in any proceedings before petitioners, they will be subjected to the discriminatory practices that petitioners are alleged to have followed." We could not find a case or controversy in those circumstances: the threat to the plaintiffs was not "sufficiently real and immediate to show an existing controversy simply because they anticipate violating lawful criminal statutes and being tried for their offenses. . . ." It was to be assumed "that [plaintiffs] will conduct their activities within the law and so avoid prosecution and conviction as well as exposure to the challenged course of conduct said to be followed by petitioners."

We further observed that case or controversy considerations "obviously shade into those determining whether the complaint states a sound basis for equitable relief," and went on to hold that even if the complaint presented an existing case or controversy, an adequate basis for equitable relief against petitioners had not been demonstrated:

> [Plaintiffs] have failed, moreover, to establish the basic requisites of the issuance of equitable relief in these circumstances — the likelihood of substantial and immediate irreparable injury, and the inadequacy of remedies at law. We have already canvassed the necessarily conjectural nature of the threatened injury to which [plaintiffs] are allegedly subjected. And if any of the [plaintiffs] are ever prosecuted and face trial, or if they are illegally sentenced, there are available state and federal procedures which could provide relief from the wrongful conduct alleged.

Another relevant decision for present purposes is *Rizzo v. Goode* (1976), a case in which plaintiffs alleged widespread illegal and unconstitutional police conduct aimed at minority citizens and against City residents in general. The Court reiterated the holding in *O'Shea* that past wrongs do not in themselves amount to that real and immediate threat of injury necessary to make out a case or controversy. The claim of injury rested upon "what one or a small, unnamed minority of policemen might do to them in the future because of that unknown policeman's perception" of departmental procedures. This hypothesis was "even more attenuated than those allegations of future injury found insufficient in *O'Shea* to warrant [the] invocation of federal jurisdiction." The Court also held that plaintiffs' showing at trial of a relatively few instances of violations by individual police officers, without any showing of a deliberate policy on behalf of the named defendants, did not provide a basis for equitable relief.

Golden v. Zwickler (1969), a case arising in an analogous situation, is directly apposite. Congressman Zwickler sought a declaratory judgment that a New York statute prohibiting anonymous handbills directly pertaining to election campaigns was unconstitutional. Although Zwickler had once been convicted under the statute, he was no longer a Congressman apt to run for reelection. A unanimous Court held that because it was "most unlikely" that Zwickler would again be subject to the statute, no case or controversy of "sufficient immediacy and reality" was present to allow a declaratory judgment. Just as Zwickler's assertion that he could be a candidate for Congress again was "hardly a substitute for evidence that this is a prospect of 'immediacy and reality,'" Lyons' assertion that he may again be subject to an illegal chokehold does not create the actual controversy that must exist for a declaratory judgment to be entered.

IV

No extension of *O'Shea* and *Rizzo* is necessary to hold that respondent Lyons has failed to demonstrate a case or controversy with the City that would justify the equitable relief sought.

Lyons' standing to seek the injunction requested depended on whether he was likely to suffer future injury from the use of the chokeholds by police officers. Count V of the complaint alleged the traffic stop and choking incident five months before. That Lyons may have been illegally choked by the police on October 6, 1976, while presumably affording Lyons standing to claim damages against the individual officers and perhaps against the City, does nothing to establish a real and immediate threat that he would again be stopped for a traffic violation, or for any other offense, by an officer or officers who would illegally choke him into unconsciousness without any provocation or resistance on his part. The additional allegation in the complaint that the police in Los Angeles routinely apply chokeholds in situations where they are not threatened by the use of deadly force falls far short of the allegations that would be necessary to establish a case or controversy between these parties.

In order to establish an actual controversy in this case, Lyons would have had not only to allege that he would have another encounter with the police but also to make the incredible assertion either, (1) that all police officers in Los Angeles always choke any citizen with whom they happen to have an encounter, whether for the purpose of arrest, issuing a citation or for questioning or, (2) that the City ordered or authorized police officers to act in such manner. Although Count V alleged that the City authorized the use of the control holds in situations where deadly force was not threatened, it did not indicate why Lyons might be realistically threatened by police officers who acted within the strictures of the City's policy. If, for example, chokeholds were authorized to be used only to counter resistance to an arrest by a suspect, or to thwart an effort to escape, any future threat to Lyons from the City's policy or from the conduct of police officers would be no more real than the possibility that he would again have an encounter with the police and that either he would illegally resist arrest or detention or the officers would disobey their instructions and again render him unconscious without any provocation.

Under *O'Shea* and *Rizzo*, these allegations were an insufficient basis to provide a federal court with jurisdiction to entertain Count V of the complaint. This was apparently the conclusion of the District Court in dismissing Lyons' claim for injunctive relief. Although the District Court acted without opinion or findings, the Court of Appeals interpreted its action as based on lack of standing, i.e., that under *O'Shea* and *Rizzo*, Lyons must be held to have made an "insufficient showing that the police were likely to do this to the plaintiff again." For several reasons—each of them infirm, in our view—the Court of Appeals thought reliance on *O'Shea* and *Rizzo* was misplaced and reversed the District Court.

First, the Court of Appeals thought that Lyons was more immediately threatened than the plaintiffs in those cases since, according to the Court of Appeals, Lyons need only be stopped for a minor traffic violation to be subject to the strangleholds. But even assuming that Lyons would again be stopped for a traffic or other violation in the reasonably near future, it is untenable to assert, and the complaint made no such allegation, that strangleholds are applied by the Los Angeles police to every citizen who is stopped or arrested regardless of the conduct of the person stopped. We cannot agree that the "odds" that Lyons would not only again be stopped for a traffic violation but would also be subjected to a chokehold without any provocation whatsoever are sufficient to make out a federal case for equitable relief. We note that five months elapsed between October 6, 1976, and the filing of the complaint, yet there was no allegation of further unfortunate encounters between Lyons and the police.

Of course, it may be that among the countless encounters between the police and the citizens of a great city such as Los Angeles, there will be certain instances in which strangleholds will be illegally applied and injury and death unconstitutionally inflicted on the victim. As we have said, however, it is no more than conjecture to suggest that in every instance of a traffic stop, arrest, or other encounter between the police and a citizen, the police will act unconstitutionally and inflict injury without provocation or legal excuse. And it is surely no more than speculation to assert either that Lyons himself will again be involved in one of those unfortunate instances, or that he will be arrested in the future and provoke the use of a chokehold by resisting arrest, attempting to escape, or threatening deadly force or serious bodily injury.

Second, the Court of Appeals viewed *O'Shea* and *Rizzo* as cases in which the plaintiffs sought "massive structural" relief against the local law enforcement systems and therefore that the holdings in those cases were inapposite to cases such as this where the plaintiff, according to the Court of Appeals, seeks to enjoin only an "established," "sanctioned" police practice assertedly violative of constitutional rights. *O'Shea* and *Rizzo*, however, cannot be so easily confined to their facts. If Lyons has made no showing that he is realistically threatened by a repetition of his experience of October, 1976, then he has not met the requirements for seeking an injunction in a federal court, whether the injunction contemplates intrusive structural relief or the cessation of a discrete practice.

The Court of Appeals also asserted that Lyons "had a live and active claim" against the City "if only for a period of a few seconds" while the stranglehold was being applied to him and that for two reasons the claim had not become moot so as to disentitle Lyons to injunctive relief: First, because under normal rules of equity, a case does not become moot merely because the complained of conduct has ceased; and second, because Lyons' claim is "capable of repetition but evading review" and therefore should be heard. We agree that Lyons had a live controversy with the City. Indeed, he still has a claim for damages against the City that appears to meet all Article III requirements. Nevertheless, the issue here is not whether that claim has become moot but whether Lyons meets the preconditions for asserting an injunctive claim in a federal forum. The equitable doctrine that cessation of the challenged conduct does not bar an injunction is of little help in this respect, for Lyons' lack of standing does not rest on the termination of the police practice but on the speculative nature of his claim that he will again experience injury as the result of that practice even if continued.

The rule that a claim does not become moot where it is capable of repetition, yet evades review, is likewise inapposite. Lyons' claim that he was illegally strangled remains to be litigated in his suit for damages; in no sense does that claim "evade" review. Furthermore, the capable-of-repetition doctrine applies only in exceptional situations, and generally only where the named plaintiff can make a reasonable showing that he will again be subjected to the alleged illegality. As we have indicated, Lyons has not made this demonstration.

The record and findings made on remand do not improve Lyons' position with respect to standing. The District Court, having been reversed, did not expressly address Lyons' standing to seek injunctive relief, although the City was careful to preserve its position on this question. There was no finding that Lyons faced a real and immediate threat of again being illegally choked. The City's policy was described as authorizing the use of the strangleholds "under circumstances where no one is threatened with death or grievous bodily harm." That policy was not further described, but the record before the court contained the department's existing policy with respect to the employment of chokeholds. Nothing in that policy, contained in a Police Department manual, suggests that the chokeholds, or other kinds of force for that matter, are authorized absent some resistance or other provocation by the arrestee or other suspect. On the contrary, police officers were instructed to use chokeholds only when lesser degrees of force do not suffice and then only "to gain control of a suspect who is violently resisting the officer or trying to escape."

Our conclusion is that the Court of Appeals failed to heed *O'Shea*, *Rizzo*, and other relevant authority, and that the District Court was quite right in dismissing Count V.

V

Lyons fares no better if it be assumed that his pending damages suit affords him Article III standing to seek an injunction as a remedy for the claim arising out of the October 1976 events.

The equitable remedy is unavailable absent a showing of irreparable injury, a requirement that cannot be met where there is no showing of any real or immediate threat that the plaintiff will be wronged again—a "likelihood of substantial and immediate irreparable injury." The speculative nature of Lyons' claim of future injury requires a finding that this prerequisite of equitable relief has not been fulfilled.

Nor will the injury that Lyons allegedly suffered in 1976 go unrecompensed; for that injury, he has an adequate remedy at law. Contrary to the view of the Court of Appeals, it is not at all "difficult" under our holding "to see how anyone can ever challenge police or similar administrative practices." The legality of the violence to which Lyons claims he was once subjected is at issue in his suit for damages and can be determined there.

Absent a sufficient likelihood that he will again be wronged in a similar way, Lyons is no more entitled to an injunction than any other citizen of Los Angeles; and a federal court may not entertain a claim by any or all citizens who no more than assert that certain practices of law enforcement officers are unconstitutional. This is not to suggest that such undifferentiated claims should not be taken seriously by local authorities. Indeed, the interest of an alert and interested citizen is an essential element of an effective and fair government, whether on the local, state or national level. A federal court, however, is not the proper forum to press such claims unless the requirements for entry and the prerequisites for injunctive relief are satisfied.

We decline the invitation to slight the preconditions for equitable relief; for as we have held, recognition of the need for a proper balance between state and federal authority counsels restraint in the issuance of injunctions against state officers engaged in the administration of the states' criminal laws in the absence of irreparable injury which is both great and immediate *Mitchum v. Foster* (1972) held that suits brought under 42 U.S.C. § 1983 are exempt from the flat ban against the issuance of injunctions directed at state court proceedings. But this holding did not displace the normal principles of equity, comity and federalism that should inform the judgment of federal courts when asked to oversee state law enforcement authorities. In exercising their equitable powers federal courts must recognize "[t]he special delicacy of the adjustment to be preserved between federal equitable power and State administration of its own law." The Court of Appeals failed to apply these factors properly and therefore erred in finding that the District Court had not abused its discretion in entering an injunction in this case.

As we noted in *O'Shea*, withholding injunctive relief does not mean that the "federal law will exercise no deterrent effect in these circumstances." If Lyons has suffered an injury barred by the Federal Constitution, he has a remedy for damages under § 1983. Furthermore, those who deliberately deprive a citizen of his constitutional rights risk conviction under the federal criminal laws.

Beyond these considerations the state courts need not impose the same standing or remedial requirements that govern federal court proceedings. The individual states may permit their courts to use injunctions to oversee the conduct of law enforcement authorities on a continuing basis. But this is not the role of a federal court absent far more justification than Lyons has proffered in this case.

The judgment of the Court of Appeals is accordingly
Reversed.

[Justices Marshall, Brennan, Blackmun, and Stevens dissented.]

NOTES AND QUESTIONS

1. *Lyons* was in one sense an easier kind of § 1983 case than either *Harris* or *Connick* because the challenge was to a city policy and there was therefore no need to proceed on a "failure to train" theory and demonstrate "deliberate indifference. The district court found, and it was not disputed on appeal, that the city permitted officers to use chokeholds even when they were not in situations where death or serious harm were threatened. Accordingly, the policy was in violation of the Fourth Amendment, as the Supreme Court held in *Tennessee v. Garner*, 471 U.S. 1 (1985).

2. The Court's use of the standing doctrine in *Lyons* was unprecedented. As the dissent points out, the Court had never before "fragmented" the concept of standing to require a separate type of standing for injunctive relief on top of the standing Lyons undeniably had — he was subjected to an unconstitutional chokehold — with respect to his damages claims.

Chokehold representation

3. The doctrine of standing flows from the Article III requirement that the judicial power can only be exercised in a "case or controversy." Professor Richard Fallon has observed that the conception of standing in *Lyons*, which he labels "remedial standing," is inconsistent with traditional understandings of the term "case," which the Court has held includes all claims arising out of "a common nucleus of operative fact." *UMW v. Gibbs*, 333 U.S. 715 (1966) (a federal court having federal question jurisdiction can exercise pendent jurisdiction over state law claims arising out of the same facts, as the state claims are part of the same "case" for Article III purposes). *See* Richard H. Fallon Jr., *Of Justiciability, Remedies, and Public Law Litigation: Notes on the Jurisprudence of* Lyons, 59 N.Y.U. L. Rev. 1, 22 & n.115 (1984).

4. The Court says that Lyons is no more likely than anyone else in Los Angeles to be subjected to an unconstitutional chokehold. Does this mean that literally no one could bring the injunctive claim Lyons brought?

Further, does this framing simply ignore the disproportionate use of chokeholds on Black people? Does it ignore that Lyons has also alleged an equal protection claim?

5. The Court claims that *O'Shea* and *Rizzo* support the result in *Lyons*. Do you see meaningful distinctions between *Lyons* and those cases?

Was the nature of the equitable relief sought by Lyons distinguishable from the relief sought by the plaintiffs in *O'Shea* and *Rizzo*?

Was the nature of Lyons's "case" as a whole distinguishable from the cases of the plaintiffs in *O'Shea* and *Rizzo*?

6. Professor Vicki Jackson asks an interesting "what if" about *Lyons* and the professed virtues of equitable restraint that it endorsed. It was less than eight years after the decision in *Lyons* that Rodney King was savagely beaten by Los Angeles police officers, which lead to a state court trial in which the officers were acquitted, precipitating riots, 45 deaths, and hundreds of injuries. It also resulted in a federal criminal prosecution of the officers. Might any of this have been avoided if in the 1980s the Los Angeles Police Department had been under some period of federal court supervision or monitoring of its operations through an injunctive decree? *See* Vicki C. Jackson, *Standing and the Role of Federal Courts: Triple Error Decisions in* Clapper v. Amnesty International USA *and* City of Los Angeles v. Lyons, 23 Wm. & Mary Bill Rts. J. 127, 122, 134 (2014).

Shortly after the Rodney King beating an independent commission headed by Warren Christopher issued a searing report on the LAPD, finding rampant use of excessive force, racist attitudes at all ranks in the department, and an utter failure to investigate and discipline officer misconduct. *Id. See generally* Warren Christopher et al., Report of the Independent Commission on the Los Angeles Police Department (1991).

7. The Court concludes its opinion in *Lyons* with this penultimate paragraph:

> As we noted in *O'Shea*, . . . withholding injunctive relief does not mean that the "federal law will exercise no deterrent effect in these circumstances." If Lyons has suffered an injury barred by the Federal Constitution, he has a remedy for damages under § 1983. Furthermore, those who deliberately deprive a citizen of his constitutional rights risk conviction under the federal criminal laws. *Ibid.*

461 U.S. at 112. Is it clear that Lyons has a remedy for damages here? Could the city defend against liability on the basis that the chokehold policy was not implemented at a high enough level in the police department to be attributable to the city under *Monell*?

The passage in *O'Shea* the Court cites makes specific reference to 18 U.S.C. § 242, which authorizes federal criminal prosecutions for deprivations of constitutional rights. Indeed, this is the statute under which the LAPD officers responsible for the beating of Rodney King were prosecuted and convicted in the federal trial. Does the Court mean to suggest that the federal criminal prosecution of a local police officer is less offensive to principles of federalism than a federal injunction?

In the next case a federal district judge is able to overcome the high hurdles imposed by *Monell* and *Lyons* in a class action challenging the New York City Police Department's stop-and-frisk policies.

Floyd v. City of New York

959 F. Supp. 2d 540 (S.D.N.Y. 2013)

Shira A. Scheindlin, District Judge:

I. INTRODUCTION

New Yorkers are rightly proud of their city and seek to make it as safe as the largest city in America can be. New Yorkers also treasure their liberty. Countless individuals have come to New York in pursuit of that liberty. The goals of liberty and safety may be in tension, but they can coexist—indeed the Constitution mandates it.

This case is about the tension between liberty and public safety in the use of a proactive policing tool called "stop and frisk." The New York City Police Department ("NYPD") made 4.4 million stops between January 2004 and June 2012. Over 80% of these 4.4 million stops were of blacks or Hispanics. In each of these stops a person's life was interrupted. The person was detained and questioned, often on a public street. More than half of the time the police subjected the person to a frisk.

Plaintiffs—blacks and Hispanics who were stopped—argue that the NYPD's use of stop and frisk violated their constitutional rights in two ways: (1) they were stopped without a legal basis in violation of the Fourth Amendment, and (2) they were targeted for stops because of their race in violation of the Fourteenth Amendment. Plaintiffs do not seek to end the use of stop and frisk. Rather, they argue that it must be reformed to comply with constitutional limits. Two such limits are paramount here: first, that all stops be based on "reasonable suspicion" as defined by the Supreme Court of the United States; and second, that stops be conducted in a racially neutral manner.

I emphasize at the outset, as I have throughout the litigation, that this case is not about the effectiveness of stop and frisk in deterring or combating crime. This Court's mandate is solely to judge the constitutionality of police behavior, not its effectiveness as a law enforcement tool. Many police practices may be useful for fighting crime—preventive detention or coerced confessions, for example—but because they are unconstitutional they cannot be used, no matter how effective. "The enshrinement of constitutional rights necessarily takes certain policy choices off the table."

This case is also not primarily about the nineteen individual stops that were the subject of testimony at trial. Rather, this case is about whether the City has a policy or custom of violating the Constitution by making unlawful stops and conducting unlawful frisks.

The Supreme Court has recognized that "the degree of community resentment aroused by particular practices is clearly relevant to an assessment of the quality of the intrusion upon reasonable expectations of personal security." In light of the very active and public debate on the issues addressed in this Opinion—and the passionate positions taken by both sides—it is important to recognize the human toll of unconstitutional stops. While it is true that any one stop is a limited intrusion in duration and deprivation of liberty, each stop is also a demeaning and humiliating experience. No one should live in fear of being stopped whenever he leaves his home to go about the activities of daily life. Those who are routinely subjected to stops are overwhelmingly people of color, and they are justifiably troubled to be singled out when many of them have done nothing to attract the unwanted attention. Some plaintiffs testified that stops make them feel unwelcome in some parts of the City, and distrustful of the police. This alienation cannot be good for the police, the community, or its leaders. Fostering trust and confidence between the police and the community would be an improvement for everyone.

Plaintiffs requested that this case be tried to the Court without a jury. Because plaintiffs seek only injunctive relief, not damages, the City had no right to demand a jury. As a result, I must both find the facts and articulate the governing law. I have endeavored to exercise my judgment faithfully and impartially in making my findings of fact and conclusions of law based on the nine-week trial held from March through May of this year.

I begin with an Executive Summary of the most important points in the Opinion. Next, I address the legal standards governing the ability of police to conduct stops and frisks. I provide a statistical overview of the 4.4 million stops made between January 2004 and June 2012, followed by a discussion of the expert analyses of those stops. I then address the question of whether the City had notice of allegations of racial profiling in the conduct of stops and frisks, and the institutional response to that notice in terms of monitoring, supervision, training, and discipline. After addressing these big picture issues, I make findings of fact with respect to each of the nineteen stops of the twelve class members who provided testimony at trial.

Finally, I present my conclusions of law based on my findings of fact. I will address the question of remedies in a separate opinion, because the remedies overlap with a different case involving stop and frisk in which I have already found that preliminary injunctive relief is warranted.

It is important that this Opinion be read synergistically. Each section of the Opinion is only a piece of the overall picture. Some will quarrel with the findings in one section or another. But, when read as a whole, with an understanding of the interplay between each section, I hope that this Opinion will bring more clarity and less disagreement to this complex and sensitive issue.

II. EXECUTIVE SUMMARY

Plaintiffs assert that the City, and its agent the NYPD, violated both the Fourth Amendment and the Equal Protection Clause of the Fourteenth Amendment of the United States Constitution. In order to hold a municipality liable for the violation of a constitutional right, plaintiffs "must prove that 'action pursuant to official municipal policy' caused the alleged constitutional injury." "Official municipal policy includes the decisions of a government's lawmakers, the acts of its policymaking officials, and practices so persistent and widespread as to practically have the force of law."

The Fourth Amendment protects all individuals against unreasonable searches or seizures. The Supreme Court has held that the Fourth Amendment permits the police to "stop and briefly detain a person for investigative purposes if the officer has a reasonable suspicion supported by articulable facts that criminal activity 'may be afoot,' even if the officer lacks probable cause." "Reasonable suspicion is an objective standard; hence, the subjective intentions or motives of the officer making the stop are irrelevant." The test for whether a stop has taken place in the context of a police encounter is whether a reasonable person would have felt free to terminate the encounter. "'[T]o proceed from a stop to a frisk, the police officer must reasonably suspect that the person stopped is armed and dangerous.'"

The Equal Protection Clause of the Fourteenth Amendment guarantees to every person the equal protection of the laws. It prohibits intentional discrimination based on race. Intentional discrimination can be proved in several ways, two of which are relevant here. A plaintiff can show: (1) that a facially neutral law or policy has been applied in an intentionally discriminatory manner; or (2) that a law or policy expressly classifies persons on the basis of race, and that the classification does not survive strict scrutiny. Because there is rarely direct proof of discriminatory intent, circumstantial evidence of such intent is permitted. "The impact of the official action—whether it bears more heavily on one race than another—may provide an important starting point."

The following facts, discussed in greater detail below, are uncontested:

- Between January 2004 and June 2012, the NYPD conducted over 4.4 million *Terry* stops.
- The number of stops per year rose sharply from 314,000 in 2004 to a high of 686,000 in 2011.
- 52% of all stops were followed by a protective frisk for weapons. A weapon was found after 1.5% of these frisks. In other words, in 98.5% of the 2.3 million frisks, no weapon was found.
- 8% of all stops led to a search into the stopped person's clothing, ostensibly based on the officer feeling an object during the frisk that he suspected to be a weapon, or immediately perceived to be contraband other than a weapon. In 9% of these searches, the felt object was in fact a weapon. 91% of the time, it was not. In 14% of these searches, the felt object was in fact contraband. 86% of the time it was not.

- 6% of all stops resulted in an arrest, and 6% resulted in a summons. The remaining 88% of the 4.4 million stops resulted in no further law enforcement action.
- In 52% of the 4.4 million stops, the person stopped was black, in 31% the person was Hispanic, and in 10% the person was white.
- In 2010, New York City's resident population was roughly 23% black, 29% Hispanic, and 33% white.
- In 23% of the stops of blacks, and 24% of the stops of Hispanics, the officer recorded using force. The number for whites was 17%.
- Weapons were seized in 1.0% of the stops of blacks, 1.1% of the stops of Hispanics, and 1.4% of the stops of whites.
- Contraband other than weapons was seized in 1.8% of the stops of blacks, 1.7% of the stops of Hispanics, and 2.3% of the stops of whites.
- Between 2004 and 2009, the percentage of stops where the officer failed to state a specific suspected crime rose from 1% to 36%.

Both parties provided extensive expert submissions and testimony that is also discussed in detail below. Based on that testimony and the uncontested facts, I have made the following findings with respect to the expert testimony.

With respect to plaintiffs' Fourth Amendment claim, I begin by noting the inherent difficulty in making findings and conclusions regarding 4.4 million stops. Because it is impossible to individually analyze each of those stops, plaintiffs' case was based on the imperfect information contained in the NYPD's database of forms ("UF-250s") that officers are required to prepare after each stop. The central flaws in this database all skew toward underestimating the number of unconstitutional stops that occur: the database is incomplete, in that officers do not prepare a UF-250 for every stop they make; it is one-sided, in that the UF-250 only records the officer's version of the story; the UF-250 permits the officer to merely check a series of boxes, rather than requiring the officer to explain the basis for her suspicion; and many of the boxes on the form are inherently subjective and vague (such as "furtive movements"). Nonetheless, the analysis of the UF-250 database reveals that at least 200,000 stops were made without reasonable suspicion.

The actual number of stops lacking reasonable suspicion was likely far higher, based on the reasons stated above, and the following points: (1) Dr. Fagan was unnecessarily conservative in classifying stops as "apparently unjustified." For example, a UF-250 on which the officer checked only Furtive Movements (used on roughly 42% of forms) and High Crime Area (used on roughly 55% of forms) is not classified as "apparently unjustified." The same is true when only Furtive Movements and Suspicious Bulge (used on roughly 10% of forms) are checked. Finally, if an officer checked only the box marked "other" on either side of the form (used on roughly 26% of forms), Dr. Fagan categorized this as "ungeneralizable" rather than "apparently unjustified." (2) Many UF-250s did not identify any suspected crime (36% of all UF-250s in 2009). (3) The rate of arrests arising from stops is low (roughly 6%), and the yield of seizures of guns or other contraband is even lower (roughly 0.1% and 1.8% respectively). (4) "Furtive Movements," "High Crime Area," and "Suspicious Bulge" are vague and subjective terms. Without an accompanying narrative explanation for the stop, these checkmarks cannot reliably demonstrate individualized reasonable suspicion.

With respect to plaintiffs' Fourteenth Amendment claim, I reject the testimony of the City's experts that the race of crime suspects is the appropriate benchmark for measuring racial bias in stops. The City and its highest officials believe that blacks and Hispanics should be stopped at the same rate as their proportion of the local criminal suspect population. But this reasoning is flawed because the stopped population is overwhelmingly innocent — not criminal. There is no basis for assuming that an innocent population shares the same characteristics as the criminal suspect population in the same area. Instead, I conclude that the benchmark used by plaintiffs' expert—a combination of local population demographics and local crime rates (to account for police deployment) is the most sensible.

Based on the expert testimony I find the following: (1) The NYPD carries out more stops where there are more black and Hispanic residents, even when other relevant variables are held constant. The racial composition of a precinct or census tract predicts the stop rate above and beyond the crime rate. (2) Blacks and Hispanics are more likely than whites to be stopped within precincts and census tracts, even after controlling for other relevant variables. This is so even in areas with low crime rates, racially heterogenous populations, or predominately white populations. (3) For the period 2004 through 2009, when any law enforcement action was taken following a stop, blacks were 30% more likely to be arrested (as opposed to receiving a summons) than whites, for the same suspected crime. (4) For the period 2004 through 2009, after controlling for suspected crime and precinct characteristics, blacks who were stopped were about 14% more likely—and Hispanics 9% more likely—than whites to be subjected to the use of force. (5) For the period 2004 through 2009, all else being equal, the odds of a stop resulting in any further enforcement action were 8% lower if the person stopped was black than if the person stopped was white. In addition, the greater the black population in a precinct, the less likely that a stop would result in a sanction. Together, these results show that blacks are likely targeted for stops based on a lesser degree of objectively founded suspicion than whites.

With respect to both the Fourth and Fourteenth Amendment claims, one way to prove that the City has a custom of conducting unconstitutional stops and frisks is to show that it acted with deliberate indifference to constitutional deprivations caused by its employees—here, the NYPD. The evidence at trial revealed significant evidence that the NYPD acted with deliberate indifference.

As early as 1999, a report from New York's Attorney General placed the City on notice that stops and frisks were being conducted in a racially skewed manner. Nothing was done in response. In the years following this report, pressure was placed on supervisors to increase the number of stops. Evidence at trial revealed that officers have been pressured to make a certain number of stops and risk negative consequences if they fail to achieve the goal. Without a system to ensure that stops are justified, such pressure is a predictable formula for producing unconstitutional stops. As one high ranking police official noted in 2010, this pressure, without a comparable emphasis on ensuring that the activities are legally justified, "could result in an officer taking enforcement action for the purpose of meeting a quota rather than because a violation of the law has occurred."

In addition, the evidence at trial revealed that the NYPD has an unwritten policy of targeting "the right people" for stops. In practice, the policy encourages the targeting of young black and Hispanic men based on their prevalence in local crime complaints. This is a form of racial profiling. While a person's race may be important if it fits the description of a particular crime suspect, it is impermissible to subject all members of a racially defined group to heightened police enforcement because some members of that group are criminals. The Equal Protection Clause does not permit race-based suspicion.

Much evidence was introduced regarding inadequate monitoring and supervision of unconstitutional stops. Supervisors routinely review the productivity of officers, but do not review the facts of a stop to determine whether it was legally warranted. Nor do supervisors ensure that an officer has made a proper record of a stop so that it can be reviewed for constitutionality. Deficiencies were also shown in the training of officers with respect to stop and frisk and in the disciplining of officers when they were found to have made a bad stop or frisk. Despite the mounting evidence that many bad stops were made, that officers failed to make adequate records of stops, and that discipline was spotty or non-existent, little has been done to improve the situation.

One example of poor training is particularly telling. Two officers testified to their understanding of the term "furtive movements." One explained that "furtive movement is a very broad concept," and could include a person "changing direction," "walking in a certain way," "[a]cting a little suspicious," "making a movement that is not regular," being "very fidgety," "going in and out of his pocket," "going in and out of a location," "looking back and forth constantly," "looking over their shoulder," "adjusting their hip or their belt," "moving in and out of a car too quickly," "[t]urning a part of their body away from you," "[g]rabbing at a certain pocket or something at their waist," "getting a little nervous, maybe shaking," and "stutter[ing]." Another officer explained that "usually" a furtive movement is someone "hanging out in front of [a] building, sitting on the benches or something like that" and then making a "quick movement," such as "bending down and quickly standing back up," "going inside the lobby . . . and then quickly coming back out," or "all of a sudden becom[ing] very nervous, very aware." If officers believe that the behavior described above constitutes furtive movement that justifies a stop, then it is no surprise that stops so rarely produce evidence of criminal activity.

I now summarize my findings with respect to the individual stops that were the subject of testimony at trial. Twelve plaintiffs testified regarding nineteen stops. In twelve of those stops, both the plaintiffs and the officers testified. In seven stops no officer testified, either because the officers could not be identified or because the officers dispute that the stop ever occurred. I find that nine of the stops and frisks were unconstitutional — that is, they were not based on reasonable suspicion. I also find that while five other stops were constitutional, the frisks following those stops were unconstitutional. Finally, I find that plaintiffs have failed to prove an unconstitutional stop (or frisk) in five of the nineteen stops. The individual stop testimony corroborated much of the evidence about the NYPD's policies and practices with respect to carrying out and monitoring stops and frisks.

In making these decisions I note that evaluating a stop in hindsight is an imperfect procedure. Because there is no contemporaneous recording of the stop (such as could be achieved through the use of a body-worn camera), I am relegated to finding facts based on the often conflicting testimony of eyewitnesses. This task is not easy, as every witness has an interest in the outcome of the case, which may consciously or unconsciously affect the veracity of his or her testimony. Nonetheless, a judge is tasked with making decisions and I judged the evidence of each stop to the best of my ability. I am also aware that a judge deciding whether a stop is constitutional, with the time to reflect and consider all of the evidence, is in a far different position than officers on the street who must make split-second decisions in situations that may pose a danger to themselves or others. I respect that police officers have chosen a profession of public service involving dangers and challenges with few parallels in civilian life.

In conclusion, I find that the City is liable for violating plaintiffs' Fourth and Fourteenth Amendment rights. The City acted with deliberate indifference toward the NYPD's practice of making unconstitutional stops and conducting unconstitutional frisks. Even if the City had not been deliberately indifferent, the NYPD's unconstitutional practices were sufficiently widespread as to have the force of law. In addition, the City adopted a policy of indirect racial profiling by targeting racially defined groups for stops based on local crime suspect data. This has resulted in the disproportionate and discriminatory stopping of blacks and Hispanics in violation of the Equal Protection Clause. Both statistical and anecdotal evidence showed that minorities are indeed treated differently than whites. For example, once a stop is made, blacks and Hispanics are more likely to be subjected to the use of force than whites, despite the fact that whites are more likely to be found with weapons or contraband. I also conclude that the City's highest officials have turned a blind eye to the evidence that officers are conducting stops in a racially discriminatory manner. In their zeal to defend a policy that they believe to be effective, they have willfully ignored overwhelming proof that the policy of targeting "the right people" is racially discriminatory and therefore violates the United States Constitution. One NYPD official has even suggested that it is permissible to stop racially defined groups just to instill fear in them that they are subject to being stopped at any time for any reason—in the hope that this fear will deter them from carrying guns in the streets. The goal of deterring crime is laudable, but this method of doing so is unconstitutional.

I recognize that the police will deploy their limited resources to high crime areas. This benefits the communities where the need for policing is greatest. But the police are not permitted to target people for stops based on their race. Some may worry about the implications of this decision. They may wonder: if the police believe that a particular group of people is disproportionately responsible for crime in one area, why should the police not target that group with increased stops? Why should it matter if the group is defined in part by race? Indeed, there are contexts in which the Constitution permits considerations of race in law enforcement operations. What is clear, however, is that the Equal Protection Clause prohibits the practices described in this case. A police department may not target a racially defined group for stops in general—that is, for stops based on suspicions of general criminal wrongdoing—simply because members of that group appear frequently in the police department's suspect data. The Equal Protection Clause does not permit the police to target a racially defined group as a whole because of the misdeeds of some of its members.

To address the violations that I have found, I shall order various remedies including, but not limited to, an immediate change to certain policies and activities of the NYPD, a trial program requiring the use of body-worn cameras in one precinct per borough, a community-based joint remedial process to be conducted by a court-appointed facilitator, and the appointment of an independent monitor to ensure that the NYPD's conduct of stops and frisks is carried out in accordance with the Constitution and the principles enunciated in this Opinion, and to monitor the NYPD's compliance with the ordered remedies.

NOTES AND QUESTIONS

1. *Floyd* arose out of New York City's notorious stop-and-frisk police tactics (Stop and Frisk) that began as early as the 1990s in response to surging crime rates. Rudolph Giuliani was elected mayor in 1993 and appointed William Bratton as police commissioner. Bratton famously implemented a "broken windows" theory of policing that involved pouring resources into policing minor offenders (e.g., subway fare evaders) in the hope that a decrease in low-level disorder will result in a decrease of more serious crime. In connection with but not directly related to this policing theory, the NYPD in the 1990s also began aggressively conducting investigative stops to detect and deter the carrying of guns. Aggressive use of stop and frisk correlated with significant lowered crime and incarceration rates in New York in the first decade of the twenty-first century. *See generally* Jeffrey Bellin, *The Inverse Relationship Between the Constitutionality and Effectiveness of Stop and Frisk*, 94 B.U. L. Rev. 1495, 1496-99 (2014). This relationship may have been recognized by Judge Scheindlin, who notes in the introduction to her opinion that "this case is not about the effectiveness of stop and frisk in deterring or combating crime." 959 F. Supp. 2d at 557.

2. Consider the raw data on the 4.4 million stops in the UF-250 database. Do you agree with the district court that the expert's analysis of the database underestimated the number of unconstitutional stops, that is, stops unjustified by "reasonable suspicion" under *Terry v. Ohio*, 392 U.S. 1 (1968)?

What do you make of the fact that only 6 percent of stops result in arrests?

Note that 36 percent of the forms do not identify a "suspected crime." Why does the form require the officer to identify a "suspected crime"?

(COMPLETE ALL CAPTIONS)

STOP, QUESTION AND FRISK REPORT WORKSHEET
PD344-151A (Rev. 11-02)

Pct. Serial No. | Date | Pct. Of Occ.
Time Of Stop | Period Of Observation Prior To Stop | Radio Run/Sprint #
Address/Intersection Or Cross Streets Of Stop
☐ Inside ☐ Outside | ☐ Transit ☐ Housing | Type Of Location Describe:
Specify Which Felony/P.L. Misdemeanor Suspected | Duration Of Stop

What Were Circumstances Which Led To Stop?
(MUST CHECK AT LEAST ONE BOX)
☐ Carrying Objects In Plain View Used In Commission Of Crime e.g., Slim Jim/Pry Bar, etc.
☐ Fits Description.
☐ Actions Indicative Of "Casing" Victim Or Location.
☐ Actions Indicative of Acting As A Lookout.
☐ Suspicious Bulge/Object (Describe)
☐ Actions Indicative Of Engaging In Drug Transaction.
☐ Furtive Movements.
☐ Actions Indicative Of Engaging In Violent Crimes.
☐ Wearing Clothes/Disguises Commonly Used In Commission Of Crime.
☐ Other Reasonable Suspicion Of Criminal Activity (Specify)

Name Of Person Stopped | Nickname/Street Name | Date Of Birth
Address | Apt. No. | Tel. No.
Identification: ☐ Verbal ☐ Photo I.D. ☐ Refused ☐ Other (Specify)
Sex: ☐ Male ☐ Female | Race: ☐ White ☐ Black ☐ White Hispanic ☐ Black Hispanic ☐ Asian/Pacific Islander ☐ American Indian/Alaskan Native
Age | Height | Weight | Hair | Eyes | Build
Other (Scars, Tattoos, Etc.)
Did Officer Explain Reason For Stop ☐ Yes ☐ No | If No, Explain:
Were Other Persons Stopped/Questioned/Frisked? ☐ Yes ☐ No | If Yes, List Pct. Serial Nos.
If Physical Force Was Used, Indicate Type:
☐ Hands On Suspect
☐ Suspect On Ground
☐ Pointing Firearm At Suspect
☐ Handcuffing Suspect
☐ Suspect Against Wall/Car
☐ Drawing Firearm
☐ Baton
☐ Pepper Spray
☐ Other (Describe)
Was Suspect Arrested? ☐ Yes ☐ No | Offense | Arrest No.
Was Summons Issued? ☐ Yes ☐ No | Offense | Summons No.
Officer In Uniform? ☐ Yes ☐ No | If No, How Identified? ☐ Shield ☐ I.D. Card ☐ Verbal

Was Person Frisked? ☐ Yes ☐ No IF YES, MUST CHECK AT LEAST ONE BOX
☐ Inappropriate Attire - Possibly Concealing Weapon
☐ Verbal Threats Of Violence By Suspect
☐ Knowledge Of Suspects Prior Criminal Violent Behavior/Use Of Force/Use Of Weapon
☐ Other Reasonable Suspicion of Weapons (Specify)
☐ Furtive Movements
☐ Actions Indicative Of Engaging In Violent Crimes
☐ Refusal To Comply With Officer's Direction(s) Leading To Reasonable Fear For Safety
☐ Violent Crime Suspected
☐ Suspicious Bulge/Object (Describe)
Was Person Searched? ☐ Yes ☐ No IF YES, MUST CHECK AT LEAST ONE BOX ☐ Hard Object ☐ Admission Of Weapons Possession
☐ Outline Of Weapon ☐ Other Reasonable Suspicion of Weapons (Specify)
Was Weapon Found? ☐ Yes ☐ No If Yes, Describe: ☐ Pistol/Revolver ☐ Rifle/Shotgun ☐ Assault Weapon ☐ Knife/Cutting Instrument
☐ Machine Gun ☐ Other (Describe)
Was Other Contraband Found? ☐ Yes ☐ No If Yes, Describe Contraband And Location
Demeanor Of Person After Being Stopped
Remarks Made By Person Stopped
Additional Circumstances/Factors: (Check All That Apply)
☐ Report From Victim/Witness
☐ Area Has High Incidence Of Reported Offense Of Type Under Investigation
☐ Time Of Day, Day Of Week, Season Corresponding To Reports Of Criminal Activity
☐ Suspect Is Associating With Persons Known For Their Criminal Activity
☐ Proximity To Crime Location
☐ Other (Describe)
☐ Evasive, False Or Inconsistent Response To Officer's Questions
☐ Changing Direction At Sight Of Officer/Flight
☐ Ongoing Investigations, e.g., Robbery Pattern
☐ Sights And Sounds Of Criminal Activity, e.g., Bloodstains, Ringing Alarms
Pct. Serial No. | Additional Reports Prepared: Complaint Rpt. No. ___ Juvenile Rpt. No. ___ Aided Rpt. No. ___ Other Rpt. (Specify) ___
REPORTED BY: Rank, Name (Last, First, M.I.) Print ___ Signature ___ Tax# ___ Command ___
REVIEWED BY: Rank, Name (Last, First, M.I.) Print ___ Signature ___ Tax# ___ Command ___

Copy of blank UF-250 Form used by the NYPD

3. As was expected, the defendants contested the standing of the named plaintiffs based on *Lyons*. The standing of only a single named plaintiff was necessary to meet the "case or controversy" requirement, and as to plaintiff David Ourlicht, the district court was able to distinguish *Lyons*; significantly, unlike Lyons's single chokehold experience, plaintiff Ourlicht had been stopped three times in 2008 and once after the lawsuit was filed in 2010, and thus recurring injury was not "speculative." The court also distinguished the 10 deaths attributed to the LAPD's chokehold policy from the NYPD's 2.8 million stops over 6 years, of which at least 60,000 were unconstitutional (30 facially unconstitutional stops a day). The court also noted that Mr. Ourlicht was stopped while just going about his day — on the sidewalk, in a park, getting into a car — and thus unlike Lyons did not need to disobey the law to suffer a recurrent injury. *See Floyd v. City of New York*, 283 F.R.D. 153, 169-70 (S.D.N.Y. 2012) (finding New York City liable under § 1983 for NYPD's racially motivated stop-and-frisk policies that violated plaintiff's Fourteenth and Fifth Amendment rights).

Floyd was settled before the Second Circuit was called on to pass on the case's merits. Do you think the district court's standing decision would have held up on appeal?

4. Note that liability under *Monell* was also a hotly litigated issue in *Floyd*. The Court notes in its executive summary that the plaintiffs established "deliberate indifference" under *Monell* and *Harris* through a combination of a report from the attorney general's office that put the city on notice of illegal stop and frisks, widespread pressure by supervisors to increase officers' number of stops, poor training of officers on performing and documenting stops, and failure to discipline officers for improper stops.

How do you think the plaintiffs were able to use the discovery process and other investigative means to put together the type of factual record necessary to support these conclusions?

5. The district court found an equal protection violation based on the NYPD's admitted but unwritten policy to target for stops "the right people," who were young Black and Hispanic men based on their prevalence in local criminal complaints.

Is it a defense that the officers honestly believed, based on their own experiences, that young Black and Hispanic men were more likely to be carrying guns than whites?

6. The merits of Judge Scheindlin's decision never made it to the Second Circuit. William DiBlasio was elected mayor in 2012 and the case was settled, with reforms implemented. The case was reassigned to another judge after Judge Scheindlin made statements at a hearing in a related case and in media interviews that caused the Second Circuit to conclude that the "appearance of impartiality" had been compromised such that "reassignment is advisable to preserve the appearance of justice." *Ligon v. City of New York*, 736 F.3d 118, 129 (2d Cir. 2013). And that didn't end the legal drama either. Several police unions attempted to intervene in the case to prevent the settlement, which required another trip to the Second Circuit affirming the denial of their intervention motion. *Floyd v. City of New York*, 770 F.3d 1051, 1056 (2d Cir. 2014).

C. QUALIFIED IMMUNITY

The next set of cases considers the Supreme Court's creation of a doctrine of qualified immunity to protect state and federal public official defendants, including police officers, from suit and liability under both § 1983 and in "*Bivens* actions." The doctrine seemed benign in its original incarnation but eventually became an unruly beast, cutting potentially meritorious lawsuits off at their knees and developing a strange, symbiotic relationship with traditional procedural rules as the Supreme Court took increasingly more extreme measures to protect individual police officers and other public officials from liability and even from litigation.

Pierson v. Ray

386 U.S. 547 (1967)

Mr. Chief Justice Warren delivered the opinion of Court.

These cases present issues involving the liability of local police officers and judges under s 1 of the Civil Rights Act of 1871, now 42 U.S.C. s 1983. Petitioners in No. 79 were members of a group of 15 white and Negro Episcopal clergymen who attempted to use segregated facilities at an interstate bus terminal in Jackson, Mississippi, in 1961. They were arrested by respondents Ray, Griffith, and Nichols, policemen of the City of Jackson, and charged with violating s 2087.5 of the Mississippi Code, which makes guilty of a misdemeanor anyone who congregates with others in a public place under circumstances such that a breach of the peace may be occasioned thereby, and refuses to move on when ordered to do so by a police officer. Petitioners waived a jury trial and were convicted of the offense by respondent Spencer, a municipal police justice. They were each given the maximum sentence of four months in jail and a fine of $200. On appeal petitioner Jones was accorded a trial de novo in the County Court, and after the city produced its evidence the court granted his motion for a directed verdict. The cases against the other petitioners were then dropped.

Having been vindicated in the County Court, petitioners brought this action for damages in the United States District Court for the Southern District of Mississippi, Jackson Division, alleging that respondents had violated s 1983, supra, and that respondents were liable at common law for false arrest and imprisonment. A jury returned verdicts for respondents on both counts. On appeal, the Court of Appeals for the Fifth Circuit held that respondent Spencer was immune from liability under both s 1983 and the common law of Mississippi for acts committed within his judicial jurisdiction. As to the police officers, the court noted that s 2087.5 of the Mississippi Code was held unconstitutional as applied to similar facts in *Thomas v. Mississippi*. Although Thomas was decided years after the arrest involved in this trial, the court held that the policemen would be liable in a suit under s 1983 for an unconstitutional arrest even if they acted in good faith and with probable cause in making an arrest under a state statute not yet held invalid. The court believed that this stern result was required by *Monroe v. Pape* (1961). Under the count based on the common law of Mississippi, however, it held that the policemen would not be liable if they had probable cause to believe that the statute had been violated, because Mississippi law does not require police officers to predict at their peril which state laws are constitutional and which are not. Apparently dismissing the common-law claim, the Court of Appeals reversed and remanded for a new trial on the s 1983 claim against the police officers because defense counsel had been allowed to cross-examine the ministers on various irrelevant and prejudicial matters, particularly including an alleged convergence of their views on racial justice with those of the Communist Party. At the new trial, however, the court held that the ministers could not recover if it were proved that they went to Mississippi anticipating that they would be illegally arrested because such action would constitute consent to the arrest under the principle of volenti non fit injuria, he who consents to a wrong cannot be injured.

We granted certiorari in No. 79 to consider whether a local judge is liable for damages under s 1983 for an unconstitutional conviction and whether the ministers should be denied recovery against the police officers if they acted with the anticipation that they would be illegally arrested. We also granted the police officers' petition in No. 94 to determine if the Court of Appeals correctly held that they could not assert the defense of good faith and probable cause to an action under s 1983 for unconstitutional arrest.

The evidence at the federal trial showed that petitioners and other Negro and white Episcopal clergymen undertook a "prayer pilgrimage" in 1961 from New Orleans to Detroit. The purpose of the pilgrimage was to visit church institutions and other places in the North and South to promote racial equality and integration, and, finally, to report to a church convention in Detroit. Letters from the leader of the group to its members indicate that the clergymen intended from the beginning to go to Jackson and attempt to use segregated facilities at the bus terminal there, and that they fully expected to be arrested for doing so. The group made plans based on the assumption that they would be arrested if they attempted peacefully to exercise their right as interstate travelers to use the waiting rooms and other facilities at the bus terminal, and the letters discussed arrangements for bail and other matters relevant to arrests.

The ministers stayed one night in Jackson, and went to the bus terminal the next morning to depart for Chattanooga, Tennessee. They entered the waiting room, disobeying a sign at the entrance that announced "White Waiting Room Only— By Order of the Police Department." They then turned to enter the small terminal restaurant but were stopped by two Jackson police officers, respondents Griffith and Nichols, who had been awaiting their arrival and who ordered them to "move on." The ministers replied that they wanted to eat and refused to move on. Respondent Ray, then a police captain and now the deputy chief of police, arrived a few minutes later. The ministers were placed under arrest and taken to the jail.

All witnesses including the police officers agreed that the ministers entered the waiting room peacefully and engaged in no boisterous or objectionable conduct while in the "White

Only" area. There was conflicting testimony on the number of bystanders present and their behavior. Petitioners testified that there was no crowd at the station, that no one followed them into the waiting room, and that no one uttered threatening words or made threatening gestures. The police testified that some 25 to 30 persons followed the ministers into the terminal, that persons in the crowd were in a very dissatisfied and ugly mood, and that they were mumbling and making unspecified threatening gestures. The police did not describe any specific threatening incidents, and testified that they took no action against any persons in the crowd who were threatening violence because they "had determined that the ministers was the cause of the violence if any might occur," although the ministers were concededly orderly and polite and the police did not claim that it was beyond their power to control the allegedly disorderly crowd. The arrests and convictions were followed by this lawsuit.

We find no difficulty in agreeing with the Court of Appeals that Judge Spencer is immune from liability for damages for his role in these convictions. The record is barren of any proof or specific allegation that Judge Spencer played any role in these arrests and convictions other than to adjudge petitioners guilty when their cases came before his court. Few doctrines were more solidly established at common law than the immunity of judges from liability for damages for acts committed within their judicial jurisdiction, as this Court recognized when it adopted the doctrine, in *Bradley v. Fisher* (1872). This immunity applies even when the judge is accused of acting maliciously and corruptly, and it "is not for the protection or benefit of a malicious or corrupt judge, but for the benefit of the public, whose interest it is that the judges should be at liberty to exercise their functions with independence and without fear of consequences." It is a judge's duty to decide all cases within his jurisdiction that are brought before him, including controversial cases that arouse the most intense feelings in the litigants. His errors may be corrected on appeal, but he should not have to fear that unsatisfied litigants may hound him with litigation charging malice or corruption. Imposing such a burden on judges would contribute not to principled and fearless decisionmaking but to intimidation.

We do not believe that this settled principle of law was abolished by s 1983, which makes liable "every person" who under color of law deprives another person of his civil rights. The legislative record gives no clear indication that Congress meant to abolish wholesale all common-law immunities. Accordingly, this Court held in *Tenney v. Brandhove* (1951), that the immunity of legislators for acts within the legislative role was not abolished. The immunity of judges for acts within the judicial role is equally well established, and we presume that Congress would have specifically so provided had it wished to abolish the doctrine.

The common law has never granted police officers an absolute and unqualified immunity, and the officers in this case do not claim that they are entitled to one. Their claim is rather that they should not be liable if they acted in good faith and with probable cause in making an arrest under a statute that they believed to be valid. Under the prevailing view in this country a peace officer who arrests someone with probable cause is not liable for false arrest simply because the innocence of the suspect is later proved. Restatement, Second, Torts s 121 (1965); 1 Harper & James, The Law of Torts s 3.18, at 277-278 (1956); *State of Missouri ex rel. and to Use of, Ward v. Fidelity & Deposit Co. of Maryland* (C.A. 8th Cir. 1950). A policeman's lot is not so unhappy that he must choose between being charged with dereliction of duty if he does not arrest when he has probable cause, and being mulcted in damages if he does. Although the matter is not entirely free from doubt, the same consideration would seem to require excusing him from liability for acting under a statute that he reasonably believed to be valid but that was later held unconstitutional on its face or as applied.

The Court of Appeals held that the officers had such a limited privilege under the common law of Mississippi, and indicated that it would have recognized a similar privilege under s 1983 except that it felt compelled to hold otherwise by our decision in *Monroe v. Pape*. *Monroe v. Pape* presented no question of immunity, however, and none was decided. The complaint in that case alleged that "13 Chicago police officers broke into petitioners' home in the early morning, routed them from bed, made them stand naked in the living room, and ransacked every room, emptying drawers and ripping mattress covers. It further allege(d) that Mr. Monroe was then taken to the police station and detained on 'open' charges for 10 hours, while he was interrogated about a two-day-old murder, that he was not taken before a magistrate, though one was accessible, that he was not permitted to call his family or attorney, that he was subsequently released without criminal charges being preferred against him." The police officers did not choose to go to trial and defend the case on the hope that they could convince a jury that they believed in good faith that it was their duty to assault Monroe and his family in this manner. Instead, they sought dismissal of the complaint, contending principally that their activities were so plainly illegal under state law that they did not act "under color of any statute, ordinance, regulation, custom, or usage, of any State or Territory" as required by s 1983. In rejecting this argument we in no way intimated that the defense of good faith and probable cause was foreclosed by the statute. We also held that the complaint should not be dismissed for failure to state that the officers had "a specific intent to deprive a person of a federal right," but this holding, which related to requirements of pleading, carried no implications as to which defenses would be available to the police officers. As we went on to say in the same paragraph, s 1983 "should be read against the background of tort liability that makes a man responsible for the natural consequences of his actions." Part of the background of tort liability, in the case of police officers making an arrest, is the defense of good faith and probable cause.

We hold that the defense of good faith and probable cause, which the Court of Appeals found available to the officers in the common-law action for false arrest and imprisonment, is also available to them in the action under s 1983. This holding does not, however, mean that the count based thereon should be dismissed. The Court of Appeals ordered dismissal of the common-law count on the theory that the police officers were not required to predict our decision in *Thomas v. Mississippi*. We agree that a police officer is not charged with predicting the future course of constitutional law. But the petitioners in this case did not simply argue that they were arrested under a statute later held unconstitutional. They claimed and attempted to prove that the police officers arrested them solely for attempting to use the "White Only" waiting room, that no crowd was present, and that no one threatened violence or seemed about to cause a disturbance. The officers did not defend on the theory that they believed in good faith that it was constitutional to arrest the ministers solely for using the waiting room. Rather, they claimed and attempted to prove that they did not arrest the ministers for the purpose of preserving the custom of segregation in Mississippi, but solely for the purpose of preventing violence. They testified, in contradiction to the ministers, that a crowd gathered and that imminent violence was likely. If the jury believed the testimony of the officers and disbelieved that of the ministers, and if the jury found that the officers reasonably believed in good faith that the arrest was constitutional, then a verdict for the officers would follow even though the arrest was in fact unconstitutional. The jury did resolve the factual issues in favor of the officers but, for reasons previously stated, its verdict was influenced by irrelevant and prejudicial evidence. Accordingly, the case must be remanded to the trial court for a new trial.

It is necessary to decide what importance should be given at the new trial to the substantially undisputed fact that the petitioners went to Jackson expecting to be illegally arrested. We do not agree with the Court of Appeals that they somehow consented to the arrest because of their anticipation that they would be illegally arrested, even assuming that they went to the Jackson bus terminal for the sole purpose of testing their rights to unsegregated public accommodations. The case contains no proof or allegation that they in any way tricked or goaded the officers into arresting them. The petitioners had the right to use the waiting room of the

Jackson bus terminal, and their deliberate exercise of that right in a peaceful, orderly, and inoffensive manner does not disqualify them from seeking damages under s 1983.

The judgment of the Court of Appeals is affirmed in part and reversed in part, and the cases are remanded for further proceedings consistent with this opinion.

NOTES AND QUESTIONS

1. Note the materials the Court purports to rely on as a basis for finding immunity for the police officers: two treatises on tort law and a federal case applying Missouri law. Would the legislative history of § 1983—discussed at length in *Monroe v. Pape* and relied on by Justice Douglas in his dissent here on judicial immunity—be informative? Note also the Court's reference to "the background of tort liability," which it claims to have relied on before in *Monroe* and again here in finding police officer immunity.

Shouldn't this "background of tort liability" have led the Court to adopt the well-settled "background" principles of respondeat superior liability when that issue came up in *Monell* or other cases? *See supra.*

And wouldn't the operative "background" immunity question have required an analysis of the extent of immunity for police officers in 1871, when § 1983 was enacted?

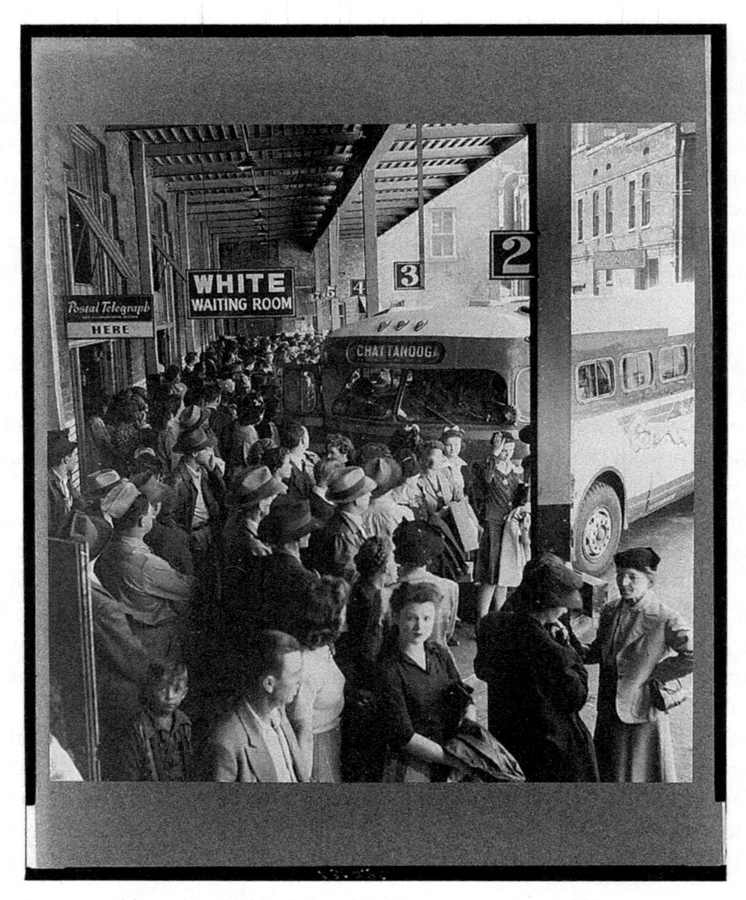

Segregated bus terminal in Memphis, Tennessee, circa 1943

2. The plaintiffs' theory of liability for the police officers at trial was that the officers arrested them for attempting to use the "whites only" waiting room and not because they believed the plaintiffs were violating the Mississippi ordinance under which they were charged. Is it relevant to the officers' defense in the retrial that 14 of the 15 plaintiffs pleaded guilty to the charges under the ordinance? Are the reasons why the charges were dropped relevant in the retrial? Is it relevant whether a prosecutor was involved in deciding whether to make and/or drop the charges?

3. The Court does not state definitively whether the "good faith and probable cause" immunity defense that it adopts applies outside of the "false arrest" variety of § 1983 violations, although it implies that this might have been available to the officers in *Monroe v. Pape*. How would the defense work in the Fourth Amendment context? For example, how would it have worked in *Monroe* itself?

How would the defense work in a Fifth Amendment context where a plaintiff is challenging police officers' use of coercive interrogation techniques?

4. The Mississippi ordinance at issue here was, as the Court notes, held unconstitutional in 1965, four years after the charges here were made. But that decision, *Thomas v. Mississippi*, 380 U.S. 524 (1965), is a per curiam opinion containing one sentence: "The petition for writ of certiorari is granted and the judgments are reversed," followed by a cite to *Boynton v. Virginia*, 364 U.S. 454 (1960). Does this suggest that the unconstitutionality of the Mississippi ordinance should have been readily apparent to the officers and to Judge Spencer as of when *Boynton* was decided, which was before the events here took place? Does the scope of the judicial immunity recognized by the Court cover judicial enforcement of a statute that a judge knew or should have known was unconstitutional? Would it insulate from liability a judge who judicially enforced a statute even after that very statute was declared unconstitutional by a higher court?

Justice Douglas dissents from the Court's holding on judicial immunity based on language in the legislative history of § 1983 indicating that Congress was concerned about state judges being involved in civil rights violations. The Court would later hold that the doctrine of absolute judicial immunity should not mean that the "federal law will exercise no deterrent effect" on lawless judges, whose immunity would not protect them from criminal exposure under 18 U.S.C. § 242, which criminalizes deprivations of rights "under color of law." *O'Shea v. Littleton*, 414 U.S. 488, 503 (1974).

5. Note that the only policy reason identified by the Court as supporting immunity for police officers is to prevent them from "being mulcted in damages." And although the Court does use the word "immunity," it leaves no doubt that "good faith and probable cause" is a defense that police officers must assert and prove. Indeed, the Court remands for a new trial where the officers will be able to use the defense.

The Supreme Court would not return to the issue of police officer immunity under § 1983 for over two decades. In the meantime, amid the tumult of the war in Vietnam and the Nixon Administration, several questions of immunity for other executive branch personnel came before the Court. In *Scheuer v. Rhodes*, 416 U.S. 232 (1974), the estates of students slain by the Ohio National Guard in the 1970 massacre at Kent State University brought a § 1983 action against Ohio governor James Rhodes and his top aides. The Court rejected the defendants' assertion of absolute immunity and held that they were sufficiently protected by a qualified immunity. *Id.* at 247-48. In *Butz v. Economou*, 438 U.S. 478 (1978), similarly, the Court rejected the absolute immunity claims of Department of Agriculture officials who allegedly commenced an administrative proceeding against a plaintiff in retaliation for his criticism of the agency. The Court found that qualified immunity was sufficient protection, and again expressed confidence in district judges' ability to use the Federal Rules of Civil Procedure to protect defendants against frivolous lawsuits. Both cases mentioned *Pierson v. Ray* only in passing, perhaps because the duties of police officers were so different than those of the defendants in these cases.

These cases set the stage for the next case, also arising out of alleged misconduct by officials in the Nixon Administration, and also resting on allegations of retaliation.

Harlow v. Fitzgerald

457 U.S. 800 (1982)

Justice Powell delivered the opinion of the Court.

The issue in this case is the scope of the immunity available to the senior aides and advisers of the President of the United States in a suit for damages based upon their official acts.

I

In this suit for civil damages petitioners Bryce Harlow and Alexander Butterfield are alleged to have participated in a conspiracy to violate the constitutional and statutory rights of the respondent A. Ernest Fitzgerald. Respondent avers that petitioners entered the conspiracy in their capacities as senior White House aides to former President Richard M. Nixon. As the alleged conspiracy is the same as that involved in *Nixon v. Fitzgerald*, the facts need not be repeated in detail.

Respondent claims that Harlow joined the conspiracy in his role as the Presidential aide principally responsible for congressional relations. At the conclusion of discovery the supporting evidence remained inferential. As evidence of Harlow's conspiratorial activity respondent relies heavily on a series of conversations in which Harlow discussed Fitzgerald's dismissal with Air Force Secretary Robert Seamans. The other evidence most supportive of Fitzgerald's claims consists of a recorded conversation in which the President later voiced a tentative recollection that Harlow was "all for canning" Fitzgerald.

Disputing Fitzgerald's contentions, Harlow argues that exhaustive discovery has adduced no direct evidence of his involvement in any wrongful activity. He avers that Secretary Seamans advised him that considerations of efficiency required Fitzgerald's removal by a reduction in force, despite anticipated adverse congressional reaction. Harlow asserts he had no reason to believe that a conspiracy existed. He contends that he took all his actions in good faith.

Petitioner Butterfield also is alleged to have entered the conspiracy not later than May 1969. Employed as Deputy Assistant to the President and Deputy Chief of Staff to H. R. Haldeman, Butterfield circulated a White House memorandum in that month in which he claimed to have learned that Fitzgerald planned to "blow the whistle" on some "shoddy purchasing practices" by exposing these practices to public view. Fitzgerald characterizes this memorandum as evidence that Butterfield had commenced efforts to secure Fitzgerald's retaliatory dismissal. As evidence that Butterfield participated in the conspiracy to conceal his unlawful discharge and prevent his reemployment, Fitzgerald cites communications between Butterfield and Haldeman in December 1969 and January 1970. After the President had promised at a press conference to inquire into Fitzgerald's dismissal, Haldeman solicited Butterfield's recommendations. In a subsequent memorandum emphasizing the importance of "loyalty," Butterfield counseled against offering Fitzgerald another job in the administration at that time.

For his part, Butterfield denies that he was involved in any decision concerning Fitzgerald's employment status until Haldeman sought his advice in December 1969—more than a month after Fitzgerald's termination had been scheduled and announced publicly by the Air Force. Butterfield states that he never communicated his views about Fitzgerald to any official of the Defense Department. He argues generally that nearly eight years of discovery have failed to turn up any evidence that he caused injury to Fitzgerald.

Together with their codefendant Richard Nixon, petitioners Harlow and Butterfield moved for summary judgment on February 12, 1980. In denying the motion the District Court upheld the legal sufficiency of Fitzgerald's *Bivens* claim under the First Amendment and his "inferred" statutory causes of action under 5 U.S.C. § 7211 and 18 U.S.C. § 1505. The court found that genuine issues of disputed fact remained for resolution at trial. It also ruled that petitioners were not entitled to absolute immunity.

Independently of former President Nixon, petitioners invoked the collateral order doctrine and appealed the denial of their immunity defense to the Court of Appeals for the District of Columbia Circuit. The Court of Appeals dismissed the appeal without opinion. Never having determined the immunity available to the senior aides and advisers of the President of the United States, we granted certiorari.

As we reiterated today in *Nixon v. Fitzgerald*, our decisions consistently have held that government officials are entitled to some form of immunity from suits for damages. As recognized at common law, public officers require this protection to shield them from undue interference with their duties and from potentially disabling threats of liability.

Our decisions have recognized immunity defenses of two kinds. For officials whose special functions or constitutional status requires complete protection from suit, we have recognized the defense of "absolute immunity." The absolute immunity of legislators, in their legislative functions, and of judges, in their judicial functions, now is well settled. Our decisions also have extended absolute immunity to certain officials of the Executive Branch. These include prosecutors and similar officials, executive officers engaged in adjudicative functions and the President of the United States.

For executive officials in general, however, our cases make plain that qualified immunity represents the norm. Without discounting the adverse consequences of denying high officials an absolute immunity from private lawsuits alleging constitutional violations, we emphasized our expectation that insubstantial suits need not proceed to trial:

> Insubstantial lawsuits can be quickly terminated by federal courts alert to the possibilities of artful pleading. Unless the complaint states a compensable claim for relief . . ., it should not survive a motion to dismiss. Moreover, the Court recognized in *Scheuer* that damages suits concerning constitutional violations need not proceed to trial, but can be terminated on a properly supported motion for summary judgment based on the defense of immunity. . . . In responding to such a motion, plaintiffs may not play dog in the manger; and firm application of the Federal Rules of Civil Procedure will ensure that federal officials are not harassed by frivolous lawsuits.

Butz continued to acknowledge that the special functions of some officials might require absolute immunity. But the Court held that "federal officials who seek absolute exemption from personal liability for unconstitutional conduct must bear the burden of showing that public policy requires an exemption of that scope." This we reaffirmed today in *Nixon v. Fitzgerald.*

• • •

Even if they cannot establish that their official functions require absolute immunity, petitioners assert that public policy at least mandates an application of the qualified immunity standard that would permit the defeat of insubstantial claims without resort to trial. We agree.

The resolution of immunity questions inherently requires a balance between the evils inevitable in any available alternative. In situations of abuse of office, an action for damages may offer the only realistic avenue for vindication of constitutional guarantees. It is this recognition that has required the denial of absolute immunity to most public officers. At the same time, however, it cannot be disputed seriously that claims frequently run against the innocent as well as the guilty—at a cost not only to the defendant officials, but to society as a whole. These social costs include the expenses of litigation, the diversion of official energy from pressing public issues, and the deterrence of able citizens from acceptance of public office. Finally, there is the danger that fear of being sued will "dampen the ardor of all but the most resolute, or the most irresponsible [public officials], in the unflinching discharge of their duties."

In identifying qualified immunity as the best attainable accommodation of competing values, we relied on the assumption that this standard would permit "[i]nsubstantial lawsuits [to] be quickly terminated." Yet petitioners advance persuasive arguments that the dismissal of insubstantial lawsuits without trial—a factor presupposed in the balance of competing interests struck by our prior cases—requires an adjustment of the "good faith" standard established by our decisions.

Qualified or "good faith" immunity is an affirmative defense that must be pleaded by a defendant official. Decisions of this Court have established that the "good faith" defense has both an "objective" and a "subjective" aspect. The objective element involves a presumptive knowledge of and respect for "basic, unquestioned constitutional rights." The subjective component refers to "permissible intentions." Characteristically the Court has defined these elements by identifying the circumstances in which qualified immunity would not be available. Referring both to the objective and subjective elements, we have held that qualified immunity would be defeated if an official "knew or reasonably should have known that the action he took within his sphere of official responsibility would violate the constitutional rights of the [plaintiff], or if he took the action with the malicious intention to cause a deprivation of constitutional rights or other injury. . . ."

The subjective element of the good-faith defense frequently has proved incompatible with our admonition in *Butz* that insubstantial claims should not proceed to trial. Rule 56 of the Federal Rules of Civil Procedure provides that disputed questions of fact ordinarily may not be decided on motions for summary judgment. And an official's subjective good faith has been considered to be a question of fact that some courts have regarded as inherently requiring resolution by a jury.

In the context of *Butz*' attempted balancing of competing values, it now is clear that substantial costs attend the litigation of the subjective good faith of government officials. Not only are there the general costs of subjecting officials to the risks of trial—distraction of officials from their governmental duties, inhibition of discretionary action, and deterrence of able people from public service. There are special costs to "subjective" inquiries of this kind. Immunity generally is available only to officials performing discretionary functions. In contrast with the thought processes accompanying "ministerial" tasks, the judgments surrounding discretionary action almost inevitably are influenced by the decisionmaker's experiences, values, and emotions. These variables explain in part why questions of subjective intent so rarely can be decided by summary judgment. Yet they also frame a background in which there often is no clear end to the relevant evidence. Judicial inquiry into subjective motivation therefore may entail broad-ranging discovery and the deposing of numerous persons, including an official's professional colleagues. Inquiries of this kind can be peculiarly disruptive of effective government.

Consistently with the balance at which we aimed in *Butz*, we conclude today that bare allegations of malice should not suffice to subject government officials either to the costs of trial or to the burdens of broad-reaching discovery. We therefore hold that government officials performing discretionary functions generally are shielded from liability for civil damages insofar as their conduct does not violate clearly established statutory or constitutional rights of which a reasonable person would have known.

Reliance on the objective reasonableness of an official's conduct, as measured by reference to clearly established law, should avoid excessive disruption of government and permit the resolution of many insubstantial claims on summary judgment. On summary judgment, the judge appropriately may determine, not only the currently applicable law, but whether that law was clearly established at the time an action occurred. If the law at that time was not clearly established, an official could not reasonably be expected to anticipate subsequent legal developments, nor could he fairly be said to "know" that the law forbade conduct not previously identified as unlawful. Until this threshold immunity question is resolved, discovery should not be allowed. If the law was clearly established, the immunity defense ordinarily should fail, since a reasonably competent public official should know the law governing his conduct. Nevertheless, if the official pleading the defense claims extraordinary circumstances and can prove that he neither knew nor should have known of the relevant legal standard, the defense should be sustained. But again, the defense would turn primarily on objective factors.

By defining the limits of qualified immunity essentially in objective terms, we provide no license to lawless conduct. The public interest in deterrence of unlawful conduct and in compensation of victims remains protected by a test that focuses on the objective legal reasonableness of an official's acts. Where an official could be expected to know that certain conduct would violate statutory or constitutional rights, he should be made to hesitate; and a person who suffers injury caused by such conduct may have a cause of action. But where an official's duties legitimately require action in which clearly established rights are not implicated, the public interest may be better served by action taken "with independence and without fear of consequences." *Pierson v. Ray* (1967).

In this case petitioners have asked us to hold that the respondent's pretrial showings were insufficient to survive their motion for summary judgment. We think it appropriate, however, to remand the case to the District Court for its reconsideration of this issue in light of this opinion. The trial court is more familiar with the record so far developed and also is better situated to make any such further findings as may be necessary.

The judgment of the Court of Appeals is vacated, and the case is remanded for further action consistent with this opinion.

NOTES AND QUESTIONS

1. This case has an abstract quality about it. The underlying legal claim is barely explained; all that the Court seems to want the reader to know about the lawsuit is that it was "insubstantial" and that defendant's summary judgment motion nonetheless was denied, perhaps because of disputed factual issues about defendant's state of mind (although that's not clear either). The companion lawsuit of *Nixon v. Fitzgerald*, 457 U.S. 731 (1982), explains that the plaintiff, a management analyst in the Department of the Air Force, was allegedly retaliated against by President Nixon and other executive officials after he testified before a congressional subcommittee about enormous cost overruns on a military air transport project. His discharge sufficiently concerned Congress that it held hearings about his discharge after it occurred.

Might there be better candidates than *Harlow* for a case in which to make out of whole cloth a new standard for qualified immunity premised on the protection of officials from frivolous lawsuits?

2. The Court quite candidly admits that it is changing the substantive rules of qualified immunity in order to permit defendants to more easily obtain summary judgment under Fed. R. Civ. P. 56. In doing so, the Court—again candidly—relies on nothing other than pure policy reasons, costs to "society as a whole," that support a more robust immunity. The Court identifies four specific costs engendered by "insubstantial" lawsuits "against the innocent": the diversion of executive energy from public affairs, the expense of litigation, the deterrence of persons from public service, and diminished aggressiveness by public officials.

Which of these social costs seem most persuasive? Least persuasive?

Why do you think the Court doesn't explicitly mention liability exposure as a social cost? Is it implicit in any of the others? Recall the Court's explicit reference in *Pierson* to the possibility of a police officer being "mulcted in damages" absent immunity.

3. The Court's overarching concern is with the "subjective good faith" element of the existing qualified immunity standard. Due to the aforementioned "social costs," and the concerns about allowing for summary judgment, the Court simply eliminates that component and redefines qualified immunity to exist based solely on the "objective reasonableness" of the official's conduct, good faith or not.

Could the goal have been accomplished by simply tweaking rather than eliminating the intent element? If so, how?

4. Summing up, the Court concludes that "bare allegations of malice should not suffice to subject government officials to either the costs of trial or to the burdens of far-reaching discovery." This formulation of the holding reflects at least one and probably two misunderstandings about civil procedure, at least based on civil procedure as you have learned it. What are they?

5. *Harlow* is a "*Bivens* action," inasmuch as the plaintiff's claims are levied against federal officials and not against state officials under § 1983. Should the Court have more latitude in determining the metes and bounds of an immunity defense to a *Bivens* claim than it does to a claim brought under § 1983? Why or why not?

In a footnote the Court notes that in *Butz v. Economou* it had previously held that it would be "untenable to draw a distinction for purposes of immunity law between suits brought against state officials under § 1983 and suits brought directly under the Constitution against federal officials." 438 U.S. at 504. Why would such a result be untenable?

Alexander Butterfield

6. Is it clear that the holding of *Harlow*—that officials enjoy immunity insofar as their conduct "does not violate clearly established statutory or constitutional rights of which a reasonable person would have known"—applies to police officers? Note that *Pierson v. Ray* is only mentioned once at the tail end of the opinion and very much in passing.

How would the *Harlow* immunity formulation apply to the police officers in *Pierson*?

7. One of Bryce Harlow's co-defendants was Alexander Butterfield, deputy assistant to President Richard Nixon. Butterfield transformed the Watergate investigation into the Nixon White House when he acknowledged in Senate testimony in July 1973 that White House communications involving President Nixon were routinely tape-recorded. Butterfield was never charged with any wrongdoing in connection with the Watergate scandal.

The Court returned to the issue of police officer immunity under § 1983 in the next case, where plaintiffs alleged that the defendant officers violated the statute in connection with submitting affidavits to a magistrate upon which arrest warrants were based.

Malley v. Briggs
475 U.S. 335 (1986)

Justice White delivered the opinion of the Court.

This case presents the question of the degree of immunity accorded a defendant police officer in a damages action under 42 U.S.C. § 1983 when it is alleged that the officer caused the plaintiffs to be unconstitutionally arrested by presenting a judge with a complaint and a supporting affidavit which failed to establish probable cause.

In December 1980, the Rhode Island State Police were conducting a court-authorized wiretap on the telephone of one Paul Driscoll, an acquaintance of respondents' daughter. On December 20, the police intercepted a call to Driscoll from an unknown individual who identified himself as "Dr. Shogun." The police logsheet summarizes the call as follows: "General conversation re. a party they went to last night . . . caller says I can't believe I was token [sic] in front of Jimmy Briggs—caller states he passed it to Louisa . . . Paul says Nancy was sitting in his lap rolling her thing."

Petitioner Edward Malley (hereafter petitioner) was the Rhode Island state trooper in charge of the investigation of Driscoll. After reviewing the logsheet for December 20, petitioner decided that the call from "Dr. Shogun" was incriminating, because in drug parlance "toking" means smoking marihuana and "rolling her thing" refers to rolling a marihuana cigarette. Petitioner also concluded that another call monitored the same day showed that the party discussed by Driscoll and "Dr. Shogun" took place at respondents' house. On the basis of these two calls, petitioner drew up felony complaints charging that respondents and Paul Driscoll "did unlawfully conspire to violate the uniform controlled substance act of the State of Rhode Island by having [marihuana] in their possession. . . ." These complaints were presented to a State District Court Judge in February 1981, after the wiretap of Driscoll's phone had been terminated. Accompanying the complaints were unsigned warrants for each respondent's arrest, and supporting affidavits describing the two intercepted calls and petitioner's interpretation of them. The judge signed warrants for the arrest of respondents and 20 other individuals charged by petitioner as a result of information gathered through the wiretap.

Respondents were arrested at their home shortly before six o'clock on the morning of March 19, 1981. They were taken to a police station, booked, held for several hours, arraigned, and released. Local and statewide newspapers published the fact that respondents, who are prominent members of their community, had been arrested and charged with drug possession. The charges against respondents were subsequently dropped when the grand jury to which the case was presented did not return an indictment.

Respondents brought an action under 42 U.S.C. § 1983 in the United States District Court for the District of Rhode Island charging, inter alia, that petitioner, in applying for warrants for their arrest, violated their rights under the Fourth and Fourteenth Amendments. The case was tried to a jury, and at the close of respondents' evidence, petitioner moved for and was granted a directed verdict. The District Court's primary justification for directing a verdict was that the act of the judge in issuing the arrest warrants for respondents broke the causal chain between petitioner's filing of a complaint and respondents' arrest. The court also stated that an officer who believes that the facts stated in his affidavit are true and who submits them to a neutral magistrate may thereby be entitled to immunity under the "objective reasonableness" standard of *Harlow v. Fitzgerald* (1982).

The United States Court of Appeals for the First Circuit reversed, holding that an officer who seeks an arrest warrant by submitting a complaint and supporting affidavit to a judge is not entitled to immunity unless the officer has an objectively reasonable basis for believing that the facts alleged in his affidavit are sufficient to establish probable cause. We granted certiorari in order to review the First Circuit's application of the "objective reasonableness" standard in this context. We affirm.

II

Petitioner urges reversal on two grounds: first, that in this context, he is absolutely immune from liability for damages; second, that he is at least entitled to qualified immunity in this case. We reject both propositions and address first the absolute immunity issue.

A

Our general approach to questions of immunity under § 1983 is by now well established. Although the statute on its face admits of no immunities, we have read it "in harmony with general principles of tort immunities and defenses rather than in derogation of them." Our initial inquiry is whether an official claiming immunity under § 1983 can point to a common-law counterpart to the privilege he asserts. If "an official was accorded immunity from tort actions at common law when the Civil Rights Act was enacted in 1871, the Court next considers whether § 1983's history or purposes nonetheless counsel against recognizing the same immunity in § 1983 actions." Thus, while we look to the common law for guidance, we do not assume that Congress intended to incorporate every common-law immunity into § 1983 in unaltered form.

Our cases also make plain that "[f]or executive officers in general, . . . qualified immunity represents the norm." Like federal officers, state officers who "seek absolute exemption from personal liability for unconstitutional conduct must bear the burden of showing that public policy requires an exemption of that scope."

B

Although we have previously held that police officers sued under § 1983 for false arrest are qualifiedly immune, *Pierson*, petitioner urges that he should be absolutely immune because his function in seeking an arrest warrant was similar to that of a complaining witness. The difficulty with this submission is that complaining witnesses were not absolutely immune at common law. In 1871, the generally accepted rule was that one who procured the issuance of an arrest warrant by submitting a complaint could be held liable if the complaint was made maliciously and without probable cause. Given malice and the lack of probable cause, the complainant enjoyed no immunity. The common law thus affords no support for petitioner.

Nor are we moved by petitioner's argument that policy considerations require absolute immunity for the officer applying for a warrant. As the qualified immunity defense has evolved, it provides ample protection to all but the plainly incompetent or those who knowingly violate the law. At common law, in cases where probable cause to arrest was lacking, a complaining witness' immunity turned on the issue of malice, which was a jury question. Under the *Harlow* standard, on the other hand, an allegation of malice is not sufficient to defeat immunity if the defendant acted in an objectively reasonable manner. The *Harlow* standard is specifically designed to "avoid excessive disruption of government and permit the resolution of many insubstantial claims on summary judgment," and we believe it sufficiently serves this goal. Defendants will not be immune if, on an objective basis, it is obvious that no reasonably competent officer would have concluded that a warrant should issue; but if officers of reasonable competence could disagree on this issue, immunity should be recognized.

C

As an alternative ground for claiming absolute immunity, petitioner draws an analogy between an officer requesting a warrant and a prosecutor who asks a grand jury to indict a suspect. Like the prosecutor, petitioner argues, the officer must exercise a discretionary judgment based on the evidence before him, and like the prosecutor, the officer may not exercise his best judgment if the threat of retaliatory lawsuits hangs over him. Thus, petitioner urges us to read § 1983 as giving the officer the same absolute immunity enjoyed by the prosecutor.

We reemphasize that our role is to interpret the intent of Congress in enacting § 1983, not to make a freewheeling policy choice, and that we are guided in interpreting Congress' intent by the common-law tradition. In *Imbler, supra*, we concluded that at common law "[t]he general rule was, and is, that a prosecutor is absolutely immune from suit for malicious prosecution." We do not find a comparable tradition of absolute immunity for one whose complaint causes a warrant to issue. While this observation may seem unresponsive to petitioner's policy argument, it is, we believe, an important guide to interpreting § 1983. Since the statute on its face does not provide for any immunities, we would be going far to read into it an absolute immunity for conduct which was only accorded qualified immunity in 1871.

Even were we to overlook the fact that petitioner is inviting us to expand what was a qualified immunity at common law into an absolute immunity, we would find his analogy between himself and a prosecutor untenable. We have interpreted § 1983 to give absolute immunity to functions "intimately associated with the judicial phase of the criminal process," not from an exaggerated esteem for those who perform these functions, and certainly not from a desire to shield abuses of office, but because any lesser degree of immunity could impair the judicial process itself. We intend no disrespect to the officer applying for a warrant by observing that his action, while a vital part of the administration of criminal justice, is further removed from the judicial phase of criminal proceedings than the act of a prosecutor in seeking an indictment. Furthermore, petitioner's analogy, while it has some force, does not take account of the fact that the prosecutor's act in seeking an indictment is but the first step in the process of seeking a conviction. Exposing the prosecutor to liability for the initial phase of his prosecutorial work could interfere with his exercise of independent judgment at every phase of his work, since the prosecutor might come to see later decisions in terms of their effect on his potential liability. Thus, we shield the prosecutor seeking an indictment because any lesser immunity could impair the performance of a central actor in the judicial process.

In the case of the officer applying for a warrant, it is our judgment that the judicial process will on the whole benefit from a rule of qualified rather than absolute immunity. We do not believe that the *Harlow* standard, which gives ample room for mistaken judgments, will frequently deter an officer from submitting an affidavit when probable cause to make an arrest is present. True, an officer who knows that objectively unreasonable decisions will be actionable may be motivated to reflect, before submitting a request for a warrant, upon whether he has a reasonable basis for believing that his affidavit establishes probable cause. But such reflection is desirable, because it reduces the likelihood that the officer's request for a warrant will be premature. Premature requests for warrants are at best a waste of judicial resources; at worst, they lead to premature arrests, which may injure the innocent or, by giving the basis for a suppression motion, benefit the guilty.

Furthermore, it would be incongruous to test police behavior by the "objective reasonableness" standard in a suppression hearing, while exempting police conduct in applying for an arrest or search warrant from any scrutiny whatsoever in a § 1983 damages action. While we believe the exclusionary rule serves a necessary purpose, it obviously does so at a considerable cost to society as a whole, because it excludes evidence probative of guilt. On the other hand, a damages remedy for an arrest following an objectively unreasonable request for a warrant imposes a cost directly on the officer responsible for the unreasonable request, without the side effect of hampering a criminal prosecution. Also, in the case of the § 1983 action, the likelihood is obviously greater than at the suppression hearing that the remedy is benefiting the victim of police misconduct one would think most deserving of a remedy—the person who in fact has done no wrong, and has been arrested for no reason, or a bad reason.

Accordingly, we hold that the same standard of objective reasonableness that we applied in the context of a suppression hearing in *Leon*, supra, defines the qualified immunity accorded an officer whose request for a warrant allegedly caused an unconstitutional arrest. Only where the warrant application is so lacking in indicia of probable cause as to render official belief in its existence unreasonable, will the shield of immunity be lost.

III

We also reject petitioner's argument that if an officer is entitled to only qualified immunity in cases like this, he is nevertheless shielded from damages liability because the act of applying for a warrant is per se objectively reasonable, provided that the officer believes that the facts alleged in his affidavit are true. Petitioner insists that he is entitled to rely on the judgment of a judicial officer in finding that probable cause exists and hence issuing the warrant. This view of objective reasonableness is at odds with our development of that concept in *Harlow* and *Leon*. In *Leon*, we stated that "our good-faith inquiry is confined to the objectively ascertainable question whether a reasonably well-trained officer would have known that the search was illegal despite the magistrate's authorization." The analogous question in this case is whether a reasonably well-trained officer in petitioner's position would have known that his affidavit failed to establish probable cause and that he should not have applied for the warrant. If such was the case, the officer's application for a warrant was not objectively reasonable, because it created the unnecessary danger of an unlawful arrest. It is true that in an ideal system an unreasonable request for a warrant would be harmless, because no judge would approve it. But ours is not an ideal system, and it is possible that a magistrate, working under docket pressures, will fail to perform as a magistrate should. We find it reasonable to require the officer applying for the warrant to minimize this danger by exercising reasonable professional judgment.

The judgment of the Court of Appeals is affirmed, and the case is remanded for further proceedings consistent with this opinion.

NOTES AND QUESTIONS

1. The Court acknowledges *Pierson v. Ray* but makes no effort to apply *Pierson*'s immunity formulation to the case at hand, treating the case as if it, at most, retains utility in the limited context of an allegedly false arrest. *Harlow* is the new sheriff in town; any doubt about whether *Harlow* applies to police officers is removed.

Is there an argument that the type of immunity *Harlow* recognized for senior executive branch officials is not necessarily appropriate for police officers in the field, whose day-to-day duties are much different than such executives?

2. In rejecting the defendant officer's claim for absolute immunity, the Court trumpets the virtues of qualified immunity under *Harlow*, as if to say "who needs absolute immunity when you've got qualified immunity under *Harlow*?" To put a bow on the point, the Court says that the qualified immunity defense under *Harlow* "provides ample protection to all but the plainly incompetent or those who knowingly violate the law."

Having said this, the Court affirms the First Circuit's reversal of the district court's granting of a directed verdict to the defendant police officer, impliedly finding that the jury could have found that the defendant was either "plainly incompetent" or "knowingly violated" the law.

Seriously: How should the district judge instruct the jury on defendant's qualified immunity defense?

3. *Malley* has an abstract air about it similar to *Harlow*. We know the following: the plaintiffs were arrested on marijuana charges on the basis of arrest warrants issued by a judge that were, in turn, based on complaints submitted by Officer Malley; plaintiffs' arrest received widespread press coverage; the charges were dropped after the grand jury (presumably applying the same probable cause standard as would be applicable to the arrest warrants) refused to indict plaintiffs. What we don't know, critically, is what the complaints submitted by Officer Malley *actually said*. We also aren't told anything about the evidence at the § 1983 trial.

The Court holds that the complaint and supplemental affidavit did not establish probable cause. Can you tell why from the opinion? Was it because the facts in the complaints were false or exaggerated (and the grand jury later found that this was the case)? Was it because the facts in the complaints were true but failed to rise to a sufficient level to establish probable cause? Was it because the officer failed to appreciate a relevant legal standard?

4. The district judge, in granting a directed verdict for Officer Malley, found that the state judge's issuance of the arrest warrants "broke the causal chain" between the officer's complaint and the plaintiffs' arrest. Is that necessarily the case? What is a scenario in which it would be the case?

5. In the interim between *Pierson* and *Harlow* the Court had held in *Imbler v. Pachtman*, 424 U.S. 409 (1976), that prosecutors were generally entitled to absolute immunity from suits under § 1983 when acting within the scope of their duties in initiating a prosecution. Isn't initiating a prosecution a fair description of what Trooper Malley did here? Why shouldn't he receive the same protection as a prosecutor? Suppose that an assistant district attorney had reviewed the complaints before they were presented to the judge. What immunity defenses would Trooper Malley and the ADA have in that scenario?

6. What do you make of the Court's comment, in rejecting defendant's argument for qualified immunity, that: "We reemphasize that our role is to interpret the intent of Congress in enacting § 1983, not to make a freewheeling policy choice, and that we are guided in interpreting Congress' intent by the common-law tradition."

7. Note that the result in *Malley* is a remand for a new trial where, presumably, the jury will decide the qualified immunity issue. This result was itself unremarkable at the time. But as Professor William Baude noted in 2018, in the 30 times the Supreme Court applied the *Harlow* objective reasonableness standard between 1982 and 2017, *Malley* is one of only four cases that counts as even an arguable victory for a plaintiff. William Baude, *Is Qualified Immunity Unlawful?*, 106 Calif. L. Rev. 45, 82-83 (2018).

Anderson v. Creighton

483 U.S. 635 (1987)

Justice Scalia delivered the opinion of the Court.

The question presented is whether a federal law enforcement officer who participates in a search that violates the Fourth Amendment may be held personally liable for money damages if a reasonable officer could have believed that the search comported with the Fourth Amendment.

I

Petitioner Russell Anderson is an agent of the Federal Bureau of Investigation. On November 11, 1983, Anderson and other state and federal law enforcement officers conducted a warrantless search of the home of respondents, the Creighton family. The search was conducted because Anderson believed that Vadaain Dixon, a man suspected of a bank robbery committed earlier that day, might be found there. He was not.

The Creightons later filed suit against Anderson in a Minnesota state court, asserting among other things a *Bivens* claim for money damages under the Fourth Amendment. After removing the suit to Federal District Court, Anderson filed a motion to dismiss or for summary judgment, arguing that the *Bivens* claim was barred by Anderson's qualified immunity from civil damages liability. Before any discovery took place, the District Court granted summary judgment on the ground that the search was lawful, holding that the undisputed facts revealed that Anderson had had probable cause to search the Creighton's home and that his failure to obtain a warrant was justified by the presence of exigent circumstances.

The Creightons appealed to the Court of Appeals for the Eighth Circuit, which reversed. The Court of Appeals held that the issue of the lawfulness of the search could not properly be decided on summary judgment, because unresolved factual disputes made it impossible to determine as a matter of law that the warrantless search had been supported by probable cause and exigent circumstances. The Court of Appeals also held that Anderson was not entitled to summary judgment on qualified immunity grounds, since the right Anderson was alleged to have violated—the right of persons to be protected from warrantless searches of their home unless the searching officers have probable cause and there are exigent circumstances—was clearly established.

Anderson filed a petition for certiorari, arguing that the Court of Appeals erred by refusing to consider his argument that he was entitled to summary judgment on qualified immunity grounds if he could establish as a matter of law that a reasonable officer could have believed the search to be lawful. We granted the petition to consider that important question.

II

When government officials abuse their offices, "action[s] for damages may offer the only realistic avenue for vindication of constitutional guarantees." On the other hand, permitting damages suits against government officials can entail substantial social costs, including the risk that fear of personal monetary liability and harassing litigation will unduly inhibit officials in the discharge of their duties. Our cases have accommodated these conflicting concerns by generally providing government officials performing discretionary functions with a qualified immunity, shielding them from civil damages liability as long as their actions could reasonably have been thought consistent with the rights they are alleged to have violated. Somewhat more concretely, whether an official protected by qualified immunity may be held personally liable for an allegedly unlawful official action generally turns on the "objective legal reasonableness" of the action assessed in light of the legal rules that were "clearly established" at the time it was taken.

The operation of this standard, however, depends substantially upon the level of generality at which the relevant "legal rule" is to be identified. For example, the right to due process of law is quite clearly established by the Due Process Clause, and thus there is a sense in which any action that violates that Clause (no matter how unclear it may be that the particular action is a violation) violates a clearly established right. Much the same could be said of any other constitutional or statutory violation. But if the test of "clearly established law" were to be applied at this level of generality, it would bear no relationship to the "objective legal reasonableness" that is the touchstone of *Harlow*. Plaintiffs would be able to convert the rule of qualified immunity that our cases plainly establish into a rule of virtually unqualified liability simply by alleging violation of extremely abstract rights. *Harlow* would be transformed from a guarantee of immunity into a rule of pleading. Such an approach, in sum, would destroy "the balance that our cases strike between the interests in vindication of citizens' constitutional rights and in public officials' effective performance of their duties," by making it impossible for officials "reasonably [to] anticipate when their conduct may give rise to liability for damages." It should not be surprising, therefore, that our cases establish that the right the official is alleged to have violated must have been "clearly established" in a more particularized, and hence more relevant, sense: The contours of the right must be sufficiently clear that a reasonable official would understand that what he is doing violates that right. This is not to say that an official action is protected by qualified immunity unless the very action in question has previously been held unlawful, but it is to say that in the light of pre-existing law the unlawfulness must be apparent.

Anderson contends that the Court of Appeals misapplied these principles. We agree. The Court of Appeals' brief discussion of qualified immunity consisted of little more than an assertion that a general right Anderson was alleged to have violated—the right to be free from warrantless searches of one's home unless the searching officers have probable cause and there are exigent circumstances—was clearly established. The Court of Appeals specifically refused to consider the argument that it was not clearly established that the circumstances with which Anderson was confronted did not constitute probable cause and exigent circumstances. The previous discussion should make clear that this refusal was erroneous. It simply does not follow immediately from the conclusion that it was firmly established that warrantless searches not supported by probable cause and exigent circumstances violate the Fourth Amendment that Anderson's search was objectively legally unreasonable. We have recognized that it is inevitable that law enforcement officials will in some cases reasonably but mistakenly conclude that probable cause is present, and we have indicated that in such cases those officials—like other officials who act in ways they reasonably believe to be lawful—should not be held personally liable. The same is true of their conclusions regarding exigent circumstances.

It follows from what we have said that the determination whether it was objectively legally reasonable to conclude that a given search was supported by probable cause or exigent circumstances will often require examination of the information possessed by the searching officials. But contrary to the Creightons' assertion, this does not reintroduce into qualified immunity analysis the inquiry into officials' subjective intent that *Harlow* sought to minimize. The relevant question in this case, for example, is the objective (albeit fact-specific) question whether a reasonable officer could have believed Anderson's warrantless search to be lawful, in light of clearly established law and the information the searching officers possessed. Anderson's subjective beliefs about the search are irrelevant.

The principles of qualified immunity that we reaffirm today require that Anderson be permitted to argue that he is entitled to summary judgment on the ground that, in light of the clearly established principles governing warrantless searches, he could, as a matter of law, reasonably have believed that the search of the Creightons' home was lawful.

III

In addition to relying on the reasoning of the Court of Appeals, the Creightons advance three alternative grounds for affirmance. All of these take the same form, i.e., that even if Anderson is entitled to qualified immunity under the usual principles of qualified immunity law we have just described, an exception should be made to those principles in the circumstances of this case. We note at the outset the heavy burden this argument must sustain to be successful. We have emphasized that the doctrine of qualified immunity reflects a balance that has been struck "across the board." Although we have in narrow circumstances provided officials with an absolute immunity, we have been unwilling to complicate qualified immunity analysis by making the scope or extent of immunity turn on the precise nature of various officials' duties or the precise character of the particular rights alleged to have been violated. An immunity that has as many variants as there are modes of official action and types of rights would not give conscientious officials that assurance of protection that it is the object of the doctrine to provide. With that observation in mind, we turn to the particular arguments advanced by the Creightons.

First, and most broadly, the Creightons argue that it is inappropriate to give officials alleged to have violated the Fourth Amendment—and thus necessarily to have unreasonably searched or seized—the protection of a qualified immunity intended only to protect reasonable official action. It is not possible, that is, to say that one "reasonably" acted unreasonably. The short answer to this argument is that it is foreclosed by the fact that we have previously extended qualified immunity to officials who were alleged to have violated the Fourth Amendment. Even if that were not so, however, we would still find the argument unpersuasive. Its surface appeal is attributable to the circumstance that the Fourth Amendment's guarantees have been expressed in terms of "unreasonable" searches and seizures. Had an equally serviceable term, such as "undue" searches and seizures been employed, what might be termed the "reasonably unreasonable" argument against application of *Harlow* to the Fourth Amendment would not be available—just as it would be available against application of *Harlow* to the Fifth Amendment if the term "reasonable process of law" had been employed there. The fact is that, regardless of the terminology used, the precise content of most of the Constitution's civil-liberties guarantees rests upon an assessment of what accommodation between governmental need and individual freedom is reasonable, so that the Creightons' objection, if it has any substance, applies to the application of *Harlow* generally. We have frequently observed, and our many cases on the point amply demonstrate, the difficulty of determining whether particular searches or seizures comport with the Fourth Amendment. Law enforcement officers whose judgments in making these difficult determinations are objectively legally reasonable should no more be held personally liable in damages than should officials making analogous determinations in other areas of law.

Finally, we reject the Creightons' narrowest and most procrustean proposal: that no immunity should be provided to police officers who conduct unlawful warrantless searches of innocent third parties' homes in search of fugitives. Although it is true that we have observed that our determinations as to the scope of official immunity are made in the light of the "common-law tradition," we have never suggested that the precise contours of official immunity can and should be slavishly derived from the often arcane rules of the common law. That notion is plainly contradicted by *Harlow*, where the Court completely reformulated qualified immunity along principles not at all embodied in the common law, replacing the inquiry into subjective malice so frequently required at common law with an objective inquiry into the legal reasonableness of the official action. As we noted before, *Harlow* clearly expressed the understanding that the general principle of qualified immunity it established would be applied "across the board."

The general rule of qualified immunity is intended to provide government officials with the ability "reasonably [to] anticipate when their conduct may give rise to liability for damages." Where that rule is applicable, officials can know that they will not be held personally liable as long as their actions are reasonable in light of current American law. That security would be utterly defeated if officials were unable to determine whether they were protected by the rule without entangling themselves in the vagaries of the English and American common law. We are unwilling to Balkanize the rule of qualified immunity by carving exceptions at the level of detail the Creightons propose. We therefore decline to make an exception to the general rule of qualified immunity for cases involving allegedly unlawful warrantless searches of innocent third parties' homes in search of fugitives.

For the reasons stated, we vacate the judgment of the Court of Appeals and remand the case for further proceedings consistent with this opinion.

[Justices Stevens, Marshall, and Brennan dissented.]

NOTES AND QUESTIONS

1. Why would law enforcement officers not be incentivized to go to the trouble of getting a search warrant for the search of a home where, as here, they believed a suspect in a case unrelated to the occupants of the home could be found?

2. The district court granted summary judgment for the defendant FBI agent Anderson, before any discovery had occurred, on the ground that the "undisputed facts" showed that he had probable cause to search the home based on exigent circumstances. The court of appeals reversed, finding factual disputes regarding both the probable cause and exigent circumstances inquiries.

How could the facts be undisputed prior to any discovery taking place?

3. The Eighth Circuit also rejected Anderson's qualified immunity claim because the right allegedly violated by defendant — the right of persons to be protected from warrantless searches of their homes absent probable cause and exigent circumstances — was a "clearly established" right within the meaning of *Harlow*.

Why was this conclusion erroneous? Why doesn't the Supreme Court identify the appropriate level of generality at which the "objective legal reasonableness" of Anderson's conduct should be considered? Is this determination purely a function of case law? What case law?

4. The Court here identifies an additional "social cost" of suits against public officials, not mentioned in *Harlow*: "the risk that fear of personal monetary liability . . . will unduly inhibit officials in the discharge of their duties." To the extent this is an important underpinning of the qualified immunity doctrine, should it matter whether any liability (as well as litigation expense) is actually borne by the official as opposed to the employer? *See infra*.

And on the subject of "social costs," aren't these more properly a subject for legislatures to evaluate and not courts?

5. The Court makes an impressively packaged concession in connection with rejecting an argument plaintiffs made based on English precedent: "[W]e have never suggested that the precise contours of official immunity can and should be slavishly derived from the often arcane rules of the common law." What is the Court trying to say here? That we're just making this up as we go along?

6. The dissent makes the point that the Court's decision requires applying a "double standard of reasonableness" in cases such as this one, determining whether a police officer acted reasonably in making the required Fourth Amendment evaluation. Is the standard objectionable as a matter of logic as well as because it unduly insulates police officers from liability?

The "double standard of reasonableness" issue will recur in § 1983 and *Bivens* claims based on police use of excessive force, which the Supreme Court definitively identified as a Fourth Amendment violation in *Graham v. Connor*, 490 U.S. 386 (1989). In the meantime, however, the Court was making sure that civil rights action defendants were given special procedural protections not enjoyed by other litigants.

In 1985, shortly after *Harlow* but before *Malley* and *Anderson*, the Court concluded that the normally applicable procedural rules — which *Harlow* changed the immunity doctrine to avoid — still weren't doing enough to protect § 1983 defendants. It saw an opportunity in *Mitchell v. Forsyth*, 472 U.S. 511 (1985), a claim against former Nixon Administration Attorney General John Mitchell alleging illegal wiretapping under 18 U.S.C. § 2511(3), a provision in Title III of the Omnibus Crime Control and Safe Streets Act of 1968, 18 U.S.C. §§ 2510-2520, a federal statute that for the first time had established comprehensive standards governing the use of wiretaps and electronic surveillance by both governmental and private agents.

In *Mitchell*, the Court repurposed qualified immunity as "an immunity from suit rather than a mere defense to liability." And under this reasoning the Court held that federal district court summary judgment decisions denying a defendant's claim of qualified immunity—though interlocutory—could be immediately appealed under the "collateral order" exception to the final judgment rule. *Id.* at 530. It so held despite such claims not being "conceptually distinct" from the merits, the usual requirement for the exception, and despite its characterization just three years earlier as an "affirmative defense," which normally must be asserted and proven at trial. Indeed, the Court continued even after *Mitchell* to describe qualified immunity as an affirmative defense. *See Corr. Servs. Corp. v. Malesko*, 534 U.S. 61, 69 (2001) (describing qualified immunity as an "affirmative defense"); *Siegert v. Gilley*, 500 U.S. 226, 231 (1991) ("Qualified immunity is a defense that must be pleaded by a defendant official.").

So just to review: In *Harlow* the Court completely transforms the substance of qualified immunity to make it easier for defendants to prevail on summary judgment under Rule 56. And then five years later in *Mitchell* the Court loosens the contours of the collateral order doctrine to allow defendants to circumvent the normal appellate rules.

The interplay between the qualified immunity doctrine and procedural norms was not over. In *Wyatt v. Cole*, 504 U.S. 158 (1992), in a concurring opinion, Justice Kennedy acknowledged that *Harlow* had "depart[ed] from history in the name of policy," and implied that that departure may have been premature inasmuch as just four years after *Harlow* the Court clarified that summary judgment can be granted even in cases where state-of-mind issues such as good faith can be dispositive. *Id.* at 171-72 (citing *Celotex Corp. v. Catrett*, 477 U.S. 317, 322 (1986)).

Many commentators, moreover, attribute the heightened pleading standards imposed by the Supreme Court in *Ashcroft v. Iqbal*, 556 U.S. 662 (2009), to the fact that the underlying claim was a *Bivens* action potentially implicating qualified immunity. *See, e.g.*, John M. Greabe, Iqbal, al-Kidd *and Pleading Past Qualified Immunity: What the Cases Mean and How They Demonstrate a Need to Eliminate the Immunity Doctrines from Constitutional Tort Law*, 20 Wm. & Mary Bill Rts. J. 1, 7-12 (2011).

In the next case the Supreme Court also imposes an unusual procedural requirement. In addressing qualified immunity for the first time in the context of a Fourth Amendment excessive force claim, the Court dictates to district courts the precise sequence in which issues should be decided.

Saucier v. Katz

533 U.S. 194 (2001)

Justice KENNEDY delivered the opinion of the Court.

In this case a citizen alleged excessive force was used to arrest him. The arresting officer asserted the defense of qualified immunity. The matter we address is whether the requisite analysis to determine qualified immunity is so intertwined with the question whether the officer used excessive force in making the arrest that qualified immunity and constitutional violation issues should be treated as one question, to be decided by the trier of fact. The Court of Appeals held the inquiries do merge into a single question. We now reverse and hold that the ruling on qualified immunity requires an analysis not susceptible of fusion with the question whether unreasonable force was used in making the arrest.

I

In autumn of 1994, the Presidio Army Base in San Francisco was the site of an event to celebrate conversion of the base to a national park. Among the speakers was Vice President

Albert Gore, Jr., who attracted several hundred observers from the military and the general public. Some in attendance were not on hand to celebrate, however. Respondent Elliot Katz was concerned that the Army's Letterman Hospital would be used for conducting experiments on animals. (Katz was president of a group called In Defense of Animals. Although both he and the group are respondents here, the issues we discuss center upon Katz, and we refer to him as "respondent.") To voice opposition to the possibility that the hospital might be used for experiments, respondent brought with him a cloth banner, approximately 4 by 3 feet, that read "Please Keep Animal Torture Out of Our National Parks." In the past, as respondent was aware, members of the public had been asked to leave the military base when they engaged in certain activities, such as distributing handbills; and he kept the banner concealed under his jacket as he walked through the base.

The area designated for the speakers contained seating for the general public, separated from the stage by a waist-high fence. Respondent sat in the front row of the public seating area. At about the time Vice President Gore began speaking, respondent removed the banner from his jacket, started to unfold it, and walked toward the fence and speakers' platform.

Petitioner Donald Saucier is a military police officer who was on duty that day. He had been warned by his superiors of the possibility of demonstrations, and respondent had been identified as a potential protester. Petitioner and Sergeant Steven Parker — also a military police officer, but not a party to the suit — recognized respondent and moved to intercept him as he walked toward the fence. As he reached the barrier and began placing the banner on the other side, the officers grabbed respondent from behind, took the banner, and rushed him out of the area. Each officer had one of respondent's arms, half-walking, half-dragging him, with his feet "barely touching the ground." Respondent was wearing a visible, knee-high leg brace, although petitioner later testified he did not remember noticing it at the time. Saucier and Parker took respondent to a nearby military van, where, respondent claims, he was shoved or thrown inside. Id., at 25. The reason for the shove remains unclear. It seems agreed that respondent placed his feet somewhere on the outside of the van, perhaps the bumper, but there is a dispute whether he did so to resist. As a result of the shove, respondent claims, he fell to the floor of the van, where he caught himself just in time to avoid any injury. The officers drove respondent to a military police station, held him for a brief time, and then released him. Though the details are not clear, it appears that at least one other protester was also placed into the van and detained for a brief time.

Respondent brought this action in the United States District Court for the Northern District of California against petitioner and other officials pursuant to *Bivens*, alleging, inter alia, that defendants had violated respondent's Fourth Amendment rights by using excessive force to arrest him. The District Court granted the defendants' motions for summary judgment on the grounds of qualified immunity on all claims other than the excessive force claim against Saucier. It held a dispute on a material fact existed concerning whether excessive force was used to remove respondent from the crowd and place him into the van. The District Court held that the law governing excessive force claims was clearly established at the time of the arrest, and that "[i]n the Fourth Amendment context, the qualified immunity inquiry is the same as the inquiry made on the merits." As a result, it ruled, petitioner was not entitled to summary judgment.

In the United States Court of Appeals for the Ninth Circuit petitioner filed an interlocutory appeal from the denial of qualified immunity. The Court of Appeals affirmed, noting at the outset its two-part analysis for qualified immunity questions. First, the Court of Appeals considers "whether the law governing the official's conduct was clearly established." If it was not, that ends the matter, and the official is entitled to immunity. If, however, the law was clearly established when the conduct occurred, the Court of Appeals' second step is to determine if a reasonable officer could have believed, in light of the clearly established law, that his conduct was lawful. As to the first step of its analysis, the court observed that *Graham v. Connor*, 490 U.S. 386 (1989), sets forth the objective reasonableness test for evaluating excessive force claims, a principle the Court of Appeals concluded was clearly established for qualified immunity purposes. The court then concluded that the second step of the qualified immunity inquiry and the merits of the Fourth Amendment excessive force claim are identical, since both concern the objective reasonableness of the officer's conduct in light of the circumstances the officer faced on the scene. On this reasoning, summary judgment based on qualified immunity was held inappropriate.

Saucier, represented by the Government of the United States, sought review here, arguing the Court of Appeals erred in its view that the qualified immunity inquiry is the same as the constitutional inquiry and so becomes superfluous or duplicative when excessive force is alleged. We granted certiorari.

II

The Court of Appeals ruled first that the right was clearly established; and second that the reasonableness inquiry into excessive force meant that it need not consider aspects of qualified immunity, leaving the whole matter to the jury. This approach cannot be reconciled with *Anderson v. Creighton* (1987), however, and was in error in two respects. As we shall explain, the first inquiry must be whether a constitutional right would have been violated on the facts alleged; second, assuming the violation is established, the question whether the right was clearly established must be considered on a more specific level than recognized by the Court of Appeals.

In a suit against an officer for an alleged violation of a constitutional right, the requisites of a qualified immunity defense must be considered in proper sequence. Where the defendant seeks qualified immunity, a ruling on that issue should be made early in the proceedings so that the costs and expenses of trial are avoided where the defense is dispositive. Qualified immunity is "an entitlement not to stand trial or face the other burdens of litigation." The privilege is "an immunity from suit rather than a mere defense to liability; and like an absolute immunity, it is effectively lost if a case is erroneously permitted to go to trial." As a result, "we repeatedly have stressed the importance of resolving immunity questions at the earliest possible stage in litigation."

A court required to rule upon the qualified immunity issue must consider, then, this threshold question: Taken in the light most favorable to the party asserting the injury, do the facts alleged show the officer's conduct violated a constitutional right? This must be the initial inquiry. In the course of determining whether a constitutional right was violated on the premises alleged, a court might find it necessary to set forth principles which will become the basis for a holding that a right is clearly established. This is the process for the law's elaboration from case to case, and it is one reason for our insisting upon turning to the existence or nonexistence of a constitutional right as the first inquiry. The law might be deprived of this explanation were a court simply to skip ahead to the question whether the law clearly established that the officer's conduct was unlawful in the circumstances of the case.

If no constitutional right would have been violated were the allegations established, there is no necessity for further inquiries concerning qualified immunity. On the other hand, if a violation could be made out on a favorable view of the parties' submissions, the next, sequential step is to ask whether the right was clearly established. This inquiry, it is vital to note, must be undertaken in light of the specific context of the case, not as a broad general proposition; and it too serves to advance understanding of the law and to allow officers to avoid the burden of trial if qualified immunity is applicable.

In this litigation, for instance, there is no doubt that *Graham v. Connor, supra*, clearly establishes the general proposition that use of force is contrary to the Fourth Amendment if it is excessive under objective standards of reasonableness. Yet that is not enough. Rather, we emphasized in Anderson "that the right the official is alleged to have violated must have been 'clearly established' in a more particularized, and hence more relevant, sense: The contours of the right must be sufficiently clear that a reasonable official would understand that what he is doing violates that right." The relevant, dispositive inquiry in determining whether a right is clearly established is whether it would be clear to a reasonable officer that his conduct was unlawful in the situation he confronted.

The approach the Court of Appeals adopted—to deny summary judgment any time a material issue of fact remains on the excessive force claim—could undermine the goal of qualified immunity to "avoid excessive disruption of government and permit the resolution of many insubstantial claims on summary judgment." If the law did not put the officer on notice that his conduct would be clearly unlawful, summary judgment based on qualified immunity is appropriate.

This is not to say that the formulation of a general rule is beside the point, nor is it to insist the courts must have agreed upon the precise formulation of the standard. Assuming, for instance, that various courts have agreed that certain conduct is a constitutional violation under facts not distinguishable in a fair way from the facts presented in the case at hand, the officer would not be entitled to qualified immunity based simply on the argument that courts had not agreed on one verbal formulation of the controlling standard.

The Court of Appeals concluded that qualified immunity is merely duplicative in an excessive force case, eliminating the need for the second step where a constitutional violation could be found based on the allegations. In *Anderson*, a warrantless search case, we rejected the argument that there is no distinction between the reasonableness standard for warrantless searches and the qualified immunity inquiry. We acknowledged there was some "surface appeal" to the argument that, because the Fourth Amendment's guarantee was a right to be free from "unreasonable" searches and seizures, it would be inconsistent to conclude that an officer who acted unreasonably under the constitutional standard nevertheless was entitled to immunity because he "'reasonably' acted unreasonably." This superficial similarity, however, could not overcome either our history of applying qualified immunity analysis to Fourth Amendment claims against officers or the justifications for applying the doctrine in an area where officers perform their duties with considerable uncertainty as to "whether particular searches or seizures comport with the Fourth Amendment." With respect, moreover, to the argument made in *Anderson* that an exception should be made for Fourth Amendment cases, we observed "the heavy burden this argument must sustain to be successful," since "the doctrine of qualified immunity reflects a balance that has been struck 'across the board.'" We held that qualified immunity applied in the Fourth Amendment context just as it would for any other claim of official misconduct.

Faced, then, with the heavy burden of distinguishing *Anderson* and of carving out an exception to the typical qualified immunity analysis applied in other Fourth Amendment contexts, the primary submission by respondent in defense of the Court of Appeals' decision is that our decision in *Graham v. Connor* somehow changes matters. *Graham*, in respondent's view, sets forth an excessive force analysis indistinguishable from qualified immunity, rendering the separate immunity inquiry superfluous and inappropriate. Respondent asserts that, like the qualified immunity analysis applicable in other contexts, the excessive force test already affords officers latitude for mistaken beliefs as to the amount of force necessary, so that "*Graham* has addressed for the excessive force area most of the concerns expressed in *Anderson*." Respondent points out that *Graham* did not address the interaction of excessive force claims and qualified immunity, since the issue was not raised; and respondent seeks to distinguish *Anderson* on the theory that the issue of probable cause implicates evolving legal standards and resulting legal uncertainty, a subject raising recurrent questions of qualified immunity. By contrast, respondent says, excessive force is governed by the standard established in *Graham*, a standard providing ample guidance for particular situations. Finally, respondent adopts the suggestion made by one Court of Appeals that the relevant distinction is that probable cause is an ex post inquiry, whereas excessive force, like qualified immunity, should be evaluated from an ex ante perspective.

These arguments or attempted distinctions cannot bear the weight respondent seeks to place upon them. *Graham* did not change the qualified immunity framework explained in *Anderson*. The inquiries for qualified immunity and excessive force remain distinct, even after *Graham*.

In *Graham*, we held that claims of excessive force in the context of arrests or investigatory stops should be analyzed under the Fourth Amendment's "objective reasonableness standard," not under substantive due process principles. Because "police officers are often forced to make split-second judgments — in circumstances that are tense, uncertain, and rapidly evolving — about the amount of force that is necessary in a particular situation," the reasonableness of the officer's belief as to the appropriate level of force should be judged from that on-scene perspective. We set out a test that cautioned against the "20/20 vision of hindsight" in favor of deference to the judgment of reasonable officers on the scene. *Graham* sets forth a list of factors relevant to the merits of the constitutional excessive force claim, "requir[ing] careful attention to the facts and circumstances of each particular case, including the severity of the crime at issue, whether the suspect poses an immediate threat to the safety of the officers or others, and whether he is actively resisting arrest or attempting to evade arrest by flight." If an officer reasonably, but mistakenly, believed that a suspect was likely to fight back, for instance, the officer would be justified in using more force than in fact was needed.

The qualified immunity inquiry, on the other hand, has a further dimension. The concern of the immunity inquiry is to acknowledge that reasonable mistakes can be made as to the legal constraints on particular police conduct. It is sometimes difficult for an officer to determine how the relevant legal doctrine, here excessive force, will apply to the factual situation the officer confronts. An officer might correctly perceive all of the relevant facts but have a mistaken understanding as to whether a particular amount of force is legal in those circumstances. If the officer's mistake as to what the law requires is reasonable, however, the officer is entitled to the immunity defense.

Graham does not always give a clear answer as to whether a particular application of force will be deemed excessive by the courts. This is the nature of a test which must accommodate limitless factual circumstances. This reality serves to refute respondent's claimed distinction between excessive force and other Fourth Amendment contexts; in both spheres the law must be elaborated from case to case. Qualified immunity operates in this case, then, just as it does in others, to protect officers from the sometimes "hazy border between excessive and acceptable force," and to ensure that before they are subjected to suit, officers are on notice their conduct is unlawful.

Graham and *Anderson* refute the excessive force/probable cause distinction on which much of respondent's position seems to depend. The deference owed officers facing suits for alleged excessive force is not different in some qualitative respect from the probable-cause inquiry in *Anderson*. Officers can have reasonable, but mistaken, beliefs as to the facts establishing the existence of probable cause or exigent circumstances, for example, and in those situations courts will not hold that they have violated the Constitution. Yet, even if a court were to hold that the officer violated the Fourth Amendment by conducting an unreasonable, warrantless search, *Anderson* still operates to grant officers immunity for reasonable mistakes as to the legality of their actions. The same analysis is applicable in excessive force cases, where in addition to the deference officers receive on the underlying constitutional claim, qualified immunity can apply in the event the mistaken belief was reasonable.

III

The case was presented to the Court of Appeals on the assumption that respondent's seizure and brief detention did not violate clearly established First Amendment privileges and did not violate the Fourth Amendment right to be free from arrest without probable cause, as distinct from the force used to detain. The sole question, then, is whether the force used violated a clearly established Fourth Amendment protection so that petitioner was not entitled to immunity.

Our instruction to the district courts and courts of appeals to concentrate at the outset on the definition of the constitutional right and to determine whether, on the facts alleged, a constitutional violation could be found is important. As we have said, the procedure permits courts in appropriate cases to elaborate the constitutional right with greater degrees of specificity. Because we granted certiorari only to determine whether qualified immunity was appropriate, however, and because of the limits imposed upon us by the questions on which we granted review, we will assume a constitutional violation could have occurred under the facts alleged based simply on the general rule prohibiting excessive force, then proceed to the question whether this general prohibition against excessive force was the source for clearly established law that was contravened in the circumstances this officer faced. There was no contravention under this standard. Though it is doubtful that the force used was excessive, we need not rest our conclusion on that determination. The question is what the officer reasonably understood his powers and responsibilities to be, when he acted, under clearly established standards.

Respondent's excessive force claim for the most part depends upon the "gratuitously violent shove" allegedly received when he was placed into the van, although respondent notes as well that the alleged violation resulted from the "totality of the circumstances," including the way he was removed from the speaking area.

These circumstances, however, disclose substantial grounds for the officer to have concluded he had legitimate justification under the law for acting as he did. In *Graham* we noted that "[o]ur Fourth Amendment jurisprudence has long recognized that the right to make an arrest or investigatory stop necessarily carries with it the right to use some degree of physical coercion or threat thereof to effect it." A reasonable officer in petitioner's position could have believed that hurrying respondent away from the scene, where the Vice President was speaking and respondent had just approached the fence designed to separate the public from the speakers, was within the bounds of appropriate police responses.

Petitioner did not know the full extent of the threat respondent posed or how many other persons there might be who, in concert with respondent, posed a threat to the security of the Vice President. There were other potential protesters in the crowd, and at least one other individual was arrested and placed into the van with respondent. In carrying out the detention, as it has been assumed the officers had the right to do, petitioner was required to recognize the necessity to protect the Vice President by securing respondent and restoring order to the scene. It cannot be said there was a clearly established rule that would prohibit using the force petitioner did to place respondent into the van to accomplish these objectives.

As for the shove respondent received when he was placed into the van, those same circumstances show some degree of urgency. We have approved the observation that "[n]ot every push or shove, even if it may later seem unnecessary in the peace of a judge's chambers, violates the Fourth Amendment." Ibid. (citations omitted). Pushes and shoves, like other police conduct, must be judged under the Fourth Amendment standard of reasonableness.

In the circumstances presented to this officer, which included the duty to protect the safety and security of the Vice President of the United States from persons unknown in number, neither respondent nor the Court of Appeals has identified any case demonstrating a clearly established rule prohibiting the officer from acting as he did, nor are we aware of any such rule. Our conclusion is confirmed by the uncontested fact that the force was not so excessive that respondent suffered hurt or injury. On these premises, petitioner was entitled to qualified immunity, and the suit should have been dismissed at an early stage in the proceedings.

The judgment of the Court of Appeals is reversed, and the case is remanded for further proceedings consistent with this opinion.

NOTES AND QUESTIONS

1. Does the Court's description of the excessive force claim here — an uncalled-for "shove" — telegraph how this case is going to come out?

2. *Saucier* resolved a circuit split over how to analyze qualified immunity in the context of excessive force claims under *Graham v. Connor*, 490 U.S. 386 (1989). Prior to *Saucier*, a majority of circuits had held that a qualified immunity defense was unavailable in excessive force cases under the theory that the substantive reasonableness component of the merits claim is coterminous with the reasonableness standard in the defense. *See, e.g., Jackson v. Hoylman*, 933 F.2d 401, 402-03 (6th Cir. 1991) (affirming the district court's determination that "qualified immunity turns on the same objective reasonableness standard that the claim of excessive force turns on . . ."); *see generally* Osagie K. Obasogie & Anna Zaret, *Plainly Incompetent: How Qualified Immunity Became an Exculpatory Doctrine of Police Excessive Force*, 170 U. Pa. L. Rev. 407 (2022) (discussing qualified immunity in excessive force cases).

3. In siding with the minority side of the circuit split the Court endorses a "double standard of reasonableness" similar to the one it found appropriate in *Anderson v. Creighton, supra*. Are there meaningful distinctions between a police officer's actions in assessing probable cause and in exercising force that could justify a different outcome in the latter context? Put differently, in which context should police officers be entitled to a greater amount of leeway?

4. In decreeing the sequence in which lower courts must decide the merits and immunity issues, the Court suggests that the purpose of this requirement is the development of a body of constitutional law. Is this a sufficient justification for imposing such a burden on the lower courts?

If a district court or a court of appeals finds (a) that a complaint adequately alleges a violation of a constitutional right but also finds (b) that the right was not "clearly established," is the former decision dicta?

Is the Court's decree inconsistent with the general rule that constitutional questions should be avoided where possible?

5. The sequencing aspect of *Saucier* was effectively overruled just eight years later in *Pearson v. Callahan*, 555 U.S. 223, 227 (2009), where the Court held that the sequencing it had decreed in *Saucier* was no longer mandatory. Among other things, the Court noted that the opinions resulting from adherence to *Saucier* "often fail to make a meaningful contribution" to the development of constitutional precedent.

Why is that not surprising?

In the next case the Court considers the application of qualified immunity in the context of a police officer's use of deadly force.

Mullenix v. Luna

577 U.S. 7 (2015)

Per Curiam.

On the night of March 23, 2010, Sergeant Randy Baker of the Tulia, Texas Police Department followed Israel Leija, Jr., to a drive-in restaurant, with a warrant for his arrest. When Baker approached Leija's car and informed him that he was under arrest, Leija sped off, headed for Interstate 27. Baker gave chase and was quickly joined by Trooper Gabriel Rodriguez of the Texas Department of Public Safety (DPS).

Leija entered the interstate and led the officers on an 18-minute chase at speeds between 85 and 110 miles per hour. Twice during the chase, Leija called the Tulia Police dispatcher, claiming to have a gun and threatening to shoot at police officers if they did not abandon their pursuit. The dispatcher relayed Leija's threats, together with a report that Leija might be intoxicated, to all concerned officers.

As Baker and Rodriguez maintained their pursuit, other law enforcement officers set up tire spikes at three locations. Officer Troy Ducheneaux of the Canyon Police Department manned the spike strip at the first location Leija was expected to reach, beneath the overpass at Cemetery Road. Ducheneaux and the other officers had received training on the deployment of spike strips, including on how to take a defensive position so as to minimize the risk posed by the passing driver.

DPS Trooper Chadrin Mullenix also responded. He drove to the Cemetery Road overpass, initially intending to set up a spike strip there. Upon learning of the other spike strip positions, however, Mullenix began to consider another tactic: shooting at Leija's car in order to disable it. Mullenix had not received training in this tactic and had not attempted it before, but he radioed the idea to Rodriguez. Rodriguez responded "10-4," gave Mullenix his position, and said that Leija had slowed to 85 miles per hour. Mullenix then asked the DPS dispatcher to inform his supervisor, Sergeant Byrd, of his plan and ask if Byrd thought it was "worth doing." Before receiving Byrd's response, Mullenix exited his vehicle and, armed with his service rifle, took a shooting position on the overpass, 20 feet above I-27. Respondents allege that from this position, Mullenix still could hear Byrd's response to "stand by" and "see if the spikes work first."

As Mullenix waited for Leija to arrive, he and another officer, Randall County Sheriff's Deputy Tom Shipman, discussed whether Mullenix's plan would work and how and where to shoot the vehicle to best carry it out. Shipman also informed Mullenix that another officer was located beneath the overpass.

Approximately three minutes after Mullenix took up his shooting position, he spotted Leija's vehicle, with Rodriguez in pursuit. As Leija approached the overpass, Mullenix fired six shots. Leija's car continued forward beneath the overpass, where it engaged the spike strip, hit the median, and rolled two and a half times. It was later determined that Leija had been killed by Mullenix's shots, four of which struck his upper body. There was no evidence that any of Mullenix's shots hit the car's radiator, hood, or engine block.

Respondents sued Mullenix under 42 U.S.C. § 1983, alleging that he had violated the Fourth Amendment by using excessive force against Leija. Mullenix moved for summary judgment on the ground of qualified immunity, but the District Court denied his motion, finding that "[t]here are genuine issues of fact as to whether Trooper Mullenix acted recklessly, or acted as a reasonable, trained peace officer would have acted in the same or similar circumstances."

Mullenix appealed, and the Court of Appeals for the Fifth Circuit affirmed. The court agreed with the District Court that the "immediacy of the risk posed by Leija is a disputed fact that a reasonable jury could find either in the plaintiffs' favor or in the officer's favor, precluding us from concluding that Mullenix acted objectively reasonably as a matter of law."

Judge King dissented. She described the "'fact issue' referenced by the majority" as "simply a restatement of the objective reasonableness test that applies to Fourth Amendment excessive force claims," which, she noted, the Supreme Court has held "'is a pure question of law.'" Turning to that legal question, Judge King concluded that Mullenix's actions were objectively reasonable. When Mullenix fired, she emphasized, he knew not only that Leija had threatened to shoot the officers involved in his pursuit, but also that Leija was seconds away from encountering such an officer beneath the overpass. Judge King also dismissed the notion that Mullenix should have given the spike strips a chance to work. She explained that because spike strips are often ineffective, and because officers operating them are vulnerable to gunfire from passing cars, Mullenix reasonably feared that the officers manning them faced a significant risk of harm.

We address only the qualified immunity question, not whether there was a Fourth Amendment violation in the first place, and now reverse.

• • •

In this case, Mullenix confronted a reportedly intoxicated fugitive, set on avoiding capture through high-speed vehicular flight, who twice during his flight had threatened to shoot police officers, and who was moments away from encountering an officer at Cemetery Road. The relevant inquiry is whether existing precedent placed the conclusion that Mullenix acted unreasonably in these circumstances "beyond debate." The general principle that deadly force requires a sufficient threat hardly settles this matter.

Far from clarifying the issue, excessive force cases involving car chases reveal the hazy legal backdrop against which Mullenix acted. In *Brosseau* itself, the Court held that an officer did not violate clearly established law when she shot a fleeing suspect out of fear that he endangered "other officers on foot who [she] believed were in the immediate area," "the occupied vehicles in [his] path," and "any other citizens who might be in the area." The threat Leija posed was at least as immediate as that presented by a suspect who had just begun to drive off and was headed only in the general direction of officers and bystanders. By the time Mullenix fired, Leija had led police on a 25-mile chase at extremely high speeds, was reportedly intoxicated, had twice threatened to shoot officers, and was racing towards an officer's location.

This Court has considered excessive force claims in connection with high-speed chases on only two occasions since *Brosseau.* In *Scott v. Harris*, the Court held that an officer did not violate the Fourth Amendment by ramming the car of a fugitive whose reckless driving "posed an actual and imminent threat to the lives of any pedestrians who might have been present, to other civilian motorists, and to the officers involved in the chase." And in *Plumhoff v. Rickard* (2014), the Court reaffirmed *Scott* by holding that an officer acted reasonably when he fatally shot a fugitive who was "intent on resuming" a chase that "pose[d] a deadly threat for others on the road." The Court has thus never found the use of deadly force in connection with a dangerous car chase to violate the Fourth Amendment, let alone to be a basis for denying qualified immunity. Leija in his flight did not pass as many cars as the drivers in *Scott* or *Plumhoff*; traffic was light on I-27. At the same time, the fleeing fugitives in *Scott* and *Plumhoff* had not verbally threatened to kill any officers in their path, nor were they about to come upon such officers. In any event, none of our precedents "squarely governs" the facts here. Given Leija's conduct, we cannot say that only someone "plainly incompetent" or who "knowingly violate[s] the law" would have perceived a sufficient threat and acted as Mullenix did.

• • •

Because the constitutional rule applied by the Fifth Circuit was not "'beyond debate,'" we grant Mullenix's petition for certiorari and reverse the Fifth Circuit's determination that Mullenix is not entitled to qualified immunity.

NOTES AND QUESTIONS

1. The Court emphasizes multiple times that Leija had stated to the dispatcher that he would kill police officers, a fact that may have been necessary to bring the defendant's conduct within the ambit of the rule announced by the Court in *Tennessee v. Garner*, 471 U.S. 1 (1985).

Would the result here have been different if those threats had not been made?

What if Mullenix had admitted at his deposition that he was unaware of those threats? Or that he would have done everything the same even if those threats had not been made?

2. Justice Scalia, concurring, rejects the formulation of the facts here as "application of deadly force." Do you agree? Is it dispositive of this issue that Mullenix fired shots from his rifle in order to stop the car and not to hit the driver?

3. In finding that the defendant had violated clearly established law the Fifth Circuit had relied in part on one of its precedents—*Lytle v. Bexar County*, 560 F.3d 404 (5th Cir. 2009), where it had denied qualified immunity to an officer who had fired at a fleeing car and killed a passenger. The Supreme Court rejects the notion that this precedent did not make what Mullenix did a violation of clearly established law because the car in this case was not fleeing but coming at him.

What does this tell you about the Court's view of the appropriate level of generality at which the immunity inquiry must take place?

Lower courts have no choice against this backdrop but to look for precedent that is right on point. *See Baxter v. Bracey*, 751 F. App'x 869, 870 (6th Cir. 2018), *cert. denied*, 140 S. Ct. 1862 (2020) (defendant officer entitled to qualified immunity in excessive force case for decision to release a police dog on a defendant who was surrendering with his hands up because the nearest precedent only found a violation where police had released their dog on an individual who was lying down).

4. In dissent in *Mullenix* Justice Sotomayor offers an additional fact that she concedes has no significance to the appropriate legal analysis in the case but does have "big picture" import:

> When Mullenix confronted his superior officer after the shooting, his first words were, "How's that for proactive?" (Mullenix was apparently referencing an earlier counseling session in which Byrd suggested that he was not enterprising enough. [577 U.S. at 25-26]) The glib comment does not impact our legal analysis; an officer's actual intentions are irrelevant to the Fourth Amendment's "objectively reasonable" inquiry. But the comment seems to me revealing of the culture this Court's decision supports when it calls it reasonable—or even reasonably reasonable—to use deadly force for no discernible gain and over a supervisor's express order to "stand by." By sanctioning a "shoot first, think later" approach to policing, the Court renders the protections of the Fourth Amendment hollow.

The Supreme Court seems to have singled out cases involving uses of deadly force, such as *Mullenix*, for particular deference in recent years. *See, e.g., Brosseau v. Haugen*, 543 U.S. 194, 195-97 (2004) (per curiam) (overturning lower court decision denying qualified immunity to a police officer who shot plaintiff in the back); *Plumhoff v. Rickard*, 572 U.S. 765, 768-70 (2014) (granting qualified immunity to police officers who shot and killed the driver and passenger in a "dangerous" fleeing car); *City and County of San Francisco v. Sheehan*, 575 U.S. 600, 603-06, 617 (2015) (granting qualified immunity to officers who shot a mentally ill woman in her group home when she would not drop a knife); *White v. Pauly*, 580 U.S. 73 (2017) (per curiam) (granting immunity to an officer who shot an armed home occupant during a standoff); *Kisela v. Hughes*, 584 U.S. 100, 101-08 (2018) (per curiam) (granting immunity to an officer who shot a mentally ill woman armed with a kitchen knife). *But see City of Escondido v. Emmons*, 586 U.S. 38, 39-44 (2019) (per curiam) (reversing lower court decision to grant immunity to an officer who forcibly took a man to the ground as he attempted to walk past them); *City of Tahlequah v. Bond*, 595 U.S. 9, 10-11 (2021) (per curiam) (reversing lower court decision to deny qualified immunity to police who shot man wielding a hammer). *See Kisela*, 584 U.S. at 121 (Sotomayor, J., dissenting) (noting the Court has "unflinching willingness to summarily reverse courts for wrongly denying officers the protection of qualified immunity but rarely intervene[s] where courts wrongly afford officers the benefit of qualified immunity in these same cases").

Notwithstanding all of the above, a leading academic on the subject has suggested there may be "cracks in qualified immunity's armor." Joanna C. Schwartz, *The Case Against Qualified Immunity*, 93 Notre Dame L. Rev. 1797 (2018). Perhaps the most significant crack is the following concurring opinion by Justice Thomas.

Ziglar v. Abbasi

582 U.S. 120 (2017)

THOMAS, J., concurring.

As for respondents' claims under 42 U.S.C. § 1985(3), I join Part V of the Court's opinion, which holds that respondents are entitled to qualified immunity. The Court correctly applies our precedents, which no party has asked us to reconsider. I write separately, however, to note my growing concern with our qualified immunity jurisprudence.

The Civil Rights Act of 1871, of which § 1985(3) and the more frequently litigated § 1983 were originally a part, established causes of action for plaintiffs to seek money damages from Government officers who violated federal law. Although the Act made no mention of defenses or immunities, "we have read it in harmony with general principles of tort immunities and defenses rather than in derogation of them." We have done so because "[c]ertain immunities were so well established in 1871 . . . that 'we presume that Congress would have specifically so provided had it wished to abolish' them." Immunity is thus available under the statute if it was "historically accorded the relevant official" in an analogous situation "at common law," unless the statute provides some reason to think that Congress did not preserve the defense.

In some contexts, we have conducted the common-law inquiry that the statute requires. For example, we have concluded that legislators and judges are absolutely immune from liability under § 1983 for their official acts because that immunity was well established at common law in 1871. *Tenney v. Brandhove* (1951) (legislators); *Pierson v. Ray* (1967) (judges). We have similarly looked to the common law in holding that a prosecutor is immune from suits relating to the "judicial phase of the criminal process." *Imbler.*

In developing immunity doctrine for other executive officers, we also started off by applying common-law rules. In *Pierson*, we held that police officers are not absolutely immune from a § 1983 claim arising from an arrest made pursuant to an unconstitutional statute because the common law never granted arresting officers that sort of immunity. Rather, we concluded that police officers could assert "the defense of good faith and probable cause" against the claim for an unconstitutional arrest because that defense was available against the analogous torts of "false arrest and imprisonment" at common law.

In further elaborating the doctrine of qualified immunity for executive officials, however, we have diverged from the historical inquiry mandated by the statute. In the decisions following *Pierson*, we have "completely reformulated qualified immunity along principles not at all embodied in the common law." *Anderson v. Creighton* (1987) (discussing *Harlow v. Fitzgerald* (1982)). Instead of asking whether the common law in 1871 would have accorded immunity to an officer for a tort analogous to the plaintiff's claim under § 1983, we instead grant immunity to any officer whose conduct "does not violate clearly established statutory or constitutional rights of which a reasonable person would have known." We apply this "clearly established" standard "across the board" and without regard to "the precise nature of the various officials' duties or the precise character of the particular rights alleged to have been violated." We have not attempted to locate that standard in the common law as it existed in 1871, however, and some evidence supports the conclusion that common-law immunity as it existed in 1871 looked quite different from our current doctrine. *See generally* Baude, Is Qualified Immunity Unlawful? 106 Cal. L. Rev. (forthcoming 2018).

Because our analysis is no longer grounded in the common-law backdrop against which Congress enacted the 1871 Act, we are no longer engaged in "interpret[ing] the intent of Congress in enacting" the Act. Our qualified immunity precedents instead represent precisely the sort of "freewheeling policy choice[s]" that we have previously disclaimed the power to make. We have acknowledged, in fact, that the "clearly established" standard is designed to "protec[t] the balance between vindication of constitutional rights and government officials' effective performance of their duties." The Constitution assigns this kind of balancing to Congress, not the Courts.

In today's decision, we continue down the path our precedents have marked. We ask "whether it would have been clear to a reasonable officer that the alleged conduct was unlawful in the situation he confronted," rather than whether officers in petitioners' positions would have been accorded immunity at common law in 1871 from claims analogous to respondents'. Even if we ultimately reach a conclusion consistent with the common-law rules prevailing in 1871, it is mere fortuity. Until we shift the focus of our inquiry to whether immunity existed at common law, we will continue to substitute our own policy preferences for the mandates of Congress. In an appropriate case, we should reconsider our qualified immunity jurisprudence.

Another significant potential "crack" in qualified immunity's armor is that two of the most important policy reasons that led the Supreme Court to create the doctrine in the first place—protecting police officers and other officials from the expense of litigation and judgments—have proven over time to be fallacious. In a study of dozens of police departments Professor Schwartz concluded that police officers almost never pay for defense counsel or damages, sometimes because of their employer's indemnification obligations and sometimes because of custom and practice. Schwartz, *The Case Against Qualified Immunity*, *supra* at 1804-07. *See Richardson v. McKnight*, 521 U.S. 399, 408-12 (1997) (rejecting qualified immunity claim of prison guards at a private, for-profit prison in part because the private character of the guards' employer "increases the likelihood of employee indemnification"). The other policy reasons the Court identified in *Harlow* as justifications for robust immunity—not discouraging people from public service, and ensuring that public officials are not unduly timid—are largely a function of the expense issue. That leaves only the "distraction of litigation" as a valid policy justification. If the President of the United States is required to defend against civil litigation while in office, *Clinton v. Jones*, 520 U.S. 681 (1997), why shouldn't police officers be required to do the same?

There is also a remote possibility of legislative reform. In the wake of the George Floyd murder in 2020, the House passed several bills modifying or eliminating qualified immunity. *See* Qualified Immunity Act of 2021, H.R. 288, 117th Cong. (2021); Ending Qualified Immunity Act, H.R. 1470, 117th Cong. (2021); Ending Qualified Immunity Act, S. 492, 117th Cong. (2021).

D. THE DEPARTMENT OF JUSTICE AND STRUCTURAL REFORM LITIGATION

Why can't the Department of Justice—Justice!—do something about local police misconduct besides just occasionally prosecuting police officers for constitutional violations? After all, such one-off criminal prosecutions are crude vehicles for changing the behavior of police departments, where misconduct may be endemic. It's not that it hasn't tried. In the 1970s the DOJ filed a civil action against Philadelphia alleging a litany of abusive and racist police practices that deprived persons of their due process rights. *United States v. City of Philadelphia*, 644 F.2d 187 (3d Cir. 1980). As authority for its suit, the Department claimed an implied right of action based on 18 U.S.C. §§ 241 and 242 and/or its authority under Article II, § 3 of the Constitution to "take care that the laws be faithfully executed," citing *Bivens* among other things. The Third Circuit rejected both arguments and dismissed the lawsuit.

Eleven years later there was videotape. On March 3, 1991, LAPD officers were captured on videotape viciously beating Black motorist Rodney King and landing dozens of blows even after King was submissive and then motionless. A grainy black-and-white videotape of the beating, which began recording after King had resisted the officers and the beatings had begun, was made with an early version of a "camcorder" by plumber George Holliday, a resident of an apartment complex across the street from where King was apprehended, who just happened to be out on his balcony. After being rebuffed by the local branch of the LAPD, Holliday took the tape to Los Angeles news station KTLA, which immediately aired the videotape, as eventually did television stations around the world.

Congress was spurred into action, and the consequence was the passage of 42 U.S.C. § 14141. The statute authorizes the Department of Justice to seek equitable or declaratory relief, *id.* § 14141(b), against any government authority or agent of such authority that engages in a "pattern or practice" of conduct that violates the Constitution or laws of the United States, *id.* § 14141(a). The statute was praised by scholars as a potentially revolutionary reform. *See, e.g.*, Barbara E. Armacost, *Organizational Culture and Police Misconduct*, 72 Geo. Wash. L. Rev. 453, 464-65 (2004) (describing § 14141 as "perhaps the most promising legal mechanism" for reducing police misconduct); William J. Stuntz, *The Pathological Politics of Criminal Law*, 100 Mich. L. Rev. 505, 538-39 n.134 (2001) (describing § 14141 as possibly "more significant, in the long run, than *Mapp v. Ohio*"). (42 U.S.C. § 14141 has been reclassified as § 12601 of Title 34 of the United States Code. To remain consistent with cited works and to avoid confusion, § 14141 will be used throughout this section.)

For reasons that will be explained below, there is almost never litigation under the statute. The City of Columbus, Ohio, however, did bring an early challenge to the department's authority under the statute, and the decision rejecting the challenge nicely explains the statute's text and backdrop.

United States v. City of Columbus

2000 WL 1133166 (S.D. Ohio Aug. 3, 2000)

REPORT AND RECOMMENDATION

King, Magistrate J.

This is an action for injunctive and declaratory relief, instituted under the provisions of 42 U.S.C. § 14141, in which the United States alleges that officers of the Columbus Division of Police have engaged in a pattern or practice of conduct violative of federal law and that the defendant city has tolerated the alleged misconduct by failing to implement adequate policies, training, supervision, monitoring and incident investigation procedures. This matter is now before the Court on the motion to dismiss filed by the defendant city and on the motion for judgment on the pleadings filed by the defendant-intervenor, the Fraternal Order of Police, City Lodge No. 9.

In their motions, the movants argue, first, that the Court is without subject matter jurisdiction over the claims asserted in the action because Congress exceeded its constitutional authority in promulgating the statute upon which the complaint is based, 42 U.S.C. § 14141. Movants argue, in the alternative, that the original complaint fails to state a claim upon which relief can be granted because it purports to impose vicarious liability on the defendant city, because it fails to allege with specificity the claimed wrongdoing of the defendant city or its police officers, and because its allegations are, in whole or in part, untimely. Although plaintiff has filed a motion for leave to amend the complaint in order to assert an additional claim of racially discriminatory conduct, that motion remains pending. The Court will therefore consider the movants' motions solely by reference to the original complaint.

• • •

II. THE ORIGINAL COMPLAINT

The original complaint alleges that Columbus police officers have engaged in, and continue to engage in, a pattern or practice of using excessive force, Complaint, ¶ 6, falsely arresting individuals, Id., ¶ 7, and falsifying official reports and conducting searches either without lawful authority or in an improper manner. Id., ¶ 8(a), (b). The complaint further alleges that the City of Columbus has "tolerated the misconduct of individual officers," Id., ¶ 9, by failing "to implement a policy on use of force that appropriately guides the actions of individual officers," Id., ¶ 9(a), by failing to adequately "train," "supervise," and "monitor" officers, Id., ¶ 9(b)-(d), and by failing to "establish a procedure whereby citizen complaints are adequately investigated," Id., ¶ 9(e), "investigate adequately incidents in which a police officer uses lethal or non-lethal force," Id., ¶ 9(f), "fairly and adequately adjudicate or review citizen complaints, and incidents in which an officer uses lethal or non-lethal force," Id., ¶ 9(g), and "discipline adequately . . . officers who engage in misconduct." Id., ¶ 9(h). The complaint seeks a declaration that the city "is engaged in a pattern or practice by . . . officers of depriving persons of rights, privileges, or immunities secured or protected by the Constitution or laws of the United States," and asks that the Court enjoin the city "from engaging in any of the predicate acts forming the basis of the pattern or practice of conduct as described . . ." and order the city "to adopt and implement policies, practices, and procedures to remedy the pattern or practice of conduct described . . . and to prevent officers from depriving persons of rights, privileges or immunities secured or protected by the Constitution or laws of the United States. . . ."

III. THE STATUTE

The original complaint asserts claims under 42 U.S.C. § 14141. That statute, enacted as part of the Violent Crime Control and Law Enforcement Act of 1994, reads in full as follows:

Cause of Action

(a) Unlawful Conduct

It shall be unlawful for any governmental authority, or any agent thereof, or any person acting on behalf of a governmental authority, to engage in a pattern or practice of conduct by law enforcement officers or by officials or employees of any governmental agency with responsibility for the administration of juvenile justice or the incarceration of juveniles that deprives persons of rights, privileges, or immunities secured or protected by the Constitution or laws of the United States.

(b) Civil Action by Attorney General

Whenever the Attorney General has reasonable cause to believe that a violation of paragraph (1) has occurred, the Attorney General, for or in the name of the United States, may in a civil action obtain appropriate equitable and declaratory relief to eliminate the pattern or practice.

The parties agree that § 14141, which has no direct legislative history and which has never been construed by any court, is a successor to an earlier, nearly identical, provision of the Omnibus Crime Control Act of 1991, which was never actually promulgated. All parties also refer to the legislative history of that provision in their discussion of 42 U.S.C. § 14141.

Like § 14141, the earlier statute was intended to confer standing on the United States Attorney General to obtain civil injunctive relief against governmental authorities for patterns or practices of unconstitutional police practices. In considering the need for such legislation, the House Subcommittee on Civil and Constitutional Rights held two days of hearings and, in its report, the Committee on the Judiciary specifically referred to the Rodney King incident in Los Angeles, and to alleged misconduct within the Boston, New York City and Reynoldsburg, Ohio, Police Departments. Although recognizing that police misconduct violates the United States Constitution and, under 18 U.S.C. §§ 241, 242, can give rise to federal criminal liability, the Committee also noted that, under *United States v. City of Philadelphia*, 644 F.2d 187 (3d Cir. 1980), the United States had neither statutory nor constitutional authority to sue a police department itself "to correct the underlying policy." The problem was compounded, the Committee concluded, by the Supreme Court's holding, in *Los Angeles v. Lyons*, 461 U.S. 95 (1983), that, although a private citizen victimized by police misconduct could recover monetary relief under 42 U.S.C. § 1983, future injunctive relief remained unavailable absent a showing of likely future harm to that particular plaintiff. The proposed statute, the committee stated in its report, "would close this gap in the law, authorizing the Attorney General . . . to sue for injunctive relief against abusive police practices." Significantly, the Committee went on to explain:

> The Act does not increase the responsibilities of police departments or impose any new standards of conduct on police officers. The standards of conduct under the Act are the same as those under the Constitution, presently enforced in damage actions under section 1983. The Act merely provides another tool for a court to use, after a police department is held responsible for a pattern or practice of misconduct that violates the Constitution or laws of the United States.
>
> Because the Act imposes no new standard of conduct on law enforcement agencies, it should not increase the amount of litigation against police departments. Individuals aggrieved by the use of excessive force already can and do sue under 42 U.S.C. § 1983 for monetary damages. With adoption of this section, such persons will be able to seek injunctive relief as well, if their injury is the product of a pattern or practice of misconduct. [N.B. A provision in the statute authorizing private individuals to enforce it was removed from the final version after opposition from police groups and the George H. W. Bush administration. Marshall Miller, Note, Police Brutality, 17 Yale L. & Policy Rev. 149, 163 (1998).]

This provision may in fact decrease the number of lawsuits against police departments. Currently, changes in a police department's policy are prompted by successive criminal cases or damage actions; the cumulative weight of convictions or adverse monetary judgments may lead the police leadership to conclude that change is necessary. This is an inefficient way to enforce the Constitution and is not always effective. Some police departments have shown they are willing to absorb millions of dollars of damage payments per year without changing their policies. If there is a pattern of abuse, this section can bring it to an end with a single legal action.

IV. CONGRESSIONAL AUTHORITY TO PROMULGATE § 14141

• • •

As the House Committee report makes clear, and as all parties to this action appear to concede, the grant of authority to the Attorney General reflected in both the Police Accountability Act of 1991 and in § 14141 was drafted in light of and was intended to remedy the inadequacies of 42 U.S.C. § 1983. That statute provides in pertinent part:

> Every person who, under color of any statute, ordinance, regulation, custom, or usage, of any State or Territory or the District of Columbia subjects, or causes to be subjected, any citizen of the United States or other person within the jurisdiction thereof to the deprivation of any rights, privileges, or immunities secured by the Constitution and laws, shall be liable to the party injured in an action at law, suit in equity, or other proper proceeding for redress.

Section 1983 does not impose vicarious liability solely on the basis of an employment relationship between a governmental agency and a tortfeasor. Before a city can be held liable under § 1983, some "action pursuant to official municipal policy of some nature [must have] caused a constitutional tort." *Monell.* Simply put, cities are not subject to liability under § 1983 on a theory of respondeat superior.

That having been said, cities can nevertheless be held liable under § 1983 for more than just the most direct and egregious violations of an individual's Fourteenth Amendment rights. For example, if the constitutional violation is the result of inadequate police training, the city may be held liable under § 1983 if "the failure to train amounts to deliberate indifference to the rights of persons with whom the police come into contact." Liability under § 1983 can be imposed on a municipality where "'a deliberate choice to follow a course of action is made from among various alternatives' by city policy makers."

The Supreme Court based its relatively narrow construction of § 1983 on the express language of the statute, its legislative history, *Monell*, and "perceived constitutional difficulties" on the part of the drafters of the statute.

This Court concludes that § 14141 is properly construed to similar effect. Its language does not unambiguously contemplate the possibility of vicarious liability and such legislative history as exists manifests a congressional intent to conform its substantive provisions to the standards of § 1983.

As so construed, the Court concludes that § 14141 is a valid and proper exercise of congressional authority under § 5 of the Fourteenth Amendment. As the House Committee report makes clear, the authority conferred on the Attorney General by § 14141 was intended to "close [the] gap in the law" as it had developed in litigation under § 1983 by providing the remedy of broad injunctive relief where "appropriate." The remedy authorized by § 14141 is clearly responsive to the constitutional harm identified in the House Committee report and is no more expansive than is necessary to address that harm. The statute therefore reflects a valid exercise of Congress' constitutional mandate to identify, remedy and even prevent substantive violations of the Fourteenth Amendment. As so construed, § 14141 is neither incongruent nor disproportionate to Congress' constitutional prerogative and responsibility.

To the extent that the complaint seeks to posit liability against the City of Columbus on a theory of respondeat superior, the original complaint is deficient. However, the United States asks that, in such event, "the Court grant the United States sufficient time to amend the complaint to remedy any identified deficiency." The Court will grant that request.

NOTES AND QUESTIONS

1. Does it make sense for the court to interpret § 14141 in light of interpretations of § 1983 simply because they are aimed at the same evil? Is it relevant that the two statutes were enacted 123 years apart?

2. Does the limitation on municipal liability that the court reads into the statute, based on *Monell*, necessarily hamper DOJ's use of § 14141?

3. If *Monell* had recognized traditional respondeat superior liability under § 1983, would § 14141 be necessary? Would the doctrine of qualified immunity be necessary?

The DOJ selects its target police departments from a number of sources. *See generally* Stephen Rushin, *Federal Enforcement of Police Reform*, 82 Fordham L. Rev. 3189, 3219-24 (2014) (identifying sources based on interviews with stakeholders in the "structural police reform process," including former DOJ employees). These include existing civil litigation or investigations initiated by private interest groups; media reports of police misconduct; research studies; police department whistleblowers; and extreme individual examples of police misconduct. *Id.* Based on such sources, the DOJ will start with what it calls a "preliminary inquiry," to determine whether there is reason to believe the police department was or is engaging in systemic misconduct. *Id.* at 3225. If so, a formal investigation will be opened, a step DOJ does not take lightly as formal investigations have proven to be expensive and time-consuming. *Id.* at 3226-28.

Formal investigations usually result in settlement agreements, often with the nominal filing of a lawsuit and the entry of a settlement agreement that is embodied into a consent decree that is judicially enforceable. No one wants to litigate under § 14141. DOJ has resource and financial concerns, and the only remedy it can seek and cares about is essentially accomplished by a settlement agreement embodied in a consent decree. Police departments, similarly, prefer to avoid the expense of litigation as well as the bad publicity it can engender. Settlement agreements typically require police departments to undergo significant reforms in areas such as officer use of force, complaint management, training, bias-free policing, community-oriented policing, line-up procedures, canine deployment, and crisis intervention. Stephen Rushin & Griffin Edwards, *De-Policing*, 102 Cornell L. Rev. 721, 749 (2017). Between its enactment in 1994 through 2016, DOJ has investigated 61 police departments and reached settlements with 31 of them, including large cities such as New York, Los Angeles, Chicago, Washington, D.C., Seattle, Albuquerque, Cincinnati, New Orleans, Newark, Buffalo, Columbus, Pittsburgh, and Cleveland. *Id.* There are approximately 18,000 separate police departments in the United States, *id.*; some may have little need for DOJ intervention.

One issue that comes up in connection with settling investigations under § 14141, even when litigation is unnecessary, is ensuring a meaningful role for nonparty police departments and community organizations. Recall that in the City of Columbus litigation described above as well as in the *Floyd* litigation involving the NYPD, police departments intervened under Fed. R. Civ. P. 24 in litigation against the city. *See generally* Kami Chavis Simmons, *The Politics of Policing: Ensuring Stakeholder Collaboration in the Federal Reform of Local Law Enforcement Agencies*, 98 J. Crim. L. & Criminology 489 (2008) (advocating for inclusion of all stakeholders in the settlement process); Alexandra Holmes, *Bridging the Information Gap: The Department of Justice's "Pattern or Practice" Suits and Community Organizations*, 92 Tex. L. Rev. 1241 (2014) (similar).

Unsurprisingly different presidential administrations have varied in the vigor with which they use § 14141. Rushin, *Federal Enforcement*, *supra* at 3233-36. The Clinton and Obama Administrations aggressively lobbied for increased funding and personnel for these actions. The George W. Bush Administration preferred the use of nonbinding "technical assistance letters" to full-blown investigations. The Trump Administration renounced the use of § 14141 altogether. On March 31, 2017, Attorney General Jeff Sessions issued a two-page memorandum declaring that "[i]t is not the responsibility of the federal government to manage non-federal law enforcement agencies." It declared the "[t]he misdeeds of individual bad actors should not impugn or undermine the legitimate and honorable work that law enforcement officers and agencies perform in keeping American communities safe." And, it ordered the deputy attorney general and associate attorney general to begin a review of existing and contemplated agreements that the DOJ had reached with American police departments during the Obama Administration.

Section 14141 is not without its critics, although most advocate for better and more effective use of this potent weapon. Professor Rushin argues for a more transparent case selection process, Rushin, *Federal Enforcement*, *supra* at 3240, as does Professor Rachel Harmon. *See* Rachel A. Harmon, *Promoting Civil Rights Through Proactive Policing Reform*, 62 Stan. L. Rev. 1, 27 (2009). Professor Rushin also argues for grafting a private right of action onto the statute as a means for increasing the number of cases, although he cautions that this approach may be precluded by *Lyons, Federal Enforcement, supra.* Professor Monica Bell suggests that DOJ should include in § 14141 settlement agreements remedies aimed at promoting "anti-segregation" policing. Monica C. Bell, *Anti-Segregation Policing*, 95 N.Y.U. L. Rev. 650, 756-57 (2020).

A student commentator suggests allowing potential misconduct victims to make use in private litigation of the factfinding generated under § 14144 investigations, although acknowledging this would not increase the number of police departments investigated and would be a disincentive to settlement. Matthew J. Silveira, Comment, *An Unexpected Application of 42 U.S.C. § 14141: Using Investigative Findings for § 1983 Litigation*, 52 UCLA L. Rev. 601 (2004).

The most interesting suggestion is Professor Harmon's. Her proposal for getting more bang for the buck out of § 14141 centers on a "safe harbor" enforcement model. Under this approach, police departments that have been targeted by DOJ through preliminary inquiries could voluntarily opt in to an agreed-upon set of "best practice" reforms, perhaps less draconian than those typically reached after an investigation, and thereby avoid the expense and disruption of a plenary investigation. The proposal would require the development of a national database that could allow DOJ to identify the most deficient departments, as well as a means of enforcing the safe harbor set of reforms. *See* Rachel A. Harmon, *Promoting Civil Rights Through Proactive Policing Reform*, *supra* at 2-7.

CHAPTER VII

GRAND JURY

The grand jury, in a constitutional sense, is associated with a "right," a right expressly spelled out in the Bill of Rights no less. The Fifth Amendment provides that "[n]o person shall be held to answer for a capital, or otherwise infamous crime, unless on a presentment or indictment of a Grand Jury." Yet the "right" to indictment only by a grand jury is the only core criminal procedural right in the Bill of Rights that has not been "incorporated," via the Due Process Clause of the Fourteenth Amendment, so as to apply to the States. *Hurtado v. California*, 110 U.S. 516 (1884). No matter how the different attributes of incorporation-worthy rights have been articulated over the years—rights "so rooted in the traditions and conscience of our people so as to be ranked as fundamental," rights that are "the very essence of a scheme of ordered liberty," rights essential to "a fair and enlightened system of justice"—the grand jury right has not passed muster. *See* Roger A. Fairfax Jr., *Interrogating the Nonincorporation of the Grand Jury Clause*, 43 Cardozo L. Rev. 855 (2022).

The grand jury right, in short, is the ugly duckling of the Bill of Rights.

The truth is that Americans soured on the grand jury over the course of the nineteenth century, finding it inefficient and cumbersome, antidemocratic in its traditional secrecy requirements, and a threat to individual liberty in its inquisitorial powers. John F. Decker, *Legislating New Federalism: The Call for Grand Jury Reform in the States*, 58 Okla. L. Rev. 341, 346-47 (2005). Even before *Hurtado* some states had eliminated the grand jury requirement altogether, permitting prosecutions to be commenced by either grand jury indictment or by the prosecutor filing charges with the court that were contained in a document called an "information," which would be reviewed by a magistrate in a preliminary examination. *Id.* After *Hurtado*, the next six states admitted to the union did not guarantee the right to grand jury indictment in their constitutions. *Id.* Today, there is no grand jury indictment requirement in approximately half of the states, and in those states charges can be brought by information or an equivalent procedure. *Id.* at 354-55. In the remaining half, a grand jury indictment is required for the commencement of at least certain types of crimes. *Id.*

Ugly duckling or not, where it exists the grand jury is a critical part of the criminal process. Federally, and in many states as well, a grand jury indictment is the necessary first step in a criminal prosecution. And in the federal system and in many states the grand jury's investigative ability—to subpoena witnesses and documents, to confer immunity from prosecution—is its true power. The term "its power" is used loosely—as will be seen the grand jury is in essence a tool of the prosecutor, and the powers "it" has are in truth enjoyed by and deployed by the prosecutor. So not only does the grand jury have a sort of junior varsity status in the Bill of Rights, it is of interest less as a source of "rights" than as a source of "power"—and powers, no less, that are not really its own.

Section A of this chapter is introductory, further reflecting on the grand jury's second-tier constitutional status. Section B looks at the issue of race and the composition of the grand jury. Section C explores two central attributes of the grand jury—its historic independence and informality—attributes that are still recognized today, and which make it a particularly powerful investigative force in service of the prosecutor. Section D takes a close look at the grand jury's power to subpoena documents and other records, power that is virtually unfettered in comparison to other public bodies or to a private litigant's ability to get information from an adversary through the discovery process. Section E considers the rules of grand jury secrecy, which are often misconstrued by prosecutors and the public alike. Section F examines the rights, if any, of grand jury witnesses, including the Department of Justice's policies on grand jury witnesses. Section G looks into how the government can abuse the grand jury power for improper purposes. Section H looks at the grand jury's output—indictments. And finally, Section I takes a brief look at the grand jury's role in police misconduct cases.

Almost all of the cases in this section are federal. Where it exists under state law, the grand jury in most respects functions in substance similarly to its federal counterpart. There are numerous administrative variances among state grand juries and as compared to federal practice, however. For example, in federal grand jury practice, governed to a significant extent by Rule 6 of the Federal Rules of Criminal Procedure, there are 23 people on a federal grand jury with 16 votes required for an indictment; state grand jury sizes range from 5 to 23, with the percentage requirements for an indictment varying from a simple majority to near unanimity. Decker, *Legislating New Federalism*, *supra* at 341, 354-55.

A. INTRODUCTION: GRAND JURY MYTHOS

As if to compensate for the grand jury's exile from the land of incorporation, the Supreme Court has consistently exalted the grand jury in hagiographic terms, describing its historical conception and function in passages that read like—pick your term—paeans, odes, love songs, hosannas. This excerpt from *United States v. Calandra*, 414 U.S. 338 (1974), is representative:

> The institution of the grand jury is deeply rooted in Anglo-American history. In England, the grand jury served for centuries both as a body of accusers sworn to discover and present for trial persons suspected of criminal wrongdoing and as a protector of citizens against arbitrary and oppressive governmental action. In this country the Founders thought the grand jury so essential to basic liberties that they provided in the Fifth Amendment that federal prosecution for serious crimes can only be instituted by "a presentment or indictment of a Grand Jury." The grand jury's historic functions survive to this day. Its responsibilities continue to include both the determination whether there is probable cause to believe a crime has been committed and the protection of citizens against unfounded criminal prosecutions.
>
> Traditionally the grand jury has been accorded wide latitude to inquire into violations of criminal law. No judge presides to monitor its proceedings. It deliberates in secret and may determine alone the course of its inquiry. The grand jury may compel the production of evidence or the testimony of witnesses as it considers appropriate, and its operation generally is unrestrained by the technical procedural and evidentiary rules governing the conduct of criminal trials. It is a grand inquest, a body with powers of investigation and inquisition, the scope of whose inquiries is not to be limited narrowly by questions of propriety or forecasts of the probable result of the investigation, or by doubts whether any particular individual will be found properly subject to an accusation of crime.

Id. at 342-43. By retelling this and other versions of the grand jury myth the Court seems to give itself permission to ignore how the grand jury operates in the real world, particularly with respect to its independence. For example, it has been common knowledge for decades that the grand jury is essentially a tool of the prosecutor. *United States v. Mara*, 410 U.S. 19, 23 (1973) (Douglas, J., dissenting). *See generally* Wayne L. Morse, *A Survey of the Grand Jury System*, 10 Or. L. Rev. 101, 101 (1931) (noting the criticism that the grand jury was "merely a rubber stamp for the district attorney"). Yet the Court has never stopped insisting upon the grand jury's independence, and deciding cases based upon that fiction.

The Court's mythologizing also serves to obscure the formidable power of a prosecutor-led grand jury. "Save for torture, it would be hard to find a more effective tool of tyranny than the power of unlimited and unchecked ex parte examination." *United States v. Remington*, 208 F. 2d 567, 573 (2d Cir. 1953) (L. Hand, J., dissenting), *cert. denied*, 347 U.S. 913 (1954). Yet as in the above passage from *Calandra*, the Court's hosannas consistently sing of the grand jury's dual functions as "sword" and "shield." The cases before the Court, however, almost always focus only on the sword—the grand jury's role as an investigatory or inquisitory body.

B. RACE AND GRAND JURY COMPOSITION

As was the case with its fancier-named cousin the petit jury, the grand jury historically in the United States excluded minorities. The next two cases look at how that began to change.

Castaneda v. Partida

430 U.S. 482 (1977)

Mr. Justice Blackmun delivered the opinion of the Court.

The sole issue presented in this case is whether the State of Texas, in the person of petitioner, the Sheriff of Hidalgo County, successfully rebutted respondent prisoner's prima facie showing of discrimination against Mexican-Americans in the state grand jury selection process. In his brief, petitioner, in claiming effective rebuttal, asserts:

> This list (of the grand jurors that indicted respondent) indicates that 50 percent of the names appearing thereon were Spanish. The record indicates that 3 of the 5 jury commissioners, 5 of the grand jurors who returned the indictment, 7 of the petit jurors, the judge presiding at the trial, and the Sheriff who served notice on the grand jurors to appear had Spanish surnames.

I

This Court on prior occasions has considered the workings of the Texas system of grand jury selection. Texas employs the "key man" system, which relies on jury commissioners to select prospective grand jurors from the community at large. The procedure begins with the state district judge's appointment of from three to five persons to serve as jury commissioners. The commissioners then "shall select not less than 15 nor more than 20 persons from the citizens of different portions of the county" to compose the list from which the actual grand jury will be drawn. When at least 12 of the persons on the list appear in court pursuant to summons, the district judge proceeds to "test their qualifications." . . . A grand juror must be a citizen of Texas and of the county, be a qualified voter in the county, be "of sound mind and good moral character," be literate, have no prior felony conviction, and be under no pending indictment "or other legal accusation for theft or of any felony." Interrogation under oath is the method specified for testing the prospective juror's qualifications. . . . After the court finds 12 jurors who meet the statutory qualifications, they are impaneled as the grand jury.

II

Respondent, Rodrigo Partida, was indicted in March 1972 by the grand jury of the 92d District Court of Hidalgo County for the crime of burglary of a private residence at night with intent to rape. Hidalgo is one of the border counties of southern Texas. After a trial before a petit jury, respondent was convicted and sentenced to eight years in the custody of the Texas Department of Corrections. He first raised his claim of discrimination in the grand jury selection process on a motion for new trial in the State District Court. In support of his motion, respondent testified about the general existence of discrimination against Mexican-Americans in that area of Texas and introduced statistics from the 1970 census and the Hidalgo County grand jury records. The census figures show that in 1970, the population of Hidalgo County was 181,535. Persons of Spanish language or Spanish surname totaled 143,611. On the assumption that all the persons of Spanish language or Spanish surname were Mexican-Americans, these figures show that 79.1% of the county's population was Mexican-American.

Respondent's data compiled from the Hidalgo County grand jury records from 1962 to 1972 showed that over that period, the average percentage of Spanish-surnamed grand jurors was 39%. In the 2½-year period during which the District Judge who impaneled the jury that indicted respondent was in charge, the average percentage was 45.5%. On the list from which the grand jury that indicted respondent was selected, 50% were Spanish surnamed. The last set of data that respondent introduced, again from the 1970 census, illustrated a number of ways in which Mexican-Americans tend to be underprivileged, including poverty-level incomes, less desirable jobs, substandard housing, and lower levels of education. The State offered no evidence at all either attacking respondent's allegations of discrimination or demonstrating that his statistics were unreliable in any way. The State District Court, nevertheless, denied the motion for a new trial.

On appeal, the Texas Court of Criminal Appeals affirmed the conviction. Reaching the merits of the claim of grand jury discrimination, the court held that respondent had failed to make out a prima facie case. In the court's view, he should have shown how many of the females who served on the grand juries were Mexican-Americans married to men with Anglo-American surnames, how many Mexican-Americans were excused for reasons of age or health, or other legal reasons, and how many of those listed by the census would not have met the statutory qualifications of citizenship, literacy, sound mind, moral character, and lack of criminal record or accusation. Quite beyond the uncertainties in the statistics, the court found it impossible to believe that discrimination could have been directed against a Mexican-American, in light of the many elective positions held by Mexican-Americans in the county and the substantial representation of Mexican-Americans on recent grand juries. In essence, the court refused to presume that Mexican-Americans would discriminate against their own kind.

After exhausting his state remedies, respondent filed his petition for habeas corpus in the Federal District Court, alleging a denial of due process and equal protection, guaranteed by the Fourteenth Amendment, because of gross under-representation of Mexican-Americans on the Hidalgo County grand juries. At a hearing at which the state transcript was introduced, petitioner presented the testimony of the state judge who selected the jury commissioners who had compiled the list from which respondent's grand jury was taken. The judge first reviewed the State's grand jury selection process. In selecting the jury commissioners, the judge stated that he tried to appoint a greater number of Mexican-Americans than members of other ethnic groups. He testified that he instructed the commissioners about the qualifications of a grand juror and the exemptions provided by law. The record is silent, however, with regard to instructions dealing with the potential problem of discrimination directed against any identifiable group. The judge admitted that the actual results of the selection process had not produced grand jury lists that were "representative of the ethnic balance in the community." The jury commissioners themselves, who were the only ones in a position to explain the apparent substantial underrepresentation of Mexican-Americans and to provide information on the actual operation of the selection process, were never called.

On the basis of the evidence before it, the court concluded that respondent had made out a "bare prima facie case" of invidious discrimination with his proof of "a long continued disproportion in the composition of the grand juries in Hidalgo County." Based on an examination of the reliability of the statistics offered by respondent, however, despite the lack of evidence in the record justifying such an inquiry, the court stated that the prima facie case was weak. The court believed that the census statistics did not reflect the true situation accurately, because of recent changes in the Hidalgo County area and the court's own impression of the demographic characteristics of the Mexican-American community. On the other hand, the court recognized that the Texas key-man system of grand jury selection was highly subjective, and was "archaic and inefficient," and that this was a factor arguing for less tolerance in the percentage differences. On balance, the court's doubts about the reliability of the statistics, coupled with its opinion that Mexican-Americans constituted a "governing majority" in the county, caused it to conclude that the prima facie case was rebutted. The "governing majority" theory distinguished respondent's case from all preceding cases involving similar disparities. On the basis of those findings, the court dismissed the petition.

The United States Court of Appeals for the Fifth Circuit reversed. It agreed with the District Court that respondent had succeeded in making out a prima facie case. It found, however, that the State had failed to rebut that showing. The "governing majority" theory contributed little to the State's case in the absence of specific proof to explain the disparity. In light of the State's abdication of its responsibility to introduce controverting evidence, the court held that respondent was entitled to prevail.

We granted certiorari to consider whether the existence of a "governing majority" in itself can rebut a prima facie case of discrimination in grand jury selection, and, if not, whether the State otherwise met its burden of proof.

III

A

This Court has long recognized that "it is a denial of the equal protection of the laws to try a defendant of a particular race or color under an indictment issued by a grand jury . . . from which all persons of his race or color have, solely because of that race or color, been excluded by the State." While the earlier cases involved absolute exclusion of an identifiable group, later cases established the principle that substantial underrepresentation of the group constitutes a constitutional violation as well, if it results from purposeful discrimination. Recent cases have established the fact that an official act is not unconstitutional solely because it has a racially disproportionate impact. Nevertheless, as the Court recognized in *Arlington Heights*, "(s)ometimes a clear pattern, unexplainable on grounds other than race, emerges from the effect of the state action even when the governing legislation appears neutral on its face." In *Washington v. Davis*, the application of these principles to the jury cases was considered:

> It is also clear from the cases dealing with racial discrimination in the selection of juries that the systematic exclusion of Negroes is itself such an "unequal application of the law . . . as to show intentional discrimination." . . . A prima facie case of discriminatory purpose may be proved as well by the absence of Negroes on a particular jury combined with the failure of the jury commissioners to be informed of eligible Negro jurors in a community, . . . or with racially non-neutral selection procedures. . . . With a prima facie case made out, "the burden of proof shifts to the State to rebut the presumption of unconstitutional action by showing that permissible racially neutral selection criteria and procedures have produced the monochromatic result."

Thus, in order to show that an equal protection violation has occurred in the context of grand jury selection, the defendant must show that the procedure employed resulted in substantial underrepresentation of his race or of the identifiable group to which he belongs. The first step is to establish that the group is one that is a recognizable, distinct class, singled out for different treatment under the laws, as written or as applied. Next, the degree of underrepresentation must be proved, by comparing the proportion of the group in the total population to the proportion called to serve as grand jurors, over a significant period of time. This method of proof, sometimes called the "rule of exclusion," has been held to be available as a method of proving discrimination in jury selection against a delineated class. Finally, as noted above, a selection procedure that is susceptible of abuse or is not racially neutral supports the presumption of discrimination raised by the statistical showing. Once the defendant has shown substantial underrepresentation of his group, he has made out a prima facie case of discriminatory purpose, and the burden then shifts to the State to rebut that case.

B

In this case, it is no longer open to dispute that Mexican-Americans are a clearly identifiable class. The statistics introduced by respondent from the 1970 census illustrate disadvantages to which the group has been subject. Additionally, the selection procedure is not racially neutral with respect to Mexican-Americans; Spanish surnames are just as easily identifiable as race was from the questionnaires in *Alexander* or the notations and card colors in *Whitus v. Georgia* and *Avery v. Georgia*.

The disparity proved by the 1970 census statistics showed that the population of the county was 79.1% Mexican-American, but that, over an 11-year period, only 39% of the persons summoned for grand jury service were Mexican-American. This difference of 40% is greater than that found [in other cases]. Since the State presented no evidence showing why the 11-year period was not reliable, we take it as the relevant base for comparison. The mathematical disparities that have been accepted by this Court as adequate for a prima facie case have all been within the range presented here. For example, in *Whitus v. Georgia* (1967), the number of Negroes listed on the tax digest amounted to 27.1% of the taxpayers, but only 9.1% of those on the grand jury venire. The disparity was held to be sufficient to make out a prima facie case of discrimination. We agree with the District Court and the Court of Appeals that the proof in this case was enough to establish a prima facie case of discrimination against the Mexican-Americans in the Hidalgo County grand jury selection.

Supporting this conclusion is the fact that the Texas system of selecting grand jurors is highly subjective. The facial constitutionality of the key-man system, of course, has been accepted by this Court. Nevertheless, the Court has noted that the system is susceptible of abuse as applied. Additionally, as noted, persons with Spanish surnames are readily identifiable.

The showing made by respondent therefore shifted the burden of proof to the State to dispel the inference of intentional discrimination. Inexplicably, the State introduced practically no evidence. The testimony of the State District Judge dealt principally with the selection of the jury commissioners and the instructions given to them. The commissioners themselves were not called to testify. A case such as *Swain v. Alabama* illustrates the potential usefulness of such testimony, when it sets out in detail the procedures followed by the commissioners. The opinion of the Texas Court of Criminal Appeals is particularly revealing as to the lack of rebuttal evidence in the record:

> How many of those listed in the census figures with Mexican-American names were not citizens of the state, but were so-called "wet-backs" from the south side of the Rio Grande; how many were migrant workers and not residents of Hidalgo County; how many were illiterate and could not read and write; how many were not of sound mind and good moral character, how many had been convicted of a felony or were under indictment or legal accusation for theft or a felony; none of these facts appear in the record.

In fact, the census figures showed that only a small part of the population reported for Hidalgo County was not native born. Without some testimony from the grand jury commissioners about the method by which they determined the other qualifications for grand jurors prior to the statutory time for testing qualifications, it is impossible to draw any inference about literacy, sound mind and moral character, and criminal record from the statistics about the population as a whole. These are questions of disputed fact that present problems not amenable to resolution by an appellate court. We emphasize, however, that we are not saying that the statistical disparities proved here could never be explained in another case; we are simply saying that the State did not do so in this case.

C

In light of our holding that respondent proved a prima facie case of discrimination that was not rebutted by any of the evidence presently in the record, we have only to consider whether the District Court's "governing majority" theory filled the evidentiary gap. In our view, it did not dispel the presumption of purposeful discrimination in the circumstances of this case. Because of the many facets of human motivation, it would be unwise to presume as a matter of law that human beings of one definable group will not discriminate against other members of their group. . . . The problem is a complex one, about which widely differing views can be held, and, as such, it would be somewhat precipitate to take judicial notice of one view over another on the basis of a record as barren as this.

Furthermore, the relevance of a governing majority of elected officials to the grand jury selection process is questionable. The fact that certain elected officials are Mexican-American demonstrates nothing about the motivations and methods of the grand jury commissioners who select persons for grand jury lists. The only arguably relevant fact in this record on the issue is that three of the five jury commissioners in respondent's case were Mexican-American. Knowing only this, we would be forced to rely on the reasoning that we have rejected that human beings would not discriminate against their own kind in order to find that the presumption of purposeful discrimination was rebutted. Without the benefit of this simple behavioral presumption, discriminatory intent can be rebutted only with evidence in the record about the way in which the commissioners operated and their reasons for doing so. It was the State's burden to supply such evidence, once respondent established his prima facie case. The State's failure in this regard leaves unchallenged respondent's proof of purposeful discrimination.

Finally, even if a "governing majority" theory has general applicability in cases of this kind, the inadequacy of the record in this case does not permit such an approach. Among the evidentiary deficiencies are the lack of any indication of how long the Mexican-Americans have enjoyed "governing majority" status, the absence of information about the relative power inherent in the elective offices held by Mexican-Americans, and the uncertain relevance of the general political power to the specific issue in this case. Even for the most recent time period, when presumably the political power of Mexican-Americans was at its greatest, the discrepancy between the number of Mexican-Americans in the total population and the number on the grand jury lists was substantial. Thus, under the facts presented in this case, the "governing majority" theory is not developed fully enough to satisfy the State's burden of rebuttal.

IV

Rather than relying on an approach to the jury discrimination question that is as faintly defined as the "governing majority" theory is on this record, we prefer to look at all the facts that bear on the issue, such as the statistical disparities, the method of selection, and any other relevant testimony as to the manner in which the selection process was implemented. Under this standard, the proof offered by respondent was sufficient to demonstrate a prima facie case of discrimination in grand jury selection. Since the State failed to rebut the presumption of purposeful discrimination by competent testimony, despite two opportunities to do so, we affirm the Court of Appeals' holding of a denial of equal protection of the law in the grand jury selection process in respondent's case.

It is so ordered.

NOTES AND QUESTIONS

1. Consider the operation of Texas's "key man" system for the selection of grand jurors. The Court notes that while the facial constitutionality of such a system has been upheld, the system is "highly subjective" and "is susceptible to abuse as applied." How many different layers of discretion are built into the system?

2. The Court finds that the defendant made out a "prima facie case" of discrimination in violation of the Equal Protection Clause. What is the significance of a "prima facie case" in this context? Is this methodology an alternative to proving intentional discrimination? What are the components of defendant's prima facie case? What does the Court mean by "the rule of exclusion"?

3. In response to defendant's federal habeas challenge the state offered only testimony from the state district judge who selected the jury commissioners in the key man system, and not from the commissioners themselves or the persons the commissioners enlisted to compile juror lists. The Court finds the state's response "inexplicabl[e]," *id.* at 498. What might the explanation be? What showing by the state might be sufficient to rebut the statistical force of the prima facie case?

4. The district court found that the defendant had made out a "weak" prima facie case of discrimination but dismissed the claim nonetheless, in part because Mexican Americans constituted a "governing majority" in the county in light of their substantial presence in elective positions. Both the Court and Justice Marshall, concurring, strongly criticize reliance on this factor. Can you imagine a scenario where such evidence might be relevant, for example, if the jury commissioners themselves were Mexican Americans?

5. While it does not acknowledge the racist diatribe by the Texas Court of Criminal Appeals, *id.* at 498, which the majority opinion calls "revealing," the dissenting opinion of Justice Burger also faults the defendant for not providing a "meaningful statistical disparity" in that there is no showing that "disproportionately large numbers of eligible individuals were excluded systematically from grand jury service." *Id.* at 505. What is eligibility supposed to mean in this context? How could such a statistical disparity be demonstrated?

Vasquez v. Hillery

474 U.S. 254 (1986)

Justice Marshall delivered the opinion of the Court.

The Warden of San Quentin State Prison asks this Court to retire a doctrine of equal protection jurisprudence first announced in 1880. The time has come, he urges, for us to abandon the rule requiring reversal of the conviction of any defendant indicted by a grand jury from which members of his own race were systematically excluded.

I

In 1962, the grand jury of Kings County, California, indicted respondent, Booker T. Hillery, for a brutal murder. Before trial in Superior Court, respondent moved to quash the indictment on the ground that it had been issued by a grand jury from which blacks had been systematically excluded. A hearing on respondent's motion was held by Judge Meredith Wingrove, who was the sole Superior Court Judge in the county and had personally selected all grand juries, including the one that indicted respondent, for the previous seven years. Absolving himself of any discriminatory intent, Judge Wingrove refused to quash the indictment. Respondent was subsequently convicted of first-degree murder.

For the next 16 years, respondent pursued appeals and collateral relief in the state courts, raising at every opportunity his equal protection challenge to the grand jury that indicted him. Less than one month after the California Supreme Court foreclosed his final avenue of state relief in 1978, respondent filed a petition for a writ of habeas corpus in federal court, raising that same challenge. The District Court concluded that respondent had established discrimination in the grand jury, and granted the writ.

II

• • •

Several affidavits challenged here as "new" evidence supported respondent's allegations that no black had ever served on the grand jury in Kings County and that qualified blacks in the county were available to serve, which he had pressed in his pretrial motion to quash in Superior Court and throughout the state proceedings. The California Supreme Court found that the total absence of blacks from the grand jury in the history of Kings County was an undisputed fact. That fact was entitled, therefore, to a presumption of correctness on federal review. The California Supreme Court also discussed Judge Wingrove's consideration of blacks' qualifications, and found that blacks had served as petit jurors, minimum eligibility requirements for which were substantially the same as for grand jurors. . . .

The remaining "new" evidence under attack, a computer analysis submitted in response to the District Court's request, assessed the mathematical probability that chance or accident could have accounted for the exclusion of blacks from the Kings County grand jury over the years at issue. Petitioner would have us conclude that the "sophisticated computer techniques" rendered respondent's claim a "wholly different animal." These statistical estimates, however, added nothing to the case that this Court has not considered intrinsic to the consideration of any grand jury discrimination claim. As early as 1942, this Court rejected a contention that absence of blacks on the grand jury was insufficient to support an inference of discrimination, summarily asserting that "chance or accident could hardly have accounted for the continuous omission of negroes from the grand jury lists for so long a period as sixteen years or more." This proposition, which the Court derived solely on the basis of judicial intuition, is precisely what respondent sought to establish by methods now considered somewhat more reliable.

More recently, in reviewing a habeas corpus proceeding, this Court independently applied general statistical principles to the evidence on the record in order to assess the role of chance in the exclusion of Mexican-Americans from a grand jury in Texas. *Castaneda v. Partida* (1977). Form would indeed triumph over substance were we to allow the question of exhaustion to turn on whether a federal judge has relied on educated conjecture or has sought out a more sophisticated interpretative aid to accomplish the same objective.

We emphasize that the District Court's request for further information was evidently motivated by a responsible concern that it provide the meaningful federal review of constitutional claims that the writ of habeas corpus has contemplated throughout its history. Respondent had initially submitted only the evidence that had been considered in state court, and subsequently complied with the court's request by furnishing materials no broader than necessary to meet the needs of the court. Accordingly, the circumstances present no occasion for the Court to consider a case in which the prisoner has attempted to expedite federal review by deliberately withholding essential facts from the state courts. We hold merely that the supplemental evidence presented by respondent did not fundamentally alter the legal claim already considered by the state courts, and, therefore, did not require that respondent be remitted to state court for consideration of that evidence.

III

On the merits, petitioner urges this Court to find that discrimination in the grand jury amounted to harmless error in this case, claiming that the evidence against respondent was overwhelming and that discrimination no longer infects the selection of grand juries in Kings County. Respondent's conviction after a fair trial, we are told, purged any taint attributable to the indictment process. Our acceptance of this theory would require abandonment of more than a century of consistent precedent.

In 1880, this Court reversed a state conviction on the ground that the indictment charging the offense had been issued by a grand jury from which blacks had been excluded. We reasoned that deliberate exclusion of blacks "is practically a brand upon them, affixed by the law, an assertion of their inferiority, and a stimulant to that race prejudice which is an impediment to securing to individuals of the race that equal justice which the law aims to secure to all others." *Strauder v. West Virginia* (1880).

Thereafter, the Court has repeatedly rejected all arguments that a conviction may stand despite racial discrimination in the selection of the grand jury. Only six years ago, the Court explicitly addressed the question whether this unbroken line of case law should be reconsidered in favor of a harmless-error standard, and determined that it should not. We reaffirmed our conviction that discrimination on the basis of race in the selection of grand jurors "strikes at the fundamental values of our judicial system and our society as a whole," and that the criminal defendant's right to equal protection of the laws has been denied when he is indicted by a grand jury from which members of a racial group purposefully have been excluded.

Petitioner argues here that requiring a State to retry a defendant, sometimes years later, imposes on it an unduly harsh penalty for a constitutional defect bearing no relation to the fundamental fairness of the trial. Yet intentional discrimination in the selection of grand jurors is a grave constitutional trespass, possible only under color of state authority, and wholly within the power of the State to prevent. Thus, the remedy we have embraced for over a century—the only effective remedy for this violation—is not disproportionate to the evil that it seeks to deter. If grand jury discrimination becomes a thing of the past, no conviction will ever again be lost on account of it.

Nor are we persuaded that discrimination in the grand jury has no effect on the fairness of the criminal trials that result from that grand jury's actions. The grand jury does not determine only that probable cause exists to believe that a defendant committed a crime, or that it does not. In the hands of the grand jury lies the power to charge a greater offense or a lesser offense; numerous counts or a single count; and perhaps most significant of all, a capital offense or a noncapital offense—all on the basis of the same facts. Moreover, "[t]he grand jury is not bound to indict in every case where a conviction can be obtained." Thus, even if a grand jury's determination of probable cause is confirmed in hindsight by a conviction on the indicted offense, that confirmation in no way suggests that the discrimination did not impermissibly infect the framing of the indictment and, consequently, the nature or very existence of the proceedings to come.

When constitutional error calls into question the objectivity of those charged with bringing a defendant to judgment, a reviewing court can neither indulge a presumption of regularity nor evaluate the resulting harm. Accordingly, when the trial judge is discovered to have had some basis for rendering a biased judgment, his actual motivations are hidden from review, and we must presume that the process was impaired. Similarly, when a petit jury has been selected upon improper criteria or has been exposed to prejudicial publicity, we have required reversal of the conviction because the effect of the violation cannot be ascertained. Like these fundamental flaws, which never have been thought harmless, discrimination in the grand jury undermines the structural integrity of the criminal tribunal itself, and is not amenable to harmless-error review.

Just as a conviction is void under the Equal Protection Clause if the prosecutor deliberately charged the defendant on account of his race, a conviction cannot be understood to cure the taint attributable to a charging body selected on the basis of race. Once having found discrimination in the selection of a grand jury, we simply cannot know that the need to indict would have been assessed in the same way by a grand jury properly constituted. The overriding imperative to eliminate this systemic flaw in the charging process, as well as the difficulty of assessing its effect on any given defendant, requires our continued adherence to a rule of mandatory reversal.

The judgment of the Court of Appeals, accordingly, is affirmed.

• • •

It is so ordered.

NOTES AND QUESTIONS

1. The factual findings relevant here are set forth in an opinion of the district court. *See Hillery v. Pulley*, 563 F. Supp. 1228 (E.D. Cal. 1983). The population of Kings County was 4 percent Black in 1950 and 5 percent Black in 1960. *Id.* at 1231. No Black person had ever served on a Kings County grand jury. *Id.* The state court judge who had personally selected all of the county's grand jurors during the relevant period testified at the state court hearing on defendant's motion. He denied any prejudice or any attempt to exclude Black people; he said he just tried to select grand jurors of "the better type" of people. *Id.* The district court found, following *Castaneda*, that this methodology was "susceptible to abuse as applied." A statistician testified that the probability that the total exclusion of Black jurors was due to chance was 2 in 1,000. *Id.* at 1242.

2. The Court rejects the state's argument that reversal of the conviction is unwarranted because any discrimination in the grand jury selection process was harmless error inasmuch as the defendant was convicted at trial and thus any "taint" was purged. The premise of this argument seems to be that if defendant was convicted by a petit jury in a trial requiring a unanimous verdict under a reasonable doubt standard, then, as a matter of logic, he necessarily would have been indicted by any grand jury on a probable cause standard, even one including Black jurors, where unanimity was not required.

Is this premise unassailable?

3. The Court rejects the defendant's harmless error argument on essentially three grounds: (a) that reversal is "the only effective remedy for this violation"; (b) that discrimination in the grand jury may have infected the framing of the indictment, independent of its effect on the finding of probable cause; and (c) that the error undermines the structural integrity of the criminal process and is thus not amenable to harmless error analysis.

Which of these arguments do you find most and least persuasive? What does the Court mean by the "structural integrity" of the criminal process? What other types of improper influences on the grand jury might undermine the "structural integrity" of the criminal process?

4. The State argues, with some support from the dissent, that it is unfair to require it to retry the defendant 24 years after the fact. The Court responds that "intentional discrimination in the selection of grand jurors is a grave constitutional trespass, possible only under color of state authority, and wholly within the power of the State to prevent." *Id.* at 262. What else might the Court have said in response to the state's "unfairness" argument?

C. GRAND JURY INDEPENDENCE AND INFORMALITY

Many of the Supreme Court's passages on the grand jury laud its independence, noting that it is not technically a part of any of the three branches of the federal government. In a similar vein, praise is given to the free-spirited nature of its inquiries, unburdened by legal formalities and technicalities. Consider as you read the next set of cases whether these descriptions are accurate and, to the extent they are, whether these are virtues or vices.

United States v. Costello

350 U.S. 359 (1956)

Mr. Justice BLACK delivered the opinion of the Court.

We granted certiorari in this case to consider a single question: "May a defendant be required to stand trial and a conviction be sustained where only hearsay evidence was presented to the grand jury which indicted him?"

Petitioner, Frank Costello, was indicted for wilfully attempting to evade payment of income taxes due the United States for the years 1947, 1948 and 1949. The charge was that petitioner falsely and fraudulently reported less income than he and his wife actually received during the taxable years in question. Petitioner promptly filed a motion for inspection of the minutes of the grand jury and for a dismissal of the indictment. His motion was based on an affidavit stating that he was firmly convinced there could have been no legal or competent evidence before the grand jury which indicted him since he had reported all his income and paid all taxes due. The motion was denied. At the trial which followed the Government offered evidence designed to show increases is Costello's net worth in an attempt to prove that he had received more income during the years in question than he had reported. To establish its case the Government called and examined 144 witnesses and introduced 368 exhibits. All of the testimony and documents related to business transactions and expenditures by petitioner and his wife. The prosecution concluded its case by calling three government agents. Their investigations had produced the evidence used against petitioner at the trial. They were allowed to summarize the vast amount of evidence already heard and to introduce computations showing, if correct, that petitioner and his wife had received far greater income than they had reported. We have held such summarizations admissible in a "net worth" case like this.

Counsel for petitioner asked each government witness at the trial whether he had appeared before the grand jury which returned the indictment. This cross-examination developed the fact that the three investigating officers had been the only witnesses before the grand jury. After the Government concluded its case, petitioner again moved to dismiss the indictment on the ground that the only evidence before the grand jury was "hearsay," since the three officers had no firsthand knowledge of the transactions upon which their computations were based. Nevertheless the trial court again refused to dismiss the indictment, and petitioner was convicted. The Court of Appeals affirmed, holding that the indictment was valid even though the sole evidence before the grand jury was hearsay. Petitioner here urges: (1) that an indictment based solely on hearsay evidence violates that part of the Fifth Amendment providing that "No person shall be held to answer for a capital, or otherwise infamous crime, unless on a presentment or indictment of a Grand Jury . . ." and (2) that if the Fifth Amendment does not invalidate an indictment based solely on hearsay we should now lay down such a rule for the guidance of federal courts.

The Fifth Amendment provides that federal prosecutions for capital or otherwise infamous crimes must be instituted by presentments or indictments of grand juries. But neither the Fifth Amendment nor any other constitutional provision prescribes the kind of evidence upon which grand juries must act. The grand jury is an English institution, brought to this country by the early colonists and incorporated in the Constitution by the Founders. There is every reason to believe that our constitutional grand jury was intended to operate substantially like its English progenitor. The basic purpose of the English grand jury was to provide a fair method for instituting criminal proceedings against persons believed to have committed crimes. Grand jurors were selected from the body of the people and their work was not hampered by rigid procedural or evidential rules. In fact, grand jurors could act on their own knowledge and were free to make their presentments or indictments on such information as they deemed satisfactory. Despite its broad power to institute criminal proceedings the grand jury grew in popular favor with the years. It acquired an independence in England free from control by the Crown or judges. Its adoption in our Constitution as the sole method for preferring charges in serious criminal cases shows the high place it held as an instrument of justice. And in this country as in England of old the grand jury has convened as a body of laymen, free from technical rules, acting in secret, pledged to indict no one because of prejudice and to free no one because of special favor. As late as 1927 an English historian could say that English grand juries were still free to act on their own knowledge if they pleased to do so. And in 1852 Mr. Justice Nelson on circuit could say "No case has been cited, nor have we been able to find any, furnishing an authority for looking into and revising the judgment of the grand jury upon the evidence, for the purpose of determining whether or not the finding was founded upon sufficient proof. . . ."

In *Holt v. United States*, this Court had to decide whether an indictment should be quashed because supported in part by incompetent evidence. Aside from the incompetent evidence "there was very little evidence against the accused." The Court refused to hold that such an indictment should be quashed, pointing out that "The abuses of criminal practice would be enhanced if indictments could be upset on such a ground." The same thing is true where as here all the evidence before the grand jury was in the nature of "hearsay." If indictments were to be held open to challenge on the ground that there was inadequate or incompetent evidence before the grand jury, the resulting delay would be great indeed. The result of such a rule would be that before trial on the merits a defendant could always insist on a kind of preliminary trial to determine the competency and adequacy of the evidence before the grand jury. This is not required by the Fifth Amendment. An indictment returned by a legally constituted and unbiased grand jury, like an information drawn by the prosecutor, if valid on its face, is enough to call for trial of the charge on the merits. The Fifth Amendment requires nothing more.

Petitioner urges that this Court should exercise its power to supervise the administration of justice in federal courts and establish a rule permitting defendants to challenge indictments on the ground that they are not supported by adequate or competent evidence. No persuasive reasons are advanced for establishing such a rule. It would run counter to the whole history of the grand jury institution, in which laymen conduct their inquiries unfettered by technical rules. Neither justice nor the concept of a fair trial requires such a change. In a trial on the merits, defendants are entitled to a strict observance of all the rules designed to bring about a fair verdict. Defendants are not entitled, however, to a rule which would result in interminable delay but add nothing to the assurance of a fair trial.

Affirmed.

Mr. Justice Clark and Mr. Justice Harlan took no part in the consideration or decision of this case.

Mr. Justice Burton, concurring.

I agree with the denial of the motion to quash the indictment. In my view, however, this case does not justify the breadth of the declarations made by the Court. I assume that this Court would not preclude an examination of grand-jury action to ascertain the existence of bias or prejudice in an indictment. Likewise, it seems to me that if it is shown that the grand jury had before it no substantial or rationally persuasive evidence upon which to base its indictment, that indictment should be quashed. To hold a person to answer to such an empty indictment for a capital or otherwise infamous federal crime robs the Fifth Amendment of much of its protective value to the private citizen.

Here, as in *Holt v. United States*, substantial and rationally persuasive evidence apparently was presented to the grand jury. We may fairly assume that the evidence before that jury included much of the testimony later given at the trial by the three government agents who said that they had testified before the grand jury. At the trial, they summarized financial transactions of the accused about which they were not qualified to testify of their own knowledge. To use Justice Holmes' phrase in the *Holt* case, such testimony, standing alone, was "incompetent by circumstances," and yet it was rationally persuasive of the crime charged and provided a substantial basis for the indictment. At the trial, with preliminary testimony laying the foundation for it, the same testimony constituted an important part of the competent evidence upon which the conviction was obtained.

To sustain this indictment under the above circumstances is well enough, but I agree with Judge Learned Hand that "if it appeared that no evidence had been offered that rationally established the facts, the indictment ought to be quashed; because then the grand jury would have in substance abdicated." Accordingly, I concur in this judgment, but do so for the reasons stated in the opinion of the Court of Appeals and subject to the limitations there expressed.

NOTES AND QUESTIONS

1. Note that defendant was unable before trial to get access to the transcripts of grand jury testimony. Had he been prosecuted just two years later, he would have been able to get access to the grand jury testimony at least of the witnesses who testified against him at trial under the Jencks Act. Yet that may not have been as useful as he likely expected inasmuch as the only witnesses who testified in the grand jury were law enforcement agents.

Why would the prosecutors have proceeded this way, putting their entire case to the grand jury by way of hearsay in the form of summary witness testimony? *See* Fed. R. Evid. 1006 (authorizing use of summary exhibits or testimony). What are the pros and cons from a prosecutor's perspective of calling percipient witnesses to testify in the grand jury as opposed to relying on hearsay, as they did in *Costello*?

2. As usual, the Court provides background on the history of the grand jury "institution." This particular ode to the grand jury focuses on its independence and informality, its amateurish quality—"a body of laymen, free from technical rules." The Court even claims that recently "grand juries were still free to act on their own knowledge."

Isn't it especially ironic that the Court relies on this myth based on the facts of *Costello*? Is the rule against hearsay a "technical rule"?

3. Defendant Frank Costello was at the time of his indictment in this case the boss of the Lucky Luciano branch of New York's organized crime families. Might this have influenced how the prosecutors approached their decision making about which witnesses they called into the grand jury?

On the tax evasion charge at issue here Costello was convicted and sentenced to five years in prison. Costello later served 18 months in federal prison on a contempt of Congress charge arising out of his testimony before Senate hearings investigating organized crime. After he was

Frank Costello testifying before Congress in 1950 or 1951

released from prison, Vito Genovese ordered his assassination in 1957. Although Costello survived the attempt, he subsequently took early retirement, relinquishing power to the Genovese family.

4. The Court notes that permitting challenges to indictments on hearsay grounds would result in "delay." What sort of delay does the Court seem to have in mind? Are there even more serious issues than delay from the prosecution's perspective? The concurrence suggests that an indictment could be challenged where "no evidence had been offered that rationally established the facts." *Id.* at 365. What might this mean? How could such a rule be enforced?

5. As it does in other contexts, the Court relies on the grand jury/trial dichotomy to support its position, noting that "neither justice nor the concept of a fair trial" require permitting challenges to indictments based on hearsay.

Why does the Court view fairness as something to be reserved only for trials?

Does a fair trial extinguish unfairness in the grand jury?

6. The Court does seem to acknowledge that an indictment could be susceptible to challenge if it is not "valid on its face." What do you think this means? Note that current Fed. R. Crim. P. 12(b)(3)(B)(v) contemplates the filing of a pretrial motion challenging an indictment's "failure to state an offense."

The next case addresses whether a judicially imposed requirement that exculpatory evidence be presented to the grand jury would compromise the grand jury's historical mission.

United States v. Williams

504 U.S. 36 (1992)

Justice Scalia delivered the opinion of the Court.

The question presented in this case is whether a district court may dismiss an otherwise valid indictment because the Government failed to disclose to the grand jury "substantial exculpatory evidence" in its possession.

I

On May 4, 1988, respondent John H. Williams, Jr., a Tulsa, Oklahoma, investor, was indicted by a federal grand jury on seven counts of "knowingly mak[ing] [a] false statement or report . . . for the purpose of influencing . . . the action [of a federally insured financial institution]," in violation of 18 U.S.C. § 1014 (1988 ed., Supp. II). According to the indictment, between September 1984 and November 1985 Williams supplied four Oklahoma banks with "materially false" statements that variously overstated the value of his current assets and interest income in order to influence the banks' actions on his loan requests.

Williams' misrepresentation was allegedly effected through two financial statements provided to the banks, a "Market Value Balance Sheet" and a "Statement of Projected Income and Expense." The former included as "current assets" approximately $6 million in notes receivable from three venture capital companies. Though it contained a disclaimer that these assets were carried at cost rather than at market value, the Government asserted that listing them as "current assets"—i.e., assets quickly reducible to cash—was misleading, since Williams knew that none of the venture capital companies could afford to satisfy the notes in the short term. The second document—the Statement of Projected Income and Expense—allegedly misrepresented Williams' interest income, since it failed to reflect that the interest payments received on the notes of the venture capital companies were funded entirely by Williams' own loans to those companies. The Statement thus falsely implied, according to the Government, that Williams was deriving interest income from "an independent outside source."

Shortly after arraignment, the District Court granted Williams' motion for disclosure of all exculpatory portions of the grand jury transcripts. Upon reviewing this material, Williams demanded that the District Court dismiss the indictment, alleging that the Government had failed to fulfill its obligation under the Tenth Circuit's prior decision in *United States v. Page* (1987), to present "substantial exculpatory evidence" to the grand jury (emphasis omitted). His contention was that evidence which the Government had chosen not to present to the grand jury—in particular, Williams' general ledgers and tax returns, and Williams' testimony in his contemporaneous Chapter 11 bankruptcy proceeding—disclosed that, for tax purposes and otherwise, he had regularly accounted for the "notes receivable" (and the interest on them) in a manner consistent with the Balance Sheet and the Income Statement. This, he contended, belied an intent to mislead the banks, and thus directly negated an essential element of the charged offense.

The District Court initially denied Williams' motion, but upon reconsideration ordered the indictment dismissed without prejudice. It found, after a hearing, that the withheld evidence was "relevant to an essential element of the crime charged," created "'a reasonable doubt about [respondent's] guilt,'" and thus "render[ed] the grand jury's decision to indict gravely suspect." Upon the Government's appeal, the Court of Appeals affirmed the District Court's order, following its earlier decision in *Page*, supra. It first sustained as not "clearly erroneous" the District Court's determination that the Government had withheld "substantial exculpatory evidence" from the grand jury. It then found that the Government's behavior "'substantially influence[d]'" the grand jury's decision to indict, or at the very least raised a "'grave doubt that the decision to indict was free from such substantial influence.'" Under these circumstances, the Tenth Circuit concluded, it was not an abuse of discretion for the District Court to require the Government to begin anew before the grand jury.

• • •

III

Respondent does not contend that the Fifth Amendment itself obliges the prosecutor to disclose substantial exculpatory evidence in his possession to the grand jury. Instead, building on our statement that the federal courts "may, within limits, formulate procedural rules not specifically required by the Constitution or the Congress," he argues that imposition of the Tenth Circuit's disclosure rule is supported by the courts' "supervisory power." We think not. *Hasting*, and the cases that rely upon the principle it expresses, deal strictly with the courts' power to control their own procedures. That power has been applied not only to improve the truth-finding process of the trial, but also to prevent parties from reaping benefit or incurring harm from violations of substantive or procedural rules (imposed by the Constitution or laws) governing matters apart from the trial itself. Thus, *Bank of Nova Scotia v. United States* (1988), makes clear that the supervisory power can be used to dismiss an indictment because of misconduct before the grand jury, at least where that misconduct amounts to a violation of one of those "few, clear rules which were carefully drafted and approved by this Court and by Congress to ensure the integrity of the grand jury's functions."

We did not hold in *Bank of Nova Scotia*, however, that the courts' supervisory power could be used, not merely as a means of enforcing or vindicating legally compelled standards of prosecutorial conduct before the grand jury, but as a means of prescribing those standards of prosecutorial conduct in the first instance—just as it may be used as a means of establishing standards of prosecutorial conduct before the courts themselves. It is this latter exercise that respondent demands. Because the grand jury is an institution separate from the courts, over whose functioning the courts do not preside, we think it clear that, as a general matter at least, no such "supervisory" judicial authority exists, and that the disclosure rule applied here exceeded the Tenth Circuit's authority.

A

"[R]ooted in long centuries of Anglo–American history," the grand jury is mentioned in the Bill of Rights, but not in the body of the Constitution. It has not been textually assigned, therefore, to any of the branches described in the first three Articles. It "'is a constitutional fixture in its own right.'" In fact the whole theory of its function is that it belongs to no branch of the institutional Government, serving as a kind of buffer or referee between the Government and the people. Although the grand jury normally operates, of course, in the courthouse and under judicial auspices, its institutional relationship with the Judicial Branch has traditionally been, so to speak, at arm's length. Judges' direct involvement in the functioning of the grand jury has generally been confined to the constitutive one of calling the grand jurors together and administering their oaths of office.

The grand jury's functional independence from the Judicial Branch is evident both in the scope of its power to investigate criminal wrongdoing and in the manner in which that power is exercised. "Unlike [a] [c]ourt, whose jurisdiction is predicated upon a specific case or controversy, the grand jury 'can investigate merely on suspicion that the law is being violated, or even because it wants assurance that it is not.'" It need not identify the offender it suspects, or even "the precise nature of the offense" it is investigating. The grand jury requires no authorization from its constituting court to initiate an investigation, nor does the prosecutor require leave of court to seek a grand jury indictment. And in its day-to-day functioning, the grand jury generally operates without the interference of a presiding judge. It swears in its own witnesses, and deliberates in total secrecy.

True, the grand jury cannot compel the appearance of witnesses and the production of evidence, and must appeal to the court when such compulsion is required. And the court will refuse to lend its assistance when the compulsion the grand jury seeks would override rights accorded by the Constitution, or even testimonial privileges recognized by the common law. Even in this setting, however, we have insisted that the grand jury remain "free to pursue its investigations unhindered by external influence or supervision so long as it does not trench upon the legitimate rights of any witness called before it." Recognizing this tradition of independence, we have said that the Fifth Amendment's "constitutional guarantee presupposes an investigative body 'acting independently of either prosecuting attorney or judge'. . . ."

No doubt in view of the grand jury proceeding's status as other than a constituent element of a "criminal prosecutio[n]," U.S. Const., Amdt. 6, we have said that certain constitutional protections afforded defendants in criminal proceedings have no application before that body. The Double Jeopardy Clause of the Fifth Amendment does not bar a grand jury from returning an indictment when a prior grand jury has refused to do so. We have twice suggested, though not held, that the Sixth Amendment right to counsel does not attach when an individual is summoned to appear before a grand jury, even if he is the subject of the investigation. And although "the grand jury may not force a witness to answer questions in violation of [the Fifth Amendment's] constitutional guarantee" against self-incrimination, our cases suggest that an indictment obtained through the use of evidence previously obtained in violation of the privilege against self-incrimination "is nevertheless valid."

Given the grand jury's operational separateness from its constituting court, it should come as no surprise that we have been reluctant to invoke the judicial supervisory power as a basis for prescribing modes of grand jury procedure. Over the years, we have received many requests to exercise supervision over the grand jury's evidence-taking process, but we have refused them all, including some more appealing than the one presented today. In *United States v. Calandra*, a grand jury witness faced questions that were allegedly based upon physical evidence the Government had obtained through a violation of the Fourth Amendment; we rejected the proposal that the exclusionary rule be extended to grand jury proceedings, because of "the potential injury to the historic role and functions of the grand jury." In *Costello* we declined to enforce the hearsay rule in grand jury proceedings, since that "would run counter to the whole history of the grand jury institution, in which laymen conduct their inquiries unfettered by technical rules."

These authorities suggest that any power federal courts may have to fashion, on their own initiative, rules of grand jury procedure is a very limited one, not remotely comparable to the power they maintain over their own proceedings. It certainly would not permit judicial reshaping of the grand jury institution, substantially altering the traditional relationships between the prosecutor, the constituting court, and the grand jury itself. As we proceed to discuss, that would be the consequence of the proposed rule here.

B

Respondent argues that the Court of Appeals' rule can be justified as a sort of Fifth Amendment "common law," a necessary means of assuring the constitutional right to the judgment "of an independent and informed grand jury." Respondent makes a generalized appeal to functional notions: Judicial supervision of the quantity and quality of the evidence relied upon by the grand jury plainly facilitates, he says, the grand jury's performance of its twin historical responsibilities, i.e., bringing to trial those who may be justly accused and shielding the innocent from unfounded accusation and prosecution. We do not agree. The rule would neither preserve nor enhance the traditional functioning of the institution that the Fifth Amendment demands. To the contrary, requiring the prosecutor to present exculpatory as well as inculpatory evidence would alter the grand jury's historical role, transforming it from an accusatory to an adjudicatory body.

It is axiomatic that the grand jury sits not to determine guilt or innocence, but to assess whether there is adequate basis for bringing a criminal charge. That has always been so; and to make the assessment it has always been thought sufficient to hear only the prosecutor's side. As Blackstone described the prevailing practice in 18th-century England, the grand jury was "only to hear evidence on behalf of the prosecution[,] for the finding of an indictment is only in the nature of an enquiry or accusation, which is afterwards to be tried and determined So also in the United States. According to the description of an early American court, three years before the Fifth Amendment was ratified, it is the grand jury's function not "to enquire . . . upon what foundation [the charge may be] denied," or otherwise to try the suspect's defenses, but only to examine "upon what foundation [the charge] is made" by the prosecutor. As a consequence, neither in this country nor in England has the suspect under investigation by the grand jury ever been thought to have a right to testify or to have exculpatory evidence presented.

Imposing upon the prosecutor a legal obligation to present exculpatory evidence in his possession would be incompatible with this system. If a "balanced" assessment of the entire matter is the objective, surely the first thing to be done — rather than requiring the prosecutor to say what he knows in defense of the target of the investigation — is to entitle the target to tender his own defense. To require the former while denying (as we do) the latter would be quite absurd. It would also be quite pointless, since it would merely invite the target to circumnavigate the system by delivering his exculpatory evidence to the prosecutor, whereupon it would have to be passed on to the grand jury — unless the prosecutor is willing to take the chance that a court will not deem the evidence important enough to qualify for mandatory disclosure.

Respondent acknowledges (as he must) that the "common law" of the grand jury is not violated if the grand jury itself chooses to hear no more evidence than that which suffices to convince it an indictment is proper. Thus, had the Government offered to familiarize the grand jury in this case with the five boxes of financial statements and deposition testimony alleged to contain exculpatory information, and had the grand jury rejected the offer as pointless, respondent would presumably agree that the resulting indictment would have been valid. Respondent insists, however, that courts must require the modern prosecutor to alert the grand jury to the nature and extent of the available exculpatory evidence, because otherwise the grand jury "merely functions as an arm of the prosecution." We reject the attempt to convert a nonexistent duty of the grand jury itself into an obligation of the prosecutor. The authority of the prosecutor to seek an indictment has long been understood to be "coterminous with the authority of the grand jury to entertain [the prosecutor's] charges." If the grand jury has no obligation to consider all "substantial exculpatory" evidence, we do not understand how the prosecutor can be said to have a binding obligation to present it.

There is yet another respect in which respondent's proposal not only fails to comport with, but positively contradicts, the "common law" of the Fifth Amendment grand jury. Motions to quash indictments based upon the sufficiency of the evidence relied upon by the grand jury were unheard of at common law in England. And the traditional American practice was described by Justice Nelson, riding circuit in 1852, as follows:

> No case has been cited, nor have we been able to find any, furnishing an authority for looking into and revising the judgment of the grand jury upon the evidence, for the purpose of determining whether or not the finding was founded upon sufficient proof, or whether there was a deficiency in respect to any part of the complaint.

We accepted Justice Nelson's description in *Costello*, where we held that "[i]t would run counter to the whole history of the grand jury institution" to permit an indictment to be challenged "on the ground that there was inadequate or incompetent evidence before the grand jury." And we reaffirmed this principle recently in *Bank of Nova Scotia*, where we held that "the mere fact that evidence itself is unreliable is not sufficient to require a dismissal of the indictment," and that "a challenge to the reliability or competence of the evidence presented to the grand jury" will not be heard. It would make little sense, we think, to abstain from reviewing the evidentiary support for the grand jury's judgment while scrutinizing the sufficiency of the prosecutor's presentation. A complaint about the quality or adequacy of the evidence can always be recast as a complaint that the prosecutor's presentation was "incomplete" or "misleading." Our words in *Costello* bear repeating: Review of facially valid indictments on such grounds "would run counter to the whole history of the grand jury institution[,] [and] [n]either justice nor the concept of a fair trial requires [it]."

Echoing the reasoning of the Tenth Circuit in *United States v. Page*, respondent argues that a rule requiring the prosecutor to disclose exculpatory evidence to the grand jury would, by removing from the docket unjustified prosecutions, save valuable judicial time. That depends, we suppose, upon what the ratio would turn out to be between unjustified prosecutions eliminated and grand jury indictments challenged — for the latter as well as the former consume "valuable judicial time." We need not pursue the matter; if there is an advantage to the proposal, Congress is free to prescribe it. For the reasons set forth above, however, we conclude that courts have no authority to prescribe such a duty pursuant to their inherent supervisory authority over their own proceedings. The judgment of the Court of Appeals is accordingly reversed, and the cause is remanded for further proceedings consistent with this opinion.

So ordered.

Justice STEVENS, with whom Justice BLACKMUN and Justice O'CONNOR join, and with whom Justice THOMAS joins as to Parts II and III, dissenting.

• • •

II

Like the Hydra slain by Hercules, prosecutorial misconduct has many heads. Some are cataloged in Justice Sutherland's classic opinion for the Court in *Berger*:

> That the United States prosecuting attorney overstepped the bounds of that propriety and fairness which should characterize the conduct of such an officer in the prosecution of a criminal offense is clearly shown by the record. He was guilty of misstating the facts in his cross-examination of witnesses; of putting into the mouths of such witnesses things which they had not said; of suggesting by his questions that statements had been made to him personally out of court, in respect of which no proof was offered; of pretending to understand that a witness had said something which he had not said and persistently cross-examining the witness upon that basis; of assuming prejudicial facts not in evidence; of bullying and arguing with witnesses; and in general, of conducting himself in a thoroughly indecorous and improper manner. . . .
> The prosecuting attorney's argument to the jury was undignified and intemperate, containing improper insinuations and assertions calculated to mislead the jury.

This, of course, is not an exhaustive list of the kinds of improper tactics that overzealous or misguided prosecutors have adopted in judicial proceedings. The reported cases of this Court alone contain examples of the knowing use of perjured testimony, the suppression of evidence favorable to an accused person, and misstatements of the law in argument to the jury, to name just a few.

Nor has prosecutorial misconduct been limited to judicial proceedings: The reported cases indicate that it has sometimes infected grand jury proceedings as well. The cases contain examples of prosecutors presenting perjured testimony, questioning a witness outside the presence of the grand jury and then failing to inform the grand jury that the testimony was exculpatory, failing to inform the grand jury of its authority to subpoena witnesses, operating under a conflict of interest, misstating the law, and misstating the facts on cross-examination of a witness.

Justice Sutherland's identification of the basic reason why that sort of misconduct is intolerable merits repetition:

> "The United States Attorney is the representative not of an ordinary party to a controversy, but of a sovereignty whose obligation to govern impartially is as compelling as its obligation to govern at all; and whose interest, therefore, in a criminal prosecution is not that it shall win a case, but that justice shall be done. As such, he is in a peculiar and very definite sense the servant of the law, the twofold aim of which is that guilt shall not escape or innocence suffer. He may prosecute with earnestness and vigor—indeed, he should do so. But, while he may strike hard blows, he is not at liberty to strike foul ones. It is as much his duty to refrain from improper methods calculated to produce a wrongful conviction as it is to use every legitimate means to bring about a just one." *Berger v. United States.*

It is equally clear that the prosecutor has the same duty to refrain from improper methods calculated to produce a wrongful indictment. Indeed, the prosecutor's duty to protect the fundamental fairness of judicial proceedings assumes special importance when he is presenting evidence to a grand jury. As the Court of Appeals for the Third Circuit recognized, "the costs of continued unchecked prosecutorial misconduct" before the grand jury are particularly substantial because there

> the prosecutor operates without the check of a judge or a trained legal adversary, and virtually immune from public scrutiny. The prosecutor's abuse of his special relationship to the grand jury poses an enormous risk to defendants as well. For while in theory a trial provides the defendant with a full opportunity to contest and disprove the charges against him, in practice, the handing up of an indictment will often have a devastating personal and professional impact that a later dismissal or acquittal can never undo. Where the potential for abuse is so great, and the consequences of a mistaken indictment so serious, the ethical responsibilities of the prosecutor, and the obligation of the judiciary to protect against even the appearance of unfairness, are correspondingly heightened.

In his dissent in *United States v. Ciambrone* (CA2 1979), Judge Friendly also recognized the prosecutor's special role in grand jury proceedings:

> As the Supreme Court has noted, "the Founders thought the grand jury so essential to basic liberties that they provided in the Fifth Amendment that federal prosecution for serious crimes can only be instituted by 'a presentment or indictment of a Grand Jury.'" Before the grand jury the prosecutor has the dual role of pressing for an indictment and of being the grand jury adviser. In case of conflict, the latter duty must take precedence.
>
> The ex parte character of grand jury proceedings makes it peculiarly important for a federal prosecutor to remember that, in the familiar phrase, the interest of the United States "in a criminal prosecution is not that it shall win a case, but that justice shall be done."

The standard for judging the consequences of prosecutorial misconduct during grand jury proceedings is essentially the same as the standard applicable to trials. In *United States v. Mechanik* (1986), we held that there was "no reason not to apply [the harmless error rule] to 'errors, defects, irregularities, or variances' occurring before a grand jury just as we have applied it to such error occurring in the criminal trial itself." We repeated that holding in *Bank of Nova Scotia v. United States* (1988), when we rejected a defendant's argument that an indictment should be dismissed because of prosecutorial misconduct and irregularities in proceedings before the grand jury. Referring to the prosecutor's misconduct before the grand jury, we "concluded that our customary harmless-error inquiry is applicable where, as in the cases before us, a court is asked to dismiss an indictment prior to the conclusion of the trial." Moreover, in reviewing the instances of misconduct in that case, we applied precisely the same standard to the prosecutor's violations and to his violations of the general duty of fairness that applies to all judicial proceedings. This point is illustrated by the Court's comments on the prosecutor's abuse of a witness:

> The District Court found that a prosecutor was abusive to an expert defense witness during a recess and in the hearing of some grand jurors. Although the Government concedes that the treatment of the expert tax witness was improper, the witness himself testified that his testimony was unaffected by this misconduct. The prosecutors instructed the grand jury to disregard anything they may have heard in conversations between a prosecutor and a witness, and explained to the grand jury that such conversations should have no influence on its deliberations. In light of these ameliorative measures, there is nothing to indicate that the prosecutor's conduct toward this witness substantially affected the grand jury's evaluation of the testimony or its decision to indict.

Unquestionably, the plain implication of that discussion is that if the misconduct, even though not expressly forbidden by any written rule, had played a critical role in persuading the jury to return the indictment, dismissal would have been required.

In an opinion that I find difficult to comprehend, the Court today repudiates the assumptions underlying these cases and seems to suggest that the court has no authority to supervise the conduct of the prosecutor in grand jury proceedings so long as he follows the dictates of the Constitution, applicable statutes, and Rule 6 of the Federal Rules of Criminal Procedure. The Court purports to support this conclusion by invoking the doctrine of separation of powers and citing a string of cases in which we have declined to impose categorical restraints on the grand jury. Needless to say, the Court's reasoning is unpersuasive.

Although the grand jury has not been "textually assigned" to "any of the branches described in the first three Articles" of the Constitution, it is not an autonomous body completely beyond the reach of the other branches. Throughout its life, from the moment it is convened until it is discharged, the grand jury is subject to the control of the court. As Judge Learned Hand recognized over 60 years ago, "a grand jury is neither an officer nor an agent of the United States, but a part of the court." This Court has similarly characterized the grand jury:

> A grand jury is clothed with great independence in many areas, but it remains an appendage of the court, powerless to perform its investigative function without the court's aid, because powerless itself to compel the testimony of witnesses. It is the court's process which summons the witness to attend and give testimony, and it is the court which must compel a witness to testify if, after appearing, he refuses to do so.

This Court has, of course, long recognized that the grand jury has wide latitude to investigate violations of federal law as it deems appropriate and need not obtain permission from either the court or the prosecutor. Correspondingly, we have acknowledged that "its operation generally is unrestrained by the technical procedural and evidentiary rules governing the conduct of criminal trials." But this is because Congress and the Court have generally thought it best not to impose procedural restraints on the grand jury; it is not because they lack all power to do so.

To the contrary, the Court has recognized that it has the authority to create and enforce limited rules applicable in grand jury proceedings. Thus, for example, the Court has said that the grand jury "may not itself violate a valid privilege, whether established by the Constitution, statutes, or the common law." And the Court may prevent a grand jury from violating such a privilege by quashing or modifying a subpoena, or issuing a protective order forbidding questions in violation of the privilege. Moreover, there are, as the Court notes, a series of cases in which we declined to impose categorical restraints on the grand jury. In none of those cases, however, did we question our power to reach a contrary result.

Although the Court recognizes that it may invoke its supervisory authority to fashion and enforce privilege rules applicable in grand jury proceedings, ibid., and suggests that it may also invoke its supervisory authority to fashion other limited rules of grand jury procedure, it concludes that it has no authority to prescribe "standards of prosecutorial conduct before the grand jury," because that would alter the grand jury's historic role as an independent, inquisitorial institution. I disagree.

We do not protect the integrity and independence of the grand jury by closing our eyes to the countless forms of prosecutorial misconduct that may occur inside the secrecy of the grand jury room. After all, the grand jury is not merely an investigatory body; it also serves as a "protector of citizens against arbitrary and oppressive governmental action." Explaining why the grand jury must be both "independent" and "informed," the Court wrote in *Wood v. Georgia* (1962):

> Historically, this body has been regarded as a primary security to the innocent against hasty, malicious and oppressive persecution; it serves the invaluable function in our society of standing between the accuser and the accused, whether the latter be an individual, minority group, or

other, to determine whether a charge is founded upon reason or was dictated by an intimidating power or by malice and personal ill will.

It blinks reality to say that the grand jury can adequately perform this important historic role if it is intentionally misled by the prosecutor—on whose knowledge of the law and facts of the underlying criminal investigation the jurors will, of necessity, rely.

Unlike the Court, I am unwilling to hold that countless forms of prosecutorial misconduct must be tolerated—no matter how prejudicial they may be, or how seriously they may distort the legitimate function of the grand jury—simply because they are not proscribed by Rule 6 of the Federal Rules of Criminal Procedure or a statute that is applicable in grand jury proceedings. Such a sharp break with the traditional role of the federal judiciary is unprecedented, unwarranted, and unwise. Unrestrained prosecutorial misconduct in grand jury proceedings is inconsistent with the administration of justice in the federal courts and should be redressed in appropriate cases by the dismissal of indictments obtained by improper methods.

III

What, then, is the proper disposition of this case? I agree with the Government that the prosecutor is not required to place all exculpatory evidence before the grand jury. A grand jury proceeding is an ex parte investigatory proceeding to determine whether there is probable cause to believe a violation of the criminal laws has occurred, not a trial. Requiring the prosecutor to ferret out and present all evidence that could be used at trial to create a reasonable doubt as to the defendant's guilt would be inconsistent with the purpose of the grand jury proceeding and would place significant burdens on the investigation. But that does not mean that the prosecutor may mislead the grand jury into believing that there is probable cause to indict by withholding clear evidence to the contrary. I thus agree with the Department of Justice that "when a prosecutor conducting a grand jury inquiry is personally aware of substantial evidence which directly negates the guilt of a subject of the investigation, the prosecutor must present or otherwise disclose such evidence to the grand jury before seeking an indictment against such a person." U.S. Dept. of Justice, United States Attorneys' Manual ¶ 9-11.233, p. 88 (1988).

Although I question whether the evidence withheld in this case directly negates respondent's guilt, I need not resolve my doubts because the Solicitor General did not ask the Court to review the nature of the evidence withheld. Instead, he asked us to decide the legal question whether an indictment may be dismissed because the prosecutor failed to present exculpatory evidence. Unlike the Court and the Solicitor General, I believe the answer to that question is yes, if the withheld evidence would plainly preclude a finding of probable cause. I therefore cannot endorse the Court's opinion.

NOTES AND QUESTIONS

1. Note the charge and the government's theory of the case against defendant. Does this strike you as a particularly strong case for the government? What weaknesses do you see? Why do you think the Court bothers to explain the charge and theory?

2. How does Williams get access to the grand jury transcripts? What is his argument that the prosecution has violated the Tenth Circuit's rule in *Page*? Is this argument persuasive?

3. The district court dismissed the indictment without prejudice, that is, it ruled that the government was free to attempt to re-indict Willams but it would have to re-present its case, along with the exculpatory evidence, to the grand jury. Why do you think the government did not take advantage of that opportunity, especially given that its pursuit of appeals in the Tenth Circuit and the Supreme Court delayed the prosecution by several years? Did the government fear that the grand jury might not return an indictment if the exculpatory evidence were presented to it? Why might a reasonable prosecutor have been willing to present this exculpatory evidence to the grand jury?

4. The Court emphasizes the grand jury's "operational separateness" in holding that the supervisory power does not authorize a federal court to prescribe modes of prosecutorial conduct before the grand jury. Does the Court exaggerate the grand jury's "operational separateness"? Is it accurate to say, as the Court does, that "[j]udges' direct involvement in the functioning of the grand jury has generally been confined to the constitutive one of calling the grand jurors together and administering their oaths of office"? Is it more accurate to call the grand jury an "appendage of the court" as the dissent does? Outside the narrow context of the exercise of judicial supervisory power, is the entire argument about the grand jury's relationship to the judiciary a red herring in view of the grand jury's total dependence on the prosecutor?

5. The Court also claims that requiring a grand jury to consider exculpatory evidence would alter its historical role as an "accusatory body." The dissent responds by recalling the sword/shield nature of the grand jury's historical powers, citing dicta from *Calandra* that the grand jury also functions as a "protector of citizens against arbitrary and oppressive action." *Id.* at 68. In any event, isn't the grand jury an accusatory body primarily in the sense that its output is accusations as opposed to determinations? Is there something inherently wrong with an "accusatory body" considering more than one version of events before it levels its accusations?

6. The dissent notes that the ethical obligations of a prosecutor to "do justice" are heightened by the one-sided nature of grand jury proceedings. If anything, the dissent understates this point. In the grand jury the prosecutor is omnipotent: no judge presides; the witnesses do not have counsel, and no one can object to the prosecutor's questions; the prosecutor decides what witnesses to call, what to ask them, and what documents to show them; and the grand jurors are simply a captive witness until the prosecutor lets them go home.

7. Note the difference between the "substantial exculpatory evidence" standard in the *Page* rule and the DOJ rule requiring disclosure of "substantial evidence that directly negates guilt." What are the practical differences between the two rules? Did the undisclosed evidence here satisfy either standard? Both standards?

8. The Tenth Circuit's decision in *United States v. Page*, 808 F.2d 723, 728 (10th Cir. 1987), only required disclosure of exculpatory evidence the government "discovered in" the course of its investigation, obviating the dissent's concern about requiring the government to "ferret out" such evidence. Having said that, aren't responsible prosecutors always going to be on the lookout for potential exculpatory evidence if, for no other reason, so they won't be surprised at trial?

Presentments. The Fifth Amendment provides that "[n]o person shall be held to answer for a capital, or otherwise infamous crime, unless on a *presentment* or indictment of a Grand Jury." A presentment, historically, was a public charge the grand jury would bring on its own, independent of the prosecutor, often against government officials. The prosecutor would have to sign or otherwise ratify the presentment document in order to commence a prosecution. Presentments were famously issued by grand juries in connection with two different investigations of Aaron Burr, who was suspected of treason by his political enemies. Grand juries in Kentucky and Mississippi were empaneled at the instigation of those enemies, and both declined to indict Burr. The Kentucky grand jury issued a written declaration to the court criticizing the lack of evidence against Burr and the Mississippi grand jury returned presentments condemning the accusations against Burr as vindictive. *See* Roger Roots, *If It's Not a Runaway It's Not a Real Grand Jury*, 33 Creighton L. Rev. 821, 840-41 (2000).

Notwithstanding that the word "presentment" is right there in the text of the Fifth Amendment, presentments are now almost entirely of historical interest, as in 1946 the Federal Rules of Criminal Procedure consigned them to the ashbin of history. Rule 7, governing indictments and informations — the means by which federal prosecutions normally begin — makes no mention of presentments. The Advisory Committee's Notes state that "[p]resentment is not included as an additional type of formal accusation, since presentments as a method of initiating prosecutions are obsolete, at least as concerns the Federal courts." Some commentators believe the Rules overstate the obsolescence of presentments, and have urged their return. *See* Roots, *If It's Not a Runaway, supra*; Renee Lettow, *Reviving Grand Jury Presentments*, 103 Yale L.J. 1333 (1994). Another commentator observed, shortly after the Rules were enacted, that retention of the presentment power "might encourage the use of the 'run-away' grand jury as the grand jury could act from their own knowledge or observation and not only from charges made by the United States attorney." Lester B. Oldfeld, *The Federal Grand Jury*, 22 F.R.D. 343, 346 (1958).

Runaway Grand Juries. Despite their banishment by the Federal Rules, presentments and also runaway grand juries reentered the public discourse briefly during the 1990s. A special grand jury was empaneled to investigate environmental crimes at a Rockwell International plutonium trigger manufacturing plant in Rocky Flats, Colorado, a Denver suburb. The plant was on land owned by the Department of Energy, and Rockwell made parts for use in nuclear weapons under a federal contract. After a lengthy investigation the grand jurors were unhappy with the decision of the lead assistant U.S. attorney not to recommend the indictment of individual officials of Rockwell or DOE. When the grand jury rejected a proposed indictment of the corporation only, the AUSA proceeded by way of a criminal information (often used when a defendant is pleading guilty and will waive indictment), bypassing the grand jury, under which Rockwell pled guilty and paid an $18.5 million fine. End of case.

Not so easy. The grand jurors went rogue. They did legal research. They found a prosecutor's manual, and proceeded to draft "indictments" against five Rockwell employees and three DOE officials. They also issued those charges as "presentments" and wrote a report criticizing the prosecutors. The district court sealed all these documents pursuant to Rule 6, but the jurors leaked information to the press, which published accounts of the grand jury proceedings. Then things got even more adversarial: The district court asked the Justice Department to investigate the jurors for violations of their secrecy oath; the jurors wrote to then-President-elect Clinton requesting appointment of a special prosecutor to investigate the AUSA; jurors held press conferences on the courthouse steps; and the jurors hired a lawyer, a Georgetown law professor. A congressional investigation was commenced. Immunity deals for the grand jurors were negotiated. *See generally* Lettow, *Reviving Grand Jury Presentments, supra* at 1333.

The reasons the Rocky Flats grand jury turned into a runaway are complex but by no means so singular as to not recur. By all accounts it was a cocktail of prosecutorial arrogance, some generalized antigovernment populist sentiment, a charismatic foreperson, and a collection of jurors who took both themselves and their mission seriously. For example, the grand jurors pointedly recalled their initial instruction when they were sworn in by the district court: "You must remember that you are not the prosecutor's agent. . . . You must not yield your powers nor forgo your independence of spirit. . . . You would perform a disservice if you did not indict where the evidence warranted an indictment." The grand jurors' spirit was summed up by the grand jury foreperson, rancher Wesley McKinley, who declared at one point: "If you're going to let one government chickenshit lawyer tell you what to do, you're not part of America." It's also worth considering whether the dynamics of a "special grand jury" — empaneled to investigate one case only, and doing so for two and a half years—contributed to the grand jurors' aggressiveness, a dynamic sometimes shared by special prosecutors. *See generally* Lettow, *Reviving Grand Jury Presentments*, *supra* at 1333, 1349-53.

Wesley McKinley

Courts' commitment to the grand jury's independence can be somewhat situational even in less dramatic contexts than a runaway. In *United States v. Marcucci*, 299 F.3d 1156 (9th Cir. 2002), defendants appealed on the ground that the grand jury that indicted them was not instructed that it could refuse to indict even if probable cause existed. Rather, it was instructed in part as follows:

> [Y]our task is to determine whether the government's evidence as presented to you is sufficient to cause you to conclude that there is probable cause to believe that the accused is guilty of the offense charged. To put it another way, you should vote to indict where the evidence presented to you is sufficiently strong to warrant a reasonable person's believing that the accused is probably guilty of the offense with which the accused is charged.

Id. at 1158. Defendants relied on dicta in *Vasquez v. Hillery*, 474 U.S. 254, 263 (1986), where the Supreme Court had stated that "[t]he grand jury is not bound to indict in every case where a conviction can be obtained." A divided panel of the Ninth Circuit found that whatever historical independence the grand jury may have once had in earlier British and American times was no longer an actual feature of its function. Further, the instruction that it was given afforded the grand jury some discretion by charging only that it "should" indict—not "must" or "shall" indict—on a showing of probable cause.

As we have seen and will continue to see, the Supreme Court decides most grand jury issues on the basis of the institution's historical conception, and not on present-day realities. What harm could come from instructing the grand jury in accordance with its historical pedigree?

The next case considers an entirely different angle on grand jury independence, and the respective relationships of the executive and the judiciary vis-à-vis the grand jury. The context is the civil rights movement and litigation in federal court in Mississippi.

United States v. Cox

342 F.2d 167 (5th Cir. 1965)

Jones, Circuit Judge:

On October 22, 1964, an order of the United States District Court for the Southern District of Mississippi, signed by Harold Cox, a judge of that Court, was entered. The order, with caption and formal closing omitted, is as follows:

> THE GRAND JURY, duly elected, impaneled and organized, for the Southern District of Mississippi, reconvened on order of the Court at 9:00 a.m., October 21, 1964, in Court Room Number 2 in Jackson, Mississippi, for the general dispatch of its business. The grand jury was fully instructed as to their duties, powers and responsibilities and retired to the grand jury room number 538 in the Federal Building at Jackson to do its work. The United States Attorney (and one of his assistants) sat with the grand jury throughout the day on October 21 and explained in detail to the grand jury the perjury laws and the Court's construction of such laws for their information. The grand jury heard witnesses throughout the day on October 21, 1964. On the morning of October 22, 1964, the grand jury, through its foreman, made known to the Court in open court that they had requested Robert E. Hauberg, United States Attorney, to prepare certain indictments which they desired to bring against some of the persons under consideration and about which they had heard testimony, and the United States Attorney refused to draft or sign any such indictments on instructions of the Acting Attorney General of the United States; whereupon the Court ordered and directed said United States Attorney to draft such true bills or no bills as the grand jury may have duly voted and desired to report and to sign such instruments as required by law under penalty of contempt. The United States Attorney was afforded one hour within which to decide as to whether or not he would abide by the instructions and order of the Court in such respect. At the end of such time, the Court re-convened and the United States Attorney was specifically asked in open court as to whether or not he intended to conform with the order and direction of the Court in said respects whereupon the United States Attorney answered that he respectfully declined to do so on instructions from Nicholas deB. Katzenbach, Acting Attorney General. He was thereupon duly adjudged by the Court to be in civil contempt of the Court and was afforded an opportunity to make any statement which he desired to make to the Court before sentence; whereupon the United States Attorney reiterated his inability to comply with the order of the Court upon express and direct instructions from Nicholas deB. Katzenbach, Acting Attorney General of the United States.
>
> WHEREFORE, IT IS ORDERED AND ADJUDGED by the Court that Robert E. Hauberg, United States Attorney, is guilty of civil contempt of this Court and in the presence of the Court for his said refusal to obey its said order and he is ordered into custody of the United States Marshal to be confined by him in the Hinds County, Mississippi, jail, there to remain until he purges himself of this contempt by agreeing to conform to said order by performing his official duty for the grand jury as requested in the several (about five) pending cases before them on October 21 and October 22, 1964.
>
> IT IS FURTHER ORDERED by the Court that a citation issue to Nicholas deB. Katzenbach, Acting Attorney General of the United States, directing him to appear before this Court and show cause why he should not be adjudged guilty of contempt of this Court for his instructions and directions to the United States Attorney to disregard and disobey the orders of this Court in the respects stated.
>
> The United States Attorney requested a stay of enforcement of this order and further proceedings herein for five days after this date to enable him to apply to the United States Court of Appeals for the Fifth Circuit for a writ of prohibition and such request is granted; and these proceedings and enforcement of this order in its entirety is stayed for five days, subject to the further orders of the United States Court of Appeals on said application; and for the enforcement of all of which, let proper process issue.

The United States Attorney, Robert E. Hauberg, and the Acting Attorney General, Nicholas deB. Katzenbach, have appealed from the order and they, joined by the United States, seek a writ of prohibition against the District Judge from enforcing the Court's order, and from asserting jurisdiction to require the Attorney General or the United States Attorney "to institute criminal prosecutions or to take any steps in regard thereto." The facts recited in the order are uncontroverted. No further facts are essential to a decision of the issues before this Court. Although the issues here presented arose, in part at least, as an incident of a civil rights matter, no civil rights questions are involved in the rather broad inquiry which we are called upon to make.

The constitutional requirement of an indictment or presentment as a predicate to a prosecution for capital or infamous crimes has for its primary purpose the protection of the individual from jeopardy except on a finding of probable cause by a group of his fellow citizens, and is designed to afford a safeguard against oppressive actions of the prosecutor or a court. The constitutional provision is not to be read as conferring on or preserving to the grand jury, as such, any rights or prerogatives. The constitutional provision is, as has been said, for the benefit of the accused. The constitutional provision is not to be read as precluding, as essential to the validity of an indictment, the inclusion of requisites which did not exist at common law.

Traditionally, the Attorney for the United States had the power to enter a nolle prosequi of a criminal charge at any time after indictment and before trial, and this he could have done without the approval of the court or the consent of the accused. It may be doubted whether, before the adoption of the Federal Rules of Criminal Procedure, he had any authority to prevent the return of an indictment by a grand jury. There would be no constitutional barrier to a requirement that the signature of a United States Attorney upon an indictment is essential to its validity.

It is now provided by the Federal Rules of Criminal Procedure that the Attorney General or the United States Attorney may by leave of court file a dismissal of an indictment. Rule 48(a) Fed. Rules Crim. Proc. 18 U.S.C.A. In the absence of the Rule, leave of court would not have been required. The purpose of the Rule is to prevent harassment of a defendant by charging, dismissing and re-charging without placing a defendant in jeopardy. Rule 7 eliminates the necessity for the inclusion in an indictment of many of the technical and prolix averments which were required at common law, by providing that the indictment shall be a plain, concise and definite written statement of the essential facts constituting the offense charged. The Rule also provides that "It shall be signed by the attorney for the government." Rule 7(c) Fed. Rules Crim. Proc. 18 U.S.C.A.

The judicial power of the United States is vested in the federal courts, and extends to prosecutions for violations of the criminal laws of the United States. The executive power is vested in the President of the United States, who is required to take care that the laws be faithfully executed. The Attorney General is the hand of the President in taking care that the laws of the United States in legal proceedings and in the prosecution of offenses, be faithfully executed. The role of the grand jury is restricted to a finding as to whether or not there is probable cause to believe that an offense has been committed. The discretionary power of the attorney for the United States in determining whether a prosecution shall be commenced or maintained may well depend upon matters of policy wholly apart from any question of probable cause. Although as a member of the bar, the attorney for the United States is an officer of the court, he is nevertheless an executive official of the Government, and it is as an officer of the executive department that he exercises a discretion as to whether or not there shall be a prosecution in a particular case. It follows, as an incident of the constitutional separation of powers, that the courts are not to interfere with the free exercise of the discretionary powers of the attorneys of the United States in their control over criminal prosecutions. The provision of Rule 7, requiring the signing of the indictment by the attorney for the Government, is a recognition of the power of Government counsel to permit or not to permit the bringing of an indictment. If the attorney refuses to sign, as he has the discretionary power of doing, we conclude that there is no valid indictment. It is not to be supposed that the signature of counsel is merely an attestation of the act of the grand jury. The signature of the foreman performs that function. It is not to be supposed that the signature of counsel is a certificate that the indictment is in proper form to charge an offense. The sufficiency of the indictment may be tested before the court. Rather, we think, the requirement of the signature is for the purpose of evidencing the joinder of the attorney for the United States with the grand jury in instituting a criminal proceeding in the court. Without the signature there can be no criminal proceeding brought upon an indictment. Substantial compliance rather than technical exactness meets the requirement of the rule. There seems to be no authority for the statement that the absence of a signature is not fatal.

If it were not for the discretionary power given to the United States Attorney to prevent an indictment by withholding his signature, there might be doubt as to the constitutionality of the requirement of Rule 48 for leave of court for a dismissal of a pending prosecution.

Because, as we conclude, the signature of the Government attorney is necessary to the validity of the indictment and the affixing or withholding of the signature is a matter of executive discretion which cannot be coerced or reviewed by the courts, the contempt order must be reversed. It seems that, since the United States Attorney cannot be required to give validity to an indictment by affixing his signature, he should not be required to indulge in an exercise of futility by the preparation of the form of an indictment which he is unwilling to vitalize with his signature. Therefore he should not be required to prepare indictments which he is unwilling and under no duty to sign.

Judges Tuttle, Jones, Brown and Wisdom join in the conclusion that the signature of the United States Attorney is essential to the validity of an indictment. Judge Brown, as appears in his separate opinion, is of the view that the United States Attorney is required, upon the request of the grand jury, to draft forms of indictments in accordance with its desires. The order before us for review is in the conjunctive; it requires the United States Attorney to prepare and sign. A majority of the court, having decided that the direction to sign is erroneous, the order on appeal will be reversed.

• • •

Wisdom, Circuit Judge (concurring specially):

The dissenters show judicial craftsmanship of the highest order in writing persuasively about "the traditional sphere" of the grand jury while not turning up one case holding that a court may compel a prosecutor to prepare and sign a bill of indictment requested by a grand jury. Not one case in all the years between 1166 and 1965. I submit that the result reached in the dissent is the product of a misunderstanding of the historical meaning of "presentment and indictment," a failure to give effect to the difference between the sword and the shield of the grand jury, and an abstract approach that disregards the factual setting in which the issue is presented.

Nothing in the position of any of the judges in the majority "ignores" or tends to diminish the purely inquisitorial role of the federal grand jury. But when that role goes beyond inquiry and report and becomes accusatorial, no aura of traditional or constitutional sanctity surrounds the grand jury. The Grand Jury earned its place in the Bill of Rights by its shield, not by its sword.

• • •

II

Because recognition of the grand jury's shield-like function is lodged in the Bill of Rights, the bedrock of basic rights, it is fair to say that national policy favors a liberal construction of the power of the grand jury to protect the individual against official tyranny. No such policy favors the grand jury in its accusatorial role. Accordingly, we look for and should expect to find a check on its unjust accusations similar to the grand jury's check on the government's unjust accusations.

If there is one aspect of the doctrine of Separation of Powers that the Founding Fathers agreed upon, it is the principle, as Montesquieu stated it: "To prevent the abuse of power, it is necessary that by the very disposition of things, power should be a check to power." Taking their institutions as they found them, the framers wove a web of checks and balances designed to prevent abuse of power, regardless of the age, origin, and character of the institution. At the same time, the framers were too sophisticated to believe that the three branches of government were absolutely separate, air-tight departments. It does not matter, therefore, whether the grand jury is regarded as an arm of the court, as the Federal Grand Jury Handbook states, or is regarded as a sui generis institution derived from the people. What does matter is that the power of the executive not to prosecute, and therefore not to take steps necessarily leading to prosecution, is the appropriate curb on a grand jury in keeping with the constitutional theory of checks and balances. Such a check is especially necessary, if there is any question of the grand jury's and the district court's being in agreement; if they differ, of course the district court may dismiss the grand jury. The need is rendered more acute if there is a possibility that community hostility against the suspected offenders, individually or as a race, may jeopardize justice before the petit jury. In short, if we give the same meaning to "presentment or indictment" that Madison and others gave to these terms when Madison introduced the Bill of Rights in the First Congress, the grand jury provision in the Bill of Rights cuts both ways: it prevents harassment and intimidation and oppression through unjust prosecution—by the Grand Jury or by the Government.

III

The prosecution of offenses against the United States is an executive function within the exclusive prerogative of the Attorney General. "There shall be at the seat of government an executive department to be known as the Department of Justice, and an Attorney General, who shall be the head thereof." 5 U.S.C. § 291. That official, the chief law-enforcement officer of the Federal Government is "the hand of the president in taking care that the laws of the United States in protection of the interests of the United States in legal proceedings and in the prosecution of offenses be faithfully executed." He "has the authority, and it is made his duty, to supervise the conduct of all suits brought by or against the United States," including the authority "to begin criminal prosecution." He "is invested with the general superintendence of all such suits, and all the district attorneys who do bring them in the various courts in the country are placed under his immediate direction and control."

"The district attorney has absolute control over criminal prosecutions, and can dismiss or refuse to prosecute, any of them at his discretion. The responsibility is wholly his." The determination of whether and when to prosecute "is a matter of policy for the prosecuting officer and not for the determination of the courts." As another court has stated it:

> All of these considerations point up the wisdom of vesting broad discretion in the United States Attorney. The federal courts are powerless to interfere with his discretionary power. The Court cannot compel him to prosecute a complaint, or even an indictment, whatever his reasons for

> not acting. The remedy for any dereliction of his duty lies, not with the courts, but, with the executive branch of our government and ultimately with the people.

• • •

The functions of prosecutor and judge are incompatible. In *United States v. Thompson*, for example, the Supreme Court reversed a lower court for attempting to prevent a United States Attorney from instituting criminal prosecution by resubmitting the matter to a grand jury. The Court's decision was expressly based upon "the absolute right of the United States to prosecute," and upon "the right of the Government to initiate prosecutions for crime," a right not subject to control by judicial discretion. Similarly, the Court has held that a district court was without jurisdiction to refuse to issue a warrant of arrest upon an indictment by a grand jury upon the application of the United States Attorney, because such refusal would bar "the absolute right of the United States to prosecute" and would bar "the lawful authority of the United States Attorney."

In *Goldberg v. Hoffman*, a petition for mandamus was filed against the Attorney General, an Assistant Attorney General, and the United States Attorney, to compel them to relieve the petitioner of an indictment. The Court of Appeals dismissed as to the Attorney General and Assistant Attorney General for lack of jurisdiction:

> Our adjudication of the issues raised must be guided by considerations inherent in the well-settled principle of the separation of the powers vested in the three branches of government, which is the keynote of our constitutional mandate. We must bear in mind that the United States Attorney is an officer of the executive branch responsible primarily to the President, and, through him, to the electorate, and that the remedy sought against Tieken is a broad one, to-wit, a direct mandate from this court compelling him to take, or refrain from taking, a specific course of action with respect to the indictment pending against petitioner. More specifically, we are asked to review the exercise of administrative discretion, overrule the decision of the executive and direct the course which that discretion must take. We think such judicial control of an executive officer is beyond the power of this court.

• • •

Rule 48(a) does not directly apply to the present case, because there has been no indictment, information, or complaint, but since the rule preserves the prosecutor's discretion to dismiss a complaint before indictment, the drafters of the Rules must have intended to preserve the discretion not to prosecute. In this case, the prosecutor cannot move to dismiss; there is nothing to dismiss. What he can do, however, is to refuse to prepare and sign the indictment. Under this theory, Rule 7(c), requiring that the indictment be signed by the United States Attorney, preserves the prosecutor's traditional discretion as to whether to initiate prosecution.

The reason for vesting discretion to prosecute in the Executive, acting through the Attorney General is two-fold. First, in the interests of justice and the orderly, efficient administration of the law, some person or agency should be able to prevent an unjust prosecution. The freedom of the petit jury to bring in a verdict of not guilty and the progressive development of the law in the direction of making more meaningful the guarantees of an accused person's constitutional rights give considerable protection to the individual before and after trial. They do not protect against a baseless prosecution. This is a harassment to the accused and an expensive strain on the machinery of justice. The appropriate repository for authority to prevent a baseless prosecution is the chief law-enforcement officer whose duty, unlike the grand jury's duty, is to collect evidence on both sides of a case.

Second, when, within the context of law-enforcement, national policy is involved, because of national security, conduct of foreign policy, or a conflict between two branches of government, the appropriate branch to decide the matter is the executive branch. The executive is charged with carrying out national policy on law-enforcement and, generally speaking, is informed on more levels than the more specialized judicial and legislative branches. In such a situation, a decision not to prosecute is analogous to the exercise of executive privilege. The executive's absolute and exclusive discretion to prosecute may be rationalized as an illustration of the doctrine of separation of powers, but it would have evolved without the doctrine and exists in countries that do not purport to accept this doctrine.

IV

This brings me to the facts. They demonstrate, better than abstract principles or legal dicta, the imperative necessity that the United States, through its Attorney General, have uncontrollable discretion to prosecute.

The crucial fact here is that Goff and Kendrick, two Negroes, testified in a suit by the United States against the Registrar of Clarke County, Mississippi, and the State of Mississippi, to enforce the voting rights of Negroes under the Fourteenth Amendment and the Civil Rights Act.

Goff and Kendrick testified that some seven years earlier at Stonewall, Mississippi, the registrar had refused to register them or give them application forms. They said that they had seen white persons registering, one of whom was a B. Floyd Jones. Ramsey, the registrar, testified that Jones had not registered at that time or place, but had registered the year before in Enterprise, Mississippi. He testified also that he had never discriminated against Negro applicants for registration. Jones testified that he was near the registration table in Stonewall in 1955, had talked with the registrar, and had shaken hands with him. The presiding judge, Judge W. Harold Cox, stated from the bench that Goff and Kendrick should be "bound over to await the action of the grand jury for perjury."

In January 1963 attorneys of the Department of Justice requested the Federal Bureau of Investigation to investigate the possible perjury. The FBI completed a full investigation in March 1963 and referred the matter to the Department's Criminal Division. In June 1963 the Criminal Division advised the local United States Attorney, Mr. Hauberg, that the matter presented "no basis for a perjury prosecution." Mr. Hauberg informed Judge Cox of the Department's decision. Judge Cox stated that in his view the matter was clearly one for the grand jury and that he would be inclined, if necessary, to appoint an outside attorney to present the matter to the grand jury. (I find no authority for a federal judge to displace the United States Attorney by appointing a special prosecutor.) On receiving this information, the Criminal Division again reviewed its files and concluded that the charge of perjury could not be sustained. General Katzenbach, then Deputy Attorney General, after reviewing the files, concurred in the Criminal Division's decision. In September 1963 General Katzenbach called on Judge Cox as a courtesy to explain why the Department had arrived at the conclusion that no perjury was involved. Judge Cox, unconvinced, requested the United States Attorney to present to the grand jury the Goff and Kendrick cases, which he regarded as cases of "palpable perjury."

In October 1963 Goff and Kendrick were arrested, jailed for two days, and placed on a $3,000 bond for violations of State law for falsely testifying in federal court. After their indictment by a state grand jury, the Department of Justice filed suit against the State District Attorney, United States v. Warner, (Civ. No. 1219, S.D. Miss.), seeking to enjoin the state prosecution on the grounds that: (1) the States have no authority to prosecute for alleged perjury committed while testifying in a federal court; (2) the purpose and effect of the State's prosecution was to threaten and intimidate Goff and Kendrick and to inhibit them and other Negroes from registering to vote. The district court (per Mize, J.) ruled in favor of the United States.

The Federal Grand Jury, originally convened on September 9, 1963, was reconvened on September 21, 1964. September 28, 1964, the Foreman of the Grand Jury advised the Government Attorney who was presenting matters to the Grand Jury that Judge Cox had asked the Foreman to hear several witnesses. September 29, 1964, Mr. Riddell, attorney for the Registrar, and the district attorney for the Second Circuit District for the State of Mississippi, Mr. Holleman, came to the courthouse to appear before the Grand Jury. Judge Mize, in a special charge to the Grand Jury stated—in open court— that Judge Cox had informed him, before leaving for his vacation, that:

> . . . he wanted the Grand Jury to call before it Mr. Boyce Holleman of Gulfport, Mississippi and Mr. Talley Riddell of Quitman, Mississippi as witnesses, because it was his impression that they had some matters that ought to be investigated at least and that they should be permitted to appear.

Judge Mize stated that he was not familiar with the matters "other than just what Judge Cox requested me to do, to see to it that these two witnesses had an opportunity to appear before the Grand Jury." Judge Mize advised the Grand Jury that they had a right to hear the testimony of Messrs. Riddell and Holleman, but requested them not to do so until October 21, 1964, the day after Judge Cox was to return from his vacation.

October 20 Mr. Katzenbach talked with Judge Cox by telephone, reiterating the Department's position. He also instructed Mr. Hauberg not to prepare or sign indictments. October 22 the foreman of the grand jury in open court informed Judge Cox that Mr. Hauberg had declined to assist in preparing true bills. The United States Attorney stated that "the Department of Justice and the United States felt as if that the law and the fact was not sufficient to constitute perjury and that an indictment thereon would be no good." Judge Cox said:

> I here and now order and direct you to disregard your instructions from the Department of Justice and to prepare true bills or no bills as this Grand Jury may direct you to do and to sign those bills or no bills, as the Grand Jury may decide under penalty of contempt. . . ."

Judge Cox recessed court for one hour. During this recess Mr. Hauberg and Mr. Katzenbach conferred by telephone; the Attorney General directed the United States Attorney not to prepare or sign perjury indictments of Goff and Kendrick. Court reopened. Mr. Hauberg respectfully declined to comply with the court's order. Judge Cox forthwith adjudged him "guilty of civil contempt," ordered him confined to a jail in Hinds County, ordered the issuance of a citation to the Acting Attorney General to appear before the court to show cause why he should not be held in contempt; and stayed the order for a period of five days.

Against the backdrop of Mississippi versus the Nation in the field of civil rights, we have a heated but bona fide difference of opinion between Judge Cox and the Attorney General as to whether two Negroes, Goff and Kendrick, should be prosecuted for perjury. Taking a narrow view of the case, we would be justified in holding that the Attorney General's implied powers, by analogy to the express powers of Rule 48(a), give him discretion to prosecute. Here there was a bona fide, reasonable exercise of discretion made after a full investigation and long consideration of the case—both sides of the case, not just the evidence tending to show guilt. If the grand jury is dissatisfied with that administrative decision, it may exercise its inquisitorial power and make a presentment in open court. It could be said, that is all there is to the case. But there is more to the case.

This Court, along with everyone else, knows that Goff and Kendrick, if prosecuted, run the risk of being tried in a climate of community hostility. They run the risk of a punishment that may not fit the crime. The Registrar, who provoked the original litigation, runs no risk, notwithstanding the fact that the district court, in effect, found that Ramsay did not tell the truth on the witness stand. In these circumstances, the very least demands of justice require that the discretion to prosecute be lodged with a person or agency insulated from local prejudices and parochial pressures. This is not the hard case that makes bad law. This is the type of case that comes up, in one way or another, whenever the customs, beliefs, or interests of a region collide with national policy as fixed by the Constitution or by Congress. It is not likely that the men who devised diversity jurisdiction expected to turn over to local juries the discretionary power to bring federal prosecutions. This case is unusual only for the clarity with which the facts, speaking for themselves, illuminate the imperative necessity in American Federalism that the discretion to prosecute be lodged in the Attorney General of United States.

The decision not to prosecute represents the exercise of a discretion analogous to the exercise of executive privilege. As a matter of law, the Attorney General has concluded that there is not sufficient evidence to prove perjury. As a matter of fact, the Attorney General has concluded, as he pleaded in *United States v. Warner*, that trial for perjury would have the effect of inhibiting not only Goff and Kendrick but other Negroes in Mississippi from registering to vote. There is a conflict, therefore, between society's interest in law enforcement (diluted in this case by the Attorney General's conclusion that the evidence does not support the charge of guilt) and the national policy, set forth in the Constitution and the Civil Rights Acts, of outlawing racial discrimination. It is unthinkable that resolution of this important conflict affecting the whole Nation should lie with a majority of twenty-three members of a jury chosen from the Southern District of Mississippi. The nature of American Federalism, looking to the differences between the Constitution and the Articles of Confederation, requires that the power to resolve this question lie in the unfettered discretion of the President of United States or his deputy for law enforcement, the Attorney General.

My memory, too, goes back to the days, pointedly referred to by the dissenters, when we had "an Attorney General suspected of being corrupt." But I am not aware that we have had more lawless Attorneys General than lawless juries.

NOTES AND QUESTIONS

1. Judge Cox's order, the subject of the appeal, purports to require the United States attorney to draft and sign the bills requested by the grand jury. The order also reveals that Judge Cox appears to have had other involvement with this particular grand jury. How else does he seem to have been involved? Was such involvement permissible? What additional involvement is revealed in Judge Wisdom's opinion? Does a district court judge have any legitimate recourse if he believes a witness is committing perjury in his courtroom?

2. Rule 7(c) of the Federal Rules of Criminal Procedure appears to address purely matters of form, dispensing with technical requirements (much like its civil analogue, Fed. R. Civ. P. 8) and providing, seemingly by way of housekeeping, that it "shall be signed an attorney for the government." Was this rule really intended to carry the weight the court assigns it here?

3. Note that the opinion of the court does not address the underlying facts. Why not?

4. Judge Wisdom opens his opinion by declaring that "[t]he grand jury earned its place in the Bill of Rights by its shield, not its sword." What point is he trying to make here? In the same passage he contrasts the "inquisitorial" and "accusatorial" roles of the grand jury, and notes that in the latter role "no aura of traditional or constitutionality sanctity surrounds the grand jury." *Id.* at 186. How does this compare with the Supreme Court's view of the grand jury decades later in *Williams*?

5. Judge Wisdom finds ample legal authority for the proposition that the prosecution of federal crimes is the "exclusive prerogative" of the executive function, further expressed by statute in Rules 7(c) and 48(a) of the Federal Rules of Criminal Procedure. He also views this allocation as wise insofar as the executive branch is the best-suited body for making prosecutorial decisions when matters of "national policy" are involved. What sort of "national policy" is he referring to? Does this sentiment amount to an endorsement of a role for politics in prosecutorial decision making?

6. Here, the DOJ concluded that there was no basis for a perjury prosecution of Goff and Kendrick. (That is not surprising, as it was fellow DOJ lawyers who elicited their testimony.) What if instead the DOJ had doubts about the veracity of their testimony, and believed they may have committed perjury? Was nonprosecution nonetheless justified because of the chilling effect such a prosecution might have on other potential government witnesses in voting rights cases? Was nonprosecution justified by the "lawless juries" likely to be empaneled for such a prosecution?

7. Judge Wisdom states that if the grand jury is dissatisfied with the prosecutor's decision not to indict, its recourse is to "exercise its inquisitorial power and make a presentment in open court." *Id.* at 196. Do you agree that the grand jury has that power?

The presiding district court judge here, Harold Cox, was roommates at the University of Mississippi with James Eastland, who would go on to be a United States senator from Mississippi from 1943 to 1978, leading southern resistance to integration for four decades. Supposedly, President Kennedy's nomination of Cox to a federal judgeship in the early 1960s was a quid pro quo for Eastland's agreement not to oppose Thurgood Marshall's contemporaneous nomination to the Second Circuit. Iconic NAACP civil rights lawyer and future federal judge Constance Baker Motley, who spent much of her life in the early 1960s litigating in federal court in Mississippi, including in connection with James Meredith's efforts to gain admission to the University of Mississippi, called Judge Cox "the most openly racist judge to ever sit on a federal court bench." Constance Baker Motley, Equal Justice Under Law: An Autobiography 180 (1999).

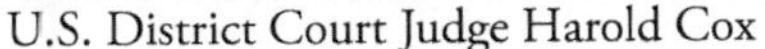

U.S. District Court Judge Harold Cox

Nicholas Katzenbach

D. GRAND JURY SUBPOENA POWER

The grand jury does its work through subpoenas. Grand jury subpoenas for documents are analogous to their civil counterparts—*see* Fed. R. Civ. P. 34 & 45—in that they purport to require the recipient to produce materials at the location of the grand jury room at a specified date. The similarities largely end there. There are no geographical limits on the grand jury's service of subpoenas, and there is no provision in the Federal Rules for "objecting" to grand jury subpoenas, although most prosecutors—remember, these are really the prosecutors' subpoenas—will usually be reasonable about the terms of compliance. The next two cases consider the breadth of the grand jury's subpoena power.

United States v. Dionisio

410 U.S. 1 (1973)

Mr. Justice Stewart delivered the opinion of the Court.

A special grand jury was convened in the Northern District of Illinois in February 1971, to investigate possible violations of federal criminal statutes relating to gambling. In the course of its investigation, the grand jury received in evidence certain voice recordings that had been obtained pursuant to court orders.

The grand jury subpoenaed approximately 20 persons, including the respondent Dionisio, seeking to obtain from them voice exemplars for comparison with the recorded conversations that had been received in evidence. Each witness was advised that he was a potential defendant in a criminal prosecution. Each was asked to examine a transcript of an intercepted conversation, and to go to a nearby office of the United States Attorney to read the transcript into a recording device. The witnesses were advised that they would be allowed to have their attorneys present when they read the transcripts. Dionisio and other witnesses refused to furnish the voice exemplars, asserting that these disclosures would violate their rights under the Fourth and Fifth Amendments.

The Government then filed separate petitions in the United States District Court to compel Dionisio and the other witnesses to furnish the voice exemplars to the grand jury. The petitions stated that the exemplars were "essential and necessary" to the grand jury investigation, and that they would "be used solely as a standard of comparison in order to determine whether or not the witness is the person whose voice was intercepted. . . ."

Following a hearing, the District Judge rejected the witnesses' constitutional arguments and ordered them to comply with the grand jury's request. He reasoned that voice exemplars, like handwriting exemplars or fingerprints, were not testimonial or communicative evidence, and that consequently the order to produce them would not compel any witness to testify against himself. The District Judge also found that there would be no Fourth Amendment violation, because the grand jury subpoena did not itself violate the Fourth Amendment, and the order to produce the voice exemplars would involve no unreasonable search and seizure within the proscription of that Amendment:

> The witnesses are lawfully before the grand jury pursuant to subpoena. The Fourth Amendment prohibition against unreasonable search and seizure applies only where identifying physical characteristics, such as fingerprints, are obtained as a result of unlawful detention of a suspect, or when an intrusion into the body, such as a blood test, is undertaken without a warrant, absent an emergency situation.

When Dionisio persisted in his refusal to respond to the grand jury's directive, the District Court adjudged him in civil contempt and ordered him committed to custody until he obeyed the court order, or until the expiration of 18 months.

The Court of Appeals for the Seventh Circuit reversed. It agreed with the District Court in rejecting the Fifth Amendment claims, but concluded that to compel the voice recordings would violate the Fourth Amendment. In the court's view, the grand jury was "seeking to obtain the voice exemplars of the witnesses by the use of its subpoena powers because probable cause did not exist for their arrest or for some other, less unusual, method of compelling the production of the exemplars." The court found that the Fourth Amendment applied to grand jury process, and that "under the fourth amendment law enforcement officials may not compel the production of physical evidence absent a showing of the reasonableness of the seizure."

In *Davis* this Court held that it was error to admit the petitioner's fingerprints into evidence at his trial for rape, because they had been obtained during a police detention following a lawless wholesale roundup of the petitioner and more than 20 other youths. Equating the procedures followed by the grand jury in the present case to the fingerprint detentions in Davis, the Court of Appeals reasoned that "(t)he dragnet effect here, where approximately twenty persons were subpoenaed for purposes of identification, has the same invidious effect on fourth amendment rights as the practice condemned in *Davis*."

I

The Court of Appeals correctly rejected the contention that the compelled production of the voice exemplars would violate the Fifth Amendment. It has long been held that the compelled display of identifiable physical characteristics infringes no interest protected by the privilege against compulsory self-incrimination. In *Holt v. United States*, Mr. Justice Holmes, writing for the Court, dismissed as an "extravagant extension of the Fifth Amendment" the argument that it violated the privilege to require a defendant to put on a blouse for identification purposes. He explained that "the prohibition of compelling a man in a criminal court to be witness against himself is a prohibition of the use of physical or moral compulsion to extort communications from him, not an exclusion of his body as evidence when it may be material."

More recently, in *Schmerber* we relied on *Holt*, and noted that:

> (B)oth federal and state courts have usually held that (the privilege) it offers no protection against compulsion to submit to fingerprinting, photographing, or measurements, to write or speak for identification, to appear in court, to stand, to assume a stance, to walk, or to make a particular gesture. The distinction which has emerged, often expressed in different ways, is that the privilege is a bar against compelling "communications" or "testimony," but that compulsion which makes a suspect or accused the source of "real or physical evidence" does not violate it.

The Court held that the extraction and chemical analysis of a blood sample involved no "shadow of testimonial compulsion upon or enforced communication by the accused."

These cases led us to conclude in *Gilbert v. California* that handwriting exemplars were not protected by the privilege against compulsory self-incrimination. While "(o)ne's voice and handwriting are, of course, means of communication," we held that a "mere handwriting exemplar, in contrast to the content of what is written, like the voice or body itself, is an identifying physical characteristic outside its protection." And similarly in *United States v. Wade* we found no error in compelling a defendant accused of bank robbery to utter in a lineup words that had allegedly been spoken by the robber. The accused there was "required to use his voice as an identifying physical characteristic, not to speak his guilt."

Wade and *Gilbert* definitively refute any contention that the compelled production of the voice exemplars in this case would violate the Fifth Amendment. The voice recordings were to be used solely to measure the physical properties of the witnesses' voices, not for the testimonial or communicative content of what was to be said.

II

The Court of Appeals held that the Fourth Amendment required a preliminary showing of reasonableness before a grand jury witness could be compelled to furnish a voice exemplar, and that in this case the proposed "seizures" of the voice exemplars would be unreasonable because of the large number of witnesses summoned by the grand jury and directed to produce such exemplars. We disagree.

The Fourth Amendment guarantees that all people shall be "secure in their persons, houses, papers, and effects, against unreasonable searches and seizures. . . ." Any Fourth Amendment violation in the present setting must rest on a lawless governmental intrusion upon the privacy of "persons" rather than on interference with "property relationships or private papers." In *Terry v. Ohio* the Court explained the protection afforded to "persons" in terms of the statement in *Katz v. United States*, that "the Fourth Amendment protects people, not places," and concluded that "wherever an individual may harbor a reasonable 'expectation of privacy,' . . . he is entitled to be free from unreasonable governmental intrusion."

As the Court made clear in *Schmerber*, supra, the obtaining of physical evidence from a person involves a potential Fourth Amendment violation at two different levels — the "seizure" of the "person" necessary to bring him into contact with government agents, and the subsequent search for and seizure of the evidence. In *Schmerber*, we found the initial seizure of the accused justified as a lawful arrest, and the subsequent seizure of the blood sample from his body reasonable in light of the exigent circumstances. And in *Terry*, we concluded that neither the initial seizure of the person, an investigatory "stop" by a policeman, nor the subsequent search, a "patdown" of his outer clothing for weapons, constituted a violation of the Fourth and Fourteenth Amendments. The constitutionality of the compulsory production of exemplars from a grand jury witness necessarily turns on the same dual inquiry — whether either the initial compulsion of the person to appear before the grand jury, or the subsequent directive to make a voice recording is an unreasonable "seizure" within the meaning of the Fourth Amendment.

It is clear that a subpoena to appear before a grand jury is not a "seizure" in the Fourth Amendment sense, even though that summons may be inconvenient or burdensome. Last Term we again acknowledged what has long been recognized, that "(c)itizens generally are not constitutionally immune from grand jury subpoenas. . . ." We concluded that:

> Although the powers of the grand jury are not unlimited and are subject to the supervision of a judge, the longstanding principle that "the public . . . has a right to every man's evidence," except for those persons protected by a constitutional, common law, or statutory privilege is particularly applicable to grand jury proceedings.

These are recent reaffirmations of the historically grounded obligation of every person to appear and give his evidence before the grand jury. "The personal sacrifice involved is a part of the necessary contribution of the individual to the welfare of the public." And while the duty may be "onerous" at times, it is "necessary to the administration of justice."

The compulsion exerted by a grand jury subpoena differs from the seizure effected by an arrest or even an investigative "stop" in more than civic obligation. For, as Judge Friendly wrote for the Court of Appeals for the Second Circuit:

> The latter is abrupt, is effected with force or the threat of it and often in demeaning circumstances, and, in the case of arrest, results in a record involving social stigma. A subpoena is served in the same manner as other legal process; it involves no stigma whatever; if the time for appearance is inconvenient, this can generally be altered; and it remains at all times under the control and supervision of a court.

Thus the Court of Appeals for the Seventh Circuit correctly recognized in a case subsequent to the one now before us, that a "grand jury subpoena to testify is not that kind of governmental intrusion on privacy against which the Fourth Amendment affords protection once the Fifth Amendment is satisfied."

This case is thus quite different from *Davis v. Mississippi*, supra, on which the Court of Appeals primarily relied. For in *Davis* it was the initial seizure — the lawless dragnet detention — that violated the Fourth and Fourteenth Amendments, not the taking of the fingerprints. We noted that "(i)nvestigatory seizures would subject unlimited numbers of innocent persons to the harassment and ignominy incident to involuntary detention," and we left open the question whether, consistently with the Fourth and Fourteenth Amendments, narrowly circumscribed procedures might be developed for obtaining fingerprints from people when there was no probable cause to arrest them. *Davis* is plainly inapposite to a case where the initial restraint does not itself infringe the Fourth Amendment.

This is not to say that a grand jury subpoena is some talisman that dissolves all constitutional protections. The grand jury cannot require a witness to testify against himself. It cannot require the production by a person of private books and records that would incriminate him. The Fourth Amendment provides protection against a grand jury subpoena duces tecum too sweeping in its terms "to be regarded as reasonable." *Hale v. Henkel.* And last Term, in the context of a First Amendment claim, we indicated that the Constitution could not tolerate the transformation of the grand jury into an instrument of oppression: "Official harassment of the press undertaken not for purposes of law enforcement but to disrupt a reporter's relationship with his news sources would have no justification. Grand juries are subject to judicial control and subpoenas to motions to quash. We do not expect courts will forget that grand juries must operate within the limits of the First Amendment as well as the Fifth."

But we are here faced with no such constitutional infirmities in the subpoena to appear before the grand jury or in the order to make the voice recordings. There is, as we have said, no valid Fifth Amendment claim. There was no order to produce private books and papers, and no sweeping subpoena duces tecum. And even if *Branzburg* be extended beyond its First Amendment moorings and tied to a more generalized *due* process concept, there is still no indication in this case of the kind of harassment that was of concern there.

The Court of Appeals found critical significance in the fact that the grand jury had summoned approximately 20 witnesses to furnish voice exemplars. We think that fact is basically irrelevant to the constitutional issues here. The grand jury may have been attempting to identify a number of voices on the tapes in evidence, or it might have summoned the 20 witnesses in an effort to identify one voice. But whatever the case, "(a) grand jury's investigation is not fully carried out until every available clue has been run down and all witnesses examined in every proper way to find if a crime has been committed. . . ." As the Court recalled last Term, "Because its task is to inquire into the existence of possible criminal conduct and to return only well-founded indictments, its investigative powers are necessarily broad." The grand jury may well find it desirable to call numerous witnesses in the course of an investigation. It does not follow that each witness may resist a subpoena on the ground that too many witnesses have been called. Neither the order to Dionisio to appear nor the order to make a voice recording was rendered unreasonable by the fact that many others were subjected to the same compulsion.

But the conclusion that Dionisio's compulsory appearance before the grand jury was not an unreasonable "seizure" is the answer to only the first part of the Fourth Amendment inquiry here. Dionisio argues that the grand jury's subsequent directive to make the voice recording was itself an infringement of his rights under the Fourth Amendment. We cannot accept that argument.

In *Katz v. United States* we said that the Fourth Amendment provides no protection for what "a person knowingly exposes to the public, even in his own home or office. . . ." The physical characteristics of a person's voice, its tone and manner, as opposed to the content of a specific conversation, are constantly exposed to the public. Like a man's facial characteristics, or handwriting, his voice is repeatedly produced for others to hear. No person can have a reasonable expectation that others will not know the sound of his voice, any more than he can reasonably expect that his face will be a mystery to the world. As the Court of Appeals for the Second Circuit stated:

> Except for the rare recluse who chooses to live his life in complete solitude, in our daily lives we constantly speak and write, and while the content of a communication is entitled to Fourth Amendment protection . . . the underlying identifying characteristics—the constant factor throughout both public and private communications—are open for all to see or hear. There is no basis for constructing a wall of privacy against the grand jury which does not exist in casual contacts with strangers. Hence no intrusion into an individual's privacy results from compelled execution of handwriting or voice exemplars; nothing is being exposed to the grand jury that has not previously been exposed to the public at large.

The required disclosure of a person's voice is thus immeasurably further removed from the Fourth Amendment protection than was the intrusion into the body effected by the blood extraction in *Schmerber*. "The interests in human dignity and privacy which the Fourth Amendment protects forbid any such intrusions on the mere chance that desired evidence might be obtained." Similarly, a seizure of voice exemplars does not involve the "severe, though brief, intrusion upon cherished personal security," effected by the "pat down" in *Terry*—"surely . . . an annoying, frightening, and perhaps humiliating experience." Rather, this is like the fingerprinting in *Davis*, where, though the initial dragnet detentions were constitutionally impermissible, we noted that the fingerprinting itself "involves none of the probing into an individual's private life and thoughts that marks an interrogation or search."

Since neither the summons to appear before the grand jury nor its directive to make a voice recording infringed upon any interest protected by the Fourth Amendment, there was no justification for requiring the grand jury to satisfy even the minimal requirement of "reasonableness" imposed by the Court of Appeals. A grand jury has broad investigative powers to determine whether a crime has been committed and who has committed it. The jurors may act on tips, rumors, evidence offered by the prosecutor, or their own personal knowledge. No grand jury witness is "entitled to set limits to the investigation that the grand jury may conduct." And a sufficient basis for an indictment may only emerge at the end of the investigation when all the evidence has been received.

> It is impossible to conceive that . . . the examination of witnesses must be stopped until a basis is laid by an indictment formally preferred, when the very object of the examination is to ascertain who shall be indicted.

Since Dionisio raised no valid Fourth Amendment claim, there is no more reason to require a preliminary showing of reasonableness here than there would be in the case of any witness who, despite the lack of any constitutional or statutory privilege, declined to answer a question or comply with a grand jury request. Neither the Constitution nor our prior cases justify any such interference with grand jury proceedings.

The Fifth Amendment guarantees that no civilian may be brought to trial for an infamous crime "unless on a presentment or indictment of a Grand Jury." This constitutional guarantee presupposes an investigative body "acting independently of either prosecuting attorney or judge," *Stirone v. United States*, whose mission is to clear the innocent, no less than to bring to trial those who may be guilty. Any holding that would saddle a grand jury with minitrials and preliminary showings would assuredly impede its investigation and frustrate the public's interest in the fair and expeditious administration of the criminal laws. The grand jury may not always serve its historic role as a protective bulwark standing solidly between the ordinary citizen and an overzealous prosecutor, but if it is even to approach the proper performance of its constitutional mission, it must be free to pursue its investigations unhindered by external influence or supervision so long as it does not trench upon the legitimate rights of any witness called before it.

Since the Court of Appeals found an unreasonable search and seizure where none existed, and imposed a preliminary showing of reasonableness where none was required, its judgment is reversed and this case is remanded to that court for further proceedings consistent with this opinion.

It is so ordered.

Judgment reversed and case remanded.

NOTES AND QUESTIONS

1. No specific Rule of the Federal Rules of Criminal Procedure governs grand jury subpoenas, an issue that we consider more thoroughly in connection with *United States v. R. Enterprises, Inc.*, 498 U.S. 292 (1991), *infra*. But consider exactly what the grand jury subpoenas here purport to require of the witnesses: reading from a transcript at a United States attorney's office. The witnesses are not even appearing personally before the grand jury. Does the grand jury have the power to require a witness to testify before another person? Should it?

The government apparently was sensitive to the odd nature of this request as it permitted the witnesses' attorneys to be present during the reading, which would normally be a violation of grand jury secrecy laws governing who may be present during grand jury testimony. *See infra*. And in its motion to compel enforcement of the subpoenas the government had no problem telling the court exactly why it needed the voice exemplars, information prosecutors often refuse to disclose in court due to "grand jury secrecy" concerns. Is the government's description of the basic nature of an investigation really a violation of grand jury secrecy?

2. The Court rejects the defendant's Fifth Amendment argument that the compelled voice exemplars violated his right against self-incrimination, reasoning that they were not "testimonial" but merely "the compelled display of physical characteristics." Do you agree? Is the compelled reading of a transcript (of unknown length) simply a revealing of a physical characteristic? Both of the dissenters disagree with the "testimonial" limit on Fifth Amendment compulsion, but do you have to go that far to disagree with the majority in this case? Are the witnesses here being asked merely for "exemplars"?

3. The Court also rejects the argument that a grand jury subpoena is a "seizure" for Fourth Amendment purposes, and in particular rejects the analogy to the "investigative seizure" condemned by the Court in *Davis v. Mississippi*, 394 U.S. 721 (1969). Justice Douglas's dissent in a companion case to *Dionisio*, *United States v. Mara*, 410 U.S. 19 (1973), on the other hand, finds the "dragnet effect" at issue to be "just the kind of invasion that the *Davis* case sought to prevent." *Id.* at 26-27. Do you agree? Is it relevant to this issue that Dionisio and Mara were among 20 people that were subpoenaed?

4. In rejecting the seizure argument the Court concedes that the Fourth Amendment at least provides protection against grand jury subpoenas that are unreasonably broad. *Dionisio*, 410 U.S. at 11-12. In reaching this conclusion the Court relied on the venerable case of *Hale v. Henkel*, 201 U.S. 43, 77 (1906), which held that a subpoena lacking in particularity is "equally indefensible as a search warrant would be if couched in similar terms," and that in such cases a showing of "some necessity" may be required of the government.

How is any such overbreadth argument to be analyzed in the typical case where the government has revealed little about the subject of the grand jury's investigation? Were the subpoenas here unreasonably broad, either individually or when analyzed as a group of 20?

5. Justice Douglas begins his *Mara* dissent with the following quotation from United States District Court Judge William Campbell, who has been on the federal court in Chicago for over 32 years:

> This great institution of the past has long ceased to be the guardian of the people for which purpose it was created at Runnymede. Today it is but a convenient tool for the prosecutor — too often used solely for publicity. Any experienced prosecutor will admit that he can indict anybody at any time for almost anything before any grand jury.

Mara, 410 U.S. at 23. This is the earliest public acknowledgment by a Supreme Court Justice that the federal grand jury — no matter how it was conceived or envisioned by the Founders — may not be what the Court says it is. Yet the love songs continued well after *Dionisio*.

United States v. R. Enterprises, Inc.

498 U.S. 292 (1991)

Justice O'Connor delivered the opinion of the Court.

This case requires the Court to decide what standards apply when a party seeks to avoid compliance with a subpoena duces tecum issued in connection with a grand jury investigation.

I

Since 1986, a federal grand jury sitting in the Eastern District of Virginia has been investigating allegations of interstate transportation of obscene materials. In early 1988, the grand jury issued a series of subpoenas to three companies — Model Magazine Distributors, Inc. (Model), R. Enterprises, Inc., and MFR Court Street Books, Inc. (MFR). Model is a New York distributor of sexually oriented paperback books, magazines, and videotapes. R. Enterprises, which distributes adult materials, and MFR, which sells books, magazines, and videotapes, are also based in New York. All three companies are wholly owned by Martin Rothstein. The grand jury subpoenas sought a variety of corporate books and records and, in Model's case, copies of 193 videotapes that Model had shipped to retailers in the Eastern District of Virginia. All three companies moved to quash the subpoenas, arguing that the subpoenas called for production of materials irrelevant to the grand jury's investigation and that the enforcement of the subpoenas would likely infringe their First Amendment rights.

The District Court, after extensive hearings, denied the motions to quash. As to Model, the court found that the subpoenas for business records were sufficiently specific and that production of the videotapes would not constitute a prior restraint. As to R. Enterprises, the court found a "sufficient connection with Virginia for further investigation by the grand jury." The court relied in large part on the statement attributed to Rothstein that the three companies were "all the same thing, I'm president of all three." Ibid. Additionally, the court explained in denying MFR's motion to quash that it was "inclined to agree" with "the majority of the jurisdictions," which do not require the Government to make a "threshold showing" before a grand jury subpoena will be enforced. Even assuming that a preliminary showing of relevance was required, the court determined that the Government had made such a showing. It found sufficient evidence that the companies were "related entities," at least one of which "certainly did ship sexually explicit material into the Commonwealth of Virginia." Ibid. The court concluded that the subpoenas in this case were "fairly standard business subpoenas" and "ought to be complied with." Notwithstanding these findings, the companies refused to comply with the subpoenas. The District Court found each in contempt and fined them $500 per day, but stayed imposition of the fine pending appeal.

The Court of Appeals for the Fourth Circuit upheld the business records subpoenas issued to Model, but remanded the motion to quash the subpoena for Model's videotapes. Of particular relevance here, the Court of Appeals quashed the business records subpoenas issued to R. Enterprises and MFR. In doing so, it applied the standards set out by this Court in *United States v. Nixon* (1974). The court recognized that *Nixon* dealt with a trial subpoena, not a grand jury subpoena, but determined that the rule was "equally applicable" in the grand jury context. Accordingly, it required the Government to clear the three hurdles that *Nixon* established in the trial context—relevancy, admissibility, and specificity—in order to enforce the grand jury subpoenas. The court concluded that the challenged subpoenas did not satisfy the *Nixon* standards, finding no evidence in the record that either company had ever shipped materials into, or otherwise conducted business in, the Eastern District of Virginia. The Court of Appeals specifically criticized the District Court for drawing an inference that, because Rothstein owned all three businesses and one of them had undoubtedly shipped sexually explicit materials into the Eastern District of Virginia, there might be some link between the Eastern District of Virginia and R. Enterprises or MFR. It then noted that "any evidence concerning Mr. Rothstein's alleged business activities outside of Virginia, or his ownership of companies which distribute allegedly obscene materials outside of Virginia, would most likely be inadmissible on relevancy grounds at any trial that might occur," and that the subpoenas therefore failed "to meet the requirements [sic] that any documents subpoenaed under [Federal] Rule [of Criminal Procedure] 17(c) must be admissible as evidence at trial." The Court of Appeals did not consider whether enforcement of the subpoenas duces tecum issued to respondents implicated the First Amendment.

We granted certiorari to determine whether the Court of Appeals applied the proper standard in evaluating the grand jury subpoenas issued to respondents. We now reverse.

II

The grand jury occupies a unique role in our criminal justice system. It is an investigatory body charged with the responsibility of determining whether or not a crime has been committed. Unlike this Court, whose jurisdiction is predicated on a specific case or controversy, the grand jury "can investigate merely on suspicion that the law is being violated, or even just because it wants assurance that it is not." The function of the grand jury is to inquire into all information that might possibly bear on its investigation until it has identified an offense or has satisfied itself that none has occurred. As a necessary consequence of its investigatory function, the grand jury paints with a broad brush. "A grand jury investigation 'is not fully carried out until every available clue has been run down and all witnesses examined in every proper way to find if a crime has been committed.'"

A grand jury subpoena is thus much different from a subpoena issued in the context of a prospective criminal trial, where a specific offense has been identified and a particular defendant charged. "[T]he identity of the offender, and the precise nature of the offense, if there be one, normally are developed at the conclusion of the grand jury's labors, not at the beginning." In short, the Government cannot be required to justify the issuance of a grand jury subpoena by presenting evidence sufficient to establish probable cause because the very purpose of requesting the information is to ascertain whether probable cause exists.

This Court has emphasized on numerous occasions that many of the rules and restrictions that apply at a trial do not apply in grand jury proceedings. This is especially true of evidentiary restrictions. The same rules that, in an adversary hearing on the merits, may increase the likelihood of accurate determinations of guilt or innocence do not necessarily advance the mission of a grand jury, whose task is to conduct an ex parte investigation to determine whether or not there is probable cause to prosecute a particular defendant. In *Costello* this

Court declined to apply the rule against hearsay to grand jury proceedings. Strict observance of trial rules in the context of a grand jury's preliminary investigation "would result in interminable delay but add nothing to the assurance of a fair trial." In *Calandra* we held that the Fourth Amendment exclusionary rule does not apply to grand jury proceedings. Permitting witnesses to invoke the exclusionary rule would "delay and disrupt grand jury proceedings" by requiring adversary hearings on peripheral matters, and would effectively transform such proceedings into preliminary trials on the merits. The teaching of the Court's decisions is clear: A grand jury "may compel the production of evidence or the testimony of witnesses as it considers appropriate, and its operation generally is unrestrained by the technical procedural and evidentiary rules governing the conduct of criminal trials."

This guiding principle renders suspect the Court of Appeals' holding that the standards announced in *Nixon* as to subpoenas issued in anticipation of trial apply equally in the grand jury context. The multifactor test announced in *Nixon* would invite procedural delays and detours while courts evaluate the relevancy and admissibility of documents sought by a particular subpoena. We have expressly stated that grand jury proceedings should be free of such delays. "Any holding that would saddle a grand jury with minitrials and preliminary showings would assuredly impede its investigation and frustrate the public's interest in the fair and expeditious administration of the criminal laws. Additionally, application of the *Nixon* test in this context ignores that grand jury proceedings are subject to strict secrecy requirements. See Fed. Rule Crim. Proc. 6(e). Requiring the Government to explain in too much detail the particular reasons underlying a subpoena threatens to compromise "the indispensable secrecy of grand jury proceedings." Broad disclosure also affords the targets of investigation far more information about the grand jury's internal workings than the Federal Rules of Criminal Procedure appear to contemplate.

III

A

The investigatory powers of the grand jury are nevertheless not unlimited. Grand juries are not licensed to engage in arbitrary fishing expeditions, nor may they select targets of investigation out of malice or an intent to harass. In this case, the focus of our inquiry is the limit imposed on a grand jury by Federal Rule of Criminal Procedure 17(c), which governs the issuance of subpoenas duces tecum in federal criminal proceedings. The Rule provides that "[t]he court on motion made promptly may quash or modify the subpoena if compliance would be unreasonable or oppressive."

This standard is not self-explanatory. As we have observed, "what is reasonable depends on the context." In *Nixon*, this Court defined what is reasonable in the context of a jury trial. We determined that, in order to require production of information prior to trial, a party must make a reasonably specific request for information that would be both relevant and admissible at trial. But, for the reasons we have explained above, the *Nixon* standard does not apply in the context of grand jury proceedings. In the grand jury context, the decision as to what offense will be charged is routinely not made until after the grand jury has concluded its investigation. One simply cannot know in advance whether information sought during the investigation will be relevant and admissible in a prosecution for a particular offense.

To the extent that Rule 17(c) imposes some reasonableness limitation on grand jury subpoenas, however, our task is to define it. In doing so, we recognize that a party to whom a grand jury subpoena is issued faces a difficult situation. As a rule, grand juries do not announce publicly the subjects of their investigations. A party who desires to challenge a grand jury subpoena thus may have no conception of the Government's purpose in seeking production of the requested information. Indeed, the party will often not know whether he or she is a primary target of the investigation or merely a peripheral witness. Absent even minimal information, the subpoena recipient is likely to find it exceedingly difficult to persuade a court that "compliance would be unreasonable." As one pair of commentators has summarized it, the challenging party's "unenviable task is to seek to persuade the court that the subpoena that has been served on [him or her] could not possibly serve any investigative purpose that the grand jury could legitimately be pursuing."

Our task is to fashion an appropriate standard of reasonableness, one that gives due weight to the difficult position of subpoena recipients but does not impair the strong governmental interests in affording grand juries wide latitude, avoiding minitrials on peripheral matters, and preserving a necessary level of secrecy. We begin by reiterating that the law presumes, absent a strong showing to the contrary, that a grand jury acts within the legitimate scope of its authority. Consequently, a grand jury subpoena issued through normal channels is presumed to be reasonable, and the burden of showing unreasonableness must be on the recipient who seeks to avoid compliance. Indeed, this result is indicated by the language of Rule 17(c), which permits a subpoena to be quashed only "on motion" and "if *compliance* would be unreasonable" (emphasis added). To the extent that the Court of Appeals placed an initial burden on the Government, it committed error. Drawing on the principles articulated above, we conclude that where, as here, a subpoena is challenged on relevancy grounds, the motion to quash must be denied unless the district court determines that there is no reasonable possibility that the category of materials the Government seeks will produce information relevant to the general subject of the grand jury's investigation. Respondents did not challenge the subpoenas as being too indefinite nor did they claim that compliance would be overly burdensome. The Court of Appeals accordingly did not consider these aspects of the subpoenas, nor do we.

B

It seems unlikely, of course, that a challenging party who does not know the general subject matter of the grand jury's investigation, no matter how valid that party's claim, will be able to make the necessary showing that compliance would be unreasonable. After all, a subpoena recipient "cannot put his whole life before the court in order to show that there is no crime to be investigated." Consequently, a court may be justified in a case where unreasonableness is alleged in requiring the Government to reveal the general subject of the grand jury's investigation before requiring the challenging party to carry its burden of persuasion. We need not resolve this question in the present case, however, as there is no doubt that respondents knew the subject of the grand jury investigation pursuant to which the business records subpoenas were issued. In cases where the recipient of the subpoena does not know the nature of the investigation, we are confident that district courts will be able to craft appropriate procedures that balance the interests of the subpoena recipient against the strong governmental interests in maintaining secrecy, preserving investigatory flexibility, and avoiding procedural delays. For example, to ensure that subpoenas are not routinely challenged as a form of discovery, a district court may require that the Government reveal the subject of the investigation to the trial court in camera, so that the court may determine whether the motion to quash has a reasonable prospect for success before it discloses the subject matter to the challenging party.

IV

Applying these principles in this case demonstrates that the District Court correctly denied respondents' motions to quash. It is undisputed that all three companies—Model, R. Enterprises, and MFR—are owned by the same person, that all do business in the same area, and that one of the three, Model, has shipped sexually explicit materials into the Eastern District of Virginia. The District Court could have concluded from these facts that there was a reasonable possibility that the business records of R. Enterprises and MFR would produce information relevant to the grand jury's investigation into the interstate transportation of obscene materials. Respondents' blanket denial of any connection to Virginia did not suffice to render the District Court's conclusion invalid. A grand jury need not accept on faith the self-serving assertions of those who may have committed criminal acts. Rather, it is entitled to determine for itself whether a crime has been committed.

Both in the District Court and in the Court of Appeals, respondents contended that these subpoenas sought records relating to First Amendment activities, and that this required the Government to demonstrate that the records were particularly relevant to its investigation. The Court of Appeals determined that the subpoenas did not satisfy Rule 17(c) and thus did not pass on the First Amendment issue. We express no view on this issue and leave it to be resolved by the Court of Appeals.

The judgment is reversed insofar as the Court of Appeals quashed the subpoenas issued to R. Enterprises and MFR, and the case is remanded for further proceedings consistent with this opinion.

It is so ordered.

NOTES AND QUESTIONS

Attorney General Edwin Meese

1. The investigation at issue in *R. Enterprises* was part of the effort of the Reagan Administration's Department of Justice, led by Attorney General Edwin Meese, to crack down on the child pornography industry. *See* Jim Duffy & Brian McGee, Main Justice: The Men and Women Who Enforce the Nation's Laws and Guard Its Liberties 279-300 (1996). As part of this effort the DOJ changed its internal guidelines for commencing actions in multiple jurisdictions against the same party.

Is its prioritizing this issue an example of the DOJ being improperly "political"?

2. The Fourth Circuit can be rightly criticized for relying on the trial subpoena standard of *United States v. Nixon*, 418 U.S. 683 (1974), in analyzing a motion to quash a grand jury subpoena, as the three-part showing required in that case — "relevancy, admissibility, and specificity," *id.* at 699-700 — makes little sense in the grand jury context, where there is no charged crime, no defendant, and not even any defined facts or issues. And in fact, *Nixon* was addressing the standard for a subpoena returnable "prior to trial," as opposed to at or during trial, making the analogy even weaker.

But isn't the Supreme Court's reliance on Rule 17 of the Federal Rules of Criminal Procedure equally mystifying? Look at its language. Isn't Rule 17 also designed to govern procedures for trial subpoenas and not grand jury subpoenas?

3. The *R. Enterprises* version of the grand jury love song emphasizes the breadth of the grand jury's investigative powers, an aspect that has been touched on but was never the primary focus of earlier versions. In so doing, the Court relies on dicta from two cases that were themselves supported by no precedent whatsoever. First, the Court observes that the grand jury "can investigate merely on suspicion that the law is being violated, or even just because it wants assurance that it is not" (citing *United States v. Morton Salt Co.*, 338 U.S. 632, 642-43

(1950)). *Id.* at 296. The quote is accurate but *Morton Salt* has nothing to do with the grand jury; the Court was simply analogizing to the grand jury in justifying the Federal Trade Commission's authority to require corporations to file reports demonstrating their compliance with a consent decree. And isn't this observation flatly contradicted in *R. Enterprises* itself by the Court's subsequent statement, *id.* at 302, that grand juries "are not licensed to engage in arbitrary fishing expeditions"?

Isn't an investigation to obtain "assurance" that the law is not being violated in substance a description of a fishing exhibition? If the Court's "assurance" language is taken literally, is there any substantive limit to grand jury subpoenas?

4. The Court also relies on dicta from a Second Circuit case, cited by the Court in *Branzburg v. Hayes*, 408 U.S. 665 (1972): "A grand jury investigation 'is not fully carried out until every available clue has been run down and all witnesses examined in every proper way to find if a crime has been committed.'" *Id.* at 701 (quoting *United States v. Stone*, 429 F.2d 138, 140 (2d Cir. 1970)). *Stone* was a two-page decision that included the quoted statement, without any citation, in responding to an argument by the defendant (Sam Stone) that his perjury conviction should be reversed because his false testimony was not "material" to the grand jury.

Doesn't this language also condone fishing exhibitions?

5. It is on the backs of these ill-conceived and never-applied conceptions of the grand jury—as an amorphous and omnivorous investigative blob—that the Court proceeds to determine what "reasonableness" requires under Rule 17. Accordingly, the Court fashions the following test for challenging a grand jury subpoena on relevance grounds: "the motion to quash must be denied unless the district court determines that there is no reasonable possibility that the category of materials the Government seeks will produce information relevant to the general subject of the grand jury's investigation." *Id.* at 301. But of course that definition must also be informed by Rule 6's secrecy requirements, which prevent the government from "explain[ing] in too much detail the particular reasons underlying a subpoena."

6. Did the district court properly deny the motions to quash on relevance grounds under this standard? What does the Court mean by saying that the "grand jury need not accept on faith" the respondents' blanket denial of any connection to Virginia? Does the district court have the discretion in ruling on a motion to quash to simply reject factual contentions made by the movant? Consider the dissent's comments on the relationship between "unreasonable" and "oppressive" under Rule 17. How would you make a combined relevance and burdensomeness argument on these facts?

Note that the superficially straightforward term "grand jury subpoena" is somewhat misleading. On the one hand, it is true that a grand jury subpoena is a document with a court caption that requires the production of materials under the authority of the grand jury's powers. On the other hand, a grand jury subpoena is usually entirely the product of the prosecutor: it is issued by the prosecutor, requiring no approval by the court or even by the grand jury itself; the grand jury may not even be aware of the subpoena's existence; and the grand jury may never even be shown the documents that were produced in response to the subpoena.

E. GRAND JURY SECRECY

Grand jury secrecy has, among its purposes, the protection from public knowledge of the identities of persons who testify in the grand jury as well as the identities of persons under investigation who end up not being charged with a crime. These purposes are important. But sometimes prosecutors invoke the concept of grand jury secrecy overbroadly to impermissibly shield their investigations from public scrutiny.

United States v. Sells Engineering, Inc.

463 U.S. 418 (1983)

BRENNAN, Justice.

The question in this case is under what conditions attorneys for the Civil Division of the Justice Department, their paralegal and secretarial staff, and all other necessary assistants, may obtain access to grand jury materials, compiled with the assistance and knowledge of other Justice Department attorneys, for the purpose of preparing and pursuing a civil suit. We hold that such access is permissible only when the Government moves for court-ordered disclosure under Federal Rule of Criminal Procedure 6(e)(3)(C)(i) and makes the showing of particularized need required by that Rule.

I

Respondents Peter A. Sells and Fred R. Witte were officers of respondent Sells Engineering, Inc. That company had contracts with the United States Navy to produce airborne electronic devices designed to interfere with enemy radar systems. In 1974, a Special Agent of the Internal Revenue Service began a combined criminal and civil administrative investigation of respondents. The Agent issued administrative summonses for certain corporate records of Sells Engineering. When the corporation refused to comply, the Agent obtained a district court order enforcing the summonses. Enforcement was stayed, however, pending appeal.

While the enforcement case was pending in the Court of Appeals, a federal grand jury was convened to investigate charges of criminal fraud on the Navy and of evasion of federal income taxes. The grand jury subpoenaed, and respondents produced, many of the same materials that were the subject of the IRS administrative summonses. The grand jury indicted all three respondents on two counts of conspiracy to defraud the United States and nine counts of tax fraud. Respondents moved to dismiss the indictment, alleging grand jury misuse for civil purposes. Before the motion was decided, however, the parties reached a plea bargain. The individual respondents each pleaded guilty to one count of conspiracy to defraud the Government by obstructing an IRS investigation. All other counts were dismissed, and respondents withdrew their charges of grand jury misuse.

Thereafter, the Government moved for disclosure of all grand jury materials to attorneys in the Justice Department's Civil Division, their paralegal and secretarial assistants, and certain Defense Department experts, for use in preparing and conducting a possible civil suit against respondents under the False Claims Act, 31 U.S.C. § 231 et seq. Respondents opposed the disclosure, renewing their allegations of grand jury misuse. The District Court granted the requested disclosure, concluding that attorneys in the Civil Division are entitled to disclosure as a matter of right under Rule 6(e)(3)(A)(i). The Court also stated that disclosure to Civil Division attorneys and their non-attorney assistants was warranted because the Government had shown particularized need for disclosure. The Court of Appeals vacated and remanded, holding that Civil Division attorneys could obtain disclosure only by showing particularized need under Rule 6(e)(3)(C)(i), and that the District Court had not applied a correct standard of particularized need.

We granted certiorari. We now affirm.

II

A

The grand jury has always occupied a high place as an instrument of justice in our system of criminal law — so much so that it is enshrined in the Constitution. It serves the "dual function of determining if there is probable cause to believe that a crime has been committed and of protecting citizens against unfounded criminal prosecutions." It has always been extended extraordinary powers of investigation and great responsibility for directing its own efforts:

> Traditionally the grand jury has been accorded wide latitude to inquire into violations of criminal law. No judge presides to monitor its proceedings. It deliberates in secret and may determine alone the course of its inquiry. The grand jury may compel the production of evidence or the testimony of witnesses as it considers appropriate, and its operation generally is unrestrained by the technical procedural and evidentiary rules governing the conduct of criminal trials. "It is a grand inquest, a body with powers of investigation and inquisition, the scope of whose inquiries is not to be limited narrowly by questions of propriety or forecasts of the probable result of the investigation, or by doubts whether any particular individual will be found properly subject to an accusation of crime."

These broad powers are necessary to permit the grand jury to carry out both parts of its dual function. Without thorough and effective investigation, the grand jury would be unable either to ferret out crimes deserving of prosecution, or to screen out charges not warranting prosecution.

The same concern for the grand jury's dual function underlies the "long-established policy that maintains the secrecy of the grand jury proceedings in the federal courts."

> We consistently have recognized that the proper functioning of our grand jury system depends upon the secrecy of grand jury proceedings. In particular, we have noted several distinct interests served by safeguarding the confidentiality of grand jury proceedings. First, if preindictment proceedings were made public, many prospective witnesses would be hesitant to come forward voluntarily, knowing that those against whom they testify would be aware of that testimony. Moreover, witnesses who appeared before the grand jury would be less likely to testify fully and frankly, as they would be open to retribution as well as to inducements. There also would be the risk that those about to be indicted would flee, or would try to influence individual grand jurors to vote against indictment. Finally, by preserving the secrecy of the proceedings, we assure that persons who are accused but exonerated by the grand jury will not be held up to public ridicule.

Grand jury secrecy, then, is "as important for the protection of the innocent as for the pursuit of the guilty." Both Congress and this Court have consistently stood ready to defend it against unwarranted intrusion. In the absence of a clear indication in a statute or Rule, we must always be reluctant to conclude that a breach of this secrecy has been authorized.

B

Rule 6(e) of the Federal Rules of Criminal Procedure codifies the traditional rule of grand jury secrecy. Paragraph 6(e)(2) provides that grand jurors, government attorneys and their assistants, and other personnel attached to the grand jury are forbidden to disclose matters occurring before the grand jury. Witnesses are not under the prohibition unless they also happen to fit into one of the enumerated classes. Paragraph 6(e)(3) sets forth four exceptions to this nondisclosure rule.

Subparagraph 6(e)(3)(A) contains two authorizations for disclosure as a matter of course, without any court order. First, under subparagraph 6(e)(3)(A)(i), disclosure may be made without a court order to "an attorney for the government for use in the performance of such attorney's duty" (referred to hereinafter as "(A)(i) disclosure"). "Attorney for the government" is defined in Rule 54(c) in such broad terms as potentially to include virtually every attorney in the Department of Justice. Second, under subparagraph 6(e)(3)(A)(ii), grand jury materials may likewise be provided to "government personnel . . . [who] assist an attorney for the government in the performance of such attorney's duty to enforce federal criminal law" ("(A)(ii) disclosure"). Subparagraph 6(e)(3)(B) further regulates (A)(ii) disclosure, forbidding use of grand jury materials by "government personnel" for any purpose other than assisting an attorney for the Government in his enforcement of criminal law, and requiring that the names of such personnel be provided to the district court.

Subparagraph 6(e)(3)(C) also authorizes courts to order disclosure. Under subparagraph 6(e)(3)(C)(i), a court may order disclosure "preliminarily to or in connection with a judicial proceeding" (a "(C)(i) order"). Under subparagraph 6(e)(3)(C)(ii), a court may order disclosure under certain conditions at the request of a defendant.

The main issue in this case is whether attorneys in the Justice Department may obtain automatic (A)(i) disclosure of grand jury materials for use in a civil suit, or whether they must seek a (C)(i) court order for access. If a (C)(i) order is necessary, we must address the dependent question of what standards should govern issuance of the order.

III

The Government contends that all attorneys in the Justice Department qualify for automatic disclosure of grand jury materials under (A)(i), regardless of the nature of the litigation in which they intend to use the materials. We hold that (A)(i) disclosure is limited to use by those attorneys who conduct the criminal matters to which the materials pertain. This conclusion is mandated by the general purposes and policies of grand jury secrecy, by the limited policy reasons why government attorneys are granted access to grand jury materials for criminal use, and by the legislative history of Rule 6(e).

A

The Government correctly contends that attorneys for the Civil Division of the Justice Department are within the class of "attorneys for the government" to whom (A)(i) allows disclosure without a court order. Rule 54(c) defines the phrase expansively, to include "authorized assistants to the Attorney General"; 28 U.S.C. § 515(a) provides that the Attorney General may direct any attorney employed by the Department to conduct "any kind of legal proceeding, civil or criminal, including grand jury proceedings. . . ." *See also* § 518(b). In short, as far as Rules 6 and 54 are concerned, it is immaterial that certain attorneys happen to be assigned to a unit called the Civil Division, or that their usual duties involve only civil cases. If, for example, the Attorney General (for whatever reason) were to detail a Civil Division attorney to conduct a criminal grand jury investigation, nothing in Rule 6 would prevent that attorney from doing so; he need not secure a transfer out of the Civil Division.

It does not follow, however, that any Justice Department attorney is free to rummage through the records of any grand jury in the country, simply by right of office. Disclosure under (A)(i) is permitted only "in the performance of such attorney's duty." The heart of the primary issue in this case is whether performance of duty, within the meaning of (A)(i), includes preparation and litigation of a civil suit by a Justice Department attorney who had no part in conducting the related criminal prosecution.

Given the strong historic policy of preserving grand jury secrecy, one might wonder why government attorneys are given any automatic access at all. The draftsmen of the original Rule 6 provided the answer:

> Government attorneys are entitled to disclosure of grand jury proceedings, other than the deliberations and the votes of the jurors, inasmuch as they may be present in the grand jury room during the presentation of evidence. The rule continues this practice.

Advisory Committee's Notes on Federal Rule of Criminal Procedure 6(e), 18 U.S.C. App., p. 1411.

This is potent evidence that Rule 6(e) was never intended to grant free access to grand jury materials to attorneys not working on the criminal matters to which the materials pertain.

The Advisory Committee's explanation strongly suggests that automatic access to grand jury materials is available only to those attorneys for the Government who would be entitled to appear before the grand jury. But government attorneys are allowed into grand jury rooms, not for the general and multifarious purposes of the Department of Justice, but because both the grand jury's functions and their own prosecutorial duties require it. As the Advisory Committee suggested, the same reasoning applies to disclosure of grand jury materials outside the grand jury room.

The purpose of the grand jury requires that it remain free, within constitutional and statutory limits, to operate "independently of either prosecuting attorney or judge." Nevertheless, a modern grand jury would be much less effective without the assistance of the prosecutor's office and the investigative resources it commands. The prosecutor ordinarily brings matters to the attention of the grand jury and gathers the evidence required for the jury's consideration. Although the grand jury may itself decide to investigate a matter or to seek certain evidence, it depends largely on the prosecutor's office to secure the evidence or witnesses it requires. The prosecutor also advises the lay jury on the applicable law. The prosecutor in turn needs to know what transpires before the grand jury in order to perform his own duty properly. If he considers that the law and the admissible evidence will not support a conviction, he can be expected to advise the grand jury not to indict. He must also examine indictments, and the basis for their issuance, to determine whether it is in the interests of justice to proceed with prosecution.

None of these considerations, however, provides any support for breaching grand jury secrecy in favor of government attorneys other than prosecutors—either by allowing them into the grand jury room, or by granting them uncontrolled access to grand jury materials. An attorney with only civil duties lacks both the prosecutor's special role in supporting the grand jury, and the prosecutor's own crucial need to know what occurs before the grand jury.

Of course, it would be of substantial help to a Justice Department civil attorney if he had free access to a storehouse of evidence compiled by a grand jury; but that is of a different order from the prosecutor's need for access. The civil lawyer's need is ordinarily nothing more than a matter of saving time and expense. The same argument could be made for access on behalf of any lawyer in another government agency, or indeed, in private practice. We have consistently rejected the argument that such savings can justify a breach of grand jury secrecy. In most cases, the same evidence that could be obtained from the grand jury will be available through ordinary discovery or other routine avenues of investigation.

Not only is disclosure for civil use unjustified by the considerations supporting prosecutorial access, but it threatens to do affirmative mischief. The problem is threefold.

First, disclosure to government bodies raises much the same concerns that underlie the rule of secrecy in other contexts. Not only does disclosure increase the number of persons to whom the information is available (thereby increasing the risk of inadvertent or illegal release to others), but it renders considerably more concrete the threat to the willingness of witnesses to come forward and to testify fully and candidly. If a witness knows or fears that his testimony before the grand jury will be routinely available for use in governmental civil litigation or administrative action, he may well be less willing to speak for fear that he will get himself into trouble in some other forum.

Second, because the Government takes an active part in the activities of the grand jury, disclosure to government attorneys for civil use poses a significant threat to the integrity of the grand jury itself. If prosecutors in a given case knew that their colleagues would be free to use the materials generated by the grand jury for a civil case, they might be tempted to manipulate the grand jury's powerful investigative tools to root out additional evidence useful in the civil suit, or even to start or continue a grand jury inquiry where no criminal prosecution seemed likely. Any such use of grand jury proceedings to elicit evidence for use in a civil case is improper per se. We do not mean to impugn the professional characters of Justice

Department lawyers in general; nor do we express any view on the allegations of misuse that have been made in this case. Our concern is based less on any belief that grand jury misuse is in fact widespread than on our concern that, if and when it does occur, it would often be very difficult to detect and prove. Moreover, as the legislative history discussed infra shows our concern over possible misappropriation of the grand jury itself was shared by Congress when it enacted the present version of Rule 6(e). Such a potential for misuse should not be allowed absent a clear mandate in the law.

Third, use of grand jury materials by government agencies in civil or administrative settings threatens to subvert the limitations applied outside the grand jury context on the Government's powers of discovery and investigation. While there are some limits on the investigative powers of the grand jury, there are few if any other forums in which a governmental body has such relatively unregulated power to compel other persons to divulge information or produce evidence. Other agencies, both within and without the Justice Department, operate under specific and detailed statutes, rules, or regulations conferring only limited authority to require citizens to testify or produce evidence. Some agencies have been granted special statutory powers to obtain information and require testimony in pursuance of their duties. Others (including the Civil Division) are relegated to the usual course of discovery under the Federal Rules of Civil Procedure. In either case, the limitations imposed on investigation and discovery exist for sound reasons—ranging from fundamental fairness to concern about burdensomeness and intrusiveness. If government litigators or investigators in civil matters enjoyed unlimited access to grand jury material, though, there would be little reason for them to resort to their usual, more limited avenues of investigation. To allow these agencies to circumvent their usual methods of discovery would not only subvert the limitations and procedural requirements built into those methods, but would grant to the Government a virtual ex parte form of discovery, from which its civil litigation opponents are excluded unless they make a strong showing of particularized need. In civil litigation as in criminal, "it is rarely justifiable for the [Government] to have exclusive access to a storehouse of relevant fact." We are reluctant to conclude that the draftsmen of Rule 6 intended so remarkable a result.

In short, if grand juries are to be granted extraordinary powers of investigation because of the difficulty and importance of their task, the use of those powers ought to be limited as far as reasonably possible to the accomplishment of the task. The policies of Rule 6 require that any disclosure to attorneys other than prosecutors be judicially supervised rather than automatic.

NOTES AND QUESTIONS

1. The love song to the grand jury in *Sells* is different than some we have seen as it explicitly focuses on the "dual function" of the grand jury. Neither function is necessarily implicated by the specific disclosure questions at issue in *Sells*, although the Court does note that both "sword" and "shield" interests are served by the grand jury's secrecy requirements.

Which of the "several distinct interests" for secrecy that are noted by the Court are most compelling? Least compelling?

2. Note that witnesses in the grand jury are not among the persons bound by Rule 6(e)'s secrecy requirements. Bear this in mind next time you read about "grand jury leaks." Sometimes information about grand jury proceedings becomes public by perfectly legal disclosures from a witness or witness's counsel. Why do you think witnesses are exempted from the secrecy requirements?

3. The Court interprets the disclosure-permitting language in Rule 6(e)(3)(A)(i) to permit disclosure only to DOJ attorneys conducting criminal matters. Is this a defensible interpretation of the Rule's language? The Court advances three reasons why permitting disclosure to DOJ non-prosecutors "threatens to do affirmative mischief": (a) witnesses will be less truthful if they believe their testimony will be routinely available for noncriminal purposes; (b) it abuses the grand jury to use it as an adjunct to aid civil enforcement; and (c) civil enforcement lawyers might take advantage of the breadth of grand jury powers to subvert discovery limitations in civil matters.

Are each of these reasons equally persuasive? How does the Court's consciously naïve description of the role of prosecutors in grand jury proceedings advance its argument?

4. *Sells* was a tax case, investigated by agents of the Internal Revenue Service, an agency that has both criminal and civil investigative authority. Note that the investigation appears to have begun as a civil investigation, which stalled due to litigation of a civil discovery dispute, during which time a grand jury investigation was commenced regarding issues that were related, at a minimum, to the civil investigation. Is this the sort of fact pattern that suggests the potential for the second variety of "affirmative mischief" noted above?

5. Tax is an area of the law, like many areas — antitrust, securities fraud, health care fraud, etc. — where the same or substantially similar conduct can violate both civil and criminal laws. Does the existence of these areas of substantive overlap militate for more or less ease of criminal-civil disclosure? *See United States v. Procter & Gamble*, 356 U.S. 677 (1958) (reversing district court's order granting broad disclosure of grand jury testimony to defendants in civil antitrust action, which apparently was made due to the district court's belief that the government had used the grand jury to develop evidence for the civil case; Court noted, however, that it would have been illegal for the government to have used the grand jury for a purpose other than criminal investigation).

While *Sells* is a case about who can rightfully gain access to grand jury materials there is often litigation about what constitutes "a matter occurring before the grand jury" within the meaning of Rule 6(e)(2)(B). For example, in *Hodge v. FBI*, 703 F.3d 575 (D.C. Cir. 2013), a prisoner brought a claim under the federal Freedom of Information Act (FOIA) seeking documents relating to the federal investigation that led to his prosecution. In interpreting one of the FOIA exemptions that cross-references Rule 6(e), the D.C. Circuit found that Rule 6(e) applies if the disclosed material would "tend to reveal some secret aspect of the grand jury's investigation," including "the identities of witnesses or jurors, the substance of testimony, the strategy or direction of the investigation," or "the deliberations or questions of jurors." *Id.* at 580. Prosecutors will often unfurl the banner of "grand jury secrecy" when they don't want to inform a witness or even a court about the nature of an investigation, but cases like *Hodge* make clear that Rule 6(e) sweeps less broadly.

Consider the following hypothetical:

> An investigation of ABC corporation begins with a grand jury subpoena of the company for documents. The documents are produced by ABC to the government and reviewed and analyzed by the prosecution team. As a result of that review, twenty individuals who are current or former employees of ABC are served with grand jury subpoenas. Ten of these individuals show up pursuant to their subpoenas and testify in the grand jury. The other ten, after negotiations between their counsel and the prosecutor, are interviewed by the prosecutor and agents outside the presence of the grand jury. All twenty witnesses are examined about the subjects reflected in the documents produced in response to the grand jury subpoena.

Which of these witnesses were questioned in the "grand jury investigation"?

Would a statement by the AUSA to the press that "we've talked to many company employees" be a Rule 6(e) violation?

United States v. Bryant

655 F.3d 232 (3d Cir. 2011)

AMBRO, Circuit Judge.

This case involves the federal crimes of honest services fraud, mail fraud, and bribery. Appellants Wayne Bryant and R. Michael Gallagher were charged with six counts of honest services fraud, in violation of 18 U.S.C. §§ 1341, 1343 and 1346 (the "honest services fraud counts"), and one count each of bribery in connection with a state agency that receives federal funds, in violation of 18 U.S.C. § 666(a) (the "bribery counts"), all in connection with a scheme to defraud the citizens of the State of New Jersey of Bryant's honest services as a State Senator. Counts 9-13 charged Bryant with mail fraud, in violation of 18 U.S.C. § 1341, in connection with a second scheme involving his state pension application. A jury convicted Bryant on all counts and Gallagher on all counts but one, which dealt with the mailing of Bryant's 2003 Financial Disclosure statement. Their sentences included imprisonment—48 months for Bryant and 18 months for Gallagher—and joint restitution in the amount of $113,167. For the reasons that follow, we affirm their convictions and the restitution order.

I. BACKGROUND

Gallagher was formerly Dean of the School of Osteopathic Medicine ("SOM") of the University of Medicine and Dentistry of New Jersey ("UMDNJ"). Bryant, as noted, was a New Jersey State Senator. They were indicted in 2007. The charges stemmed from an alleged quid pro quo arrangement in which Gallagher gave Bryant a "low-show" job at SOM (meaning he provided only minimal or nominal services) as a "Program Support Coordinator," in which position he received an annual salary of $35,000 (and a $5,000 bonus), in exchange for Bryant's efforts as Chairman of the Senate Appropriations Committee to funnel State funding to SOM. The quo was a "success": during Bryant's tenure at SOM, the institution gained an additional $10 million in funding over three years. Based on that same scheme, Bryant and Gallagher were also charged under the federal bribery statute—Bryant for corruptly soliciting and demanding the SOM salary and Gallagher for corruptly giving the salary.

In a second scheme, involving only Bryant, the Government alleged that he also attempted to use a "no-show" job (meaning he personally provided no services at all) as an attorney for the Gloucester County Board of Social Services (the "Social Services Board") to increase his pension benefits. Specifically, the Government introduced evidence at trial showing that Bryant falsely reported that he had worked numerous hours providing legal services to the Social Services Board when he had not provided those services at all but had delegated his work to associates at his private law firm. In other words, Bryant claimed pensionable time credit for work he did not do. In New Jersey, the amount of pension benefits for which a public servant is eligible depends on the number of public sector jobs held. Thus, by accumulating public sector jobs, but not actually performing the duties commensurate with the positions, the Government argued that Bryant fraudulently inflated his pension eligibility.

After Appellants' convictions in November 2008, the District Court denied their motions for a judgment of acquittal or a new trial and this appeal followed. The District Court had jurisdiction under 18 U.S.C. § 3231. We have jurisdiction under 28 U.S.C. § 1291.

Appellants challenge their convictions on the following grounds: they argue that the Government violated their due process rights by interfering with their access to potential witnesses in the pretrial phase of the case. . . .

II. DISCUSSION

A. The Prosecutorial Misconduct Claim

During its investigation of Appellants, the Government issued grand jury subpoenas to potential witnesses with the following language placed on the front of each subpoena:

> Disclosure of the nature and existence of this subpoena could obstruct and impede a criminal investigation into alleged violations of federal law. Therefore, the United States Attorney requests that you do not disclose the existence of this subpoena.

Appellants argued to the District Court that this language, and the Government's requests during the grand jury proceedings that witnesses voluntarily not disclose "any matters" that occur during those proceedings, interfered with the defense's access to witnesses. They claim that this violated due process and Federal Rule of Criminal Procedure 6(e)(2)(A), which prohibits the Government from imposing an obligation of secrecy on witnesses. The District Court denied their pretrial motion to dismiss the indictment on those grounds. Instead, it ordered the Government to write to the witnesses and inform them that they were under no legal obligation to keep the subpoena secret.

On appeal, Appellants again argue that the Government's conduct—including both the subpoena language and its requests to witnesses to preserve the secrecy of the proceeding—violated Rule 6(e)(2)(A) and due process. They claim that the Government's actions restricted the "free choice" of potential witnesses to speak to defense counsel and effectively imposed an obligation of secrecy on those witnesses. We disagree.

We review a district court's decision regarding a motion to dismiss an indictment because of prosecutorial misconduct for abuse of discretion. Generally, because witnesses "belong" neither to the defense nor to the prosecution, both must have equal access to witnesses before trial. If the prosecution impermissibly interferes with the defense's access to a witness during a criminal trial, that conduct violates due process insofar as it undermines the fundamental fairness of the proceeding. In connection with a grand jury proceeding, Rule 6(e)(2) also provides that the Government may not impose an obligation of secrecy on a witness absent limited exceptions, none of which applies here.

However, there is an important difference between requesting nondisclosure and discretion on the part of witnesses and artificially restricting defense counsel's access to witnesses by, for example, instructing the latter not to communicate with the former. Merely requesting that witnesses practice discretion does not violate a defendant's due process rights. Here, the record demonstrates that the Government requested, but never required, witnesses not to disclose the subpoena or the grand jury proceedings. Aside from those requests, it took no affirmative steps to restrict or stop witnesses from conferring with the defense.

Appellants argue that the language, emblazoned on the subpoena, gave an appearance of a judicial imprimatur that suggested to witnesses they were legally obligated to comply with the Government's secrecy request. Certainly, many forthright citizens would comply with such a request, given the context in which it was made. However, we will not say what occurred here imposed an obligation of secrecy.

Nor do we think that the Government's actions infected the fairness of the proceeding. Notably, Appellants did not identify to the District Court (nor do they now) any witnesses who claim that they would have spoken to the defense but were deterred from doing so because of the Government's nondisclosure requests. Rather, those witnesses who declined to speak with the defense did so on the advice of counsel. But "[n]o right of a defendant is violated when a potential witness freely chooses not to talk; a witness may of his own free will refuse to be interviewed by either the prosecution or the defense."

Even if there were witnesses (about whom we do not know) with the mistaken impression that they could not speak to the defense, the District Court took measures to clarify such a misunderstanding well before trial. In response to Appellants' motion to dismiss, the Court instructed the Government to send a letter to all subpoena recipients five months before the start of trial, stating that the witnesses had "an absolute right to speak to anyone . . . about anything [they] know about any of the matters under investigation, including the fact that [they] were subpoenaed and . . . testified before the grand jury." In particular, that letter confirmed that the Government "[would] not take any adverse action against [the witness] or [his or her] employer because [he or she chose] to speak to the defense or anyone else about these matters."

In these circumstances, we believe that Appellants have not shown that, because of the Government's conduct, there was an "absence of . . . fairness [that] fatally infected the trial." Accordingly, we conclude that Appellants were not denied due process of law or the protections of Rule 6(e)(2)(A) and we decline to vacate their convictions for those reasons.

NOTES AND QUESTIONS

1. This is an especially overt example of the government attempting to convert the limited secrecy provisions of Rule 6 into a means of intimidating grand jury witnesses from sharing information about the investigation with others, specifically, the defense team. Note that the broad language on the subpoena could even conceivably deter a witness from seeking legal advice regarding the subpoena. Was the district court's order sufficient to cure the prosecutor's violation? Short of dismissing the indictment, what more could it have done?

2. The Third Circuit notes that the government merely requested, but never required, that the witness not disclose the existence of the subpoena. Is there a meaningful difference in this context? Presumably the most important witnesses in this investigation—a classic public corruption case—were those who worked closely with the defendants and had firsthand knowledge about the allegedly illicit arrangements. These would of course have been the same people who had concern about their own criminal exposure. How firmly did they need to be told about the government's "request" for secrecy? Do you think the prosecutor's "corrective" letter had any effect on them?

3. The Third Circuit also faults the defendants for failing to identify any witnesses who would have spoken to them but for the prosecution's interference. Is this realistic? How could the defense possibly have made that showing?

4. The Court cites other cases where federal prosecutors have improperly instructed grand jury witnesses to keep the proceedings secret. Should the fact that this is recurring misconduct by DOJ prosecutors have affected the district court's remedy or the court of appeals' decision? Could the district court have enlisted Fed. R. Crim. P. 15, which (in its current form) permits a party to "move that a prospective witness be deposed in order to preserve testimony for trial." The court may grant the motion because of exceptional circumstances and in the interest of justice.

F. WITNESSES IN THE GRAND JURY

The next two cases consider whether a witness who faces potential criminal exposure by testifying in the grand jury has a right to receive any sort of warnings—akin to *Miranda* warnings—from the prosecutor before testifying. The *Miranda* analogy is imperfect: The grand jury setting may be coercive but it is not custodial in the classical sense, and a witness's attendance at the grand jury is compelled by subpoena but not (at least initially) by force.

The Department of Justice responded to these cases by issuing internal policies regulating the treatment of certain witnesses in the grand jury, which will be discussed after the cases.

United States v. Mandujano

425 U.S. 564 (1976)

Mr. Chief Justice BURGER announced the judgment of the Court in an opinion in which Mr. Justice WHITE, Mr. Justice POWELL, and Mr. Justice REHNQUIST join.

This case presents the question whether the warnings called for by *Miranda*, must be given to a grand jury witness who is called to testify about criminal activities in which he may have been personally involved; and whether, absent such warnings, false statements made to the grand jury must be suppressed in a prosecution for perjury based on those statements.

(1)

During the course of a grand jury investigation into narcotics traffic in San Antonio, Tex., federal prosecutors assigned to the Drug Enforcement Administration Task Force learned of an undercover narcotics officer's encounter with respondent in March 1973. At that time, the agent had received information that respondent, who was employed as a bartender at a local tavern, was dealing in narcotics. The agent, accompanied by an informant, met respondent at the tavern and talked for several hours. During the meeting, respondent agreed to obtain heroin for the agent, and to that end placed several phone calls from the bar. He also requested and received $650 from the agent to make the purchase. Respondent left the tavern with the money so advanced to secure the heroin. However, an hour later respondent returned to the bar without the narcotics and returned the agent's money. Respondent instructed the agent to telephone him at the bar that evening to make arrangements for the transaction. The agent tried but was unable to contact respondent as directed. The record provides no explanation for respondent's failure to keep his appointment. No further action was taken by the agent, and the investigatory file on the matter was closed. The agent did, however, report the information to federal prosecutors. At that time, the Government was seeking information on local drug traffic to present to a special grand jury investigating illicit traffic in the area.

Respondent was subpoenaed to testify before the grand jury on May 2, 1973; this was approximately six weeks after the abortive narcotics transaction at the tavern where respondent was employed. When called into the grand jury room and after preliminary statements, the following colloquy occurred between the prosecutor and respondent:

Q. . . . Now, you are required to answer all the questions that I ask you except for the ones that you feel would tend to incriminate you. Do you understand that?

A. Do I answer all the questions you ask?

Q. You have to answer all the questions except for those you think will incriminate you in the commission of a crime. Is that clear?

A. Yes, sir.

Q. You don't have to answer questions which would incriminate you. All other questions you have to answer openly and truthfully. And, of course, if you do not answer those (questions) truthfully, in other words if you lie about certain questions, you could possibly be charged with perjury. Do you understand that?

A. Yes, sir.

Q. Have you contacted a lawyer in this matter?

A. I don't have one. I don't have the money to get one.

Q. Well, if you would like to have a lawyer, he cannot be inside this room. He can only be outside. You would be free to consult with him if you so chose. Now, if during the course of this investigation, the questions that we ask you, if you feel like you would like to have a lawyer outside to talk to, let me know.

During the questioning respondent admitted that he had previously been convicted of distributing drugs, that he had recently used heroin himself, and that he had purchased heroin as recently as five months previously. Despite this admitted experience with San Antonio's heroin traffic, respondent denied knowledge of the identity of any dealers, save for a streetcorner source named Juan. Respondent steadfastly denied either selling or attempting to sell heroin since the time of his conviction 15 years before.

Respondent specifically disclaimed having discussed the sale of heroin with anyone during the preceding year and stated that he would not even try to purchase an ounce of heroin for $650. Respondent refused to amplify on his testimony when directly confronted by the prosecutor:

Q. Mr. Mandujano, our information is that you can tell us more about the heroin business here in San Antonio than you have today. Is there anything you would like to add telling us more about who sells heroin?

A. Well, sir, I couldn't help you because, you know, I don't get along with the guys and I just can't tell you, you know.

Following this appearance, respondent was charged by a grand jury on June 13, 1973, in a two-count indictment with attempting to distribute heroin in violation of 21 U.S.C. ss 841(a)(1), 846, and for willfully and knowingly making a false material declaration to the grand jury in violation of 18 U.S.C. s 1623. The falsity of his statements was conceded; his sole claim was that the testimony before the grand jury should be suppressed because the Government failed to provide the warnings called for by *Miranda*. Following an evidentiary hearing, the District Court granted respondent's motion to suppress. The court held that respondent was a "putative" or "virtual" defendant when called before the grand jury; respondent had therefore been entitled to full *Miranda* warnings.

The Court of Appeals affirmed. It recognized that certain warnings had in fact been given to respondent at the outset of his grand jury appearance. But the court agreed with the District Court that "full *Miranda* warnings should have been accorded Mandujano who was in the position of a virtual or putative defendant." The essence of the Court of Appeals' holding is:

> In order to deter the prosecuting officers from bringing a putative or virtual defendant before the grand jury, for the purpose of obtaining incriminating or perjur(i)ous testimony, the accused must be adequately apprised of his rights, or all of his testimony, incriminating and perjur(i)ous, will be suppressed.

In so ruling, the court undertook to distinguish its own holding in *United States v. Orta* (1958), in which Judge Rives, speaking for the court, stated:

> (A grand jury witness) might answer truthfully and thereafter assert the constitutional guaranty. Under no circumstances, however, could he commit perjury and successfully claim that the Constitution afforded him protection from prosecution for that crime. ". . .[T]he immunity afforded by the constitutional guaranty relates to the past, and does not endow the person who testifies with a license to commit perjury."

In the *Orta* opinion, Judge Rives went on to observe:

> The only debatable question is one of the supervision of the conduct of Government representatives in the interest of fairness. In *United States v. Scully*, the Court of Appeals for the Second Circuit held:

> the mere possibility that the witness may later be indicted furnishes no basis for requiring that he be advised of his rights under the Fifth Amendment, when summoned to give testimony before a Grand Jury.
>
> That holding is applicable to the present record. There is no showing that the Grand Jury before which Orta testified was seeking to indict him or any other person already identified.

The Court of Appeals concluded that the "totality of the circumstances" commanded suppression of all the testimony on which the charge of perjury rested.

We agree with the views expressed by Judge Rives in *Orta*, supra, and disagree with the Court of Appeals in the instant case; accordingly, we reverse.

(2)

The grand jury is an integral part of our constitutional heritage which was brought to this country with the common law. The Framers, most of them trained in the English law and traditions, accepted the grand jury as a basic guarantee of individual liberty; notwithstanding periodic criticism, much of which is superficial, overlooking relevant history, the grand jury continues to function as a barrier to reckless or unfounded charges. "Its adoption in our Constitution as the sole method for preferring charges in serious criminal cases shows the high place it held as an instrument of justice." Its historic office has been to provide a shield against arbitrary or oppressive action, by insuring that serious criminal accusations will be brought only upon the considered judgment of a representative body of citizens acting under oath and under judicial instruction and guidance.

Earlier we noted that the law vests the grand jury with substantial powers, because "(t) he grand jury's investigative power must be broad if its public responsibility is adequately to be discharged. Indispensable to the exercise of its power is the authority to compel the attendance and the testimony of witnesses, and to require the production of evidence.

When called by the grand jury, witnesses are thus legally bound to give testimony. This principle has long been recognized. In *United States v. Burr*, Mr. Chief Justice Marshall drew on English precedents, aptly described by Lord Chancellor Hardwicke in the 18th century, and long accepted in America as a hornbook proposition: "The public has a right to every man's evidence." This Court has repeatedly invoked this fundamental proposition when dealing with the powers of the grand jury.

The grand jury's authority to compel testimony is not, of course, without limits. The same Amendment that establishes the grand jury also guarantees that "no person . . . shall be compelled in any criminal case to be a witness against himself. . . ." The duty to give evidence to a grand jury is therefore conditional; every person owes society his testimony, unless some recognized privilege is asserted.

Under settled principles, the Fifth Amendment does not confer an absolute right to decline to respond in a grand jury inquiry; the privilege does not negate the duty to testify but simply conditions that duty. The privilege cannot, for example, be asserted by a witness to protect others from possible criminal prosecution. Nor can it be invoked simply to protect the witness' interest in privacy. "Ordinarily, of course, a witness has no right of privacy before the grand jury."

The very availability of the Fifth Amendment privilege to grand jury witnesses, recognized by this Court in *Counselman v. Hitchcock* (1892), suggests that occasions will often arise when potentially incriminating questions will be asked in the ordinary course of the jury's investigation. Probing questions to all types of witnesses is the stuff that grand jury investigations are made of; the grand jury's mission is, after all, to determine whether to make a presentment or return an indictment. "The basic purpose of the English grand jury was to provide a fair method for instituting criminal proceedings against persons believed to have committed crimes."

It is in keeping with the grand jury's historic function as a shield against arbitrary accusations to call before it persons suspected of criminal activity, so that the investigation can be complete. This is true whether the grand jury embarks upon an inquiry focused upon individuals suspected of wrongdoing, or is directed at persons suspected of no misconduct but who may be able to provide links in a chain of evidence relating to criminal conduct of others, or is centered upon broader problems of concern to society. It is entirely appropriate indeed imperative to summon individuals who may be able to illuminate the shadowy precincts of corruption and crime. Since the subject matter of the inquiry is crime, and often organized, systematic crime as is true with drug traffic it is unrealistic to assume that all of the witnesses capable of providing useful information will be pristine pillars of the community untainted by criminality.

The Court has never ignored this reality of law enforcement. Speaking for the Court in *Kastigar v. United States*, Mr. Justice Powell said:

> (M)any offenses are of such a character that the only persons capable of giving useful testimony are those implicated in the crime.

Mr. Justice White made a similar observation in the context of a state investigation:

> (T)he very fact that a witness is called . . . is likely to be based upon knowledge, or at least a suspicion based on some information, that the witness is implicated in illegal activities. . . .

Moreover, the Court has expressly recognized that "(t)he obligation to appear is no different for a person who may himself be the subject of the grand jury inquiry."

There is nothing new about the Court's recognition of this reality of grand jury inquiries. In one of the early cases dealing with the Fifth Amendment privilege, the Court observed: "(I) t is only from the mouths of those having knowledge of the (unlawful conduct) that the facts can be ascertained."

Accordingly, the witness, though possibly engaged in some criminal enterprise, can be required to answer before a grand jury, so long as there is no compulsion to answer questions that are self-incriminating; the witness can, of course, stand on the privilege, assured that its protection "is as broad as the mischief against which it seeks to guard." The witness must invoke the privilege, however, as the "Constitution does not forbid the asking of criminative questions."

> The (Fifth) Amendment speaks of compulsion. It does not preclude a witness from testifying voluntarily in matters which may incriminate him. If, therefore, he desires the protection of the privilege, he must claim it or he will not be considered to have been "compelled" within the meaning of the Amendment.

Absent a claim of the privilege, the duty to give testimony remains absolute.

The stage is therefore set when the question is asked. If the witness interposes his privilege, the grand jury has two choices. If the desired testimony is of marginal value, the grand jury can pursue other avenues of inquiry; if the testimony is thought sufficiently important, the grand jury can seek a judicial determination as to the bona fides of the witness' Fifth Amendment claim, in which case the witness must satisfy the presiding judge that the claim of privilege is not a subterfuge. If in fact "'there is reasonable ground to apprehend danger to the witness from his being compelled to answer,'" the prosecutor must then determine whether the answer is of such overriding importance as to justify a grant of immunity to the witness.

If immunity is sought by the prosecutor and granted by the presiding judge, the witness can then be compelled to answer, on pain of contempt, even though the testimony would implicate the witness in criminal activity. The reason for this is not hard to divine; Mr. Justice

Frankfurter indicated as much in observing that immunity is the quid pro quo for securing an answer from the witness: "Immunity displaces the danger. Based on this recognition, federal statutes conferring immunity on witnesses in federal judicial proceedings, including grand jury investigations, are so familiar that they have become part of our "'constitutional fabric.'" Immunity is the Government's ultimate tool for securing testimony that otherwise would be protected; unless immunity is conferred, however, testimony may be suppressed, along with its fruits, if it is compelled over an appropriate claim of privilege. On the other hand, when granted immunity, a witness once again owes the obligation imposed upon all citizens the duty to give testimony since immunity substitutes for the privilege.

In this constitutional process of securing a witness' testimony, perjury simply has no place whatever. Perjured testimony is an obvious and flagrant affront to the basic concepts of judicial proceedings. Effective restraints against this type of egregious offense are therefore imperative. The power of subpoena, broad as it is, and the power of contempt for refusing to answer, drastic as that is and even the solemnity of the oath cannot insure truthful answers. Hence, Congress has made the giving of false answers a criminal act punishable by severe penalties; in no other way can criminal conduct be flushed into the open where the law can deal with it.

Similarly, our cases have consistently indeed without exception allowed sanctions for false statements or perjury; they have done so even in instances where the perjurer complained that the Government exceeded its constitutional powers in making the inquiry.

In *Bryson*, a union officer was required by federal labor law to file an affidavit averring that he was not a Communist. The affidavit was false in material statements. In a collateral attack on his conviction, Bryson argued that since the statute required him either to incriminate himself or lie, he could not lawfully be imprisoned for failure to comply. This Court rejected the contention:

> (I)t cannot be thought that as a general principle of our law a citizen has a privilege to answer fraudulently a question that the Government should not have asked. Our legal system provides methods for challenging the Government's right to ask questions lying is not one of them.

Even where a statutory scheme granted blanket immunity from further use of testimony, the Court has found perjured statements to fall outside the grant. In *Glickstein*, a bankrupt was indicted for perjury committed in the course of a bankruptcy proceeding. The Bankruptcy Act expressly conferred broad immunity on a bankrupt: "(N)o testimony given by him shall be offered in evidence against him in any criminal proceeding." The Court rejected the bankrupt's literalistic interpretation of the statute as conferring immunity from prosecution for perjury:

> (T)he sanction of an oath and the imposition of a punishment for false swearing are inherently a part of the power to compel the giving of testimony, they are included in that grant of authority and are not prohibited by the immunity as to self-incrimination. . . . (I)t cannot be conceived that there is power to compel the giving of testimony where no right exists to require that the testimony shall be given under such circumstances and safeguards as to compel it to be truthful. . . . (T)he immunity afforded by the constitutional guarantee relates to the past and does not endow the person who testifies with a license to commit perjury.

(3)

In this case, the Court of Appeals required the suppression of perjured testimony given by respondent, as a witness under oath, lawfully summoned before an investigative grand jury and questioned about matters directly related to the grand jury's inquiry. The court reached this result because the prosecutor failed to give *Miranda* warnings at the outset of Mandujano's interrogation. Those warnings were required, in the Court of Appeals' view, because Mandujano was a "virtual" or "putative" defendant that is, the prosecutor had specific information concerning Mandujano's participation in an attempted sale of heroin and the focus of the grand jury interrogation, as evidenced by the prosecutor's questions, centered on Mandujano's involvement in narcotics traffic. The fundamental error of the prosecutor, in the court's view, was to treat respondent in such a way as to "'smack' of entrapment"; as a consequence, the court concluded that "elemental fairness" required the perjured testimony to be suppressed.

The court's analysis, premised upon the prosecutor's failure to give *Miranda* warnings, erroneously applied the standards fashioned by this Court in *Miranda*. Those warnings were aimed at the evils seen by the Court as endemic to police interrogation of a person in custody. *Miranda* addressed extrajudicial confessions or admissions procured in a hostile, unfamiliar environment which lacked procedural safeguards. The decision expressly rested on the privilege against compulsory self-incrimination; the prescribed warnings sought to negate the "compulsion" thought to be inherent in police station interrogation. But the *Miranda* Court simply did not perceive judicial inquiries and custodial interrogation as equivalents: "(T)he compulsion to speak in the isolated setting of the police station may well be greater than in courts or other official investigations, where there are often impartial observers to guard against intimidation or trickery."

The Court thus recognized that many official investigations, such as grand jury questioning, take place in a setting wholly different from custodial police interrogation. Indeed, the Court's opinion in *Miranda* reveals a focus on what was seen by the Court as police "coercion" derived from "factual studies (relating to) police violence and the 'third degree' . . . physical brutality beating, hanging, whipping and to sustained and protracted questioning incommunicado in order to extort confessions. . . . " To extend these concepts to questioning before a grand jury inquiring into criminal activity under the guidance of a judge is an extravagant expansion never remotely contemplated by this Court in *Miranda*; the dynamics of constitutional interpretation do not compel constant extension of every doctrine announced by the Court.

The marked contrasts between a grand jury investigation and custodial interrogation have been commented on by the Court from time to time. Mr. Justice Marshall observed that the broad coercive powers of a grand jury are justified, because "in contrast to the police it is not likely that (the grand jury) will abuse those powers."

(4)

The warnings volunteered by the prosecutor to respondent in this case were more than sufficient to inform him of his rights and his responsibilities and particularly of the consequences of perjury. To extend the concepts of *Miranda*, as contemplated by the Court of Appeals, would require that the witness be told that there was an absolute right to silence, and obviously any such warning would be incorrect, for there is no such right before a grand jury. Under *Miranda*, a person in police custody has, of course, an absolute right to decline to answer any question, incriminating or innocuous, whereas a grand jury witness, on the contrary, has an absolute duty to answer all questions, subject only to a valid Fifth Amendment claim. And even when the grand jury witness asserts the privilege, questioning need not cease, except as to the particular subject to which the privilege has been addressed. Other lines of inquiry may properly be pursued.

Respondent was also informed that if he desired he could have the assistance of counsel, but that counsel could not be inside the grand jury room. That statement was plainly a correct recital of the law. No criminal proceedings had been instituted against respondent, hence the Sixth Amendment right to counsel had not come into play. A witness "before a grand jury cannot insist, as a matter of constitutional right, on being represented by his counsel. . . ."

Under settled principles the witness may not insist upon the presence of his attorney in the grand jury room. Fed. Rule Crim. Proc. 6(d).

Respondent, by way of further explanation, was also warned that he could be prosecuted for perjury if he testified falsely. Since respondent was already under oath to testify truthfully, this explanation was redundant; it served simply to emphasize the obligation already imposed by the oath.

> Once a witness swears to give truthful answers, there is no requirement to "warn him not to commit perjury or, conversely to direct him to tell the truth." It would render the sanctity of the oath quite meaningless to require admonition to adhere to it.

Similarly, a witness subpoenaed to testify before a petit jury and placed under oath has never been entitled to a warning that, if he violates the solemn oath to "tell the truth," he may be subject to a prosecution for perjury, for the oath itself is the warning. Nor has any case been cited to us holding that the absence of such warnings before a petit jury provides a shield against use of false testimony in a subsequent prosecution for perjury or in contempt proceedings.

In any event, a witness sworn to tell the truth before a duly constituted grand jury will not be heard to call for suppression of false statements made to that jury, any more than would be the case with false testimony before a petit jury or other duly constituted tribunal. In another context, this Court has refused to permit a witness to protect perjured testimony by proving a *Miranda* violation. In *Harris v. New York* (1971), the Court held that notwithstanding a *Miranda* violation

> (The Fifth Amendment) privilege cannot be construed to include the right to commit perjury.

More recently, the Court reaffirmed this salutary principle:

> (T)he shield provided by *Miranda* is not to be perverted to a license to testify inconsistently, or even perjuriously, free from the risk of confrontation with prior inconsistent utterances.

The fact that here the grand jury interrogation had focused on some of respondent's specific activities does not require that these important principles be jettisoned; nothing remotely akin to "entrapment" or abuse of process is suggested by what occurred here. Assuming arguendo, that respondent, was indeed a "putative defendant," that fact would have no bearing on the validity of a conviction for testifying falsely.

The grand jury was appropriately concerned about the sources of narcotics in the San Antonio area. The attempted heroin sale by respondent provided ample reason to believe that he had knowledge about local heroin suppliers. It was, therefore, entirely proper to question him with respect to his knowledge of narcotics trafficking. Respondent was free at every stage to interpose his constitutional privilege against self-incrimination, but perjury was not a permissible option. As the Tenth Circuit has held, the law provides "other methods for challenging the government's right to ask questions."

The judgment of the Court of Appeals is therefore reversed, and the cause is remanded for further proceedings consistent with this opinion.

NOTES AND QUESTIONS

1. Judging by the questioning reproduced in the opinion, what was the government's primary purpose in subpoenaing Mandujano to testify in the grand jury?

2. Mandujano apparently conceded the falsity of his grand jury testimony. Did he have to? What's the strongest case for defending against the perjury charge on the ground that the testimony was not false?

3. The court of appeals held that Mandujano should have been given full-blown *Miranda* warnings because he was a "putative or virtual" defendant. What does that mean? How does this status compare to that of a suspect in a custodial interrogation setting where *Miranda* warnings are required? Do you agree that he was a "putative or virtual" defendant? Should this status require *Miranda* warnings?

4. The grand jury love song here, again unironically, focuses on the "shield" role of the grand jury. *Id.* at 571-73. The Court observes:

> It is in keeping with the grand jury's historic function as a shield against arbitrary accusations to call before it persons suspected of criminal activity, so that the investigation can be complete. This is true whether the grand jury embarks upon an inquiry focused upon individuals suspected of wrongdoing, or is directed at persons suspected of no misconduct but who may be able to provide links in a chain of evidence relating to criminal conduct of others, or is centered upon broader problems of concern to society.

Id. at 573. However accurate this historic description may be, how does it reflect the grand jury's function "as a shield"? Who's being shielded in this scenario? Aren't those people who can "provide links in a chain" as to the criminality of others likely to themselves have some degree of criminal exposure?

5. No one is a proponent of perjury. It is, and should be, a federal crime, such as the one Mandujano was prosecuted under, 18 U.S.C. § 1623. But the Court here seems almost morally offended by the fact that the defendant lied in the grand jury.

> In this constitutional process of securing a witness' testimony, perjury simply has no place whatever. Perjured testimony is an obvious and flagrant affront to the basic concepts of judicial proceedings.

Id. at 577. Does the fact of defendant's perjury affect the result here? Does this case possibly come out differently if the Court was confronted only with the abstract issue whether a person the government intends to indict must be given *Miranda* warnings if he is subpoenaed to the grand jury? Note that the Court seems to concede that some warnings must be given in this context. *Id.* at 580.

6. In a concurring opinion Justice Brennan proposes a caveat to the Court's rule for situations where the government calls before a grand jury a person whom "it has probable cause . . . to suspect of committing a crime" to testify regarding that crime. *Id.* at 599. In such cases, Justice Brennan opines, there must be some form of "intentional and intelligent waiver" of the right against self-incrimination. *Id.* Is this rule enforceable? And why is this a concurrence and not a dissent?

United States v. Washington

431 U.S. 181 (1977)

Mr. Chief Justice Burger delivered the opinion of the Court.

The question presented in this case is whether testimony given by a grand jury witness suspected of wrongdoing may be used against him in a later prosecution for a substantive criminal offense when the witness was not informed in advance of his testimony that he was a potential defendant in danger of indictment.

(1)

The facts are not in dispute. Zimmerman and Woodard were driving respondent's van truck when a Washington, D.C., policeman stopped them for a traffic offense. Seeing a motorcycle in the rear of the van which he identified as stolen, the officer arrested both men and impounded respondent's vehicle. When respondent came to reclaim the van, he told police that Zimmerman and Woodard were friends who were driving the van with his permission.

He explained the presence of the stolen motorcycle by saying that while driving the van himself he had stopped to assist an unknown motorcyclist whose machine had broken down. Respondent then allowed the motorcycle to be placed in his van to take it for repairs. Soon after this the van stalled and he walked to a nearby gasoline station to call Zimmerman and Woodard for help, leaving the van with the unknown motorcyclist. After reaching Zimmerman by phone, respondent waited at the gasoline station for his friends, then returned to the spot he had left the van when they failed to appear; by that time the van had disappeared. Respondent said he was not alarmed, assuming his friends had repaired the van and driven it away. Shortly thereafter, Zimmerman and Woodard were arrested with the stolen motorcycle in the van.

Not surprisingly, the officer to whom respondent related this tale was more than a little skeptical; he told respondent he did not believe his story, and advised him not to repeat it in court, "because you're liable to be in trouble if you (do so)." The officer also declined to release the van. Respondent then repeated this story to an Assistant United States Attorney working on the case. The prosecutor, too, was dubious of the account; nevertheless, he released the van to respondent. At the same time, he served respondent with a subpoena to appear before the grand jury investigating the motorcycle theft.

When respondent appeared before the grand jury, the Assistant United States Attorney in charge had not yet decided whether to seek an indictment against him. The prosecutor was aware of respondent's explanation, and was also aware of the possibility that respondent could be indicted by the grand jury for the theft if his story was not believed.

The prosecutor did not advise respondent before his appearance that he might be indicted on a criminal charge in connection with the stolen motorcycle. But respondent, after reciting the usual oath to tell the truth, was given a series of other warnings, as follows:

> **Q.** . . . .
> You have a right to remain silent. You are not required to say anything to us in this Grand Jury at any time or to answer any question.
> Anything you say can be used against you in Court.
> You have the right to talk to a lawyer for advice before we question you and have him outside the Grand Jury during any questioning.
> If you cannot afford a lawyer and want one a lawyer will be provided for you.
> If you want to answer questions now without a lawyer present you will still have the right to stop answering at any time.
> You also have the right to stop answering at any time until you talk to a lawyer.
> Now, do you understand those rights, sir?
>
> **A.** Yes, I do.
>
> **Q.** And do you want to answer questions of the Grand Jury in reference to a stolen motorcycle that was found in your truck?
>
> **A.** Yes, sir.
>
> **Q.** And do you want a lawyer here or outside the Grand Jury room while you answer those questions?
>
> **A.** No, I don't think so.

In response to questions, respondent again related his version of how the stolen motorcycle came to be in the rear of his van. Subsequently, the grand jury indicted respondent, Zimmerman, and Woodard for grand larceny and receiving stolen property.

Respondent moved to suppress his testimony and quash the indictment, arguing that it was based on evidence obtained in violation of his Fifth Amendment privilege against compelled self-incrimination. The Superior Court for the District of Columbia suppressed the testimony and dismissed the indictment, holding that before the Government could use respondent's grand jury testimony at trial, it had first to demonstrate that respondent had knowingly waived his privilege against compelled self-incrimination. Notwithstanding the comprehensive warnings described earlier, the court found no effective waiver had been made, holding that respondent was not properly advised of his Fifth Amendment rights. The court thought the Constitution required, at a minimum, that

> inquiry be made of the suspect to determine what his educational background is, and what his formal education is and whether or not he understands that this is a constitutional privilege and whether he fully understands the consequences of what might result in the event that he does waive his constitutional right and in the event that he does make incriminatory statements. . . .

The court also held that respondent should have been told that his testimony could lead to his indictment by the grand jury before which he was testifying, and could then be used to convict him in a criminal prosecution.

The District of Columbia Court of Appeals affirmed the suppression order. That court also took the position that "the most significant failing of the prosecutor was in not advising (respondent) that he was a potential defendant. Another shortcoming was in the prosecutor's waiting until after administering the oath in the cloister of the grand jury before undertaking to furnish what advice was given."

(2)

The implicit premise of the District of Columbia Court of Appeals' holding is that a grand jury inquiry, like police custodial interrogation, is an "interrogation of persons suspected or accused of crime (that) contains inherently compelling pressures which work to undermine the individual's will to resist and to compel him to speak where he would not otherwise do so freely." But this Court has not decided that the grand jury setting presents coercive elements which compel witnesses to incriminate themselves. Nor have we decided whether any Fifth Amendment warnings whatever are constitutionally required for grand jury witnesses; moreover, we have no occasion to decide these matters today, for even assuming that the grand jury setting exerts some pressures on witnesses generally or on those who may later be indicted, the comprehensive warnings respondent received in this case plainly satisfied any possible claim to warnings. Accordingly, respondent's grand jury testimony may properly be used against him in a subsequent trial for theft of the motorcycle.

Although it is well settled that the Fifth Amendment privilege extends to grand jury proceedings, it is also axiomatic that the Amendment does not automatically preclude self-incrimination, whether spontaneous or in response to questions put by government officials. "It does not preclude a witness from testifying voluntarily in matters which may incriminate him," for "those competent and freewilled to do so may give evidence against the whole world, themselves included." Indeed, far from being prohibited by the Constitution, admissions of guilt by wrongdoers, if not coerced, are inherently desirable. In addition to guaranteeing the right to remain silent unless immunity is granted, the Fifth Amendment proscribes only self-incrimination obtained by a "genuine compulsion of testimony." Absent some officially coerced self-accusation, the Fifth Amendment privilege is not violated by even the most damning admissions. Accordingly, unless the record reveals some compulsion, respondent's incriminating testimony cannot conflict with any constitutional guarantees of the privilege.

The Constitution does not prohibit every element which influences a criminal suspect to make incriminating admissions. Of course, for many witnesses the grand jury room engenders an atmosphere conducive to truth telling, for it is likely that upon being brought before such a body of neighbors and fellow citizens, and having been placed under a solemn oath to tell the truth, many witnesses will feel obliged to do just that. But it does not offend the guarantees of the Fifth Amendment if in that setting a witness is more likely to tell the truth than in less solemn surroundings. The constitutional guarantee is only that the witness be not compelled to give self-incriminating testimony. The test is whether, considering the totality of the circumstances, the free will of the witness was overborne.

(3)

After being sworn, respondent was explicitly advised that he had a right to remain silent and that any statements he did make could be used to convict him of crime. It is inconceivable that such a warning would fail to alert him to his right to refuse to answer any question which might incriminate him. This advice also eliminated any possible compulsion to self-incrimination which might otherwise exist. To suggest otherwise is to ignore the record and reality. Indeed, it seems self-evident that one who is told he is free to refuse to answer questions is in a curious posture to later complain that his answers were compelled. Moreover, any possible coercion or unfairness resulting from a witness' misimpression that he must answer truthfully even questions with incriminatory aspects is completely removed by the warnings given here. Even in the presumed psychologically coercive atmosphere of police custodial interrogation, *Miranda* does not require that any additional warnings be given simply because the suspect is a potential defendant; indeed, such suspects are potential defendants more often than not.

Respondent points out that unlike one subject to custodial interrogation, whose arrest should inform him only too clearly that he is a potential criminal defendant, a grand jury witness may well be unaware that he is targeted for possible prosecution. While this may be so in some situations, it is an overdrawn generalization. In any case, events here clearly put respondent on notice that he was a suspect in the motorcycle theft. He knew that the grand jury was investigating that theft and that his involvement was known to the authorities. Respondent was made abundantly aware that his exculpatory version of events had been disbelieved by the police officer, and that his friends, whose innocence his own story supported, were to be prosecuted for the theft. The interview with the prosecutor put him on additional notice that his implausible story was not accepted as true. The warnings he received in the grand jury room served further to alert him to his own potential criminal liability. In sum, by the time he testified respondent knew better than anyone else of his potential defendant status.

However, all of this is largely irrelevant, since we do not understand what constitutional disadvantage a failure to give potential defendant warnings could possibly inflict on a grand jury witness, whether or not he has received other warnings. It is firmly settled that the prospect of being indicted does not entitle a witness to commit perjury, and witnesses who are not grand jury targets are protected from compulsory self-incrimination to the same extent as those who are. Because target witness status neither enlarges nor diminishes the constitutional protection against compelled self-incrimination, potential-defendant warnings add nothing of value to protection of Fifth Amendment rights.

Respondent suggests he must prevail under *Garner v. United States.* There, the petitioner was charged with a gambling conspiracy. As part of its case, the Government introduced Garner's income tax returns, in one of which he had identified his occupation as "professional gambler," and in all of which he had reported substantial income from wagering. The Court recognized that Garner was indeed compelled by law to file a tax return, but held that this did not constitute compelled self-incrimination. The Court noted that Garner did not claim his Fifth Amendment privilege, instead making the incriminating disclosure that he was a professional gambler. *Garner* holds that the Self-Incrimination Clause is violated only when the Government compels disclosures which it knows will incriminate the declarant that is, only when it intentionally places the individual under "compulsions to incriminate, not merely compulsions to make unprivileged disclosures." But the distinction between compulsion to incriminate and compulsion to disclose what the Government is entitled to know is of no help to respondent; in this case there was no compulsion to do either.

In *Beckwith v. United States*, decided shortly after *Garner*, we reaffirmed the need for showing overbearing compulsion as a prerequisite to a Fifth Amendment violation. There, the Government agent interrogated the taxpayer for the explicit purpose of securing information that would incriminate him. There, as here, the interrogation was not conducted in an inherently coercive setting; hence the claim of compelled self-incrimination was rejected.

(4)

Since warnings were given, we are not called upon to decide whether such warnings were constitutionally required. However, the District of Columbia Court of Appeals held that whatever warnings are required are insufficient if given "in the cloister of the grand jury." That court gave no reason for its view that warnings must be given outside the presence of the jury, but respondent now advances two justifications. First, it could be thought that warnings given to respondent before the grand jury came too late, because of the short time to assimilate their significance, and because of the presence of the grand jurors. But respondent does not contend that he did not understand the warnings given here. In any event, it is purely speculative to attribute any such effects to warnings given in the presence of the jury immediately before taking the stand. If anything, the proximity of the warnings to respondent's testimony and the solemnity of the grand jury setting seem likely to increase their effectiveness.

Second, respondent argues that giving the oath in the presence of the grand jury undermines assertion of the Fifth Amendment privilege by placing the witness in fear that the grand jury will infer guilt from invocation of the privilege. But this argument entirely overlooks that the grand jury's historic role is an investigative body; it is not the final arbiter of guilt or innocence. Moreover, it is well settled that invocation of the Fifth Amendment privilege in a grand jury proceeding is not admissible in a criminal trial, where guilt or innocence is actually at stake.

The judgment of the Court of Appeals is reversed, and the cause is remanded for further proceedings not inconsistent with this opinion.

Reversed and remanded.

Mr. Justice Brennan, with whom Mr. Justice Marshall joins, dissenting.

The general rule that a witness must affirmatively claim the privilege against compulsory self-incrimination must in my view admit of an exception in the case of a grand jury witness whom the prosecutor interrogates with the express purpose of getting evidence upon which to base a criminal charge against him. In such circumstances, even warnings, before interrogation, of his right to silence do not suffice. The privilege is emptied of substance unless the witness is further advised by the prosecutor that he is a potential defendant. Only if the witness then nevertheless intentionally and intelligently waives his right to be free from compulsory self-incrimination and submits to further interrogation should use of his grand jury testimony against him be sanctioned. As I stated in *United States v. Mandujano*:

> I would hold that, in the absence of an intentional and intelligent waiver by the individual of his known right to be free from compulsory self-incrimination, the Government may not call before a grand jury one whom it has probable cause as measured by an objective standard to suspect of committing a crime, and by use of judicial compulsion compel him to testify with regard to that crime. In the absence of such a waiver, the Fifth Amendment requires that any testimony obtained in this fashion be unavailable to the Government for use at trial. Such a waiver could readily be demonstrated by proof that the individual was warned prior to questioning that he is currently subject to possible criminal prosecution for the commission of a stated crime. . . .

In this case, although respondent Washington was advised of his rights to silence and to talk to a lawyer before he appeared before the grand jury, he was "only told that he was needed as a witness in prosecuting the two who were occupants of the van at the time of its impoundment." He was never told that he was in danger of being indicted himself, even though "at the time of his grand jury appearance respondent was a potential defendant whose indictment was considered likely by the prosecution."

The ancient privilege of a witness against being compelled to incriminate himself is precious to free men as a shield against high-handed and arrogant inquisitorial practices. It has survived centuries of controversies, periodically kindled by popular impatience that its protection sometimes allows the guilty to escape punishment. But it has endured as a wise and necessary protection of the individual against arbitrary power, and the price of occasional failures of justice is paid in the larger interest of general personal security.

I would hold that a failure to warn the witness that he is a potential defendant is fatal to an indictment of him when it is made unmistakably to appear, as here, that the grand jury inquiry became an investigation directed against the witness and was pursued with the purpose of compelling him to give self-incriminating testimony upon which to indict him. I would further hold that without such prior warning and the witness' subsequent voluntary waiver of his privilege, there is such gross encroachment upon the witness' privilege as to render worthless the values protected by it unless the self-incriminating testimony is unavailable to the Government for use at any trial brought pursuant to even a valid indictment.

It should be remarked that, of course, today's decision applies only to application of the privilege against self-incrimination secured by the Fifth Amendment to the United States Constitution. The holding does not affect the authority of state courts to construe counterpart provisions of state constitutions even identically phrased provisions "to give the individual greater protection than is provided" by the federal provision. . . . See generally Brennan, State Constitutions and the Protection of Individual Rights, 90 Harv. L. Rev. 489 (1977).

A number of state courts have recognized that a defendant or potential defendant called before a grand jury is privileged against the State's using his self-incriminating testimony to procure an indictment or using it to introduce against him at trial, even in the absence of an affirmative claim of his privilege against self-incrimination. . . . One court has specifically held that interrogating a potential defendant "under (the) guise of examining him as to the guilt of someone else" is a violation of the defendant's privilege against self-incrimination. The rationale of these decisions which I would find applicable to the case now before us is that where the grand jury investigation is in fact a proceeding against the witness, or even if begun as a general investigation it becomes a proceeding against the witness, the encroachment upon the witness' privilege requires that a court deny to the prosecution the use of the witness' self-incriminating testimony.

NOTES AND QUESTIONS

1. According to the Court, at the time Washington was brought before the grand jury, the AUSA "had not yet decided whether to seek an indictment against him." *Id.* at 183. Assuming that was so, what might have been the prosecutor's purpose or purposes in subpoenaing Washington to the grand jury? Do you think it would have affected the prosecutor's decision if Washington had taken the Fifth?

2. Note that unlike the defendant in *Mandujano*, Washington was advised "[a]nything you say can be used against you in Court." Washington argues that notwithstanding the warnings' content, which he admits he understood, the warnings were deficient because (a) they were given in the presence of the grand jury and (b) they were given after he was sworn in to testify.

Is either argument persuasive as a matter of human nature? Should this matter legally?

3. The Court rejects Washington's arguments about the effectiveness of the warnings. Drawing on some unknown fount of psychological expertise, the Court states that "[i]f anything, the proximity of the warnings to respondent's testimony and the solemnity of the grand jury setting seem likely to increase their effectiveness." Effectiveness at what? The Court also observes, as to Washington's argument that the presence of the grand jurors inhibited his willingness to invoke the Fifth Amendment, "the argument entirely overlooks that the grand jury's historic role is an investigative body; it is not the final arbiter of guilt or innocence."

Whatever you think of Washington's arguments, are the Court's arguments dismissing his concerns persuasive?

4. On the psychological expertise front, note the Court's bizarre observation that "for many witnesses the grand jury room engenders an atmosphere conducive to truth telling, for it is likely that upon being brought before such a body of neighbors and fellow citizens, and having been placed under a solemn oath to tell the truth, many witnesses will feel obliged to do just that." *Id.* at 188.

One can't help wondering if anyone on the Court had ever been in a "grand jury room" or, for that matter, ever been accused of wrongdoing.

The context in the opinion for this sentiment is somewhat confusing. Does the Court seem to be contemplating witnesses who have committed crimes, and will willingly and righteously confess their sins to their "neighbors and fellow citizens"? Has the Court forgotten that a federal prosecutor, whose job is to charge people with crimes, will also be in the room?

5. The dissent reasserts the position of the dissent in *Mandujano*, and would require that a witness in Washington's position—who was "likely" to be indicted—must be warned that he "is a potential defendant." What does this add to the warnings Washington actually received? Is it relevant that a police officer who had some affiliation with the case told Washington that he disbelieved his story and warned him not to repeat it in court? Does this mean anything other than that Washington was foolish?

6. The dissent notes a fact omitted in the Court's opinion: that Washington was not told he was a potential defendant but "was only told that he was needed as a witness in prosecuting the two who were occupants of the van at the time of its impoundment." How should this statement factor into the analysis? It is unclear whether it was the prosecutor or a police officer who said this, and it matters: Prosecutors, as lawyers, are ethically bound not to make misrepresentations, while police and agents have no such obligations and often traffic in misrepresentations. Was Washington's story so inherently farfetched that he shouldn't have believed that he was only a witness regardless of what he was told?

7. In a companion case to *Washington*, *United States v. Wong*, 431 U.S. 174 (1977), the Court held that a witness who lied in the grand jury could be prosecuted for perjury based on that testimony even where the district court found that the witness was a native of China and had not understood the Fifth Amendment warnings she had been given in the grand jury.

Does nothing else matter if a witness commits perjury? Does a person who lies forfeit all rights? Is the take-away that no warning could possibly lead a witness to believe they could lie?

Department of Justice Grand Jury Policies. Notwithstanding the results in *Mandujano*, *Washington*, and *Wong*, the Department of Justice has developed internal policies regarding appropriate practices in this area, which are codified in the DOJ Justice Manual. One of these is JM § 9-11.150, "Subpoenaing Targets of the Investigation." The DOJ definition of "target," in turn, is found in JM 9-11.151: "a person as to whom the prosecutor or the grand jury has substantial evidence linking him or her to the commission of a crime and who, in the judgment of the prosecutor, is a putative defendant."

Do you think the DOJ really means "putative" or is just using that word because it has been used in the case law? Are any dictionary definitions of "putative" helpful here? Under the DOJ definition would you say that Mandujano was a "target" at the time of his grand jury appearance? Was Washington?

As far as subpoenaing targets to the grand jury, the Justice Manual provides:

> A grand jury may properly subpoena a subject or a target of the investigation and question the target about his or her involvement in the crime under investigation. *See United States v. Wong*, 431 U.S. 174, 179 n. 8 (1977); *United States v. Washington*, 431 U.S. 181, 190 n.6 (1977); *United States v. Mandujano*, 425 U.S. 564, 573-75 and 584 n.9 (1976); *United States v. Dionisio*, 410 U.S. 1, 10 n.8 (1973). However, in the context of particular cases such a subpoena may carry the appearance of unfairness. Because the potential for misunderstanding is great, before a known "target" (as defined in JM 9-11.151) is subpoenaed to testify before the grand jury about his or her involvement in the crime under investigation, an effort should be made to secure the target's voluntary appearance. If a voluntary appearance cannot be obtained, the target should be subpoenaed only after the United States Attorney or the responsible Assistant Attorney General have approved the subpoena.

The JM goes on to suggest that approval of such a subpoena should be based on factors such as the need for the testimony in the overall scheme of the investigation and whether the questioning likely implicates any privileges.

Given that by definition a "target" already has exhibited "substantial evidence" of criminality, what factors could account for a "need" for the target's testimony?

Note that the Justice Manual acknowledges the "appearance" of unfairness. How effective do you think this policy would be in limiting the subpoenaing of targets into the grand jury? Suppose you were a supervising AUSA and a junior colleague came to you and requested approval to subpoena Mandujano to the grand jury, based on the facts as recounted in the case prior to the grand jury appearance. How would you analyze the issue?

Why does the policy require an effort to secure the target's voluntary appearance? How likely is it that a target, who was aware of that status, would "voluntarily appear" before the grand jury?

The Justice Manual also has a policy regarding "Advice of 'Rights" to Grand Jury Witnesses," set forth at JM § 9-11.151:

> It is the policy of the Department of Justice to advise a grand jury witness of his or her rights if such witness is a "target" or "subject" of a grand jury investigation.
>
> A "target" [see definition above]
>
> A "subject" of an investigation is a person whose conduct is within the scope of the grand jury's investigation.
>
> The Supreme Court declined to decide whether a grand jury witness must be warned of his or her Fifth Amendment privilege against compulsory self-incrimination before the witness's grand jury testimony can be used against the witness. *See United States v. Washington*, 431 U.S. 181, 186 and 190-191 (1977); *United States v. Wong*, 431 U.S. 174 (1977); *United States v. Mandujano*, 425 U.S. 564, 582 n.7. (1976). In *Mandujano* the Court took cognizance of the fact that Federal prosecutors customarily warn "targets" of their Fifth Amendment rights before grand jury questioning begins. Similarly, in *Washington*, the Court pointed to the fact that Fifth Amendment warnings were administered as negating "any possible compulsion to self-incrimination which might otherwise exist" in the grand jury setting. *See Washington*, 431 U.S. at 188.
>
> Notwithstanding the lack of a clear constitutional imperative, it is the policy of the Department that an "Advice of Rights" form be appended to all grand jury subpoenas to be served on any "target" or "subject" of an investigation. See advice of rights below.
>
> In addition, these "warnings" should be given by the prosecutor on the record before the grand jury and the witness should be asked to affirm that the witness understands them.
>
> Although the Court in *Washington, supra*, held that "targets" of the grand jury's investigation are entitled to no special warnings relative to their status as "potential defendant(s)," the

> Department of Justice continues its longstanding policy to advise witnesses who are known "targets" of the investigation that their conduct is being investigated for possible violation of Federal criminal law. This supplemental advice of status of the witness as a target should be repeated on the record when the target witness is advised of the matters discussed in the preceding paragraphs.
>
> When a district court insists that the notice of rights not be appended to a grand jury subpoena, the advice of rights may be set forth in a separate letter and mailed to or handed to the witness when the subpoena is served.
>
> Advice of Rights:
>
> The grand jury is conducting an investigation of possible violations of Federal criminal laws involving: (State here the general subject matter of inquiry, e.g., conducting an illegal gambling business in violation of 18 U.S.C. § 1955).
>
> You may refuse to answer any question if a truthful answer to the question would tend to incriminate you.
>
> Anything that you do say may be used against you by the grand jury or in a subsequent legal proceeding.
>
> If you have retained counsel, the grand jury will permit you a reasonable opportunity to step outside the grand jury room to consult with counsel if you so desire.
>
> Additional Advice to be Given to Targets: If the witness is a target, the above advice should also contain a supplemental warning that the witness's conduct is being investigated for possible violation of federal criminal law.

JM § 9-11.151. How much does the additional advice for targets add to the advice given to subjects? Under the DOJ's own definitions, is the additional advice for targets equally applicable to persons categorized as subjects?

Much of the content in these particular Justice Manual provisions is academic. Targets almost never testify in the grand jury. But the DOJ definitions of "target" and "subject"—and by negative implication a third category of "witness," persons of interest only as sources of information about others—are part of the everyday discourse between defense counsel and AUSAs.

The first question a defense attorney will ask an AUSA about a client who has received a grand jury subpoena is what is the witness's status: that is, is the client a target, subject, or witness? The answer to this question, although often heavily caveated (e.g., "just a witness for now"), will guide defense counsel's advice to the client about how to respond to the subpoena.

If the client is a target, the advice is simple: Do not testify. Take the Fifth if the AUSA insists on an appearance.

Next simplest is the "witness" category. If the client is truly just a witness—based on the AUSA's representation, which defense counsel is able to confirm by interviewing the client and perhaps from other sources of information—it may be permissible for the client simply to appear and testify in response to the subpoena. This is never a good idea unless there is 100 percent confidence the client is only a witness (e.g., a recordkeeper from a bank).

The client who is a "subject"—that is, the client's "conduct is within the scope of the grand jury's investigation"—is more complicated.

Can you negotiate an immunity grant for the client? This is always the ideal solution. But the AUSA will be reluctant to grant immunity if the client has significant exposure (and the AUSA believes the client should plead guilty) or if the AUSA is unsure the client can help the investigation, usually by implicating others in criminal conduct.

Take the Fifth? This strategy will often be necessary when the client is a subject. But this is risky. Sometimes AUSAs will require the client to assert the Fifth on a question-by-question basis. The client will be in the grand jury alone, and asserting the Fifth too broadly can result in collateral litigation over the scope of the privilege, while asserting it too narrowly can result in waiver or exposure.

Negotiate a proffer agreement? Under such an arrangement, the client can be interviewed informally by the AUSA and agents outside the grand jury, with a very limited form of immunity. Sometimes this is better than simply taking the Fifth. Sometimes it isn't.

G. PROSECUTORIAL ABUSE OF THE GRAND JURY'S POWERS

The next cases focus on prosecutors' use of the grand jury for an improper purpose, that is, a purpose other than investigating whether a crime has been committed. We saw a variation on this theme in *Sells Engineering*, *supra*, where the Court was concerned about the grand jury being used to develop evidence for use in a civil suit. The following cases consider whether the grand jury may be used to develop evidence to use in a case that has already been indicted and whether the grand jury can be used to induce a person to commit perjury in the grand jury.

United States v. Doe

455 F.2d 1270 (1st Cir. 1972)

IN THE MATTER OF GRAND JURY PROCEEDING: APPLICATION OF DANIEL ELLSBERG FOR PROTECTIVE ORDER

Coffin, Circuit Judge.

Daniel Ellsberg, a defendant in a pending criminal prosecution initiated by an indictment in the Central District of California, seeks a protective order barring a grand jury sitting in the District of Massachusetts (Boston) from gathering evidence which would be relevant to his trial in California. The district court denied the motion, basing its decision on the prosecution's representation "that its purpose in calling witnesses [in Boston] is not to obtain testimony or other evidence tending to prove the charge or charges [in California] but to determine whether any offense or offenses against the United States may have been committed within the District of Massachusetts." Movant now asks for a stay of the denial pending appeal.

The California indictment charges Ellsberg with unlawful possession of classified government documents (18 U.S.C. § 793(e)) and with unlawful conversion of such documents to his own use (18 U.S.C. § 641). In addition, Ellsberg, Anthony Russo and "others unknown" are charged with entering into a conspiracy with two other named but unindicted co-conspirators "to defraud the United States . . . [by] defeating its lawful governmental function of controlling the dissemination of classified Government studies," more specifically, by receiving the Pentagon Papers, copying them, and communicating them to unauthorized persons. Trial is scheduled to commence in from six to ten weeks.

The protective order which movant seeks would bar the prosecution from asking any witness subpoenaed to testify before the Boston grand jury questions bearing on the charge that he, Ellsberg, had conspired to communicate the Pentagon Papers to unauthorized persons, as broadly charged in the California indictment. The request is based on movant's assertion that use of the powerful and essentially unreviewable grand jury process in Boston to aid preparation of the government's case in California would subvert the protections accorded a defendant by the Federal Rules of Criminal Procedure and would consequently jeopardize his right to a fair trial on the pending charges. Although movant's argument, so put, contains due process elements, he appeals principally for an exercise of this court's general supervisory powers.

Although the attorneys for the government—the same three being responsible for both the presentation before the Boston grand jury and the California trial jury—have stated that the principal purpose of the Boston proceedings is to ascertain whether offenses against the United States, other than those already charged in the California indictment, have been committed and have expressly disavowed any intent to utilize the Boston grand jury "to extract testimony for use . . . in Los Angeles," they candidly admit that the investigation here may turn up some evidence relevant to the California proceedings. As long as such evidence remains a necessary—though usable—byproduct of the Boston investigation and is not allowed to disturb the focus of that investigation, however, the government contends that such evidence is properly usable in the California trial. It also believes that the Boston grand jury is not foreclosed from inquiring into events in Boston which "suggest other aspects" of the conspiracy alleged in the California indictment or "separate conspiracies involving Daniel Ellsberg as a central figure."

• • •

The nature of movant's claim is a large and compendious one. The rule, as accurately stated by Professor Moore, does not differ markedly from the general position staked out by the government: "It is improper to use the grand jury for the purpose of preparing an already pending indictment for trial. But the courts have generally held that where another purpose is predominant, the fact that the government may derive incidental benefit from a grand jury proceeding does not preclude its use." The classic case dealt with a grand jury subpoenaing the same witnesses and documents as had a prior grand jury which issued an indictment, where the court's compelled conclusion was that the "dominating, if not the only, object" was to prepare for trial of the earlier indictment. In another case, the Supreme Court refused to interfere with government use of a grand jury transcript in the preparation of a civil suit, even though no indictment was returned, in the absence of a finding that the grand jury had been used as a short cut or that criminal procedure had been subverted. In *United States v. Dardi* (1964), the test was thus stated: "It is improper to utilize a Grand Jury for the sole or dominating purpose of preparing an already pending indictment for trial."

Movant's claim of taint, therefore, would be the expansive one that the Boston grand jury, as a whole, had, as its sole or dominating purpose, preparation for trial of the California criminal prosecution. This claim could be tested only by a comprehensive viewing of the entire Boston grand jury minutes. But Rule 6(e) of the Federal Rules of Criminal Procedure gives movant no right to disclosure, except upon a showing of grounds for dismissal of the indictment. Moreover, the 1970 amendments to the Jencks Act, 18 U.S.C. § 3500, make clear that a defendant has no right to compel pre-trial disclosure of grand jury minutes. And, we cannot envisage the California District Court, even in camera, reviewing months of testimony.

But the same problem of immensity of claim that inclines us to take appellate jurisdiction also poses the most serious problem in structuring an intervention in such a way as to respect the independent role of the grand jury while at the same time giving absolute protection to movant. We cannot, for example, subscribe to the protective order requested and attempt to bar the grand jury from inquiring of a witness whether movant communicated the Pentagon Papers to an unauthorized person. In the first place, such a transaction could be a separate crime committed in Massachusetts, implicating additional prospective defendants, as well as being germane to the California trial. In the second place, we give credence to the government attorneys when they say that they do not know in advance what testimony will be forthcoming from a witness. And, finally, we recognize the futility both of barring questions which might occur to the jurors themselves and of policing the questions which could be put. . . .

We recognize, in short, that grand jury proceedings cannot be policed in any detail. It is a price we pay for grand jury independence that sometimes people are indicted on the basis of evidence tainted in part by hearsay, or of illegally obtained evidence. Nor is a grand jury narrowly confined in its objectives. And, even when a grand jury produces evidence but does not return an indictment, that is insufficient to embargo its fruits.

On the other hand, we are sensitive to the possibilities of abuse of the grand jury process which are inherent in the present situation. As Moore has observed, "The government has at its disposal one of the most effective discovery mechanisms yet devised—the grand jury. This body may call witnesses under compulsory process and examine them in secret under oath, unhampered by the rules of evidence or an adversary counsel's cross-examination, or in the case of a 'prospective defendant' by Fifth Amendment immunity [citations omitted]."

The problem is akin to that of using the wide-ranging discovery procedure available under the Federal Rules of Civil Procedure to gather evidence for a criminal prosecution. This practice has been the subject of critical comment but is not easily forbidden. The Court in *Kordel*, however, specifically noted that the issue there faced was not one in which the government brought a civil action "solely to obtain evidence for its criminal prosecution." Here we confront not only a broadly-phrased indictment in California, and a grand jury inquiry on the home ground of the movant, but an identity of prosecutors in the two proceedings. The difficulties they face in not confusing their roles, with the consequent potential for distortion of the role of the grand jury, cannot be dismissed as unreal.

We conclude that there is a modest though necessarily incomplete, protection which we can give movant, consistent with our respect for the integrity of the Boston grand jury. While, in the absence of a compelling showing of the probability of abuse, a total review, either here or there, of that jury's proceedings before movant's trial in California is not warranted, the record will be available here in the event that disciplinary action against the prosecutors should ever be called for. More important from the movant's point of view is the possibility of the California trial court's own scrutiny, pre-trial, of the testimony of such witnesses before the Boston grand jury as are expected to be called as witnesses at the California trial.

It is of course clear that the recent amendments to the Jencks Act, the restrictions surrounding the disclosure of grand jury proceedings in Rule 6(e), F. R. Crim. P., and even the proposed amendment to Rule 6(a)(3) give a defendant no right in the ordinary course to grand jury minutes. But Rule 6(e) itself authorizes a court "preliminarily to or in connection with a judicial proceeding" to direct disclosure. The Supreme Court in *Dennis v. United States* (1966), referring to this power, quoted the statement, "after the grand jury's functions are ended, disclosure is wholly proper where the ends of justice require it."

Were transcripts of the Boston grand jury testimony available to the California trial court, it would be possible for such pre-trial scrutiny to be made, in camera. Cf. Rule 16(e), F. R. Crim. P.; 18 U.S.C. § 3500. In the unlikely event that scrutiny of a number of witnesses' transcripts led the court to suspect that the Boston grand jury might in fact have been used dominantly to prepare for the California trial, it could conduct a more comprehensive review. The court might at some point conclude that the ends of justice would be served by such full disclosure. Short of this, the court could proscribe the calling of a witness whose testimony in Boston appeared to have been elicited chiefly for its contribution to the trial in California. This partial proscription would have been the result in *United States v. Dardi* (1964), had the trial court concluded that a witness had been called before a grand jury largely to gather evidence for an ongoing trial. To be sure, such an inquiry may not uncover fruits stemming from Boston disclosures, but, as the Second Circuit observed a motion for suppression of evidence may seek to encompass such fruits, "which is often quite as difficult of ascertainment as the benefits of the Government's allegedly improper discovery would be here."

In saying what we have said, we most particularly do not wish to be understood as asserting any competence to advise another federal court about the conduct of its business. All we seek is to assure the availability of testimony to the California court if it should see fit to make use of it. We do have and therefore exercise our power here to require the prosecutors who are presenting matters to the Boston grand jury to make available to the District Court of Central California the transcripts of testimony of each witness, if any, whom the government intends to call at trial in California, as seasonably as feasible. This will allow that court the opportunity, if it wishes to avail itself of it, to survey the proposed testimony to judge whether, at least as to the putative witnesses, the Boston grand jury was decoyed into serving primarily as a discovery device for the government's trial preparation.

Subject to this requirement, we deny the motion for stay.

NOTES AND QUESTIONS

1. The court describes "the rule" at issue in this case as straightforward: "It is improper to use the grand jury for the purpose of preparing an already pending indictment for trial." Easily stated, but what aspect or aspects of the grand jury's historic function make this use improper? How is such use inconsistent with the grand jury's broad inquisitorial and investigative powers?

2. Suppose a defendant is indicted but is tipped off and flees the jurisdiction before he can be arrested. The defendant, in other words, is a fugitive. Would it be permissible to use the grand jury to obtain testimony from the defendant's known acquaintances and family members in an attempt to find information regarding the defendant's whereabouts so he can be apprehended? Are there other reasons why these witnesses could be subpoenaed to the grand jury? *See* 18 U.S.C. § 1071 (criminalizing the harboring of a fugitive).

3. The court takes the defendant's allegations of potential grand jury abuse here quite seriously, despite its acknowledged lack of ability or authority to police the grand jury in any meaningful way. How important was it that the same three AUSAs were responsible for both the California trial and the presentation to the Boston grand jury? Note the high quality of the lawyering on both sides here. The defense attorneys make an aggressive and creative argument based on a hardly obvious attribute of the grand jury. And the prosecutors, while claiming they intend to use the Boston grand jury proceedings to investigate crimes other than those charged in California, candidly admit that the Boston grand jury investigation might unearth evidence that is relevant to the California trial.

Can the prosecutors properly use the Boston grand jury to investigate whether other additional crimes or additional persons should be added to the California charges?

4. The civil outcome of Daniel Ellsberg's famous leak of the Pentagon Papers is well known: The Supreme Court ruled in *New York Times v. United States*, 403 U.S. 713 (1971), that the *New York Times* and *Washington Post* could not be enjoined from publishing them. Ellsberg's subsequent indictment by the Nixon Justice Department, at issue here, is less well known. Ultimately, the federal court in California dismissed the Ellsberg indictment on multiple grounds of prosecutorial misconduct. *See* Melville B. Nimmer, *National Security Secrets v. Free Speech: The Issues Left Undecided in the Ellsberg Case*, 26 Stan. L. Rev. 311 (1973).

Somewhat analogous to the improper use of the grand jury to find evidence for an existing indictment is the use of the grand jury for the sole or primary—which adjective applies is unclear—purpose of inducing a witness to commit perjury in the grand jury. Using the grand jury for this purpose is sometimes called a "perjury trap." *See generally* Bennett L. Gershman, *The Perjury Trap*, 129 U. Pa. L. Rev. 624, 683 (1981) ("The prosecutor's use of the grand jury, not to uncover antecedent crime, but to cause perjury to be committed, implicates fundamental notions of fairness. The awesome powers of investigating grand juries, the limited rights of witnesses, the secrecy of the interrogation, and the harsh intolerance of perjured testimony, all provide a natural setting for oppression and deceit. In such circumstances, the protections offered by the due process clause seem especially appropriate, and perhaps necessary.").

People v. Tyler

385 N.E.2d 1224 (N.Y. Ct. App. 1978)

BREITEL, Chief Judge.

Based on testimony he gave before a Grand Jury, defendant, a Supreme Court Justice, was convicted after jury trial on three counts of perjury in the first degree (Penal Law, s 210.15). He was sentenced to probation. The Special Prosecutor appeals from the Appellate Division's unanimous reversal and dismissal of the indictment.

There should be an affirmance.

Involved are defendant's false answers to questions limited to the outward details of place and time of a single meeting between defendant and a reputed criminal character. The primary issue is whether a prosecution for perjury may be based on such false answers where the prosecutor, in his questioning, demonstrated no palpable interest in eliciting facts material to the authorized substantive investigation of antecedent crime or official misconduct. A secondary issue is whether the false answers about peripheral details of the single meeting may support a perjury prosecution without the prosecutor laying enough of a foundation to recall to the witness' mind what, without some prodding, may have in truth escaped the witness' recollection. In resolving the issues it is concluded that the conviction may not stand, and the indictment was properly dismissed as a matter of law.

First elected to the Civil Court in 1967, defendant became a Supreme Court Justice in January, 1970. Admitted to the Bar sometime after World War II, for the 18 years before he became a Judge defendant had been a lawyer practicing largely on his own and devoting about 50% of his time to criminal matters.

In February, 1975 an Extraordinary Grand Jury was charged, among other things, with investigating the relationship of defendant with certain known gambling figures. The inquiry, which included 20 sessions at which 22 witnesses were heard, was not concluded until October, 1976. Among the gamblers was one Raymond Marquez, also known as "Spanish" Raymond, the reputed head of one of the largest illegal gambling operations in New York. The Grand Jury was informed that Marquez, who was released from Federal prison in April, 1975, had been convicted of both Federal and State crimes, including interstate racketeering, gambling policy, and contempt.

Each of the counts charged in the instant indictment for perjury before the Grand Jury arises out of defendant's answers to questions concerning a single meeting with Marquez. According to the acting forewoman of the Grand Jury, the inquiry was aimed at uncovering any bribery, bribe receiving, or official misconduct.

Three police officers involved in an extensive personal surveillance of defendant testified to the Grand Jury that on May 16, 1975, after the Grand Jury had been convened, they saw Marquez in defendant's company. According to the officers, after some activity that suggested he may have been waiting for someone, defendant met Marquez and his wife near Lincoln Center in Manhattan. They drove about 10 blocks in defendant's automobile to Patsy's Restaurant on West 56th Street, and remained there for over an hour. Upon leaving, defendant and Marquez allegedly spoke for 10 minutes, while Mrs. Marquez sat in defendant's automobile. Defendant then drove the two back to where their own automobile was garaged. Substantially the same testimony was given by the officers at trial.

Defendant appeared before the Grand Jury on four occasions, and on two was questioned about Marquez. Other areas of inquiry were defendant's background and how he came to be a Judge, defendant's acquaintance with other reputed gamblers, and bail applications granted by defendant out of the ordinary courtroom setting.

On March 2, 1976, defendant's second appearance, defendant testified that he knew Marquez as a man who had been convicted "some years ago for policy," and recalled representing him as a lawyer "in the fifties" in a case that "had something to do with gambling." When asked about contacts with Marquez since defendant had become a Supreme Court Justice, defendant denied communicating with him. He remembered, however, that as he was going to his courthouse chambers one day he saw Marquez being escorted by Marshals to Federal court.

Marquez was not mentioned when defendant appeared before the Grand Jury for the third time on May 18, 1976. In his final appearance two days later, however, Marquez was again the subject of inquiry. This time, when asked about communications with Marquez, defendant, who later explained at trial that a discussion he had had with his wife following his earlier appearance had refreshed his recollection, recalled the May 16 meeting:

Q. (Y)ou testified before that you saw him on occasion when he was being transported by federal marshals. You said that was the only time you'd seen him since you'd become a judge. Is that the occasion you're talking about?
A. No, that's not the occasion I'm talking about.
Q. What is the occasion that you're talking about?
A. I saw him on an occasion when he was with his wife on 58th Street in Manhattan.
Q. When was that?
A. I couldn't fix the dates. Probably somewhere around May. May of '75, somewhere around there.
Q. Can you describe that in any more detail, that meeting or encounter or whatever it was on 58th Street?
A. Yes. It was outside of Patsy's Restaurant. I think that's where it was.
Q. What were you doing? Were you walking down the street, driving, in the restaurant? What was
A. I was on my way into Patsy's.
Q. What happened?
A. I saw him and his wife.
Q. What did you do?
A. We greeted each other, asked him how he was. He asked me how I was. Asked me how things were getting along, and I asked him the same thing.
Q. This was out on the street?
A. That was on the street.
Then they walked into Patsy's and I walked into Patsy's.
Q. Were you alone or with anyone else?
A. I was alone. I was waiting for my daughter.
Q. What happened after you went into Patsy's?
A. I think I had a drink.
Q. Was there a bar there, or did you have it at the table?
A. Sitting right at the entrance of the door, I had a drink at the door.
Q. Did you have a drink alone?
A. No. He and his wife sat down.
Q. How long did that take?
A. About ten or fifteen minutes.
Q. What happened then?
A. I got up and left.
Q. And they remained in the place?
A. I believe so.

Q. Did you have a previous arrangement to meet with Mr. Marquez at that location?
A. No, sir.
Q. It was purely chance?
A. Yes, sir.
Q. When you arrived there did you withdrawn. What did you discuss during the course of that meeting with Mr. Marquez?
A. How he was, basically.
Q. Had he recently come out of prison?
A. I understood that he had, yes.
Q. Was that part of the discussion?
A. Yes.
Q. Anything else except his health?
A. That's all. Health and what he planned to do.
Q. Did he tell you what he planned to do?
A. He said he intended to take it easy.
Q. And that was the extent of the conversation?
A. In substance.
Q. Can you remember anything else that was discussed?
A. No, I can't, because it was just chit-chat.
Q. Did he discuss with you any matters that were in the courts at that time?
A. No, sir.
Q. Did you discuss any of the did he discuss the fact that the people in his organization had been arrested?
A. No, sir.

At this final appearance, defendant also corrected his earlier testimony to reflect that his former representation of Marquez related not to gambling, but to a violation of probation arising out of an assault.

A four-count indictment for perjury in the first degree followed. As noted, the charges are entirely based on defendant's answers to questions about the single meeting with Marquez. The first count charges defendant with falsely stating that he had not "talked to Marquez" since becoming a Supreme Court Justice. That count, presumably because of defendant's later recantation, resulted in an acquittal, but defendant was convicted of the three remaining counts. Count two alleges that "upon being asked where he saw Marquez for the first time on May 16, 1975 (defendant) testified that it was in front of Patsy's Restaurant." Under count three, it is asserted that defendant testified that his meeting with Marquez "had lasted about ten to fifteen minutes." The fourth count alleges that "upon being asked what happened after conversing with Marquez in Patsy's Restaurant, (defendant) testified that . . . he exited the Restaurant and left Marquez inside the premises." The surveillance team, as observed earlier, had testified that defendant, after driving the couple 10 blocks to the restaurant, talked to them there for over an hour, and upon leaving, but before driving them to their garage, spoke to Mr. Marquez while Mrs. Marquez waited in defendant's automobile.

Among the grounds for reversal adopted by the Appellate Division were that in counts two and three the materiality necessary to a conviction for perjury in the first degree was lacking and that in counts two and four the falsity of the statements alleged was insufficiently proved. Since the challenged interrogation amounted, on the whole, to an impermissible "perjury trap," neither ambiguity nor insufficiency of evidence, usually issues of fact resolvable by the jury, need be discussed. Nor need materiality be discussed.

The primary function of the Grand Jury is to uncover crimes and misconduct in public office for the purpose of prosecution. False testimony before the Grand Jury, then, especially by the holder of public office, is a grave matter affecting the public interest and the administration of justice. It is not properly a principal aim of the Grand Jury, however, to "create" new crimes in the course of its proceedings. Thus, where a prosecutor exhibits no palpable interest in eliciting facts material to a substantive investigation of crime or official misconduct and substantially tailors his questioning to extract a false answer, a valid perjury prosecution should not lie. Since no legitimate investigatory function is discernible in questioning designed primarily or solely to support a perjury prosecution against the witness, it cannot be said that the responsive testimony, albeit false, frustrates any authorized purpose of the Grand Jury.

It is not unprecedented for an improper purpose to invalidate that which is otherwise lawful. There is an analogy in the tort field. Where there is an "abuse of process," that is, a "misuse or perversion of regularly issued legal process for a purpose not justified by the nature of the process," a cause of action will lie. It has also been suggested that abuse of the power of the Grand Jury to investigate and indict for criminal acts may fatally infect the proceeding. Recognized is that it is not just the target of the abuse who is offended, but the administration of justice.

The absence of a legitimate purpose to the inquiry also makes suspect the administration of the oath to the defendant. It is elementary that there must be a validly administered oath to establish perjury. Where the questioning is not intended to further the Grand Jury investigation, but, instead, is aimed substantially at trapping the witness into giving false testimony, the validity of the oath previously administered is questionable.

Ordinarily, whether a trap primarily or solely to support a prosecution for perjury against the witness was set by the prosecutor raises a question of fact. The questioning in the instant case, however, was an unmitigated effort to trap the witness on minor outward details of a single meeting with a reputed criminal figure. There was no attempt to establish that the meeting was pertinent to a proper substantive goal of Grand Jury investigation. The meeting might well have been a chance encounter at which the former lawyer chatted with his ex-client. Or, it might have been planned to discuss matters inappropriate between one now a Judge and the other a convicted gambler, even if he were a former client. More to the point, the meeting would then have had more of a suspect character and probably would have related to the substantive criminal investigatory goals of the Grand Jury.

The prosecutor evinced minimal or no interest in establishing the materiality of the meeting. Almost as if he were conducting only a quiz to test memory or recall, he devoted most of his questions, as the excerpt quoted earlier indicates, to the logistical details of the May 16 encounter, facts contemporaneously documented by the surveillance team.

It is true that after an extended series of questions about where defendant and Marquez met, how long they were together, and how they parted, defendant was asked what they spoke about. And, some directed, if isolated, questions, such as whether they discussed matters then in the courts or that people in "the organization" had been arrested, were posed. Seemingly content with defendant's description of an innocuous encounter, however, at no time did the prosecutor, either by repetition, restatement, or elaboration, press defendant into giving a convincing narrative of what indeed went on at the restaurant. Yet, it is the content of the meeting which would determine whether the outward details were of any significance and, more important, whether substantive inquiry should be pursued. In sum, there is demonstrated no palpable effort to establish, either from the Grand Jury testimony or from the evidence at the trial, that the meeting was material to the Grand Jury investigation. In such a context, false answers to questions limited to peripheral details of time and place may not support a prosecution for perjury.

Also critical is that, upon hearing defendant's version of the outward details of the May 16 meeting, the prosecutor failed to confront defendant, or otherwise stimulate his memory, if only by limited cues, with some of the contrary facts acquired from the surveillance team. Such cues are not to inform the witness of the information already acquired, but to make certain that the witness is not failing sincerely to recall details of no memorable significance. To establish that defendant's assertion that he first met Marquez "outside of Patsy's Restaurant" was knowingly false, and not just a lapse in memory, some slight effort to stimulate defendant's recollection should have been made. The same may be said of defendant's assertion that he sat with the Marquezes for only 10 or 15 minutes, and that when he left the restaurant the Marquez couple remained.

It is not so much that the witness deserves an opportunity to refresh his recollection; it is that the foundation established by stimulation of recollection bears on resolution of the ultimate issue: whether defendant is deliberately falsifying. Indeed, if the meeting were no more than benign but questionable socializing between former lawyer and client, details would not likely be remembered or easily recalled. This does not mean that the kind of foundation required to impeach a witness with a prior inconsistent statement is indicated. Much less is indicated, simply enough to exclude the innocent lack of recollection or memory of a peripheral detail not likely to be memorable.

That is not to say that a witness suspected of falsifying must be wetnursed, or that in every case a "last clear chance" to tell the truth must be afforded. A rigid rule would deny the prosecutor the right to exercise judgment. In inquisitorial investigations particularly, just as on trial cross-examination, indirect questioning is characteristic and permissible. But the nature, and especially the intrinsic significance, or insignificance, of the event to be recalled will, almost invariably, be critical in determining the cues, if any, the prosecutor should provide for the witness, if it is the truth that is being sought.

It is true that when defendant met with Marquez, the Grand Jury investigation had already been underway, and inquiry concerning bail applications handled by defendant was being made by the State Commission on Judicial Conduct. That is hardly enough to compel the conclusion that the meeting, albeit between a Supreme Court Justice and a recently released Federal prisoner, was other than harmless, even if perhaps indiscreet. And no more was established by the prosecutor. But even if the encounter between former lawyer and client should have been memorable, either because it involved a transaction of significance, or because it was at that point so unusual for defendant in light of his then experience and associations, it is unrealistic to expect defendant's recollection of the surrounding details to equal that of the surveillance officers who were making contemporaneous notes of defendant's every step.

Put another way, it is not suggested that full disclosure of the information known to the prosecutor must have been made to defendant, especially if disclosure would reveal too much of how the investigation was conducted and how far it has proceeded. Yet, the examiner has an inescapable burden to provide a transcript which demonstrates that the witness is testifying falsely intentionally, rather than mistakenly, whether it is with respect to surrounding neutral details or to substantive matters relevant to an authorized investigation. The record in this case does not establish either intentional falsity or purposeful substantive inquiry. Thus, the only rational explanation for the tactics employed is the unacceptable one: that a perjury indictment, rather than the ascertainment of facts leading to substantive goals, was the object.

Nor is it suggested that defendant would have answered a more disciplined interrogation differently. That cannot be known. Nor should it be supposed that the mere anticipation of perjury in an inquiry would invalidate an indictment for the anticipated perjury. That would be unrealistic, and a boon to which perjurers are not entitled. How defendant might otherwise have responded, or whether a prosecutor could reasonably have hoped for more illuminating testimony, is not what ultimately determines the issues. Dispositive in this case is that the preoccupation with trapping defendant into committing perjury is unmitigated by substantive investigative goals. There was not even that little which might have presented a question of fact for the jury to decide. Dismissal of the indictment as a matter of law was thus proper.

• • •

Accordingly, the order of the Appellate Division should be affirmed, and the indictment stand dismissed.

NOTES AND QUESTIONS

1. "It is not properly a principal aim of the Grand Jury, however, to 'create' new crimes in the course of its proceedings." If there was ever any doubt about whether a pure perjury trap was a legitimate use of the grand jury, this delightfully understated sentence would seem to eliminate it. The court finds in *Tyler* that the grand jury examination of the defendant had "no legitimate investigatory function." What does that mean? Is there any whiff in the examination of legitimate investigation? How easy would it have been for the prosecutor here, if his intention was to get the defendant to commit perjury, to fake some "legitimate investigatory function"? How would the prosecutor have done so?

2. Apart from the prosecutor's apparent apathy about the content of the defendant's meeting with Marquez, the court also sees it as important "that, upon hearing defendant's version of the outward details of the May 16 meeting, the prosecutor failed to confront defendant, or otherwise stimulate his memory, if only by limited cues, with some of the contrary facts acquired from the surveillance team." How could this have been done without tipping the prosecutor's hand, for example, by suggesting that the defendant had been (and might still be) under surveillance? Is the Court suggesting that the prosecutor's willingness to be satisfied with a weak perjury case is probative of a perjury trap?

3. Consider again the facts of *Mandujano*. What are the arguments for and against a perjury trap defense based on the grand jury testimony in the opinion?

4. *Tyler* is one of the few reported cases upholding a perjury trap defense. Might it have been relevant—either as a matter of experience, institutional fidelity, or motivation—that the prosecutor in *Tyler* was a "Special Counsel," presenting a case to an Extraordinary Grand Jury?

Many federal courts have acknowledged the potential existence of a "perjury trap" defense, but the defense has rarely been litigated and has apparently never succeeded in federal court. *See United States v. Regan*, 103 F.3d 1072, 1079 (2d Cir. 1997) ("[W]e find that the facts of this case 'render the perjury trap defense inapplicable' and thus do not decide whether this defense is available in the Second Circuit."); *United States v. Chevoor*, 526 F.2d 178, 185 (1st Cir. 1975) ("We cannot say that calling Chevoor in these circumstances even in the anticipation that he would perjure himself is beyond the pale of permissible prosecutorial conduct."); *United States v. Nickels*, 502 F.2d 1173, 1176 (7th Cir. 1974) ("Since the questions were material to the grand jury's investigation, we doubt that we can inquire into the motivation for asking them."); *United States v. Lazaros*, 480 F.2d 174, 177 (6th Cir. 1973) ("Regardless of the actual beliefs of the United States Attorney, the grand jury was entitled to hear Lazaros's testimony."). *See* Billy Joe McLain, *Debunking the Perjury-Trap Myth*, 88 Tex. L. Rev. 883 (2010) (arguing inter alia that since a necessary element of the perjury trap defense—the immateriality of the allegedly perjured testimony—is also a defense to perjury on the merits, the perjury trap defense is superfluous).

As for the difficulties of establishing a viable perjury trap defense in a specific case, consider *United States v. Chen*, 933 F.3d 793 (9th Cir. 1991). In a grand jury investigation of potential corruption within the Public Utility Agency of Guam, two agency employees testified they had been paid bribes by one Chen. When Chen was subsequently subpoenaed before the grand jury, he denied paying the bribes and, subsequently, was indicted for perjury on the basis of that testimony.

Chen had one strong fact in his favor: The statute of limitations on any bribe charges had already run at the time he testified in the grand jury. So he raised the defense of perjury trap, arguing that he had been called to testify in the grand jury only for the purpose of eliciting false testimony for which he could be indicted. On appeal, the court acknowledged the theoretical availability of the defense but rejected it, finding that the scope of the grand jury's investigation was wider than just the relationship between Chen and the two agency employees he had testified about, and that the questioning had a legitimate investigative purpose.

H. THE INDICTMENT

An indictment is, above all, a document. As a written instrument, the indictment is critical to a defendant's Sixth Amendment right to be "informed of the nature and cause of the accusation." *Hamling v. United States*, 418 U.S. 87 (1974). Yet the legal requirements of a sufficient indictment are minimal. The Court further stated in *Hamling*: "It is generally sufficient that an indictment set forth the offense in the words of the statute itself . . . provided that it also includes such a statement of the facts and circumstances as will inform the accused of the specific offence, coming under the general description, with which he is charged." Rule 7(c)(1) of the Federal Rules of Criminal Procedure, similarly, merely states that "[t]he indictment or information must be a plain, concise, and definite written statement of the essential facts constituting the offense charged."

Note the similarity between Fed. R. Crim. P. 7(c)(1) and Fed. R. Civ. P. 8(a)(2), which requires only that a complaint set forth "a short and plain statement of the claim showing that the pleader is entitled to relief." In the civil context, however, unlike the criminal, the Supreme Court has by case law aggressively fortified such notice requirements. *See Ashcroft v. Iqbal*, 556 U.S. 662 (2009) (complaint that offers labels and conclusions or formulaic recitation of elements of cause of action will not do, nor does complaint suffice if it tenders naked assertions devoid of further factual enhancement). *Bell Atlantic Corp. v. Twombly*, 550 U.S. 544 (2007) (complaint must "plausibly" allege a claim). Labels, conclusions, and naked assertions are the standard fare of indictments. How is it that a civil defendant is entitled to more notice of the allegations against him than a criminal defendant?

In a similar vein, under Fed. R. Civ. P. 9(b) allegations of fraud must be stated "with particularity." Fed. R. Crim. P. 7 has no equivalent provision pertaining to an indictment's allegations of fraud, which, of course, are the heart of indictments charging defendants with violating one of the many federal criminal fraud statutes (mail, wire, bank, health care, securities, etc.). Rule 9(b) is a potent weapon for civil defendants in all manner of cases premised on fraud, from securities fraud to claims under the federal False Claims Act. *See, e.g., U.S. ex rel. Clausen v. Lab. Corp. of Am.*, 290 F.3d 1301 (11th Cir. 2002). Civil Rule 9(b)'s tepid criminal counterpart, if you can call it that, is Fed. R. Crim. P. 7(f), which provides that the court "may" direct the government to file a bill of particulars, fleshing out the details of an indictment's generalized allegations. Bills of particulars are totally within the trial court's discretion, however, and a decision denying a motion for a bill of particulars will be reviewed only for an abuse of that discretion. *United States v. Mejia*, 448 U.S. 436 (D.C. Cir. 2006).

The grand jury's indictment decision must be based on a finding of probable cause. But given how that finding of probable cause may be arrived at, as we have seen, should that finding have any collateral consequences? The next case considers this issue in the criminal forfeiture context.

Kaley v. United States

571 U.S. 320 (2014)

Justice KAGAN delivered the opinion of the Court.

A federal statute, 21 U.S.C. § 853(e), authorizes a court to freeze an indicted defendant's assets prior to trial if they would be subject to forfeiture upon conviction. In *United States v. Monsanto* (1989) we approved the constitutionality of such an order so long as it is "based on a finding of probable cause to believe that the property will ultimately be proved forfeitable." And we held that standard to apply even when a defendant seeks to use the disputed property to pay for a lawyer.

In this case, two indicted defendants wishing to hire an attorney challenged a pre-trial restraint on their property. The trial court convened a hearing to consider the seizure's legality under *Monsanto*. The question presented is whether criminal defendants are constitutionally entitled at such a hearing to contest a grand jury's prior determination of probable cause to believe they committed the crimes charged. We hold that they have no right to relitigate that finding.

I

A

Criminal forfeitures are imposed upon conviction to confiscate assets used in or gained from certain serious crimes. *See* 21 U.S.C. § 853(a). Forfeitures help to ensure that crime does not pay: They at once punish wrongdoing, deter future illegality, and "lessen the economic power" of criminal enterprises. The Government also uses forfeited property to recompense victims of crime, improve conditions in crime-damaged communities, and support law enforcement activities like police training. Accordingly, "there is a strong governmental interest in obtaining full recovery of all forfeitable assets."

In line with that interest, § 853(e)(1) empowers courts to enter pre-trial restraining orders or injunctions to "preserve the availability of [forfeitable] property" while criminal proceedings are pending. Such an order, issued "[u]pon application of the United States," prevents a defendant from spending or transferring specified property, including to pay an attorney for legal services. In *Monsanto*, our principal case involving this procedure, we held a pre-trial asset restraint constitutionally permissible whenever there is probable cause to believe that the property is forfeitable. That determination has two parts, reflecting the requirements for forfeiture under federal law: There must be probable cause to think (1) that the defendant has committed an offense permitting forfeiture, and (2) that the property at issue has the requisite connection to that crime. See § 853(a). The *Monsanto* Court, however, declined to consider "whether the Due Process Clause requires a hearing" to establish either or both of those aspects of forfeitability.

Since *Monsanto*, the lower courts have generally provided a hearing to any indicted defendant seeking to lift an asset restraint to pay for a lawyer. In that hearing, they have uniformly allowed the defendant to litigate the second issue stated above: whether probable cause exists to believe that the assets in dispute are traceable or otherwise sufficiently related to the crime charged in the indictment. But the courts have divided over extending the hearing to the first issue. Some have considered, while others have barred, a defendant's attempt to challenge the probable cause underlying a criminal charge. This case raises the question whether an indicted defendant has a constitutional right to contest the grand jury's prior determination of that matter.

B

The grand jury's indictment in this case charges a scheme to steal prescription medical devices and resell them for profit. The indictment accused petitioner Kerri Kaley, a sales representative for a subsidiary of Johnson & Johnson, and petitioner Brian Kaley, her husband, with transporting stolen medical devices across state lines and laundering the proceeds of that activity. The Kaleys have contested those allegations throughout this litigation, arguing that the medical devices at issue were unwanted, excess hospital inventory, which they could lawfully take and market to others.

Immediately after obtaining the indictment, the Government sought a restraining order under § 853(e)(1) to prevent the Kaleys from transferring any assets traceable to or involved in the alleged offenses. Included among those assets is a $500,000 certificate of deposit that the Kaleys intended to use for legal fees. The District Court entered the requested order. Later, in response to the Kaleys' motion to vacate the asset restraint, the court denied a request for an evidentiary hearing and confirmed the order, except as to $63,000 that it found (based on the parties' written submissions) was not connected to the alleged offenses.

On interlocutory appeal, the Eleventh Circuit reversed and remanded for further consideration of whether some kind of evidentiary hearing was warranted. The District Court then concluded that it should hold a hearing, but only as to "whether the restrained assets are traceable to or involved in the alleged criminal conduct." The Kaleys informed the court that they no longer disputed that issue; they wished to show only that the "case against them is 'baseless.'" Accordingly, the District Court affirmed the restraining order, and the Kaleys took another appeal. The Eleventh Circuit this time affirmed, holding that the Kaleys were not entitled at a hearing on the asset freeze "to challenge the factual foundation supporting the grand jury's probable cause determination[ ]"—that is, "the very validity of the underlying indictment."

We granted certiorari in light of the Circuit split on the question presented, and we now affirm the Eleventh Circuit.

II

This Court has twice considered claims, similar to the Kaleys', that the Fifth Amendment's right to due process and the Sixth Amendment's right to counsel constrain the way the federal forfeiture statute applies to assets needed to retain an attorney. We begin with those rulings not as mere background, but as something much more. On the single day the Court decided both those cases, it cast the die on this one too.

In *Caplin & Drysdale*, we considered whether the Fifth and Sixth Amendments exempt from forfeiture money that a convicted defendant has agreed to pay his attorney. We conceded a factual premise of the constitutional claim made in the case: Sometimes "a defendant will be unable to retain the attorney of his choice," if he cannot use forfeitable assets. Still, we held, the defendant's claim was "untenable." "A defendant has no Sixth Amendment right to spend another person's money" for legal fees—even if that is the only way to hire a preferred lawyer. Consider, we submitted, the example of a "robbery suspect" who wishes to "use funds he has stolen from a bank to retain an attorney to defend him if he is apprehended." That money is "not rightfully his." Accordingly, we concluded, the Government does not violate the Constitution if, pursuant to the forfeiture statute, "it seizes the robbery proceeds and refuses to permit the defendant to use them" to pay for his lawyer.

And then, we confirmed in *Monsanto* what our "robbery suspect" hypothetical indicated: Even prior to conviction (or trial)—when the presumption of innocence still applies—the Government could constitutionally use § 853(e) to freeze assets of an indicted defendant "based on a finding of probable cause to believe that the property will ultimately be proved forfeitable." In *Monsanto*, too, the defendant wanted to use the property at issue to pay a lawyer, and maintained that the Fifth and Sixth Amendments entitled him to do so. We disagreed. We first noted that the Government may sometimes "restrain persons where there is a finding of probable cause to believe that the accused has committed a serious offense." Given that power, we could find "no constitutional infirmity in § 853(e)'s authorization of a similar restraint on [the defendant's] property" in order to protect "the community's interest" in recovering "ill-gotten gains." Nor did the defendant's interest in retaining a lawyer with the disputed assets change the equation. Relying on *Caplin & Drysdale*, we reasoned: "[I]f the Government may, post-trial, forbid the use of forfeited assets to pay an attorney, then surely no constitutional violation occurs when, after probable cause is adequately established, the Government obtains an order barring a defendant from frustrating that end by dissipating his assets prior to trial." So again: With probable cause, a freeze is valid.

The Kaleys little dispute that proposition; their argument is instead about who should have the last word as to probable cause. A grand jury has already found probable cause to think that the Kaleys committed the offenses charged; that is why an indictment issued. No one doubts that those crimes are serious enough to trigger forfeiture. Similarly, no one contests that the assets in question derive from, or were used in committing, the offenses. The only question is whether the Kaleys are constitutionally entitled to a judicial re-determination of the conclusion the grand jury already reached: that probable cause supports this criminal prosecution (or alternatively put, that the prosecution is not "baseless," as the Kaleys believe). And that question, we think, has a ready answer, because a fundamental and historic commitment of our criminal justice system is to entrust those probable cause findings to grand juries.

This Court has often recognized the grand jury's singular role in finding the probable cause necessary to initiate a prosecution for a serious crime. "[A]n indictment 'fair upon its face,' and returned by a 'properly constituted grand jury,'" we have explained, "conclusively determines the existence of probable cause" to believe the defendant perpetrated the offense alleged. And "conclusively" has meant, case in and case out, just that. We have found no "authority for looking into and revising the judgment of the grand jury upon the evidence, for the purpose of determining whether or not the finding was founded upon sufficient proof." To the contrary, "the whole history of the grand jury institution" demonstrates that "a challenge to the reliability or competence of the evidence" supporting a grand jury's finding of probable cause "will not be heard." The grand jury gets to say — without any review, oversight, or second-guessing — whether probable cause exists to think that a person committed a crime.

And that inviolable grand jury finding, we have decided, may do more than commence a criminal proceeding (with all the economic, reputational, and personal harm that entails); the determination may also serve the purpose of immediately depriving the accused of her freedom. If the person charged is not yet in custody, an indictment triggers "issuance of an arrest warrant without further inquiry" into the case's strength. Alternatively, if the person was arrested without a warrant, an indictment eliminates her Fourth Amendment right to a prompt judicial assessment of probable cause to support any detention. In either situation, this Court — relying on the grand jury's "historical role of protecting individuals from unjust persecution" — has "let [that body's] judgment substitute for that of a neutral and detached magistrate." The grand jury, all on its own, may effect a pre-trial restraint on a person's liberty by finding probable cause to support a criminal charge.

The same result follows when, as here, an infringement on the defendant's property depends on a showing of probable cause that she committed a crime. If judicial review of the grand jury's probable cause determination is not warranted (as we have so often held) to put a defendant on trial or place her in custody, then neither is it needed to freeze her property. The grand jury that is good enough — reliable enough, protective enough — to inflict those other grave consequences through its probable cause findings must needs be adequate to impose this one too. Indeed, *Monsanto* already noted the absence of any reason to hold property seizures to different rules: As described earlier, the Court partly based its adoption of the probable cause standard on the incongruity of subjecting an asset freeze to any stricter requirements than apply to an arrest or ensuing detention. By similar token, the probable cause standard, once selected, should work no differently for the single purpose of freezing assets than for all others. So the longstanding, unvarying rule of criminal procedure we have just described applies here as well: The grand jury's determination is conclusive.

And indeed, the alternative rule the Kaleys seek would have strange and destructive consequences. The Kaleys here demand a do-over, except with a different referee. They wish a judge to decide anew the exact question the grand jury has already answered—whether there is probable cause to think the Kaleys committed the crimes charged. But suppose the judge performed that task and came to the opposite conclusion. Two inconsistent findings would then govern different aspects of one criminal proceeding: Probable cause would exist to bring the Kaleys to trial (and, if otherwise appropriate, hold them in prison), but not to restrain their property. And assuming the prosecutor continued to press the charges, the same judge who found probable cause lacking would preside over a trial premised on its presence. That legal dissonance, if sustainable at all, could not but undermine the criminal justice system's integrity—and especially the grand jury's integral, constitutionally prescribed role. For in this new world, every prosecution involving a pre-trial asset freeze would potentially pit the judge against the grand jury as to the case's foundational issue.

The Kaleys counter that apparently inconsistent findings are not really so, because the prosecutor could have presented scantier evidence to the judge than he previously offered the grand jury. Suppose, for example, that at the judicial hearing the prosecutor put on only "one witness instead of all five"; then, the Kaleys maintain, the judge's decision of no probable cause would mean only that "the Government did not satisfy its burden[ ] on that one day in time." But we do not think that hypothetical solves the problem. As an initial matter, it does not foreclose a different fact pattern: A judge could hear the exact same evidence as the grand jury, yet respond to it differently, thus rendering what even the Kaleys must concede is a contradictory finding. And when the Kaleys' hypothetical is true, just what does it show? Consider that the prosecutor in their example has left home some of the witnesses he took to the grand jury—presumably because, as we later discuss, he does not yet wish to reveal their identities or likely testimony. The judge's ruling of no probable cause therefore would not mean that the grand jury was wrong: As the Kaleys concede, the grand jury could have heard more than enough evidence to find probable cause that they committed the crimes charged. The Kaleys would win at the later hearing despite, not because of, the case's true merits. And we would then see still less reason for a judge to topple the grand jury's (better supported) finding of probable cause.

Our reasoning so far is straightforward. We held in *Monsanto* that the probable cause standard governs the pre-trial seizure of forfeitable assets, even when they are needed to hire a lawyer. And we have repeatedly affirmed a corollary of that standard: A defendant has no right to judicial review of a grand jury's determination of probable cause to think a defendant committed a crime. In combination, those settled propositions signal defeat for the Kaleys because, in contesting the seizure of their property, they seek only to relitigate such a grand jury finding.

• • •

Chief Justice ROBERTS, with whom Justice BREYER and Justice SOTOMAYOR join, dissenting.

An individual facing serious criminal charges brought by the United States has little but the Constitution and his attorney standing between him and prison. He might readily give all he owns to defend himself.

We have held, however, that the Government may effectively remove a defendant's primary weapon of defense—the attorney he selects and trusts—by freezing assets he needs to pay his lawyer. That ruling is not at issue. But today the Court goes further, holding that a defendant may be hobbled in this way without an opportunity to challenge the Government's decision to freeze those needed assets. I cannot subscribe to that holding and respectfully dissent.

I

The facts of this case are important. They highlight the significance to a defendant of being able to hire his counsel of choice, and the potential for unfairness inherent in giving the prosecutor the discretion to take that right away. Kerri Kaley worked as a sales representative for a Johnson & Johnson subsidiary, selling prescription medical devices. Kaley and other sales representatives occasionally obtained outmoded or surplus devices from staff members at the medical facilities they served, when, for example, those devices were no longer needed because they had been superseded by newer models. Kaley sold the unwanted devices to a Florida company, dividing the proceeds among the sales representatives.

Kaley learned in January 2005 that a federal grand jury was investigating those activities as a conspiracy to sell stolen prescription medical devices. Kaley and her husband (who allegedly helped ship the products to Florida) retained counsel, who immediately set to work preparing their defense against any impending charges. Counsel regularly discussed the investigation with the Kaleys, helped review documents demanded by the grand jury, and met with prosecutors in an attempt to ward off an indictment. Nonetheless preparing for the worst, the Kaleys applied for a $500,000 equity line of credit on their home to pay estimated legal fees associated with a trial. They used that money to purchase a $500,000 certificate of deposit, which they set aside until it would be needed to pay their attorneys for the trial.

In February 2007, the grand jury returned a seven-count indictment charging the Kaleys and another sales representative, Jennifer Gruenstrass, with violations of federal law. The indictment alleged that a "money judgment" of over $2 million and the $500,000 certificate of deposit were subject to forfeiture under 18 U.S.C. § 981(a)(1)(C) because those assets constituted "proceeds" of the alleged crimes. Armed with this indictment, the prosecution obtained an ex parte order pursuant to 21 U.S.C. § 853(e), thereby freezing all of the Kaleys' assets listed in the indictment, including the certificate of deposit set aside for legal fees. The Government did not seek to freeze any of Gruenstrass's assets.

The Kaleys moved to vacate the order, requesting a hearing at which they could argue that there was no probable cause to believe their assets were forfeitable, because their alleged conduct was not criminal. They argued they were entitled to such a hearing because the restraining order targeted funds they needed and had set aside to retain for trial the same counsel who had been preparing their defense for two years. And they contended that the prosecution was baseless because the Government could not identify anyone who claimed ownership of the medical devices alleged to have been "stolen." During a telephone conference with a Magistrate Judge on the motion, the prosecution conceded that it had been able to trace only $140,000 in allegedly criminal proceeds to the Kaleys, which led the Magistrate Judge to question the lawfulness of restraining the listed assets.

Just two business days after that conference, the Government obtained a superseding indictment that added a count of conspiracy to commit money laundering under 18 U.S.C. § 1956(h). Adding that charge enabled the Government to proceed under a much broader forfeiture provision than the one in the original indictment. While the civil forfeiture provision in § 981(a)(1)(C) authorized forfeiture of property that "constitutes or is derived from proceeds traceable to" a qualifying criminal violation, the criminal forfeiture provision now invoked by the Government—§ 982(a)(1)—authorizes forfeiture of property "involved in" a qualifying offense, or "any property traceable to such property." The superseding indictment alleged that a sum of more than $2 million, the certificate of deposit reserved to pay legal expenses, and now the Kaleys' home were subject to forfeiture. And again, the Government sought an order freezing substantially all those assets.

The Kaleys objected, repeating the arguments they had previously raised, and also contending that the prosecutors were being vindictive in adding the money laundering charge and seeking broader forfeiture. The District Court nonetheless entered the broader order requested by the Government, and the restraint on the Kaleys' assets remains in place.

While the Kaleys' appeal from that denial was pending, the Government proceeded to trial separately against their codefendant Gruenstrass. As the Government had not sought to freeze Gruenstrass's assets, she was represented by her chosen counsel. Her counsel argued that the Government was pitching a fraud without a victim, because no Government witness took the stand to claim ownership of the allegedly stolen devices. The jury acquitted Gruenstrass on all charges in less than three hours—a good omen for the Kaleys and their counsel as they prepared for their own trial.

II

The issues at stake here implicate fundamental constitutional principles. The Sixth Amendment provides that "[i]n all criminal prosecutions, the accused shall enjoy the right . . . to have the Assistance of Counsel for his defence." In many ways, this is the most precious right a defendant has, because it is his attorney who will fight for the other rights the defendant enjoys. And more than 80 years ago, we found it "hardly necessary to say that, the right to counsel being conceded, a defendant should be afforded a fair opportunity to secure counsel of his own choice."

Indeed, we recently called the "right to select counsel of one's choice . . . the root meaning of the constitutional guarantee" of the Sixth Amendment. *United States v. Gonzalez-Lopez* (2006). The Amendment requires "that a particular guarantee of fairness be provided—to wit, that the accused be defended by the counsel he believes to be best." An individual's right to counsel of choice is violated "whenever the defendant's choice is wrongfully denied," and such error "pervades the entire trial." A violation of this right is therefore a "structural error," that is, one of the very few kinds of errors that "undermine the fairness of a criminal proceeding as a whole." *United States v. Davila* (2013).

It is of course true that the right to counsel of choice is (like most rights) not absolute. A defendant has no right to choose counsel he cannot afford, counsel who is not a member of the bar, or counsel with an impermissible conflict of interest. And a district court need not always shuffle its calendar to accommodate a defendant's preferred counsel if it has legitimate reasons not to do so. But none of those limitations is imposed at the unreviewable discretion of a prosecutor—the party who wants the defendant to lose at trial.

This Court has held that the prosecution may freeze assets a defendant needs to retain his counsel of choice upon "a finding of probable cause to believe that the assets are forfeitable." The Kaleys do not challenge that holding here. But the Court in *Monsanto* acknowledged and reserved the crucial question whether a defendant had the right to be heard before the Government could take such action.

There was good reason for that caution. The possibility that a prosecutor could elect to hamstring his target by preventing him from paying his counsel of choice raises substantial concerns about the fairness of the entire proceeding. "A fair trial in a fair tribunal is a basic requirement of due process." Issues concerning the denial of counsel of choice implicate the overall fairness of the trial because they "bear[ ] directly on the 'framework within which the trial proceeds.'"

III

Notwithstanding the substantial constitutional issues at stake, the majority believes that syllogistic-type reasoning effectively resolves this case. The majority's reasoning goes like this: First, to freeze assets prior to trial, the Government must show probable cause to believe that a defendant has committed an offense giving rise to forfeiture. Second, grand jury determinations of probable cause are nonreviewable. Therefore, the Kaleys cannot "relitigate [the] grand jury finding" of probable cause to avoid a pretrial restraint of assets they need to retain their counsel of choice. I do not view the matter as nearly so "straightforward," and neither did the multiple Courts of Appeals since *Monsanto* that have granted defendants the type of hearing the Kaleys request.

To begin with, the majority's conclusion is wrong on its own terms. To freeze assets prior to trial, the Government must show probable cause to believe both that (1) a defendant has committed an offense giving rise to forfeiture and (2) the targeted assets have the requisite connection to the alleged criminal conduct. 21 U.S.C. § 853(e)(1)(A). The Solicitor General concedes — and all Courts of Appeals to have considered the issue have held — that "defendants are entitled to show that the assets that are restrained are not actually the proceeds of the charged criminal offense," that is, that the second prong of the required showing is not satisfied. But by listing property in the indictment and alleging that it is subject to forfeiture — as required to restrain assets before trial under § 853(e)(1)(A) — the grand jury found probable cause to believe those assets were linked to the charged offenses, just as it found probable cause to believe the Kaleys committed the underlying crimes. Neither the Government nor the majority gives any reason why the District Court may reconsider the grand jury's probable cause finding as to traceability — and in fact constitutionally must, if asked — but may not do so as to the underlying charged offenses.

In any event, the hearing the Kaleys seek would not be mere relitigation of the grand jury proceedings. At that hearing, the District Court would consider the merits of the prosecution to determine whether there is probable cause to believe the Kaleys' assets are forfeitable, not to determine whether the Kaleys may be tried at all. If the judge agrees with the Kaleys, he will merely hold that the Government has not met its burden at that hearing to justify freezing the assets the Kaleys need to pay their attorneys. The Government may proceed with the prosecution, but the Kaleys will have their chosen counsel at their side.

Even though the probable cause standard applies at both the indictment stage and the pretrial asset restraint hearing, the judge's determination will be based on different evidence than that previously presented to the grand jury. For its part, the Government may choose to put on more or less evidence at the hearing than it did before the grand jury. And of course the Kaleys would have the opportunity to tell their side of the story — something the grand jury never hears. Here, much of what the Kaleys want to present comes from Gruenstrass's trial — evidence that the grand jury obviously could not have considered. So even if the judge determined that probable cause to justify the pretrial asset restraint had not been adequately established, that determination would not in any way amount to "looking into and revising the judgment of the grand jury upon the evidence, for the purpose of determining whether or not the finding was founded upon sufficient proof." The judge's decision based on the evidence presented at the hearing would have no necessary legal or logical consequence for the underlying prosecution because it would be based on different evidence and used for a different purpose.

The majority warns that allowing a judge to consider the underlying merits of the prosecution for purposes of determining whether a defendant's assets may be restrained pretrial could create "legal dissonance" with the grand jury's indictment, which "could not but undermine the criminal justice system's integrity." But as explained, such a judicial finding based on different evidence with both sides present would not contradict the grand jury's probable cause finding based on what was before it. That finding would still suffice to accomplish its purpose — to call for a trial on the merits of the charges. Rather than creating "dissonance," the traditional roles of the principal actors in our justice system would remain respected: The grand jury decides whether a defendant should be required to stand trial, the judge decides pretrial matters and how the trial should proceed, and the jury decides whether the defendant is guilty of the crime.

Indeed, in the bail context — the pretrial determination that is perhaps the closest analogue to the pretrial restraint of assets at issue here — we allow judicial inquiries into the underlying merits of the indicted charges, without concern about intruding into the province of the grand jury. An indictment charging sufficiently serious crimes gives rise to a rebuttable presumption that a defendant is not eligible for pretrial release. See 18 U.S.C. §§ 3142(e)(3) and (f). Such a defendant is nonetheless entitled to an evidentiary hearing at which he may contest (among other things) "the weight of the evidence against" him, § 3142(g)(2). Yet no one would say that the district court encroached on the grand jury's role if the court determined that it would not authorize pretrial detention because of the weakness of the prosecution's case. That makes sense, because the district court has considered the underlying merits of the charges based on different information and for a different purpose than the grand jury did. Such a defendant would be granted pretrial release, but would still have to show up for trial.

In any event, few things could do more to "undermine the criminal justice system's integrity" than to allow the Government to initiate a prosecution and then, at its option, disarm its presumptively innocent opponent by depriving him of his counsel of choice — without even an opportunity to be heard. That is the result of the Court's decision in this case, and it is fundamentally at odds with our constitutional tradition and basic notions of fair play.

NOTES AND QUESTIONS

1. The Court and the government concede that a defendant has a right to a hearing on the issue of whether there is probable cause to believe restrained property is forfeitable, the second of the two questions deferred in *Monsanto*, even though the grand jury indictment makes allegations both in this regard as well as alleging the commission of a crime. Is the Court's description of the restraint allegations as "a technical matter far removed from the grand jury's core competence" persuasive? Does Chief Justice Roberts's dissenting opinion have the better view of this issue? What is the "core competence" of this body of laypersons?

2. The Court notes that since the grand jury's finding of probable cause is sufficient in itself to justify a person's arrest and to create a presumption of pretrial detention it should therefore also be enough to justify a pretrial asset restraint. Do you agree? How is a pretrial asset restraint distinguishable?

3. Chief Justice Roberts says in dissent that "[t]he facts of this case are important." Of course they are. They always are. But he has a point: It is hard to imagine a better set of facts — a specified bucket of prospective legal fees, a defense counsel known to the prosecution, a not guilty verdict at the trial of a codefendant, a reactive and potentially vindictive action by the prosecutor with regard to forfeiture — on which to litigate this issue. What is the significance of each of these facts?

4. The Court states that if the issue of probable cause could be litigated in the asset restraint context, every such case "would potentially pit the judge against the grand jury as to the case's foundational issue." Do you agree?

Do jury trials likewise "pit" the petit jury against the grand jury on a foundational issue, and in an even starker competition?

Are the defendants really requesting a "do over," as the Court puts it?

Would a contrary judicial finding as to probable cause truly "undermine the criminal justice system's integrity"?

Did the not guilty verdict of the Kaleys' codefendant at trial similarly undermine the criminal justice system's integrity inasmuch as she, too, was indicted by a grand jury?

5. Whether "probable cause" was the original Founding-era standard for the commencement of criminal charges — as has long been assumed, *see Kaley*, 571 U.S. at 328 — has been called into question by Professor William Ortman. William Ortman, *Probable Cause Revisited*, 68 Stan. L. Rev. 511 (2015). Professor Ortman presents a strong case that many Founding-era grand juries were instructed to return indictments only upon a higher evidentiary showing (sometimes a "certainty") due to the summary nature of criminal trials at the time. *Id.* at 514-15. Probable cause appeared to emerge as the governing standard over the course of the nineteenth century as a corollary of the formalization of the criminal trial during the same period. *Id.* at 515. The probable cause standard endured, paradoxically, even as plea bargaining and not trials became the predominant means of resolving criminal cases over the second half of the nineteenth century. *Id.* at 515-16.

6. Suppose the Supreme Court were to embrace Professor Ortmann's "originalist" understanding of the grand jury probable cause requirement. What would be the practical consequences of such a shift?

I. THE GRAND JURY AND INVESTIGATION OF POLICE MISCONDUCT

Among the recent criticisms of the grand jury has been that it has selectively exercised its "shield" function to protect police officers charged with racial violence. Roger A. Fairfax Jr., *Interrogating the Nonincorporation of the Grand Jury Clause*, 43 Cardozo L. Rev. 855, 909-12 (2022). *See also* Roger A. Fairfax Jr., *The Grand Jury and Police Violence Against Black Men*, in Policing the Black Man 209-33 (Angela J. Davis ed., 2017). Grand juries have failed to return indictments against police officers in several high-profile cases, including the killings of Michael Brown (shot and killed by former officer Darren Wilson), Eric Garner (killed by a chokehold administered by former officer Daniel Pantaleo), Tamir Rice (shot and killed by former officer Tim Loehman), and Breonna Taylor (shot and killed by multiple Louisville police officers).

It is impossible to know exactly why grand juries did not indict these police officers. Grand jury secrecy rules make such proceedings largely invisible; note that in many cases misconduct that occurred in the grand jury is uncovered only due to the prosecutor's obligation, at trial, to disclose the prior testimony of witnesses. When a grand jury does not indict, there is no trial and no disclosure obligation ever arises. We do know, of course, that grand jury investigations of police misconduct, like all grand jury investigations, are normally led by prosecutors, who work with and rely on the police officers under investigation. At a minimum, such prosecutors will find it awkward to seek a grand jury indictment of a police officer.

Several other institutional factors make grand jury indictments of police officers difficult. First, member of the general public — that is, grand jurors — tend to respect and sympathize with police officers, public servants who have dangerous jobs. Second, police officers are experienced in the criminal process and are unlikely to make the sort of unforced errors — for example, talking to investigators without lawyering up — that can make indictment and prosecution easy. *See* Kate Levine, *How We Prosecute the Police*, 104 Geo. L.J. 745, 762-63 (2016). Third, and perhaps most important, in a typical police misconduct case — use of excessive force, for example — it is extremely unlikely that any other police officers at the scene will corroborate the victim's version of events. *See, e.g.*, Gabriel J. Chin & Scott C. Wells, *The "Blue Wall of Silence" as Evidence of Bias and Motive to Lie: A New Approach to Police Perjury*, 59 U. Pitt. L. Rev. 233, 237 (1998) ("Police officers . . . lie under oath because of the 'blue wall of silence,' an unwritten code in many departments which prohibits . . . testifying truthfully if the facts would implicate the conduct of a fellow officer.").

It also seems that prosecutors tend to be atypically "thorough"in grand jury investigations of police officers. Levine, *How We Prosecute the Police*, *supra* at 762-66. This was actually confirmed to be the case in the investigation of the killing of Michael Brown by Ferguson, Missouri, police officer Darren Wilson. In that case, St. Louis County prosecuting attorney Robert McCulloch took the unusual step of releasing the grand jury transcripts after the decision not to indict had been made. What the transcripts showed was a grand jury process that was anything but business as usual. Far from the wholly inquisitory and often imbalanced inquiry you have become familiar with throughout this chapter, the investigation of Darren Wilson was exhaustive, stretching over months and involving 62 witnesses. *Id.* at 766. Two things in particular stuck out from the transcripts. One, Darren Wilson testified at some length but was not cross-examined by the prosecutor, although the prosecutor cross-examined many other witnesses. Two, the grand jury was told at the outset that it would be presented with "every statement" and "every bit of evidence" and that the proceeding would be "like a trial." *Id.*

What inference might the grand jurors have drawn from the prosecutor's failure to cross-examine Darren Wilson? How might the instruction that the proceeding would be "like a trial" have affected the grand jury's deliberations?

The point is not necessarily that the Ferguson grand jury was wrong. Indeed, the Department of Justice reached a similar conclusion. *See* Dept. of Justice, Report Regarding the Criminal Investigation into the Shooting Death of Michael Brown by Ferguson, Missouri Police Officer Darren Wilson 86. The point is that putative police officer defendants appear to be getting preferential treatment in the grand jury process.

Michael Brown

An unusual civil lawsuit in the aftermath of Ferguson sheds light on this point. In *Doe v. McCulloch*, 2015 WL 2092492 (E.D. Mo. 2015), a woman who had served on the St. Louis County grand jury investigating Officer Wilson sued the county prosecuting attorney, seeking a declaration that Missouri laws that criminalized a juror's disclosure of information about her experience on the state grand jury violated her free speech rights. *Id.* at *1. Specifically, the woman apparently wanted the freedom to speak publicly about the differential manner in the presentation of evidence between other investigations and the investigation of Officer Wilson. She noted that the presentation to the grand jury was different in significant ways from previous cases; the investigation had a stronger emphasis on the victim than in other cases; and the "presentation of the law to which the grand jurors were to apply the facts was made in a muddled and untimely manner." *Id.* at *2. The lawsuit was dismissed on abstention grounds.

A good example of differential process by legislative command—not just prosecutorial choice—can be seen in Georgia law prior to 2016. *See* Roger A. Fairfax Jr., *The Grand*

Jury's Role in the Prosecution of Unjustified Police Killings—Challenges and Solutions, 52 Harv. C.R.-C.L. L. Rev. 397, 413-14 (2017). Georgia had an especially dismal record on fatal police shootings: Half of the over 180 people shot and killed by police between 2010 and 2015 were either unarmed or were shot by police in the back; in only 9 of those cases did the prosecutor ask for an indictment; in only one case was an indictment returned. *Id.* The explanation may be at least partially found in Georgia law that gave police officers the right to be present during the entirety of the grand jury proceeding and listen to and observe—in person—all of the witness testimony against them, and at the conclusion of the grand jury presentation, to make a statement to the grand jurors without any rebuttal by the prosecutor. *Id.*

TABLE OF CASES

Principal cases are indicated by italics.

INDEX